W9-CJO-313

WEB SITES FOR ACCOUNTANTS

Standard Setting:

Financial Accounting Standards Board, http://www.fasb.org
Governmental Finance Officers Association, http://www.gfoa.org
International Accounting Standards Board, http://www.iasb.org

Regulatory:

Internal Revenue Service, http://www.irs.gov
Public Company Accounting Oversight Board, http://www.pcaobus.org
Securities and Exchange Commission, http://www.sec.gov

Other:

American Institute of Certified Public Accountants, http://www.aicpa.org
Association of Certified Fraud Examiners, http://www.cfenet.com
Center for Corporate Financial Leadership, http://www.ccflinfo.org
Financial Executives International, http://www.fei.org
Financial Planning Interactive, http://www.financial-planning.com
Information Systems Audit and Control Association, http://www.isaca.org
Institute of Internal Auditors, http://www.theiia.org
Institute of Management Accountants, http://www.imanet.org
International Federation of Accountants, http://www.ifac.org
National Association of Corporate Directors, http://www.nacdonline.org
Rutgers Accounting Web, http://www.accounting.rutgers.edu
Tax Web, http://www.taxweb.com
Yahoo Finance, http://www.finance.yahoo.com

9e

Advanced Accounting

Paul Marcus Fischer, PhD, CPA
Professor of Accounting
University of Wisconsin, Milwaukee

William James Taylor, PhD, CPA, CVA
Assistant Professor of Accounting
Univerisity of Wisconsin, Milwaukee

Rita Hartung Cheng, PhD, CPA
Professor of Accounting
University of Wisconsin, Milwaukee

THOMSON
SOUTH-WESTERN

Australia · Brazil · Canada · Mexico · Singapore · Spain · United Kingdom · United States

THOMSON
SOUTH-WESTERN

Advanced Accounting, 9th edition
Paul M. Fischer, William J. Taylor, Rita H. Cheng

VP/Editorial Director
Jack W. Calhoun

Publisher
Rob Dewey

Acquisitions Editor
Matthew Filimonov

Developmental Editor
Leslie Kauffman

Marketing Manager
Chris McNamee

Sr. Production Project Manager
Tim Bailey

Production Technology Project Manager
Peggy Buskey

Manager of Technology, Editorial
Vicky True

Technology Project Editor
Sally Nieman

Web Coordinator
Scott Cook

Manufacturing Coordinator
Doug Wilke

Art Director
Chris Miller

Cover Designer
Stratton Design

Cover Photo
Stone/Robin Smith

Production
LEAP Publishing Services, Inc.

Composition
Cadmus Professional Communications

Printer
Quebecor World
Taunton, MA

COPYRIGHT © 2006
Thomson South-Western, a part of The Thomson Corporation. Thomson, the Star logo, and South-Western are trademarks used herein under license.

Printed in the United States of America
1 2 3 4 5 09 08 07 06 05

Student Edition ISBN:
0-324-30411-0
Student Edition with CD ISBN:
0-324-30401-3

ALL RIGHTS RESERVED.
No part of this work covered by the copyright hereon may be reproduced or used in any form or by any means—graphic, electronic, or mechanical, including photocopying, recording, taping, Web distribution or information storage and retrieval systems, or in any other manner—without the written permission of the publisher.

For permission to use material from this text or product, submit a request online at http://www.thomsonrights.com.

Library of Congress Control Number:
2005928967

For more information about our products, contact us at:

Thomson Learning Academic Resource Center

1-800-423-0563

Thomson Higher Education
5191 Natorp Boulevard
Mason, OH 45040
USA

Portions of GASB Statement No. 14, The Financial Reporting Entity, and GASB Statement No. 32, Basic Financial Statements—and Management's Discussion and Analysis—for State and Local Governments, copyright by the Governmental Accounting Standards Board, 401 Merritt 7, Norwalk, CT 06856, U.S.A., are reproduced with permission. Complete copies of these documents are available from the GASB.

Material from the Uniform CPA Examination Questions and Unofficial Answers, Copyright © 1975 through 1995 by the American Institute of Certified Public Accountants, Inc., is reprinted (or adapted) with permission.

Advanced Leadership

INNOVATION

The ninth edition of *Advanced Accounting* by Paul Fischer, William Taylor, and Rita Cheng raises the standard in accounting education. Providing the most innovative and comprehensive coverage of advanced financial accounting topics on the market today, the ninth edition incorporates pedagogically strong elements throughout. The end result is a valuable and useful resource for both the present and the future. Fischer/Taylor/Cheng's *Advanced Accounting* offers the learner the ability to understand and apply new knowledge like no other advanced accounting text available. Leading the way are these unique, innovative and helpful features:

- **Excelling with ease—An easy-to-follow Excel tutorial and convenient electronic working papers on CD:**
    - This unique tutorial teaches a step-by-step process for completing consolidations worksheets in an Excel-based environment. The tutorial makes it possible to master consolidations worksheets more quickly.
    - The tutorial guides the student through the creation of Excel worksheets. Each chapter of the tutorial adds the consolidations processes to parallel those presented in Chapters 2-6 and Chapter 11 of the text.
    - The electronic working papers in Excel format provide students with the basic worksheet structure for selected assignments throughout the text. These assignments are identified in the text by the icon shown here.

- **Comprehending through consistency—Common coding for the worksheets:**
    - All consolidations worksheets use a common coding for the eliminations and adjustments. A complete listing of the codes is presented on the inside of the front cover. Students are now able to quickly recall worksheet adjustments as they move from one chapter to the next.
    - Within the chapter narrative, the worksheet eliminations and adjustments are shown in journal entry form and are referenced using the same coding. This provides consistent reinforcement of the consolidations process and aids students in their understanding of the worksheet procedures.

(CY1)	Eliminate current-year equity income:		
	Subsidiary Income	60,000	
	Investment in Company S		60,000
(EL)	Eliminate 80% of subsidiary equity against investment in subsidiary account:		
	Common Stock ($10 par), Company S	80,000	
	Retained Earnings, January 1, 20X1, Company S	56,000	
	Investment in Company S		136,000
(IS)	Eliminate intercompany merchandise sales:		
	Sales	100,000	
	Cost of Goods Sold		100,000

- The same codes are continued in the Excel tutorial, the worksheet solutions, and the Student Companion Book.

- **Preparing for new consolidations rules—A new appendix to explain the FASB Exposure Drafts issued June 30, 2005, that will impact accounting for business combinations:**
  - The FASB issued two new exposure drafts on business combinations in June 2005, and a new standard is expected in 2006.
  - Major changes may include the elimination of proration for bargain purchases, recognizing 100% of fair values in less than 100% purchases, new rules for block purchases, and changes in ownership interest.
  - All major expected changes are explained and demonstrated in a new appendix, Special Appendix 2, that encompasses all of the business combination chapters.
  - The text web site at http://fischer.swlearning.com will keep adopters posted on the progress of the Exposure Draft.

- **Taming a tough topic—Coverage of derivatives and related accounting issues in a module:**
  - A comprehensive module deals with derivative instruments and related accounting issues. This module, located just before Chapter 10, sets forth the basic characteristics of derivative financial instruments and explains the features of common types of derivatives. Accounting for derivatives held as an investment and as a part of a hedging strategy is discussed.
  - Fair value and cash flow hedges are clearly defined, and the special accounting given such hedges is set forth in a clear and concise manner. Options, futures, and interest rate swaps are used to demonstrate accounting for fair value hedges and cash flow hedges.
  - New explanations, examples, and end-of-chapter problems have been added to help simplify this complex topic.
  - The more complex complications that are associated with the use of forward contracts are introduced in the module and then fully addressed in Chapter 10. Thus, Chapter 10's discussion of hedging foreign currency transactions is more streamlined and less cumbersome.
  - Most of the chapter's discussion of hedging foreign currency transactions involves the use of forward contracts. The focus is on the use of such contracts to hedge foreign currency transactions, commitments, and forecasted transactions.

- **Accounting for change—Coverage of new government reporting model and estate tax planning:**
  - Comprehensive coverage of governmental standards through GASB Statement No. 41, including the historic changes to the reporting model.
  - Government and not-for-profit chapters include material for CPA exam preparation.
  - Chapters are designed for use in advanced accounting courses or in standalone governmental and not-for-profit courses.
  - Text materials have been revised to reflect the most recent estate tax rates, unified credit, and planning strategies.

1

OBJECTIVE

Explain why transactions between members of a consolidated firm should not be reflected in the consolidated financial statements.

- **Measuring student mastery—Learning Objectives:**
  - Each chapter begins with a list of measurable learning objectives, which are repeated in the margin near the related coverage.
  - The exercises and problems at the end of the chapter indicate the specific learning objectives that they reinforce. This helpful indicator, along with the assignment titles, provides a quick reference for both student and instructor.

- **Communicating the core content—Reflection:**
  - Concluding every main section is a reflection on the core information contained in that section.

REFLECTION

- Merchandise sales between affiliated companies are eliminated; only the purchase and sale to the "outside world" should remain in the statements.
- The profit must be removed from beginning inventory by reducing the cost of goods sold and the retained earnings.

◆ These reflections provide students with a clear picture of the key points they should grasp and give them a helpful tool for quick review.

◆ **Thinking it through—Understanding the Issues:**

◆ These questions at the end of the chapter emphasize and reinforce the core main issues of the chapter.

UNDERSTANDING THE ISSUES

5. Company P had internally generated net income of $200,000 (excludes share of subsidiary income). Company P has 100,000 shares of outstanding common stock. Subsidiary Company S has a net income of $60,000 and 40,000 shares of outstanding common stock. Company P owns 100% of the Company S shares. What is consolidated diluted EPS, if:

   a. Company S has outstanding stock options for Company S shares, which cause a dilutive effect of 2,000 additional shares of Company S shares?
   b. Company S has outstanding stock options for Company P shares, which cause a dilutive effect of 2,000 additional shares of Company P shares?
   c. Company P has outstanding stock options for Company P shares, which cause a dilutive effect of 2,000 additional shares of Company P shares?

6. Company S is an 80%-owned subsidiary of Company P. For 20X1, Company P reports internally generated income before tax of $100,000. Company S reports an income before tax of $40,000. A 30% tax rate applies to both companies. Calculate consolidated net income (after taxes) and the distribution of income to the controlling and noncontrolling interests, if:

   a. The consolidated firm meets the requirements of an affiliated firm and files a consolidated tax return.
   b. The consolidated firm does not meet the requirements of an affiliated firm and files separate tax returns. Assume an 80% dividend exclusion rate.

◆ They encourage students to think in greater depth about the topics and expand their reasoning skills. Discussion skills are also developed through use of the questions as springboards for class interaction.

THEORY BLENDED WITH APPLICATION

With a strong tradition of combining sound theoretical foundations with a hands-on, learn-by-example approach, the ninth edition continues its prominent leadership position in advanced accounting classrooms across the country. The authors build on *Advanced Accounting's* clear writing style, comprehensive coverage, and focus on conceptual understanding.

Realizing that students reap the greatest benefits when they can visualize the application of theories, *Advanced Accounting* closely links theory and practice by providing examples through relevant exhibits and tables that are common to real-world accounting. When students can visualize the concept being discussed and apply it directly to an example, their understanding greatly improves. This focus on conceptual understanding makes even the most complex topics approachable.

Assignments are clearly defined. Questions are used to reinforce theory, and exercises are short, focused applications of specific topics in the chapter. These exercises are very helpful when students use them as preparations for class presentation. The book's problems—more comprehensive than the exercises—often combine topics and are designed to work well as after-class assignments. For group projects, the cases found in the business combinations chapters provide an innovative way to blend theoretical and numerical analysis.

ENHANCED COVERAGE

Advanced Accounting reflects changes in accounting procedures and standards while improving on those features that aid in student comprehension.

- **Comprehensive coverage of the impact of the latest FASB statements, including:**
  - New to ninth edition of *Advanced Accounting* is Special Appendix 2, Analysis of FASB Exposure Drafts for Business Combinations. This new appendix is based on the Exposure Drafts: Consolidated Financial Statements, Including Accounting and Reporting of Noncontrolling Interests in Subsidiaries – a replacement of ARB No. 51, and Business Combinations – a replacement of FASB No. 141. The appendix summarizes the major changes of these new accounting procedures and demonstrates how these changes impact the accounting procedures taught in the text. Exercises and problems that utilize the new accounting procedures are included.
  - Discussion of the FASB's convergence project, designed to move toward a common set of international accounting standards, is included.

- **Updated coverage of governmental and not-for-profit accounting:**
  - Chapter 15 has been updated to incorporate the latest guidance on accounting for revenues of nonexchange transactions, post-retirement benefits other than pensions, and investments.
  - The authors have included a chapter (Chapter 17) to focus on the new reporting model for state and local governments.
  - Chapters 18 and 19 have been updated to better present this challenging area of accounting. Since many of the not-for-profit organizations also have government counterparts and GASB standards prohibit governments from applying the FASB not-for-profit standards, the text separates the discussion of college and university, health-care organizations, voluntary health and welfare, and other not-for-profit organizations.

- **Comprehensive coverage of the impact of the latest GASB statements, including:**
  - A complete explanation and presentation of the comprehensive annual financial report (CAFR) provides students with a strong basis for understanding the reporting requirements as set forth in GASB Statement Nos. 34, 35, and 37.
  - The authors have provided a comprehensive presentation of revenue recognition requirements for nonexchange transactions, found in GASB Statement Nos. 33 and 36.
  - The note disclosure requirements in GASB Statement No. 38 are described.
  - Coverage of additional guidance on post-retirement benefits other than pensions (GASB Statement Nos. 43 and 45) and content on the statistical section (GASB Statement No. 44) are included.

FLEXIBILITY

The book's flexible coverage of topics allows for professors to teach their course at their own pace and in their preferred order. There are no dependencies between major sections of the text except that coverage of consolidations should precede multinational accounting if one is to understand accounting for foreign subsidiaries. It is also advisable that students master the module on derivatives before advancing to the chapter on foreign currency transactions. The book contains enough coverage to fill two advanced courses, but when only one semester is available, many professors find it ideal to cover the first four to six chapters in business combinations.

The text is divided into the following major topics:

Business Combinations—Basic Topics (Chapters 1–6)

Chapter 1 demonstrates the FASB rules, under Statement Nos. 141 and 142, for allocating the cost of a purchased company to its assets and liabilities. Goodwill impairment replaces amortization and is fully explained.

Chapters 2 through 5 cover the basics of preparing a consolidated income statement and balance sheet. In 1977, we introduced two schedules that have been much appreciated by students and faculty alike—the Determination and Distribution of Excess Schedule and Income Distribution Schedule. The determination and distribution schedule (quickly termed the D&D schedule by students) analyzes the difference between the price paid in a purchase and the underlying equity of the subsidiary. It provides a check figure for all subsequent years' worksheets, details all information for the distribution of differences between book and market values, and reveals all data for the amortization of the differences. The schedule provides rules for all types of purchase situations and for alternative consolidation theories. The income distribution schedule (known as the IDS) is a set of T accounts that distributes income between the noncontrolling and controlling interests. It also provides a useful check function to ensure that all intercompany eliminations are properly accounted for. These chapters give the student all topics needed for the CPA Exam. (For easy reference, the text contains an icon in the margin, as shown here, that ties the narrative to the worksheets. All demonstration worksheets appear both in the text, just before the assignment material, and in the Student Companion Book. In addition, the related narrative pages are indicated in the upper right side of each worksheet. This allows the reader to quickly locate important explanations.)

worksheet

With regard to the alternative worksheet methods and why we follow the approaches we do, consider the method used to record the investment in the subsidiary's and the parent's books. There are two key points of general agreement. The first is that it doesn't really matter which method is used, since the investment account is eliminated. Second, when the course is over, a student should know how to handle each method: simple equity, full (we call it sophisticated) equity, and cost. The real issue is which method is the easiest one to learn first. We believe the winner is simple equity, since it is totally symmetric with the equity accounts of the subsidiary. It simplifies elimination of subsidiary equity against the investment account. Every change in subsidiary equity is reflected, on a pro rata basis, in the parent's investment account. Thus, the simple equity method becomes the mainline method of the text. We teach the student to convert investments maintained under the cost method to the simple equity method. In practice, most firms and the majority of the problems in the text use the cost method. This means that the simple equity method is employed to solve problems that begin as either simple equity or cost method problems.

We also cover the sophisticated equity method, which amortizes the excess of cost or book value through the investment account. This method should also adjust for intercompany profits through the investment account. The method is cumbersome because it requires the student to deal with amortizations of excess and intercompany profits in the investment account before getting to the consolidated worksheet, which is designed to handle these topics. This means teaching consolidating procedures without the benefit of a worksheet. We cover the method after the student is proficient with a worksheet and the other methods. Thorough understanding of the sophisticated method is important so that it can be applied to influential investments that are not consolidated.

Another major concern among advanced text professors has to do with the worksheet style used. There are three choices: the horizontal (trial balance) format, the vertical (stacked) method, and the balance sheet only. Again, we do cover all three, but the horizontal format is our main method. Horizontal is by far the most appealing to students. They have used it in both introductory and intermediate accounting. It is also the most likely method to be found in practice. On this basis, we use it initially to develop all topics. We cover the vertical format but not until the student is proficient with the horizontal format. There is no difference in the elimination entries; only the worksheet logistics differ. It takes only one problem assignment to teach the students this approach so they are prepared for its possible appearance on the CPA Exam. The balance-sheet-only format has no reason to exist other than its use as a CPA Exam testing shortcut. We cover it in an appendix.

Chapter 6 may be more essential for those entering practice than it is for the CPA Exam. It contains cash flow for consolidated firms, taxation issues, and the use of the sophisticated equity method for influential investments. Support schedules guide the worksheet procedures for consolidated companies, which are taxed as separate entities. Taxation is the most difficult application of consolidation procedures. Every intercompany transaction is a tax allocation issue. Teaching the tax allocation issues with every topic as it is introduced is very confusing to students. We prefer to have the students fully understand worksheet procedures without taxes and then introduce taxes.

Business Combinations—Specialized Topics (Chapters 7 and 8)

These chapters deal with topics that occasionally surface in practice and have not appeared on the CPA Exam for over 18 years. Studying these chapters perfects the students' understanding of consolidations and stockholders' equity accounting, thus affording a valuable experience. Chapter 7 deals with piecemeal acquisitions of an investment in a subsidiary, sale of the parent's investment, and the impact of preferred stock in the subsidiary's equity structure. Chapter 8 deals with the impact of subsidiary equity transactions including stock dividends, sale of common stock shares, and subsidiary reacquisitions of shares. The chapter also considers indirect or three-tier ownership structures and reciprocal holdings where the subsidiary owns parent shares. Both Chapters 7 and 8 would be radically changed by the possible new FASB statement on business combinations. Following Chapter 8, a Special Appendix explores accounting for leveraged buyouts. This is a popular topic and is easily mastered using consolidation techniques. Students enjoy mastering it, since it is a common business phenomenon that sounds difficult but really is not. It appeals particularly to students with an interest in financial management.

A new special appendix, following the one on leveraged buyouts, to accompany the consolidations chapters explains and demonstrates the changes that may occur as a result of the new FASB Exposure Drafts issued June 30, 2005. The changes would include:

- Expensing direct acquisition costs.
- Eliminating allocation to nonpriority accounting in a bargain purchase. A gain would be recorded when the price paid is less than the amount assigned to net identifiable assets.
- Adjusting subsidiary assets to 100% of fair value no matter what the size of the controlling interest.
- Reflecting changes in the rules for block purchases. An initial noncontrolling interest would be rolled in (at fair value) to the price paid for the later controlling interest. A purchase made after control is achieved would be treated as a retirement of the shares.
- Adjusting of the rules for changes in the ownership interest of the parent caused by subsidiary stock transactions. There would not be any opportunity for a gain or loss on these transactions.

Multinational Accounting and Other Reporting Concerns (Chapters 9–11 and Module)

As business has developed beyond national boundaries, the discipline of accounting also has evolved internationally. As our global economy develops, so, too, does the demand for reliable and comparable financial information. Chapter 9 discusses the international accounting environment and compares accounting principles among several countries. This comparison illustrates the need for accounting standards to be in harmony with each other. Approaches to the harmonization of standards and the various organizations involved are identified.

The use of derivative financial instruments and the related accounting is a very complex subject that is discussed in a separate module. The principles set forth in FASB Statement Nos. 133 and 137 are set forth in a clear manner. The module may be used to support a standalone topic dealing with derivatives or as a preface to the multinational chapter dealing with foreign currency transactions. Regardless of how one chooses to use the module, students will benefit from an understanding of this important topic. The nature of derivatives is discussed along with a more in-depth look at the common types of derivative instruments. The basic accounting for derivatives held as an investment is illustrated. Options, futures, and interest rate swaps are used for illustrative purposes. The accounting for derivatives that are designated as a hedge is illustrated for both fair value and cash flow hedges. More specifically, the use of a derivative to hedge a recognized transaction (asset or liability), an unrecognized firm commitment, or a forecasted transaction is discussed and illustrated. Throughout the module, illustrative entries and graphics are used to improve the students' understanding of this topic.

Chapter 10 discusses the accounting for transactions that are denominated or settled in a foreign currency. Following this discussion, the hedging of such transactions with the use of forward contracts is introduced. Hedging foreign currency recognized transactions, unrecognized firm commitments, and forecasted transactions is discussed in order to illustrate the business purpose and special accounting associated with such hedging strategies in an international setting. The chapter is not overly complicated, given the fact that the concept of hedging and the special accounting given hedges has already been discussed in a separate module on derivatives and related accounting issues.

Chapter 11 demonstrates the remeasurement and/or translation of a foreign entity's financial statements into a U.S. investor's currency. Wherever possible, examples of footnote disclosure relating to international accounting issues are presented.

The usefulness of financial information naturally increases if it is communicated on a timely basis. Therefore, interim financial statements and reporting requirements are now widely accepted. In Chapter 12, the concept of an interim period as an integral part of a larger annual accounting period is set forth as a basis for explaining the specialized accounting principles of interim reporting. Particular attention is paid to the determination of the interim income tax provision including the tax implications of net operating losses. Chapter 12 also examines segmental reporting and the various disclosure requirements. A worksheet format for developing segmental data is used, and students are able to review the segmental footnote disclosure for a large public company. The section on segmental reporting is based on the principles of accounting set forth in FASB Statement No. 131.

Accounting for Partnerships (Chapters 13 and 14)

Chapters 13 and 14 take students through the entire life cycle of a partnership, beginning with formation and ending in liquidation. Although new forms of organization such as the limited liability corporation are available, partnerships continue to be a common form of organization. Practicing accountants must be aware of the characteristics of this form of organization and the unique accounting principles. The accounting aspects of profit and loss agreements, changes in the composition of partners (admissions and withdrawals), and partnership liquidations are fully illustrated. In addition to accounting principles, certain income tax principles relating to partnerships are set forth. The end-of-chapter material in this area focuses on evaluating various alternative strategies available to partners, for example, deciding whether it would be better to liquidate a partnership or admit a new partner.

Governmental and Not-for-Profit Accounting (Chapters 15–19)

Chapters 15–19 provide comprehensive coverage of accounting and financial reporting of state and local governments, colleges and universities, health-care entities, and not-for-profit organizations. Since the eighth edition of this text was released, standards-setting bodies have issued several accounting, auditing, and financial reporting standards that impact topics covered in these chapters. This new edition discusses recent developments in state and local government accounting and financial reporting, including the Governmental Accounting Standards Board's (GASB's) new financial reporting model (GASB Statement Nos. 34 and 35).

Chapter 15 covers the unique accounting and financial reporting issues of state and local governments. This chapter has been updated to cover the basics of accounting and financial reporting of the general fund and account groups. The chapter incorporates GASB guidance on accounting for revenues and expenditures using a financial resources measurement focus and a modified accrual basis of accounting. The unique ways of accounting for capital assets and long-term debt are detailed.

Chapter 16 details accounting for the specialized funds of government, e.g., those established to account for restricted operating resources, long-term construction projects or acquisition of major fixed assets, and servicing of principal and interest on long-term debt. The chapter also covers the unique accounting for various trust funds, including permanent funds and proprietary (business-type) funds. Accounting for pensions, post-retirement benefits other than pensions, recognition of assets and liabilities and related disclosures arising from securities lending transactions, accounting for certain investments at fair value, and accounting for landfill operations are illustrated.

Chapter 17 presents the government's basic financial statements required in the new reporting model. The unique features of the *funds-based statements*, which maintain the traditional measurement focus and basis of accounting for both governmental and proprietary funds, and the *government-wide statements*, which use the flow of economic resources measurement focus and full accrual basis of accounting for both the government and proprietary activities, are detailed. The chapter includes a discussion of the requirement for governments to report all capital assets, including retroactive reporting of infrastructure assets. Detailed illustrations help to clarify the new requirements to report depreciation or use the modified approach. The chapter contains a sample government-wide statement of net assets that reports governmental and proprietary activities in separate columns and a program- or function-oriented statement of activities. The requirements for the *management's discussion and analysis* (MD&A) are highlighted. Additional coverage surrounds key issues in governmental audit, including the single audit requirements, from AICPA, OMB, and GAO authoritative sources.

Chapter 18 begins with an overall summary of the accounting and financial reporting standards as they apply to all not-for-profit organizations. Coverage of FASB Statement Nos. 116, 117, 124, and 136 is included. Expanded illustrations enable the student to better grasp the unique requirements for revenue and expense recognition of not-for-profit organizations. External financial statements are illustrated without a funds structure. Since the FASB standards have shifted financial reporting away from fund accounting, funds are viewed as internal control and management tools throughout this chapter. The appendix to the chapter includes a discussion of the fund structure traditionally used in not-for-profit organizations and illustrates financial statements incorporating the funds.

Chapter 19 offers a complete description of accounting for private and governmental universities and private and governmental health-care organizations. The concepts from Chapters 15–18 are applied to the college and university accounting. A comparison of the governmental and nongovernmental reporting requirements and/or practices are highlighted to enable the student to gain a better understanding of differences between them. Updated illustrations and end-of-chapter materials are also designed to compare and contrast the government and private-sector requirements.

Fiduciary Accounting (Chapters 20 and 21)

The role of estate planning and the use of trusts are important to many individuals and present some unique accounting principles. The tax implications of estate planning are discussed so that the student has a basic understanding of this area. Various accounting reports necessary for the administration of an estate or trust are illustrated in Chapter 20.

No business is immune from financial difficulty. Chapter 21 discusses various responses to such difficulties, including troubled debt restructuring, quasi-reorganizations, corporate liquidations, and corporate reorganizations.

UNPARALLELED SUPPORT

Supplementary Materials for the Instructor:

Instructor's Resource CD (0-324-30406-4). The IRCD provides instructors with a convenient and complete source of support materials. It contains all of the **solutions manual** files (in Word and Excel), the **test bank** files (in Word and ExamView®), the **solutions transparency masters** files (in Word), the **Excel solutions** to the Excel tutorial, and the **PowerPoint®** files.

Solutions Manual (0-324-30403-X). This manual provides answers to all end-of-chapter "Understanding the Issues" questions and solutions to all exercises, problems, and cases, as well as the problems in the new end-of-text appendix. The electronic files for this printed ancillary can be found on the Instructor's Resource CD and in the Instructor Resources section of the text's Web site (http://fischer.swlearning.com).

Test Bank. Consisting of a variety of multiple-choice questions and short problems and the related solutions, this test bank had been newly updated and revised by Roy Weatherwax (University of Wisconsin—Whitewater). The content includes testing questions for the text chapters and the derivatives module. The test bank is available in electronically in Word and ExamView® on the Instructor's Resource CD.

Solution Transparencies (0-324-30405-6). The solutions to problems in Chapters 1–8 and 11 are provided on acetate transparencies upon request only. These are duplicates of the solutions in the solutions manual. The files for these are provided in Word on the Instructor's Resource CD.

Dedicated Product Web Site (http://fischer.swlearning.com). The Instructor Resources section contains:

- **PowerPoint® Presentations.** Author-developed electronic slides are available to enrich classroom teaching of concepts and practice.
- **Solutions Manual files, in Microsoft® Word and Excel.** The Excel files include the solutions to the Excel working papers.
- **Solutions Transparencies files, in Microsoft® Word.** Files are provided for the solutions transparencies for Chapters 1-8 and Chapter 11.
- **Check Figures.** A list of helpful check figures to the end-of-chapter problems is provided. Instructors may share these with their students, if desired.
- **Updates for new FASB and GASB statements.**
- **See below for the content of the Student Resources section.**

Valuable Supplementary Materials for the Student:

Student Companion Book. This support book, packaged free with each new copy of the text, contains the worksheets from Chapters 2–8 and Chapter 11. It also contains financial statements from the City of Milwaukee for use with Chapter 17. An icon in the margin indicates the worksheets that appear in this support book.

Excel Tutorial and Working Papers on CD. This CD, provided free with each new copy of the text, contains a step-by-step tutorial that carefully guides students as they learn how to set up worksheets in Excel and apply their consolidations knowledge learned in Chapters 2–6 and 11 of the text. In addition, Excel working papers for selected text problems are provided to assist students in completing homework. These selected end-of-chapter assignments are identified in the text by the icon shown here.

Study Guide (0-324-30402-1). New to the ninth edition, a comprehensive study guide provides students with various opportunities to review and practice text concepts. Each study guide chapter includes a chapter outline for review, true/false and multiple-choice questions, and practice problems. Solutions are given in the back of the study guide to allow students to check their work.

WebTutor™ ToolBox on WebCT™ or Blackboard®. Available free with the purchase of a new textbook, WebTutor ToolBox provides students with links to the rich content from the book companion web site. Available for WebCT and Blackboard only.

Dedicated Product Web Site (http://fischer.swlearning.com). The Student Resources section contains:

- **PowerPoint® Presentations**. Author-developed electronic slides are available to enrich classroom teaching of concepts and practice.
- **City of Milwaukee Financial Statements**. These statements provide a helpful reference for coverage in the governmental chapters.
- **Learning Objectives and Reflections**. These are repeated here to serve as a study aid.
- **Chapter Quizzes.**
- **Glossary.**
- **Content Updates relevant to changes in FASB standards.**

Acknowledgments

In preparation for the new edition, over one hundred Advanced Accounting instructors provided helpful responses to our survey. We thank them all for their timely information. In addition, the following individuals shared detailed ideas and suggestions for changes and improvements, of which many have been implemented in this ninth edition text and supplements.

Earl H. Godfrey, Jr., Gardner-Webb University
Paul D. Hutchison, University of North Texas
Cynthia Jeffrey, Iowa State University
Thomas D. Klein, University of Arizona
Heibatollah Sami, Temple University
Wesley A. Tucker, Austin Community College
Scott Whisenant, University of Houston

We thank the following ancillary writers and verifiers for their conscientious effort to make sure the support materials are accurate and tie closely to the text's up-to-date content.

Writers:
Test Bank and Web Quizzes: Roy Weatherwax (University of Wisconsin—Whitewater)

PowerPoint: Anne M. Oppegard (Augustana College)

Verifiers:
Solutions Manual: Dianne Feldman

Study Guide: Sara Wilson

Test Bank: James Emig

Their patience in the revision process is greatly appreciated.

Finally, a special thank you goes to Carol Fischer (University of Wisconsin—Waukesha) for her many hours of extensive, creative work on developing the Excel tutorial materials. This product provides easy-to-follow assistance to students as they learn the worksheet process.

Paul Fischer
William Taylor
Rita Cheng

About the Authors

Paul M. Fischer is the Jerry Leer Professor of Accounting and Director of Undergraduate Programs at the University of Wisconsin, Milwaukee. He teaches intermediate and advanced financial accounting and has received both the AMOCO Outstanding Professor Award and the School of Business Administration Advisory Council Teaching Award. He also teaches continuing education classes and provides executive training courses for several large corporations. He earned his undergraduate accounting degree at Milwaukee and earned an MBA and Ph.D. at the University of Wisconsin, Madison. Dr. Fischer is a CPA and is a member of the American Institute of CPAs, the Wisconsin Institute of CPAs, and the American Accounting Association. He is a past president of the Midwest Region of the American Accounting Association. Dr. Fischer has previously authored *Cost Accounting: Theory and Applications* (with Frank), *Financial Dimensions of Marketing Management* (with Crissy and Mossman), journal articles, and computer software. He actively pursues research and consulting interests in the areas of leasing, pension accounting, and business combinations.

William J. Taylor primarily teaches financial accounting and auditing at both the undergraduate and graduate levels. In addition, he is involved in providing executive training courses for several large corporations and through an executive MBA program. He has been recognized for his teaching excellence and has received both the AMOCO Outstanding Professor Award and the School of Business Administration Advisory Council Teaching Award. He earned his Ph.D. from Georgia State University and is a CPA and a CVA (Certified Valuation Analyst). His professional experience includes working for Deloitte and Touche and Arthur Andersen & Co. in their audit practices. His private consulting activities include business valuations, litigation services, and issues affecting closely held businesses. Dr. Taylor is a member of the American Institute of CPAs, the Wisconsin Institute of CPAs, and the National Association of Certified Valuation Analysts. He serves as a director and officer for a number of organizations.

Rita H. Cheng is Professor of Accounting at the University of Wisconsin, Milwaukee. She teaches government and not-for-profit accounting and advanced financial accounting. She has published numerous journal articles and technical reports and is often asked to speak on government and not-for-profit accounting topics. She has been recognized for her teaching excellence and is a recipient of the School of Business Administration Advisory Council Outstanding Teaching Award. She earned her Ph.D. in Accounting from Temple University. She is a CPA and a Certified Government Financial Manager. Dr. Cheng is actively involved in research focusing on the quality of accounting and financial reporting by state and local governments and the influence of accounting regulation on corporate business competitiveness. She is an active member of the Government and Nonprofit Section of the American Accounting Association and has served as the section's president. She has also testified before the Governmental Accounting Standards Board and coordinated the academic response to several proposed standards.

Brief Contents

Contents

Part 1
Combined Corporate Entities and Consolidations

PART

1 Combined Corporate Entities and Consolidations

The acquisition of one company by another is a commonplace business activity. Frequently, a company is groomed for sale. Also, the recent proliferation of new technology businesses and financial services firms that merge into larger companies is an expected, and often planned for, occurrence. For three decades, prior to 2001, accounting standards for business combinations had remained stable. Two models of recording combinations had coexisted. The pooling-of-interests method brought over the assets and liabilities of the acquired company at existing book values. The purchase method brought the acquired company's assets and liabilities to the acquiring firm's books at fair market value. FASB Statement No. 141, issued in July of 2001, ended the use of the pooling method and gave new guidance for recording business combinations under purchase accounting principles.

There are two types of accounting transactions to accomplish a combination. The first is to acquire the assets and liabilities of a company directly from the company itself by paying cash or by issuing bonds or stock. This is called a *direct asset acquisition* and is studied in Chapter 1. All of the theory involving combinations is first explained in this context.

The more common way to achieve control is to acquire a controlling interest, usually over 50%, in the voting common stock of another company. When two companies are under common control, a single set of *consolidated statements* must be prepared. Chapters 2 through 8 provide the methods for consolidating the separate statements of the affiliated firms into a consolidated set of financial statements. The consolidation process becomes a continuous activity, which is further complicated by continuing transactions between the affiliated companies.

On June 30, 2005, the FASB published two exposure drafts: "Consolidated Financial Statements, Including Accounting and Reporting of Noncontrolling Interests in Subsidiaries – A Replacement of ARB No. 51" and "Business Combinations – A Replacement of FASB No. 141." Special Appendix 2 analyzes and applies the provisions of these exposure drafts to Chapters 1–3 and 6–8.

CHAPTER 1

Business Combinations: America's Most Popular Business Activity, Bringing an End to the Controversy

"There are few areas of accounting that need improvement more than the accounting for business combinations. The current accounting literature allows two economically similar business combinations to be accounted for using different accounting methods that produce dramatically different financial results, which is confusing to investors."

Edmund L. Jenkins, Chairman of the Financial Accounting Standards Board
Testimony before the U.S. House of Representative, May 4, 2000

Learning Objectives

When you have completed this chapter, you should be able to

1. **Describe the major economic advantages of business combinations.**
2. **Differentiate between a purchase of assets and the purchase of a controlling interest of a company in terms of accounting procedures.**
3. **Demonstrate an understanding of the major difference between purchase and pooling-of-interests accounting.**
4. **Allocate the purchase cost to the assets and liabilities of the acquired company.**
5. **Account for assets and liabilities included in a business combination that involves goodwill.**
6. **Account for acquired assets and liabilities subsequent to a purchase, and apply impairment testing to goodwill.**
7. **Use zone analysis to account for purchases made at a price below the fair value of the company's net assets.**
8. **Explain the special issues that may arise in a purchase, and show how to account for them.**
9. **Be aware of transition rules for the use of pooling of interests and the procedures for existing goodwill.**
10. **(Appendix) Estimate the value of goodwill.**

Business combinations have been a common business transaction since the start of commercial activity. The concept is simple: A business combination is the group acquisition of all of a company's assets at a single price. *Business combinations* is a comprehensive term covering all acquisitions of one firm by another. Business combinations can be further categorized as either mergers or consolidations. The term *merger* applies when an existing company acquires another company and combines that company's operations with its own. The term *consolidation* applies when two or more previously separate firms merge into one new, continuing company. Business combinations make headlines not only in the business press but also in the local newspapers of the communities where the participating companies are located. While investors may delight in the price received for their interest, employees become concerned about continued employment, and local citizens worry about a possible relocation of the business.

The popularity of business combinations grew exponentially during the 1990s but peaked in the year 2001. From then until 2003, activity slowed considerably, with the dollar amount of deals falling even more than the number of deals. Exhibit 1-1 includes the Merger Completion Record covering 1995 through 2004. The drastic change in business combinations can be attributed to several causes.

- The growth period prior to 2001 reflects, in part, the boom economy of that period, especially in high-tech industries. There was also a motivation to complete acquisitions prior to July 1, 2001, when FASB Statement 141, Business Combinations, became effective. FASB Statement 141 eliminated the pooling-of-interests method. Pooling allowed companies to record the acquired assets at existing book value. This meant less depreciation and amortization charges in later periods. When the alternative purchase method was used prior to 2001, goodwill that was recorded could be amortized over four years. After 2001, FASB Statement 141 required goodwill impairment testing, which meant there was a risk of a major goodwill impairment loss in a future period.
- The decline in acquisition activity could also be attributed to the soft economy during the post-2001 period. The high-tech sector of the economy, which had been a hotbed of combinations, was especially weak. Add to it the increased scrutiny of companies being acquired, as caused by the accounting and business scandals of the period, and the motivation to acquire was lessened.
- Aside from broad-based accounting infractions, there arose specific allegations of *"precombination beautification."* It became clear that adjustments were made to the books of the company being acquired to make it look more valuable as a takeover candidate. This included arranging in advance to meet the pooling-of-interests criteria and making substantial write-offs to enhance postacquisition income. In the fall of 1999, it was alleged that Tyco International arranged to have acquired companies take major write-downs before being acquired by Tyco. This concern caused a major decline in the value of Tyco shares and led to stockholder suits against the company.

Exhibit 1-1
Merger Completion Record 1995–2004

10-Year Merger Completion Record 1995 to 2004

Year	No. of Deals	% Change	Value ($bil.)	% Change
1995	6,714	–	$389.8	–
1996	7,839	16.8%	565.6	45.1%
1997	9,127	16.4	776.1	37.2
1998	10,825	18.6	1,369.6	76.5
1999	9,641	-10.9	1,427.2	4.2
2000	9,313	-3.4	1,780.4	24.7
2001	6,577	-29.4	1,148.7	-35.5
2002	5,776	-12.2	622.0	-48.9
2003	6,173	6.9	518.3	-16.7
2004	6,919	12.1	823.5	58.9

Source: Mergers and Acquisitions Alamanac, February 2005, p. 25.

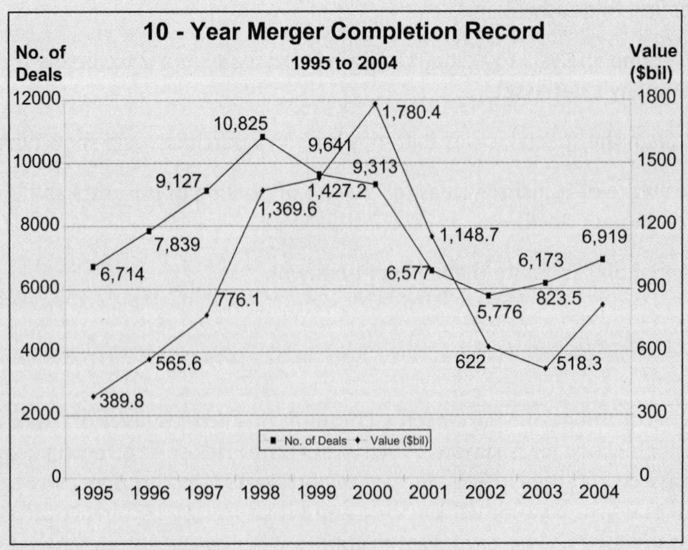

ECONOMIC ADVANTAGES OF COMBINATIONS

1

OBJECTIVE

Describe the major economic advantages of business combinations.

Business combinations are typically viewed as a way to jump-start economies of scale. Savings may result from the elimination of duplicative assets. Perhaps both companies will utilize common facilities and share fixed costs. There may be further economies as one management team replaces two separate sets of managers. It may be possible to better coordinate production, marketing, and administrative actions.

Horizontal combinations involve those where competitors serving similar functions hope to economize by combining those functions, such as the SBC acquisition of Ameritech Corporation. The following comments from the 1999 Annual Report of SBC Communications Inc. refer to its acquisition of Ameritech Corporation:

> *We grew our customer base significantly through the acquisition of Ameritech Corporation, which made us the local communications provider to about 53 million American homes and businesses. Being the incumbent provider is a huge advantage in a marketplace where customers increasingly look to one company to provide all their communications needs. This much larger customer base gives us the scope to achieve significant merger synergies and expand to 30 new major U.S. markets within the next two years.*[1]

Vertical combinations are the combinations of companies that were at different levels within the marketing chain. An example would be the acquisition of a food distribution company by a restaurant chain. The intended benefit of the vertical combination is the closer coordination of different levels of activity in a given industry. Recently, manufacturers have purchased retail dealers to control the distribution of their products. For example, the major automakers have been actively acquiring auto dealerships.

Conglomerates are combinations of dissimilar businesses. A company may want to diversify by entering a new industry. The purchase of Nabisco Holdings Corporation, a food product company, by Philip Morris, a tobacco company, was just such a diversification.

Tax Advantages of Combinations

Perhaps the most universal economic benefit in business combinations is a possible tax advantage. The owners of a small business, whether sole proprietors, partners, or shareholders, may wish to retire from active management of the company. If they were to sell their interest for cash or accept debt instruments, they would have an immediate taxable gain. If, however, they accept the common stock of another corporation in exchange for their interest and carefully craft the transaction as a "tax-free reorganization," they may account for the transaction as a tax-free exchange. No taxes are paid until the shareholders sell the shares received in the business combination. The shareholder records the new shares received (for tax purposes) at the book value of the exchanged shares.

In early 2005, SBC proposed to acquire AT&T. The following information was proposed to shareholders:

> *AT&T shareholders will receive .7792 shares of SBC common stock for each share of AT&T. Based on SBC's closing stock price on January 28, 2005, this exchange ratio equals $18.41 per share. In addition, at the time of closing, AT&T will pay its shareholders a special dividend of $1.30 per share. The stock consideration in the transaction is expected to be tax free to AT&T shareholders.*

Further tax advantages exist when the target company has reported losses on its tax returns in prior periods. Section 172 (b) of the Internal Revenue Code provides that operating losses can be carried back two years to obtain a refund of taxes paid in previous years. Should the loss not be offset by income in the two prior years, the loss may be carried forward up to 20 years to offset

1 SBC Communications Inc. Annual Report 1999, p. 2, San Antonio, Texas, 2000.

future taxable income, thus eliminating or reducing income taxes that would otherwise be payable. These loss maneuvers have little or no value to a target company that has not had income in the two prior years and does not expect profitable operations in the near future. However, tax losses are transferable in a business combination. To an acquiring company that has a profit in the current year and/or expects profitable periods in the future, the tax losses of a target company may have real value. That value, viewed as an asset by the acquiring company, will be reflected in the price paid. However, the acquiring company must exercise caution in anticipating the benefits of tax loss carryovers. The realization of the tax benefits may be denied if it can be shown that the primary motivation for the combination was the transfer of the tax loss benefit.

A tax benefit may also be available in a subsequent period as a single consolidated tax return is filed by the single remaining corporation. The losses of one of the affiliated companies can be used to offset the net income of another affiliated company to lessen the taxes that would otherwise be paid by the profitable company. In some cases, it may be disadvantageous to file as a consolidated company. Companies with low incomes may fare better by being taxed separately due to the progressive income tax rate structure. The marginal tax rate of each company may be lower than that resulting when the incomes of the two companies are combined.[2]

REFLECTION

- Business combinations may have economic advantages for a firm desiring to expand horizontally or vertically or may be a means of diversifying risk by purchasing dissimilar businesses.
- Potential sellers may be motivated by the tax advantages available to them in a business combination.

OBTAINING CONTROL

2
OBJECTIVE

Differentiate between a purchase of assets and the purchase of a controlling interest of a company in terms of accounting procedures.

Control of another company may be achieved by either acquiring the assets of the target company or purchasing a controlling interest (typically over 50%) in the target company's voting common stock. In an acquisition of assets, *all* of the company's assets are acquired *directly* from the company. In most cases, existing liabilities of the acquired company also are assumed. When assets are acquired and liabilities are assumed, we refer to the transaction as an acquisition of "net assets." Payment could be made in cash, exchanged property, or issuance of either debt or equity securities. It is common to issue securities, since this avoids depleting cash or other assets that may be needed in future operations. Legally, a *statutory consolidation* refers to the combining of two or more previously independent legal entities into one new legal entity. The previous companies are dissolved and are then replaced by a single continuing company. A *statutory merger* refers to the absorption of one or more former legal entities by another company that continues as the sole surviving legal entity. The absorbed company ceases to exist as a legal entity but may continue as a division of the surviving company.

In a *stock acquisition*, a controlling interest (typically, more than 50%) of another company's voting common stock is acquired. The company making the acquisition is termed the *parent*, and the company acquired is termed a *subsidiary*. Both the parent and the subsidiary remain separate legal entities and maintain their own financial records and statements. However, for external financial reporting purposes, the companies usually will combine their individual financial statements into a single set of consolidated statements. Thus, a consolidation may refer to a statutory combination or, more commonly, to the consolidated statements of a parent and its subsidiary.

There may be several advantages to obtaining control by purchasing a controlling interest in stock. Most obvious is that the total cost is lower, since only a controlling interest in the assets,

2 See Chapter 6, "Cash Flow, EPS, Taxation, and Unconsolidated Investments," pp. 329 to 388 .

and not the total assets, must be acquired. In addition, control through stock ownership may be simpler to achieve, since no formal negotiations or transactions with the acquired company's management are necessary. Further advantages may result from maintaining the separate legal identity of the former company. First of all, risk is lowered because the legal liability of each corporation is limited to its own assets. Secondly, separate legal entities may be desirable when only one of the companies is subject to government control. Lastly, there may be tax advantages resulting from the preservation of the legal entities.

Stock acquisitions are said to be "friendly" when the stockholders of the target corporation, as a group, decide to sell or exchange their shares. In such a case, an offer may be made to the board of directors by the acquiring company. If the directors approve, they will recommend acceptance of the offer to the shareholders, who are likely to approve the transaction. Often, a two-thirds vote is required. Once approval is gained, the exchange of shares will be made with the individual shareholders. If the officers decline the offer, or if no offer is made, the acquiring company may deal directly with individual shareholders in an attempt to secure a controlling interest. Frequently, the acquiring company may make a formal *tender offer.* The tender offer typically will be published in newspapers and will offer a greater-than-market price for shares made available by a stated date. The acquiring company may reserve the right to withdraw the offer if an insufficient number of shares are made available to it. Where management and/or a significant number of shareholders oppose the purchase of the company by the intended buyer, the acquisition is viewed as *hostile.* Unfriendly offers are so common that several standard defensive mechanisms have evolved. Following are the common terms used to describe these defensive moves:

Greenmail. The target company may pay a premium price ("greenmail") to purchase treasury shares. It may either buy shares already owned by a potential acquiring company or purchase shares from a current owner who, it is feared, would sell to the acquiring company. The price paid for these shares in excess of their market price may not be deducted from stockholders' equity; instead, it is expensed.[3]

White Knight. The target company locates a different company to acquire a controlling interest. This could occur when the original acquiring company is in a similar industry and it is feared that current management of the target company would be displaced. The replacement acquiring company, the "white knight," might be in a different industry and could be expected to keep current management intact.

Poison Pill. The "poison pill" involves the issuance of stock rights to existing shareholders to purchase additional shares at a price far below fair value. However, the rights are exercisable only when an acquiring company purchases or makes a bid to purchase a stated number of shares. The effect of the options is to substantially raise the cost to the acquiring company. If the attempt fails, there is at least a greater gain for the original shareholders.

Selling the Crown Jewels. This approach has the management of the target company selling vital assets (the "crown jewels") of the target company to others to make the company less attractive to the acquiring company.

Leveraged Buyouts. The management of the existing target company attempts to purchase a controlling interest in that company. Often, substantial debt will be incurred to raise the funds needed to purchase the stock, hence the term "leveraged buyout." When bonds are sold to provide this financing, the bonds may be referred to as "junk bonds," since they are often high-interest and high-risk due to the high debt-to-equity ratio of the resulting corporation.

Further protection against takeovers is offered by federal and state law. The Clayton Act of 1914 (section 7) is a federal law that prohibits business combinations in which "the effect of such acquisition may be substantially to lessen competition or to tend to create a monopoly."

---

3 Financial Accounting Standards Board, FASB Technical Bulletin, Nos. 85 and 86, *Accounting for a Purchase of Treasury Shares at a Price Significantly in Excess of the Current Market Price of the Shares* and the *Income Statement Classification of Costs Incurred in Defending Against a Takeover Attempt* (Stamford, CT, 1985).

The Williams Act of 1968 is a federal law that regulates tender offers; it is enforced by the SEC. Several states also have enacted laws to discourage hostile takeovers. These laws are motivated, in part, by the fear of losing employment and taxes.

Accounting Ramifications of Control

When control is achieved through an asset acquisition, the acquiring company records on its books the assets and assumed liabilities of the acquired company. From the acquisition date on, all transactions of both the acquiring and acquired company are recorded in one combined set of accounts. The only new skill one needs to master is the proper recording of the acquisition when it occurs. **Once the initial acquisition is properly recorded, subsequent accounting procedures are the same as for any single accounting entity.** Combined statements of the new, larger company for periods following the combination are automatic.

Accounting procedures are more involved when control is achieved through a stock acquisition. The controlling company, the parent, will record only an investment account to reflect its interest in the controlled company, the subsidiary. Both the parent and the subsidiary remain separate legal entities with their own separate sets of accounts and separate financial statements. Accounting theory holds that where one company has effective control over another, there is only one economic entity, and there should be only one set of financial statements that combines the activities of the entities under common control. The accountant will prepare a worksheet, referred to as the *consolidated worksheet*, that starts with the separate accounts of the parent and the subsidiary. Various adjustments and eliminations will be made on this worksheet to merge the separate accounts of the two companies into a single set of financial statements, which are called *consolidated statements*.

This chapter discusses business combinations resulting from asset acquisitions, since the accounting principles are more easily understood in this context. The principles developed are applied directly to stock acquisitions that are presented in the chapters that follow.

REFLECTION

- Control of another company is gained by either acquiring all of that firm's assets (and usually its liabilities) or by purchasing a controlling interest in that company's voting common stock.
- Control through an acquisition of assets requires the correct initial recording of the purchase. Combined statements for future periods are automatically produced.

3

OBJECTIVE

Demonstrate an understanding of the major difference between purchase and pooling-of-interests accounting.

PURCHASE VERSUS POOLING

Prior to the issuance of FASB Statement No. 141,[4] in 2001, there were two methods available to record the acquisition of a company. The primary method, applicable to most acquisitions, was the purchase method. Purchase accounting recorded all assets and liabilities at their estimated fair values. When the price exceeded the sum of the fair values for individual, identifiable assets, the excess was attributed to goodwill. Prior to July 2001, goodwill was amortized up to 40 years. With the issuance of FASB Statement No. 142,[5] goodwill is no longer amortized. It is now tested for, and, if necessary, adjusted for impairment. Under the pooling method, all assets and liabilities were transferred to the acquiring company at existing book values, and no goodwill could be created.

4 FASB Statement No. 141, *Business Combinations* (Norwalk, CT: Financial Accounting Standards Board, June 2001).

5 FASB Statement No. 142, *Goodwill and Other Intangible Assets* (Norwalk, CT: Financial Accounting Standards Board, June 2001).

Purchase and pooling were not meant to be alternative methods available for any acquisition. It was intended that pooling would apply only to a "merger of equals." Toward this objective, in 1970, *APB Opinion No. 16*[6] restricted the use of pooling to transactions that met a strict set of criteria. The most important of the criteria required that 90% of the acquired firm's common stock shares be received in exchange for the acquiring company's common stock. All shareholders had to be treated equally in the distribution of shares. Over time, many business combinations were "managed" so that they would meet the pooling criteria. This meant that the acquiring company would receive the more favorable accounting treatment. Several perceived advantages led firms to try to use the pooling method. Below is a summary of the major differences between pooling and purchases.

Differences in Accounting	Pooling Advantage
Asset valuation: Under purchase accounting, assets are recorded at fair value, and goodwill may be recorded. Under pooling, assets were recorded at existing book value (which is generally lower than fair value), and no goodwill was created.	◆ Reported income is higher because depreciation expense is lower and there was no new goodwill amortization. (Goodwill was amortized over 40 years or less prior to FASB Statement No. 142.) ◆ Return on assets is greater as a higher income is divided by a lower asset base.
Current-year income: Under purchase accounting, the acquired firm's income is added to the acquiring firm's income statement starting on the purchase date. Under pooling, the acquired firm's income was added as of the first day of the reporting period (no matter when the acquisition occurs).	◆ Assuming that the acquired firm is profitable, the acquiring firm was able to include the acquired firm's income, along with its own, for the entire year even if the pooling occurred on the last day of the reporting period.
Retained earnings: In a purchase, the acquired firm's retained earnings cannot be added to that of the purchasing company. Under pooling, the retained earnings of the acquired firm were added to that of the acquiring firm (with some rare exceptions).	◆ There was an instant increase in retained earnings, which made prior periods look more profitable. ◆ Prior-year income statements were retroactively combined; thus, the acquiring firm "pulled in" the income of the acquired firm in its prior-year statements.
Direct acquisition costs: In a purchase, these costs are added to the cost of the company purchased. They are typically included in goodwill, which used to increase goodwill amortization in later periods. Now these costs could increase impairment losses in future periods. In a pooling, these costs were expensed in the period of the purchase.	◆ Income could have been higher in later periods, since there was no amortization of these costs. However, pooling income was decreased in the period of the acquisition, since these costs were expensed in the period of acquisition.
Total equity: In a purchase, the fair value of the shares issued to pay for the purchase must be added to the equity of the acquiring firm. In a pooling, the book value of the acquired firm's equity was assigned to the shares issued by the acquiring firm.	◆ Total equity was usually lower. Return on equity was greater, since a higher income was divided by a lower equity amount.

6 Accounting Principles Board Opinion No. 16, *Business Combinations* (New York: American Institute of Certified Public Accountants, 1970).

The financial statement advantages incurred by the pooling method and the increased "gaming" to use the pooling method led to its elimination in July 2001 with the issuance of FASB Statement No. 141. The FASB held that fair values should be used in all combinations. The lack of comparability due to financial statement distortions, which resulted from companies using alternative methods, could no longer be tolerated. Even before the statement was issued, companies were reluctant to use pooling. In the fall of 1999, Tyco International was criticized for stimulating earnings growth through the use of the pooling method. This precipitated a significant decline in the value of Tyco's shares. Tyco later announced that it would no longer acquire companies as a pooling of interests.

Some foreign countries still allow the use of the pooling method when similar-size firms combine; it is difficult to determine the buyer versus the seller in such cases. There were, of course, many combinations in the United States, prior to July 2001, that used the pooling method.

REFLECTION

- Purchase and pooling created very different account values and caused significant differences in income.
- Pooling generally resulted in more favorable income statements in periods following the combination.
- Pooling accounting will no longer be allowed in the future.

4

OBJECTIVE

Allocate the purchase cost to the assets and liabilities of the acquired company.

VALUATION UNDER THE PURCHASE METHOD

The purchase of another business is viewed as a group purchase of assets. In most cases, the purchasing firm assumes the liabilities of the acquired company. This means that the purchaser will record the liabilities on its books and pay them as they become due. Where liabilities are assumed, the purchase is termed a *purchase of net assets.*

All assets acquired and liabilities assumed are to be recorded at individually determined fair values. *Fair value* is the amount that the asset or liability could be bought or sold for in a current, normal (nonforced) sale between willing parties. The preferred measure is quoted fair value, where an active market for the item exists. When there is not an active market, independent appraisals, discounted cash flow analysis, and other types of valuations are used to determine fair values. The list of assets includes intangible assets that may or may not be recorded on the selling company's books. If the price paid for the entire company exceeds the values assigned to individually identifiable net assets, the remaining balance is recorded as goodwill.

Assigning Value to Assets and Liabilities

The allocation of value begins by determining the fair value of tangible assets, including accounts such as receivables, inventory, investments, and fixed assets. Fair values are also established for liabilities. Typically, current liabilities are recorded at book value, since this tends to approximate fair value. However, long-term liabilities may have fair values at variance with recorded book value due to changes in interest rates.

The next step is to identify and value intangible assets. In order to record an intangible asset, the intangible must meet the general requirements to be recognized as an asset under FASB Conceptual Statements Nos. 5 and 6. An asset must have "probable future economic benefits defined or controlled by a particular entity as a result of past transactions and events."[7] In addi-

7 Statement of Financial Accounting Concepts No. 6, *Elements of Financial Statements* (Stamford, CT: Financial Accounting Standards Board, December 1985), par. 25.

tion, the attributes must be able to be reliably measured.[8] FASB Statement No. 141 further requires that an intangible asset meet one of the two following criteria:[9]

- Contractual or other legal rights assure control over future economic benefits. This includes rights that cannot be separated or transferred individually apart from other assets. For example, the Pepsi trademark could have a separate value even though, in reality, it could not be separated from the recipe and production process.
- The asset can be separated or divided so that it can be sold, exchanged, licensed, rented, or transferred. This does not require that a market for the asset currently exists. An intangible asset meets this test even if it could only be sold, exchanged, licensed, rented, or transferred with a group of other related assets or liabilities. For example, a client list of a service firm might have little value without the transfer of the company name in the same transaction.

Exhibit 1-2 contains examples of intangible assets that meet the criteria for recognition apart from goodwill.[10]

One of the intangible assets identified may be research and development (R&D). Value is assigned to R&D as though it was an asset, but the amount is usually expensed in the period of the purchase. The only case in which R&D can be treated as an asset and not immediately expensed is when there are R&D assets with multiple future uses.[11] Multiple-use R&D is later allocated to benefiting projects. A major purchase of R&D occurred in 1995 when IBM purchased Lotus Development Corporation for $2.9 billion. A $1.84 billion amount was assigned to R&D, which was immediately expensed. Imagine telling stockholders that it was prudent to buy this expense!

Recording Goodwill

When the price paid for a business exceeds the sum of the values assigned to identifiable assets, including intangible assets, the excess price is recorded as goodwill. Goodwill cannot be recorded unless the price paid for a company exceeds the total fair values assigned to all identifiable assets, net of liabilities assumed. Goodwill reflects intangible assets that could not be measured separately. It also includes the future benefits from other factors, such as excess earnings ability and achieving economies of scale. In this sense, goodwill is a residual value used to account for the price paid that cannot be assigned to other assets.

Prior to establishing the final price to be paid for a company, the buyer may want to estimate the value of goodwill attributable to anticipated excess earnings. Estimating the amount by which future income exceeds the amount considered normal for the industry can provide a reasonable value. The expected excess future income may be valued by multiplying it by the number of years it is expected to occur or by discounting the excess incomes to their present value. The appendix at the end of this chapter includes methods for estimating goodwill. In the final recording of goodwill, any estimate made becomes irrelevant. **Recorded goodwill is the excess of the price paid over the values assigned to all other net identifiable assets.**

8 Statement of Financial Accounting Concepts No. 5, *Recognition and Measurement in Financial Statements of Business Enterprises* (Stamford, CT: Financial Accounting Standards Board, December 1984), par. 63.
9 FASB Statement No. 141, *Business Combinations* (Norwalk, CT: Financial Accounting Standards Board, June 2001), par. 39.
10 Ibid., par. A14.
11 Financial Accounting Standards Board Interpretation No. 4, *Applicability of FASB Statement No. 2 to Business Combinations* (Stamford, CT: Financial Accounting Standards Board, 1975).

Exhibit 1-2
Examples of Intangibles

Examples of Intangibles	Meet the Contractual-Legal Criterion*	Meet the Separability Criterion
Marketing-related intangible assets:		
Trademarks, tradenames	X	
Service marks, collective marks, certification marks	X	
Trade dress (unique color, shape, or package design)	X	
Newspaper mastheads	X	
Internet domain names	X	
Noncompetition agreements	X	
Customer-related intangible assets:		
Customer lists		X
Order or production backlog	X	
Customer contracts and related customer relationships	X	
Noncontractual customer relationships		X
Artistic-related intangible assets:		
Plays, operas, ballets	X	
Books, magazines, newspapers, other literary works	X	
Musical works such as compositions, song lyrics, advertising jingles	X	
Pictures, photographs	X	
Video and audiovisual material, including motion pictures, music videos, television programs	X	
Contract-based intangible assets:		
Licensing, royalty, standstill agreements	X	
Advertising, construction, management, service or supply contracts	X	
Lease agreements	X	
Construction permits	X	
Franchise agreements	X	
Operating and broadcast rights	X	
Use rights such as drilling, water, air, mineral, timber cutting, and route authorities	X	
Servicing contracts, such as mortgage servicing contracts	X	
Employment contracts	X	
Technology-based intangible assets:		
Patented technology	X	
Computer software and mask work	X	
Unpatented technology		X
Databases, including title plants		X
Trade secrets, such as formulas, processes, and recipes	X	

* Some intangibles listed may also meet the separability criterion.

REFLECTION

- Under the purchase method, assets and liabilities generally are recorded at fair value.
- Identifiable intangible assets are included in the assets recorded at fair value.
- Goodwill is the excess of the price paid over the amount assigned to identifiable net assets.

RECORDING A PURCHASE WITH GOODWILL

5 OBJECTIVE

Account for assets and liabilities included in a business combination that involves goodwill.

When the purchase of an existing company is being considered, a thorough appraisal should be made to determine the fair value of the company's assets and liabilities. A complete appraisal will usually precede negotiations over the price to be paid. Generally, the prospective purchaser will seek the seller's permission to conduct a preacquisition audit. The audit will determine whether all assets and liabilities are properly recorded. The purchaser knows that, while book values may be indicative of the fair values of most current assets, they seldom represent a reasonable fair value for fixed and intangible assets. Even among current assets, an inventory valued on a LIFO basis has value unrelated to fair value. Fixed and intangible assets are recorded at historical cost less an arbitrary estimate of accumulated depreciation or amortization, which has little to do with fair value. Intangible assets, such as customer lists, brand names, and favorable lease agreements, may exist yet not be recorded. Some liabilities may not be recorded at an amount that represents fair value because the fair value of liabilities changes as interest rates change.

The company being purchased may have goodwill on its books (arising from a prior purchase of another company). **Existing goodwill is assigned no value in a purchase.** The only goodwill recorded is that caused by the current purchase.

Acknowledging the limitations of (and for some assets, the absence of) recorded book values, the purchaser will typically engage an independent consultant to estimate the fair value of the individual assets to be acquired and the liabilities to be assumed. These estimates of fair value are of primary consideration when determining the price to be paid for the entire company.

To illustrate, assume that Acquisitions Inc. is considering the purchase of Johnson Company. The audited balance sheet on the date of purchase, December 31, 20X1, and a comparison of fair and book values follows:

Johnson Company
Balance Sheet
December 31, 20X1

Assets			Liabilities and Equity		
Current assets:					
Accounts receivable	$28,000		Current liabilities	$ 5,000	
Inventory	40,000		Bonds payable	20,000	
Total current assets		$ 68,000	Total liabilities		$ 25,000
Long-term assets:					
Land	$10,000				
Buildings (net)	40,000		Stockholders' equity:		
Equipment (net)	20,000		Common stock, $1 par	$ 1,000	
Patent (net)	15,000		Paid-in capital in excess of par	59,000	
Goodwill (existing)	20,000		Retained earnings	88,000	

(continued)

Assets		Liabilities and Equity	
Total long-term assets	105,000	Total stockholders' equity.	148,000
Total assets	$173,000	Total liabilities and equity	$173,000

Johnson Company
Fair Values
December 31, 20X1

Assets	Book Value	Fair Value	Liabilities and Equity	Book Value	Fair Value
Current assets:					
Accounts receivable.	$ 28,000	$ 28,000	Current liabilities	$ 5,000	$ 5,000
Inventory	40,000	45,000	Bonds payable	20,000	21,000
Total current assets	$ 68,000	$ 73,000	Total liabilities	$ 25,000	$ 26,000
Long-lived assets:					
Land	$ 10,000	$ 50,000			
Buildings (net)	40,000	80,000			
Equipment (net)	20,000	50,000			
Patent (net)	15,000	30,000			
Brand-name copyright* . . .	—	**40,000**			
Goodwill (preexisting)	20,000				
Total long-lived assets	$105,000	$250,000	Value of net assets		
Total assets	$173,000	$323,000	(assets – liabilities)	$148,000	$297,000

*Previously unrecorded assets.

Let us assume that the price to be paid to the seller for the net assets is $350,000. Direct acquisition costs of $10,000 are added to the purchase price (see below). The total price paid is $360,000. Prior to the issuance of FASB Statement No. 141, it would have been common to seek fair value for only the existing recorded accounts and to treat any price paid in excess of their total as goodwill. In the above example, the fair value of the net recorded assets (without the copyright) is $257,000 ($297,000 net assets – $40,000 copyright). The remaining price of $103,000 ($360,000 price – $257,000) could have been recorded as goodwill. But under FASB Statement No. 141, goodwill exists only to the extent that the price paid exceeds the fair values assigned to all identifiable assets including intangible assets that may not have existed on the books of the selling company. Notice that the sum of the fair values assigned to identifiable net assets is **$297,000** ($323,000 assets – $26,000 liabilities). Thus, at a price of $360,000, **goodwill would be recorded at $63,000,** the excess of the $360,000 total price over the $297,000 assigned to all net assets, including identifiable intangible assets, at fair value.

Entry to Record the Purchase

Assume that Acquisitions Inc. has agreed to pay $350,000 to Johnson Company for its net assets. Payment could be made in cash or by issuing bonds or stocks to Johnson's shareholders. For our initial analysis, we will assume that $350,000 cash is paid to Johnson Company and that another $10,000 is paid to independent attorneys and accountants for direct acquisition costs. The journal entry to record the purchase would be as follows:

Accounts Receivable	28,000	
Inventory	45,000	

Land	50,000	
Building	80,000	
Equipment	50,000	
Patent	30,000	
Brand-Name Copyright	40,000	
Goodwill (based on current purchase)	**63,000**	
Current Liabilities		5,000
Bonds Payable		20,000
Premium on Bonds Payable		1,000
Cash (for direct acquisition costs)		10,000
Cash (payment to Johnson Company)		350,000
Dr. = Cr. Check Totals	*386,000*	*386,000*

Note that all fixed and intangible assets are recorded at their estimated fair value, with no allowance for accumulated depreciation or amortization. Any adjustment of bonds payable is accomplished using a premium (in this case) or discount account. This is done to maintain a record of the legal face value.

The more common method of payment is for the purchaser to issue additional shares of its common stock. This preserves both cash and future borrowing ability. Let us assume that Acquisitions Inc. will issue $1 par value shares with a fair value of $50 per share. Acquisitions Inc. would have to issue 7,000 shares ($350,000/$50 per share). The journal entry to record the purchase follows. Note that the only difference between this and the preceding entry is the replacement of the credit to cash (for the payment to Johnson) with a credit to the buyers' paid-in equity accounts.

Accounts Receivable	28,000	
Inventory	45,000	
Land	50,000	
Building	80,000	
Equipment	50,000	
Patent	30,000	
Brand-Name Copyright	40,000	
Goodwill	**63,000**	
Current Liabilities		5,000
Bonds Payable		20,000
Premium on Bonds Payable		1,000
Cash (for direct acquisition costs)		10,000
Common Stock ($1 par, 7,000 shares)		7,000
Paid-In Capital in Excess of Par ($350,000 – 7,000 par)		343,000
Dr. = Cr. Check Totals	*386,000*	*386,000*

Issue costs resulting from the issuance of stock as consideration given in a purchase arrangement are not included in the cost of the company purchased. Instead, issue costs are subtracted from the amount assigned to the stock issued. Issue costs could always be recorded in a separate entry so that there is no opportunity to confuse them with the price paid for the company purchased. If the issue costs were $5,000 in the above example, the added entry would be as follows:

Paid-In Capital in Excess of Par (reduced for issue costs)	5,000	
Cash (for payment of issue costs)		5,000

Required Disclosure

For the period in which a purchase occurs, a schedule must be presented in the notes to the statements that discloses the fair value to the accounts of the company purchased. The schedule would be prepared as follows for the purchase of Johnson Company:

Schedule of Assigned Values
Johnson Company Purchase
December 31, 20X1

Accounts	Assigned Value
Accounts Receivable	$ 28,000
Inventory	45,000
Land	50,000
Building	80,000
Equipment	50,000
Patent	30,000
Brand-Name Copyright	40,000
Goodwill	63,000
Current Liabilities	(5,000)
Bonds Payable	(20,000)
Premium on Bonds Payable	(1,000)
Net assets acquired	**$360,000**

The following additional information must be included in the notes to the financial statements of the acquiring company in the period the purchase occurs:

1. Name and description of the firm purchased and the percentage of voting shares purchased.
2. The primary reason for the purchase and the factors that led to the price if goodwill is recorded.
3. The portion of the financial reporting period for which the results of the purchased firm are included.
4. The cost of the company purchased and, if stock was issued as payment, the value assigned to the shares including a description of how the value per share was determined.
5. Disclosure of contingent payment agreements, options, or commitments included in the purchase agreement and the accounting methods that would be used if the contingency occurs.
6. The amount of in-process R&D purchased and written off during the period.
7. Disclosures as to any purchase price allocation that has not been finalized and an explanation as to why it has not been completed. In subsequent periods, any adjustment to the allocation is to be disclosed.

When the amount of goodwill recorded is significant with respect to other assets acquired, disclosure is also required as to:

1. The amount of goodwill related to each reporting segment (under FASB Statement No. 131).
2. The amount of acquired goodwill that is tax deductible.

Pro Forma Income Disclosures. Pro forma income disclosure is also required in the period in which the purchase occurs. The disclosure seeks to provide consistency over the current and prior periods by showing what the income would have been had the purchase occurred at the *start of the prior accounting period.* The following pro forma disclosures are made:

1. Results of operations for the current period as if the purchase occurred at the beginning of the period (unless the purchase was at or near the beginning of the period).
2. Results of operations for the immediately prior period if comparative statements are issued.

The statements themselves are not adjusted. The footnote must include, at a minimum, revenue, income before extraordinary items and cumulative effect of accounting changes, net income and earnings per share. This disclosure would include the impact of the values assigned to accounts in the purchase transaction. Exhibit 1-3 presents the disclosure for business combinations from the 2004 Annual Report of Quest Diagnostics Inc.

Exhibit 1-3
Quest Diagnostics Incorporated and Subsidiaries
Notes to consolidated Financial Statements
(dollars in thousands unless otherwise indicated)

3. Business Acquisitions

Acquisition of Unilab Corporation

On February 28,2003, the Company completed the acquisition of Unilab Corporation ("Unilab"), the leading commercial clinical laboratory in California. In connection with the acquisition, the Company paid $297 million in cash and issued 7.1 million shares of Quest Diagnostics common stock to acquire all of the outstanding capital stock of Unilab. In addition, the Company reserved approximately 0.3 million shares of Quest Diagnostics common stock for outstanding stock options of Unilab which were converted upon the completion of the acquisition into options to acquire shares of Quest Diagnostics common stock (the "converted options").

The aggregate purchase price of $698 million included the cash portion of the purchase price of $297 million and transaction costs of approximately $20 million, with the remaining portion of the purchase price paid through the issuance of 7.1 million shares of Quest Diagnostics common stock (valued at $372 million or $52.80 per share, based on the average closing stock price of Quest Diagnostics common stock for the five trading days ended March 4, 2003) and the issuance of approximately 0.3 million converted options (valued at approximately $9 million, based on the Black Scholes option-pricing model). Of the total transaction costs incurred, approximately $8 million was paid during fiscal 2002.

In conjunction with the acquisition of Unilab, the Company repaid $220 million of debt, representing substantially all of Unilab's then existing outstanding debt, and related accrued interest. Of the $220 million, $124 million represents payments related to the Company's cash tender offer, which was completed on March 7, 2003, for all of the outstanding $101 million principal amount and related accrued interest of Unilab's $12\frac{3}{4}$% Senior Subordinated Notes due 2009 and $23 million of related tender premium and associated tender offer costs.

The Company financed the cash portion of the purchase price and related transaction costs, and the repayment of substantially all of Unilab's outstanding debt and related accrued interest, with the proceeds from a new $450 million amortizing term loan due June 2007 and cash on-hand. During 2003, the Company repaid $145 million of principal outstanding under the term loan due June 2007. During 2004, the Company refinanced the remaining $305 million of principal outstanding under the term loan due June 2007 (see Note 10).

As part of the Unilab acquisition, Quest Diagnostics acquired all of Unilab's operations, including its primary testing facilities in Los Angeles, San Jose and Sacramento, California, and approximately 365 patient service centers and 35 rapid response laboratories and approximately 4,100 employees. As the leading commercial clinical laboratory in California, the acquisition of Unilab further solidified the Company's leading position within the clinical laboratory testing industry, and further enhanced its national network and access to its comprehensive range of services for physicians, hospitals, patients, and healthcare insurers.

In connection with the acquisition of Unilab, as part of a settlement agreement with the United States Federal Trade Commission, the Company entered into an agreement to sell to Laboratory Corporation of America Holdings, Inc., ("LabCorp"), certain assets in northern California for $4.5 million, including the assignment of agreements with four independent physician associations ("IPA") and leases for 46 patient service centers [five of which also serve as rapid response laboratories (the "Divestiture")]. Approximately $27 million in annual net revenues were generated by capitated fees under the IPA agreements and associated fee-for-service testing for physicians whose patients use these patient service centers, as well as from specimens received directly from the IPA physicians. The Company completed the transfer of assets and assignment of the IPA agreements to LabCorp and recorded a $1.5 million gain in the third quarter of 2003 in connection with the Divestiture, which is included in "other operating expense (income), net" within the consolidated statements of operations.

The acquisition of Unilab was accounted for under the purchase method of accounting. As such, the cost to acquire Unilab has been allocated to the assets and liabilities acquired based on estimated fair values as of the closing date. The consolidated financial statements include the results of operations of Unilab subsequent to the closing of the acquisition.

(continued)

Exhibit 1-3 *(Continued)*

The following table summarizes the Company's purchase price allocation related to the acquisition of Unilab based on the estimated fair value of the assets acquired and liabilities assumed on the acquisition date.

	Fair Values as of February 28, 2003
Current assets	$193,798
Property, plant and equipment	10,855
Goodwill	735,853
Other assets	47,777
Total assets acquired	988,283
Current liabilities	62,002
Long-term liabilities	7,369
Long-term debt	221,291
Total liabilities assumed	290,662
Net assets acquired	$697,621

Based on management's review of the net assets acquired and consultations with third-party valuation specialists, no intangible assets meeting the criteria under SFAS No. 141, "Business Combinations," were identified. Of the $736 million allocated to goodwill, approximately $85 million is expected to be deductible for tax purposes.

Acquisition of American Medical Laboratories, Incorporated

On April 1, 2002, the Company completed its acquisition of all of the outstanding voting stock of American Medical Laboratories, Incorporated ("AML"), and an affiliated company of AML, LabPortal, Inc. ("LabPortal"), a provider of electronic connectivity products, in an all-cash transaction with a combined value of approximately $500 million, which included the assumption of approximately $160 million in debt.

Through the acquisition of AML, Quest Diagnostics acquired all of AML's operations, including two full-service laboratories, 51 patient service centers, and hospital sales, service, and logistics capabilities. The all-cash purchase price of approximately $335 million and related transaction costs, together with the repayment of approximately $150 million of principal and related accrued interest, representing substantially all of AML's debt, was financed by Quest Diagnostics with cash on-hand, $300 million of borrowings under its secured receivables credit facility, and $175 million of borrowings under its unsecured revolving credit facility. During 2002, Quest Diagnostics repaid all of the $475 million in borrowings related to the acquisition of AML.

The acquisition of AML was accounted for under the purchase method of accounting. As such, the cost to acquire AML has been allocated to the assets and liabilities acquired based on estimated fair values as of the closing date. The consolidated financial statements include the results of operations of AML subsequent to the closing of the acquisition.

The following table summarizes the Company's purchase price allocation related to the acquisition of AML based on the estimated fair value of the assets acquired and liabilities assumed on the acquisition date.

	Fair Values as of April 1, 2002
Current assets	$ 83,403
Property, plant and equipment	31,475
Goodwill	426,314
Other assets	8,211
Total assets acquired	549,403

(continued)

Exhibit 1-3 *(Continued)*

	Fair Values as of April 1, 2002
Current portion of long-term debt	$ 11,834
Other current liabilities	51,403
Long-term debt	139,465
Other liabilities	4,925
Total liabilities assumed	207,627
Net assets acquired	$341,776

Based on management's review of the net assets acquired and consultations with valuation specialists, no intangible assets meeting the criteria under SFAS No. 141, "Business Combinations," were identified. Of the $426 million allocated to goodwill, approximately $17 million is expected to be deductible for tax purposes.

Acquisition of LabPortal

The all-cash purchase price for LabPortal of approximately $4 million and related transaction costs, together with the repayment of all of LabPortal's outstanding debt of approximately $7 million and related accrued interest, was financed by Quest Diagnostics with cash on-hand. The acquisition of LabPortal was accounted for under the purchase method of accounting. As such, the cost to acquire LabPortal has been allocated to the assets and liabilities acquired based on estimated fair values as of the closing date, including approximately $8 million of goodwill. The consolidated financial statements include the results of operations of LabPortal subsequent to the closing of the acquisition.

Pro Forma Combined Financial Information

The following unaudited pro forma combined financial information for the years ended December 31, 2003 and 2002 assumes that the Unilab and AML acquisitions and the Divestiture were completed on January 1, 2002 (in thousands, except per share data):

	2003	2002
Net revenues	$4,803,875	$4,607,242
Net income	444,944	365,448
Basic earnings per common share:		
Net income	$ 4.26	$ 3.53
Weighted averaged common shares outstanding—basic	104,552	103,522
Diluted earnings per common share:		
Net income	$ 4.08	$ 3.36
Weighted average common shares outstanding—diluted	109,936	109,783

The pro forma combined financial information presented above reflects certain reclassifications to the historical financial statements of Unilab and AML to conform the acquired companies' accounting policies and classification of certain costs and expenses to that of Quest Diagnostics. These adjustments had no impact on pro forma net income. Pro forma results for the year ended December 31, 2003, exclude $14.5 million of direct transaction costs, which were incurred and expensed by Unilab in conjunction with its acquisition by Quest Diagnostics. Pro forma results for the year ended December 31, 2002, exclude $14.5 million and $6.3 million, respectively, of direct transaction costs, which were incurred and expensed by AML and Unilab, respectively, in conjunction with their acquisitions by Quest Diagnostics.

4. Integration of Acquired Businesses

In July 2002, the FASB issued SFAS No. 146, " Accounting for Costs Associated with Exit or Disposal Activities " ("SFAS 146"). SFAS 146, which the Company adopted effective January 1, 2003,

Exhibit 1-3 *(Continued)*

requires that a liability for a cost associated with an exit activity, including those related to employee termination benefits and contractual obligations, be recognized when the liability is incurred, and not necessarily the date of an entity's commitment to an exit plan, as under previous accounting guidance. The provisions of SFAS 146 apply to integration costs associated with actions that impact the employees and operations of Quest Diagnostics. Costs associated with actions that impact the employees and operations of an acquired company, such as Unilab, are accounted for as a cost of the acquisition and included in goodwill in accordance with EITF No. 95-3, "Recognition of Liabilities in Connection with a Purchase Business Combination."

Integration of Unilab Corporation

During the fourth quarter of 2003, the Company finalized its plan related to the integration of Unilab into Quest Diagnostics' laboratory network. As part of the plan, following the sale of certain assets to LabCorp as part of the Divestiture, the Company closed its previously owned clinical laboratory in the San Francisco Bay area and completed the integration of remaining customers in the northern California area to Unilab's laboratories in San Jose and Sacramento. The Company currently operates two laboratories in the Los Angeles metropolitan area. As part of the integration plan, the Company plans to open a new regional laboratory in the Los Angeles metropolitan area into which it will integrate all of its business in the area.

During 2003, the company recorded $9 million of costs associated with executing the Unilab integration plan. The majority of these integration costs related to employee severance and contractual obligations associated with leased facilities and equipment. Employee groups affected as a result of this plan include those involved in the collection and testing of specimens, as well as administrative and other support functions. Of the $9 million in costs, $7.9 million was recorded in the fourth quarter of 2003 and related to actions that impact the employees and operations of Unilab, was accounted for as a cost of the Unilab acquisition and included in goodwill. Of the $7.9 million, $6.8 million related to employee severance benefits for approximately 150 employees, with the reminder primarily related to contractual obligations. In addition, $1.1 million of integration costs, related to actions that impact Quest Diagnostics' employees and operations and comprised principally of employee severance benefits for approximately 30 employees, were accounted for as a charge to earnings in the third quarter of 2003 and included in "other operating expense (income), net" within the consolidated statements of operations. As of December 31, 2004 and 2003, accruals related to the Unilab integration plan totaled $3.0 million and $6.6 million, respectively. The remaining accruals at December 31, 2004, substantially all of which represented severance costs, are expected to be paid in 2005.

Integration of American Medical Laboratories, Incorporated

During the third quarter of 2002, the Company finalized its plan related to the integration of AML into Quest Diagnostics' laboratory network. The plan focused principally on improving customer service by enabling the Company to perform esoteric testing on the east and west coasts of the United States, and redirecting certain physician testing volumes within its national network to provide more local testing. As part of the plan, the Company's Chantilly, Virginia laboratory, acquired as part of the AML acquisition, has become the primary esoteric testing laboratory and hospital service center for the eastern United States, complementing the Company's Nichols Institute esoteric testing facility in San Juan Capistrano, California. Esoteric testing volumes have been redirected within the Company's national network to provide customers with improved turnaround time and customer service. The Company has completed the transition of certain routine clinical laboratory testing previously performed in the Chantilly, Virginia laboratory to other testing facilities within the Company's regional laboratory network. A reduction in staffing occurred as the Company executed the integration plan and consolidated duplicate or overlapping functions and facilities. Employee groups affected as a result of this plan included those involved in the collection and testing of specimens, as well as administrative and other support functions.

In connection with the AML integration plan, the Company recorded $11 million of costs associated with executing the plan. The majority of these integration costs related to employee severance and contractual obligations associated with leased facilities and equipment. Of the total costs indicated above, $9.5 million, related to actions that impact the employees and operations of AML, was accounted for as a cost of the AML acquisition and included in goodwill. Of the $9.5 million, $5.9 million related to employee severance benefits for approximately 200 employees, with

Exhibit 1-3 *(Concluded)*

the remainder primarily related to contractual obligations associated with leased facilities and equipment. In addition, $1.5 million of integration costs, related to actions that impact Quest Diagnostics' employees and operations and comprised principally of employee severance benefits for approximately 100 employees, were accounted for as a charge to earnings in the third quarter of 2002 and included in "other operating expense (income), net" within the consolidated statements of operations. As of December 31, 2003, accruals related to the AML integration plan totaled $4.1 million. The actions associated with the AML integration plan, including those related to severed employees, were completed in 2003. The remaining accruals associated with the AML integration were not material at December 31, 2004.

Integration of Clinical Diagnostic Services, Inc.

During 2001, the Company acquired Clinical Diagnostics Services, Inc. ("CDS"), which operated a diagnostic testing laboratory and more than 50 patient service centers in New York and New Jersey. During the fourth quarter of 2002, the Company finalized its plan related to the integration of CDS into Quest Diagnostics' laboratory network in the New York metropolitan area. Of the $13.3 million of costs recorded in the fourth quarter of 2002 in connection with the execution of the CDS integration plan, all of which were associated with actions impacting the employees and operations of CDS, $3 million related to employee severance benefits for approximately 150 employees with the remainder primarily associated with remaining contractual obligations under facility and equipment leases. The costs outlined above were recorded as a cost of the acquisition and included in goodwill. As of December 31, 2004 and 2003, accruals related to the CDS integration plan totaled $4.0 million and $5.3 million, respectively. The actions associated with the CDS integration plan, including those related to severed employees, were completed in 2003. The remaining accruals at December 31, 2004, substantially all of which represented remaining contractual obligations under facility leases, have terms extending beyond 2005.

Source: Quest Diagnostics Inc. 10-K 2004-12-31.

Accounting for the Purchase by the Selling Company

The goodwill recorded by the buyer is not tied to the gain (or loss) recorded by the seller. The seller records the removal of net assets at their book values. The excess of the price received by the seller ($350,000[12]) over the sum of the net asset book values ($173,000 assets − $25,000 liabilities) is recorded as a gain on the sale. In this case, the gain is $202,000. The entry on Johnson's books would be as follows:

Investment in Acquisitions Inc. Stock	350,000	
Current Liabilities	5,000	
Bonds Payable	20,000	
Accounts Receivable		28,000
Inventory		40,000
Land		10,000
Buildings (net)		40,000
Equipment (net)		20,000
Patent (net)		15,000
Goodwill (preexisting)		20,000
Gain on Sale of Business		202,000
Dr. = Cr. Check Totals	*375,000*	*375,000*

12 Remember that the $10,000 in direct acquisition costs is paid by the purchaser to a third party, not to the seller.

The only remaining asset of Johnson Company is cash. Johnson would typically distribute the stock received to its shareholders and cease operations.

REFLECTION

- The buyer records all accounts, including identifiable assets, at fair value.
- Existing book values, including existing goodwill, do not affect the amount assigned to accounts.
- In the period of the purchase, the amounts assigned to accounts must be disclosed.
- The entry of the seller is based on book values and records a gain for the excess of the price over the net book value of the assets transferred.

6

OBJECTIVE

Account for acquired assets and liabilities subsequent to a purchase, and apply impairment testing to goodwill.

ACCOUNTING FOR THE ACQUIRED ASSETS AND LIABILITIES AFTER THE PURCHASE

Normal depreciation and amortization procedures are applied to the newly acquired identifiable tangible assets and to the liabilities. FASB Statement No. 142 requires special amortization and impairment procedures for intangible assets. Goodwill is not subject to amortization but has unique impairment testing procedures.

Tangible Assets and All Liabilities

All tangible asset accounts are considered newly acquired and are accounted for based on their assigned values and, when applicable, anticipated lives. The accounting procedures for the acquired tangible accounts are as follows:

Inventory—Maintained at assigned fair value until sold. Upon sale, the fair value is assigned to the cost of goods sold.

Receivables—Accounts and notes receivable may be adjusted to a lower amount by using an allowance for bad debts. Once created, the allowance is accounted for in the normal manner. Adjustments to notes receivable and other debt investments may be necessary due to a change in interest rates. An adjustment to reflect a change in interest rates is amortized as a premium or discount over the remaining term of the investment.

Equity Investments—They are adjusted to a new fair value that will be their cost for all subsequent fair value adjustments and sales.

Fixed Assets—These are fixed assets used by the business, such as land, buildings, and equipment. Except for land, depreciation will be calculated on the newly assigned value, using the newly estimated salvage value and remaining life. Any appropriate depreciation method may be used. Long-lived assets are also subject to impairment testing under FASB Statement No. 121. Impairment testing requires that assets, or groups of assets, be tested for future cash flows upon the occurrence of certain events that could suggest a decline in value. When the anticipated, undiscounted, future cash flows are less than carrying value, the assets are adjusted down to their fair value.[13]

Liabilities—Current liabilities are recorded at the amounts that are expected to be paid. Long-term liabilities are recorded at their legal face value, and a premium or discount is recorded and then amortized over the life of the liability.

13 FASB Statement No. 121, *Impairment Testing of Long-lived Assets and for Long-lived Assets to Be Disposed of* (Norwalk, CT: Financial Accounting Standards Board, 1995), pars. 4–11.

Separately Identified Intangible Assets

Intangible assets with a determinable life are to be amortized over their useful economic lives. Where a residual value at the end of the economic life can be estimated, it is subtracted from the amount to be amortized. There is no maximum amortization period. The amortization method should reflect the pattern of benefits conveyed by the asset, but if the pattern cannot be reliably determined, the straight-line method is to be used. As with other long-lived assets, intangible assets are subject to normal asset impairment testing under FASB Statement No. 121.

In the period that the purchase occurs, there must be a footnote disclosure of the following information if intangible assets were a material amount of the price paid:

- For intangible assets subject to amortization, disclose the following:
  1. The total amount assigned to intangible assets and the amounts assigned to each major class of intangible assets.
  2. The amount of any significant residual values in total and by major classes of intangible assets.
  3. The weighted average amortization period applicable to all intangible assets and to major classes of intangible assets.
- For intangible assets not subject to amortization, disclose the total amount assigned to these assets and to each major class of such intangible assets.

FASB Statement No. 142 states that "If no legal, regulatory, contractual, competitive, economic, or other factors limit the useful life of the intangible asset to the reporting entity, the useful life of the asset shall be considered to be indefinite."[14]

Intangible assets with indefinite economic lives are not amortized until a determinable life can be established. An indefinite economic life is not synonymous with an infinite life; rather, it means that the life extends beyond the foreseeable horizon. Intangible assets not subject to amortization are subject to separate impairment testing on an annual basis or on an interim basis if it appears that impairment has occurred. An impairment loss is recorded if the fair value of the intangible asset is less than the book value.

The notes to each period's financial statements must include total carrying amounts and cumulative amortization for each major class of identifiable intangible asset subject to amortization. Amortization expense must also be disclosed for the period. The notes must also include the estimated annual amortization expense for each of the next five fiscal periods.

Example of Future Effects

At the time of the purchase, amortization procedures will be determined for all assets and liabilities acquired. Let us assume that Acquisitions Inc. adopted the following amortization policies for the assets and liabilities acquired in the purchase of Johnson Company. [The asterisk (*) identifies an adjustment that applies only to the year following the purchase.]

Accounts	Assigned Value	Amortization Procedure	Amortization Amount
Accounts receivable	$ 28,000	None	
Inventory	45,000	Sold during the first year	$45,000*
Land.	50,000	Not amortized; realized when sold	
Building	80,000	$0 salvage, 20 years, straight-line	4,000
Equipment	50,000	$10,000 salvage, 5 years, straight-line . .	8,000
Patent.	30,000	No salvage, 4-year estimated useful life, straight-line	7,500

(continued)

14 FASB Statement No. 142, *Goodwill and Other Intangible Assets*, par. 11.

Accounts	Assigned Value	Amortization Procedure	Amortization Amount
Brand-name copyright	40,000	No salvage, 10-year estimated useful life, straight-line	4,000
Goodwill	63,000	No amortization (will be subject to impairment procedures)	
Current liabilities	(5,000)	None	
Notes payable	(21,000)	$1,000 premium amortized over 5 years straight-line, reduces interest expense . .	(200)
Net assets acquired	**$360,000**		

Acquisitions Inc. might also do a pro forma analysis of what the impact of the purchase will be on future income. Future financial statements will be based on the combined transactions of both companies. There will no longer be separate accounts maintained for each of the former companies. Thus, all of the above adjustments will be included in the accounts of Acquisitions Inc.

Acquisitions Inc.
Pro Forma Income Statement
For the Year Ending December 31, 20X2

Adjustments Necessary Due to
Purchase of Johnson Company

Sales revenue		$350,000
Less: Cost of goods sold (includes $45,000 Johnson inventory)		130,000
Gross profit		$220,000
Selling expenses (includes $4,000, copyright amortization)	$44,000	
Administrative expenses	63,000	
Depreciation—building (includes $4,000, Johnson building)	25,000	
Depreciation—equipment (includes $8,000, Johnson equipment)	18,000	
Patent amortization (for Johnson patents)	7,500	
Total operating expenses		157,500
Operating income		$ 62,500
Less: Interest expense (minus $200 premium amortization)		9,800
Income before taxes		$ 52,700
Provision for income tax (40%)		(21,080)
Net income		$ 31,620

Goodwill Impairment

Goodwill is not amortized but is subject to separate and distinct impairment procedures. Five specific concerns need to be addressed:

1. Goodwill must be allocated to reporting units if the purchased company contains more than one reporting unit.
2. A reporting unit valuation plan must be established within one year of a purchase. This sets forth the procedures that will be used to measure the fair value of reporting units in future periods.
3. Impairment testing is normally done on an annual basis. There are, however, exceptions to annual testing and some cases where testing may be required *between* annual testing dates.
4. The procedure for determining if impairment has occurred must be established.
5. The procedure for determining the amount of the impairment loss, which is also the decrease in the goodwill amount recorded, must be established.

Allocating Goodwill to Reporting Units. In most cases, the company purchased will be made up of more than one reporting unit. For purposes of segment reporting, under FASB Statement No. 131,[15] a reporting unit is either the same level or one level lower than an operating segment. To be a reporting unit, one level below an operating unit, *both* of the following criteria must be met:

- Segment managers measure and review performance at this level.
- The unit has separate financial information available and has economic characteristics that distinguish it from other units of the operating segment.

All assets and liabilities are to be allocated to the underlying reporting units. Goodwill is allocated to the reporting segments by subtracting the identifiable net assets of the unit from the estimated fair value of the entire reporting unit. The method of estimating the fair value of the reporting unit should be documented. In essence, an estimate must be made of the price that would have been paid for only the specific reporting unit. In only limited cases would a reporting unit have its own equity issues that would allow fair value to be inferred from the fair value of the shares. Even if a unit had its own stock, this would not have to be the sole determinant of its fair value.

Reporting Unit Valuation Procedures. The steps in the reporting unit measurement process will be illustrated with the following example of the purchase of Johnson Company, which is a purchase of a single operating unit.

A. Determine the valuation method and estimated fair value of the identifiable assets, goodwill, and all liabilities of the reporting unit.

At the time of purchase, the valuations of Johnson Company's identifiable assets, liabilities, and goodwill were as shown below. [The asterisk (*) indicates numbers have been rounded for presentation purposes.]

Assets	Comments	Valuation Method	Fair Value
Inventory	Replacement cost available	Market replacement cost for similar items	$ 45,000
Accounts receivable	Recorded amount is adjusted for estimated bad debts	Aging schedule used for valuation	28,000
Land	Per-acre value well established	Five acres at $10,000 per acre	50,000
Building	Most reliable measure is rent potential	Rent estimated at $20,000 per year for 20 years, discounted at 14% return for similar properties; present value of $132,463 reduced for $50,000 land value	80,000*
Equipment	Cost of replacement capacity can be estimated	Estimated purchase cost of equipment with similar capacity	50,000

(continued)

15 FASB Statement No. 131, *Disclosure about Segments of an Enterprise and Related Information* (Norwalk, CT: Financial Accounting Standards Board, 1997). See Chapter 12 for detailed coverage of accounting for segments of a business.

Assets	Comments	Valuation Method	Fair Value
Patent	Recorded by seller at only legal cost; has significant future value	Added profit made possible by patent is $11,600 per year for four years; discounted at risk adjusted rate for similar investments of 20% per year; PV equals $30,029	$ 30,000*
Brand-name copyright	Not recorded by seller value	Estimated sales value	40,000
Current liabilities	Recorded amounts are accurate	Recorded value	(5,000)
Bonds payable	Specified interest rate is above market rate	Discount at market interest rate	(21,000)
Net identifiable assets at fair value			297,000
Price paid for reporting unit			360,000
Goodwill	Believed to exist based on reputation and customer list	Implied by price paid	63,000

B. Measure the fair value of the reporting unit and document assumptions and models used to make the measurement.

If the stock of the reporting unit is publicly traded, the market capitalization of the reporting unit may be indicative of its fair value, but it need not be the only measure considered. The price paid to acquire all of the shares or a controlling interest could exceed the product of the fair value per share times the number of shares outstanding. A common method used to estimate fair value is to determine the present value of the unit's future cash flows. The following is an example of that approach.

Assumptions:

1. The reporting unit will provide operating cash flows, net of tax, of $40,000 during the next reporting period.
2. Operating cash flows will increase at the rate of 10% per year for the next four reporting periods and then will remain steady for 15 more years.
3. Forecast cash flows will be adjusted for capital expenditures needed to maintain market position and productive capacity.
4. Cash flows defined as net of cash from operations less capital expenditures will be discounted at an after-tax discount rate of 12%. An annual rate of 12% is a reasonable risk-adjusted rate of return for investments of this type.
5. An estimate of salvage value (net of tax effect of gains or losses) of the assets at the end of 20 years will be used to approximate salvage value. This is a conservative assumption, since the unit may be operated after that period.

Schedule of net tax cash flows:

Year	Net of Tax Operating Flow	Capital Expenditure	Salvage Value	Net Cash Flow
1	$40,000			$ 40,000
2	44,000			44,000
3	48,400			48,400
4	53,240			53,240
5	58,564	$(25,000)		33,564
6	58,564			58,564
7	58,564			58,564
8	58,564			58,564
9	58,564			58,564
10	58,564	(30,000)		28,564
11	58,564			58,564
12	58,564			58,564
13	58,564			58,564
14	58,564			58,564
15	58,564	(35,000)		23,564
16	58,564			58,564
17	58,564			58,564
18	58,564			58,564
19	58,564			58,564
20	58,564		$75,000	133,564
Net present value at 12% annual rate				376,173

C. Compare fair value of reporting unit with amounts assigned to identifiable net assets plus goodwill.

Estimated fair value of reporting unit	$376,173
Estimated fair value of identifiable net assets, plus goodwill.	360,000
Excess of fair value of reporting unit over net assets.	**$ 16,173**

An excess of the fair value of the reporting unit over the value of the net assets indicated that the price paid was reasonable and below a theoretical maximum purchase price. It requires no adjustment of assigned values. If, however, the fair value of the net assets exceeds the fair value of the reporting unit, the model used to determine the fair value of the reporting unit should be reassessed. If the reestimation of the values assigned to the net assets and the reporting unit still indicates an excess of the value of the net assets over the value of the reporting unit, goodwill is to be tested for impairment. This would likely result in an impairment loss being recorded on the goodwill.

Frequency of Impairment Testing. The normal procedure is to do impairment testing of goodwill on an annual basis. Testing need not be at period end; it can be done on a consistent, scheduled, annual basis during the reporting period.

The annual impairment test is not needed if all the following criteria are met:

- The assets and liabilities of the unit have not significantly changed since the last valuation;
- The last calculation of the unit's fair value far exceeded book value, thus making it unlikely that the unit's fair value could now be less than book value; and
- No adverse events have occurred since the last valuation, indicating that the fair value of the unit has fallen below book value.

There may also be instances when goodwill must be impairment tested sooner than the normal annual measurement date. These situations include the occurrence of an adverse event that could diminish the unit's fair value, the likelihood that the unit will be disposed of, the impairment of a group of the unit's assets (under FASB Statement No. 121), or a goodwill impairment loss that is recorded in a higher level organization of which the unit is a part.

Impairment Testing. **Goodwill is considered to be impaired if the implied fair value of the reporting unit is less than the carrying value of the reporting unit's net assets** (including goodwill). Let us revisit the Johnson Company example. Assume that the following new estimates were made at the end of the first year:

Estimated implied fair value of reporting unit, based on analysis of projected cash flow (discounted at 12% annual rate)	$320,000
Existing *net book value* of reporting unit (including goodwill)	345,000

Since the recorded net book value of the reporting unit exceeds its implied fair value, goodwill is considered to be impaired. If the estimated fair value exceeds the existing book value, there is no loss to be calculated.

Goodwill Impairment Loss. If the above test indicates impairment, the impairment loss must be estimated. **The impairment loss for goodwill is the excess of the implied fair value of the reporting unit over the fair value of the reporting unit's identifiable net assets (excluding goodwill) on the impairment date.** These are the values that would be assigned to those accounts if the reporting unit were purchased on the date of impairment measurement.

Two important issues must be understood at this point:

1. The **impairment test** compares the implied fair value of the reporting unit to the unit's **book value (including goodwill)**. The **impairment loss calculation** compares the implied fair value of the reporting unit to the unit's estimated **fair values (excluding goodwill)** on the impairment date.
2. While fair values of net assets are used to measure the impairment loss, they are not recorded. The existing book values on the impairment date remain in place (unless they are adjusted for their own impairment loss).

For our example, the following calculation was made for the impairment loss:

Estimated implied fair value of reporting unit, based on cash flow analysis discounted at a 12% annual rate	$320,000
Less: Fair value of net assets on the date of measurement, Exclusive of goodwill	285,000
Implied fair value of goodwill	$ 35,000
Existing recorded goodwill	63,000
Estimated impairment loss	$ (28,000)

The following journal entry would be made:

Goodwill Impairment Loss	28,000	
Goodwill		28,000

The impairment loss will be shown as a separate line item within the operating section unless it is identified with a discontinued operation, in which case, it is part of the gain or loss on disposal. **Once goodwill is written down, it cannot be adjusted to a higher amount.**

Significant disclosure requirements for goodwill exist in any period in which goodwill changes. A note must accompany the balance sheet in any period that has a change in goodwill.

The note would explain the goodwill acquired, the goodwill impairment losses, and the goodwill written off as part of a disposal of a reporting unit. It is further required that information be included that provides the details of any impairment loss recorded during the period. The information would include the reporting unit involved, the circumstances leading to the impairment, and the possibility of further adjustments.

REFLECTION

- Tangible assets and liabilities are expensed, depreciated, or amortized based on their fair values recorded on the purchase date.
- Identifiable intangible assets are amortized unless they can be shown to have an indefinite life.
- Goodwill is not amortized but is subject to precise impairment testing procedures.

RECORDING A BARGAIN PURCHASE

7

OBJECTIVE

Use zone analysis to account for purchases made at a price below the fair value of the company's net assets.

A *bargain purchase* occurs when the price paid for the company is less than the total estimated fair value of the net assets purchased. In the preceding example for the purchase of Johnson Company, a **price below $297,000** ($323,000 assets – $26,000 liabilities assumed) would be a bargain. Obviously, no goodwill is recorded in a bargain purchase. Certain *priority accounts* are *always* recorded at fair value, no matter what the price. The remaining *nonpriority accounts* are discounted below their fair values in a bargain purchase. In an extreme case, the price paid for a company could be less than the sum of its net priority accounts. Should this occur, the excess of the fair value of the net priority accounts over the price paid is recorded as an extraordinary gain.

Priority Accounts

Priority accounts are recorded at full fair value, no matter how low the price paid for the company is. These accounts include **all current assets and all liabilities plus the following assets that would not otherwise qualify as current assets:**

- All investments, except for influential investments accounted for under the equity method.
- Assets to be disposed of by sale (excess assets included in the purchase).
- Deferred tax assets (as well as deferred tax liabilities).
- Prepaid assets relating to pension plans and other postretirement benefit plans.

Typically, priority accounts should have readily determinable fair values and will not be discounted no matter what price is paid. Should the price paid be less than the sum of the values assigned to the priority accounts, the excess of their fair value over the price is recorded as an **extraordinary gain.** Prior to FASB Statement No. 141, this amount would be recorded as a deferred credit and amortized over a period not to exceed 40 years (the amortization amount would increase income).

Applying the Priorities

Zone analysis is used to guide the assignment of the price paid to purchase a company. The zones and their application to the Johnson Company example are as follows:

Account Groups	Accounts Included	Fair Value	Group Total	Cumulative Group Totals
Priority	Accounts receivable	$ 28,000		
	Inventory	45,000		
	Current liabilities	(5,000)		
	Bonds payable	(21,000)	$ 47,000	$ 47,000
Nonpriority	Land	$ 50,000		
	Buildings (net)	80,000		
	Equipment (net)	50,000		
	Patent (net)	30,000		
	Brand-name copyright	40,000	$250,000	$297,000

Notice that existing goodwill is not considered. Now, consider alternative prices and the assignment of value that would occur. For each price, the number of $50 fair value shares will be adjusted to equal the price tested.

Premium Price (over $297,000). All accounts are at full fair value, and the amount above $297,000 is recorded as goodwill. That is the case in the example given earlier at a price of $360,000, where goodwill is $63,000.

Bargain (greater than $47,000, but less than $297,000). Priority accounts are recorded at full fair value. The nonpriority accounts receive the amount by which the price exceeds $47,000. For example, assume that 4,000 shares of common stock, with a fair value of $50 each, were issued as consideration. The total price paid would be $210,000, which is $200,000 (4,000 shares × $50) of stock plus $10,000 of direct acquisition costs. This leaves $163,000 ($210,000 − $47,000) available for the nonpriority accounts. The $163,000 would be allocated as follows:

Nonpriority Accounts	Fair Value	Percent of Nonpriority Total	Amount to Allocate	Allocated Value
Land	$ 50,000	20%	$163,000	**$ 32,600**
Buildings (net)	80,000	32	163,000	**52,160**
Equipment (net)	50,000	20	163,000	**32,600**
Patent (net)	30,000	12	163,000	**19,560**
Brand-name copyright	40,000	16	163,000	**26,080**
Total	$250,000	100%		$163,000

The journal entry to record the purchase would be as follows:

Accounts Receivable (book and fair value)	28,000	
Inventory (fair value)	45,000	
Land (allocation)	**32,600**	
Building (allocation)	**52,160**	
Equipment (allocation)	**32,600**	
Patent (allocation)	**19,560**	
Brand-Name Copyright (allocation)	**26,080**	
Current Liabilities (book and fair value)		5,000
Bond Payable (face value)		20,000
Premium on Bond Payable (adjust bonds to fair value)		1,000
Common Stock ($1 par, 4,000 shares)		4,000
Paid-In Capital in Excess of Par ($200,000 – $4,000 par)		196,000
Cash (for direct acquisition costs)		10,000
Dr. = Cr. Check Totals	*236,000*	*236,000*

Notice that when the price is a bargain, no amount is recorded for goodwill, because the price paid does not exceed the fair value of the net assets acquired.

Extraordinary Gain (price less than $47,000). Priority accounts are still recorded at full fair value. No amount is available for nonpriority accounts or for goodwill. The excess value of the priority accounts over the price paid will be recorded as an extraordinary gain. For example, assume that 600 shares of common stock, with a fair value of $50 each, were issued as consideration. The total price paid would be $40,000, which is $30,000 (600 shares × $50) of stock plus $10,000 of direct acquisition costs. The $40,000 is $7,000 less than the amount assigned to priority accounts, resulting in an extraordinary gain of $7,000. No allocations are needed, and the following entry is recorded:

Accounts Receivable (book and fair value)	28,000	
Inventory	45,000	
Current Liabilities (book and fair value)		5,000
Bond Payable (face value)		20,000
Premium on Bond Payable (adjust bonds to fair value)		1,000
Extraordinary Gain		**7,000**
Common Stock ($1 par, 600 shares)		600
Paid-In Capital in Excess of Par ($30,000 – $600 par)		29,400
Cash (for direct acquisition costs)		10,000
Dr. = Cr. Check Totals	*73,000*	*73,000*

No amounts are recorded for nonpriority accounts or for goodwill.

The **Excel tutorial, provided on a CD with this text,** assists you in building an Excel template to allocate price to accounts under all possible price scenarios. An example of its application is included in the Summary Problem at the end of this chapter.

REFLECTION

- If a price paid is less than the net assets at fair value, there is no goodwill. The nonpriority accounts are discounted. Current assets, all liabilities, investments (other than investments under the equity method), deferred taxes, and prepaid pension assets are priority accounts and are not discounted.
- If the price paid is less than the sum of the net priority accounts, there is an extraordinary gain.

PURCHASE ACCOUNTING: ADDED CONSIDERATIONS

8
OBJECTIVE
Explain the special issues that may arise in a purchase, and show how to account for them.

Several complications may arise in a purchase, such as the following:

1. Substantial expenditures may be incurred to accomplish the business combination. These expenditures must be recorded properly.
2. Debt issuances outstanding may need to be recorded at fair value. This will require the application of present value analysis.
3. The acquired company may be a lessee or a lessor. This requires a consideration of the classification of the leases and the resulting assets and/or liabilities that need to be recorded.
4. Frequently, purchases are structured as tax-free exchanges for the seller. This means that the seller may, for tax purposes, assign the book value of the net assets sold to the stock received from the buyer. No tax is due until the shares are sold.

5. The purchased company may have existing tax loss carryovers. The resulting tax savings are an asset to be considered in the recording of the purchase.
6. Finally, there may be contingent consideration. This is an agreement to pay additional consideration (pay more cash or issue additional securities) at a later date if certain future events occur.

Expenditures to Accomplish Business Combination

Three categories of expenditures may be involved in negotiating and consummating the purchase of another company. These categories and their recording are as follows:

Category	Examples	Accounting
Direct costs	Paid to outside parties such as lawyers, consultants, brokers, and CPAs. Could include preaudit, broker's fees, and legal fees.	Included in the price paid for the company purchased and, therefore, is included in amounts assigned to assets and, possibly, goodwill.
Indirect costs	Allocation of existing expenses of the acquiring firm connected to negotiating and consummating the purchase. Could include salaries for employees who worked on the acquisition and related overhead expenses.	They remain an expense of the period and are not included in the price paid.
Issue costs	Costs connected with issuing the stock or bonds used as payment for the acquisition.	Recorded as a separate asset or deducted from the value of the issued stock or bonds, since they relate to the method of payment. Not included in the price paid.

Direct costs may also include the costs of integrating the operating activities of the acquired company with those of the purchasing company. These costs could include expenses related to revising information systems, terminating employees, and closing duplicative facilities. A liability may be established for these costs at the time of the purchase. Subsequent payments for these costs would reduce the estimated liability account.

Revaluation of Long-Term Liabilities

Liabilities that are assumed by the buyer in a purchase transaction must always be recorded at their current fair value. When interest rates have increased since the original issue of the debt, the fair value of the debt will be less than the book value, and a discount will be recorded. If interest rates have decreased since issuance of the debt, the debt will have a value in excess of book value and a premium will be recorded. For large corporations with publicly traded debt securities, the fair value of the debt is easily secured. In those cases where quoted market prices are not available, the current value of the debt instrument is imputed using the market rate of interest for similar debt instruments. Consider the following example of imputing the current value of an existing bond. The company being acquired has outstanding a $100,000, 8% bond with five years remaining to maturity. Interest is paid annually each December 31. The acquisition date is January 1, 20X1. The current interest rate for a similar bond is 6%. The current value of the debt would be imputed as follows:

Present value of interest payments at 6%	
($8,000 annual interest × 5-year, 6% present value of annuity factor of 4.2124)	$ 33,699
Present value of principal ($100,000 × 5-year present value factor of 0.7473)	74,730
Imputed market value of liability	$108,429

The purchase entry would include the following credits:

Bonds payable	100,000
Premium on bonds payable...	8,429

The premium will be amortized over the remaining 5-year term using either the effective interest or straight-line amortization methods. Had the current interest rate exceeded the original face rate of 8%, the bonds would have a fair value below $100,000, and a discount would result.

Lease Agreements

Special analysis of the purchase price in a business combination is necessary when the company acquired in a purchase transaction is bound contractually by existing leases as either a lessee or lessor. Sometimes, the terms of the lease may be modified as a result of the combination. These modifications would require the consent of the third party (lessee or lessor). When the terms of the lease are modified to the extent that a new lease is created, the new lease is classified and recorded according to the requirements of FASB Statement No. 13.[16] It is more common, however, to find that the contractual terms of a lease are not altered as a result of the purchase. In such cases, it is necessary to record only the fair value of the acquired firm's existing rights and obligations under the lease.

When the company acquired is a lessee under an operating lease, it has recorded rent as an expense but has not recorded any asset or long-term liability. Thus, there is no existing recorded asset or liability to adjust. At acquisition, if the contractual rent under the remaining lease term is materially below fair rental value, an asset should be recorded equal to the value of the rent savings. The asset should be amortized over the lease term as an adjustment to rent expense. If the contractual rent exceeds the fair rental value, a liability should be credited, equal to the value of the excess rent, using an appropriate market interest rate. The liability should be amortized as a reduction of rent expense in future periods. Under both situations, future rent expense would reflect fair rental value as of the date of the combination.[17]

When the acquired company is a lessee under a capital lease, it has recorded the asset as well as the liability under that lease. At the time of the purchase, both the asset and the liability should be analyzed independently and recorded at their separate fair values.

When the acquired company is a lessor under an operating lease, it has recorded the cost of the leased asset less accumulated depreciation. In the purchase transaction, the asset should be recorded at its current fair value. However, the fair value may be based partly on the present value of the rents due under existing leases.

When the acquired company is a lessor under a capital lease, it has recorded only a receivable due for future rents and perhaps an unguaranteed residual value. In the purchase transaction, the receivable should be recorded at its fair value based on prevailing current interest rates. The unguaranteed residual value should be estimated and discounted to its present value, using the same current interest rate.

Nontaxable Exchanges

The selling company may wish to structure the purchase so as to avoid a taxable gain at the time of the combination. Section 368(a)(1) of the Tax Code authorizes seven types of reorganizations that qualify as tax-free exchanges. For asset acquisitions, the tax-free exchange status is accomplished by exchanging the common stock of the purchasing company for substantially all the assets of the acquired company. After the exchange, the acquired corporation

16 FASB Statement No. 13, *Accounting for Leases* (Stamford, CT: Financial Accounting Standards Board, 1976), par. 9.

17 Accounting Principles Board Opinion No. 16, *Business Combinations* (New York: American Institute of Certified Public Accountants, 1970), par. 88.

liquidates by distributing the shares received to its shareholders. The shareholders of the acquired company do not record a gain for tax purposes until the shares received are sold. The purchasing company in a nontaxable exchange inherits the book values of the assets purchased for use in future tax calculations. This means that only the net book value on the books of the acquired company are used as the tax basis of the assets acquired when they are later sold or depreciated. This results in the recording of a deferred tax liability because the depreciation and amortization expense recorded on the financial statements will be higher than what is recorded on the tax return.

As an example, assume that in a nontaxable exchange the tax basis of a given fixed asset is \$50,000, and its fair value at acquisition is \$150,000. Depreciation on the \$100,000 difference will be deducted in the financial statements but not in the tax return. If the purchasing company is in a 35% tax bracket, the future tax payments will be \$35,000 greater than the recorded tax expense. This added tax burden is recognized by recording a deferred tax liability to be amortized over the life of the asset.

The goodwill arising in a tax-free exchange is also not deductible. This means that a deferred tax liability also arises applicable to the goodwill. Suppose that after recording all other assets and liabilities at fair value, \$65,000 of unallocated cost remains. This represents the "net value" of goodwill. The gross amount of goodwill (GG) is calculated as follows:

$$\$65{,}000 = GG - (0.35 \times GG)$$

$$\$65{,}000 = 0.65 \times GG$$

$$\$65{,}000 \div 0.65 = \$100{,}000$$

Thus, the goodwill is recorded at a gross value of \$100,000 (\$65,000 ÷ 0.65), and a deferred tax liability of \$35,000 is recorded.

Tax Loss Carryovers

Tax law provides that an existing company with a tax loss may first carry the loss back to the previous two years to offset income and thus receive a refund of taxes paid in the preceding years. If the loss exceeds income available in the prior 2-year period, the loss can be carried forward up to 20 years to offset future income and therefore reduce the taxes which otherwise would be paid. The acquired company may have unused tax loss carryovers that it has not been able to utilize due to an absence of sufficient income in prior years. This becomes a benefit for which the purchasing company will pay. Tax provisions limit the amount of the NOL (net operating loss) available to the acquiring company to discourage business combinations that are motivated primarily by tax loss carryovers. The purchaser is allowed to use the acquired company's tax loss carryovers to offset its own income in the current and future periods subject to the following limitations:

1. None of the target company's NOL can be used to refund taxes paid in prior years.
2. Section 381 of the Tax Code restricts the use of the target company's NOL in the tax year of the acquisition. The NOL that can be used cannot exceed

$$\text{Income from acquiring company} \times \frac{\text{Number of days in year after the acquisition}}{\text{Number of days in the tax year}}$$

   Thus, if the target company was acquired on July 1, the acquiring company could not use an NOL in excess of 50% of its income for the year.

3. For years subsequent to the acquisition, Section 382 of the Tax Code restricts the use of the NOL from an acquired company to an amount not greater than the product of total fair value of the acquired company's stock multiplied by the long-term, tax-exempt interest rate on U.S. obligations. Thus, if the fair value of the acquired company's stock was \$2 million

and the U.S. tax-exempt rate was 6%, the NOL used in any one year could not exceed $120,000.

The value of the expected future tax loss carryovers is recorded as *Deferred Tax Asset (DTA)* on the date of the acquisition. It is, however, necessary to attempt to determine whether there will be adequate future tax liabilities to support the value of the deferred tax asset. The accountant would have to consider existing evidence to make this determination. If it is likely that some or all of the deferred tax asset will not be realized, the contra account Allowance for Unrealizable Tax Assets would be used to reduce the deferred tax asset to an estimated amount to be realized.[18] This may have the practical effect of the contra account's totally offsetting the deferred tax asset. The inability to record a net deferred tax asset often will result in the consideration paid for the NOL carryover being assigned to goodwill. This occurs because the price paid will exceed the value of the assets that are allowed to be recorded.

Consider an example of a purchase that includes both of the previous tax ramifications. Farlow Inc. is purchasing Granada Company, which has the following balance sheet on the purchase date:

Assets		Liabilities and Equity	
Inventory	$ 50,000	Liabilities	$ 80,000
Land	100,000	Common stock ($10 par)	100,000
Building	270,000	Retained earnings	170,000
Accumulated depreciation	(70,000)		
Total assets	$350,000	Total liabilities and equity	$350,000

The fair values of the land and building are $100,000 and $300,000, respectively. Granada has an NOL carryover totaling $200,000. Granada has not recorded the deferred tax asset applicable to the NOL carryover, since it does not foresee adequate future tax liabilities. Farlow Inc. issued 8,500, $10 par value common shares with a fair value of $50 each for the net assets of Granada in a transaction structured as a tax-free exchange. Farlow also paid $10,000 in direct acquisition costs. Farlow has a 30% tax rate and believes that the NOL carryovers will be fully realized. The following zone analysis is prepared:

Account Groups	Accounts Included	Fair Value	Group Total	Cumulative Group Totals
Priority	Inventory	$ 50,000		
	Deferred tax asset—NOL, 30% × $200,000	60,000		
	Liabilities	(80,000)	$ 30,000	$ 30,000
Nonpriority	Land	$100,000		
	Building (net)	300,000		
	Deferred tax liability—building, 30% × ($300,000 fair value − $200,000 book value)	(30,000)	$370,000	$400,000

Theoretically, deferred tax assets and liabilities are priority accounts. However, in this case, the *deferred tax liability (DTL)* only exists to the extent that the building is valued in excess of its existing book value. Since it is proportionate to the amount of value assigned in excess of existing book value, it has the same priority as the asset itself.

The price paid exceeds the cumulative sum of all identifiable assets, less liabilities. The amount assigned to goodwill is determined as follows:

18 FASB Statement No. 109, *Accounting for Income Taxes* (Norwalk, CT: Financial Accounting Standards Board, 1992), par. 17.

Market value of shares issued ($50 × 8,500 shares)	$425,000
Direct acquisition costs	10,000
Total cost	$435,000
Total amount assigned to identifiable assets, less liabilities	400,000
Excess remaining for goodwill, net of tax	$ 35,000
Goodwill, divide by (1 − tax rate) = (1.0 − 0.3) = 0.7	50,000
Deferred tax liability applicable to goodwill (30% × $50,000)	$ (15,000)

The journal entry to record the purchase is as follows:

Inventory	50,000	
Land	100,000	
Building	300,000	
Deferred Tax Asset (on NOL)	60,000	
Goodwill	50,000	
Liabilities		80,000
Deferred Tax Liability ($30,000 building + $15,000 goodwill)		45,000
Common Stock ($10 par, 8,500 shares)		85,000
Paid-In Capital in Excess of Par (8,500 shares × $40)		340,000
Cash (for direct acquisition costs)		10,000
Dr. = Cr. Check Totals	*560,000*	*560,000*

Procedures get complicated if the tax-free exchange occurs at a bargain price. If the total value given had been only $350,000 (6,800 shares issued plus $10,000 direct acquisition costs), the zone analysis above would make only $320,000 ($350,000 total − $30,000 for priority accounts) available for the land and the building. The $320,000 would be the total amount available, net of the tax adjustment. In this case, the $200,000 book value of the building can be recorded in full. However, any fair value adjustment is subject to a 30% tax adjustment. Allocation of the excess would be as follows:

Nonpriority Accounts	Fair Value	Percent of Nonpriority Total	Amount to Allocate	Allocated Net Value
Land	$100,000	25%	$320,000	**$ 80,000**
Building (net)	300,000	75	320,000	**240,000**
Total	$400,000	100%		$ 320,000

The gross amount of the adjustment and the DTA (DTL) would be calculated as follows, where G equals "gross," and the DTA (DTL) is equal to 30% of the difference between the gross and book values:

Account	Calculation	Gross	Net	DTA (DTL)
Land	$80,000 = G + 0.3($100,000 − G)	$ 71,429	$ 80,000	$ 8,571
Building (net)	$240,000 = G − 0.3(G − $200,000)	257,143	240,000	(17,143)
Total		$328,572	$320,000	$ (8,572)

The building, land, and related tax amounts would be recorded as follows:

Inventory	50,000	
Land	71,429	
Deferred Tax Asset (on land)	8,571	
Building	257,143	
Deferred Tax Asset (on NOL)	60,000	
Liabilities		80,000
Deferred Tax Liability (on building)		17,143
Common Stock ($10 par, 6,800 shares)		68,000
Paid-In Excess of Par (6,800 shares × $40)		272,000
Cash (for direct acquisition costs)		10,000
Dr. = Cr. Check Totals	*447,143*	*447,143*

Contingent Consideration Included in the Purchase Agreement

A purchase agreement may provide that the purchaser will transfer additional consideration to the seller, contingent upon the occurrence of specified future events or transactions. This consideration could involve the transfer of cash or other assets or the issuance of additional securities. During the period preceding the date on which the contingency is resolved, the purchaser has a contingent liability that is disclosed in a footnote to the financial statements but is not recorded.[19] On the date that the contingency is resolved, the contingent liability ceases, and the purchaser records any additional consideration as an adjustment to the original purchase transaction. The method used to make the adjustment is dependent upon the nature of the contingency.

Contingent Consideration Based on Earnings. A purchaser may agree to make a final payment contingent upon the earnings of the acquired company during a specified future time period. If, during this period, the earnings of the acquired company reach or exceed an agreed-upon amount, further payment will be made at the end of the contingency period. In essence, the value of all or part of the goodwill is to be confirmed before full payment is made. Clearly, when an earnings contingency exists, the total price to be paid for the acquired company is not known until the end of the contingency period. As is the case for the initial payment, the purchaser must record the fair value of the consideration given, including the fair value of additional securities issued. Normally, the amount of the additional payment will result in an increased amount of goodwill.[20] Adjustments to other assets would be made only if the contingency was based on their value.

To illustrate, assume that Company A acquires the assets of Company B on January 1, 20X2, in exchange for Company A's common stock. Also, Company A agrees to issue 10,000 additional common shares to the former stockholders of Company B on January 1, 20X5, if the acquired company's average annual income before taxes for the three years, 20X2 through 20X4, reaches or exceeds $50,000. During the contingency period, Company A will disclose the contingent liability in the footnotes to its financial statements. If the earnings condition is met, Company A will record the final payment on January 1, 20X5, by increasing the goodwill account. Assuming the 10,000 shares have a par value of $1 and a fair value of $8 per share on January 1, 20X5, the following entry would be made:

Goodwill ($8 fair value × 10,000 shares)	80,000	
Common Stock ($1 par × 10,000 shares)		10,000
Paid-In Capital in Excess of Par		70,000

19 APB Opinion No. 16 (par. 78) provides that a liability is to be recorded if the amount of the contingent liability is determinable at the date of the acquisition. Of course, doing so would increase the price paid for the firm and would impact values assigned to the assets.

20 When the contingency involves the value of an asset other than goodwill, that asset's value is to be adjusted as a result of the contingent payment. For example, with a contingency involving the value of a building, the value would be adjusted at the time the contingency was resolved and the added payment made.

The additional goodwill is added to existing goodwill, and the resulting total is subject to impairment testing.

Special procedures are needed when there is contingent consideration, based on performance, in a purchase that is at a price (before the contingent consideration) below the fair value of net identifiable assets. For example, the price paid on the purchase date is $600,000, the net priority assets total $100,000, and the nonpriority assets total $700,000. If the contingent consideration is less than the price deficiency of $200,000, the amount of possible contingent consideration is recorded as a liability. If the possible contingent consideration was $150,000, the following summary entry would record the purchase:

Net Priority Assets	100,000	
Nonpriority Assets ($700,000 less $50,000 bargain)	650,000	
Estimated Liability (for contingent consideration)		150,000
Cash (for original payment)		600,000

If the amount is paid, the liability is debited. If the amount is not paid, nonpriority accounts gain is credited as follows:

Estimated Liability (for contingent consideration)	150,000	
Nonpriority Accounts		150,000

If the possible contingent payment exceeds the price deficiency, the liability recorded is limited to the deficiency. Thus, if the possible contingent payment was $300,000, only a $200,000 liability would be recorded as follows:

Net Priority Assets	100,000	
Nonpriority Assets	700,000	
Estimated Liability (for contingent consideration)		200,000
Cash (for original payment)		600,000

If the $300,000 contingent payment was made the summary entry would be:

Estimated Liability (for contingent consideration)	200,000	
Goodwill	100,000	
Cash		300,000

If the contingent payment were not made, the liability would be removed, and the nonpriority accounts would be recorded as follows:

Estimated Liability (for contingent consideration)	200,000	
Nonpriority Accounts		200,000

Contingent Consideration Based on Issuer's Security Prices. In exchange for its assets, a seller may be reluctant to accept the securities of the purchasing company. This reluctance is caused by the seller's fear of a possible future decline in the fair value of the securities. When a stock issuance is involved, the concern may be based, in part, on the dilutive effect of a significant increase in the number of shares outstanding. To combat this apprehension, the purchaser may guarantee the total value of the securities on a given future date. The purchaser agrees to transfer additional assets or issue additional securities on that date, for the amount by which the guaranteed value exceeds the fair value on the date selected. For example, on January 1, 20X2, Company C issues 100,000 shares of its common stock, which has a $1 par value and a $12 fair value per share, in exchange for the assets of Company D. The following summarized entry would be recorded:

Net Assets ($12 fair value × 100,000 shares)	1,200,000	
Common Stock ($1 par × 100,000 shares)		100,000
Paid-In Capital in Excess of Par		1,100,000

Company C guarantees the value of the stock at $12 per share as of January 1, 20X3. If necessary, additional consideration will be paid in cash. During the contingency period, Company C must disclose the contingent liability in a footnote. Should the market price of the common stock be less than $12 per share on January 1, 20X3, additional consideration will be recorded.

Assume that on January 1, 20X3, the fair value is $10 per share. Then, $200,000 (100,000 shares × $2 per share deficiency) is the amount by which the guaranteed value of the shares exceeds the total fair value. Company C will have to pay an additional $200,000 in cash. How should the payment be recorded? The payment is not based on a revaluation of the purchase price, as is the case with an earnings contingency. Instead, the payment reflects the fact that the value assigned to the original security issuance was only an estimate, with the final amount to be determined later. To record the adjustment of the estimate, the original credit to Paid-In Capital in Excess of Par should be decreased as shown by the following entry:

Paid-In Capital in Excess of Par	200,000	
Cash		200,000

In the preceding example, the value guaranteed was satisfied in cash. More often, the satisfaction will involve the issuance of additional securities. In that case, Company C would issue 20,000 additional shares ($200,000 fair value deficiency ÷ $10 current fair value per share). Company C will now need 120,000 shares to equal the $1,200,000 original consideration, rather than the 100,000 shares previously issued. Accordingly, the $1,200,000 originally assigned to the 100,000 shares must be reassigned to 120,000 shares. The following entry will accomplish the reassignment:

Paid-In Capital in Excess of Par	20,000	
Common Stock ($1 par × 20,000 shares)		20,000

REFLECTION

- The direct costs of a purchase are included in the price allocated to accounts. Indirect costs are expensed. Issue costs are either separately capitalized or subtracted from the amount assigned to the securities issued.
- Leases retain their classification unless terms are changed. Fair value is used for all existing, lease-related accounts.
- Assets acquired in a nontaxable exchange are recorded at full fair value, and a separate deferred tax liability is recorded equal to the dollar value of the forfeited depreciation or amortization deductions.
- Net operating loss carryforwards are booked as an asset less an allowance for nonrealization. If part or all of the NOL is not recorded, it becomes a part of goodwill. If included in goodwill and later realized, goodwill is reduced.
- Contingent consideration that arises from an earnings contingency results in more goodwill. Contingent consideration caused by a price guarantee applicable to stock issued as payment is an adjustment of the amount previously assigned to the stock issued.

9

OBJECTIVE

Be aware of transition rules for the use of pooling of interests and the procedures for existing goodwill.

TRANSITION ISSUES

The pooling-of-interests method continues to be applied to business combinations that occurred before July 1, 2001, if they met the pooling criteria at the time of the transaction. The pooling method may also be used for transactions that were initiated prior to July 1, 2001, but were not competed until after that date. APB Opinion No. 16 (par. 46) defines the initiation date for a business combination. If, however, the terms of the combination were altered after June 30, 2001, the pooling method is not allowed.

For transactions initiated prior to July 1, 2001, that did not then qualify as a pooling of interests, the new purchase accounting procedures are applied if the transaction was completed on or after July 1, 2001.

The most universal transition concern applies to purchase transactions completed prior to July 1, 2001, that resulted in the recording of intangible assets and/or goodwill. The following rules apply to fiscal years starting after December 15, 2001 (with some exceptions for early adoption):

1. The remaining book value of an existing intangible asset that no longer meets the criteria for a separately identifiable intangible asset is added to goodwill.
2. If a portion of a purchase price was assigned to an intangible asset that now meets the test for separate recording was included in goodwill, the carrying value of such an asset is to be removed from goodwill and recorded as a separate intangible asset.
3. Prior to FASB Statement No. 141, a price below the sum of the priority accounts resulted in recording a "deferred credit." This credit was amortized as an addition to income over a period not to exceed 40 years. Any balance of such a deferred credit is recorded as income from a change in accounting principle.
4. The remaining book value of existing goodwill and the goodwill created by a transfer of an intangible asset balance must be assigned to reporting units.
5. The first step of the goodwill impairment test that compares the fair value of the reporting unit with its book value must be completed within six months of adoption of the Statement. The measurement uses values on the first day of the reporting period. If impairment is indicated, the impairment loss is measured as of the first day of the period and is included in that year's financial statements. The loss is recorded as a change in accounting principle and included in the first interim period reports. If an event occurs during the initial period that would lead to impairment, that loss is separately measured and is reported as a loss on impairment.
6. Annual goodwill impairment testing is applied in addition to the transitional impairment test applied on the adoption date.
7. Intangible assets that are subject to amortization should have their remaining lives reconsidered. Existing intangible assets that are no longer subject to amortization remain at their existing book values.
8. Statements included in comparative results covering periods prior to the adoption of FASB Statement Nos. 141 and 142 shall include footnote disclosure of the impact of applying the new statements to those periods. The disclosure should include income before extraordinary items, net income, and earnings per share.

REFLECTION

- Poolings initiated prior to July 2001 remain in effect.
- Goodwill existing on July 1, 2001, will no longer be amortized but will be impairment tested.

APPENDIX: CALCULATING AND RECORDING GOODWILL

10

OBJECTIVE

(Appendix) Estimate the value of goodwill.

A purchaser may attempt to forecast the future income of a target company in order to arrive at a logical purchase price. Goodwill is often, at least in part, a payment for above-normal expected future earnings. A forecast of future income may start by projecting recent years' incomes into the future. When this is done, it is important to factor out "one-time" occurrences that will not likely recur in the near future. Examples would include the cumulative effect of changes in accounting principles, extraordinary items, discontinued operations, or any other unusual event. Expected future income is compared to "normal" income. Normal income is the product of the appropriate industry rate of return on assets times the fair value of the gross assets (no deduction for liabilities) of the acquired company. Gross assets include specifically identifiable intangible assets such as patents and copyrights but do not include existing goodwill. The following calculation of earnings in excess of normal might be made for the Johnson Company example on page 11:

Expected average future income		$40,000
Less normal return on assets:		
Fair value of total identifiable assets	$345,000	
Industry normal rate of return	× 10%	
Normal return on assets		34,500
Expected annual earnings in excess of normal		$ 5,500

There are several methods that use the expected annual earnings in excess of normal to estimate goodwill. A common approach is to pay for a given number of years' excess earnings. For instance, Acquisitions Inc. might offer to pay for four years of excess earnings, which would total $22,000. Alternatively, the excess earnings could be viewed as an annuity. The most optimistic purchaser might expect the excess earnings to continue forever. If so, the buyer might capitalize the excess earnings as a perpetuity at the normal industry rate of return according to the following formula:

$$\text{Goodwill} = \frac{\text{Annual excess earnings}}{\text{Industry normal rate of return}}$$

$$= \frac{\$5{,}500}{0.10}$$

$$= \$55{,}000$$

Another estimation method views the factors that produce excess earnings to be of limited duration, such as 10 years, for example. This purchaser would calculate goodwill as follows:

$$\begin{aligned}\text{Goodwill} &= \text{Discounted present value of a \$5,500-per-year annuity for 10 years at 10\%}\\ &= \$5{,}500 \times \text{10-year, 10\% present value of annuity factor}\\ &= \$5{,}500 \times 6.145\\ &= \$33{,}798\end{aligned}$$

Other analysts view the normal industry earning rate to be appropriate only for identifiable assets and not goodwill. Thus, they might capitalize excess earnings at a higher rate of return to reflect the higher risk inherent in goodwill.

All calculations of goodwill are only estimates used to assist in the determination of the price to be paid for a company. For example, Acquisitions might add the $33,798 estimate of goodwill to the $319,000 fair value of Johnson's other net assets to arrive at a tentative maximum price of $352,798. However, estimates of goodwill may differ from actual negotiated goodwill. If the final agreed-upon price for Johnson's assets was $350,000, the actual negotiated goodwill would be $31,000, which is the price paid less the fair value of the net assets acquired.

REFLECTION

- Goodwill valuation is often based on an estimation of the future earnings of the target company.

UNDERSTANDING THE ISSUES

1. Identify each of the following business combinations as being vertical, horizontal, or conglomerate:
   a. An inboard marine engine company is acquired by an outboard engine manufacturer.
   b. A cosmetics manufacturer purchases a drug store chain.
   c. A medical clinic purchases an apartment complex.
2. Abrams Company is a sole proprietorship. The book value of its identifiable net assets is $400,000, and the fair value of the same net assets is $600,000. It is agreed that the business is worth $850,000. What advantage might there be for the seller if the company were exchanged for the common stock of another corporation as opposed to receiving cash? Consider both the immediate and future impact.
3. Major Corporation is acquiring Abrams Company by issuing its common stock in a tax-free exchange. Major is issuing common stock with a fair value of $850,000 for net identifiable assets with book and fair values of $400,000 and $600,000, respectively. What values will Major assign to the identifiable assets, to goodwill, and to the deferred tax liability? Assume a 40% tax rate.
4. Panther Company is about to acquire a 100% interest in Snake Company. Snake has identifiable net assets with book and fair values of $300,000 and $500,000, respectively. Panther will issue common stock as payment with a fair value of $750,000. When and how would the fair value of the net assets and goodwill be recorded if the acquisition is:
   a. A purchase of net assets.
   b. A purchase of Snake's common stock and Snake remains a separate legal entity.
5. Puncho Company is acquiring Semos Company in exchange for common stock valued at $900,000. Semos' identifiable net assets have book and fair values of $400,000 and $800,000, respectively. Compare accounting for the purchase (including assignment of the price paid) by Puncho with accounting for the sale by Semos.
6. Pallos Company is purchasing the net assets of Shrilly Company. The book and fair values of Shrilly's accounts are as follows:

Accounts	Book	Fair
Current assets	$100,000	$120,000
Land	50,000	80,000
Building and equipment	300,000	400,000
Customer list	0	20,000
Liabilities	100,000	100,000

What values will be assigned to **current assets, land, building and equipment, the customer list, liabilities, goodwill, and extraordinary gain** under each of the following purchase price scenarios?
   a. $800,000
   b. $450,000
   c. $15,000

7. Pablo Company incurred the following expenses to consummate the purchase of a subsidiary:
   a. $30,000 paid to a legal firm to structure and record the transaction.
   b. $35,000 preacquisition audit of subsidiary company accounts prior to purchase to determine purchase price.
   c. $10,000 paid to American Appraisal Company to determine fair values of assets acquired.
   d. $20,000 paid to All States Investment Company to issue common stock used as consideration to pay for subsidiary.
   e. Pablo Company's controller has allocated $56,000 of Pablo payroll costs to the purchase.

   How would Pablo account for each of the above costs?

8. What are the accounting ramifications of each of the two following situations involving the payment of contingent consideration in a purchase?
   a. P Company issued 100,000 shares of its $50 fair value common stock as payment to buy S Company on January 1, 20X1. P agreed to issue 10,000 additional shares of its stock two years later if S income exceeded an income target. The target was exceeded.
   b. P Company issued 100,000 shares of its $50 fair value common stock as payment to buy S Company on January 1, 20X1. P agreed to issue additional shares two years later if the fair value of P shares fell below $50 per share. Two years later, the stock had a value far below $50, and added shares were issued to S.

EXERCISES

Exercise 1 *(LO 3)* **Historical comparison—income effect of purchase versus pooling.** World Corporation acquired the net assets of Globe Company on July 1, 1998. In exchange for Globe's net assets, World issued 10,000 shares of its $5 par common stock, which had a $40 fair value on the date of acquisition. Globe Company had the following balance sheet on the date of acquisition:

Globe Company
Balance Sheet
July 1, 1998

Assets		Liabilities and Equity	
Accounts receivable	$ 50,000	Total liabilities	$450,000
Inventory	100,000	Common stock ($5 par)	125,000
Buildings (net)	300,000	Paid-in capital in excess of par	25,000
Equipment (net)	200,000	Retained earnings	50,000
Total assets	$650,000	Total liabilities and equity	$650,000

Appraisals have determined that fair values agree with the book values of the net assets.

Reported income amounts for both World and Globe for the year ended December 31, 1998, are as follows:

Income Statement
For the Year Ended December 31, 1998

	World	Globe
Sales	$ 800,000	$ 500,000
Less: Cost of goods sold	(400,000)	(300,000)
Operating expenses	(150,000)	(75,000)
Other expenses	(50,000)	(25,000)
Net income	$ 200,000	$ 100,000

No goodwill is reflected in the above income statement. At this point in time, goodwill was amortized. World amortized goodwill over 10 years. Assuming that income is earned evenly throughout the year, compare combined current-year income using the purchase method and the pooling method.

Exercise 2 *(LO 4, 5)* **Asset versus stock purchase.** Benz Company is contemplating the purchase of the net assets of Cardinal Company for $800,000 cash. To complete the transaction, direct acquisition costs are $15,000. The balance sheet of Cardinal Company on the purchase date is as follows:

Cardinal Company
Balance Sheet
December 31, 20X1

Assets		Liabilities and Equity	
Current assets	$ 80,000	Liabilities	$100,000
Land	50,000	Common stock ($10 par)	100,000
Building	450,000	Paid-in capital in excess of par	150,000
Accumulated depreciation, building	(200,000)	Retained earnings	230,000
Equipment	300,000		
Accumulated depreciation, equipment	(100,000)		
Total assets	$ 580,000	Total liabilities and equity	$580,000

The following fair values have been obtained for Cardinal's assets and liabilities:

Current assets	$100,000
Land	75,000
Building	300,000
Equipment	275,000
Liabilities	102,000

1. Record the purchase of the net assets of Cardinal Company on Benz Company's books.
2. Record the sale of the net assets on the books of Cardinal Company.
3. Record the purchase of 100% of the common stock of Cardinal Company on Benz's books. Cardinal Company will remain a separate legal entity.

Exercise 3 *(LO 5)* **Purchase with goodwill.** Smith Company was acquired by Rogers Corporation on July 1, 20X1. Rogers exchanged 60,000 shares of its $5 par stock, with a fair value of $20 per share, for the net assets of Smith Company.

Rogers incurred the following costs as a result of this transaction:

Direct acquisition costs	$25,000
Indirect acquisition costs	30,000
Stock registration and issuance costs	10,000
Total costs	$65,000

The balance sheet of Smith Company, on the day of the acquisition, was as follows:

Smith Company
Balance Sheet
July 1, 20X1

Assets			Liabilities and Equity		
Cash		$ 100,000	Current liabilities		$ 80,000
Inventory		300,000	Bonds payable		550,000
Property, plant, and equipment:			Stockholders' equity:		
Land	$200,000		Common stock	$200,000	
Buildings (net)	250,000		Paid-in capital in excess of par	100,000	
Equipment (net)	200,000	650,000	Retained earnings	120,000	420,000
Total assets		$1,050,000	Total liabilities and equity		$1,050,000

The appraised fair values as of July 1, 20X1, are as follows:

Inventory	$250,000
Equipment	220,000
Land	180,000
Buildings	300,000
Current liabilities	80,000
Bonds payable	410,000

Record the purchase of Smith Company on the books of Rogers Corporation.

Exercise 4 *(LO 6)* **Income after a purchase.** On December 31, 20X1, Panama Corporation acquired the net assets of Keyes Corporation. On the date of acquisition, book values agreed with fair values of the net assets, with the following exceptions:

	Book Value	Fair Value
Inventory	$100,000	$125,000
Land	200,000	250,000
Equipment (net)	350,000	380 000
Buildings (net)	400,000	475,000

Despite these markups, there was still an excess of purchase price over fair values, and goodwill of $75,000 was recorded by Panama Corporation. The following pro forma income statement for 20X2 was prepared just prior to the acquisition:

	Panama	Keyes
Sales	$ 400,000	$ 300,000
Less: Cost of goods sold	(200,000)	(140,000)
Operating expenses	(100,000)	(85,000)
Other expenses	(30,000)	(20,000)
Net income	$ 70,000	$ 55,000

Prepare an adjusted 20X2 pro forma income statement for the combined company. Fixed assets are depreciated using the straight-line method over a 20-year life.

Exercise 5 *(LO 7)* **Bargain purchase.** Nectar Corporation has agreed to purchase the net assets of Pyramid Corporation. Just prior to the purchase, Pyramid's balance sheet was as follows:

Pyramid Corporation
Balance Sheet
January 1, 20X1

Assets		Liabilities and Equity		
Accounts receivable	$200,000	Current liabilities	$ 80,000	
Inventory	270,000	Mortgage payable	250,000	$330,000
Equipment (net)	100,000	Stockholders' equity:		
		Common stock ($10 par)	$100,000	
		Retained earnings	140,000	240,000
Total assets	$570,000	Total liabilities and equity		$570,000

Fair values agree with book values except for the equipment, which has an estimated fair value of $40,000. Also, it has been determined that brand-name copyrights have an estimated value of $15,000. Nectar Corporation paid $10,000 in direct acquisition costs and $15,000 in indirect acquisition costs to consummate the transaction.

Record the purchase on the books of Nectar Corporation assuming the cash paid to Pyramid Corporation was $180,000.

Suggestion: Use zone analysis to guide your calculations and entries.

Exercise 6 *(LO 7)* **Purchase below value of priority accounts.** Use the facts of Exercise 5 for the acquisition of Pyramid Corporation by Nectar Corporation. Record the purchase on the books of Nectar Corporation assuming the cash paid to Pyramid Corporation was $125,000. Use zone analysis to guide your calculations and entries.

Exercise 7 *(LO 7)* **Bargain purchase with allocation.** Carp Corporation is purchasing the net assets of Bass Company on December 31, 20X6, when Bass Company has the following balance sheet:

Assets		Liabilities and Equity	
Current assets	$100,000	Liabilities	$ 90,000
Land	50,000	Common stock ($10 par)	200,000
Buildings (net)	200,000	Retained earnings	140,000
Equipment (net)	60,000		
Patents	20,000		
Total assets	$430,000	Total liabilities and equity	$430,000

Carp has obtained the following fair values for Bass Company accounts:

Current assets	$120,000
Land	80,000
Buildings	250,000
Equipment	150,000
Liabilities	92,000
Patents	20,000

Direct acquisition costs are $18,000, and indirect acquisition costs are $5,000.

Prepare the entries to record the purchase of Bass Company assuming the cash payment by Carp Corporation to Bass Company is $400,000. Carp Corporation will assume the liabilities of Bass Company. Zone analysis is recommended.

Exercise 8 *(LO 7)* **Bargain purchase, extraordinary gain.** Use the facts of Exercise 7 for the acquisition of Bass Company by Carp Corporation. Prepare the entries to record the purchase of Bass Company assuming the cash paid by Carp Corporation to Bass Company is $5,000. Use zone analysis to guide your calculations and entries.

Exercise 9 *(LO 6, 7)* **Goodwill impairment.** Anton Company purchased the net assets of Hair Company on January 1, 20X1, for $600,000. Using a business valuation model, the estimated value of Anton Company was $650,000 immediately after the purchase. The fair value of Anton's net assets was $400,000.

1. What amount of goodwill was recorded by Anton Company when it purchased Hair Company?
2. Using the information above, answer the questions posed in the following two independent situations:
   a. On December 31, 20X2, there were indications that goodwill might have been impaired. At that time, the existing recorded book value of Anton Company's net assets, including goodwill, was $500,000. The fair value of the net assets, exclusive of goodwill, was estimated to be $340,000. The value of the business was estimated to be $520,000. Is goodwill impaired? If so, what adjustment is needed?
   b. On December 31, 20X4, there were indications that goodwill might have been impaired. At that time, the existing recorded book value of Anton Company's net assets, including goodwill, was $450,000. The fair value of the net assets, exclusive of goodwill, was estimated to be $340,000. The value of the business was estimated to be $400,000. Is goodwill impaired? If so, what adjustment is needed?

Exercise 10 *(LO 8)* **Deferred tax liability.** Your client, Lewison International, has informed you that it has reached an agreement with Herro Company for the purchase of all of Herro's assets. This transaction will be accomplished through the issue of Lewison's common stock.

After your examination of the financial statements and the purchase agreement, you have discovered the following important facts.

The Lewison common stock issued has a fair value of $800,000. The fair value of Herro's assets, net of all liabilities, is $700,000. All asset book values equaled their fair values except for one machine valued at $200,000. This machine was originally purchased two years ago by Herro for $180,000. This machine has been depreciated using the straight-line method with an assumed useful life of 10 years and no salvage value. The acquisition is to be considered a tax-free exchange for tax purposes.

Assuming a 30% tax rate, what amounts will be recorded for the machine, deferred tax liability, and goodwill?

Exercise 11 *(LO 8)* **Tax loss carryover.** Lake Company had the following balance sheet on December 31, 20X1, when it was purchased for $900,000 in cash by Atlantic Corporation:

Lake Company
Balance Sheet
December 31, 20X1

Assets		Liabilities and Equity		
Current assets	$100,000	Current liabilities		$ 60,000
Equipment (net)	200,000	Stockholders' equity:		
Building (net)	270,000	Common stock ($5 par)	$100,000	
		Retained earnings	410,000	510,000
Total assets	$570,000	Total liabilities and equity		$570,000

All assets have fair values equal to their book values. The combination is structured as a tax-free exchange. Lake Company has a tax loss carryforward of $400,000, which it has not recorded. The balance of the $400,000 tax loss carryover is considered fully realizable. Atlantic is taxed at a rate of 30%.

Record the purchase of Lake Company by Atlantic Corporation.

Exercise 12 *(LO 8)* **Contingent consideration.** Gonring Company purchased the net assets of Helm Company on January 1, 20X1, and made the following entry to record the purchase:

Current Assets	100,000	
Equipment	150,000	
Land	50,000	
Buildings	300,000	
Goodwill	100,000	
Liabilities		80,000
Common Stock ($1 par)		100,000
Paid-In Capital in Excess of Par		520,000

Make the required entry on January 1, 20X3, for each of the two following independent contingency agreements:

1. An additional cash payment would be made on January 1, 20X3, equal to twice the amount by which average annual earnings of the Helm Division exceed $25,000 per year, prior to January 1, 20X3. Net income was $50,000 in 20X1 and $60,000 in 20X2.
2. Added shares would be issued on January 1, 20X3, to compensate for any fall in the value of Gonring common stock below $6 per share. The settlement would be to cure the deficiency by issuing added shares based on their fair value on January 1, 20X3. The market price of the shares on January 1, 20X3, was $4.

APPENDIX EXERCISE

Exercise 1A-1 *(LO 9)* **Estimating goodwill.** Green Company is considering acquiring the assets of Gold Corporation by assuming Gold's liabilities and by making a cash payment. Gold Corporation has the following balance sheet on the date negotiations occur:

Gold Corporation
Balance Sheet
December 31, 20X6

Assets		Liabilities and Equity	
Accounts receivable	$100,000	Total liabilities	$200,000
Inventory	100,000	Capital stock ($10 par)	100,000
Land	100,000	Paid-in capital in excess of par	200,000
Buildings (net)	220,000	Retained earnings	300,000
Equipment (net)	280,000		
Total assets	$800,000	Total liabilities and equity	$800,000

Appraisals indicate that the inventory is undervalued by $25,000, the building is undervalued by $80,000, and the equipment is overstated by $30,000. Past earnings have been considered above average and were as follows:

Year	Net Income
20X1	$ 90,000
20X2	110,000
20X3	120,000
20X4	140,000*
20X5	130,000

*Includes extraordinary gain of $40,000.

It is assumed that the average operating income of the past five years will continue. In this industry, the average return on assets is 12% on the fair value of the total identifiable assets.

1. Prepare an estimate of goodwill based on each of the following assumptions:
   a. The purchasing company paid for five years of excess earnings.
   b. Excess earnings will continue indefinitely and are to be capitalized at the industry normal return.
   c. Excess earnings will continue for only five years and should be capitalized at a higher rate of 16%, which reflects the risk applicable to goodwill.
2. Determine the actual goodwill recorded if Green pays $900,000 cash for the net assets of Gold Corporation and assumes all existing liabilities.

PROBLEMS

Problem 1-1 *(LO 3)* **Zone analysis, alternative prices.** Browne Corporation agreed to purchase the net assets of White Corporation on January 1, 20X1. White had the following balance sheet on the date of acquisition:

White Corporation
Balance Sheet
January 1, 20X1

Assets		Liabilities and Equity	
Accounts receivable	$ 79,000	Current liabilities	$145,000
Inventory	112,000	Bonds payable	100,000
Other current assets	55,000	Common stock	200,000
Equipment (net)	294,000	Paid-in capital in excess of par	50,000
Trademark	30,000	Retained earnings	75,000
Total assets	$570,000	Total liabilities and equity	$570,000

An appraiser determines that In-Process R&D exists and has an estimated value of $14,000. The appraisal indicates that the following assets had fair values that differed from their book values:

	Fair Value
Inventory	$120,000
Equipment	307,000
Trademark	27,000

◄◄◄◄◄ **Required**

Use zone analysis to prepare the entry on the books of Browne Corporation to purchase the net assets of White Corporation under each of the following purchase price scenarios:

a. $500,000
b. $250,000
c. $5,000

Problem 1-2 *(LO 3)* **Purchase of two companies with goodwill.** Barker Corporation has been looking to expand its operations and has decided to acquire the assets of Verk Company and Kent Company. Barker will issue 30,000 shares of its $10 par common stock to acquire the net assets of Verk Company and will issue 15,000 shares to acquire the net assets of Kent Company.

Verk and Kent have the following balance sheets as of December 31, 20X1:

Assets	Verk	Kent
Accounts receivable	$ 200,000	$ 80,000
Inventory	150,000	85,000
Property, plant, and equipment:		
Land	150,000	50,000
Building	500,000	300,000
Accumulated depreciation	(150,000)	(110,000)
Total assets	$ 850,000	$ 405,000

Liabilities and Equity	Verk	Kent
Current liabilities	$160,000	$ 55,000
Bonds payable	100,000	100,000
Stockholders' equity:		
Common stock ($10 par)	300,000	100,000
Retained earnings	290,000	150,000
Total liabilities and equity	$850,000	$405,000

The following fair values are agreed upon by the two firms:

Assets	Verk	Kent
Inventory	$200,000	$100,000
Bonds payable	90,000	95,000
Land	300,000	80,000
Buildings	450,000	400,000

Barker's stock is currently trading at $40 per share. Barker will incur $5,000 of direct acquisition costs in Verk and $4,000 of direct acquisition costs in Kent. Barker also incurred $13,000 of indirect acquisition costs and $15,000 of registration and issuance costs.

Barker stockholders' equity is as follows:

Common stock, $10 par	$1,200,000
Paid-in capital in excess of par	800,000
Retained earnings	750,000

Required ▶ ▶ ▶ ▶ ▶ Record the acquisition on the books of Barker Corporation, using purchase accounting principles. Zone analysis is suggested to guide your work.

Problem 1-3 *(LO 4, 7)* **Pro forma income after a purchase.** Molitor Company is contemplating the acquisition of Yount Inc. on January 1, 20X1. If Molitor proceeded to acquire Yount, it would pay $730,000 in cash to Yount and direct acquisition costs of $20,000.

The January 1, 20X1, balance sheet of Yount Inc. is anticipated to be as follows:

Yount Inc.
Pro Forma Balance Sheet
January 1, 20X1

Assets		Liabilities and Equity	
Cash equivalents	$100,000	Current liabilities	$ 30,000
Accounts receivable	120,000	Long-term liabilities	165,000
Inventory	50,000	Common stock ($10 par)	80,000
Depreciable fixed assets	200,000	Retained earnings	115,000
Accumulated depreciation	(80,000)		
Total assets	$390,000	Total liabilities and equity	$390,000

Fair values agree with book values except for the inventory and the depreciable fixed assets, which have fair values of $70,000 and $400,000, respectively.

Your projections of the combined operations for 20X1 are as follows:

Combined sales	$200,000
Combined cost of goods sold, including beginning inventory of Yount at book value which will be sold in 20X1	120,000
Other expenses not including depreciation of Yount assets	25,000

Depreciation on Yount fixed assets is straight-line using a 20-year life.

◄◄◄◄◄ **Required**

1. Prepare a zone analysis for the purchase, and record the purchase.
2. Prepare a pro forma income statement for the combined firm for 20X1. Show supporting calculations for consolidated income. Ignore tax issues.

Problem 1-4 *(LO 7)* **Alternate consideration, bargain.** Kent Corporation is considering the purchase of Williams Incorporated. Kent has asked you, its accountant, to evaluate the various offers it might make to Williams Incorporated. The December 31, 20X1, balance sheet of Williams is as follows:

Williams Incorporated
Balance Sheet
December 31, 20X1

Assets			Liabilities and Equity		
Current assets:			Accounts payable		$ 40,000
Accounts receivable	$ 50,000				
Inventory	300,000				
		$350,000	Stockholders' equity:		
Noncurrent assets:			Common stock	$ 40,000	
Land	$ 20,000		Paid-in capital in excess of par	110,000	
Building (net)	70,000	90,000	Retained earnings	250,000	400,000
Total assets		$440,000	Total liabilities and equity		$440,000

The following fair values differ from existing book values:

Inventory	$250,000
Land	40,000
Building	120,000

Required ▶ ▶ ▶ ▶ ▶ Record the purchase entry for Kent Corporation that would result under each of the alternative offers. Price zone analysis is suggested.

1. Kent Corporation issues 20,000 of its $10 par common stock with a fair value of $25 per share for the net assets of Williams Incorporated.
2. Kent Corporation pays $385,000 in cash.

Problem 1-5 *(LO 4, 7)* **Revaluation of assets.** Jansen Company is a corporation that was organized on July 1, 20X1. The June 30, 20X6, balance sheet for Jansen is as follows:

Assets		
Investments		$ 400,500
Accounts receivable	$1,250,000	
Allowance for doubtful accounts	(300,000)	950,000
Inventory		1,500,000
Prepaid insurance		18,000
Land		58,000
Machinery and equipment (net)		1,473,500
Goodwill		100,000
Total assets		$4,500,000

Liabilities and Equity	
Current liabilities	$1,475,000
Common stock, $10 par	1,200,000
Retained earnings	1,825,000
Total liabilities and equity	$4,500,000

Machinery was purchased in fiscal years 20X2, 20X4, and 20X5 for $500,000, $850,000, and $660,000, respectively. The straight-line method of depreciation and a 10-year estimated life with no salvage value have been used for all machinery, with a half-year of depreciation taken in the year of acquisition. The experience of other companies over the last several years indicates that the machinery can be sold at 125% of its book value.

An analysis of the accounts receivable indicates that the allowance for doubtful accounts should be increased to $337,500. An independent appraisal made in June 20X1 valued the land at $70,000. Using the lower-of-cost-or-market rule, inventory is to be restated at $1,200,000.

To be exchanged are 16,000 shares of Clark Corporation for 120,000 Jansen shares. During June 20X6, the fair value of a share of Clark Corporation was $265. The stockholders' equity account balances of Clark Corporation as of June 30, 20X6, were as follows:

Common stock, $10 par	$2,000,000
Additional paid-in capital	580,000
Retained earnings	2,496,400
Total stockholders' equity	$5,076,400

Direct acquisition costs are $12,000.

Required ▶ ▶ ▶ ▶ ▶ Assuming the books of Clark Corporation are to be retained, prepare the necessary journal entry (or entries) to effect the business combination on July 1, 20X6, as a purchase. Use zone analysis to support the purchase entries.

Problem 1-6 *(LO 7)* **Cash purchase, several of each priority, with goodwill.** Tweedy Corporation is contemplating the purchase of the net assets of Sylvester Corporation in anticipation of expanding its operations. The balance sheet of Sylvester Corporation on December 31, 20X1, is as follows:

Sylvester Corporation
Balance Sheet
December 31, 20X1

Current assets:			**Current liabilities:**		
Notes receivable	$ 24,000		Accounts payable	$ 45,000	
Accounts receivable	56,000		Payroll and benefit-related liabilities	12,500	
Inventory	31,000		Debt maturing in one year	10,000	
Other current assets	18,000				
Total current assets		$129,000	Total current liabilities		$ 67,500
Investments		65,000			
Fixed assets:			**Other liabilities:**		
Land	$ 32,000		Long-term debt	$248,000	
Building	245,000		Payroll and benefit-related liabilities	156,000	
Equipment	387,000				
Total fixed assets		664,000	Total other liabilities		404,000
Intangibles:			**Stockholders' equity:**		
Goodwill	$ 45,000		Common stock	$100,000	
Patents	23,000		Paid-in capital in excess of par	250,000	
Trade names	10,000		Retained earnings	114,500	
Total intangibles		78,000	Total equity		464,500
Total assets		$936,000	Total liabilities and equity		$936,000

An appraiser for Tweedy determined the fair values of the assets and liabilities to be as follows:

Assets		Liabilities	
Notes receivable	$ 24,000	Accounts payable	$ 45,000
Accounts receivable	56,000	Payroll and benefit-related liabilities	12,500
Inventory	30,000	Debt maturing in one year	10,000
Other current assets	15,000		
Investments	63,000		
Land	55,000	Long-term debt	248,000
Building	275,000	Payroll and benefit-related liabilities—long-term	156,000
Equipment	426,000		
Goodwill	—		
Patents	20,000		
Trade names	15,000		

The agreed-upon purchase price was $580,000 in cash. Direct acquisition costs paid in cash totaled $20,000.

◄◄◄◄◄ **Required**

Using the above information, do zone analysis, and prepare the entry on the books of Tweedy Corporation to purchase the net assets of Sylvester Corporation on December 31, 20X1.

Problem 1-7 *(LO 5, 7)* **Stock purchase, goodwill.** HT Corporation is contemplating the acquisition of the net assets of Smith Company on December 31, 20X1. It is considering making an offer, which would include a cash payout of $290,000 along with giving 10,000 shares of its $2 par value common stock that is currently selling for $20 per share. The balance sheet of Smith Company is given below, along with estimated fair values of the net assets to be acquired.

Smith Company
Balance Sheet
December 31, 20X1

	Book Value	Fair Value		Book Value	Fair Value
Current assets:			**Current liabilities:**		
Notes receivable	$ 33,000	$ 33,000	Accounts payable	$ 63,000	$ 63,000
Inventory	89,000	80,000	Taxes payable	15,000	15,000
Prepaid expenses	15,000	15,000	Interest payable	3,000	3,000
Total current assets	$137,000	$128,000	Total current liabilities	$ 81,000	$ 81,000
Investments	$ 36,000	$ 55,000			
Fixed assets:			**Other liabilities:**		
Land	$ 15,000	$ 90,000	Bonds payable	$250,000	$250,000
Buildings	115,000	170,000	Discount on bonds payable	(18,000)	(30,000)
Equipment	256,000	250,000			
Vehicles	32,000	25,000			
Total fixed assets	$418,000	$535,000	Total other liabilities	$232,000	$220,000
Intangibles:			**Stockholders' equity:**		
Franchise	$ 56,000	$ 70,000	Common stock	$ 50,000	
			Paid-in capital in excess of par	200,000	
			Retained earnings	84,000	
			Total equity	$334,000	
Total assets	$647,000	$788,000	Total liabilities and equity	$647,000	

Required ▶ ▶ ▶ ▶ ▶ Do zone analysis and prepare the entry on the books of HT Corporation to record the acquisition of Smith Company.

Problem 1-8 *(LO 5, 7)* **Cash purchase, extraordinary gain, allocate to nonpriority accounts.** James Company owned by Howard and Jane James has been experiencing financial difficulty for the past several years. Both Howard and Jane have not been in good health and have decided to find a buyer. J&K International, after being approached by Howard and Jane and reviewing the financial statements for the previous three years, has decided to make an offer of $23,000 for the net assets of James Company on January 1, 20X2. The balance sheet as of this date is as follows:

James Company
Balance Sheet
January 1, 20X2

Current assets:		**Current liabilities:**	
Accounts receivable	$ 87,000	Accounts payable	$ 56,000
Inventory	36,000	Accrued liabilities	14,000

Other current assets	14,000		
Total current assets	$137,000	Total current liabilities	$ 70,000
Fixed assets:		**Other liabilities:**	
Equipment	$105,000	Notes payable	$ 30,000
Vehicles	69,000		
Total fixed assets	$174,000	Total liabilities	$100,000
Intangibles:		**Stockholders' equity:**	
Mailing lists	$ 4,000	Common stock	$ 60,000
		Paid-in capital in excess of par	100,000
		Retained earnings	55,000
		Total equity	$215,000
Total assets	$315,000	Total liabilities and equity	$315,000

In reviewing the above balance sheet, J&K's appraiser felt the liabilities were stated at their fair values. He placed the following fair values on the assets of the company.

James Company
Fair Values
January 1, 20X2

Current assets:	
Accounts receivable	$ 87,000
Inventory	30,000
Other current assets	8,000
Total current assets	$125,000
Fixed assets:	
Equipment	$ 80,000
Vehicles	71,000
Total fixed assets	$151,000
Intangibles:	
Mailing lists	$ 0
Total intangibles	$ 0
Total assets	$276,000

◀◀◀◀◀ **Required**

1. Using this information, do zone analysis, and prepare the entry to record the purchase of the net assets of James Company on the books of J&K International.
2. Howard and Jane were disappointed in J&K International's offer and initially rejected it. J&K International then offered them $45,000 in cash. Assuming this offer is accepted, do zone analysis, and prepare the entry that should be made on J&K International's books. (Assume that the fair values of the net assets have not changed.)

Problem 1-9 *(LO 6)* **Pro forma income after purchase.** On January 1, 20X1, Arthur Enterprises acquired Ann's Tool Company. Prior to the merger of the two companies, each company had prepared an estimate of its income for the year ended December 31, 20X1. These estimates are as follows:

(continued)

Income Statement Accounts		Arthur Enterprises		Ann's Tool Company
Sales revenue		$550,000		$140,000
Cost of goods sold		200,000		50,000
Gross profit		$350,000		$ 90,000
Selling expenses	$125,000		$30,000	
Administrative expenses	150,000		45,000	
Depreciation expense	13,800		7,500	
Amortization expense	5,600		2,000	
Total operating expenses		294,400		84,500
Operating income		$ 55,600		$ 5,500
Nonoperating revenues and expenses:				
Interest expense				4,000
Interest income		7,000		
Dividend income		4,000		
Income before taxes		$ 66,600		$ 1,500
Provision for income taxes (30% rate)		19,980		450
Net income		$ 46,620		$ 1,050

An analysis of the merger agreement revealed that the purchase price exceeded the fair value of all assets by $40,000. The book and fair values of Ann's Tool Company are given in the table below along with an estimate of the useful lives of each of these asset categories.

Asset Account	Book Value	Fair Value	Useful Life
Inventory	$30,000	$ 28,000	Sold during 20X1
Land	50,000	80,000	Unlimited
Buildings	75,000	125,000	25 years
Equipment	32,000	56,000	8 years
Truck	1,000	3,000	2 years
Patent	12,000	18,000	6 years
Computer software	0	10,000	2 years
Copyright	0	20,000	10 years

Management believes the company will be in a combined tax bracket of 30%. The company uses the straight-line method of computing depreciation and amortization and assigns a zero salvage value.

Required ▶ ▶ ▶ ▶ ▶ Using the above information, prepare a pro forma income statement for the combined companies.

Problem 1-10 *(LO 5, 7)* **Issue stock, several of each priority account, goodwill, purchase entry and pro forma income.**

Part A. Garden International has been looking to expand its operations and has decided to acquire the net assets of Iris Company. Garden will be issuing 10,000 shares of its $5 par value common stock for the net assets of Iris. Garden's stock is currently selling for $27 per share. In addition, Garden paid $10,000 in direct acquisition costs. A balance sheet for Iris Company as of December 31, 20X1, is as follows:

Current assets:		**Current liabilities:**	
Accounts receivable	$ 15,000	Accounts payable	$ 22,000
Inventory	38,000	Interest payable	2,000
Prepaid expenses	12,000		
Total current assets	$ 65,000	Total current liabilities	$ 24,000
Investments	19,000		

Fixed assets:			**Other liabilities:**		
Land	$30,000		Long-term notes payable		40,000
Building	70,000				
Equipment	56,000				
Total fixed assets		156,000	Total liabilities		$ 64,000
Intangibles:			**Stockholders' equity:**		
Patent	$17,000		Common stock	$ 40,000	
Copyrights	22,000		Paid-in capital in excess of par	120,000	
Goodwill	8,000		Retained earnings	63,000	
Total intangibles		47,000	Total equity		223,000
Total assets		$287,000	Total liabilities and equity		$287,000

In reviewing Iris's balance sheet and in consulting with various appraisers, Garden has determined that the inventory is understated by $2,000, the land is understated by $10,000, the building is understated by $15,000, and the copyrights are understated by $4,000. Garden has also determined that the equipment is overstated by $6,000, and the patent is overstated by $5,000.

The investments have a fair value of $33,000 on December 31, 20X1, and the amount of goodwill (if any) must be determined.

Part A. Using the information above, do zone analysis, and record the acquisition of Iris Company on Garden International's books. ◄◄◄◄◄ **Required**

Part B. Garden International wishes to estimate its net income after the acquisition of Iris. Projected income statements for 20X2 are as follows:

Income Statement Accounts	Garden International	Iris Company
Sales revenue	$(350,000)	$(125,000)
Cost of goods sold	147,000	55,000
Gross profit	$(203,000)	$ (70,000)
Selling expenses*	$ 100,000	$ 20,000
Administrative expenses*	50,000	30,000
Depreciation expense	12,500	8,600
Amortization expense	1,000	3,900
Total operating expenses	$ 163,500	$ 62,500
Operating income	$ (39,500)	$ (7,500)
Nonoperating revenues and expenses:		
Interest expense		3,000
Investment income	(12,000)	(4,500)
Income before taxes	$ (51,500)	$ (9,000)
Provision for income taxes (40% rate)	20,600	3,600
Net income	$ (30,900)	$ (5,400)

*Does not include depreciation or amortization expense.

Garden International estimates that the following amount of depreciation and amortization should be taken on the revalued assets of Iris Company.

Building depreciation	$4,000
Equipment depreciation	5,000
Patent amortization	1,200
Copyright amortization	2,600

Required ▶ ▶ ▶ ▶ ▶ **Part B.** Using the above information, prepare a pro forma income statement for Garden International combined with Iris Company for the year ended December 31, 20X2.

Problem 1-11 *(LO 8)* **Revaluation of leases.** Sentry Inc. purchased for $2,300,000 in cash the net assets of New Equipment Leasing Company. The purchase was made on December 31, 20X1, at which time New Equipment had prepared the following balance sheet:

New Equipment Leasing Company
Balance Sheet
December 31, 20X1

Assets		Liabilities and Equity	
Current assets	$ 100,000	Current liabilities	$ 150,000
Assets under operating leases	520,000	Obligation under capital lease of equipment	35,000
Net investment in direct financing (capital leases)	730,000	Common stock ($5 par)	100,000
Leased equipment under capital lease (net)	40,000	Paid-in capital in excess of par	400,000
Buildings (net)	200,000	Retained earnings	955,000
Land	50,000		
Total assets	$1,640,000	Total liabilities and equity	$1,640,000

The following information is available concerning the assets and liabilities of New Equipment:

a. Current assets and liabilities are stated fairly. No payments resulting from leases are included in current accounts, since all payments are due each December 31 and payment for 20X1 has been made.
b. Assets under operating leases have an estimated value of $580,000. This figure includes consideration of remaining rents and the value of the assets at the end of the lease terms.
c. The net investment in direct financing leases represents receivables at their discounted present values. All leases are written at the current market interest rate of 12%, except one equipment lease requiring payments of $50,000 per year for five remaining years. The $50,000 payments include interest at 8%.
d. The buildings and the land have appraised fair values of $400,000 and $100,000, respectively.
e. The leased equipment under the capital lease pertains to a computer used by New Equipment. The obligation under the capital lease of equipment includes the present value of five remaining payments of $9,233 due at the end of each year and discounted at 10%. The current interest rate for this type of transaction is 12%. The fair value of the equipment under the lease is $60,000.
f. New Equipment has expended $100,000 on R&D leading to new equipment applications. Sentry estimates the value of this work to be $200,000.
g. New Equipment has been named in a $200,000 lawsuit involving an accident by a lessee using its equipment. It is likely that New Equipment will be found liable in the amount of $50,000.

Required ▶ ▶ ▶ ▶ ▶ Record the purchase of New Equipment Leasing Company by Sentry Inc. Carefully support your entry. You may assume that the price will allow goodwill to be recorded.

Problem 1-12 *(LO 8)* **Tax-free exchange, tax loss carryover.** Gusty Company issued 10,000 shares of $10 par common stock for the net assets of Marco Incorporated on December 31, 20X2. The stock has a fair value of $60 per share. Direct acquisition costs were $10,000, and the cost of issuing the stock was $3,000. At the time of the purchase, Marco had the following summarized balance sheet:

Assets		Liabilities and Equity	
Current assets	$150,000	Bonds payable	$200,000
Equipment (net)	200,000	Common stock ($10 par)	100,000
Land and buildings (net)	250,000	Retained earnings	300,000
Total assets	$600,000	Total liabilities and equity	$600,000

The only fair value differing from book value is equipment, which is worth $300,000. Marco has $120,000 in operating losses in prior years. The previous asset values are also the tax basis of the assets, which will be the tax basis for Gusty, since the acquisition is a tax-free exchange. Gusty is confident that it will recover the entire tax loss carryforward applicable to the past losses of Marco. The applicable tax rate is 30%.

Record the purchase of the net assets of Marco Incorporated by Gusty Company. You may assume the price paid will allow goodwill to be recorded. ◄◄◄◄◄ **Required**

Problem 1-13 *(LO 8)* **Contingent consideration.** Dodd Corporation is purchasing the net assets, exclusive of cash, of Walsh Company as of January 1, 20X1, at which time Walsh Company's balance sheet is as follows:

Assets		
Current assets:		
Cash	$ 30,000	
Accounts receivable	50,000	$ 80,000
Noncurrent assets:		
Investments in marketable securities	$120,000	
Land	600,000	
Buildings (net)	450,000	
Equipment (net)	800,000	
Goodwill	100,000	2,070,000
Total assets		$2,150,000

Liabilities and Stockholders' Equity		
Current liabilities:		
Accounts payable	$ 150,000	
Income tax payable	190,000	$ 340,000
Equity:		
Common stock ($5 par)	$1,200,000	
Retained earnings	610,000	1,810,000
Total liabilities and equity		$2,150,000

Dodd Corporation feels that the following fair values should be substituted for Walsh's book values:

Accounts receivable	$ 60,000
Investment in marketable securities	150,000
Land	450,000
Buildings	450,000
Equipment	600,000
Accounts payable	120,000

(continued)

Dodd will issue 20,000 shares of its common stock with a \$2 par value and a quoted fair value of \$60 per share on January 1, 20X1, to Walsh Company to acquire the net assets. Dodd also agrees that two years from now it will issue additional securities to compensate Walsh for any decline in value below that on the date of issue.

Required ▶ ▶ ▶ ▶ ▶

1. Record the purchase on the books of Dodd Corporation on January 1, 20X1. Include support for calculations used to arrive at the values assigned to the assets and liabilities. Use price zone analysis to aid your solution.
2. Indicate the disclosure that would be necessary in the financial statements of Dodd Corporation on December 31, 20X1, assuming the quoted value of the stock is \$62 per share.
3. Record payment (if any) of contingent consideration on January 1, 20X3, assuming that the quoted value of the stock is \$57.50. (Round shares to nearest whole share.)

APPENDIX PROBLEM

Problem 1A-1 *(LO 9)* **Estimate goodwill, record purchase.** Caswell Company is contemplating the purchase of LaBelle Company as of January 1, 20X6. LaBelle Company has provided the following current balance sheet:

Assets		Liabilities and Equity	
Cash and receivables	\$ 150,000	Current liabilities	\$120,000
Inventory	180,000	9% bonds payable	300,000
Land	50,000	Common stock (\$5 par)	100,000
Building	600,000	Paid-in capital in excess of par	200,000
Accumulated depreciation	(150,000)	Retained earnings	150,000
Goodwill	40,000		
Total assets	\$ 870,000	Total liabilities and equity	\$870,000

The following information exists relative to balance sheet accounts:

a. The inventory has a fair value of \$200,000.
b. The land is appraised at \$100,000 and the building at \$600,000.
c. The 9% bonds payable have five years to maturity and pay annual interest each December 31. The current interest rate for similar bonds is 8% per year.
d. It is likely that there will be a payment for goodwill based on projected income in excess of the industry average, which is 10% on total assets. Caswell will project the average past five years' operating income and will pay for excess income based on an assumption of a 5-year life and a risk rate of return of 16%. The past five years' net incomes for LaBelle are as follows:

20X1	\$ 120,000
20X2	140,000
20X3	150,000
20X4	200,000 (includes \$40,000 extraordinary gain)
20X5	180,000

Required ▶ ▶ ▶ ▶ ▶

1. Provide an estimate of fair value for the bonds and for goodwill.
2. Using the values derived in Requirement 1, record the purchase on the Caswell books.

The High Price of Cookies — *Case 1-1*

Part A. In June of 2000, Philip Morris Companies Inc., the large food and tobacco conglomerate, announced it would purchase Nabisco Holdings Corp. for $55 per share. Philip Morris chairman and chief executive Geoffrey Bible said in a statement that the purchase at $55 per share would greatly expand the firm's food offerings. "The combination of Kraft and Nabisco will create the most dynamic company in the food industry, both in terms of earnings levels and the revenues and earnings growth rates."

Philip Morris purchased the net assets of Nabisco and assumed all of Nabisco's debt. The price of a Nabisco share increased from $30 per share in April 2000 to $51.62, just prior to the purchase announcement.

Exhibit A shows a balance sheet for Nabisco Holdings Corp. as of March 31, 2000. The goodwill shown is from prior purchases made by Nabisco and does not reflect the purchase of the company by Philip Morris. The purchase included all of the Class A and Class B common stock shown on the balance sheet.

Exhibit A

Nabisco Holdings Corp.
Nabisco, Inc.
Consolidated Condensed Balance Sheets
(dollars in millions)

	March 31, 2000		December 31, 1999	
	Nabisco Holdings	Nabisco	Nabisco Holdings	Nabisco
ASSETS				
Current assets:				
Cash and cash equivalents	$ 94	$ 94	$ 110	$ 110
Accounts receivable, net	553	553	681	681
Deferred income taxes	100	100	116	116
Inventories	964	964	898	898
Prepaid expenses and other current assets	82	82	79	79
Total current assets	1,793	1,793	1,884	1,884
Property, plant and equipment—at cost	5,087	5,087	5,053	5,053
Less accumulated depreciation	(2,030)	(2,030)	(1,966)	(1,966)
Net property, plant and equipment	3,057	3,057	3,087	3,087
Trademarks, net of accumulated amortization of $1,242 and $1,214, respectively	3,414	3,414	3,443	3,443
Goodwill, net of accumulated amortization of $1,032 and $1,007, respectively	3,151	3,151	3,159	3,159
Other assets and deferred charges	163	163	134	134
	$11,578	$11,578	$11,707	$11,707

(continued)

Exhibit A *(Concluded)*

	March 31, 2000		December 31, 1999	
	Nabisco Holdings	Nabisco	Nabisco Holdings	Nabisco
LIABILITIES AND STOCKHOLDERS' EQUITY				
Current liabilities:				
Notes payable	$ 72	$ 72	$ 39	$ 39
Accounts payable	403	403	642	642
Accrued liabilities	982	932	1,020	970
Intercompany payable to Nabisco Holdings	—	7	—	7
Current maturities of long-term debt	11	11	158	158
Income taxes accrued	121	121	104	104
Total current liabilities	1,589	1,546	1,963	1,920
Long-term debt (less current maturities)	4,094	4,094	3,892	3,892
Other noncurrent liabilities	770	770	744	744
Deferred income taxes	1,180	1,180	1,176	1,176
Stockholders' equity:				
Class A common stock (51,412,707 shares issued and outstanding at March 31, 2000 and December 31, 1999)	1	—	1	—
Class B common stock (213,250,000 shares issued and outstanding at March 31, 2000 and December 31, 1999)	2	—	2	—
Paid-in capital	4,093	4,141	4,093	4,141
Retained earnings	158	137	148	127
Treasury stock, at cost	(17)	—	(17)	—
Accumulated other comprehensive income (loss)	(290)	(290)	(293)	(293)
Notes receivable on common stock purchases	(2)	—	(2)	—
Total stockholders' equity	3,945	3,988	3,932	3,975
	$11,578	$11,578	$11,707	$11,707

Required (Part A):

Calculate the price paid for the net assets of Nabisco and compare it to book value. By what amount will net assets have to be increased to reflect the price paid for Nabisco?

Part B. For the year ended December 31, 1999, Nabisco reported a net income of $357 million or $1.35 per share. The interesting issue is, will this influx of income have a favorable effect on Philip Morris's reported income? For the year ended December 31, 1999, Philip Morris reported a net income of $7.75 billion on 2,339 billion shares of common stock. Earnings per share, after various adjustments, was $3.91 per share.

Assume that the excess of the price paid for Nabisco over the book value of its net assets is primarily attributable to goodwill. At the time of the purchase, the amortization period for goodwill was 40 years. Further assume that the added goodwill amortization expense is tax deductible at a rate of 38%.

Required (Part B):

Assuming that Nabisco has the same income (prior to asset adjustments resulting from the purchase) in years after the purchase, how much net income will Nabisco add to Philip Morris using a 40-year amortization period for goodwill? What would the income increment be if goodwill is not amortized?

Structured Example of Goodwill Impairment

Case 1-2

Modern Company purchased the net assets of the Frontier Company for $1,300,000 on January 1, 20X1. A business valuation consultant arrived at the price and deemed it to be a good value.

Part 1. The following list of fair values was provided to you by the consultant:

Assets and Liabilities	Comments	Valuation Method	Fair Value
Cash equivalents	Sellers values are accepted.	Existing book value.	$ 80,000
Inventory	Replacement cost is available.	Market replacement cost for similar items is used.	150,000
Accounts receivable	Asset is adjusted for estimated bad debts.	Aging schedule is used for valuation.	180,000
Land	Per-acre value is well established.	Calculation is based on 20 acres at $10,000 per acre.	200,000
Building	Most reliable measure is rent potential.	Rent is estimated at $80,000 per year for 20 years, discounted at 14% return for similar properties. Present value is reduced for land value.	329,850
Equipment	Cost of replacement capacity can be estimated.	Estimated purchase cost of equipment with similar capacity is used.	220,000
Patent	Recorded by seller at only legal cost; has significant future value.	Added profit made possible by patent is $40,000 per year for 4 years. Discounted at risk-adjusted rate for similar investments of 20% per year.	103,550
Current liabilities	Recorded amounts are accurate.	Recorded value is used.	(120,000)
Mortgage payable	Specified interest rate is below market rate.	Discount the $50,000 annual payments for 5 years at annual market rate of 7%.	(205,010)
Net identifiable assets at fair value			$ 938,390
Price paid for reporting unit			1,300,000
Goodwill	Believed to exist based on reputation and customer list.	Implied by price paid.	$ 361,610

(continued)

Required:

1. Using the information in the preceding table, confirm the accuracy of the present value calculations made for the building, patent, and mortgage payable.

Part 2. Frontier did not have publicly traded stock. You made an estimate of the value of the company based on the following assumptions that will later be included in the reporting unit valuation procedure:

1. Frontier will provide operating cash flows, net of tax, of $150,000 during the next fiscal year.
2. Operating cash flows will increase at the rate of 10% per year for the next 4 fiscal years and then will remain steady for 15 more years.
3. Cash flows, defined as net of cash from operations less capital expenditures, will be discounted at an after-tax discount rate of 12%. An annual rate of 12% is a reasonable risk-adjusted rate of return for investments of this type.
4. Added capital expenditures will be $100,000 after 5 years, $120,000 for 10 years, and $130,000 after 15 years.
5. An estimate of salvage value (net of the tax effect of gains or losses) of the assets after 20 years is estimated to be $300,000. This is a conservative assumption, since the unit may be operated after that period.

Required:

2. Prepare a schedule of net-of-tax cash flows for Frontier and discount them to present value.
3. Compare the estimated fair value of the reporting unit with amounts assigned to identifiable assets plus goodwill less liabilities.
4. Record the purchase.

Part 3. Revisit the information in Part 1 that illustrates the reporting unit valuation procedure.

Assume that by fiscal year-end, December 31, 20X1, events have occurred suggesting goodwill could be impaired. You have the following information. These new estimates were made at the end of the first year:

Net book value of Frontier Company including goodwill	$1,300,000
Estimated implied fair value of the reporting unit, based on cash flow analysis discounted at a 12% annual rate	1,200,000
Estimated fair value of identifiable net assets using methods excluding goodwill	1,020,000

Required:

5. Has goodwill been impaired? Perform the impairment testing procedure. If goodwill has been impaired, calculate the adjustment to goodwill and make the needed entry.

Consolidated Statements: Date of Acquisition

CHAPTER

2

Learning Objectives

When you have completed this chapter, you should be able to

1. **Differentiate among the accounting methods used for investments, based on the level of common stock ownership in another company.**
2. **State the traditional criteria for presenting consolidated statements, and explain why disclosure of separate subsidiary financial information might be important.**
3. **Explain when control might exist without majority ownership.**
4. **Demonstrate the worksheet procedures needed to eliminate the investment account.**
5. **Demonstrate the worksheet procedures needed to merge subsidiary accounts.**
6. **Apply zone and price analyses to guide the adjustment process to reflect the price paid for the controlling interest.**
7. **Create a determination and distribution of excess (D&D) schedule.**
8. **Explain the impact of a noncontrolling interest on worksheet procedures and financial statement preparation.**
9. **Show the impact of preexisting goodwill on the consolidation process.**
10. **Define push-down accounting, and explain when it may be used and its impact.**

The preceding chapter dealt with business combinations that are accomplished as asset acquisitions. The net assets of an entire company are purchased and recorded directly on the books of the purchasing company. Consolidation of the two companies is automatic because all subsequent transactions are recorded on a single set of books.

A company will commonly purchase a large enough interest in another company's voting common stock to obtain control of operations. The company owning the controlling interest is termed the *parent*, while the controlled company is termed the *subsidiary.* Legally, the parent company has only an investment in the stock of the subsidiary and will only record an investment account in its accounting records. The subsidiary will continue to prepare its own financial statements. However, accounting principles require that when one company has effective control over another, a single set of *consolidated statements* must be prepared for the companies under common control. The consolidated statements present the financial statements of the parent and its subsidiaries as those of a single economic entity. Worksheets are prepared to merge the separate statements of the parent and its subsidiary(s) into a single set of consolidated statements.

This chapter is the first of several that will show how to combine the separate statements of a parent and its subsidiaries. The theory of purchase accounting, developed in Chapter 1, is applied in the consolidation process. In fact, the consolidated statements of a parent and its 100% owned subsidiary look exactly like they would have had the net assets been purchased. **This chapter contains only the procedures necessary to prepare consolidated statements**

on the day that the controlling investment is acquired. The procedures for consolidating controlling investments in periods subsequent to the purchase date will be developed in Chapter 3. The effect of operating activities between the parent and its subsidiaries, such as intercompany loans, merchandise sales, and fixed asset sales, will be discussed in Chapters 4 and 5. Later chapters deal with taxation issues and changes in the level of ownership.

1

OBJECTIVE

Differentiate among the accounting methods used for investments, based on the level of common stock ownership in another company.

LEVELS OF INVESTMENT

The purchase of the voting common stock of another company receives different accounting treatments depending on the level of ownership and the amount of influence or control caused by the stock ownership. The ownership levels and accounting methods can be summarized as follows:

Level of Ownership	Initial Recording	Recording of Income
Passive—generally under 20% ownership.	At cost including brokers' fees.	Dividends as declared (except stock dividends).
Influential—generally 20% to 50% ownership.	At cost including brokers' fees.	Ownership share of income (or loss) as reported. Shown as investment income on financial statements. (Dividends declared are distributions of income already recorded; they reduce the investment account.)
Controlling—generally over 50% ownership.	At cost including all direct acquisition costs.	Ownership share of income (or loss). (Some adjustments are explained in later chapters.) Accomplished by merging the subsidiary income statement accounts with those of the parent in the consolidation process.

To illustrate the differences in reporting the income applicable to the common stock shares owned, consider the following example based on the reported income of the investor and investee (company whose shares are owned by investor):

Account	Investor*	Investee
Sales	$500,000	$300,000
Less: Cost of goods sold	250,000	180,000
Gross profit	$250,000	$120,000
Less: Selling and administrative expenses	100,000	80,000
Net income	$150,000	$ 40,000

*Does not include any income from investee.

Assume that the investee company paid $10,000 in cash dividends. The investor would prepare the following income statements, depending on the level of ownership:

Level of Ownership	10% Passive	30% Influential	80% Controlling
Sales	$ 500,000	$ 500,000	$ 800,000
Less: Cost of goods sold	250,000	250,000	430,000
Gross profit	$ 250,000	$ 250,000	$ 370,000
Less: Selling and administrative expenses	100,000	100,000	180,000

(continued)

Level of Ownership	10% Passive	30% Influential	80% Controlling
Operating income	$ 150,000	$ 150,000	
Dividend income (10% × $10,000 dividends)	1,000		
Investment income (30% × $40,000 reported income)		12,000	
Net income	**$151,000**	**$162,000**	$ 190,000
Noncontrolling interest (20% × $40,000 reported income)			$ 8,000
Controlling interest			**$182,000**

With a 10% passive interest, the investor included only its share of the dividends declared by the investee as its income. With a 30% influential ownership interest, the investor reported 30% of the investee income as a separate source of income. With an 80% controlling interest, the investor (now termed the parent) merges the investee's (now a subsidiary) nominal accounts with its own amounts. Dividend and investment income no longer exist. The essence of consolidated reporting is the portrayal of the separate legal entities as a single economic entity. If the parent owned a 100% interest, net income would simply be reported as $190,000. Since this is only an 80% interest, the net income must be shown as allocated between the noncontrolling and controlling interests. The noncontrolling interest is the 20% of the subsidiary not owned by the parent. The controlling interest is the parent income, plus 80% of the subsidiary income.

REFLECTION

- An influential investment (generally over 20% ownership) requires recording the investor's share of income as it is earned as a single line item amount.
- A controlling investment (generally over 50% ownership) requires that subsidiary income statement accounts be combined with those of the parent company.

THE FUNCTION OF CONSOLIDATED STATEMENTS

2

OBJECTIVE

State the traditional criteria for presenting consolidated statements, and explain why disclosure of separate subsidiary financial information might be important.

Consolidated financial statements are designed to present the results of operations, cash flow, and the balance sheet of both the parent and its subsidiaries as if they were a single company. Generally, consolidated statements are the most informative to the stockholders of the controlling company. Yet, consolidated statements do have their shortcomings. The rights of the noncontrolling shareholders are limited to only the company they own, and, therefore, they get little value from consolidated statements. They really need the separate statements of the subsidiary. Similarly, creditors of the subsidiary need its separate statements, because they may look only to the legal entity that is indebted to them for satisfaction of their claims. The parent's creditors should be content with the consolidated statements, since the investment in the subsidiary will produce cash flows that can be used to satisfy their claims.

Consolidated statements have been criticized for being too aggregated. Unprofitable subsidiaries may not be very obvious, because, when consolidated, their performance is combined with that of other affiliates. However, this shortcoming is easily overcome. One option is to prepare separate statements of the subsidiary as supplements to the consolidated statements. The second option, which may be required, is to provide disclosure for major business segments. When subsidiaries are in businesses distinct from the parent, the definition of a segment may parallel that of a subsidiary.

Traditional Criteria for Consolidated Statements

Generally, statements are to be consolidated when a parent firm owns over 50% of the voting common stock of another company. There may be instances where consolidation is appropriate even though less than 51% of the voting common stock is owned by the parent. SEC Regulation S-X defines control in terms of power to direct or cause the direction of management and policies of a person, whether through the ownership of voting securities, by contract, or otherwise. Thus, control has been said to exist when a less than 51% ownership interest exists but where there is no other large ownership interest that can exert influence on management. The exception to consolidating when control exists is if control is only temporary or does not rest with the majority owner. For example, control would be presumed not to reside with the majority owner when the subsidiary is in bankruptcy, in legal reorganization, or when foreign exchange restrictions or foreign government controls cast doubt on the ability of the parent to exercise control over the subsidiary.

Prior to 1988, it was acceptable to exclude subsidiaries from consolidation when their operations were not homogeneous with those of the parent. It was common for a manufacturing-based parent to exclude from consolidations those subsidiaries involved in banking, financing, real estate, or leasing activities, but this exception for "nonhomogeneity" came under criticism. Frequently, firms diversified and excluded some types of subsidiaries from consolidation. This meant that a significant amount of assets, liabilities, and cash flows were not presented. The option of not consolidating selected subsidiaries was often considered a form of "off-balance sheet" financing. For instance, Ford, General Motors, and Chrysler did not consolidate their financing company subsidiaries; this meant that millions of dollars of debt did not appear on the consolidated balance sheets of these firms. Stockholders are interested in the total financial position of the corporation, regardless of how diversified the operations have become. Based on their concerns and the divergence in practice as to consolidation policy, the nonhomogeneity exception was eliminated by FASB Statement No. 94.[1] In addition, the Statement eliminated less commonly used exceptions for large noncontrolling interests and foreign locations. There is a concern that the combining of unlike operations will cloud the interpretation of financial statements. In response to this concern, many corporations are preparing classified balance sheets that separate the assets and liabilities of the nonhomogeneous operations. Ford Motor Company segregates its financial services subsidiaries, which in the past had not been consolidated.

Nonconsolidated subsidiaries now have become a rarity. When they do exist, they are accounted for as an investment under the equity method. The accounting methods for such an investment are discussed in Chapter 6.

3

OBJECTIVE

Explain when control might exist without majority ownership.

Consolidation Based on Control

The SEC has suggested that consolidation may be appropriate where control exists without majority (over 50%) ownership of controlling shares. A revised FASB Exposure Draft, issued in 1999, also recommends consolidation where control is achieved with less than majority ownership. Under the latest modification to the Exposure Draft in 2000, the FASB would presume that control exists, without majority ownership, if one of several possible situations exists:

- The parent company has the right to appoint or elect a majority of the members of the governing board. This could occur without owning a majority of the common voting shares because of a voting trust, the controlled corporation's charter or bylaws, or through other similar devices.
- The parent company has the ability to elect a majority of the members of the governing board of an entity through a large noncontrolling (less than 50%) voting interest. Again, this can be accomplished by owning a large noncontrolling interest through an agreement, a trust, or a stipulation in the entity's charter or bylaws. A large noncontrolling interest is one that is expected to cast at least 50% of the votes actually cast (not the total that could theoretically be cast) in an election of the governing board. No other party or group may

1 Statement of Financial Accounting Standards No. 94, *Consolidation of All Majority-Owned Subsidiaries* (Stamford: Financial Accounting Standards Board, 1987).

own a significant interest. An interest is assumed to be significant if it exceeds one-third the size of the parent company interest. For example, if the parent holds a 40% interest, no other party or group may own more than 13%.

- The parent has the ability to elect a majority of the members of the governing board of an entity through the ownership of securities that can be exercised or converted to obtain sufficient shares of voting common stock.
- The parent company is the only general partner in a limited partnership, and no other partner group may dissolve the partnership or remove the general partner.
- The parent has the unilateral ability to assume the role of general partner in a limited partnership through the present ownership of convertible securities or other rights that are currently exercisable.

There has been a common practice of not consolidating a newly acquired subsidiary if control was only temporary. This practice would no longer be allowed under the current FASB proposal.

REFLECTION

- There are many circumstances where control will exist and consolidation will be required without a greater than 50% ownership interest in a subsidiary's voting common stock.

TECHNIQUES OF CONSOLIDATION

4

OBJECTIVE

Demonstrate the worksheet procedures needed to eliminate the investment account.

This chapter builds an understanding of the techniques used to consolidate the separate balance sheets of a parent and its subsidiary immediately subsequent to the acquisition. The consolidated balance sheet as of the acquisition date is discussed first. The impact of consolidations on operations after the acquisition date is discussed in Chapters 3 through 8.

Chapter 1 emphasized that there are two means of achieving control over the assets of another company. A company may directly acquire the assets of another company, or it may acquire a controlling interest in the other company's voting common stock. In an *asset acquisition*, the company whose assets were purchased is dissolved. The assets acquired are recorded directly on the books of the purchaser, and consolidation of balance sheet amounts is automatic. Where control is achieved through a *stock acquisition*, the acquired company (the subsidiary) remains as a separate legal entity with its own financial statements. While the initial accounting for the two types of acquisitions differs significantly, a 100% stock acquisition and an asset acquisition have the same effect of creating one larger single reporting entity and should produce the same consolidated balance sheet. There is, however, a difference if the stock acquisition is less than 100%. Then, there will be a noncontrolling interest in the consolidated balance sheet which is not possible when the assets are purchased directly.

In the following discussion, the recording of an asset acquisition and a 100% stock acquisition are compared, and the balance sheets that result from each type of acquisition are studied. Then, the chapter deals with the accounting procedures needed when there is less than a 100% stock ownership and a noncontrolling equity interest exists.

Reviewing an Asset Acquisition

Illustration 2-1 demonstrates an asset acquisition of Company S by Company P for cash. Part A of the exhibit presents the balance sheets of the two companies just prior to the acquisition. Part B shows the entry to record Company P's payment of $500,000 in cash for the net assets of

Company S. The book values of the assets and liabilities acquired are assumed to be representative of their fair values, and no goodwill is acknowledged. The assets and liabilities of Company S are added to those of Company P to produce the balance sheet for the combined company, shown in Part C. Since account balances are combined in recording the acquisition, **statements for the single combined reporting entity are produced automatically, and no consolidation process is needed.**

Illustration 2-1
Asset Acquisition

A. Balance sheets of Companies P and S prior to acquisition:

Company P Balance Sheet

Assets		Liabilities and Equity	
Cash	$ 800,000	Current liabilities	$ 150,000
Accounts receivable	300,000	Bonds payable	500,000
Inventory	100,000	Common stock	100,000
Equipment (net)	150,000	Retained earnings	600,000
Total	$1,350,000	Total	$1,350,000

Company S Balance Sheet

Assets		Liabilities and Equity	
Accounts receivable	$ 200,000	Current liabilities	$ 100,000
Inventory	100,000	Common stock	200,000
Equipment (net)	300,000	Retained earnings	300,000
Total	$ 600,000	Total	$ 600,000

B. Entry on Company P's books to record acquisition of the net assets of Company S by Company P:

Accounts Receivable	200,000	
Inventory	100,000	
Equipment	300,000	
Current Liabilities		100,000
Cash		500,000

C. Balance sheet of Company P subsequent to asset acquisition:

Company P Balance Sheet

Assets		Liabilities and Equity	
Cash	$ 300,000	Current liabilities	$ 250,000
Accounts receivable	500,000	Bonds payable	500,000
Inventory	200,000	Common stock	100,000
Equipment (net)	450,000	Retained earnings	600,000
Total	$1,450,000	Total	$1,450,000

Consolidating a Stock Acquisition

In a stock acquisition, the acquiring company deals only with existing shareholders, not the company itself. Assuming the same facts as those used in Illustration 2-1, except that Company P will purchase all the outstanding stock of Company S from its shareholders for $500,000, Company P would make the following entry:

Investment in Subsidiary S	500,000	
Cash		500,000

This entry does not record the individual underlying assets and liabilities over which control is achieved. Instead, the acquisition is recorded in an investment account that represents the controlling interest in the net assets of the subsidiary. If no further action was taken, the investment in the subsidiary account would appear as a long-term investment on Company P's balance sheet. However, such a presentation is permitted only if consolidation were not required.

Assuming consolidated statements are required, the balance sheet of the two companies must be combined into a single consolidated balance sheet. The consolidation process is separate from the existing accounting records of the companies and requires completion of a worksheet. No journal entries are actually made to the parent's or subsidiary's books, so the elimination process starts anew each year.

The first example of a consolidated worksheet, Worksheet 2-1, appears later in the chapter on page 91. (The icon in the margin indicates the location of the worksheet at the end of the chapter. The worksheets are also repeated in the Student Companion Book.) The first two columns of the worksheet include the trial balances (balance sheet only for this chapter) for Companies P and S. The trial balances and the consolidated balance sheet are presented in single columns to save space. Credit balances are shown in parentheses. Obviously, since there are no nominal accounts listed, the income statement accounts have already been closed to retained earnings.

worksheet
Worksheet 2-1: page 91

The consolidated worksheet requires elimination of the investment account balance because the two companies will be treated as one. (How can a company have an investment in itself?) Similarly, the subsidiary's stockholders' equity accounts are eliminated because its assets and liabilities belong to the parent, not to outside equity owners. In general journal form, the elimination entry is as follows:

(EL)	Common Stock, Company S	200,000	
	Retained Earnings, Company S.	300,000	
	Investment in Company S.		500,000

Note that the key "EL" will be used in all future worksheets. Keys, once introduced, will be assigned to all similar items throughout the text. The balances in the consolidated balance sheet column (the last column) are exactly the same as in the balance sheet prepared for the preceding asset acquisition example—as they should be.

REFLECTION

- Consolidation is required for any company that is controlled, even in cases where less than 50% of the company's shares is owned by the parent.
- Consolidation produces the same balance sheet that would result in an asset acquisition.
- Consolidated statements are separate but derived from the individual statements of the parent and its subsidiaries.

5

OBJECTIVE

Demonstrate the worksheet procedures needed to merge subsidiary accounts.

ADJUSTMENT OF SUBSIDIARY ACCOUNTS

In the last example, the price paid for the investment in the subsidiary was equal to the net book value of the subsidiary (which means the price was also equal to the subsidiary's stockholders' equity). In most purchases, the price will exceed the book value of the subsidiary's net assets. Typically, fair values will exceed the recorded book values of assets. The price may also reflect unrecorded intangible assets including goodwill. Let us revisit the last example and assume that instead of paying $500,000 cash, Company P paid $700,000 cash for all the common stock shares of Company S and made the following entry for the purchase:

Investment in Subsidiary S	700,000	
Cash		700,000

Use the same Company S balance sheet as in Illustration 2-1, with the following additional information on fair values:

Company S Book and Estimated Fair Values
December 31, 20X1

Assets	Book Value	Fair Value	Liabilities and Equity	Book Value	Fair Value
Accounts receivable	$ 200,000	$ 200,000	Current liabilities	$ 100,000	$ 100,000
Inventory	100,000	120,000			
Equipment (net)	300,000	400,000	**Market value of net**		
Total assets	**$600,000**	**$720,000**	**assets (assets – liabilities)**	**$500,000**	**$620,000**

If this were an asset acquisition, the identifiable assets and liabilities would be recorded at fair value and goodwill at $80,000 (price paid of $700,000 minus $620,000 fair value of net assets). Adding fair values to Company P's accounts, the new balance sheet would appear as follows:

Company P
Consolidated Balance Sheet
December 31, 20X1

Assets			Liabilities and Equity		
Current assets:			Current liabilities	$250,000	
Cash	$100,000		Bonds payable	500,000	
Accounts receivable	500,000		Total liabilities		$ 750,000
Inventory	220,000				
Total		$ 820,000			

(continued)

Assets			Liabilities and Equity		
Long-term assets:			Stockholders' equity:		
Equipment (net)	$550,000		Common stock	$100,000	
Goodwill	80,000		Retained earnings	600,000	
Total		630,000	Total		700,000
Total assets		$1,450,000	Total liabilities and equity		$1,450,000

As before, the consolidated worksheet should produce a consolidated balance sheet that looks exactly the same as the preceding balance sheet for an asset acquisition. Worksheet 2-2, on page 92, shows how this is accomplished.

worksheet

Worksheet 2-2: page 92

- The (EL) entry is the same as before; $500,000 of subsidiary equity is eliminated against the investment account.
- Entry (**D**) distributes the remaining cost of $200,000 to the acquired assets to bring them from book to fair value and to record goodwill of $80,000.

In general journal entry form, the elimination entries are as follows:

(EL)	Common Stock, Company S	200,000	
	Retained Earnings, Company S	300,000	
	Investment in Company S		500,000
(D1)	Inventory (to increase from $100,000 to $120,000)	20,000	
(D2)	Equipment (to increase from $300,000 to $400,000)	100,000	
(D3)	Goodwill ($700,000 price minus $620,000 fair value assets)	80,000	
(D)	Investment in Company S ($700,000 price minus $500,000 book value eliminated above)		200,000

The balance sheet column of Worksheet 2-2 includes the subsidiary accounts at full fair value and reflects the $80,000 of goodwill included in the purchase price. The formal balance sheet for Company P, based on the worksheet, would be exactly the same as shown above for the asset acquisition.

Purchase of a subsidiary at a price in excess of the fair values of the subsidiary equity is as simple as the case just presented, especially where there are a limited number of assets to adjust to fair value. For more involved purchases, where there are many accounts to adjust and/or the price paid is not high enough to adjust all accounts to full fair value, a more complete analysis is needed. We will now proceed to develop these tools.

Analysis of Complicated Purchases—100% Interest

6

OBJECTIVE

Apply zone and price analyses to guide the adjustment process to reflect the price paid for the controlling interest.

The previous examples assumed the purchase of the subsidiary for cash. However, most purchases are accomplished by the parent issuing common stock (or, less often, preferred stock) in exchange for the subsidiary common shares being acquired. This avoids the depletion of cash and, if other criteria are met, allows the subsidiary shareholders to have a tax-free exchange. In most cases, the shares are issued by a publicly traded parent company which provides a readily determinable market price for the shares issued. The investment in the subsidiary is then recorded at the fair value of the shares issued. Less frequently, a nonpublicly traded parent may issue shares to subsidiary shareholders. In these cases, the fair values are determined for the net assets of the subsidiary company, and the total estimated fair value of the subsidiary company is recorded as the cost of the investment.

In order to illustrate the complete procedures used to record the investment in and the consolidation of a subsidiary, we will revisit the Johnson Company example used in Chapter 1 (page 11). This will also allow us to continue to compare the procedures used for a stock purchase with those used for an asset acquisition in Chapter 1. The balance sheet of the Johnson Company on December 31, 20X1, when Acquisitions Inc. purchased 100% of its shares, was as follows:

Johnson Company Balance Sheet
December 31, 20X1

Assets			Liabilities and Equity		
Current assets:			Current liabilities	$ 5,000	
Accounts receivable.	$28,000		Bonds payable	20,000	
Inventory	40,000		Total liabilities		$ 25,000
Total		$ 68,000			
Long-term assets:			Stockholders' equity:		
Land	$10,000		Common stock, $1 par . . .	$ 1,000	
Buildings (net)	40,000		Paid-in capital in excess		
Equipment (net)	20,000		of par	59,000	
Patent (net)	15,000		Retained earnings	68,000	
Total		85,000	Total		128,000
Total assets		$153,000	Total liabilities and equity . . .		$153,000

Assume that Acquisitions Inc. exchanges 7,000 shares of its common stock for the 1,000 shares of Johnson common stock (7 to 1 exchange ratio). The fair value per share is $50, and the par value is $1 per share. Acquisitions Inc. also makes the following additional payments:

1. $10,000 to attorneys and accountants for direct acquisition costs.
2. $5,000 to a brokerage company for stock issuance costs.

Johnson could also attribute significant *indirect* costs to the purchase, but they are expensed and cannot be included in the cost of the Johnson Company shares. Acquisitions Inc. would record the investment as follows:

Investment in Johnson Company (7,000 shares × $50 fair value per share + $10,000 direct acquisition cost)	360,000	
Common Stock, $1 Par (7,000 shares × $1)		7,000
Paid-In Capital in Excess of Par ($350,000 – $7,000 par)		343,000
Cash (for direct acquisition costs).		10,000

The payment of the issue costs would reduce the amount assigned to the shares issued as follows:

Paid-In Capital in Excess of Par	5,000	
Cash (to investment company).		5,000

Acquisitions Inc. is aware that it will have to consolidate this investment into its financial statements. It realizes that the $360,000 price paid does not agree with the book value of the underlying equity ($128,000). When consolidating, it will be eliminating a $360,000 investment against a stockholders' equity of $128,000. The difference is the amount of adjustment that will be needed for the subsidiary's accounts. Knowing this, Johnson would prepare a comparison of recorded book versus estimated fair values for assets and liabilities. Assets will be arranged by their priorities as follows:

Johnson Company Book and Estimated Fair Values
December 31, 20X1

Assets	Book Value	Fair Value	Liabilities and Equity	Book Value	Fair Value
Priority assets:					
Accounts receivable.	$ 28,000	$ 28,000	Current liabilities	$ 5,000	$ 5,000
Inventory	40,000	45,000	Bonds payable	20,000	21,000
Total priority assets . . .	**$ 68,000**	**$ 73,000**	**Total liabilities**.	**$ 25,000**	**$ 26,000**
Nonpriority assets:					
Land.	$ 10,000	$ 50,000			
Buildings (net)	40,000	80,000			
Equipment (net)	20,000	50,000			
Patent (net).	15,000	30,000			
*Brand-name copyright**	*0*	*40,000*			
Total nonpriority assets	**$ 85,000**	**$250,000**	**Value of net assets**		
Total assets	**$153,000**	**$323,000**	**(assets – liabilities)**	**$128,000**	**$297,000**

*Previously unrecorded assets.

The comparison includes the priorities or the accounts as discussed in Chapter 1.

Zone Analysis. A *zone analysis*, based on fair values, used in Chapter 1 (page 28) is prepared as follows:

Zone Analysis	Group Total	Cumulative Total
Priority accounts (fair value priority assets – liabilities).	$ 47,000	$ 47,000
Nonpriority accounts (at fair value)	250,000	297,000

From the zone analysis, we can do a *price analysis.*

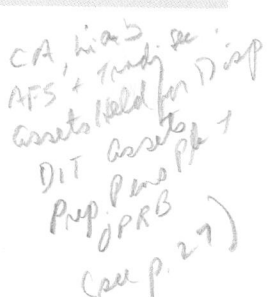

Price Analysis

- **Extraordinary gain:** A price **below $47,000** will have no value assigned to nonpriority accounts or to goodwill. Only the priority accounts will be recorded at fair value. The amount below $47,000 would result in an extraordinary gain.
- **Bargain:** A price **between $47,000 and $297,000** will allow priority accounts to be recorded at full fair value, lead to nonpriority accounts being assigned less than full fair value, and result in no goodwill being recorded.
- **Premium price:** A price **above $297,000** will allow all identifiable accounts to be adjusted to full fair value and lead to recording goodwill for any excess of the price paid over $297,000.

A *price analysis schedule* compares the price paid to the above cumulative zone limits and determines the amount available to each group of assets. For this example, the price paid exceeds the total, including nonpriority accounts, by $63,000, leading to the following price analysis:

Price (including direct acquisition costs)	**$360,000**	
Assign to priority accounts	$ 47,000	Full value
Assign to non-priority accounts	250,000	Full value
Goodwill	**63,000**	
Extraordinary gain	**0**	

The price analysis schedule indicates that all the accounts can be fully adjusted to fair value; therefore, no allocation will be needed.

worksheet

Worksheet 2-3: page 93

Examine Worksheet 2-3 on page 93 for Acquisitions Inc. and its subsidiary, Johnson Company, as it would be prepared immediately after the purchase. Notice that entry (EL) eliminated total stockholders' equity of $128,000 against an investment balance of $360,000. The entry in general journal form is as follows:

(EL)	Common Stock, $1 Par	1,000	
	Paid-In Capital in Excess of Par	59,000	
	Retained Earnings	68,000	
	Investment in Johnson Company		128,000

7

OBJECTIVE

Create a determination and distribution of excess (D&D) schedule.

Determination and Distribution of Excess Schedule. After the (EL) entry, there is an excess of cost over book value of $232,000 ($360,000 cost − $128,000 subsidiary equity). This amount reflects the undervaluation of Johnson's accounts and is the amount of write-up to fair value that must be made in the consolidation process. The *determination and distribution of excess (D&D) schedule* compares the price paid with the subsidiary equity to predetermine the imbalance that will occur on the consolidated worksheet when the investment account amount is eliminated against the underlying subsidiary equity. The schedule then uses the price analysis schedule to guide the adjustment of subsidiary accounts. In this example, the price analysis indicated that every account can be fully adjusted to fair value.

Price paid for investment (including direct acquisition costs)		**$360,000**	
Less book value of interest purchased:			
Common stock, $1 par	$ 1,000		
Paid-in capital in excess of par	59,000		
Retained earnings	68,000		
Total equity		128,000	
Excess of cost over book value		**$232,000**	Cr.
Adjustments:			
Accounts receivable	$ 0		
Inventory ($45,000 fair − $40,000 book)	5,000		Dr.
Current liabilities	0		
Premium on bonds payable (new account)	(1,000)		Cr.
Land ($50,000 fair − $10,000 book)	40,000		Dr.
Buildings (net) ($80,000 fair − $40,000 book)	40,000		Dr.
Equipment (net) ($50,000 fair − $20,000 book)	30,000		Dr.
Patent (net) ($30,000 fair − $15,000 book)	15,000		Dr.
Brand-name copyright (new account)	40,000		Dr.
Goodwill (new account)	63,000		Dr.
Total adjustments		**$232,000**	

This schedule is then used to distribute the excess in Worksheet 2-3, entry series (D), as follows in journal entry form:

(D1)	Inventory	5,000	
(D2)	Premium on Bonds Payable		1,000
(D3)	Land	40,000	
(D4)	Buildings (net)	40,000	
(D5)	Equipment (net)	30,000	
(D6)	Patent (net)	15,000	
(D7)	Brand-Name Copyright	40,000	
(D8)	Goodwill	63,000	
(D)	Investment in Johnson Company (balance)		232,000

The adjustments to the building (D4) and equipment (D5) are made by increasing the asset cost amount, rather than by decreasing accumulated depreciation. A more complex solution would be to restate the assets at their net fair value and eliminate all accumulated depreciation. This causes more complications in worksheets of future periods than is typically warranted.

The same D&D will be a necessary support schedule for all future worksheets because, as noted earlier, the worksheet eliminations and adjustments are not recorded on the books of either the subsidiary or the parent. The D&D prepared on the purchase date will always drive the distribution of excess entry. Separate adjustments to depreciate or amortize the adjustments will be described and recorded in Chapter 3.

The consolidated balance sheet includes the book value of parent accounts and the fair value of subsidiary accounts. The following formal consolidated balance sheet would be prepared on December 31, 20X1:

Acquisitions Inc.
Consolidated Balance Sheet
December 31, 20X1

Assets			Liabilities and Equity		
Current assets:			Current liabilities	$ 94,000	
Cash	$ 51,000		Bonds payable	120,000	
Accounts receivable	70,000		Prem. on bonds payable	1,000	
Inventory	140,000		Total liabilities		$ 215,000
Total		$ 261,000			
Long-term assets:					
Land	$110,000				
Buildings	600,000				
Accumulated depreciation	(70,000)				
Equipment	120,000		Stockholders' equity:		
Accumulated depreciation	(34,000)		Common stock, $1 par	$ 20,000	
Patent (net)	30,000		Paid-in capital in excess of par	480,000	
Brand-name copyright	40,000				
Goodwill	63,000		Retained earnings	405,000	
Total		859,000	Total		905,000
Total assets		$1,120,000	Total liabilities and equity		$1,120,000

Bargain Purchases—100% Interest

A *bargain purchase* is one in which the price paid does not allow nonpriority accounts to be recorded at fair value. There is no excess available for goodwill. The previous zone analysis shows that this would occur at a price less than $297,000, but greater than $47,000.

We will assume that 4,000 shares of Acquisitions Inc. common stock are issued as payment with a fair value of $50 each. We will again assume that there are direct acquisition costs of $10,000 and issue costs of $5,000. The entries to record the purchase would be as follows:

Investment in Johnson Company (4,000 shares × $50 fair value per share + $10,000 direct acquisition cost)	210,000	
Common Stock, $1 Par (4,000 shares × $1)		4,000
Paid-In Capital in Excess of Par ($200,000 – $4,000 par)		196,000
Cash (for direct acquisition costs)		10,000
Paid-In Capital in Excess of Par	5,000	
Cash (to investment company)		5,000

The price of $210,000 is compared to the same zone analysis used in the previous example:

Zone Analysis	Group Total	Cumulative Total
Priority accounts (net of liabilities)	$ 47,000	$ 47,000
Nonpriority accounts	250,000	297,000

A price analysis schedule compares the price paid to the cumulative totals in the zone analysis and determines the amount available to each group of assets. For this example, the price analysis would be as follows:

Price (including direct acquisition costs)	**$210,000**	
Assign to priority accounts	$ 47,000	Full value
Assign to nonpriority accounts	163,000	Allocate
Goodwill	**0**	
Extraordinary gain	**0**	

The price analysis indicates that full value will be assigned to priority accounts and the $163,000 will be used to adjust the nonpriority accounts as follows:

Allocation to Nonpriority Accounts:	Fair Value	Percent	Amount to Allocate	Allocated Amount	Book Value	Adjustment
Land	$ 50,000	20%	$163,000	$ 32,600	$10,000	$22,600
Buildings (net)	80,000	32	163,000	52,160	40,000	12,160
Equipment (net)	50,000	20	163,000	32,600	20,000	12,600
Patent	30,000	12	163,000	19,560	15,000	4,560
Brand-name copyright	40,000	16	163,000	26,080	0	26,080
Total	$250,000			$163,000	$85,000	$78,000

Note that the total adjustment is for $78,000, because the subsidiary's books already included $85,000 of the total $163,000 to be allocated to this group of assets.

The determination and distribution schedule will proceed to adjust the priority accounts to full fair value and will distribute $78,000 to the nonpriority assets. The schedule is prepared as follows:

Price paid for investment (including direct acquisition costs)		**$210,000**	
Less book value of interest purchased:			
Common stock, $1 par	$ 1,000		
Paid-in capital in excess of par	59,000		
Retained earnings	68,000		
Total equity		128,000	
Excess of cost over book value		**$ 82,000**	Cr.
Adjustments:			
Accounts receivable	$ 0		
Inventory ($45,000 fair – $40,000 book)	5,000		Dr.
Current liabilities	0		
Premium on bonds payable (new account)	(1,000)		Cr.
Land (from allocation schedule)	22,600		Dr.
Buildings (net) (from allocation schedule)	12,160		Dr.
Equipment (net) (from allocation schedule)	12,600		Dr.
Patent (net) (from allocation schedule)	4,560		Dr.
Brand-name copyright (from allocation schedule)	26,080		Dr.
Total adjustments		**$ 82,000**	

Examine Worksheet 2-4 on page 94 for Acquisitions Inc. and its subsidiary, Johnson Company. Notice that entry (EL) eliminated total stockholders' equity of $128,000 against an investment balance of $210,000. The worksheet entry in journal entry form is as follows:

worksheet
Worksheet 2-4: page 94

(EL)	Common Stock, $1 Par	1,000	
	Paid-In Capital in Excess of Par	59,000	
	Retained Earnings	68,000	
	Investment in Johnson Company		128,000

The D&D schedule is then used to distribute the excess in Worksheet 2-4, entry series (D), in journal entry form as follows:

(D1)	Inventory	5,000	
(D2)	Premium on Bonds Payable		1,000
(D3)	Land	22,600	
(D4)	Buildings (net)	12,160	
(D5)	Equipment (net)	12,600	
(D6)	Patent (net)	4,560	
(D7)	Brand-Name Copyright	26,080	
(D)	Investment in Johnson Company (balance)		82,000

The consolidated balance sheet values include the book value of the parent plus the adjusted values of the subsidiary accounts. Notice that there is no investment in the subsidiary on the consolidated balance sheet. The following formal consolidated balance sheet would be prepared on December 31, 20X1:

Acquisitions Inc.
Consolidated Balance Sheet
December 31, 20X1

Assets			Liabilities and Equity		
Current assets:			Current liabilities	$ 94,000	
Cash	$ 51,000		Bonds payable	120,000	
Accounts receivable	70,000		Prem. on bonds payable	1,000	
Inventory	140,000		Total liabilities		$215,000
Total		$261,000			
Long-term assets:					
Land	$ 92,600				
Buildings	572,160				
Accumulated depreciation	(70,000)		Stockholders' equity:		
Equipment	102,600		Common stock, $1 par	$ 17,000	
Accumulated depreciation	(34,000)		Paid-in capital in excess of par	333,000	
Patent (net)	19,560				
Brand-name copyright	26,080		Retained earnings	405,000	
Total		709,000	Total		755,000
Total assets		$970,000	Total liabilities and equity		$970,000

Extraordinary Gain—100% Interest

We will assume that 500 shares of Acquisitions Inc. common stock are issued as payment with a fair value of $50 each. We will again assume that there are direct acquisition costs of $10,000 and issue costs of $5,000. The entries to record the purchase would be as follows:

Investment in Johnson Company (500 shares × $50 fair value per share + $10,000 direct acquisition cost)	35,000	
Common Stock, $1 Par (500 shares × $1)		500
Paid-In Capital in Excess of Par ($25,000 – $500 par)		24,500
Cash (for direct acquisition costs)		10,000
Paid-In Capital in Excess of Par	5,000	
Cash (to investment company)		5,000

The price of $35,000 is compared to the same zone analysis used in the previous examples as follows:

Zone Analysis	Group Total	Cumulative Total
Priority accounts (net of liabilities)	$ 47,000	$ 47,000
Nonpriority accounts	250,000	297,000

A price analysis schedule compares the price paid to the cumulative totals in the zone analysis and determines the amount available to each group of assets. For this example, the price analysis would be as follows:

Price (including direct acquisition costs)	**$ 35,000**	
Assign to priority accounts	$ 47,000	Full value
Assign to nonpriority accounts	0	No value
Goodwill	**0**	
Extraordinary gain	**(12,000)**	

The determination and distribution schedule will proceed to adjust the priority accounts to full fair value. Since no value will be assigned to nonpriority accounts, the book value applicable to them is removed. An extraordinary gain becomes part of the distribution. The schedule is prepared as follows:

Price paid for investment (including direct acquisition costs)		**$ 35,000**	
Less book value of interest purchased:			
Common stock, $1 par	$ 1,000		
Paid-in capital in excess of par	59,000		
Retained earnings	68,000		
Total equity	$ 128,000		
Ownership interest	× 100%	128,000	
Excess of cost over book value (book value exceeds cost)		**$(93,000)**	Dr.
Adjustments:			
Accounts receivable	$ 0		
Inventory ($45,000 fair – $40,000 book)	5,000		Dr.
Current liabilities	0		
Premium on bonds payable (new account)	(1,000)		Cr.
Land (remove book value)	(10,000)		Cr.
Buildings (net) (remove book value)	(40,000)		Cr.
Equipment (net) (remove book value)	(20,000)		Cr.
Patent (net) (remove book value)	(15,000)		Cr.
Brand-name copyright (no amount available)	0		
Extraordinary gain	(12,000)		Cr.
Total adjustments		**$(93,000)**	

Examine Worksheet 2-5 on page 95 for Acquisitions Inc. and its subsidiary, Johnson Company, as it would be prepared immediately after the purchase. Notice that entry (EL) eliminated total stockholders' equity of $128,000 against an investment balance of $35,000. The worksheet entry in general journal form is as follows:

worksheet
Worksheet 2-5: page 95

(EL)	Common Stock, $1 Par	1,000	
	Paid-In Capital in Excess of Par	59,000	
	Retained Earnings	68,000	
	Investment in Johnson Company		128,000

The investment account is overeliminated by $93,000 ($35,000 cost less $128,000 elimination). This requires that subsidiary assets be reduced and an extraordinary gain be recorded. The D&D schedule is then used to distribute this overelimination in Worksheet 2-5, entry series (D), as follows:

(D1)	Inventory	5,000	
(D2)	Premium on Bonds Payable		1,000
(D3)	Land		10,000
(D4)	Buildings (net)		40,000
(D5)	Equipment (net)		20,000
(D6)	Patent (net)		15,000
(D8)	Extraordinary Gain (Parent retained earnings)		12,000
(D)	Investment in Johnson Company (balance)	93,000	

The consolidated balance sheet values include the book value of the parent plus the adjusted values of the subsidiary accounts. The following formal consolidated balance sheet would be prepared on December 31, 20X1:

Acquisitions Inc.
Consolidated Balance Sheet
December 31, 20X1

Assets			Liabilities and Equity		
Current assets:			Current liabilities	$ 94,000	
Cash	$ 51,000		Bonds payable	120,000	
Accounts receivable	70,000		Prem. on bonds payable	1,000	
Inventory	140,000		Total liabilities		$215,000
Total		$261,000			
Long-term assets:					
Land	$ 60,000		Stockholders' equity:		
Buildings	520,000		Common stock, $1 par	$ 13,500	
Accumulated depreciation	(70,000)		Paid-in capital in excess of par	161,500	
Equipment	70,000				
Accumulated depreciation	(34,000)		Retained earnings	417,000	
Total		546,000	Total		592,000
Total assets		$807,000	Total liabilities and equity		$807,000

Notice that there is no goodwill on the consolidated balance sheet. There has been no value added to the parent's accounts for all subsidiary nonpriority accounts. Since only a balance sheet is being prepared, the extraordinary gain has been added to the parent's retained earnings.

REFLECTION

- A difference will usually exist between the price paid for a 100% interest and the underlying book value of subsidiary accounts. The difference is the total adjustment that must be made to subsidiary accounts when consolidating.
- A premium price is high enough to adjust all accounts to full fair value. Any unallocated excess is considered goodwill.

- A bargain price allows priority accounts (current assets, other marketable investments, and liabilities) to be recorded at fair value. The value remaining is not sufficient to record non-priority assets at full fair value; instead, they are allocated the cost remaining after recording the priority accounts at fair value.
- An extraordinary gain occurs when the price paid is less than the amount assigned to the priority accounts (which are never discounted).

CONSOLIDATING A LESS THAN 100% INTEREST

8

OBJECTIVE

Explain the impact of a noncontrolling interest on worksheet procedures and financial statement preparation.

Consolidation of financial statements is required whenever the parent company controls a subsidiary. In other words, a parent company could consolidate far less than a 100% ownership interest. Several important ramifications may arise when less than 100% interest is consolidated.

- The parent's investment account is eliminated against only its ownership percentage of the underlying subsidiary equity accounts. The noneliminated portion of the subsidiary equity is termed the *noncontrolling interest (NCI).* The NCI is typically shown on the consolidated balance sheet in total and is not broken into par, paid-in capital in excess of par, and retained earnings. In the past, the NCI has been displayed on the consolidated balance sheet as a liability, as equity, or in some cases has appeared between the liability and equity sections of the balance sheet. A 2005 FASB Exposure Draft on Consolidated Financial Statements[2] would require the noncontrolling interest to be displayed as a part of stockholders' equity. This text will follow the proposal.
- The entire amount of every subsidiary nominal (income statement) account is merged with the nominal accounts of the parent to calculate consolidated income. *The noncontrolling interest is allocated its percentage ownership times the reported income of the subsidiary only.* The precise methods and display of this interest are discussed in Chapter 3. In the past, this share of income has often been treated as an other expense in the consolidated income statement. The 2005 FASB Exposure Draft would require that it not be shown as an expense, but rather as a distribution of consolidated income. (See prior page 81.)
- Current practice is to *adjust subsidiary accounts to fair value only for the parent's percentage interest.* Thus, if the book value of a subsidiary asset is $50,000 and the fair value is $80,000, an 80% parent owner would adjust the asset by only $24,000 (80% × $30,000 book/fair value difference). This text will use this idea which is called the "Proprietary Theory of Consolidation." The 2005 exposure draft suggests adjusting subsidiary assets to 100% of their fair value.

Analysis of Complicated Purchase—Less than 100% Interest

When less than a 100% interest is purchased, zone analysis, price analysis, and the determination and distribution of excess procedures are applied only to the percentage interest purchased. We will now revisit the example involving the purchase of an interest in the Johnson Company, as found on pages 72 to 73. We will assume that Acquisitions Inc. exchanges 5,600 shares of its common stock for 800 shares (an 80% interest) of Johnson Company stock (7 to 1 exchange ratio). The fair value of the shares issued is $50, and the par value is $1. The following additional payments are again made:

1. $10,000 to attorneys and accountants for direct acquisition costs.
2. $5,000 to a brokerage company for stock issuance costs.

---

2 FASB Exposure Draft, "Consolidated Financial Statements, Including Accounting and Reporting of Noncontrolling Interests in Subsidiaries – a replacement of ARB. 51" (Proposed Statements of the Financial Accounting Standards Board) June 30, 2005.

Acquisitions Inc. would record the investment as follows:

Investment in Johnson Company (5,600 shares × $50 fair value per share + $10,000 direct acquisition cost)	290,000	
Common Stock, $1 Par (5,600 shares × $1)		5,600
Paid-In Capital in Excess of Par ($280,000 – $5,600 par)		274,400
Cash (for direct acquisition costs)		10,000

The payment of the issue costs would again reduce the amount assigned to the shares issued as follows:

Paid-In Capital in Excess of Par	5,000	
Cash (to investment company)		5,000

Zone analysis is now performed on the 80% interest using the fair values shown on page 73. Adding an *ownership portion* modifies the zone analysis schedule. The parent may adjust only 80% of each account to fair value. The cumulative totals are also based on an 80% interest.

Zone Analysis	Group Total	Ownership Portion	Cumulative Total
Ownership percentage		80%	
Priority accounts (net of liabilities)	$ 47,000	$ 37,600	$ 37,600
Nonpriority accounts	250,000	200,000	237,600

Premium Price. A price analysis schedule compares the price paid to the zone limits (used for the prior example) and determines the amount available to each group of assets. For this example, the price analysis would be as follows:

Price (including direct acquisition costs)	**$290,000**	
Assign to priority accounts, controlling share	$ 37,600	Full value
Assign to nonpriority accounts, controlling share	200,000	Full value
Goodwill	**52,400**	
Extraordinary gain	**0**	

The price analysis schedule indicates that the parent's share of all accounts can be fully adjusted to fair value. Goodwill is recorded for the excess of the $290,000 price over the $237,600 fair value of the parent's share of the subsidiary's net assets.

Examine Worksheet 2-6 on page 96 for Acquisitions Inc. and its subsidiary, Johnson Company. Notice that entry (EL) eliminated only 80% of the subsidiary's equity ($102,400) against an investment balance of $290,000. The worksheet entry in journal form is as follows:

worksheet

Worksheet 2-6: page 95

(EL)	Common Stock, $1 Par, 80%	800	
	Paid-In Capital in Excess of Par, 80%	47,200	
	Retained Earnings, 80%	54,400	
	Investment in Johnson Company		102,400

There is an excess of cost over book value of $187,600 ($290,000 price – $102,400 equity). As before, this amount reflects the undervaluation of the parent's share of Johnson's accounts and is the amount of write-up to fair value that must be made in the consolidation process. The D&D schedule compares the price paid with 80% of the subsidiary equity. Notice that a new line was added to the schedule to reduce the total subsidiary equity to the portion owned by the parent. The D&D then uses the price analysis schedule to guide the adjustment of subsidiary accounts. In this example, the parent's share of every account can be adjusted to fair value as follows:

Price paid for investment (including direct acquisition costs)		**$290,000**	
Less book value of interest purchased:			
Common stock, $1 par	$ 1,000		
Paid-in capital in excess of par	59,000		
Retained earnings	68,000		
Total equity	$ 128,000		
Ownership interest	× 80%	102,400	
Excess of cost over book value		**$187,600**	Cr.
Adjustments:			
Accounts receivable	$ 0		
Inventory, 80% of ($45,000 fair – $40,000 book)	4,000		Dr.
Current liabilities	0		
Premium on bonds payable, 80% of $1,000	(800)		Cr.
Land, 80% of ($50,000 fair – $10,000 book)	32,000		Dr.
Buildings (net), 80% of ($80,000 fair – $40,000 book)	32,000		Dr.
Equipment (net), 80% of ($50,000 fair – $20,000 book)	24,000		Dr.
Patent (net), 80% of ($30,000 fair – $15,000 book)	12,000		Dr.
Brand-name copyright, 80% of $40,000	32,000		Dr.
Goodwill	52,400		Dr.
Total adjustments		**$187,600**	

The D&D schedule is then used to distribute this overelimination in Worksheet 2-6, entry series (D), in journal entry form as follows:

(D1)	Inventory	4,000	
(D2)	Premium on Bonds Payable		800
(D3)	Land	32,000	
(D4)	Buildings (net)	32,000	
(D5)	Equipment (net)	24,000	
(D6)	Patent (net)	12,000	
(D7)	Brand-Name Copyright	32,000	
(D8)	Goodwill	52,400	
(D)	Investment in Johnson Company (balance)		187,600

The consolidated balance sheet values are the book value of the parent plus the adjusted values of the subsidiary's accounts. In this case, the parent's 80% interest in subsidiary accounts is at fair value, and the 20% NCI remains at book value. The following formal consolidated balance sheet would be prepared on December 31, 20X1:

Acquisitions Inc.
Consolidated Balance Sheet
December 31, 20X1

Assets			Liabilities and Equity		
Current assets:			Current liabilities	$ 94,000	
Cash	$ 51,000		Bonds payable	120,000	
Accounts receivable	70,000		Prem. on bonds payable	800	
Inventory	139,000		Total liabilities		$ 214,800
Total		$ 260,000			

(continued)

Assets			Liabilities and Equity		
Long-term assets:					
Land	$102,000				
Buildings	592,000				
Accumulated depreciation	(70,000)				
Equipment	114,000		Stockholders' equity:		
Accumulated depreciation	(34,000)		**Noncontrolling interest**	**$ 25,600**	
Patent (net)	27,000		Common stock, $1 par	18,600	
Brand-name copyright	32,000		Paid-in capital in excess of par	411,400	
Goodwill	52,400		Retained earnings	405,000	
Total		815,400	Total		860,600
Total assets		$1,075,400	Total liabilities and equity		$1,075,400

Notice that the NCI is shown only in the aggregate as a subdivision of stockholders' equity.

Bargain Purchase. The procedures for a bargain purchase with less than a 100% interest are basically the same as that for a 100% interest, except that all adjustments are limited to the ownership percentage interest. As an example, assume that Acquisitions Inc. issued only 4,000 shares of its common stock for an 80% interest in Johnson Company and incurred the same direct acquisition and issue costs. The entries to record the purchase would be as follows:

Investment in Johnson Company (4,000 shares × $50 fair value per share + $10,000 direct acquisition cost)	210,000	
Common Stock, $1 Par (4,000 shares × $1)		4,000
Paid-In Capital in Excess of Par ($200,000 – $4,000 par)		196,000
Cash (for direct acquisition costs)		10,000

The payment of the issue costs would again reduce the amount assigned to the shares issued as follows:

Paid-In Capital in Excess of Par	5,000	
Cash (to investment company)		5,000

A price analysis schedule compares the price paid to the cumulative totals in the previous zone analysis and determines the amount available to each group of assets. For this example, the price analysis would be as follows:

Price (including direct acquisition costs)	**$210,000**	
Assign to priority accounts, controlling share	$ 37,600	Full value
Assign to nonpriority accounts, controlling share	172,400	Allocate
Goodwill	**0**	
Extraordinary gain	**0**	

The price analysis schedule indicates that the parent's share of nonpriority accounts will be discounted and that there will be no goodwill. The *allocation schedule* for nonpriority accounts is as follows:

	Fair Value	Percent	Amount to Allocate	Allocated Amount	80% Book Value	Adjustment
Allocation to nonpriority accounts:						
Land	$ 50,000	20%	$172,400	$ 34,480	$ 8,000	$ 26,480
Buildings (net)	80,000	32	172,400	55,168	32,000	23,168
Equipment (net)	50,000	20	172,400	34,480	16,000	18,480
Patent	30,000	12	172,400	20,688	12,000	8,688
Brand-name copyright	40,000	16	172,400	27,584	0	27,584
Total	$250,000			$172,400	$68,000	$104,400

Note that the *amount to allocate* applies to only the controlling share of all accounts. Therefore, this amount must be compared to only 80% of the subsidiary recorded book value. The NCI remains at book value as in the prior example.

Examine Worksheet 2-7 on page 97 for Acquisitions Inc. and its subsidiary, Johnson Company. Notice that entry (EL) eliminated 80% of the subsidiary's equity of $102,400 against an investment balance of $210,000. The worksheet entry in journal form is as follows:

Worksheet 2-7: page 97

		Dr.	Cr.
(EL)	Common Stock, $1 Par, 80%	800	
	Paid-In Capital in Excess of Par, 80%	47,200	
	Retained Earnings, 80%	54,400	
	Investment in Johnson Company		102,400

There is an excess of cost over book value of $107,600. This amount reflects the undervaluation of the parent's share of Johnson's accounts and is the amount of write-up to fair value that must be made in the consolidation process. The determination and distribution of excess schedule compares the price paid with 80% of the subsidiary.

Price paid for investment (including direct acquisition costs)		**$210,000**	
Less book value of interest purchased:			
Common stock, $1 par	$ 1,000		
Paid-in capital in excess of par	59,000		
Retained earnings	68,000		
Total equity	$ 128,000		
Ownership interest	× 80%	102,400	
Excess of cost over book value		**$107,600**	Cr.
Adjustments:			
Accounts receivable	$ 0		
Inventory, 80% × ($45,000 fair − $40,000 book)	4,000		Dr.
Current liabilities	0		
Premium on bonds payable, 80% × $1,000	(800)		Cr.
Land (from allocation schedule)	26,480		Dr.
Buildings (net) (from allocation schedule)	23,168		Dr.
Equipment (net) (from allocation schedule)	18,480		Dr.
Patent (net) (from allocation schedule)	8,688		Dr.
Brand-name copyright (from allocation schedule)	27,584		Dr.
Total adjustments		**$107,600**	

This schedule is then used to distribute the excess in Worksheet 2-7, entry series (D), as follows:

(D1)	Inventory	4,000	
(D2)	Premium on Bonds Payable		800
(D3)	Land	26,480	
(D4)	Buildings (net)	23,168	
(D5)	Equipment (net)	18,480	
(D6)	Patent (net)	8,688	
(D7)	Brand-Name Copyright	27,584	
(D)	Investment in Johnson Company (balance)		107,600

Extraordinary Gain. We will assume that 400 shares of Acquisitions Inc. common stock are issued as payment with a fair value of $50 each. We will again assume that there are direct acquisition costs of $10,000 and issue costs of $5,000. The entries to record the purchase would be as follows:

Investment in Johnson Company (400 shares × $50 fair value per share + $10,000 direct acquisition cost)	30,000	
Common Stock, $1 Par (400 shares × $1)		400
Paid-In Capital in Excess of Par ($20,000 – $400 par)		19,600
Cash (for direct acquisition costs)		10,000
Paid-In Capital in Excess of Par	5,000	
Cash (to investment company)		5,000

A price analysis schedule compares the price paid to the cumulative totals in the zone analysis and determines the amount available to each group of assets. For this example, the price analysis would be as follows:

Price (including direct acquisition costs)	**$30,000**	
Assign to priority accounts, controlling share	$ 37,600	Full value
Assign to nonpriority accounts, controlling share	0	
Goodwill	**0**	
Extraordinary gain	**7,600**	

The determination and distribution schedule will proceed to adjust the controlling share of priority accounts to fair value. Since no value will be assigned to nonpriority accounts, the 80% (controlling share) book value applicable to them is removed. An extraordinary gain becomes part of the distribution. The schedule is prepared as follows:

Price paid for investment (including direct acquisition costs)		**$ 30,000**	
Less book value of interest purchased:			
Common stock, $1 par	$ 1,000		
Paid-in capital in excess of par	59,000		
Retained earnings	68,000		
Total equity	$ 128,000		
Ownership interest	× 80%	102,400	
Excess of cost over book value (book value exceeds cost)		**$(72,400)**	Dr.

(continued)

Adjustments:			
Accounts receivable	$ 0		
Inventory, 80% × ($45,000 fair – $40,000 book)	4,000		Dr.
Current liabilities	0		
Premium on bonds payable (80% × $1,000)	(800)		Cr.
Land (remove 80% of book value)	(8,000)		Cr.
Buildings (net) (remove 80% of book value)	(32,000)		Cr.
Equipment (net) (remove 80% of book value)	(16,000)		Cr.
Patent (net) (remove 80% of book value)	(12,000)		Cr.
Brand-name copyright (no amount available)	0		
Extraordinary gain	(7,600)		Cr.
Total adjustments		**$(72,400)**	

80% of the nonpriority accounts would be eliminated on the consolidated worksheet. Only the 20% NCI share of the subsidiary nonpriority accounts would be extended to the consolidated balance sheet.

REFLECTION

- A less than 100% interest requires that zone and price analyses use only the parent ownership portion of all subsidiary accounts.
- Account adjustments are limited to the parent interest times the fair/book value difference.
- The noncontrolling interest percentage of all subsidiary assets remains at book value.
- The noncontrolling share of subsidiary equity appears as a single line item amount within the equity section of the balance sheet.

PREEXISTING GOODWILL

9

OBJECTIVE

Show the impact of preexisting goodwill on the consolidation process.

If a subsidiary is purchased and it has goodwill on its books, it is ignored in the zone and price analyses, since it has no priority. The only complication caused by existing goodwill is that the D&D schedule will adjust existing goodwill, rather than only recording new goodwill. Let us return to the example involving the Johnson Company on page 72 and change only two facts: assume Johnson had goodwill of $40,000 and that its retained earnings was $40,000 greater. The modified comparison of values would be as follows:

Johnson Company Book and Estimated Fair Values
December 31, 20X1

Assets	Book Value	Fair Value	Liabilities and Equity	Book Value	Fair Value
Priority assets:					
Accounts receivable	$ 28,000	$ 28,000	Current liabilities	$ 5,000	$ 5,000
Inventory	40,000	45,000	Bonds payable	20,000	21,000
Total priority assets	**$ 68,000**	**$ 73,000**	**Total liabilities**	**$ 25,000**	**$ 26,000**

(continued)

Assets	Book Value	Fair Value	Liabilities and Equity	Book Value	Fair Value
Nonpriority assets:					
Land	$ 10,000	$ 50,000			
Buildings (net)	40,000	80,000			
Equipment (net)	20,000	50,000			
Patent (net)	15,000	30,000			
*Brand-name copyright**	*0*	*40,000*			
Goodwill	**40,000**	**?**			
Total nonpriority assets	**$125,000**	**$250,000**	**Value of net assets**		
Total assets	**$193,000**	**$323,000**	**(assets − liabilities)**	**$168,000**	**$297,000**

*Previously unrecorded asset.

No amount is entered for the fair value of goodwill since that is determined by the price paid. Zone analysis is based only on priority accounts and nonpriority accounts remaining other than goodwill, so it remains unchanged.

Let us revisit the example on page 81, where an 80% interest is purchased for $290,000. There would be absolutely no change in the zone and price analyses on page 82. There would, however, be some modifications to the determination and distribution of excess schedule as shown below:

Price paid for investment (including direct acquisition costs)		$290,000	
Less book value of interest purchased:			
Common stock, $1 par	$ 1,000		
Paid-in capital in excess of par	59,000		
Retained earnings **(greater by $40,000)**	108,000		
Total equity	$ 168,000		
Ownership interest	× 80%	134,400	
Excess of cost over book value		**$155,600**	Cr.
Adjustments:			
Accounts receivable	$ 0		
Inventory, 80% of $5,000	4,000		Dr.
Current liabilities	0		
Premium on bonds payable, 80% of $1,000	(800)		Cr.
Land, 80% of $40,000	32,000		Dr.
Buildings (net), 80% of $40,000	32,000		Dr.
Equipment (net), 80% of $30,000	24,000		Dr.
Patent (net), 80% of $15,000	12,000		Dr.
Brand-name copyright, 80% of $40,000	32,000		Dr.
Goodwill ($52,400 − existing 80% × 40,000)	20,400		Dr.
Total adjustments		**$155,600**	

Note that instead of goodwill being recorded for the full $52,400 indicated in the price analysis, the controlling interest in goodwill is adjusted *to $52,400.* Total subsidiary existing goodwill is $40,000. The NCI portion of goodwill (20% × $40,000) cannot be adjusted. The parent's share of existing goodwill is $32,000. It must be adjusted by $20,400 to bring it to the required $52,400 balance.

Existing Goodwill in a Bargain

Let us assume that the price paid for the 80% interest in Johnson was $210,000 (same as example on page 100). Again, the price analysis and the nonpriority account allocation schedules on pages 100 and 101 remain unchanged. The modified determination and distribution of excess schedule would appear as follows:

Price paid for investment (including direct acquisition costs)		**$210,000**	
Less book value of interest purchased:			
Common stock, $1 par	$ 1,000		
Paid-in capital in excess of par	59,000		
Retained earnings ($40,000 greater)	108,000		
Total equity	$ 168,000		
Ownership interest	× 80%	134,400	
Excess of cost over book value		**$ 75,600**	Cr.
Adjustments:			
Accounts receivable	$ 0		
Inventory, 80% × $5,000	4,000		Dr.
Current liabilities	0		
Premium on bonds payable, 80% × $1,000	(800)		Cr.
Land (from allocation schedule)	26,480		Dr.
Buildings (net) (from allocation schedule)	23,168		Dr.
Equipment (net) (from allocation schedule)	18,480		Dr.
Patent (net) (from allocation schedule)	8,688		Dr.
Brand-name copyright (from allocation schedule)	27,584		Dr.
Goodwill (remove 80% × $40,000 existing)	**(32,000)**		**Cr.**
Total adjustments		**$ 75,600**	

Notice that goodwill, applicable to the controlling interest, is entirely eliminated. No goodwill can be applicable to the parent's interest unless all other accounts have been adjusted to full fair value for the parent's ownership portion.

REFLECTION

- Goodwill on the subsidiary's books at the time of the purchase is ignored in zone and price analyses.
- The D&D schedule shows an adjustment for the difference between total goodwill (from price analysis) and the parent's share of existing goodwill.

10

OBJECTIVE

Define push-down accounting, and explain when it may be used and its impact.

PUSH-DOWN ACCOUNTING

Thus far, it has been assumed that the subsidiary's statements are unaffected by the parent's purchase of a controlling interest in the subsidiary. None of the subsidiary's accounts is adjusted on the subsidiary's books. In all preceding examples, adjustments to reflect fair value are made only on the consolidated worksheet. This is the most common but not the only accepted method.

Some accountants object to the inconsistency of using book values in the subsidiary's separate statements while using fair value adjusted values when the same accounts are included in the consolidated statements. They would advocate *push-down accounting*, whereby the subsidiary's accounts are adjusted to reflect the fair value adjustments. In accordance with the new basis of accounting, retained earnings are eliminated, and the balance (as adjusted for fair value adjustments) is added to paid-in capital. It is argued that the purchase of a controlling interest gives rise to a new basis of accountability for the interest traded, and the subsidiary accounts should reflect those values.

If the push-down method were applied to the example of a 100% purchase for $360,000 on page 72, the following entry would be made by the subsidiary on its books:

Inventory	5,000	
Premium on Bonds Payable		1,000
Land	40,000	
Buildings	40,000	
Equipment	30,000	
Patent	15,000	
Brand-Name Copyright	40,000	
Goodwill	63,000	
Paid-In Capital in Excess of Par		232,000

This entry would raise the subsidiary equity to $360,000. The $360,000 investment account would be eliminated against the $360,000 subsidiary equity with no excess remaining. If there is a noncontrolling interest, adjustments on the subsidiary books would be limited to the controlling ownership percentage.

The SEC staff has adopted a policy of requiring push-down accounting, in some cases, for the separately published statements of a subsidiary. The existence of any significant noncontrolling interests (usually above 5%) and/or significant publicly held debt or preferred stock generally eliminates the requirement to use push-down accounting. **Note that the consolidated statements are unaffected by this issue.** The only difference is in the placement of the adjustments from the determination and distribution of excess schedule. The conventional approach, which is used in this text, makes the adjustments on the consolidated worksheet. The push-down method makes the same adjustments directly on the books of the subsidiary. Under the push-down method, the adjustments are already made when consolidation procedures are applied. Since all accounts are adjusted to reflect fair values, the investment account is eliminated against subsidiary equity with no excess. The difference in methods affects only the presentation on the subsidiary's separate statements.

REFLECTION

- Push-down accounting revalues subsidiary accounts directly on the books of the subsidiary based on adjustments indicated in the D&D schedule.
- Since assets are revalued before the consolidation process starts, no distribution of excess (to adjust accounts) is required on the consolidated worksheet.

Worksheet 2-1

100% Interest; Price Equals Book Value
Company P and Subsidiary Company S
Worksheet for Consolidated Balance Sheet
December 31, 20X1

Worksheet 2-1 (see page 69)

		Trial Balance		Eliminations & Adjustments		Consolidated Balance Sheet	
		Company P	Company S	Dr.	Cr.		
1	Cash	300,000				300,000	1
2	Accounts Receivable	300,000	200,000			500,000	2
3	Inventory	100,000	100,000			200,000	3
4	Investment in Company S	500,000			(EL) 500,000		4
5							5
6	Equipment (net)	150,000	300,000			450,000	6
7	Goodwill						7
8	Current Liabilities	(150,000)	(100,000)			(250,000)	8
9	Bonds Payable	(500,000)				(500,000)	9
10	Common Stock—Company S		(200,000)	(EL) 200,000			10
11	Retained Earnings—Company S		(300,000)	(EL) 300,000			11
12	Common Stock—Company P	(100,000)				(100,000)	12
13	Retained Earnings—Company P	(600,000)				(600,000)	13
14	Totals	0	0	500,000	500,000	0	14

Eliminations and Adjustments:

(EL) Eliminate the investment in the subsidiary against the subsidiary equity accounts.

Worksheet 2-2

100% Interest; Price Exceeds Book Value
Company P and Subsidiary Company S
Worksheet for Consolidated Balance Sheet
December 31, 20X1

Worksheet 2-2 (see page 71)

		Trial Balance		Eliminations & Adjustments		Consolidated Balance Sheet	
		Company P	Company S	Dr.	Cr.		
1	Cash	100,000				100,000	1
2	Accounts Receivable	300,000	200,000			500,000	2
3	Inventory	100,000	100,000	**(D1) 20,000**		220,000	3
4	Investment in Company S	700,000			(EL) 500,000		4
5					**(D) 200,000**		5
6	Equipment (net)	150,000	300,000	**(D2) 100,000**		550,000	6
7	Goodwill			**(D3) 80,000**		80,000	7
8	Current Liabilities	(150,000)	(100,000)			(250,000)	8
9	Bonds Payable	(500,000)				(500,000)	9
10	Common Stock—Company S		(200,000)	(EL) 200,000			10
11	Retained Earnings—Company S		(300,000)	(EL) 300,000			11
12	Common Stock—Company P	(100,000)				(100,000)	12
13	Retained Earnings—Company P	(600,000)				(600,000)	13
14	Totals	0	0	700,000	700,000	0	14

Eliminations and Adjustments:

(EL) Eliminate the investment in the subsidiary against the subsidiary equity accounts.
(D) Distribute $200,000 excess of cost over book value as follows:
(D1) Inventory, $20,000.
(D2) Equipment, $100,000.
(D3) Goodwill, $80,000.

Worksheet 2-3

100% Interest; Price Exceeds Market Value of Identifiable Net Assets
Acquisitions Inc. and Subsidiary Johnson Company
Worksheet for Consolidated Balance Sheet
December 31, 20X1

Worksheet 2-3 (see page 74)

		Trial Balance		Eliminations & Adjustments		Consolidated Balance Sheet	
		Acquisitions	Johnson	Dr.	Cr.		
1	Cash	51,000	0			51,000	1
2	Accounts Receivable	42,000	28,000			70,000	2
3	Inventory	95,000	40,000	(D1) 5,000		140,000	3
4	Investment in Johnson Company	360,000			(EL) 128,000		4
5					(D) 232,000		5
6	Land	60,000	10,000	**(D3) 40,000**		110,000	6
7	Buildings	500,000	60,000	**(D4) 40,000**		600,000	7
8	Accumulated Depreciation	(50,000)	(20,000)			(70,000)	8
9	Equipment	60,000	30,000	(D5) 30,000		120,000	9
10	Accumulated Depreciation	(24,000)	(10,000)			(34,000)	10
11	Patent (net)		15,000	**(D6) 15,000**		30,000	11
12	Brand-Name Copyright			**(D7) 40,000**		40,000	12
13	Goodwill			(D8) 63,000		63,000	13
14	Current Liabilities	(89,000)	(5,000)			(94,000)	14
15	Bonds Payable	(100,000)	(20,000)			(120,000)	15
16	Discount (premium)				**(D2) 1,000**	(1,000)	16
17	Common Stock—Johnson		(1,000)	(EL) 1,000			17
18	Paid-In Capital in Excess of Par—Johnson		(59,000)	(EL) 59,000			18
19	Retained Earnings—Johnson		(68,000)	(EL) 68,000			19
20	Common Stock—Acquisitions	(20,000)				(20,000)	20
21	Paid-In Capital in Excess of Par—Acquisitions	(480,000)				(480,000)	21
22	Retained Earnings—Acquisitions	(405,000)				(405,000)	22
23	Totals	0	0	361,000	361,000	0	23

Eliminations and Adjustments:

(EL) Eliminate investment in subsidiary against subsidiary equity accounts.
(D) Distribute $232,000 excess of cost over book value as follows:
(D1) Inventory, $5,000.
(D2) Premium on bonds payable, ($1,000).
(D3) Land, $40,000.
(D4) Buildings, $40,000.
(D5) Equipment, $30,000.
(D6) Patent, $15,000.
(D7) Brand-name copyright, $40,000.
(D8) Goodwill, $63,000.

Worksheet 2-4

100% Interest; Price Exceeds Fair Value of Priority Accounts
Acquisitions Inc. and Subsidiary Johnson Company
Worksheet for Consolidated Balance Sheet
December 31, 20X1

Worksheet 2-4 (see page 77)

		Trial Balance		Eliminations & Adjustments		Consolidated Balance Sheet	
		Acquisitions	Johnson	Dr.	Cr.		
1	Cash	51,000	0			51,000	1
2	Accounts Receivable	42,000	28,000			70,000	2
3	Inventory	95,000	40,000	(D1) 5,000		140,000	3
4	Investment in Johnson	210,000			(EL) 128,000		4
5					(D) 82,000		5
6	Land	60,000	10,000	(D3) 22,600		92,600	6
7	Buildings	500,000	60,000	(D4) 12,160		572,160	7
8	Accumulated Depreciation	(50,000)	(20,000)			(70,000)	8
9	Equipment	60,000	30,000	(D5) 12,600		102,600	9
10	Accumulated Depreciation	(24,000)	(10,000)			(34,000)	10
11	Patent (net)		15,000	(D6) 4,560		19,560	11
12	Brand-Name Copyright			(D7) 26,080		26,080	12
13	Goodwill			**(D8) 0**			13
14	Current Liabilities	(89,000)	(5,000)			(94,000)	14
15	Bonds Payable	(100,000)	(20,000)			(120,000)	15
16	Discount (premium)				(D2) 1,000	(1,000)	16
17	Common Stock—Johnson		(1,000)	(EL) 1,000			17
18	Paid-In Capital in Excess of Par—Johnson		(59,000)	(EL) 59,000			18
19	Retained Earnings—Johnson		(68,000)	(EL) 68,000			19
20	Common Stock—Acquisitions	(17,000)				(17,000)	20
21	Paid-In Capital in Excess of Par—Acquisitions	(333,000)				(333,000)	21
22	Retained Earnings—Acquisitions	(405,000)				(405,000)	22
23	Totals	0	0	211,000	211,000	0	23

Eliminations and Adjustments:

(EL) Eliminate investment in subsidiary against subsidiary equity accounts.
(D) Distribute $82,000 excess of cost over book value as follows:
(D1) Inventory, $5,000.
(D2) Premium on bonds payable, ($1,000).
(D3) Land, $22,600.
(D4) Buildings, $12,160.
(D5) Equipment, $12,600.
(D6) Patent, $4,560.
(D7) Brand-name copyright, $26,080.
(D8) No amount available for goodwill.

Worksheet 2-5

100% Interest; Price Is Less than Fair Value of Priority Accounts
Acquisitions Inc. and Subsidiary Johnson Company
Worksheet for Consolidated Balance Sheet
December 31, 20X1

Worksheet 2-5 (see page 79)

		Trial Balance		Eliminations & Adjustments		Consolidated	
		Acquisitions	Johnson	Dr.	Cr.	Balance Sheet	
1	Cash	51,000	0			51,000	1
2	Accounts Receivable	42,000	28,000			70,000	2
3	Inventory	95,000	40,000	(D1) 5,000		140,000	3
4	Investment in Johnson	35,000			(EL) 128,000		4
5				(D) 93,000			5
6	Land	60,000	10,000		(D3) 10,000	60,000	6
7	Buildings	500,000	60,000		(D4) 40,000	520,000	7
8	Accumulated Depreciation	(50,000)	(20,000)			(70,000)	8
9	Equipment	60,000	30,000		(D5) 20,000	70,000	9
10	Accumulated Depreciation	(24,000)	(10,000)			(34,000)	10
11	Patent (net)		15,000		(D6) 15,000		11
12	Brand-Name Copyright			**(D7) 0**			12
13	Goodwill						13
14	Current Liabilities	(89,000)	(5,000)			(94,000)	14
15	Bonds Payable	(100,000)	(20,000)			(120,000)	15
16	Discount (premium)				(D2) 1,000	(1,000)	16
17	Common Stock—Johnson		(1,000)	(EL) 1,000			17
18	Paid-In Capital in Excess of Par—Johnson		(59,000)	(EL) 59,000			18
19	Retained Earnings—Johnson		(68,000)	(EL) 68,000			19
20	Common Stock—Acquisitions	(13,500)				(13,500)	20
21	Paid-In Capital in Excess of Par—Acquisitions	(161,500)				(161,500)	21
22	Retained Earnings—Acquisitions	(405,000)			**(D8) 12,000**	(417,000)	22
23	Totals	0	0	226,000	226,000	0	23

Eliminations and Adjustments:

(EL) Eliminate investment in subsidiary against subsidiary equity accounts.
(D) Distribute $93,000 excess of book value over cost as follows:
(D1) Inventory, $5,000.
(D2) Premium on bonds payable, ($1,000).
(D3) Land, ($10,000).
(D4) Building is eliminated; no value available.
(D5) Equipment is eliminated; no value available.
(D6) Patent is eliminated; no value available.
(D7) No amount available for brand-name copyright.
(D8) No goodwill; record extraordinary gain. Since this is a balance sheet only, extraordinary gain is credited to retained earnings.

Worksheet 2-6

80% Interest; Price Exceeds Fair Value of Priority Accounts
Acquisitions Inc. and Subsidiary Johnson Company
Worksheet for Consolidated Balance Sheet
December 31, 20X1

Worksheet 2-6 (see page 82)

		Trial Balance		Eliminations & Adjustments		NCI	Consolidated Balance Sheet	
		Acquisitions	Johnson	Dr.	Cr.			
1	Cash	51,000	0				51,000	1
2	Accounts Receivable	42,000	28,000				70,000	2
3	Inventory	95,000	40,000	(D1) 4,000			139,000	3
4	Investment in Johnson	290,000			(EL) 102,400			4
5					(D) 187,600			5
6	Land	60,000	10,000	(D3) 32,000			102,000	6
7	Buildings	500,000	60,000	(D4) 32,000			592,000	7
8	Accumulated Depreciation	(50,000)	(20,000)				(70,000)	8
9	Equipment	60,000	30,000	(D5) 24,000			114,000	9
10	Accumulated Depreciation	(24,000)	(10,000)				(34,000)	10
11	Patent (net)		15,000	(D6) 12,000			27,000	11
12	Brand-Name Copyright			(D7) 32,000			32,000	12
13	Goodwill			**(D8) 52,400**			52,400	13
14	Current Liabilities	(89,000)	(5,000)				(94,000)	14
15	Bonds Payable	(100,000)	(20,000)				(120,000)	15
16	Discount (premium)				(D2) 800		(800)	16
17	Common Stock—Johnson		(1,000)	(EL) 800		(200)		17
18	Paid-In Capital in Excess of Par—Johnson		(59,000)	(EL) 47,200		(11,800)		18
19	Retained Earnings—Johnson		(68,000)	(EL) 54,400		(13,600)		19
20	Common Stock—Acquisitions	(18,600)					(18,600)	20
21	Paid-In Capital in Excess of Par—Acquisitions	(411,400)					(411,400)	21
22	Retained Earnings—Acquisitions	(405,000)					(405,000)	22
23	Noncontrolling Interest						(25,600)	23
24	Totals	0	0	290,800	290,800	(25,600)	0	24

Eliminations and Adjustments:

(EL) Eliminate investment in subsidiary against 80% of the subsidiary's equity accounts.
(D) Distribute $187,600 excess of cost over book value as follows:
(D1) Inventory, $4,000.
(D2) Premium on bonds payable, ($800).
(D3) Land, $32,000.
(D4) Buildings, $32,000.
(D5) Equipment, $24,000.
(D6) Patent, $12,000.
(D7) Brand-name copyright, $32,000.
(D8) Goodwill, $52,400.

Worksheet 2-7

80% Purchase, Bargain
Acquisitions Inc. and Subsidiary Johnson Company
Worksheet for Consolidated Balance Sheet
December 31, 20X1

Worksheet 2-7 (see page 85)

		Trial Balance		Eliminations & Adjustments			
		Acquisitions	Johnson	Dr.	Cr.	NCI	Consolidated Balance Sheet	
1	Cash	51,000	0				51,000	1
2	Accounts Receivable	42,000	28,000				70,000	2
3	Inventory	95,000	40,000	(D1) 4,000			139,000	3
4	Investment in Johnson	210,000			(EL) 102,400			4
5					(D) 107,600			5
6	Land	60,000	10,000	(D3) 26,480			96,480	6
7	Buildings	500,000	60,000	(D4) 23,168			583,168	7
8	Accumulated Depreciation	(50,000)	(20,000)				(70,000)	8
9	Equipment	60,000	30,000	(D5) 18,480			108,480	9
10	Accumulated Depreciation	(24,000)	(10,000)				(34,000)	10
11	Patent (net)		15,000	(D6) 8,688			23,688	11
12	Brand-Name Copyright			(D7) 27,584			27,584	12
13	Goodwill			(D8) 0				13
14	Current Liabilities	(89,000)	(5,000)				(94,000)	14
15	Bonds Payable	(100,000)	(20,000)				(120,000)	15
16	Discount (premium)				(D2) 800		(800)	16
17	Common Stock—Johnson		(1,000)	(EL) 800		(200)		17
18	Paid-In Capital in Excess of Par—Johnson		(59,000)	(EL) 47,200		(11,800)		18
19	Retained Earnings—Johnson		(68,000)	(EL) 54,400		(13,600)		19
20	Common Stock—Acquisitions	(17,000)					(17,000)	20
21	Paid-In Capital in Excess of Par—Acquisitions	(333,000)					(333,000)	21
22	Retained Earnings—Acquisitions	(405,000)					(405,000)	22
23	Noncontrolling Interest						(25,600)	23
24	Totals	0	0	210,800	210,800	(25,600)	0	24

Eliminations and Adjustments:

(EL) Eliminate investment in subsidiary against 80% of the subsidiary's equity accounts.
(D) Distribute $107,600 excess of cost over book value as follows:
(D1) Inventory, $4,000.
(D2) Land, $26,480.
(D3) Premium on bonds payable, ($800).
(D4) Buildings, $23,168.
(D5) Equipment, $18,480.
(D6) Patent, $8,688.
(D7) Brand-name copyright, $27,584.

UNDERSTANDING THE ISSUES

1. Johnson Company is considering an investment in the common stock of Bickler Company. What are the accounting issues surrounding the recording of income in future periods if Johnson purchases:

   a. 10% of Bickler's outstanding shares.
   b. 30% of Bickler's outstanding shares.
   c. 100% of Bickler's outstanding shares.
   d. 80% of Bickler's outstanding shares.

2. A parent must normally consolidate a company if it owns over 50% of the outstanding voting common stock of that company. In your own words, explain how a parent could gain control without an over 50% interest in a company.

3. What does the elimination process accomplish?

4. Padro Company purchases a controlling interest in Salto Company. Salto had identifiable net assets with a cost of $400,000 and a fair value of $600,000. It was agreed that the total fair value of Salto's common stock was $900,000. What adjustments will be made to Salto's accounts, and what new accounts and amounts will be recorded if:

   a. Padro purchases 100% of Salto's common stock for $900,000.
   b. Padro purchases 80% of Salto's common stock for $720,000.

5. Pillow Company is purchasing a 100% interest in the common stock of Sleep Company. Sleep's balance sheet amounts at book and fair value are as follows:

Account	Book Value	Fair Value
Current assets	$ 200,000	$ 250,000
Fixed assets	350,000	800,000
Liabilities	(200,000)	(200,000)

   What adjustments to recorded values of Sleep Company's accounts will be made in the consolidation process (including the creation of new accounts), if the price paid for the 100% is:

   a. $1,000,000.
   b. $500,000.
   c. $30,000.

6. Pillow Company is purchasing an 80% interest in the common stock of Sleep Company. Sleep's balance sheet amounts at book and fair value are as follows:

Account	Book Value	Fair Value
Current assets	$ 200,000	$ 250,000
Fixed assets	350,000	800,000
Liabilities	(200,000)	(200,000)

   What adjustments to recorded values of Sleep Company's accounts will be made in the consolidation process (including the creation of new accounts), if the price paid for the 100% is:

   a. $800,000.
   b. $600,000.
   c. $30,000.

7. Pillow Company is purchasing an 80% interest in the common stock of Sleep Company. Sleep's balance sheet amounts at book and fair value are as follows:

Account	Book Value	Fair Value
Current assets	$ 200,000	$ 250,000
Fixed assets	350,000	800,000
Liabilities	(200,000)	(200,000)

What will be the amount of the noncontrolling interest in the consolidated balance sheet, and how will it be displayed in the consolidated balance sheet?

EXERCISES

Exercise 1 *(LO 1)* **Investment recording methods.** Solara Corporation is considering investing in Focus Corporation, but is unsure about what level of ownership should be undertaken. Solara and Focus have the following reported incomes:

	Solara	Focus
Sales	$640,000	$370,000
Cost of goods sold	300,000	230,000
Gross profit	$340,000	$140,000
Selling and administrative expenses	120,000	75,000
Net income	$220,000	$ 65,000

Focus paid $15,000 in cash dividends to its investors. Prepare a pro forma income statement for Solara Corporation that compares income under 10%, 20%, and 70% ownership levels.

Exercise 2 *(LO 4)* **Asset compared to stock purchase.** Glass Company is thinking about acquiring Plastic Company. Glass Company is considering two methods of accomplishing control and is wondering how the accounting treatment will differ under each method. Glass Company has estimated that the fair values of Plastic's net assets are equal to their book values, except for the equipment which is understated by $20,000.

The following balance sheets have been prepared on the date of acquisition:

Assets	Glass	Plastic
Cash	$540,000	$ 20,000
Accounts receivable	50,000	70,000
Inventory	50,000	100,000
Property, plant, and equipment (net)	230,000	270,000
Total assets	$870,000	$460,000
Liabilities and Equity		
Current liabilities	$140,000	$ 80,000
Bonds payable	250,000	100,000
Stockholders' equity:		
Common stock, ($100 par)	200,000	150,000
Retained earnings	280,000	130,000
Total liabilities and equity	$870,000	$460,000

1. Assume Glass Company purchased the net assets directly from Plastic Company for $530,000.

   a. Prepare the entry that Glass Company would make to record the purchase.
   b. Prepare the balance sheet for Glass Company immediately following the purchase.

2. Assume that 100% of the outstanding stock of Plastic Company is purchased from the former stockholders for a total of $530,000.

   a. Prepare the entry that Glass Company would make to record the purchase.
   b. State how the investment would appear on Glass's unconsolidated balance sheet prepared immediately after the purchase.
   c. Indicate how the consolidated balance sheet would appear.

Exercise 3 *(LO 6)* **Simple price zone analysis.** Flower Company is considering the cash purchase of 100% of the outstanding stock of Vase Company. The terms are not set, and alternative prices are being considered for negotiation. The balance sheet of Vase Company shows the following values:

Assets		Liabilities and Equity	
Cash equivalents	$ 60,000	Current liabilities	$ 60,000
Inventory	120,000	Common stock ($5 par)	100,000
Land	50,000	Paid-in capital in excess of par	150,000
Building (net)	200,000	Retained earnings	120,000
Total assets	$430,000	Total liabilities and equity	$430,000

Appraisals reveal that the inventory has a fair value of $160,000 and that the land and building have fair values of $100,000 and $300,000, respectively. The questions to be answered concern the price to be paid for Vase's common stock:

1. Above what price would goodwill be recorded?
2. Below what price would fixed assets be recorded at less-than-full fair value?
3. Below what price would an extraordinary gain be recorded?

Exercise 4 *(LO 6, 7)* **Recording purchase with goodwill.** Wood'n Wares Inc. purchased all the outstanding stock of Pine Inc. for $950,000. Wood'n Wares also paid $10,000 in direct acquisition costs and $3,000 for indirect acquisition costs. Just before the investment, the two companies had the following balance sheets:

Assets	Wood'n Wares Inc.	Pine Inc.
Accounts receivable	$ 900,000	$ 500,000
Inventory	600,000	200,000
Depreciable fixed assets (net)	1,500,000	600,000
Total assets	$3,000,000	$1,300,000

Liabilities and Equity		
Current liabilities	$ 950,000	$ 400,000
Bonds payable	500,000	200,000
Common stock ($10 par)	400,000	300,000
Paid-in capital in excess of par	500,000	380,000
Retained earnings	650,000	20,000
Total liabilities and equity	$3,000,000	$1,300,000

Appraisals for the assets of Pine Inc. indicate that fair values differ from recorded book values for the inventory and for the property, plant, and equipment which have fair values of $250,000 and $700,000, respectively.

1. Prepare the entry to record the purchase of the Pine Inc. common stock including all acquisition costs.
2. Prepare a zone analysis and a determination and distribution of excess schedule for the investment in Pine Inc.
3. Prepare the elimination entries that would be made on a consolidated worksheet.

Exercise 5 *(LO 6, 7)* **Purchase at alternative prices.** Libra Company is purchasing 100% of the outstanding stock of Gemini Company, which has the following balance sheet on the date of acquisition:

Assets		Liabilities and Equity	
Accounts receivable	$ 300,000	Current liabilities	$ 250,000
Inventory	200,000	Bonds payable	200,000
Property, plant, and		Common stock ($5 par)	200,000
equipment (net)	500,000	Paid-in capital in excess of par	300,000
Computer software	125,000	Retained earnings	175,000
Total assets	$1,125,000	Total liabilities and equity	$1,125,000

Appraisals indicate that the following fair values should be acknowledged:

Inventory	$215,000
Property, plant, and equipment	700,000
Bonds payable	210,000
Computer software	130,000

1. Above what price would goodwill be recorded?
2. Below what price would an extraordinary gain be recorded?

Prepare the zone analysis, the determination and distribution of excess schedule, and the worksheet elimination entries that would be made if:

3. The price paid for the 100% interest was $1,000,000.
4. The price paid for the 100% interest was $810,000.

Exercise 6 *(LO 6, 7, 9)* **Bargain purchase, allocation.** Lancaster Company is purchasing 100% of the outstanding common stock of Villard Company for $600,000 plus $20,000 of direct acquisition costs. The following balance sheet was prepared for Villard on the date of the purchase:

Assets		Liabilities and Equity	
Inventory	$ 50,000	Current liabilities	$150,000
Mineral rights	250,000	Common stock ($5 par)	100,000
Equipment (net)	150,000	Paid-in capital in excess of par	300,000
Goodwill	50,000	Retained earnings	(50,000)
Total assets	$500,000	Total liabilities and equity	$500,000

Appraisals are as follows for the assets of Villard Company:

Inventory	$ 10,000
Mineral rights	700,000
Equipment	100,000

Based on the preceding facts,

1. Prepare a zone analysis and a determination and distribution of excess schedule.
2. Prepare the elimination entries that would be made on a consolidated worksheet prepared on the date of purchase.

Exercise 7 *(LO 6, 7, 8)* **80% purchase, goodwill.** Quincy Company purchased 80% of the common stock of Cooker Company for $700,000 plus direct acquisition costs of $30,000. At the time of the purchase, Cooker Company had the following balance sheet:

Assets		Liabilities and Equity	
Cash equivalents	$ 120,000	Current liabilities	$ 200,000
Inventory	200,000	Bonds payable	400,000
Land	100,000	Common stock ($5 par)	100,000
Building (net)	450,000	Paid-in capital in excess of par	150,000
Equipment (net)	230,000	Retained earnings	250,000
Total assets	$1,100,000	Total liabilities and equity	$1,100,000

Fair values differ from book values for all assets other than cash equivalents. The fair values are as follows:

Inventory	$300,000
Land	200,000
Building	600,000
Equipment	200,000

Based on the preceding facts,

1. Prepare a zone analysis and a determination and distribution of excess schedule.
2. Prepare the elimination entries that would be made on a consolidated worksheet prepared on the date of purchase.

Exercise 8 *(LO 6, 7, 8)* **80% purchase, alternative prices.** Venus Company purchased 8,000 shares of Saturn Company for $82 per share. Just prior to the purchase, Saturn Company had the following balance sheet:

Assets		Liabilities and Equity	
Cash	$ 20,000	Current liabilities	$250,000
Inventory	280,000	Common stock ($5 par)	50,000
Property, plant, and equipment (net)	400,000	Paid-in capital in excess of par	130,000
Goodwill	100,000	Retained earnings	370,000
Total assets	$800,000	Total liabilities and equity	$800,000

Venus Company believes that the inventory has a fair value of $400,000 and that the property, plant, and equipment is worth $500,000. Business consultants have suggested that the goodwill is worth no more than $50,000. Based on these facts,

1. Prepare a zone analysis and a determination and distribution of excess schedule.
2. Prepare the elimination entries that would be made on a consolidated worksheet prepared on the date of acquisition.
3. Prepare the elimination entries that would be made on a consolidated worksheet prepared on the date of acquisition assuming Venus pays $64 per share.

Exercise 9 *(LO 10)* **Push-down accounting.** On January 1, 20X7, Knight Corporation purchased all the outstanding shares of Craig Company for $950,000. It has been decided that Craig Company will use push-down accounting principles to account for this transaction. The current balance sheet is stated at historical cost.

The following balance sheet was prepared for Craig Company on January 1, 20X7:

Assets			Liabilities and Equity		
Current assets:			Current liabilities		$ 90,000
Cash	$ 80,000		Long-term liabilities:		
Accounts receivable	260,000		Bonds payable	$300,000	
			Deferred taxes	50,000	350,000
Prepaid expenses	20,000	$ 360,000	Stockholders' equity:		
Property, plant, and equipment:			Common stock ($10 par)	$300,000	
Land	$200,000		Retained earnings	420,000	720,000
Building (net)	600,000	800,000			
Total assets		$1,160,000	Total liabilities and equity		$1,160,000

Knight Corporation received the following appraisals for Craig Company's assets and liabilities:

Accounts receivable	$280,000
Land	230,000
Building (net)	700,000
Bonds payable	280,000
Deferred tax liability	40,000

1. Record the investment.
2. Record the adjustments on the books of Craig Company.
3. Prepare the entries that would be made on the consolidated worksheet to eliminate the investment.

PROBLEMS

Problem 2-1 *(LO 4, 5, 6, 7)* **100% purchase, goodwill, consolidated balance sheet.** On July 1, 20X6, Rose Company exchanged 18,000 of its $35 fair value ($10 par value) shares for all the outstanding shares of Daisy Company. Rose paid direct acquisition costs of $20,000 and $5,000 in stock issuance costs. The two companies had the following balance sheets on July 1, 20X6:

Assets	Rose	Daisy
Other current assets	$ 50,000	$ 70,000
Inventory	120,000	60,000
Land	100,000	40,000
Buildings (net)	300,000	120,000
Equipment (net)	430,000	110,000
Total assets	$1,000,000	$400,000
Liabilities and Equity		
Current liabilities	$ 180,000	$ 60,000
Common stock ($10 par)	400,000	200,000
Retained earnings	420,000	140,000
Total liabilities and equity	$1,000,000	$400,000

(continued)

The following fair values differ from book values for Daisy's assets:

Inventory	$ 65,000
Land	100,000
Building	150,000
Equipment	75,000

Required ▶ ▶ ▶ ▶ ▶

1. Record the investment in Daisy Company and any other entry necessitated by the purchase.
2. Prepare a zone analysis and a determination and distribution of excess schedule.
3. Prepare a consolidated balance sheet for July 1, 20X6, immediately subsequent to the purchase.

Problem 2-2 *(LO 4, 5, 6, 7, 8)* **80% purchase, goodwill, consolidated balance sheet.** Using the data given in Problem 2-1, assume that Rose Company exchanged 18,000 of its $35 fair value ($10 par value) shares for 16,000 of the outstanding shares of Daisy Company.

Required ▶ ▶ ▶ ▶ ▶

1. Record the investment in Daisy Company and any other entry necessitated by the purchase.
2. Prepare a determination and distribution of excess schedule.
3. Prepare a consolidated balance sheet for July 1, 20X6, immediately subsequent to the purchase.

Problem 2-3 *(LO 4, 5, 6, 7)* **100% purchase, bargain, elimination entries only.** On March 1, 20X6, Carlson Enterprises purchased a 100% interest in Express Corporation for $400,000.

Express Corporation had the following balance sheet on February 28, 20X5:

Express Corporation
Balance Sheet
For the Month Ended February 28, 20X5

Assets		Liabilities and Equity	
Accounts receivable	$ 60,000	Current liabilities	$ 50,000
Inventory	80,000	Bonds payable	100,000
Land	40,000	Common stock	50,000
Buildings	300,000	Paid-in capital in excess of par	250,000
Accum. depr.—building	(120,000)	Retained earnings	70,000
Equipment	220,000		
Accum. depr.—equipment	(60,000)		
Total assets	$ 520,000	Total liabilities and equity	$520,000

Carlson Enterprises received an independent appraisal on the fair values of Express Corporation's assets. The controller has reviewed the following figures and accepts them as reasonable.

Inventory	$100,000
Land	40,500
Building	202,500
Equipment	162,000
Bonds payable	95,000

Required ▶ ▶ ▶ ▶ ▶

1. Record the investment in Express Corporation.
2. Prepare a zone analysis and a determination and distribution of excess schedule.
3. Prepare the elimination entries that would be made on a consolidated worksheet prepared on the date of acquisition.

Problem 2-4 *(LO 6, 7, 10)* **100% purchase, goodwill, push-down accounting.** On March 1, 20X5, Collier Enterprises purchased a 100% interest in Robby Corporation for $480,000. It was decided that Robby Corporation will apply push-down accounting principles to account for this acquisition.

Robby Corporation had the following balance sheet on February 28, 20X5:

Robby Corporation
Balance Sheet
For the Month Ended February 28, 20X5

Assets		Liabilities and Equity	
Accounts receivable	$ 60,000	Current liabilities	$ 50,000
Inventory	80,000	Bonds payable	100,000
Land	40,000	Common stock	50,000
Buildings	300,000	Paid-in capital in excess of par	250,000
Accum. depr.—building	(120,000)	Retained earnings	70,000
Equipment	220,000		
Accum. depr.—equipment	(60,000)		
Total assets	$ 520,000	Total liabilities and equity	$520,000

Collier Enterprises received an independent appraisal on the fair values of Robby Corporation's assets. The controller has reviewed the following figures and accepts them as reasonable.

Inventory	$100,000
Land	55,000
Building	200,000
Equipment	150,000
Bonds payable	98,000

◀◀◀◀◀ **Required**

1. Record the investment in Robby Corporation.
2. Prepare a zone analysis and a determination and distribution of excess schedule.
3. Give Robby Corporation's adjusting entry.

Problem 2-5 *(LO 4, 5, 6, 7)* **100% purchase, goodwill, worksheet.** On December 31, 20X1, Adam Company purchased 100% of the common stock of Scott Company for $475,000. On this date, any excess of cost over book value was attributed to accounts with fair values that differed from book values. These accounts of the Scott Company had the following fair values:

?

Inventory	$140,000
Land	45,000
Buildings and equipment	225,000
Bonds payable	105,000
Copyrights	25,000

The following comparative balance sheets were prepared for the two companies immediately after the purchase:

	Adam	Scott
Cash	$ 160,000	$ 40,000
Accounts receivable	70,000	30,000
Inventory	130,000	120,000

(continued)

	Adam	Scott
Investment in Scott Company	$ 475,000	
Land	50,000	$ 35,000
Building and equipment	350,000	230,000
Accumulated depreciation	(100,000)	(50,000)
Copyrights	40,000	10,000
Total assets	$1,175,000	$415,000
Current liabilities	$ 192,000	$ 65,000
Bonds payable		100,000
Common stock ($10 par), Adam	100,000	
Common stock ($5 par), Scott		50,000
Paid-in capital in excess of par	250,000	70,000
Retained earnings	633,000	130,000
Total liabilities and equity	$1,175,000	$415,000

Required ▶ ▶ ▶ ▶ ▶

1. Prepare zone and price analyses and a determination and distribution of excess schedule for the investment in Scott Company.
2. Complete a consolidated worksheet for Adam Company and its subsidiary Scott Company as of December 31, 20X1.

Problem 2-6 *(LO 4, 5, 6, 7, 8)* **80% purchase, goodwill, worksheet.** Using the data given in Problem 2-5, assume that Adam Company purchased 80% of the common stock of Scott Company for $475,000.

Required ▶ ▶ ▶ ▶ ▶

1. Prepare zone and price analyses and a determination and distribution of excess schedule for the investment in Scott Company.
2. Complete a consolidated worksheet for Adam Company and its subsidiary Scott Company as of December 31, 20X1.

Use the following information for Problems 2-7 through 2-10:
In an attempt to expand its operations, Pantera Company acquired Sader Company on January 1, 20X6. Pantera paid cash in exchange for the common stock of Sader. On the date of acquisition, Sader had the following balance sheet:

Sader Company
Balance Sheet
January 1, 20X1

Assets		Liabilities and Equity	
Accounts receivable	$ 20,000	Current liabilities	$ 40,000
Inventory	50,000	Bonds payable	100,000
Land	40,000	Common stock, $1 par	10,000
Buildings	200,000	Paid-in capital in excess	
Accumulated depreciation	(50,000)	of par	90,000
Equipment	60,000	Retained earnings	60,000
Accumulated depreciation	(20,000)		
Total assets	$300,000	Total liabilities and equity	$300,000

An appraisal indicates that the following assets exist and have fair values that differed from their book values:

Inventory	$ 55,000
Land	70,000
Buildings	250,000
Equipment	60,000
Copyright	50,000

Problem 2-7 *(LO 4, 5, 6, 7)* **100% purchase, goodwill, limited adjustments, worksheet.** Use the preceding information for Pantera's purchase of Sader common stock. Assume Pantera purchased 100% of the common stock for $410,000. Pantera had the following balance sheet immediately after the purchase:

template cd

?

Pantera Company
Balance Sheet
January 1, 20X1

Assets		Liabilities and Equity	
Cash	$ 51,000	Current liabilities	$ 80,000
Accounts receivable	65,000	Bonds payable	200,000
Inventory	80,000	Common stock	20,000
Land	100,000	Paid-in capital in excess of par	180,000
Investment in Sader	410,000	Retained earnings	446,000
Buildings	250,000		
Accumulated depreciation	(80,000)		
Equipment	90,000		
Accumulated depreciation	(40,000)		
Total assets	$926,000	Total liabilities and equity	$926,000

◄◄◄◄◄ **Required**

1. Prepare a zone analysis and a determination and distribution of excess schedule for the investment in Sader.
2. Complete a consolidated worksheet for Pantera Company and its subsidiary Sader Company as of January 1, 20X1.

Problem 2-8 *(LO 4, 5, 6, 7)* **100% purchase, bargain, limited adjustments, worksheet.** Use the preceding information for Pantera's purchase of Sader common stock. Assume Pantera purchased 100% of the common stock for $250,000. Pantera had the following balance sheet immediately after the purchase:

template cd

Pantera Company
Balance Sheet
January 1, 20X1

Assets		Liabilities and Equity	
Cash	$211,000	Current liabilities	$ 80,000
Accounts receivable	65,000	Bonds payable	200,000
Inventory	80,000	Common stock	20,000
Land	100,000	Paid-in capital in excess of par	180,000
Investment in Sader	250,000	Retained earnings	446,000
Buildings	250,000		
Accumulated depreciation	(80,000)		
Equipment	90,000		
Accumulated depreciation	(40,000)		
Total assets	$926,000	Total liabilities and equity	$926,000

(continued)

Required ▶ ▶ ▶ ▶ ▶

1. Prepare a zone analysis and a determination and distribution of excess schedule for the investment in Sader.
2. Complete a consolidated worksheet for Pantera Company and its subsidiary Sader Company as of January 1, 20X1.

Problem 2-9 *(LO 4, 5, 6, 7, 8)* **80% purchase, goodwill, limited adjustments, worksheet.** Use the preceding information for Pantera's purchase of Sader common stock. Assume Pantera purchased 80% of the common stock for $360,000. Pantera had the following balance sheet immediately after the purchase:

Pantera Company
Balance Sheet
January 1, 20X1

Assets		Liabilities and Equity	
Cash	$101,000	Current liabilities	$ 80,000
Accounts receivable	65,000	Bonds payable	200,000
Inventory	80,000	Common stock	20,000
Land	100,000	Paid-in capital in excess of par	180,000
Investment in Sader	360,000	Retained earnings	446,000
Buildings	250,000		
Accumulated depreciation	(80,000)		
Equipment	90,000		
Accumulated depreciation	(40,000)		
Total assets	$926,000	Total liabilities and equity	$926,000

Required ▶ ▶ ▶ ▶ ▶

1. Prepare a zone analysis and a determination and distribution of excess schedule for the investment in Sader.
2. Complete a consolidated worksheet for Pantera Company and its subsidiary Sader Company as of January 1, 20X1.

Problem 2-10 *(LO 4, 5, 6, 7, 8)* **80% purchase, bargain, limited adjustments, worksheet.** Use the preceding information for Pantera's purchase of Sader common stock. Assume Pantera purchased 80% of the common stock for $200,000. Pantera had the following balance sheet immediately after the purchase:

Pantera Company
Balance Sheet
January 1, 20X1

Assets		Liabilities and Equity	
Cash	$261,000	Current liabilities	$ 80,000
Accounts receivable	65,000	Bonds payable	200,000
Inventory	80,000	Common stock	20,000
Land	100,000	Paid-in capital in excess of par	180,000
Investment in Sader	200,000	Retained earnings	446,000
Buildings	250,000		
Accumulated depreciation	(80,000)		
Equipment	90,000		
Accumulated depreciation	(40,000)		
Total assets	$926,000	Total liabilities and equity	$926,000

◄◄◄◄◄ **Required**

1. Prepare a zone analysis and a determination and distribution of excess schedule for the investment in Sader.
2. Complete a consolidated worksheet for Pantera Company and its subsidiary Sader Company as of January 1, 20X1.

Use the following information for Problems 2-11 through 2-14:
Purnell Corporation acquired Soma Corporation on December 31, 20X1. Soma had the following balance sheet on the date of acquisition:

Soma Corporation
Balance Sheet
December 31, 20X1

Assets		Liabilities and Equity	
Accounts receivable	$ 50,000	Current liabilities	$ 90,000
Inventory	120,000	Bonds payable	200,000
Land	100,000	Common stock, $1 par	10,000
Buildings	300,000	Paid-in capital in excess	
Accumulated depreciation	(100,000)	of par	190,000
Equipment	140,000	Retained earnings	140,000
Accumulated depreciation	(50,000)		
Patent	10,000		
Goodwill	60,000		
Total assets	$ 630,000	Total liabilities and equity	$630,000

An appraisal has been performed to determine whether the book values of Soma's net assets reflect their fair values. The appraiser also determined that several intangible assets existed, although they were not recorded. The following assets and liabilities had fair values that differed from their book values:

Inventory	$150,000
Land	200,000
Buildings	400,000
Equipment	200,000
Patent	150,000
Computer software	50,000
Bonds payable	210,000

Problem 2-11 *(LO 4, 5, 6, 7, 9)* **100% purchase, goodwill, several adjustments, worksheet.** Use the preceding information for Purnell's purchase of Soma common stock. Assume Purnell exchanged 24,000 shares of its own stock for 100% of the common stock of Soma. The stock had a market value of $50 per share and a par value of $1. Purnell had the following trial balance immediately after the purchase:

template cd

(continued)

Purnell Company
Trial Balance
December 31, 20X1

Cash	170,000
Accounts Receivable	300,000
Inventory	410,000
Land	800,000
Investment in Soma	1,200,000
Buildings	2,800,000
Accumulated Depreciation	(500,000)
Equipment	600,000
Accumulated Depreciation	(230,000)
Current Liabilities	(150,000)
Bonds Payable	(300,000)
Common Stock ($1 par)	(100,000)
Paid-In Capital in Excess of Par	(3,900,000)
Retained Earnings	(1,100,000)
Total	0

Required ▶ ▶ ▶ ▶ ▶

1. Prepare a zone analysis and a determination and distribution of excess schedule for the investment in Soma.
2. Complete a consolidated worksheet for Purnell Company and its subsidiary Soma Company as of December 31, 20X1.

template cd

Problem 2-12 *(LO 4, 5, 6, 7, 9)* **100% purchase, bargain, several adjustments, worksheet.** Use the preceding information for Purnell's purchase of Soma common stock. Assume Purnell exchanged 16,000 shares of its own stock for 100% of the common stock of Soma. The stock had a market value of $50 per share and a par value of $1. Purnell had the following trial balance immediately after the purchase:

Purnell Company
Trial Balance
December 31, 20X1

Cash	170,000
Accounts Receivable	300,000
Inventory	410,000
Land	800,000
Investment in Soma	800,000
Buildings	2,800,000
Accumulated Depreciation	(500,000)
Equipment	600,000
Accumulated Depreciation	(230,000)
Current Liabilities	(150,000)
Bonds Payable	(300,000)
Common Stock ($1 par)	(92,000)
Paid-In Capital in Excess of Par	(3,508,000)
Retained Earnings	(1,100,000)
Total	0

Required ▶ ▶ ▶ ▶ ▶

1. Prepare a zone analysis and a determination and distribution of excess schedule for the investment in Soma.
2. Complete a consolidated worksheet for Purnell Company and its subsidiary Soma Company as of December 31, 20X1.

Problem 2-13 *(LO 4, 5, 6, 7, 8, 9)* **80% purchase, goodwill, several adjustments, worksheet.** Use the preceding information for Purnell's purchase of Soma common stock. Assume Purnell exchanged 19,000 shares of its own stock for 80% of the common stock of Soma. The stock had a market value of $50 per share and a par value of $1. Purnell had the following trial balance immediately after the purchase:

Purnell Company
Trial Balance
December 31, 20X1

Cash	170,000
Accounts Receivable	300,000
Inventory	410,000
Land	800,000
Investment in Soma	950,000
Buildings	2,800,000
Accumulated Depreciation	(500,000)
Equipment	600,000
Accumulated Depreciation	(230,000)
Current Liabilities	(150,000)
Bonds Payable	(300,000)
Common Stock ($1 par)	(95,000)
Paid-in Capital in Excess of Par	(3,655,000)
Retained Earnings	(1,100,000)
Total	0

◄◄◄◄◄ **Required**

1. Prepare a zone analysis and a determination and distribution of excess schedule for the investment in Soma.
2. Complete a consolidated worksheet for Purnell Company and its subsidiary Soma Company as of December 31, 20X1.

Problem 2-14 *(LO 4, 5, 6, 7, 8, 9)* **80% purchase, bargain, several adjustments, worksheet.** Use the preceding information for Purnell's purchase of Soma common stock. Assume Purnell exchanged 10,000 shares of its own stock for 80% of the common stock of Soma. The stock had a market value of $50 per share and a par value of $1. Purnell had the following trial balance immediately after the purchase:

Purnell Company
Trial Balance
December 31, 20X1

Cash	170,000
Accounts Receivable	300,000
Inventory	410,000
Land	800,000
Investment in Soma	500,000
Buildings	2,800,000
Accumulated Depreciation	(500,000)
Equipment	600,000
Accumulated Depreciation	(230,000)
Current Liabilities	(150,000)
Bonds Payable	(300,000)

(continued)

Common Stock ($1 par)	(86,000)
Paid-In Capital in Excess of Par	(3,214,000)
Retained Earnings	(1,100,000)
Total	0

Required ▶ ▶ ▶ ▶ ▶

1. Prepare a zone analysis and a determination and distribution of excess schedule for the investment in Soma.
2. Complete a consolidated worksheet for Purnell Company and its subsidiary Soma Company as of December 31, 20X1.

Case 2-1 *Consolidating a Bargain Purchase*

Your client, Best Value Hardware Stores, has come to you for assistance in evaluating an opportunity to purchase a controlling interest in a hardware store in a neighboring city. The store under consideration is a closely held family corporation. Owners of 60% of the shares are willing to sell you the 60% interest, 30,000 common stock shares in exchange for 7,500 of Best Value shares, which have a fair value of $40 each and a par value of $10 each.

Your client sees this as a good opportunity to enter a new market. The controller of Best Value knows, however, that all is not well with the store being considered. The store, Al's Hardware, has not kept pace with the market and has been losing money. It also has a major lawsuit against it stemming from alleged faulty electrical components it supplied which caused a fire. The store is not insured for the loss. Legal counsel advises that the store will likely pay $300,000 in damages.

The following balance sheet was provided by Al's Hardware as of December 31, 20X1:

Assets		Liabilities and Equity	
Cash	$ 180,000	Current liabilities	$ 425,000
Accounts receivable	460,000	8% Mortgage payable	600,000
Inventory	730,000	Common stock ($5 par)	250,000
Land	120,000	Paid-In capital in	
Building	630,000	excess of par	750,000
Accum. depr.—building	(400,000)	Retained earnings	(80,000)
Equipment	135,000		
Accum. depr.—equipment	(85,000)		
Goodwill	175,000		
Total assets	$1,945,000	Total liabilities and equity	$1,945,000

Your analysis raises substantial concerns about the values shown. You have gathered the following information:

1. Aging of the accounts receivable reveals the need for a $110,000 allowance for bad debts.
2. The inventory has many obsolete items; the fair value is $600,000.
3. Appraisals for long-lived assets are as follows:

Land	$100,000
Building	300,000
Equipment	100,000

4. The goodwill resulted from the purchase of another hardware store that has since been consolidated into the existing location. The goodwill was attributed to customer loyalty.
5. Liabilities are fairly stated except that there should be a provision for the estimated loss on the lawsuit.

On the basis of your research, you are convinced that the statements of Al's Hardware are not representative and need major restatement. Your client is not interested in being associated with statements that are not accurate.

Your client asks you to make recommendations on two concerns:

1. Does the price asked seem to be a real bargain? It is suggested that you consider the fair value of the entire equity of Al's Hardware and then decide if the price is reasonable for a 60% interest.
2. If the deal were completed, what accounting methods would you recommend either on the books of Al's Hardware or in the consolidation process? Al's Hardware would remain a separate legal entity with a substantial noncontrolling interest.

Consolidated Statements: Subsequent to Acquisition

CHAPTER

3

Learning Objectives

When you have completed this chapter, you should be able to

1. **Show how an investment in a subsidiary account is maintained under the simple equity, sophisticated equity, and cost methods.**
2. **Complete a consolidated worksheet using the simple equity method for the parent's investment account.**
3. **Complete a consolidated worksheet using the cost method for the parent's investment account.**
4. **Describe the special worksheet procedures that are used for an investment maintained under the sophisticated equity method.**
5. **Distribute and amortize multiple adjustments resulting from the difference between the price paid for an investment in a subsidiary and the subsidiary equity eliminated.**
6. **Demonstrate the worksheet procedures used for investments purchased during the financial reporting period.**
7. **Demonstrate an understanding of when goodwill impairment loss exists and how it is calculated.**
8. **(Appendix A) Consolidate a subsidiary using vertical worksheet format.**
9. **(Appendix B) Explain the impact of tax-related complications arising on the purchase date.**

This chapter's mission is to teach the procedures needed to prepare consolidated income statements, retained earnings statements, and balance sheets in periods subsequent to the acquisition of a subsidiary. There are several worksheet models to master. This variety is caused primarily by the alternative methods available to a parent for maintaining its investment in a subsidiary account. Accounting principles do not address the method used by a parent to record its investment in a subsidiary that is to be consolidated. The method used is of no concern to standard setters since the investment account is always eliminated when consolidating. Thus, the method chosen to record the investment usually is based on convenience.

In the preceding chapter, worksheet procedures included asset and liability adjustments to reflect fair values on the date of the purchase. This chapter discusses the subsequent depreciation and amortization of these asset and liability revaluations in conjunction with its analysis of worksheet procedures for preparing consolidated financial statements. Appendix A, page 141, explains the vertical worksheet as an alternative approach to the horizontal worksheet used in this chapter for developing consolidated statements.

This chapter does not deal with the income tax issues of the consolidated company except to the extent that they are reflected in the original acquisition price. Appendix B, pages 142 to 147, considers tax issues that arise as part of the original purchase. These include recording procedures for deferred tax liabilities arising in a tax-free exchange and tax loss carryovers. A full discussion of tax issues in consolidations is included in Chapter 6.

1

OBJECTIVE

Show how an investment in a subsidiary account is maintained under the simple equity, sophisticated equity, and cost methods.

ACCOUNTING FOR THE INVESTMENT IN A SUBSIDIARY

A parent may choose one of two basic methods when accounting for its investment in a subsidiary: the *equity method* or the *cost method.* The equity method records as income an ownership percentage of the reported income of the subsidiary, whether or not it was received by the parent. The cost method treats the investment in the subsidiary like a passive investment by recording income only when dividends are declared by the subsidiary.

Equity Method

The equity method views the earning of income by a controlled subsidiary as sufficient reason to record the parent's share of that income.

The equity method records as income the parent's ownership interest percentage multiplied by the subsidiary reported net income. The income is added to the parent's investment account. In a like manner, the parent records its share of a subsidiary loss and lowers its investment account for its share of the loss. Dividends received from the subsidiary are viewed as a conversion of a portion of the investment account into cash; thus, dividends reduce the investment account balance. The investment account at any point in time can be summarized as follows:

Investment in Subsidiary (equity method)

	Original cost	less:	Ownership interest × Reported losses of subsidiary since acquisition
plus:	Ownership interest × Reported income of subsidiary since acquisition	less:	Ownership interest × Dividends declared by subsidiary since acquisition
equals:	Equity-adjusted balance		

The real advantage of using the simple equity method when consolidating is that every dollar of change in the stockholders' equity of the subsidiary is recorded on a pro rata basis in the investment account. This method expedites the elimination of the investment account in the consolidated worksheets in future periods. It is favored in this text because of its simplicity.

For some unconsolidated investments, the sophisticated equity method is required by APB Opinion No. 18, *The Equity Method of Accounting for Investments in Common Stock.* According to this Opinion, a company's investment should be adjusted for amortizations when the investor has an "influential" investment of 20% or more of another company's voting stock. For example, assume that the price paid for an investment in a subsidiary exceeded underlying book value and that the determination and distribution of excess schedule attributed the entire excess to a building. Just as a building will decrease in value and should be depreciated, so should that portion of the price paid for the investment attributed to the building also be amortized. If the estimated life of the building is 10 years, then the portion of the investment price attributed to the building should be amortized over 10 years. This would be accomplished by reducing the investment income each year by the amortization, which means that the income posted to the investment account each year is also less by the amount of the amortization.

The sophisticated equity method is required for influential investments (normally 20% to 50% interests) and for those rare subsidiaries that are not consolidated. Its use for these types of investments is fully discussed in Chapter 6. The sophisticated equity method also is used by some parent companies to maintain the investment in a subsidiary that is to be consolidated. This better reflects the investment account in the parent-only statements, but such statements may not be used as the primary statements for external reporting purposes. Parent-only statements may be used as supplemental statements only when the criteria for consolidated statements are met. The use of this method for investments to be consolidated makes recording the investment income and the elimination of the investment account more difficult than under the simple equity method.

Cost Method

When the cost method is used, the investment in subsidiary account is retained at its original cost-of-acquisition balance. No adjustments are made to the account for income as it is earned by the subsidiary. Income on the investment is limited to dividends received from the subsidiary. The cost method is acceptable for subsidiaries that are to be consolidated because, in the consolidation process, the investment account is eliminated entirely.

The cost method is the most common method used in practice by parent companies. It is simple to use during the accounting period and avoids the risk of incorrect adjustments. Typically, the correct income of the subsidiary is not known until after the end of the accounting period. Awaiting its determination would delay the parent company's closing procedures. Companies that use the cost method may convert to the simple equity method as part of the consolidation process.

Example of the Equity and Cost Methods

The simple equity, sophisticated equity, and cost methods will be illustrated by an example covering two years. This example, which will become the foundation for several consolidated worksheets in this chapter, is based on the following facts:

1. The following D&D schedule was prepared on the date of purchase. This schedule is similar to that of the preceding chapter but is modified to indicate the period over which adjustments to the subsidiary book values will be allocated. This expanded format will be used in preparing all future worksheets.
2. Income during 20X1 was $30,000 for Company S; dividends declared by Company S at the end of 20X1 totaled $10,000.
3. During 20X2, Company S had a loss of $10,000 and declared dividends of $5,000.
4. The balance in Company S's retained earnings account on December 31, 20X2, is $55,000.

Company P and Subsidiary Company S
Determination and Distribution of Excess Schedule
January 1, 20X1

	Total	Controlling		Amort. Periods	Controlling Amort.
Price paid for investment		$ 145,000			
Less book value interest acquired:					
Common stock	$ 100,000				
Retained earnings	50,000				
Total stockholders' equity	$ 150,000				
Interest acquired	× 90%	135,000			
Excess of cost over book value (debit)		**$ 10,000**			
Patent		**$ 10,000**	**Dr.**	**10**	**$1,000**

	Event	Simple Equity Method		
20X1 Jan. 1	Purchase of stock	Investment in Company S	145,000	
		Cash		145,000
Dec. 31	Subsidiary income of $30,000 reported to parent	Investment in Company S	27,000	
		Subsidiary Income		27,000
31	Dividends of $10,000 declared by subsidiary	Dividends Receivable	9,000	
		Investment in Company S...............		9,000
		Investment Balance, Dec. 31, 20X1 ...		**$163,000**
20X2 Dec. 31	Subsidiary loss of $10,000 reported to parent	Loss on Subsidiary Operations	9,000	
		Investment in Company S...............		9,000
31	Dividends of $5,000 declared by subsidiary	Dividends Receivable	4,500	
		Investment in Company S...............		4,500
		Investment Balance, Dec. 31, 20X2 ...		**$149,500**

The journal entries and resulting investment account balances shown above and on page 135 record this information on the books of Company P using the simple equity, cost, and sophisticated equity methods. Note that the only difference between the sophisticated and simple equity methods is that the former reduces investment income each year for an amount equal to the amortization of the patent ($1,000).

REFLECTION

- The simple equity method records investment income equal to the parent ownership interest multiplied by the reported subsidiary income.
- The sophisticated equity method records investment income equal to the parent ownership interest multiplied by the reported subsidiary income and deducts amortizations of excess related to the price paid for the investment.
- The cost method records only dividends as received.

2

OBJECTIVE

Complete a consolidated worksheet using the simple equity method for the parent's investment account.

ELIMINATION PROCEDURES

Worksheet procedures necessary to prepare consolidated income statements, retained earnings statements, and balance sheets are examined in the following section. **Recall that the consolidation process is performed independently each year since the worksheet eliminations of previous years are never recorded by the parent or subsidiary.**

Cost Method			Sophisticated Equity Method		
Investment in Company S	145,000		Investment in Company S	145,000	
Cash......................		145,000	Cash		145,000
No entry.			Investment in Company S	26,000[a]	
			Subsidiary Income..........		26,000
Dividends Receivable	9,000		Dividends Receivable	9,000	
Subsidiary (Dividend) Income ..		9,000	Investment in Company S......		9,000
Investment Balance, Dec. 31, 20X1		**$145,000**	**Investment Balance, Dec. 31, 20X1**		**$162,000**
No entry.			Loss on Subsidiary Operations ...	10,000[b]	
			Investment in Company S......		10,000
Dividends Receivable	4,500		Dividends Receivable	4,500	
Subsidiary (Dividend) Income ..		4,500	Investment in Company S......		4,500
Investment Balance, Dec. 31, 20X2		**$145,000**	**Investment Balance, Dec. 31, 20X2**		**$147,500**

[a]Parent's share of subsidiary income less amortization of excess of $1,000 per year.

[b]Parent's share of subsidiary loss (90% × $10,000) = $9,000 plus amortization of excess of $1,000 per year.

The illustrations that follow are based on the facts concerning the investment in Company S, as detailed in the previous example. The procedures for consolidating an investment maintained under the simple equity method will be discussed first, followed by an explanation of how procedures would differ under the cost and sophisticated equity methods. (See the inside front cover for a complete listing of the elimination codes used in this text.)

Effect of Simple Equity Method on Consolidation

Examine Worksheet 3-1 on pages 148 and 149, noting that the worksheet trial balances for Company P and Company S are pre-closing trial balances and, thus, include the income statement accounts of both companies. Look at Company P's trial balance and note that Investment in Company S is now at the equity-adjusted cost at the end of the year. The balance reflects the following information:

worksheet
Worksheet 3-1: page 148

Cost	$145,000
Plus equity income (90% × $30,000 Company S income)........................	27,000
Less dividends received (90% × $10,000 dividends paid by Company S)	(9,000)
Balance	$163,000

If we are going to eliminate the subsidiary equity against the investment account and get the correct excess, **the investment account and subsidiary equity must be at the same point in time.** Right now, the investment account is adjusted through the end of the year, and the subsidiary retained earnings is still at its January 1 balance. Eliminating the entries that affected the investment balance during the current year creates date alignment. First, entry for (CY1) [for Current Year entry #1] eliminates the subsidiary income recorded against the investment account as follows:

	Eliminate current-year investment income:		
(CY1)	Subsidiary Income (Company P account)	27,000	
	Investment in Company S.		27,000

This elimination also removes the subsidiary income account. This is appropriate because we will, instead, be including the income statement accounts of the subsidiary. The intercompany dividends paid by the subsidiary to the parent will be eliminated next as follows with entry (CY2):

	Eliminate intercompany dividends:		
(CY2)	Investment in Company S	9,000	
	Dividends Declared (Company S account)		9,000

After this entry, only subsidiary dividends paid to the noncontrolling shareholders will remain. These are dividends paid to the "outside world" and, as such, belong in the consolidated statements.

Once you have created date alignment, it is appropriate to eliminate 90% of the subsidiary equity against the investment account with entry (EL) [for Elimination entry]. This entry is the same as described in Chapter 2.

	Eliminate 90% subsidiary equity against investment account:		
(EL)	Common Stock ($10 par), Company S (90% eliminated).	90,000	
	Retained Earnings, January 1, 20X1, Company S (90% eliminated)	45,000	
	Investment in Company S.		135,000

The excess ($145,000 balance after eliminating current year entries − $135,000) should always agree with that indicated by the D&D schedule. The next procedure is to distribute the excess with entry (D) [for Distribute entry] as indicated by the D&D schedule as follows:

	Distribute excess investment account balance to accounts to be adjusted:		
(D)	Patent.	10,000	
	Investment in Company S (remaining balance)		10,000

The D&D schedule indicated that the life of the patent was 10 years. It must now be amortized for the first year with entry (A) [for Amortization entry]:

	Amortize excess for current year:		
(A)	Patent Amortization Expense ($10,000/10 years)	1,000	
	Patent.		1,000

Patent amortization expense should be maintained in a separate account, so that it will be available for the income statement as a separate item.

The Consolidated Income Statement column follows the Eliminations & Adjustments columns. The adjusted income statement accounts of the constituent companies are used to calculate the *consolidated net income* of $69,000. This income is distributed to the controlling interest and NCI. Note that the NCI receives 10% of the $30,000 reported net income of the subsidiary, or $3,000. The controlling interest receives the balance of the consolidated net income, or $66,000.

The distribution of income is handled best by using *income distribution schedules (IDS)* which appear at the end of Worksheet 3-1. The subsidiary IDS is a "T account" which begins with the reported net income of the subsidiary. This income is termed *internally generated net income*, which connotes the income of only the company being analyzed without consideration of income derived from other members of the affiliated group. Until Chapter 8, when the subsidiary owns an interest in the parent, the subsidiary's internally generated net income is the same as its net income. In Worksheet 3-1, the subsidiary net income is multiplied by the noncontrolling ownership percentage to calculate the NCI share of income. A similar T account is used for the parent IDS. The parent's share of subsidiary net income is added to the internally generated net income of the parent, and amortizations of excess are deducted. Patent amortization is borne entirely by the controlling interest. Note that this is true for *all* excess cost over book value situations. Under the parent company theory, only the portion applicable to the purchaser's interest is acknowledged; thus, the amortization of excess affects only the controlling interest. The balance in the parent T account is the controlling share of the consolidated net income. **The IDS is a valuable self-check procedure since the sum of the income distributions should equal the consolidated net income on the worksheet.**

The NCI column of the worksheet summarizes the total ownership interest of noncontrolling stockholders on the balance sheet date. The noneliminated portion of subsidiary common stock at par, additional paid-in capital in excess of par, beginning retained earnings, the NCI share of income, and dividends declared is extended to this column. The total of this column is then extended to the consolidated balance sheet column as the noncontrolling interest. The formal balance sheet will typically show only the total NCI and will not provide information on the components of this balance.

The Controlling Retained Earnings column produces the controlling retained earnings balance on the balance sheet date. The beginning parent retained earnings balance, as adjusted by eliminations and adjustments, is extended to this column. Dividends declared by the parent are also extended to this column. The controlling share of consolidated income is extended to this column to produce the ending balance. The balance is extended to the balance sheet column as the retained earnings of the consolidated company.

The Consolidated Balance Sheet column includes the consolidated asset and liability balances. The paid-in equity balances of the parent are extended as the consolidated paid-in capital balance. As mentioned above, the aggregate balances of the NCI and the Controlling Retained Earnings are also extended to the balance sheet column.

Separate debit and credit columns may be used for the consolidated balance sheet. This arrangement may minimize errors and aid analysis. Single columns are not advocated but are used to facilitate the inclusion of lengthy worksheets in a summarized fashion.

The information for the following formal statements is taken directly from Worksheet 3-1:

Company P
Consolidated Income Statement
For Year Ended December 31, 20X1

Revenue	$ 180,000
Expenses	(110,000)
Patent amortization	(1,000)
Consolidated net income	$ 69,000
Distributed to:	
Noncontrolling interest	$ 3,000
Controlling interest	$ 66,000

Company P
Consolidated Retained Earnings Statement
For Year Ended December 31, 20X1

	Controlling
Retained earnings, January 1, 20X1	$123,000
Consolidated net income (Company P share)	66,000
Balance, December 31, 20X1	$189,000

Company P
Consolidated Balance Sheet
December 31, 20X1

Assets		Stockholders' Equity		
Net tangible assets	$397,000	Noncontrolling interest		$ 17,000
Patent	9,000	Controlling interest:		
		Common stock	$200,000	
		Retained earnings	189,000	389,000
Total assets	$406,000	Total stockholders' equity		$406,000

There are several features of the consolidated statements that you should notice:

- Consolidated net income is the total income earned by the consolidated entity. The consolidated net income is then distributed to the noncontrolling interest (NCI) and the controlling interest. This is consistent with the FASB Exposure Draft on liabilities and equity.[1] In the past, it was common to find the NCI portion of consolidated net income treated as an expense. The controlling share of income was then incorrectly labeled "consolidated net income."
- The retained earnings statement shows only the controlling interest. The beginning balance is only the parent retained earnings balance, the income added is only the controlling share of consolidated net income, and, if the parent paid dividends, the parent's dividends declared would be deducted. Detail as to the subsidiary retained earnings appears only in the separate statements of the subsidiary.
- The consolidated balance sheet shows the NCI as a subdivision of stockholders' equity as discussed in Chapter 2. The NCI is shown only as a total and is not itemized.

Now consider consolidation procedures for 20X2 as they would apply to Companies P and S under the simple equity method. This will provide added practice in preparing worksheets and will emphasize that, at the end of each year, consolidation procedures are applied to the separate statements of the constituent firms. In essence, **each year's consolidation procedures begin as if there had never been a previous consolidation.** However, reference to past worksheets is used commonly to save time.

The separate trial balances of Companies P and S are displayed in the first two columns of Worksheet 3-2, pages 150 and 151. The investment in subsidiary account includes the simple-equity-adjusted investment balance as calculated on page 118. Note that the balances in the retained earnings accounts of Companies P and S are for January 1, 20X2, because these are the pre-closing trial balances. The retained earnings amounts are calculated as follows:

worksheet

Worksheet 3-2: page 150

Company P:	January 1, 20X1, balance	$123,000
	Net income, 20X1 (including Company P's share of subsidiary income under simple equity method)	67,000
	Balance, January 1, 20X2	$190,000
Company S:	January 1, 20X1, balance	$ 50,000
	Net income, 20X1	30,000
	Dividends declared	(10,000)
	Balance, January 1, 20X2	$ 70,000

1 2000 FASB Exposure Draft, *Accounting for Financial Instruments with Characteristics of Liabilities, Equity, or Both* (Norwalk, CT: Financial Accounting Standards Board), October 27, 2000.

As before, entry (CY1) eliminates the subsidiary income recorded by the parent, and entry (CY2) eliminates the intercompany dividends. Neither subsidiary income or dividends declared by the subsidiary to the parent should remain in the consolidated statements. In journal form, the entries are as follows:

	Create date alignment and eliminate current-year subsidiary income:		
(CY1)	Investment in Company S	9,000	
	Subsidiary Loss		9,000
(CY2)	Investment in Company S	4,500	
	Dividends Declared (Company S account)		4,500

At this point, the investment account balance is returned to \$163,000 (\$149,500 on the trial balance + \$9,000 loss + \$4,500 dividends), which is the balance on January 1, 20X2. Date alignment now exists, and elimination of the investment account may proceed. Entry (EL) eliminates 90% of the subsidiary equity accounts against the investment account. Entry (EL) differs in amount from the prior year's (20X1) entry only because Company S's retained earnings balance has changed. Always eliminate the subsidiary's equity balances as they appear on the worksheet, not in the original D&D schedule. In journal form, entry (EL) is as follows:

	Eliminate investment account at beginning of the year balance:		
(EL)	Common Stock, Company S	90,000	
	Retained Earnings, January 1, 20X2, Company S	63,000	
	Investment in Company S		153,000

Entry (D) is exactly the same as it was on the 20X1 worksheet. It will be necessary to make this same entry every year until the mark-up caused by the purchase is fully amortized or the asset is sold. In entry form, entry (D) is as follows:

	Distribute excess of cost (patent):		
(D)	Patent	10, 000	
	Investment in Company S		10,000

Finally, entry (A) includes amortization of the patent for 20X1 and 20X2. The expense for 20X1 is charged to Company P retained earnings since it relates to prior-year income. The charge is made only to the parent's retained earnings because the asset adjustment applies only to the controlling interest. In journal form, the entry is as follows:

	Amortize patent for current and prior year:		
(A)	Retained Earnings, January 1, 20X2, Company P	1,000	
	Patent Amortization Expense	1,000	
	Patent		2,000

Note that the 20X3 worksheet will include three total years of amortization, and so **the entries made in prior periods' worksheets have not been recorded in either the parent's or subsidiary's books.** Even in later years, when the patent is past its 10-year life, it will be necessary to use a revised entry (D), which would adjust all prior years' amortizations to the patent as follows:

Retained Earnings, Company P (10 years × \$1,000)	10,000	
Investment in Company S (the excess)		10,000

Note that the original D&D schedule prepared on the date of acquisition becomes the foundation for all subsequent worksheets. Once prepared, the schedule is used without modification.

3

OBJECTIVE

Complete a consolidated worksheet using the cost method for the parent's investment account.

Effect of Cost Method on Consolidation

Recall that parent companies often may choose to record their investments in a subsidiary under the cost method, whereby the investments are maintained at their original costs. Income from the investments are recorded only when dividends are declared by the subsidiary. The use of the cost method means that the investment account does not reflect changes in subsidiary equity. Rather than develop a new set of procedures for the elimination of an investment under the cost method, **the cost method investment will be converted to its simple equity balance at the beginning of the period** to create date alignment. Then, the elimination procedures developed earlier can be applied.

worksheet
Worksheet 3-3: page 152

Worksheet 3-3, pages 152 and 153, is a consolidated financial statements worksheet for Companies P and S for the first year of combined operations. The worksheet is based upon the entries made under the cost method, as shown on page 119. Reference to Company P's Trial Balance column in Worksheet 3-3 reveals that the investment in the subsidiary account at year-end still is stated at the original $145,000 cost and the income recorded by the parent as a result of subsidiary ownership is limited to $9,000, or 90% of the dividends declared by the subsidiary. When the cost method is used, the account title *Dividend Income* may be used in place of *Subsidiary Income.*

There is no need for an equity conversion at the end of the first year. Date alignment is automatic; the investment in Company S account and the subsidiary retained earnings are both as of January 1, 20X1. There is no entry (CY1) under the cost method; only entry (CY2) is needed to eliminate intercompany dividends. All remaining eliminations are the same as for 20X1 under the equity method. In journal form, the complete set of entries for 20X1 are as follows:

	Eliminate current-year dividends:		
(CY2)	Subsidiary Income	9,000	
	Dividends Declared (Company S account)		9,000
	Eliminate investment account at beginning of the year balance:		
(EL)	Common Stock, Company S	90,000	
	Retained Earnings, January 1, 20X1, Company S	45,000	
	Investment in Company S.		135,000
	Distribute excess of cost (patent):		
(D)	Patent.	10,000	
	Investment in Company S.		10,000
	Amortize patent for current year:		
(A)	Patent Amortization Expense.	1,000	
	Patent.		1,000

The last four columns of Worksheet 3-3 are exactly the same as those for Worksheet 3-1, resulting in the same consolidated statements.

worksheet
Worksheet 3-4: page 154

For periods after 20X1 (first year of consolidation), date alignment will not exist, and an equity conversion entry will be needed. Worksheet 3-4 on pages 154 and 155 is such an example. The worksheet is for 20X2 and parallels Worksheet 3-2 except that the cost method is in use. The balance in the investment account is still the original cost of $145,000. The retained earnings of the subsidiary is, however, at its January 1, 20X2, balance of $70,000. Note that the parent's January 1, 20X2, retained earnings balance is $18,000 less than in Worksheet 3-2 because it does not include the 20X1 undistributed subsidiary income of $18,000 ($27,000 income less $9,000 dividends received). In order to get date alignment, an equity conversion entry, (CV), is made to convert the investment account to its January 1, 20X2, simple equity balance. This conversion entry is always calculated as follows:

	Date	Amount
Retained earnings, Company S, start of current year	Jan. 1, 20X2	$70,000
Retained earnings, date of purchase	Jan. 1, 20X1	50,000
Change in subsidiary retained earnings		$20,000
Parent ownership interest		× 90%
Equity conversion adjustment (parent share of change)		$18,000

Based on this calculation, the conversion entry on Worksheet 3-4 is as follows in journal entry form:

	Convert investment to simple equity method as of Jan. 1, 20X2:		
(CV)	Investment in Company S	18,000	
	Retained Earnings, Jan. 1, 20X2, Company P		18,000

With date alignment created, remaining eliminations parallel Worksheet 3-2 except that there is no entry (CY1) for current-year equity income. Entry (CY2) is still used to eliminate intercompany dividends. In journal form, the remaining entries for Worksheet 3-4 are as follows:

	Eliminate current-year dividends:		
(CY2)	Subsidiary Income	4,500	
	Dividends Declared (Company S account)		4,500
	Eliminate investment account at beginning of the year balance:		
(EL)	Common Stock, Company S	90,000	
	Retained Earnings, Jan. 1, 20X2, Company S	63,000	
	Investment in Company S		153,000
	Distribute excess of cost (patent):		
(D)	Patent	10,000	
	Investment in Company S		10,000
	Amortize patent for current and prior years:		
(A)	Retained Earnings, Jan. 1, 20X2, Company P	1,000	
	Patent Amortization Expense	1,000	
	Patent		2,000

The last four columns of Worksheet 3-4 are exactly the same as those for Worksheet 3-2, as are the consolidated financial statements for 20X2.

The simplicity of this technique of converting from the cost to the simple equity method should be appreciated. At any future date, in order to convert to the simple equity method, it is necessary only to compare the balance of the subsidiary retained earnings account on the worksheet trial balance with the balance of that account on the original date of acquisition (included in the D&D schedule). Specific reference to income earned and dividends paid by the subsidiary in each intervening year is unnecessary. The only complications occur when stock dividends have been issued by the subsidiary or when the subsidiary has issued or retired stock. These complications are examined in Chapter 8.

4

OBJECTIVE

Describe the special worksheet procedures that are used for an investment maintained under the sophisticated equity method.

Effect of Sophisticated Equity Method on Consolidation

In some cases, a parent may desire to prepare its own separate statements as a supplement to the consolidated statements. In this situation, the investment in the subsidiary must be shown on the parent's separate statements at the sophisticated equity balance. This requirement may lead the parent to maintain its subsidiary investment account under the sophisticated equity method. Two ramifications occur when such an investment is consolidated. First, the current year's equity adjustment is net of excess amortizations; second, the investment account contains only the remaining unamortized excess applicable to the investment.

The use of the sophisticated equity method complicates the elimination of the investment account in that the worksheet distribution and amortization of the excess procedures are altered. However, there is no impact on the other consolidation procedures. To illustrate, the information given in Worksheet 3-2 will be used as the basis for an example. The trial balance of Company P will show the following changes as a result of using the sophisticated equity method:

1. The Investment in Company S will be carried at $147,500 ($149,500 simple equity balance less 2 years' amortization of excess at $1,000 per year).
2. The January 1, 20X2, balance for Company P Retained Earnings will be $189,000 ($190,000 under simple equity less 1 year's amortization of excess of $1,000).
3. The subsidiary loss account of the parent will have a balance of $10,000 ($9,000 share of the subsidiary loss plus $1,000 amortization of excess).

Based on these changes, a partial worksheet under the sophisticated equity method follows:

Company P and Subsidiary Company S
Partial Worksheet for Consolidated Financial Statements
For Year Ended December 31, 20X2

(Credit balance amounts are in parentheses.)	Trial Balance		Eliminations & Adjustments			
	Company P	Company S	Dr.		Cr.	
Investment in Company S	**147,500**		**(CY1)**	**10,000**	(EL)	153,000
			(CY2)	**4,500**	**(D)**	**9,000**
Patent			**(D)**	**9,000**	**(A)**	**1,000**
Retained Earnings, January 1, 20X2, Company P	**(189,000)**					
Common Stock ($10 par), Company S		(100,000)	(EL)	90,000		
Retained Earnings, January 1, 20X2, Company S		(70,000)	(EL)	63,000		
Revenue	(100,000)	(50,000)				
Expenses	80,000	60,000	**(A)**	**1,000**		
Patent Amortization						
Subsidiary Loss	**10,000**				**(CY1)**	**10,000**
Dividends Declared		5,000			**(CY2)**	**4,500**

Eliminations and Adjustments:

(CY1) Eliminate the current-year entries made in the investment account to record the subsidiary loss. The loss account now includes the $1,000 excess amortization.
(CY2) Eliminate intercompany dividends.
(EL) Using the balances at the beginning of the year, eliminate 90% of the Company S equity balances against the remaining investment account.
(D) Distribute the remaining unamortized excess on January 1, 20X2 ($10,000 on purchase date less $1,000 20X1 amortization) to the patent account.
(A) Amortize the patent for the current year only; prior-year amortization has been recorded in the parent's investment account.

The sophisticated equity method essentially is a modification of simple equity procedures. The major difference in the consolidation procedures under the two methods is that, subsequent to the acquisition, the original excess calculated on the determination and distribution of excess schedule does not appear when the sophisticated equity method is used. Only the remaining unamortized excess appears. Since the investment account is eliminated in the consolidation process, the added complexities of the sophisticated method are not justified for most companies and seldom are applied to consolidated subsidiaries.

Determination of the Method Being Used

Before you attempt to prepare a consolidated worksheet, you need to know which of the three methods is being used by the parent to record its investment in the subsidiary. You cannot begin to eliminate the intercompany investment until that is determined. The most efficient approach is to

1. Test for the use of the cost method. If the cost method is used:
   a. *The investment account will be at the original cost shown on the determination and distribution of excess schedule.*
   b. *The parent will have recorded as its share of subsidiary income its ownership interest times the dividends declared by the subsidiary. In most cases, this income will be called "subsidiary dividend income," but some may call it "subsidiary income" or "dividend income." Therefore, do not rely on the title of the account.*
2. If the method used is not cost, check for the use of simple equity as follows:
   a. *The investment account will not be at the original cost.*
   b. *The parent will have recorded as subsidiary income its ownership percentage times the reported net income of the subsidiary.*
3. If the method used is neither cost nor simple equity, it must be the sophisticated equity method. Confirm that it is by noting that
   a. *The investment account will not be at the original cost.*
   b. *The parent will have recorded as subsidiary income its ownership percentage times the reported net income of the subsidiary minus the amortizations of excess for the current period.*

REFLECTION

- Date alignment is needed before an investment can be eliminated.
- For an equity method investment, date alignment means removing current–year entries to return to the beginning of the year investment balance.
- For a cost method investment, date alignment means converting the investment account to its equity-adjusted balance at the start of the year.
- Many distributions of excess must be followed by amortizations that cover the current and prior years.
- The consolidated net income derived on a worksheet is allocated to the controlling and noncontrolling interests using an income distribution schedule.

5

OBJECTIVE

Distribute and amortize multiple adjustments resulting from the difference between the price paid for an investment in a subsidiary and the subsidiary equity eliminated.

COMPLICATED PURCHASE, SEVERAL DISTRIBUTIONS OF EXCESS

In Worksheets 3-1 through 3-4, it was assumed that the entire excess of cost over book value was attributable to a patent. In reality, the excess will seldom apply to a single asset. The following example illustrates a more complicated purchase.

Paulos Company paid $690,000 to obtain 8,000 shares (80% interest) of Carlos Company on January 1, 20X1. In addition, $10,000 of direct acquisition costs were paid by Paulos. At the time of the purchase, Carlos had the following summarized balance sheet:

Carlos Company Balance Sheet
January 1, 20X1

Assets			Liabilities and Equity		
Current assets:			Current liabilities	$ 50,000	
Inventory		$ 75,000	Bonds payable, 6%, due December 31, 20X4	200,000	
Long-term assets:			Total liabilities		$250,000
Land	$ 150,000				
Buildings	600,000		Stockholders' equity:		
Accumulated depreciation. . .	(300,000)		Common stock, $10 par	$100,000	
Equipment	150,000		Paid-in capital in excess of par . . .	150,000	
Accumulated depreciation. . .	(50,000)		Retained earnings	250,000	
Patent (net)	125,000		Total		500,000
Total		675,000			
Total assets		$750,000	Total liabilities and equity		$750,000

The entry to record the purchase would be as follows:

Investment in Carlos Company ($690,000 + $10,000 direct acquisition costs)	700,000	
Cash (for purchase of Carlos shares)		690,000
Cash (for direct acquisition costs).		10,000

An analysis of book versus fair values is prepared as follows:

Carlos Company Book and Estimated Fair Values
December 31, 20X1

Assets	Book Value	Fair Value	Liabilities and Equity	Book Value	Fair Value
Priority assets:					
			Current liabilities	$ 50,000	$ 50,000
Inventory	$ 75,000	$ 80,000	Bonds payable*	200,000	186,750
Total priority assets	**$ 75,000**	**$ 80,000**	**Total liabilities**	**$250,000**	**$236,750**
Nonpriority accounts:					
Land	$ 150,000	$ 200,000			
Buildings (net)	300,000	500,000			
Equipment (net)	100,000	80,000			
Patent (net)	125,000	150,000			
Total nonpriority assets . . .	**$675,000**	**$ 930,000**	**Market value of net assets**		
Total assets	**$750,000**	**$1,010,000**	**(assets − liabilities)**	**$500,000**	**$773,250**

*The bonds pay 6% nominal interest annually. There are four years to maturity. The current market interest rate is 8%. Discounting the $12,000 per year cash interest plus the $200,000 maturity value at 8% annual interest provides a present value of $186,751 (rounded to $186,750 to eliminate partial dollars when amortizing).

Zone analysis is now performed on the 80% interest using the fair values as follows:

Zone Analysis	Group Total	Ownership Portion	Cumulative Total
Ownership percentage		80%	
Priority accounts (net of liabilities)	$(156,750)	$(125,400)	$(125,400)
Nonpriority accounts	930,000	744,000	618,600

Price analysis would be as follows:

Price (including direct acquisition costs)	**$700,000**	
Assign to priority accounts, controlling share	(125,400)	Full value
Assign to nonpriority accounts, controlling share	744,000	Full value
Goodwill	**81,400**	
Extraordinary gain	**0**	

The price analysis schedule indicates that the parent's share of all accounts can be fully adjusted to fair value.

From this information, a determination and distribution excess is prepared. *Columns have been added that indicate the period of time over which the excess will be amortized and the annual amortization amount.* The schedule will now appear as follows:

Price paid for investment (including direct acquisition costs)		**$700,000**			
Less book value of interest purchased:					
Common stock, $10 par	$ 100,000				
Paid-in capital in excess of par	150,000				
Retained earnings	250,000				
Total equity	$ 500,000				
Ownership interest	× 80%	400,000			
Excess of cost over book value		**$300,000**	Credit/Key	**Amort. Period**	**Amort. Amount**
Adjustments:					
Inventory, 80% of $5,000 fair-book value	$ 4,000		Debit D1	1	$ 4,000
Land, 80% of $50,000 fair-book value	40,000		Debit D2	None	
Discount on bonds payable, 80% of $13,250 fair-book value	10,600		Debit D3	4	2,650
Buildings (net), 80% of $200,000 fair-book value	160,000		Debit D4	20	8,000
Equipment (net), 80% of ($20,000) fair-book value	(16,000)		Credit D5	5	(3,200)
Patent (net), 80% of $25,000 fair-book value	20,000		Debit D6	10	2,000
Goodwill	81,400		Debit D7		
Total adjustments		**$300,000**			

The following observations need to be made relative to the above determination and distribution of excess schedule:

- It is assumed that the inventory will be sold in the first year after the purchase. A total of $4,000 would therefore be added to the cost of goods sold for 20X1. In later periods, this adjustment will be made to controlling retained earnings.
- The discount on the bonds payable is being amortized on a straight-line basis over four years. If effective interest amortization were used, the amounts over the four years would be $2,352, $2,540, $2,743, and $2,965, respectively.
- Equipment depreciation will be reduced each year by $3,200 for five years.
- Theoretically, adjustments to plant and equipment should eliminate all accumulated depreciation applicable to the controlling interest. The parent's share of the assets would then start with a new basis. For the sake of simplicity, the assets are adjusted directly.

- Goodwill is not amortized in this and the following examples. Impairment testing is required and could lead to impairment losses in any given period.

A summary of depreciation and amortization adjustments follows:

Account Adjustments	Life	Annual Amount	Current Year	Prior Years	Total	Key
Inventory	1	$ 4,000	$ 4,000	$0	$ 4,000	(D1)
Subject to amortization:						
Bonds payable	4	$ 2,650	$ 2,650	$0	$ 2,650	(A3)
Buildings	20	8,000	8,000	0	8,000	(A4)
Equipment	5	(3,200)	(3,200)	0	(3,200)	(A5)
Patent (net)	10	2,000	2,000	0	2,000	(A6)
Total		$ 9,450	$ 9,450	$0	$ 9,450	

It is assumed that the method and life used for depreciation of fixed assets and amortization of the patent are the same as those used by the subsidiary. If that were not the case, the parent would have to recompute depreciation and patent amortization, based on their life and method and then adjust amounts recorded by the subsidiary. The "same method and life assumption" allows us to just depreciate or amortize the adjustment made in consolidation.

Examine Worksheet 3-5, on pages 156 to 157, for Paulos and Carlos companies on December 31, 20X1, the end of the first year of consolidated operations. The simple equity method was used to record the investment. The investment account balance on December 31, 20X1, is as follows:

worksheet
Worksheet 3-5: page 156

Original cost	$700,000
80% of 20X1 Carlos reported income of $60,000.	48,000
80% of $20,000 dividends declared by Carlos	(16,000)
Investment balance, December 31, 20X1	$732,000

The eliminations on Worksheet 3-5 are as follows in journal entry form:

	Eliminate subsidiary income recorded by parent company:		
(CY1)	Subsidiary Income	48,000	
	Investment in Carlos		48,000
	Eliminate dividends paid by Carlos to Paulos:		
(CY2)	Investment in Carlos.	16,000	
	Dividends Declared by Carlos		16,000
	Eliminate 80% of Carlos equity against Investment in Carlos:		
(EL)	Common Stock, Carlos	80,000	
	Paid-In Capital in Excess of Par, Carlos	120,000	
	Retained Earnings, Carlos	200,000	
	Investment in Carlos		400,000
	Distribute excess of cost over book value:		
(D1)	Cost of Goods Sold (inventory on January 1 has been sold) . . .	4,000	
(D2)	Land	40,000	
(D3)	Discount on Bonds Payable	10,600	
(D4)	Buildings	160,000	
(D5)	Equipment		16,000
(D6)	Patent	20,000	

(D7)	Goodwill	81,400	
(D)	Investment in Carlos (noneliminated excess)		300,000
	Amortize excess for current year as shown on preceding schedule:		
(A3)	Interest Expense	2,650	
	Discount on Bonds Payable		2,650
(A4)	Depreciation Expense—Building	8,000	
	Accumulated Depreciation—Building		8,000
(A5)	Accumulated Depreciation—Equipment	3,200	
	Depreciation Expense—Equipment		3,200
(A6)	Other Expenses (patent amortization)	2,000	
	Patent		2,000

When all the adjustments and eliminations have been made, the remaining columns in the worksheet are completed by summing across the parent and subsidiary trial balances and adding or subtracting the adjusting and eliminating entries. (This is called cross-footing.) Each of the income statement accounts goes to the Consolidated Net Income column, which is then totaled and allocated to either the NCI or the Controlling Retained Earnings column based on the IDS which is located after the worksheet. Note that all of the amortizations of excess (including the inventory adjustment) are subtracted from the controlling interest in the IDS. Recall that only the parent's share of account adjustments is recorded, thus the parent must absorb all the remaining amortizations.

The NCI portion of consolidated net income is extended to the NCI column that also includes any remaining subsidiary equity accounts and the dividends declared balances (by the subsidiary). The controlling share of consolidated net income is extended to the Controlling Retained Earnings column which also includes the parent's retained earnings and dividends declared balances.

Now examine Worksheet 3-6, on pages 160 to 161, for Paulos and Carlos for 20X2, the second year of consolidated operations. Paulos has the following investment account balance for Carlos on December 31, 20X2:

Worksheet 3-6: page 160

Investment balance, December 31, 20X1	$732,000
80% of 20X2 Carlos income of $100,000	80,000
80% of $20,000 dividends declared by Carlos	(16,000)
Balance, December 31, 20X2	$796 000

Eliminations in journal entry form are as follows:

	Eliminate subsidiary income recorded by the parent company:		
(CY1)	Subsidiary Income	80,000	
	Investment in Carlos		80,000
	Eliminate dividends paid by Carlos to Paulos:		
(CY2)	Investment in Carlos	16,000	
	Dividends Declared by Carlos		16,000
	Eliminate 80% of Carlos equity against Investment in Carlos:		
(EL)	Common Stock, Carlos	80,000	
	Paid-In Capital in Excess of Par, Carlos	120,000	
	Retained Earnings, Carlos	232,000	
	Investment in Carlos		432,000

(continued)

	Distribute excess of cost over book value:		
(D1)	Retained Earnings, Paulos (inventory sold in prior period) . . .	4,000	
(D2)	Land.	40,000	
(D3)	Discount on Bonds Payable	10,600	
(D4)	Buildings	160,000	
(D5)	Equipment		16,000
(D6)	Patent.	20,000	
(D7)	Goodwill	81,400	
(D)	Investment in Carlos (noneliminated excess)		300,000
	Amortize excess for current year as shown on preceding schedule:		
(A3)	Interest Expense.	2,650	
	Retained Earnings, Paulos (included in entries A3–A6).	2,650	
	Discount on Bonds Payable		5,300
(A4)	Depreciation Expense—Building.	8,000	
	Retained Earnings, Paulos (included in entries A3–A6).	8,000	
	Accumulated Depreciation—Building		16,000
(A5)	Accumulated Depreciation—Equipment	6,400	
	Retained Earnings, Paulos (included in entries A3–A6). . . .		3,200
	Depreciation Expense—Equipment.		3,200
(A6)	Other Expenses (patent amortization)	2,000	
	Retained Earnings, Paulos (included in entries A3–A6).	2,000	
	Patent.		4,000

Take note of the following differences in Worksheet 3-6 as compared to Worksheet 3-5:

- The adjustment of the inventory, at the time of the purchase on January 1, 20X1, now goes to retained earnings since it is a correction of the 20X1 cost of goods sold.
- Amortizations of excess are made for both the current and prior years, using the following schedule:

Account Adjustments	Life	Annual Amount	Current Year	Prior Years	Total	Key
Inventory	1	$ 4,000	$ 0	$ 4,000	$ 4,000	(D1)
Subject to amortization:						
Bonds payable	4	$ 2,650	$ 2,650	$ 2,650	$ 5,300	(A3)
Buildings	20	8,000	8,000	8,000	16,000	(A4)
Equipment	5	(3,200)	(3,200)	(3,200)	(6,400)	(A5)
Patent (net).	10	2,000	2,000	2,000	4,000	(A6)
Total.		$ 9,450	$ 9,450	$ 9,450	$18,900	

The amortizations of excess for prior periods and the inventory adjustment are carried to controlling retained earnings. Since only the controlling share of asset adjustments was recorded, amortizations are borne only by the controlling interest.

- The controlling retained earnings balance is adjusted for the above amortizations of excess before it is extended to the Retained Earnings column.

If a worksheet were prepared for December 31, 20X3, the prior years' amortizations of excess would cover two prior years as follows:

Account Adjustments	Life	Annual Amount	Current Year	Prior Years	Total	Key
Inventory	1	$ 4,000	$ 0	$ 4,000	$ 4,000	(D1)
Subject to amortization:						
Bonds payable	4	$ 2,650	$ 2,650	$ 5,300	$ 7,950	(A3)
Buildings	20	8,000	8,000	16,000	24,000	(A4)
Equipment	5	(3,200)	(3,200)	(6,400)	(9,600)	(A5)
Patent (net)	10	2,000	2,000	4,000	6,000	(A6)
Total		$ 9,450	$ 9,450	$18,900	$28,350	

Exhibit 3-1 contains the formal consolidated financial statements for Paulos Company for 20X2. Note the following features of the statements:

- All nominal accounts are merged, as adjusted, for amortizations to arrive at consolidated net income. The consolidated net income is then distributed to the noncontrolling and controlling interests, using the amounts from the income distribution schedules.

Exhibit 3-1
Consolidated Financial Statements for Paulos Company

Paulos Company
Consolidated Income Statement
Period Ending December 31, 20X2

Sales revenue		$700,000
Less cost of goods sold		320,000
Gross profit		$380,000
Less operating expenses:		
Depreciation expense (building and equipment)	$ 99,800	
Other operating expenses	125,000	224,800
Operating income		$155,200
Interest expense		14,650
Consolidated net income		$140,550
Distributed to noncontrolling interest		$ 20,000
Distributed to controlling interest		$120,550

Paulos Company
Retained Earnings Statement
Period Ending December 31, 20X2

Retained earnings, balance, December 31, 20X2	$714,550
Net income (controlling share of consolidated net income)	120,550
Balance, December 31, 20X2	$835,100

(continued)

Exhibit 3-1 *(Concluded)*

Paulos Company
Consolidated Balance Sheet
December 31, 20X2

Assets			Liabilities and Equity		
Current assets:			Current liabilities	$ 190,000	
Cash	$ 472 000		Bonds payable, 6%, due Dec. 31, 20X4	200,000	
Inventory	330,000		Discount on bonds payable	(5,300)	
Total current assets		$ 802,000	Total liabilities		$ 384,700
Long-term assets:					
Land	$ 390,000				
Buildings	1,560,000				
Accumulated depreciation	(466,000)				
Equipment	534,000		Stockholders' equity:		
Accumulated depreciation	(173,600)		Noncontrolling interest	$ 124,000	
Patent (net)	116,000		Common stock	1,500,000	
Goodwill	81,400		Retained earnings	835,100	
Total long-term assets		2,041,800	Total equity		2,459,100
Total assets		$2,843,800	Total liabilities and equity		$2,843,800

- The statement of retained earnings only shows the changes in the controlling retained earnings. The beginning balance reflects the parent company balance as adjusted for prior years' amortization of excess amounts.
- The total NCI is shown as a single amount under stockholders' equity in the consolidated balance sheet.

REFLECTION

- There may be many asset (and possibly liability) adjustments resulting from the D&D schedule. Each adjustment is distributed as a part of the elimination procedure.
- Most distribution adjustments will require amortization, each over the appropriate life. The amortizations should be keyed to the distribution entry.

6

OBJECTIVE

Demonstrate the worksheet procedures used for investments purchased during the financial reporting period.

INTRAPERIOD PURCHASE UNDER THE SIMPLE EQUITY METHOD

The accountant will be required to apply special procedures when consolidating a controlling investment in common stock that is acquired during the fiscal year. The D&D schedule must be based on the subsidiary stockholders' equity on the interim purchase date, including the subsidiary retained earnings balance on that date. Also, the consolidated income of the consolidated company, as derived on the worksheet, is to include only subsidiary income earned subsequent to the purchase date.

There are two options available for consolidating an intraperiod purchase. The first option is to require the subsidiary to close its books as of the purchase date. This procedure would make retained earnings on the acquisition date available for use in the determination and distribution of excess schedule and would mean that the consolidated worksheet would include only the operations of the subsidiary subsequent to the purchase date. The second and more realistic option is to modify the determination and distribution of excess schedule to include the purchased share of undistributed income for the portion of the year prior to the purchase. Then, it is possible to include the operations of the subsidiary for the entire fiscal year in the consolidated worksheet.

Option 1: Subsidiary Books Closed. Company S has the following trial balance on July 1, 20X1, the date of an 80% purchase by Company P:

Current Assets	68,000	
Equipment	80,000	
Accumulated Depreciation		30,000
Liabilities		10,000
Common Stock ($10 par)		50,000
Retained Earnings, January 1, 20X1		45,000
Dividends Declared	5,000	
Sales		90,000
Cost of Goods Sold	60,000	
Expenses	12,000	
Total	225,000	225,000

If Company P requires Company S to close its nominal accounts as of July 1, Company S would increase its retained earnings account by $13,000 with the following entries:

Sales	90,000	
Cost of Goods Sold		60,000
Expenses		12,000
Retained Earnings		18,000
Retained Earnings	5,000	
Dividends Declared		5,000

Assume Company P pays $106,400 for its 80% interest in Company S. Assume also that all assets have fair values equal to book value and that any excess is attributed to goodwill. The zone analysis would be as follows:

Zone Analysis	Group Total	Ownership Portion	Cumulative Total
Ownership percentage		80%	
Priority accounts (net of liabilities)	$58,000	$46,400	$46,400
Nonpriority accounts	50,000	40,000	86,400

Price analysis would be as follows:

Price (including direct acquisition costs)	**$106,400**	
Assign to priority accounts, controlling share	46,400	Full value
Assign to nonpriority accounts, controlling share	40,000	Full value
Goodwill	**20,000**	
Extraordinary gain	**0**	

From this information, a D&D schedule would be prepared as follows:

Determination and Distribution of Excess Schedule	Total	Controlling
Price paid for investment		$106,400
Less book value interest acquired:		
Common stock ($10 par)	$ 50 000	
Retained earnings, July 1, 20X1	58,000	
Total stockholders' equity	$108,000	
Interest acquired	× 80%	86,400
Excess of cost over book value (debit)		$ 20,000
Goodwill		**$ 20,000**

Proceeding to the end of the year, assume that the operations of Company S for the last six months result in a net income of $20,000 and dividends of $5,000 are declared by Company S on December 31. Worksheet 3-7, pages 164 to 165, includes Company S nominal accounts for only the second 6-month period since the nominal accounts were closed on July 1. Company S Retained Earnings shows the July 1, 20X1, balance. The trial balance of Company P includes operations for the entire year. The subsidiary income listed by Company P includes 80% of the subsidiary's $20,000 second 6-months' income. Company P's investment account balance shows the following:

worksheet

Worksheet 3-7: page 164

Original cost	$106,400
80% of subsidiary's second six-months' income of $20,000	16,000
80% of $5,000 dividends declared by subsidiary on Dec. 31	(4,000)
Investment balance, Dec. 31, 20X1	$118,400

In conformance with purchase theory, the Consolidated Income Statement column of Worksheet 3-7 includes only subsidiary income earned after the acquisition date. Likewise, only subsidiary income earned after the purchase date is distributed to the NCI and controlling interest. Income earned and dividends declared prior to the purchase date by Company S are reflected in its July 1, 20X1, retained earnings balance, of which the minority is granted its share. The notes to the statements would have to disclose what the income of the consolidated company would have been had the purchase occurred at the start of the year.

Option 2: Subsidiary Books Not Closed. Usually, a subsidiary does not close its books as a result of the parent company's securing a controlling interest in its stock. Normally, the parent company is able to ascertain the income earned by the subsidiary between the beginning of the year and the date control is achieved. If the subsidiary has already declared dividends as of the time of the acquisition, these dividends would be deducted in arriving at the total subsidiary equity interest as of that date.

Assume the parent had access to the Company S trial balance shown in Option 1, but Company S did not close its books as of July 1, 20X1. Company P would prepare the same zone analysis as follows:

Zone Analysis	Group Total	Ownership Portion	Cumulative Total
Ownership percentage		80%	
Priority accounts (net of liabilities)	$58,000	$46,400	$46,400
Nonpriority accounts	50,000	40,000	86,400

Price analysis would be as follows:

Price (including direct acquisition costs)	**$106,400**	
Assign to priority accounts, controlling share	46,400	Full value
Assign to nonpriority accounts, controlling share	40,000	Full value
Goodwill	**20,000**	
Extraordinary gain	**0**	

From this information, a D&D schedule would be prepared as follows:

Determination and Distribution of Excess Schedule	Total	Controlling
Price paid for investment		$106,400
Less book value interest acquired:		
Common stock ($10 par)	$ 50 000	
Retained earnings, Jan. 1, 20X1	45 000	
Income of Company S, Jan. 1–July 1	**18,000**	
Dividends declared, Jan. 1–July 1	**(5,000)**	
Total stockholders' equity	$108,000	
Interest acquired	× 80%	86,400
Excess of cost over book value (debit)		$ 20,000
Goodwill		**$ 20,000**

Since the subsidiary did not close its books as of July 1, 20X1, Worksheet 3-8, pages 166 to 167, includes the Company S trial balance reflecting the entire year's operations. The Company S retained earnings account is dated January 1, 20X1. The Company P investment and subsidiary income accounts are identical to those in Worksheet 3-7.

Worksheet 3-8: page 166

The challenge is to create date alignment. The investment account balance and the retained earnings of the subsidiary must be adjusted to the same point in time. The investment account is as of July 1, 20X1, while the retained earnings of the subsidiary are as of January 1, 20X1. This problem is solved by using a temporary account, *Purchased Income*, to record the current-year subsidiary income already earned as of July 1 by the subsidiary that was **purchased by** the parent. This would be 80% of the $18,000 subsidiary income earned during the first six months. Purchased income is included in step **(EL)**, which can be explained in journal entry form as follows:

Common Stock, Company S	40,000	
Retained Earnings, **Jan. 1, 20X1**, Company S	36,000	
Purchased Income*	14,400	
Dividends Declared**		4,000
Investment in Company S		86,400

*Parent share of income earned in the first six months which was included in the equity interest purchased (80% × $18,000)

**Prior to the purchase date and deducted from subsidiary equity at time of purchase (80% × $5,000)

In Worksheet 3-8, the nominal accounts of the subsidiary for the entire year are included in the Consolidated Income column. Since 80% of the income earned in the first half of the year belonged to outside interests (shareholders that are no longer members of the affiliated group), Purchased Income is deleted to arrive at the consolidated income. As with the income, 80% of the dividends declared by the subsidiary prior to the purchase also belonged to outside interests and must be eliminated. Note that the noncontrolling interest existed for the entire year; thus, it is permitted a **20% share** of subsidiary income and dividends declared for the **full** year. Worksheet 3-8 leads to the following unique income statement:

Company P and Subsidiary Company S
Consolidated Income Statement
For Year Ended December 31, 20X1

Sales	$ 682,000
Cost of goods sold	(470,000)
Gross profit	$ 212,000
Other expenses	(94,000)
Total net income of Company P and Company S for year 20X1	$ 118,000
Income earned by outside interests existing prior to Company P purchase	**(14,400)**
Consolidated net income	$ 103,600
NCI	$ 7,600
Controlling interest	$ 96,000

The format of this income statement has the advantage of disclosing the total net income of the two companies for the year and the consolidated net income. The total net income for the year becomes the basis for a pro forma statement of what income would have been if the combination had occurred at the beginning of the year.

Special care must be taken in consolidating an intraperiod purchase in subsequent periods. It is common to find that a company has made an error by taking a full year's share of equity income in the period of acquisition rather than including only income earned after the date of acquisition. When this error is found, a correcting entry should be recorded by the parent.

Intraperiod Purchase under the Cost Method

There are only two variations of the procedures discussed in the preceding section if the cost method is used by the parent company to record its investment in the subsidiary:

1. During the year of acquisition, the parent would record as income only its share of dividends declared by the subsidiary. Thus, eliminating entries would be confined to the intercompany dividends.
2. For years after the purchase, the cost-to-equity conversion adjustment would be based on the change in the subsidiary retained earnings balance **from the intraperiod purchase date** to the beginning of the year for which the worksheet is being prepared.

REFLECTION

- Purchases during the year require the D&D schedule to be based on the subsidiary equity on the "during the year" purchase date.
- The parent's share of subsidiary income that was earned prior to the purchase date was earned by stockholders that are not members of the consolidated company. This income is not included in consolidated income.

SUMMARY: WORKSHEET TECHNIQUE

At this point, it is wise to review the overall mechanical procedures used to prepare a consolidated worksheet. It will help you to have this set of procedures at your side for the first few worksheets you do. Later, the process will become automatic. The following procedures are designed to provide for both efficiency and correctness:

1. When recopying the trial balances, always sum them and make sure they balance before proceeding with the eliminations. At this point, you want to be sure that there are no errors in transporting figures to the worksheet. An amazing number of students' consolidated balance sheets are out of balance because their trial balances did not balance to begin with.
2. Carefully key all eliminations to aid future reference. It is suggested that a symbol, a little "p" for parent or a little "s" for subsidiary, be used to identify each worksheet adjustment entry that affects consolidated net income. This identification will make it easier to locate the adjustments that must be posted later to the income distribution schedules. Recall that any adjustment to income must be assigned to one of the company's income distribution schedules. This second step will become particularly important in the next two chapters where there will be many adjustments to income.
3. Sum the eliminations to be sure that they balance before you begin to extend the account totals.
4. Now that the eliminations are completed, crossfoot account totals and then extend them to the appropriate worksheet column. Extend each account in the order that it appears on the trial balance. Do not select just the accounts needed for a particular statement. For example, do not work only on the income statement. This can lead to errors. There may be some accounts that you will forget to extend, and you may not be aware of the errors until your balance sheet column total fails to equal zero. Extending each account in order assures that none will be overlooked and allows careful consideration of the appropriate destination of each account balance.
5. Calculate consolidated net income.
6. Prepare income distribution schedules. Verify that the sum of the distributions equals the consolidated net income on the worksheet. Distribute the NCI in income to the NCI column and distribute the controlling interest in income to the Controlling Retained Earnings column.
7. Sum the NCI column and extend that total to the Consolidated Balance Sheet column. Sum the Controlling Retained Earnings column and extend that total to the Consolidated Balance Sheet column as well.
8. Verify that the Consolidated Balance Sheet column total equals zero (or that the totals are equal if two columns are used).

GOODWILL IMPAIRMENT LOSSES

7

OBJECTIVE

Demonstrate an understanding of when goodwill impairment loss exists and how it is calculated.

When circumstances indicate that the goodwill may have become impaired (see Chapter 1), the remaining goodwill will be estimated. If the resulting estimate is less than the book value of the goodwill, a *goodwill impairment loss* is recorded. The impairment loss is reported in the consolidated income statement for the period in which it occurs. It is presented on a before-tax basis as part of continuing operations and may appear under the caption "other gains and losses."

The parent company could handle the impairment loss in two ways:

1. The parent could record the impairment loss on its books and credit the investment in subsidiary account. This would automatically reduce the excess available for distribution, including the amount available for goodwill. This would mean that the impairment loss would already exist before consolidation procedures start. The loss would automatically be extended to the Consolidated Income column. On the controlling IDS schedule, the loss would appear as a debit in periods subsequent to the impairment, the controlling retained

earnings would already have been reduced on the parent's books, and no adjustment would be needed.

2. The impairment loss could be recorded only on the consolidated worksheet. This would adjust consolidated net income and produce a correct balance sheet. The only complication affects consolidated worksheets in periods subsequent to the impairment. The investment account, resulting goodwill, and the controlling retained earnings would be overstated. Thus, on the worksheet, an adjustment reducing the goodwill account and the controlling retained earnings would be needed.

The procedure used in this text will be to follow Option 1 and directly adjust the investment account on the parent's books. This approach would mean the price used in the D&D schedule would be reduced by the amount of the impairment.

The impairment loss is applicable only to the interest owned in the subsidiary. The impairment test must use the sophisticated equity investment balance (simple equity balance less amortizations of excess to date). For example, suppose Company P purchased an 80% interest in Company S in 20X2 and the price resulted in goodwill of $165,000. On a future balance sheet date, say December 31, 20X4, the following information would apply to Company S:

Sophisticated equity method investment balance on December 31, 20X4	$800,000
Estimated fair value of Company S	900,000
Estimated fair value of net identifiable assets	850,000

Determining if goodwill has been impaired would be calculated as shown here:

Sophisticated equity method investment balance on December 31, 20X4	$800 000
Estimated fair value of investment (80% × $900,000)	720,000

Because the investment amount exceeds the fair value, goodwill is impaired, and a loss must be calculated.

The impairment loss would be calculated as follows:

Estimated fair value of Company S	$ 900,000
Estimated fair value of net identifiable assets	850,000
Estimated goodwill	$ 50,000
80% ownership interest (80% × $50,000)	$ 40,000
Existing goodwill	165,000
Goodwill impairment loss	$(125,000)

The impairment entry on Company P's books would be as follows:

Goodwill Impairment Loss	125,000	
Investment in Company S		125,000

REFLECTION

- When the fair value of an investment is less than the sophisticated equity balance of that investment, any goodwill arising from the investment purchase is impaired, and a related loss must be recognized.

APPENDIX A: THE VERTICAL WORKSHEET

8

OBJECTIVE

Consolidate a subsidiary using vertical worksheet format.

This chapter has used the *horizontal format* for its worksheet examples. Columns for eliminations and adjustments, consolidated income, NCI, controlling retained earnings, and the balance sheet are arranged horizontally in adjacent columns. This format makes it convenient to extend account balances from one column to the next. This is the format that you used for trial balance working papers in introductory and intermediate accounting. It is also the most common worksheet format used in practice. The horizontal format will be used in all nonappendix worksheets in subsequent chapters and in all worksheet problems unless otherwise stated.

The alternative format is the *vertical format.* Rather than beginning the worksheet with the trial balances of the parent and the subsidiary, this format begins with the completed income statements, statements of retained earnings, and the balance sheets of the parent and subsidiary. This method, which is seldom used in practice and harder to master, commonly has been used on the CPA Exam.

The vertical format is used in Worksheet 3-9 on pages 168 and 169. This worksheet is based on the same facts used for Worksheet 3-6 (an equity method example for the second year of a purchase with a complicated distribution of excess cost). Worksheet 3-9 is based on the determination and distribution of excess schedule shown on page 129.

worksheet

Worksheet 3-9: page 168

Note that the original separate statements are stacked vertically upon each other. Be sure to follow the carrydown procedure as it is applied to the separate statements. The net income from the income statement is carried down to the retained earnings statement. Then, the ending retained earnings balance is carried down to the balance sheet. Later, this same carrydown procedure is applied to the consolidated statements.

Understand that there are no differences in the elimination and adjustment procedures as a result of this alternative format. Compare the elimination entries to those in Worksheet 3-6. Even though there is no change in the eliminations, there are two areas of caution. First, the order in which the accounts appear is reversed; that is, nominal accounts precede balance sheet accounts. This difference in order will require care in making eliminations. Second, the eliminations to retained earnings must be made against the January 1 beginning balances, not the December 31 ending balances. The ending retained earnings balances are never adjusted but are derived after all eliminations have been made.

The complicated aspect of the vertical worksheet is the carrydown procedure used to create the retained earnings statement and the balance sheet. Arrows are used in Worksheet 3-9 to emphasize the carrydown procedure. Note that the net income line in the retained earnings statement and the retained earnings lines on the balance sheet are never available to receive eliminations. These balances are always carried down. The net income balances are derived from the same income distribution schedules used in Worksheet 3-6.

REFLECTION

- On vertical worksheets for consolidations subsequent to acquisition, the income statement accounts appear at the top, followed by the retained earnings statement accounts, and then the balance sheet accounts appear in the bottom section.
- Net income is carried down to the retained earnings section.
- Ending retained earnings is then carried down to the balance sheet section.

9

OBJECTIVE

Explain the impact of tax-related complications arising on the purchase date.

APPENDIX B: TAX-RELATED ADJUSTMENTS

Recall from Chapter 1 that a deferred tax liability results when the fair value of an asset may not be used in future depreciation calculations for tax purposes. (This occurs when the purchase is a *tax-free exchange* to the seller.) In this situation, future depreciation charges for tax purposes must be based on the book value of the asset, and a liability should be acknowledged in the determination and distribution of excess schedule by creating a deferred tax liability account. Consider the following determination and distribution of excess schedule for a subsidiary that has a building with a book value for tax purposes of $120,000 and a fair value of $200,000. Assuming a tax rate of 30%, there is a deferred tax liability of $24,000 ($80,000 excess of fair value over tax basis × 30%).

As is true in all determination and distribution of excess schedules, any remaining unallocated value becomes goodwill. In the case of a tax-free exchange, the remaining unallocated value is the amount available for goodwill **less the applicable deferred tax liability.** In the example which follows, the remaining unallocated value on the determination and distribution of excess schedule is $44,000. The $44,000 excess is what is left after a 30% deferred tax liability is recorded. The goodwill to be recorded is, therefore, $44,000 divided by the net of tax rate of 70% which equals $62,857. The deferred tax liability is 30% of the goodwill recorded (30% × $62,857 = $18,857).

Price paid for investment		$ 600,000	
Less interest acquired:			
Common stock	$ 100,000		
Retained earnings	400,000		
Total stockholders' equity	$ 500 000		
Interest acquired	× 100%	500,000	
Excess of cost over book value (debit balance)		$ 100,000	
Available for long-lived assets:			
Building		80,000	Dr.
Deferred tax liability, building		**(24,000)**	**Cr.**
Goodwill (net of deferred tax liability)		**$ 44,000**	**Dr.**
Distributed as follows:			
Goodwill ($44,000 ÷ 70%)		$ 62,857	
Deferred tax liability (30% × $62,857)		**(18,857)**	
Net goodwill		$ 44,000	

The worksheet entry to distribute the excess of cost over book value would be as follows:

Building (to fair value)	80,000	
Goodwill (balance of excess)	62,857	
Deferred Tax Liability (**$24,000 + $18,857**)		42,857
Investment in Subsidiary S (excess cost after elimination of subsidiary equity)		100,000

Worksheet eliminations will be simpler if each deferred tax liability is recorded below the asset to which it relates. It is possible that inventory could have a fair value in excess of its book value used for tax purposes. This, too, would require the recognition of a deferred tax liability.

Recall the general rule that the fair values of the liabilities are acknowledged in full even in a bargain purchase. There is an exception to this rule with respect to the deferred tax liability that results from recording the fair value adjustments made in a purchase: **The deferred tax liability has the same priority as the asset to which it relates.** For instance, since inventory always is adjusted to full fair value, the deferred tax liability related to inventory is recognized fully as well. In the case of a depreciable asset, only a portion of the difference between book and fair value is recorded in a bargain purchase; thus, the deferred tax liability is limited to the portion of the fair-book value disparity that is recorded.

The need to recognize the deferred tax liability may complicate the distribution of the excess. Assume we have an asset that has a fair value estimated to exceed its book value by $150,000, but there is only $70,000 of excess available to distribute to the asset. Assuming a 30% tax rate, the excess would be divided by 70%, or the net-of-tax percentage, to arrive at the amount to allocate to the asset itself—in this case, $100,000 ($70,000 ÷ 70%); thus, 30% of the $100,000 would be recognized as related deferred tax liability. The $70,000 excess of cost would be distributed as follows:

Excess of cost over book value available		$70,000
Adjustment of depreciable assets:		
Asset	$100,000	
Deferred tax liability	(30 000)	70,000
		$ 0

A second tax complication arises when the subsidiary has tax loss carryovers. To the extent that the tax loss carryovers are not recorded or are reduced by a valuation allowance by the subsidiary on its balance sheet, the carryovers may be an asset to be considered in the determination and distribution of excess schedule. When a tax-free exchange occurs during the accounting period, a portion of the tax loss carryover may be used during that period.[2] The amount that may be used is the acquiring company's tax liability for the year times the percentage of the year that the companies were under common control. If, for example, the acquiring company's tax liability was $100,000 and the purchase occurred on April 1, 3/4 of $100,000, or $75,000, of the tax loss carryover could be utilized. The current portion of the tax loss carryover is recorded as *Current Deferred Tax Expense.* Any remaining carryover is carried forward and recorded as a noncurrent asset using the account, *Noncurrent Deferred Tax Expense.* If it is probable that the deferred tax expense will not be fully realized, a contra-valuation allowance is provided. These are monetary accounts and, thus, are priority accounts.

Let us consider the example of a subsidiary that has the following tax loss carryovers on the date of purchase:

Tax loss carryover to be used in current period	$100,000
Tax loss carryover to be used in future periods	200,000

Assume that the parent has anticipated future tax liabilities against which the tax loss carryovers may be offset and has a 30% tax rate. A zone and price analyses would be prepared as follows:

Zone Analysis	Group Total	Ownership Portion	Cumulative Total
Ownership percentage		80%	
Priority accounts (net of liabilities)	$125,000	$100,000	$100,000
Nonpriority accounts	862,500	690,000	790,000

2 Section 381 (c)(1)(B) of the Federal Tax Code.

Price analysis would be as follows:

Price (including direct acquisition costs)	**$895,000**	
Assign to priority accounts, controlling share	100,000	Full value
Assign to nonpriority accounts, controlling share	690,000	Full value
Goodwill (net of deferred tax liability)	**105,000**	
Extraordinary gain	**0**	

From this information, a D&D schedule would be prepared as follows:

	Total	Controlling		Amort. Periods	Controlling Amortization
Price paid for investment		$ 895,000			
Less book value interest acquired:					
Common stock	$ 300,000				
Retained earnings	400,000				
Total stockholders' equity	$ 700,000				
Interest acquired	× 100%	700,000			
Excess of cost over book value (debit)		**$195,000**			
Priority accounts:					
Current deferred tax expense (30% × $100,000)		**30 000**	**Dr.**	**1**	
Noncurrent deferred tax expense (30% × $200,000)		**60,000**	**Dr.**	**Note 1**	
Goodwill (net of deferred tax liability)		$ 105,000			
Goodwill adjustment distributed as follows:					
Goodwill, gross ($105,000 ÷ 70%)		$ 150,000			
Deferred tax liability (30% × $150,000)		(45,000)			
Net goodwill		$ 105,000			

Note 1: Depends on income in future periods.

The worksheet entry to distribute the excess would be as follows:

Current Deferred Tax Expense	30,000	
Noncurrent Deferred Tax Expense	60,000	
Goodwill	150,000	
Investment in Subsidiary S (excess after elimination of subsidiary equity)		195,000
Deferred Tax Liability (applicable to goodwill)		45,000

Comprehensive Example. Both of the preceding tax issues will complicate the consolidated worksheet. Our example will consider the distribution of the tax adjustments on the worksheet and the resulting amortization adjustments needed to calculate consolidated net income. We will consider a nontaxable exchange with fixed asset and goodwill adjustments in addition to a tax loss carryover.

Assume that Paro Company purchased an 80% interest in Sunstran Corporation on January 1, 20X1. Paro expects to utilize $100,000 of tax loss carryovers in the current period and $250,000 in future periods.[3] The following zone analysis was prepared:

Zone Analysis	Group Total	Ownership Portion	Cumulative Total
Ownership percentage		80%	
Priority accounts (net of liabilities)	$280,000	$224,000	$224,000
Nonpriority accounts	765,000	612,000	836,000

Price analysis would be as follows:

Price (including direct acquisition costs)	**$990,000**	
Assign to priority accounts, controlling share	224,000	Full value
Assign to nonpriority accounts, controlling share	612,000	Full value
Goodwill (net of deferred tax liability)	**154,000**	
Extraordinary gain	**0**	

From this information, a D&D schedule would be prepared as follows:

	Total	Controlling		Amort. Periods	Controlling Amortization
Price paid for investment		$990,000			
Less book value interest acquired:					
Common stock ($10 par)	$100,000				
Paid-in capital in excess of par	300,000				
Retained earnings	400,000				
Total stockholders' equity	$800,000				
Interest acquired	× 80%	640,000			
Excess of cost over book value (debit)		$350,000			
Priority accounts:					
Current deferred tax expense (30% × 80% interest × $100,000)		24,000	Dr.	1	$24,000
Noncurrent deferred tax expense (30% × 80% interest × $250,000)		60,000	Dr.	Note 1	
Nonpriority accounts:					
Building (80% × $200,000)		160,000	Dr.	20	8,000
Deferred tax liability—Building (30% × $160,000)		**(48,000)**	**Cr.**	**20**	**(2,400)**
Goodwill (net of deferred tax liability)		$154,000			
Goodwill adjustment distributed as follows:					
Goodwill, gross ($154,000 ÷ 70%)		$220,000			
Deferred tax liability (30% × $220,000)		(66,000)			
Net goodwill		$154,000			

Note 1: Depends on income in future periods but must be consumed in 20 years or less.

3 Considers tax limitations and assumes full realizability of tax loss carryovers.

Worksheet 3-10: page 170

Worksheet 3-10, pages 170 to 171, is the consolidated worksheet for Paro Company and its subsidiary, Sunstran Corporation, at the end of 20X1. Unlike previous worksheets, the nominal accounts of both firms include a 30% provision for tax on internally generated net income (Paro does not include a tax on subsidiary income recorded). The calculation of the tax liabilities for affiliated firms is discussed further in Chapter 6. It should be noted, however, that Paro has reduced its tax provision for the benefit of the current deferred tax asset of $24,000 that resulted from the purchase ($100,000 current tax loss carryover × 80% interest × 30%). Paro's income before tax is $800,000. The 30% tax provision would be $240,000. The $240,000 has been reduced $24,000 for the benefit of the tax savings attributable to the current tax loss carryover. Since the deferred tax asset had not been recorded on the separate books, the tax savings was subtracted from the current year's provision. Since the deferred tax asset results from the purchase of the subsidiary, it is first recorded on the consolidated worksheet. The tax provision recorded by the subsidiary was also calculated using depreciation based on the building's book value.

The procedures to eliminate the investment account are the same as for previous examples using the equity method. In journal entry form, the eliminations are as follows:

	Eliminate subsidiary income recorded by parent company:		
(CY1)	Subsidiary Income	84,000	
	Investment in Sunstran		84,000
	Eliminate dividends paid by Sunstran to Paro:		
(CY2)	Investment in Sunstran	16,000	
	Dividends Declared (by Sunstran)		16,000
	Eliminate 80% of Sunstran equity against Investment in Sunstran:		
(EL)	Common Stock, Sunstran	80,000	
	Paid-In Capital in Excess of Par, Sunstran	240,000	
	Retained Earnings, Sunstran	320,000	
	Investment in Sunstran		640,000
	Distribute excess of cost over book value:		
(D1)	Provision for Tax	24,000	
(D2)	Noncurrent Deferred Tax Expense	60,000	
(D3)	Building	160,000	
(D3t)	Deferred Tax Liability (applicable to building)		48,000
(D4)	Goodwill	220,000	
(D4t)	Deferred Tax Liability (applicable to goodwill)		66,000
(D)	Investment in Sunstran (noneliminated excess)		350,000
	Amortize excess for current year as shown on the following schedule:		
(A3)	Expenses (for depreciation)	8,000	
	Accumulated Depreciation—Buildings		8,000
(A3t)	Deferred Tax Liability	2,400	
	Provision for Tax		2,400

Amortizations of excess are made for the current year using the following schedule:

Account Adjustments to Be Amortized	Life	Annual Amount	Current Year	Prior Years	Total	Key
Buildings	20	$ 8,000	$ 8,000		$ 8,000	(A3)
Deferred tax liability (building)	20	(2,400)	(2,400)		(2,400)	(A3t)
Total (excluding inventory)		$ 5,600	$ 5,600		$ 5,600	

Notice that entry (D1) distributes $24,000 to the provision for tax account. The deferred tax asset amount has already been recorded by the parent as a reduction of its tax expense. The parent, not having recorded the deferred tax asset previously, viewed the $24,000 as a tax savings in the current period. Entry (D1) increases the tax provision and properly records the $24,000 as the consumption of the $24,000 deferred tax asset included in the purchase price. Entry (D2) records the noncurrent portion of the tax loss carryforward. Entry (D3) increases the building by $160,000, and entry (D3t) records the deferred tax liability applicable to the building adjustment. Entry (D4) records goodwill of $220,000, and entry (D4t) records the deferred tax liability applicable to goodwill.

As a result of the increase in the value of the building, entry (A3) increases the deprecation for the building by $8,000. Given the 30% tax rate, entry (A3t) reduces the provision for tax account by $2,400 as a result of the depreciation adjustment. This entry is not a reduction in the current taxes payable. Instead, it is a reduction in the deferred tax liability recorded as part of the distribution of excess [entry (D3)]. Remember that the deferred tax liability reflects the loss of future tax deductions caused by the difference between the building's higher fair value and its lower book value on the date of the purchase. Thus, the net result of the entry is to record the tax provision as if the deductions were allowable (for tax purposes) without changing the tax payable for the current period. There is no amortization of the noncurrent deferred tax asset since it is not used in the current period. All amortizations of excess and all tax adjustments are carried to the parent's income distribution schedule. This is again the case, since only the controlling share of all adjustments is recorded.

REFLECTION

- One of the assets that may be included in the purchase is a tax loss carryover. It should be separated into its current and noncurrent components.
- When assets are part of a tax-free exchange, they must be accompanied by a deferred tax liability equal to the value of the forfeited tax deduction.

Worksheet 3-1

Simple Equity Method
Company P and Subsidiary Company S
Worksheet for Consolidated Financial Statements
For Year Ended December 31, 20X1

	(Credit balance amounts are in parentheses.)	Trial Balance	
		Company P	Company S
1	**Investment in Company S**	**163,000**	
2			
3			
4	**Patent**		
5	Other Assets (net of liabilities)	227,000	170,000
6	Common Stock ($10 par), Company P	(200,000)	
7	Retained Earnings, January 1, 20X1, Company P	(123,000)	
8	Common Stock ($10 par), Company S		(100,000)
9	Retained Earnings, January 1, 20X1, Company S		(50,000)
10	Revenue	(100,000)	(80,000)
11	**Expenses**	60,000	50,000
12	**Patent Amortization**		
13	**Subsidiary Income**	**(27,000)**	
14	**Dividends Declared**		**10,000**
15		0	0
16	**Consolidated Net Income**		
17	**To NCI (see distribution schedule)**		
18	**Balance to Controlling Interest (see distribution schedule)**		
19	Total NCI		
20	Retained Earnings, Controlling Interest, December 31, 20X1		
21			

Eliminations and Adjustments:

(CY1) Eliminate subsidiary income against the investment account.
(CY2) Eliminate dividends paid by subsidiary to parent. After (CY1) and (CY2), the investment account and subsidiary retained earnings are at a common point in time. Then, elimination of the investment account can proceed.
(EL) Eliminate the pro rata share of Company S equity balances *at the beginning of the year* against the investment account. The elimination of the parent's share of subsidiary stockholders' equity leaves only the noncontrolling interest in each element of the equity.
(D) Distribute the $10,000 excess cost as required by the D&D schedule on page 117. In this example, Patent is recorded for $10,000.
(A) Amortize the resulting patents over the 10-year period. The current portion is $1,000 per year ($10,000 ÷ 10 years).

Worksheet 3-1 (see page 119)

Eliminations & Adjustments Dr.		Eliminations & Adjustments Cr.		Consolidated Income Statement	NCI	Controlling Retained Earnings	Consolidated Balance Sheet	
(CY2)	**9,000**	**(CY1)**	**27,000**					1
		(EL)	135,000					2
		(D)	10,000					3
(D)	10,000	**(A)**	**1,000**				9,000	4
							397,000	5
							(200,000)	6
						(123,000)		7
(EL)	90,000				(10,000)			8
(EL)	45,000				(5,000)			9
				(180,000)				10
				110,000				11
(A)	**1000**			**1,000**				12
(CY1)	**27,000**							13
		(CY2)	**9,000**		**1,000**			14
	182,000		182,000					15
				(69,000)				16
				3,000	**(3,000)**			17
				66,000		**(66,000)**		18
					(17,000)		(17,000)	19
						(189,000)	(189,000)	20
							0	21

Subsidiary Company S Income Distribution

		Internally generated net income	$ 30,000
		Adjusted income	$ 30,000
		NCI share	× 10%
		NCI	**$ 3,000**

Parent Company P Income Distribution

Patent amortization . . . . **(A)**	**$1,000**	Internally generated net income	$ 40,000
		90% × Company S adjusted income of $30,000.	27,000
		Controlling interest	**$66,000**

Worksheet 3-2

Simple Equity Method, Second Year
Company P and Subsidiary Company S
Worksheet for Consolidated Financial Statements
For Year Ended December 31, 20X2

	(Credit balance amounts are in parentheses.)	Trial Balance	
		Company P	Company S
1	**Investment in Company S**	**149,500**	
2			
3	**Patent**		
4	Other Assets (net of liabilities)	251,500	155,000
5	Common Stock ($10 par), Company P	(200,000)	
6	**Retained Earnings, January 1, 20X2, Company P**	**(190,000)**	
7	Common Stock ($10 par), Company S		(100,000)
8	Retained Earnings, January 1, 20X2, Company S		(70,000)
9	Revenue	(100,000)	(50,000)
10	Expenses	80,000	60,000
11	**Patent Amortization**		
12	**Subsidiary Loss**	**9,000**	
13	**Dividends Declared**		**5,000**
14		0	0
15	**Consolidated Net Income**		
16	**To NCI (see distribution schedule)**		
17	**Balance to Controlling Interest (see distribution schedule)**		
18	Total NCI		
19	Retained Earnings, Controlling Interest, December 31, 20X2		
20			

Eliminations and Adjustments:

(CY1) Eliminate controlling share of subsidiary loss.
(CY2) Eliminate dividends paid by subsidiary to parent. The investment account is now returned to its January 1, 20X2, balance so that elimination may proceed.
(EL) Using balances *at the beginning of the year,* eliminate 90% of the Company S equity balances against the remaining investment account.
(D) Distribute the $10,000 excess cost as indicated by the D&D schedule that was prepared on the date of acquisition.
(A) Amortize the patent over the selected 10-year period. It is necessary to record the amortization *for current and past periods,* because asset adjustments resulting from the consolidation process do not appear on the separate statements of the constituent companies. Thus, entry (A) reduces Patent by $2,000 for the 20X1 and 20X2 amortizations. The amount for the current year is expensed, while the cumulative amortization for prior years is deducted from the beginning controlling retained earnings account. The NCI does not share in the adjustments because the only patent originally acknowledged is that which is applicable to the controlling interest.

Worksheet 3-2 (see page 122)

Eliminations & Adjustments Dr.		Eliminations & Adjustments Cr.		Consolidated Income Statement	NCI	Controlling Retained Earnings	Consolidated Balance Sheet	
(CY1)	**9,000**	(EL)	153,000					1
(CY2)	**4,500**	(D)	10,000					2
(D)	10,000	**(A)**	**2,000**				8,000	3
							406,500	4
							(200,000)	5
(A)	**1,000**					(189,000)		6
(EL)	90,000				(10,000)			7
(EL)	63,000				(7,000)			8
				(150,000)				9
				140,000				10
(A)	**1,000**			**1,000**				11
		(CY1)	**9,000**					12
		(CY2)	**4,500**		500			13
	178,500		178,500					14
				(9,000)				15
				(1,000)	**1,000**			16
				10,000		**(10,000)**		17
					(15,500)		**(15,500)**	18
						(199,000)	**(199,000)**	19
							0	20

Subsidiary Company S Income Distribution

Internally generated **loss**	$ 10,000	
Adjusted income	$ 10,000	
NCI share	× 10%	
NCI	**$ 1,000**	

Parent Company P Income Distribution

Patent amortization . . . .**(A)**	**$1,000**	Internally generated net income	$ 20,000
90% × Company S adjusted income of $10,000	9,000		
		Controlling interest	**$10,000**

Worksheet 3-3

Cost Method
Company P and Subsidiary Company S
Worksheet for Consolidated Financial Statements
For Year Ended December 31, 20X1

	(Credit balance amounts are in parentheses.)	Trial Balance	
		Company P	Company S
1	**Investment in Company S**	**145,000**	
2			
3	**Patent**		
4	Other Assets (net of liabilities)	227,000	170,000
5	Common Stock ($10 par), Company P	(200,000)	
6	Retained Earnings, January 1, 20X1, Company P	(123,000)	
7	Common Stock ($10 par), Company S		(100,000)
8	Retained Earnings, January 1, 20X1, Company S		(50,000)
9	Revenue	(100,000)	(80,000)
10	Expenses	60,000	50,000
11	**Patent Amortization**		
12	**Subsidiary (Dividend) Income**	**(9,000)**	
13	**Dividends Declared**		**10,000**
14		0	0
15	Consolidated Net Income		
16	To NCI (see distribution schedule)		
17	Balance to Controlling Interest (see distribution schedule)		
18	Total NCI		
19	Retained Earnings, Controlling Interest, December 31, 20X1		
20			

Eliminations and Adjustments:

(CY2) Eliminate intercompany dividends.
(EL) Eliminate 90% of the Company S equity balances at the beginning of the year against the investment account.
(D) Distribute the $10,000 excess cost as indicated by the D&D schedule on page 120.
(A) Amortize the patent for the current year.

Worksheet 3-3 (see page 124)

Eliminations & Adjustments Dr.		Eliminations & Adjustments Cr.		Consolidated Income Statement	NCI	Controlling Retained Earnings	Consolidated Balance Sheet	
		(EL)	135,000					1
		(D)	10,000					2
(D)	10,000	(A)	1,000				9,000	3
							397,000	4
							(200,000)	5
						(123,000)		6
(EL)	90,000				(10,000)			7
(EL)	45,000				(5,000)			8
				(180,000)				9
				110,000				10
(A)	1,000			1,000				11
(CY2)	**9,000**							12
		(CY2)	**9,000**		**1,000**			13
	155,000		155,000					14
				(69,000)				15
				3,000	(3,000)			16
				66,000		(66,000)		17
					(17,000)		(17,000)	18
						(189,000)	(189,000)	19
							0	20

Subsidiary Company S Income Distribution

	Internally generated net income	$30,000
	Adjusted income	$30,000
	NCI share	× 10%
	NCI	**$ 3,000**

Parent Company P Income Distribution

Patent amortization (A)	$1,000	Internally generated net income	$ 40,000
		90% × Company S adjusted income of $30,000	27,000
		Controlling interest	**$66,000**

Worksheet 3-4

Cost Method, Second Year
Company P and Subsidiary Company S
Worksheet for Consolidated Financial Statements
For Year Ended December 31, 20X2

	(Credit balance amounts are in parentheses.)	Trial Balance	
		Company P	Company S
1	**Investment in Company S**	**145,000**	
2			
3	Patent		
4	Other Assets (net of liabilities)	251,500	155,000
5	Common Stock ($10 par), Company P	(200,000)	
6	**Retained Earnings, January 1, 20X2, Company P**	**(172,000)**	
7	Common Stock ($10 par), Company S		(100,000)
8	Retained Earnings, January 1, 20X2, Company S		(70,000)
9	Revenue	(100,000)	(50,000)
10	Expenses	80,000	60,000
11	Patent Amortization		
12	**Subsidiary (Dividend) Income**	**(4,500)**	
13	**Dividends Declared**		**5,000**
14		0	0
15	Consolidated Net Income		
16	To NCI (see distribution schedule)		
17	Balance to Controlling Interest (see distribution schedule)		
18	Total NCI		
19	Retained Earnings, Controlling Interest, December 31, 20X2		
20			

Eliminations and Adjustments:

(CV) Convert to simple equity method as of January 1, 20X2.
(CY2) Eliminate the current-year intercompany dividends.
(EL) Eliminate 90% of the Company S equity balances at the beginning of the year against the investment account.
(D) Distribute the $10,000 excess cost as indicated by the D&D schedule that was prepared on the date of acquisition.
(A) Amortize the patent for the current year and one previous year.

Worksheet 3-4 (see page 124)

Eliminations & Adjustments				Consolidated Income Statement	NCI	Controlling Retained Earnings	Consolidated Balance Sheet	
Dr.		Cr.						
(CV)	**18,000**	(EL)	153,000					1
		(D)	10,000					2
(D)	10,000	(A)	2,000				8,000	3
							406,500	4
							(200,000)	5
(A)	1,000	**(CV)**	**18,000**			(189,000)		6
(EL)	90,000				(10,000)			7
(EL)	63,000				(7,000)			8
				(150,000)				9
				140,000				10
(A)	1,000			1,000				11
(CY2)	**4,500**							12
		(CY2)	**4,500**		**500**			13
	187,500		187,500					14
				(9,000)				15
				(1,000)	1,000			16
				10,000		(10,000)		17
					(15,500)		(15,500)	18
						(199,000)	(199,000)	19
							0	20

Subsidiary Company S Income Distribution

Internally generated **loss**	$ 10,000	
Adjusted income	$ 10,000	
NCI share	× 10%	
NCI	**$ 1,000**	

Parent Company P Income Distribution

Patent amortization . . . . (A)	$1,000	Internally generated net income	$ 20,000
90% × Company S adjusted income of $10,000	9,000		
		Controlling interest	**$10,000**

Worksheet 3-5

Simple Equity Method, First Year
Paulos Company and Subsidiary Carlos Company
Worksheet for Consolidated Financial Statements
For Year Ended December 31, 20X1

	(Credit balance amounts are in parentheses.)	Trial Balance	
		Paulos	Carlos
1	Cash	100,000	50,000
2	Inventory	226,000	62,500
3	Land	200,000	150,000
4	Investment in Carlos	732,000	
5			
6			
7	Buildings	800,000	600,000
8	Accumulated Depreciation	(80,000)	(315,000)
9	Equipment	400,000	150,000
10	Accumulated Depreciation	(50,000)	(70,000)
11	Patent (net)		112,500
12	Goodwill		
13	Current Liabilities	(100,000)	
14	Bonds Payable		(200,000)
15	Discount (premium)		
16	Common Stock, Carlos		(100,000)
17	Paid-In Capital in Excess of Par, Carlos		(150,000)
18	Retained Earnings, January 1, 20X1, Carlos		(250,000)
19	Common Stock, Paulos	(1,500,000)	
20	Retained Earnings, January 1, 20X1, Paulos	(600,000)	
21	Sales	(350,000)	(200,000)
22	Cost of Goods Sold	150,000	80,000
23	Depreciation Expense—Building	40,000	15,000
24	Depreciation Expense—Equipment	20,000	20,000
25	Other Expenses	60,000	13,000
26	Interest Expense		12,000
27	Subsidiary Income	(48,000)	
28	Dividends Declared		20,000
29	Totals	0	0
30	Consolidated Net Income		
31	NCI Share		
32	Controlling Share		
33	Total NCI		
34	Retained Earnings, Controlling Interest, Dec. 31, 20X1		
35	Totals		

Worksheet 3-5 (see page 130)

Eliminations & Adjustments Dr.	Eliminations & Adjustments Cr.	Consolidated Income Statement	NCI	Controlling Retained Earnings	Consolidated Balance Sheet	
					150,000	1
					288,500	2
(D2) 40,000					390,000	3
(CY2) 16,000	(CY1) 48,000					4
	(EL) 400,000					5
	(D) 300,000					6
(D4) 160,000					1,560,000	7
	(A4) 8,000				(403,000)	8
	(D5) 16,000				534,000	9
(A5) 3,200					(116,800)	10
(D6) 20,000	(A6) 2,000				130,500	11
(D7) 81,400					81,400	12
					(100,000)	13
					(200,000)	14
(D3) 10,600	(A3) 2,650				7,950	15
(EL) 80,000			(20,000)			16
(EL) 120,000			(30,000)			17
(EL) 200,000			(50,000)			18
					(1,500,000)	19
				(600,000)		20
		(550,000)				21
(D1) 4,000		234,000				22
(A4) 8,000		63,000				23
	(A5) 3,200	36,800				24
(A6) 2,000		75,000				25
(A3) 2,650		14,650				26
(CY1) 48,000						27
	(CY2) 16,000		4,000			28
795,850	795,850					29
		(126,550)				30
		12,000	(12,000)			31
		114,550		(114,550)		32
			(108,000)		(108,000)	33
				(714,550)	(714,550)	34
					0	35

Eliminations and Adjustments:

(CY1) Eliminate current-year entries made to record subsidiary income.
(CY2) Eliminate dividends paid by Carlos to Paulos. The investment is now at its January 1, 20X1, balance.
(EL) Eliminate 80% of subsidiary equity against the investment account.
(D) Distribute $300,000 excess as follows:
(D1) Cost of goods sold for inventory adjustment at time of purchase.
(D2) Land adjustment.
(D3) Record discount on bonds payable.
(D4) Adjust building.
(D5) Adjust equipment.
(D6) Adjust patent.
(D7) Record goodwill.

(A3–A6) Account Adjustments to Be Amortized	Life	Annual Amount	Current Year	Prior Years	Total	Key
Bonds payable	4	$ 2,650	$ 2,650	0	$ 2,650	(A3)
Buildings	20	8,000	8,000	0	8,000	(A4)
Equipment	5	(3,200)	(3,200)	0	(3,200)	(A5)
Patent (net)	10	2,000	2,000	0	2,000	(A6)
Total	0	$ 9,450	$ 9,450	0	$ 9,450	

Subsidiary Carlos Company Income Distribution

		Internally generated net income	$60,000
		Adjusted income	$60,000
		NCI share	× 20%
		NCI	$12,000

Parent Paulos Company Income Distribution

Amortizations of excess (Elim. A) (A3–A6)	$9,450	Internally generated net income	$ 80,000
Inventory adjustment (D1)	4,000	80% × Carlos adjusted income	48,000
		Controlling interest	$114,550

Worksheet 3-6

Simple Equity Method, Second Year
Paulos Company and Subsidiary Carlos Company
Worksheet for Consolidated Financial Statements
For Year Ended December 31, 20X2

	(Credit balance amounts are in parentheses.)	Trial Balance	
		Paulos	Carlos
1	Cash	312,000	160,000
2	Inventory	210,000	120,000
3	Land	200,000	150,000
4	Investment in Carlos	796,000	
5			
6			
7	Buildings	800,000	600,000
8	Accumulated Depreciation	(120,000)	(330,000)
9	Equipment	400,000	150,000
10	Accumulated Depreciation	(90,000)	(90,000)
11	Patent (net)		100,000
12	Goodwill		
13	Current Liabilities	(150,000)	(40,000)
14	Bonds Payable		(200,000)
15	Discount (premium)		
16	Common Stock, Carlos		(100,000)
17	Paid-In Capital in Excess of Par, Carlos		(150,000)
18	Retained Earnings, Jan. 1, 20X2, Carlos		(290,000)
19	Common Stock, Paulos	(1,500,000)	
20	Retained Earnings, Jan. 1, 20X2, Paulos	(728,000)	
21			
22	Sales	(400,000)	(300,000)
23	Cost of Goods Sold	200,000	120,000
24	Depr. Expense—Building	40,000	15,000
25	Depreciation Exp.—Equipment	20,000	20,000
26	Other Expenses	90,000	33,000
27	Interest Expense		12,000
28	Subsidiary Income	(80,000)	
29	Dividends Declared		20,000
30	Totals	0	0
31	Consolidated Net Income		
32	NCI Share		
33	Controlling Share		
34	Total NCI		
35	Retained Earnings, Controlling Interest, Dec. 31, 20X2		
36	Totals		

Worksheet 3-6 (see page 131)

Eliminations & Adjustments Dr.		Eliminations & Adjustments Cr.		Consolidated Income Statement	NCI	Controlling Retained Earnings	Consolidated Balance Sheet	
							472,000	1
							330,000	2
(D2)	40,000						390,000	3
(CY2)	16,000	(CY1)	80,000					4
		(EL)	432,000					5
		(D)	300,000					6
(D4)	160,000						1,560,000	7
		(A4)	16,000				(466,000)	8
		(D5)	16,000				534,000	9
(A5)	6,400						(173,600)	10
(D6)	20,000	(A6)	4,000				116,000	11
(D7)	81,400						81,400	12
							(190,000)	13
							(200,000)	14
(D3)	10,600	(A3)	5,300				5,300	15
(EL)	80,000				(20,000)			16
(EL)	120,000				(30,000)			17
(EL)	232,000				(58,000)			18
							(1,500,000)	19
(D1)	4,000							20
(A3–A6)	9,450					(714,550)		21
				(700,000)				22
				320,000				23
(A4)	8,000			63,000				24
		(A5)	3,200	36,800				25
(A6)	2,000			125,000				26
(A3)	2,650			14,650				27
(CY1)	80,000							28
		(CY2)	16,000		4,000			29
	872,500		872,500					30
				(140,550)				31
				20,000	(20,000)			32
				120,550		(120,550)		33
					(124,000)		(124,000)	34
						(835,100)	(835,100)	35
							0	36

Eliminations and Adjustments:

(CY1) Eliminate current-year entries made to record subsidiary income.
(CY2) Eliminate dividends paid by Carlos to Paulos. The investment is now at its January 1, 20X2, balance.
(EL) Eliminate 80% of subsidiary equity against the investment account.
(D) Distribute $300,000 excess as follows:
(D1) Cost of goods sold for inventory adjustment at time of purchase.
(D2) Land adjustment.
(D3) Record discount on bonds payable.
(D4) Adjust building.
(D5) Adjust equipment.
(D6) Adjust patent.
(D7) Record goodwill.

(A3–A6) Account Adjustments to Be Amortized	Life	Annual Amount	Current Year	Prior Years	Total	Key
Bonds payable	4	$ 2,650	$ 2,650	$ 2,650	$ 5,300	(A3)
Buildings	20	8,000	8,000	8,000	16,000	(A4)
Equipment	5	(3,200)	(3,200)	(3,200)	(6,400)	(A5)
Patent (net)	10	2,000	2,000	2,000	4,000	(A6)
Total		$ 9,450	$ 9,450	$ 9,450	$18,900	

Subsidiary Carlos Company Income Distribution

		Internally generated net income	$ 100,000
		Adjusted income	$ 100,000
		NCI share	× 20%
		NCI	$ 20,000

Parent Paulos Company Income Distribution

Amortizations of excess (Elim. A) ....(A3–A6)	$9,450	Internally generated net income	$ 50,000
		80% × Carlos adjusted income	80,000
		Controlling interest	$120,550

Worksheet 3-7

Intraperiod Purchase; Subsidiary Books Closed on Purchase Date
Company P and Subsidiary Company S
Worksheet for Consolidated Financial Statements
For Year Ended December 31, 20X1

	(Credit balance amounts are in parentheses.)	Trial Balance	
		Company P	Company S
1	Current Assets	187,600	87,500
2	**Investment in Company S**	**118,400**	
3			
4			
5	Goodwill		
6	Equipment	400,000	80,000
7	Accumulated Depreciation	(200,000)	(32,500)
8	Liabilities	(60,000)	(12,000)
9	Common Stock, Company P	(250,000)	
10	Retained Earnings, **Jan. 1, 20X1, Company P**	(100,000)	
11	Common Stock, Company S		(50,000)
12	Retained Earnings, **July 1, 20X1, Company S**		(58,000)
13	Sales	(500,000)	(92,000)
14	Cost of Goods Sold	350,000	60,000
15	Expenses	70,000	12,000
16	**Subsidiary Income**	**(16,000)**	
17	Dividends Declared		5,000
18		0	0
19			
20			
21	Consolidated Net Income		
22	To NCI (see distribution schedule)		
23	Balance to Controlling Interest (see distribution schedule)		
24	Total NCI		
25	Retained Earnings, Controlling Interest, Dec. 31, 20X1		
26			

Eliminations and Adjustments:

(CY1) Eliminate the entries made in the investment in Company S account and in the subsidiary income account to record the parent's 80% controlling interest in the subsidiary's second *six months' income.*
(CY2) Eliminate intercompany dividends. This restores the investment account to its balance as of the July 1, 20X1, investment date.
(EL) Eliminate 80% of the subsidiary's *July 1, 20X1,* equity balances against the *balance* of the investment account.
(D) Distribute the excess of cost over book value of $20,000 to Goodwill in accordance with the D&D schedule.

Worksheet 3-7 (see page 136)

Eliminations & Adjustments Dr.		Eliminations & Adjustments Cr.		Consolidated Income Statement	NCI	Controlling Retained Earnings	Consolidated Balance Sheet	
							275,100	1
(CY2)	4,000	(CY1)	16,000					2
		(EL)	86,400					3
		(D)	20,000					4
(D)	20,000						20,000	5
							480,000	6
							(232,500)	7
							(72,000)	8
							(250,000)	9
						(100,000)		10
(EL)	40,000				(10,000)			11
(EL)	46,400				(11,600)			12
				(592,000)				13
				410,000				14
				82,000				15
(CY1)	16,000							16
		(CY2)	4,000		1,000			17
								18
	126,400		126,400					19
								20
				(100,000)				21
				4,000	(4,000)			22
				96,000		(96,000)		23
					(24,600)		(24,600)	24
						(196,000)	(196,000)	25
							0	26

Subsidiary Company S Income Distribution

Internally generated net income **(last six months)** . . .	**$20,000**
Adjusted income . . .	$ 20,000
NCI share . . .	× 20%
NCI . . .	**$ 4,000**

Parent Company P Income Distribution

Internally generated net income . . .	$ 80,000
80% × Company S adjusted income of $20,000 **(last six months)** . . .	**16,000**
Controlling interest . . .	**$96,000**

Worksheet 3-8

Intraperiod Purchase; Subsidiary Books Not Closed on Purchase Date
Company P and Subsidiary Company S
Worksheet for Consolidated Financial Statements
For Year Ended December 31, 20X1

	(Credit balance amounts are in parentheses.)	Trial Balance	
		Company P	Company S
1	Current Assets	187,600	87,500
2	**Investment in Company S**	**118,400**	
3			
4			
5	Goodwill		
6	Equipment	400,000	80,000
7	Accumulated Depreciation	(200,000)	(32,500)
8	Liabilities	(60,000)	(12,000)
9	Common Stock, Company P	(250,000)	
10	Retained Earnings, **Jan. 1, 20X1, Company P**	(100,000)	
11	Common Stock, Company S		(50,000)
12	Retained Earnings, **Jan. 1, 20X1, Company S**		(45,000)
13	Sales	(500,000)	(182,000)
14	Cost of Goods Sold	350,000	120,000
15	Expenses	70,000	24,000
16	**Subsidiary Income**	**(16,000)**	
17	**Dividends Declared**		**10,000**
18			
19	**Purchased Income**		
20		0	0
21			
22	Consolidated Net Income		
23	To NCI (see distribution schedule)		
24	Balance to Controlling Interest (see distribution schedule)		
25	Total NCI		
26	Retained Earnings, Controlling Interest, Dec. 31, 20X1		
27			

Eliminations and Adjustments:

(CY1) Eliminate the entries made in the investment account and in the subsidiary income account (same as Worksheet 3-7).
(CY2) Eliminate intercompany dividends. Notice that Company P's share of the subsidiary dividends declared are from those declared *after* the purchase.
(EL) Eliminate 80% of the subsidiary equity balances at the beginning of the year plus 80% of Company S's income earned as of July 1, 20X1, against the investment account. The share of preacquisition income is entered as *Purchased Income* to emphasize that this income was earned prior to the date of purchase by Company P. For elimination purposes, this account may be viewed as a supplement to retained earnings. Since the subsidiary also declared dividends *prior to July 1, 20X1*, the controlling percentage of those dividends should be eliminated in this entry by crediting Dividends Declared.
(D) Distribute the $20,000 excess of cost over book value (same as Worksheet 3-7).

Worksheet 3-8 (see page 137)

Eliminations & Adjustments Dr.	Eliminations & Adjustments Cr.	Consolidated Income Statement	NCI	Controlling Retained Earnings	Consolidated Balance Sheet	
					275,100	1
(CY2) 4,000	(CY1) 16,000					2
	(EL) 86,400					3
	(D) 20,000					4
(D) 20,000					20,000	5
					480,000	6
					(232,500)	7
					(72,000)	8
					(250,000)	9
				(100,000)		10
(EL) 40,000			(10,000)			11
(EL) 36,000			(9,000)			12
		(682,000)				13
		470,000				14
		94,000				15
(CY1) 16,000						16
	(CY2) 4,000		2,000			17
	(EL) 4,000					18
(EL) 14,400		**14,400**				19
130,400	130,400					20
						21
		(103,600)				22
		7,600	(7,600)			23
		96,000		(96,000)		24
			(24,600)		(24,600)	25
				(196,000)	(196,000)	26
					0	27

Subsidiary Company S Income Distribution

Internally generated net income **entire year**	**$38,000**
Adjusted income	$ 38,000
NCI share	× 20%
NCI	**$ 7,600**

Parent Company P Income Distribution

Internally generated net income	$ 80,000
80% × Company S adjusted income of $20,000 **(last six months)**	**16,000**
Controlling interest	**$96,000**

Worksheet 3-9

Vertical Format, Simple Equity Method
Paulos Company and Subsidiary Carlos Company
Worksheet for Consolidated Financial Statements
For Year Ended December 31, 20X2

Worksheet 3-9 (see page 141)

	Compare this worksheet to Worksheet 3-6. Note that eliminations and adjustments, explanations, as well as income distribution schedules are the same for Worksheet 3-9 as for Worksheet 3-6.	Financial Statements: Paulos	Financial Statements: Carlos	Eliminations & Adjustments: Dr.	Eliminations & Adjustments: Cr.	NCI	Consolidated Balance Sheet	
1	**Income Statement**							1
2	Sales	(400,000)	(300,000)				(700,000)	2
3	Cost of Goods Sold	200,000	120,000				320,000	3
4	Depreciation Expense—Building	40,000	15,000	(A4) 8,000			63,000	4
5	Depreciation Expense—Equipment	20,000	20,000		(A5) 3,200		36,800	5
6	Other Expenses	90,000	33,000	(A6) 2,000			125,000	6
7	Subsidiary Income	(80,000)		(CY1) 80,000				7
7a								7a
7b	Interest Expense		12,000	(A3) 2,650			14,650	7b
8	Net Income	**(130,000)**	**(100,000)**					8
9	Consolidated Net Income						(140,550)	9
10								10
11	NCI (see income distribution schedule)					**(20,000)**		11
12	Controlling Interest (see income distribution schedule)						**(120,550)**	12
13								13
14	**Retained Earnings Statement:**							14
15	Retained Earnings, Jan. 1, 20X2, Paulos	(728,000)		(D1) 4,000			(714,550)	15
16				(A3–A6) 9,450				16
17								17
18								18
19								19
20	Retained Earnings, Jan. 1, 20X2, Carlos		(290,000)	(EL) 232,000		(58,000)		20
21	Net Income (carrydown)	(130,000)	(100,000)			(20,000)	(120,550)	21
22	Dividends Declared		20,000		(CY2) 16,000	4,000		22
23	Retained Earnings, Dec. 31, 20X2	**(858,000)**	**(370,000)**					23
24								24
25	Retained Earnings, NCI, Dec. 31, 20X2					**(74,000)**		25

26										26
27	Retained Earn., Controlling Interest, Dec. 31, 20X2								**(835,100)**	27
28										28
29	**Balance Sheet:**									29
30	Cash	312,000	160,000						472,000	30
31	Inventory	210,000	120,000						330,000	31
32	Land	200,000	150,000	(D2)	40,000				390,000	32
33	Building	800,000	600,000	(D4)	160,000				1,560,000	33
34	Accumulated Depreciation—Building	(120,000)	(330,000)			(A4)	16,000		(466,000)	34
35	Equipment	400,000	150,000			(D5)	16,000		534,000	35
36	Accumulated Depreciation—Equipment	(90,000)	(90,000)	(A5)	6,400				(173,600)	36
37	Investment in Carlos Company	796,000		(CY2)	16,000	(CY1)	80,000			37
38						(EL)	432,000			38
39						(D)	300,000			39
40	Patent		100,000	(D6)	20,000	(A6)	4,000		116,000	40
40a	Goodwill			(D7)	81,400				81,400	40a
41	Current Liabilities	(150,000)	(40,000)						(190,000)	41
42	Bonds Payable		(200,000)						(200,000)	42
43	Discount/Premium			(D3)	10,600	(A3)	5,300		5,300	43
44	Common Stock, Paulos	(1,500,000)							(1,500,000)	44
45	Common Stock, Carlos		(100,000)	(EL)	80,000			(20,000)		45
46	Paid-In Capital in Excess of Par, Carlos		(150,000)	(EL)	120,000			(30,000)		46
47	Retained Earnings, Dec. 31, 20X2 (carrydown)	(858,000)	(370,000)							47
48	Retained Earn., Controlling Interest, Dec. 31, 20X2								(835,100)	48
49										49
50	Retained Earnings, NCI, Dec. 31, 20X2							(74,000)		50
51	Total NCI							(124,000)	(124,000)	51
52	Total	0	0		872,500		872,500		0	52

Worksheet 3-10

Equity Method, Tax Issues
Paro Company and Subsidiary Sunstran Corporation
Worksheet for Consolidated Financial Statements
For Year Ended December 31, 20X1

	(Credit balance amounts are in parentheses.)	Trial Balance	
		Paro	Sunstran
1	Cash	324,000	30,000
2	Accounts Receivable (net)	354,000	95,000
3	Inventory	540,000	100,000
4	Land	100,000	30,000
5	Building	1,300,000	950,000
6	Accumulated Depreciation, Building	(400,000)	(300,000)
7	**Noncurrent Deferred Tax Expense**		
8	Investment in Sunstran Company	1,058,000	
9			
10			
11	Goodwill		
12	Current Liabilities	(248,000)	(20,000)
13	**Deferred Tax Liability**		
14			
15	Common Stock, Paro	(510,000)	
16	Retained Earnings, Jan. 1, 20X1, Paro	(1,950,000)	
17			
18	Common Stock, Sunstran		(100,000)
19	Paid-In Capital in Excess of Par, Sunstran		(300,000)
20	Retained Earnings, Jan. 1, 20X1, Sunstran		(400,000)
21			
22	Sales	(3,400,000)	(900,000)
23	Cost of Goods Sold	2,070,000	600,000
24	Expenses	530,000	150,000
25			
26	Subsidiary Income	(84,000)	
27	Provision for Tax	216,000	45,000
28			
29	Dividends Declared	100,000	20,000
30		0	0
31	Consolidated Net Income		
32	To NCI (see distribution schedule)		
33	Balance to Controlling Interest (see distribution schedule)		
34	Total NCI		
35	Retained Earnings, Controlling Interest, Dec. 31, 20X1		
36			

Worksheet 3-10 (see page 146)

Eliminations & Adjustments				Consolidated Income Statement	NCI	Controlling Retained Earnings	Consolidated Balance Sheet	
Dr.		Cr.						
							354,000	1
							449,000	2
							640,000	3
							130,000	4
							2,250,000	5
(D3)	160,000	(A3)	8,000				(548,000)	6
(D2)	**60,000**						60,000	7
(CY2)	16,000	(CY1)	84,000					8
		(EL)	640,000					9
		(D)	350,000					10
(D4)	220,000						220,000	11
							(268,000)	12
(A3t)	**2,400**	**(D3t)**	**48,000**				(111,600)	13
		(D4t)	**66,000**					14
							(510,000)	15
						(1,950,000)		16
								17
(EL)	80,000				(20,000)			18
(EL)	240,000				(60,000)			19
(EL)	320,000				(80,000)			20
								21
				(4,300,000)				22
				2,670,000				23
(A3)	8,000			688,000				24
								25
(CY1)	84,000							26
(D1)	**24,000**	**(A3t)**	**2,400**	282,600				27
								28
		(CY2)	16,000		4,000	100,000		29
	1,214,400		1,214,400					30
				(659,400)				31
				21,000	(21,000)			32
				638,400		(638,400)		33
					(177,000)		(177,000)	34
						(2,488,400)	(2,488,400)	35
							0	36

Eliminations and Adjustments:

(CY1) Eliminate the parent's share of subsidiary income.
(CY2) Eliminate the current-year intercompany dividends. The investment account is adjusted now to its January 1, 20X2, balance so that it may be eliminated.
(EL) Eliminate the 80% ownership portion of the subsidiary equity accounts against the investment. A $350,000 excess cost remains.
(D) Distribute the $350,000 excess cost as follows, in accordance with the determination and distribution of excess schedule:
(D1) Record the current portion of tax loss carryover used this period. It is assumed the parent reduced its provision for the carryover used.
(D2) Record the noncurrent portion of the tax loss carryover.
(D3) Increase the building by $160,000 by lowering accumulated depreciation.
(D3t) Record the deferred tax liability related to the building increase.
(D4) Record the goodwill.
(D4t) Record the deferred tax liability applicable to goodwill.
(A3) Record the annual increase in building depreciation; $160,000 net increase in the building divided by its 20-year life equals $8,000.
(A3t) Reduce the provision for tax account by 30% of the increase in depreciation expense ($2,400).

Subsidiary Sunstran Company Income Distribution

		Internally generated net income	$ 105,000
		Adjusted income	$ 105,000
		NCI share	× 20%
		NCI	**$ 21,000**

Parent Paro Company Income Distribution

Building depreciation **(A3)**	$ 8,000	Internally generated net income	$ 584 000
Current tax carryover **(D1)**	24,000	80% × Sunstran Company adjusted income of $105,000	84,000
		Decrease in provision for tax: (A3t)	**2,400**
		Controlling interest	**$638,400**

UNDERSTANDING THE ISSUES

1. A parent company paid $400,000 for a 100% interest in a subsidiary. At the end of the first year, the subsidiary reported net income of $30,000 and paid $5,000 in dividends. The price paid reflected understated equipment of $50,000, which will be amortized over 10 years. What would be the subsidiary income reported on the parent's unconsolidated income statement, and what would the parent's investment balance be at the end of the first year under each of these methods?

   a. The simple equity method
   b. The sophisticated equity method
   c. The cost method

2. What is meant by date alignment? Does it exist on the consolidated worksheet under the following methods, and if not, how is it created prior to elimination of the investment account under each of these methods?

   a. The simple equity method
   b. The sophisticated equity method
   c. The cost method

3. What is the noncontrolling share of consolidated net income? Does it reflect adjustments based on fair values at the purchase date? How has it been displayed in income statements in the past, and how should it be displayed?

4. A parent company purchased an 80% interest in a subsidiary on July 1, 20X1. The subsidiary reported net income of $60,000 for 20X1, earned evenly during the year. The parent's net income, exclusive of any income of the subsidiary, was $140,000. The price paid for the subsidiary exceeded book value by $100,000. The entire difference was attributed to a patent with a 10-year life.

   a. What is consolidated net income for 20X1?
   b. What is the noncontrolling share of net income for 20X1?

5. A parent company purchased an 80% interest in a subsidiary on January 1, 20X1, at a price high enough to result in goodwill. Included in the assets of the subsidiary are inventory with a book value of $50,000 and a fair value of $60,000 and equipment with a book value of $100,000 and a fair value of $150,000. The equipment has a 5-year remaining life. What impact would the inventory and equipment, acquired in the purchase, have on consolidated net income in 20X1 and 20X2?

6. You are working on a consolidated trial balance of a parent and an 80%-owned subsidiary. What components will enter into the total noncontrolling interest, and how will it be displayed in the consolidated balance sheet?

7. It seems as if consolidated net income is always less than the sum of the parent's and subsidiary's separately calculated net incomes. Is it possible that the consolidated net income of the two affiliated companies could actually *exceed* the sum of their individual net incomes?

8. How would push-down accounting simplify consolidated worksheet procedures?

EXERCISES

Exercise 1 *(LO 1)* **Compare alternative methods for recording income.** Cooke Company purchased an 80% interest in Hill Company common stock for $360,000 cash on January 1, 20X1. At that time, Hill Company had the following balance sheet:

Assets		Liabilities and Equity	
Current assets	$ 60,000	Accounts payable	$ 60,000
Land	100,000	Common stock ($5 par)	50,000
Equipment	350,000	Paid-in capital in excess of par	100,000
Accumulated depreciation	(150,000)	Retained earnings	150,000
Total assets	$ 360,000	Total liabilities and equity	$360,000

Appraisals indicated that accounts are fairly stated except for the equipment which has a fair value of $225,000 and a remaining life of five years. Any remaining excess is goodwill.

Hill Company experienced the following changes in retained earnings during 20X1 and 20X2:

Retained earnings, January 1, 20X1		$150,000
Net income, 20X1	$ 60,000	
Dividends paid in 20X1	(10,000)	50,000
Balance, December 31, 20X1		$200,000
Net income, 20X2	$ 40,000	
Dividends paid in 20X2	(10,000)	30,000
Balance, December 31, 20X2		$230,000

Prepare a determination and distribution of excess schedule for the investment in Hill Company. Prepare journal entries that Cooke Company would make on its books to record income earned and/or dividends received on its investment in Hill Company during 20X1 and 20X2 under the following methods: simple equity, sophisticated equity, and cost.

Exercise 2 *(LO 1)* **Alternative investment models, more complex D&D.** Mast Corporation purchased a 75% interest in the common stock of Shaw Company on January 1, 20X4, for $462,500 cash. Shaw had the following balance sheet on that date:

Assets		Liabilities and Equity	
Current assets	$ 80,000	Current liabilities	$ 50,000
Inventory	40,000	Common stock ($5 par)	50,000
Land	100,000	Paid-in capital in excess of par	150,000
Buildings and equipment (net)	200,000	Retained earnings	200,000
Patent	30,000		
Total assets	$450,000	Total liabilities and equity	$450,000

Appraisals indicated that the book values for inventory, buildings and equipment, and patent are below fair values. The inventory had a fair value of $50,000 and was sold during 20X4. The buildings and equipment have an appraised fair value of $300,000 and a remaining life of 20 years. The patent, which has a 10-year life, has an estimated fair value of $50,000. Any remaining excess is goodwill.

Shaw Company reported the following income earned and dividends paid during 20X4 and 20X5:

Retained earnings, January 1, 20X4		$200,000
Net income, 20X4	$ 70,000	
Dividends paid in 20X4	(20,000)	50,000
Balance, December 31, 20X4		$250,000
Net income, 20X5	$ 48,000	
Dividends paid in 20X5	(20,000)	28,000
Balance, December 31, 20X5		$278,000

Prepare a determination and distribution of excess schedule for the investment in Shaw Company and determine the balance in the Investment in Shaw Company on Mast Company's books as of December 31, 20X5, under the following methods that could be used by the parent, Mast Company: simple equity, sophisticated equity, and cost.

Exercise 3 *(LO 2)* **Equity method, first year, eliminations, statements.** Pepper Company purchased an 80% interest in Salt Company for $250,000 in cash on January 1, 20X1, when Salt Company had the following balance sheet:

Assets		Liabilities and Equity	
Current assets	$100,000	Current liabilities	$ 50,000
Depreciable fixed assets	200,000	Common stock ($10 par).	100,000
		Retained earnings	150,000
Total assets.	$300,000	Total liabilities and equity . . .	$300,000

Any excess of the price paid over book value is attributable only to the fixed assets, which have a 10-year remaining life. Pepper Company uses the simple equity method to record its investment in Salt Company.

The following trial balances of the two companies were prepared on December 31, 20X1:

	Pepper	Salt
Current Assets	60,000	130,000
Depreciable Fixed Assets	400,000	200,000
Accumulated Depreciation	(106,000)	(20,000)
Investment in Salt Company	266,000	
Current Liabilities.	(60,000)	(40,000)
Common Stock ($10 par)	(300,000)	(100,000)
Retained Earnings, January 1, 20X1.	(200,000)	(150,000)
Sales	(150,000)	(100,000)
Expenses	110,000	75,000
Subsidiary Income.	(20,000)	
Dividends Declared.		5,000
Total.	0	0

1. Prepare a determination and distribution of excess schedule for the investment.
2. Prepare all the eliminations and adjustments that would be made on the 20X1 consolidated worksheet.
3. Prepare the 20X1 consolidated income statement and its related income distribution schedules.
4. Prepare the 20X1 consolidated balance sheet.

Exercise 4 *(LO 2)* **Equity method, second year, eliminations, statements.** The trial balances of Pepper and Salt companies of Exercise 3 for December 31, 20X2, are presented as follows:

	Pepper	Salt
Current Assets	152,000	115,000
Depreciable Fixed Assets	400,000	200,000
Accumulated Depreciation	(130,000)	(40,000)
Investment in Salt Company	270,000	
Current Liabilities.	(80,000)	
Common Stock ($10 par)	(300,000)	(100,000)

(continued)

	Pepper	Salt
Retained Earnings, January 1, 20X2	(260,000)	(170,000)
Sales	(200,000)	(100,000)
Expenses	160,000	85,000
Subsidiary Income	(12,000)	
Dividends Declared		10,000
Total	0	0

Pepper Company continued to use the simple equity method.

1. Prepare all the eliminations and adjustments that would be made on the 20X2 consolidated worksheet.
2. Prepare the 20X2 consolidated income statement and its related income distribution schedules.

Exercise 5 *(LO 4)* **Sophisticated equity method, first year, eliminations, statements.** *(Note: Read carefully. This is not the same as Exercise 3.)* Pepper Company purchased an 80% interest in Salt Company for $250,000 on January 1, 20X1, when Salt Company had the following balance sheet:

Assets		Liabilities and Equity	
Current assets	$100,000	Current liabilities	$ 50,000
Depreciable fixed assets	200,000	Common stock ($10 par)	100,000
		Retained earnings	150,000
Total assets	$300,000	Total liabilities and equity	$300,000

Any excess of the price paid over book value is attributable only to the fixed assets, which have a 10-year remaining life. Pepper uses the sophisticated equity method to record the investment in Salt Company.

The following trial balances of the two companies were prepared on December 31, 20X1:

	Pepper	Salt
Current Assets	60,000	130,000
Depreciable Fixed Assets	400,000	200,000
Accumulated Depreciation	(106,000)	(20,000)
Investment in Salt Company	261,000	
Current Liabilities	(60,000)	(40,000)
Common Stock ($10 par)	(300,000)	(100,000)
Retained Earnings, January 1, 20X1	(200,000)	(150,000)
Sales	(150,000)	(100,000)
Expenses	110,000	75,000
Subsidiary Income (from Salt Company)	(15,000)	
Dividends Declared		5,000
Total	0	0

1. If you did not solve Exercise 3, prepare a determination and distribution of excess schedule for the investment.
2. Prepare all the eliminations and adjustments that would be made on the 20X1 consolidated worksheet.
3. If you did not solve Exercise 3, prepare the 20X1 consolidated income statement and its related income distribution schedule.
4. If you did not solve Exercise 3, prepare the 20X1 consolidated balance sheet.

Exercise 6 *(LO 4)* **Sophisticated equity method, second year, eliminations, statements.** The trial balances of Pepper and Salt companies of Exercise 5 for December 31, 20X2, are presented as follows:

	Pepper	Salt
Current Assets	152,000	115,000
Depreciable Fixed Assets	400,000	200,000
Accumulated Depreciation	(130,000)	(40,000)
Investment in Salt Company	260,000	
Current Liabilities	(80,000)	
Common Stock ($10 par)	(300,000)	(100,000)
Retained Earnings, January 1, 20X2	(255,000)	(170,000)
Sales	(200,000)	(100,000)
Expenses	160,000	85,000
Subsidiary Income (from Salt Company)	(7,000)	
Dividends Declared		10,000
Total	0	0

Pepper Company continued to use the sophisticated equity method.

1. Prepare all the eliminations and adjustments that would be made on the 20X2 consolidated worksheet.
2. If you did not solve Exercise 4, prepare the 20X2 consolidated income statement and its related income distribution schedules.

Exercise 7 *(LO 3)* **Cost method, first year, eliminations, statements.** *(Note: Read carefully. This is not the same as Exercise 3 or 5.)* Pepper Company purchased an 80% interest in Salt Company for $250,000 in cash on January 1, 20X1, when Salt Company had the following balance sheet:

Assets		Liabilities and Equity	
Current assets	$100,000	Current liabilities	$ 50,000
Depreciable fixed assets	200,000	Common stock ($10 par)	100,000
		Retained earnings	150,000
Total assets	$300,000	Total liabilities and equity	$300,000

Any excess of the price paid over book value is attributable only to the fixed assets, which have a 10-year remaining life. Pepper Company uses the cost method to record its investment in Salt Company.

The following trial balances of the two companies were prepared on December 31, 20X1:

	Pepper	Salt
Current Assets	60,000	130,000
Depreciable Fixed Assets	400,000	200,000
Accumulated Depreciation	(106,000)	(20,000)
Investment in Salt Company	250,000	
Current Liabilities	(60,000)	(40,000)
Common Stock ($10 par)	(300,000)	(100,000)
Retained Earnings, January 1, 20X2	(200,000)	(150,000)
Sales	(150,000)	(100,000)
Expenses	110,000	75,000
Dividend Income (from Salt Company)	(4,000)	
Dividends Declared		5,000
Total	0	0

1. If you did not solve Exercise 3 or 5, prepare a determination and distribution of excess schedule for the investment.
2. Prepare all the eliminations and adjustments that would be made on the 20X1 consolidated worksheet.
3. If you did not solve Exercise 3 or 5, prepare the 20X1 consolidated income statement and its related income distribution schedules.
4. If you did not solve Exercise 3 or 5, prepare the 20X1 consolidated balance sheet.

Exercise 8 *(LO 3)* **Cost method, second year, eliminations, statements.** The trial balances of Pepper and Salt companies of Exercise 7 for December 31, 20X2, are presented as follows:

	Pepper	Salt
Current Assets	152,000	115,000
Depreciable Fixed Assets	400,000	200,000
Accumulated Depreciation	(130,000)	(40,000)
Investment in Salt Company	250,000	
Current Liabilities	(80,000)	
Common Stock ($10 par)	(300,000)	(100,000)
Retained Earnings, January 1, 20X2	(244,000)	(170,000)
Sales	(200,000)	(100,000)
Expenses	160,000	85,000
Dividend Income (from Salt Company)	(8,000)	
Dividends Declared		10,000
Total	0	0

Pepper Company continued to use the cost method.

1. Prepare all the eliminations and adjustments that would be made on the 20X2 consolidated worksheet.
2. If you did not solve Exercise 4 or 6, prepare the 20X2 consolidated income statement and its related income distribution schedules.

Exercise 9 *(LO 5)* **Amortization procedures, several years.** Walt Company purchased an 80% interest in Mitchell Company common stock on January 1, 20X1. Appraisals of Mitchell's assets and liabilities were performed, and Walt ended up paying an amount that was greater than the fair value of Mitchell's net assets. The following determination and distribution of excess schedule was created on December 31, 20X1, to assist in putting together the consolidated financial statements:

Determination and Distribution of Excess Schedule			
Price paid for investment		$1,100,000	
Less book value interest acquired:			
Common stock	$ 100,000		
Paid-in capital in excess of par	150,000		
Retained earnings	350,000		
Total equity	$ 600,000		
Interest acquired	× 80%	480,000	
Excess of cost over book value (debit)		$ 620,000	
Adjustments to first priority accounts:			Life
Inventory		$ 5,000	1
Investments		20,000	5
Land		40,000	—
Bonds payable		10,000	5

Buildings (net)	200,000	20
Equipment (net)	138,000	5
Patent	18,000	10
Trademark	16,000	10
Goodwill	173,000	
Total adjustments	$ 620,000	

Prepare an amortization schedule for the years 20X1, 20X2, 20X3, and 20X4.

Exercise 10 *(LO 6)* **Purchase during the year, elimination entries, income statement.** Karen Company had the following balance sheet on January 1, 20X2:

Assets		Liabilities and Equity	
Current assets	$200,000	Current liabilities	$100,000
Equipment (net)	300,000	Common stock ($10 par)	100,000
		Retained earnings	300,000
Total assets	$500,000	Total liabilities and equity	$500,000

Between January 1 and July 1, 20X2, Karen Company estimated its net income to be $30,000. On July 1, 20X2, Neiman Company purchased 80% of the outstanding common stock of Karen Company for $310,000. Any excess of book value over cost was attributed to the equipment which had an estimated 5-year life. Karen Company did not close its books on July 1.

On December 31, 20X2, Neiman Company and Karen Company prepared the following trial balances:

	Neiman	Karen
Current Assets	220,000	250,000
Equipment	500,000	300,000
Accumulated Depreciation—Equipment	(140,000)	(20,000)
Investment in Karen Company	310,000	
Current Liabilities	(200,000)	(70,000)
Common Stock ($10 par)	(200,000)	(100,000)
Retained Earnings, Jan. 1, 20X2	(430,000)	(300,000)
Sales	(300,000)	(200,000)
Cost of Goods Sold	180,000	90,000
General Expenses	60,000	50,000
Total	0	0

1. Prepare a determination and distribution of excess schedule for the investment.
2. Prepare all the eliminations and adjustments that would be made on the December 31, 20X2, consolidated worksheet.
3. Prepare the 20X2 consolidated income statement and its related income distribution schedules.

Exercise 11 *(LO 7)* **Impairment loss.** The Albers Company purchased an 80% interest in the Baker Company on January 1, 20X1, for $850,000. The following determination and distribution of excess schedule was prepared at the time of purchase:

Price paid		$850,000
Stockholders' equity	$600,000	
Interest acquired	× 80%	480,000
Excess of cost over book value		$370,000

(continued)

Attributed to:	
Building, 80% × $200,000 undervaluation, 20-year life.	160,000
Goodwill	$210,000

Albers used the simple equity method for its investment in Baker. As of December 31, 20X5, Baker had earned $200,000 since it was purchased by Albers. Baker paid no dividends during 20X1–20X5.

On December 31, 20X5, the following values were available:

Fair value of Baker's identifiable net assets (100%)	$ 900,000
Estimated fair value of Baker Company (net of liabilities)	1,000,000

Determine if goodwill is impaired. If not, explain your reasoning. If so, calculate the adjustment needed to the investment account. (Albers will directly adjust its investment account for any impairment losses.)

APPENDIX EXERCISES

Exercise 3B-1 *(LO 9)* **D&D for nontaxable exchange.** Rainman Corporation is considering the acquisition of Lamb Company through the purchase of Lamb's common stock. Rainman Corporation will issue 20,000 shares of its $5 par common stock, with a fair value of $25 per share, in exchange for all 10,000 outstanding shares of Lamb Company's voting common stock.

The acquisition meets the criteria for a tax-free exchange as to the seller. Because of this, Rainman Corporation will be limited for future tax returns to the book value of the depreciable assets. Rainman Corporation falls into the 30% tax bracket.

The appraisal of the assets of Lamb Company showed that the inventory has a fair value of $120,000, and the depreciable fixed assets have a fair value of $270,000. Any excess is attributed to goodwill. Lamb Company had the following balance sheet just before the acquisition:

Lamb Company
Balance Sheet
December 31, 20X5

Assets		Liabilities and Equity		
Cash	$ 40,000	Current liabilities		$ 70,000
Accounts receivable	150,000	Bonds payable		100,000
Inventory	100,000	Stockholders' equity:		
Depreciable fixed assets	210,000	Common stock ($10 par). . .	$100,000	
		Retained earnings	230,000	330,000
Total assets	$500,000	Total liabilities and equity		$500,000

1. Record the acquisition of Lamb Company by Rainman Corporation.
2. Prepare a determination and distribution of excess schedule.
3. Prepare the elimination entries that would be made on the consolidated worksheet.

Exercise 3B-2 *(LO 9)* **D&D and income statement for nontaxable exchange.** Lucy Company issued securities with a fair value of $465,000 for a 90% interest in Desmond Company on January 1, 20X1, at which time Desmond Company had the following balance sheet:

Assets		Liabilities and Equity	
Accounts receivable	$ 50,000	Current liabilities	$ 70,000
Inventory	80,000	Common stock ($5 par)	100,000
Land	20,000	Paid-in capital in excess of par	130,000
Building (net)	200,000	Retained earnings	50,000
Total assets	$350,000	Total liabilities and equity	$350,000

It was believed that the inventory and the building were undervalued by $20,000 and $50,000, respectively. The building had a 10-year remaining life; the inventory on hand January 1, 20X1, was sold during the year. The deferred tax liability associated with the asset revaluations was to be reflected in the consolidated statements. Each company has an income tax rate of 30%. Any remaining excess is goodwill.

The separate income statements of the two companies prepared for 20X1 are as follows:

	Lucy	Desmond
Sales	$ 400,000	$150,000
Cost of goods sold	(200,000)	(90,000)
Gross profit	$ 200 000	$ 60 000
General expenses	(50 000)	(25 000)
Depreciation expense	(60 000)	(15,000)
Operating income	$ 90 000	$ 20 000
Subsidiary income	18,000	
Net income before income tax	$ 108,000	$ 20,000
Provision for tax (does not include tax on subsidiary income)	(27,000)	(6,000)
Net income	$ 81,000	$ 14,000

1. Prepare a determination and distribution of excess schedule for the investment.
2. Prepare the 20X1 consolidated income statement and its related income distribution schedules.

Exercise 3B-3 *(LO 9)* **D&D for nontaxable exchange with tax loss carryforward.** Palto issued 20,000 of its $5 par value common stock shares, with a fair value of $35 each, for a 100% interest in the Sarge Company on January 1, 20X1. The balance sheet of the Sarge Company on that date was as follows:

Assets		Liabilities and Equity	
Current assets	$100,000	Current liabilities	$ 50,000
Buildings and equipment (net)	300,000	Common stock, par	250,000
		Retained earnings	100,000
Total assets	$400,000	Total liabilities and equity	$400,000

On the purchase date, the buildings and equipment were understated $50,000 and had a remaining life of 10 years. Sarge had tax loss carryovers of $200,000. They are believed to be fully realizable at a tax rate of 30%. $40,000 of the tax loss carryovers will be utilized in 20X1. The purchase is a tax-free exchange. The tax rate applicable to all transactions is 30%. Any remaining excess is attributed to goodwill.

Prepare a determination and distribution of excess schedule for this investment.

PROBLEMS

Problem 3-1 *(LO 1)* **Alternative investment account methods, effect on eliminations.** On January 1, 20X1, Peter Company purchased an 80% interest in Saul Company by issuing 10,000 of its common stock shares with a par value of $10 per share and a fair value of $72 per share. The direct acquisition costs were $20,000. At the time of the purchase, Saul had the following balance sheet:

Assets		Liabilities and Equity	
Current assets	$100,000	Current liabilities	$ 80,000
Investments	150,000	Bonds payable	250,000
Land	120,000	Common stock ($10 par)	100,000
Building (net)	350,000	Paid-in capital in excess of par	200,000
Equipment (net)	160,000	Retained earnings	250,000
Total assets	$880,000	Total liabilities and equity	$880,000

Appraisals indicate that book values are representative of fair values with the exception of land and buildings. The land has a fair value of $190,000, and the building is appraised at $450,000. The building has an estimated remaining life of 20 years. Any remaining excess is goodwill.

The following summary of Saul's retained earnings applies to 20X1 and 20X2:

Balance, January 1, 20X1	$250,000
Net income for 20X1	60,000
Dividends paid in 20X1	(10,000)
Balance, December 31, 20X1	$300,000
Net income for 20X2	45,000
Dividends paid in 20X2	(10,000)
Balance, December 31, 20X2	$335,000

Required ▶ ▶ ▶ ▶ ▶

1. Prepare a determination and distribution of excess schedule for the investment in Saul Company. As a part of the schedule, indicate annual amortization of excess adjustments.
2. For 20X1 and 20X2, prepare the entries that Peter would make concerning its investment in Saul under the simple equity, sophisticated equity, and cost methods. It is suggested that you set up a worksheet with side-by-side columns for each method so that you can easily compare the entries.
3. For 20X1 and 20X2, prepare the worksheet elimination that would be made on a consolidated worksheet under the simple equity, sophisticated equity, and cost methods. It is suggested that you set up a worksheet with side-by-side columns for each method so that you can easily compare the entries.

template cd

Problem 3-2 *(LO 2)* **Equity method adjustments, consolidated worksheet.** On January 1, 20X1, Peres Company purchased 80% of the common stock of Soil Company for $308,000. On this date, Soll had common stock, other paid-in capital, and retained earnings of $50,000, $100,000, and $150,000, respectively. Net income and dividends for two years for Soll Company were as follows:

	20X1	20X2
Net income	$60,000	$90,000
Dividends	20,000	30,000

On January 1, 20X1, the only tangible assets of Soll that were undervalued were inventory and the building. Inventory, for which FIFO is used, was worth $10,000 more than cost. The inventory was sold in 20X1. The building, which is worth $25,000 more than book value, has a remaining life of 10 years, and straight-line depreciation is used. The remaining excess of cost over book value is attributable to goodwill.

◀◀◀◀◀ **Required**

1. Using this information or the information in the following trial balances, prepare a determination and distribution of excess schedule.
2. Peres Company carries the investment in Soll Company under the simple equity method. In general journal form, record the entries that would be made to apply the equity method in 20X1 and 20X2.
3. Compute the balance that should appear in Investment in Soll Company and in Soll Income on December 31, 20X2 (the second year). Fill in these amounts on Peres Company's trial balance for 20X2.
4. Complete a worksheet for consolidated financial statements for 20X2. Include columns for eliminations and adjustments, consolidated income, NCI, controlling retained earnings, and balance sheet.

	Peres Company	Soll Company
Inventory, December 31	100,000	50,000
Other Current Assets	148,000	180,000
Investment in Soll Company	Note 1	
Land	50,000	50,000
Buildings and Equipment	350,000	320,000
Accumulated Depreciation	(100,000)	(60,000)
Goodwill		
Other Intangibles	20,000	
Current Liabilities	(120,000)	(40,000)
Bonds Payable		(100,000)
Other Long-Term Liabilities	(200,000)	
Common Stock, P Company	(200,000)	
Other Paid-In Capital, P Company	(100,000)	
Retained Earnings, P Company	(214,000)	
Common Stock, S Company		(50,000)
Other Paid-In Capital, S Company		(100,000)
Retained Earnings, S Company		(190,000)
Net Sales	(520,000)	(450,000)
Cost of Goods Sold	300,000	260,000
Operating Expenses	120,000	100,000
Soll Income	Note 1	
Dividends Declared, P Company	50,000	
Dividends Declared, S Company		30,000

Note 1: To be calculated.

Problem 3-3 *(LO 4)* **Sophisticated equity method adjustments, consolidated worksheet.** (This is the same as Problem 3-2, except the sophisticated equity method is used.) On January 1, 20X1, Peres Company purchased 80% of the common stock of Soll Company for $308,000. On this date, Soll had common stock, other paid-in capital, and retained earnings of $50,000, $100,000, and $150,000, respectively. Net income and dividends for two years for Soll Company were as follows:

template cd

	20X1	20X2
Net income	$60,000	$90,000
Dividends	20,000	30,000

On January 1, 20X1, the only tangible assets of Soll that were undervalued were inventory and the building. Inventory, for which FIFO is used, was worth $10,000 more than cost. The inventory was sold in 20X1. The building, which is worth $25,000 more than book value, has a remaining life of 10 years, and straight-line depreciation is used. The remaining excess of cost over book value is attributable to goodwill.

Required ▶ ▶ ▶ ▶ ▶

1. Using this information or the information in the following trial balances, prepare a determination and distribution of excess schedule.
2. Peres Company carries the investment in Soll Company under the sophisticated equity method. In general journal form, record the entries that would be made to apply the equity method in 20X1 and 20X2.
3. Compute the balance that should appear in Investment in Soll Company and in Soll Income on December 31, 20X2 (the second year). Fill in these amounts on Peres Company's trial balance for 20X2.
4. Complete a worksheet for consolidated financial statements for 20X2. Include columns for eliminations and adjustments, consolidated income, NCI, controlling retained earnings, and balance sheet.

	Peres Company	Soll Company
Inventory, December 31	100,000	50,000
Other Current Assets	148,000	180,000
Investment in Soll Company	Note 1	
Land	50,000	50,000
Buildings and Equipment	350,000	320,000
Accumulated Depreciation	(100,000)	(60,000)
Goodwill		
Other Intangibles	20,000	
Current Liabilities	(120,000)	(40,000)
Bonds Payable		(100,000)
Other Long-Term Liabilities	(200,000)	
Common Stock, P Company	(200, 000)	
Other Paid-In Capital, P Company	(100,000)	
Retained Earnings, P Company	(204, 000)	
Common Stock, S Company		(50,000)
Other Paid-In Capital, S Company		(100,000)
Retained Earnings, S Company		(190,000)
Net Sales	(520, 000)	(450,000)
Cost of Goods Sold	300,000	260,000
Operating Expenses	120,000	100,000
Soll Income	Note 1	
Dividends Declared, P Company	50,000	
Dividends Declared, S Company		30,000

Note 1: To be calculated.

Problem 3-4 *(LO 3)* **Cost method, consolidated statements.** The trial balances of Chango Company and its subsidiary, Lhasa Inc., are as follows on December 31, 20X3:

	Chango	Lhasa
Current Assets	530,000	130,000
Depreciable Fixed Assets	1,805,000	440,000
Accumulated Depreciation	(405,000)	(70,000)
Investment in Lhasa Inc.	460,000	
Liabilities	(900,000)	(225,000)
Common Stock ($1 par)	(220,000)	
Common Stock ($5 par)		(50,000)
Paid-In Capital in Excess of Par	(1,040,000)	(15,000)
Retained Earnings, January 1, 20X3	(230,000)	(170,000)
Revenues	(460,000)	(210,000)
Expenses	450,000	170,000
Dividends Declared	10,000	
Total	0	0

On January 1, 20X1, Chango Company exchanged 20,000 shares of its common stock, with a fair value of $23 per share, for all the outstanding stock of Lhasa Inc. Any excess of cost over book value was attributed to goodwill. The stockholders' equity of Lhasa Inc. on the purchase date was as follows:

Common stock ($5 par)	$ 50,000
Paid-in capital in excess of par	15,000
Retained earnings	135,000
Total equity	$200,000

◄◄◄◄◄ **Required**

1. Prepare a determination and distribution of excess schedule for the investment.
2. Prepare the 20X3 consolidated statements, including the income statement, retained earnings statement, and balance sheet. (A worksheet is not required.)

Problem 3-5 *(LO 3)* **Cost method, worksheet, statements.** Bell Corporation purchased all of the outstanding stock of Stockdon Corporation for $220,000 in cash on January 1, 20X7. On the purchase date, Stockdon Corporation had the following condensed balance sheet:

Assets		Liabilities and Equity	
Cash	$ 60,000	Liabilities	$150,000
Inventory	40,000	Common stock ($10 par)	100,000
Land	120,000	Paid-in capital in excess of par	50,000
Building (net)	180,000	Retained earnings	100,000
Total assets	$400,000	Total liabilities and equity	$400,000

Any excess of book value over cost was attributable to the building, which is currently overstated on Stockdon's books. All other assets and liabilities have book values equal to fair values. The building has an estimated 10-year life with no salvage value.

The trial balances of the two companies on December 31, 20X7, appear as follows:

	Bell	Stockdon
Cash	180,000	143,000
Inventory	60,000	30,000
Land	120,000	120,000
Buildings (net)	600,000	162,000
Investment in Stockdon Corp.	220,000	
Accounts Payable	(405,000)	(210,000)
Common Stock ($3 par)	(300,000)	
Common Stock ($10 par)		(100,000)
Paid-In Capital in Excess of Par	(180,000)	(50,000)
Retained Earnings, Jan. 1, 20X7	(255,000)	(100,000)
Sales	(210,000)	(40,000)
Cost of Goods Sold	120,000	35,000
Other Expenses	45,000	10,000
Dividends Declared	5,000	
Total	0	0

Required ▶ ▶ ▶ ▶ ▶

1. Prepare a determination and distribution of excess schedule for the investment.
2. Prepare the 20X7 consolidated worksheet. Include columns for the eliminations and adjustments, the consolidated income statement, the controlling retained earnings, and the consolidated balance sheet.
3. Prepare the 20X7 consolidated statements, including the income statement, retained earnings statement, and balance sheet.

Problem 3-6 *(LO 2)* **Equity method, 80% interest, worksheet, statements.** Scully Company prepared the following balance sheet on January 1, 20X1:

Assets		Liabilities and Equity	
Current assets	$ 50,000	Liabilities	$140,000
Land	75,000	Common stock ($10 par)	100,000
Buildings	350,000	Paid-in capital in excess of par	120,000
Accumulated depreciation —Buildings	(140,000)	Retained earnings (deficit)	(25,000)
Total assets	$ 335,000	Total liabilities and equity	$335,000

On this date, Prescott Company purchased 8,000 shares of Scully Company's outstanding stock for a total price of $270,000. Also on this date, the buildings were understated by $40,000 and had a 10-year remaining life. Any remaining discrepancy between the price paid and book value was attributed to goodwill. Since the purchase, Prescott Company has used the simple equity method to record the investment and its related income.

Prescott Company and Scully Company have prepared the following separate trial balances on December 31, 20X2:

	Prescott	Scully
Current Assets	180,000	115,000
Land	150,000	75,000
Buildings	590,000	350,000
Accumulated Depreciation—Buildings	(265,000)	(182,000)
Investment in Scully Company	294,000	
Liabilities	(175,000)	(133,000)
Common Stock ($10 par)	(200,000)	(100,000)
Paid-In Capital in Excess of Par		(120,000)

Retained Earnings, Jan. 1, 20X2	(503,000)	15,000
Sales	(360,000)	(120,000)
Cost of Goods Sold	179,000	50,000
Expenses	120,000	45,000
Subsidiary Income	(20,000)	
Dividends Declared	10,000	5,000
Total	0	0

Required

1. Prepare a determination and distribution of excess schedule for the investment.
2. Prepare the 20X2 consolidated worksheet. Include columns for the eliminations and adjustments, the consolidated income statement, the NCI, the controlling retained earnings, and the consolidated balance sheet. Prepare supporting income distribution schedules.
3. Prepare the 20X2 consolidated statements including the income statement, retained earnings statement, and the balance sheet.

Problem 3-7 *(LO 6)* **Interperiod purchase.** Jeter Corporation purchased 80% of the outstanding stock of Summer Company for $275,000 on May 1, 20X1. Summer Company had the following stockholders' equity:

Common stock ($5 par)	$150,000
Retained earnings	50,000
Total equity	$200 000

The fair values of Summer's assets and liabilities agreed with the book values, except for the equipment and the building. The equipment was undervalued by $10,000 and was thought to have a 5-year life; the building was undervalued by $50,000 and was thought to have a 20-year life. The remaining excess of cost over book value is attributable to goodwill. Jeter Corporation uses the simple equity method to record its investments.

Since the purchase date, both firms have operated separately, and no intercompany transactions have occurred. Summer Company did not close its books on the date of acquisition. Therefore, the income amounts in the trial balance reflect amounts earned during the whole year. Income is earned evenly throughout the year.

The separate trial balances of the firms on December 31, 20X1, are as follows:

	Jeter Corp.	Summer Co.
Cash	296,600	97,000
Land	160,000	90,000
Buildings	225,000	135,000
Accumulated Depreciation—Building	(100,000)	(50,000)
Equipment	450,000	150,000
Accumulated Depreciation—Equipment	(115,000)	(60,000)
Investment in Summer Company	284,600	
Liabilities	(480,000)	(150,000)
Common Stock ($100 par)	(400,000)	
Common Stock ($5 par)		(150,000)
Paid-In Capital in Excess of Par	(40,000)	
Retained Earnings, January 1, 20X1	(251,600)	(50,000)
Sales	(460,000)	(120,000)
Cost of Goods Sold	220,000	60,000
Other Expenses	210,000	48,000
Subsidiary Income	(9,600)	
Dividends Declared	10,000	
Total	0	0

Required ▶ ▶ ▶ ▶ ▶

1. Prepare a determination and distribution of excess schedule for the investment.
2. Prepare the 20X1 consolidated worksheet. Include columns for the eliminations and adjustments, the consolidated income statement, the NCI, the controlling retained earnings, and the consolidated balance sheet. Prepare supporting income distribution schedules as well.
3. Prepare the 20X1 consolidated statements, including the income statement, retained earnings statement, and balance sheet.

Problem 3-8 *(LO 3, 5)* **Cost method, 80% interest, worksheet, several adjustments.** Detner International purchased 80% of the outstanding stock of Hughes Company for $1,600,000 plus $8,000 of direct acquisition costs on January 1, 20X5. At the purchase date, the inventory, the equipment, and the patents of Hughes Company had fair values of $10,000, $50,000, and $100,000, respectively, in excess of their book values. The other assets and liabilities of Hughes Company had book values equal to their fair values. The inventory was sold during the month following the purchase. The two companies agreed that the equipment had a remaining life of eight years and the patents, 10 years. On the purchase date, the owners' equity of Hughes Company was as follows:

Common stock ($10 stated value)	$1,000,000
Additional paid-in capital	300,000
Retained earnings	400,000
Total equity	$1,700,000

During the next two years, Hughes Company had income and paid dividends as follows:

	Income	Dividends
20X5	$ 90,000	$30,000
20X6	150,000	30,000

The trial balances of the two corporations as of December 31, 20X7, are as follows:

	Detner International	Hughes Company
Current Assets	624,000	505,000
Equipment (net)	1,320,000	940,000
Patents	100,000	35,000
Other Assets	1,620,000	730,000
Investment in Hughes	1,608,000	
Accounts Payable	(658,000)	(205,000)
Common Stock ($5 par)	(2,000,000)	
Common Stock ($10 par)		(1,000,000)
Paid-In Capital in Excess of Par	(1,200,000)	(300,000)
Retained Earnings, Jan. 1, 20X7	(1,255,000)	(580,000)
Sales	(905,000)	(425,000)
Cost of Goods Sold	470,000	170,000
Other Expenses	250,000	100,000
Dividend Income	(24,000)	
Dividends Declared	50,000	30,000
Total	0	0

Required ▶ ▶ ▶ ▶ ▶

The remaining excess of cost over book value is attributable to goodwill.

1. Prepare the original determination and distribution of excess schedule for the investment.
2. Prepare the 20X7 consolidated worksheet for December 31, 20X7. Include columns for the

eliminations and adjustments, the consolidated income statement, the controlling retained earnings, and the consolidated balance sheet.

Use the following information for Problems 3-9 through 3-12:
Pcraft Corporation builds powerboats. On January 1, 20X1, Pcraft acquired Sailair Corporation, a company that manufactures sailboats. Pcraft paid cash in exchange for Sailair common stock. Sailair had the following balance sheet on January 1, 20X1:

Sailair Corporation
Balance Sheet
January 1, 20X1

Assets		Liabilities and Equity	
Accounts receivable	$ 32,000	Current liabilities	$ 90,000
Inventory	40,000	Bonds payable	100,000
Land	60,000	Common stock, $1 par	10,000
Buildings	250,000	Paid-in capital in excess of par	90,000
Accumulated depreciation	(50,000)	Retained earnings	112,000
Equipment	100,000		
Accumulated depreciation	(30,000)		
Total assets	$402,000	Total liabilities and equity	$402,000

An appraisal indicated that the following assets and liabilities had fair values that differed from their book values:

Inventory (sold during 20X1)	$ 38,000
Land	150,000
Buildings (20-year life)	300,000
Equipment (5-year life)	100,000
Bonds payable (5-year life)	96,000

Any remaining excess is attributed to goodwill.

Problem 3-9 *(LO 2, 5)* **100%, equity method worksheet, several adjustments, third year.** Refer to the preceding information for Pcraft's acquisition of Sailair's common stock. Assume that Pcraft paid $500,000 for 100% of Sailair common stock. Pcraft uses the simple equity method to account for its investment in Sailair. Pcraft and Sailair had the following trial balances on December 31, 20X3:

	Pcraft	Sailair
Cash	80,000	60,000
Accounts Receivable	90,000	55,000
Inventory	120,000	86,000
Land	100,000	60,000
Investment in Sailair	595,000	
Buildings	800,000	300,000
Accumulated Depreciation	(220,000)	(80,000)
Equipment	150,000	100,000
Accumulated Depreciation	(90,000)	(72,000)

(continued)

	Pcraft	Sailair
Current Liabilities	(60,000)	(102,000)
Bonds Payable		(100,000)
Common Stock	(100,000)	(10,000)
Paid-In Capital in Excess of Par	(900,000)	(90,000)
Retained Earnings, Jan. 1, 20X3	(385,000)	(182,000)
Sales	(800,000)	(350,000)
Cost of Goods Sold	450,000	210,000
Depreciation Expense—Buildings	30,000	15,000
Depreciation Expense—Equipment	15,000	14,000
Other Expenses	140,000	68,000
Interest Expense		8,000
Subsidiary Income	(35,000)	
Dividends Declared	20,000	10,000
Total	0	0

Required ▶ ▶ ▶ ▶ ▶

1. Prepare a zone analysis and a determination and distribution of excess schedule for the investment in Sailair.
2. Complete a consolidated worksheet for Pcraft Corporation and its subsidiary Sailair Corporation as of December 31, 20X3. Prepare supporting amortization and income distribution schedules.

template cd

Problem 3-10 *(LO 3, 5)* **100%, cost method worksheet, several adjustments, third year.** Refer to the preceding information for Pcraft's acquisition of Sailair's common stock. Assume that Pcraft paid $500,000 for 100% of Sailair common stock. Pcraft uses the cost method to account for its investment in Sailair. Pcraft and Sailair had the following trial balances on December 31, 20X3:

	Pcraft	Sailair
Cash	80,000	60,000
Accounts Receivable	90,000	55,000
Inventory	120,000	86,000
Land	100,000	60,000
Investment in Sailair	500,000	
Buildings	800,000	300,000
Accumulated Depreciation	(220,000)	(80,000)
Equipment	150,000	100,000
Accumulated Depreciation	(90,000)	(72,000)
Current Liabilities	(60,000)	(102,000)
Bonds Payable		(100,000)
Common Stock	(100,000)	(10,000)
Paid-In Capital in Excess of Par	(900,000)	(90,000)
Retained Earnings, Jan. 1, 20X3	(315,000)	(182,000)
Sales	(800,000)	(350,000)
Cost of Goods Sold	450,000	210,000
Depreciation Expense—Buildings	30,000	15,000
Depreciation Expense—Equipment	15,000	14,000
Other Expenses	140,000	68,000
Interest Expense		8,000
Dividend Income	(10,000)	
Dividends Declared	20,000	10,000
Total	0	0

◄◄◄◄◄ **Required**

1. Prepare a zone analysis and a determination and distribution of excess schedule for the investment in Sailair.
2. Complete a consolidated worksheet for Pcraft Corporation and its subsidiary Sailair Corporation as of December 31, 20X3. Prepare supporting amortization and income distribution schedules.

Problem 3-11 *(LO 3, 5)* **70%, cost method worksheet, several adjustments, first year.** Refer to the preceding information for Pcraft's acquisition of Sailair's common stock. Assume that Pcraft paid $400,000 for 70% of Sailair common stock. Pcraft uses the cost method to account for its investment in Sailair. Pcraft and Sailair had the following trial balances on December 31, 20X1:

template cd

	Pcraft	Sailair
Cash	177,000	31,000
Accounts Receivable	80,000	35,000
Inventory	90,000	52,000
Land	100,000	60,000
Investment in Sailair	400,000	
Buildings	800,000	250,000
Accumulated Depreciation	(200,000)	(60,000)
Equipment	150,000	100,000
Accumulated Depreciation	(75,000)	(44,000)
Current Liabilities	(50,000)	(88,000)
Bonds Payable		(100,000)
Common Stock	(100,000)	(10,000)
Paid-In Capital in Excess of Par	(900,000)	(90,000)
Retained Earnings, Jan. 1, 20X1	(300,000)	(112,000)
Sales	(750,000)	(300,000)
Cost of Goods Sold	400,000	180,000
Depreciation Expense—Buildings	30,000	10,000
Depreciation Expense—Equipment	15,000	14,000
Other Expenses	120,000	54,000
Interest Expense		8,000
Dividend Income	(7,000)	
Dividends Declared	20,000	10,000
Total	0	0

◄◄◄◄◄ **Required**

1. Prepare a zone analysis and a determination and distribution of excess schedule for the investment in Sailair.
2. Complete a consolidated worksheet for Pcraft Corporation and its subsidiary Sailair Corporation as of December 31, 20X1. Prepare supporting amortization and income distribution schedules.

Problem 3-12 *(LO 3, 5)* **70%, cost method worksheet, several adjustments, third Year.** Refer to the preceding information for Pcraft's acquisition of Sailair's common stock. Assume that Pcraft paid $400,000 for 70% of Sailair common stock. Pcraft uses the cost method to account for its investment in Sailair. Pcraft and Sailair had the following trial balances on December 31, 20X3:

template cd

	Pcraft	Sailair
Cash	177,000	60,000
Accounts Receivable	90,000	55,000

(continued)

	Pcraft	Sailair
Inventory	120,000	86,000
Land	100,000	60,000
Investment in Sailair	400,000	
Buildings	800,000	300,000
Accumulated Depreciation	(220,000)	(80,000)
Equipment	150,000	100,000
Accumulated Depreciation	(90,000)	(72,000)
Current Liabilities	(60,000)	(102,000)
Bonds Payable		(100,000)
Common Stock	(100,000)	(10,000)
Paid-In Capital in Excess of Par	(900,000)	(90,000)
Retained Earnings, Jan. 1, 20X3	(315,000)	(182,000)
Sales	(800,000)	(350,000)
Cost of Goods Sold	450,000	210,000
Depreciation Expense—Buildings	30,000	15,000
Depreciation Expense—Equipment	15,000	14,000
Other Expenses	140,000	68,000
Interest Expense		8,000
Dividend Income	(7,000)	
Dividends Declared	20,000	10,000
Total	0	0

Required ▶ ▶ ▶ ▶ ▶

1. Prepare a zone analysis and a determination and distribution of excess schedule for the investment in Sailair.
2. Complete a consolidated worksheet for Pcraft Corporation and its subsidiary Sailair Corporation as of December 31, 20X3. Prepare supporting amortization and income distribution schedules.

template cd

Problem 3-13 *(LO 4, 5)* **100%, sophisticated equity method, several excesses, third year.** Refer to the preceding information for Pcraft's acquisition of Sailair's common stock. Assume that Pcraft paid $500,000 for 100% of Sailair common stock. Pcraft uses the sophisticated equity method to account for its investment in Sailair. Pcraft and Sailair had the following trial balances on December 31, 20X3:

	Pcraft	Sailair
Cash	80,000	60,000
Accounts Receivable	90,000	55,000
Inventory	120,000	86,000
Land	100,000	60,000
Investment in Sailair	561,600	
Buildings	800,000	300,000
Accumulated Depreciation	(220,000)	(80,000)
Equipment	150,000	100,000
Accumulated Depreciation	(90,000)	(72,000)
Current Liabilities	(60,000)	(102,000)
Bonds Payable		(100,000)
Common Stock	(100,000)	(10,000)
Paid-In Capital in Excess of Par	(900,000)	(90,000)
Retained Earnings, Jan. 1, 20X3	(363,400)	(182,000)
Sales	(800,000)	(350,000)
Cost of Goods Sold	450,000	210,000
Depreciation Expense—Buildings	30,000	15,000
Depreciation Expense—Equipment	15,000	14,000

Other Expenses	140,000	68,000
Interest Expense		8,000
Subsidiary Income	(23,200)	
Dividends Declared	20,000	10,000
Total	0	0

1. Prepare a zone analysis and a determination and distribution of excess schedule for the investment in Sailair. ◄◄◄◄◄ **Required**
2. Complete a consolidated worksheet for Pcraft Corporation and its subsidiary Sailair Corporation as of December 31, 20X3. Prepare supporting amortization and income distribution schedules.

Use the following information for Problems 3-14 through 3-18:

Fast Cool Company and HD Air Company are both manufacturers of air conditioning equipment. On January 1, 20X1, Fast Cool acquired the common stock of HD Air by exchanging its own $1 par, $20 fair value common stock. On the date of acquisition, HD Air had the following balance sheet:

HD Air Company
Balance Sheet
January 1, 20X1

Assets		Liabilities and Equity	
Accounts receivable	$ 40,000	Current liabilities	$ 30,000
Inventory	60,000	Mortgage payable	200,000
Land	50,000	Common stock, $1 par	100,000
Buildings	400,000	Paid-in capital in excess of par	200,000
Accumulated depreciation	(50,000)	Retained earnings	180,000
Equipment	150,000		
Accumulated depreciation	(30,000)		
Patent (net)	40,000		
Goodwill	50,000		
Total assets	$710,000	Total liabilities and equity	$710,000

Fast Cool requested that an appraisal be done to determine whether the book value of HD Air's net assets reflected their fair values. The appraiser determined that several intangible assets existed, although they were unrecorded. If the intangible assets did not have an observable market, the appraiser estimated their value. The following are the fair values and estimates determined by the appraiser:

Inventory (sold during 20X1)	$ 65,000
Land	100,000
Buildings (20-year life)	500,000
Equipment (5-year life)	100,000
Patent (5-year life)	50,000
Mortgage payable (5-year life)	205,000
Production backlog (2-year life)	10,000

Any remaining excess is attributed to goodwill.

Problem 3-14 *(LO 2, 5)* **100%, complicated excess, first year.** Refer to the preceding information for Fast Cool's acquisition of HD Air's common stock. Assume Fast Cool issued 40,000 shares of its $20 fair value common stock for 100% of HD Air's common stock. Fast Cool uses the simple equity method to account for its investment in HD Air. Fast Cool and HD Air had the following trial balances on December 31, 20X1:

	Fast Cool	HD Air
Cash	147,000	37,000
Accounts Receivable	70,000	100,000
Inventory	150,000	60,000
Land	60,000	50,000
Investment in HD Air	837,500	
Buildings	1,200,000	400,000
Accumulated Depreciation	(176,000)	(67,500)
Equipment	140,000	150,000
Accumulated Depreciation	(68,000)	(54,000)
Patent (net)		32,000
Goodwill		50,000
Current Liabilities	(80,000)	(40,000)
Mortgage Payable		(200,000)
Common Stock	(100,000)	(100,000)
Paid-In Capital in Excess of Par	(1,500,000)	(200,000)
Retained Earnings, Jan. 1, 20X1	(400,000)	(180,000)
Sales	(700,000)	(400,000)
Cost of Goods Sold	380,000	210,000
Depreciation Expense—Buildings	10,000	17,500
Depreciation Expense—Equipment	7,000	24,000
Other Expenses	50,000	85,000
Interest Expense		16,000
Subsidiary Income	(47,500)	
Dividends Declared	20,000	10,000
Total	0	0

Required ▶ ▶ ▶ ▶ ▶

1. Prepare a zone analysis and a determination and distribution of excess schedule for the investment in HD Air.
2. Complete a consolidated worksheet for Fast Cool Company and its subsidiary D Air Company as of December 31, 20X1. Prepare supporting amortization and income distribution schedules.

Problem 3-15 *(LO 2, 5)* **100%, complicated excess, equity, second year.** Refer to the preceding information for Fast Cool's acquisition of HD Air's common stock. Assume Fast Cool issued 40,000 shares of its $20 fair value common stock for 100% of HD Air's common stock. Fast Cool uses the simple equity method to account for its investment in HD Air. Fast Cool and HD Air had the following trial balances on December 31, 20X2:

	Fast Cool	HD Air
Cash	396,000	99,000
Accounts Receivable	200,000	120,000
Inventory	120,000	95,000
Land	60,000	50,000
Investment in HD Air	895,000	
Buildings	1,200,000	400,000
Accumulated Depreciation	(200,000)	(85,000)
Equipment	140,000	150,000

Accumulated Depreciation	(80,000)	(78,000)
Patent (net)		24,000
Goodwill		50,000
Current Liabilities	(150,000)	(50,000)
Mortgage Payable		(200,000)
Common Stock	(100,000)	(100,000)
Paid-In Capital in Excess of Par	(1,500,000)	(200,000)
Retained Earnings, Jan. 1, 20X2	(680,500)	(217,500)
Sales	(700,000)	(500,000)
Cost of Goods Sold	380,000	260,000
Depreciation Expense—Buildings	10,000	17,500
Depreciation Expense—Equipment	7,000	24,000
Other Expenses	50,000	115,000
Interest Expense		16,000
Subsidiary Income	(67,500)	
Dividends Declared	20,000	10,000
Total	0	0

◄◄◄◄◄ **Required**

1. Prepare a zone analysis and a determination and distribution of excess schedule for the investment in HD Air.
2. Complete a consolidated worksheet for Fast Cool Company and its subsidiary HD Air Company as of December 31, 20X2. Prepare supporting amortization and income distribution schedules.

Problem 3-16 *(LO 2, 5)* **100% bargain, complicated equity, second year.** Refer to the preceding information for Fast Cool's acquisition of HD Air's common stock. Assume Fast Cool issued 25,000 shares of its $20 fair value common stock for 100% of HD Air's common stock. Fast Cool uses the simple equity method to account for its investment in HD Air. Fast Cool and HD Air had the following trial balances on December 31, 20X2:

	Fast Cool	HD Air
Cash	396,000	99,000
Accounts Receivable	200,000	120,000
Inventory	120,000	95,000
Land	60,000	50,000
Investment in HD Air	595,000	
Buildings	1,200,000	400,000
Accumulated Depreciation	(200,000)	(85,000)
Equipment	140,000	150,000
Accumulated Depreciation	(80,000)	(78,000)
Patent (net)		24,000
Goodwill		50,000
Current Liabilities	(150,000)	(50,000)
Mortgage Payable		(200,000)
Common Stock	(85,000)	(100,000)
Paid-In Capital in Excess of Par	(1,215,000)	(200,000)
Retained Earnings, Jan. 1, 20X2	(680,500)	(217,500)
Sales	(700,000)	(500,000)
Cost of Goods Sold	380,000	260,000
Depreciation Expense—Buildings	10,000	17,500

(continued)

	Fast Cool	HD Air
Depreciation Expense—Equipment	7,000	24,000
Other Expenses	50,000	115,000
Interest Expense		16,000
Subsidiary Income	(67,500)	
Dividends Declared	20,000	10,000
Total	0	0

Required ▶ ▶ ▶ ▶ ▶

1. Prepare a zone analysis and a determination and distribution of excess schedule for the investment in HD Air.
2. Complete a consolidated worksheet for Fast Cool Company and its subsidiary HD Air Company as of December 31, 20X2. Prepare supporting amortization and income distribution schedules.

template cd

Problem 3-17 *(LO 2, 5)* **80%, first year, complicated excess.** Refer to the preceding information for Fast Cool's acquisition of HD Air's common stock. Assume Fast Cool issued 35,000 shares of its $20 fair value common stock for 80% of HD Air's common stock. Fast Cool uses the simple equity method to account for its investment in HD Air. Fast Cool and HD Air had the following trial balances on December 31, 20X1:

	Fast Cool	HD Air
Cash	145,000	37,000
Accounts Receivable	70,000	100,000
Inventory	150,000	60,000
Land	60,000	50,000
Investment in HD Air	730,000	
Buildings	1,200,000	400,000
Accumulated Depreciation	(176,000)	(67,500)
Equipment	140,000	150,000
Accumulated Depreciation	(68,000)	(54,000)
Patent (net)		32,000
Goodwill		50,000
Current Liabilities	(80,000)	(40,000)
Mortgage Payable		(200,000)
Common Stock	(95,000)	(100,000)
Paid-In Capital in Excess of Par	(1,405,000)	(200,000)
Retained Earnings, Jan. 1, 20X1	(400,000)	(180,000)
Sales	(700,000)	(400,000)
Cost of Goods Sold	380,000	210,000
Depreciation Expense—Buildings	10,000	17,500
Depreciation Expense—Equipment	7,000	24,000
Other Expenses	50,000	85,000
Interest Expense		16,000
Subsidiary Income	(38,000)	
Dividends Declared	20,000	10,000
Total	0	0

Required ▶ ▶ ▶ ▶ ▶

1. Prepare a zone analysis and a determination and distribution of excess schedule for the investment in HD Air.
2. Complete a consolidated worksheet for Fast Cool Company and its subsidiary HD Air Company as of December 31, 20X1. Prepare supporting amortization and income distribution schedules.

Problem 3-18 *(LO 2, 5)* **80%, second year, complicated excess.** Refer to the preceding information for Fast Cool's acquisition of HD Air's common stock. Assume Fast Cool issued 35,000 shares of its $20 fair value common stock for 80% of HD Air's common stock. Fast Cool uses the simple equity method to account for its investment in HD Air. Fast Cool and HD Air had the following trial balances on December 31, 20X2:

template cd

	Fast Cool	HD Air
Cash	392,000	99,000
Accounts Receivable	200,000	120,000
Inventory	120,000	95,000
Land	60,000	50,000
Investment in HD Air	776,000	
Buildings	1,200,000	400,000
Accumulated Depreciation	(200,000)	(85,000)
Equipment	140,000	150,000
Accumulated Depreciation	(80,000)	(78,000)
Patent (net)		24,000
Goodwill		50,000
Current Liabilities	(150,000)	(50,000)
Mortgage Payable		(200,000)
Common Stock	(95,000)	(100,000)
Paid-In Capital in Excess of Par	(1,405,000)	(200,000)
Retained Earnings, Jan. 1, 20X2	(671,000)	(217,500)
Sales	(700,000)	(500,000)
Cost of Goods Sold	380,000	260,000
Depreciation Expense—Buildings	10,000	17,500
Depreciation Expense—Equipment	7,000	24,000
Other Expenses	50,000	115,000
Interest Expense		16,000
Subsidiary Income	(54,000)	
Dividends Declared	20,000	10,000
Total	0	0

◄◄◄◄◄ **Required**

1. Prepare a zone analysis and a determination and distribution of excess schedule for the investment in HD Air.
2. Complete a consolidated worksheet for Fast Cool Company and its subsidiary HD Air Company as of December 31, 20X2. Prepare supporting amortization and income distribution schedules.

APPENDIX PROBLEMS

Problem 3A-1 *(LO 2, 8)* **Equity method adjustments, vertical consolidated worksheet.** (Same as Problem 3-2 except vertical format worksheet is used.) On January 1, 20X1, Peres Company purchased 80% of the common stock of Soll Company for $308,000. On this date, Soll had common stock, other paid-in capital, and retained earnings of $50,000, $100,000, and $150,000, respectively. Net income and dividends for two years for Soll Company were as follows:

template cd

	20X1	20X2
Net income	$60,000	$90,000
Dividends	20,000	30,000

(continued)

On January 1, 20X1, the only tangible assets of Soll that were undervalued were inventory and the building. Inventory, for which FIFO is used, was worth $10,000 more than cost. The inventory was sold in 20X1. The building, which is worth $25,000 more than book value, has a remaining life of 10 years, and straight-line depreciation is used. The remaining excess of cost over book value is attributable to goodwill.

Required ▶ ▶ ▶ ▶ ▶

1. Using this information or the information in the following statements, prepare a determination and distribution of excess schedule.
2. Peres Company carries the Investment in Soll Company under the simple equity method. In general journal form, record the entries that would be made to apply the equity method in 20X1 and 20X2.
3. Complete the vertical worksheet for consolidated financial statements for 20X2.

Statement—Accounts	Peres Company	Soll Company
Income Statement:		
Net Sales	(520,000)	(450,000)
Cost of Goods Sold	300,000	260,000
Operating Expenses	120,000	100,000
Subsidiary Income	(72,000)	
Noncontrolling Interest in Income		
Net Income	(172,000)	(90,000)
Retained Earnings Statement:		
Balance, Jan. 1, 20X2, P Company	(214,000)	
Balance, Jan. 1, 20X2, S Company		(190,000)
Net Income (from above)	(172,000)	(90,000)
Dividends Declared, P Company	50,000	
Dividends Declared, S Company		30,000
Balance, December 31, 20X2	(336,000)	(250,000)
Consolidated Balance Sheet:		
Inventory, December 31	100,000	50,000
Other Current Assets	148,000	180,000
Investment in Soll Company	Note 1	
Land	50,000	50,000
Building and Equipment	350,000	320,000
Accumulated Depreciation	(100,000)	(60,000)
Goodwill		
Other Intangibles	20,000	
Current Liabilities	(120,000)	(40,000)
Bonds Payable		(100,000)
Other Long-Term Liabilities	(200,000)	
Common Stock, P Company	(200,000)	
Other Paid-In Capital, P Company	(100,000)	
Common Stock, S Company		(50,000)
Other Paid-In Capital, S Company		(100,000)
Retained Earnings, December 31, 20X2 (from above)	(336,000)	(250,000)
Total	0	0

Note 1: To be calculated.

Problem 3A-2 *(LO 2, 6, 8)* **Equity method, later period, vertical worksheet, several excess adjustments.** Booker Enterprises purchased an 80% interest in Kobe International for $850,000 on January 1, 20X5. Booker Enterprises also paid $4,000 in direct acquisition costs. On the purchase date, Kobe International had the following stockholders' equity:

Common stock ($10 par)	$150,000
Paid-in capital in excess of par	200,000
Retained earnings	400,000
	$750,000

Also on the purchase date, it was determined that Kobe International's assets were understated as follows:

Equipment, 10-year remaining life	$80,000
Land	20,000
Building, 20-year remaining life	60,000

The remaining excess of cost over book value was attributed to goodwill.

The following summarized statements of Booker Enterprises and Kobe International are for the year ended December 31, 20X7:

	Booker Enterprises	Kobe International
Income Statements:		
Sales	(650,000)	(320,000)
Cost of Goods Sold	260,000	240,000
Operating Expenses	170,000	70,000
Depreciation Expense	65,000	30,000
Subsidiary (Income)/Loss	16,000	
Net (Income)/Loss	(139,000)	20,000
Retained Earnings:		
Retained Earnings, Jan. 1, 20X7, Booker	(625,000)	
Retained Earnings, Jan. 1, 20X7, Kobe		(460,000)
Net (Income)/Loss	(139,000)	20,000
Dividends Declared		10,000
Retained Earnings, Dec. 31, 20X7	(764,000)	(430,000)
Balance Sheets:		
Cash	334,000	170,000
Inventory	135,000	400,000
Land	145,000	150,000
Buildings	900,000	500,000
Accumulated Depreciation—Building	(345,000)	(360,000)
Equipment	350,000	250,000
Accumulated Depreciation—Equipment	(135,000)	(90,000)
Investment in Kobe International	828,000	
Liabilities	(248,000)	(40,000)

(continued)

	Booker Enterprises	Kobe International
Balance Sheets *(cont'd.)*:		
Bonds Payable		(200,000)
Common Stock, Booker	(1,200,000)	
Common Stock, Kobe		(150,000)
Paid-In Capital in Excess of Par		(200,000)
Retained Earnings, Dec. 31, 20X7	(764,000)	(430,000)
Balance	0	0

Required ▶▶▶▶▶ Using the vertical format, prepare a consolidated worksheet for December 31, 20X7. Precede the worksheet with a determination and distribution of excess schedule. Include income distribution schedules to allocate the consolidated net income to the noncontrolling and controlling interests.

Suggestion: Remember that all adjustments to retained earnings are to beginning retained earnings, and it is the beginning balance of the subsidiary retained earnings account which is subject to elimination. Carefully follow the "carrydown" procedure to calculate the ending retained earnings balances.

Problem 3A-3 *(LO 5, 8)* **Cost method, later period, vertical worksheets.** Harvard Company purchased a 90% interest in Benz Company for $740,000 on January 1, 20X1. The investment has been accounted for under the cost method. At the time of the purchase, a building owned by Benz was understated by $180,000; it had a 20-year remaining life on the purchase date. The remaining excess was attributed to goodwill. The stockholders' equity of Benz Company on the purchase date was as follows:

Common stock ($10 par)	$350,000
Retained earnings	200,000
Total equity	$550,000

The following summarized statements are for the year ending December 31, 20X2. (Credit balance amounts are in parentheses.)

	Harvard	Benz
Income Statements:		
Sales	(580,000)	(280,000)
Cost of Goods Sold	285,000	155,000
Operating Expenses	140,000	55,000
Depreciation Expense	72,000	30,000
Dividend Income	(9,000)	
Net Income	(92,000)	(40,000)
Retained Earnings Statements:		
Retained Earnings, Jan. 1, 20X2, Harvard	(484,000)	
Retained Earnings, Jan. 1, 20X2, Benz		(320,000)
Net Income	(92,000)	(40,000)
Dividends Declared	20,000	10,000
Retained Earnings, Dec. 31, 20X2	(556,000)	(350,000)
Balance Sheets:		
Cash	310,000	170,000
Inventory	260,000	340,000

Land	99,000	150,000
Building	800,000	500,000
Accumulated Depreciation—Building	(380,000)	(360,000)
Equipment	340,000	250,000
Accumulated Depreciation—Equipment	(190,000)	(90,000)
Investment in Benz Company	740,000	
Current Liabilities	(123,000)	(60,000)
Bonds Payable		(200,000)
Common Stock, Harvard	(800,000)	
Paid-In Capital in Excess of Par, Harvard	(500,000)	
Common Stock, Benz		(350,000)
Retained Earnings, Dec. 31, 20X2	(556,000)	(350,000)
Balance	0	0

◄◄◄◄◄ **Required**

Using the vertical format, prepare a consolidated worksheet for December 31, 20X2. Precede the worksheet with a determination and distribution of excess schedule. Include income distribution schedules to allocate the consolidated net income to the noncontrolling and controlling interests.

Suggestion: Remember that all adjustments to retained earnings are to beginning retained earnings, and it is the beginning balance of the subsidiary retained earnings account which is subject to elimination. One of the adjustments to the parent retained earnings account is the cost-to-equity conversion entry. Be sure to follow the carrydown procedure to calculate the ending retained earnings balances.

Problem 3B-1 *(LO 9)* **D&D only, nontaxable exchange, tax loss carryover.** On December 31, 20X5, Bryant Company exchanged 10,000 of its $10 par value shares for a 90% interest in Joshua Company. The purchase was recorded at the $80 per share fair value of Bryant shares. Joshua Company had the following balance sheet on the date of the purchase:

template cd

Assets		Liabilities and Equity	
Cash	$ 100,000	Current liabilities	$ 130,000
Accounts receivable	200,000	Deferred rental income	120,000
Inventory	150,000	Bonds payable	250,000
Investment in marketable securities	150,000	Common stock ($10 par)	100,000
Depreciable fixed assets	400,000	Paid-in capital in excess of par	150,000
		Retained earnings	250,000
Total assets	$1,000,000	Total liabilities and equity	$1,000,000

It was determined that the following fair values differed from book values for the assets of Joshua Company:

Inventory	$200,000
Depreciable fixed assets (net)	500,000
Investment in marketable securities	170,000

(continued)

The purchase is a tax-free exchange to the seller, which means Bryant Company will use the book value of Joshua's assets for tax purposes. Joshua Company has $200,000 of tax loss carryovers. Bryant will be able to utilize $40,000 of the losses to offset taxes to be paid in 20X6. The balance of the tax loss carryover will not be used within a year but is considered fully realizable in the future. The tax rate for both firms is 30%.

Required ▶ ▶ ▶ ▶ ▶ Record the investment and prepare a determination and distribution of excess schedule.

Suggestion: Asset adjustments should be accompanied by the appropriate deferred tax liability.

Problem 3B-2 *(LO 2, 9)* **Worksheet for nontaxable exchange with tax loss carryover.** The balance sheets of Tip Company and Kim Company as of December 31, 20X6, are as follows:

	Tip	Kim
Cash	$ 1,200,000	$ 50,000
Accounts receivable	2,400,000	300,000
Inventory	11,200,000	1,500,000
Prepayments	422,000	47,000
Depreciable fixed assets	18,978,000	2,100,000
Investment in Kim Company	2,400,000	
Total assets	$36,600,000	$3,997,000
Payables	$ 7,200,000	$1,750,000
Accruals	1,615,000	400,000
Common stock ($100 par)	10,000,000	1,000,000
Retained earnings	17,785,000	847,000
Total liabilities and equity	$36,600,000	$3,997,000

An appraisal on December 31, 20X6, which was considered carefully and approved by the boards of directors of both companies, placed a total replacement value, less depreciation, of $3,000,000 on Kim's depreciable fixed assets.

Tip Company offered to purchase all the assets of Kim Company, subject to its liabilities, as of December 31, 20X6, for $3,000,000. However, 20% of the stockholders of Kim Company objected to the price because it did not include any consideration for goodwill, which they believed to be worth at least $500,000. A counterproposal was made, and a final agreement was reached. In exchange for its own shares, Tip acquired 80% of the common stock of Kim at the agreed-upon fair value of $300 per share. The purchase is structured as a tax-free exchange to the seller; thus, Tip will use the book value of the assets for future tax purposes. The tax rate for both companies is 30%.

Required ▶ ▶ ▶ ▶ ▶ Prepare a consolidated worksheet and a consolidated balance sheet as of December 31, 20X6. Include a determination and distribution schedule.

(AICPA adapted)

Problem 3B-3 *(LO 2, 9)* **Worksheet for nontaxable exchange with tax loss carryover.** The trial balances of Campton Corporation and Deer Corporation as of December 31, 20X1, are as follows:

	Campton Corporation	Deer Corporation
Current Assets	167,000	80,000
Land	400,000	100,000
Building and Equipment (net)	900,000	240,000
Investment in Deer Corporation	625,600	
Current Tax Liability	(4,200)	(6,000)
Other Current Liabilities	(130,000)	(100,000)
Common Stock ($5 par)	(500,000)	
Common Stock ($50 par)		(200,000)
Paid-In Capital in Excess of Par	(750,000)	
Retained Earnings, January 1, 20X1	(650,000)	(100,000)
Sales	(309,000)	(150,000)
Subsidiary Income	(12,600)	
Cost of Goods Sold	170,000	80,000
Expenses	89,000	50,000
Provision for Tax	4,200*	6,000
Total	0	0

*$15,000 tax liability ($50,000 income × 30%) – $10,800 tax loss carryover ($40,000 × 90% × 30%).

On January 1, 20X1, Campton purchased 90% of the outstanding stock of Deer Corporation for $600,000, plus direct acquisition costs of $13,000. The acquisition was a tax-free exchange for the seller. At the purchase date, Deer's equipment was undervalued by $100,000 and had a remaining life of 10 years. All other assets had book values that approximated their fair values. Deer Corporation had a tax loss carryover of $200,000, of which $40,000 was utilizable in 20X1 and the balance in future periods. The tax loss carryover is expected to be fully utilized. Any remaining excess is considered to be goodwill. A tax rate of 30% applies to both companies.

◀◀◀◀◀ **Required**

1. Prepare a determination and distribution of excess schedule for the investment.
2. Prepare the 20X1 consolidated worksheet. Include columns for the eliminations and adjustments, the consolidated income statement, the NCI, the controlling retained earnings, and the consolidated balance sheet. Prepare supporting income distribution schedules as well.
3. Prepare the 20X1 consolidated statements, including the income statement, retained earnings statement, and balance sheet.

Suggestion: A deferred tax liability results from the increase in the fair value of the equipment. As the added depreciation is recognized on the equipment, the deferred tax liability becomes payable. Note that income distribution schedules record net-of-tax income. Therefore, be sure that any adjustments to the income distribution schedules consider tax where appropriate.

Intercompany Transactions: Merchandise, Plant Assets, and Notes

CHAPTER

4

Learning Objectives

When you have completed this chapter, you should be able to

1. **Explain why transactions between members of a consolidated firm should not be reflected in the consolidated financial statements.**
2. **Defer intercompany profits on merchandise sales when appropriate and eliminate the double counting of sales between affiliates.**
3. **Defer profits on intercompany sales of long-term assets and realize the profits over the period of use and/or at the time of sale to a firm outside the consolidated group.**
4. **Demonstrate an understanding of the profit deferral issues for intercompany sales of assets under long-term construction contracts.**
5. **Eliminate intercompany loans and notes.**
6. **Discuss the complications intercompany profits create for the use of the sophisticated equity method.**
7. **(Appendix) Apply intercompany profit eliminations on a vertical worksheet.**

The elimination of the parent's investment in a subsidiary and the adjustments that may result from the elimination process are only the start of the procedures that are necessary to consolidate a parent and a subsidiary. It is common for affiliated companies to transact business with one another. The more integrated the affiliates are with respect to operations, the more common intercompany transactions become. This chapter considers the most often encountered types of intercompany transactions. These include intercompany sales of merchandise and fixed assets as well as loans between members of the consolidated group.

Transactions between the separate legal and accounting entities must be recorded on each affiliate's books. The consolidation process starts with the assumption that these transactions are recorded properly on the separate books of the parent and the subsidiary. However, consolidated statements are those that portray the parent and its subsidiary as a single economic entity. There should not be any intercompany transactions found in these consolidated statements. Only the effect of those transactions between the consolidated company and the companies outside the consolidated company should appear in the consolidated statements. Intercompany transactions must be eliminated as part of the consolidation process. For each type of intercompany transaction, sound reasoning will be developed to support the worksheet procedures. The guiding principle shall come from answering this question: **From the standpoint of a single consolidated company, what accounts and amounts should remain in the financial statements?**

The worksheet eliminations for intercompany transactions are the same no matter what method is used by the parent to maintain its investment in the subsidiary account. The examples in this chapter assume the use of the simple equity method. This is done because any investment that is maintained under the cost method is converted to the simple equity method on the consolidation worksheet. The impact of intercompany transactions on the investment account under the sophisticated equity method is considered in the appendix to this chapter. Note, however, that even where the sophisticated equity method is used, there is no change in the procedures for the individual intercompany transactions.

1

OBJECTIVE

Explain why transactions between members of a consolidated firm should not be reflected in the consolidated financial statements.

INTERCOMPANY MERCHANDISE SALES

It is common to find that the goods sold by one member of an affiliated group have been purchased from another member of the group. One company may produce component parts that are assembled by its affiliate that sells the final product. In other cases, the product may be produced entirely by one member company and sold on a wholesale basis to another member company that is responsible for selling and servicing the product to the final users. Taken as a whole, these different examples of merchandise sales represent the most common type of intercompany transaction and must be understood as a basic feature of consolidated reporting.

Sales between affiliated companies will be recorded in the normal manner on the books of the separate companies. Remember that each company is a separate legal entity maintaining its own accounting records. Thus, sales to and purchases from an affiliated company are recorded as if they were transactions made with a company outside the consolidated group, and the separate financial statements of the affiliated companies will include these purchase and sale transactions. However, when the statements of the affiliates are consolidated, such sales become transfers of goods within the consolidated entity. Since these sales do not involve parties outside the consolidated group, they cannot be acknowledged in consolidated statements.

Following are the procedures for consolidating affiliated companies engaged in intercompany merchandise sales:

1. The intercompany sale must be eliminated to avoid double counting. To understand this requirement, assume that Company P sells merchandise costing $1,000 to a subsidiary, Company S, for $1,200. Company S, in turn, sells the merchandise to an outside party for $1,500. If no elimination is made, the consolidated income statement would show the following with respect to the two transactions:

Sales	$2,700	($1,500 outside sale plus $1,200 sale to Company S)
Less cost of goods sold.	2,200	($1,000 cost to Company P plus $1,200 purchase by Company S)
Gross profit	$ 500	(18.5% gross profit rate)

While the gross profit is correct, sales and the cost of goods sold are inflated because they are included twice. As a result, the gross profit percentage is understated, since the $500 gross profit appears to relate to $2,700 of sales rather than to the outside sale of $1,500. The intercompany sale must be eliminated from the consolidated statements. All that should remain on the consolidated income statement with respect to the two transactions is as follows:

Sales	$1,500	(only the final sale to the outside party)
Less cost of goods sold.	1,000	(only the purchase from the outside party)
Gross profit	$ 500	(33⅓% gross profit rate)

When the goods sold between the affiliated companies are manufactured by the selling affiliate, the consolidated cost of goods sold includes only those costs that can be inventoried, such as labor, materials, and overhead, and may not include any profit.

The intercompany sale, though eliminated, does have an effect on the distribution of consolidated net income to the controlling interest and NCI. This is true because the reported net income of the subsidiary reflects the intercompany sales price, and the subsidiary's separate income statement becomes the base from which the noncontrolling share of income is calculated. In effect, the intercompany transfer price becomes an agreement as to how a portion of combined net income will be divided. For example, if Company S is an 80%-owned subsidiary, the NCI will receive 20% of the $300 profit made on the final sale by Company S, or $60. If the intercompany transfer price is increased from $1,200 to $1,300 and the final sales price remains at $1,500, Company S would earn only $200, and the NCI would receive 20% of $200, or $40.

2. Often, intercompany sales will be made on credit. Thus, intercompany trade balances will appear in the separate accounts of the affiliated companies. From a consolidated viewpoint, intercompany receivables and payables represent internal agreements to transfer funds. As such, **this internal debt should not appear on consolidated statements and must be eliminated.** Only debt transactions with entities *outside* the consolidated group should appear on the consolidated balance sheet.
3. **No profit on intercompany sales may be recognized until the profit is realized by a sale to an *outside* party.** This means that any profit contained in the ending inventory of intercompany goods must be eliminated and its recognition deferred until the period in which the goods are sold to outsiders. In the example described in item 1, assume that the sale by Company P to Company S was made on December 30, 20X1, and that Company S did not sell the goods until March 20X2. From a consolidated viewpoint, there can be no profit recognized until the outside sale occurs in March of 20X2. At that time, consolidation theory will acknowledge a $500 profit, of which $200 will be distributed to Company P and $300 will be distributed to Company S as part of the 20X2 consolidated net income. However, until that time, the $200 profit on the intercompany sale recorded by Company P must be deferred. In addition, not only must the $1,200 intercompany sale be eliminated, but the inventory on December 31, 20X1, must be reduced by $200 (the amount of the intercompany profit) to its $1,000 cost to the consolidated companies.

Care must be taken in calculating the profit applicable to intercompany inventory. It is most convenient when the gross profit rate is provided so that it can be multiplied by the inventory value to arrive at the intercompany profit. In some instances, however, the profit on sales may be stated as a percentage of cost. For example, one might be told that the cost of units is "marked up" 25% to arrive at the intercompany sales price. If the inventory sales price is $1,000, it cannot be multiplied by 25% to calculate the intercompany profit because the 25% applies to the *cost* and not the sales price, at which the inventory is stated. Instead, the gross profit rate, which is a percentage of sales price, should be calculated. The easiest method of accomplishing this is to pick the theoretical cost of $1 and mark it up by 25% (the given percentage of cost) to $1.25 and ask: "What is the gross profit percentage?" In this example, it is $0.25 ÷ $1.25, or 20%. From this point, the $1,000 inventory value can be multiplied by 20% to arrive at the intercompany profit of $200.

The worksheet procedures to eliminate the effects of intercompany inventory sales are discussed in the next four sections as follows:

1. There are no intercompany goods in the beginning or ending inventories.
2. Intercompany goods remain in the ending inventory.
3. There are intercompany goods in the ending inventory, and there were intercompany goods in the beginning inventory. This is the most common situation.
4. Instead of the perpetual inventory method assumed in sections 1-3 above, the companies use the periodic inventory method. There are intercompany goods in the ending inventory, and there were intercompany goods in the beginning inventory.

No Intercompany Goods in Purchasing Company's Inventories

In the simplest case, which is illustrated in Worksheet 4-1, pages 228 and 229, all goods sold between the affiliates have been sold, in turn, to outside parties by the end of the accounting period. Worksheet 4-1 is based on the following assumptions:

worksheet

Worksheet 4-1: page 228

1. Company S is an 80%-owned subsidiary of Company P. On January 1, 20X1, Company P purchased its interest in Company S at a price equal to its pro rata share of Company S's book value. Company P uses the equity method to record the investment.
2. Companies P and S had the following separate income statements for 20X1:

	Company P	Company S
Sales	$700,000	$500,000
Less cost of goods sold	510,000	350,000
Gross profit	$190,000	$150,000
Other expenses	(90,000)	(75,000)
Subsidiary income	60,000	
Net income	$160,000	$ 75,000

Note that under the equity method, Company P's income includes 80% of the reported income of Company S.

3. During the year, Company S sold goods that cost $80,000 to Company P for $100,000 (a 20% gross profit). Company P then sold all of the goods purchased from Company S to outside parties for $150,000. Company P had not paid $25,000 of the invoices received from Company S for the goods. (Note that it is assumed in this and Worksheets 4-2 and 4-3 that a **perpetual** inventory system is used.) Consider the journal entries made by each affiliate:

Company S

Accounts Receivable (from Company P)	100,000	
Sales (to Company P)		100,000
Cost of Goods Sold (to Company P)	80,000	
Inventory		80,000
Cash	75,000	
Accounts Receivable (from Company P)		75,000

Company P

Inventory	100,000	
Accounts Payable (to Company S)		100,000
Accounts Receivable (from outside parties)	150,000	
Sales (to outside parties)		150,000
Cost of Goods Sold (to outside parties)	100,000	
Inventory		100,000
Accounts Payable (to Company S)	75,000	
Cash		75,000

The elimination entries for Worksheet 4-1 in journal entry form are as follows:

(CY1)	Eliminate current-year equity income:		
	Subsidiary Income	60,000	
	Investment in Company S		60,000
(EL)	Eliminate 80% of subsidiary equity against investment in subsidiary account:		
	Common Stock ($10 par), Company S	80,000	
	Retained Earnings, January 1, 20X1, Company S	56,000	
	Investment in Company S		136,000
(IS)	Eliminate intercompany merchandise sales:		
	Sales	100,000	
	Cost of Goods Sold		100,000

(IA)	Eliminate intercompany unpaid trade balances at year-end:		
	Accounts Payable	25,000	
	Accounts Receivable		25,000

Entry (IS) is a simplified summary entry that can be further analyzed with the following entry:

Sales (to Company P)	100,000	
Cost of Goods Sold (by Company S to Company P—the intercompany sale)		80,000
Cost of Goods Sold (by Company P to outside parties—the profit recorded by Company S)		20,000

The preceding expanded entry removes the cost of goods sold with respect to the intercompany sale and removes the intercompany profit from the sales made by the parent to outside parties. Note that the parent recorded the cost of the goods sold to outside parties at $100,000, which contains $20,000 of Company S's profit. As shown in the expanded (IS) entry above, the true cost of the goods to the consolidated company is $80,000 ($100,000 less the 20% internal gross profit).

Entry (IA) eliminates the intercompany receivables/payables still remaining unpaid at the end of the year. Income distribution schedules are used in Worksheet 4-1 to distribute the $175,000 of consolidated net income to the noncontrolling and controlling interests. It should be noted that all of the above procedures remain unchanged if the parent is the seller of the intercompany goods.

Intercompany Goods in Purchasing Company's Ending Inventory

2

OBJECTIVE

Defer intercompany profits on merchandise sales when appropriate and eliminate the double counting of sales between affiliates.

Let us now change the example in Worksheet 4-1 to assume that Company P did not resell $40,000 of the total of $100,000 of goods it purchased from Company S. This means that $40,000 of goods purchased from Company S remain in Company P's ending inventory. As shown below, Company S (the intercompany seller) will have the same entries as presented on page 208, and Company P will have the following revised entries:

Company S

Accounts Receivable (from Company P)	100,000	
Sales (to Company P)		100,000
Cost of Goods Sold (to Company P)	80,000	
Inventory		80,000
Cash	75,000	
Accounts Receivable (from Company P)		75,000

Company P

Inventory	100,000	
Accounts Payable (to Company S)		100,000
Accounts Receivable (from outside parties)	90,000	
Sales (to outside parties)		90,000
Cost of Goods Sold (to outside parties)	60,000	
Inventory		60,000
Accounts Payable (to Company S)	75,000	
Cash		75,000

Let us now consider what has happened to the $100,000 of goods sold to Company P by Company S:

$80,000 is the original cost of the goods sold by Company S that should be removed from the consolidated cost of goods sold since it is derived from the intercompany sale and not the outside sale.

$12,000 is the intercompany profit included in the goods sold by Company P to outside parties. The cost of these sales should be reduced by $12,000 (20% × $60,000) to arrive at the true cost of the goods to the consolidated company.

$8,000 is the intercompany profit remaining in the Company P ending inventory. This inventory, now at $40,000, should be reduced by $8,000 (20% × $40,000) to $32,000. Another way to view this is that 60% of the original intercompany goods (60% × $100,000 = $60,000) have been sold to outside parties. Thus, only the profit on these sales (20% × $60,000 = $12,000) has been realized.

If we follow the above analysis to the letter, we would make the following elimination in entry form:

Sales (by Company S to Company P)	100,000	
Cost of Goods Sold (by Company S)		80,000
Cost of Goods Sold (by Company P)		12,000
Inventory, December 31, 20X1 (held by Company P)		8,000

In practice, this entry is cumbersome in that it requires an analysis of the destiny of all intercompany sales. The approach used in Worksheet 4-2, pages 230 and 231, is simplified first to eliminate the intercompany sales under the assumption that all goods have been resold, and then to adjust for those goods still remaining in the inventory. This method simplifies worksheet procedures, including the distribution of combined net income. In journal form, the simplified entries are:

worksheet
Worksheet 4-2: page 230

(CY1)	Eliminate current-year equity income:		
	Subsidiary Income	60,000	
	Investment in Company S		60,000
(EL)	Eliminate 80% of subsidiary equity against investment in subsidiary account:		
	Common Stock ($10 par), Company S	80,000	
	Retained Earnings, January 1, 20X1, Company S	56,000	
	Investment in Company S		136,000
(IS)	Eliminate intercompany merchandise sales:		
	Sales	100,000	
	Cost of Goods Sold		100,000
(EI)	Eliminate intercompany profit in ending inventory:		
	Cost of Goods Sold	8,000	
	Inventory, December 31, 20X1		8,000
(IA)	Eliminate intercompany unpaid trade balance at year-end:		
	Accounts Payable	25,000	
	Accounts Receivable		25,000

The $8,000 is viewed as the unrealized intercompany inventory profit that may not be realized until a later period when the goods are sold to outside parties.

The unrealized intercompany profit is subtracted from the seller's income distribution schedule. In the income distribution schedules for Worksheet 4-2, the unrealized profit of $8,000 is deducted from the subsidiary's internally generated net income of $75,000. The adjusted net income of $67,000 is apportioned, with $13,400 (20%) distributed to the noncontrolling interest and $53,600 (80%) distributed to the controlling interest.

There is no change in worksheet elimination procedures if the parent is the seller and the subsidiary has intercompany goods in its ending inventory. Only the distribution of combined net income changes. To illustrate, assume the parent, Company P, is the seller of the intercompany goods. The income distribution schedules would be prepared as follows:

Subsidiary Company S Income Distribution

		Internally generated net income	$ 75,000
		Adjusted income	$ 75,000
		NCI share	× 20%
		NCI	$ 15,000

Parent Company P Income Distribution

Unrealized profit in ending inventory	**(EI) $8,000**	Internally generated net income	$100,000
		80% × Company S adjusted income of $75,000	60,000
		Controlling interest	$152,000

Intercompany Goods in Purchasing Company's Beginning and Ending Inventories

When intercompany goods are included in the purchaser's beginning inventory, the inventory value includes the profit made by the seller. The intercompany seller of the goods has included in the prior period such sales in its separate income statement as though the transactions were consummated. Thus, the beginning retained earnings balance of the seller also includes the profit on these goods. While this profit should be reflected on the separate books of the affiliates, it should not be recognized when a consolidated view is taken. Remember: **Profit must not be recognized in consolidated statement until it is realized in the subsequent period through the sale of goods to an outside party.** Therefore, in the consolidating process, the beginning inventory of intercompany goods must be reduced to its cost to the consolidated company. Likewise, the retained earnings of the consolidated entity must be reduced by deleting the profit that was recorded in prior periods on intercompany goods contained in the buyer's beginning inventory.

To illustrate, using the example of Company P and Company S from Worksheet 4-3 on pages 232 to 233, assume the two companies have the following individual income data for **20X2**:

worksheet
Worksheet 4-3: page 232

	Company P	Company S
Sales	$ 800,000	$ 600,000
Less cost of goods sold	610,000	440,000
Gross profit	$ 190,000	$ 160,000
Other expenses	(120,000)	(100,000)
Subsidiary income	48,000	
Net income	$ 118,000	$ 60,000

Assume the following additional facts:

1. Company P's 20X2 beginning inventory includes $40,000 of the goods purchased from Company S in **20X1**. The gross profit rate on the sale was 20%.
2. Company S sold $120,000 of goods to Company P during **20X2**.
3. Company S recorded a 20% gross profit on these sales.
4. At the end of **20X2**, Company P still owed $60,000 to Company S for the purchases.
5. Company P also had $30,000 of the intercompany purchases in its **20X2** ending inventory.

Worksheet 4-3 contains the **20X2** year-end trial balances of Company P and Company S. The elimination entries in journal entry form are as follows:

(CY1)	Eliminate current-year equity income:		
	Subsidiary Income	48,000	
	Investment in Company S		48,000

(EL)	Eliminate subsidiary equity against investment in subsidiary account:		
	Common Stock ($10 par), Company S	80,000	
	Retained Earnings, January 1, 20X2, Company S	116,000	
	Investment in Company S		196,000
(BI)	Eliminate intercompany profit in beginning inventory and reduce current-year cost of goods sold:		
	Retained Earnings, January 1, 20X2, Company P	6,400	
	Retained Earnings, January 1, 20X2, Company S	1,600	
	Cost of Goods Sold		8,000
(IS)	Eliminate intercompany merchandise sales:		
	Sales	120,000	
	Cost of Goods Sold		120,000
(EI)	Eliminate intercompany profit in ending inventory:		
	Cost of Goods Sold	6,000	
	Inventory, December 31, 20X2		6,000
(IA)	Eliminate intercompany unpaid trade balance at year-end:		
	Accounts Payable	60,000	
	Accounts Receivable		60,000

Entry (BI) adjusts for the intercompany profit contained in the beginning inventory. At the start of 20X2, Company P included $40,000 of goods purchased from Company S in its beginning inventory. During 20X2, the inventory was debited to the cost of goods sold at $40,000. The cost of goods sold must now be reduced to cost by removing the $8,000 intercompany profit. The intercompany profit also was included in last year's income by the subsidiary. That income was closed to retained earnings. Thus, the beginning retained earnings of Company S are overstated by $8,000. That $8,000 is divided between the noncontrolling and controlling interest in retained earnings. Subsidiary retained earnings have been 80% eliminated, and only the 20% noncontrolling interest remains. The other 80% of beginning retained earnings is included in Company P's retained earnings through the use of the equity method.

Note that once the controlling share of subsidiary retained earnings is eliminated, there is a transformation of what was **subsidiary** retained earnings into what now is **NCI** in retained earnings. Entries (IS), (EI), and (IA) eliminate the intercompany sales, ending inventory, and trade accounts in the same manner as was done in Worksheet 4-2. After all eliminations and adjustments are made, the consolidated net income of $132,000 is distributed as shown in the income distribution schedules. **The adjustments for intercompany inventory profits are reflected in the *selling company's schedule.***

It might appear that the intercompany goods in the beginning inventory are always assumed to be sold in the current period, since the deferred profit of the previous period is realized during the current period as reflected by the seller's income distribution schedule. That assumption need not be made, however. Even if part of the beginning inventory is unsold at year-end, it still would be a part of the $30,000 ending inventory, on which $6,000 of profit is deferred. Note that the use of the LIFO method for inventories could cause a given period's inventory profit to be deferred indefinitely. Unless otherwise stated, the examples and problems of this text will assume a FIFO flow.

Worksheet 4-3 assumed the intercompany merchandise sales were made by the subsidiary. Procedures would differ as follows if the sales were made by the parent:

1. The beginning inventory profit would be subtracted entirely from the beginning controlling retained earnings since only the parent recorded the profit.
2. The adjustments for the beginning and ending inventory profits would be included in the parent income distribution schedule and not in the subsidiary schedule.

Eliminations for Periodic Inventories

In Worksheet 4-1 through 4-3, the cost of goods sold was included in the trial balances, since both the parent and the subsidiary used a perpetual inventory system. However, in Worksheet 4-4 on pages 234 to 235, a periodic inventory system is used. In this illustration, which is based on the same facts as Worksheet 4-3, the following differences in worksheet procedures result from the use of a periodic inventory system:

Worksheet 4-4: page 234

1. The 20X2 beginning inventories of $70,000 and $40,000, rather than the ending inventories, appear as assets in the trial balances. The beginning inventories less the intercompany profit in Company P's beginning inventory are extended to the consolidated income statement column as a debit.
2. The purchases accounts, rather than the cost of goods sold, appear in the trial balances and, after adjustment, are extended to the consolidated income statement column.
3. Entry (BI) credits the January 1 inventory to eliminate the intercompany profit.
4. Entry (IS) credits the purchases account, which is still open under the periodic method, and makes the usual debit to the sales account.
5. The ending inventories of both Company P and Company S are entered in each company's trial balances as both a debit (the balance sheet amount) and a credit (the adjustment to the cost of goods sold). These inventories are recorded at the price paid for them, which, for intercompany goods, includes the intercompany sales profit. Entry (EI) removes the $6,000 intercompany profit applicable to the ending inventory. The balance sheet inventory is reduced to $104,000. The $104,000 credit balance is extended to the consolidated income statement column.

The elimination entries in journal entry form are as follows:

(CY1)	Eliminate current-year equity income:		
	Subsidiary Income	48,000	
	Investment in Company S		48,000
(EL)	Eliminate subsidiary equity against investment in subsidiary account:		
	Common Stock ($10 par), Company S	80,000	
	Retained Earnings, January 1, 20X2, Company S	116,000	
	Investment in Company S		196,000
(BI)	Eliminate intercompany profit in beginning inventory and reduce current-year cost of goods sold:		
	Retained Earnings, January 1, 20X2, Company P	6,400	
	Retained Earnings, January 1, 20X2, Company S	1,600	
	Cost of Goods Sold		8,000
(IS)	Eliminate intercompany merchandise sales:		
	Sales	120,000	
	Purchases		120,000
(EI)	Eliminate intercompany profit in ending inventory:		
	Cost of Goods Sold	6,000	
	Inventory, December 31, 20X2, Asset		6,000
(IA)	Eliminate intercompany unpaid trade balance at year-end:		
	Accounts Payable	60,000	
	Accounts Receivable		60,000

Effect of Lower-of-Cost-or-Market Method on Inventory Profit

Intercompany inventory in the hands of the purchaser may have been written down by the purchaser to a market value below its intercompany transfer cost. Assume that, for $50,000, Company S purchased goods that cost its parent company $40,000. Assume further that Company S has all the goods in its ending inventory but has written them down to $42,000, the lower market value at the end of the period. As a result of this markdown, the inventory needs to be reduced by only another $2,000 to reflect its cost to the consolidated company ($40,000). The only remaining issue is how to defer the $2,000 inventory profit in the income distribution schedules. As before, such profit is deferred by entering it as a debit on the intercompany seller's schedule. In the subsequent period, the profit will be realized by the seller.

It may seem strange that the $8,000 of profit written off is realized, in effect, by the seller, since it is not deducted in the seller's distribution schedule. This procedure is proper, however, since the loss recognized by the buyer is offset. Had the inventory been written down to $40,000 or less, there would be no need to defer the offsetting profit in the consolidated worksheet or in the income distribution schedules.

Losses on Intercompany Sales

Assume a parent sells goods to a subsidiary for $5,000 and the goods cost the parent $6,000. If the market value of the goods is $5,000 or less, the loss may be recognized in the consolidated income statement, even if the goods remain in the subsidiary's ending inventory. Such a loss can be recognized under the lower-of-cost-or-market principle that applies to inventory. However, if the intercompany sales price is below market value, the part of the loss that results from the price being below market value cannot be recognized until the subsidiary sells the goods to an outside party. Elimination procedures would be similar, but opposite in direction, to those used for unrealized gains.

REFLECTION

- Merchandise sales between affiliated companies are eliminated; only the purchase and sale to the "outside world" should remain in the statements.
- The profit must be removed from beginning inventory by reducing the cost of goods sold and the retained earnings.
- The profit must be removed from the ending inventory both by reducing the inventory and by increasing the cost of goods sold. The deduction of the inventory from the goods available for sale is too great prior to this adjustment.
- Unpaid intercompany trade payables/receivables resulting from intercompany merchandise sales are eliminated.

3

OBJECTIVE

Defer profits on intercompany sales of long-term assets and realize the profits over the period of use and/or at the time of sale to a firm outside the consolidated group.

INTERCOMPANY PLANT ASSET SALES

Any plant asset may be sold between members of an affiliated group, and such a sale may result in a gain for the seller. The buyer will record the asset at a price that includes the gain, and when the sale involves a depreciable asset, the buyer will base future depreciation charges on the price paid. While these recordings are proper for the companies as separate entities, they must not be reflected in the consolidated statements. Consolidation theory views the sale as an *internal transfer of assets*. There is no basis for recognizing a gain at the time of the internal transfer. A gain on the sale of a nondepreciable asset cannot be recorded on the consolidated statements until the asset is resold to the outside world. However, the recognition of a gain on the sale of a depreciable asset does not have to wait until resale occurs. Instead, the intercompany gain is amortized over the depreciable life of the asset. The buyer's normal intent is to use the asset, not to resell it. Since the asset is overstated by the amount of the intercompany gain, subsequent depreciation is overstated as well. The consolidation process reduces depreciation in future years so that depreciation charges in the consolidated statements reflect the original cost of the asset to the consolidated company. While the gain is deferred in the year of sale, it is realized later through the increased combined net income resulting from the reduction in depreciation expense in subsequent periods. The decrease in depreciation expense for each and every period is equal to the difference between the depreciation based on the intercompany sales price and the depreciation based on the book value of the asset on the sale date.

Intercompany Sale of a Nondepreciable Asset

One member of an affiliated group may sell land to another affiliate and record a gain. For consolidating purposes, there has been no sale; thus, there is no cause to recognize a gain. Since the asset is not depreciable, the entire gain must be deferred until the land is sold to an outside party. This deferment may be permanent if there is no intent to sell at a later date. For example, assume that in 20X1 Company S (80% owned) sells land to its parent company, Company P. The sale price is $30,000, and the original cost of the land to Company S was $20,000. Consolidation theory would rule that, until Company P sells the land to an outside party, recognition of the $10,000 profit must be deferred. Elimination (LA) eliminates the intercompany gain in the year of sale.

	Partial Trial Balance		Eliminations & Adjustments	
	Company P	Company S	Dr.	Cr.
Land	30,000			**(LA) 10,000**
Gain on Sale of Land		(10,000)	**(LA) 10,000**	

As usual, the selling company's income distribution schedule would reflect the deferment of the gain.

In subsequent years, assuming the land is not sold by Company P, the gain must be removed from the consolidated retained earnings. Since the sale was made by Company S, which is an 80%-owned subsidiary of Company P, the controlling interest must absorb 80% of the deferment, while the noncontrolling interest must absorb 20%. For example, the adjustments in 20X2 would be as follows:

	Partial Trial Balance		Eliminations & Adjustments	
	Company P	Company S	Dr.	Cr.
Land	30,000			**(LA) 10,000**
Retained Earnings, January 1, 20X2, Company P	(100,000)*		**(LA) 8,000**	
Retained Earnings, January 1, 20X2, Company S		(20,000)*	**(LA) 2,000**	

*arbitrary balance

Now, assume Company P sells the land in 20X3 to an outside party for $45,000, recording a gain of $15,000. When this sale occurs, the $10,000 intercompany gain also is realized. The following elimination would remove the previously unrealized gain from the consolidated retained earnings and would add it to the gain already recorded by Company P. The retained earnings adjustment is allocated 80% to the controlling interest and 20% to the noncontrolling interest, since the original sale was made by the subsidiary.

	Partial Trial Balance		Eliminations & Adjustments	
	Company P	Company S	Dr.	Cr.
Gain on Sale of Land	(15,000)			**(LA) 10,000**
Retained Earnings, January 1, 20X3, Company P	(120,000)*		**(LA) 8,000**	
Retained Earnings, January 1, 20X3, Company S		(15,000)*	**(LA) 2,000**	

*arbitrary balance

The income distribution schedule would add the $10,000 gain to the 20X3 internally generated net income of Company S. At this point, it should be clear that the gain on the intercompany sale was deferred, not eliminated. The original gain of $10,000 eventually is credited to the subsidiary. Thus, the gain does affect the noncontrolling share of consolidated net income at a future date. Any sale of a nondepreciable asset should be viewed as an agreement between the controlling and noncontrolling interests regarding the future distribution of consolidated net income.

When a parent sells a nondepreciable asset to a subsidiary, the worksheet procedures are the same, except for these areas:

1. The deferment of the gain in the year of the intercompany sale and the recognition of the gain in the year of the sale of the asset to an outside party flow through only the parent company income distribution schedule.
2. In the years subsequent to the intercompany sale through the year the land is sold to an external company, the related adjustment is made exclusively through the controlling retained earnings.

Intercompany Sale of a Depreciable Asset

Turning to the case where a depreciable plant asset is sold between affiliates, the following example illustrates the worksheet procedures necessary for the **deferment of a gain on the sale *over the asset's useful life.*** Assume that the parent, Company P, sells a machine to a subsidiary, Company S, for $30,000 on January 1, 20X1. Originally, the machine cost $32,000. Accumulated depreciation as of January 1, 20X1, is $12,000. Therefore, the book value of the machine is $20,000, and the reported gain on the sale is $10,000. Further assume that Company S (*the buyer*) believes the asset has a 5-year remaining life; thus, it records straight-line depreciation of $6,000 ($30,000 cost ÷ 5 years) annually.

The eliminations recognize the gain over the 5-year life of the asset by reducing annual depreciation charges. For consolidated reporting purposes, depreciation is based on the asset's $20,000 book value to the consolidated company. Worksheet 4-5, on pages 236 and 237, is based on the following additional facts:

Worksheet 4-5: page 236

1. Company P owns an 80% investment in Company S. The amount paid for the investment was equal to the book value of Company S's underlying equity. The simple equity method is used by Company P to record its investment.
2. There were no beginning or ending inventories, and the companies had the following separate income statements for 20X1:

	Company P	Company S
Sales	$ 200,000	$100,000
Cost of goods sold	(150,000)	(59,000)
Gross profit	$ 50,000	$ 41,000
Depreciation expense	(30,000)	(16,000)
Gain on sale of machine	10,000	
Subsidiary income (80%)	20,000	
Net income	$ 50,000	$ 25,000

The elimination entries in journal entry form are:

(CY1)	Eliminate current-year equity income:		
	Subsidiary Income	20,000	
	Investment in Company S		20,000
(EL)	Eliminate subsidiary equity against investment in subsidiary account:		
	Common Stock ($10 par), Company S	40,000	
	Retained Earnings, January 1, 20X1, Company S	60,000	
	Investment in Company S		100,000
(F1)	Eliminate intercompany gain on machine sale and reduce machine to cost:		
	Gain on Sale of Machinery	10,000	
	Machinery		10,000
(F2)	Reduce machinery depreciation to amount based on book value:		
	Accumulated Depreciation—Machinery	2,000	
	Depreciation Expense		2,000

Entry (F1) eliminates the $10,000 intercompany gain and restates the asset at its book value of $20,000 on the date of the intercompany sale.

Entry (F2) reduces the depreciation expense for the year by the difference between depreciation based on:

1. The book value [($32,000 − $12,000 = $20,000 depreciable base) ÷ 5 years = $4,000] and
2. The intercompany sales price ($30,000 depreciable base ÷ 5 years = $6,000).

The allocation of consolidated net income of $47,000 is shown in the income distribution schedules. Note that Company S (the buyer in this example) must absorb depreciation based on the agreed-upon sales price, and it is the controlling interest that realizes the benefit of the reduced depreciation as the asset is used. Also, note that the realizable profit for Company P (the seller) in any year is the depreciation absorbed by the buyer minus the depreciation for consolidated purposes ($6,000 − $4,000). If the sale had been made by Company S, the profit deferment and recognition entries would flow through its income distribution schedule.

Worksheets for periods subsequent to the sale of the machine must correct the current-year nominal accounts and remove the unrealized profit in the beginning consolidated retained earnings. Worksheet 4-6, on pages 238 to 239, portrays a consolidated worksheet for 20X2, based on the following separate income statements of Company P and Company S:

worksheet

Worksheet 4-6: page 238

	Company P	Company S
Sales	$ 250,000	$120,000
Cost of goods sold	(180,000)	(80,000)
Gross profit	$ 70,000	$ 40,000
Depreciation expense	(20,000)	(16,000)
Subsidiary income (80%)	19,200	
Net income	$ 69,200	$ 24,000

The elimination entries in journal entry form are as follows:

(CY1)	Eliminate current-year equity income:		
	Subsidiary Income	19,200	
	Investment in Company S		19,200
(EL)	Eliminate subsidiary equity against investment in subsidiary account:		
	Common Stock ($10 par), Company S	40,000	
	Retained Earnings, January 1, 20X2, Company S	80,000	
	Investment in Company S		120,000

(continued)

(F1)	Eliminate remaining intercompany gain on machine sale, reduce machine to cost, and adjust accumulated depreciation for prior year:		
	Retained Earnings, Company P, January 1, 20X2	8,000	
	Accumulated Depreciation—Machinery.	2,000	
	Machinery		10,000
(F2)	Reduce current-year machinery depreciation to amount based on book value:		
	Accumulated Depreciation—Machinery.	2,000	
	Depreciation Expense		2,000

Entry (F1) in this worksheet corrects the asset's net book value, accumulated depreciation, and retained earnings as of the beginning of the year. Since the sale was by the parent, only the controlling interest in beginning retained earnings is adjusted. Had the sale been by the subsidiary, the adjustment would have been split 20/80 to the noncontrolling and controlling interests, respectively, in beginning retained earnings.

Entry (F2) corrects the depreciation expense, and the accumulated depreciation accounts for the current year. The resulting consolidated net income of $76,000 is distributed as shown in the income distribution schedules that follow Worksheet 4-6. During each year, Company S must absorb the larger depreciation expense that resulted from its purchase of the asset. Company P has the right to realize $2,000 more of the original deferred profit.

It may occur that an asset purchased from an affiliate is sold before it is fully depreciated. To illustrate this possibility, assume that Company S of the previous example sells the asset to a third party for $14,000 at the end of the second year. Since Company S's asset cost is $30,000, with $12,000 of accumulated depreciation, the loss recorded by Company S is $4,000 ($14,000 − $18,000 net book value). However, on a consolidated basis, the $4,000 loss becomes a $2,000 gain, determined as follows:

	On Books of Company S		For Consolidated Entity	
Selling price of machine sold by Company S		$14,000		$14,000
Less book value at end of second year following sale to Company S:				
Cost of machine	$ 30,000		$20,000*	
Accumulated depreciation.	(12,000)	18,000	(8,000)	12,000
Gain (loss)		$ (4,000)		$ 2,000

*($32,000 − $12,000) = the net book value on January 1, 20X1, the date of intercompany sale.

Worksheet 4-7: page 240

Worksheet 4-7, on pages 240 and 241, is a revision of the previous worksheet so that Company S's subsequent sale of the depreciable asset at the end of the second year is included.

The elimination entries in journal entry form are as follows:

(CY1)	Eliminate current-year equity income:		
	Subsidiary Income.	16,000	
	Investment in Company S.		16,000
(EL)	Eliminate subsidiary equity against investment in subsidiary account:		
	Common Stock ($10 par), Company S.	40,000	
	Retained Earnings, January 1, 20X2, Company S	80,000	
	Investment in Company S.		120,000

(F3)	Eliminate remaining machinery gain as January 1, 20X2, and adjust recorded loss on sale to reflect book value at the time of sale:		
	Retained Earnings, Company P, January 1, 20X2	8,000	
	Depreciation Expense		2,000
	Loss on Sale of Machine (as recorded by Company S)		4,000
	Gain on Sale of Machine (on consolidated basis)		2,000

Entry (F3) removes the $8,000 remaining intercompany profit on the asset sale from controlling retained earnings, adjusts current depreciation by $2,000, and converts the $4,000 loss on the sale recorded by the subsidiary into a $2,000 gain on the consolidated statements.

However, a loss on an intercompany sale of plant assets does not have to be deferred if the loss could have been recorded in the absence of a sale. Where there has been an impairment in the value of a fixed asset, it may be written down to a lower market value. Where, however, the asset is sold to an affiliated company at a price below fair market value, the loss is to be deferred in the same manner as an intercompany gain. The loss would be deferred over the depreciation life of the asset. If the asset were sold to a nonaffiliated company, the remaining deferred loss would be recognized at the time of the sale.

Intercompany Long-Term Construction Contracts

4

OBJECTIVE

Demonstrate an understanding of the profit deferral issues for intercompany sales of assets under long-term construction contracts.

One member of an affiliated group of companies may construct a plant asset for another affiliate over an extended period of time. The company constructing the asset will record progress under the completed-contract method or the percentage-of-completion method. During construction, special adjustments may be necessary when consolidating, depending on which of the two methods is used to record the contract by the constructing affiliate. From a consolidated viewpoint, such activity amounts to the self-construction of an asset to be used by the consolidated entity. Once the asset has been sold to an affiliate, consolidation procedures are similar to those used for a normal intercompany sale of a plant asset.

Completed-Contract Method. The constructing affiliate using the completed-contract method records no profit on the asset until it is completed and transferred to the purchasing affiliate. However, costs incurred to date on the contract are capitalized in a special account, such as *Cost of Construction in Progress*. This account will appear on the trial balance of the constructing affiliate. This account should be eliminated and re-recorded as *Assets Under Construction*, which is the usual account for the cost of an asset being constructed for a company's own use.

The constructing affiliate may bill the purchasing affiliate for work done prior to the completion of the asset. When this occurs, the constructing affiliate will record billed amounts by debiting *Contracts Receivable* and crediting *Billings on Long-Term Contracts*. The billings account acts as a contra-account to Cost of Construction in Progress. The purchasing affiliate would debit *Assets Under Construction* and credit *Contracts Payable* for billings received. Consolidation procedures require that the constructing affiliate's account Billings on Long-Term Contracts be eliminated against Cost of Construction in Progress. Any excess of cost incurred over the amount of billings is closed to the purchaser's account, Assets Under Construction. In addition, it is necessary to eliminate any remaining intercompany receivable and payable amounts recorded on the long-term contract.

Percentage-of-Completion Method. This method allows the constructing company to recognize a portion of the total estimated profit on the contract as construction progresses. During the construction period, the contracting company debits an account usually entitled *Construction in Progress* for costs that are incurred to outside companies. The contractor also debits Construction in Progress and credits *Earned Income on Long-Term Contracts* for the estimated profit earned during each accounting period. Thus, the construction in progress account includes accumulated costs and estimated earnings. When the purchaser is billed, the contractor will debit the amount billed to Contracts Receivable and credit Billings on Construction in Progress, while the purchaser will debit Assets Under Construction and credit Contracts Payable.

To illustrate the elimination procedures when the percentage-of-completion method is used, assume a subsidiary, Company S, enters into a contract to construct a building for its parent company, Company P, for $500,000 and Company S estimates the cost of the building to be $400,000. During 20X1, the building is 50% completed and $200,000 of cost has been incurred as of December 31, 20X1, but only $150,000 has been billed. The contract is completed in 20X2 at an additional cost of $200,000. The entries on the books of the separate affiliates for December 20X1 are as follows:

Company S

Construction in Progress	200,000	
Payables (to outsiders)		200,000
To record costs incurred for the long-term contract under the percentage-of-completion method.		
Construction in Progress	50,000	
Earned Income on Long-Term Contracts		50,000
To record pro rata share of estimated profit [50% × ($500,000 – $400,000)].		
Contracts Receivable	150,000	
Billings on Construction in Progress		150,000
To record billing to parent for the portion of amount due under the contract.		

Company P

Assets Under Construction	150,000	
Contracts Payable		150,000
To record billing from subsidiary for amount due.		

The subsidiary's balance sheet prepared at the end of 20X1 would list a net current asset of $100,000, as the $150,000 balance in Billings on Construction in Progress would be offset against the $250,000 balance in Construction in Progress. If billings exceed the amount recorded for construction in progress, a net current liability would be shown on the balance sheet.

The following partial consolidated worksheet for 20X1 shows the relevant accounts and the eliminations that would appear for this example. The elimination procedures are complex and involve answering this question: What should remain on the consolidated statements? From a consolidated viewpoint, a self-constructed asset is in progress and $200,000 has been spent to date. *All that should remain on the consolidated statements is a $200,000 asset under construction and a $200,000 payable to outside interests.* The income distribution schedule of the constructing affiliate would reflect the profit deferral through a debit for $50,000.

Company P and Subsidiary Company S
Partial Worksheet for Consolidated Financial Statements
For Year Ended December 31, 20X1

(Credit balance amounts are in parentheses.)	Partial Trial Balance		Eliminations & Adjustments			
	Company P	Company S	Dr.		Cr.	
Assets Under Construction	150,000		(LT3)	50,000		
Contracts Receivable		150,000			(LT1)	150,000
Billings on Construction in Progress		(150,000)	(LT3)	150,000		
Construction in Progress		250,000			(LT2)	50,000
					(LT3)	200,000
Earned Income on Long-Term Contracts		(50,000)	(LT2)	50,000		
Contracts Payable	(150,000)		(LT1)	150,000		
Payables (to outsiders)		(200,000)				

Eliminations and Adjustments:

(LT1) Eliminate the intercompany debt and receivable resulting from the long-term contract.
(LT2) Eliminate the income recorded on the long-term intercompany contract and remove the profit from Construction in Progress.
(LT3) Eliminate the balances of Construction in Progress and Billings on Construction in Progress, and increase Assets Under Construction for the unbilled costs on the long-term intercompany contract.

As is true with all intercompany sales of plant assets, any intercompany profit is deferred until realized through the subsequent sale or use of the asset. Thus, the intercompany profit resulting from a long-term construction contract should be realized as the asset is depreciated. The unrealized profit will result in an adjustment to retained earnings in subsequent years.

REFLECTION

- The gain on an intercompany sale of land cannot be recognized until (if ever) the land is sold to the "outside world." The gain is deducted from the land account. In the year of intercompany sale, the gain is eliminated; in later periods, retained earnings is reduced for the amount of the gain.
- A gain on the intercompany sale of a fixed asset is eliminated in the period of sale. The gain is recognized over the depreciable life of the asset as a reduction in each period's depreciation expense.
- Any fixed asset gain, not amortized through depreciation adjustments, is recognized if the asset is later sold to the "outside world."
- Under the percentage-of-completion method for long-term projects, gains may be recorded prior to completion. Any such gains on an intercompany construction project must also be eliminated and later recognized through depreciation adjustments.

INTERCOMPANY DEBT

5
OBJECTIVE
Eliminate intercompany loans and notes.

Typically, a parent company is larger than any one of its subsidiaries and can secure funds under more favorable terms. Because of this, a parent company often will advance cash to a subsidiary. The parent may accept a note from the subsidiary as security for the loan, or the parent may discount a note that the subsidiary received from a customer. In most cases, the parent will charge a competitive interest rate for the funds advanced to the subsidiary.

In the examples that follow, the more common situation in which the parent is the lender is assumed. If the subsidiary were the lender, the theory and practice would be identical, with the only differences being the books on which the applicable accounts appear and the procedure for the distribution of combined net income.

Assume that on July 1, 20X1, an 80%-owned subsidiary, Company S, borrows $10,000 from its parent, Company P, signing a 1-year, 8% note, with interest payable on the due date. This intercompany loan will cause the following accounts and their balances to appear on the December 31, 20X1, trial balances of the separate affiliated companies:

Parent Company P		Subsidiary Company S	
Notes Receivable.	10,000	Notes Payable.	(10,000)
Interest Income.	(400)	Interest Expense.	400
Interest Receivable.	400	Interest Payable	(400)

While this information is required on the books of the separate companies, it should not appear on the consolidated statements. The procedures needed to eliminate this intercompany note and its related interest amounts are demonstrated in Worksheet 4-8, pages 242 and 243.

The elimination entries in journal entry form are as follows:

Worksheet 4-8: page 242

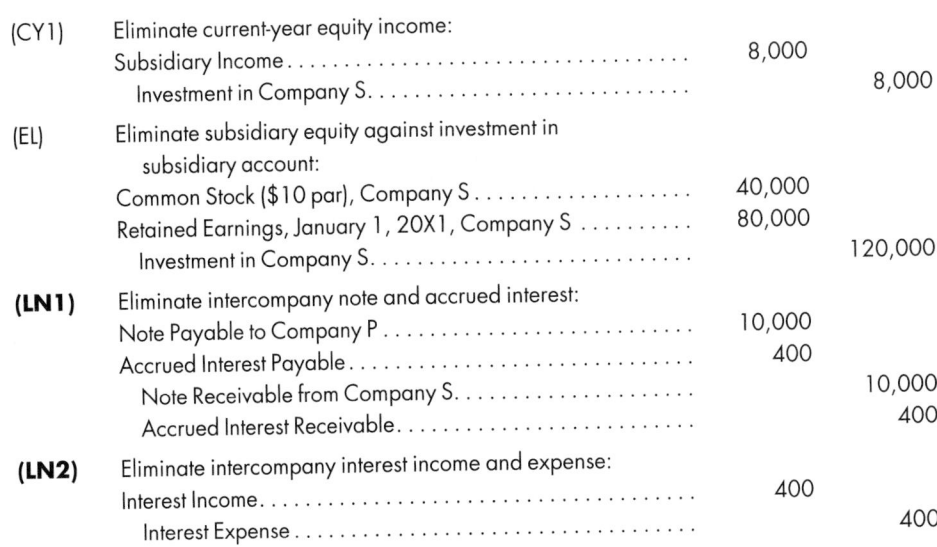

(CY1)	Eliminate current-year equity income:		
	Subsidiary Income.	8,000	
	Investment in Company S.		8,000
(EL)	Eliminate subsidiary equity against investment in subsidiary account:		
	Common Stock ($10 par), Company S.	40,000	
	Retained Earnings, January 1, 20X1, Company S	80,000	
	Investment in Company S.		120,000
(LN1)	Eliminate intercompany note and accrued interest:		
	Note Payable to Company P	10,000	
	Accrued Interest Payable.	400	
	Note Receivable from Company S.		10,000
	Accrued Interest Receivable.		400
(LN2)	Eliminate intercompany interest income and expense:		
	Interest Income.	400	
	Interest Expense		400

Entry (LN1) eliminates the intercompany receivable and payable for the note and the accrued interest on the note. Entry (LN2) eliminates the intercompany interest income and expense amounts. In this worksheet, it is assumed that the intercompany note is the only note recorded. However, sometimes an intercompany note and its related interest expense, revenue, and accruals are commingled with notes to outside parties. Before the trial balances are entered on the worksheet and before consolidation is attempted, intercompany interest expense and revenue must be accrued properly on the books of the parent and subsidiary.

After all the necessary worksheet eliminations are made, the effect of the note on the distribution of consolidated net income must be considered. There might be a temptation to increase the noncontrolling share of consolidated net income by $400 as a result of eliminating the interest expense on the intercompany note, but it is not correct to do so. Even though the interest does not appear on the consolidated income statement, it is a legitimate expense for Company S as a separate entity and a legitimate revenue for Company P as a separate entity. In essence, Company S has agreed to transfer $400 to Company P for interest during 20X1, and the NCI must respect this agreement when calculating its share of consolidated net income. Thus, the basis for calculating the noncontrolling share is the net income of Company S as a separate entity. The NCI receives 20% of this $10,000 net income which is net of the $400 of intercompany interest expense.

A parent receiving a note from a subsidiary subsequently may discount the note at a nonaffiliated financial institution in order to receive immediate cash. This results in a note receivable discounted being recorded by the parent. From a consolidated viewpoint, there is a note payable to outside parties. Consolidation procedures should eliminate the internal note receivable against the note receivable discounted. This elimination will result in the note, now payable to an outside party, being extended to the consolidated balance sheet. Intercompany interest accrued prior to the discounting is eliminated. Interest paid by the subsidiary subsequent to the discounting is paid to the outside party and is not eliminated. The net interest expense or revenue on the discounting of the note is a transaction between the parent and the outside party and, thus, is not eliminated. When consolidated statements are prepared, however, it is desirable to net the interest expense on the note recorded by the maker subsequent to the discounting of the note against the net interest expense or revenue on the discounting transaction.

REFLECTION

- Intercompany debt balances, including accrued interest receivable/payable, are eliminated.
- Intercompany interest expense/revenue is also eliminated. These amounts are equal; thus, there is no effect on consolidated net income.

SOPHISTICATED EQUITY METHOD: INTERCOMPANY TRANSACTIONS

6

OBJECTIVE

Discuss the complications intercompany profits create for the use of the sophisticated equity method.

Chapter 3 demonstrated the use of the sophisticated equity method for the parent's recording of its investment in a subsidiary. Recall that one major difference between the simple and sophisticated equity methods was that the latter records subsidiary income net of amortizations of excess. In contrast, the simple equity method ignores amortizations and records as income for the parent the subsidiary reported income multiplied by the parent's percentage of ownership. Some companies using the sophisticated equity method will proceed to the next level of complexity. Instead of adjusting for their share of the income reported by the subsidiary (as under the simple equity method), they will adjust for their share of subsidiary income after it is adjusted for intercompany profits. This means that, before the parent can make an equity adjustment for income of the subsidiary, it must prepare an income distribution schedule for the subsidiary company. **The adjusted net income derived in the income distribution schedule will become the income to which the parent ownership percentage is applied to arrive at equity income.**

The added complexity of the sophisticated equity method is unwarranted when statements are to be consolidated, since the subsidiary income and the investment in subsidiary accounts are eliminated entirely. However, this procedure must be used in the rare case when a subsidiary is not to be consolidated or when parent-only statements are to be prepared as a supplement to the consolidated statements.

Unrealized Profits of the Current Period

The case of intercompany profits generated only during the current period will be considered first. Although the same procedure applies to all types of subsidiary-generated unrealized intercompany profits and losses of the current period, the impact of the sophisticated equity method will be demonstrated assuming only the existence of inventory profits.

The following example is based on the information presented in Worksheet 4-2, but this time the parent is using the sophisticated equity method. Because of this fact, the parent has to prepare a subsidiary income distribution schedule before it can record its share of subsidiary income. This schedule is shown on the following page. Note that, instead of recording **on its books** a subsidiary income of $60,000, the parent would have recorded $53,600:

Equity Income: Subsidiary Company S

Unrealized profit in ending inventory	$8,000	Internally generated net income	$ 75,000
		Adjusted income	$ 67,000
		Controlling share	× **80%**
		Controlling interest	**$ 53,600***

*This is the same amount that is shown in the parent's income distribution schedule for Worksheet 4-2.

The only elimination procedure in this example that differs from Worksheet 4-2 is entry (CY1), which eliminates the entry made by the parent to record its share of the subsidiary current period income. There is no impact on the other worksheet procedures, and the balance of Worksheet 4-2 would be unchanged. A portion of the revised worksheet is shown on page 225.

Unrealized Profits of Current and Prior Periods

The effect of the sophisticated equity method when there are intercompany profits from current and prior periods is demonstrated in the following example, which is based on the information given in Worksheet 4-3. The subsidiary income reported by the parent in 20X2 under the sophisticated equity method is calculated as follows:

Equity Income: Subsidiary Company S

Unrealized profit in ending inventory	$6,000	Internally generated net income	$ 60,000
		Realized profit in beginning inventory	8,000
		Adjusted income	$ 62,000
		Controlling share	× **80%**
		Controlling interest	**$ 49,600**

The elimination procedures illustrated in the following partial worksheets are applicable to all types of subsidiary-generated intercompany profits and losses of prior and current periods. The differences in the parent's trial balance are explained in the notes that follow the partial worksheet on page 226.

Company P and Subsidiary Company S
Partial Worksheet
For Year Ended December 31, **20X1**

(Credit balance amounts are in parentheses.)	Partial Trial Balance		Eliminations & Adjustments	
	Company P	Company S	Dr.	Cr.
Accounts Receivable	110,000	150,000		(IA) 25,000
Inventory, December 31, 20X1	70,000	40,000		(EI) 8,000
Investment in Company S	**(b) 189,600**			**(CY1) 53,600**
				(EL) 136,000
Other Assets	314,000	155,000		
Accounts Payable	(80,000)	(100,000)	(IA) 25,000	
Common Stock ($10 par), Co. P	(200,000)			
Retained Earnings, January 1, 20X1, Co. P	(250,000)			
Common Stock ($10 par), Co. S		(100,000)	(EL) 80,000	
Retained Earnings, January 1, 20X1, Co. S		(70,000)	(EL) 56,000	
Sales	(700,000)	(500,000)	(IS) 100,000	
Cost of Goods Sold	510,000	350,000	(EI) 8,000	(IS) 100,000
Expenses	90,000	75,000		
Subsidiary Income	**(a) (53,600)**		**(CY1) 53,600**	
	0	0	322,600	322,600

Notes to Trial Balance:

(a) See the previously prepared income distribution schedule.
(b) $136,000 beginning-of-year balance + $53,600 sophisticated equity method income.

Eliminations and Adjustments:

(CY1) Eliminate the entry recording the parent's share (80%) of the subsidiary net income under the sophisticated equity method.
(EL, IS, EI, and IA) Same as Worksheet 4-2.

Company P and Subsidiary Company S
Partial Worksheet
For Year Ended December 31, **20X2**

(Credit balance amounts are in parentheses.)	Partial Trial Balance		Eliminations & Adjustments	
	Company P	Company S	Dr.	Cr.
Accounts Receivable	160,000	170,000		(IA) 60,000
Inventory, December 31, 20X2	60,000	50,000		(EI) 6,000
Investment in Company S	**(c) 239,200**			**(CY1) 49,600**
				(EL) 189,600
Other Assets	354,000	165,000		
Accounts Payable	(90,000)	(80,000)	(IA) 60,000	
Common Stock ($10 par), Co. P	(200,000)			
Retained Earnings, January 1, 20X2, Co. P	**(b) (403,600)**			
Common Stock ($10 par), Co. S		(100,000)	**(EL) 80,000**	
Retained Earnings, January 1, 20X2, Co. S		(145,000)	**(Adj) 8,000**	
			(EL) 109,600	
Sales	(800,000)	(600,000)	(IS) 120,000	
Cost of Goods Sold	610,000	440,000	(EI) 6,000	**(Adj) 8,000**
				(IS) 120,000
Expenses	120,000	100,000		
Subsidiary Income	**(a) (49,600)**		**(CY1) 49,600**	
	0	0	433,200	433,200

Notes to Trial Balance:

(a) See the previously prepared income distribution schedule.
(b) $410,000 simple equity balance – (80% × $8,000 subsidiary beginning inventory profit).
(c) $136,000 original balance + $53,600 sophisticated equity method income for 20X1 + $49,600 sophisticated equity method income for 20X2.

Eliminations and Adjustments:

(Adj) Eliminate the $8,000 beginning inventory profit from the cost of goods sold and the subsidiary beginning retained earnings accounts. This entry replaces entry (BI) of Worksheet 4-3.
(CY1) Eliminate the entry recording the parent's share (80%) of the subsidiary net income under the sophisticated equity method.
(EL) Eliminate 80% of the subsidiary equity balances against the investment account. The elimination of Retained Earnings is 80% of the adjusted balance of $137,000 ($145,000 – $8,000).
(IS, EI, and IA) Same as Worksheet 4-3.

When the sophisticated equity method is used, the worksheet elimination of the parent's investment account against the stockholders' equity of the subsidiary is more complicated because there is an inconsistency between the parent's accounts and those of the subsidiary. In the 20X2 partial worksheet illustrated, the parent's investment and retained earnings accounts do not reflect the $8,000 beginning inventory profit recorded by the subsidiary. The intercompany profit was removed in the prior period before the parent's share of the subsidiary's net income was recorded. The subsidiary's trial balance does include the $8,000 beginning inventory profit in the January 1 retained earnings balance, and the parent's beginning inventory, now in the cost of goods sold, does include the profit. The inconsistency is removed on the worksheet by making an adjustment, coded "Adj," that removes the intercompany profit from the subsidiary's beginning retained earnings and the parent's beginning inventory. This entry replaces entry (BI) in Worksheet 4-3.

Entry (CY1) of the partial worksheet removes the subsidiary income as recorded by the parent. Entry (EL) reflects the adjustment of the subsidiary's Retained Earnings. The remaining entries and worksheet procedures are identical to those in Worksheet 4-3.

REFLECTION

- When used properly, the sophisticated equity method should record annual subsidiary income net of all intercompany profits.
- The parent's beginning retained earnings will not include prior periods' intercompany profits, but the subsidiary's beginning retained earnings does. The subsidiary's beginning retained earnings must be adjusted for these profits prior to its elimination.

APPENDIX: INTERCOMPANY PROFIT ELIMINATIONS ON THE VERTICAL WORKSHEET

7

OBJECTIVE

Apply intercompany profit eliminations on a vertical worksheet.

worksheet

Worksheet 4-9: page 244

In keeping with the overall worksheet format approach of this text, all previous examples in this chapter have been presented using the horizontal worksheet style. Worksheet 4-9, page 244, provides the reader an opportunity to study the vertical worksheet when intercompany merchandise and plant asset transactions are involved. This worksheet is based on the following facts:

1. Company P purchased an 80% interest in Company S on January 1, 20X1. At that time, the following determination and distribution of excess schedule was prepared:

Price paid		$500,000
Less interest acquired:		
Common stock ($5 par)	$ 200,000	
Retained earnings, January 1, 20X1	350,000	
Total stockholders' equity	$ 550,000	
Interest acquired	× 80%	440,000
Excess of cost over book value attributed to goodwill		$ 60,000

2. Company P accounts for the investment under the simple equity method.
3. Company S sells merchandise to Company P to yield a gross profit of 20%. Sales totaled $150,000 during 20X2. There were $40,000 of such goods in Company P's beginning inventory and $50,000 of such goods in Company P's ending inventory. As of December 31, 20X2, Company P had not paid the $20,000 owed for the purchases.
4. On July 1, 20X1, Company P sold a new machine that cost $20,000 to Company S for $25,000. At that time, both companies believed that the machine had a 5-year remaining life; both companies use straight-line depreciation.
5. Company S declared and paid $20,000 in dividends during 20X2.

Notice that the eliminations in Worksheet 4-9 are identical to those required for the horizontal format. Also, when working with the vertical format, keep in mind the cautions that are stated in Appendix A of Chapter 3: (a) the nominal accounts are presented above the balance sheet accounts, and (b) the eliminations are made only to the *beginning* retained earnings accounts. The carrydown procedures for the vertical worksheet are the same as those presented in Appendix A of Chapter 3.

REFLECTION

- On a vertical worksheet, the eliminating and adjusting entries are the same as those on a trial balance worksheet.

Worksheet 4-1

Intercompany Sales; No Intercompany Goods in Inventories
Company P and Subsidiary Company S
Worksheet for Consolidated Financial Statements
For Year Ended December 31, **20X1**

	(Credit balance amounts are in parentheses.)	Trial Balance	
		Company P	Company S
1	**Accounts Receivable**	**110,000**	**150,000**
2	Inventory, December 31, 20X1	70,000	40,000
3	Investment in Company S	196,000	
4			
5	Other Assets	314,000	155,000
6	**Accounts Payable**	**(80,000)**	**(100,000)**
7	Common Stock ($10 par), Company P	(200,000)	
8	Retained Earnings, January 1, 20X1, Company P	(250,000)	
9	Common Stock ($10 par), Company S		(100,000)
10	Retained Earnings, January 1, 20X1, Company S		(70,000)
11	**Sales**	**(700,000)**	**(500,000)**
12	**Cost of Goods Sold**	**510,000**	**350,000**
13	Expenses	90,000	75,000
14	Subsidiary Income	(60,000)	
15		0	0
16	Consolidated Net Income		
17	To NCI (see distribution schedule)		
18	Balance to Controlling Interest (see distribution schedule)		
19	Total NCI		
20	Retained Earnings, Controlling Interest, December 31, 20X1		
21			

Eliminations and Adjustments:

(CY1) Eliminate the entry recording the parent's share of subsidiary net income.
(EL) Eliminate against the investment in Company S account the pro rata portion of the subsidiary equity balances (80%) owned by the parent. To simplify the elimination, there is no discrepancy between the cost and book values of the investment in this example. Also, note that the worksheet process is expedited by always eliminating the intercompany investment first.
(IS) Eliminate the intercompany sales to avoid double counting. Now only Company S's original purchase from third parties and Company P's final sale to third parties remain in the consolidated income statement.
(IA) Eliminate the $25,000 intercompany trade balances resulting from the intercompany sale.

Worksheet 4-1 (see page 207)

Eliminations & Adjustments Dr.		Eliminations & Adjustments Cr.		Consolidated Income Statement	NCI	Controlling Retained Earnings	Consolidated Balance Sheet	
		(IA)	**25,000**				235,000	1
							110,000	2
		(CY1)	60,000					3
		(EL)	136,000					4
							469,000	5
(IA)	**25,000**						(155,000)	6
							(200,000)	7
						(250,000)		8
(EL)	80,000				(20,000)			9
(EL)	56,000				(14,000)			10
(IS)	**100,000**			(1,100,000)				11
		(IS)	**100,000**	760,000				12
				165,000				13
(CY1)	60,000							14
	321,000		321,000					15
				(175,000)				16
				15,000	(15,000)			17
				160,000		(160,000)		18
					(49,000)		(49,000)	19
						(410,000)	(410,000)	20
							0	21

Subsidiary Company S Income Distribution

	Internally generated net income	$ 75,000
	Adjusted income	$ 75,000
	NCI share	× 20%
	NCI	$ 15,000

Parent Company P Income Distribution

	Internally generated net income	$100,000
	80% × Company S adjusted income of $75,000	60,000
	Controlling interest	$160,000

Worksheet 4-2

Intercompany Goods in Ending Inventory
Company P and Subsidiary Company S
Worksheet for Consolidated Financial Statements
For Year Ended December 31, **20X1**

	(Credit balance amounts are in parentheses.)	Trial Balance	
		Company P	Company S
1	Accounts Receivable	110,000	150,000
2	**Inventory, December 31, 20X1**	**70,000**	**40,000**
3	Investment in Company S	196,000	
4			
5	Other Assets	314,000	155,000
6	Accounts Payable	(80,000)	(100,000)
7	Common Stock ($10 par), Company P	(200,000)	
8	Retained Earnings, January 1, 20X1, Company P	(250,000)	
9	Common Stock ($10 par), Company S		(100,000)
10	Retained Earnings, January 1, 20X1, Company S		(70,000)
11	Sales	(700,000)	(500,000)
12	**Cost of Goods Sold**	**510,000**	**350,000**
13	Expenses	90,000	75,000
14	Subsidiary Income	(60,000)	
15		0	0
16	Consolidated Net Income		
17	To NCI (see distribution schedule)		
18	Balance to Controlling Interest (see distribution schedule)		
19	Total NCI		
20	Retained Earnings, Controlling Interest, December 31, 20X1		
21			

Eliminations and Adjustments:

(CY1) Eliminate the entry recording the parent's share of subsidiary net income.
(EL) Eliminate 80% of the subsidiary equity balances against the investment in Company S account. There is no excess of cost or book value in this example.
(IS) Eliminate the intercompany sale.
(EI) Eliminate intercompany profit in ending inventory.
(IA) Eliminate the intercompany trade balances.

Worksheet 4-2 (see page 210)

Eliminations & Adjustments Dr.		Eliminations & Adjustments Cr.		Consolidated Income Statement	NCI	Controlling Retained Earnings	Consolidated Balance Sheet	
		(IA)	25,000				235,000	1
		(EI)	**8,000**				102,000	2
		(CY1)	60,000					3
		(EL)	136,000					4
							469,000	5
(IA)	25,000						(155,000)	6
							(200,000)	7
						(250,000)		8
(EL)	80,000				(20,000)			9
(EL)	56,000				(14,000)			10
(IS)	100,000			(1,100,000)				11
(EI)	**8,000**	(IS)	100,000	768,000				12
				165,000				13
(CY1)	60,000							14
	329,000		329,000					15
				(167,000)				16
				13,400	(13,400)			17
				153,600		(153,600)		18
					(47,400)		(47,400)	19
						(403,600)	(403,600)	20
							0	21

Subsidiary Company S Income Distribution

Unrealized profit in ending inventory .... **(EI)**	**$8,000**	Internally generated net income	$ 75,000
		Adjusted income	$ 67,000
		NCI share	× 20%
		NCI	$ 13,400

Parent Company P Income Distribution

	Internally generated net income	$100,000
	80% × Company S adjusted income of $67,000	53,600
	Controlling interest	$153,600

Worksheet 4-3

Intercompany Goods in Beginning and Ending Inventories
Company P and Subsidiary Company S
Worksheet for Consolidated Financial Statements
For Year Ended December 31, **20X2**

	(Credit balance amounts are in parentheses.)	Trial Balance	
		Company P	Company S
1	Accounts Receivable	160,000	170,000
2	**Inventory, December 31, 20X2**	**60,000**	**50,000**
3	Investment in Company S	244,000	
4			
5	Other Assets	354,000	165,000
6	Accounts Payable	(90,000)	(80,000)
7	Common Stock ($10 par), Company P	(200,000)	
8	**Retained Earnings, January 1, 20X2, Company P**	**(410,000)**	
9	Common Stock ($10 par), Company S		(100,000)
10	**Retained Earnings, January 1, 20X2, Company S**		**(145,000)**
11			
12	Sales	(800,000)	(600,000)
13	**Cost of Goods Sold**	**610,000**	**440,000**
14			
15	Expenses	120,000	100,000
16	Subsidiary Income	(48,000)	
17		0	0
18	Consolidated Net Income		
19	To NCI (see distribution schedule)		
20	Balance to Controlling Interest (see distribution schedule)		
21	Total NCI		
22	Retained Earnings, Controlling Interest, December 31, 20X2		
23			

Eliminations and Adjustments:

(CY1) Eliminate the entry recording the parent's share of subsidiary net income.
(EL) Eliminate 80% of the subsidiary equity balances against the investment in Company S account. There is no excess of cost or book value in this example.
(BI) Eliminate the intercompany profit of $8,000 (20% × $40,000) in the beginning inventory by reducing both the cost of goods sold and the beginning retained earnings accounts. 20% of the decrease in retained earnings is shared by the noncontrolling interest, since, in this case, the *selling company was the subsidiary*. If the parent had been the seller, only the controlling interest in retained earnings would be decreased. It should be noted that the $8,000 profit is shifted from 20X1 to 20X2, since, as a result of the entry, the 20X2 consolidated cost of goods sold balance is reduced by $8,000. This procedure emphasizes the concept that intercompany inventory profit is not eliminated but only deferred until inventory is sold to an outsider.
(IS) Eliminate the intercompany sales to avoid double counting.
(EI) Eliminate the intercompany profit of $6,000 (20% × $ 30,000) recorded by Company S for the intercompany goods contained in Company P's ending inventory, and increase the cost of goods sold balance by this same amount.
(IA) Eliminate the intercompany trade balances.

Worksheet 4-3 (see page 211)

Eliminations & Adjustments Dr.		Eliminations & Adjustments Cr.		Consolidated Income Statement	NCI	Controlling Retained Earnings	Consolidated Balance Sheet	
		(IA)	60,000				270,000	1
		(EI)	**6,000**				104,000	2
		(CY1)	48,000					3
		(EL)	196,000					4
							519,000	5
(IA)	60,000						(110,000)	6
							(200,000)	7
(BI)	**6,400**					(403,600)		8
(EL)	80,000				(20,000)			9
(EL)	116,000							10
(BI)	**1,600**				(27,400)			11
(IS)	120,000			(1,280,000)				12
(EI)	**6,000**	**(BI)**	**8,000**					13
		(IS)	120,000	928,000				14
				220,000				15
(CY1)	48,000							16
	438,000		438,000					17
				(132,000)				18
				12,400	(12,400)			19
				119,600		(119,600)		20
					(59,800)		(59,800)	21
						(523,200)	(523,200)	22
							0	23

Subsidiary Company S Income Distribution

Unrealized profit in ending inventory, 20% × $30,000 . . . .(EI) $6,000	Internally generated net income	$ 60,000
	Realized profit in beginning inventory, 20% × $40,000 . . . . (BI)	**8,000**
	Adjusted income	$ 62,000
	NCI share	× 20%
	NCI	$ 12,400

Parent Company P Income Distribution

	Internally generated net income	$ 70,000
	80% × Company S adjusted income of $62,000	49,600
	Controlling interest	$119,600

Worksheet 4-4

Intercompany Goods in Beginning and Ending Inventories; Periodic Inventory
Company P and Subsidiary Company S
Worksheet for Consolidated Financial Statements
For Year Ended December 31, **20X2**

	(Credit balance amounts are in parentheses.)	Trial Balance	
		Company P	Company S
1	Accounts Receivable	160,000	170,000
2	**Inventory, January 1, 20X2**	**70,000**	**40,000**
3	Investment in Company S	244,000	
4			
5	Other Assets	354,000	165,000
6	Accounts Payable	(90,000)	(80,000)
7	Common Stock ($10 par), Company P	(200,000)	
8	**Retained Earnings, January 1, 20X2, Company P**	**(410,000)**	
9	Common Stock ($10 par), Company S		(100,000)
10	**Retained Earnings, January 1, 20X2, Company S**		**(145,000)**
11			
12	Sales	(800,000)	(600,000)
13	**Purchases**	**600,000**	**450,000**
14	**Inventory, December 31, 20X2: Asset**	**60,000**	**50,000**
15	**Cost of Goods Sold**	**(60,000)**	**(50,000)**
16	Expenses	120,000	100,000
17	Subsidiary Income	(48,000)	
18		0	0
19	Consolidated Net Income		
20	To NCI (see distribution schedule)		
21	Balance to Controlling Interest (see distribution schedule)		
22	Total NCI		
23	Retained Earnings, Controlling Interest, December 31, 20X2		
24			

Eliminations and Adjustments:

(CY1) Eliminate the entry recording the parent's share of subsidiary net income.
(EL) Eliminate 80% of the subsidiary equity balances against the investment in Company S account. There is no excess of cost or book value in this example.
(BI) Eliminate the intercompany profit of $8,000 (20% × $40,000) in the beginning inventory by reducing both the cost of goods sold and the beginning retained earnings accounts. 20% of the decrease in retained earnings is shared by the noncontrolling interest, since, in this case, the *selling company was the subsidiary*. If the parent had been the seller, only the controlling interest in retained earnings would be decreased. It should be noted that the $8,000 profit is shifted from 20X1 to 20X2, since, as a result of the entry, the 20X2 consolidated cost of goods sold balance is reduced by $8,000. This procedure emphasizes the concept that intercompany inventory profit is not eliminated but only deferred until inventory is sold to an outsider.
(IS) Eliminate the intercompany sales to avoid double counting.
(EI) Enter the combined ending inventories of Company P and Company S, $60,000 and $50,000, respectively, less the intercompany profit of $6,000 (20% × $30,000) recorded by Company S for the intercompany goods contained in Company P's ending inventory.
(IA) Eliminate the intercompany trade balances.

Worksheet 4-4 (see page 213)

Eliminations & Adjustments				Consolidated Income Statement	NCI	Controlling Retained Earnings	Consolidated Balance Sheet	
Dr.		Cr.						
		(IA)	60,000				270,000	1
		(BI)	**8,000**	102,000				2
		(CY1)	48,000					3
		(EL)	196,000					4
							519,000	5
(IA)	60,000						(110,000)	6
							(200,000)	7
(BI)	**6,400**					(403,600)		8
(EL)	80,000				(20,000)			9
(EL)	116,000							10
(BI)	**1,600**				(27,400)			11
(IS)	**120,000**			(1,280,000)				12
		(IS)	**120,000**	930,000				13
		(EI)	**6,000**				104,000	14
(EI)	**6,000**			(104,000)				15
				220,000				16
(CY1)	48,000							17
	438,000		438,000					18
				(132,000)				19
				12,400	(12,400)			20
				119,600		(119,600)		21
					(59,800)		(59,800)	22
						(523,200)	(523,200)	23
							0	24

Subsidiary Company S Income Distribution

Unrealized profit in ending inventory, 20% × $30,000 .... **(EI)**	**$6,000**	Internally generated net income	$ 60,000[a]
		Realized profit in beginning inventory, 20% × $40,000 .... **(BI)**	**8,000**
		Adjusted income	$ 62,000
		NCI share	× 20%
		NCI	$ 12,400

[a][$600,000 – ($40,000 + $450,000 – $50,000) – $100,000 = $60,000]

Parent Company P Income Distribution

	Internally generated net income	$ 70,000[b]
	80% × Company S adjusted income of $62,000	49,600
	Controlling interest	$119,600

[b][$800,000 – ($70,000 + $600,000 – $60,000) – $120,000 = $70,000]

Worksheet 4-5

Intercompany Sale of Depreciable Asset
Company P and Subsidiary Company S
Worksheet for Consolidated Financial Statements
For Year Ended December 31, **20X1**

	(Credit balance amounts are in parentheses.)	Trial Balance		
		Company P		Company S
1	Current Assets	15,000		20,000
2	**Machinery**	50,000	**(a)**	**230,000**
3	**Accumulated Depreciation—Machinery**	(25,000)	**(b)**	**(100,000)**
4	Investment in Company S	120,000		
5				
6	Common Stock ($10 par), Company P	(100,000)		
7	Retained Earnings, January 1, 20X1, Company P	(10,000)		
8	Common Stock ($10 par), Company S			(50,000)
9	Retained Earnings, January 1, 20X1, Company S			(75,000)
10	Sales	(200,000)		(100,000)
11	Cost of Goods Sold	150,000		59,000
12	**Depreciation Expense**	30,000	**(b)**	**16,000**
13	**Gain on Sale of Machine**	**(10,000)**		
14	Subsidiary Income	(20,000)		
15		0		0
16	Consolidated Net Income			
17	To NCI (see distribution schedule)			
18	Balance to Controlling Interest (see distribution schedule)			
19	Total NCI			
20	Retained Earnings, Controlling Interest, December 31, 20X1			
21				

Notes to Trial Balance:

(a) Includes machine purchased for $30,000 from Company P on January 1, 20X1.
(b) Includes $6,000 depreciation on machine purchased from Company P on January 1, 20X1.

Eliminations and Adjustments:

(CY1) Eliminate the entry recording the parent's share of subsidiary net income for the current year.
(EL) Eliminate 80% of the subsidiary equity balances against the investment account. There is no excess to be distributed.
(F1) Eliminate the $10,000 gain on the intercompany sale of the machine, and reduce machine to book value.
(F2) Reduce the depreciation expense and accumulated depreciation accounts to reflect the depreciation ($4,000 per year) based on the consolidated book value of the machine, rather than the depreciation ($6,000 per year) based on the sales price.

Worksheet 4-5 (see page 216)

Eliminations & Adjustments Dr.	Eliminations & Adjustments Cr.	Consolidated Income Statement	NCI	Controlling Retained Earnings	Consolidated Balance Sheet	
					35,000	1
	(F1) 10,000				270,000	2
(F2) 2,000					(123,000)	3
	(CY1) 20,000					4
	(EL) 100,000					5
					(100,000)	6
				(10,000)		7
(EL) 40,000			(10,000)			8
(EL) 60,000			(15,000)			9
		(300,000)				10
		209,000				11
	(F2) 2,000	44,000				12
(F1) 10,000						13
(CY1) 20,000						14
132,000	132,000					15
		(47,000)				16
		5,000	(5,000)			17
		42,000		(42,000)		18
			(30,000)		(30,000)	19
				(52,000)	(52,000)	20
					0	21

Subsidiary Company S Income Distribution

	Internally generated net income	$25,000
	Adjusted income	$25,000
	NCI share	× 20%
	NCI	$ 5,000

Parent Company P Income Distribution

Unrealized gain on sale of machine (F1)	**$10,000**	Internally generated net income (including sale of machine)	$30,000
		80% × Company S adjusted income of $25,000	20,000
		Gain realized through use of machine sold to subsidiary (F2)	**2,000**
		Controlling interest	$42,000

Worksheet 4-6

Intercompany Sale of Depreciable Asset
Company P and Subsidiary Company S
Worksheet for Consolidated Financial Statements
For Year Ended December 31, **20X2**

	(Credit balance amounts are in parentheses.)	Trial Balance		
		Company P		Company S
1	Current Assets	85,000		60,000
2	**Machinery**	50,000	(a)	**230,000**
3	**Accumulated Depreciation—Machinery**	(45,000)	(b)	**(116,000)**
4				
5	Investment in Company S	139,200		
6				
7	Common Stock ($10 par), Company P	(100,000)		
8	**Retained Earnings, January 1, 20X2, Company P**	**(60,000)**		
9	Common Stock ($10 par), Company S			(50,000)
10	Retained Earnings, January 1, 20X2, Company S			(100,000)
11	Sales	(250,000)		(120,000)
12	**Cost of Goods Sold**	180,000		80,000
13	**Depreciation Expense**	20,000	(c)	**16,000**
14	Subsidiary Income	(19,200)		
15		0		0
16	Consolidated Net Income			
17	To NCI (see distribution schedule)			
18	Balance to Controlling Interest (see distribution schedule)			
19	Total NCI			
20	Retained Earnings, Controlling Interest, December 31, 20X2			
21				

Notes to Trial Balance:

(a) Includes machine purchased for $30,000 from Company P on January 1, 20X1.
(b) Includes $12,000 accumulated depreciation ($6,000 per year) on machine purchased from Company P on January 1, 20X1.
(c) Includes $6,000 depreciation on machine purchased from Company P on January 1, 20X1.

Eliminations and Adjustments:

(CY1) Eliminate the entry recording the parent's share of subsidiary net income for the current year.
(EL) Eliminate 80% of the subsidiary equity balances against the investment account. There is no excess to be distributed.
(F1) Eliminate the gain on the intercompany sale as it is reflected in beginning retained earnings on the parent's trial balance. Since the sale was made by the *parent*, Company P, the entire unrealized gain at the beginning of the year (now $8,000) is removed from the controlling retained earnings beginning balance. If the sale had been made by the subsidiary, the adjustment of beginning retained earnings would be split 80% to the controlling interest and 20% to the noncontrolling interest.
(F2) Reduce the depreciation expense and accumulated depreciation accounts to reflect the depreciation based on the consolidated book value of the asset on the date of sale. This entry will bring the accumulated depreciation account to its correct consolidated year-end balance.

Worksheet 4-6 (see page 217)

Eliminations & Adjustments				Consolidated Income Statement	NCI	Controlling Retained Earnings	Consolidated Balance Sheet	
Dr.		Cr.						
							145,000	1
		(F1)	**10,000**				270,000	2
(F1)	**2,000**						(157,000)	3
(F2)	**2,000**							4
		(CY1)	19,200					5
		(EL)	120,000					6
							(100,000)	7
(F1)	**8,000**					(52,000)		8
(EL)	40,000				(10,000)			9
(EL)	80,000				(20,000)			10
				(370,000)				11
				260,000				12
		(F2)	**2,000**	34,000				13
(CY1)	19,200							14
	151,200		151,200					15
				(76,000)				16
				4,800	(4,800)			17
				71,200		(71,200)		18
					(34,800)		(34,800)	19
						(123,200)	(123,200)	20
							0	21

Subsidiary Company S Income Distribution

	Internally generated net income	$24,000
	Adjusted income	$24,000
	NCI share	× 20%
	NCI	$ 4,800

Parent Company P Income Distribution

	Internally generated net income	$50,000
	80% of Company S adjusted income of $24,000	19,200
	Gain realized through use of machine sold to subsidiary .... **(F2)**	**2,000**
	Controlling interest	$71,200

Worksheet 4-7

Intercompany Sale of a Depreciable Asset; Subsequent Sale of Asset to an Outside Party
Company P and Subsidiary Company S
Worksheet for Consolidated Financial Statements
For Year Ended December 31, **20X2**

	(Credit balance amounts are in parentheses.)	Trial Balance	
		Company P	Company S
1	Current Assets	85,000	74,000
2	Machinery	50,000	200,000
3	Accumulated Depreciation—Machinery	(45,000)	(104,000)
4	Investment in Company S	136,000	
5			
6	Common Stock ($10 par), Company P	(100,000)	
7	**Retained Earnings, January 1, 20X2, Company P**	**(60,000)**	
8	Common Stock ($10 par), Company S		(50,000)
9	Retained Earnings, January 1, 20X2, Company S		(100,000)
10	Sales	(250,000)	(120,000)
11	Cost of Goods Sold	180,000	80,000
12	**Depreciation Expense**	20,000	**16,000**
13	**Loss on Sale of Machine**		**4,000**
14	Subsidiary Income	(16,000)	
15	**Gain on Sale of Machine**		
16		0	0
17	Consolidated Net Income		
18	To NCI (see distribution schedule)		
19	Balance to Controlling Interest (see distribution schedule)		
20	Total NCI		
21	Retained Earnings, Controlling Interest, December 31, 20X2		
22			

Eliminations and Adjustments:

(CY1) Eliminate the entry recording the parent's share of subsidiary net income for the current year.
(EL) Eliminate 80% of the subsidiary equity balances against the investment account. There is no excess to be distributed.
(F3) Eliminate the gain on the intercompany sale as it is reflected in the parent's beginning retained earnings account, adjust the current year's depreciation expense, and revise the recording of the sale of the equipment to an outside party to reflect the net book value of the asset to the consolidated company.

Worksheet 4-7 (see page 218)

Eliminations & Adjustments Dr.		Eliminations & Adjustments Cr.		Consolidated Income Statement	NCI	Controlling Retained Earnings	Consolidated Balance Sheet	
							159,000	1
							250,000	2
							(149,000)	3
		(CY1)	16,000					4
		(EL)	120,000					5
							(100,000)	6
(F3)	**8,000**					(52,000)		7
(EL)	40,000				(10,000)			8
(EL)	80,000				(20,000)			9
				(370,000)				10
				260,000				11
		(F3)	**2,000**	34,000				12
		(F3)	**4,000**					13
(CY1)	16,000							14
		(F3)	**2,000**	(2,000)				15
	144,000		144,000					16
				(78,000)				17
				4,000	(4,000)			18
				74,000		(74,000)		19
					(34,000)		(34,000)	20
						(126,000)	(126,000)	21
							0	22

Subsidiary Company S Income Distribution

	Internally generated net income	$20,000
	Adjusted income	$20,000
	NCI share	× 20%
	NCI	$ 4,000

Parent Company P Income Distribution

	Internally generated net income	$50,000
	80% × Company S adjusted income of $20,000	16,000
	Gain realized on sale of machine (F3)	**8,000**[a]
	Controlling interest	$74,000

[a]$10,000 original gain − $2,000 realized in 20X1

Worksheet 4-8

Intercompany Notes
Company P and Subsidiary Company S
Worksheet for Consolidated Financial Statements
For Year Ended December 31, **20X1**

	(Credit balance amounts are in parentheses.)	Trial Balance	
		Company P	Company S
1	Cash	35,000	20,400
2	**Note Receivable from Company S**	**10,000**	
3	**Interest Receivable**	**400**	
4	Property, Plant, and Equipment (net)	140,000	150,000
5	Investment in Company S	128,000	
6			
7	**Note Payable to Company P**		**(10,000)**
8	**Interest Payable**		**(400)**
9	Common Stock, Company P	(100,000)	
10	Retained Earnings, January 1, 20X1, Company P	(200,000)	
11	Common Stock, Company S		(50,000)
12	Retained Earnings, January 1, 20X1, Company S		(100,000)
13	Sales	(120,000)	(50,000)
14	**Interest Income**	**(400)**	
15	Subsidiary Income	(8,000)	
16	Cost of Goods Sold	75,000	20,000
17	Other Expenses	40,000	19,600
18	**Interest Expense**		**400**
19		0	0
20	Consolidated Net Income		
21	To NCI (see distribution schedule)		
22	Balance to Controlling Interest (see distribution schedule)		
23	Total NCI		
24	Retained Earnings, Controlling Interest, December 31, 20X5		
25			

Eliminations and Adjustments:

(CY1) Eliminate the parent's share (80%) of subsidiary net income.
(EL) Eliminate the controlling portion (80%) of the Company S January 1, 20X1, stockholders' equity against the investment in Company S account. No excess results.
(LN1) Eliminate the intercompany note and accrued interest applicable to the note. This entry removes the *internal note* from the consolidated balance sheet.
(LN2) Eliminate the intercompany interest expense and revenue. Since an equal amount of expense and revenue is eliminated, there is no change in the combined net income as a result of this entry.

Worksheet 4-8 (see page 222)

Eliminations & Adjustments Dr.	Eliminations & Adjustments Cr.	Consolidated Income Statement	NCI	Controlling Retained Earnings	Consolidated Balance Sheet	
					55,400	1
	(LN1) 10,000					2
	(LN1) 400					3
					290,000	4
	(CY1) 8,000					5
	(EL) 120,000					6
(LN1) 10,000						7
(LN1) 400						8
					(100,000)	9
				(200,000)		10
(EL) 40,000			(10,000)			11
(EL) 80,000			(20,000)			12
		(170,000)				13
(LN2) 400						14
(CY1) 8,000						15
		95,000				16
		59,600				17
	(LN2) 400					18
138,800	138,800					19
		(15,400)				20
		2,000	(2,000)			21
		13,400		(13,400)		22
			(32,000)		(32,000)	23
				(213,400)	(213,400)	24
					0	25

Subsidiary Company S Income Distribution

Internally generated net income	$10,000
Adjusted income	$10,000
NCI share	× 20%
NCI	$ 2,000

Parent Company P Income Distribution

Internally generated net income	$ 5,400
80% × Company S adjusted income of $10,000	8,000
Controlling interest	$13,400

Worksheet 4-9

Vertical Worksheet Alternative
Company P and Subsidiary Company S
Worksheet for Consolidated Financial Statements
For Year Ended December 31, **20X2**

Worksheet 4-9 (see page 227)

	(Credit balance amounts are in parentheses.)	Trial Balance		Eliminations & Adjustments						
		Company P	Company S	Dr.		Cr.		NCI	Consolidated	
1	**Income Statement**									1
2	Sales	(600,000)	(530,000)	**(IS)**	**150,000**				(980,000)	2
3	Cost of goods sold	400,000	280,000	**(EI)**	**10,000**	**(IS)**	**150,000**			3
4						**(BI)**	**8,000**		532,000	4
5	Depreciation expense	40,000	50,000			**(F2)**	**1,000**		89,000	5
6	Other expenses	60,000	70,000						130,000	6
7	Subsidiary income	(104,000)		(CY1)	104,000					7
8	**Net income**	**(204,000)**	**(130,000)**						(227,500)	8
9	NCI (see distribution schedule)							**(25,600)**		9
10	Controlling interest (see distribution schedule)								**(203,400)**	10
11										11
12	**Retained Earnings Statement**									12
13	Retained earnings, January 1, 20X2, Company P	(600,000)								13
14				**(BI)**	**6,400**					14
15				**(F1)**	**4,500**				(589,100)	15
16	Retained earnings, January 1, 20X2, Company S		(400,000)	(EL)	320,000					16
17				**(BI)**	**1,600**			(78,400)		17
18	**Net income (carrydown)**	**(204,000)**	**(130,000)**					**(25,600)**	**(203,400)**	18
19	Dividends declared		20,000			(CY2)	16,000	4,000		19
20	**Retained earnings, December 31, 20X2**	**(804,000)**	**(510,000)**							20
21	NCI, retained earnings, December 31, 20X2							**(100,000)**		21
22	Controlling interest, retained earnings, December 31, 20X2								**(792,500)**	22
23										23
24	**Balance Sheet**									24
25	Inventory	300,000	250,000			**(EI)**	**10,000**		540,000	25
26	Accounts receivable	120,000	180,000			**(IA)**	**20,000**		280,000	26
27	Plant assets	236,000	400,000			**(F1)**	**5,000**		631,000	27
28	Accumulated depreciation	(100,000)	(60,000)	**(F1)**	**500**					28
29				**(F2)**	**1,000**				(158,500)	29
30	Investment in Company S	628,000		(CY2)	16,000	(CY1)	104,000			30
31						(EL)	480,000			31
32						(D)	60,000			32
33	Goodwill			(D)	60,000				60,000	33
34	Current liabilities	(80,000)	(60,000)	**(IA)**	**20,000**				(120,000)	34
35	Common stock ($5 par), Company S		(200,000)	(EL)	160,000			(40,000)		35
36	Common stock ($10 par), Company P	(300,000)							(300,000)	36
37	**Retained earnings (carrydown)**	**(804,000)**	**(510,000)**							37
38	Retained earnings, controlling interest, December 31, 20X2								**(792,500)**	38
39	Retained earnings, NCI, December 31, 20X2							**(100,000)**		38
40	Total NCI							(140,000)	(140,000)	40
41	Totals	0	0		854,000		854,000		0	41

Eliminations and Adjustments:

(CY1) Eliminate the current-year entries recording the parent's share (80%) of subsidiary net income.
(CY2) Eliminate intercompany dividends.
(EL) Eliminate the pro rata portion of the subsidiary equity balances owned by the parent (80%) against the balance of the investment account.
(D) Distribute the excess to the goodwill account according to the determination and distribution of excess schedule.
(IS) Eliminate the intercompany sales made during 20X2.
(BI) Eliminate the intercompany profit in the beginning inventory, 20% (0.25 ÷ 1.25) multiplied by $40,000. Since it was a subsidiary sale, the profit is shared 20% by the NCI.
(EI) Eliminate the intercompany profit (20%) applicable to the $50,000 of intercompany goods in the ending inventory.
(IA) Eliminate the intercompany trade balances.
(F1) Eliminate the intercompany gain remaining on January 1, 20X2, applicable to the sale of the machine by Company P ($5,000 original gain less one-half-year's gain of $500).
(F2) Reduce the depreciation expense and accumulated depreciation accounts ($1,000 for the current year) in order to reflect depreciation based on the original cost.

Subsidiary Company S Income Distribution

Unrealized profit in ending inventory (20% × $50,000) . . . . . (EI)	$10,000	Internally generated net income		$ 130,000
		Realized profit in beginning inventory (20% × $40,000)	(BI)	8,000
		Adjusted income		$ 128,000
		NCI share		× 20%
		NCI		**$ 25,600**

Parent Company P Income Distribution

		Internally generated net income		$ 100,000
		Gain realized on sale of machine	(F2)	1,000
		80% × Company S adjusted income of $128,000		102,400
		Controlling interest		**$203,400**

UNDERSTANDING THE ISSUES

1. During 20X1, Company P sold $40,000 of goods to subsidiary Company S at a profit of $10,000. One-fourth of the goods remain unsold at year-end. If there were no adjustments made on the consolidated worksheet, what would be incorrect on the consolidated income statement and balance sheet?
2. During 20X1, Company P sold $40,000 of goods to subsidiary Company S at a profit of $10,000. One-fourth of the goods remain unsold at year-end. What specific procedures are needed on the consolidated worksheet to deal with these issues?
3. Company S is 80% owned by Company P. Near the end of 20X1, Company S sold merchandise with a cost of $4,000 to Company P for $6,000. Company P sold the merchandise to a nonaffiliated firm in 20X2 for $10,000. How much total profit should be recorded on the consolidated income statements in 20X1 and 20X2? How much profit should be awarded to the controlling and noncontrolling interests in 20X1 and 20X2?
4. Subsidiary Company S is 80% owned by Company P. Company S sold a machine with a book value of $100,000 to Company P for $150,000. The asset has a 5-year life and is depreciated under the straight-line method. The president of Company S thinks it has scored a $50,000 immediate profit for the noncontrolling interest. Explain how much profit the noncontrolling interest will realize and when it will be awarded.
5. On January 1, 20X1, Company P sold a machine to its 70%-owned subsidiary, Company S, for $60,000. The book value of the machine was $40,000. The machine was depreciated straight-line, over 5 years. On December 31, 20X3, Company S sold the machine to a nonaffiliated firm for $35,000. On the consolidated statements, how much gain or loss on the intercompany machine sale should be recognized in 20X1, 20X2, and 20X3?
6. Company S is a 70%-owned subsidiary of Company P. Company S is building a ship to be used by Company P. The ship was 40% completed in 20X1 and 100% completed in 20X2. The actual and budgeted profit on the ship was $100,000. Company S uses the percentage-of-completion method for its long-term construction projects. The ship went into service for Company P on January 1, 20X3, and is depreciated straight-line over 20 years. How much profit was recorded by Company S in 20X1, 20X2, and 20X3? How much profit will appear in the consolidated statements for the ship in 20X1, 20X2, and 20X3?
7. Company S is an 80%-owned subsidiary of Company P. Company S needed to borrow $500,000 on January 1, 20X1. The best interest rate it could secure was 10% annual. Company P has a better credit rating and decided to borrow the funds needed from a bank at 8% annual and then loaned the money to Company S at 9.5% annual.
   a. Is Company S better off as a result of borrowing the funds from Company P?
   b. What are the interest revenue and expense amounts recorded by Company P and Company S during 20X2?
   c. How much interest expense and/or interest revenue should appear in the 20X1 consolidated income statement?

EXERCISES

Exercise 1 *(LO 1, 2)* **Gross profit: separate firms versus consolidated.** Solvent is an 80%-owned subsidiary of the Painter Company. The two affiliates had the following separate income statements for 20X1 and 20X2:

	Solvent Company		Painter Company	
	20X1	20X2	20X1	20X2
Sales revenue	$250,000	$300,000	$500,000	$540,000
Cost of goods sold	150,000	180,000	310,000	360,000
Gross profit	$100,000	$120,000	$190,000	$180,000
Expenses	45,000	56,000	120,000	125,000
Net income	$ 55,000	$ 64,000	$ 70,000	$ 55,000

Solvent sells at the same gross profit percentage to all customers. During 20X1, Solvent sold goods to Painter for the first time in the amount of $100,000. $20,000 of these sales remained in Painter's ending inventory. During 20X2, sales to Painter by Solvent were $110,000, of which $30,000 sales were still in Painter's December 31, 20X2, inventory.

Prepare consolidated income statements including the distribution of income to the controlling and noncontrolling interests for 20X1 and 20X2.

Exercise 2 *(LO 2)* **Inventory profits with lower-of-cost-or-market adjustment.** Hide Corporation is a wholly owned subsidiary of Seek Company. During 20X1, Hide sold all of its production to Seek Company for $400,000, a price that includes a 20% gross profit. 20X1 is the first year that such intercompany sales were made. By year-end, Seek sold 80% of the goods it had purchased for $416,000. The balance of the intercompany goods, $80,000, remained in the ending inventory and was adjusted to a lower fair value of $70,000. The adjustment was a charge to the cost of goods sold.

1. Determine the gross profit on sales recorded by both companies.
2. Determine the gross profit to be shown on the consolidated income statement.

Exercise 3 *(LO 2)* **Distribution of income with inventory profits.** Nick Company is an 80%-owned subsidiary of Van Corporation. The separate income statements of the two companies for 20X2 are as follows:

	Van Corporation	Nick Company
Sales	$ 220,000	$120,000
Cost of goods sold	(150,000)	(90,000)
Gross profit	$ 70,000	$ 30,000
Other expenses	(40,000)	(12,000)
Other income	5,000	
Operating income	$ 35,000	$ 18,000
Subsidiary income	14,400	
Net income	$ 49,400	$ 18,000

The following facts apply to 20X2:

a. Nick Company sold $70,000 of goods to Van Corporation. The gross profits on sales to Van and to unrelated companies are equal and have not changed from the previous years.
b. Van Corporation held $15,000 of the goods purchased from Nick Company in its beginning inventory and $20,000 of such goods in ending inventory.
c. Van Corporation billed Nick Company $5,000 for computer services. The charge was expensed by Nick Company and treated as other income by Van Corporation.

Prepare the consolidated income statement for 20X2, including the distribution of the consolidated net income to the controlling and noncontrolling interests. The supporting income distribution schedules should be prepared as well.

Exercise 4 *(LO 3)* **Machinery sale.** On January 1, 20X2, Jungle Company sold a machine to Safari Company for $30,000. The machine had an original cost of $24,000, and accumulated depreciation on the asset was $9,000 at the time of the sale. The machine has a 5-year remaining life and will be depreciated on a straight-line basis with no salvage value. Safari Company is an 80%-owned subsidiary of Jungle Company.

1. Explain the adjustments that would have to be made to arrive at consolidated net income for the years 20X2 through 20X6 as a result of this sale.
2. Prepare the elimination that would be required on the December 31, 20X2, consolidated worksheet as a result of this sale.
3. Prepare the entry for the December 31, 20X3, worksheet as a result of this sale.

Exercise 5 *(LO 3)* **Land and building profit.** Wavemasters Inc. owns an 80% interest in Sayner Development Company. In a prior period, Sayner Development purchased a parcel of land for $50,000. During 20X1, it constructed a building on the land at a cost of $500,000. The land and building were sold to Wavemasters at the very end of 20X1 for $750,000, of which $100,000 was for the land. It is estimated that the building has a 20-year life with no salvage value.

1. Prepare all worksheet eliminations that would be made on the 20X1 consolidated worksheet as a result of the real estate sale.
2. Prepare all worksheet eliminations that would be made on the 20X3 consolidated worksheet as a result of the 20X1 real estate sale.

Exercise 6 *(LO 3)* **Resale of intercompany asset.** Hilton Corporation sold a press to its 80%-owned subsidiary, Agri Fab Inc., for $5,000 on January 1, 20X2. The press originally was purchased by Hilton on January 1, 20X1, for $20,000, and $6,000 of depreciation for 20X1 had been recorded. The fair value of the press on January 1, 20X2, was $10,000. Agri Fab proceeded to depreciate the press on a straight-line basis, using a 5-year life and no salvage value. On December 31, 20X3, Agri Fab, having no further need for the machine, sold it for $2,000 and recorded a loss on the sale.

Explain the adjustments that would have to be made to the separate income statements of the two companies to arrive at the consolidated income statements for 20X2 and 20X3.

Exercise 7 *(LO 4)* **Completed-contract method.** Janis Company contracted with its 80%-owned subsidiary, Essuman Equipment Company, for the construction of two stamping machines. The first machine was completed and put into operation on July 1, 20X1. It cost Essuman $60,000 and has a 5-year estimated life with no salvage value. The contract price was $75,000. The machine is being depreciated on a straight-line basis. The second machine, with an estimated total cost of $90,000 and a contract price of $120,000, was 80% complete on December 31, 20X1. To date, costs on the second contract total $72,000. By the statement date, Janis had completely paid for the first machine and still owed $3,000 of the $60,000 billed to date on the second machine. Essuman uses the completed-contract method to account for its long-term construction contracts.

1. Prepare the necessary eliminations for the consolidated worksheet on December 31, 20X1.
2. What are the effects of these contracts on the income distribution schedules?

Exercise 8 *(LO 4)* **Percentage-of-completion method.** Apple Contractors, an 80%-owned subsidiary, is constructing a warehouse for its parent, Plum Corporation. The following information is available on December 31, 20X1:

Percent of completion	60%
Costs incurred to date	$120,000
Estimated costs to complete	80,000
Contract price	250,000
Amount billed to date (no amounts collected)	150,000

Apple uses the percentage-of-completion method to account for its long-term contracts.

Record the journal entries that each of the two companies would have made relative to the construction. Prepare a partial trial balance using the data from your entries, and show the eliminations relating to the contract for the December 31, 20X1, consolidated worksheet.

Exercise 9 *(LO 3)* **Fixed asset sales by parent and subsidiary.** The separate income statements of Dark Company and its 90%-owned subsidiary, Light Company, for the year ended December 31, 20X2, are as follows:

	Dark Company	Light Company
Sales	$ 700,000	$ 280,000
Cost of goods sold	(450,000)	(190,000)
Gross profit	$ 250,000	$ 90,000
Other expenses	(180,000)	(70,000)
Other income	20,000	
Operating income	$ 90,000	$ 20,000
Subsidiary income	18,000	
Net income	$ 108,000	$ 20,000

The following additional facts apply:

a. On January 1, 20X1, Light Company purchased a building, with a book value of $100,000 and an estimated 20-year life, from Dark Company for $180,000. The building was being depreciated on a straight-line basis with no salvage value.
b. On January 1, 20X2, Light Company sold a machine with a book value of $50,000 to Dark Company for $60,000. The machine had an expected life of 5 years and is being depreciated on a straight-line basis with no salvage value. Light Company is a dealer for the machine.

Prepare the December 31, 20X2, consolidated income statement and supporting income distribution schedules.

Exercise 10 *(LO 2, 3)* **Merchandise and fixed asset sale.** Peninsula Company owns an 80% controlling interest in the Sandbar Company. Sandbar regularly sells merchandise to Peninsula, which then sold to outside parties. The gross profit on all such sales is 40%. On January 1, 20X1, Peninsula sold land and a building to Sandbar. Tax assessments divide the value of the parcel 20% to land and 80% to structures. Pertinent information for the companies is summarized:

	Peninsula	Sandbar
Internally generated net income, 20X1	$520,000	$250,000
Internally generated net income, 20X2	340,000	235,000
Intercompany merchandise sales, 20X1		100,000
Intercompany merchandise sales, 20X2		120,000
Intercompany inventory, December 31, 20X1		15,000
Intercompany inventory, December 31, 20X2		20,000
Cost of real estate sold on January 1, 20X1	600,000	
Sale price for real estate on January 1, 20X1	800,000	
Depreciable life of building		20 years

Prepare income distribution schedules for 20X1 and 20X2 for Peninsula and Sandbar as they would be prepared to distribute income to the noncontrolling and controlling interests in support of consolidated worksheets.

Exercise 11 *(LO 5)* **Intercompany note.** Saratoga Company owns 80% of the outstanding common stock of Windsor Company. On May 1, 20X3, Windsor Company arranged a 1-year, $50,000 loan from Saratoga Company. The loan agreement specified that interest would accrue at the rate of 6% per annum and that all interest would be paid on the maturity date of the loan.

The financial reporting period ends on December 31, 20X3, and the note originating from the loan remains outstanding.

1. Prepare the entries that both companies would have made on their separate books, including the accrual of interest.
2. Prepare the eliminations, in entry form, that would be made on a consolidated worksheet prepared as of December 31, 20X3.

Exercise 12 *(LO 5)* **Intercompany note discounted.** Assume the same facts as in Exercise 11, but in addition, assume that Saratoga was itself in need of cash. It discounted the note received from Windsor at the First Bank on July 1, 20X3, at a discount rate of 8% per annum.

1. Prepare the entries that both companies would make on their separate books, including interest accruals.
2. Prepare the eliminations, in entry form, that would be made on a consolidated worksheet prepared as of December 31, 20X3.

PROBLEMS

Problem 4-1 *(LO 2)* **100%, equity, ending inventory.** On January 1, 20X1, 100% of the outstanding stock of Solid Company was purchased by Plaid Corporation for $3,200,000. At that time, the fair value and book value of Solid's net assets equaled $2,800,000. The excess is attributable to equipment with a 10-year life.

The following trial balances of Plaid Corporation and Solid Company were prepared on December 31, 20X1:

	Plaid Corporation	Solid Company
Cash	810,000	170,000
Accounts Receivable	425,000	365,000
Inventory	600,000	275,000
Property, Plant, and Equipment (net)	4,000,000	2,300,000
Investment in Solid Company	3,410,000	
Accounts Payable	(35,000)	(100,000)
Common Stock ($10 par)	(1,000,000)	(400,000)
Paid-In Capital in Excess of Par	(1,500,000)	(200,000)
Retained Earnings, January 1, 20X1	(5,500,000)	(2,200,000)
Sales	(12,000,000)	(1,000,000)
Cost of Goods Sold	7,000,000	750,000
Other Expenses	4,000,000	40,000
Subsidiary Income	(210,000)	
Total	0	0

Throughout 20X1, sales to Plaid Corporation made up 40% of Solid's revenue and produced a 30% gross profit rate. At year-end, Plaid Corporation had sold $300,000 of the goods purchased from Solid Company and still owed Solid $25,000. None of the Solid products were in Plaid's January 1, 20X1, beginning inventory.

Required ▶ ▶ ▶ ▶ ▶ Prepare the worksheet necessary to produce the consolidated income statement and balance sheet of Plaid Corporation and its subsidiary for the year ended December 31, 20X1. Include the determination and distribution of excess schedule.

Problem 4-2 *(LO 2)* **80%, cost, beginning and ending inventory.** On April 1, 20X1, Baxter Corporation purchased 80% of the outstanding stock of Crystal Company for $425,000. A condensed balance sheet of Crystal Company at the purchase date follows:

Assets		Liabilities and Equity	
Current assets	$180,000	Liabilities	$100,000
Long-lived assets (net)	320,000	Equity	400,000
Total assets	$500,000	Total liabilities and equity	$500,000

All book values approximated fair values on the purchase date. Any excess cost is attributed to goodwill.

The following information has been gathered pertaining to the first 2 years of operation since Baxter's purchase of Crystal Company stock:

a. Intercompany merchandise sales are summarized as follows:

Date	Transaction	Sales	Gross Profit	Merchandise Remaining in Purchaser's Ending Inventory
April 1, 20X1 to March 31, 20X2	Baxter to Crystal	$35,000	15%	$9,000
	Crystal to Baxter	20,000	20	3,500
April 1, 20X2 to March 31, 20X3	Baxter to Crystal	32,000	22	6,000
	Crystal to Baxter	30,000	25	3,000

b. On March 31, 20X3, Baxter owed Crystal $10,000, and Crystal owed Baxter $5,000 as a result of the intercompany sales.

c. Baxter paid $25,000 in cash dividends on March 20, 20X2 and 20X3. Crystal paid its first cash dividend on March 10, 20X3, giving each share of outstanding common stock a $0.15 cash dividend.

d. The trial balances of the two companies as of March 31, 20X3, follow:

	Baxter Corporation	Crystal Company
Cash	216,200	44,300
Accounts Receivable (net)	290,000	97,000
Inventory	310,000	80,000
Investment in Crystal Company	425,000	
Land	1,081,000	150,000
Building and Equipment	1,850,000	400,000
Accumulated Depreciation	(940,000)	(210,000)
Goodwill	60,000	
Accounts Payable	(242,200)	(106,300)
Bonds Payable	(400,000)	
Common Stock ($0.50 par)	(250,000)	
Common Stock ($1 par)		(200,000)
Paid-In Capital in Excess of Par	(1,250,000)	(100,000)
Retained Earnings, April 1, 20X2	(1,105,000)	(140,000)
Sales	(880,000)	(630,000)
Dividend Income (from Crystal Company)	(24,000)	
Cost of Goods Sold	704,000	504,000
Other Expenses	130,000	81,000
Dividends Declared	25,000	30,000
Total	0	0

1. Prepare the worksheet necessary to produce the consolidated financial statements of Baxter Corporation and its subsidiary for the year ended March 31, 20X3. Include the determination and distribution of excess schedule and the income distribution schedules. ◄◄◄◄◄ **Required**

2. Prepare the formal consolidated income statement for the fiscal year 20X2–20X3.

Use the following information for Problems 4-3 and 4-4:

On January 1, 20X1, Panther Corporation acquired 70% of the common stock of Spider Corporation for $350,000. On this date, Spider had the following balance sheet:

Spider Corporation
Balance Sheet
January 1, 20X1

Assets		Liabilities and Equity	
Accounts receivable	$ 60,000	Accounts payable	$ 40,000
Inventory	40,000	Bonds payable	100,000
Land	60,000	Common stock, $1 par	10,000
Buildings	200,000	Paid-in capital in excess of par	90,000
Accumulated depreciation	(50,000)	Retained earnings	112,000
Equipment	72,000		
Accumulated depreciation	(30,000)		
Total assets	$352,000	Total liabilities and equity	$352,000

Buildings, which have a 20-year life, are understated by $150,000. Equipment, which has a 5-year life, is understated by $58,000. Any remaining excess is considered to be goodwill. Panther uses the simple equity method to account for its investment in Spider.

Panther and Spider had the following trial balances on December 31, 20X2:

	Panther Corporation	Spider Corporation
Cash	116,000	132,000
Accounts Receivable	90,000	45,000
Inventory	120,000	56,000
Land	100,000	60,000
Investment in Spider	378,000	
Buildings	800,000	200,000
Accumulated Depreciation	(220,000)	(65,000)
Equipment	150,000	72,000
Accumulated Depreciation	(90,000)	(46,000)
Accounts Payable	(60,000)	(102,000)
Bonds Payable		(100,000)
Common Stock	(100,000)	(10,000)
Paid-In Capital in Excess of Par	(800,000)	(90,000)
Retained Earnings, January 1, 20X2	(325,000)	(142,000)
Sales	(800,000)	(350,000)
Cost of Goods Sold	450,000	208,500
Depreciation Expense—Buildings	30,000	7,500
Depreciation Expense—Equipment	15,000	8,000
Other Expenses	140,000	98,000
Interest Expense		8,000
Subsidiary Income	(14,000)	
Dividends Declared	20,000	10,000
Totals	0	0

Problem 4-3 *(LO 2)* **70%, equity, beginning and ending inventory, subsidiary seller.** Refer to the preceding facts for Panther's acquisition of Spider common stock. On January 1, 20X2, Panther held merchandise acquired from Spider for $8,000. This beginning inventory had an applicable gross profit of 25%. During 20X2, Spider sold $30,000 worth of merchandise to Panther. Panther held $6,000 of this merchandise at December 31, 20X2. This ending inventory had an applicable gross profit of 30%. Panther owed Spider $6,000 on December 31 as a result of these intercompany sales.

template cd

◄◄◄◄◄ **Required**

1. Prepare a zone analysis and a determination and distribution of excess schedule for the investment in Spider.
2. Complete a consolidated worksheet for Panther Corporation and its subsidiary Spider Corporation as of December 31, 20X2. Prepare supporting amortization and income distribution schedules.

Problem 4-4 *(LO 2)* **70%, equity, beginning and ending inventory, parent and subsidiary seller.** Refer to the preceding facts for Panther's acquisition of Spider common stock. On January 1, 20X2, Panther held merchandise acquired from Spider for $10,000. This beginning inventory had an applicable gross profit of 25%. During 20X2, Spider sold $40,000 worth of merchandise to Panther. Panther held $6,000 of this merchandise at December 31, 20X2. This ending inventory had an applicable gross profit of 30%. Panther owed Spider $11,000 on December 31 as a result of this intercompany sale.

template cd

On January 1, 20X2, Spider held merchandise acquired from Panther for $15,000. This beginning inventory had an applicable gross profit of 40%. During 20X2, Panther sold $60,000 worth of merchandise to Spider. Spider held $22,000 of this merchandise at December 31, 20X2. This ending inventory had an applicable gross profit of 35%. Spider owed Panther $12,000 on December 31 as a result of this intercompany sale.

◄◄◄◄◄ **Required**

1. Prepare a zone analysis and a determination and distribution of excess schedule for the investment in Spider.
2. Complete a consolidated worksheet for Panther Corporation and its subsidiary Spider Corporation as of December 31, 20X2. Prepare supporting amortization and income distribution schedules.

Problem 4-5 *(LO 2)* **80%, equity, beginning and ending inventory, write-down, note.** On January 1, 20X1, Silvio Corporation exchanged on a 1-for-3 basis common stock it held in its treasury for 80% of the outstanding stock of Jenkins Company. Silvio Corporation common stock had a market price of $40 per share on the exchange date.

template cd

On the date of the acquisition, the stockholders' equity section of Jenkins Company was as follows:

Common stock ($5 par)	$ 450,000
Paid-in capital in excess of par	180,000
Retained earnings	370,000
Total	$1,000,000

Also on that date, Jenkins Company's book values approximated fair values, except for the land, which was undervalued by $75,000. The remaining excess is attributable to goodwill.

Information regarding intercompany transactions for 20X3 follows:

a. Silvio Corporation sells merchandise to Jenkins Company, realizing a 30% gross profit. Sales during 20X3 were $140,000. Jenkins had $25,000 of the 20X2 purchases in its beginning inventory for 20X3 and $35,000 of the 20X3 purchases in its ending inventory for 20X3.
b. Jenkins signed a 12%, 4-month, $10,000 note to Silvio in order to cover the remaining balance of its payables on November 1, 20X3. No new merchandise was purchased after this date.
c. Jenkins wrote down to $28,000 the merchandise purchased from Silvio Corporation and remaining in its 20X3 ending inventory.

The trial balances of Silvio Corporation and Jenkins Company as of December 31, 20X3, are as follows:

	Silvio Corporation	Jenkins Company
Cash	140,000	205,200
Accounts Receivable	285,000	110,000
Interest Receivable	1,500	
Notes Receivable	50,000	
Inventory	470,000	160,000
Land	350,000	300,000
Depreciable Fixed Assets	1,110,000	810,000
Accumulated Depreciation	(500,000)	(200,000)
Intangibles	60,000	
Investment in Jenkins Company	1,128,000	
Accounts Payable	(611,500)	(175,000)
Interest Payable		(200)
Common Stock ($1 par)	(400,000)	
Common Stock ($5 par)		(450,000)
Paid-In Capital in Excess of Par	(1,235,000)	(180,000)
Retained Earnings, January 1, 20X3	(958,500)	(470,000)
Treasury Stock (at cost)	315,000	
Sales	(1,020,000)	(500,000)
Interest Income	(1,500)	
Subsidiary Income	(88,000)	
Cost of Goods Sold	705,000	300,000
Other Expenses	200,000	90,000
Totals	0	0

Required ▶ ▶ ▶ ▶ ▶ Prepare the worksheet necessary to produce the consolidated financial statements of Silvio Corporation and its subsidiary for the year ended December 31, 20X3. Include the determination and distribution of excess schedule and the income distribution schedules.

Problem 4-6 *(LO 3)* **80%, equity, fixed asset sales by subsidiary and parent.** On September 1, 20X1, Parcel Corporation purchased 80% of the outstanding common stock of Sack Corporation for $152,000. On that date, Sack's net book values equaled fair values, and there was no excess of cost or book value resulting from the purchase. Parcel has been maintaining its investment under the simple equity method.

Over the next 3 years, the intercompany transactions between the companies were as follows:

a. On September 1, 20X1, Sack sold its 4-year-old delivery truck to Parcel for $14,000 in cash. At that time, Sack had depreciated the truck, which had cost $15,000, to its $5,000 salvage value. Parcel estimated on the date of the sale that the asset had a remaining useful life of 3 years and no salvage value.
b. On September 1, 20X2, Parcel sold equipment to Sack for $103,000. Parcel originally paid $80,000 for the equipment and planned to depreciate it over 20 years, assuming no salvage value. However, Parcel had the property for only 10 years and carried it at a net book value of $40,000 on the sale date. Sack will use the equipment for 10 years, at which time Sack expects no salvage value.

Both companies use straight-line depreciation for all assets.

Trial balances of Parcel Corporation and Sack Corporation as of the August 31, 20X3, year-end are as follows:

	Parcel Corporation	Sack Corporation
Cash	120,000	50,000
Accounts Receivable (net)	115,000	18,000
Notes Receivable		10,000
Inventory	175,000	34,000
Investment in Sack Corporation	217,440	
Plant and Equipment	990,700	295,000
Accumulated Depreciation	(170,000)	(85,000)
Other Assets	28,000	
Accounts Payable	(80,000)	(50,200)
Notes Payable	(25,000)	
Bonds Payable, 12%	(300,000)	
Common Stock ($10 par)	(290,000)	(70,000)
Paid-In Capital in Excess of Par	(110,000)	(62,000)
Retained Earnings, September 1, 20X2	(498,850)	(118,000)
Sales	(920,000)	(240,000)
Cost of Goods Sold	598,000	132,000
Selling and General Expenses	108,000	80,000
Subsidiary Income	(23,040)	
Interest Income		(800)
Interest Expense	37,750	
Gain on Sale of Equipment	(63,000)	
Dividends Declared	90,000	7,000
Totals	0	0

Prepare the worksheet necessary to produce the consolidated financial statements of Parcel Corporation and its subsidiary for the year ended August 31, 20X3. Include the income distribution schedules. ◄◄◄◄◄ **Required**

Use the following information for Problems 4-7 and 4-8:

On January 1, 20X1, Polka Company acquired Salsa Company. Polka paid $440,000 for 80% of Salsa's common stock. On the date of acquisition, Salsa had the following balance sheet:

Salsa Company
Balance Sheet
January 1, 20X1

Assets		Liabilities and Equity	
Accounts receivable	$ 60,000	Accounts payable	$ 40,000
Inventory	40,000	Bonds payable	100,000
Land	60,000	Common stock, $1 par	10,000
Buildings	200,000	Paid-in capital in excess of par	90,000
Accumulated depreciation	(50,000)	Retained earnings	112,000
Equipment	72,000		
Accumulated depreciation	(30,000)		
Total assets	$352,000	Total liabilities and equity	$352,000

Buildings, which have a 20-year life, are understated by $100,000. Equipment, which has a 5-year life, is understated by $38,000. Any remaining excess is considered goodwill. Polka uses the simple equity method to account for its investment in Salsa.

(continued)

Polka and Salsa had the following trial balances on December 31, 20X2:

	Polka Company	Salsa Company
Cash	24,000	132,000
Accounts Receivable	90,000	45,000
Inventory	120,000	56,000
Land	100,000	60,000
Investment in Salsa	472,000	
Buildings	800,000	200,000
Accumulated Depreciation	(220,000)	(65,000)
Equipment	150,000	72,000
Accumulated Depreciation	(90,000)	(46,000)
Accounts Payable	(60,000)	(102,000)
Bonds Payable		(100,000)
Common Stock	(100,000)	(10,000)
Paid-In Capital in Excess of Par	(800,000)	(90,000)
Retained Earnings, January 1, 20X2	(325,000)	(142,000)
Sales	(800,000)	(350,000)
Cost of Goods Sold	450,000	208,500
Depreciation Expense—Buildings	30,000	7,500
Depreciation Expense—Equipment	15,000	8,000
Other Expenses	160,000	98,000
Gain on Fixed Asset Sale	(20,000)	
Interest Expense		8,000
Subsidiary Income	(16,000)	
Dividends Declared	20,000	10,000
Totals	0	0

template cd

Problem 4-7 *(LO 3)* **80%, equity, several excess distributions, fixed asset sale.** Refer to the preceding facts for Polka's acquisition of Salsa common stock. On January 1, 20X2, Polka held merchandise sold to it from Salsa for $12,000. This beginning inventory had an applicable gross profit of 25%. During 20X2, Salsa sold merchandise to Polka for $75,000. On December 31, 20X2, Polka held $18,000 of this merchandise in its inventory. This ending inventory had an applicable gross profit of 30%. Polka owed Salsa $20,000 on December 31 as a result of this intercompany sale.

On January 1, 20X2, Polka sold equipment with a book value of $30,000 to Salsa for $50,000. During 20X2, the equipment was used by Salsa. Depreciation is computed over a 5-year life, using the straight-line method.

Required ▶ ▶ ▶ ▶ ▶

1. Prepare a zone analysis and a determination and distribution of excess schedule for the investment in Salsa.
2. Complete a consolidated worksheet for Polka Company and its subsidiary Salsa Company as of December 31, 20X2. Prepare supporting amortization and income distribution schedules.

template cd

Problem 4-8 *(LO 3)* **80%, equity, several excess distributions, fixed asset sale by parent and subsidiary.** Refer to the preceding facts for Polka's acquisition of Salsa common stock. On January 1, 20X2, Salsa held merchandise sold to it from Polka for $20,000. During 20X2, Polka sold merchandise to Salsa for $100,000. On December 31, 20X2, Salsa held $25,000 of this merchandise in its inventory. Polka has a gross profit of 30%. Salsa owed Polka $15,000 on December 31 as a result of this intercompany sale.

On January 1, 20X1, Salsa sold equipment to Polka at a profit of $30,000. Depreciation is computed over a 6-year life, using the straight-line method. The gain shown for 20X2 is on sales to outside parties.

◄◄◄◄◄ **Required**

1. Prepare a zone analysis and a determination and distribution of excess schedule for the investment in Salsa.
2. Complete a consolidated worksheet for Polka Company and its subsidiary Salsa Company as of December 31, 20X2. Prepare supporting amortization and income distribution schedules.

Problem 4-9 *(LO 2, 3, 4)* **100%, cost, merchandise sales, percentage-of-completion contracts.** Pardon Inc. purchased 100% of the common stock of Slarno Corporation for $150,000 in cash on June 30, 20X1. At that date, Slarno's stockholders' equity was as follows:

Common stock ($1 par)	$100,000
Retained earnings	50,000
Total	$150,000

The fair values of the assets and liabilities did not differ materially from their book values. Slarno has made no adjustments on its books to reflect the purchase by Pardon. On December 31, 20X1, Pardon and Slarno prepared consolidated financial statements.

The transactions that occurred between Pardon and Slarno during the next year included the following:

a. On January 3, 20X2, land with a $10,000 book value was sold by Pardon to Slarno for $15,000. Slarno made a $3,000 down payment and signed an 8% mortgage note, payable in 12 equal quarterly payments of $1,135, including interest, beginning March 31, 20X2.
b. Slarno produced equipment for Pardon under 2 separate contracts. The first contract, which was for office equipment, was begun and completed during the year at a cost to Slarno of $17,500. Pardon paid $22,000 in cash for the equipment on April 17, 20X2. The second contract was begun on February 15, 20X2, but will not be completed until May 20X3. Slarno has incurred $45,000 of costs as of December 31, 20X2, and anticipates an additional $30,000 of costs to complete the $95,000 contract. Slarno accounts for all contracts under the percentage-of-completion method. Pardon has made no account on its books for this uncompleted contract as of December 31, 20X2.
c. Pardon depreciates all of its equipment over a 10-year estimated economic life, with no salvage value. Pardon takes one-half-year's depreciation in the year of purchase.
d. Pardon sells merchandise to Slarno at an average markup of 12% on cost. During the year, Pardon charged Slarno $238,000 for merchandise purchased, of which Slarno paid $211,000. Slarno has $11,200 of this merchandise on hand on December 31, 20X2.

Trial balances of Pardon Inc. and its subsidiary as of December 31, 20X2, are as follows:

	Pardon Inc.	Slarno Corporation
Cash	45,000	31,211
Accounts Receivable	119,000	73,500
Billings on Construction in Progress		(1,201,900)
Mortgage Receivable	8,311	
Unsecured Notes Receivable	18,000	
Inventories	217,000	117,500
Land	34,000	42,000
Building and Equipment (net)	717,000	408,000
Investment in Slarno Corporation	150,000	
Accounts Payable	(203,000)	(147,000)
Mortgages Payable	(592,000)	(397,311)
Common Stock	(250,000)	(100,000)
Retained Earnings, January 1, 20X2	(139,311)	(70,000)
Sales	(1,800,000)	

(continued)

	Pardon Inc.	Slarno Corporation
Earned Income on Long-Term Contracts		(437,000)
Cost of Goods Sold	1,155,000	
Construction in Progress		1,289,000
Selling, General, and Administrative Expenses	497,000	360,000
Interest Income	(20,000)	
Interest Expense	49,000	32,000
Gain on Sale of Land	(5,000)	
Totals	0	0

Required ▶ ▶ ▶ ▶ ▶ Prepare the worksheet necessary to produce the consolidated financial statements of Pardon Inc. and its subsidiary for the year ended December 31, 20X2. Assume both companies have made all the adjusting entries required for separate financial statements unless an obvious discrepancy exists. Include the determination and distribution of excess schedule.

(AICPA adapted)

Problem 4-10 *(LO 2, 5)* **90%, cost, merchandise, note payable.** The December 31, 20X2, trial balances of the Pettie Corporation and its 90%-owned subsidiary Sunny Corporation are as follows:

	Pettie Corporation	Sunny Corporation
Cash	75,000	45,500
Accounts and Other Current Receivables	410,900	170,000
Inventory	920,000	739,400
Property, Plant, and Equipment (net)	1,000,000	400,000
Investment in Sunny Corporation	1,200,000	
Accounts Payable and Other Current Liabilities	(140,000)	(305,900)
Common Stock ($10 par)	(500,000)	
Common Stock ($10 par)		(200,000)
Retained Earnings, January 1, 20X2	(2,800,000)	(650,000)
Dividends Declared		1,000
Sales	(2,000,000)	(650,000)
Dividend Income	(900)	
Interest Expense		5,000
Interest Income	(5,000)	
Cost of Goods Sold	1,500,000	400,000
Other Expenses	340,000	45,000
Totals	0	0

Pettie's investment in Sunny was purchased for $1,200,000 in cash on January 1, 20X1, and is accounted for by the cost method. On January 1, 20X1, Sunny had the following equity balances:

Common stock	$200,000
Retained earnings	600,000
Total equity	$800,000

Pettie's excess of cost over book value on Sunny's investment has been identified appropriately as goodwill.

Sunny borrowed $100,000 from Pettie on June 30, 20X2, with the note maturing on June 30, 20X3, at 10% interest. Correct accruals have been recorded by both companies.

During 20X2, Pettie sold merchandise to Sunny at an aggregate invoice price of $300,000, which included a profit of $75,000. As of December 31, 20X2, Sunny had not paid Pettie for

$90,000 of these purchases, and 10% of the total merchandise purchased from Pettie still remained in Sunny's inventory.

Sunny declared a $1,000 cash dividend in December 20X2 payable in January 20X3.

◀◀◀◀◀ **Required**

Prepare the worksheet required to produce the consolidated statements of Pettie Corporation and its subsidiary, Sunny Corporation, for the year ending December 31, 20X2. Include the determination and distribution of excess schedule and the income distribution schedules.

(AICPA adapted)

Problem 4-11 *(LO 2, 3)* **80%, equity, several excess distributions, merchandise, equipment sales.** On January 1, 20X1, Peanut Company acquired 80% of the common stock of Sam Company for $200,000. On this date, Sam had total owners' equity of $200,000. During 20X1 and 20X2, Peanut has appropriately accounted for its investment in Sam using the simple equity method.

template cd

Any excess of cost over book value is attributable to inventory (worth $12,500 more than cost), to equipment (worth $25,000 more than book value), and to goodwill. FIFO is used for inventories. The equipment has a remaining life of 4 years, and straight-line depreciation is used. On January 1, 20X2, Peanut held merchandise acquired from Sam for $20,000. During 20X2, Sam sold merchandise to Peanut for $40,000, $10,000 of which is still held by Peanut on December 31, 20X2. Sam's usual gross profit is 50%.

On December 31, 20X1, Peanut sold equipment to Sam at a gain of $15,000. During 20X2, the equipment was used by Sam. Depreciation is being computed using the straight-line method, a 5-year life, and no salvage value.

The following trial balances were prepared for the Peanut and Sam companies for December 31, 20X2:

	Peanut Company	Sam Company
Inventory, December 31	130,000	50,000
Other Current Assets	241,000	235,000
Investment in Sam Company	308,000	
Other Long-Term Investments	20,000	
Land	140,000	80,000
Buildings and Equipment	375,000	200,000
Accumulated Depreciation	(120,000)	(30,000)
Other Intangibles		20,000
Current Liabilities	(150,000)	(70,000)
Bonds Payable		(100,000)
Other Long-Term Liabilities	(200,000)	(50,000)
Common Stock, Peanut Company	(200,000)	
Other Paid-In Capital, Peanut Company	(100,000)	
Retained Earnings, Peanut Company	(320,000)	
Common Stock, Sam Company		(50,000)
Other Paid-In Capital, Sam Company		(50,000)
Retained Earnings, Sam Company		(150,000)
Net Sales	(600,000)	(315,000)
Cost of Goods Sold	350,000	150,000
Operating Expenses	150,000	60,000
Subsidiary Income	(84,000)	
Dividends Declared, Peanut Company	60,000	
Dividends Declared, Sam Company		20,000
Totals	0	0

◀◀◀◀◀ **Required**

Complete the worksheet for consolidated financial statements for the year ended December 31, 20X2. Include the necessary determination and distribution of excess schedule and income distribution schedules.

Problem 4-12 *(LO 2, 3)* **80%, cost, several excess distributions, merchandise, equipment sales.** (This is the same as Problem 4-11 except for use of the cost method.) On January 1, 20X1, Peanut Company acquired 80% of the common stock of Sam Company for $200,000. On this date, Sam had total owners' equity of $200,000, which included retained earnings of $100,000. During 20X1 and 20X2, Peanut has accounted for its investment in Sam using the cost method.

Any excess of cost over book value is attributable to inventory (worth $12,500 more than cost), to equipment (worth $25,000 more than book value), and to goodwill. FIFO is used for inventories. The equipment has a remaining life of 4 years, and straight-line depreciation is used.

On January 1, 20X2, Peanut held merchandise acquired from Sam for $20,000. During 20X2, Sam sold merchandise to Peanut for $40,000, $10,000 of which is still held by Peanut on December 31, 20X2. Sam's usual gross profit is 50%.

On December 31, 20X1, Peanut sold equipment to Sam at a gain of $15,000. During 20X2, the equipment was used by Sam. Depreciation is being computed using the straight-line method, a 5-year life, and no salvage value.

The following trial balances were prepared for the Peanut and Sam companies for December 31, 20X2:

	Peanut Company	Sam Company
Inventory, December 31	130,000	50,000
Other Current Assets	241,000	235,000
Investment in Sam Company	200,000	
Other Long-Term Investments	20,000	
Land	140,000	80,000
Buildings and Equipment	375,000	200,000
Accumulated Depreciation	(120,000)	(30,000)
Other Intangibles		20,000
Current Liabilities	(150,000)	(70,000)
Bonds Payable		(100,000)
Other Long-Term Liabilities	(200,000)	(50,000)
Common Stock, Peanut Company	(200,000)	
Other Paid-In Capital, Peanut Company	(100,000)	
Retained Earnings, Peanut Company	(280,000)	
Common Stock, Sam Company		(50,000)
Other Paid-In Capital, Sam Company		(50,000)
Retained Earnings, Sam Company		(150,000)
Net Sales	(600,000)	(315,000)
Cost of Goods Sold	350,000	150,000
Operating Expenses	150,000	60,000
Dividend Income	(16,000)	
Dividends Declared, Peanut Company	60,000	
Dividends Declared, Sam Company		20,000
Totals	0	0

Required ▶ ▶ ▶ ▶ ▶ Complete the worksheet for consolidated financial statements for the year ended December 31, 20X2. Include any necessary determination and distribution of excess schedule and income distribution schedules.

Problem 4-13 *(LO 2, 3, 6)* **80%, sophisticated equity, several excess distributions, merchandise, equipment sales.** (This is the same as Problem 4-11 except for use of the sophisticated equity method.) On January 1, 20X1, Peanut Company acquired 80% of the common stock of Sam Company for $200,000. On this date, Sam had total owners' equity of $200,000. During 20X1 and 20X2, Peanut has appropriately accounted for its investment in Sam using the sophisticated equity method.

Any excess of cost over book value is attributable to inventory (worth $12,500 more than cost), to equipment (worth $25,000 more than book value), and to goodwill. FIFO is used for inventories. The equipment has a remaining life of 4 years, and straight-line depreciation is used.

On January 1, 20X2, Peanut held merchandise acquired from Sam for $20,000. During 20X2, Sam sold merchandise to Peanut for $40,000, $10,000 of which is still held by Peanut on December 31, 20X2. Sam's usual gross profit is 50%.

On December 31, 20X1, Peanut sold equipment to Sam at a gain of $15,000. During 20X2, the equipment was used by Sam. Depreciation is being computed using the straight-line method, a 5-year life, and no salvage value.

The following trial balances were prepared for the Peanut and Sam companies for December 31, 20X2:

	Peanut Company	Sam Company
Inventory, December 31	130,000	50,000
Other Current Assets	241,000	235,000
Investment in Sam Company	284,000	
Other Long-Term Investments	20,000	
Land	140,000	80,000
Buildings and Equipment	375,000	200,000
Accumulated Depreciation	(120,000)	(30,000)
Other Intangibles		20,000
Current Liabilities	(150,000)	(70,000)
Bonds Payable		(100,000)
Other Long-Term Liabilities	(200,000)	(50,000)
Common Stock, Peanut Company	(200,000)	
Other Paid-In Capital, Peanut Company	(100,000)	
Retained Earnings, Peanut Company	(297,000)	
Common Stock, Sam Company		(50,000)
Other Paid-In Capital, Sam Company		(50,000)
Retained Earnings, Sam Company		(150,000)
Net Sales	(600,000)	(315,000)
Cost of Goods Sold	350,000	150,000
Operating Expenses	150,000	60,000
Subsidiary Income	(83,000)	
Dividends Declared, Peanut Company	60,000	
Dividends Declared, Sam Company		20,000
Totals	0	0

Complete the worksheet for consolidated financial statements for the year ended December 31, 20X2. Include any necessary determination and distribution of excess schedule and income distribution schedules. ◄◄◄◄◄ **Required**

Use the following information for Problems 4-14 and 4-15:

On January 1, 20X1, Purple Company acquired Simple Company. Purple paid $300,000 for 80% of Simple's common stock. On the date of acquisition, Simple had the following balance sheet:

Simple Company
Balance Sheet
January 1, 20X1

Assets		Liabilities and Equity	
Accounts receivable	$ 50,000	Accounts payable	$ 60,000
Inventory	60,000	Bonds payable	200,000
Land	100,000	Common stock, $1 par	10,000
Buildings	150,000	Paid-in capital in excess of par	90,000
Accumulated depreciation	(50,000)	Retained earnings	60,000
Equipment	100,000		
Accumulated depreciation	(30,000)		
Goodwill	40,000		
Total assets	$420,000	Total liabilities and equity	$420,000

Buildings, which have a 20-year life, are understated by $100,000. Equipment, which has a 5-year life, is understated by $50,000. Any remaining excess is goodwill. Purple uses the simple equity method to account for its investment in Simple.

Problem 4-14 *(LO 2, 3)* **80%, equity, several excess distributions, inventory, fixed assets, parent and subsidiary sales.** Refer to the preceding facts for Purple's acquisition of Simple common stock. On January 1, 20X2, Simple held merchandise sold to it from Purple for $14,000. This beginning inventory had an applicable gross profit of 40%. During 20X2, Purple sold merchandise to Simple for $60,000. On December 31, 20X2, Simple held $12,000 of this merchandise in its inventory. This ending inventory had an applicable gross profit of 35%. Simple owed Purple $8,000 on December 31 as a result of this intercompany sale.

Purple held $12,000 worth of merchandise in its beginning inventory from sales from Simple. This beginning inventory had an applicable gross profit of 25%. During 20X2, Simple sold merchandise to Purple for $30,000. Purple held $16,000 of this inventory at the end of the year. This ending inventory had an applicable gross profit of 30%. Purple owed Simple $6,000 on December 31 as a result of this intercompany sale.

On January 1, 20X1, Purple sold equipment to Simple at a profit of $40,000. Depreciation on this equipment is computed over an 8-year life, using the straight-line method.

On January 1, 20X2, Simple sold equipment with a book value of $30,000 to Purple for $54,000. This equipment has a 6-year life and is depreciated using the straight-line method.

Purple and Simple had the following trial balances on December 31, 20X2:

	Purple Company	Simple Company
Cash	92,400	65,500
Accounts Receivable	130,000	36,000
Inventory	105,000	76,000
Land	100,000	100,000
Investment in Simple	387,600	
Buildings	800,000	150,000
Accumulated Depreciation	(250,000)	(60,000)
Equipment	210,000	220,000
Accumulated Depreciation	(115,000)	(80,000)
Goodwill		40,000

Accounts Payable	(70,000)	(78,000)
Bonds Payable		(200,000)
Common Stock	(100,000)	(10,000)
Paid-In Capital in Excess of Par	(800,000)	(90,000)
Retained Earnings, January 1, 20X2	(325,000)	(142,000)
Sales	(800,000)	(350,000)
Cost of Goods Sold	450,000	208,500
Depreciation Expense—Buildings	30,000	5,000
Depreciation Expense—Equipment	25,000	23,000
Other Expenses	140,000	92,000
Gain on Fixed Asset Sale		(24,000)
Interest Expense		8,000
Subsidiary Income	(30,000)	
Dividends Declared	20,000	10,000
Totals	0	0

◄◄◄◄◄ Required

1. Prepare a zone analysis and a determination and distribution of excess schedule for the investment in Simple.
2. Complete a consolidated worksheet for Purple Company and its subsidiary Simple Company as of December 31, 20X2. Prepare supporting amortization and income distribution schedules.

Problem 4-15 *(LO 2, 3)* **80%, equity, several excess distributions, inventory, fixed assets, parent and subsidiary sales.** Refer to the preceding facts for Purple's acquisition of Simple common stock. On January 1, 20X3, Simple held merchandise sold to it from Purple for $12,000. This beginning inventory had an applicable gross profit of 35%. During 20X3, Purple sold merchandise to Simple for $60,000. On December 31, 20X3, Simple held $10,000 of this merchandise in its inventory. This ending inventory had an applicable gross profit of 40%. Simple owed Purple $8,000 on December 31 as a result of this intercompany sale.

Purple held $16,000 worth of merchandise in its January 1, 20X3, inventory from sales from Simple. This beginning inventory had an applicable gross profit of 30%. During 20X3, Simple sold merchandise to Purple for $30,000. Purple held $20,000 of this inventory at the end of the year. This ending inventory had an applicable gross profit of 35%. Purple owed Simple $6,000 on December 31 as a result of this intercompany sale.

On January 1, 20X1, Purple sold equipment to Simple at a profit of $40,000. Depreciation on this equipment is computed over an 8-year life, using the straight-line method.

On January 1, 20X2, Simple sold equipment with a book value of $30,000 to Purple for $54,000. This equipment has a 6-year life and is depreciated using the straight-line method.

Purple and Simple had the following trial balances on December 31, 20X3:

	Purple Company	Simple Company
Cash	195,400	53,500
Accounts Receivable	140,000	53,000
Inventory	140,000	81,000
Land	100,000	60,000
Investment in Simple	443,600	
Buildings	800,000	150,000
Accumulated Depreciation	(280,000)	(65,000)

(continued)

	Purple Company	Simple Company
Equipment	150,000	220,000
Accumulated Depreciation	(115,000)	(103,000)
Goodwill		40,000
Accounts Payable	(25,000)	(50,000)
Bonds Payable		(100,000)
Common Stock	(100,000)	(10,000)
Paid-In Capital in Excess of Par	(800,000)	(90,000)
Retained Earnings, January 1, 20X3	(510,000)	(169,500)
Sales	(850,000)	(500,000)
Cost of Goods Sold	480,000	290,000
Depreciation Expense—Buildings	30,000	5,000
Depreciation Expense—Equipment	15,000	23,000
Other Expenses	210,000	94,000
Interest Expense		8,000
Subsidiary Income	(64,000)	
Dividends Declared	40,000	10,000
Totals	0	0

Required ▶ ▶ ▶ ▶ ▶

1. Prepare a zone analysis and a determination and distribution of excess schedule for the investment in Simple.
2. Complete a consolidated worksheet for Purple Company and its subsidiary Simple Company as of December 31, 20X3. Prepare supporting amortization and income distribution schedules.

APPENDIX PROBLEMS

template cd

Problem 4A-1 *(LO 2, 3, 7)* **Vertical worksheet, 100%, cost, fixed asset and merchandise sales.** Arther Corporation acquired all of the outstanding $10 par voting common stock of Trent Inc. on January 1, 20X2, in exchange for 50,000 shares of its $10 par voting common stock. On December 31, 20X1, the common stock of Arther had a closing market price of $15 per share on a national stock exchange. The retained earnings balance of Trent Inc. was $156,000 on the date of the acquisition. The acquisition was accounted for appropriately as a purchase. Both companies continued to operate as separate business entities maintaining separate accounting records with years ending December 31.

On December 31, 20X4, after year-end adjustments but before the nominal accounts were closed, the companies had the following condensed statements:

	Arther Corporation	Trent Inc.
Income Statement:		
Sales	$(1,900,000)	$(1,500,000)
Dividend Income (from Trent Inc.)	(40,000)	
Cost of Goods Sold	1,180,000	870,000
Operating Expenses (includes depreciation)	550,000	440,000
Net Income	$ (210,000)	$ (190,000)
Retained Earnings:		
Retained Earnings, January 1, 20X4	$ (250,000)	$ (206,000)
Net Income	(210,000)	(190,000)
Dividends Paid		40,000
Balance, December 31, 20X4	$ (460,000)	$ (356,000)

(continued)

Balance Sheet:

Cash	$ 285,000	$ 150,000
Accounts Receivable (net)	430,000	350,000
Inventories	530,000	410,000
Land, Building, and Equipment	660,000	680,000
Accumulated Depreciation	(185,000)	(210,000)
Investment in Trent Inc. (at cost)	750,000	
Accounts Payable and Accrued Expenses	(670,000)	(544,000)
Common Stock ($10 par)	(1,200,000)	(400,000)
Additional Paid-In Capital	(140,000)	(80,000)
Retained Earnings, December 31, 20X2	(460,000)	(356,000)
Totals	$ 0	$ 0

Additional information is as follows:

a. There have been no changes in the common stock and additional paid-in capital accounts since the one necessitated in 20X2 by Arther's acquisition of Trent Inc.
b. At the acquisition date, the market value of Trent's machinery exceeded book value by $54,000. This excess is being amortized over the asset's estimated average remaining life of 6 years. The fair values of Trent's other assets and liabilities were equal to book values. Any remaining excess is goodwill.
c. On July 1, 20X2, Arther sold a warehouse facility to Trent for $129,000 in cash. At the date of sale, Arther's book values were $33,000 for the land and $66,000 for the undepreciated cost of the building. Trent allocated the $129,000 purchase price to the land for $43,000 and to the building for $86,000. Trent is depreciating the building over its estimated 5-year remaining useful life by the straight-line method with no salvage value.
d. During 20X4, Arther purchased merchandise from Trent at an aggregate invoice price of $180,000, which included a 100% markup on Trent's cost. At December 31, 20X4, Arther owed Trent $75,000 on these purchases, and $36,000 of the merchandise purchased remained in Arther's inventory.

◄◄◄◄◄ **Required**

Complete the vertical worksheet necessary to prepare the consolidated income statement and retained earnings statement for the year ended December 31, 20X4, and a consolidated balance sheet as of December 31, 20X4, for Arther Corporation and its subsidiary. Formal consolidated statements and journal entries are not required. Include the determination and distribution of excess schedule and the income distribution schedules.

(AICPA adapted)

Problem 4A-2 *(LO 2, 3, 7)* **Vertical worksheet, 80%, cost, several excess distributions, merchandise, equipment sales.** (This is similar to Problem 4-11; it uses the simple equity method and vertical worksheet format.) On January 1, 20X1, Peanut Company acquired 80% of the common stock of Sam Company for $200,000. On this date, Sam had total owners' equity of $200,000, which included retained earnings of $100,000. During 20X1 and 20X2, Peanut has accounted for its investment in Sam using the simple equity method.

Any excess of cost over book value is attributable to inventory (worth $12,500 more than cost), to equipment (worth $25,000 more than book value), and to goodwill. FIFO is used for inventories. The equipment has a remaining life of 4 years, and straight-line depreciation is used. Any remaining excess is attributed to goodwill.

On January 1, 20X2, Peanut held merchandise acquired from Sam for $20,000. During 20X2, Sam sold merchandise to Peanut for $40,000, $10,000 of which is still held by Peanut on December 31, 20X2. Sam's usual gross profit is 50%.

On December 31, 20X1, Peanut sold equipment to Sam at a gain of $15,000. During 20X2, the equipment was used by Sam. Depreciation is being computed using the straight-line method, a 5-year life, and no salvage value.

The following condensed statements were prepared for the Peanut and Sam companies for December 31, 20X2.

	Peanut Company	Sam Company
Income Statement:		
Net Sales	$ (600,000)	$(315,000)
Cost of Goods Sold	350,000	150,000
Operating Expenses	150,000	60,000
Subsidiary Income	(84,000)	
Net Income	$ (184,000)	$(105,000)
Retained Earnings Statement:		
Balance, January 1, 20X2, Peanut Company	$ (320,000)	
Balance, January 1, 20X2, Sam Company		$(150,000)
Net Income (from above)	(184,000)	(105,000)
Dividends Declared, Peanut Company	60,000	
Dividends Declared, Sam Company		20,000
Balance, December 31, 20X2	$ (444,000)	$(235,000)
Consolidated Balance Sheet:		
Inventory, December 31	$ 130,000	$ 50,000
Other Current Assets	241,000	235,000
Investment in Sam Company	308,000	
Other Long-Term Investments	20,000	
Land	140,000	80,000
Building and Equipment	375,000	200,000
Accumulated Depreciation	(120,000)	(30,000)
Other Intangibles		20,000
Current Liabilities	(150,000)	(70,000)
Bonds Payable		(100,000)
Other Long-Term Liabilities	(200,000)	(50,000)
Common Stock, Peanut Company	(200,000)	
Other Paid-In Capital, Peanut Company	(100,000)	
Common Stock, Sam Company		(50,000)
Other Paid-In Capital, Sam Company		(50,000)
Retained Earnings, December 31, 20X2	(444,000)	(235,000)
Totals	$ 0	$ 0

Required ▶ ▶ ▶ ▶ ▶ Complete the worksheet for consolidated financial statements for the year ended December 31, 20X2. Include any necessary determination and distribution of excess schedule and income distribution schedules.

Case 4-1 *The Noncontrolling Interest's Concern with Intercompany Transactions*

Henderson Window Company was a privately held corporation until January 1, 20X1. On January 1, 20X1, Cool Glass Company purchased a 70% interest in Henderson at a price well in excess of book value. There were some minor differences between book and fair values, but the bulk of the excess was attributed to goodwill. In its consolidated statements, Cool Glass is amortizing the goodwill over 10 years.

Harvey Henderson did not sell his shares to Cool Glass as a part of the January 1, 20X1, Cool Glass purchase. He wanted to remain a Henderson shareholder since he felt Henderson was a more profitable and stable company than was Cool Glass. Harvey remains an employee of Henderson Window, working in an accounting capacity.

Harvey is concerned about some accounting issues that he feels are detrimental to his ownership interest. Harvey told you that Henderson always bought most of its glass from Cool Glass. He never felt the prices charged for the glass were unreasonable. Since the purchase of Henderson by Cool Glass, he feels the price charged to Henderson by Cool Glass has risen dramatically and that it is out of step with what would be paid to other glass suppliers.

The second concern is the sale of a large Henderson warehouse to Cool Glass for less than what Harvey would consider to be the market value. Harvey agrees that the sale is reasonable since the new just-in-time order system has made the space unnecessary. He just feels the sale price is below market.

Harvey did make his concerns known to the president of Cool Glass. The president made several points. First, she said that the price charged for the glass was a little high, but Harvey should consider its high quality. She went on to say that the transfer price washes out in the annual report, and it has no impact on reported net income of the corporation. She also stated that the warehouse sale was at a low price, but there was a reason. It was a good year, and a large gain wasn't needed. She would rather have lower depreciation in future years. Her last point was: "We paid a big price for Henderson, and we are stuck with big goodwill amortization expenses. We should get some benefits from it!"

◄◄◄◄◄ Required

Write a memo to Harvey Henderson suggesting how he might respond to the president's comments.

Intercompany Transactions: Bonds and Leases

CHAPTER

5

Learning Objectives

When you have completed this chapter, you should be able to

1. **Explain the alternatives a parent company has if it wishes to acquire outstanding subsidiary bonds from outside owners.**
2. **Follow the procedures used to retire intercompany bonds on a consolidated worksheet.**
3. **Explain why a parent company would lease assets to the subsidiary.**
4. **Show how to eliminate intercompany operating lease transactions from the consolidated statements.**
5. **Eliminate intercompany capital leases on the consolidated worksheet.**
6. **Demonstrate an understanding of the process used to defer intercompany profits on sales-type leases.**
7. **(Appendix) Explain the complications caused by unguaranteed residual values with intercompany leases.**

This chapter focuses on intercompany transactions that create a long-term debtor-creditor relationship between the members of a consolidated group. The usual impetus for these transactions is the parent's ability to borrow larger amounts of capital at more favorable terms than would be available to the subsidiary. In addition, the parent company may desire to manage all capital needs of the consolidated company for better control of all capital sources. Intercompany leasing with the parent as the lessor also may be motivated by centralized asset management and credit control.

Intercompany bond holdings will be analyzed first. Here, one member of the consolidated group, usually the subsidiary, has issued bonds which appear on its balance sheet as long-term liabilities. Another member may purchase the bonds and list them on its balance sheet as an investment. However, when consolidated statements are prepared, the intercompany purchase, in effect, should be viewed as a retirement of the bonds. Consideration of intercompany leasing of assets will follow the bond coverage. In this case, one member of the consolidated group purchases the asset and leases it to another member. While the leasing transaction is recorded as such on the separate books of the affiliates, the lease has no substance from a consolidated viewpoint. Only a lease that involves a nonaffiliated company may appear in the consolidated statements.

INTERCOMPANY INVESTMENT IN BONDS

To secure long-term funds, one member of a consolidated group may sell its bonds directly to another member of the group. Clearly, such a transaction results in intercompany debt which must be eliminated from the consolidated statements. On the worksheet, the investment in bonds recorded by one company must be eliminated against the bonds payable of the other. In

1
OBJECTIVE

Explain the alternatives a parent company has if it wishes to acquire outstanding subsidiary bonds from outside owners.

addition, the applicable interest expense recorded by one affiliate must be eliminated against the applicable interest revenue recorded by the other affiliate. Interest accruals recorded on the books of the separate companies must be eliminated as well.

There are situations where one affiliate (usually the subsidiary) has outstanding bonds that have been purchased by parties that are not members of the affiliated group, and a decision is made by another affiliate (usually the parent) to obtain these bonds. The simplest way to accomplish the removal of subsidiary bonds from outsiders is for the parent to advance funds to the subsidiary so that the subsidiary may retire the bonds. From an accounting standpoint, this transaction is easy to record. The former debt is retired and a new, long-term intercompany debt originates. The only procedures required on future consolidated worksheets involve the elimination of the resulting intercompany debt.

A more complicated method is to have the parent purchase the subsidiary bonds from the outside parties and to hold them as an investment. This method creates an intercompany investment in bonds, where each affiliate continues to accrue and record interest on the bonds. While the intercompany bonds are treated as a liability on one set of books and as an investment on the other set, from a consolidated viewpoint the bonds have been retired and the debt to outside parties has been liquidated. The purchase of intercompany bonds has the following ramifications when consolidating:

1. Consolidated statements prepared for the period in which the bonds are purchased must portray the intercompany purchase as a retirement of the bonds. It is possible, but unlikely, that the bonds will be purchased at book value. There usually will be a gain or loss on retirement; this gain or loss is deemed to be an ordinary gain or loss and is recognized on the consolidated income statement.
2. For all periods during which the intercompany investment exists, the intercompany bonds, interest accruals, and interest expense/revenue must be eliminated since the bonds no longer exist from a consolidated viewpoint.

The complexity of the elimination procedures depends on whether the bonds originally were issued at face value or at a premium or discount. Additionally, one must exercise extra care in the application of elimination procedures when only a portion of the outstanding bonds is purchased intercompany.

2
OBJECTIVE

Follow the procedures used to retire intercompany bonds on a consolidated worksheet.

Bonds Originally Issued at Face Value

When bonds are sold at face value by a subsidiary to outside parties, contract (nominal) interest agrees with the effective, or market, interest, and no amortizations of issuance premiums or discounts need to be recorded. However, subsequent to the issuance, the market rate of interest most likely will deviate from the contract rate. Thus, while there is no original issuance premium or discount, there will be what could be termed an *investment premium* or *discount* resulting from the intercompany purchase of the bonds.

To illustrate the procedures required for intercompany bonds originally issued at face value, assume a subsidiary, Company S, issued 5-year, 8% bonds at face value of $100,000 to outside parties on January 1, 20X1. Interest is paid on January 1 for the preceding year. On January 2, 20X3, the parent, Company P, purchased the bonds from the outside parties for $103,600.

Company S will continue to list the $100,000 bonded debt and to record interest expense of $8,000 during 20X3, 20X4, and 20X5. However, Company P will record a bond investment of $103,600 and will amortize $1,200 per year, for the remaining life of the bond, by reducing the investment account and adjusting interest revenue. Though the interest method of amortization is preferable, the straight-line method is permitted if results are not materially different. This initial example and most others in this chapter use the straight-line method in order to simplify analysis. A summary example is used to demonstrate the interest method of amortization.

Although the investment and liability accounts continue to exist on the separate books of the affiliated companies, retirement has occurred from a consolidated viewpoint. Debt with a book value of $100,000 was retired by a payment of $103,600, and there is a $3,600 extraordinary loss on retirement. If a consolidated worksheet is prepared on the day the bonds are purchased, Bonds Payable would be eliminated against Investment in Company S Bonds, and a *loss on retirement* would be reported on the consolidated income statement. The following abbreviated worksheet displays the procedures used to retire the bonds as part of the elimination process:

	Partial Trial Balance		Eliminations & Adjustments	
	Co. P	Co. S	Dr.	Cr.
Investment in Company S Bonds	103,600			(B) 103,600
Bonds Payable		(100,000)	(B) 100,000	
Loss on Bond Retirement			(B) 3,600	

This partial worksheet, prepared on January 2, 20X3, is only hypothetical since, in reality, there will be no consolidated worksheet prepared until December 31, 20X3, the end of the period. During 20X3, Companies P and S will record the transactions for interest as follows:

Company P			Company S		
Interest Receivable	8,000		Interest Expense	8,000	
Investment in Company S Bonds		1,200	Interest Payable		8,000
Interest Income		6,800	To record interest expense.		
To record interest revenue net of $1,200 per year premium amortization.					

These entries will be reflected in the trial balances of the December 31, 20X3, consolidated worksheet, shown in Worksheet 5-1 on pages 288 to 289. Note that Investment in Company S Bonds reflects the premium amortization since the balance is $102,400 ($103,600 original cost −$1,200 amortization). In this worksheet, it is assumed that Investment in Company S Stock reflects a 90% interest purchased at a price equal to the book value of the underlying equity, and the simple equity method is used by Company P to record the investment in stock.

worksheet
Worksheet 5-1: page 288

Entries (CY1) and (EL) eliminate the intercompany stock investment. Entry (B1) eliminates the intercompany bonds at their year-end balances and the intercompany interest expense and revenue recorded during the year. In journal entry form, elimination entries are as follows:

(CY1)	*Eliminate current-year equity income:*		
	Subsidiary Income	10,800	
	Investment in Company S Stock		10,800
(EL)	*Eliminate 90% of subsidiary equity:*		
	Common Stock ($10 par), Company S	72,000	
	Retained Earnings, January 1, 20X3, Company S	18,000	
	Investment in Company S Stock		90,000
(B1)	*Eliminate intercompany bonds and interest expense:*		
	Bonds Payable	100,000	
	Investment in Company S Bonds		102,400
	Interest Income	6,800	
	Interest Expense		8,000
	Loss on Bond Retirement	3,600	
(B2)	*Eliminate intercompany accrued interest:*		
	Interest Payable	8,000	
	Interest Receivable		8,000

The amount of the gain or loss is the sum of the difference between the remaining book value of the investment on bonds compared to the debt and the difference between interest expense and debt. For this example

Investment in Bonds Balance, December 31, 20X3	$102,400	
Bonds Payable, December 31, 20X3	100,000	$2,400
Interest Expense, 20X3	$ 8,000	
Interest Revenue, 20X3	6,800	1,200
Loss, January 2, 20X3		$3,600

As a result of the elimination entries, the consolidated income statement will include the retirement loss but will exclude intercompany interest payments and accruals. The consolidated balance sheet will not list the intercompany bonds payable or investment in bonds accounts.

The only remaining problem is the distribution of consolidated net income to the controlling and noncontrolling interests. The income distribution schedule shows Company S absorbing all of the retirement loss. It is most common to view the purchasing affiliate as a mere agent of the issuing affiliate. Therefore, it is the issuer, not the purchaser, that must bear the entire gain or loss on retirement. Even though the debt is retired from a consolidated viewpoint, it still exists internally. Company P has a right to collect the interest as part of its share of Company S's operations. Based on the value of the debt on January 2, 20X3, the interest expense/revenue is $6,800. The interest cost of $8,000 recorded by Company S must be corrected to reflect the internal interest expense of $6,800. The income distribution schedule increases the income of Company S to reflect the adjustment ($1,200) to interest expense. It should be noted that the retirement loss borne by Company S will entirely offset the adjustments to interest expense by the time the bonds mature. If the parent, Company P, had issued the bonds to outside parties and if the subsidiary, Company S, later had purchased them, the only change would be that the income distribution schedule of Company P would absorb the loss on retirement and the interest adjustment.

The worksheet procedures that would be needed at the end of 20X4 are shown in Worksheet 5-2 on pages 290 to 291. The interest revenue and expense have been recorded on the books of the separate companies. The investment in Company S bonds account on the parent's books reflects its book value at the end of 20X4.

worksheet

Worksheet 5-2: page 290

The eliminations in journal entry form are as follows:

(CY1)	*Eliminate current-year equity income:*		
	Subsidiary Income	19,800	
	Investment in Company S Stock		19,800
(EL)	*Eliminate 90% of subsidiary equity:*		
	Common Stock ($10 par), Company S	72,000	
	Retained Earnings, January 1, 20X4, Company S	28,800	
	Investment in Company S Stock		100,800
(B1)	*Eliminate intercompany bonds and interest expense:*		
	Bonds Payable	100,000	
	Investment in Company S Bonds		101,200
	Interest Income	6,800	
	Interest Expense		8,000
	Retained Earnings, January 1, 20X4, Company P	2,160	
	Retained Earnings, January 1, 20X4, Company S	240	
(B2)	*Eliminate intercompany accrued interest:*		
	Interest Payable	8,000	
	Interest Receivable		8,000

Entry (B1) eliminates the intercompany bonds at their year-end balances and the intercompany interest expense and revenue. Recall that the original retirement loss was $3,600 when the bonds had 3 years to maturity. By the start of the second period, 20X4, $1,200 of that loss was already amortized on the separate books of the affiliates. The loss remaining is $2,400 [it is verified in the explanation to entry (B1) in Worksheet 5-2]. This remaining loss is debited to Retained Earnings since the retirement occurred in a prior period. The adjustment is allocated to noncontrolling and controlling beginning retained earnings since the bonds were issued by the subsidiary.

The 20X4 consolidated income statement will not include intercompany interest. The income distribution schedules for Worksheet 5-2 reflect the fact that the debt still existed internally during the period. However, the interest expense recorded by Company S is reduced to reflect the interest cost based on the January 2, 20X3, purchase price.

If Company S was the purchaser and Company P the issuer of the bonds, Worksheet 5-2 would differ as follows:

1. The January 1, 20X4, retained earnings adjustment would be absorbed completely by the controlling retained earnings, since the parent company would be the issuer absorbing the loss.
2. The income distribution schedule of the parent would contain the interest adjustment.

Bonds Not Originally Issued at Face Value

The principles of eliminating intercompany investments in bonds are not altered by the existence of a premium or discount stemming from original issuance. The numerical calculations just become more complex. To illustrate, assume Company S issued $100,000 of 5-year, 8% bonds on January 1, 20X1. The market interest rate approximated 9% and, as a result, the bonds sold at a discount of $3,890. Interest is paid each December 31. On each interest payment date, the discount is amortized $778 ($3,890 ÷ 5 years) by decreasing the discount and by increasing interest expense. On December 31, 20X3, the balance of the discount is $1,556 [$3,890 − (3 × $778 annual amortization)].

The parent, Company P, purchased the bonds for $103,600 on December 31, 20X3, after interest had been paid. The parent will amortize $1,800 of the investment each subsequent December 31, reducing the parent's interest income to $6,200 ($8,000 cash − $1,800 amortization) for 20X4 and 20X5.

The following abbreviated December 31, 20X3 (date of purchase) worksheet lists the investment in Company S bonds account, the bonds payable account, and the remaining issuance discount. Eliminating the $103,600 price paid for the bonds by Company P against the book value of $98,444 ($100,000 − $1,556) creates a loss on retirement of $5,156 which is carried to consolidated net income. Worksheet procedures may be aided by linking the bonds payable and the related discount or premium on the worksheet. This is done on our worksheets by circling the amounts in the trial balance and in the eliminations.

	Partial Trial Balance		Eliminations & Adjustments	
	Company P	Company S	Dr.	Cr.
Investment in Company S Bonds	103,600			(B) 103,600
Bonds Payable, 8%		(100,000)	(B) 100,000	
Discount on Bonds Payable		1,556		(B) 1,556
Loss on Bond Retirement			(B) 5,156	
Interest Expense		8,778*		

*$8,000 cash + $778 straight-line amortization.

Interest expense on the books of Company S is extended to the consolidated income statement, since this interest was incurred as a result of transactions with outside parties. There would be no interest adjustment for 20X3, since the bonds were not purchased by the parent until December 31, 20X3. The income distribution schedules accompanying the worksheet would assess the retirement loss against the issuer, Company S.

The implications of these intercompany bonds on the 20X4 consolidated worksheet are reflected in Worksheet 5-3 on pages 292 to 293. Assume Company P acquired a 90% interest in the common stock of Company S at a price equal to the book value of the underlying equity. The simple equity method is used by the parent to record the investment in the stock of Company S. The trial balances include the following items:

Worksheet 5-3: page 292

1. The investment in Company S bonds at its amortized December 31, 20X4, balance of \$101,800 (\$103,600 − \$1,800 amortization),
2. The interest revenue (adjusted for amortization) of \$6,200 on the books of Company P,
3. The discount on bonds account at its amortized December 31, 20X4, balance of \$778, and
4. The interest expense (adjusted for discount amortization) of \$8,778 (\$8,000 cash + \$778 amortization) on the books of Company S.
5. There is no accrued interest receivable/payable since interest was paid on December 31, 20X4.

The eliminations in journal entry form are as follows:

(CY1)	*Eliminate current-year equity income:*		
	Subsidiary Income	8,874	
	Investment in Company S Stock		8,874
(EL)	*Eliminate 90% of subsidiary equity:*		
	Common Stock (\$10 par), Company S	36,000	
	Retained Earnings, January 1, 20X4, Company S	99,000	
	Investment in Company S Stock		135,000
(B)	*Eliminate intercompany bonds and interest expense:*		
	Bonds Payable	100,000	
	Discount on Bonds		778
	Investment in Company S Bonds		101,800
	Interest Income	6,200	
	Interest Expense		8,778
	Retained Earnings, January 1, 20X4, Company P	4,640	
	Retained Earnings, January 1, 20X4, Company S	516	

Entry (B) eliminates the investment in bonds against the bonds payable and the applicable remaining discount. Entry (B) also eliminates interest expense and revenue. Be sure to understand the calculation of the adjustment to beginning retained earnings which is explained in the entry (B) information. The loss at the start of the year is the sum of the loss remaining at year-end and the loss amortized on the books of the separate affiliates during the year.

Again, the consolidated income statement does not include intercompany interest. However, the Company S income distribution schedule does reflect the adjustment of Company S's interest expense. The original \$8,778 interest expense has been replaced by a \$6,200 expense, based on the purchase price paid by Company P. The smaller interest expense compensates the subsidiary for the retirement loss absorbed in a previous period.

Purchase of Only a Portion of the Bonds

The preceding examples assume that the parent company purchases all of the outstanding bonds of the subsidiary. In such cases, all of the bonds are retired on the worksheet. There may be cases, however, where the parent purchases only a portion of the subsidiary's outstanding bonds. Suppose, for example, that the parent purchased 80% of the subsidiary's outstanding bonds. Only the 80% interest in the bonds would be eliminated on the consolidated worksheet, and only the interest expense and revenue applicable to 80% of the bonds would be eliminated on the worksheet. **The 20% interest in the subsidiary bonds owned by persons outside the control group remains as a valid debt of the consolidated company and should not be eliminated.** It is a common error for students to eliminate the 80% interest in intercompany bonds owned by a parent against 100% of the bonds issued by the subsidiary. Such a mistake improperly eliminates valid debt and greatly miscalculates the gain or loss on retirement. It also should be noted that the interest paid to persons outside the control group should remain a part of the consolidated statements. Only the interest paid to the affiliated company is to be eliminated.

Interest Method of Amortization

The procedures used to eliminate intercompany bonds are not altered by the interest method of amortization; only the dollar values change. To illustrate the calculations, assume that Company S issued $100,000 of 5-year, 8% bonds on January 1, 20X1. The market interest rate on that date was 9%, so that the bonds sold at a discount of $3,890. Interest on the bonds is paid each December 31. The discount amortization for the term of the bonds follows:

Year	Debt Balance, January 1	Effective Interest	Nominal Interest	Discount Amortization
20X1	$96,110	$8,650 (0.09 × $96,110)	$8,000	$ 650
20X2	96,760 ($96,110 + $650)	8,708 (0.09 × $96,760)	8,000	708
20X3	97,468 ($96,760 + $708)	8,772 (0.09 × $97,468)	8,000	772
20X4	98,240 ($97,468 + $772)	8,842 (0.09 × $98,240)	8,000	842
20X5	99,082 ($98,240 + $842)	8,918* (0.09 × $99,082)	8,000	918
*Includes $1 rounding error.				$3,890

On December 31, 20X3, after interest had been paid, the bonds were purchased by parent Company P at a price to yield 6%. Based on present value computations, $103,667 was paid for the bonds. The premium on the bonds would be amortized by Company P as follows:

Year	Investment Balance, January 1	Effective Interest	Nominal Interest	Premium Amortization
20X4	$103,667	$6,220 (0.06 × $103,667)	$8,000	$1,780
20X5	101,887 ($103,667 − $1,780)	6,113 (0.06 × $101,887)	8,000	1,887
				$3,667

The following abbreviated December 31, 20X3 (date of purchase) worksheet lists the investment in Company S bonds account, the bonds payable account, and the remaining issuance discount. Eliminating the $103,667 price paid by Company P against the book value of $98,240 ($100,000 − $1,760) creates a loss on retirement of $5,427 that is carried to consolidated net income.

	Partial Trial Balance		Eliminations & Adjustments	
	Company P	Company S	Dr.	Cr.
Investment in Company S Bonds	103,667			(B) 103,667
Bonds Payable, 8%		(100,000)	(B) 100,000	
Discount on Bonds Payable		1,760		(B) 1,760
Loss on Bond Retirement			(B) 5,427	
Interest Expense		8,772*		

*See preceding discount amortization schedule for issuer.

worksheet

Worksheet 5-4: page 294

The differences in the 20X4 consolidated worksheet caused by the interest method of amortization are shown in Worksheet 5-4 on pages 294 to 295. Note particularly the change in the Company S income distribution schedule. The original 9% interest, totaling $8,842, has been replaced by the $6,220 of interest calculated using the 6% rate.

The eliminations in journal entry form are as follows:

(CY1)	*Eliminate current-year equity income:*		
	Subsidiary Income	8,820	
	Investment in Company S Stock		8,820
(EL)	*Eliminate 90% of subsidiary equity:*		
	Common Stock ($10 par), Company S	36,000	
	Retained Earnings, January 1, 20X4, Company S	99,180	
	Investment in Company S Stock		135,180
(B)	*Eliminate intercompany bonds and interest expense:*		
	Bonds Payable	100,000	
	Discount on Bonds		918
	Investment in Company S Bonds		101,887
	Interest Income	6,220	
	Interest Expense		8,842
	Retained Earnings, January 1, 20X4, Company P	4,884	
	Retained Earnings, January 1, 20X4, Company S	543	

REFLECTION

- The parent can effectively retire subsidiary bonds by lending money to the subsidiary and letting the subsidiary purchase the bonds from existing owners or by simply buying the bonds from existing owners.
- When the parent buys subsidiary bonds, the bonds cease to exist, from a consolidated viewpoint. They are retired on the consolidated worksheet by elimination.
- When the intercompany bonds are eliminated, there will be a difference between the amortized cost and the price paid; this creates a gain or loss on retirement.
- In periods subsequent to the intercompany purchase, the bonds must continue to be eliminated, and retained earnings is adjusted for the remaining retirement gain or loss that has not already been amortized.

- Intercompany interest expense/revenue and accrued interest receivable/payable are also eliminated.

INTERCOMPANY LEASES

3

OBJECTIVE

Explain why a parent company would lease assets to the subsidiary.

Intercompany leases have become one of the most frequently encountered types of transactions between affiliated companies. It is particularly common for parent companies with substantial financial resources to acquire major assets and to lease the assets to their subsidiaries. This action may occur because the financially stronger parent may be able to both purchase and finance assets on more favorable terms. Also, the parent company may desire close control over plant assets and may prefer centralized ownership and management of assets. Leasing becomes a mechanism through which the parent can convey the use of centrally owned assets to subsidiaries. Some companies achieve centralized asset management by forming separate leasing subsidiaries whose major function is to lease assets to affiliated companies. When such subsidiaries exist, they are consolidated automatically with the parent regardless of the ownership percentage of the parent.[1]

Operating Leases

4

OBJECTIVE

Show how to eliminate intercompany operating lease transactions from the consolidated statements.

Consolidation procedures for intercompany leases depend on the original recording of the lease by the separate companies. When an operating lease exists, the lessor has recorded the purchase of the asset and depreciates it. The lessor records rent revenue, while the lessee records rent expense. In such cases, it is necessary in the consolidation process to eliminate the intercompany rent expense/revenue and any related rent receivable/payable. The lessor's asset and related accumulated depreciation should be reclassified as a normal productive asset rather than as property under an operating lease. As an example, assume the parent, Company P, has both productive equipment used in its own operations and equipment that is under operating lease to a subsidiary, Company S. The following partial worksheet may be used to analyze required consolidation procedures:

	Partial Trial Balance		Eliminations & Adjustments	
	Company P	Company S	Dr.	Cr.
Equipment	800,000			
Accumulated Depreciation—Equipment	(300,000)			
Rent Receivable	1,200			(OL2) 1,200
Rent Payable		(1,200)	(OL2) 1,200	
Rent Income	(14,400)		(OL1) 14,400	
Rent Expense		14,400		(OL1) 14,400
Depreciation Expense	50,000			

Eliminations and Adjustments:

(OL1) Eliminate intercompany rent expense and revenue of $1,200 per month.
(OL2) Eliminate one month's accrued rent.

1 Statement of Financial Accounting Standards No. 13, *Accounting for Leases* (Stamford: Financial Accounting Standards Board, 1976), par. 31.

No adjustments are made in the income distribution schedules as a result of operating leases. The eliminations made on the worksheet do not change the amount of income or the distribution of income between the noncontrolling and controlling interests.

5

OBJECTIVE

Eliminate intercompany capital leases on the consolidated worksheet.

Capitalized Leases

Consolidation procedures become more complicated when the lease is recorded as a capital lease by the lessee and as a direct-financing or sales-type lease by the lessor. The lessee records both an asset and intercompany long-term debt. Generally, the criteria for determining when a lease requires such accounting treatment are the same for affiliated companies as for independent companies. However, when the terms of the lease are significantly affected by the fact that the lessee and lessor are affiliates, the usual criteria for classification of leases do not apply. Lease terms could be considered "significantly affected" when they could not reasonably be expected to occur between independent companies.[2] For example, a parent might lease to its subsidiary at a rent far below the market rate, or a parent might rent a highly specialized machine to its subsidiary on a month-to-month basis. Typically, such specialized machinery would be leased only on a long-term lease promising a full recovery of cost to the lessor, since there would be no use for the machine by other lessees if it were returned to the lessor. The month-to-month lease is possible only because the parent's control of the subsidiary assures a continued flow of rent payments. When, in the accountant's judgment, the terms of the lease are affected significantly by the parent-subsidiary relationship, the normal criteria are not used and the transaction is recorded so as to reflect its true economic substance.[3] Usually in these circumstances, the lessee is viewed as having purchased the asset using funds borrowed from the lessor.

Consolidation Procedures for Direct-Financing Leases. A direct-financing lease is viewed as a unique type of asset transfer by the lessor, who accepts a long-term receivable from the lessee as consideration for the asset received by the lessee. There is no profit or loss to the lessor on the transfer, only future interest revenue as payments become due.

Prior to studying consolidated worksheet procedures, the entries made by the affiliated lessee and lessor will be analyzed. In its simplest form, a direct-financing lease is recorded by the lessee as an asset, and debt is recorded to recognize the lease obligation. The lessor records the lease as a receivable from the lessee. If all payments to be received by the lessor will come from or are guaranteed by the original lessee, the present value of the net receivable recorded by the lessor will equal the present value of the payable recorded by the lessee, and the interest rates used to amortize the debt will be equal.

To illustrate, assume Company S is an 80%-owned subsidiary of Company P. On January 1, 20X1, Company P purchased a machine for $5,851 and leased it to Company S. The terms of the direct-financing lease provide for rental payments of $2,000 per year at the beginning of each period and allow the lessee to exercise an option to purchase the machine for $1,000 at the end of 20X3. The $1,000 purchase option is considered a bargain purchase option that will be exercised and is included in the minimum lease payments. The implicit interest rate (which equates all payments, including the bargain purchase option, to the lessor's purchase cost) is 16%. The lessee will depreciate the capitalized cost of the machine over 5 years, using the straight-line method. The lessee may use a 5-year life, despite the 3-year lease term, because it is assumed that the bargain purchase option will be exercised and that the asset will be used for 5 years.

The amortization of the debt at the implicit 16% interest rate is as follows:

2 *Ibid.*, par. 29.
3 *Ibid.*

Date	Payment	Interest at 16% on Previous Balance	Reduction of Principal	Principal Balance
January 1, 20X1	$2,000		$2,000	$3,851*
January 1, 20X2	2,000	$ 616	1,384	2,467
January 1, 20X3	2,000	395	1,605	862
December 31, 20X3	1,000	138	862	
Total	$7,000	$1,149	$5,851	

*Purchase price of $5,851 – $2,000 initial payment.

The journal entries for the separate companies would be as follows for the first two years:

Date	Company S (Lessee)			Company P (Lessor)		
20X1						
Jan. 1	Assets Under Capital Lease	5,851		Minimum Lease Payments Receivable	5,000	
	Obligations Under Capital Lease		3,851	Cash	2,000	
	Cash		2,000	Unearned Interest Income		1,149
				Accounts Payable (for asset)		5,851
Dec. 31	Interest Expense (at 16%)	616		Unearned Interest Income	616	
	Interest Payable		616	Interest Income (at 16%)		616
	Depreciation Expense (1/5 × $5,851)	1,170				
	Accumulated Depreciation—Assets Under Capital Lease		1,170			
20X2						
Jan. 1	Obligations Under Capital Lease	1,384		Cash	2,000	
	Interest Payable	616		Minimum Lease Payments Receivable		2,000
	Cash		2,000			
Dec. 31	Interest Expense (at 16%)	395		Unearned Interest Income	395	
	Interest Payable		395	Interest Income (at 16%)		395
	Depreciation Expense	1,170				
	Accumulated Depreciation—Assets Under Capital Lease		1,170			

At the end of each period, consolidation procedures would be needed to eliminate the intercompany transactions. In substance, there appears on the separate records of the affiliates an intercompany transfer of a plant asset with resulting intercompany debt. The intercompany debt, related interest expense/revenue, and interest accruals must be eliminated. Also, it is necessary to reclassify the assets under capital leases as productive assets owned by the consolidated group. The adjusted partial worksheets (pages 280 and 281) illustrate consolidation procedures at the end of 20X1 and 20X2.

A review of the worksheet eliminations and adjustments reveals that **consolidated net income is not changed because equal amounts of interest expense and revenue were eliminated.** Therefore, no adjustments are required in the income distribution schedules.

Partial Worksheet
For Year Ended December 31, 20X1

	Trial Balance		Eliminations & Adjustments	
	Company P	Company S	Dr.	Cr.
Assets Under Capital Lease		5,851		(CL3) 5,851
Accumulated Depreciation—Assets Under Capital Lease		(1,170)	(CL3) 1,170	
Property, Plant, and Equipment	200,000	120,000	(CL3) 5,851	
Accumulated Depreciation—Property, Plant, and Equipment	(80,000)	(50,000)		(CL3) 1,170
Obligations Under Capital Lease		(3,851)	**(CL2)** 3,851	
Interest Payable		(616)	**(CL2)** 616	
Minimum Lease Payments Receivable	5,000			**(CL2)** 5,000
Unearned Interest Income	(533)		**(CL2)** 533*	
Interest Expense		616		(CL1) 616
Interest Income	(616)		(CL1) 616	

Eliminations and Adjustments:

(CL1) Eliminate intercompany Interest Expense/Revenue of $616.
(CL2) Eliminate the intercompany debt recorded by the lessee (obligation under capital lease plus accrued interest payable) against the net intercompany receivable of the lessor (minimum lease payments receivable less unearned interest income).
(CL3) Reclassify the asset under capital lease and its related accumulated depreciation as a productive asset owned by the consolidated company.

*From the amortization table on page 279; $533 = $395 + $138

Some capital leases will designate a portion of the annual rent as being applicable to executory costs, such as property taxes or maintenance, incurred by the lessor. Such payments for executory costs are not included in the obligation of the lessee or the minimum lease payments receivable recorded by the lessor. Instead, such payments are recorded as rent expense and revenue in each period. In the consolidation process, that portion of rent applicable to executory costs is eliminated like any other charge for intercompany services.

The preceding example has a bargain purchase option. This means that all payments to be received by the lessor would come from the original lessee. Equality of payments for both parties to a lease between affiliates is the most common case. However, there may be intercompany leases where there is an unguaranteed residual value for the lessor. This means that a portion of the total payments to be received by the lessor will come from parties outside the control group. Therefore, the stream of payments to be received by the lessor exceeds the stream of payments to be paid by the lessee. This complicates the consolidation process. (The appendix to this chapter illustrates a revised version of the preceding example that deals with an unequal stream of payments.)

6

OBJECTIVE

Demonstrate an understanding of the process used to defer intercompany profits on sales-type leases.

Consolidation Procedures for Sales-Type Leases. Under a sales-type lease, a lessor records a sales profit or loss at the inception of the lease. The sales profit or loss is the difference between the fair value of the asset at the inception of the lease and the cost of an asset purchased (or the net book value of an asset previously used by the seller) for the lessor. Consolidation procedures do not allow recognition of this intercompany profit or loss at the inception of the lease. This is exactly the same as the procedure for the deferral of gains and losses on fixed asset sales in Chapter 4. Instead, the profit or loss is deferred and then amortized over the lessee's period of usage. This period will be the lease term unless there is a bargain purchase or bargain renewal option, in which case the asset's useful life would be used.

Partial Worksheet
For Year Ended December 31, 20X2

	Trial Balance		Eliminations & Adjustments	
	Company P	Company S	Dr.	Cr.
Assets Under Capital Lease		5,851		(CL3) 5,851
Accumulated Depreciation—Assets Under Capital Lease		(2,340)	(CL3) 2,340	
Property, Plant, and Equipment	200,000	120,000	(CL3) 5,851	
Accumulated Depreciation—Property, Plant, and Equipment	(100,000)	(60,000)		(CL3) 2,340
Obligations Under Capital Lease		(2,467)	(CL2) 2,467	
Interest Payable		(395)	(CL2) 395	
Minimum Lease Payments Receivable	3,000			(CL2) 3,000
Unearned Interest Income	(138)		(CL2) 138	
Interest Expense		395		(CL1) 395
Interest Income	(395)		(CL1) 395	

Eliminations and Adjustments:

(CL1) Eliminate intercompany Interest Expense/Revenue of $395.
(CL2) Eliminate intercompany debt and net receivable.
(CL3) Reclassify the asset under the capital lease and its related accumulated depreciation as a productive asset owned by the consolidated company.

To illustrate, assume that in the previous example the asset leased to Company S had a cost to Company P of $4,951. Company P would have recorded the following entry at the inception of the sales-type lease:

Minimum Lease Payments Receivable	5,000	
Cash	2,000	
Unearned Interest Income		1,149
Asset (cost of asset leased)		4,951
Sales Profit on Leases		900

This entry differs from that of the previous example only to the extent of recording the gain and transferring an existing asset. None of the lessor's subsequent entries recording the earning of interest and the payment of the receivable would change. The lessee's entries are unaffected by the existence of the sales profit.

Consolidation procedures for a sales-type lease, however, do require added steps to those already illustrated. The sales profit is similar to a profit on the sale of a plant asset. The $900 profit in this example must be deferred over the 3-year lease term. Thus, the asset and its related depreciation accounts must be adjusted to reflect the original sales profit.

The following added adjustments on the 20X1 partial consolidated worksheet (page 280) would be needed for the original $900 sales profit:

(F1)	Sales Profit on Leases	900	
	Property, Plant, and Equipment		900
	To reduce cost of asset for gain on sales-type lease.		
(F2)	Accumulated Depreciation—Property, Plant, and Equipment	300	
	Depreciation Expense		300
	To reduce depreciation expense at the rate of $300 per year.		

The income distribution schedule of the parent (lessor) would reflect the deferral of the original $900 profit in the year of the sale and would recognize $300 per year during the asset's life.

For the 20X2 partial consolidated worksheet (page 281), the following added adjustments would be required if a sales-type lease were involved:

(F1)	Retained Earnings—Controlling Interest	600	
	Accumulated Depreciation—Property, Plant, and Equipment	300	
	Property, Plant, and Equipment		900
	To adjust the remaining sales profit at the beginning of the period.		
(F2)	Accumulated Depreciation—Property, Plant, and Equipment	300	
	Depreciation Expense		300
	To reduce depreciation expense at the rate of $300 per year.		

REFLECTION

- Intercompany leases provide the opportunity for the parent company to control the assets used by a subsidiary.
- Intercompany operating leases are the most common type of lease and are easy to eliminate. Intercompany rent expense/revenue is eliminated with no effect on consolidated income. The leased assets should also be reclassified as productive, rather than leased assets.
- An intercompany capital lease creates an intercompany receivable/payable that must be eliminated along with the resulting intercompany interest expense/revenue and the intercompany accrued interest, all of which must be eliminated. The asset under the capital lease must also be reclassified as a productive asset.
- An intercompany sales-type lease requires all of the same elimination procedures of a capital lease. In addition, the intercompany sales profit must be eliminated and deferred over the life of the asset in the same manner as was a profit on fixed assets in Chapter 4.

INTERCOMPANY TRANSACTIONS PRIOR TO BUSINESS COMBINATION

It is possible that the companies involved in a business combination may have had dealings with each other prior to the acquisition of one company by another. Under purchase accounting procedures, profits made prior to the purchase are allowed to stand and require no adjustment. However, debt and lease instruments between the parties change their nature on the purchase date. Amounts that were due between separate entities now become intercompany debt or leases, and they must be eliminated. Consider the following examples:

1. Trade receivables/payables of the former independent companies become intercompany trade debt on the purchase date. If still existing on the balance sheet date, they are eliminated. Only interest expense/revenue applicable to the period after the purchase is eliminated.
2. Bonds of one of the affiliates that are owned by another affiliate were valid when the firms were not affiliated. Once the purchase occurs, the bonds become intercompany bonds and are eliminated on the consolidated worksheet. Interest expense/revenue prior to the purchase stand, but interest expense/revenue applicable to the period after the purchase is eliminated.

3. Operating leases may have existed between the affiliated companies prior to the purchase. Once the purchase occurs, rent expense/revenue for periods after the purchase becomes intercompany and must be eliminated.
4. If there were capitalized leases between the companies prior to the purchase date, the capital lease amounts remaining in each company's accounts must be eliminated after the purchase date. The interest expense/revenue for periods after the purchase is also eliminated.

All of the above eliminations of amounts that become intercompany, after the purchase occurs, do not affect income or balance sheet amounts for periods prior to the purchase. No restatement of prior-period statements is required.

It should be noted that pooling-of-interests accounting did require restatement of prior-period statements, as if the acquisition had occurred prior to the period covered in the entire set of comparative statements. This meant that all intercompany transactions had to be retroactively eliminated in prior-period statements. The formerly independent, now affiliated companies would change incomes of prior periods to the extent that there were merchandise sales, fixed asset sales, or bond holdings between the now affiliated companies.

REFLECTION

- When an acquisition was a purchase, prior sales between the two entities do not impact the consolidated worksheet.
- Debt and lease instruments between the parties change their nature on the purchase date and become intercompany relationships that must be eliminated when consolidating.
- When an acquisition was a pooling, prior sales between the two entities had to be adjusted on the consolidated worksheet.

APPENDIX: INTERCOMPANY LEASES WITH UNGUARANTEED RESIDUAL VALUE

7

OBJECTIVE

Explain the complications caused by unguaranteed residual values with intercompany leases.

The intercompany lease may contain an unguaranteed residual value. This means that the original intercompany lessee will supply only a portion of the total cash flow to be received by the lessor. At the end of the original lease term, the lessor may lease the asset again or sell it. In either case, there is no obligation on the part of the lessee to renew the lease or to purchase the asset. Since the original lessee is contractually bound to provide only a portion of the payments to be received by the lessor, the lessee will record as its lease obligation only the present value of the minimum lease payments for which it is obligated. The lessee must calculate the present value of the minimum lease payments using its incremental borrowing rate, unless the lessee knows the lessor's implicit rate (and the implicit rate is lower). Since it is an intercompany lease, the interest rate used would normally be the implicit rate of the lessor. As part of the consolidation process, if any other rate is used, the present value of the payments would be adjusted to reflect the implicit lessor rate.

The lessor records the gross investment in the lease, which is the sum of the minimum lease payments receivable and the unguaranteed residual value. Unearned interest income is recorded as a contra account at an amount that reduces the gross investment to the market value of the asset at the inception of the lease. Unearned interest is amortized using the implicit rate of the lessor. The implicit rate of the lessor thus equates the present value of all payments expected, including the unguaranteed residual value, to the market value of the asset.

The recording methods used by the lessee and lessor for leases with an unguaranteed residual value present a complication to the consolidation process. The amount of the asset under the capital lease recorded by the lessee will be less than the asset's market value, since the present value of the lease payments recorded by the lessee will not include the asset's unguaranteed residual value. To understand this complication, the previous example may be used with one change. Instead of the $1,000 bargain purchase option that was included in the set of minimum lease payments, assume there is a $1,000 unguaranteed residual value. Since the residual value is not guaranteed, it is not part of the minimum lease payments. The revised facts are as follows:

1. Cost of asset to lessor: $5,851.
2. Lease terms: Three annual payments of $2,000, due at the start of each year. Unguaranteed residual value of $1,000 to lessor at the end of 20X3.
3. Lessor implicit rate: 16% equates the three $2,000 payments plus the unguaranteed residual value to $5,851.
4. Lessee interest rate: 16% (lessor implicit rate) which, when applied only to the lease payments, results in a present value of $5,210.
5. Depreciation: Straight-line over the 3-year lease term, since the contractual use of the asset is for three years.
6. Amortization tables:

Lessor (16%)

Date	Payment	Interest at 16% on Previous Balance	Reduction of Principal	Principal Balance
January 1, 20X1	$2,000		$2,000	$3,851*
January 1, 20X2	2,000	$ 616	1,384	2,467
January 1, 20X3	2,000	395	1,605	862
December 31, 20X3	1,000	138	862	
Total	$7,000	$1,149	$5,851	

*Purchase price of $5,851 – $2,000 initial payment.

Lessee (16%)

Date	Payment	Interest at 16% on Previous Balance	Reduction of Principal	Principal Balance
January 1, 20X1	$2,000		$2,000	$3,210**
January 1, 20X2	2,000	$514	1,486	1,724
January 1, 20X3	2,000	276	1,724	
Total	$6,000	$790	$5,210	

**Present value of $5,210 – $2,000 initial payment.

The journal entries for the separate companies would be as follows for the first two years:

Date	Company S (Lessee)			Company P (Lessor)		
20X1						
Jan. 1	Assets Under Capital Lease	5,210		Minimum Lease Payments Receivable . .	4,000	
	Cash		2,000	Unguaranteed Residual Value.	1,000	
	Obligations Under Capital Lease . .		3,210	Cash	2,000	
				Unearned Interest Income		1,149
Dec. 31	Interest Expense (at 16%)	514		Accounts Payable (for asset)		5,851
	Interest Payable		514	Unearned Interest Income	616	
	Depreciation Expense			Interest Income (at 16%)		616
	(1/3 × $5,210).	1,737				
	Accumulated Depreciation—Assets Under Capital Lease.		1,737			
20X2						
Jan. 1	Obligations Under Capital Lease	1,486		Cash	2,000	
	Interest Payable	514		Minimum Lease Payments Receivable		2,000
	Cash		2,000			
Dec. 31	Interest Expense (at 16%)	276		Unearned Interest Income	395	
	Interest Payable		276	Interest Income (at 16%)		395
	Depreciation Expense	1,737				
	Accumulated Depreciation—Assets Under Capital Lease.		1,737			

A comparison of the lessor and lessee's amortization tables shows the following difference between the lessee's interest expense and the lessor's interest income each period:

Year Ending December 31	16% Lessor Implicit Interest	16% Lessee Interest	Difference
20X1	$ 616	$514	$102
20X2	395	276	119
20X3	138		138
Total	$1,149	$790	$359

The difference is the interest on the unguaranteed residual value, which is recorded only by the lessor. This can be demonstrated as follows:

Date	16% Implicit Interest	Difference in Principal Balances
January 1, 20X1		$ 641*
December 31, 20X1	$102	743
December 31, 20X2	119	862
December 31, 20X3	138	1,000
Total	$359	$3,246

*$5,851 – $5,210.

In the consolidation process, the intercompany debt and all interest applicable to the lease are eliminated. Even the interest income recorded on the unguaranteed residual value is eliminated, since it is a ramification of a lease that, from a consolidated viewpoint, does not exist. The asset recorded by the lessee and the unguaranteed residual value recorded by the lessor are eliminated and replaced by a productive asset recorded by the consolidated company.

Worksheet 5-5: page 296

Worksheet 5-5, pages 296 to 297, contains the detailed steps for the elimination of the intercompany lease at the end of 20X1. In this worksheet, it is assumed that the interest in the 80%-owned subsidiary was purchased at its book value.

The eliminations in journal entry form are as follows:

(CY1)	*Eliminate current-year equity income:*		
	Subsidiary Income	15,634	
	Investment in Company S Stock		15,634
(EL)	*Eliminate 80% of subsidiary equity:*		
	Common Stock ($10 par), Company S	32,000	
	Retained Earnings, January 1, 20X4, Company S	40,000	
	Investment in Company S Stock		72,000
(CL1)	*Eliminate intercompany interest and restore unearned interest on unguaranteed residual:*		
	Interest Income	616	
	Interest Expense		514
	Unearned Interest Income		102
(CL2)	*Eliminate intercompany debt, unguaranteed residual value and restate asset as owned asset:*		
	Property, Plant, and Equipment	5,851	
	Asset Under Capital Lease		5,210
	Unearned Interest Income	635	
	Minimum Lease Payments Receivable		4,000
	Unguaranteed Residual Value		1,000
	Obligation Under Capital Lease	3,210	
	Interest Payable	514	
(CL3)	*Adjust and reclassify depreciation:*		
	Accumulated Depreciation—Asset Under Capital Lease	1,737	
	Accumulated Depreciation—Property, Plant, and Equipment		1,617
	Depreciation Expense		120

Entry (CL1) eliminates the \$616 of interest income against the \$514 of interest expense. The \$102 disparity reflects the interest applicable to the unguaranteed residual value and is returned to unearned interest income. Entry (CL2) eliminates the intercompany debt applicable to the lease. The \$359 disparity reflects the interest applicable to the unguaranteed residual value over the life of the lease. This amount is used to reduce the unguaranteed residual value to its original present value of \$641. The \$641, combined with the \$5,210 asset under capital lease, is eliminated and replaced by an owned asset and recorded at the \$5,851 original cost to the consolidated company. Entry (CL3) adjusts the depreciation to reflect the cost and the residual value of the asset to the consolidated company. The accumulated depreciation also is reclassified as that applicable to an owned asset.

In Worksheet 5-6 on pages 300 to 301, the consolidation procedures for the second year of the lease term are illustrated.

worksheet

Worksheet 5-6: page 300

REFLECTION

- An unguaranteed residual value causes the present value of the lease for the lessor to exceed that of the lessee. The interest applicable to the unguaranteed residual value is allowed to remain in the consolidated statements, since it will come from the outside world.
- All remaining procedures parallel those used for ordinary capital leases.

Worksheet 5-1

Intercompany Investment in Bonds, Year of Acquisition; Straight-Line Method of Amortization
Company P and Subsidiary Company S
Worksheet for Consolidated Balance Sheet
For Year Ended December 31, 20X3

	(Credit balance amounts are in parentheses.)	Trial Balance	
		Company P	Company S
1	Other Assets	56,400	220,000
2	**Interest Receivable**	**8,000**	
3	Investment in Company S Stock (90%)	100,800	
4			
5	**Investment in Company S Bonds (100%)**	**102,400**	
6	**Interest Payable**		**(8,000)**
7	**Bonds Payable, 8%**		**(100,000)**
8	Common Stock ($10 par), Company P	(100,000)	
9	Retained Earnings, January 1, 20X3, Company P	(120,000)	
10	Common Stock ($10 par), Company S		(80,000)
11	Retained Earnings, January 1, 20X3, Company S		(20,000)
12	Operating Revenue	(100,000)	(80,000)
13	Operating Expense	70,000	60,000
14	**Interest Income**	**(6,800)**	
15	**Interest Expense**		**8,000**
16	Subsidiary Income	(10,800)	
17	**Loss on Bond Retirement**		
18		0	0
19	Consolidated Net Income		
20	To NCI (see distribution schedule)		
21	Balance to Controlling Interest (see distribution schedule)		
22	Total NCI		
23	Retained Earnings, Controlling Interest, December 31, 20X3		
24			

Eliminations and Adjustments:

(CY1) Eliminate the entry recording the parent's share of subsidiary net income for the current year. This entry returns the investment in Company S stock account to its January 1, 20X3, balance to aid the elimination process.

(EL) Eliminate 90% of the subsidiary equity balances of January 1, 20X3, against the investment in stock account. No excess results.

(B1) Eliminate intercompany interest revenue and expense. Eliminate the balance of the investment in bonds against the bonds payable. Note that the investment in bonds is at its end-of-the-year amortized balance. The loss on retirement at the date the bonds were purchased is calculated as follows:

Loss remaining at year-end:		
Investment in bonds at December 31, 20X3	$102,400	
Less: Carrying value of bonds at December 31, 20X3	100,000	$2,400
Loss amortized during year:		
Interest expense eliminated	$ 8,000	
Less: Interest revenue eliminated	6,800	1,200
Loss at January 2, 20X3		$3,600

(B2) Eliminate intercompany interest payable and receivable.

Worksheet 5-1 (see page 271)

Eliminations & Adjustments Dr.		Eliminations & Adjustments Cr.		Consolidated Income Statement	NCI	Controlling Retained Earnings	Consolidated Balance Sheet	
							276,400	1
		(B2)	**8,000**					2
		(CY1)	10,800					3
		(EL)	90,000					4
		(B1)	**102,400**					5
(B2)	**8,000**							6
(B1)	**100,000**							7
							(100,000)	8
						(120,000)		9
(EL)	72,000				(8,000)			10
(EL)	18,000				(2,000)			11
				(180,000)				12
				130,000				13
(B1)	**6,800**							14
		(B1)	**8,000**					15
(CY1)	10,800							16
(B1)	**3,600**			3,600				17
	219,200		219,200					18
				(46,400)				19
				960	(960)			20
				45,440		(45,440)		21
					(10,960)		(10,960)	22
						(165,440)	(165,440)	23
							0	24

Subsidiary Company S Income Distribution

Loss on bond retirement .... **(B1)**	**$3,600**	Internally generated net income, **including interest expense**	**$12,000**
		Interest adjustment ($3,600 ÷ 3) .... **(B1)**	**1,200**
		Adjusted income	$ 9,600
		NCI share	× 10%
		NCI	$ 960

Parent Company P Income Distribution

Internally generated net income, **including interest revenue**................	**$36,800**
90% × Company S adjusted income of $9,600	8,640
Controlling interest	$ 45,440

Worksheet 5-2

Intercompany Investment in Bonds, Year Subsequent to Acquisition; Straight-Line Method of Amortization
Company P and Subsidiary Company S
Worksheet for Consolidated Financial Statements
For Year Ended December 31, 20X4

	(Credit balance amounts are in parentheses.)	Trial Balance	
		Company P	Company S
1	Other Assets	94,400	242,000
2	Interest Receivable	8,000	
3	Investment in Company S Stock (90%)	120,600	
4			
5	**Investment in Company S Bonds (100%)**	**101,200**	
6	Interest Payable		(8,000)
7	Bonds Payable, 8%		(100,000)
8	Common Stock ($10 par), Company P	(100,000)	
9	**Retained Earnings, January 1, 20X4, Company P**	**(167,600)**	
10	Common Stock ($10 par), Company S		(80,000)
11	**Retained Earnings, January 1, 20X3, Company S**		**(32,000)**
12			
13	Operating Revenue	(130,000)	(100,000)
14	Operating Expense	100,000	70,000
15	Subsidiary Income	(19,800)	
16	Interest Expense		8,000
17	Interest Income	(6,800)	
18		0	0
19	Consolidated Net Income		
20	To NCI (see distribution schedule)		
21	Balance to Controlling Interest (see distribution schedule)		
22	Total NCI		
23	Retained Earnings, Controlling Interest, December 31, 20X4		
24			

Eliminations and Adjustments:

(CY1) Eliminate the entry recording the parent's share of subsidiary net income for the current year.
(EL) Eliminate 90% of the subsidiary equity balances of January 1, 20X4, against the investment in stock account. There is no excess to be distributed.
(B1) Eliminate intercompany interest revenue and expense. Eliminate the balance of the investment in bonds against the bonds payable. Note that the investment in bonds is at its end-of-the-year amortized balance. The remaining unamortized loss on retirement at the start of theyear is calculated as follows:

Loss remaining at year-end:		
Investment in bonds at December 31, 20X4	$101,200	
Less: Carrying value of bonds at December 31, 20X4	100,000	$1,200
Loss amortized during year:		
Interest expense eliminated	$ 8,000	
Less: Interest revenue eliminated	6,800	1,200
Remaining loss at January 1, 20X4		$2,400

The remaining unamortized loss of $2,400 on January 1, 20X4, is allocated 90% to the controlling retained earnings and 10% to the noncontrolling retained earnings since the bonds were issued by the subsidiary.
(B2) Eliminate intercompany interest payable and receivable.

Worksheet 5-2 (see page 272)

Eliminations & Adjustments Dr.		Eliminations & Adjustments Cr.		Consolidated Income Statement	NCI	Controlling Retained Earnings	Consolidated Balance Sheet	
							336,400	1
		(B2)	8,000					2
		(CY1)	19,800					3
		(EL)	100,800					4
		(B1)	**101,200**					5
(B2)	8,000							6
(B1)	**100,000**							7
							(100,000)	8
(B1)	**2,160**					(165,440)		9
(EL)	72,000				(8,000)			10
(EL)	28,800				(2,960)			11
(B1)	**240**							12
				(230,000)				13
				170,000				14
(CY1)	19,800							15
		(B1)	**8,000**					16
(B1)	**6,800**							17
	237,800		237,800					18
				(60,000)				19
				2,320	(2,320)			20
				57,680		(57,680)		21
					(13,280)		(13,280)	22
						(223,120)	(223,120)	23
							0	24

Subsidiary Company S Income Distribution

	Internally generated net income, including interest expense	$22,000
	Interest adjustment ($3,600 ÷ 3) **(B1)**	1,200
	Adjusted income	$23,200
	NCI share	× 10%
	NCI	$ 2,320

Parent Company P Income Distribution

	Internally generated net income, including interest revenue	$36,800
	90% × Company S adjusted income of $23,200	20,880
	Controlling interest	$57,680

Worksheet 5-3

Intercompany Bonds, Subsequent Period; Straight-Line Method of Amortization
Company P and Subsidiary Company S
Worksheet for Consolidated Financial Statements
For Year Ended December 31, 20X4

	(Credit balance amounts are in parentheses.)	Trial Balance	
		Company P	Company S
1	Other Assets	59,400	259,082
2	Investment in Company S Stock	143,874	
3			
4	Investment in Company S Bonds	101,800	
5	Bonds Payable		(100,000)
6	**Discount on Bonds**		**778**
7	Common Stock, Company P	(100,000)	
8	**Retained Earnings, January 1, 20X4, Company P**	**(160,000)**	
9	Common Stock, Company S		(40,000)
10	**Retained Earnings, January 1, 20X4, Company S**		**(110,000)**
11			
12	Sales	(80,000)	(50,000)
13	**Interest Income**	**(6,200)**	
14	Cost of Goods Sold	50,000	31,362
15	**Interest Expense**		**8,778**
16	Subsidiary Income	(8,874)	
17		0	0
18	Consolidated Net Income		
19	To NCI (see distribution schedule)		
20	Balance to Controlling Interest (see distribution schedule)		
21	Total NCI		
22	Retained Earnings, Controlling Interest, December 31, 20X4		
23			

Eliminations and Adjustments:

(CY1) Eliminate the entry recording the parent's share of subsidiary net income for the current year.
(EL) Eliminate 90% of the January 1, 20X4, subsidiary equity balances against the January 1, 20X4, investment in Company S stock balance. No excess results.
(B) Eliminate intercompany interest revenue and expense. Eliminate the balance of the investment in bonds against the bonds payable. Note that the investment in bonds and the discount on bonds are at their end-of-the-year amortized balances. The remaining unamortized loss on retirement at the start of the year is calculated as follows:

Loss remaining at year-end:			
Investment in bonds at December 31, 20X4		$101,800	
Less: Bonds payable at December 31, 20X4	$100,000		
Discount on bonds at December 31, 20X4	(778)	99,222	$2,578
Loss amortized during year:			
Interest expense eliminated		$ 8,778	
Less: Interest revenue eliminated		6,200	2,578
Remaining loss at January 1, 20X4			$5,156

Since from the consolidated viewpoint the bonds were retired in the prior year and since the bonds were issued by the subsidiary, the remaining unamortized loss of $5,156 on January 1, 20X4, is allocated 90% to the controlling retained earnings and 10% to the noncontrolling retained earnings.

Worksheet 5-3 (see page 274)

Eliminations & Adjustments Dr.		Eliminations & Adjustments Cr.		Consolidated Income Statement	NCI	Controlling Retained Earnings	Consolidated Balance Sheet	
							318,482	1
		(CY1)	8,874					2
		(EL)	135,000					3
		(B)	**101,800**					4
(B)	**100,000**							5
		(B)	**778**					6
							(100,000)	7
(B)	**4,640**					(155,360)		8
(EL)	36,000				(4,000)			9
(EL)	99,000				(10,484)			10
(B)	**516**							11
				(130,000)				12
(B)	**6,200**							13
				81,362				14
		(B)	**8,778**					15
(CY1)	8,874							16
	255,230		255,230					17
				(48,638)				18
				1,244	(1,244)			19
				47,394		(47,394)		20
					(15,728)		(15,728)	21
						(202,754)	(202,754)	22
							0	23

Subsidiary Company S Income Distribution

Internally generated net income, including interest expense	$ 9,860
Interest adjustment ($8,778–$6,200) . . . . **(B)**	**2,578**
Adjusted income	$12,438
NCI share	× 10%
NCI	$ 1,244

Parent Company P Income Distribution

Internally generated net income, including interest revenue	$36,200
90% × Company S adjusted income of $12,438	11,194
Controlling interest	$47,394

Worksheet 5-4

Intercompany Bonds; Interest Method of Amortization
Company P and Subsidiary Company S
Worksheet for Consolidated Financial Statements
For Year Ended December 31, 20X4

	(Credit balance amounts are in parentheses.)	Trial Balance	
		Company P	Company S
1	Other Assets	59,333	259,082
2	Investment in Company S Stock	144,000	
3			
4	**Investment in Company S Bonds**	**101,887**	
5	**Bonds Payable**		**(100,000)**
6	**Discount on Bonds**		**918**
7	Common Stock, Company P	(100,000)	
8	Retained Earnings, January 1, 20X4, Company P	(160,180)	
9	Common Stock, Company S		(40,000)
10	Retained Earnings, January 1, 20X4, Company S		(110,200)
11			
12	Sales	(80,000)	(50,000)
13	**Interest Income**	**(6,220)**	
14	Cost of Goods Sold	50,000	31,358
15	**Interest Expense**		**8,842**
16			
17	Subsidiary Income	(8,820)	
18		0	0
19	Consolidated Net Income		
20	To NCI (see distribution schedule)		
21	Balance to Controlling Interest (see distribution schedule)		
22	Total NCI		
23	Retained Earnings, Controlling Interest, December 31, 20X4		
24			

Eliminations and Adjustments:

(CY1) Eliminate the entry recording the parent's share of subsidiary net income for the current year.

(EL) Eliminate 90% of the January 1, 20X4, subsidiary equity balances against the January 1, 20X4, investment in Company S stock balance. No excess results.

(B) Eliminate intercompany interest revenue and expense. Eliminate the balance of the investment in bonds against the bonds payable. Note that the investment in bonds and the discount on bonds are at their end-of-the-year amortized balances. The remaining unamortized loss on retirement at the start of the year is calculated as follows:

Loss remaining at year-end:			
Investment in bonds at December 31, 20X4		$101,887	
Less: Bonds payable at December 31, 20X4.	$100,000		
Discount on bonds at December 31, 20X4	(918)	99,082	$2,805
Loss amortized during year:			
Interest expense eliminated		$ 8,842	
Less: Interest revenue eliminated		6,220	2,622
Remaining loss at January 1, 20X4			$5,427

Since from the consolidated viewpoint the bonds were retired in the prior year and since the bonds were issued by the subsidiary, the remaining unamortized loss of $5,427 on January 1, 20X4, is allocated 90% to the controlling retained earnings and 10% to the noncontrolling retained earnings.

Worksheet 5-4 (see page 276)

Eliminations & Adjustments Dr.		Eliminations & Adjustments Cr.		Consolidated Income Statement	NCI	Controlling Retained Earnings	Consolidated Balance Sheet	
							318,415	1
		(CY1)	8,820					2
		(EL)	135,180					3
		(B)	**101,887**					4
(B)	**100,000**							5
		(B)	**918**					6
							(100,000)	7
(B)	**4,884**					(155,296)		8
(EL)	36,000				(4,000)			9
(EL)	99,180				(10,477)			10
(B)	**543**							11
				(130,000)				12
(B)	**6,220**							13
				81,358				14
		(B)	**8,842**					15
								16
(CY1)	8,820							17
	255,647		255,647					18
				(48,642)				19
				1,242	(1,242)			20
				47,400		(47,400)		21
					(15,719)		(15,719)	22
						(202,696)	(202,696)	23
							0	24

Subsidiary Company S Income Distribution

	Internally generated net income, including interest expense	$ 9,800
	Interest adjustment ($8,842 – $6,220) . . . . **(B)**	**2,622**
	Adjusted income	$ 12,422
	NCI share	× 10%
	NCI	$ 1,242

Parent Company P Income Distribution

	Internally generated net income, including interest revenue	$36,220
	90% × Company S adjusted income of $12,422	11,180
	Controlling interest	$47,400

Worksheet 5-5

Intercompany Capital Lease
Company P and Subsidiary Company S
Worksheet for Consolidated Financial Statements
For Year Ended December 31, 20X1

	(Credit balance amounts are in parentheses.)	Trial Balance	
		Company P	Company S
1	Accounts Receivable	30,149	44,793
2	**Minimum Lease Payments Receivable**	**4,000**	
3	**Unguaranteed Residual Value**	**1,000**	
4	**Unearned Interest Income**	**(533)**	
5	**Assets Under Capital Lease**		**5,210**
6	**Accumulated Depreciation—Assets Under Capital Lease**		**(1,737)**
7	Property, Plant, and Equipment	200,000	120,000
8	Accumulated Depreciation—Property, Plant, and Equipment	(80,000)	(50,000)
9	Investment in Company S	87,634	
10			
11	Accounts Payable	(21,000)	(5,000)
12	**Obligations Under Capital Lease**		**(3,210)**
13	**Interest Payable**		**(514)**
14	Common Stock ($10 par), Company P	(50,000)	
15	Retained Earnings, January 1, 20X1, Company S	(120,000)	
16	Common Stock ($5 par), Company S		(40,000)
17	Retained Earnings, January 1, 20X1, Company S		(50,000)
18	Sales	(120,000)	(70,000)
19	**Interest Income**	**(616)**	
20	Subsidiary Income	(15,634)	
21	Operating Expense	65,000	38,207
22	**Interest Expense**		**514**
23	Depreciation Expense	20,000	11,737
24		0	0
25	Consolidated Net Income		
26	To NCI (see distribution schedule)		
27	Balance to Controlling Interest (see distribution schedule)		
28	Total NCI		
29	Retained Earnings, Controlling Interest, December 31, 20X1		
30			

Worksheet 5-5 (see page 286)

Eliminations & Adjustments Dr.		Eliminations & Adjustments Cr.		Consolidated Income Statement	NCI	Controlling Retained Earnings	Consolidated Balance Sheet	
							74,942	1
		(CL2)	**4,000**					2
		(CL2)	**1,000**					3
(CL2)	**635**	**(CL1)**	**102**					4
		(CL2)	**5,210**					5
(CL3)	**1,737**							6
(CL2)	**5,851**						325,851	7
		(CL3)	**1,617**				**(131,617)**	8
		(CY1)	15,634					9
		(EL)	72,000					10
							(26,000)	11
(CL2)	**3,210**							12
(CL2)	**514**							13
							(50,000)	14
						(120,000)		15
(EL)	32,000				(8,000)			16
(EL)	40,000				(10,000)			17
				(190,000)				18
(CL1)	**616**							19
(CY1)	15,634							20
				103,207				21
		(CL1)	**514**					22
		(CL3)	**120**	31,617				23
	100,197		100,197					24
				(55,176)				25
				3,908	(3,908)			26
				51,268		(51,268)		27
					(21,908)		(21,908)	28
						(171,268)	(171,268)	29
							0	30

Eliminations and Adjustments:

(CY1) Eliminate the parent company's entry recording its share of Company S net income. This step returns the investment account to its January 1, 20X1, balance to aid the elimination process.

(EL) Eliminate 80% of the January 1, 20X1, Company S equity balances against the investment in Company S balance.

(CL1) Eliminate the interest income recorded by the lessor, $616, and the interest expense recorded by the lessee, $514. The $102 disparity reflects the interest recorded on the unguaranteed residual value. This amount is returned to the unearned interest income.

(CL2) Eliminate the intercompany debt and the unguaranteed residual value. Eliminate the asset under capital lease and record the owned asset. The amounts are reconciled as follows:

Disparity in recorded debt:	
Lessor balance, **$4,000 – $635** unearned interest income	$ 3,365
Lessee balance, **$3,210 + $514** accrued interest	3,724
Interest applicable to unguaranteed residual value	$ (359)
Unguaranteed residual value	**1,000**
Net original present value of unguaranteed residual value	$ 641
Asset under capital lease	**5,210**
Owned asset at original cost	$ 5,851

(CL3) Reclassify accumulated depreciation and adjust the depreciation expense to acknowledge cost of asset. The adjustment to depreciation expense is determined as follows:

Capitalized cost by lessee		$5,210
Depreciable cost:		
Cost	$5,851	
Less residual (salvage) value	1,000	4,851
Decrease in depreciable cost		$ 359
Adjustment to depreciation expense ($359 ÷ 3-year lease term)		**$ 120**

Subsidiary Company S Income Distribution

		Internally generated net income, **including interest income on lease**	$19,542
		Adjusted income	$19,542
		NCI share	× 20%
		NCI	$ 3,908

Parent Company P Income Distribution

Net interest eliminated . . . (CL1)	**$102**	Internally generated net income, **including interest income on lease**	$35,616
		80% × Company S adjusted income of $19,542	15,634
		Decrease in depreciation . . . (CL3)	**120**
		Controlling interest	$51,268

Worksheet 5-6

Intercompany Capital Lease, Subsequent Period
Company P and Subsidiary Company S
Worksheet for Consolidated Financial Statements
For Year Ended December 31, 20X2

	(Credit balance amounts are in parentheses.)	Trial Balance	
		Company P	Company S
1	Accounts Receivable	102,149	82,925
2	**Minimum Lease Payments Receivable**	**2,000**	
3	**Unguaranteed Residual Value**	**1,000**	
4	**Unearned Interest Income**	**(138)**	
5			
6	**Assets Under Capital Lease**		**5,210**
7	**Accumulated Depreciation—Assets Under Capital Lease**		**(3,474)**
8	Property, Plant, and Equipment	200,000	120,000
9	Accumulated Depreciation—Property, Plant, and Equipment	(100,000)	(60,000)
10	Investment in Company S	102,129	
11			
12	Accounts Payable	(41,000)	(15,000)
13	**Obligations Under Capital Lease**		**(1,724)**
14	**Interest Payable**		**(276)**
15	Common Stock ($10 par), Company P	(50,000)	
16	**Retained Earnings, January 1, 20X2, Company P**	**(171,250)**	
17	Common Stock ($5 par), Company S		(40,000)
18	Retained Earnings, January 1, 20X2, Company S		(69,542)
19	Sales	(150,000)	(80,000)
20	**Interest Income**	**(395)**	
21	Subsidiary Income	(14,495)	
22	Operating Expense	100,000	49,868
23	**Interest Expense**		**276**
24	Depreciation Expense	20,000	11,737
25		0	0
26	Consolidated Net Income		
27	To NCI (see distribution schedule)		
28	Balance to Controlling Interest (see distribution schedule)		
29	Total NCI		
30	Retained Earnings, Controlling Interest, December 31, 20X2		
31			

Worksheet 5-6 (see page 287)

Eliminations & Adjustments				Consolidated Income Statement	NCI	Controlling Retained Earnings	Consolidated Balance Sheet	
Dr.		Cr.						
							185,074	1
		(CL2)	**2,000**					2
		(CL2)	**1,000**					3
(CL2)	**359**	**(CL1a)**	**119**					4
		(CL1b)	**102**					5
		(CL2)	**5,210**					6
(CL3)	**3,474**							7
(CL2)	**5,851**						325,851	8
		(CL3)	**3,234**				(163,234)	9
		(CY1)	14,495					10
		(EL)	87,634					11
							(56,000)	12
(CL2)	**1,724**							13
(CL2)	**276**							14
							(50,000)	15
(CL1b)	**102**	**(CL3)**	**120**			(171,268)		16
(EL)	32,000				(8,000)			17
(EL)	55,634				(13,908)			18
				(230,000)				19
(CL1a)	**395**							20
(CY1)	14,495							21
				149,868				22
		(CL1)	**276**					23
		(CL3)	**120**	31,617				24
	114,310		114,310					25
				(48,515)				26
				3,624	(3,624)			27
				44,891		(44,891)		28
					(25,532)		(25,532)	29
						(216,159)	(216,159)	30
							0	31

Eliminations and Adjustments:

(CY1) Eliminate the parent company's entry recording its share of Company S net income.
(EL) Eliminate 80% of the January 1, 20X2, Company S equity balances against the investment in Company S balance.
(CL1a) Eliminate the interest income recorded by the lessor, $395, and the interest expense recorded by the lessee, $276. The $119 disparity reflects the interest recorded on the unguaranteed residual value. This amount is returned to the unearned interest income.
(CL1b) Adjust the unearned income and the parent's retained earnings for the $102 interest recorded in 20X1 on the unguaranteed residual value.
(CL2) Eliminate the intercompany debt and the unguaranteed residual value. Eliminate the asset under capital lease and record the owned asset. The amounts are reconciled as follows:

Disparity in recorded debt:	
Lessor balance, **$2,000 − $359** unearned interest income	$ 1,641
Lessee balance, **$1,724 + $276** accrued interest	2,000
Interest applicable to unguaranteed residual value	$ (359)
Unguaranteed residual value	**1,000**
Net original present value of unguaranteed residual value	$ 641
Asset under capital lease	**5,210**
Owned asset at original cost	$ 5,851

(CL3) Reclassify accumulated depreciation. Adjust the depreciation expense for the current year and the controlling retained earnings for the preceding year to acknowledge cost of asset. The adjustment to the depreciation expense and the retained earnings is determined as follows:

Capitalized cost by lessee		$5,210
Depreciable cost:		
Cost	$5,851	
Less residual (salvage) value	1,000	4,851
Decrease in depreciable cost		$ 359
Adjustment to depreciation expense and retained earnings ($359 ÷ 3-year lease term)		**$ 120**

Subsidiary Company S Income Distribution

		Internally generated net income, **including interest on lease**	$18,119
		Adjusted income	$18,119
		NCI share	× 20%
		NCI	$ 3,624

Parent Company P Income Distribution

Net interest eliminated .... **(CL1a)**	**$119**	Internally generated net income, **including interest income on lease**	$30,395
		80% × Company S adjusted income of $18,119	14,495
		Decrease in depreciation .... **(CL3)**	**120**
		Controlling interest	$44,891

UNDERSTANDING THE ISSUES

1. Subsidiary Company S has $1,000,000 of bonds outstanding. The bonds have 10 years to maturity and pay interest at 12% annually. The parent has an average annual borrowing cost of 9% and wishes to reduce the interest cost of the consolidated company. What methods could be used to maintain the subsidiary as the debtor?

2. Subsidiary Company S has $1,000,000 of bonds outstanding at 12% annual interest. The bonds have 10 years to maturity. If the parent, Company P, is able to purchase the bonds at a price that reflects 10% annual interest, what effect will the purchase have on income in the current and future years? What would the effects be if the purchase price reflected a 13% annual interest rate? Your response need not be quantified.

3. Subsidiary Company S has $1,000,000 of bonds outstanding at 12% annual interest. The bonds have 10 years to maturity. If the parent, Company P, is able to purchase the bonds at a price that reflects 10% annual interest, how will the noncontrolling interest be affected in the current and future years? Your response need not be quantified.

4. Company P purchased $100,000 of subsidiary Company S's bonds for $95,000 on January 1, 20X1. The bonds were issued at face value, pay interest at 10% annually, and have 5 years to maturity. What will the impact of this transaction be on consolidated net income for the current and future 4 years? Assuming a 20% noncontrolling interest, how will the NCI be affected in the current and next 4 years? Quantify your response.

5. Your friend is a noncontrolling interest shareholder in a large company. He knows that the subsidiary company leases most of its assets from the parent company under operating leases. He further believes that the lease rates are in excess of market rates. He made his concern known to the parent company management. Their response was, "Don't worry about it; it washes out in the consolidation process and ends up having no effect on income." Your friend wants to know if this is true and if he was wrong to be concerned.

6. A parent company may want to shift profits to the controlling interest and may use intercompany capital leases to accomplish that end. Is there an opportunity to do that with both direct financing and sales-type leases? What are the differences between the two types of leases with respect to income shifting?

7. A parent company is a producer of production equipment, some of which is acquired and used by the parent's subsidiary companies. The parent offers a discount to the subsidiaries but still earns a significant profit on the sales of equipment to a subsidiary. Is there any difference in the consolidated company's ability to recognize the profit on these sales if, instead of selling equipment to the subsidiaries, the equipment is leased to them under capital leases? Are there any other profit opportunities for the controlling interest in leasing as opposed to selling equipment to the subsidiaries?

EXERCISES

Exercise 1 *(LO 1)* **Options to lower interest cost.** Marcus Engineering is a large corporation with the ability to obtain financing by selling its bonds at favorable rates. Currently, it pays 7% interest on its 10-year bond issues. In the past year, Marcus purchased an 80% interest in a subsidiary, Patel Industries. Patel Industries has $1,000,000 of bonds outstanding that mature in 6 years. Interest is paid annually at a stated rate of 10%. The bonds were issued at face value.

Interest rates have come down, but Patel Industries could still expect to pay 9% to 9.5% interest on a long-term issue. Patel Industries is a smaller company with a lower credit rating than Marcus.

Marcus would like to reduce interest costs on the Patel Industries debt. The company has asked your advice on whether it should purchase the bonds or loan Patel Industries the money to retire its own debt. Compare the options with a focus on the impact on consolidated statements.

Exercise 2 *(LO 1)* **Effect of intercompany bonds on income.** Dennis Company is an 80%-owned subsidiary of Kay Industries. Dennis Company issued 10-year, 8% bonds in the amount of $1,000,000 on January 1, 20X1. The bonds were issued at face value, and interest is payable each January 1. On January, 1, 20X3, Kay Industries purchased all of the Dennis bonds for $968,000. Kay will amortize the discount on a straight-line basis. For the years ending (a) December 31, 20X3, and (b) December 31, 20X4, determine the effects of this transaction

1. On consolidated net income.
2. On the distribution of income to the controlling and noncontrolling interests.

Exercise 3 *(LO 2)* **Bond eliminations, straight-line.** Casper Company is an 80%-owned subsidiary of Dien Corporation. Casper Company issued $100,000 of 9%, 10-year bonds for $95,000 on January 1, 20X1. Annual interest is paid on January 1. Dien Corporation purchased the bonds on January 1, 20X5, for $101,800. Both companies are using the straight-line method to amortize the premium/discount on the bonds.

1. Prepare the eliminations and adjustments that would be made on the December 31, 20X5, consolidated worksheet as a result of this purchase.
2. Prepare the eliminations and adjustments that would be made on the December 31, 20X6, consolidated worksheet.

Exercise 4 *(LO 2)* **Bond eliminations, effective interest.** On January 1, 20X4, Dunbar Corporation, an 85%-owned subsidiary of Garfield Industries, received $48,055 for $50,000 of 8%, 5-year bonds it issued when the market rate was 9%. When Garfield Industries purchased these bonds for $47,513 on January 2, 20X6, the market rate was 10%. Given the following effective interest amortization schedules for both companies, calculate the gain or loss on retirement and the interest adjustments to the issuer's income distribution schedules over the remaining term of the bonds.

Dunbar (issuer)

Date	Effective Interest (9%)	Nominal Interest	Discount Amortization	Balance
1/1/X4				$48,055
1/1/X5	$4,325	$4,000	$325	48,380
1/1/X6	4,354	4,000	354	48,734
1/1/X7	4,386	4,000	386	49,120
1/1/X8	4,421	4,000	421	49,541
1/1/X9	4,459	4,000	459	50,000

Garfield (purchaser)

Date	Effective Interest (10%)	Nominal Interest	Discount Amortization	Balance
1/1/X6				$47,513
1/1/X7	$4,751	$4,000	$751	48,264
1/1/X8	4,826	4,000	826	49,091
1/1/X9	4,909	4,000	909	50,000

Exercise 5 *(LO 2)* **Bond eliminations, partial purchase.** Carlton Company is an 80%-owned subsidiary of Mirage Company. On January 1, 20X1, Carlton sold $100,000 of 10-year, 7% bonds for $101,000. Interest is paid annually on January 1. The market rate for this type of bond was 9% on January 2, 20X3, when Mirage purchased 60% of the Carlton bonds for $53,600. Discounts may be amortized on a straight-line basis.

1. Prepare the eliminations and adjustments required for this bond purchase on the December 31, 20X3, consolidated worksheet.
2. Prepare the eliminations and adjustments required on the December 31, 20X4, consolidated worksheet.

Exercise 6 *(LO 2)* **Bond calculations, effective interest.** Lift Industries, a 90%-owned subsidiary of Shark Incorporated, issued $100,000 of 12-year, 8% bonds on January 1, 20X5, to yield 7% interest. Interest is paid annually on January 1. The effective interest method is used to amortize the premium. Shark purchased the bonds for $94,005 on January 2, 20X8, when the market rate of interest was 9%. On the purchase date, the remaining premium on the bonds was $6,516. Lift's 20X8 net income was $500,000.

1. Prepare the eliminations and adjustments required for this purchase on the December 31, 20X8, consolidated worksheet.
2. Prepare the 20X8 income distribution schedule for the NCI.

Exercise 7 *(LO 4)* **Operating lease, entries, and eliminations.** Grande Machinery Company purchased, for cash, a $60,000 custom machine on January 1, 20X1. The machine has an estimated 5-year life and will be straight-line depreciated with no salvage value. The machine was then leased to Sunshine Engineering Company, an 80%-owned subsidiary, under a 5-year operating lease for $15,000 per year, payable each January 1.

1. Record the 20X1 entries for the purchase of the machine and the lease to Sunshine Engineering Company on the books of Grande Machinery Company.
2. Record the 20X1 entries for the transaction on the books of Sunshine Engineering Company.
3. Provide the elimination entries that would be made on the 20X1 consolidated worksheet.

Exercise 8 *(LO 5)* **Direct-financing lease eliminations.** On January 1, 20X1, Traylor Company, an 80%-owned subsidiary of Parker Electronics Inc., signed a 4-year direct-financing lease with its parent for the rental of electronic equipment. The lease agreement requires a $12,000 payment on January 1 of each year, and title transfers to Traylor on January 1, 20X5. The equipment originally cost $40,822 and had an estimated remaining life of 5 years at the start of the lease term. The lessor's implicit interest rate is 12%. The lessee also used the 12% rate to record the transaction.

1. Prepare the eliminations and adjustments required for this lease on the December 31, 20X1, consolidated worksheet.
2. Prepare the eliminations and adjustments for the December 31, 20X2, consolidated worksheet.

Exercise 9 *(LO 6)* **Sales-type lease eliminations.** The Auto Clinic is a wholly owned subsidiary of Fast-Check Equipment Company. Fast-Check Equipment sells and leases 4-wheel alignment machines. The usual selling price of each machine is $35,000; it has a cost to Fast-Check Equipment of $25,000. On January 1, 20X1, Fast-Check Equipment leased such a machine to Auto Clinic. The lease provided for payments of $9,096 at the start of each year for 5 years. The payments include $1,000 per year for maintenance to be provided by the seller. There is a bargain purchase price of $2,000 at the end of the fifth year. The implicit interest rate in the lease is 10% per year. The equipment is being depreciated over 8 years.

The amortization schedule for the lease prepared by Fast-Check Equipment is as follows:

Date	Payment	Interest at 10% on Previous Balance	Reduction of Principal	Principal Balance
1/1/X1	$8,096		$8,096	$26,904
1/1/X2	8,096	$2,691	5,405	21,499
1/1/X3	8,096	2,150	5,946	15,553
1/1/X4	8,096	1,556	6,540	9,013
1/1/X5	8,096	901	7,195	1,818
12/31/X5	2,000	182	1,818	0

Prepare the eliminations and adjustments, in entry form, that would be required on a consolidated worksheet prepared on December 31, 20X1.

PROBLEMS

Problem 5-1 *(LO 2)* **Eliminations, equity, 100%, bonds with straight-line.** Since its 100% acquisition of Drew Corporation stock on December 31, 20X2, Justin Corporation has maintained its investment under the equity method. However, due to Drew's earning potential, the price included a $40,000 payment for goodwill. At the time of the purchase, the fair value of Drew's assets equaled their book value.

On January 2, 20X4, Drew Corporation issued 10-year, 9% bonds at a face value of $50,000. The bonds pay interest each December 31. On January 2, 20X6, Justin Corporation purchased all of Drew Corporation's outstanding bonds for $48,400. The premium is amortized on a straight-line basis. They have been included in Justin's long-term investment in bonds account. Below are the trial balances of both companies on December 31, 20X6:

	Justin Corp.	Drew Corp.
Cash	71,100	67,500
Accounts Receivable	450,000	75,000
Inventory	200,000	65,000
Investment in Bonds	48,600	
Plant and Equipment (net)	2,420,000	196,000
Investment in Drew Corporation	350,000	
Accounts Payable	(275,000)	(18,000)
Bonds Payable (9%)		(50,000)
Common Stock, Justin ($ 10 par)	(1,000,000)	
Paid-In Capital in Excess of Par, Justin	(750,000)	
Retained Earnings, Justin, January 1, 20X6	(730,000)	
Common Stock, Drew ($ 10 par)		(100,000)
Paid-In Capital in Excess of Par, Drew		(130,000)
Retained Earnings, Drew, January 1, 20X6		(80,000)
Sales	(2,500,000)	(540,000)
Cost of Goods Sold	1,000,000	405,000
Other Expenses	720,000	105,000
Interest Income	(4,700)	
Interest Expense	0	4,500
Total	0	0

Required ▶ ▶ ▶ ▶ ▶

1. Prepare the worksheet entries needed to eliminate the intercompany debt on December 31, 20X6.
2. Prepare a consolidated income statement for the year ended December 31, 20X6.

Note: No worksheet is required.

Problem 5-2 *(LO 2)* **Cost method, 90%, straight-line bonds.** On January 1, 20X1, Patrick Company purchased 90% of the common stock of Stuart Company for $350,000. On this date, Stuart had common stock, other paid-in capital, and retained earnings of $100,000, $40,000, and $210,000, respectively. The excess of cost over book value is due to goodwill. In both 20X1 and 20X2, Patrick has accounted for the investment in Stuart using the cost method.

On January 1, 20X1, Stuart sold $100,000 par value of 10-year, 8% bonds for $94,000. The bonds pay interest semiannually on January 1 and July 1 of each year. On December 31, 20X1, Patrick purchased all of Stuart's bonds for $96,400. The bonds are still held on December 31, 20X2. Both companies have correctly recorded all entries relative to bonds and interest, using straight-line amortization for premium or discount.

The trial balances of Patrick Company and its subsidiary were as follows on December 31, 20X2:

	Patrick Company	Stuart Company
Interest Receivable	4,000	
Other Current Assets	249,200	315,200
Investment in Stuart Company	350,000	
Investment in Stuart Bonds	96,800	
Land	80,000	60,000
Buildings and Equipment	400,000	280,000
Accumulated Depreciation	(120,000)	(60,000)
Interest Payable		(4,000)
Other Current Liabilities	(98,000)	(56,000)
Bonds Payable, 8%		(100,000)
Discount on Bonds Payable		4,800
Other Long-Term Liabilities	(200,000)	
Common Stock, Patrick Company	(100,000)	
Other Paid-In Capital, Patrick Company	(200,000)	
Retained Earnings, Patrick Company	(365,000)	
Common Stock, Stuart Company		(100,000)
Other Paid-In Capital, Stuart Company		(40,000)
Retained Earnings, Stuart Company		(260,000)
Net Sales	(640,000)	(350,000)
Cost of Goods Sold	360,000	200,000
Operating Expenses	168,400	71,400
Interest Expense		8,600
Interest Income	(8,400)	
Divdend Income	(27,000)	
Dividends Declared	50,000	30,000
Total	0	0

Required Prepare the worksheet necessary to produce the consolidated financial statements of Patrick and its subsidiary Stuart for the year ended December 31, 20X2. Round all computations to the nearest dollar.

Problem 5-3 *(LO 2)* **80%, cost method, straight-line bonds, fixed asset sale.** On January 1, 20X3, Warehouse Outlets had the following balances in its stockholders' equity accounts: Common Stock ($10 par), $800,000; Paid-In Capital in Excess of Par, $625,000; and Retained Earnings, $450,000. General Appliances purchased 64,000 shares of Warehouse Outlets' common stock for $1,700,000 on that date. Any excess of cost over book value was attributed to goodwill.

Warehouse Outlets issued $500,000 of 8-year, 11% bonds on December 31, 20X2. The bonds sold for $476,000. General Appliances purchased one-half of these bonds in the market on January 1, 20X5, for $259,000. Both companies use the straight-line method of amortization of premiums and discounts.

On July 1, 20X6, General Appliances sold to Warehouse Outlets an old building with a book value of $167,500, remaining life of 10 years, and $30,000 salvage value, for $195,000. The building is being depreciated on a straight-line basis. Warehouse Outlets paid $20,000 in cash and signed a mortgage note with its parent for the balance. Interest, at 11% of the unpaid balance, and principal payments are due annually beginning July 1, 20X7. (For convenience, the mortgage balances are not divided into current and long-term portions.)

The trial balances of the two companies at December 31, 20X6, are as follows:

	General Appliances	Warehouse Outlets
Cash	401,986	72,625
Accounts Receivable (net)	752,500	105,000
Interest Receivable	9,625	
Inventory	1,950,000	900,000
Investment in Warehouse Outlets	1,700,000	
Investment in 11% Bonds	256,000	
Investment in Mortgage	175,000	
Property, Plant, and Equipment	9,000,000	2,950,000
Accumulated Depreciation	(1,695,000)	(940,000)
Accounts Payable	(670,000)	(80,000)
Interest Payable	(18,333)	(9,625)
Bonds Payable, 11%	(2,000,000)	(500,000)
Discount on Bonds Payable	10,470	12,000
Mortgage Payable		(175,000)
Common Stock ($5 par)	(3,200,000)	
Common Stock ($10 par)		(800,000)
Paid-In Capital in Excess of Par	(4,550,000)	(625,000)
Retained Earnings, January 1, 20X6	(1,011,123)	(770,000)
Sales	(9,800,000)	(3,000,000)
Gain on Sale of Building	(27,500)	
Interest Income	(35,625)	
Dividend Income	(48,000)	
Cost of Goods Sold	4,940,000	1,700,000
Depreciation Expense	717,000	95,950
Interest Expense	223,000	67,544
Other Expenses	2,600,000	936,506
Dividends Declared	320,000	60,000
Total	0	0

Required ▶ ▶ ▶ ▶ ▶

Prepare the worksheet necessary to produce the consolidated financial statements of General Appliances and its subsidiary for the year ended December 31, 20X6. Include the determination and distribution of excess and income distribution schedules.

Use the following information for Problems 5-4 and 5-5:

On January 1, 20X4, Packard Company acquired an 80% interest in the common stock of Stackner Company for $350,000. Stackner had the following balance sheet on the date of acquisition:

Stackner Company
Balance Sheet
January 1, 20X4

Assets		Liabilities and Equity	
Accounts receivable	$ 40,000	Accounts payable	$ 42,297
Inventory	20,000	Bonds payable	100,000
Land.	35,000	Discount on bonds payable. . .	(2,297)
Buildings	250,000	Common stock, $10 par	10,000
Accumulated depreciation . . .	(50,000)	Paid-in capital in excess	
Equipment	120,000	of par	90,000
Accumulated depreciation . . .	(60,000)	Retained earnings	115,000
Total assets.	$355,000	Total liabilities and equity . .	$355,000

Buildings (20-year life) are undervalued by $75,000. Equipment (5-year life) is undervalued by $60,000. Any remaining excess is considered to be goodwill.

Problem 5-4 *(LO 2)* **80%, equity, straight-line bonds purchased this year, inventory profits.** Refer to the preceding facts for Packard's acquisition of 80% of Stackner's common stock. Packard uses the simple equity method to account for its investment in Stackner. On January 1, 20X5, Stackner held merchandise acquired from Packard for $15,000. During 20X5, Packard sold $50,000 worth of merchandise to Stackner . Stackner held $20,000 of this merchandise at December 31, 20X5. Stackner owed Packard $10,000 on December 31 as a result of these intercompany sales. Packard has a gross profit rate of 30%.

Stackner issued $100,000 of 8%, 10-year bonds for $96,719 on January 1, 20X1. Annual interest is paid on December 31. Packard purchased the bonds on January 1, 20X5, for $100,930. Both companies use the straight-line method to amortize the premium/discount on the bonds. Packard and Stackner used the following bond amortization schedules:

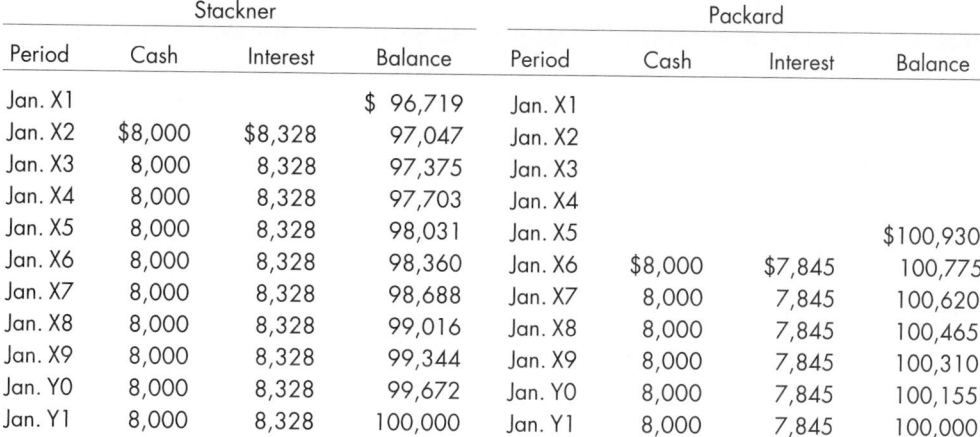

Stackner				Packard			
Period	Cash	Interest	Balance	Period	Cash	Interest	Balance
Jan. X1			$ 96,719	Jan. X1			
Jan. X2	$8,000	$8,328	97,047	Jan. X2			
Jan. X3	8,000	8,328	97,375	Jan. X3			
Jan. X4	8,000	8,328	97,703	Jan. X4			
Jan. X5	8,000	8,328	98,031	Jan. X5			$100,930
Jan. X6	8,000	8,328	98,360	Jan. X6	$8,000	$7,845	100,775
Jan. X7	8,000	8,328	98,688	Jan. X7	8,000	7,845	100,620
Jan. X8	8,000	8,328	99,016	Jan. X8	8,000	7,845	100,465
Jan. X9	8,000	8,328	99,344	Jan. X9	8,000	7,845	100,310
Jan. Y0	8,000	8,328	99,672	Jan. Y0	8,000	7,845	100,155
Jan. Y1	8,000	8,328	100,000	Jan. Y1	8,000	7,845	100,000

Packard and Stackner had the following trial balances on December 31, 20Y0:

	Packard Company	Stackner Company
Cash	71,070	32,032
Accounts Receivable	90,000	60,000
Inventory	100,000	30,000
Land.	150,000	45,000

(continued)

	Packard Company	Stackner Company
Investment in Stackner	385,738	
Investment in Stackner Bonds	100,775	
Buildings	500,000	250,000
Accumulated Depreciation	(300,000)	(70,000)
Equipment	200,000	120,000
Accumulated Depreciation	(100,000)	(84,000)
Accounts Payable	(55,000)	(25,000)
Bonds Payable		(100,000)
Discount on Bonds Payable		1,640
Common Stock	(100,000)	(10,000)
Paid-In Capital in Excess of Par	(600,000)	(90,000)
Retained Earnings, January 1, 20X5	(400,000)	(145,000)
Sales	(600,000)	(220,000)
Cost of Goods Sold	410,000	120,000
Depreciation Expense—Buildings	30,000	10,000
Depreciation Expense—Equipment	15,000	12,000
Other Expenses	110,000	45,000
Interest Revenue	(7,845)	
Interest Expense		8,328
Subsidiary Income	(19,738)	
Dividends Declared	20,000	10,000
Total	0	0

Required ▶ ▶ ▶ ▶ ▶ Prepare the worksheet necessary to produce the consolidated financial statements for Packard Company and its subsidiary Stackner Company for the year ended December 31, 20X5. Include the determination and distribution of excess and income distribution schedules.

Problem 5-5 *(LO 2)* **80%, equity, straight-line bonds purchased last year, inventory profits.** Refer to the preceding facts for Packard's acquisition of 80% of Stackner's common stock. Packard uses the simple equity method to account for its investment in Stackner. On January 1, 20X6, Stackner held merchandise acquired from Packard for $20,000. During 20X6, Packard sold $60,000 worth of merchandise to Stackner. Stackner held $25,000 of this merchandise at December 31, 20X6. Stackner owed Packard $12,000 on December 31 as a result of these intercompany sales. Packard has a gross profit rate of 30%.

Stackner issued $100,000 of 8%, 10-year bonds for $96,719 on January 1, 20X1. Annual interest is paid on December 31. Packard purchased the bonds on January 1, 20X5, for $100,930. Both companies use the straight-line method to amortize the premium/discount on the bonds. Packard and Stackner used the following bond amortization schedules:

Stackner				Packard			
Period	Cash	Interest	Balance	Period	Cash	Interest	Balance
Jan. X1			$ 96,719	Jan. X1			
Jan. X2	$8,000	$8,328	97,047	Jan. X2			
Jan. X3	8,000	8,328	97,375	Jan. X3			
Jan. X4	8,000	8,328	97,703	Jan. X4			
Jan. X5	8,000	8,328	98,031	Jan. X5			$100,930
Jan. X6	8,000	8,328	98,360	Jan. X6	$8,000	$7,845	100,775
Jan. X7	8,000	8,328	98,688	Jan. X7	8,000	7,845	100,620
Jan. X8	8,000	8,328	99,016	Jan. X8	8,000	7,845	100,465
Jan. X9	8,000	8,328	99,344	Jan. X9	8,000	7,845	100,310
Jan. Y0	8,000	8,328	99,672	Jan. Y0	8,000	7,845	100,155
Jan. Y1	8,000	8,328	100,000	Jan. Y1	8,000	7,845	100,000

Packard and Stackner had the following trial balances on December 31, 20X6:

	Packard Company	Stackner Company
Cash	101,710	61,032
Accounts Receivable	110,000	60,000
Inventory	120,000	45,000
Land	150,000	45,000
Investment in Stackner	403,075	
Investment in Stackner Bonds	100,620	
Buildings	500,000	250,000
Accumulated Depreciation	(330,000)	(80,000)
Equipment	200,000	120,000
Accumulated Depreciation	(115,000)	(96,000)
Accounts Payable	(35,000)	(25,000)
Bonds Payable		(100,000)
Discount on Bonds Payable		1,312
Common Stock	(100,000)	(10,000)
Paid-In Capital in Excess of Par	(600,000)	(90,000)
Retained Earnings, January 1, 20X6	(442,223)	(159,672)
Sales	(700,000)	(230,000)
Cost of Goods Sold	480,000	125,000
Depreciation Expense—Buildings	30,000	10,000
Depreciation Expense—Equipment	15,000	12,000
Other Expenses	125,000	43,000
Interest Revenue	(7,845)	
Interest Expense		8,328
Subsidiary Income	(25,337)	
Dividends Declared	20,000	10,000
Total	0	0

Prepare the worksheet necessary to produce the consolidated financial statements for Packard Company and its subsidiary Stackner Company for the year ended December 31, 20X6. Include the determination and distribution of excess and income distribution schedules. ◄◄◄◄◄ **Required**

Use the following information for Problems 5-6 and 5-7:

On January 1, 20X4, Postman Company acquired Sparkle Company. Postman paid $400,000 for 80% of Sparkle's common stock. On the date of acquisition, Sparkle had the following balance sheet:

Sparkle Company
Balance Sheet
January 1, 20X4

Assets		Liabilities and Equity	
Accounts receivable	$ 90,000	Accounts payable	$ 17,352
Inventory	50,000	Bonds payable	100,000
Land	60,000	Premium on bonds payable	2,648
Buildings	100,000	Common stock, $1 par	10,000
Accumulated depreciation	(30,000)	Paid-in capital in excess of par	90,000
Equipment	80,000		
Accumulated depreciation	(30,000)	Retained earnings	100,000
Total assets	$320,000	Total liabilities and equity	$320,000

(continued)

Buildings, which have a 20-year life, are undervalued by $130,000. Equipment, which has a 5-year life, is undervalued by $50,000. Any remaining excess is considered to be goodwill.

Problem 5-6 *(LO 2)* **80%, equity, effective interest bonds purchased this year, inventory profits.** Refer to the preceding facts for Postman's acquisition of 80% of Sparkle's common stock. Postman uses the simple equity method to account for its investment in Sparkle. On January 1, 20X5, Postman held merchandise acquired from Sparkle for $9,000. During 20X5, Sparkle sold $20,000 worth of merchandise to Postman. Postman held $12,000 of this merchandise at December 31, 20X5. Postman owed Sparkle $7,000 on December 31 as a result of these intercompany sales. Sparkle has a gross profit rate of 25%.

Sparkle issued $100,000 of 8%, 10-year bonds for $103,432 on January 1, 20X1, when the market rate was 7.5%. Annual interest is paid on December 31. Postman purchased the bonds for $95,514 on January 1, 20X5, when the market rate was 9%. Both companies use the effective interest method to amortize the premium/discount on the bonds. Postman and Sparkle prepared the following bond amortization schedules:

Sparkle				Postman			
Period	Cash	Interest	Balance	Period	Cash	Interest	Balance
Jan. X1			$103,432.04	Jan. X1			
Jan. X2	$8,000	$7,757.40	103,189.44	Jan. X2			
Jan. X3	8,000	7,739.21	102,928.65	Jan. X3			
Jan. X4	8,000	7,719.65	102,648.30	Jan. X4			
Jan. X5	8,000	7,698.62	102,346.92	Jan. X5			$ 95,514.08
Jan. X6	8,000	7,676.02	102,022.94	Jan. X6	$8,000	$8,596.27	96,110.35
Jan. X7	8,000	7,651.72	101,674.66	Jan. X7	8,000	8,649.93	96,760.28
Jan. X8	8,000	7,625.60	101,300.26	Jan. X8	8,000	8,708.43	97,468.71
Jan. X9	8,000	7,597.52	100,897.78	Jan. X9	8,000	8,772.18	98,240.89
Jan. Y0	8,000	7,567.33	100,465.12	Jan. Y0	8,000	8,841.68	99,082.57
Jan. Y1	8,000	7,534.88	100,000.00	Jan. Y1	8,000	8,917.43	100,000.00

Postman and Sparkle had the following trial balances on December 31, 20X5:

	Postman	Sparkle
Cash	144,486	99,347
Accounts Receivable	90,000	60,000
Inventory	120,000	55,000
Land	200,000	60,000
Investment in Sparkle	429,859	
Investment in Sparkle Bonds	96,110	
Buildings	600,000	100,000
Accumulated Depreciation	(310,000)	(40,000)
Equipment	150,000	80,000
Accumulated Depreciation	(90,000)	(50,000)
Accounts Payable	(55,000)	(25,000)
Bonds Payable		(100,000)
Discount on Bonds Payable		(2,023)
Common Stock	(100,000)	(10,000)
Paid-In Capital in Excess of Par	(800,000)	(90,000)
Retained Earnings, January 1, 20X5	(300,000)	(120,000)
Sales	(850,000)	(320,000)
Cost of Goods Sold	500,000	200,000

Depreciation Expense—Buildings	30,000	5,000
Depreciation Expense—Equipment	15,000	10,000
Other Expenses	140,000	70,000
Interest Revenue	(8,596)	
Interest Expense		7,676
Subsidiary Income	(21,859)	
Dividends Declared	20,000	10,000
Total	0	0

Prepare the worksheet necessary to produce the consolidated financial statements for Postman Company and its subsidiary Sparkle Company for the year ended December 31, 20X5. Include the determination and distribution of excess and income distribution schedules. ◄◄◄◄◄ **Required**

Problem 5-7 *(LO 2)* **80%, equity, effective interest bonds purchased last year, inventory profits.** Refer to the preceding facts for Postman's acquisition of 80% of Sparkle's common stock. Postman uses the simple equity method to account for its investment in Sparkle. On January 1, 20X6, Postman held merchandise acquired from Sparkle for $12,000. During 20X6, Sparkle sold $25,000 worth of merchandise to Postman. Postman held $10,000 of this merchandise at December 31, 20X6. Postman owed Sparkle $6,000 on December 31 as a result of these intercompany sales. Sparkle has a gross profit rate of 25%.

template cd

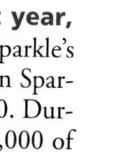

Sparkle issued $100,000 of 8%, 10-year bonds for $103,432 on January 1, 20X1, when the market rate was 7.5%. Annual interest is paid on December 31. Postman purchased the bonds for $95,514 on January 1, 20X5, when the market rate was 9%. Both companies use the effective interest method to amortize the premium/discount on the bonds. Postman and Sparkle prepared the following bond amortization schedules:

Sparkle				Postman			
Period	Cash	Interest	Balance	Period	Cash	Interest	Balance
Jan. X1			$103,432.04	Jan. X1			
Jan. X2	$8,000	$7,757.40	103,189.44	Jan. X2			
Jan. X3	8,000	7,739.21	102,928.65	Jan. X3			
Jan. X4	8,000	7,719.65	102,648.30	Jan. X4			
Jan. X5	8,000	7,698.62	102,346.92	Jan. X5			$ 95,514.08
Jan. X6	8,000	7,676.02	102,022.94	Jan. X6	$8,000	$8,596.27	96,110.35
Jan. X7	8,000	7,651.72	101,674.66	Jan. X7	8,000	8,649.93	96,760.28
Jan. X8	8,000	7,625.60	101,300.26	Jan. X8	8,000	8,708.43	97,468.71
Jan. X9	8,000	7,597.52	100,897.78	Jan. X9	8,000	8,772.18	98,240.89
Jan. Y0	8,000	7,567.33	100,465.12	Jan. Y0	8,000	8,841.68	99,082.57
Jan. Y1	8,000	7,534.88	100,000.00	Jan. Y1	8,000	8,917.43	100,000.00

Postman and Sparkle had the following trial balances on December 31, 20X6:

	Postman Company	Sparkle Company
Cash	290,486	99,347
Accounts Receivable	120,000	91,000
Inventory	140,000	55,000
Land	200,000	60,000
Investment in Sparkle	435,737	
Investment in Sparkle Bonds	96,760	
Buildings	600,000	100,000
Accumulated Depreciation	(340,000)	(45,000)
Equipment	150,000	80,000

(continued)

	Postman Company	Sparkle Company
Accumulated Depreciation	(105,000)	(60,000)
Accounts Payable	(40,000)	(34,000)
Bonds Payable		(100,000)
Premium on Bonds Payable		(1,675)
Common Stock	(100,000)	(10,000)
Paid-In Capital in Excess of Par	(800,000)	(90,000)
Retained Earnings, January 1, 20X6	(475,455)	(137,324)
Sales	(900,000)	(350,000)
Cost of Goods Sold	530,000	230,000
Depreciation Expense—Buildings	30,000	5,000
Depreciation Expense—Equipment	15,000	10,000
Other Expenses	155,000	80,000
Interest Revenue	(8,650)	
Interest Expense		7,652
Subsidiary Income	(13,878)	
Dividends Declared	20,000	10,000
Total	0	0

Required ▶ ▶ ▶ ▶ ▶ Prepare the worksheet necessary to produce the consolidated financial statements for Postman Company and its subsidiary Sparkle Company for the year ended December 31, 20X6. Include the determination and distribution of excess and income distribution schedules.

Problem 5-8 *(LO 2)* **CPA Objective, equipment, merchandise, bonds.** The problem below is an example of a question of the CPA "Other Objective Format" type as it was applied to the consolidations area. A mark-sensing answer sheet was used on the exam. You may just supply the answer which should be accompanied by calculations where appropriate.

Presented below are selected amounts from the separate unconsolidated financial statements of Poe Corporation and its 90%-owned subsidiary, Shaw Company, at December 31, 20X2. Additional information follows:

	Poe Corporation	Shaw Company
Selected income statement amounts:		
Sales	$ 710,000	$ 530,000
Cost of goods sold	490,000	370,000
Gain on the sale of equipment		21,000
Earnings from investment in subsidiary (sophisticated equity)	61,000	
Interest expense		16,000
Depreciation	25,000	20,000
Selected balance sheet amounts:		
Cash	50,000	15,000
Inventories	229,000	150,000
Equipment	440,000	360,000
Accumulated depreciation	(200,000)	(120,000)
Investment in Shaw (sophisticated equity balance)	189,000	
Investment in bonds	(100,000)	
Discount on bonds	(9,000)	
Bonds payable		(200,000)
Common stock	(100,000)	(10,000)
Additional paid-in capital	(250,000)	(40,000)
Retained earnings	(402,000)	(140,000)

Selected statement of retained earnings amounts:		
Beginning balance, December 31, 20X1	272,000	100,000
Net income	210,000	70,000
Dividends paid	80,000	30,000

Additional information is as follows:

1. On January 2, 20X2, Poe purchased 90% of Shaw's 100,000 outstanding common stock for cash of $155,000. On that date, Shaw's stockholders' equity equaled $150,000, and the fair values of Shaw's assets and liabilities equaled their carrying amounts. Poe has accounted for the acquisition as a purchase. Any remaining excess is considered to be goodwill.
2. On September 4, 20X2, Shaw paid cash dividends of $30,000.
3. On December 31, 20X2, Poe recorded its equity in Shaw's earnings.

◄◄◄◄◄ **Required**

1. Items (a) through (c) below represent transactions between Poe and Shaw during 20X2. Determine the dollar amount effect of the consolidating adjustment on 20X2 consolidated net income. Ignore income tax considerations.

   Items to be answered:

   a. On January 3, 20X2, Shaw sold equipment with an original cost of $30,000 and a carrying value of $15,000 to Poe for $36,000. The equipment had a remaining life of 3 years and was depreciated using the straight-line method by both companies.
   b. During 20X2, Shaw sold merchandise to Poe for $60,000, which included a profit of $20,000. At December 31, 20X2, half of this merchandise remained in Poe's inventory.
   c. On December 31, 20X2, Poe paid $91,000 to purchase 50% of the outstanding bonds issued by Shaw. The bonds mature on December 31, 20X8, and were originally issued at par. The bonds pay interest annually on December 31, and the interest was paid to the prior investor immediately before Poe's purchase of the bonds.

2. Items (a) through (1) below refer to accounts that may or may not be included in Poe's and Shaw's consolidated financial statements. The list on the right refers to the various possibilities of those amounts to be reported in Poe's consolidated financial statements for the year ended December 31, 20X2. Consider all transactions stated above in determining your answer. Ignore income tax considerations.

Items to be answered:

a. Cash
b. Equipment
c. Investment in subsidiary
d. Bonds payable
e. NCI
f. Common stock
g. Beginning retained earnings
h. Dividends paid
i. Gain on retirement of bonds
j. Cost of goods sold
k. Interest expense
l. Depreciation expense

Responses to be selected:

1. Sum of amounts on Poe's and Shaw's separate unconsolidated financial statements.
2. Less than the sum of amounts on Poe's and Shaw's separate unconsolidated financial statements, but not the same as the amount on either.
3. Same as amount for Poe only.
4. Same as amount for Shaw only.
5. Eliminated entirely in consolidation.
6. Shown in consolidated financial statements but not in separate unconsolidated financial statements.
7. Neither in consolidated nor in separate unconsolidated financial statements.

(AICPA adapted)

Problem 5-9 *(LO 2)* **90%, cost, machine, merchandise, effective interest bonds.** Princess Company acquired a 90% interest in Superstar Company on January 1, 20X1, for $660,000. Any excess of cost over book value was due to goodwill.

(continued)

Capital balances of Superstar Company on January 1, 20X1, were:

Common stock ($10 par)	$200,000
Paid-in capital in excess of par	100,000
Retained earnings	300,000
Total equity	$600,000

Superstar Company sold a machine to Princess for $30,000 on January 1, 20X4. It cost Superstar $20,000 to build the machine, which had a 5-year remaining life on the date of the sale and is subject to straight-line depreciation.

Princess purchased one-half of the outstanding 9% bonds of Superstar for $89,186 (to yield 12%) on December 31, 20X5. The bonds were sold originally by Superstar to yield 10% to outside parties. The discount on the bonds was $7,582 on December 31, 20X5. The effective interest method of amortization is used.

During 20X6, Princess Company sold merchandise to Superstar for $50,000. Princess recorded a 30% gross profit on the sales price. $20,000 of the merchandise purchased from Princess remains unsold at the end of the year.

The trial balances of Princess and its subsidiary, Superstar, are as follows on December 31, 20X6:

	Princess Company	Superstar Company
Inventory	40,000	80,000
Equipment	371,190	1,522,413
Accumulated Depreciation	(200,000)	(600,000)
Investment in Superstar Stock	660,000	
Investment in Superstar Bonds	90,888	
Bonds Payable, 9%		(200,000)
Discount on Bonds Payable		6,345
Common Stock ($10 par)	(200,000)	(200,000)
Paid-In Capital in Excess of Par	(300,000)	(100,000)
Retained Earnings, January 1, 20X6	(401,376)	(500,000)
Sales	(300,000)	(260,000)
Cost of Goods Sold	100,000	72,000
Interest Income	(10,702)	
Other Expenses	150,000	160,000
Interest Expense		19,242
Total	0	0

Required ▶ ▶ ▶ ▶ ▶ Prepare the worksheet necessary to produce the consolidated financial statements of Princess Company and its subsidiary for the year ended December 31, 20X6. Include the determination and distribution of excess and income distribution schedules.

Problem 5-10 *(LO 4)* **100%, cost, operating lease.** Sym Corporation, a wholly owned subsidiary of Paratec Corporation, leased equipment from its parent company on August 1, 20X6. The terms of the agreement clearly do not require the lease to be accounted for as a capital lease. Both entities are accounting for the lease as an operating lease. The lease payment is $12,000 per year, paid in advance each August 1.

Paratec purchased its investment in Sym on December 31, 20X1, when Sym had a retained earnings balance of $150,000. Paratec is accounting for its investment in Sym under the cost method. Included in the original purchase price was a $50,000 premium attributable to Sym's history of exceptional earnings.

The December 31, 20X8, trial balances of Paratec and its subsidiary are presented below:

	Paratec Corporation	Sym Corporation
Cash	190,000	40,000
Accounts Receivable (net)	738,350	142,000
Inventory	500,000	75,000
Prepaid Rent on Equipment		7,000
Investment in Bonds	250,000	65,000
Investment in Sym Corporation	400,000	
Land	250,000	85,000
Plant and Equipment	1,950,000	295,000
Accumulated Depreciation—Plant and Equipment	(250,000)	(60,000)
Equipment Under Operating Lease	120,000	
Accumulated Depreciation—Assets Under Operating Lease	(36,000)	
Accounts Payable	(385,000)	(52,000)
Deferred Rent Revenue	(7,000)	
Common Stock (no par)	(2,000,000)	(200,000)
Retained Earnings, January 1, 20X8	(1,076,350)	(310,000)
Sales	(4,720,000)	(500,000)
Rent Income	(12,000)	
Cost of Goods Sold	3,068,000	300,000
Rent Expense		12,000
Other Expenses	725,000	101,000
Dividends Declared	295,000	
Total	0	0

◄◄◄◄◄ **Required**

Prepare the worksheet necessary to produce the consolidated income statement and balance sheet of Paratec Corporation and its subsidiary for the year ended December 31, 20X8.

Use the following information for Problems 5-11 through 5-14:

On January 1, 20X1, Press Company acquired 80% of Sabre Company's common stock for $450,000. On the date of the acquisition, Sabre had the following balance sheet:

Sabre Company
Balance Sheet
January 1, 20X1

Assets		Liabilities and Equity	
Accounts receivable	$ 40,000	Accounts payable	$ 80,000
Inventory	60,000	Common stock, $1 par	10,000
Land	100,000	Paid-in capital in excess	
Buildings	400,000	of par	190,000
Accumulated depreciation	(200,000)	Retained earnings	190,000
Equipment	100,000		
Accumulated depreciation	(30,000)		
Total assets	$ 470,000	Total liabilities and equity	$470,000

Buildings, which have a 20-year life, are undervalued by $100,000. Any excess cost is considered to be goodwill.

Problem 5-11 *(LO 5)* **80%, equity, financing lease, merchandise.** Refer to the preceding facts for Press's acquisition of Sabre common stock. Press uses the simple equity method to account for its investment in Sabre. On January 1, 20X2, Press held merchandise acquired from Sabre for $10,000. During 20X2, Sabre sold $40,000 worth of merchandise to Press. Press held $12,000 of this merchandise at December 31, 20X2. Press owed Sabre $6,000 on December 31 as a result of this intercompany sale. Sabre has a gross profit rate of 25%.

On January 1, 20X2, Sabre signed a 5-year lease with Press for the rental of equipment, which has a 5-year life. Payments of $23,363 are due each January 1, and there is a guaranteed residual value of $10,000 at the end of the 5 years. The market value of the equipment at the inception of the lease was $100,000. Press has a 12% implicit rate on the lease. The following amortization table was prepared for the lease:

Period	Payment	Interest	Principal	Balance
Jan. 1, 20X2	$23,363		$(23,363)	$76,637
Jan. 1, 20X3	23,363	$9,196	(14,167)	62,470
Jan. 1, 20X4	23,363	7,496	(15,867)	46,603
Jan. 1, 20X5	23,363	5,592	(17,771)	28,832
Jan. 1, 20X6	23,363	3,460	(19,903)	8,929
Jan. 1, 20X7	10,000	1,071	(8,929)	0

Press and Sabre had the following trial balances on December 31, 20X2:

	Press Company	Sabre Company
Cash	72,363	73,637
Accounts Receivable	72,000	45,000
Inventory	120,000	56,000
Land	100,000	100,000
Investment in Sabre	506,643	
Minimum Lease Payments Receivable	103,452	
Unearned Interest	(17,619)	
Buildings	800,000	400,000
Accumulated Depreciation	(220,000)	(220,000)
Equipment	150,000	100,000
Accumulated Depreciation	(90,000)	(50,000)
Equipment—Capital Lease		100,000
Accumulated Depreciation—Capital Lease		(18,000)
Accounts Payable	(60,000)	(40,000)
Obligation Under Capital Lease		(76,637)
Accrued Interest—Capital Lease		(9,196)
Common Stock	(100,000)	(10,000)
Paid-In Capital in Excess of Par	(800,000)	(190,000)
Retained Earnings, January 1, 20X2	(450,000)	(230,000)
Sales	(800,000)	(400,000)
Cost of Goods Sold	450,000	240,000
Depreciation Expense—Buildings	30,000	10,000
Depreciation Expense—Equipment	15,000	28,000
Other Expenses	140,000	72,000
Interest Revenue	(9,196)	
Interest Expense		9,196
Subsidiary Income	(32,643)	
Dividends Declared	20,000	10,000
Total	0	0

Required ▶ ▶ ▶ ▶ ▶ Prepare the worksheet necessary to produce the consolidated financial statements for Press Company and its subsidiary Sabre Company for the year ended December 31, 20X2. Include the determination and distribution of excess and income distribution schedules.

template cd

Problem 5-12 *(LO 5)* **80%, equity, financing lease, merchandise, later year.** Refer to the preceding facts for Press's acquisition of Sabre common stock. Press uses the simple equity method to account for its investment in Sabre. On January 1, 20X3, Press held merchandise acquired from Sabre for $12,000. During 20X3, Sabre sold $35,000 worth of merchandise to Press. Press held $8,000 of this merchandise at December 31, 20X3. Press owed Sabre $7,000 on December 31 as a result of this intercompany sale. Sabre has a gross profit rate of 25%.

On January 1, 20X2, Sabre signed a 5-year lease with Press for the rental of equipment, which has a 5-year life. Payments of $23,363 are due each January 1, and there is a guaranteed residual value of $10,000 at the end of the 5 years. The market value of the equipment at the inception of the lease was $100,000. Press has a 12% implicit rate on the lease. The following amortization table was prepared for the lease:

Period	Payment	Interest	Principal	Balance
Jan. 1, 20X2	$23,363		$(23,363)	$76,637
Jan. 1, 20X3	23,363	$9,196	(14,167)	62,470
Jan. 1, 20X4	23,363	7,496	(15,867)	46,603
Jan. 1, 20X5	23,363	5,592	(17,771)	28,832
Jan. 1, 20X6	23,363	3,460	(19,903)	8,929
Jan. 1, 20X7	10,000	1,071	(8,929)	0

Press and Sabre had the following trial balances on December 31, 20X3:

	Press Company	Sabre Company
Cash	140,000	78,274
Accounts Receivable	87,000	55,000
Inventory	170,000	66,000
Land	168,726	100,000
Investment in Sabre	516,646	
Minimum Lease Payments Receivable	80,089	
Unearned Interest	(10,123)	
Buildings	800,000	400,000
Accumulated Depreciation	(250,000)	(230,000)
Equipment	150,000	100,000
Accumulated Depreciation	(105,000)	(60,000)
Equipment—Capital Lease		100,000
Accumulated Depreciation—Capital Lease		(36,000)
Accounts Payable	(60,000)	(30,000)
Obligation Under Capital Lease		(62,470)
Accrued Interest—Capital Lease		(7,496)
Common Stock	(100,000)	(10,000)
Paid-In Capital in Excess of Par	(800,000)	(190,000)
Retained Earnings, January 1, 20X3	(636,839)	(260,804)
Sales	(900,000)	(450,000)
Cost of Goods Sold	550,000	290,000
Depreciation Expense—Buildings	30,000	10,000
Depreciation Expense—Equipment	15,000	28,000
Other Expenses	160,000	92,000
Interest Revenue	(7,496)	
Interest Expense		7,496
Subsidiary Income	(18,003)	
Dividends Declared	20,000	10,000
Total	0	0

Required Prepare the worksheet necessary to produce the consolidated financial statements for Press Company and its subsidiary Sabre Company for the year ended December 31, 20X3. Include the determination and distribution of excess and income distribution schedules.

Problem 5-13 *(LO 5, 6)* **80%, equity, sales-type lease, merchandise.** Refer to the preceding facts for Press's acquisition of Sabre common stock. Press uses the simple equity method to account for its investment in Sabre. On January 1, 20X2, Press held merchandise acquired from Sabre for $10,000. During 20X2, Sabre sold $40,000 worth of merchandise to Press. Press held $12,000 of this merchandise at December 31, 20X2. Press owed Sabre $6,000 on December 31 as a result of this intercompany sale. Sabre has a gross profit rate of 25%.

On January 1, 20X2, Sabre signed a 5-year lease with Press for the rental of equipment, which has a 5-year life. Payments of $23,363 are due each January 1, and there is a guaranteed residual value of $10,000 at the end of the 5 years. The market value of the equipment at the inception of the lease was $100,000. The cost of the equipment to Press was $85,000. Press has a 12% implicit rate on the lease. The following amortization table was prepared for the lease:

Period	Payment	Interest	Principal	Balance
Jan. 1, 20X2	$23,363		$(23,363)	$76,637
Jan. 1, 20X3	23,363	$9,196	(14,167)	62,470
Jan. 1, 20X4	23,363	7,496	(15,867)	46,603
Jan. 1, 20X5	23,363	5,592	(17,771)	28,832
Jan. 1, 20X6	23,363	3,460	(19,903)	8,929
Jan. 1, 20X7	10,000	1,071	(8,929)	0

Press and Sabre had the following trial balances on December 31, 20X2:

	Press Company	Sabre Company
Cash	72,363	73,637
Accounts Receivable	72,000	45,000
Inventory	120,000	56,000
Land	100,000	100,000
Investment in Sabre	506,643	
Minimum Lease Payments Receivable	103,452	
Unearned Interest	(17,619)	
Buildings	800,000	400,000
Accumulated Depreciation	(220,000)	(220,000)
Equipment	150,000	100,000
Accumulated Depreciation	(90,000)	(50,000)
Equipment—Capital Lease		100,000
Accumulated Depreciation—Capital Lease		(18,000)
Accounts Payable	(60,000)	(40,000)
Obligation Under Capital Lease		(76,637)
Accrued Interest—Capital Lease		(9,196)
Common Stock	(100,000)	(10,000)
Paid-In Capital in Excess of Par	(800,000)	(190,000)
Retained Earnings, January 1, 20X2	(450,000)	(230,000)
Sales	(800,000)	(400,000)
Cost of Goods Sold	465,000	240,000
Depreciation Expense—Buildings	30,000	10,000
Depreciation Expense—Equipment	15,000	28,000
Other Expenses	140,000	72,000
Interest Revenue	(9,196)	
Interest Expense		9,196
Gain on Fixed Asset Sale	(15,000)	
Subsidiary Income	(32,643)	
Dividends Declared	20,000	10,000
Total	0	0

Prepare the worksheet necessary to produce the consolidated financial statements for Press Company and its subsidiary Sabre Company for the year ended December 31, 20X2. Include the determination and distribution of excess and income distribution schedules. ◄◄◄◄◄ **Required**

Problem 5-14 *(LO 5, 6)* **80%, equity, sales-type lease, merchandise, later year.** Refer to the preceding facts for Press's acquisition of Sabre common stock. Press uses the simple equity method to account for its investment in Sabre. On January 1, 20X3, Press held merchandise acquired from Sabre for $12,000. During 20X3, Sabre sold merchandise to Press for $35,000. Press held $8,000 of this merchandise at December 31, 20X3. Press owed Sabre $7,000 on December 31 as a result of this intercompany sale. Sabre has a gross profit rate of 25%.

template cd

On January 1, 20X2, Sabre signed a 5-year lease with Press for the rental of equipment, which has a 5-year life. Payments of $23,363 are due each January 1, and there is a guaranteed residual value of $10,000 at the end of the 5 years. The market value of the equipment at the inception of the lease was $100,000. The cost of the equipment to Press was $85,000. Press has a 12% implicit rate on the lease. The following amortization table was prepared for the lease:

Period	Payment	Interest	Principal	Balance
Jan. 1, 20X2	$23,363		$(23,363)	$76,637
Jan. 1, 20X3	23,363	$9,196	(14,167)	62,470
Jan. 1, 20X4	23,363	7,496	(15,867)	46,603
Jan. 1, 20X5	23,363	5,592	(17,771)	28,832
Jan. 1, 20X6	23,363	3,460	(19,903)	8,929
Jan. 1, 20X7	10,000	1,071	(8,929)	0

Press and Sabre had the following trial balances on December 31, 20X3:

	Press Company	Sabre Company
Cash	140,000	78,274
Accounts Receivable	87,000	55,000
Inventory	170,000	66,000
Land	168,726	100,000
Investment in Sabre	516,646	
Minimum Lease Payments Receivable	80,089	
Unearned Interest	(10,123)	
Buildings	800,000	400,000
Accumulated Depreciation	(250,000)	(230,000)
Equipment	150,000	100,000
Accumulated Depreciation	(105,000)	(60,000)
Equipment—Capital Lease		100,000
Accumulated Depreciation—Capital Lease		(36,000)
Accounts Payable	(60,000)	(30,000)
Obligation Under Capital Lease		(62,470)
Accrued Interest—Capital Lease		(7,496)
Common Stock	(100,000)	(10,000)
Paid-In Capital in Excess of Par	(800,000)	(190,000)
Retained Earnings, January 1, 20X3	(636,839)	(260,804)
Sales	(900,000)	(450,000)
Cost of Goods Sold	550,000	290,000
Depreciation Expense—Buildings	30,000	10,000
Depreciation Expense—Equipment	15,000	28,000
Other Expenses	160,000	92,000
Interest Revenue	(7,496)	
Interest Expense		7,496
Subsidiary Income	(18,003)	
Dividends Declared	20,000	10,000
Total	0	0

Required ▶ ▶ ▶ ▶ ▶ Prepare the worksheet necessary to produce the consolidated financial statements for Press Company and its subsidiary Sabre Company for the year ended December 31, 20X3. Include the determination and distribution of excess and income distribution schedules.

Problem 5-15 *(LO 5, 6)* **80%, cost, financing and sales-type leases.** Plessor Industries acquired 80% of the outstanding common stock of Slessee Company on January 1, 20X1, for $320,000. On that date, Slessee's book values approximated fair values, and the balance of its retained earnings account was $80,000. Any excess was attributed to goodwill. Slessee's net income was $20,000 for 20X1 and $30,000 for 20X2. No dividends were paid in either year.

On January 1, 20X2, Slessee signed a 5-year lease with Plessor for the rental of a small factory building with a 10-year life. Payments of $25,000 are due each January 1, and Slessee is expected to exercise the $5,000 bargain purchase option at the end of the fifth year. The fair value of the factory was $103,770 at the start of the lease term. Plessor's implicit rate on the lease is 12%.

A second lease agreement, for the rental of production equipment with an 8-year life, was signed by Slessee on January 1, 20X3. The terms of this 4-year lease require a payment of $15,000 each January 1. The present value of the lease payments at Plessor's 12% implicit rate was equal to the fair value of the equipment, $52,298, when the lease was signed. The cost of the equipment to Plessor was $45,000, and there is a $2,000 bargain purchase option. Eight-year, straight-line depreciation is being used, with no salvage value.

The following trial balances were prepared by the separate companies at December 31, 20X3:

	Plessor Industries	Slessee Company
Cash	60,000	40,745
Accounts Receivable	97,778	76,000
Inventory	140,000	120,000
Minimum Lease Payments Receivable	127,000	
Unearned Interest Income	(14,417)	
Investment in Slessee Company	320,000	
Assets Under Capital Lease		156,068
Accumulated Depreciation—Assets Under Capital Lease		(27,291)
Property, Plant, and Equipment	1,900,000	310,000
Accumulated Depreciation—Property, Plant, and Equipment	(1,077,000)	(72,000)
Accounts Payable	(148,000)	(45,065)
Obligations Under Capital Lease		(100,520)
Common Stock ($10 par)	(700,000)	(300,000)
Paid-In Capital in Excess of Par	(325,000)	
Retained Earnings, January 1, 20X3	(295,000)	(130,000)
Sales	(1,400,000)	(600,000)
Sales Profit on Leases	(7,298)	
Interest Income	(12,063)	
Cost of Goods Sold	780,000	380,000
Interest Expense		12,063
Other Expenses	510,000	165,000
Dividend Income	(12,000)	
Dividends Declared	56,000	15,000
Total	0	0

Required ▶ ▶ ▶ ▶ ▶ Prepare the worksheet necessary to produce the consolidated financial statements of Plessor Industries and its subsidiary for the year ended December 31, 20X3. Include the determination and distribution of excess and income distribution schedules.

Problem 5-16 *(LO 4, 5, 6)* **80%, cost, operating, sales-type and financing leases.** Patter Inc. purchased an 80% interest in Swampy Company for $480,000 on January 1, 20X1, when Swampy had the following stockholders' equity:

Common stock ($10 par)	$100,000
Additional paid-in capital	300,000
Retained earnings	100,000
Total equity	$500,000

Any excess was attributed to goodwill.

The trial balances of Patter Inc. and Swampy Company were prepared on December 31, 20X5.

	Patter Inc.	Swampy Company
Cash	91,013	26,050
Inventory	70,000	20,000
Property, Plant, and Equipment	320,000	50,000
Accumulated Depreciation—Property, Plant, and Equipment	(70,000)	(20,000)
Assets Under Capital Lease	40,676	
Accumulated Depreciation—Assets Under Capital Lease	(10,796)	
Assets Under Operating Lease		420,000
Accumulated Depreciation—Assets Under Operating Lease		(80,000)
Minimum Lease Payments Receivable		412,000
Unearned Interest Income on Leases		(4,000)
Investment in Swampy Company	480,000	
Accounts Payable	(130,000)	(180,000)
Obligations Under Capital Lease	(24,560)	
Interest Payable	(4,440)	
Common Stock ($10 par)	(200,000)	(100,000)
Paid-In Capital in Excess of Par	(300,000)	(300,000)
Retained Earnings, January 1, 20X5	(278,333)	(226,610)
Sales	(300,000)	(130,000)
Rent Income		(34,000)
Interest Income—Capital Lease		(4,440)
Depreciation Expense	41,000	23,000
Interest Expense	4,440	
Selling and General Expense	70,000	38,000
Cost of Goods Sold	190,000	90,000
Rent Expense	11,000	
Total	0	0

The following intercompany leases have been written by Swampy since the acquisition:

1. On January 1, 20X3, Swampy purchased for $140,000 land and a building, which it leased to Patter Inc. under a 5-year operating lease. Payments of $11,000 per year are required at the beginning of each year. The $120,000 building cost is being depreciated over 20 years on a straight-line basis.
2. On January 1, 20X4, Swampy purchased a machine for $14,000 and leased it to Patter Inc. The 4-year lease qualifies as a capital lease. The rentals are $5,000 per year, payable at the beginning of each year. There is a bargain purchase option whereby Patter will purchase the machine at the end of 4 years for $2,000.

(continued)

The fair value of the machine was $17,560 at the start of the lease term. The lease payments, including the purchase option, yield an implicit rate of 15% to the lessor. Patter is depreciating the machine over 7 years on a straight-line basis with no salvage value.

3. On January 1, 20X5, Swampy purchased a truck for $23,116 and leased it to Patter Inc. under a 3-year capital lease. Payments of $8,000 per year are required at the beginning of each year. There is a bargain purchase agreement for $5,000. Patter Inc. is depreciating the truck over 4 years, straight-line, with no salvage value. The lease has a lessor implicit rate of 20%.
4. Patter Inc. has accrued interest in 20X5 on its capital lease obligations. Swampy has recognized earned interest for the year on its capital leases.

Required ▶ ▶ ▶ ▶ ▶ Prepare the worksheet necessary to produce the consolidated financial statements of Patter Inc. and its subsidiary for the year ended December 31, 20X5. Include the determination and distribution of excess and income distribution schedules.

APPENDIX PROBLEMS

Problem 5A-1 *(LO 7)* **80%, equity, financing leases with unguaranteed residual, fixed asset profit.** Steven Truck Company has been an 80%-owned subsidiary of Paulz Heavy Equipment since January 1, 20X3, when Paulz purchased 128,000 shares of Steven common stock for $832,000, an amount equal to the book value of Steven's net assets at that date. Steven's net income and dividends paid since acquisition are as follows:

Year	Net Income	Dividends
20X3	$70,000	$25,000
20X4	75,600	25,000
20X5	81,650	30,000

On January 1, 20X5, Paulz leased a truck from Steven. The 3-year financing-type lease provides for payments of $10,000 each January 1. On January 1, 20X5, the present value of the truck at Steven's 8% implicit rate, including the unguaranteed residual value of $6,000 at the end of the third year, was $32,596. Paulz also has used the 8% implicit rate to record the lease. The truck is being depreciated on a straight-line basis.

On January 1, 20X6, Steven signed a 4-year financing-type lease with Paulz for the rental of specialized production machinery with an 8-year life. There is a $7,000 purchase option at the end of the fourth year. The lease agreement requires lease payments of $30,000 each January 1 plus $1,500 for maintenance of the equipment. It also calls for contingent payments equal to 10% of Steven's cost savings through the use of this equipment, as reflected in any increase in net income (excluding gains or losses on sale of assets) above the previous growth rate of Steven's net income. The present value of the equipment on January 1, 20X6, at Paulz's 10% implicit rate was $109,388.

On October 1, 20X6, Steven sold Paulz a warehouse having a 20-year remaining life, a book value of $135,000, and an estimated salvage value of $20,000. Paulz paid $195,000 for the building, which is being depreciated on a straight-line basis.

The trial balances were prepared by the separate companies on December 31, 20X6.

	Paulz Heavy Equipment	Steven Truck Company
Cash	90,485	123,307
Accounts Receivable (net)	228,000	120,000
Inventory	200,000	140,000
Minimum Lease Payments Receivable	97,000	10,000
Unguaranteed Residual Value		6,000

	Paulz Heavy Equipment	Steven Truck Company
Unearned Interest Income	(9,673)	(444)
Assets Under Capital Lease	27,833	109,388
Accumulated Depreciation—Assets Under Capital Lease	(18,556)	(13,674)
Property, Plant, and Equipment	2,075,000	1,145,000
Accumulated Depreciation—Property, Plant, and Equipment	(713,000)	(160,000)
Investment in Steven Truck Company	1,045,800	
Accounts Payable	(100,000)	(85,000)
Interest Payable	(740)	(7,939)
Obligations Under Capital Lease	(9,260)	(79,388)
Common Stock ($5 par)	(1,800,000)	(800,000)
Retained Earnings, January 1, 20X6	(864,834)	(387,250)
Sales	(3,200,000)	(1,400,000)
Gain on Sale of Assets		(60,000)
Interest Income	(7,939)	(1,152)
Rent Income	(2,182)	
Cost of Goods Sold	1,882,000	770,000
Interest Expense	740	7,939
Depreciation Expense	135,000	45,000
Other Expenses	924,326	483,213
Subsidiary Income	(124,000)	
Dividends Declared	144,000	35,000
Total	0	0

Prepare the worksheet necessary to produce the consolidated financial statements of Paulz Heavy Equipment and its subsidiary for the year ended December 31, 20X6. Include income distribution schedules. ◄◄◄◄◄ **Required**

Problem 5A-2 *(LO 7)* **Eliminations only, sales-type lease with unguaranteed residual value.** Penn Company leased a production machine to its 80%-owned subsidiary, Smith Company. The lease agreement, dated January 1, 20X1, requires Smith to pay $18,000 each January 1 for three years. There is an unguaranteed residual value of $5,000. The machine cost $50,098. The present value of the machine at Penn's 16% implicit interest rate was $50,098 on January 1, 20X1. Smith also uses the 16% lessor implicit rate to record the lease. The machine is being depreciated over 3 years on a straight-line basis with a $5,000 salvage value. Lease payment amortization schedules are as follows:

Penn (16%)

Date	Payment	Interest at 16% on Previous Balance	Reduction of Principal	Principal Balance
Jan. 1, 20X1				$50,098
Jan. 1, 20X1	$18,000		$18,000	32,098
Jan. 1, 20X2	18,000	$5,136	12,864	19,234
Jan. 1, 20X3	18,000	3,078	14,922	4,312
Jan. 1, 20X4	5,000	688	4,312	
Total	$59,000	$8,902	$50,098	

(continued)

Smith (16%)

Date	Payment	Interest at 16% on Previous Balance	Reduction of Principal	Principal Balance
Jan. 1, 20X1				$46,894
Jan. 1, 20X1	$18,000		$18,000	28,894
Jan. 1, 20X2	18,000	$4,623	13,377	15,517
Jan. 1, 20X3	18,000	2,483	15,517	
Total	$54,000	$7,106	$46,894	

Required ▶ ▶ ▶ ▶ ▶

1. Prepare the eliminations and adjustments required for this lease on the December 31, 20X1, consolidated worksheet.
2. Prepare the eliminations and adjustments for the December 31, 20X2, consolidated worksheet.

Case 5-1 *Methods of Eliminating Subsidiary Debt*

Power Pro Inc. is a large manufacturer of marine engines. In recent years, Power Pro, like other engine manufacturers, has purchased independent boat builders. The intent of the acquisitions is to control the engine choice of the boat builder. By including the outboard engine in the boat package, it is not necessary to sell to and finance many small dealers.

Power Pro purchased Swift-Craft during the last year. Swift-Crafts are built in California and are sold only in western states. Power Pro wants to build the boats in the Midwest as well, so as to expand sales without paying major shipping costs from the West. A new plant will cost $1,000,000 to build and another $1,500,000 to equip for production.

Currently, Swift-Craft has $800,000 in long-term debt. It has 11% annual interest bonds outstanding in the hands of local investors. Current investors have no interest in lending any more funds. The interest rate Swift-Craft pays is high due to its size and credit rating.

Power Pro has ready access to the bond market and borrows at 7.5% annual interest. Power Pro also has expertise in constructing and equipping new facilities since it has built many new plants. Power Pro also has a sophisticated fixed asset accounting system. Power Pro would prefer to build the new plant and turn it over to Swift-Craft when it is complete. It is considering either selling the building to Swift-Craft and taking back the mortgage or leasing the asset to Swift-Craft under a long-term capital lease.

Power Pro would like you to cover the options it has in using its borrowing ability and asset management experience in assisting Swift-Craft. There is a concern as to existing debt and with respect to funds needed to finance the new plant. Your discussion should consider the impact of alternatives on the consolidation process and on NCI shareholders.

Case 5-2 *Impact of Alternative Methods to Retire Subsidiary Debt*

Magna Company is the parent company which owns an 80% interest in Metros Company. The interest was purchased at book value, and the simple equity method is used to record the ownership interest. The trial balances of the two companies on December 31, 20X6, are as follows:

	Magna Company	Metros Company
Cash	258,000	100,000
Other Current Assets	50,000	200,000
Investment in Metros	316,000	
Plant and Equipment	800,000	500,000
Accumulated Depreciation	(300,000)	(200,000)

Current Liabilities	(40,000)	(5,000)
Bonds Payable		(200,000)
Common Stock, Par	(300,000)	(100,000)
Retained Earnings	(746,000)	(285,000)
Sales	(150,000)	(170,000)
Cost of Goods Sold	90,000	130,000
Expenses	30,000	10,000
Interest Expense		20,000
Subsidiary Income	(8,000)	
Total	0	0

As of December 31, 20X6, the Magna Company was considering acquiring the $200,000 of Metros' 10% bonds from the current owner. Based on a 12% current interest rate for bonds of this risk, the purchase price of the bonds would be $185,000. There are two possible options:

1. Magna could lend $185,000 to Metros at 8% annual interest. Metros would then use the funds to retire the bonds.
2. Magna could buy the bonds and hold them as an investment and enjoy the high interest rate.

◄◄◄◄◄ **Required**

1. Prepare a pro forma consolidated income statement and balance sheet for 20X6 assuming option 1 is used.
2. Indicate how your solution to Requirement 1 would change if the second option were used.

Alternative Ways to Transfer Asset to Subsidiary — *Case 5-3*

Pannier Company is the parent company which owns an 80% interest in Jodestar Company. The interest was purchased at book value, and the simple equity method is used to record the ownership interest. The trial balances of the two companies on December 31, 20X6, are as follows:

	Pannier Company	Jodestar Company
Cash	258,000	100,000
Inventory	150,000	40,000
Other Current Assets	50,000	160,000
Investment in Metros	316,000	
Plant and Equipment	650,000	500,000
Accumulated Depreciation	(300,000)	(200,000)
Current Liabilities	(40,000)	(5,000)
Long-Term Debt		(200,000)
Common Stock, Par	(300,000)	(100,000)
Retained Earnings	(746,000)	(285,000)
Sales	(150,000)	(170,000)
Cost of Goods Sold	90,000	130,000
Expenses	30,000	10,000
Interest Expense		20,000
Subsidiary Income	(8,000)	
Total	0	0

As the year ended, Pannier was planning to transfer a major piece of equipment to Jodestar. The equipment was just purchased by Pannier and is included in its inventory account. The equipment cost Pannier $100,000 and would be transferred to Jodestar for $125,000. There are two options:

1. Sell the equipment to Jodestar for $125,000 and finance it with a 5-year, 10% interest installment note.
2. Lease the equipment to Jodestar on a 5-year lease requiring payments of $29,977 in advance.

Required ▶ ▶ ▶ ▶ ▶

1. Make the journal entries for both companies if the intercompany sale was consummated on December 31.
2. Prepare a consolidated income statement and balance sheet for the company for 20X6.
3. Make the journal entries for both companies if the intercompany lease was executed on December 31.
4. If the lease were used, how would the consolidated statements differ from those in Requirement 2?

Cash Flow, EPS, Taxation, and Unconsolidated Investments

CHAPTER

6

Learning Objectives

When you have completed this chapter, you should be able to

1. **Demonstrate an understanding of the effect of a business combination on cash flow in and after the period of the purchase.**
2. **Compute earnings per share for a consolidated firm.**
3. **Calculate and prepare a consolidated worksheet where the consolidated firm is an "affiliated group" and pays a single consolidated tax.**
4. **Prepare a consolidated worksheet where the parent and subsidiary are separately taxed by employing tax allocation procedures.**
5. **Apply consolidation-type procedures to influential investments.**

This chapter contains the remaining consolidation issues that affect the vast majority of consolidated companies and extends consolidation concepts to nonconsolidated investments that are accounted for under the sophisticated equity method.

We begin with the procedures necessary to prepare a consolidated statement of cash flows. Fortunately, this requires only minor changes in the procedures used in your prior accounting courses. Also, only minor adjustments of typical earnings per share procedures are needed for consolidated companies. The final consolidation issue is taxation of the consolidated company. Prior worksheets are now enhanced to include the provision for tax. This is quite simple when the affiliated companies are taxed as a single entity. Procedures are a bit more involved when the individual companies are taxed separately.

This chapter concludes with a discussion of the use of the sophisticated equity method for investments that are not consolidated. These investments require the use of procedures that parallel those used in consolidations. The end result is that the income reported from the investee is the same as if the investee were consolidated and the controlling interest in subsidiary income was calculated.

CONSOLIDATED STATEMENT OF CASH FLOWS

1

OBJECTIVE

Demonstrate an understanding of the effect of a business combination on cash flow in and after the period of the purchase.

FASB Statement of Financial Accounting Standards No. 95 requires that a statement of cash flows accompany a company's published income statement and balance sheet. The process of preparing a consolidated statement of cash flows is similar to that which is used for a single company, a topic covered in depth in intermediate accounting texts. Since the analysis of changes in cash of a consolidated entity begins with consolidated statements, intercompany transactions will have been eliminated and, thus, will not cause any complications. However, because of the parent–subsidiary relationship, there are some situations that require special consideration. These situations are discussed in the following paragraphs.

Cash Acquisition of Controlling Interest

The cash purchase of a controlling interest in a company is considered an *investing activity* and would appear as a cash outflow in the cash flows from investing activities section of the statement of cash flows. It also is necessary to explain the total increase in consolidated assets and the addition of the NCI to the consolidated balance sheet. This is a result of the requirement that the statement of cash flows disclose investing and *financing activities* that affect the company's financial position even though they do not impact cash.

To illustrate the disclosure required, consider an example of a cash purchase of an 80% interest in a company. Assume Company S had the following balance sheet on January 1, 20X1, when Company P acquired an 80% interest for $540,000 in cash:

Assets		Liabilities and Equity	
Cash and cash equivalents	$ 50,000	Long-term liabilities	$150,000
Inventory	60,000	Common stock ($10 par)	200,000
Equipment (net)	190,000	Retained earnings	350,000
Building (net)	400,000		
Total assets	$700,000	Total liabilities and equity	$700,000

Assume the fair values of the equipment and building are $250,000 and $425,000, respectively, and any remaining excess of cost is attributed to goodwill. The estimated remaining life of the equipment is 5 years and of the building is 10 years.

The following zone analysis would be prepared:

	Group Total	Ownership Portion	Cumulative Total
Ownership percentage		80%	
Priority accounts (net of liabilities)	$ (40,000)	$ (32,000)	$ (32,000)
Nonpriority accounts	675,000	540,000	508,000

Price Analysis

Price (including direct acquisition costs)	$540,000	
Assign to priority accounts, controlling share	(32,000)	Full value
Assign to nonpriority accounts, controlling share	540,000	Full value
Goodwill	32,000	

The price analysis schedule indicates that the parent's share of all accounts can be fully adjusted to fair value.

From this information, a determination and distribution of excess would be prepared:

	Company	Controlling Interest		Amortization Periods	Controlling Amortization
Price paid for investment including direct acquisition costs		$540,000			
Less book value of interest purchased:					
Common stock ($10 par)	$200,000				
Retained earnings	350,000				
Total equity	$550,000				
Ownership interest	× 80%	440,000			
Excess of cost over book value adjustments		$100,000	Cr.		
Equipment (net), 80% of $60,000		(48,000)	Dr.	5	$9,600
Buildings (net), 80% of $25,000		(20,000)	Dr.	10	2,000
Goodwill		$ 32,000	Dr.		

The effect of the purchase on the balance sheet accounts of the consolidated company for 20X1 would be as follows:

	Debit	Credit
Cash ($540,000 paid – $50,000 subsidiary cash)		490,000
Inventory	60,000	
Equipment ($190,000 book value + $48,000 excess)	238,000	
Building ($400,000 book value + $20,000 excess)	420,000	
Goodwill	32,000	
Long-term liabilities		150,000
Noncontrolling interest (20% × $550,000 subsidiary equity)		110,000
Total	750,000	750,000

The disclosure of the purchase on the statement of cash flows would be summarized as follows:

Under the heading "Cash flows from investing activities":

Payment for purchase of Company S, net of cash acquired	$(490,000)

In the supplemental schedule of noncash financing and investing activity:

Company P purchased 80% of the common stock of Company S for $540,000. In conjunction with the acquisition, liabilities were assumed and an NCI was created as follows:

Adjusted value of assets acquired ($700,000 book value + $100,000 excess)	$800,000
Cash paid for common stock	540,000
Balance (noncash)	$260,000
Liabilities assumed	$150,000
NCI	$110,000

Noncash Acquisition of Controlling Interest

Suppose that instead of paying cash for its controlling interest, Company P issued 10,000 shares of its $10 par stock for the controlling interest. Further assume the shares had a market value of $54 each. Since the acquisition price is the same ($540,000), the determination and distribution of excess schedule would not change. The analysis of balance sheet account changes would be as follows:

	Debit	Credit
Cash ($50,000 subsidiary cash)	50,000	
Inventory	60,000	
Equipment($190,000 book value + $48,000 excess)	238,000	
Building ($400,000 book value + $20,000 excess)	420,000	
Goodwill	32,000	
Long-term liabilities		150,000
Noncontrolling interest (20% × $550,000 subsidiary equity)		110,000
Common stock, $10 par, Company P		100,000
Paid-in capital in excess of par, Company P		440,000
Total	800,000	800,000

The disclosure of the purchase on the statement of cash flows would be summarized as follows:

Under the heading "Cash flows from investing activities":

Cash acquired in purchase of Company S	$50,000

In the supplemental schedule of noncash financing and investing activity:

Company P acquired 80% of the common stock of Company S in exchange for 10,000 shares of Company P common stock valued at $540,000. In conjunction with the acquisition, liabilities were assumed and a noncontrolling interest was created as follows:

Adjusted value of assets acquired ($700,000 book value + $100,000 excess).	$800,000
Common stock issued	$540,000
Liabilities assumed.	$150,000
Noncontrolling interest	$110,000

In the past, when an acquisition qualified as a pooling of interests, all prior financial statements were consolidated retroactively which required that cash flow analyses proceed from a comparison of the consolidated balance sheets of the current and previous periods. Due to the retroactive application of the pooling of interests, there was no difference between the comparative statements as a result of the pooling. The impact of the pooling on the consolidated stockholders' equity was disclosed in the period the pooling was consummated.

Adjustments Resulting from Business Combinations

A business combination will have ramifications on the statements of cash flows prepared in subsequent periods. A purchase may create amortizations of excess deductions (noncash items) which need to be adjusted. In addition, there may be impact resulting from additional purchases of subsidiary shares and/or dividend payments by the subsidiary. Intercompany bonds and nonconsolidated investments also need to be considered for their impact.

Amortization of Excesses. Income statements prepared for periods including or following a purchase of another company will include the amortization of the excesses that are shown on the determination and distribution of excess schedule as well as book value depreciation and amortization recorded by both the parent and subsidiary. These amortizations of the excesses, while reflected in consolidated net income, do not require the use of cash; thus, under the indirect method, they must be included as an adjustment to consolidated net income to arrive at cash flows from operating activities. Using the facts of the preceding examples, the following adjustments would appear on the cash flows statement for 20X1:

Cash from operating activities:	
Consolidated net income	$XXX,XXX
Add amortizations resulting from business combination:	
Depreciation on equipment ($48,000 ÷ 5)	9,600
Depreciation on building ($20,000 ÷ 10).	2,000

In addition, cash from operating activities would be adjusted for depreciation and amortizations of book value recorded by the constituent companies on their separate books.

Purchase of Additional Subsidiary Shares. The purchase of additional shares directly from the subsidiary results in no added cash flowing into the consolidated company. The transfer of cash within the consolidated company would not appear in the consolidated statement of cash flows. However, the purchase of additional shares from the noncontrolling interest does result in an outflow of cash. From a consolidated viewpoint, it is the equivalent of purchasing treasury shares. Thus, it would be listed under *financing activities.*

Subsidiary Dividends. Dividends paid by the subsidiary to the parent are a transfer of cash within the consolidated entity and thus would not appear in the consolidated statement of cash flows. However, dividends paid by the subsidiary to noncontrolling shareholders represent a flow of cash to parties outside the consolidated group and would appear as an outflow under the cash flows from financing activities heading of the consolidated statement of cash flows.

Purchase of Intercompany Bonds. The purchase of intercompany bonds from parties outside the consolidated company affects a cash flow from one member of the consolidated group to parties outside the consolidated entity. Recall that the purchase of intercompany bonds is viewed as a retirement of the bonds on the consolidated worksheet. The consolidated statement of cash flows also treats the purchase of the bonds as a retirement of the consolidated company's debt and includes the cash outflow under cash flows from financing activities. Since the process of constructing a cash flows statement starts with the consolidated income statement and balance sheet, intercompany interest payments and amortizations of premiums and/or discounts already are eliminated and will not enter into the analysis of consolidated cash flows. Only cash interest payments to bondholders outside the consolidated entity are important to the analysis and should be included in cash flows from *operating* activities.

Nonconsolidated Investments. Investments in the stock of companies not included in the consolidated group result in income to the consolidated entity. Where the investment is accounted for under the cost method, cash dividends received are included in cash flows from operating activities. However, where the equity method is applied, only that portion of the income received in cash may be included in cash from operating activities. For example, the investee may report income of $50,000 and pay dividends of $10,000. Assume further that the consolidated company paid $20,000 more than book value for its 30% interest and regards the excess as attributable to equipment with a 10-year life. Investment income under the equity method would be calculated as follows:

30% of reported income of $50,000	$15,000
Less amortization of excess cost ($20,000 ÷ 10)	2,000
Equity income	$13,000

Only $3,000 (30% × $10,000) was received in the form of cash dividends; thus, the $13,000 of income would be reduced to only $3,000 of cash from operating activities. The $10,000 of undistributed income would be adjusted out of net income to arrive at cash from operating activities.

Preparation of Consolidated Statement of Cash Flows

A complete example of the process of preparing a consolidated statement of cash flows is presented in this section. Assume Company P originally purchased an 80% interest in Company S on January 1, 20X1. In addition, Company P purchased a 20% interest in Company E on January 2, 20X2, and accounted for the investment under the sophisticated equity method. The following determination and distribution of excess schedules were prepared for each investment:

Price paid for investment in Company S		$365,000
Less book value interest acquired:		
Common stock ($10 par)	$ 50,000	
Paid-in capital in excess of par	150,000	
Retained earnings	100,000	
Total stockholders' equity	$300,000	
Interest acquired	× 80%	240,000

(continued)

			Amortization Periods	Controlling Amortization
Excess of cost over book value (debit)	$ 125,000			
Equipment, 80% × $31,250	**25,000**	**Dr.**	**5**	**$5,000**
Goodwill	**$100,000**			

For the January 2, 20X2, 20% investment in nonconsolidated Company E:

Price paid for investment in Company E		$255,000
Less interest acquired:		
Common stock	$ 500,000	
Retained earnings	750,000	
Total equity	$ 1,250,000	
Interest acquired	× 20%	250,000
Equipment (10-year life)		$ 5,000

Since this investment is not consolidated, there will be no recording of the increased value of the equipment. This information is used only to amortize the excess cost in future income statements. Because of this, there are no debits or credits accompanying the distribution of the excess. The following consolidated statements were prepared for Company P and its subsidiary, Company S, for 20X3:

Company P and Subsidiary Company S
Consolidated Income Statement
For Year Ended December 31, 20X3

Sales		$ 900,000
Less cost of goods sold		525,000
Gross profit		$ 375,000
Less expenses:		
General and administrative	$150,500	
Depreciation	**70,000***	**220,500**
Operating income		$ 154,500
Investment income (equity method)		**15,500****
Consolidated net income		$ 170,000
Distributed to:		
NCI		11,200
Controlling interest		$ 158,800

*Includes $5,000 of depreciation resulting from the excess of the subsidiary equipment's fair value over book value on January 1, 20X1, the date on which the 80% interest was acquired.
**20% of Company E net income of $80,000 less $500 amortization of equipment. (Dividends received were $2,000.)

Company P and Subsidiary Company S
Consolidated Retained Earnings Statement
For Year Ended December 31, 20X3

Retained earnings, January 1, 20X3	$440,000
Add distribution of consolidated net income	158,800
Less dividends declared	(50,000)
Balance, December 31, 20X3	$548,800

Company P and Subsidiary Company S
Consolidated Balance Sheet
December 31, 20X2 and 20X3

Assets	20X3	20X2
Cash and cash equivalents	$ 179,000	$ 160,000
Inventory	210,000	180,000
Accounts receivable	154,000	120,000
Property, plant, and equipment	1,330,000	1,250,000
Accumulated depreciation	(370,000)	(300,000)
Goodwill	100,000	100,000
Investment in Company E (20%)	333,500	320,000
Total assets	$1,936,500	$1,830,000
Liabilities and Stockholders' Equity		
Accounts payable	$ 156,500	$ 166,000
Bonds payable	300,000	300,000
Noncontrolling interest	79,200	72,000
Controlling interest:		
Common stock, par	200,000	200,000
Paid-in capital in excess of par	652,000	652,000
Retained earnings	548,800	440,000
Total liabilities and stockholders' equity	$1,936,500	$1,830,000

The following additional facts are available to aid in the preparation of a consolidated statement of cash flows:

1. Company P purchased a new piece of equipment during 20X3 for $80,000.
2. In 20X3, Company P declared and paid $50,000 in dividends and Company S declared and paid $20,000 in dividends.

Illustration 6-1 is a worksheet approach to calculating a statement of cash flows under the *indirect method.* Explanations 1 through 6 use changes in balance sheet accounts to analyze cash from operations. This information is taken from the income statement and is implied from changes in current assets and current liabilities. Explanation 7 reflects the only investing activity in this example. Explanations 8 and 9 show the financing activities. The worksheet provides the information needed to develop the statement of cash flows located on page 337.

If the *direct method* of disclosing cash from operating activities is used, the cash flows from operating activities section of the statement of cash flows would be prepared as follows:

Cash flows from operating activities:	
Cash from customers ($900,000 sales – $34,000 increase in accounts receivable) . .	$ 866,000
Cash from investments (dividends received)	2,000
Cash to suppliers ($525,000 cost of goods sold + $30,000 inventory increase + $9,500 decrease in accounts payable).	(564,500)
Cash for general and administrative expenses	(150,500)
Net cash provided by operating activities.	$ 153,000

Illustration 6-1
Company P and Subsidiary Company S
Worksheet for Analysis of Cash: Indirect Approach
For Year Ended December 31, 20X3

	Account Change			Explanations			
	Debit	Credit		Debit		Credit	Balance
Inventory	30,000		(4)	30,000			0
Accounts receivable	34,000		(3)	34,000			0
Property, plant, and equipment.	80,000		(7)	80,000			0
Accumulated depreciation		70,000			(2)	70,000	0
Goodwill	0						0
Investment in Company E (20%)	13,500		(6)	13,500			0
Accounts payable	9,500		(5)	9,500			0
Bonds payable							0
Noncontrolling interest		7,200	(9)	4,000	(1)	11,200	0
Controlling interest:							
Common stock, par							0
Paid-in excess of par							0
Retained earnings		108,800	(8)	50,000	(1)	158,800	0
	167,000	186,000		221,000		240,000	
Net change in cash	19,000	0		19,000		0	
Cash from Operations:							
Consolidated net income.			(1)	170,000			
Depreciation expense			(2)	70,000			
Increase in accounts receivable.					(3)	34,000	
Increase in inventory					(4)	30,000	
Decrease in accounts payable					(5)	9,500	
Equity income in excess of dividends.					(6)	13,500	
Net cash provided by operating activities.				153,000			
Cash from Investing:							
Purchase of equipment					(7)	80,000	
Net cash used in investing activities						80,000	
Cash from Financing:							
Dividend payment to controlling interest					(8)	50,000	
Dividend payment to noncontrolling interest					(9)	4,000	
Net cash used in investing activities						54,000	
Net cash provided.				19,000			

Company P and Subsidiary Company S
Consolidated Statement of Cash Flows
For Year Ended December 31, 20X3

Cash flows from operating activities:		
Consolidated net income		$170,000
Adjustments to reconcile net income to net cash:		
Depreciation expense	$ 70,000	
Increase in accounts receivable	(34,000)	
Increase in inventory	(30,000)	
Decrease in accounts payable	(9,500)	
Equity income from Company E in excess of dividends received	(13,500)	
Total adjustments		(17,000)
Net cash provided by operating activities		$153,000
Cash flows from investing activities:		
Purchase of equipment		(80,000)
Cash flows from financing activities:		
Dividend payments to controlling interests	$(50,000)	
Dividend payments to noncontrolling interest	(4,000)	
Net cash used in financing activities		(54,000)
Net increase in cash and cash equivalents		$ 19,000
Cash and cash equivalents at beginning of year		160,000
Cash and cash equivalents at year-end		$179,000

REFLECTION

- Subsequent to the period of purchase, the only impact of consolidations on cash flow is the added amortization and depreciation caused by the purchase.
- A purchase of a subsidiary for cash is in the "investing" section of the cash flow statement. The cash outflow is net of the cash received.
- A purchase of a subsidiary by issuing securities is a noncash investing/financing activity that must be disclosed in the notes to the cash flow statement. Any subsidiary cash received in the purchase is a positive cash flow under "investing."
- The parent purchase of subsidiary bonds is treated as a retirement and is a financing activity.
- The parent purchase of additional shares of subsidiary stock is viewed as a treasury stock transaction and is considered a financing activity.

CONSOLIDATED EARNINGS PER SHARE

2

OBJECTIVE

Compute earnings per share for a consolidated firm.

The computation of *consolidated earnings per share (EPS)* remains virtually the same as that for single entities. For the purpose of this discussion, all calculations will be made only on an annual basis. ***Basic earnings per share (BEPS)* is calculated by dividing only the controlling**

interest in consolidated net income by parent company outstanding stock. The calculation of *diluted earnings per share (DEPS)* is not complicated when applied to the consolidated company, provided that the subsidiary company has no dilutive securities. As long as no such securities exist, the controlling interest's share of consolidated net income is divided by the number of outstanding parent company shares. The numerator and denominator adjustments caused by parent company dilutive securities can be considered in the normal manner.

When the subsidiary has dilutive securities, the calculation of consolidated DEPS becomes a two-stage process. First, the DEPS of the subsidiary must be calculated. Then, the consolidated DEPS is calculated using as a component of the calculation the adjusted DEPS of the subsidiary. This two-stage process handles subsidiary dilutive securities which require the possible issuance of subsidiary company shares. A further complication occurs when the subsidiary has outstanding dilutive options, warrants, and/or convertible securities which may require the issuance of parent company shares.

First, consider the calculation of consolidated DEPS when the subsidiary has outstanding dilutive securities which may require the issuance of subsidiary company shares only. The EPS model for a single entity is modified in two ways:

1. Only the parent's adjusted internally generated net income, the parent's income adjusters, and the parent's share adjusters enter the formula directly.
2. The parent's share of subsidiary's income is entered indirectly by multiplying the number of equivalent subsidiary shares owned by the parent times the subsidiary DEPS.

The basic model by which to compute consolidated EPS in this situation is as follows:

$$\text{Consolidated DEPS} = \frac{\text{Parent's adjusted internally generated net income} + \text{Parent's DEPS income adjustments} + \left(\text{Parent-owned equivalent shares} \times \text{Subsidiary DEPS}\right)}{\text{Parent's common stock outstanding} + \text{Parent's share adjustments}}$$

The parent's adjusted internally generated net income includes adjustments for unrealized profits (on sales to the subsidiary) recorded during the current period and for realization of profits deferred from previous periods. It is also adjusted for the amortizations of excess resulting from the original purchase of the subsidiary. **This would be all of the adjustments that appear on the parent's income distribution schedule, except for the inclusion of the parent's share of subsidiary income.** Likewise, the income used to compute the subsidiary DEPS must be adjusted for intercompany transactions (as shown in the subsidiary income distribution schedule). To illustrate the computation of consolidated DEPS, assume the following data concerning the subsidiary:

Net income (adjusted for intercompany profits)	$22,000
Preferred stock cash dividend	$2,000
Interest paid on convertible bonds	$3,000
Common stock shares outstanding	5,000
Warrants to purchase one share of common stock	1,000
Warrants held by parent	500
Convertible bonds outstanding (convertible into 10 shares of common stock)	200
Convertible bonds held by parent	180

$$\text{Subsidiary DEPS} = \frac{\$22,000 - \underset{(1)}{\$2,000} + \underset{(2)}{\$3,000}}{5,000 + \underset{(3)}{2,000} + \underset{(4)}{500}} = \$3.07$$

(1) Dividend on nonconvertible preferred stock, none of which is owned by the parent.
(2) Income adjustment for convertible bonds which are dilutive.
(3) Share adjustment associated with convertible debentures, 200 bonds × 10 shares per bond.
(4) Share adjustment (treasury stock method—see Chapter 13) associated with the warrants. It is assumed that, using the average fair value of the stock, 500 shares could be purchased with the proceeds of the sale and that 500 additional new shares would be issued.

Assume the parent owns 80% of the subsidiary and has an adjusted internally generated net income of $40,000 and 10,000 shares of common stock outstanding. Also assume the parent has dilutive bonds outstanding which are convertible into 3,000 shares of common stock and the interest paid on these bonds was $5,000. The consolidated DEPS would be computed as follows:

$$\text{Consolidated DEPS} = \frac{\$40{,}000 + \underset{(1)}{\$5{,}000} + \underset{(2)}{\$18{,}574}}{10{,}000 + \underset{(3)}{3{,}000}} = \$4.89$$

(1) Income adjustment from interest on parent company convertible bonds, which are dilutive.
(2) Subsidiary common shares owned by parent

Subsidiary common shares owned by parent (80% × 5,000)	4,000
Parent-owned equivalent shares applicable to convertible bonds (90% × 2,000)*	1,800
Parent-owned equivalent shares applicable to warrants (50% × 500)**	250
Total parent-owned equivalent shares	6,050
Parent's interest in subsidiary income (6,050 shares × $3.07 subsidiary DEPS)	$18,574

(3) Shares assumed to be issued in exchange for parent company convertible bonds (a CSE).

*Parent owns 180 (or 90%) of 200 subsidiary bonds.
**Parent owns 500 (or 50%) of 1,000 subsidiary warrants.

If the dilutive subsidiary securities enable the holder to acquire common stock of the parent, these securities are not included in the computation of subsidiary DEPS. However, these securities must be included in the parent's share adjustment in computing consolidated DEPS. The basic model by which to compute consolidated DEPS in this situation is as follows:

$$\text{Consolidated DEPS} = \frac{\begin{matrix}\text{Parent's adjusted} \\ \text{internally generated} \\ \text{net income}\end{matrix} + \begin{matrix}\text{Parent's income} \\ \text{adjustments}\end{matrix} + \left(\begin{matrix}\text{Parent-owned} \\ \text{equivalent shares}\end{matrix} \times \begin{matrix}\text{Subsidiary} \\ \text{DEPS}\end{matrix}\right) + \begin{matrix}\text{Income adjustment resulting} \\ \text{from subsidiary securities} \\ \text{that enable holder to} \\ \text{acquire parent stock}\end{matrix}}{\begin{matrix}\text{Parent's common} \\ \text{stock outstanding}\end{matrix} + \begin{matrix}\text{Parent's share} \\ \text{adjustments}\end{matrix}}$$

To illustrate, assume the following facts for a parent owning 90% of the outstanding subsidiary shares:

Parent internally adjusted net income	$20,000
Parent company common stock shares outstanding	10,000
Parent company dilutive convertible bonds:	
Interest expense	$1,000
Shares to be issued in conversion	2,000
Subsidiary adjusted net income	$7,000
Subsidiary common stock shares outstanding	4,000
Subsidiary preferred stock convertible into parent common stock:	
Dividend requirement	$1,200
Number of preferred shares	1,000
Number of parent company common shares required	2,000
Subsidiary common stock warrants to acquire 100 parent shares	100

The first step is to calculate the subsidiary's BEPS as follows:

$$\text{Subsidiary DEPS} = \frac{\$7,000 - \$1,200 \text{ preferred dividends}}{4,000 \text{ outstanding shares}} = \$1.45$$

Note that the subsidiary convertible preferred stock and stock warrants are not satisfied with subsidiary shares and, thus, are not considered converted for the purpose of calculating subsidiary EPS. The consolidated DEPS would be computed as follows:

$$\text{Consolidated DEPS} = \frac{\$20,000 + \overset{(1)}{\$1,000} + \overset{(2)}{[3,600 \times \$1.45]} + \overset{(3)}{\$1,200}}{10,000 + \underset{(4)}{(2,000 + 2,000 + 50)}} = \$1.95$$

(1) $1,000 income adjustment associated with the parent company convertible security.

(2) The parent's share of subsidiary EPS. Again, since the subsidiary's preferred stock and warrants are not convertible into subsidiary shares, the total parent-owned equivalent shares is 90% × 4,000.

(3) Income adjustment representing the dividend on subsidiary preferred shares that would not be paid if the shares were converted into common stock of the parent. Note that 100% of the adjustment is added back, even though the parent's interest in the subsidiary is less than 100%.

(4) The parent's share adjustment consisting of 2,000 shares traceable to the parent company convertible security; 2,000 shares traceable to the subsidiary preferred stock that is convertible into parent common stock; and 50 incremental shares traceable to the subsidiary warrants to acquire parent common stock. It is assumed that 50 of the 100 shares required to satisfy the warrants can be purchased with the proceeds of the exercise and 50 new shares must be issued.

Special analysis is required in computing consolidated BEPS and DEPS when an acquisition occurs during a reporting period. When the acquisition is a pooling of interests, the computations of both BEPS and DEPS include subsidiary income and securities for the entire period. However, when the acquisition is a purchase, only subsidiary income since the acquisition date is included, and the number of subsidiary shares is weighted for the partial period.

REFLECTION

- Prior to calculating consolidated EPS, the subsidiary's EPS (including dilution adjustments that add more subsidiary shares) is calculated.

- The parent's numerator for EPS includes its own internally generated net income plus its share of subsidiary EPS.
- The parent also adjusts its numerator and denominator for dilative parent company securities and subsidiary securities that are satisfied by issuing parent company shares.

TAXATION OF CONSOLIDATED COMPANIES

3

OBJECTIVE

Calculate and prepare a consolidated worksheet where the consolidated firm is an "affiliated group" and pays a single consolidated tax.

Consolidated companies that do not meet the requirements to be an *affiliated group*, as defined by the tax law, must pay their taxes as separate entities. The tax definition of an affiliated group is less inclusive than that used in accounting theory. Section 1504(a) of the Tax Code does not allow two or more corporations to file a consolidated return or to be considered an affiliated group for tax purposes unless the parent owns

1. 80% of the voting power of all classes of stock and
2. 80% of the fair market value of all the outstanding stock of the other corporation.

For these provisions, preferred stock is not included if it (a) is not entitled to vote, (b) is limited and preferred as to dividends, and (c) does not have redemption rights beyond its issue price plus a reasonable redemption or liquidation premium and is not convertible into the other class of stock. Comparison of these criteria with those required for consolidated financial reporting indicates that many consolidated companies have no choice but to submit to separate taxation of the member companies.

Consolidated companies that meet the tax law requirements to be an affiliated group may elect to be taxed as a single entity or as separate entities. Once the election is made to file as a single entity, the permission of the Internal Revenue Service is required before the companies can be taxed separately again. Companies that elect to be taxed as a single entity file a consolidated tax return which may provide several tax advantages. For example, a consolidated return generally permits the offset of operating profits and losses and of capital gains and losses. Also, intercompany profits are not taxed until realized in later periods.

When companies that comprise an affiliated group elect not to file a consolidated return, each company within the group computes and pays its taxes independently. In some cases, there could be advantages in doing so. The first is that the companies do not have to use the same fiscal period or the same accounting method if separate tax returns are filed. Secondly, there may be intercompany losses that could be deducted in separate returns but not in consolidated returns. This is, however, quite rare since most intercompany losses are not deductible even when preparing separate returns.

Members of consolidated groups, when filing separate returns, must sum their incomes when applying graduated corporate tax rates. The lower tax rates available for low income levels can be used only once and cannot be applied by each of the companies individually.

Consolidated Tax Return

When an affiliated group elects to be taxed as a single entity, consolidated income as determined on the worksheet is the basis for the tax calculation. The affiliated companies should not record a provision for income tax based on their own separate incomes. Rather, the income tax expense is calculated as part of the consolidated worksheet process. The tax provision is based on consolidated income; intercompany profits will have been eliminated already. Thus, no special procedures are needed to deal with intercompany transactions when computing the tax provision. Once calculated, the tax provision may be recorded on the books of the separate companies.

As an example of an affiliated group's choosing to be taxed as a single entity, assume Company P purchased an 80% interest in Company S on January 1, 20X1, at which time the following determination and distribution of excess schedule was prepared:

				Amortization Periods	Controlling Amortization
Price paid for investment		$795,000			
Less book value interest acquired:					
Common stock ($10 par)	$ 500,000				
Retained earnings	400,000				
Total stockholders' equity	$ 900,000				
Interest acquired	× 80%	$720,000			
Excess of cost over book value (debit)		75,000			
Patent		$ 75,000	Dr.	15	$5,000

The following income statements are for Companies P and S for 20X3. Since the companies desire to file a consolidated tax return, neither company has recorded a provision for income tax. The corporate tax rate is 30%.

	Company P	Company S
Sales	$600,000	$400,000
Less cost of goods sold	350,000	200,000
Gross profit	$250,000	$200,000
Less expenses:		
Depreciation expense	25,000	20,000
Other operating expenses	75,000	80,000
Operating income	$150,000	$100,000
Subsidiary income	80,000	
Income before tax	$230,000	$100,000

On January 1, 20X2, Company P sold a piece of equipment, with a book value of $40,000, to Company S for $60,000. The equipment is depreciated by Company S on a straight-line basis over a 5-year life.

The following applies to 20X3 intercompany merchandise sales to Company P by Company S:

Intercompany sales in beginning inventory of Company P	$50,000
Intercompany sales in ending inventory of Company P	$70,000
Sales to Company P during 20X3	$100,000
Gross profit rate	50%
A 30% tax rate applies to both companies.	

worksheet

Worksheet 6-1: page 360

Worksheet 6-1, pages 360 to 361, contains the trial balances of Companies P and S on December 31, 20X3. Since the income tax is to be calculated on the worksheet, no provision exists on the separate books. If separate provisions appear in the trial balances, they should be eliminated as an initial procedure in consolidating.

The balance of the investment in Company S account results from the use of the simple equity method. All eliminations should be made prior to calculating the provision for tax. This will assure that the consolidated income, upon which the provision is based, is adjusted for all intercompany transactions.

All worksheet entries, other than (T) are unchanged from procedures used in prior worksheets, and the same coding is used. In journal entry form, the entries are as follows:

		Debit	Credit
(CY1)	Eliminate current-year equity income:		
	Subsidiary Income	80,000	
	Investment in Company S		80,000

(EL)	Eliminate 80% of subsidiary equity:		
	Common Stock, Company S	400,000	
	Retained Earnings, Company S	560,000	
	Investment in Company S		960,000
(D)	Distribute excess to patent:		
	Patent	75,000	
	Investment in Company S		75,000
(A)	Amortize patent for two prior years and the current year:		
	Patent Amortization Expense	5,000	
	Retained Earnings—Company P	10,000	
	Patent		15,000
(F1)	Adjust retained earnings for fixed asset profit at start of year:		
	Retained Earnings—Company P	16,000	
	Accumulated Depreciation—Equipment	4,000	
	Equipment		20,000
(F2)	Adjust current-year depreciation for gain on fixed asset sale:		
	Accumulated Depreciation—Equipment	4,000	
	Depreciation Expense		4,000
(IS)	Eliminate intercompany merchandise sales:		
	Sales	100,000	
	Cost of Goods Sold		100,000
(BL)	Adjust January 1 retained earnings for inventory profit recorded by subsidiary:		
	Retained Earnings—Company S	5,000	
	Retained Earnings—Company P	20,000	
	Cost of Goods Sold		25,000
(EL)	Adjust cost of goods sold for profit in ending inventory:		
	Cost of Goods Sold	35,000	
	Inventory, December 31, 20X3		35,000

Consolidated net income before tax is calculated on the worksheet and becomes the base for the tax provision. Entry **(T)** is not entered until this calculation is made. In journal entry form, the entry is

Provision for Income Tax	**71,700**	
Income Tax Payable		**71,700**
Explanation:		
Consolidated income before tax (from the consolidated worksheet)		$ 239,000
Tax rate		× 30%
Tax provision and liability		$ 71,700

In this case, it was assumed that the purchase was a taxable exchange to the seller and that all asset adjustments, including the patent, are deductible. As indicated in Chapter 1, there are some combinations that are nontaxable exchanges and amortizations of excess are then not deductible.[1]

1 When there are nondeductible amortizations of excess cost, there also may be a recorded deferred tax liability. Recall that an excess of fair value over cost relative to an identifiable asset requires the recording of a deferred tax liability for the amount of the tax rate times the excess. This deferred tax liability would be amortized to tax expense in proportion to the amortization of the excess.

The distribution of excess purchase price to goodwill creates a tax timing difference. Goodwill is no longer amortized for financial reporting but still is amortized for tax purposes over a 15-year life. Each year the tax deduction taken for goodwill will result in a *deferred tax liability (DTL)*. The DTL will not be utilized until either the goodwill is impairment adjusted or the company purchased is later sold. For example, assume goodwill amortization is $5,000 per year for tax purposes, and the company has a 40% tax rate. Each year the following adjustment would be made on the consolidated worksheet and on the parent company books:

Income Tax Payable	2,000	
Deferred Tax Liability.		2,000
To defer tax equal to 40% of $5,000 goodwill amortization for tax purposes only.		

After 5 years, there would be a $10,000 DTL. If, at the end of 5 years, the goodwill is reduced $20,000 for an impairment loss, the following adjustments would be made on the consolidated worksheet and on the parent company books:

Goodwill Impairment Loss	20,000	
Goodwill		20,000
To record loss on impairment of goodwill.		
Deferred Tax Liability.	8,000	
Provision for Income Taxes		8,000
To reduce tax provision for realization of tax liability resulting from prior amortization of goodwill for tax purposes.		

The amortization of goodwill built a DTL that is consumed when the goodwill impairment loss is recorded. The DTL could also be removed if the company to which it relates was sold.

The final complexity caused by a consolidated return involves the distribution of consolidated income. In the schedules that accompany Worksheet 6-1, the income distributions start with internally generated income before taxes. All adjustments to the worksheet are entered before tax effects. This procedure results in an adjusted income before tax for each company.

The income tax expense of the member companies, then, is calculated. The IDS allocate the income tax expense and proceed to calculate each company's adjusted net income. The subsidiary adjusted net income is distributed to the controlling and noncontrolling interests according to ownership percentages. There is no further tax on the controlling share of subsidiary income.

It will be necessary for each member company to record its share of the tax provision on its own books. The subsidiary, Company S, would record the following:

Provision for Income Tax	27,000	
Income Tax Payable.		27,000
To record the allocated portion of the tax provision.		

The parent, Company P, would record the following:

Subsidiary Income (80% × $27,000 tax provision)	21,600	
Investment in Company S.		21,600
To adjust Subsidiary Income for the tax expense recorded by Company S.		
Provision for Income Tax	44,700	
Income Tax Payable.		44,700
To record the allocated portion of the tax provision.		

In review: Consolidated returns are consistent with consolidated reporting procedures and do not alter in any way the procedures that have been discussed in previous chapters. It is necessary to add only new procedures to the worksheet to provide for income taxes. The procedures were explained in our example assuming the use of the simple equity method. There would not be any impact on the tax entry if the cost or sophisticated equity method were used.

Separate Tax Returns

4

OBJECTIVE

Prepare a consolidated worksheet where the parent and subsidiary are separately taxed by employing tax allocation procedures.

When separate returns are required or are elected to be filed, each member of the consolidated group must base its provision for tax on its own reported income. For the parent, taxable income may include dividends received from other corporations. When the members of the consolidated company meet the requirements of an affiliated company (this requires at least an 80% ownership interest), 100% of the dividends received are excluded from reported income. For ownership interests of at least 20% but less than 80%, 80% of the dividends received are excluded from reported income.[2] For ownership interests less than 20%, 70% of the dividends received are excluded from reported income. The full or partial exclusion of dividends applies only to dividends from domestic corporations and is intended to reduce multiple taxation of the same income.

A major complication arises in consolidating. **The provision for tax recorded by each company is based on its reported separate net income prior to eliminating intercompany transactions.** That means that there are timing differences that are created when consolidating. For example, suppose that the parent sells inventory to the subsidiary at a price that includes a 25% gross profit. If $40,000 of intercompany sales remains in the subsidiary's ending inventory, consolidation procedures defer $10,000 of intercompany profit. The problem is that the parent already recorded a 30% or $3,000 tax provision on the profit as a separate company. This $3,000 now becomes a *deferred (prepaid) tax asset (DTA)* when the profit to which it attaches is deferred on the consolidated worksheet. In the following period, the intercompany profit on the inventory is realized (assuming the inventory is sold in that period). The deferred tax asset relative to the inventory profit is then expensed as part of the current year's provision for tax. The adjustments required as a result of these tax issues are examples of applying interperiod tax allocation procedures.

The use of separate tax returns for a consolidated group leads to a complicated application of interperiod tax allocation techniques. The calculations may become cumbersome when intercompany sales of plant assets and merchandise are involved. To illustrate, assume Company P purchased a 75% interest in Company S on January 1, 20X1, at which time the following determination and distribution of excess schedule was prepared:

				Amortization Periods	Controlling Amortization
Price paid for investment		$285,000			
Less book value interest acquired:					
Common stock ($10 par)	$ 250,000				
Retained earnings	100,000				
Total stockholders' equity	$ 350,000				
Interest acquired	× 75%	$262,500			
Excess of cost over book value (debit)		22,500			
Patent		$ 22,500	Dr.	15	$1,500

The patent amortization will not appear on the separate statements of the parent or the subsidiary. It will only arise in the consolidation process. Since it has not been included in the parent's determination of income, the parent has taken no tax deduction.

Further assume that on January 1, 20X2, the subsidiary sold equipment with a cost of $60,000 to the parent for $100,000. This means that the subsidiary has included the $40,000 gain in 20X2 income and has paid the tax on it. Meanwhile, the parent is depreciating the asset over 5 years on a straight-line basis. The parent is recording depreciation of $20,000 per year using a cost of $100,000. The parent's tax is computed using the $20,000 depreciation deduction.

2 The exclusion rate is determined by current tax law and is subject to change.

The parent sells merchandise to the subsidiary to realize a gross profit of 40%. The subsidiary had a beginning inventory of goods purchased from the parent for $60,000. The parent included this amount in 20X2 income and paid the taxes on it. Sales during the year to the subsidiary, by the parent, totaled $100,000. $40,000 of intercompany goods remain in the subsidiary's ending inventory. Again, the parent has included the profit in its income and paid taxes on it.

The separate income statement of the parent and the subsidiary for 20X3 are as follows:

	Company P	Company S
Sales (includes $100,000 intercompany for P)	$430,000	$240,000
Less cost of goods sold (includes $100,000 for intercompany sales)	280,000	150,000
Gross profit	$150,000	$ 90,000
Less expenses:		
Depreciation expense (Parent provision = $100,000/5)	20,000	10,000
Other operating expenses	50,000	20,000
Operating income	$ 80,000	$ 60,000

Taxation of Separate Entities. Before Companies P and S can be consolidated, it is necessary to calculate their separate tax liabilities since the 80% test of an affiliated group for tax purposes is not met. The tax provision of the subsidiary is $18,000 (30% × $60,000 Company S income before tax). Company S would record its tax provision as follows:

Provision for Income Tax	18,000	
Income Tax Payable		18,000

The tax provision for Company P requires consideration of the tax status of subsidiary income. When the conditions for an affiliated group are not met, the parent company must include in its taxable income 20% of the dividends it receives from a subsidiary. When an affiliated group *elects* separate taxation, no dividends are included and no additional tax needs to be calculated. According to APB Opinion No. 23, subsidiary income included in the pretax income of a parent leads to a temporary difference between the earning of the income and its inclusion in the tax return as dividend income.[3] It is not necessary to account for the temporary difference if the tax law provides a means by which the investment can be recovered tax free. Company P will provide for tax expense equal to its tax rate times 20% of its share of the total subsidiary net income. It is assumed that the parent records its tax provision based on the income it records from the subsidiary. In this example, the parent records the investment under the simple equity method. Thus, the tax accrual is based on 20% of the simple equity income without any reduction for amortization of excesses. A parent using the cost method would record the tax only on dividends received and would need to accrue tax on the worksheet based on the cost-to-equity conversion.

This tax may be viewed as a *secondary tax* since it is the second taxation of subsidiary income. For 20X4, this tax liability would be calculated as follows:

Subsidiary net income	$42,000
Controlling interest, 75% × $42,000	31,500
Provision for tax on subsidiary income, 30% × (20% × $31,500)	1,890

Company P would add this amount to the tax it has provided for its internally generated income to arrive at its total tax provision for the period:

3 Opinions of the Accounting Principles Board No. 23, *Accounting for Income Taxes—Special Areas* (New York: American Institute of Certified Public Accountants, 1971), pars. 9–12, as amended by Statement of Financial Accounting Standards No. 109, *Accounting for Income Taxes* (Stamford, CT: Financial Accounting Standards Board, 1992), Appendix D.

Tax on internally generated income, 30% × \$80,000	\$24,000
Secondary tax provision for subsidiary income	1,890
Total Company P provision for tax	\$25,890

Since Company P has not received its share of the income of Company S, the secondary tax is not immediately payable, and a deferred tax liability for \$1,890 is created. Assuming that the tax on internally generated income is currently payable, Company P would make the following entry to record its 20X4 tax provision:

Provision for Income Tax	25,890	
Income Tax Payable		24,000
Deferred Tax Liability		1,890

If dividends had been paid by the subsidiary, the secondary tax applicable to the dividends received by Company P would be included in the current tax liability. Note that the secondary tax applies only to consolidated companies that do not qualify as an affiliated group. Companies that do meet the requirements would calculate only a single tax on each company's adjusted net income.

Worksheet Procedures. Worksheet 6-2, pages 364 to 365 includes the trial balances of Companies P and S. The companies do not qualify as an affiliated group for tax purposes. **Several observations should be made regarding the amounts listed in the trial balance before you study the elimination entries.**

Worksheet 6-2: page 364

1. The balance in Investment in Company S is computed according to the simple equity method, as follows:

Original cost		\$285,000
Subsidiary income, 20X1–20X3 (*after tax*):		
Company S retained earnings, January 1, 20X4	\$350,000	
Company S retained earnings, January 1, 20X1	100,000	
Net increase	\$250,000	
Controlling interest	× 75%	187,500
Controlling interest in subsidiary net income, 20X4 (75% × \$42,000)		31,500
Equity-adjusted balance, December 31, 20X4		\$504,000

2. Since the parent's share of subsidiary undistributed income has been recorded from the date of acquisition, a deferred tax liability has been recorded by Company P each year to recognize the secondary tax provision. The total deferred tax liability on December 31, 20X4, is calculated as follows:

Deferred tax liability on 20X1–20X3 income (20% × 30% × \$187,500 20X1–20X3 undistributed income)	\$11,250
Current year's additional deferment (20% × 30% × \$31,500)	1,890
Total deferred tax liability	\$13,140

3. The trial balances of both companies include their separate provisions for income tax and the current tax liabilities. **These provisions do not reflect adjustments for intercompany transactions.**

All worksheet entries, other than (Tl) and (T2) are unchanged from procedures used in prior worksheets, and the same coding is used. In journal entry form, the entries for Worksheet 6-2 are as follows:

(CY1)	Eliminate current-year equity income:		
	Subsidiary Income	31,500	
	Investment in Company S		31,500
(EL)	Eliminate 75% of subsidiary equity:		
	Common Stock, Company S	187,500	
	Retained Earnings, Company S	262,500	
	Investment in Company S		450,000
(D)	Distribute excess to patent:		
	Patent	22,500	
	Investment in Company S		22,500
(A)	Amortize patent for three prior years and the current year:		
	Patent Amortization Expense	1,500	
	Retained Earnings—Company P	4,500	
	Patent		6,000
(F1)	Adjust retained earnings for fixed asset profit at start of year:		
	Retained Earnings—Company P	24,000	
	Retained Earnings—Company S	8,000	
	Accumulated Depreciation—Equipment	8,000	
	Equipment		40,000
(F2)	Adjust current-year depreciation for gain on fixed asset sale:		
	Accumulated Depreciation—Equipment	8,000	
	Depreciation Expense		8,000
(IS)	Eliminate intercompany merchandise sales:		
	Sales	100,000	
	Cost of Goods Sold		100,000
(BI)	Adjust January 1 retained earnings for inventory profit recorded by parent:		
	Retained Earnings—Company P	24,000	
	Cost of Goods Sold		24,000
(EI)	Adjust cost of goods sold for profit in ending inventory:		
	Cost of Goods Sold	16,000	
	Inventory, December 31, 20X3		16,000
(T1)	Record deferred tax asset applicable to prior adjustments:		
	Deferred Tax Asset	19,158	
	Retained Earnings—Company S		2,400
	Retained Earnings—Company P		16,758
(T2)	Record change in deferred tax asset during current period:		
	Provision for Income Tax	4,602	
	Deferred Tax Asset		4,602

Worksheet entries (T1) and (T2) are explained in the directions that accompany the worksheet, but let us expand on them. Entry (T1) takes the position that both companies have already paid a tax on the income recorded by the companies in prior periods. If consolidation procedures change the income, for example reduce income, then the taxes are considered to have been paid in advance and the taxes paid become a deferred tax asset.

The adjustment to beginning retained earnings for taxes paid in prior periods, entry (Tl), is explained as follows:

		Total Tax	75% Parent Portion	25% NCI Portion
Subsidiary transactions:				
Remaining fixed asset profit ($40,000 on January 1, 20X2 – $8,000 realized in 20X3)	$32,000			
Tax paid on deferred profit on January 1, 20X3 (30% × $32,000)		$ 9,600	$ 7,200	$2,400
Second tax paid by parent as of January 1, 20X3 [20% included × 30% rate × 75% ownership interest × ($32,000 – $9,600 tax paid by subsidiary)]		1,008	1,008	
Parent transactions:				
Beginning inventory profit recorded last year	$24,000			
Patent amortizations prior to 20X3, 3 years × $1,500	4,500			
Total reduction in parent beginning retained earnings	$28,500			
First tax (30% × $28,500) paid prior to 20X3		8,550	8,550	
Total increase in retained earnings and DTA		$19,158	$16,758	$2,400

This means that income of prior periods has been reduced by $60,500 ($32,000 + $28,500) and the taxes already paid on these reductions are $19,158. These tax payments now create a deferred tax asset that will be consumed in future periods.

Entry (T2) considers the tax effects of adjustments made to the current year income. Let us consider an expanded version of the explanation to entry (T2) in the explanations to the worksheet.

		Total Tax	75% Parent Portion	25% NCI Portion
Subsidiary transactions:				
Fixed asset profit realized through added depreciation recorded by parent	$ (8,000)			
First tax [(30% × ($8,000)]		$(2,400)	$(1,800)	$(600)
Second tax [20% included × 30% rate × 75% ownership interest × ($8,000 – $2,400 first tax)]		(252)	(252)	
Parent transactions:				
Beginning inventory profit realized in 20X3	$(24,000)			
Ending inventory deferred to 20X4	16,000			
Patent amortization for 20X3	1,500			
Total increase in income	$ (6,500)			
First tax (30% × $6,500)		(1,950)	(1,950)	
Increase (decrease) in DTA		$(4,602)	$(4,002)	$(600)

When the entries in Worksheet 6-2 are completed, the resulting consolidated net income is $106,008, which is distributed to the controlling and noncontrolling interests. Since the firms are taxed separately, goodwill that results from a purchase has not been acknowledged for tax purposes and, thus, does not create a tax deduction for goodwill amortization and a resulting DTL as it did in the case of taxation of the consolidated company.

Let us revisit Worksheet 6-2 to discuss how it would be simplified if the consolidated company met the requirements of an affiliated company. The following procedures would be omitted from the worksheet:

1. Company P would not have recorded the deferred tax liability of $13,140 on its books. If the companies are an affiliated group, there is no tax due on the parent's share of subsidiary income. The parent's current-year provision for income tax would be only $24,000 since there would not be the secondary tax of $1,890 on the parent's share of subsidiary income.
2. Entry (Tl) would not include the secondary tax of $1,008 applicable to the intercompany equipment sale.
3. Entry (T2) would not include the secondary tax of $252 applicable to the intercompany equipment sale.
4. The parent's income distribution schedule would not deduct the secondary tax on the parent's share of subsidiary income. Instead, the parent would just include 75% of the subsidiary's after-tax income of $47,600, or $35,700.

There are some additional minor worksheet modifications required if the cost or sophisticated equity methods are used by the parent company. If the cost method is used, there needs to be a recording of the deferred tax liability for prior years' subsidiary income. The adjustment would be to multiply the net amount of the cost-to-equity conversion adjustment by the effective tax rate, to debit the parent's retained earnings, and to credit a deferred tax liability account. If the sophisticated equity method is used, the parent company's retained earnings and current-year tax provision are correct and need no adjustment. The only entry needed in consolidating is to adjust the beginning retained earnings of the subsidiary for any intercompany profits on a net-of-tax basis. The adjustment of subsidiary retained earnings on the consolidated worksheet was covered in the partial worksheet on pages 225 and 226. It still would be necessary to calculate the noncontrolling and controlling interests in combined net income on an after-tax basis when preparing the income distribution schedules. (Note that each income distribution schedule starts with net income *before* tax. This is done so that the tax provision may be recalculated on a consolidated basis.)

REFLECTION

- An "affiliated group" (under tax law) may prepare a consolidated tax return. The tax provision is computed based on the consolidated income computed on the worksheet. The provision is then allocated to the controlling and noncontrolling interests.
- When a consolidated company is subject to separate taxation, each firm has recorded its tax provision based on its own reported income. Taxes have already been paid on intercompany profits. The parent has paid the double tax on its share of subsidiary income.
- A worksheet prepared under separate taxation requires procedures for the adjustment of the separate taxes already present. The taxes applicable to intercompany gains, which are eliminated, become a deferred tax asset. Amortizations of excess (not deductible on separate tax returns) create additional deferred tax assets.
- As intercompany profits are realized through sale to the "outside world" or through amortization, the deferred tax asset is realized as an increase in the provision for taxes.

EQUITY METHOD FOR UNCONSOLIDATED INVESTMENTS

5
OBJECTIVE

Apply consolidation-type procedures to influential investments.

Prior to the 1971 issuance of APB Opinion No. 18, "The Equity Method of Accounting for Investments in Common Stock," investors could freely choose between the equity and cost methods to recognize income on their investments. When the equity method was used, it tended to be a simple equity method that recognized only a pro rata share of the investee's income without any attempt to amortize an excess of cost or book value on the investment or to defer intercompany gains and losses. The choice between these two divergent methods is not significant when consolidation is required since the investment and investment income accounts are eliminated in the consolidation process. However, the accounting profession did become concerned with the use of the cost method for major investments not subject to consolidation. The APB reasoned that, in such cases, the investor may have significant influence over the investee's dividend policy and the payment of dividends often would be unrelated to the investee's income during a given period. For example, dividend payments would be level over a period of years during which income varied significantly. This reasoning led the APB to state the following:

> *The equity method tends to be most appropriate if an investment enables the investor to influence the operating or financial decisions of the investee. The investor then has a degree of responsibility for the return on its investment, and it is appropriate to include in the results of operations of the investor its share of earnings or losses of the investee. Influence tends to be more effective as the investor's percent of ownership in the voting stock of the investee increases. Investments of relatively small percentages of voting stock of an investee tend to be passive in nature and enable the investor to have little or no influence on the operations of the investee.*[4]

APB Opinion No. 18 requires the use of the sophisticated equity method for the following types of investments

1. ***Influential investments.*** The APB defines influence as "representation on the board of directors, participation in policy-making processes, material intercompany transactions, interchange of managerial personnel, or technological dependency."[5] When the investor holds 20% or more of the voting shares of an investee, influence is assumed and the sophisticated equity method is required unless the investor takes on the burden of proof to show that influence does not exist, in which case the cost method would be used.[6] When the investment falls below 20%, the presumption is that influence does not exist, and the cost method is to be used unless the investor can show that influence does exist despite the low percentage of ownership. Since the most common use of the sophisticated equity method is for influential (20% to 50%) investments, such investments are used in subsequent illustrations.
2. ***Corporate joint ventures.*** A corporate joint venture is a separate, specific project organized for the benefit of several corporations. An example would be a research project undertaken jointly by several members of a given industry. The member corporations typically participate in the management of the venture and share the gains and losses. Since such an arrangement does not involve passive investors, the sophisticated equity method is required.
3. ***Unconsolidated subsidiaries.*** A parent may own over 50% of the shares of a subsidiary but may meet one of the exceptions (control is temporary or does not rest with the majority

4 Opinions of the Accounting Principles Board No. 18, *The Equity Method of Accounting for Investments in Common Stock* (New York: American Institute of Certified Public Accountants, 1971), par. 12.
5 *Ibid.*, par. 17.
6 For examples of situations that may overcome the presumption of influence, see FASB Interpretation No. 35, *Criteria for Applying the Equity Method of Accounting for Investments in Common Stock* (Stamford: Financial Accounting Standards Board, 1981).

owner) to the requirement that subsidiaries be consolidated. However, if influence does exist, the sophisticated equity method would be used for the investment.

As defined by APB Opinion No. 18, the use of the equity method requires that the investment in common stock appear as a single, equity-adjusted amount on the balance sheet of the investor. The investor's income statement will include the investor's share of the investee ordinary income as a single amount in the ordinary income section. The investor's share of investee discontinued operations, extraordinary items, and cumulative effects of changes in accounting principles will appear as single amounts in the sections of the investor's income statement that correspond to the placement of these items in the investee's statement.

Calculation of Equity Income

In its basic form, the equity method requires the investor to recognize its pro rata share of investee reported income. Dividends, when received, do not constitute income, but are viewed instead as a partial liquidation of the investment. In reality, however, the price paid for the investment usually will not agree with the underlying book value of the investee, which requires that any amortization of an excess of cost or book value be treated as an adjustment of the investor's pro rata share of investee income. It is very likely that the reported income of the investee will include gains and losses on transactions with the investor. As was true in consolidations, these gains and losses cannot be recognized until they are confirmed by a transaction between the affiliated group and unrelated parties. The proper application of the sophisticated equity method will mean that the income recognized by the investor will be the same as it would be under consolidation procedures. In fact, the sophisticated equity method sometimes is referred to as "one-line consolidation."

In the next two sections, the sophisticated equity method will be presented without consideration of the tax implications. Following that, the tax effect on such an investment will be addressed.

Amortization of Excesses. A determination and distribution of excess schedule is prepared for a sophisticated equity method investment just as it would be if the investment were to be consolidated. For example, assume the following schedule was prepared by Excel Corporation for a 25% interest in Flag Company acquired on January 1, 20X1:

Price paid		$250,000
Less interest acquired:		
Common stock ($10 par)	$ 200,000	
Retained earnings, January 1, 20X1	600,000	
Total stockholders' equity	$ 800,000	
Interest acquired	× 25%	200,000
Excess of cost over book value		$ 50,000
Less excess attributable to equipment with a 5-year remaining life and undervalued by $80,000, 25% × $80,000		20,000
Goodwill (not amortized)		$ 30,000

As a practical matter, APB Opinion No. 18 states that it may not be possible to relate the excess to specific assets, in which case the entire excess may be considered goodwill. However, an attempt should be made to allocate the excess in the same manner as would be done for the purchase of a controlling interest in a subsidiary.

The determination and distribution of excess schedule indicates the pattern of amortization to be followed. The required amortizations must be made directly through the investment account since the distributions shown on the schedule are not recorded in the absence of consolidation procedures. The debit and credit indicators have been dropped from the determination and distribution of excess schedule since there will not be any worksheet adjustments in the absence of consolidation. Assuming Flag Company reported net income of $60,000 for 20X1, Excel Corporation would make the following entry for 20X1:

Investment in Flag Company	11,000	
Investment Income		11,000

Income is calculated as follows:

25% × Flag reported net income of $60,000	$15,000
Less amortizations of excess cost:	
Equipment, $20,000 ÷ 5	4,000
Investment income, net of amortizations	$11,000

If an investment is acquired for less than book value, the excess of book value over cost would be amortized based on the life of assets to which it pertains. This procedure would increase investment income in the years of amortization.

Intercompany Transactions by Investee. The investee may sell inventory to the investor. As would be true if the investment were consolidated, the share of the investee's profit on goods still held by the investor at the end of a period cannot be included in income of that period. Instead, the profit must be deferred until the goods are sold by the investor. Since the two firms are separate reporting entities, the intercompany sales and related debt cannot be eliminated. Only the investor's share of the investee's profit on unsold goods in the hands of the investor is deferred. In a like manner, the investor may have plant assets that were purchased from the investee. The investor's share of the investee's gains and losses on these sales also must be deferred and allocated over the depreciable life of the asset. Profit deferments should be handled in an income distribution schedule similar to that used for consolidated worksheets. To illustrate, assume the following facts for the example of the 25% investment in Flag by Excel. Again, note that income tax is not being considered in this illustration:

1. Excel had the following merchandise acquired from Flag Company in its ending inventories:

Year	Amount	Gross Profit of Flag Company
20X1	$30,000	40%
20X2	40,000	45

2. Excel purchased a truck from Flag Company on January 1, 20X1, for $20,000. The truck is being depreciated over a 4-year life on a straight-line basis with no salvage value. The truck had a net book value of $16,000 when it was sold by Flag.
3. Flag Company had an income of $60,000 in 20X1 and $70,000 in 20X2.
4. Flag declared and paid $10,000 in dividends in 20X2.

Based on these facts, Excel Corporation would prepare the following income distribution schedules:

20X1 Income Distribution for Investment in Flag Company

Gain on sale of truck, to be amortized over 4 years	$ 4,000	Reported income of Flag Company	$60,000
Profit in Excel ending inventory, 40% × $30,000	12,000	Realization of ¼ of profit on sale of truck	1,000
		Adjusted income of Flag Company	$45,000
		Ownership interest, 25%	$11,250
		Less amortization of excess cost:	
		Equipment	4,000
		Investment income, net of amortizations	$ 7,250

20X2 Income Distribution for Investment in Flag Company

Profit in Excel ending inventory, 45% × $40,000	$18,000	Reported income of Flag Company	$70,000
		Profit in Excel beginning inventory, 40% × $30,000	12,000
		Realization of ¼ of profit on sale of truck	1,000
		Adjusted income of Flag Company	$65,000
		Ownership interest, 25%	$16,250
		Less amortization of excess cost: Equipment	4,000
		Income from investment	$12,250

The schedules would lead to the following entries to record investment income:

20X1	Investment in Flag Company	7,250	
	Investment Income		7,250
20X2	Investment in Flag Company	12,250	
	Investment Income		12,250

In addition, the following entry would be made in 20X2 to record dividends received:

Cash	2,500	
Investment in Flag Company		2,500

It should be noted that only the investor's share of intercompany gains and losses is deferred. The investee's remaining stockholders are not affected by the Excel Corporation investment.

Tax Effects of Equity Method

The investor not meeting the requirements of affiliation as defined by tax law pays income taxes on dividends received. In the case of a domestic corporation, 20% of the dividends are includable in taxable income. However, a temporary difference is created through the use of the equity method for financial reporting.[7] As a result, **the provision for tax must be based on the equity income, and a deferred tax liability must be created for undistributed investment income.** The provision may be based on the assumption that investment income will be distributed in dividends, or it will be realized via the sale of the investment. In the latter case, it is likely that the income would be taxed in the form of a capital gain. The assumption used will determine the rate to be applied to the undistributed income. The provision for tax is based on the investor's net investment income after adjustments and amortizations. However, **amortizations of excess cost are not deductible** since they have no impact on the income that could be distributed to the investor and, thus, must be added back to the net investment income to compute the tax.

The following entries are based on the previous example of Flag Company and Excel Corporation, but it is assumed that each company is subject to a 30% income tax. Excel Corporation's share of Flag Company *net* income would now be calculated as follows:

	20X1	20X2
Adjusted income of Flag Company, before tax*	$45,000	$65,000
Tax provision (30%)	13,500	19,500
Adjusted net income of Flag Company	$31,500	$45,500

(continued)

7 Opinions of the Accounting Principles Board No. 24, *Accounting for Income Taxes—Investments in Common Stock Accounted for by the Equity Method (Other than Subsidiaries and Corporate Joint Ventures)* (New York: American Institute of Certified Public Accountants, 1972), par. 7.

	20X1	20X2
Ownership interest in adjusted net income (25%)	$ 7,875	$11,375
Less amortizations of excess*	4,000	4,000
Net income from investment	$ 3,875	$ 7,375

*See the income distribution schedules in the previous section.

Note that the tax provision calculated by the investor will not agree with the provision for tax on the books of the investee. This is due to the adjustments made in the income distribution schedules to recognize the profit deferrals.

The 20X1 and 20X2 entries to record investment income and the applicable tax provision would be as follows:

20X1	Investment in Flag Company	3,875	
	Investment Income		3,875
	Provision for Income Tax [20% included × 30% tax rate × ($3,875 net income + $4,000 nondeductible amortizations of excess)]	473	
	Deferred Tax Liability		473
20X2	Investment in Flag Company	7,375	
	Investment Income		7,375
	Cash	2,500	
	Investment in Flag Company		2,500
	Provision for Income Tax [20% included × 30% tax rate × ($7,375 net income + $4,000 nondeductible amortizations of excess)]	683	
	Income Tax Payable (20% included × 30% tax rate × $2,500 dividends)		150
	Deferred Tax Liability ($683 − $150)		533

Unusual Equity Adjustments

There are several unusual situations involving the investee that require special procedures for the proper recording of investment income. These situations are described in the following paragraphs.

Investee with Preferred Stock. In the absence of consolidation, an investment in preferred stock does not require elimination. However, the existence of preferred stock in the capital structure of the investee requires that the investor's equity adjustment be based on only that portion of investee income available for common stockholders. Dividends declared on preferred stock must be subtracted from income of the investee. When the preferred stock has cumulative or participation rights, the claim of preferred stockholders must be subtracted from the investee income each period to arrive at the income available for common stockholders. The procedures for calculating this income are contained in Chapter 7.

Investee Stock Transactions. The investee corporation may engage in transactions with its common stockholders, such as issuing additional shares, retiring shares, or engaging in treasury stock transactions. Each of these transactions affects the investor's equity interest. A comparison is made of the investor's ownership interest before and after the investee stock transaction. An increase in the investor's interest is treated as a gain, while a decrease is recorded as a loss.

Write-Down to Market Value. The investment in another company is subject to reduction to a lower market value if it appears that a relatively permanent fall in value has occurred. The fact that the current market value of the shares is temporarily less than the equity-adjusted cost of the shares is not sufficient cause for a write-down. When the sophisticated equity method is used and a permanent decline in value occurs, a reduction would be made to the equity-adjusted cost. The equity method would continue to be applied subsequent to the write-down. There can be no subsequent write-ups, however, other than through normal equity adjustments.

Zero Investment Balance. It is possible that an investee will suffer losses to the extent that the continued application of the equity method could produce a negative balance in the investment account. Equity adjustments are to be discontinued when the investment balance becomes zero.[8] Further losses are acknowledged only by memo entries, which are needed to maintain the total unrecorded share of losses. If the investee again becomes profitable, the investor must not record income on the investment until its subsequent share of income equals the previously unrecorded share of losses.

To illustrate these procedures, assume Grate Corporation has a 35% investment in Dittmar Company, with a sophisticated equity-adjusted cost of $30,000 on January 1, 20X1, and Dittmar reports the following results:

Period	Income (loss)
20X1	$(80,000)
20X2	(50,000)
20X3	(20,000)
20X4	90,000

The following T-account summarizes entries for 20X1 through 20X4 (taxes are ignored):

Investment in Dittmar Company

Equity-adjusted balance, January 1, 20X1	$30,000	Equity loss for 20X1, 35% × $80,000 Dittmar loss	$28,000
		Recorded equity loss for 20X2, 35% × $50,000 Dittmar loss = $17,500; loss limited to investment balance	2,000
Balance, January 1, 20X2	$ 0	Memo entries:	
		Unrecorded 20X2 loss, $17,500 − $2,000	$15,500
Memo entry: Unrecorded share of 20X4 Dittmar income	22,500	Unrecorded loss for 20X3, 35% × $20,000 Dittmar loss	7,000
Actual entries resumed: Recorded equity income, 20X4, 35% × $90,000 Dittmar income, less amount to cover unrecorded losses ($15,500 + $7,000)	$ 9,000		
Balance, December 31, 20X4	$ 9,000		

Intercompany Transactions by Investor. An investor may sell merchandise and/or plant assets to an investee at a gain or loss. When influence is deemed to exist, it might seem appropriate to defer the entire gain or loss until the asset is resold or depreciated by the investee. However, an interpretation of APB Opinion No. 18 requires the entire gain or loss to be deferred only when the transaction is with a controlled (over 50%-owned) investee and is not at arm's length. In all other cases, it is appropriate to defer only a gain or loss that is in proportion to the investor's ownership interest.[9]

To illustrate, assume Grant Corporation, which owns a 35% interest in Hartwig Company, sold $50,000 of merchandise to Hartwig at a gross profit of 40%. Of this merchandise, $20,000 is still in Hartwig's 20X1 ending inventory. Grant needs to defer only profit equal to the $8,000 (40% × $20,000) unrealized gross profit multiplied by its 35% interest, or $2,800. Grant would make the following entry on December 31, 20X1:

8 According to APB Opinion No. 18 (par. 19i), any net advance to the investee that the investor may have on its books also is available to offset the investor's share of investee losses until the receivable is reduced to a zero balance.

9 Accounting Interpretations, *The Equity Method of Accounting for Investments in Common Stock: Accounting Interpretations of APB Opinion No. 18* (New York: American Institute of Certified Public Accountants, 1971), par. 1.

Sales	2,800	
Deferred Gross Profit on Sales to Investee		2,800

Assuming the investor recorded the provision for income tax prior to this adjustment, the tax applicable to the unrealized gain would be deferred by the following entry, which is based on a 30% tax rate:

Deferred Tax Expense (30% × $2,800)	840	
Provision for Income Tax		840

The deferred gross profit and the related tax deferment would be realized in the period in which the goods are sold to outside parties. The deferred profit and related tax effects on plant asset sales would be realized in proportion to the depreciation recorded by the investee company.

It may occur that the investor will purchase outstanding bonds of the investee. Unlike consolidation procedures, the bonds are not assumed to be retired since the investor and investee are separate reporting entities. Similarly, a purchase of investor bonds by the investee is not a retirement of the bonds. Thus, no adjustments to income are necessary as a result of intercompany bondholdings.

Gain or Loss of Influence. An investor may own less than a 20% interest in an investee, in which case the cost method ordinarily would be used to record investment income. If the investor subsequently buys sufficient additional shares to have its total interest equal or exceed 20%, the investor must retroactively apply the sophisticated equity method to the total holding period of the investment. APB Opinion No. 18 requires an adjustment of retained earnings for the period prior to the time the 20% interest is achieved.

It is possible that an investor will own 20% or more of the voting shares of the investee but will sell a portion of the shares so that the ownership interest falls below 20%. In such a case, the sophisticated equity method is discontinued as of the sale date. However, there is no adjustment back to the cost method. The balance of the investment account remains at its equity-adjusted balance on the sale date. Should influence be attained again, a retroactive ("catch-up") equity adjustment would be made.

When all or part of an investment recorded under the sophisticated equity method is sold, the gain or loss is based on the equity-adjusted balance as of the sale date. An adjustment also would be necessary for deferred tax balances applicable to the investment.

Disclosure Requirements

Since a significant portion of the investor's income may be derived from investments, added disclosures are required in order to properly inform the readers of the financial statements. For investments of 20% or more, the investor must disclose the name of each investee, the percentage of ownership in each investee, and the disparity between the cost and underlying book value for each investment. If the sophisticated equity method is not being applied, the reasons must be given. When investments are material with respect to the investor's financial position or income, the financial statements of the investees should be included as supplemental information.

When a market value for the investment is available, it should be disclosed. However, if the investor owns a relatively large block of a subsidiary's shares, quoted market values would have little relevance because the sale of an entire controlling interest would involve different motivations and would result in a unique value.

REFLECTION

- The sophisticated equity method is used for "influential" investments.
- The sophisticated equity income is based on the investee's adjusted (for intercompany profits) income less amortizations of excess from the D&D. Note that this process includes adjustment for only investee-generated intercompany transactions.

- The investor is liable for a "second tax" on its share of investee income.
- The investor must make a separate adjustment for its share of unrealized profits on sales to the investee. These adjustments also create a deferred tax asset.
- The investor cannot adjust its investment below a zero balance by recording its share of investee losses. If the investee becomes profitable, income equal to the unrecorded losses must be excluded from income.
- An initial ownership interest may not be "influential." If a second block is purchased, so as to make the total interest "influential," the prior block is retroactively converted to the sophisticated equity method.
- If an interest is sold down to a level that is no longer influential, the remaining interest stays at its equity-adjusted cost. The use of the equity method is discontinued in future periods.

UNDERSTANDING THE ISSUES

1. P Company acquired 100% of the common stock of the S Company for an agreed-upon price of $800,000. The book value of the net assets is $600,000, which includes $50,000 of subsidiary cash equivalents. How will this transaction affect the cash flow statement of the consolidated firm in the period of the purchase, if:
   a. P Company pays $800,000 cash to purchase the stock?
   b. P Company pays $500,000 cash and signs 5-year notes for $300,000? All Company S shareholders receive notes.
   c. P Company exchanges only common stock with the shareholders of Company S?
2. What will be the effect of the above purchase on cash flow statements prepared in periods after the year of the purchase?
3. (Issue 1 with a noncontrolling interest.) P Company acquired 80% of the common stock of the S Company for an agreed-upon price of $640,000. The book value of the net assets is $600,000, which includes $50,000 of subsidiary cash equivalents. How will this transaction affect the cash flow statement of the consolidated firm in the period of the purchase, if:
   a. P Company pays $640,000 cash to purchase the stock?
   b. P Company pays $400,000 cash and signs 5-year notes for $240,000? 80% of the Company S shareholders receive notes.
   c. P Company exchanges only common stock with the 80% of the shareholders of Company S?
4. Company P had internally generated net income of $200,000 (excludes share of subsidiary income). Company P has 100,000 shares of outstanding common stock. Subsidiary Company S has a net income of $60,000 and 40,000 shares of outstanding common stock. What is consolidated basic EPS, if:
   a. Company P owns 100% of the Company S shares?
   b. Company P owns 80% of the Company S shares?
5. Company P had internally generated net income of $200,000 (excludes share of subsidiary income). Company P has 100,000 shares of outstanding common stock. Subsidiary Company S has a net income of $60,000 and 40,000 shares of outstanding common stock. Company P owns 100% of the Company S shares. What is consolidated diluted EPS, if:
   a. Company S has outstanding stock options for Company S shares, which cause a dilutive effect of 2,000 additional shares of Company S shares?
   b. Company S has outstanding stock options for Company P shares, which cause a dilutive effect of 2,000 additional shares of Company P shares?

c. Company P has outstanding stock options for Company P shares, which cause a dilutive effect of 2,000 additional shares of Company P shares?

6. Company S is an 80%-owned subsidiary of Company P. For 20X1, Company P reports internally generated income before tax of $100,000. Company S reports an income before tax of $40,000. A 30% tax rate applies to both companies. Calculate consolidated net income (after taxes) and the distribution of income to the controlling and noncontrolling interests, if:

   a. The consolidated firm meets the requirements of an affiliated firm and files a consolidated tax return.
   b. The consolidated firm does not meet the requirements of an affiliated firm and files separate tax returns. Assume an 80% dividend exclusion rate.

7. Company S is an 80%-owned subsidiary of Company P. On January 1, 20X1, Company P sold equipment to Company S at a $50,000 profit. Assume a 30% corporate tax rate and an 80% dividend exclusion. The equipment has a 5-year life. The question is, would taxes have been paid on this profit and what adjustments (if needed) for the tax would be made, if:

   a. Company P and S are an "affiliated firm" and file a consolidated tax return?
   b. Company P and S are not an "affiliated firm" and file separate tax returns?

8. Company R paid $200,000 for a 30% interest in Company E on January 1, 20X1. Company E's total stockholders' equity on that date was $500,000. The excess price was attributed to equipment with a 10-year life. During 20X1, Company E reported net income of $40,000 and paid total dividends of $10,000. Calculate:

   a. Company R's investment income for 20X1.
   b. Company R's investment balance on December 31, 20X1.
   c. Explain in words the investment balance on December 31, 20X1.

9. Company R owns a 30% interest in Company E, which it acquired at book value. Company E reported net income of $50,000 for 20X1 (ignore taxes). There was an intercompany sale of equipment at a gain of $20,000 on January 1, 20X1. The equipment has a 5-year life. What is Company R's investment income for 20X1 and what adjusting entry (if any) does Company R need to make as a result of the equipment sale, if:

   a. Company E made the sale?
   b. Company R made the sale?

10. Company E reported net income of $100,000 for 20X1. Assume the income was earned evenly throughout the year. Dividends of $10,000 were paid on December 31. What will Company R report as investment income under the following ownership situations, if:

    a. Company R owned a 10% interest from 7/1 to 12/31?
    b. Company R owned a 10% interest from 1/1 to 6/30 and a 25% interest from 7/1 to 12/31?
    c. Company R owned a 30% interest from 1/1 to 6/30 and a 10% interest from 7/1 to 12/31?

11. Company R purchased a 25% interest in Company E on January 1, 1995, at its book value of $20,000. From 1995 until 1999, Company E earned a total of $200,000. From 2000 until 2004, it lost $300,000. In 20X5, Company E reported net income of $30,000. What is Company R's investment income for 20X5, and what is its balance in the investment in Company E account on December 31, 20X5?

Worksheet 6-1

Affiliates File Consolidated Income Tax Return
Company P and Subsidiary Company S
Worksheet for Consolidated Financial Statements
For Year Ended December 31, 20X3

	(Credit balance amounts are in parentheses.)	Trial Balance	
		Company P	Company S
1	Cash	205,000	380,000
2	Inventory	150,000	120,000
3	Investment in Company S	1,115,000	
4			
5			
6	Plant and Equipment	900,000	1,100,000
7	Accumulated Depreciation	(440,000)	(150,000)
8			
9	Patent		
10	Liabilities		(150,000)
11	Common Stock, Company S		(500,000)
12	Retained Earnings, January 1, 20X3, Company S		(700,000)
13			
14	Common Stock, Company P	(800,000)	
15	Retained Earnings, January 1, 20X3, Company P	(900,000)	
16			
17			
18	Sales	(600,000)	(400,000)
19	Cost of Goods Sold	350,000	200,000
20			
21	Depreciation Expense	25,000	20,000
22	Other Expenses	75,000	80,000
23	Patent Amortization Expense		
24	Subsidiary Income	(80,000)	
25	Total	0	0
26	**Consolidated Income Before Tax**		
27	**Consolidated Tax Provision**		
28	**Income Tax Payable**		
29	Consolidated Net Income		
30	NCI Share		
31	Controlling Share		
32	NCI		
33	Controlling Retained Earnings		
34	Total		

Worksheet 6-1 (see page 342)

Eliminations & Adjustments Dr.	Eliminations & Adjustments Cr.	Consolidated Income Statement	NCI	Controlling Retained Earnings	Consolidated Balance Sheet	
					585,000	1
	(EI) 35,000				235,000	2
	(CY1) 80,000					3
	(EL) 960,000					4
	(D) 75,000					5
(D)	(F1) 20,000				1,980,000	6
(F1) 4,000						7
(F2) 4,000					(582,000)	8
(D) 75,000	(A) 15,000				60,000	9
					(150,000)	10
(EL) 400,000			(100,000)			11
(EL) 560,000						12
(BI) 5,000			(135,000)			13
					(800,000)	14
(A) 10,000						15
(BI) 20,000						16
(F1) 16,000				(854,000)		17
(IS) 100,000		(900,000)				18
	(IS) 100,000					19
(EI) 35,000	(BI) 25,000	460,000				20
	(F2) 4,000	41,000				21
		155,000				22
(A) 5,000		5,000				23
(CY1) 80,000						24
1,314,000	1,314,000					25
		(239,000)				26
(T) 71,700		71,700				27
	(T) 71,700				(71,700)	28
		(167,300)				29
		12,600	(12,600)			30
		154,700		(154,700)		31
			(247,600)		(247,600)	32
				(1,008,700)	(1,008,700)	33
1,385,700	1,385,700				0	34

Eliminations and Adjustments:

(CY1) Eliminate the parent's entry recording its share of the current year's subsidiary income. This step returns the investment account to its balance on January 1, 20X3.

(EL) Eliminate 80% of the January 1, 20X3, subsidiary equity balances against the investment in Company S.

(D) Distribute the $75,000 excess of cost to the patent account.

(A) Amortize the patent at an annual amount of $5,000 for each of the past two years and for the current year.

(F1) Remove from retained earnings the undepreciated gain at the beginning of the year on the sale of the equipment. Since the sale was by the parent, the entire adjustment is removed from the controlling interest in retained earnings.

(F2) Adjust accumulated depreciation and the current year's depreciation expense for the $4,000 overstatement of depreciation caused by the original $20,000 intercompany gain.

(IS) Eliminate intercompany merchandise sales of $100,000 to avoid double counting.

(BI) Reduce the cost of goods sold by the $25,000 of intercompany profit included in the beginning inventory. Since the sale was made by the subsidiary, the reduction to retained earnings is borne 80% by the controlling interest and 20% by the NCI.

(EI) Reduce the ending inventory to its cost to the consolidated firm by decreasing it $35,000, and increase the cost of goods sold by $35,000.

(T) Record the provision for income tax, calculated as follows: $239,000 × 0.3 = $71,700.

Subsidiary Company S Income Distribution

Gross profit on ending inventory (50% × $70,000)	(EI)	$35,000	Internally generated net income before tax	$ 100,000
			Gross profit on beginning inventory (50% × $50,000) . . . (BI)	25,000
			Adjusted income before tax	$ 90,000
			Company S share of taxes (30% × $90,000) . . . (T)	**27,000**
			Company S net income	$ 63,000
			NCI share	× 20%
			NCI	$ 12,600

Parent Company P Income Distribution

Amortization of patent	(A)	$5,000	Internally generated income before tax	$150,000
			Realized profit on equipment ($20,000 × 20%) . . . (F2)	4,000
			Adjusted income before tax	$149,000
			Company P shares of taxes (30% × $149,000) . . . (T)	**44,700**
			Company P net income	$104,300
			Share of subsidiary net income (80% × $63,000)	50,400
			Controlling interest	$154,700

Worksheet 6-2

Nonaffiliated Group for Tax Purposes
Company P and Subsidiary Company S
Worksheet for Consolidated Financial Statements
For Year Ended December 31, 20X4

	(Credit balance amounts are in parentheses.)	Trial Balance	
		Company P	Company S
1	Cash	19,200	80,000
2	Inventory, December 31, 20X4	170,000	150,000
3	Investment in Company S	504,000	
4			
5			
6	Plant and Equipment	600,000	550,000
7	Accumulated Depreciation	(410,000)	(120,000)
8			
9	Patent		
10	Current Tax Liability	(24,000)	(18,000)
11	**Deferred Tax Liability**	**(13,140)**	
12			
13	Common Stock, Company S		(250,000)
14	Retained Earnings, January 1, 20X4, Company S		(350,000)
15			
16	Common Stock, Company P	(250,000)	
17	Retained Earnings, January 1, 20X4, Company P	(510,450)	
18			
19			
20	Sales	(430,000)	(240,000)
21	Cost of Goods Sold	280,000	150,000
22			
23	Depreciation Expense	20,000	10,000
24	Other Expenses	50,000	20,000
25	Patent Amortization Expense		
26	**Provision for Tax**	**25,890**	**18,000**
27	Subsidiary Income	(31,500)	
28	Total	0	0
29	Consolidated Net Income		
30	NCI Share		
31	Controlling Share		
32	NCI		
33	Controlling Retained Earnings		
34	Total		

Worksheet 6-2 (see page 347)

Eliminations & Adjustments				Consolidated Income Statement	NCI	Controlling Retained Earnings	Consolidated Balance Sheet	
Dr.		Cr.						
							99,200	1
		(EI)	16,000				304,000	2
		(CY1)	31,500					3
		(EL)	450,000					4
		(D)	22,500					5
		(F1)	40,000				1,110,000	6
(F1)	8,000						(514,000)	7
(F2)	8,000							8
(D)	22,500	(A)	6,000				16,500	9
							(42,000)	10
(T1)	**19,158**	**(T2)**	**4,602**				1,416	11
								12
(EL)	187,500				(62,500)			13
(EL)	262,500	**(T1)**	**2,400**					14
(F1)	8,000				(81,900)			15
							(250,000)	16
(A)	4,500	**(T1)**	**16,758**					17
(BI)	24,000							18
(F1)	24,000					(474,708)		19
(IS)	100,000			(570,000)				20
(EI)	16,000	(IS)	100,000					21
		(BI)	24,000	322,000				22
		(F2)	8,000	22,000				23
				70,000				24
(A)	1,500			1,500				25
(T2)	**4,602**			48,492				26
(CY1)	31,500							27
	721,760		721,760					28
				(106,008)				29
				11,900	(11,900)			30
				94,108		(94,108)		31
					(156,300)		(156,300)	32
						(568,816)	(568,816)	33
							0	34

Eliminations and Adjustments:

(CY1) Eliminate the parent's entry recording its share of subsidiary income for the current year. The entry now includes the parent's share of the subsidiary income after tax, since the companies are taxed as separate entities.

(EL) Eliminate 75% of the January 1, 20X4, subsidiary equity balances against the investment in Company S.

(D) Distribute the $22,500 excess of cost in the investment account to the patent account.

(A) Amortize the patent for the current year and the three previous years at $1,500 per year.

(F1) Eliminate the unamortized intercompany profit on the equipment sale by Company S as of January 1, 20X4. This elimination includes a $40,000 reduction in the asset account, an $8,000 decrease in accumulated depreciation, and a $32,000 (*before-tax*) decrease in beginning retained earnings. Since the sale was by the subsidiary, the retained earnings adjustment is allocated 75% to the controlling interest and 25% to the NCI.

(F2) Adjust the current year's depreciation expense and accumulated depreciation by the $8,000 current year's portion of the intercompany profit on the equipment sale.

(IS) Eliminate intercompany merchandise sales of $100,000 to avoid double counting.

(BI) Remove the gross profit on intercompany sales recorded by Company P in 20X3 from its January 1, 20X4, retained earnings. The beginning inventory of Company S included $60,000 of goods sold by Company P with a gross profit of 40%, or $24,000. On a consolidated basis, the cost of goods sold is overstated, and this entry removes $24,000 from the consolidated cost of goods sold.

(EI) Remove the $16,000 gross profit from the ending inventory and increase the cost of goods sold by the same amount. The Company S ending inventory includes $40,000 of goods sold by Company P with a gross profit of 40%.

(T1) Adjust the beginning retained earnings balances and create a deferred tax asset (DTL) on prior-period adjustments as follows:

DTA/DTL adjustments:

To beginning retained earnings:

Subsidiary transactions:		Total Tax	Parent Share	Subsidiary Share
Beginning inventory	$ 0			
Remaining fixed asset profit	32,000			
Total	$32,000			
First tax (30% × $32,000)		$ 9,600	$ 7,200	$ 2,400
Second tax [20% × 30% × 75% × ($32,000 – $9,600 first tax)]		1,008	1,008	
Parent transactions:				
Beginning inventory	$24,000			
Remaining fixed asset profit	0			
Amortizations of excess	4,500			
Total	$28,500			
First tax (30% × $28,500)		8,550	8,550	
Total increase in retained earnings and DTA		**$19,158**	**$16,758**	**$2,400**

(T2) Adjust current-year tax provision and adjust deferred tax asset (DTA) for the tax effects of current-year income adjustments:

Subsidiary transactions:		Total Tax	Parent Share	Subsidiary Share
Beginning inventory	$ 0			
Ending inventory	0			
Fixed asset sale	0			
Realized fixed asset	(8,000)			
Total	$ (8,000)			
First tax (30% × $8,000)		$ (2,400)	$ (1,800)	$ (600)
Second tax [20% × 30% × 75% × ($8,000 – $2,400 first tax)]		(252)	(252)	
Parent transactions:				
Beginning inventory	$(24,000)			
Ending inventory	16,000			
Fixed asset sale	0			
Remaining fixed asset profit	0			
Amortizations of excess	1,500			
Total	$ (6,500)			
First tax (30% × $6,500)		(1,950)	(1,950)	
Increase (decrease) in DTA		**$(4,602)**	**$(4,002)**	**$(600)**

Subsidiary Company S Income Distribution

		Internally generated income (before tax)	$ 60,000
		Realized gain on fixed asset (F2)	8,000
		Total income before tax	$ 68,000
		Tax provision (30%)	(20,400)
		Net income	$ 47,600
		NCI share (25%)	**11,900**
		Controlling share (75%)	$ 35,700

Parent Company P Income Distribution

Ending inventory profit (EI)	$16,000	Internally generated income (before tax)	$ 80,000
Patent amortization (A)	1,500	Realized beginning inventory profit (BI)	24,000
		Total income before tax	$ 86,500
		Tax provision (30%)	(25,950)
		Net income	$ 60,550
		Controlling share of subsidiary income (net of first tax)	35,700
		Second tax on share of subsidiary income (20% × 30% × $35,700)	(2,142)
		Total controlling interest	**$94,108**

EXERCISES

Exercise 1 *(LO 1)* **Cash flow, cash payment, year of purchase.** Batton Company purchased an 80% interest in Ricky Company for $500,000 cash on January 1, 20X3. Any excess of cost over book value was attributed to goodwill. To help pay for the acquisition, Batton Company issued 5,000 shares of its common stock with a fair value of $60 per share. Ricky's balance sheet on the date of the purchase was as follows:

Assets		Liabilities and Equity	
Cash	$ 20,000	Current liabilities	$110,000
Inventory	140,000	Bonds payable	100,000
Property, plant,		Common stock ($10 par)	200,000
and equipment (net)	550,000	Retained earnings	300,000
Total assets	$710,000	Total liabilities and equity	$710,000

Controlling share of net income for 20X3 was $145,000, net of the noncontrolling interest of $10,000. Batton declared and paid dividends of $10,000, and Ricky declared and paid dividends of $5,000. There were no purchases or sales of property, plant, or equipment during the year. Based on the following information, prepare a statement of cash flows using the indirect method for Batton Company and its subsidiary for the year ended December 31, 20X3. Any supporting schedules should be in good form.

	Batton Company December 31, 20X2	Consolidated December 31, 20X3
Cash	$ 300,000	$ 304,000
Inventory	220,000	454,000
Property, plant, and equipment (net)	800,000	1,230,000
Goodwill		100,000
Current liabilities	(160,000)	(284,000)
Bonds payable	(200,000)	(300,000)
Noncontrolling interest		(109,000)
Controlling common stock, $10 par	(200,000)	(250,000)
Controlling paid-in capital in excess of par	(300,000)	(550,000)
Retained earnings	(460,000)	(595,000)
Totals	$ 0	$ 0

Exercise 2 *(LO 1)* **Cash flow, issue stock, year of purchase.** Duckworth Corporation purchased an 80% interest in Poladna Corporation on January 1, 20X3, in exchange for 5,000 Duckworth shares (market value of $18) plus $155,000 cash. The appraisal showed that some of Poladna's equipment, with a 4-year estimated remaining life, was undervalued by $20,000. The excess is attributed to goodwill. The following is Poladna Corporation's balance sheet on December 31, 20X2:

Assets		Liabilities and Equity	
Cash	$ 30,000	Current liabilities	$ 30,000
Inventory	30,000	Long-term liabilities	40,000
Property, plant, and equipment	300,000	Common stock ($10 par)	150,000
Accumulated depreciation	(90,000)	Retained earnings	50,000
Total assets	$270,000	Total liabilities and equity	$270,000

Comparative balance sheet data are as follows:

	December 31, 20X2 (Parent only)	December 31, 20X3 (Consolidated)
Cash	$ 100,000	$ 95,000
Inventory	60,000	84,200
Property, plant, and equipment	950,000	1,342,000
Accumulated depreciation	(360,000)	(574,000)
Goodwill		69,000
Current liabilities	(80,000)	(115,000)
Long-term liabilities	(100,000)	(130,000)
Noncontrolling interest		(43,000)
Controlling interest:		
Common stock ($10 par)	(350,000)	(400,000)
Additional paid-in capital	(50,000)	(90,000)
Retained earnings	(170,000)	(238,200)
Totals	$ 0	$ 0

The following information relates to the activities of the two companies for 20X3:

a. Poladna paid off $10,000 of its long-term debt.
b. Duckworth purchased production equipment for $76,000.
c. Consolidated net income was $104,200; the NCI's share was $6,000. Depreciation expense taken by Duckworth and Poladna on their separate books was $92,000 and $28,000, respectively.
d. Duckworth paid $30,000 in dividends; Poladna paid $15,000.

Prepare the consolidated statement of cash flows for the year ended December 31, 20X3, for Duckworth Corporation and its subsidiary, Poladna Corporation.

Exercise 3 *(LO 1)* **Cash flow, subsequent to year of purchase.** Paridon Motors purchased an 80% interest in Super Battery Company on January 1, 20X2, for $700,000 cash. At that date, Super Battery Company had the following stockholders' equity:

Common stock ($10 par)	$100,000
Paid-in capital in excess of par	300,000
Retained earnings	250,000
Total stockholders' equity	$650,000

Any excess of cost over book value was attributed to goodwill. A statement of cash flows is being prepared for 20X5. For each of the following situations, indicate the impact on the cash flow statement for 20X5.

a. Adjustment resulting from the original purchase of the controlling interest.
b. Super Battery Company issued 2,000 shares of common stock for $90 per share on January 1, 20X5. At the time, the stockholders' equity of Super Battery was $800,000. Paridon Motors purchased 1,000 shares.
c. Paridon Motors purchased at 102, $100,000 of face value, 10% annual interest bonds issued by Super Battery Company at face value on January 1, 20X3. Paridon purchased the bonds on January 1, 20X5.
d. Super Battery purchased a production machine from Paridon Motors on July 1, 20X5, for $80,000. Paridon's cost was $60,000, and accumulated depreciation was $20,000.

Exercise 4 *(LO 3)* **Taxation as consolidated company.** On May 1, 20X6, Tuft Company purchased a 70% interest in Masat Company for $340,000. Tuft also paid $30,000 in direct acquisition costs. The following determination and distribution of excess schedule was prepared:

Price paid for investment		$370,000
Less book value of interest acquired:		
Common stock, Masat	$300,000	
Retained earnings	100,000	
Total stockholders' equity	$400,000	
Interest acquired	× 70%	280,000
Goodwill		**$ 90,000**

Goodwill will be amortized over 15 years *for tax purposes only.*

Tuft Company and Masat Company had the following separate income statements for the year ended December 31, 20X8:

	Tuft Company	Masat Company
Sales	$750,000	$560,000
Less cost of goods sold	440,000	350,000
Gross profit	$310,000	$210,000
Less other expenses	200,000	140,000
Income before dividends	$110,000	$ 70,000
Dividends received	17,500	
Income before tax	$127,500	$ 70,000

During 20X8, Masat Company paid cash dividends of $25,000.

Prepare the entry to record income tax payable on each company's books. Assume a 30% corporate income tax rate.

Exercise 5 *(LO 3)* **Consolidated taxation, intercompany profits.** Deko Company purchased an 80% interest in the common stock of Farelly Company for $850,000 on January 1, 20X7. The price was $75,000 in excess of the book value of the underlying equity, and the excess was attributed to a patent with a 10-year life.

During 20X9, Deko Company and Farelly Company reported the following internally generated income before taxes:

	Deko Company	Farelly Company
Sales	$ 300,000	$120,000
Cost of goods sold	(200,000)	(90,000)
Gain on machine	5,000	
Expenses	(40,000)	(20,000)
Income before taxes	$ 65,000	$ 10,000

Farelly Company sold goods to Deko Company for $50,000. Deko Company had $20,000 of Farelly Company's goods in its beginning inventory and $6,000 of Farelly's goods in its ending inventory. Farelly Company sells goods to Deko Company at gross profit of 40%.

Deko Company sold a new machine to Farelly Company on January 1, 20X9, for $30,000. The machine has a 5-year life, and its cost was $25,000.

The affiliated group files a consolidated tax return and is taxed at 30%.

Prepare a consolidated income statement for 20X9. Include income distribution for both companies.

Exercise 6 *(LO 4)* **Separate taxation, intercompany transactions.** *(This is the same as Exercise 5, but with separate taxation.)* Decker Company purchased an 80% interest in the common stock of Ferris Company for $850,000 on January 1, 20X7. The price was $75,000 in excess of the book value of the underlying equity, and the excess was attributed to a patent with a 10-year life.

During 20X9, Decker Company and Ferris Company reported the following internally generated income before taxes:

	Decker Company	Ferris Company
Sales	$ 300,000	$120,000
Cost of goods sold	(200,000)	(90,000)
Gain on machine	5,000	
Expenses	(40,000)	(20,000)
Income before taxes	$ 65,000	$ 10,000

Ferris Company sold goods to Decker Company for $50,000. Decker Company had $20,000 of Ferris Company's goods in its beginning inventory and $6,000 of Ferris's goods in its ending inventory. Ferris Company sells goods to Decker Company at a gross profit of 40%.

Decker Company sold a new machine to Ferris Company on January 1, 20X9, for $30,000. The machine has a 5-year life, and its cost was $25,000.

The companies file separate tax returns. Both are subject to a 30% tax rate. Decker receives an 80% dividend deduction.

Prepare a consolidated income statement for 20X9. Include income distribution for both companies.

Exercise 7 *(LO 4)* **Tax allocation with separate taxation.** The separate income statements of Cooper Company and its 60%-owned subsidiary, Vacant Company, for the year ended December 31, 20X7, are as follows:

	Cooper Company	Vacant Company
Sales	$520,000	$350,000
Less cost of goods sold	350,000	180,000
Gross profit	$170,000	$170,000
Less operating expenses	100,000	90,000
Operating income	$ 70,000	$ 80,000
Subsidiary income	12,600	
Income before tax	$ 82,600	$ 80,000
Provision for income tax	21,756	24,000
Net income	$ 60,844	$ 56,000

The following additional information is available:

a. Cooper Company purchased its interest in Vacant Company on July 1, 20X5. The price paid was $60,000 in excess of book value. This excess was attributable to equipment with a 20-year life.

(continued)

b. Vacant Company sold a machine to Cooper Company on December 31, 20X6, for $10,000. This machine had a book value of $6,000 and an estimated future life of 4 years at the purchase date. Straight-line depreciation is assumed.
c. Cooper Company sold $15,000 worth of merchandise to Vacant Company during 20X7. Cooper sells its merchandise at a price that enables it to realize a gross profit of 30%.
d. Vacant Company had $2,000 worth of this merchandise in its ending inventory.
e. A corporate income tax rate of 30% is assumed.

Prepare the worksheet adjustments pertaining to the purchase cost amortization and the intercompany transactions, and prepare the interperiod tax allocations that result from the elimination of the intercompany transactions. The companies do not qualify as an affiliated group under the tax code.

Exercise 8 *(LO 5)* **Equity income recording.** Trailer Corporation purchased a 25% interest in Like Company for $110,000 on January 1, 20X7. The following determination and distribution of excess schedule was prepared:

Price paid		$110,000
Less interest acquired:		
Common stock ($10 par)	$200,000	
Retained earnings	100,000	
Total stockholders' equity	$300,000	
Interest acquired	× 25%	75,000
Excess of cost over book value		$ 35,000
Less excess attributable to equipment, 25% × $40,000 (10-year life)		10,000
Goodwill		$ 25,000

Like Company earned income of $20,000 in 20X7 and $24,000 in 20X8. Like Company declared a 25-cent per share cash dividend on December 22, 20X8, payable January 12, 20X9, to stockholders of record on December 30, 20X8.

During 20X8, Like sold merchandise costing $10,000 to Trailer for $15,000. 20% of the merchandise was still in Trailer's ending inventory on December 31, 20X8.

Prepare the equity adjustment required by APB Opinion No. 18 on Trailer's books on December 31, 20X7, and December 31, 20X8, to account for its investment in Like Company. Assume Trailer Corporation makes no adjustment except at the end of each calendar year. Ignore income tax considerations.

Exercise 9 *(LO 5)* **Equity method investment with intercompany profits.** Turf Company purchased a 30% interest in Minnie Company for $90,000 on January 1, 20X1, when Minnie had the following stockholders' equity:

Common stock ($10 par)	$100,000
Paid-in capital in excess of par	20,000
Retained earnings	130,000
Total	$250,000

The excess cost was due to a building that is being amortized over 20 years.

Since the investment, Minnie had consistently sold goods to Turf to realize a 40% gross profit. Such sales totaled $50,000 during 20X3. Minnie had $10,000 of such goods in its beginning inventory and $40,000 in its ending inventory.

On January 1, 20X3, Turf sold a machine with a book value of $15,000 to Minnie for $20,000. The machine has a 5-year life and is being depreciated on a straight-line basis.

Minnie reported a net income of $60,000 before taxes for 20X3. Minnie paid $5,000 in dividends in 20X3.

Prepare all entries caused by Turf's investment in Minnie for 20X3 (ignore tax ramifications). Assume that Turf has recorded the tax on its internally generated income. Turf has properly recorded the investment in previous periods.

Exercise 10 *(LO 5)* **Equity income with intercompany profits.** Spancrete Corporation acquired a 30% interest in the outstanding stock of Werl Corporation on January 1, 20X5. At that time, the following determination and distribution of excess schedule was prepared:

Price paid		$125,000
Less interest acquired:		
Common stock	$ 150,000	
Retained earnings	160,000	
Total stockholders' equity	$310,000	
Interest acquired	× 30%	93,000
Excess of cost over book value attributable to equipment (10-year life)		$ 32,000

During 20X5, Spancrete purchased $200,000 of goods from Werl. $20,000 of these purchases were in the December 31, 20X5, ending inventory. During 20X6, Spancrete purchased $250,000 of goods from Werl. $30,000 of these purchases were in the December 31, 20X6, ending inventory. Werl's gross profit rate is 30%. Also, Spancrete purchased a machine from Werl for $15,000 on January 1, 20X6. The machine had a book value of $10,000 and a 5-year remaining life. Werl reported net income of $90,000 and paid $20,000 on dividends during 20X6.

Prepare an income distribution schedule for Werl, and record the entries to adjust the investment in Werl for 20X6.

Exercise 11 *(LO 5)* **Equity method, change in interest.** Hanson Corporation purchased a 10% interest in Novic Company on January 1, 20X6, and an additional 15% interest on January 1, 20X8. These investments cost Hanson Corporation $80,000 and $110,000, respectively.

The following stockholders' equities of Novic Company are available:

	December 31, 20X5	December 31, 20X7
Common stock ($10 par)	$500,000	$500,000
Retained earnings	250,000	300,000
Total equity	$750,000	$800,000

Any excess of cost over book value on the original investment was attributed to goodwill. Any excess on the second purchase is attributable to equipment with a 4-year life.

Novic Company had income of $30,000, $30,000, and $40,000 for 20X6, 20X7, and 20X8, respectively. Novic paid dividends of $.20 per share in 20X7 and 20X8.

Ignore income tax considerations, and assume adjusting entries are made at the end of the calendar year only.

1. Prepare the cost-to-equity conversion entry, as required by APB Opinion No. 18, on January 1, 20X8, when Hanson's investment in Novic Company first exceeded 20%. Any supporting schedules should be in good form.
2. Prepare the December 31, 20X8, equity adjustment on Hanson's books. Provide supporting calculations in good form.

Exercise 12 *(LO 5)* **Sale of equity method investment.** On January 1, 20X7, Lund Corporation purchased a 30% interest in Aluma-Boat Company for $200,000. At the time of the purchase, Aluma-Boat had total stockholders' equity of $400,000. Any excess of cost over the equity purchased was attributed in part to machinery worth $50,000 more than book value with a remaining useful life of 5 years. Any remaining excess would be allocated to goodwill.

Aluma-Boat reported the following income and dividend distributions in 20X7 and 20X8:

	20X7	20X8
Income	$50,000	$45,000
Dividends declared and paid	10,000	10,000

Lund sold its investment in Aluma-Boat Company on January 2, 20X9, for $230,000. Record the sale of the investments. You may ignore income taxes. Carefully schedule the investment account balance at the time of the sale.

PROBLEMS

Problem 6-1 *(LO 1)* **Cash flow, year subsequent to purchase.** Marc Company is an 80%-owned subsidiary of Luis Company. The interest in Marc was purchased on January 1, 20X1, for $640,000 cash. At that date, Marc had stockholders' equity of $650,000. The excess price was attributed to equipment with a 5-year life undervalued by $25,000 and to goodwill.

The following comparative consolidated trial balances apply to Luis Company and its subsidiary, Marc:

	December 31, 20X1	December 31, 20X2
Cash	$ 16,000	$ 39,500
Inventory	120,000	160,000
Accounts receivable	200,000	300,000
Property, plant, and equipment	3,000,000	3,350,000
Accumulated depreciation	(1,080,000)	(1,280,000)
Investment in Charles Corporation (30%)		244,500
Goodwill	100,000	100,000
Accounts payable	(117,000)	(200,000)
Bonds payable	(100,000)	(400,000)
Noncontrolling interest	(138,000)	(151,000)
Controlling interest:		
Common stock, par	(1,000,000)	(1,000,000)
Additional paid-in capital	(650,000)	(650,000)
Retained earnings	(351,000)	(513,000)
Totals	$ 0	$ 0

The following 20X2 information is available for the Luis and Marc companies:

a. Marc purchased equipment for $50,000.
b. Marc issued $300,000 of long-term bonds and later used the proceeds to purchase a new building.
c. On January 1, 20X2, Luis purchased 30% of the outstanding common stock of Charles Corporation for $230,000. This is an influential investment. Charles's stockholders' equity was $700,000 on the date of the purchase. Any excess cost is attributed to equipment with a 10-year life. Charles reported net income of $80,000 in 20X2 and paid dividends of $25,000.
d. Controlling share of consolidated income for 20X2 was $262,000; the noncontrolling interest in consolidated net income was $16,000. Luis paid $100,000 in dividends in 20X2; Marc paid $15,000 in dividends in 20X2.

Prepare the consolidated statement of cash flows for 20X2 using the indirect method. Any supporting calculations should be in good form. ◄◄◄◄◄ **Required**

Problem 6-2 *(LO 1)* **Cash flow, year of partial noncash purchase.** Billing Enterprises purchased a 90% interest in the common stock of Raush Corporation on January 1, 20X1, for an agreed-upon price of $500,000. Billing issued $400,000 of bonds to Raush shareholders plus $100,000 cash as payment. Raush's balance sheet on the acquisition date was as follows:

Assets		Liabilities and Equity	
Cash	$ 60,000	Accounts payable	$ 45,000
Accounts receivable	95,000	Long-term liabilities	120,000
Plant assets (net)	460,000	Common stock ($10 par)	150,000
		Retained earnings	300,000
Total assets	$615,000	Total liabilities and equity	$615,000

Raush's equipment was understated by $20,000 and had a remaining depreciable life of 5 years. Any remaining excess was attributed to goodwill.

In addition to the bonds issued as part of the purchase, Billing sold additional bonds in the amount of $100,000.

Consolidated net income for 20X1 was $92,700. The controlling interest was $87,700, and the noncontrolling interest was $5,000. Raush paid $10,000 in dividends to all shareholders, including Billing Enterprises.

No plant assets were purchased or sold during 20X1.

Comparative balance sheet data are as follows:

	December 31, 20X0 Parent Only	December 31, 20X1 Consolidated
Cash	$ 82,000	$ 182,700
Accounts receivable	120,000	161,000
Plant assets (net)	870,000	1,276,000
Goodwill		77,000
Accounts payable	(52,000)	(80,000)
Bonds payable		(500,000)
Long-term liabilities	(80,000)	(40,000)
Noncontrolling interest		(49,000)
Controlling interest:		
Common stock ($10 par)	(200,000)	(200,000)
Additional paid-in capital	(300,000)	(300,000)
Retained earnings	(440,000)	(527,700)
Totals	$ 0	$ 0

Prepare a consolidated statement of cash flows using the indirect method for the year ended December 31, 20X1. Supporting schedules should be in good form. ◄◄◄◄◄ **Required**

Problem 6-3 *(LO 1)* **Comprehensive cash flow, indirect method.** Presented below are the consolidated workpaper balances of Bush Inc. and its subsidiary, Dorr Corporation, as of December 31, 20X6 and 20X5:

Assets	20X6	20X5	Net Change Incr. (Decr.)
Cash	$ 313,000	$ 195,000	$118,000
Marketable equity securities (at cost)	175,000	175,000	

(continued)

Assets	20X6	20X5	Net Change Incr. (Decr.)
Allowance to reduce marketable equity securities to market	$ (13,000)	$ (24,000)	$ 11,000
Accounts receivable (net)	418,000	440,000	(22,000)
Inventories	595,000	525,000	70,000
Land	385,000	170,000	215,000
Plant and equipment	755,000	690,000	65,000
Accumulated depreciation	(199,000)	(145,000)	(54,000)
Goodwill	60,000	60,000	0
Total assets	$2,489,000	$2,086,000	$403,000
Liabilities and Stockholders' Equity			
Current portion of long-term note	$ 150,000	$ 150,000	
Accounts payable and accrued liabilities	595,000	474,000	$ 121,000
Note payable, long-term	300,000	450,000	(150,000)
Deferred income taxes	44,000	32,000	12,000
Noncontrolling interest in net assets of subsidiary	179,000	161,000	18,000
Common stock ($10 par)	580,000	480,000	100,000
Additional paid-in capital	303,000	180,000	123,000
Retained earnings	338,000	195,000	143,000
Treasury stock (at cost)		(36,000)	36,000
Total liabilities and stockholders' equity	$2,489,000	$2,086,000	$ 403,000

Additional information:

a. On January 20, 20X6, Bush Inc. issued 10,000 shares of its common stock for land having a fair value of $215,000.
b. On February 5, 20X6, Bush reissued all of its treasury stock for $44,000.
c. On May 15, 20X6, Bush paid a cash dividend of $58,000 on its common stock.
d. On August 8, 20X6, equipment was purchased for $127,000.
e. On September 30, 20X6, equipment was sold for $40,000. The equipment cost $62,000 and had a net book value of $34,000 on the date of the sale.
f. On December 15, 20X6, Dorr Corporation paid a cash dividend of $50,000 on its common stock.
g. Deferred income taxes represent timing differences relating to the use of accelerated depreciation methods for income tax reporting and the straight-line method for financial reporting.
h. Net income for 20X6 was as follows:

Controlling interest in consolidated net income	$201,000
Dorr Corporation	110,000

i. Bush Inc. owns 70% of Dorr Corporation. There was no change in ownership interest in Dorr during 20X5 and 20X6. There were no intercompany transactions other than the dividend paid to Bush by its subsidiary.

Required ▶▶▶▶▶ Prepare the statement of cash flows for the consolidated company using the indirect method. A cash analysis worksheet should be prepared to aid in the development of the statement. Any other supporting schedules should be in good form.

Problem 6-4 *(LO 2)* **Consolidated EPS.** On January 1, 20X2, Peanut Corporation acquired an 80% interest in Sunny Corporation. Information regarding the income and equity structure of the two companies as of the year ended December 31, 20X4, is as follows:

	Peanut Corporation	Sunny Corporation
Internally generated net income	$55,000	$56,000
Common shares outstanding during the year	20,000	12,000
Warrants to acquire Peanut stock, outstanding during the year	2,000	1,000
5% convertible (into Sunny's shares), $100 par preferred share, outstanding during the year		800
Nonconvertible preferred shares outstanding	1,000	

Additional information is as follows:

a. The warrants to acquire Peanut stock were issued in 20X3. Each warrant can be exchanged for one share of Peanut common stock at an exercise price of $12 per share.
b. Each share of convertible preferred stock can be converted into two shares of Sunny common stock. The preferred stock pays an annual dividend totaling $4,000. Peanut owns 60% of the convertible preferred stock.
c. The nonconvertible preferred stock was issued on July 1, 20X4, and paid a 6-month dividend totaling $500.
d. Relevant market prices per share of Peanut common stock during 20X4 are as follows:

	Average
1st Quarter	$10
2nd Quarter	12
3rd Quarter	13
4th Quarter	16

Compute the basic and diluted consolidated EPS for the year ended December 31, 20X4. Use quarterly share averaging. ◄◄◄◄◄ **Required**

Problem 6-5 *(LO 3)* **Consolidated income statement, affiliated firm for tax.** On January 1, 20X1, Delta Corporation exchanged 12,000 shares of its common stock for an 80% interest in Moore Company. The stock issued had a par value of $10 per share and a fair value of $20 per share. On the date of purchase, Moore had the following balance sheet:

Common stock ($2 par)	$ 20,000
Paid-in capital in excess of par	50,000
Retained earnings	100,000
Total equity	$170,000

On the purchase date, Moore had equipment with an 8-year remaining life that was undervalued by $20,000. Any remaining excess cost was attributed to goodwill.

There are intercompany merchandise sales. During 20X2, Delta sold $20,000 of merchandise to Moore. Moore sold $30,000 of merchandise to Delta. Moore had $2,000 of Delta goods in its beginning inventory and $4,200 of Delta goods in its ending inventory. Delta had $2,500 of Moore goods in its beginning inventory and $3,000 of Moore goods in its ending inventory. Delta's gross profit rate is 40%; Moore's is 25%.

On July 1, 20X1, Delta sold a machine to Moore for $90,000. The book value of the machine on Delta's books was $50,000 at the time of the sale. The machine has a 5-year remaining life. Depreciation on the machine is included in expenses.

The consolidated group meets the requirements of an affiliated group under the tax law and files a consolidated tax return. The original purchase was not structured as a nontaxable exchange.

Delta uses the cost method to record its investment in Moore. Since Moore has never paid dividends, Delta has not recorded any income on its investment in Moore. The two companies prepared the following income statements for 20X2:

	Delta Corporation	Moore Company
Sales	$1,000,000	$600,000
Less cost of goods sold	800,000	375,000
Gross profit	$ 200,000	$225,000
Less expenses	80,000	185,000
Income before tax	$ 120,000	$ 40,000

Required ▶ ▶ ▶ ▶ ▶ Prepare the 20X2 consolidated net income in schedule form. Include eliminations and adjustments. Provide income distribution schedules to allocate consolidated net income to the controlling and noncontrolling interests.

Problem 6-6 *(LO 3)* **Worksheet, consolidated taxation, simple equity, inventory, land.** On January 1, 20X1, Pepper Company purchased 80% of the common stock of Salt Company for $270,000. On this date, Salt had total owners' equity of $300,000. The excess of cost over book value is due to goodwill. *For tax purposes,* goodwill is amortized over 15 years.

During 20X1, Pepper has appropriately accounted for its investment in Salt using the simple equity method.

During 20X1, Pepper sold merchandise to Salt for $50,000, of which $10,000 is held by Salt on December 31, 20X1. Pepper's gross profit on sales is 40%.

During 20X1, Salt sold some land to Pepper at a gain of $10,000. Pepper still holds the land at year-end. Pepper and Salt qualify as an affiliated group for tax purposes and, thus, will file a consolidated tax return. Assume a 30% corporate income tax rate.

The following trial balances were prepared on December 31, 20X1:

	Pepper Company	Salt Company
Inventory, December 31	100,000	50,000
Other Current Assets	198,000	200,000
Investment in Salt Company	302,000	
Land	240,000	100,000
Buildings and Equipment	300,000	200,000
Accumulated Depreciation	(80,000)	(60,000)
Current Liabilities	(150,000)	(50,000)
Long-Term Liabilities	(200,000)	(100,000)
Common Stock	(100,000)	(50,000)
Paid-In Capital in Excess of Par	(180,000)	(100,000)
Retained Earnings	(320,000)	(150,000)
Sales	(500,000)	(300,000)
Cost of Goods Sold	300,000	180,000
Operating Expenses	100,000	80,000
Subsidiary Income	(40,000)	
Gain on Sale of Land		(10,000)
Dividends Declared	30,000	10,000
Total	0	0

Required ▶ ▶ ▶ ▶ ▶ Prepare a consolidated worksheet for Pepper Company and subsidiary Salt Company for the year ended December 31, 20X1. Include the determination and distribution schedule and the income determination schedules.

Problem 6-7 *(LO 3)* **Worksheet, consolidated taxation, simple equity, inventory, fixed asset sale.** On January 1, 20X1, Pillar Company purchased an 80% interest in Stone Company for $890,000. On the date of acquisition, Stone had total owners' equity of $800,000. Buildings, which have a 20-year life, were undervalued by $200,000. The remaining excess of cost over book value is attributable to goodwill. For tax purposes only, goodwill is amortized over 15 years.

template cd

On January 1, 20X1, Stone sold equipment, with a net book value of $60,000, to Pillar for $100,000. The equipment had a 5-year remaining life. Straight-line depreciation is used.

During 20X3, Pillar sold $70,000 worth of merchandise to Stone. As a result of these intercompany sales, Stone held beginning inventory of $40,000 and ending inventory of $30,000. At December 31, 20X3, Stone owed Pillar $8,000 from merchandise sales. Pillar has a gross profit rate of 50%.

Neither company has provided for income tax. The companies qualify as an affiliated group and, thus, will file a consolidated tax return based on a 30% corporate tax rate. The original purchase was not a nontaxable exchange.

Trial balances of Pillar and Stone as of December 31, 20X3, are as follows:

	Pillar Company	Stone Company
Cash	208,600	380,000
Accounts Receivable	130,000	150,000
Inventory	120,000	80,000
Investment in Stone	1,098,000	
Plant and Equipment	600,000	900,000
Accumulated Depreciation	(350,000)	(300,000)
Liabilities	(205,000)	(150,000)
Deferred Tax Liability (goodwill amortization)	(3,600)	
Common Stock	(500,000)	(300,000)
Retained Earnings, January 1, 20X3	(950,000)	(700,000)
Sales	(800,000)	(550,000)
Cost of Goods Sold	430,000	320,000
Depreciation Expense	60,000	50,000
Other Expenses	210,000	120,000
Subsidiary Income	(48,000)	
Total	0	0

◄◄◄◄◄ **Required**

Prepare a consolidated worksheet based on the trial balances. Include a provision for income tax, a determination and distribution of excess schedule, and income distribution schedules.

Use the following information for Problems 6-8 and 6-9:

On January 1, 20X1, Penstar Company acquired an 80% interest in Solar Company for $450,000. Solar had the following balance sheet on the date of acquisition:

Solar Company
Balance Sheet
January 1, 20X1

Assets		Liabilities and Equity	
Accounts receivable	$ 60,000	Accounts payable	$ 70,000
Inventory	80,000	Bonds payable	100,000
Land	120,000	Common stock	10,000
Buildings	250,000	Paid-in capital in excess	
Accumulated depreciation	(50,000)	of par	190,000

(continued)

Assets		Liabilities and Equity	
Equipment	$120,000	Retained earnings	$170,000
Accumulated depreciation	(70,000)		
Goodwill	30,000		
Total assets	$540,000	Total liabilities and equity	$540,000

Buildings, which have a 20-year life, are undervalued by $100,000. Equipment, which has a 5-year life, is undervalued by $50,000. Any remaining excess of cost over book value is attributable to goodwill, which has a 15-year life for tax purposes only.

template cd

Problem 6-8 *(LO 3)* **Worksheet, consolidated taxation, simple equity, inventory, fixed asset sale, analyze price.** Refer to the preceding facts for Penstar's acquisition of Solar common stock. Penstar uses the simple equity method to account for its investment in Solar. During 20X2, Solar sold $30,000 worth of merchandise to Penstar. As a result of these intercompany sales, Penstar held beginning inventory of $12,000 and ending inventory of $16,000 of merchandise acquired from Solar. At December 31, 20X2, Penstar owed Solar $6,000 from merchandise sales. Solar has a gross profit rate of 30%.

On January 1, 20X1, Penstar sold equipment having a net book value of $50,000 to Solar for $90,000. The equipment has a 5-year useful life and is depreciated using the straight-line method.

Neither company has provided for income tax. The companies qualify as an affiliated group and, thus, will file a consolidated tax return based on a 40% corporate tax rate. The original purchase was not a nontaxable exchange.

On December 31, 20X2, Penstar and Solar had the following trial balances:

	Penstar Company	Solar Company
Cash	94,107	54,000
Accounts Receivable	150,600	90,000
Inventory	105,000	90,000
Land	100,000	120,000
Investment in Solar	517,200	
Buildings	800,000	250,000
Accumulated Depreciation	(250,000)	(70,000)
Equipment	210,000	120,000
Accumulated Depreciation	(115,000)	(90,000)
Goodwill		30,000
Accounts Payable	(70,000)	(40,000)
Bonds Payable		(100,000)
Deferred Tax Liability (goodwill amortization)	(1,707)	
Common Stock	(100,000)	(10,000)
Paid-In Capital in Excess of Par	(600,000)	(190,000)
Retained Earnings, January 1, 20X2	(621,600)	(222,000)
Sales	(890,000)	(350,000)
Cost of Goods Sold	480,000	220,000
Depreciation Expense—Buildings	30,000	10,000
Depreciation Expense—Equipment	25,000	10,000
Other Expenses	150,000	60,000
Interest Expense		8,000
Subsidiary Income	(33,600)	
Dividends Declared	20,000	10,000
Total	0	0

◀◀◀◀◀ **Required**

1. Prepare a zone analysis and a determination and distribution of excess schedule.
2. Prepare a consolidated worksheet for the year ended December 31, 20X2. Include a provision for income tax and income distribution schedules.

Problem 6-9 *(LO 3)* **Worksheet, consolidated taxation, simple equity, inventory, fixed asset sale, analyze price, later year.** Refer to the preceding facts for Penstar's acquisition of Solar common stock. Penstar uses the simple equity method to account for its investment in Solar. During 20X3, Solar sold $40,000 worth of merchandise to Penstar. As a result of these intercompany sales, Penstar held beginning inventory of $16,000 and ending inventory of $10,000 of merchandise acquired from Solar. At December 31, 20X3, Penstar owed Solar $8,000 from merchandise sales. Solar has a gross profit rate of 30%.

template cd

During 20X3, Penstar sold $60,000 worth of merchandise to Solar. Solar held $15,000 of this merchandise in its ending inventory. Solar owed $10,000 to Penstar as a result of these intercompany sales. Penstar has a gross profit rate of 40%.

On January 1, 20X1, Penstar sold equipment having a net book value of $50,000 to Solar for $90,000. The equipment has a 5-year useful life and is depreciated using the straight-line method.

On January 1, 20X3, Solar sold equipment to Penstar at a profit of $25,000. The equipment has a 5-year useful life and is depreciated using the straight-line method.

Neither company has provided for income tax. The companies qualify as an affiliated group and, thus, will file a consolidated tax return based on a 40% corporate tax rate. The original purchase was not a nontaxable exchange.

On December 31, 20X3, Penstar and Solar had the following trial balances:

	Penstar Company	Solar Company
Cash	95,814	80,000
Accounts Receivable	150,600	100,000
Inventory	115,000	120,000
Land	100,000	120,000
Investment in Solar	554,000	
Buildings	900,000	250,000
Accumulated Depreciation	(290,000)	(80,000)
Equipment	210,000	120,000
Accumulated Depreciation	(140,000)	(100,000)
Goodwill		30,000
Accounts Payable	(50,000)	(40,000)
Bonds Payable		(100,000)
Deferred Tax Liability (goodwill amortization)	(3,414)	
Common Stock	(100,000)	(10,000)
Paid-In Capital in Excess of Par	(600,000)	(190,000)
Retained Earnings, January 1, 20X3	(745,400)	(238,000)
Sales	(950,000)	(400,000)
Cost of Goods Sold	550,000	250,000
Depreciation Expense—Buildings	40,000	10,000
Depreciation Expense—Equipment	25,000	10,000
Other Expenses	176,000	75,000
Interest Expense		8,000
Gain on Sale of Fixed Asset		(25,000)
Subsidiary Income	(57,600)	
Dividends Declared	20,000	10,000
Total	0	0

Required ▶ ▶ ▶ ▶ ▶

1. Prepare a zone analysis and a determination and distribution of excess schedule.
2. Prepare a consolidated worksheet for the year ended December 31, 20X3. Include a provision for income tax and income distribution schedules.

Problem 6-10 *(LO 4)* **Worksheet, separate tax, simple equity, inventory, fixed asset sale.** On January, 1, 20X1, Pike Company acquired 70% of the common stock of Sun Company for $340,400 in a taxable combination. On this date, Sun had total owners' equity of $422,000, including retained earnings of $222,000. The excess of cost over book value is attributable to goodwill.

During 20X1 and 20X2, Sun Company reported the following information:

	20X1	20X2
Net income before taxes	$40,000	$40,000
Dividends	0	30,000

During 20X1 and 20X2, Pike has appropriately accounted for its investment in Sun using the simple equity method, including income tax effects.

On January 1, 20X2, Pike held merchandise acquired from Sun for $10,000. During 20X2, Sun sold merchandise to Pike for $60,000, of which $20,000 is held by Pike on December 31, 20X2. Sun's usual gross profit on affiliated sales is 40%.

On December 31, 20X1, Pike sold some equipment to Sun, with a cost of $40,000 and a book value of $18,000. The sales price was $30,000. Sun is depreciating the equipment over a 3-year life, assuming no salvage value and using the straight-line method.

Pike and Sun do not qualify as an affiliated group for tax purposes and, thus, will file separate tax returns. Assume a 30% corporate tax rate and an 80% dividends-received deduction.

The following trial balances were prepared by Pike and Sun on December 31, 20X2:

	Trial Balance	
	Pike Company	Sun Company
Accounts Receivable	327,176	295,000
Inventory	110,000	85,000
Land	150,000	90,000
Investment in Sun	378,200	
Buildings	200,000	200,000
Accumulated Depreciation	(100,000)	(50,000)
Equipment	120,000	80,000
Accumulated Depreciation	(35,000)	(20,000)
Goodwill		
Accounts Payable	(120,000)	(80,000)
Current Tax Liability	(31,260)	(24,000)
Bond Payable	(200,000)	(100,000)
Discount (premium)		
Deferred Tax Liability	(2,268)	
Common Stock—Sun		(10,000)
Paid-In Capital in Excess of Par—Sun		(190,000)
Retained Earnings—Sun		(250,000)
Common Stock—Pike	(100,000)	
Paid-In Capital in Excess of Par—Pike	(200,000)	
Retained Earnings—Pike	(450,000)	
Sales	(590,000)	(370,000)
Cost of Goods Sold	340,000	220,000
Depreciation Expense—Building	15,000	8,000
Depreciation Expense—Equipment	20,000	12,000
Other Expenses	115,000	50,000

Interest Expense		
Provision for Tax	32,352	24,000
Subsidiary Income	(39,200)	
Dividends Declared—Sun		30,000
Dividends Declared—Pike	60,000	
Total	0	0

Note:

Provision for income taxes (Pike):

Current ($100,000 × 30%)	$30,000
Sun dividends ($21,000 × 20% × 30%)	1,260
	$31,260
Current deferred taxes [($39,200 – $21,000) × 20% × 30%]	1,092
Provision for income taxes	$32,352

Deferred tax liability (Pike):

Current deferred taxes [($39,200 – $21,000) × 20% × 30%]	$ 1,092
Change in Sun retained earnings [70% × ($250,000 – $222,000) × 20% × 30%]	1,176
Deferred tax liability	$ 2,268

◄◄◄◄◄ **Required**

Prepare a consolidated worksheet for Pike Company and subsidiary Sun Company for the year ended December 31, 20X2. Include the determination and distribution schedule and the income determination schedules.

Use the following information for Problems 6-11 and 6-12:

On January 1, 20X1, Penstar Company acquired an 80% interest in Solar Company for $450,000. Solar had the following balance sheet on the date of acquisition:

Solar Company
Balance Sheet
January 1, 20X1

Assets		Liabilities and Equity	
Accounts receivable	$ 60,000	Accounts payable	$ 70,000
Inventory	80,000	Bonds payable	100,000
Land	120,000	Common stock	10,000
Buildings	250,000	Paid-in capital in excess of par	190,000
Accumulated depreciation	(50,000)	Retained earnings	170,000
Equipment	120,000		
Accumulated depreciation	(70,000)		
Goodwill	30,000		
Total assets	$540,000	Total liabilities and equity	$540,000

Buildings, which have a 20-year life, are undervalued by $100,000. Equipment, which has a 5-year life, is undervalued by $50,000. Any remaining excess of cost over book value is attributable to goodwill.

template cd

Problem 6-11 *(LO 4)* **Worksheet, separate tax, simple equity, inventory, fixed asset sale, analyze price.** Refer to the preceding facts for Penstar's acquisition of Solar common stock. Penstar uses the simple equity method to account for its investment in Solar. During 20X2, Solar sold $30,000 worth of merchandise to Penstar. As a result of these intercompany sales, Penstar held beginning inventory of $12,000 and ending inventory of $16,000 of merchandise acquired from Solar. At December 31, 20X2, Penstar owed Solar $6,000 from merchandise sales. Solar has a gross profit rate of 30%.

On January 1, 20X1, Penstar sold equipment having a net book value of $50,000 to Solar for $90,000. The equipment has a 5-year useful life and is depreciated using the straight-line method.

Penstar and Solar do not qualify as an affiliated group for tax purposes, and thus, will file separate tax returns. Assume a 40% corporate tax rate and an 80% dividends-received exclusion.

On December 31, 20X2, Penstar and Solar had the following trial balances:

	Penstar Company	Solar Company
Cash	92,400	53,200
Accounts Receivable	150,600	90,000
Inventory	105,000	90,000
Land	100,000	120,000
Investment in Solar	503,120	
Buildings	800,000	250,000
Accumulated Depreciation	(250,000)	(70,000)
Equipment	210,000	120,000
Accumulated Depreciation	(115,000)	(90,000)
Goodwill		30,000
Accounts Payable	(70,000)	(40,000)
Current Tax Liability	(82,640)	(16,800)
Bonds Payable		(100,000)
Deferred Tax Liability (see note below)	(4,250)	
Common Stock	(100,000)	(10,000)
Paid-In Capital in Excess of Par	(600,000)	(190,000)
Retained Earnings, January 1, 20X2	(617,683)	(221,200)
Sales	(890,000)	(350,000)
Cost of Goods Sold	480,000	220,000
Depreciation Expense—Buildings	30,000	10,000
Depreciation Expense—Equipment	25,000	10,000
Other Expenses	150,000	60,000
Interest Expense		8,000
Provision for Income Tax (see note below)	83,613	16,800
Subsidiary Income	(20,160)	
Dividends Declared	20,000	10,000
Total	0	0

Note:

Provision for income taxes (Penstar):

Current ($205,000 × 40%)	$82,000
Solar dividends ($8,000 × 20% × 40%)	640
	$82,640
Current deferred taxes [($20,160 – $8,000) × 20% × 40%]	973
Provision for income taxes	$83,613

Deferred tax liability (Penstar):

Current deferred taxes [($20,160 – $8,000) × 20% × 40%]	$ 973
Change in Solar retained earnings [80% × ($221,200 – $170,000) × 20% × 40%]	3,277
Deferred tax liability	$ 4,250

◄◄◄◄◄ **Required**

1. Prepare a zone analysis and a determination and distribution of excess schedule.
2. Prepare a consolidated worksheet for the year ended December 31, 20X2. Include a provision for income tax and income distribution schedules.

Problem 6-12 *(LO 4)* **Worksheet, separate tax, simple equity, inventory, fixed asset sale, analyze price, later year.** Refer to the preceding facts for Penstar's acquisition of Solar common stock. Penstar accounts for its investment in Solar using the simple equity method, including income tax effects. During 20X3, Solar sold $40,000 worth of merchandise to Penstar. As a result of these intercompany sales, Penstar held beginning inventory of $16,000 and ending inventory of $10,000 of merchandise acquired from Solar. At December 31, 20X3, Penstar owed Solar $8,000 from merchandise sales. Solar has a gross profit rate of 30%.

During 20X3, Penstar sold $60,000 worth of merchandise to Solar. Solar held $15,000 of this merchandise in its ending inventory. Solar owed $10,000 to Penstar as a result of these intercompany sales. Penstar has a gross profit rate of 40%.

On January 1, 20X1, Penstar sold equipment having a net book value of $50,000 to Solar for $90,000. The equipment has a 5-year useful life and is depreciated using the straight-line method.

On January 1, 20X3, Solar sold equipment to Penstar at a profit of $25,000. The equipment has a 5-year useful life and is depreciated using the straight-line method.

Penstar and Solar do not qualify as an affiliated group for tax purposes, and thus, will file separate tax returns. Assume a 40% corporate tax rate and an 80% dividends-received exclusion.

On December 31, 20X3, Penstar and Solar had the following trial balances:

	Penstar Company	Solar Company
Cash	91,760	78,400
Accounts Receivable	150,600	100,000
Inventory	115,000	120,000
Land	100,000	120,000
Investment in Solar	529,680	
Buildings	900,000	250,000
Accumulated Depreciation	(290,000)	(80,000)
Equipment	210,000	120,000
Accumulated Depreciation	(140,000)	(100,000)
Goodwill		30,000
Accounts Payable	(50,000)	(40,000)
Current Tax Liability	(64,240)	(28,800)
Bonds Payable		(100,000)
Deferred Tax Liability (see note on following page)	(6,375)	
Common Stock	(100,000)	(10,000)
Paid-In Capital in Excess of Par	(600,000)	(190,000)
Retained Earnings, January 1, 20X3	(739,230)	(236,400)
Sales	(950,000)	(400,000)
Cost of Goods Sold	550,000	250,000
Depreciation Expense—Buildings	40,000	10,000
Depreciation Expense—Equipment	25,000	10,000

(continued)

	Penstar Company	Solar Company
Other Expenses	176,000	75,000
Interest Expense		8,000
Gain on Sale of Fixed Asset		(25,000)
Provision for Income Taxes (see note below)	66,365	28,800
Subsidiary Income	(34,560)	
Dividends Declared	20,000	10,000
Total	0	0

Note:

Provision for income taxes (Penstar):

Current ($159,000 × 40%)	$63,600
Solar dividends ($8,000 × 20% × 40%)	640
	$64,240
Current deferred taxes [($34,560 – $8,000) × 20% × 40%]	2,125
Provision for income taxes	$66,365

Deferred tax liability (Penstar):

Current deferred taxes [($34,560 – $8,000) × 20% × 40%]	$ 2,125
Change in Solar retained earnings [80% × ($236,400 – $170,000) × 20% × 40%]	4,250
Deferred tax liability	$ 6,375

Required ▶ ▶ ▶ ▶ ▶

1. Prepare a zone analysis and a determination and distribution of excess schedule.
2. Prepare a consolidated worksheet for the year ended December 31, 20X3. Include a provision for income tax and income distribution schedules.

Problem 6-13 *(LO 5)* **Equity income, inventory, fixed asset sale.** Heinrich Company purchased an influential 25% interest in Fink Company on January 1, 20X6, for $320,000. At that time, Fink's stockholders' equity was $1,000,000.

Fink Company assets had fair value similar to book value except for a building that was undervalued by $40,000. The building had an estimated remaining life of 20 years. Any remaining excess was attributed to goodwill.

The following additional information is available:

a. On July 1, 20X6, Heinrich sold a machine to Fink for $24,000. The cost of the machine to Heinrich was $16,000. The machine is being depreciated on a straight-line basis over 10 years.
b. Heinrich provides management services to Fink at a billing rate of $15,000 per year. This arrangement started in 20X6.
c. Fink has sold merchandise to Heinrich since 20X7. Sales were $10,000 in 20X7 and $25,000 in 20X8. The merchandise is sold to provide a gross profit rate of 25%. Heinrich had $2,000 of these goods in its December 31, 20X7, inventory and $3,000 of such goods in its December 31, 20X8, inventory.
d. The income earned and dividends paid by Fink are as follows:

Year	Income	Dividends
20X6	$48,000	$10,000
20X7	50,000	10,000
20X8	65,000	10,000

Prepare all entries necessitated by Heinrich's investment in Fink Company for 20X6 through 20X8 using the equity method for an influential investment. Supporting schedules should be in good form. Ignore taxes. ◄◄◄◄◄ **Required**

Problem 6-14 *(LO 5)* **Equity income, taxation, inventory, fixed asset sale.** On January 1, 20X6, Ashland Company purchased a 25% interest in Cramer Company for $195,000. Ashland Company prepared the following determination and distribution of excess schedule:

Price paid for investment		$195,000	
Less book value of interest acquired:			
Common stock ($5 par)	$ 100,000		
Paid-in capital in excess of par	200,000		
Retained earnings	150,000		
Total stockholders' equity	$ 450,000		
Interest acquired	× 25%	112,500	
Excess of cost over book value (debit)		$ 82,500	
Equipment, 25% × $30,000 (10-year life)		7,500	Dr.
Goodwill		$ 75,000	Dr.

The following additional information is available:

a. Cramer Company sold a machine to Ashland Company for $30,000 on July 1, 20X7. At this date, the machine had a book value of $25,000 and an estimated future life of 5 years. Straight-line depreciation (to the nearest month) is being used. For income tax purposes, the gain on the sale was taxable in the year of the sale.
b. The following applies to Ashland Company sales to Cramer Company for 20X7 and 20X8:

	20X7	20X8
Intercompany merchandise in beginning inventory		$4,000
Sales for the year	$10,000	$15,000
Intercompany merchandise in ending inventory	$4,000	$5,000
Gross profit on sales	40%	40%

c. Internally generated net income (before tax) for the two companies is as follows:

	20X6	20X7	20X8
Ashland Company	$140,000	$150,000	$155,000
Cramer Company	60,000	80,000	100,000

d. Cramer paid dividends of $5,000, $10,000, and $10,000 in 20X6, 20X7, and 20X8, respectively.
e. The corporate income tax rate of 30% applies to both companies. Assume an 80% dividend exclusion.

Prepare all adjustments to Ashland Company's investment in the Cramer Company account, as required by APB Opinion No. 18, on December 31, 20X6, 20X7, and 20X8. Consider income tax implications. Supporting calculations and schedules should be in good form. ◄◄◄◄◄ **Required**

Special Issues in Accounting for an Investment in a Subsidiary

CHAPTER

7

Learning Objectives

When you have completed this chapter, you should be able to

1. **Consolidate a subsidiary when a parent purchases stock directly from the subsidiary.**
2. **Account for purchases of multiple interests in the subsidiary at different points in time.**
3. **Demonstrate the accounting procedures for a complete or partial sale of the investment in a subsidiary.**
4. **Explain the issues surrounding preferred stock in the equity structure of the subsidiary, and follow the procedures used when the parent owns subsidiary preferred stock.**
5. **(Appendix) Solve balance-sheet-only problems (for CPA Exam issue).**

This chapter considers several issues concerning the acquisition and sale of a parent's interest in a subsidiary. The first concern is unique purchase situations. A parent may purchase its interest directly from the subsidiary at the time of original issue. This will require special consideration when consolidating. Procedures also are developed for ownership interests that are acquired in a series of separate purchases over time.

This chapter then will consider the issues involved when a parent company sells all or a portion of its controlling interest in a subsidiary. Not only must the sale be properly recorded, special care must also be taken in accounting for any portion of the investment retained.

The final equity concern of the chapter is the procedure needed in consolidation when the subsidiary has preferred stock in its equity structure. An apportionment of retained earnings may be needed in order to properly account for the parent's interest in common stock. If the parent owns any subsidiary preferred stock, it must be treated as retired in the consolidation process.

The chapter concludes with an appendix that provides the consolidation procedures needed when a worksheet is used to produce only a consolidated balance sheet. These procedures are really only of concern when preparing for the CPA Exam. The Exam may use this approach to save time and space. It is not a worksheet that is used in practice since the accountant must prepare a consolidated income statement, a consolidated statement of retained earnings, and a consolidated balance sheet. There would be no practical reason to use a worksheet for only one of the three statements.

PARENT ACQUISITION OF STOCK DIRECTLY FROM SUBSIDIARY

1

OBJECTIVE

Consolidate a subsidiary when a parent purchases stock directly from the subsidiary.

A parent company may organize a new corporation and supply all of the common stock equity funds in exchange for all of the newly organized company's common stock. Since the newly formed corporation receives the funds directly, there will be no difference between the price paid for the shares and the equity in assets acquired. Thus, the determination and distribution of excess schedule will show no excess of cost over book value or excess of book value over cost.

In other cases, the parent company will allow the newly organized subsidiary to sell a portion of the shares to persons outside the consolidated group. If the shares are sold to outsiders at a price equal to the price paid by the parent, the cost and book value again will be equal. However, if a price greater or less than the price paid by the parent is charged to outside parties, an excess of cost or book value will result. This excess occurs because the total price paid by the parent will not equal its ownership interest multiplied by the total subsidiary common stockholders' equity. Normally, the excess of cost is recorded as goodwill, and an excess of book value is recorded as an extraordinary gain since the only asset held by a newly organized company is cash, which is not subject to adjustment. If noncash assets are given in exchange for the subsidiary shares, these assets would be adjusted according to the normal distribution of excess procedures.

An existing corporation might sell a sufficient number of new shares to grant a controlling interest to the buying company. For example, assume Company S had the following equity balances prior to a sale of shares to Company P:

Common stock, $10 par, 10,000 shares	$100,000
Paid-in capital in excess of par	150,000
Retained earnings	220,000
Total stockholders' equity	$470,000

Assume Company S sells 30,000 additional shares directly to Company P at $50 per share, for a total of $1,500,000. Subsequent to the sale, the equity balances of Company S appear as follows:

Common stock, $10 par, 40,000 shares	$ 400,000
Paid-in capital in excess of par	1,350,000
Retained earnings	220,000
Total stockholders' equity	$1,970,000

A determination and distribution of excess schedule must be prepared for this investment as it would be for any acquisition of a controlling interest. There is no direct connection between the price paid and the interest in subsidiary equity received. The monies paid become a part of the subsidiary's total equity. The interest purchased is a 75% interest (30,000 of 40,000 shares) in the total equity after the sale of the new shares, not a 100% interest in the funds provided by the specific sale of the new shares purchased by the parent. The following determination and distribution of excess schedule would be prepared for the interest purchased by the parent:

Price paid		$1,500,000
Less interest acquired:		
Common stock ($10 par)	$ 400,000	
Paid-in capital in excess of par	1,350,000	
Retained earnings	220,000	
Total stockholders' equity	$1,970,000	
Interest acquired	× 75%	1,477,500
Excess of cost over book value		$ 22,500

The excess would be distributed using normal purchase rules. Any adjustment of existing identifiable accounts would be limited to 75% of the difference between book and fair values since only a 75% interest has been purchased. Any remaining excess would be considered goodwill.

REFLECTION

- The purchase of a controlling interest directly from the subsidiary still requires the preparation of a D&D schedule.

PIECEMEAL ACQUISITION OF INTEREST IN SUBSIDIARY

2
OBJECTIVE
Account for purchases of multiple interests in the subsidiary at different points in time.

Past examples of combinations in this text have involved an acquisition of a controlling interest in a subsidiary through its single purchase of stock. A parent also may acquire a controlling interest as a result of a series of purchases of subsidiary stock. Current practice follows the *parent company concept*, which views each block as a separate ownership interest with a different excess of cost or book value for each block. Each block is seen as having separate causal factors for the difference between the price paid and the underlying book value. Thus, each block requires a separate determination and distribution of excess schedule and separate elimination steps.

The Economic Entity Concept, advanced by the 1995 FASB Exposure Draft on Business Combinations, prepares only one determination and distribution schedule on the day that control is achieved. On that date, all accounts (with the possible exception of goodwill) are increased to their full fair values. No adjustments are made to accounts on the day that any block, not creating control, is purchased. When control is achieved on the first block, a later block is viewed as a stock reacquisition which impacts only equity accounts. When control is achieved on a later purchase, the first block is added to the second and considered as if it were a single purchase at the summed price. These procedures are included in the June 2005 FASB Exposure Draft.

Control Achieved upon Initial Investment

When control is achieved with the initial investment, consolidation procedures already are in effect when subsequent blocks are purchased. Thus, no major change in accounting methods is required. Under current GAAP, another determination and distribution of excess schedule must be prepared for each new investment, and additions to the existing consolidated worksheet procedures must be acknowledged.

Assume Company P purchases on the open market its original 60% interest in Company S on January 1, 20X1, for $126,000, when Company S has the following balance sheet:

Assets		Liabilities and Equity	
Current assets	$ 50,000	Liabilities	$ 40,000
Equipment (net)	150,000	Common stock ($10 par)	100,000
		Retained earnings	60,000
Total assets	$200,000	Total liabilities and equity	$200,000

Further assume that the current assets require no adjustment, and the equipment has a net fair value of $180,000 and a 5-year remaining life. The following determination and distribution of excess schedule would be prepared on *January 1, 20X1*, for the first acquisition:

Price paid		$126,000	
Less interest acquired:			
Common stock	$ 100,000		
Retained earnings	60,000		
Total stockholders' equity	$ 160,000		
Interest acquired	× **60%**	96,000	
Excess of cost over book value (debit balance)		$ 30,000	
Excess of cost attributable to equipment:			
60% × $30,000 undervaluation (to be amortized over **5 years**)		18,000	Dr.
Goodwill		$ 12,000	Dr.

On January 1, 20X3, Company P purchases on the open market an additional 20% interest in Company S by paying $50,000. The following balance sheet of Company S on January 1, 20X3, reflects two years of continued operations:

Assets		Liabilities and Equity	
Current assets	$ 80,000	Liabilities	$ 50,000
Building (net)	80,000	Common stock ($10 par)	100,000
Equipment (net)	90,000	Retained earnings	100,000
Total assets	$250,000	Total liabilities and equity	$250,000

Company P's analysis on January 1, 20X3, indicates that the equipment listed on Company S's balance sheet now is undervalued by $24,000 and has a 3-year remaining life. The current assets and the building appear to have fair values equal to their book values. Based on this analysis, the following determination and distribution of excess schedule would be prepared for the *January 1, 20X3,* investment:

Price paid		$50,000	
Less interest acquired:			
Common stock	$ 100,000		
Retained earnings	100,000		
Total stockholders' equity	$ 200,000		
Interest acquired	× **20%**	40,000	
Excess of cost over book value (debit balance)		$10,000	
Excess of cost attributable to equipment:			
20% × $24,000 undervaluation (to be amortized over **3 years**)		4,800	Dr.
Goodwill		$ 5,200	Dr.

Note that this determination and distribution of excess schedule is *free standing;* that is, it is completely independent of the appraisals made for the January 1, 20X1, schedule.

The additional worksheet procedures that arise from this piecemeal acquisition are shown in Worksheet 7-1 on pages 416 to 417. The trial balances of Companies P and S are shown as they would appear on December 31, 20X3. The investment in the Company S account is based on the use of the simple equity method during the current and previous years. The December 31, 20X3, balance was determined as follows:

worksheet

Worksheet 7-1: page 416

Cost of **60%** investment (January 1, 20X1)		$ 126,000
Add equity share of change in Company S retained earnings as of January 1, 20X3:		
Balance, January 1, 20X3	**$100,000**	
Balance, January 1, 20X1	**60,000**	
Increase in retained earnings	**$ 40,000** × **60%** =	24,000
Cost of **20%** investment (January 1, 20X3)		50,000
Add equity share of Company S 20X3 net income (**80%** × $35,000)		28,000
Investment account balance, December 31, 20X3. . .		**$228,000**

In journal entry form, the eliminations are as follows:

	Eliminate current-year entries to record subsidiary income:		
(CY)	Subsidiary Income	28,000	
	Investment in Company S.		28,000
(EL)	Eliminate subsidiary equity against investment account:		
	Common Stock, Company S	80,000	
	Retained Earnings, January 1, 20X3, Company S	80,000	
	Investment in Company S.		160,000
	Distribute excess on 20X1, 60% investment:		
(D1a)	Equipment	18,000	
(D1b)	Goodwill	12,000	
(D1)	Investment in Company S.		30,000
	Adjust depreciation on equipment for 60% purchase:		
(A1)	Retained Earnings—Company P (2 years × $3,600).	7,200	
	Expenses	3,600	
	Accumulated Depreciation—Equipment		10,800
	Distribute excess on 20X3, 20% investment:		
(D2a)	Equipment	4,800	
(D2b)	Goodwill	5,200	
(D2)	Investment in Company S.		10,000
	Adjust depreciation on equipment for 20% purchase:		
(A2)	Expenses	1,600	
	Accumulated Depreciation—Equipment		1,600

The consolidated net income of $79,800 is distributed to the controlling and noncontrolling interests as shown in the income distribution schedules that accompany Worksheet 7-1. **Since only the parent's share of excesses of cost or book value is recorded,** all amortizations of excess resulting from parent company purchases are deducted **only** from the controlling interest.

When investment blocks are carried **at cost,** each block must be converted separately to its simple equity balance as of the **beginning** of the year. For each block, the adjustment is based on the change in subsidiary retained earnings between the date of acquisition of the individual block and the beginning of the current year.

The determination and distribution of excess schedule for the second block should consider existing unrealized intercompany profits recorded by the subsidiary. Suppose the subsidiary of the previous example sold merchandise to the parent during 20X2, and a $2,000 subsidiary profit is included in the parent's ending inventory of merchandise and in the subsidiary retained earnings. *In theory,* the determination and distribution of excess schedule prepared for the 20% investment purchased on January 1, 20X3, should reflect the unrealized gross profit on sales applicable to the 20% interest purchased. Thus, the determination and distribution of excess schedule would be revised to distribute the excess as follows:

Excess of cost over book value	$10,000
Deferred gross profit on inventory sale (**20%**)	400
Excess of cost attributable to equipment (3-year life)	(4,800)
Goodwill	$ 5,600

The deferred gross profit on the inventory sale means that the NCI just acquired is overstated since the profit already is included in retained earnings. The decrease in the equity acquired increases the excess of cost over book value, thereby making more excess available to remaining assets.

The following entry would distribute the revised excess on the 20X3 worksheet:

Accumulated Depreciation—Equipment	4,800	
Goodwill	5,600	
Deferred Gross Profit on Inventory Sale		400
Investment in Company S		10,000

The following elimination for the $2,000 profit in the beginning inventory then would be made:

Retained Earnings—Controlling Interest (**60%** interest at time of original sale)	1,200	
Retained Earnings—NCI (20%)	400	
Deferred Gross Profit on Inventory Sale	400	
Cost of Goods Sold (beginning inventory)		2,000

In practice, the concept of materiality often will prevail, and the above procedure may not be followed. The determination and distribution of excess schedule may not recognize the deferred inventory profit which will result in less excess being available to other assets. In this case, goodwill will be down by $400. Under this practical approach, worksheets for periods subsequent to the second purchase will ignore the deferred profit existing on the purchase date and will distribute the retained earnings adjustment according to the ownership percentages existing at the time the worksheet is prepared. In this example, the 20% profit applicable to the inventory on the second purchase date would be allocated to the parent with the following adjustment on the worksheet:

Retained Earnings—Controlling Interest (**80%**)	1,600	
Retained Earnings—NCI (20%)	400	
Cost of Goods Sold (beginning inventory)		2,000

Control Not Achieved upon Initial Investment

It is not common to prepare consolidated statements when an initial investment in the stock of another company represents less than a 50% interest. Such an investment is carried under the cost or the sophisticated equity method, depending upon the percentage of interest acquired. APB Opinion No. 18 generally requires the use of the sophisticated equity method when the interest equals or exceeds 20% of the outstanding common shares of an investee corporation.[1] If a second block of stock is purchased, resulting in a total interest that exceeds 50%, consolida-

1 Opinions of the Accounting Principles Board No. 18, *The Equity Method of Accounting for Investments in Common Stock* (New York: American Institute of Certified Public Accountants, 1971), par. 17.

tion becomes appropriate. Current practice is derived from the parent company concept, which views each block as a separate ownership interest with independent causes of excess cost or book value. Thus, each block will have a separate determination and distribution of excess schedule and will have separate elimination procedures on the consolidated worksheet. Added complications arise because the original investment must be subjected to the consolidation process retroactively. The complexities involved depend on whether the original investment was recorded under the sophisticated equity method or the cost method.

Original Interest under the Equity Method. The sophisticated equity method of APB Opinion No. 18 requires that the original excess of cost over book value be amortized as an adjustment of investment income in subsequent years. The amortization pattern depends on the underlying nature of the excess. The Opinion admits that it may be difficult to ascertain the nature of the excess; thus, goodwill may be assumed to be the inferred cause of the entire excess of cost over book value of an investment.

To illustrate the sophisticated equity method, assume Company P purchases on the open market a 20% interest in Company S on *January 1, 20X1*, for $48,000. The balance sheet of Company S on January 1, 20X1, is

Assets			Liabilities and Equity	
Current assets		$ 50,000	Liabilities	$ 50,000
Building and equipment	$225,000		Common stock ($10 par)	50,000
Less accumulated depreciation	75,000	150,000	Retained earnings	100,000
Total assets		$200,000	Total liabilities and equity	$200,000

Assuming the excess of cost is attributable to a building, the determination and distribution of excess schedule would be prepared as follows:

Price paid		$48,000
Less interest acquired:		
Common stock	$ 50,000	
Retained earnings	100,000	
Total stockholders' equity	$150,000	
Interest acquired	× **20%**	30,000
Building (to be depreciated over **20** years)		$18,000

This schedule requires that the investor reduce the investment account $900 ($18,000 ÷ 20) per year. Since the building increase cannot be recorded in the absence of consolidation and is merely buried in the investment account, the depreciation required must be accomplished indirectly through the investment income account. If Company S reports income of $15,000 for 20X1, for example, Company P would record the following sophisticated equity adjustment to the $48,000 recorded investment cost:

Investment in Company S	2,100	
Investment Income		2,100
To recognize 20% of Company S reported income less depreciation of building [(20% × $15,000) – $900].		

Continuing this example, assume that on January 1, 20X2, Company P acquires an additional 60% interest in Company S on the open market for a price of $130,000. The balance sheet of Company S appears as follows on January 1, 20X2:

Assets			Liabilities and Equity	
Current assets		$ 70,000	Liabilities	$ 40,000
Building and			Common stock ($10 par). . . .	50,000
equipment.	$225,000		Retained earnings	115,000
Less accumulated				
depreciation	90,000	135,000		
Total assets		$205,000	Total liabilities and equity . . .	$205,000

If it is assumed that the current assets have book values equal to their market values and the equipment with a 9-year remaining life is undervalued by $9,000, the determination and distribution of excess schedule for the 60% acquisition on *January 1, 20X2*, would be prepared as follows:

Price paid		$130,000	
Less interest acquired:			
Common stock	$ 50,000		
Retained earnings	115,000		
Total stockholders' equity.	$ 165,000		
Interest acquired	× **60%**	99,000	
Excess of cost over book value (debit balance)		$ 31,000	
Excess of cost attributable to equipment:			
60% × $9,000 undervaluation			Dr.
(to be amortized over 9 years).		5,400	
Goodwill		$ 25,600	Dr.

Assuming Company S reports net income of $20,000 for 20X2, Company P would make the following simple equity adjustment for its entire investment:

Investment in Company S	16,000	
Subsidiary Income		16,000
To adjust for **80%** of Company S reported income of $20,000.		

Since control now has been achieved, it is appropriate to use the simple equity method. It no longer is necessary to amortize the excess resulting from the January 1, 20X1, investment through the investment account, since the amortization will be recorded on the consolidated worksheet as shown in Worksheet 7-2 on pages 420 to 421. The balance in the investment account results from the investments and income adjustments, which are summarized as follows:

worksheet
Worksheet 7-2: page 420

Cost of **20%** investment (January 1, 20X1)	$ 48,000
20X1 sophisticated equity adjustment.	2,100
Cost of **60%** investment (January 1, 20X2)	130,000
20X2 simple equity adjustment for **80%** interest	16,000
Investment balance, December 31, 20X2.	**$196,100**

In journal entry form, the eliminations are as follows:

	Eliminate current-year entries to record subsidiary income:		
(CY)	Subsidiary Income	16,000	
	Investment in Company S.		16,000
(EL)	Eliminate 80% subsidiary equity against investment account:		
	Common Stock, Company S	40,000	
	Retained Earnings, January 1, 20X2, Company S	92,000	
	Investment in Company S.		132,000
	Distribute remaining nonamortized excess on 20X1, 20% investment:		
(D1)	Building	17,100	
	Investment in Company S.		17,100
	Building depreciation on 20% purchase for current year only:		
(A1)	Depreciation Expense	900	
	Accumulated Depreciation—Building and Equipment		900
	Distribute excess on 20X2, 60% investment:		
(D2a)	Equipment	5,400	
(D2b)	Goodwill	25,600	
(D2)	Investment in Company S.		31,000
	Adjust depreciation on equipment for 60% purchase:		
(A2)	Expenses	600	
	Accumulated Depreciation—Equipment		600

If the parent wished for consistency in the recording of the investment, it could elect to remove the previous year's amortization of excess adjustments from the investment account and restore them to the parent's retained earnings. This would mean that the worksheet could include all amortization adjustments, not just those subsequent to obtaining control.

Original Interest under the Cost Method. When the investment acquired prior to obtaining control is recorded under the cost method, the easiest procedure is to convert the investment account to its simple equity balance if the later investment in the subsidiary is to be recorded under the simple equity method in future periods. Conversion to the simple equity method thus will make the prior investment compatible with the later investment made to secure control. **The conversion preferably should be made directly on the parent's books.**

Assume Company P in the previous illustration originally purchased only a 10% interest for $24,000 on January 1, 20X1, and used the cost method to record its investment in Company S. When control is achieved on January 1, 20X2, the following determination and distribution of excess schedule would be prepared for the *January 1, 20X1*, investment:

Price paid		$24,000
Less interest acquired:		
Common stock	$ 50,000	
Retained earnings	100,000	
Total stockholders' equity	$ 150,000	
Interest acquired	× **10%**	15,000
Building (to be amortized over 20 years)		$ 9,000

When control is achieved on January 1, 20X2, Company P would also convert the 10% interest to the simple equity method *on its books* as follows:

Investment in Company S	1,500	
Retained Earnings		1,500
To adjust for **10%** of the $15,000 increase in the subsidiary retained earnings during 20X1.		

It would not be necessary to amortize the $450 ($9,000 ÷ 20 years) of building depreciation through the investment account since that amortization can be done in the normal manner on the 20X2 worksheet for consolidated statements. The conversion process simplifies eliminations and adjustments because the entire original excess of cost of $9,000 will appear on the worksheet.

Alternative Procedure for Cost Method Investment. When control is not achieved on the first purchase, ARB No. 51 permits a parent to use the date on which control is achieved as the date of acquisition for both blocks.[2] Thus, a parent is excused from analyzing the cause of excess for a prior-to-achieving-control investment and is allowed to let the original investment remain under the cost method up to the date control is achieved if the result of doing so is not material. In the previous case of Companies P and S, the original 10% interest purchased for $24,000 could be added to the $130,000 cost of the second investment to produce the following determination and distribution of excess schedule on January 1, 20X2:

Price paid (January 1, 20X1 plus January 1, 20X2 investments, $24,000 + $130,000)		**$154,000**	
Less interest acquired:			
Common stock	$ 50,000		
Retained earnings	115,000		
Total stockholders' equity	$ 165,000		
Interest acquired	× **70%**	115,500	
Excess of cost over book value (debit balance)		$ 38,500	
Excess of cost attributable to equipment: **70%** × $9,000 undervaluation (to be amortized over 9 years)		6,300	Dr.
Goodwill		$ 32,200	Dr.

The procedure of lumping investments together *cannot* be recommended on theoretical grounds, since the facts surrounding the separate investments are ignored. Also, when the original investment meets or exceeds 20% of the shares of the subsidiary, this procedure would be a direct violation of APB Opinion No. 18.

The parent may use the cost method for blocks that are acquired prior to achieving control and continue to use it for blocks acquired after achieving control. In this situation, each block would be *independently converted* to the equity method as of the beginning of the year, prior to making any elimination entries. The cost-to-equity conversion technique was described in Chapter 3.

REFLECTION

- When control already exists at the time the parent purchases another block of subsidiary stock, a second D&D schedule is prepared. Separate distribution and amortizations of excess are also performed.
- If the parent owns a noncontrolling interest and then purchases a second block which (in combination with the first block) secures control, the prior interest must have a separate D&D schedule. Separate distribution and amortizations of excess are also performed for each block. The prior interest would also be converted to the simple equity method if it was previously accounted for under the cost method.

2 Accounting Research Bulletin No. 51, *Consolidated Financial Statements* (New York: American Institute of Certified Public Accountants, 1959), par. 10.

SALE OF PARENT'S INVESTMENT IN COMMON STOCK

3

OBJECTIVE

Demonstrate the accounting procedures for a complete or partial sale of the investment in a subsidiary.

A parent may sell all of its subsidiary interest or enough shares to fall below the 50% interest generally required for consolidated reporting. When control is lost, a gain or loss on the transaction is recorded. There may be other stock sales where the parent reduces its percentage interest but still has control after the sale. Current procedures record a gain or loss on such a sale, even though the sale is an intercompany sale of shares to noncontrolling interest stockholders.

Sale of Entire Investment

The sale of the entire investment in a subsidiary terminates the need for consolidated financial statements. In fact, when a sale occurs during the parent's fiscal year, the results of the subsidiary operations prior to the sale date typically are not consolidated. In recording the sale of the investment in a subsidiary, the accountant's primary concern is to adjust the carrying value of the investment so that the correct gain or loss on the sale can be recorded. The results of the subsidiary's operations up to the date of sale must be reported in one of two ways: (a) the net results of operations as a separate line item in the determination of income from continuing operations or (b) as a disposal of a segment of a business.

The accountant must determine if the sale of the investment in a subsidiary constitutes a disposal of a segment of a business as defined by APB Opinin No. 30. The Opinion states: "... the term *segment of a business* refers to a component of an entity whose activities represent a separate major line of business or class of customer."[3] The Opinion indicates that a segment can be in the form of a subsidiary. However, an interpretation of the Opinion makes it clear that not all subsidiaries qualify as segments of a business. For example, a parent may own several subsidiaries engaged in mining coal. If one subsidiary is sold, that would not constitute a sale of a major line of business since the parent still is involved in coal mining. When the sale of a subsidiary qualifies as a disposal of a business segment, both the gain or loss on the sale and the results of operations for the period are shown net of tax in a separate discontinued-segment section of the income statement. When the sale does not qualify as a disposal of a business segment, the gain or loss and the results of operations for the period usually are shown on the income statement as a part of the normal recurring operations.

The complexities of properly recording the sale of an entire subsidiary investment are shown in the following example. Suppose Company P purchased an 80% interest in Company S on January 1, 20X1, for $250,000, and the following determination and distribution of excess schedule was prepared:

Price paid		$250,000	
Less interest acquired:			
Common stock ($10 par)	$100,000		
Retained earnings, January 1, 20X1	150,000		
Total stockholders' equity	$250,000		
Interest acquired	× 80%	200,000	
Excess of cost over book value (debit balance)		$ 50,000	
Excess of cost attributable to equipment (5-year life)		20,000	Dr.
Goodwill		$ 30,000	Dr.

Company S earned $40,000 in 20X1 and $25,000 in 20X2. Company P sells the entire 80% interest on January 1, 20X3, for $320,000. Assuming the use of the simple equity method, Company P's separate statements reflect the following:

3 Opinions of the Accounting Principles Board No. 30, *Reporting the Results of Operations* (New York American Institute of Certified Public Accountants, 1973), par. 13.

Purchase price	$250,000
Share of subsidiary income, 20X1, 80% × $40,000	32,000
Share of subsidiary income, 20X2, 80% × $25,000	20,000
Investment in Company S, December 31, 20X2	$302,000

The investment account and the parent's January 1, 20X3, retained earnings balance reflect a $52,000 increase as a result of subsidiary operations in 20X1 and 20X2. On this basis, it appears that there is an $18,000 gain on the sale of the investment ($320,000 selling price less $302,000 simple-equity-adjusted cost). This result does not agree, however, with the consolidated financial statements prepared for 20X1 and 20X2, which included as expenses the amortizations of excess required by the determination and distribution of excess schedule. The parent's share of subsidiary income appeared as follows in the consolidated statements:

	20X1	20X2	Total
Share of subsidiary income to Company P (80%)	$32,000	$20,000	$52,000
Less amortization of excess of cost of investment over book value:			
Adjustment for depreciation on equipment: $20,000 ÷ 5 = $4,000 per year	(4,000)	(4,000)	(8,000)
Net increase in Company P income due to ownership of Company S investment	$28,000	$16,000	$44,000

Thus, while Company P's separate books show a $52,000 share of Company S income, the consolidated statements reflect only $44,000, the difference being caused by the $8,000 of amortizations indicated by the determination and distribution of excess schedule. Clearly, the recording of the sale of the parent's interest must be based on the $44,000 share of income, since that amount of income is shown on the prior income statements of the consolidated company. Before recording the sale of the investment, Company P must adjust its books to be consistent with prior consolidated statements. The entry needed will adjust the January 1, 20X3, retained earnings account on the separate books of the parent to the December 31, 20X2, balance of the controlling interest in retained earnings shown on the consolidated statements. The adjusting entry on the books of Company P is as follows:

Retained Earnings, January 1, 20X3	8,000	
Investment in Company S		8,000
To adjust the investment account and Company P retained earnings account for amortizations made on past consolidated statements.		

If the sophisticated equity method was used, the amortizations would be reflected already in the investment account and no adjustment would be needed. Under either equity method, the entry to record the sale then would be as follows:

Cash	320,000	
Investment in Company S ($302,000 – $8,000)		294,000
Gain on Disposal of Subsidiary		26,000
To record the gain on the sale of the 80% interest in Company S.		

Note that the $8,000 adjusting entry for the past years' amortizations of excess normally would have been made on the consolidated worksheet for 20X3. However, since there will be no further consolidations, the adjustment must be made directly on Company P's books. The gain (net of tax) on the disposal of the subsidiary will appear as a separate item on the income statement for 20X3 if the sale of the subsidiary meets the criteria for a disposal of a business segment.

In this example, if Company P had used the cost method, the investment account still would be shown at the original cost of $250,000. It then would be necessary to update the investment and retained earnings accounts on the separate books of Company P to include its $44,000 (net of amortizations) share of subsidiary income for 20X1 and 20X2. This adjustment would allow the accounts of the parent on January 1, 20X3, to conform to past consolidated statements. The following entries would be made on the books of Company P to record the sale of the parent's 80% interest:

Investment in Company S	44,000	
Retained Earnings, January 1, 20X3		44,000
To record the parent's share of subsidiary income as shown on prior years' consolidated statements.		
Cash	320,000	
Investment in Company S ($250,000 + $44,000)		294,000
Gain on Disposal of Subsidiary		26,000

It also is necessary to adjust the investment account for any unrealized intercompany gains and losses. These profits would have been deferred in the most recent consolidated statement, but under the cost or simple equity method they are not reflected in the investment account. Again, we must adjust the investment account to reflect the income reported in past consolidated statements. Suppose the parent had on hand at the sale date inventory on which the subsidiary recorded a $1,000 profit. Since the parent owns an 80% interest, the adjusting entry on the day the investment is sold would be as follows:

Retained Earnings	800	
Investment in Company S		800

Assume the investment in the previous example was sold for $320,000 on July 1, 20X3, and Company S reported income of $12,000 for the first six months of 20X3. Since Company S will not be a part of the consolidated group at the end of the period, the results of its operations will not be consolidated with those of the parent. Therefore, the parent must record its share of subsidiary income for the current period to the date of disposal. The parent's net share of subsidiary income would be calculated on a basis consistent with past consolidated statements, as follows:

Share of subsidiary income for first six months to Company P (80%)	$ 9,600
Less amortization of excess of cost over book value that would have been made on consolidated statements:	
Equipment depreciation adjustment, $4,000 per year × ½ year	(2,000)
Net share of subsidiary income	$ 7,600

The parent would proceed to record the July 1, 20X3, sale of its subsidiary investment as follows:

1. Assuming the past use of the simple equity method, the parent's investment account on January 1, 20X3, is adjusted to reflect the amortizations made on past consolidated statements (as calculated on page 400).

Retained Earnings, January 1, 20X3	8,000	
Investment in Company S		8,000

2. The parent's share of subsidiary income for the partial year is recorded. This amount is the $7,600 income net of amortizations (as calculated above).

Investment in Company S	7,600	
Operating Income of Subsidiary Disposed of During Year		7,600

3. The sale of the investment for $320,000 is recorded.

Cash	320,000	
Investment in Company S.		301,600
Gain on Disposal of Subsidiary		18,400

The adjusted cost of the investment is determined as follows:

Original cost, January 1, 20X1	$250,000
Simple equity income adjustments for 20X1 and 20X2	52,000
Amortization of excess (entry 1)	(8,000)
Share of Company S income for six months (entry 2)	7,600
Net cost, July 1, 20X3	$301,600

Sale of Portion of Investment

The sale of a portion of an investment in a subsidiary requires unique treatment, depending on whether effective control is lost as a result of the sale. Special procedures must also be used when a sale of a partial interest occurs during a reporting period.

Loss of Control. A parent may sell a portion of its investment in a subsidiary so that it loses control. This situation may occur for foreign subsidiaries when the foreign government passes a law forbidding control of its companies by nonresidents. Such a sale also may be made to avoid consolidating affiliated companies. FASB Statement No. 94 now requires the consolidation of nonhomogeneous subsidiaries that previously did not have to be consolidated.[4] Some sell-downs did occur after the issuance of that Statement to avoid adding the substantial debt of real estate and financing subsidiaries to the consolidated statements. If control is lost, consolidation procedures no longer will apply. This situation would require that the parent company books be adjusted to make them consistent with prior consolidated statements. Exactly the same adjusting entries as in the immediately preceding section are needed to adjust the parent's investment account. Note that the adjustments are made for the entire interest previously owned, not just the portion sold. If, in the preceding example, Company P sells one-half instead of all of its 80% interest, the investment account should be adjusted for the entire 80% interest in past and current years' subsidiary income, net of amortizations. The 40% interest sold must be adjusted to properly record the sale, and the 40% interest retained also must be adjusted, since it no longer will be consolidated. Past adjustments that would be handled as part of the annual consolidation process now must be made directly to the investment account, so that the investment remaining conforms with APB Opinion No. 18. The sophisticated equity method described in that Opinion should be applied to remaining interests of 20% or more.[5]

If one-half of Company P's investment of the preceding section is sold for $160,000 on July 1, 20X3, the following entries would be recorded:

1. Assuming the past use of the simple equity method, the parent's investment account on January 1, 20X3, is adjusted to reflect the amortizations made on past consolidated statements.

Retained Earnings, January 1, 20X3	8,000	
Investment in Company S.		8,000

4 Statement of Financial Accounting Standards No. 94, *Consolidation of All Majority-Owned Subsidiaries* (Stamford: Financial Accounting Standards Board, 1987), par. 9.

5 Opinions of the Accounting Principles Board No. 18, *The Equity Method of Accounting for Investments in Common Stock* (New York: American Institute of Certified Public Accountants, 1971), par. 17.

2. The parent's share of subsidiary income for the partial year is recorded. This amount is the $7,600 income net of amortizations.

Investment in Company S	7,600	
Subsidiary Income		7,600

3. The sale of one-half of the investment for $160,000 is recorded. The resulting gain is always ordinary income and never a gain from a "discontinued segment."

Cash	160,000	
Investment in Company S (½ of $301,600 adjusted cost calculated on page 402)		150,800
Gain on Sale of Investment		9,200

Note that the sale of a partial interest will not qualify as a discontinued segment. Thus, the operating results on the investment to the sale date and the gain or loss on the sale would be shown as a part of ordinary income from continuing operations.

The remaining 40% investment will not be consolidated. It will be accounted for as an "influential" investment under the sophisticated equity method.

Control Retained. A parent company may sell a portion of its investment in a subsidiary but still have an interest that provides control even after the sale. For example, assume that on January 1, 20X1, a parent purchased from outside parties 8,000 of the total 10,000 shares of a subsidiary. On January 1, 20X3, the parent sold 2,000 shares and thereby lowered its percentage of ownership to 60%. Since the parent still had control, the 2,000 shares were sold, in essence, to NCI shareholders. The 1995 FASB Exposure Draft on business combinations considers this type of sale to be the sale of additional shares to NCI shareholders. Under the *economic unit concept*, the parent has chosen to sell subsidiary shares, instead of parent shares, to raise additional equity capital. Under this concept, there can be no income statement gains or losses resulting from any stock issuances by the consolidated entity. This transaction would impact only paid-in capital.

A FASB Exposure Draft issued in October 2000 confirmed this approach by stating that "as long as a subsidiary remains consolidated, a sale of that subsidiary's shares to entities outside the consolidated group that increases the NCI is an equity transaction and shall be reported directly in equity in the consolidated financial statements."[6] Any resulting change in equity is treated as an adjustment to paid-in capital. The adjustment is made to the paid-in capital of the parent company. This position is affirmed in the June 2005 FASB Exposure Draft.

To illustrate the recording of such a partial sale, return to the example for which a determination and distribution of excess schedule was prepared on page 399. Assume that on January 1, 20X3, Company P sells 2,000 subsidiary shares to lower its total interest to 60%. Only the portion of the investment account sold is to be adjusted to the sophisticated equity method to allow the proper recording of the sale. The 60% retained need not be adjusted on Company P's books since all amortization adjustments on the 60% interest will be made on future consolidated statements. The adjustment of the 20% interest on the separate books of Company P must agree with the treatment of that interest in prior consolidated statements. Assuming the use of the simple equity method, the portion of the investment sold must be adjusted for its share of the past amortizations made on consolidated statements. Since the 20X1 and 20X2 amortizations on page 400 totaled $8,000 for an 80% interest, the amortizations for the 20% interest sold would be **one-fourth** of $8,000, or $2,000. The parent would make the following entry:

Retained Earnings, January 1, 20X3	2,000	
Investment in Company S		2,000
To adjust for amortizations made on previous consolidated statements for the portion of the subsidiary investment sold.		

6 FASB Exposure Draft, *Accounting for Financial Instruments with Characteristics of Liabilities, Equity, or Both* (Norwalk, CT: Financial Accounting Standards Board, October 2000).

To record the sale of the investment, the parent would remove from its books **one-fourth** of the simple-equity-adjusted cost of January 1, 20X3 (calculated at $302,000 on page 400), which along with the previous $2,000 adjustment nets to $73,500. If the sale price is less than $73,500, a loss would be recorded. If the sale price is greater than $73,500, a gain would be recorded, as shown in the following entry to record the sale of the investment for $80,000:

Cash	80,000	
Investment in Company S [(¼ × $302,000) – $2,000 amortization adjustment]		73,500
Paid-In Capital in Excess of Par, Company P		6,500

If the parent in the previous example had used the cost method, only the portion of the investment sold would be adjusted to the sophisticated equity method on the parent's books. The analysis on page 400 shows that the parent's 80% share of income for 20X1 and 20X2 was $44,000 on a consolidated basis, net of amortizations. The 20% interest sold must be adjusted by **one-fourth** of $44,000, or $11,000. The remaining 60% will be adjusted in future worksheets. The entry to adjust the 20% interest would be as follows:

Investment in Company S	11,000	
Retained Earnings, January 1, 20X3		11,000
To adjust for the parent's share of past consolidated income pertaining to the interest sold.		

The parent then would proceed to record the sale of the investment for $80,000 as follows:

Cash	80,000	
Investment in Company S (¼ of original $250,000 cost + $11,000 equity income)		73,500
Paid-In Capital in Excess of Par, Company P		6,500

Intraperiod Sale of a Partial Interest. When a sale of an interest during the reporting period does not result in loss of control, careful analysis is needed to ensure that the worksheet adheres to consolidation theory. Referring to the situation on page 400, assume Company P sells one-fourth of its 80% interest for $80,000 on July 1, 20X3, and subsidiary income for the first half of the year is $12,000. Assuming the use of the simple equity method, the parent would adjust its own investment and the beginning-of-the-year retained earnings accounts for **one-fourth** of the amortizations of excess cost recorded on the prior years' consolidated worksheets. The adjustment would be recorded as follows:

Retained Earnings, January 1, 20X3	2,000	
Investment in Company S		2,000
To record **one-fourth** of the $8,000 amortizations (shown on page 400) for 20X1 and 20X2.		

A parent using the cost method would adjust the retained earnings for the subsidiary income, net of amortizations, for 20X1 and 20X2 (20% × $44,000 income on a consolidated basis).

Next, the parent would calculate its share of subsidiary income for the first half of 20X3 applicable to the 20% interest sold and adjusted for partial-year amortizations of excess relating to that portion of the investment as follows:

Income on 20% interest in Company S sold (20% × $12,000)	$2,400
Less amortizations of excess of cost over book value that would be necessary on consolidated statements:	
Equipment depreciation adjustment, $4,000 per year × ½ year × ¼ interest sold	(500)
Net share of income on interest sold	$1,900

The parent then would make a sophisticated equity method adjustment for this income and record the sale as follows:

Investment in Company S	1,900	
Subsidiary Income		1,900
To record share of first 6 months' subsidiary income applicable to the 20% interest sold and adjusted for partial-year amortizations of excess relating to that portion of the investment.		
Cash	80,000	
Investment in Company S [(¼ × \$302,000) − \$2,000 amortizations + \$1,900 income]		75,400
Paid-In Capital in Excess of Par, Company P		4,600
To record sale of 20% interest in subsidiary.		

The sale of a partial interest that does not result in loss of control requires special procedures on the consolidated worksheet for the period in which the sale occurs. Worksheets of later periods would not include any complications resulting from the sale. In Worksheet 7-3 on pages 422 to 423, the following should be noted:

Worksheet 7-3: page 422

1. The investment in Company S account reflects its simple equity balance on December 31, 20X3, for the remaining 60% interest held. The balance is computed as follows:

December 31, 20X2, balance applicable to remaining (60%) interest held at year-end, ¾ × \$302,000	\$226,500
Add **60%** of subsidiary reported income of \$30,000 for 20X3	18,000
Simple equity balance, December 31, 20X3	\$244,500

2. The balance in Paid-In Capital in Excess of Par—Company P is the increase in equity from the 20% interest sold.
3. The balance in Subsidiary Income includes **60%** of the subsidiary's \$30,000 20X3 income, plus the \$1,900 earned on the **20%** interest prior to its sale.
4. The share of income applicable to the interest sold, \$2,400, is transferred to the NCI. The share of subsidiary income purchased by the NCI is not reduced for the amortizations of excess cost applicable to the parent's purchase. These amortizations apply only to the income recorded by the controlling interest. The amortizations are recorded and allocated to the parent for the portion of the year prior to the sale. Entry (NCI) on Worksheet 7-3 makes the transfer and records the partial-year amortization applicable to the interest sold.

In journal entry form, the eliminations are as follows:

	Transfer income on interest sold to NCI and record amortizations of excess on interest sold:		
(NCI)	Subsidiary Income	1,900	
	Expenses	500	
	Income Sold to NCI		2,400
	Eliminate current-year entries to record subsidiary income:		
(CY)	Subsidiary Income	18,000	
	Investment in Company S		18,000
(EL)	Eliminate subsidiary equity against investment account on 60% investment still owned:		
	Common Stock, Company S	60,000	
	Retained Earnings, January 1, 20X3, Company S	129,000	
	Investment in Company S		189,000

(continued)

	Distribute excess on remaining 60% investment:		
(D1)	Equipment	15,000	
(D2)	Goodwill	22,500	
(D)	Investment in Company S.		37,500
	Adjust depreciation on equipment:		
(A1)	Retained Earnings—Company P (2 years × $3,000)	6,000	
	Expenses	3,000	
	Accumulated Depreciation—Equipment		9,000

Carefully study the income distribution schedules for Worksheet 7-3. The NCI receives its 40% interest in subsidiary income for the entire year, but there is a deduction for the income purchased from the parent for the first 6 months. The parent company income distribution schedule claims 60% of the subsidiary income for the entire year plus a 20% interest in the first 6 months' income.

If the parent, Company P, had used the cost method, there would be few changes in Worksheet 7-3. Entry (NCI) would be unchanged; however, an entry would be needed to convert the remaining 60% interest to the simple equity method at the beginning of the year. Entry (CY) would not be applicable since there would be no current-year equity adjustment to reverse. Remaining entries would remain the same.

Complications Resulting from Intercompany Transactions. When a sale of subsidiary stock results in loss of control, the parent should adjust its investment account on the date of the sale for its share of unrealized subsidiary gains and losses resulting from intercompany transactions. When control is not lost as the result of a sale of subsidiary shares, the adjustment on the consolidated worksheet for unrealized gains and losses resulting from previous intercompany transactions need be recorded only as it applies to the interest sold. The remaining controlling interest's share of these gains and losses can be adjusted on subsequent consolidated worksheets. On these worksheets, retained earnings adjustments for unrealized gains and losses would be distributed according to the relative ownership interests existing on the dates the worksheets are prepared.

REFLECTION

- When the parent's entire investment in a subsidiary is sold, the investment must be adjusted to the sophisticated equity method to properly record the gain or loss. The gain or loss may qualify as a gain or loss on a discontinued operation.
- If a portion of the investment in a subsidiary is sold and control is lost, the entire investment is still adjusted to the sophisticated equity method. This allows the correct gain or loss to be calculated on the interest sold. The remaining investment is also then restated at the sophisticated equity balance.
- If a portion of the investment in a subsidiary is sold, but control is retained, only the block sold is adjusted to the sophisticated equity balance. This allows the correct calculation of the gain or loss on the interest sold. The remaining investment will still be consolidated and may be accounted for under the cost, equity, or sophisticated equity method. Special procedures are needed for the current-year portion of income on the interest sold.

SUBSIDIARY PREFERRED STOCK

4

OBJECTIVE

Explain the issues surrounding preferred stock in the equity structure of the subsidiary, and follow the procedures used when the parent owns subsidiary preferred stock.

The existence of preferred stock in the capital structure of a subsidiary complicates the calculation of a parent's claim on subsidiary retained earnings, both at the time of acquisition and in the preparation of subsequent consolidated statements. In previous examples, the subsidiary had only common stock outstanding, so that all retained earnings were associated with common stock, and the parent had a claim on subsidiary retained earnings in proportion to its ownership interest. When a subsidiary has preferred stock outstanding, however, the preferred stock also may have a claim on retained earnings. This claim may be caused by a liquidation value in excess of par value and/or by participation and cumulative dividend rights. When these conditions exist, the retained earnings must be divided between the preferred and common stockholder interests.

Once retained earnings are allocated between the common and preferred stockholders, the intercompany investments can be eliminated. The investment in subsidiary common stock account will be eliminated against the total equity claim of the common stockholders. If there is an investment in subsidiary preferred stock account, it will be eliminated against the preferred stockholders' total equity.

Determination of Preferred Shareholders' Claim on Retained Earnings

The allocation of the retained earnings to the preferred and common stockholder interests is accomplished by employing the procedures used to calculate the book value of preferred and common stock. Although typically covered in intermediate accounting, the topic will be reviewed briefly in the following paragraphs.

The preferred shareholders' claim on retained earnings equals the claim they would have if the company was dissolved. In addition to the par value of the preferred shares, there may be a stipulated liquidation value in excess of par and/or dividend preferences. In the rare case of a liquidation value in excess of par, an amount equal to the liquidation bonus (liquidation value less par value) must be segregated from retained earnings as a preferred shareholder claim. Liquidation values should not be confused with paid-in capital in excess of par which results from the sale of preferred shares. Such paid-in capital is not available to preferred shareholders in liquidation and is not part of the book value of preferred shares. Instead, it becomes part of the total paid-in capital that is available to common shareholders.

In addition to a liquidation bonus, there must be an analysis of any cumulative and/or participation clauses applicable to the preferred stock. Other than the effect of a liquidation bonus, if the preferred stock is noncumulative and nonparticipating, the preferred stockholders would have no claim and all the retained earnings attach to the common stock. However, if there are preferred shareholder claims resulting from cumulative and/or participation clauses, these claims reduce the retained earnings applicable to the common stock. For example, if the preferred stock is noncumulative but fully participating, the retained earnings are allocated pro rata according to the total par or stated values of the preferred and common stock. If the preferred stock is cumulative but nonparticipating and, for example, has two years' dividends in arrears, a claim on retained earnings equal to the two years of dividends exists, although there is no liability to pay the preferred dividends until a dividend is declared.

When preferred stock is both cumulative and fully participating, the arrearage for prior periods is met first. The remaining retained earnings are allocated pro rata according to the total par values of the preferred and common stock. When preferred stock is cumulative and participating but no dividends are in arrears, the analysis is the same as if the preferred stock were noncumulative but participating.

When preferred stock is cumulative and limited in participation to a percentage of par value, the arrearage for prior periods is met first and is excluded from the limited participation. The lesser of a pro rata share of the remaining retained earnings or the limiting percentage of the preferred stock's par value is allocated to the preferred claim. Any retained earnings remaining after this allocation are assigned to the common stock.

Apportionment of Retained Earnings

Additional procedures are required when a subsidiary with preferred stock that has liquidation and/or dividend preferences is consolidated, even if none of the preferred shares are owned by the parent. In this situation, allocation of retained earnings to the preferred and common stock is as follows:

1. The determination and distribution of excess schedule prepared as of the date of the parent's investment in common stock must include only that portion of retained earnings that is allocable to the common stock on the purchase date.
2. Periodic equity adjustments for the parent's investment in common stock are made only for the common shareholders' claim on income. The preferred shareholders' claim on the current year's income, including dividends paid or accumulated and any participation rights for the current year, must be deducted to arrive at income available to common shareholders. When the cost method is used, the worksheet simple equity conversion adjustment is made for the parent's share of change in the retained earnings applicable to common stock since the date of acquisition.
3. Subsidiary retained earnings must be allocated between preferred and common stockholders on consolidated worksheets. The parent's investment in common stock account then is eliminated against the parent's pro rata share of only the equity attaching to common stock.

To illustrate these procedures, assume Company S has the following stockholders' equity on January 1, 20X3, the date on which Company P purchases an 80% interest in the common stock for $150,000:

Preferred stock, $100 par, 6% cumulative	$100,000
Common stock, $10 par	100,000
Retained earnings	80,000
Total equity	$280,000

The preferred stock has a liquidation value equal to par value, and dividends are 2 years in arrears as of January 1, 20X3. Company S assets have a fair value equal to book value. Any excess purchase price is attributable to goodwill. The determination and distribution of excess schedule would be prepared as follows:

Price paid			$150,000
Less interest acquired:			
Common stock ($10 par)		$ 100,000	
Retained earnings:			
Balance, January 1, 20X3	**$80,000**		
Less preferred dividends in arrears (2 years × $6,000)	**12,000**	**68,000**	
Total equity applicable to common stock		$ 168,000	
Interest acquired		× 80%	134,400
Goodwill			$ 15,600

Assume that income is exactly $25,000 per year in future years and no dividends are paid. Each year, the following entry would be made by Company P using the simple equity method of accounting for its subsidiary investment:

Investment in Company S	15,200	
Subsidiary Income		15,200
To adjust for 80% of Company S income applicable to common stock ($25,000 reported income − $6,000 cumulative claim of preferred stock).		

Worksheet 7-4, pages 426 to 427, is a consolidated financial statements worksheet for the year ended *December 31, 20X5* (3 years subsequent to the purchase). The investment in common stock account includes the original cost of the investment plus 3 years (3 × \$15,200 = \$45,600) of simple equity adjustments for income and dividends. The worksheet is unique in that it subdivides the subsidiary retained earnings into two parts: one for the common portion and one for the preferred portion of retained earnings. Entry (PS) of Worksheet 7-4 accomplishes this apportionment.

Worksheet 7-4: page 426

In journal entry form, the eliminations are as follows:

	Distribute portion of retained earnings to preferred stockholders as of January 1, 20X5:		
(PS)	Retained Earnings, January 1, 20X5, Company S	24,000	
	Retained Earnings Allocated to Preferred Stock, January 1, 20X5, Company S		24,000
	Eliminate current-year entries to record subsidiary income:		
(CY)	Subsidiary Income	15,200	
	Investment in Company S.		15,200
(EL)	Eliminate subsidiary common stock equity against investment in common stock account:		
	Common Stock, Company S	80,000	
	Retained Earnings, January 1, 20X5, Company S	84,800	
	Investment in Common Stock of Company S		164,800
(D)	Distribute excess on 80% investment in common stock:		
	Goodwill	15,600	
	Investment in Common Stock of Company S		15,600

This division of retained earnings is only for worksheet purposes; the subsidiary will maintain only one retained earnings account.

After the eliminations and adjustments are completed, the resulting consolidated net income of \$175,000 is allocated as shown in the income distribution schedules. Since none of the preferred stock is owned by controlling shareholders, the NCI receives all applicable preferred income plus 20% of the income allocable to common stock. It should be observed that the NCI column, as well as the NCI shown on a formal balance sheet, includes the NCI in both preferred and common shares.

The worksheet just analyzed can handle all types of subsidiary preferred stockholder claims. Once the claim is determined, with supporting calculations, it can be isolated in a separate worksheet account, *Retained Earnings Allocated to Preferred Stock*.

When a parent uses the cost method to record its investment in a subsidiary, slightly different worksheet procedures are used. In the previous illustration, if Company P had used the cost method, the investment account still would be at the \$150,000 original cost. In addition, there would be no subsidiary income shown, and the January 1, 20X5, retained earnings of Company P would not reflect the 20X3 and 20X4 simple equity adjustments. As described earlier, a conversion to the simple equity method is made on the worksheet. Since the beginning-of-the-period investment balance is needed for elimination, the equity adjustment converts the investment account to the January 1, 20X5, balance, as follows:

Retained earnings, Company S, January 1, 20X5	\$130,000	
Less 4 years' arrearage of preferred dividends	24,000	
Retained earnings applicable to common stock, January 1, 20X5		**\$106,000**

(continued)

Retained earnings, Company S, January 1, 20X3	$ 80,000	
Less 2 years' arrearage of preferred dividends	12,000	
Retained earnings applicable to common stock, January 1, 20X3		**68,000**
Increase in common stock portion of retained earnings		$ 38,000
Controlling interest (80%)		$ 30,400

The conversion (CV) entry for $30,400 would debit the investment account and credit the Company P retained earnings account. The investment account now would be stated at its simple-equity-adjusted, January 1, 20X5, balance. Worksheet entries (PS), (EL), and (D) would be made just as in Worksheet 7-4. Only entry (CY) would be omitted, since it is not applicable to the cost method. The partial worksheet below includes the conversion and subsequent eliminations and adjustments under the cost method. All remaining procedures for this example would be identical to those used in Worksheet 7-4.

Subsidiary Preferred Stock, None Owned by Parent
Cost Method Used for Investment in Common Stock

	Partial Trial Balance		Eliminations & Adjustments	
	Company P	Company S	Dr.	Cr.
Investment in Common Stock of Company S	**150,000**		(CV) **30,400**	(EL) 164,800
				(D) 15,600
Goodwill			(D) 15,600	
Retained Earnings, January 1, 20X5, Company P	(309,600)			(CV) **30,400**
Preferred Stock ($100 par), Company S		(100,000)		
Retained Earnings, Allocated to Preferred Stock, January 1, 20X5, Company S				(PS) 24,000
Common Stock ($10 par), Company S		(100,000)	(EL) 80,000	
Retained Earnings, January 1, 20X5, Company S		(130,000)	(PS) 24,000	
			(EL) 84,800	
Expenses	100,000	25,000		

Eliminations and Adjustments:

(CV) The cost-to-equity conversion entry was explained prior to the partial worksheet.
(PS) Distribute the beginning-of-the-period subsidiary retained earnings into the portions allocable to common and preferred stock. The typical procedure would be to consider the stated subsidiary retained earnings as applicable to common and to remove the preferred portion. This distribution reflects four years of arrearage (as of January 1, 20X5) at $6,000 per year.
(EL) Eliminate the pro rata subsidiary common stockholders' equity at the beginning of the period against the investment account. This entry includes elimination of the 80% of subsidiary retained earnings applicable to common stock.
(D) Distribute the excess of cost according to the determination and distribution of excess schedule.

Parent Investment in Subsidiary Preferred Stock

A parent may purchase all or a portion of the preferred stock of a subsidiary. Normally, preferred stock is nonvoting; therefore, it is not considered in determining whether the parent owns a controlling interest in the subsidiary. Thus, a 100% ownership of nonvoting preferred stock and a 49% interest in voting common stock may not require the preparation of consolidated statements.

From a consolidated viewpoint, the parent's purchase of subsidiary preferred stock usually is viewed as a retirement of the stock.[7] The amount paid is compared to the sum of the original proceeds resulting from the issuance of the shares and any claim the shares have on retained earnings, and an increase or decrease in equity as a result of the retirement is calculated. When the price paid is less than the preferred equity retired, the resulting increase in equity is credited to the controlling paid-in capital account, not the retained earnings account, because it results from a transaction with the consolidated company's shareholders. A decrease in equity, which occurs when the price paid exceeds the preferred equity, would offset against the paid-in capital applicable to the preferred stock. If not enough of the preferred stock paid-in capital exists, the remaining decrease would be taken from the controlling retained earnings and viewed as a retirement dividend.

To illustrate this type of investment, assume Company P in the previous example purchased 600 shares (60%) of Company S preferred stock on January 1, 20X3, for $65,000. The increase or decrease in equity resulting from the retirement would be calculated as follows:

Price paid		$65,000
Less **preferred** interest acquired:		
Preferred stock ($100 par)	$100,000	
Claim on dividends (2 years in arrears × $6,000 per year)	12,000	
Total preferred interest	$112,000	
Interest acquired	× 60%	67,200
Increase in equity (credit Paid-In Capital)		**$ 2,200**

Though viewed as retired, the preferred stock investment account will continue to exist on the books of the parent in subsequent periods. At the end of each period, the investment must be "retired" on the consolidated worksheet. The procedures used depend on whether the parent accounts for the investment in preferred stock under the equity method or the cost method. Under the equity method, the parent adjusts the investment in preferred stock account each period for any additional claim on the subsidiary retained earnings, including any continued arrearage or participation privilege. In this example, the arrearage of dividends would be recorded each year, 20X3 to 20X5, as follows:

Investment in Company S Preferred Stock	3,600	
Subsidiary Income		3,600
To acknowledge 60% of the annual increase in the Company S preferred stock dividend arrearage.		

Assuming the equity adjustments are properly made, any original discrepancy between the price paid for the preferred shares and their book value would be maintained. The equity method also acknowledges that, even though the shares are viewed as retired in consolidated reports, the controlling interest is entitled to its proportionate share of consolidated net income based on both its common and preferred stock holdings.

Worksheet 7-5, pages 428 to 429, displays the consolidation procedures that would be used for the ownership interest in preferred stock described above. This worksheet parallels Worksheet 7-4 except that the parent owns 60% of the subsidiary preferred stock. The investment is listed at its $65,000 cost plus three years of equity adjustments to reflect the increasing dividend arrearage.

worksheet

Worksheet 7-5: page 428

7 It also would be possible to view the investment as treasury shares, in which case they would appear as a contra account to the preferred stock in the minority interest section of the consolidated balance sheet. This approach, however, does not have popular support. It could be justified only if there were an intent to reissue the shares.

All of the eliminations from Worksheet 7-4 are repeated in Worksheet 7-5. The following additional eliminations are added in Worksheet 7-5:

	Eliminate the income reported during the current year on the interest in preferred stock:		
(CYP)	Subsidiary Income—Preferred	3,600	
	Investment in Company S Preferred Stock		3,600
	Eliminate investment in preferred stock against equity applicable to parent's share of subsidiary preferred stock equity; excess of equity over investment is an increase in parent's paid-in capital in excess of par:		
(ELP)	Preferred Stock ($100 par), Company S	60,000	
	Retained Earnings Allocated to Preferred Stock, January 1, 20X5, Company S	14,400	
	Investment in Company S Preferred Stock		72,200
	Paid-In Capital in Excess of Par, Company P		2,200

Consolidated net income is distributed as shown in the income distribution schedules that accompany the worksheet. The distributions respect the controlling/NCI ownership of both common and preferred shares. The common and preferred equity interests of the NCI again are summarized on the worksheet and for presentation on the formal balance sheet.

If a parent uses the cost method for its investment in subsidiary preferred stock, the investment should be converted to its equity balance as of the beginning of the period. In this example, if the cost method is used for the investment in preferred stock, the following conversion adjustment would be made on the worksheet:

(CVP)	Preferred stock cost-to-equity conversion:		
	Investment in Company S Preferred Stock	7,200	
	Retained Earnings, January 1, 20X5, Company P		7,200

The adjustment reflects two years of arrearage at $6,000 per year times the 60% ownership interest. Eliminations and adjustments would proceed as in Worksheet 7-5, except that there would be no need for entry (CY).

This example contains only cumulative preferred stock. However, the same principles would apply to participating preferred stock, and the allocation procedures outlined earlier in this chapter would be used. Only the subdivision of the subsidiary retained earnings and the amounts of the equity adjustments would differ.

REFLECTION

- If a subsidiary has preferred stock with a claim on retained earnings (because it is cumulative or participating), the subsidiary retained earnings must be allocated between the preferred and common stock. The investment in common stock is eliminated only against the retained earnings allocated to the common stock.
- In addition, if the parent owns subsidiary preferred stock, the investment is eliminated on the worksheet against the applicable subsidiary preferred stock.

APPENDIX: WORKSHEET FOR A CONSOLIDATED BALANCE SHEET

5

OBJECTIVE

Solve balance-sheet-only problems (for CPA Exam issue).

Previous chapters displayed procedures applicable to worksheets that produced a consolidated income statement, retained earnings statement, and balance sheet. However, there may be occasions when only consolidated balance sheets are required, and the separate balance sheets of the affiliates form the starting point for consolidation procedures. Such occasions are rare in practice but are of concern to students desiring to take the CPA Exam. Past examinations have used balance-sheet-only consolidation problems as an expedient method for testing purposes. This type of problem requires less time to solve while still testing the candidates' knowledge of consolidations.

A balance sheet worksheet requires only adjustments to balance sheet accounts. No adjustments for nominal accounts are required. Your past experience often will lead you to consider the impact of an elimination on the nominal accounts, but you must adjust your thinking to cover only the remaining impact of an elimination on the balance sheet. For example, intercompany merchandise sales no longer will require an elimination of the sales and cost of goods sold relative to the transaction. The following sections examine the simplified procedures that are used on a consolidated balance sheet worksheet.

Investment Account

When the investment account is maintained under the simple equity method, it will reflect the same point in time as do the subsidiary equity balances. There is no need to eliminate the parent's entry for its share of subsidiary income. Instead, the pro rata share of subsidiary equity balances may be eliminated directly against the investment account.

Investments maintained under the sophisticated equity method are also at a common point in time and, thus, can be eliminated directly against the underlying subsidiary equity. The distributable excess, however, will be only that which remains net of the amortizations made in the current and previous periods.

Investments maintained at cost should be converted to the simple equity method as of the **end of the year** to agree in time with the subsidiary equity balances. The entire conversion adjustment is carried to the controlling retained earnings.

Excesses are distributed according to the determination and distribution of excess schedules. Once distributed, the excesses are amortized to the balance sheet date and the entire amortization is carried to the controlling retained earnings.

Merchandise Sales

Only the intercompany profit in the ending inventory needs adjustment. The profit is eliminated from the inventory and from retained earnings. The adjustment to retained earnings is allocated according to the NCI/controlling ownership percentages in effect when the subsidiary made the intercompany sale. If the parent made the sale, the adjustment is made only to the controlling retained earnings. The intercompany profit in the beginning inventory either has been realized through the subsequent sale of the merchandise to an outside party, or, if the units in the beginning inventory are still on hand at year-end, they would be included in the adjustment for intercompany profit in the ending inventory.

Plant Asset Sales

The only matter for concern in the case of intercompany plant asset sales is the adjustment of the asset and retained earnings accounts for the undepreciated portion of the intercompany gain or loss as of year-end. The asset account is adjusted to its cost to the consolidated firm; accumulated depreciation is adjusted for all periods to date; and retained earnings are adjusted for the undepreciated profit or loss that is to be deferred to future periods. If the subsidiary sold to the parent, the retained earnings adjustment is allocated to the NCI and controlling interests that existed at the time of the sale.

Investment in Bonds

The amortized balance in Investment in Company S Bonds is eliminated against the bonds payable and any related discount or premium balance. The net disparity in amounts is the net retirement gain or loss remaining at year-end, which is carried to retained earnings. When the subsidiary is the issuer, the retained earnings adjustment is allocated to the NCI and controlling interests.

Leases

For operating leases, it is necessary only to reclassify the asset and accumulated depreciation as owned assets rather than assets under operating leases. Where direct financing leases exist, the intercompany debt resulting from the capitalized lease must be eliminated. Also, it is necessary to reclassify the asset and accumulated depreciation as owned assets rather than assets under capital leases. An intercompany sales-type lease requires the same procedures as a direct-financing lease plus an additional adjustment to defer the remaining undepreciated intercompany profit on the lease. If the subsidiary leased the asset to the parent, the retained earnings adjustment is allocated to the NCI and controlling interest that existed at the inception of the lease.

Illustration

To illustrate the procedures used for the balance sheet worksheet, assume Company P purchased an 80% interest in Company S on January 1, 20X1. Company P uses the cost method to record its investment in Company S. The determination and distribution of excess schedule prepared for this purchase is as follows:

Price paid		$750,000	
Less interest acquired:			
Common stock ($10 par)	$200,000		
Retained earnings, January 1, 20X1	600,000		
Total stockholders' equity	$800,000		
Interest acquired	× 80%	640,000	
Excess of cost over book value (debit balance)		$110,000	
Excess of cost attributable to building (10-year remaining life)		30,000	Dr.
Goodwill		$ 80,000	Dr.

The facts pertaining to intercompany sales by Company S to Company P are as follows:

	20X3	20X4
Intercompany sales	$80,000	$100,000
Gross profit	30%	40%
Intercompany sales in ending inventory	$20,000	$40,000
Unpaid balance, end of the year	$30,000	$35,000

On January 1, 20X2, Company P sold a new piece of equipment that cost $10,000 to Company S for $15,000. Company S is depreciating the equipment over 5 years on a straight-line basis.

Company S has outstanding $100,000 of 20-year, 5% bonds due January 1, 20X9. Interest is payable on January 1 for the previous year. The bonds originally were sold to yield 6%. On January 1, 20X3, Company P purchased the bonds on the open market at a price to yield 8%.

Worksheet 7-6, pages 432 to 433, contains the balance sheets and eliminations and adjustments for Companies P and S on December 31, 20X4. After the worksheet entries are completed, the amounts are combined to produce the consolidated balance sheet.

Worksheet 7-6: page 432

In journal entry form, the eliminations for Worksheet 7-6 are as follows:

	Convert investment to simple equity balance on December 31, 20X4 (end of year):		
(CV)	Investment in Company S Stock	240,000	
	Retained Earnings, December 31, 20X4, Company P		240,000
	Eliminate 80% of subsidiary equity against the investment account:		
(EL)	Common Stock, Company S	160,000	
	Retained Earnings, December 31, 20X4, Company S	720,000	
	Investment in Company S Stock		880,000
	Distribute excess to buildings and goodwill:		
(D1)	Buildings	30,000	
(D2)	Goodwill	80,000	
(D)	Investment in Company S Stock		110,000
(A1)	Adjust depreciation on buildings through end of year:		
	Retained Earnings, December 31, 20X4, Company P (4 years × $3,000)	12,000	
	Accumulated Depreciation—Buildings		12,000
(1A)	Eliminate intercompany trade balances:		
	Accounts Payable	35,000	
	Accounts Receivable		35,000
	Defer ending inventory profit (40% × $40,000):		
(E1)	Retained Earnings, December 31, 20X4, Company P (80%)	12,800	
	Retained Earnings, December 31, 20X4, Company S (20%)	3,200	
	Inventory, December 31, 20X4		16,000
	Defer remaining profit on equipment sale ($^2/_5$ of $5,000):		
(F)	Retained Earnings, December 31, 20X4, Company P	2,000	
	Accumulated Depreciation (3 years × $1,000)	3,000	
	Equipment		5,000
	Retire intercompany bonds on the worksheet:		
(B)	Bonds Payable	100,000	
	Discount on Bonds Payable		3,465
	Investment in Company S Bonds		90,064
	Retained Earnings, December 31, 20X4, Company P (80% × $6,471)		5,177
	Retained Earnings, December 31, 20X4, Company S (20% × $6,471)		1,294

The time savings from the balance sheet worksheet stems from the fact that there is no consolidated net income to calculate and distribute.

Worksheet 7-1

Investment Acquired in Blocks; Immediate Control
Company P and Subsidiary Company S
Worksheet for Consolidated Financial Statements
For Year Ended December 31, 20X3

	(Credit balance amounts are in parentheses.)	Trial Balance	
		Company P	Company S
1	Current Assets	60,000	130,000
2	Investment in Company S	228,000	
3			
4			
5			
6	Building	400,000	80,000
7	Accumulated Depreciation—Building	(100,000)	(5,000)
8	Equipment		150,000
9			
10	**Accumulated Depreciation—Equipment**		(90,000)
11			
12	Goodwill		
13			
14	Liabilities	(100,000)	(30,000)
15	Common Stock, Company P	(200,000)	
16	**Retained Earnings, January 1, 20X3, Company P**	**(210,000)**	
17			
18	Common Stock, Company S		(100,000)
19	Retained Earnings, January 1, 20X3, Company S		(100,000)
20	Sales	(400,000)	(200,000)
21	Cost of Goods Sold	300,000	120,000
22	**Expenses**	**50,000**	**45,000**
23			
24	Subsidiary Income	(28,000)	
25		0	0
26	Consolidated Net Income		
27	To NCI (see distribution schedule)		
28	Balance to Controlling Interest (see distribution schedule)		
29	Total NCI		
30	Retained Earnings, Controlling Interest, December 31, 20X3		
31			

Worksheet 7-1 (see page 392)

Eliminations & Adjustments Dr.		Eliminations & Adjustments Cr.		Consolidated Income Statement	NCI	Controlling Retained Earnings	Consolidated Balance Sheet	
							190,000	1
		(CY)	28,000					2
		(EL)	160,000					3
		(D1)	**30,000**					4
		(D2)	**10,000**					5
							480,000	6
							(105,000)	7
(D1a)	**18,000**						172,800	8
(D2a)	**4,800**							9
		(A1a)	**10,800**				(102,400)	10
		(A2a)	**1,600**					11
(D1b)	**12,000**						17,200	12
(D2b)	**5,200**							13
							(130,000)	14
							(200,000)	15
(A1)	**7,200**					(202,800)		16
								17
(EL)	80,000				(20,000)			18
(EL)	80,000				(20,000)			19
				(600,000)				20
				420,000				21
(A1a)	**3,600**			100,200				22
(A2a)	**1,600**							23
(CY)	28,000							24
	240,400		240,400					25
				(79,800)				26
				7,000	(7,000)			27
				72,800		(72,800)		28
					(47,000)		(47,000)	29
						(275,600)	(275,600)	30
							0	31

Eliminations and Adjustments:

(CY) Eliminate the parent's entry recognizing 80% of the subsidiary net income for the current year. This entry restores the investment account to its balance at the beginning of the year, so that it can be eliminated against Company S beginning-of-the-year equity balances.

(EL) Eliminate the 80% controlling interest in beginning-of-the-year subsidiary accounts against the investment account. The 60% and 20% investments could be eliminated separately if desired.

(D1) The $30,000 excess of cost on the original 60% investment is distributed to the **(a)** equipment and **(b)** goodwill accounts according to the determination and distribution of excess schedule prepared on January 1, 20X1.

(A1a) Since the equipment has a 5-year remaining life on January 1, 20X1, the depreciation should be increased $3,600 per year for 3 years. This entry corrects the controlling retained earnings for the past 2 years by $7,200 and corrects the current depreciation expense by $3,600.

(D2) The $10,000 excess of cost on the 20% block is distributed to the **(a)** equipment and **(b)** goodwill accounts according to the determination and distribution of excess schedule prepared on January 1, 20X3.

(A2a) The $4,800 excess attributable to the equipment is to be depreciated over 3 years. Therefore, current expenses are increased by $1,600.

Subsidiary Company S Income Distribution

		Internally generated net income	$35,000
		Adjusted income	$35,000
		NCI share	× 20%
		NCI	$ 7,000

Parent Company P Income Distribution

Equipment depreciation:		Internally generated net income	$50,000
Block 1, 60% **(A1a)**	$3,600	80% × Company S adjusted income of $35,000	28,000
Block 2, 20% **(A2a)**	1,600		
		Controlling interest	$72,800

Worksheet 7-2

Investment Acquired in Blocks; Control Achieved with Second Block
Company P and Subsidiary Company S
Worksheet for Consolidated Financial Statements
For Year Ended December 31, 20X2

	(Credit balance amounts are in parentheses.)	Trial Balance	
		Company P	Company S
1	Current Assets	69,900	85,000
2	Investment in Company S	196,100	
3			
4			
5			
6	Building and Equipment	300,000	150,000
8			
8	**Accumulated Depreciation—Building and Equipment**	**(200,000)**	**(30,000)**
9			
10	**Goodwill**		
11	Liabilities		(20,000)
12	Common Stock, Company P	(100,000)	
13	**Retained Earnings, January 1, 20X2, Company P**	(200,000)	
14	Common Stock, Company S		(50,000)
15	Retained Earnings, January 1, 20X2, Company S		(115,000)
16	Sales	(300,000)	(100,000)
17	Cost of Goods Sold	200,000	60,000
18	**Expenses**	**50,000**	**20,000**
19			
20	Subsidiary Income	(16,000)	
21		0	0
22	Consolidated Net Income		
23	To NCI (see distribution schedule)		
24	Balance to Controlling Interest (see distribution schedule)		
25	Total NCI		
26	Retained Earnings, Controlling Interest, December 31, 20X2		
27			

Eliminations and Adjustments:

(CY) Eliminate the parent's entry recognizing 80% of the subsidiary net income under the simple equity method. This entry restores the investment account to its balance at the beginning of the year.

(EL) Eliminate the 80% controlling interest in beginning-of-the-year subsidiary equity accounts against the investment account. If desired, the two investment blocks may be eliminated separately.

(D1) The remaining excess of cost over book value on the original 20% investment is $17,100 ($18,000 less 1 year of $900 amortization). It must be remembered that under the sophisticated equity method, amortization entries prior to securing control reduce the investment account. Always remember that only the *unamortized original excess remains.* The remaining $17,100 excess is carried to the building account according to the determination and distribution of excess schedule prepared on January 1, 20X1.

(A1) Building depreciation of $900 is recorded for the current year. Recall that no depreciation is needed for periods prior to achieving control, since that depreciation was recorded previously through the parent's investment account. Thus, the controlling retained earnings are already reduced.

(D2) The excess attributable to the January 1, 20X2, 60% acquisition is distributed to the **(a)** building and equipment accumulated depreciation and **(b)** goodwill accounts according to the determination and distribution of excess schedule for this second acquisition.

(A2) Depreciation for the current year is increased $600 according to the January 1, 20X2, determination and distribution of excess schedule.

Worksheet 7-2 (see page 396)

Eliminations & Adjustments Dr.		Eliminations & Adjustments Cr.		Consolidated Income Statement	NCI	Controlling Retained Earnings	Consolidated Balance Sheet	
							154,900	1
		(CY)	16,000					2
		(EL)	132,000					3
		(D1)	**17,100**					4
		(D2)	**31,000**					5
(D1)	**17,100**						472,500	6
(D2a)	**5,400**							7
		(A1)	**900**				(231,500)	8
		(A2a)	**600**					9
(D2b)	**25,600**						25,600	10
							(20,000)	11
							(100,000)	12
						(200,000)		13
(EL)	40,000				(10,000)			14
(EL)	92,000				(23,000)			15
				(400,000)				16
				260,000				17
(A1)	**900**			71,500				18
(A2a)	**600**							19
(CY)	16,000							20
	197,600		197,600					21
				(68,500)				22
				4,000	(4,000)			23
				64,500		(64,500)		24
					(37,000)		(37,000)	25
						(264,500)	(264,500)	26
							0	27

Subsidiary Company S Income Distribution

	Internally generated net income	$ 20,000
	Adjusted income	$ 20,000
	NCI share	× 20%
	NCI	$ 4,000

Parent Company P Income Distribution

Equipment depreciation:			Internally generated net income	$50,000
Block 1, 20%	**(A1)**	$900	80% × Company S adjusted income of	
Block 2, 60%	**(A2a)**	600	$20,000	16,000
			Controlling interest	$64,500

Worksheet 7-3

Sale of Subsidiary Interest During Period; No Loss of Control
Company P and Subsidiary Company S
Worksheet for Consolidated Financial Statements
For Year Ended December 31, 20X3

	(Credit balance amounts are in parentheses.)	Trial Balance	
		Company P	Company S
1	Investment in Company S (60%)	244,500	
2			
3			
4	Equipment	600,000	100,000
5	Accumulated Depreciation—Equipment	(100,000)	(60,000)
6	Other Assets	581,500	305,000
7	Goodwill		
8	Common Stock, Company P	(500,000)	
9	Retained Earnings, January 1, 20X3, Company P	(701,500)	
10			
11	Common Stock, Company S		(100,000)
12	Retained Earnings, January 1, 20X3, Company S		(215,000)
13	Sales	(500,000)	(200,000)
14	Cost of Goods Sold	350,000	140,000
15	Expenses	50,000	30,000
16			
17	**Paid-In Capital in Excess of Par, Company P**	**(4,600)**	
18	Subsidiary Income	(19,900)	
19			
20	**Income Sold to NCI (second 20% block)**		
21		0	0
22			
23	Consolidated Net Income		
24	To NCI (see distribution schedule)		
25	Balance to Controlling Interest (see distribution schedule)		
26	Total NCI		
27	Retained Earnings, Controlling Interest, December 31, 20X3		
28			

Worksheet 7-3 (see page 405)

Eliminations & Adjustments Dr.	Eliminations & Adjustments Cr.	Consolidated Income Statement	NCI	Controlling Retained Earnings	Consolidated Balance Sheet	
	(CY) 18,000					1
	(EL) 189,000					2
	(D) 37,500					3
(D1) 15,000					715,000	4
	(A) 9,000				(169,000)	5
					886,500	6
(D2) 22,500					22,500	7
					(500,000)	8
(A) 6,000				(695,500)		9
						10
(EL) 60,000			(40,000)			11
(EL) 129,000			(86,000)			12
		(700,000)				13
		490,000				14
(NCI) 500		83,500				15
(A) 3,000						16
					(4,600)	17
(NCI) 1,900						18
(CY) 18,000						19
	(NCI) 2,400		(2,400)			20
255,900	255,900					21
						22
		(126,500)				23
		9,600	(9,600)			24
		116,900		(116,900)		25
			(138,000)		(138,000)	26
				(812,400)	(812,400)	27
					0	28

Eliminations and Adjustments:

(NCI) The income earned by the parent on the 20% interest sold on July 1, though earned by the controlling interest, now belongs to the NCI. The NCI owns 20% of the reported subsidiary income for the half-year ($12,000), which is $2,400. The NCI is unaffected by amortizations resulting from a previous price paid by the parent. Note that this entry credits the account, Income Sold to NCI, to accomplish the transfer of the income to the NCI. The offsetting debits are explained as follows:

20% of subsidiary income for the first six months, adjusted for one-fourth of the parent's half-year amortization of excess or (20% × $12,000) – (¼ × ½ × $4,000)	$1,900
Depreciation adjustment (¼ × ½ × $4,000)	500
Total debits	$2,400

Amortization based on an 80% interest for the first half of the year is proper, since the consolidation involves an 80% controlling interest for the first half of the year and a 60% controlling interest for the second half of the year.

(CY) Eliminate the parent's entry recording its 60% share of subsidiary net income of $30,000. This entry restores the 60% interest to its simple-equity-adjusted cost at the beginning of the year so that the investment can be eliminated against subsidiary equity balances at the beginning of the year.

(EL) Eliminate 60% of the subsidiary equity balances at the beginning of the year against the investment account. An excess cost of $37,500 remains. This amount is three-fourths (60% × 80%) of the original excess shown on page 399, since only a 60% interest is retained, as compared to an original investment of 80%.

(D) Since only three-fourths of the original investment remains, 75% of the excesses shown in the original determination and distribution of excess schedule on page 399 is recorded. Entry (D1) adjusts equipment and (D2) adjusts goodwill.

(A) 75% of the original $4,000 annual depreciation adjustments is recorded for the past two years and the current year. Note that the remaining depreciation adjustments applicable to the interest sold are already recorded.

Subsidiary Company S Income Distribution

		Internally generated net income	$ 30,000
		Adjusted income	$ 30,000
		NCI share	× 40%
		NCI for full year	$ 12,000
		Less income purchased (20% × $12,000, first 6 months)	**2,400**
		NCI	$ 9,600

Parent Company P Income Distribution

Depreciation adjustment on 60% interest . . . (A)	$3,000	Internally generated net income	$100,000
		Adjusted income	$ 97,000
		60% × Company S adjusted income of $30,000	18,000
		20% × Company S adjusted income for first 6 months (net of amortization)	**1,900**
		Controlling interest	$116,900

Worksheet 7-4

Subsidiary Preferred Stock, None Owned by Parent
Company P and Subsidiary Company S
Worksheet for Consolidated Financial Statements
For Year Ended December 31, 20X5

	(Credit balance amounts are in parentheses.)	Trial Balance	
		Company P	Company S
1	Current Assets	259,600	150,000
2	Property, Plant, and Equipment (net)	400,000	250,000
3	Investment in Company S Common Stock	195,600	
4			
5			
6	Goodwill		
7	Liabilities	(150,000)	(45,000)
8	Common Stock, Company P	(200,000)	
9	Retained Earnings, January 1, 20X5, Company P	(340,000)	
10	Preferred Stock ($100 par), Company S		(100,000)
11	**Retained Earnings Allocated to Preferred Stock, January 1, 20X5, Company S**		
12	Common Stock ($10 par), Company S		(100,000)
13	Retained Earnings, January 1, 20X5, Company S		(130,000)
14			
15	Sales	(450,000)	(200,000)
16	Cost of Goods Sold	200,000	150,000
17	Expenses	100,000	25,000
18	Subsidiary Income	(15,200)	
19		0	0
20			
21	Consolidated Net Income		
22	To NCI (see distribution schedule)		
23	Balance to Controlling Interest (see distribution schedule)		
24	Total NCI		
25	Retained Earnings, Controlling Interest, December 31, 20X5		
26			

Eliminations and Adjustments:

(PS) Distribute the beginning-of-the-period subsidiary retained earnings into the portions allocable to common and preferred stock. The typical procedure would be to consider the stated subsidiary retained earnings as applicable to common and to remove the preferred portion. This distribution reflects four years of arrearage (as of January 1, 20X5) at $6,000 per year.

(CY) Eliminate the parent's entry recording its share of subsidiary current income.

(EL) Eliminate the pro rata subsidiary common stockholders' equity at the beginning of the period against the investment account. This entry includes elimination of the 80% of subsidiary retained earnings applicable to common stock.

(D) Distribute the excess of cost according to the determination and distribution of excess schedule.

Worksheet 7-4 (see page 409)

Eliminations & Adjustments Dr.		Eliminations & Adjustments Cr.		Consolidated Income Statement	NCI	Controlling Retained Earnings	Consolidated Balance Sheet	
							409,600	1
							650,000	2
		(CY)	15,200					3
		(EL)	164,800					4
		(D)	15,600					5
(D)	15,600						15,600	6
							(195,000)	7
							(200,000)	8
						(340,000)		9
					(100,000)			10
		(PS)	**24,000**		(24,000)			11
(EL)	80,000				(20,000)			12
(PS)	**24,000**				(21,200)			13
(EL)	84,800							14
				(650,000)				15
				350,000				16
				125,000				17
(CY)	15,200							18
	219,600		219,600					19
								20
				(175,000)				21
				9,800	(9,800)			22
				165,200		(165,200)		23
					(175,000)		(175,000)	24
						(505,200)	(505,200)	25
							0	26

Subsidiary Company S Income Distribution

	Internally generated net income (no adjustments)	$ 25,000
	Less preferred cumulative claim to NCI	**(6,000)**
	Common stock income	**$19,000**
	NCI share	× 20%
	NCI in common income	$ 3,800
	Total NCI (**$6,000** + $3,800)	$ 9,800

Parent Company P Income Distribution

	Internally generated net income	$150,000
	80% × Company S adjusted income on common stock of $19,000	15,200
	Controlling interest	$165,200

Worksheet 7-5

Subsidiary Preferred Stock Owned by Parent
Company P and Subsidiary Company S
Worksheet for Consolidated Financial Statements
For Year Ended December 31, 20X5

	(Credit balance amounts are in parentheses.)	Trial Balance	
		Company P	Company S
1	Current Assets	194,600	150,000
2	Property, Plant, and Equipment (net)	400,000	250,000
3	Investment in Company S Common Stock	195,600	
4			
5			
6	**Investment in Company S Preferred Stock**	**75,800**	
7			
8	Goodwill		
9	Liabilities	(150,000)	(45,000)
10	Common Stock, Company P	(200,000)	
11	**Paid-In Capital in Excess of Par, Company P**		
12	Retained Earnings, January 1, 20X5, Company P	(347,200)	
13	Preferred Stock ($100 par), Company S		(100,000)
14	Retained Earnings Allocated to Preferred Stock, January 1, 20X5, Company S		
15	Common Stock ($10 par), Company S		(100,000)
16	Retained Earnings, January 1, 20X5, Company S		(130,000)
17			
18	Sales	(450,000)	(200,000)
19	Cost of Goods Sold	200,000	150,000
20	Expenses	100,000	25,000
21	Subsidiary Income—Common	(15,200)	
22	**Subsidiary Income—Preferred**	**(3,600)**	
23		0	0
24			
25	Consolidated Net Income		
26	To NCI (see distribution schedule)		
27	Balance to Controlling Interest (see distribution schedule)		
28	Total NCI		
29	Retained Earnings, Controlling Interest, December 31, 20X5		
30			

Worksheet 7-5 (see page 411)

Eliminations & Adjustments Dr.		Eliminations & Adjustments Cr.		Consolidated Income Statement	NCI	Controlling Retained Earnings	Consolidated Balance Sheet	
							344,600	1
							650,000	2
		(CY)	15,200					3
		(EL)	164,800					4
		(D)	15,600					5
		(CYP)	**3,600**					6
		(ELP)	**72,200**					7
(D)	15,600						15,600	8
							(195,000)	9
							(200,000)	10
		(ELP)	**2,200**				(2,200)	11
						(347,200)		12
(ELP)	**60,000**				(40,000)			13
(ELP)	**14,400**	(PS)	24,000		(9,600)			14
(EL)	80,000				(20,000)			15
(PS)	24,000				(21,200)			16
(EL)	84,800							17
				(650,000)				18
				350,000				19
				125,000				20
(CY)	15,200							21
(CYP)	**3,600**							22
	297,600		297,600					23
								24
				(175,000)				25
				6,200	(6,200)			26
				168,800		(168,800)		27
					(97,000)		(97,000)	28
						(516,000)	(516,000)	29
							0	30

Eliminations and Adjustments:

(PS), (CY), (EL), and (D) Same as Worksheet 7-4; the common stock investment elimination procedures are unaffected by the investment in preferred stock.

(CYP) Eliminate the entry recording the parent's share of income allocable to preferred stock. If declared, intercompany preferred dividends would also have been eliminated. This adjustment restores the investment account to its beginning-of-the-period equity balance.

(ELP) The parent's ownership portion of the par value and beginning-of-the-period retained earnings applicable to preferred stock is eliminated against the balance in the investment in preferred stock account. The difference in this case was an increase in equity, and it was carried to the controlling paid-in capital.

Subsidiary Company S Income Distribution

	Internally generated net income (no adjustments)	$ 25,000
	Less preferred cumulative claim:	
	to NCI, 40% × $6,000	(2,400)
	to controlling, 60% × $6,000	**(3,600)**
	Common stock income	$ 19,000
	NCI share	× 20%
	NCI in common income	$ 3,800
	Total NCI (**$2,400** + $3,800)	$ 6,200

Parent Company P Income Distribution

	Internally generated net income	$150,000
	60% × Company S income attributable to preferred stock	**3,600**
	80% × Company S adjusted income on common stock of $19,000	15,200
	Controlling interest	$168,800

Worksheet 7-6

Balance Sheet Only
Company P and Subsidiary Company S
Worksheet for Consolidated Balance Sheet
December 31, 20X4

	(Credit balance amounts are in parentheses.)	Trial Balance	
		Company P	Company S
1	Cash	61,936	106,535
2	Accounts Receivable	80,000	200,000
3	Inventory, December 31, 20X4	60,000	150,000
4	Land	300,000	250,000
5	Building	800,000	600,000
6	Accumulated Depreciation—Building	(400,000)	(100,000)
7	Equipment	120,000	95,000
8	Accumulated Depreciation—Equipment	(70,000)	(30,000)
9	Investment in Company S Bonds	90,064	
10	Investment in Company S Stock	750,000	
11			
12	Goodwill		
13	Accounts Payable	(92,000)	(75,000)
14	Bonds Payable		(100,000)
15	Discount on Bonds Payable		3,465
16	Common Stock, Company P	(500,000)	
17	Retained Earnings, December 31, 20X4, Company P	(1,200,000)	
18			
19			
20	Common Stock, Company S		(200,000)
21	Retained Earnings, December 31, 20X4, Company S		(900,000)
22			
23		0	0
24	Total NCI		
25			

Eliminations and Adjustments:

(CV) Investment in Company S Stock is converted to the simple equity method as of *December 31, 20X4*, as follows: 80% × $300,000 increase in retained earnings = $240,000.

(EL) 80% of the subsidiary equity balances are eliminated against the investment in stock account.

(D) The $110,000 excess of cost is distributed according to the determination and distribution of excess schedule. Entry (D1) adjusts the building account and (D2) adjusts goodwill.

(A1) The excess attributable to the building is amortized for four years at $3,000 per year.

(IA) The intercompany trade balance is eliminated.

(EI) The gross profit of $16,000 (40% × $40,000) recorded by Company S and applicable to merchandise in Company P's ending inventory is deferred by reducing the inventory and retained earnings. Since the sale was made by Company S, the adjustment is allocated to the NCI and controlling retained earnings.

(F) As of December 31, 20X4, $2,000 (2/5) of the profit on the equipment sale is still to be deferred. Since the sale was made by Company P, the controlling retained earnings absorb this adjustment, and the equipment and accumulated depreciation accounts are adjusted.

(B) Investment in Company S Bonds is eliminated against the net book value of the bonds. The net gain on the worksheet retirement is allocated to the NCI and controlling retained earnings, since the subsidiary originally issued the bonds.

Worksheet 7-6 (see page 415)

Eliminations & Adjustments Dr.		Eliminations & Adjustments Cr.		NCI	Consolidated Balance Sheet	
					168,471	1
		(IA)	35,000		245,000	2
		(EI)	16,000		194,000	3
					550,000	4
					1,430,000	5
(D1)	30,000	(A)	12,000		(512,000)	6
		(F)	5,000		210,000	7
(F)	3,000				(97,000)	8
		(B)	90,064			9
(CV)	**240,000**	(EL)	880,000			10
		(D)	110,000			11
(D2)	80,000				80,000	12
(IA)	35,000				(132,000)	13
(B)	100,000					14
		(B)	3,465			15
					(500,000)	16
(A1)	12,000	**(CV)**	**240,000**		(1,418,377)	17
(EI)	12,800	(B)	5,177			18
(F)	2,000					19
(EL)	160,000			(40,000)		20
(EL)	720,000	(B)	1,294	(178,094)		21
(EI)	3,200					22
	1,398,000		1,398,000			23
				(218,094)	(218,094)	24
					0	25

UNDERSTANDING THE ISSUES

1. Company S has 4,000 shares outstanding and a total stockholders' equity of $200,000. It is about to issue 6,000 new shares to the prospective parent company. The shares will be sold for a total of $600,000. Will there be an excess of cost over book value? If so, how will it likely be accounted for?

2. Company P purchased a 20% interest in Company S on January 1, 20X1, for $100,000 when Company P had a total equity of $400,000. The 20% investment was considered influential, and the sophisticated equity method was used to account for it. On January 1, 20X4, Company P purchased another 40% interest for $250,000. Company S's equity on January 1, 20X4, was $500,000. Company S earned $50,000 during 20X4. Company P had an internally generated net income of $100,000. For both purchases, any excess of cost over book value was attributed to equipment with a 10-year life. Calculate consolidated income for 20X4 and the distribution of consolidated income to the noncontrolling and controlling interests.

3. Company P purchases an 80% interest in Company S on January 1, 20X1, for $500,000. Company S had an equity of $450,000 on that date. On July 1, 20X6, Company P purchased another 10% interest for $150,000. Company S's equity was $550,000 on January 1, 20X6, and it earned $50,000 evenly during 20X6. For each investment, any excess of cost over book value was attributed to equipment with a 10-year life. Company P had internally generated net income of $120,000 during 20X6. Calculate consolidated income for 20X6 and the distribution of consolidated income to the noncontrolling and controlling interests.

4. Company P purchased an 80% interest (8,000 shares) in Company S for $800,000 on January 1, 20X1. Company S's equity on that date was $900,000. Any excess of cost over book value was attributed to equipment with a 10-year life. On January 1, 20X5, Company S's equity was $1,200,000. Company S earned $200,000, evenly, during 20X5. In December of 20X5, Company S paid $10,000 in dividends. Company P had internally generated net income of $150,000. On July 1, 20X5, there was a sale of Company S stock, for $150 per share, to outside interests by Company P. For each of the situations below:

   a. How will the sale be recorded?
   b. Will consolidated statements be prepared for 20X5? If so, what will be consolidated net income and what will be the distribution to the NCIs?
   c. If consolidated statements will not be prepared, what will be reported by the parent for its income from Company S?

   - Company P sells all 8,000 shares.
   - Company P sells 2,000 shares.
   - Company P sells 6,000 shares.

5. Company S has the following stockholders' equity on January 1, 20X5:

Common stock, $1 par, 100,000 shares	$100,000
6% preferred stock, $100 par, 2,000 shares	200,000
Paid-in capital in excess of par	900,000
Retained earnings	500,000

The preferred stock is cumulative and has dividends one year in arrears on January 1, 20X4.

Company P purchased an 80% interest in the common stock of Company S on January 1, 20X5, for $1,400,000. Any excess of cost over book value was attributed to goodwill. Company S earned $80,000 during 20X5 and paid no dividends. Company P had internally generated net income of $120,000.

What is consolidated net income for 20X5, and how is it distributed to the controlling and noncontrolling interests?

How would the answer differ if Company P also purchases one-half of the preferred stock of Company S for $120,000?

EXERCISES

Exercise 1 *(LO 1)* **Purchase of shares directly from subsidiary.** Prior to January 2, 20X4, Peeple and Simple were separate corporations. Simple Corporation was contemplating a major expansion and sought to be purchased by a larger corporation with available cash. Peeple Corporation issued $1,200,000 of bonds and used the proceeds to buy 30,000 newly issued Simple shares for $40 per share. Just prior to the issue of the bonds and the issue and purchase of Simple stock, Peeple and Simple had the following separate balance sheets:

Assets	Peeple Corporation	Simple Corporation
Current assets	$ 600,000	$100,000
Land	150,000	60,000
Property, plant, and equipment	700,000	400,000
Total assets	$1,450,000	$560,000
Liabilities and Stockholders' Equity		
Current liabilities	$ 250,000	$100,000
Common stock ($5 par)	400,000	100,000
Retained earnings	800,000	360,000
Total liabilities and equity	$1,450,000	$560,000

Purchasing the 30,000 new shares gave Peeple Corporation a 60% controlling interest (30,000 of a total 50,000 common shares). On the purchase date, Simple's property was undervalued by $200,000. Any remaining excess cost can be attributed only to goodwill.

Prepare a determination and distribution of excess schedule for Peeple Corporation's investment in Simple. Prepare a consolidated balance sheet for the consolidated firm immediately after the purchase by Peeple Corporation.

Exercise 2 *(LO 2)* **Block purchase, control with first block.** Barker Corporation purchased a 60% interest in Hard Knock Company on January 1, 20X1, for $150,000. On that date, Hard Knock Company had the following stockholders' equity:

Common stock ($10 par)	$100,000
Retained earnings	20,000
	$120,000

Any excess of cost over fair value was due to equipment with a 10-year life.

Barker Corporation purchased another 20% interest for $40,000 on January 1, 20X3, when Hard Knock Company had the following stockholders' equity:

Common stock ($10 par)	$100,000
Retained earnings	50,000
	$150,000

Any excess of cost over fair value was due to a patent with a 20-year life. On December 31, 20X5, Barker Corporation and Hard Knock Company had the following balance sheets:

Assets	Barker Corporation	Hard Knock Company
Current assets	$ 270,000	$ 80,000
Investment in Hard Knock Company	190,000	
Property, plant, and equipment	740,000	240,000
Total assets	$1,200,000	$320,000

Liabilities and Stockholders' Equity		
Current liabilities	$ 400,000	$100,000
Stockholders' equity:		
Common stock ($10 par)	500,000	100,000
Retained earnings	300,000	120,000
Total liabilities and stockholders' equity	$1,200,000	$320,000

Prepare the consolidated balance sheet of Barker Corporation and subsidiary Hard Knock Company on December 31, 20X5.

Exercise 3 *(LO 2)* **Block purchase, control with second block.** Boon Corporation purchased a 10% interest in Doyle Company on January 1, 20X1. The following determination and distribution of excess schedule was prepared as of the purchase date:

Price paid		$40,000
Less interest acquired:		
Common stock ($10 par)	$100,000	
Retained earnings	120,000	
Stockholders' equity	$220,000	
Interest acquired	× 10%	22,000
Building (10-year life)		$18,000

From January 1, 20X1, through December 31, 20X5, Doyle Company paid no dividends and reported the following net incomes:

20X1	$ 8,000	20X4	$25,000
20X2	10,000	20X5	30,000
20X3	20,000		

On January 1, 20X6, Boon Corporation purchased 7,000 additional shares of Doyle Company from existing shareholders for $300,000. This purchase raised Boon's interest to 80%. Doyle Company had the following balance sheet just prior to Boon's second purchase:

Assets		Liabilities and Equity	
Current assets	$138,000	Liabilities	$ 65,000
Buildings (net)	140,000	Common stock ($10 par)	100,000
Equipment (net)	100,000	Retained earnings	213,000
Total assets	$378,000	Total liabilities and equity	$378,000

At the time of the second purchase, Boon determined that Doyle's equipment was understated by $50,000 and had a 5-year remaining life. All other book values approximated fair values. Any remaining excess is attributed to goodwill.

1. Prepare a determination and distribution of excess schedule for the second purchase.
2. Record the investment made by Boon on January 1, 20X6.
3. Since control has now been achieved, Boon will use the simple equity method for its investment in Doyle. Assume that the cost method was used to account for the initial 10% interest. Convert the 10% interest to the simple equity method balance on January 1, 20X6.

Exercise 4 *(LO 2)* **Block purchase, influence, then control.** Cleft Company purchased a 20% interest in Key Industries on January 1, 20X2, for $100,000 and another 60% interest on January 1, 20X4, for $360,000. Key had the following stockholders' equity balances immediately prior to each purchase:

Stockholders' Equity	January 1, 20X2	January 1, 20X4
Common stock ($1 par)	$ 50,000	$ 50,000
Paid-in capital in excess of par	400,000	400,000
Retained earnings	20,000	100,000
Total equity	$470,000	$550,000

Cleft's analysis on the two purchase dates revealed the following: (1) On January 1, 20X2, Key's equipment was undervalued by $10,000 and had a remaining life of 5 years. (2) On January 1, 20X4, Key's equipment was undervalued by $9,000, with a 3-year remaining life. (3) Any excess is attributable to goodwill.

Key had income of $30,000 in 20X4 and $50,000 in 20X5 and paid its first dividend, a $0.20 per-share dividend to common stock, on December 30, 20X5.

1. Prepare a determination and distribution of excess schedule for each investment.
2. Assuming the cost method is used for both investments, prepare the calculations necessary to convert the investment account to its simple-equity-adjusted balance on December 31, 20X5.

Exercise 5 *(LO 3)* **Sale of interest, loss of control.** Rob Company purchased a 90% interest in Venlo Company for $415,000 on January 1, 20X3. Any excess of cost over book value was attributed to equipment, which is being depreciated over 20 years. Both companies end their reporting periods on December 31. Since the investment in Venlo Company is consolidated, Rob Company has chosen to use the cost method to maintain its investment.

On December 31, 20X6, Rob Company sold 8,000 shares of Venlo Company for $700,000. The following stockholders' equity balances of Venlo Company are available:

	January 1, 20X3	January 1, 20X6
Common stock ($10 par)	$100,000	$100,000
Retained earnings	250,000	420,000
Total equity	$350,000	$520,000

Venlo Company earned $70,000 during 20X6. Prepare a determination and distribution of excess schedule. Record the sale of the shares of Venlo Company and any other adjustments needed to the investment account.

Exercise 6 *(LO 3)* **Sale of interest, control maintained.** Carpenter Company has the following balance sheet on December 31, 20X5:

Assets		Liabilities and Equity		
Current assets	$150,000	Liabilities		$100,000
Investment in Hinkle Company	160,000	Equity: Common stock ($10 par)	$500,000	
Property, plant, and equipment (net)	390,000	Retained earnings	100,000	600,000
Total assets	$700,000	Total liabilities and equity		$700,000

The investment in Hinkle Company account reflects the original cost of an 80% interest (40,000 shares) purchased on January 1, 20X2. On the date of the purchase, Hinkle stockholders' equity had a book value of $150,000. Hinkle's other book values approximated fair values, except for a machine with a 5-year remaining life that was undervalued by $20,000. Any additional excess was attributed to goodwill.

A review of Hinkle's past financial statements reveals the following:

	Income	Dividends Paid
20X2	$ 10,000	$ 5,000
20X3	25,000	5,000
20X4	40,000	5,000
20X5	35,000	5,000
Total	$110,000	$20,000

Carpenter sold 2,000 shares of Hinkle common stock on January 1, 20X6, for $40,000.

Prepare the necessary entries on Carpenter's books to account accurately for the sale of the 2,000 Hinkle shares. Provide a determination and distribution of excess schedule along with all other necessary computations as support.

Exercise 7 *(LO 3)* **Sale of interest, alternative remaining interests.** Cecil Inc. purchased 24,000 shares of Browning Corporation, which equated to an 80% interest, on January 1, 20X5. The following determination and distribution of excess schedule was prepared:

Price paid for investment in Browning		$750,000	
Less interest acquired:			
Common stock ($10 par)	$300,000		
Retained earnings	400,000		
Total stockholders' equity	$700,000		
Interest acquired	× 80%	560,000	
Excess of cost over book (debit balance)		$190,000	
Building (80% × $50,000 undervaluation with 10-year life = $4,000 per year)		40,000	Dr.
Goodwill		$150,000	Dr.

Browning Corporation reported net income of $35,000 for the six months ended July 1, 20X8. Cecil's simple-equity-adjusted investment balance was $814,000 as of December 31, 20X7.

Prepare all entries for the sale of the Browning Corporation shares on July 1, 20X8, for each of the following situations:

a. 24,000 shares are sold for $850,000.
b. 12,000 shares are sold for $425,000.
c. 6,000 shares are sold for $212,500.

Exercise 8 *(LO 4)* **D&D with preferred stock.** On January 1, 20X2, Boelter Company purchased 80% of the outstanding common stock of Miller Corporation for $280,000. On this date, Miller Corporation stockholders' equity was as follows:

6% preferred stock (1,000 shares, $100 par)	$100,000
Common stock (20,000 shares, $10 par)	200,000
Retained earnings	90,000
Total stockholders' equity	$390,000

Prepare a determination and distribution of excess schedule under each of the following situations (any excess of cost over book value is attributable to goodwill):

a. The preferred stock is cumulative, with dividends one year in arrears at January 1, 20X2, and has a liquidation value equal to par.
b. The preferred stock is noncumulative but fully participating.
c. The preferred stock is cumulative, with dividends two years in arrears as of January 1, 20X2, and has a liquidation value equal to 110% of par.

Exercise 9 *(LO 4)* **Equity adjustments with preferred stock.** Acme Construction Company had the following stockholders' equity on January 1, 20X1, the date on which Russell Company purchased an 80% interest in the common stock for $700,000:

8% cumulative preferred stock (5,000 shares, $100 par)	$ 500,000
Common stock (40,000 shares, $20 par)	800,000
Retained earnings	100,000
Total stockholders' equity	$1,400,000

Acme Construction Company did not pay preferred dividends in 20X0.

1. Prepare a determination and distribution of excess schedule. Assume that the preferred stock's liquidation value is equal to par and that any excess of cost is attributable to goodwill.
2. Assume Acme Construction has the following net income (loss) for 20X1 and 20X2 and does not pay any dividends:

20X1	$ 60,000
20X2	(10,000)

Prepare the entries necessary on Russell Company's books to adjust its investment account to the simple equity balance at the end of 20X1 and 20X2.

Exercise 10 *(LO 4)* **Cost to equity conversion with preferred stock.** On December 31, 20X4, Zigler Corporation purchased an 80% interest in the common stock of Kip Company for $420,000. The stockholders' equity of Kip Company on December 31, 20X4, was as follows:

8% cumulative preferred stock (2,000 shares, $100 par)	$200,000
Common stock (30,000 shares, $10 stated value)	300,000
Retained earnings	160,000
Total stockholders' equity	$660,000

Any excess of cost over book value was attributable to goodwill. The common stock investment is accounted for under the cost method.

Zigler Corporation purchased 1,000 shares of the cumulative preferred stock of Kip Company on January 1, 20X5, for $90,000. Kip Company issued a total of 2,000 preferred shares on January 1, 20X1. Dividends on preferred stock were paid in 20X1 and 20X2, but not in subsequent years. Zigler Corporation accounts for its investment using the cost method.

During 20X5 and 20X6, Kip Company paid no dividends and its retained earnings balance on December 31, 20X6, was $210,000. Kip Company income during 20X7 was $60,000.

1. Calculate the preferred and common stockholders' equity claim on Kip Company's retained earnings balance at January 1, 20X7.
2. Prepare the cost-to-simple-equity conversion and the elimination that would be made on the December 31, 20X7, consolidated trial balance worksheet for the investment in preferred stock.
3. Prepare the cost-to-simple-equity conversion and the eliminations that would be made on the December 31, 20X7, consolidated trial balance worksheet for the investment in common stock. Provide a determination and distribution of excess schedule as support.

PROBLEMS

Problem 7-1 *(LO 2)* **Worksheet, blocks, control with first block.** The following determination and distribution of excess schedule was prepared on January 1, 20X2, the date on which Parish Company purchased a 60% interest in Sharper Company:

Price paid		$140,000
Less interest acquired:		
Common stock ($10 par)	$ 75,000	
Retained earnings	60,000	
Total stockholders' equity	$135,000	
Interest acquired	× 60%	81,000
Excess of cost over book value attributable to equipment (10-year life)		$ 59,000

On December 31, 20X3, Parish Company purchased an additional 20% interest in Sharper Company for $70,000. Sharper's stockholders' equity was determined to be the following at that date:

Common stock	$ 75,000
Retained earnings	85,000
Total stockholders' equity	$160,000

Any excess of cost is attributed to equipment with a 10-year life.

On December 31, 20X5, the following trial balances are available:

	Parish Company	Sharper Company
Current Assets	200,000	55,000
Investment in Sharper Company	269,000	
Property, Plant, and Equipment (net)	450,000	170,000
Current Liabilities	(110,000)	(20,000)
Common Stock ($10 par)	(500,000)	(75,000)
Retained Earnings, January 1, 20X5	(198,000)	(100,000)
Sales	(400,000)	(110,000)
Subsidiary Income	(36,000)	
Cost of Goods Sold	200,000	60,000
Other Expenses	100,000	15,000
Dividends Declared	25,000	5,000
Total	0	0

◄◄◄◄◄ **Required**

1. Prepare the determination and distribution of excess schedule for the second purchase of Sharper stock by Parish Company.
2. Prepare the worksheet necessary to produce the consolidated financial statements of Parish Company and its subsidiary as of December 31, 20X5. Include income distribution schedules.

Problem 7-2 *(LO 2)* **Worksheet, blocks, control with first block, merchandise sales.** On January 1, 20X1, James Company purchased 70% of the common stock of Chris Company for $244,000. On this date, Chris had common stock, other paid-in capital, and retained earnings of $50,000, $100,000, and $150,000, respectively.

On May 1, 20X2, James Company purchased an additional 20% of the common stock of Chris Company for $92,000.

Net income and dividends for two years for Chris Company were as follows:

	20X1	20X2
Net income for year	$60,000	$90,000
Dividends, declared in December	20,000	30,000

In 20X2, the net income of Chris from January 1 through April 30 was $30,000.

On January 1, 20X1, the only tangible asset of Chris that was undervalued was equipment, which was worth $20,000 more than book value. The equipment has a remaining life of four years, and straight-line depreciation is used. Any remaining excess is goodwill.

On May 1, 20X2, any excess of cost over book value is due to goodwill.

In the last quarter of 20X2, Chris sold $50,000 in goods to James, at a gross profit rate of 30%. On December 31, 20X2, $10,000 of these goods are in James' ending inventory.

The trial balances for the companies on December 31, 20X2, are as follows:

	James Company	Chris Company
Inventory, December 31	100,000	50,000
Other Current Assets	127,000	180,000
Investment in Chris Company	③	
Land	50,000	50,000
Buildings and Equipment	350,000	320,000
Accumulated Depreciation	(100,000)	(60,000)
Other Intangibles	20,000	
Current Liabilities	(120,000)	(40,000)
Bonds Payable		(100,000)
Other Long-Term Liabilities	(200,000)	
Common Stock—James	(200,000)	
Other Paid-In Capital—James	(100,000)	
Retained Earnings—James	(214,000)	
Common Stock—Chris		(50,000)
Other Paid-In Capital—Chris		(100,000)
Retained Earnings—Chris		(190,000)
Net Sales	(520,000)	(450,000)
Cost of Goods Sold	300,000	260,000
Operating Expenses	120,000	100,000
Subsidiary Income	③	
Dividends Declared	50,000	30,000
Total	0	0

③ To be calculated and inserted

Required ▶ ▶ ▶ ▶ ▶

1. Using this information, prepare determination and distribution of excess schedules for the two purchases.
2. James Company carries the Investment in Chris Company under the simple equity method. In general journal form, record the entries that would be made to apply the equity method in 20X1 and 20X2.
3. Compute the balance that should appear in Investment in Chris Company and in Subsidiary Income on December 31, 20X2 (the second year). Fill in these amounts on James Company's trial balance on the worksheet for 20X2.
4. Complete the worksheet for consolidated financial statements for 20X2.

Problem 7-3 *(LO 2)* **Worksheet, blocks, control with second block.** On January 1, 20X4, Madden Company purchased a 20% interest in Clayton Company for $100,000. Two years subsequent to this purchase, Madden Company acquired an additional 45% interest in Clayton Company for $250,000.

Balance sheets of Clayton Company immediately prior to these purchases were as follows:

Assets	January 1, 20X4	January 1, 20X6
Current assets	$150,000	$120,000
Land	150,000	150,000
Equipment (net)	200,000	300,000
Total assets	$500,000	$570,000

Liabilities and Equity		
Liabilities	$100,000	$110,000
Equity:		
Common stock ($5 par)	100,000	100,000
Paid-in capital in excess of par	150,000	150,000
Retained earnings	150,000	210,000
Total equity	$400,000	$460,000
Total liabilities and equity	$500,000	$570,000

On January 1, 20X4, and January 1, 20X6, Clayton's book values approximated fair values, except for the land, which was undervalued by $50,000. Any remaining excess is attributed to a patent with a 10-year life starting January 1, 20X4.

The original 20% investment had been maintained under the sophisticated equity method. Since it now will be necessary to prepare consolidated statements, the simple equity method is in use for 20X6.

On December 31, 20X6, Madden's investment in Clayton Company was determined as follows:

Original cost of 20% investment	$100,000
20X4–X5 equity adjustment, net of excess amortization	10,000
Original cost of 45% investment	250,000
65% of income, January 1, 20X6–December 31, 20X6	26,000
Investment in Clayton Company	$386,000

The following trial balances were prepared on December 31, 20X6:

	Madden Company	Clayton Company
Current Assets	250,000	225,000
Investment in Clayton Company	386,000	
Land	240,000	150,000
Building (net)	480,000	
Equipment (net)	400,000	220,000
Other Assets	20,000	5,000
Liabilities	(340,000)	(100,000)
Common Stock ($10 par)	(1,000,000)	
Common Stock ($5 par)		(100,000)
Paid-In Capital in Excess of Par		(150,000)
Retained Earnings, January 1, 20X6	(350,000)	(210,000)
Sales	(900,000)	(350,000)
Subsidiary Income	(26,000)	
Cost of Goods Sold	540,000	180,000
Other Expenses	250,000	130,000
Dividends Declared	50,000	
Total	0	0

Prepare the worksheet necessary to produce the consolidated financial statements of Madden Company and its subsidiary as of December 31, 20X6. Include the determination and distribution of excess and income distribution schedules. ◄◄◄◄◄ **Required**

Problem 7-4 *(LO 2)* **Worksheet, blocks, control with second block, fixed asset sale.** On January 1, 20X1, Prince Company purchased 20% of the common stock of Spud Company for $80,000. On this date, Spud had common stock, other paid-in capital, and retained earnings of $50,000, $100,000, and $150,000, respectively. Any excess of cost over book value is due to goodwill.

On January 1, 20X2, Prince Company purchased an additional 60% of the common stock of Spud Company for $284,000. On this date, the only tangible asset of Spud that was undervalued was land, which was worth $30,000 more than book value. Any remaining excess is attributed to goodwill.

Net income and dividends for two years for Spud Company were as follows:

	20X1	20X2
Net income for year	$60,000	$90,000
Dividends, declared in December	20,000	30,000

For 20X1, Prince accounted for its investment using the sophisticated equity method. For 20X2, Prince accounted for all of its investment using the simple equity method.

On July 1, 20X2, Spud purchased equipment for $40,000 and immediately sold it to Prince for $50,000. Prince is using the equipment and depreciating it over five years, using the straight-line method and assuming no salvage value.

The trial balances for both companies on December 31, 20X2, are as follows:

	Prince Company	Spud Company
Inventory, December 31	100,000	50,000
Other Current Assets	157,000	180,000
Investment in Spud Company	420,000	

(continued)

	Prince Company	Spud Company
Land	50,000	50,000
Buildings and Equipment	350,000	320,000
Accumulated Depreciation	(100,000)	(60,000)
Other Intangibles	20,000	
Current Liabilities	(120,000)	(40,000)
Bonds Payable		(100,000)
Other Long-Term Liabilities	(200,000)	
Common Stock—Prince	(200,000)	
Other Paid-In Capital—Prince	(100,000)	
Retained Earnings—Prince	(255,000)	
Common Stock—Spud		(50,000)
Other Paid-In Capital—Spud		(100,000)
Retained Earnings—Spud		(190,000)
Net Sales	(520,000)	(450,000)
Cost of Goods Sold	300,000	270,000
Operating Expenses	120,000	100,000
Gain on Sale of Equipment		(10,000)
Subsidiary Income	(72,000)	
Dividends Declared	50,000	30,000
Total	0	0

Required ▶ ▶ ▶ ▶ ▶

1. Using this information, prepare determination and distribution of excess schedules for the two purchases.
2. Prepare the worksheet necessary to produce the consolidated financial statements of Prince and Spud as of December 31, 20X2. Include income distribution schedules.

template cd

Problem 7-5 *(LO 2)* **Worksheet, blocks, control with first block, loans, fixed asset sales, intercompany merchandise.** During 20X7, Away Company acquired a controlling interest in Stallman Inc. Trial balances of the companies at December 31, 20X7, are as follows:

	Away Company	Stallman Inc.
Cash	100,000	78,000
Notes Receivable	100,000	
Accounts Receivable	200,000	100,000
Interest Receivable	3,000	
Dividends Receivable	4,500	
Inventories	924,000	125,000
Investment in Stallman Inc.	468,700	
Property, Plant, and Equipment	1,250,000	500,000
Accumulated Depreciation	(500,000)	(150,000)
Deferred Charges	25,000	
Patents and Licenses		50,000
Accounts Payable	(425,000)	(80,000)
Notes Payable		(75,000)
Dividends Payable		(5,000)
Capital Stock	(300,000)	(100,000)
Retained Earnings, January 1, 20X7	(1,605,000)	(400,000)

Sales and Services	(1,800,000)	(750,000)
Subsidiary Income	(43,200)	
Interest Income	(3,000)	
Cost of Goods Sold	1,350,000	525,000
Administrative and Selling Expenses	251,000	174,000
Interest Expense		3,000
Dividends Declared		5,000
Total	0	0

The following information is available regarding the transactions and accounts of the two companies:

a. An analysis of the investment in Stallman Inc. account follows:

	Description	Amount	Interest Acquired
January 1, 20X7	Investment	$325,000	70%
September 30, 20X7	Investment	105,000	20%
Total		$430,000	90%
December 31, 20X7	90% of Stallman income for 20X7	43,200	
December 31, 20X7	90% of Stallman dividends for 20X7	(4,500)	
Total		$468,700	

The net income of Stallman Inc. for the nine months ended September 30, 20X7, was $25,000.

b. The price paid by the parent on January 1, 20X7, to achieve control reflects uncertainty as to the future value of the patents. The remaining amortization is 10 years.
c. On September 30, 20X7, Away Company loaned its subsidiary $100,000 on a 1-year, 12% note. Interest and principal are payable in quarterly installments beginning December 31, 20X7. The December 31, 20X7, payment was made by Stallman but was not received by Away. Away Company has no other notes receivable outstanding.
d. Stallman Inc.'s sales principally are engineering services billed at cost plus 50%. During 20X7, Away Company was billed for $40,000, of which $16,500 was treated as a deferred charge at December 31, 20X7.
e. During the year, parent company sales to the subsidiary totaled $60,000, of which $10,000 remained in the inventory of Stallman Inc. at December 31, 20X7.
f. In 20X7, Away constructed certain tools at a cost of $15,000 and sold them to Stallman Inc. for $25,000. Stallman Inc. depreciates such tools using the straight-line method over a 5-year life. One-half year's depreciation is taken in the year of acquisition.

Prepare the worksheet necessary to produce the consolidated financial statements of Away Company and its subsidiary for the year ended December 31, 20X7. Include the determination and distribution of excess and income distribution schedules. ◄◄◄◄◄ **Required**

(AICPA adapted)

Problem 7-6 *(LO 3)* **Sale of partial, then balance of interest.** On January 1, 20X3, Cipher Corporation purchased 90% (18,000 shares) of the outstanding common stock of Dart Company for $500,000. Just prior to Cipher Corporation's purchase, Dart Company had the following stockholders' equity:

Common stock ($5 par)	$100,000
Paid-in capital in excess of par	300,000
Retained earnings	100,000
Total stockholders' equity	$500,000

At this time, Dart Company's book values approximated fair values except for buildings with a 20-year life.

On January 1, 20X7, Dart Company's retained earnings balance amounted to $200,000. No changes had taken place in the paid-in capital accounts since the original sale of common stock on July 10, 20X0.

On July 1, 20X7, Cipher Corporation sold 2,000 of its Dart Company shares to Tower Corporation for $80,000. At the time of this sale, Cipher had no intention of selling the balance of its holding in Dart Company.

In an unexpected move on December 31, 20X7, Cipher Corporation sold its remaining 80% interest in Dart Company to Tower Corporation for $500,000.

Dart Company's reported income and dividends for 20X7 are as follows:

	Income	Dividends
January 1, 20X7–July 1, 20X7	$25,000	$0.50/share
July 1, 20X7–December 31, 20X7	35,000	0.50/share

Required ▶ ▶ ▶ ▶ ▶ Prepare the determination and distribution of excess schedule for Cipher Corporation's purchase of Dart Company common stock on January 1, 20X3. Then, prepare all the entries on Cipher's books needed to reflect the changes in its investment account from January 1, 20X7, to December 31, 20X7. (Assume Cipher uses the cost method to report its investment in Dart Company.)

Problem 7-7 *(LO 2, LO 3, LO 4)* **Analysis of block acquisitions, sale of interest, preferred stock.** The following information is available regarding the investments of Billings Corporation in Chassel Company for the years 20X1–20X5:

Date	Transaction	Interest	Price
January 1, 20X1	Purchased common	10%	$ 25,000
January 1, 20X2	Purchased preferred	60	30,000
January 1, 20X3	Purchased common	50	140,000
January 1, 20X5	Purchased common	20	60,000
January 1, 20X6	Sold common	10	35,000

The stockholders' equity section of Chassel Company's balance sheet has not changed since the January 1, 20X0, original sale of preferred stock to the public, except for the balance in the retained earnings account. The stockholders' equity as of January 1, 20X5, is as follows:

6% cumulative preferred stock	
($50 par, liquidation value equals par value)	$ 50,000
Common stock ($10 par)	100,000
Paid-in capital in excess of par	20,000
Retained earnings	150,000
Total stockholders' equity	$320,000

Other relevant facts are as follows:

a. On January 1, 20X1, Chassel had a $60,000 retained earnings balance and there were no dividends in arrears on the preferred stock.
b. The excess of cost over book value on each investment in common stock was viewed as goodwill.
c. The 10% interest sold on January 1, 20X6, was the interest purchased on January 1, 20X1.
d. Income and dividends were as follows for 20X1–20X5:

	Net Income	Preferred Dividends	Common Dividends
20X1	$25,000	$3,000	None
20X2	30,000	3,000	$6,000
20X3	30,000	3,000	5,000
20X4	25,000	None	None
20X5	20,000	None	None

Billings' investment account balances for its interests in Chassel Company were calculated as follows on December 31, 20X5:

Investment in preferred stock:	
Original cost	$ 30,000
Plus dividends in arrears for 20X4	1,800
Balance, December 31, 20X5	$ 31,800
Investment in common stock:	
January 1, 20X1 purchase	$ 25,000
January 1, 20X3 purchase	140,000
20X3 Chassel income, $30,000 × 60%	18,000
20X3 Chassel dividends, $5,000 × 60%	(3,000)
20X4 Chassel income, $25,000 × 60%	15,000
January 1, 20X5 purchase	60,000
20X5 Chassel income, $20,000 × 80%	16,000
December 31, 20X5 sale	(35,000)
Balance, December 31, 20X5	$236,000

◄◄◄◄◄ Required

Assume the investment accounts are to be properly maintained under the simple equity method. Prepare all necessary correcting entries on the books of Billings Corporation as of January 1, 20X6. (Assume nominal accounts are open.) All supporting computations and schedules should be in good form.

Problem 7-8 *(LO 4)* **Worksheet, preferred stock, fixed asset sale.** Marsha Corporation purchased an 80% interest in the common stock of Trans Corporation on December 31, 20X3, for $720,000, when Trans had the following condensed balance sheet:

Assets		Liabilities and Stockholders' Equity	
Current assets	$ 500,000	Liabilities	$ 600,000
Land	100,000	Preferred stock (8% cumulative, $100 par)	100,000
Building (net)	400,000	Common stock ($20 par)	750,000
Equipment (net)	500,000	Retained earnings	50,000
Total assets	$1,500,000	Total liabilities and equity	$1,500,000

On the December 31, 20X3, purchase date, the dividends on the preferred stock were two years in arrears. Also on this date, the book values of Trans's assets approximated fair values, except for the building which was undervalued by $28,000 and had a 20-year remaining life. Any remaining excess is considered to be goodwill.

For 20X4–20X6, earnings and dividends for Trans Corporation were as follows:

	Income	Preferred Dividends	Common Dividends
20X4	$40,000		
20X5	50,000	$16,000	
20X6	80,000	24,000	$26,750

The following trial balances of the two companies were prepared on December 31, 20X6:

	Marsha Corporation	Trans Corporation
Current Assets	806,400	463,250
Investment in Trans Corporation	720,000	
Land	400,000	210,000
Building	950,000	500,000
Accumulated Depreciation—Building	(200,000)	(160,000)
Equipment	1,500,000	740,000
Accumulated Depreciation—Equipment	(400,000)	(200,000)
Liabilities	(800,000)	(550,000)
Preferred Stock, 8%		(100,000)
Common Stock ($20 par)	(2,000,000)	(750,000)
Retained Earnings, January 1, 20X6	(860,000)	(124,000)
Sales	(2,100,000)	(1,000,000)
Subsidiary Dividend Income	(21,400)	
Cost of Goods Sold	1,155,000	600,000
Other Expenses	650,000	320,000
Dividends Declared	200,000	50,750
Total	0	0

On January 1, 20X5, Marsha sold production equipment to Trans for $55,000 with a 5-year remaining life. Marsha's original cost was $80,000, and accumulated depreciation on the date sold was $50,000.

Required ▶ ▶ ▶ ▶ ▶

Prepare the worksheet necessary to produce the consolidated financial statements of Marsha Corporation and its subsidiary as of December 31, 20X6. Include the determination and distribution of excess and income distribution schedules.

template cd

Problem 7-9 *(LO 4)* **Worksheet, 2 subsidiaries, preferred stock, intercompany merchandise and fixed assets, bonds.** The following information pertains to Titan Corporation and its two subsidiaries, Boat Corporation and Motor Corporation:

a. The three corporations are all in the same industry and their operations are homogeneous. Titan Corporation exercises control over the boards of directors of Boat Corporation and Motor Corporation and has installed new principal officers in both.
b. Boat Corporation had a retained earnings balance of $92,000 at January 1, 20X7, and had income of $15,000 for the first three months of 20X7 and $20,000 for the first six months of 20X8.
c. Titan Corporation acquired 250 shares of fully participating Motor preferred stock for $7,000 and 14,000 shares of Motor common stock for $196,000 on January 2, 20X8. Motor Corporation had a net income of $20,000 in 20X8 and did not declare any dividends.

d. Motor Corporation's inventory includes $22,400 of merchandise acquired from Boat Corporation subsequent to July 20X8, for which no payment has been made. Boat Corporation marked up the merchandise 40% on cost.
e. Titan Corporation acquired in the open market twenty-five $1,000, 6% bonds of Boat Corporation for $21,400 on January 1, 20X5. Boat Corporation bonds mature December 31, 20X0. Interest is paid each June 30 and December 31. Straight-line amortization is allowed on the basis of materiality.
f. The 20X8 year-end balance in the investment in Boat Corporation stock account is composed of the items shown in the following schedule:

Date	Description	Amount
April 1, 20X7	Cost of 5,000 shares of Boat Corp. stock	$ 71,400
December 31, 20X7	20% of the dividends declared in December 20X7 by Boat Corp.	(9,000)
December 31, 20X7	20% of the 20X7 annual net income of Boat Corp.........	12,000
July 1, 20X8	Cost of 15,000 shares of Boat Corp.	226,200
December 31, 20X8	80% of the dividends declared in December 20X8 by Boat Corp.	(24,000)
December 31, 20X8	80% of the 20X8 annual net income of Boat Corp.........	32,000
December 31, 20X8	Total...	$308,600

g. The December 31, 20X8, trial balances for the three corporations appear as follows:

	Titan Corporation	Boat Corporation	Motor Corporation
Cash	100,000	87,000	95,000
Accounts Receivable	158,200	210,000	105,000
Inventories	290,000	90,000	115,000
Advance to Boat Corporation	17,000		
Dividends Receivable	24,000		
Property, Plant, and Equipment....................	777,600	325,000	470,000
Accumulated Depreciation	(180,000)	(55,000)	(160,000)
Investment in Boat Corporation:			
6% Bonds..................................	23,800		
Common Stock..............................	308,600		
Investment in Motor Corporation:			
Preferred Stock..............................	7,400		
Common Stock..............................	207,200		
Notes Payable................................	(45,000)	(14,000)	(44,000)
Accounts Payable	(170,000)	(96,000)	(86,000)
Bonds Payable................................	(285,000)	(150,000)	(125,000)
Discount on Bonds Payable	8,000		
Dividends Payable.............................	(22,000)	(30,000)	
Preferred Stock ($20 par)	(400,000)		(50,000)
Common Stock ($10 par)	(600,000)	(250,000)	(200,000)
Retained Earnings, January 1, 20X8................	(154,600)	(107,000)	(100,000)
Sales	(1,050,000)	(500,000)	(650,000)
Other Revenue................................	(2,100)		
Subsidiary Income:			
Common Stock (Boat)	(32,000)		
Preferred Stock (Motor)	(400)		
Common Stock (Motor)	(11,200)		
Cost of Goods Sold	650,000	300,000	400,000

(continued)

	Titan Corporation	Boat Corporation	Motor Corporation
Other Expenses	358,500	160,000	230,000
Dividends Declared	22,000	30,000	
Total	0	0	0

Required ▶ ▶ ▶ ▶ ▶ Prepare the worksheet necessary to produce the consolidated financial statements of Titan Corporation and its subsidiaries as of December 31, 20X8. Consolidated retained earnings should be allocated to Titan Corporation, and the NCIs should be shown separately in the consolidated balance sheet column. The consolidation is to be accounted for as a purchase. All supporting computations and schedules should be in good form.

(AICPA adapted)

template cd

Problem 7-10 *(LO 4)* **Worksheet, preferred stock, intercompany fixed assets and merchandise, sale of interest.** On January 1, 20X7, Black Jack Corporation purchased all of the preferred stock and 60% of the common stock of Zenon Company for $56,000 and $110,000, respectively. Immediately prior to the purchases, Zenon Company had the following stockholders' equity:

8% cumulative preferred stock ($100 par, two years in arrears)	$ 50,000
Common stock ($10 par)	100,000
Paid-in capital in excess of par (common stock)	20,000
Retained earnings	30,000
Total stockholders' equity	$200,000

The December 31, 20X8, trial balances of the two companies are as follows:

	Black Jack Corporation	Zenon Company
Cash	31,400	10,000
Accounts Receivable (net)	80,000	76,000
Inventories	230,000	44,000
Other Current Assets	20,000	8,000
Property, Plant, and Equipment	1,450,000	122,000
Accumulated Depreciation	(420,000)	(25,000)
Investment in Zenon Preferred Stock	56,000	
Investment in Zenon Common Stock	120,200	
Liabilities	(350,000)	(18,000)
Common Stock—Black Jack	(1,000,000)	
Retained Earnings—Black Jack	(195,000)	
Preferred Stock—Zenon ($100 par)		(50,000)
Common Stock—Zenon		(100,000)
Paid-In Capital in Excess of Par—Zenon		(20,000)
Retained Earnings—Zenon		(41,000)
Sales	(420,000)	(96,000)
Cost of Goods Sold	300,000	60,000
Other Expenses	80,000	26,000
Dividends Declared	25,000	4,000
Subsidiary Income—Preferred	(4,000)	
Subsidiary Income—Common	(3,600)	
Paid-In Capital in Excess of Par—Black Jack		
Total	0	0

Additional information:

a. Any excess of cost over book value on the investment in common stock is attributed to equipment with an 8-year life.
b. On December 30, 20X7, and December 30, 20X8, Zenon Company paid preferred stock dividends of $8 per share.
c. Zenon Company had a net income of $15,000 in 20X7 and $10,000 for 20X8.
d. Zenon Company sold a piece of equipment with a book value of $8,000 to Black Jack Corporation for $13,000 on January 2, 20X7. The machine had an estimated future life of five years, and straight-line depreciation is being used.
e. During 20X8, Black Jack sold $20,000 of goods to Zenon for cost plus 40%. Zenon had $2,800 of such purchases in its beginning inventory and $7,000 of such purchases in its ending inventory. Zenon owed Black Jack $2,000 for purchases at year-end. During 20X8, Zenon sold $8,000 of goods to Black Jack at cost plus 60%. Of these goods, $1,200 were in Black Jack's beginning inventory, and $1,600 of such goods were in its ending inventory. Black Jack owed Zenon $6,000 for purchases at year-end.
f. On January 1, 20X9, Black Jack Corporation sold its 60% interest in Zenon Company common stock for $130,000.

◄◄◄◄◄ **Required**

1. Prepare the worksheet necessary to produce the consolidated financial statements of Black Jack Corporation and its subsidiary for the year ended December 31, 20X8. Include the determination and distribution of excess and income distribution schedules.
2. Prepare the entries on Black Jack Corporation's books to reflect the sale of its investment in Zenon Company common stock on January 1, 20X9.

APPENDIX PROBLEMS

Problem 7A-1 *(LO 5)* **Balance sheet worksheet, blocks, control with first, inventory, fixed asset sales.** The December 31, 20X9, post-closing trial balances of Moot Corporation and its subsidiary, Ferris Corporation, are as follows:

	Moot Corporation	Ferris Corporation
Cash	167,250	101,000
Accounts Receivable	178,450	72,000
Notes Receivable	87,500	28,000
Dividends Receivable	36,000	
Inventories	122,000	68,000
Property, Plant, and Equipment	487,000	252,000
Accumulated Depreciation	(117,000)	(64,000)
Investment in Ferris Corporation	240,800	
Accounts Payable	(222,000)	(76,000)
Notes Payable	(79,000)	(89,000)
Dividends Payable		(40,000)
Common Stock ($10 par)	(400,000)	(100,000)
Retained Earnings	(501,000)	(152,000)
Total	0	0

The following additional information is available:

a. Moot initially acquired 60% of the outstanding common stock of Ferris in 20X7. There was no difference between the cost and book value of the net assets acquired. As of December 31, 20X9, the percentage owned is 90%. An analysis of the investment in Ferris Corporation account is as follows:

Date	Description	Amount
December 31, 20X7	Acquired 6,000 shares	$ 70,800
December 31, 20X8	60% of 20X8 net income of $78,000	46,800
September 1, 20X9	Acquired 3,000 shares	92,000
December 31, 20X9	Subsidiary income for 20X9	67,200*
December 31, 20X9	90% of dividends declared	(36,000)
Investment balance, December 31, 20X9		$240,800

*Subsidiary income for 20X9:

60% × $96,000	$57,600
30% × $96,000 × 33½%	9,600
Total	$67,200

Ferris net income is earned ratably during the year. Any excess of cost over the net assets acquired is attributable to a patent with a 5-year life.

b. On December 15, 20X9, Ferris declared a cash dividend of $4 per share of common stock, payable to shareholders on January 7, 20Y0.

c. During 20X9, Moot sold merchandise to Ferris. Moot had a 20% gross profit, and the sale was made at $80,000. Ferris's inventory at December 31, 20X9, included merchandise purchased from Moot for $30,000.

d. In December 20X8, Ferris sold merchandise to Moot for $67,000, which included a 30% gross profit. On January 1, 20X9, $54,000 of this merchandise remained in Moot's inventory. This merchandise subsequently was sold by Moot at a profit of $11,000 during 20X9.

e. On October 1, 20X9, Moot sold excess equipment to Ferris for $50,000. Data relating to this equipment are as follows:

Book value on Moot's records	$36,000
Method of depreciation	Straight-line
Estimated remaining life on October 1, 20X9	10 years

f. Near the end of 20X9, Ferris reduced the balance of its intercompany account payable to zero by transferring $8,000 to Moot. This payment still was in transit on December 31, 20X9.

Required ▶ ▶ ▶ ▶ ▶ Prepare the worksheet necessary to produce the consolidated balance sheet of Moot Corporation and its subsidiary as of December 31, 20X9. Include the determination and distribution of excess schedule for Moot's purchase of Ferris common stock on September 1, 20X9.

(AICPA adapted)

Problem 7A-2 *(LO 5)* **Balance sheet worksheet, mid-year purchase, intercompany bonds and inventory.** Book Inc. acquired all of the outstanding $25 par common stock of Cray Inc. on June 30, 20X4, in exchange for 40,000 shares of its $25 par common stock. On June 30, 20X4, Book Inc. common stock closed at $65 per share on a national stock exchange. Any excess of cost over book value is attributed to goodwill. Both corporations continued to operate as separate businesses, maintaining separate accounting records with years ending December 31.

Additional information is as follows:

a. Book Inc. uses the simple equity method to account for its investment in Cray.
b. On June 30, 20X4, Cray paid cash dividends of $4 per share on its common stock.
c. On December 10, 20X4, Book paid a cash dividend totaling $256,000 on its common stock.
d. On June 30, 20X4, immediately before the combination, the stockholders' equities were:

	Book Inc.	Cray Inc.
Common stock	$2,200,000	$1,000,000
Additional paid-in capital	1,660,000	190,000
Retained earnings	3,036,000	980,000
Total	$6,896,000	$2,170,000

e. Cray's long-term debt consisted of 10-year, 10% bonds issued at face value on March 31, 20X1. Interest is payable semiannually on March 31 and September 30. Book had purchased Cray's bonds at the face value of $320,000 in 20X1, and there has not been any change in ownership.
f. During October 20X4, Book sold merchandise to Cray at a total invoice price of $720,000, which included a profit of $180,000. At December 31, 20X4, one-half of the merchandise remained in Cray's inventory, and Cray had not paid Book for the merchandise purchased.
g. The 20X4 net income amounts per the separate books of Book and Cray were $890,000 (exclusive of equity in Cray earnings) and $580,000 ($320,000 in the first six months and $260,000 in the second six months), respectively.
h. The retained earnings balances at December 31, 20X3, were $2,506,000 and $820,000 for Book and Cray, respectively.
i. On December 31, 20X4, the companies had the following post-closing trial balances:

	Book Inc.	Cray Inc.
Cash	825,000	330,000
Accounts and Other Current Receivables	2,140,000	835,000
Inventories	2,310,000	1,045,000
Land	650,000	300,000
Depreciable Assets (net)	4,575,000	1,980,000
Investment in Cray Inc.	2,860,000	
Long-Term Investments and Other Assets	865,000	385,000
Accounts Payable and Other Current Liabilities	(2,465,000)	(1,145,000)
Long-Term Debt	(1,900,000)	(1,300,000)
Common Stock ($25 par)	(3,200,000)	(1,000,000)
Additional Paid-In Capital	(3,260,000)	(190,000)
Retained Earnings	(3,400,000)	(1,240,000)
Total	0	0

◄◄◄◄◄ **Required**

1. Prepare the worksheet necessary to produce the consolidated balance sheet of Book Inc. and its subsidiary for the year ended December 31, 20X4.
2. Prepare the formal consolidated statement of retained earnings for December 31, 20X4.

Problem 7A-3 *(LO 5)* **Balance sheet worksheet, intercompany inventory, bonds and capital lease.** On January 1, 20X1, Press Company acquired 90% of the common stock of Solid Company for $317,000. On this date, Solid had total owners' equity of $270,000, including retained earnings of $100,000.

On January 1, 20X1, any excess of cost over book value is attributable to the undervaluation of land, building, and goodwill. Land is worth $20,000 more than cost. Building is worth $40,000 more than book value. It has a remaining useful life of six years and is depreciated using the straight-line method.

During 20X1 and 20X2, Press has appropriately accounted for its investment in Solid using the simple equity method.

During 20X2, Solid sold merchandise to Press for $40,000, of which $15,000 is held by Press on December 31, 20X2. Solid's usual gross profit on affiliated sales is 40%. On December 31, 20X2, Press still owes Solid $8,000 for merchandise acquired in December.

On October 1, 20X0, Solid sold $100,000 par value of 10-year, 10% bonds for $102,000. The bonds pay interest semiannually on April 1 and October 1. Straight-line amortization is used. On October 2, 20X1, Press repurchased $60,000 par value of the bonds for $59,100. Straight-line amortization is used.

On January 1, 20X2, Press purchased equipment for $111,332 and immediately leased the equipment to Solid on a 3-year lease. The minimum lease payments of $40,000 are to be made annually on January 1, beginning immediately, for a total of three payments. The implicit interest rate is 8%. The useful life of the equipment is three years. The lease has been capitalized by both companies. Solid is depreciating the equipment using the straight-line method and assuming a salvage value of $6,332. A lease amortization schedule, applicable to both companies, follows:

Carrying Value on	Carrying Value	Interest Rate	Interest	Payment	Principal Reduction
January 1, 20X1	111,332				
	−40,000				
January 1, 20X2	71,332	8%	$5,707	$40,000	$34,293
	−34,293				
January 1, 20X3	37,039	8%	2,961*	40,000	37,039
	−37,039				
January 1, 20X4	0				

*Adjusted for rounding error.

The balance sheet for the companies on December 31, 20X2, was as follows:

Assets	Press Company	Solid Company
Accounts receivable	$ 72,000	$ 50,000
Bond interest receivable	1,500	
Minimum lease payments receivable	80,000	
Unearned interest income	(2,961)	
Inventory	86,000	80,000
Other current assets	60,236	183,668
Investment in Solid Company	344,000	
Investment in Solid bonds	59,225	
Land	60,000	30,000
Buildings and equipment	300,000	230,000
Accumulated depreciation	(100,000)	(50,000)
Equipment under capital lease		111,332
Accumulated depreciated equipment under lease		(35,000)
Totals	$ 960,000	$600,000

Liabilities and Equity	Press Company	Solid Company
Accounts payable	$ 78,000	$ 70,000
Bond interest payable		2,500
Lease interest payable		5,707
Other current liabilities	57,000	48,911
Lease obligation payable		71,332
Bonds payable	150,000	100,000
Premium on bonds		1,550
Common stock—Press	200,000	
Other paid-in capital—Press	150,000	
Retained earnings—Press	325,000	
Common stock—Solid		100,000
Other paid-in capital—Solid		70,000
Retained earnings—Solid		130,000
Totals	$960,000	$600,000

Complete the worksheet for a consolidated balance sheet as of December 31, 20X2. Round all computations to the nearest dollar. ◄◄◄◄◄ **Required**

Subsidiary Equity Transactions; Indirect and Mutual Holdings

CHAPTER

8

Learning Objectives

When you have completed this chapter, you should be able to

1. **Explain the effect of subsidiary stock dividends on elimination procedures.**
2. **Account for the effect of the subsidiary's sale of its own common stock on the parent's investment in the subsidiary.**
3. **Account for the effect of subsidiary treasury stock transactions on the parent's investment in the subsidiary.**
4. **Demonstrate accounting procedures for multilevel holdings.**
5. **Demonstrate an understanding of the alternatives used for accounting for investments in the parent company by the subsidiary.**

This chapter is concerned with subsidiary equity transactions and complicated parent ownership arrangements that affect the recording and consolidations of the parent's investment in a subsidiary. First, we will consider the impact of subsidiary equity transactions on the investment of the parent company. The subsidiary may issue stock dividends, sell additional shares of stock, or repurchase outstanding shares. Each of these transactions has an effect on the procedures used by the parent to record and to consolidate its investment in the subsidiary.

Second, this chapter will deal with more complex ownership structures. Accounting procedures will be developed for indirect holdings and mutual holdings. Indirect holdings are situations where a parent holds a controlling interest in a subsidiary and the subsidiary is, in turn, a parent of another company. A mutual holding exists when the subsidiary owns voting common stock of the parent company.

SUBSIDIARY STOCK DIVIDENDS

1

OBJECTIVE

Explain the effect of subsidiary stock dividends on elimination procedures.

A subsidiary may issue stock dividends to convert retained earnings into paid-in capital. The minimum amount to be removed from retained earnings is the par value or stated value of the shares distributed. However, according to accounting principles, when the distribution does not exceed 20% to 25% of the previously outstanding shares, an amount equal to the fair value of the shares should be removed from retained earnings and transferred to paid-in capital. The recording of stock dividends at fair value is defended by the following statement from ARB No. 43:

> *. . . a stock dividend does not, in fact, give rise to any change whatsoever in either the corporation's assets or its respective shareholders' proportionate interests therein. However, it cannot fail to be recognized that, merely as a consequence of the expressed purpose of the transaction and its characterization as a dividend in related notices to shareholders and the public at large,*

many recipients of stock dividends look upon them as distributions of corporate earnings and usually in an amount equivalent to the fair value of the additional shares received.[1]

Accounting theory, however, is not consistent when it comes to recording the receipt of dividends by an investor. Even though the false impression of the "typical" investor is sufficient reason to allow the issuing corporation to record the market value of the shares distributed, the investor is not permitted to do likewise. In fact, the investor must not record income when stock dividends are received but must acknowledge the true impact of the transaction, which is that nothing of substance has been given or received. Thus, the investor merely makes a memo entry indicating that the cost of the original investment now is allocated to a greater number of shares. The revised number of shares is important in computing cost per share if there is a subsequent partial sale of the investment.

To review the recording of a stock dividend and to provide a basis for worksheets, assume Company P acquired an 80% interest in Company S on January 1, 20X1, at which time the following determination and distribution of excess schedule was prepared:

Price paid		$200,000	
Less interest acquired:			
Common stock ($10 par)	$ 100,000		
Retained earnings	80,000		
Total stockholders' equity	$ 180,000		
Interest acquired	× 80%	144,000	
Equipment (10-year life)		$ 56,000	Dr.

On January 2, 20X3, Company S declared and distributed a 10% stock dividend. Prior to declaration of the dividend, its stockholders' equity appeared as follows:

Common stock ($10 par)	$100,000
Retained earnings	120,000
Total stockholders' equity	$220,000

In the following entry to record the stock dividend, Company S acknowledged the $25 fair value of the 1,000 shares distributed:

Retained Earnings (or Stock Dividends Declared) ($25 fair value × 1,000 shares)	25,000	
Common Stock ($10 par × 1,000 shares)		10,000
Additional Paid-In Capital from Stock Dividend (1,000 shares × $15 excess over par)		15,000

Parent Using the Simple Equity Method

Continuing the example, on January 1, 20X3 (prior to the dividend), Company P has a simple-equity-adjusted balance of $232,000 in its investment in Company S account, derived as follows:

Original cost		$200,000
Share of undistributed income:		
Company S retained earnings, January 1, 20X3	$ 120,000	
Company S retained earnings, January 1, 20X1	80,000	
Increase in retained earnings	$ 40,000	
Ownership interest	× 80%	32,000
Simple-equity-adjusted balance, January 1, 20X3		$232,000

1 Accounting Research and Terminology Bulletin No. 43, *Restatement and Revision of Accounting Research Bulletins* (New York: American Institute of Certified Public Accountants, 1961), Ch. 7, Sec. B, par. 10.

During 20X3, Company S earned $20,000 and made no other dividend declarations. Company P would make the following entries during 20X3, under the simple equity method:

Receipt of stock dividend:

Jan. 2, 20X3	Memo: Investment in Company S now includes 800 added shares for a total of 8,800 shares. The parent's interest remains at 80%.		

Recording of equity income:

Dec. 31, 20X3	Investment in Company S	16,000	
	Subsidiary Income		16,000
	To record the 80% interest in Company S $20,000 reported net income for 20X3.		

The partial worksheet below lists the investment in Company S account at the December 31, 20X3, simple-equity-adjusted cost of $248,000. Note that the partial worksheet includes the redistributed capital structure of Company S which results from the stock dividend. It should be clear that the complications arising from stock dividends pertain primarily to their recording by the separate affiliated firms. There is only a minimal effect on the consolidated worksheet.

	Trial Balance		Eliminations & Adjustments	
	Company P	Company S	Dr.	Cr.
Investment in Company S	248,000			(CY) 16,000
				(EL) 176,000
				(D) 56,000
Equipment			(D) 56,000	(A) 16,800
Common Stock, Company P	(500,000)			
Retained Earnings, Company P	(420,000)		(A) 11,200	
Common Stock ($10 par), Company S		(110,000)	**(EL) 88,000**	
Additional Paid-In Capital from Stock Dividend, Company S		(15,000)	**(EL) 12,000**	
Retained Earnings, Company S (reduced $25,000 for stock dividend)		(95,000)	**(EL) 76,000**	
Subsidiary Income	(16,000)		(CY) 16,000	
Expenses	30,000	18,000	(A) 5,600	

Eliminations and Adjustments:

(CY) Eliminate the parent's entry recording its share of subsidiary income for the current year. There is no complication caused by the stock dividend since it does not constitute income to Company P.
(EL) Eliminate 80% of Company S equity balances as restructured by the stock dividend. If the subsidiary recorded the stock dividend with a debit to Stock Dividends Declared, 80% of that account would be eliminated in this step.
(D) Distribute the excess cost to the equipment account as required by the determination and distribution of excess schedule.
(A) Depreciate the equipment for three years. Depreciation for the two prior years reduces the controlling interest in retained earnings, while the current-year depreciation reduces current consolidated net income.

Parent Using the Sophisticated Equity Method

Using the sophisticated equity method, the parent would have a balance in its investment in Company S account of $220,800, derived as follows:

Original cost		$200,000
Share of undistributed income:		
Company S retained earnings, January 1, 20X3	$120,000	
Company S retained earnings, January 1, 20X1	80,000	
Increase in retained earnings	$ 40,000	
Ownership interest	× 80%	32,000
Equipment depreciation, 2 years × $5,600		(11,200)
Sophisticated-equity-adjusted balance, January 1, 20X3		$220,800

During 20X3, Company P would make the same memo entry as under the simple equity method to record the stock dividend. The following entry would be made to record equity income for 20X3:

Dec. 31, 20X3	Investment in Company S	10,400	
	Subsidiary Income		10,400
	To record the 80% interest in Company S reported income for 20X3 less $5,600 equipment depreciation.		

The following partial worksheet would apply to the investment maintained under the sophisticated equity method.

	Trial Balance		Eliminations & Adjustments	
	Company P	Company S	Dr.	Cr.
Investment in Company S	231,200			(CY) 10,400
				(EL) 176,000
				(D) 44,800
Equipment			(D) 44,800	(A) 5,600
Common Stock, Company P	(500,000)			
Retained Earnings, Company P, January 1, 20X3	(408,800)			
Common Stock ($10 par), Company S		(110,000)	**(EL) 88,000**	
Additional Paid-In Capital from Stock Dividend, Company S		(15,000)	**(EL) 12,000**	
Retained Earnings, Company S (reduced $25,000 for stock dividend), January 1, 20X3		(95,000)	**(EL) 76,000**	
Subsidiary Income	(10,400)		(CY) 10,400	
Expenses	30,000	18,000	(A) 5,600	

Eliminations and Adjustments:

(CY) Eliminate the parent's entry recording its share of subsidiary income for the current year. There is no complication caused by the stock dividend since it does not constitute income to Company P.
(EL) Eliminate 80% of Company S equity balances as restructured by the stock dividend. If the subsidiary recorded the stock dividend with a debit to Stock Dividends Declared, 80% of that account would be eliminated in this entry.
(D) Distribute the excess cost to the equipment account as required by the determination and distribution of excess schedule.
(A) Depreciate the equipment for the current year.

Note the following special features:

1. The investment is at the sophisticated equity balance of $231,200 ($220,800 balance on January 1, 20X3, plus $10,400 equity income for 20X3).

2. The retained earnings of Company P are $408,800. This is $11,200 less than under the simple equity method since there is $5,600 per year of equipment depreciation subtracted for 20X1 and 20X2.
3. Subsidiary income is the sophisticated equity amount of $10,400.
4. Only the equipment adjustment remaining on January 1, 20X3, is entered when distributing the excess in entry (D). Recall that the prior years' depreciation has already reduced the investment account and the parent retained earnings. Note that only the current-year depreciation is made in entry (A).

Parent Using the Cost Method

In the preceding example, if the parent, Company P, had used the cost method to record its investment in Company S, no adjustments would have been made to the investment account. The investment in Company S still would be carried at its original cost of $200,000 on the December 31, 20X3, worksheet.

The declaration of a stock dividend by a subsidiary requires a more difficult process for the conversion of the parent's investment account from a cost to a simple equity basis. The conversion must reflect all the changes in subsidiary retained earnings since acquisition, including the retained earnings transferred to paid-in capital as a result of a stock dividend. The correct simple equity conversion would be made as follows for the preceding example:

Retained earnings, January 2, 20X3 (after stock dividend)	$ 95,000
Retained earnings, January 1, 20X1	80,000
Change in retained earnings balance	$ 15,000
Retained earnings transferred to paid-in capital ($25 × 1,000 shares) as a result of stock dividend	25,000
Total change in retained earnings	$ 40,000
Ownership interest	× 80%
Simple equity conversion	$ 32,000

A faster approach to the simple equity conversion is to consider the change in total subsidiary stockholders' equity available to common stockholders as follows:

Subsidiary equity, January 1, 20X3	$ 220,000
Subsidiary equity, January 1, 20X1	180,000
Net change	$ 40,000
Ownership interest	× 80%
Simple equity conversion	$ 32,000

Normally, a parent will maintain a permanent file with the needed information for this adjustment. This faster method, however, could be useful in later years if facts surrounding the stock dividend were not readily available. The faster procedure will work well, provided in the interim periods there have been no other changes in subsidiary paid-in capital, such as a subsidiary sale or retirement of its shares.

The $32,000 simple equity conversion would be the first step on a worksheet when the cost method is used for the subsidiary investment. This step converts the investment in subsidiary account to its simple equity balance at the beginning of 20X3. The entry would be:

Investment in Company S	32,000	
Retained Earnings, January 1, 20X3		32,000

The remaining worksheet procedures would not include the elimination of the current year's subsidiary income, but otherwise it would be identical to entries (EL) and (A) of the partial worksheet on page 459.

REFLECTION

- The receipt of subsidiary stock dividends requires no entry by the parent.
- Care needs to be taken when converting from cost to equity. The adjustment for the increase in equity includes amounts moved from retained earnings to paid-in capital in excess of par as a result of subsidiary stock dividends.

2

OBJECTIVE

Account for the effect of the subsidiary's sale of its own common stock on the parent's investment in the subsidiary.

SUBSIDIARY SALE OF ITS OWN COMMON STOCK

In virtually all cases where the subsidiary issues additional shares of stock, the transaction impacts the parent's investment in the subsidiary account. Even though the parent purchases none of the newly issued shares, its share of subsidiary equity has changed and consolidation procedures must acknowledge the change. When the parent purchases some of the newly issued shares, the adjustment needed depends on whether the ownership interest after the purchase is equal to, less than, or greater than the ownership interest prior to the purchase. The adjustments resulting from a subsidiary stock sale are made at the time of the sale when the equity method is used, or they are part of the cost-to-equity conversion process when the cost method is used.

Sale of Subsidiary Stock to Noncontrolling Shareholders

A parent may allow a subsidiary to sell additional shares of stock in order to raise equity funds. A sale of stock by the subsidiary to new or existing noncontrolling shareholders results in an increase in the total subsidiary stockholders' equity against which the controlling interest has a claim. However, the effect of increasing the number of subsidiary shares in the hands of noncontrolling stockholders is to lower the controlling interest ownership percentage. Thus, the controlling ownership receives a smaller portion of a larger subsidiary equity. The net effect on the value of the controlling interest depends on the price at which the shares are sold.

There has been a long debate on how to record the impact of a change in a subsidiary's equity (the sale or retirement of subsidiary shares) on the consolidated financial statements. In the past, some companies recorded a gain or a loss, while others treated these changes as a capital transaction, which affected paid-in capital in excess of par. The 2005 FASB Exposure Draft takes the position that a change in the equity of the subsidiary is to be recorded as a capital transaction with no impact on income. In most cases, the subsidiary equity change would be recorded as a change in the paid-in capital of the parent company (debit effect could impact retained earnings, when to paid-in excess exists).[2]

Parent Using the Equity Method. A parent company using either the simple or sophisticated equity method usually will need to make an adjustment to its investment account when its subsidiary sells additional shares of stock to minority shareholders. To illustrate, assume Company P has a 90% interest in Company S. The interest was purchased on January 1, 20X1, at which time the following determination and distribution of excess schedule was prepared:

Price paid		$140,000	
Less interest acquired:			
Common stock ($10 par)	$100,000		
Retained earnings, January 1, 20X1	50,000		
Total stockholders' equity	$150,000		
Interest acquired	× 90%	135,000	
Equipment (10-year life)		$ 5,000	Dr.

2 FASB Exposure Draft, "Consolidated Financial Statements, Including Accounting and Reporting of Noncontrolling Interests in Subsidiaries – a replacement of ARB. 51" (Proposed Statements of the Financial Accounting Standards Board) June 30, 2005.

On January 1, 20X4, 2,000 shares of previously unissued common stock are sold to the noncontrolling interest. As a result, the parent's interest is reduced to 75% (9,000 ÷ 12,000). An analysis of the controlling interest before and after the sale of 2,000 new subsidiary shares to noncontrolling shareholders follows. The analysis shows the three possibilities: shares sold at book value (Case 1), at more than book value (Case 2), and at less than book value (Case 3).

	Case 1	Case 2	Case 3
Sale price per share	$ 24	$ 30	$ 20
Company S shareholders' equity prior to sale	$240,000	$240,000	$240,000
Add to common stock, $10 par × 2,000 shares	20,000	20,000	20,000
Add to paid-in capital in excess of par	28,000	40,000	20,000
Company S shareholders' equity subsequent to sale	$288,000	$300,000	$280,000
Controlling interest subsequent to sale (75%)	$216,000	$225,000	$210,000
Prior controlling interest (90% × $240,000)	216,000	216,000	216,000
Net increase (decrease) in controlling interest	$ 0	$ 9,000	$ (6,000)

Based on the results of the three cases within the above table, it should be noted that no change in controlling interest occurs when a subsidiary sells new stock to noncontrolling shareholders at book value. An increase occurs when the stock is sold above book value, and a decrease results when the stock is sold below book value.

The parent would adjust its investment in subsidiary account to record the effect on controlling interest in each of the three cases as follows:

Case 1:	Memo entry only to record a change from a 90% to a 75% interest.		
Case 2:	Investment in Company S	9,000	
	Paid-In Capital in Excess of Par		9,000
	To record increase in ownership interest and change from 90% to 75% interest.		
Case 3:	Paid-In Capital in Excess of Par*	6,000	
	Investment in Company S		6,000
	To record decrease in ownership interest. It is assumed that parent additional paid-in capital exists to offset the decrease. Also record change from 90% to 75% interest.		

*Or Retained Earnings if there is no paid-in capital in excess of par.

Note that when the equity method is used, these entries would be made directly on the books of the parent; they are not worksheet adjustments.

To illustrate the effect of Case 2 on consolidation, assume subsidiary income for 20X4 was $40,000 and no dividends were declared. The investment account balance under the simple equity method would be determined as follows:

Original cost	$140,000
Simple equity income adjustments, 20X1 through 20X3, 90% × $90,000 increase in retained earnings	81,000
Increase from stock sale to NCI on January 1, 20X4	9,000
Simple equity adjustment for 20X4 subsidiary income, 75% × $40,000 income	30,000
Balance, December 31, 20X4	$260,000

In the partial worksheet shown below, for the year ended December 31, 20X4, the trial balances of Company P and Company S reflect the sale of 2,000 additional shares at $30 per share (Case 2).

Company P and Subsidiary Company S
Partial Worksheet (Simple Equity Method)
For Year Ended December 31, 20X4

	Trial Balance		Eliminations & Adjustments	
	Company P	Company S	Dr.	Cr.
Investment in Company S (75%)	260,000			(CY) 30,000
				(EL) 225,000
				(D) 5,000
Equipment			(D) 5,000	(A) 2,000
Common Stock, Company P	(400,000)			
Paid-In Capital in Excess of Par, Company P	(9,000)			
Retained Earnings, Company P	(320,000)		(A) 1,500	
Common Stock, Company S		(120,000)	(EL) 90,000	
Paid-In Capital in Excess of Par, Company S		(40,000)	(EL) 30,000	
Retained Earnings, Company S, January 1, 20X4		(140,000)	(EL) 105,000	
Subsidiary Income	(30,000)		(CY) 30,000	
Expenses	40,000	27,000	(A) 500	

Eliminations and Adjustments:

(CY) Eliminate the parent's entry recording subsidiary income for the current year. The parent's share is now **75%** of the subsidiary undistributed net income. If the sale had occurred *during the year*, the old percentage of ownership would be applied to income earned prior to the sale date.
(EL) Eliminate the parent's **75%** share of subsidiary equity balances at the beginning of the year against the investment account.
(D) Distribute to the equipment account the original excess of cost over book value as required by the January 1, 20X1, determination and distribution of excess schedule.
(A) Depreciate equipment for the past three years and the current year.

The consolidated worksheet may require the adjustment of both the controlling and noncontrolling interests in beginning retained earnings for intercompany transactions originating in previous periods. When such adjustments are necessary, the current, not the original, ownership interest percentages are used.

Parent Using the Cost Method. A parent using the cost method records only dividends received from a subsidiary. Usually, no adjustment is made for any other changes in the subsidiary stockholders' equity, including changes caused by sales of subsidiary stock. As a result, the entry to convert from the cost method to the equity method on future worksheets must consider not only the equity adjustments for the subsidiary undistributed income but also adjustments in the parent's ownership interest caused by subsidiary stock sales. A parent using the cost method still would list the subsidiary investment at its original cost.

The partial worksheet on page 465 demonstrates the consolidation procedures needed for Case 2 when the cost method is used.

To review this process, the cost-to-simple-equity conversion amount for Case 2 is determined as it would apply to the December 31, 20X5, worksheet:

Undistributed income:	
90% of change in retained earnings of Company S from January 1, 20X1, to January 1, 20X4, 90% × $90,000	$ 81,000

75% of change in retained earnings of Company S from January 1, 20X4, to January 1, 20X5, 75% × $40,000		30,000
Increase in Company P retained earnings		$111,000
Adjustment to paid-in capital:		
Controlling interest in Company S equity subsequent to sale on January 1, 20X4, 75% × $300,000	$225,000	
Controlling interest in Company S equity prior to sale on January 1, 20X4, 90% × $240,000	216,000	
Net increase in paid-in capital		9,000
Total increase in investment account		$120,000

Company P and Subsidiary Company S
Partial Worksheet (Cost Method)
For Year Ended December 31, 20X4

	Trial Balance		Eliminations & Adjustments	
	Company P	Company S	Dr.	Cr.
Investment in Company S (75%)	140,000		**(CV) 90,000**	(EL) 225,000
				(D) 5,000
Equipment			(D) 5,000	(A) 2,000
Common Stock, Company P	(400,000)			
Paid-In Capital in Excess of Par, Company P				**(CV) 9,000**
Retained Earnings, Company P ($81,000 less since no equity income was recorded), January 1, 20X4	(239,000)		(A) 1,500	**(CV) 81,000**
Common Stock, Company S		(120,000)	(EL) 90,000	
Paid-In Capital in Excess of Par, Company S		(40,000)	(EL) 30,000	
Retained Earnings, Company S, January 1, 20X4		(140,000)	(EL) 105,000	
Expenses	40,000	27,000	(A) 500	

Eliminations and Adjustments:

(CV) The simple equity conversion is recorded:

Undistributed income:		
90% of change in retained earnings of Company S from January 1, 20X1, to January 1, 20X4, 90% × $90,000		$81,000
Adjustment to paid-in capital resulting from the subsidiary stock sale:		
Controlling interest in Company S equity subsequent to sale on January 1, 20X4, 75% × $300,000	$225,000	
Controlling interest in Company S equity prior to sale on January 1, 20X4, 90% × $240,000	216,000	
Net increase in paid-in capital		9,000
Total increase in the investment account		$90,000

(EL) Eliminate 75% of the subsidiary equity balances at the beginning of the year against the investment account.
(D) Distribute the excess of cost to the equipment account as shown by the original determination and distribution of excess schedule.
(A) Depreciate the equipment for the past three years and the current year.

A dangerous shortcut might be attempted whereby the net change in the controlling ownership interest is calculated by comparing 90% of the total subsidiary equity on January 1, 20X1, to 75% of the total subsidiary equity on January 1, 20X5. This shortcut will produce the correct adjustment to the investment in subsidiary account, but it will not provide the analysis needed to distribute the adjustment to the parent's paid-in capital and retained earnings.

Parent Purchase of Newly Issued Subsidiary Stock

A parent may purchase all or a portion of the newly issued stock. The general approach in such cases is to compare the change in equity before and after the sale to the price paid for the additional interest. When the ownership interest remains the same, there will be no adjustment. When the ownership interest increases, any difference between the change in equity and the price paid is the excess of cost or book value attributable to the new block. When the ownership interest decreases, the difference between the change in equity and the price paid is viewed as a change in paid-in capital. Presented in the following table are three cases based on the previous example for which the determination and distribution of excess schedule was shown on page 462. Recall that the subsidiary is issuing 2,000 new shares of common stock for $30 per share.

	Case A Maintain Interest		Case B Increase Interest		Case C Decrease Interest	
1 Shares purchased by parent	1,800		2,000		1,000	
2 Total shares owned by parent after purchase	10,800		11,000		10,000	
3 Total subsidiary shares outstanding after issue	12,000		12,000		12,000	
4 Subsidiary equity after the sale	$300,000		$300,000		$300,000	
5 Parent's ownership percent after purchase **(2 ÷ 3)**	× 90%		× 91.67%		× 83.33%	
6 Parent's new equity interest after purchase **(4 × 5)**		$270,000		$275,000		$250,000
7 Subsidiary equity prior to the sale	$240,000		$240,000		$240,000	
8 Parent's ownership percent prior to the purchase	× 90%		× 90%		× 90%	
9 Parent's equity interest prior to purchase **(7 × 8)**		216,000		216,000		216,000
10 Change in parent's equity interest due to purchase **(6 − 9)**		$ 54,000		$ 59,000		$ 34,000
11 Price paid **($30 × 1)**		54,000		60,000		30,000
12 Increase (decrease) in parent's equity interest over price paid **(10 − 11)**		$ 0		$ (1,000)		$ 4,000

In Case A, the parent maintains its ownership interest by purchasing 90% of the newly issued shares. Note that there is no difference between the price paid by the parent for the new shares and the dollar change in the parent's ownership interest due to the purchase. Thus, no entry is needed other than to record the purchase of the shares as follows:

Investment in Company S (1,800 shares × $30)	54,000	
Cash		54,000

No new disparity between cost and underlying equity is created. As a result, **no additional equity adjustment is needed when the parent maintains its ownership interest, and the same price is paid by all buyers.**

In Case B, the parent has increased its ownership interest to 91.67%. The price paid in excess of the additional interest could be allocated to various assets and liabilities, based on differences between cost and fair value. However, the adjustments would be limited to the size of the new interest, 1.67%, times the disparities between book and fair values. Based on materiality, this new excess usually would be considered goodwill. No entry would be made at the time of the purchase other than to record the added purchase of the shares as follows:

Investment in Company S (2,000 shares × $30)	60,000	
Cash		60,000

Future eliminations would be based on the 91.67% interest; the new $1,000 of excess would require separate distribution and amortization (except for goodwill) on future worksheets.

In Case C, the parent did not buy enough shares to maintain its ownership interest. However, the parent's investment account increased by $4,000 more than the price paid for the new interest. The increase would be an addition to paid-in capital. A decrease would be a debit to existing paid-in capital. If there is no existing paid-in capital on the parent's books, retained earnings would be reduced. In Case C, the investment account increased $34,000, and the price paid was only $30,000. In addition to recording the purchase of the shares, an entry should be made to record the $4,000 increase in the parent's ownership interest. The entries for the transactions discussed would be as follows:

Investment in Company S (1,000 shares × $30)	30,000	
Cash		30,000
Investment in Company S	4,000	
Paid-In Capital in Excess of Par		4,000

This entry is made at the time of the purchase and assumes the use of the equity method. If the cost method were used, it would be made as part of the cost-to-equity conversion process.

REFLECTION

- The subsidiary may increase its equity by issuing additional shares to noncontrolling shareholders.
- A before and after comparison is used to calculate the effect of stock issuance by the subsidiary on the parent's interest.
- The adjustment is made to the paid-in capital in excess of par account of the parent. (A decrease in equity would be a reduction of the parent's retained earnings.)

SUBSIDIARY PURCHASE OF ITS OWN COMMON STOCK

3 OBJECTIVE

Account for the effect of subsidiary treasury stock transactions on the parent's investment in the subsidiary.

When a subsidiary acquires some of its own shares from the noncontrolling interest, the resulting reduction of shares outstanding effectively increases the parent's ownership percentage. Thus, such an acquisition is considered to be an indirect purchase of an additional interest in the subsidiary by its parent company.[3] From a consolidated viewpoint, the subsidiary is acting as an agent of the parent which desires the additional interest in the subsidiary. This means that another block of stock has been purchased that will require a determination and distribution of excess schedule. Typically, the subsidiary would record the purchase of the shares as treasury stock at cost. On subsequent consolidated worksheets, the treasury stock account would be eliminated against the underlying equity it represents.

3 *Accounting Interpretations of APB Opinion No. 16* (New York: American Institute of Certified Public Accountants, 1972), par. 26.

Some consolidated firms still may practice what could be termed the *retirement method*. This method has the subsidiary retire the noncontrolling shares purchased. The parent company then adjusts its subsidiary investment account for the impact of the retirement on its interest in the subsidiary.[4] The continued use of this method can be defended only on the basis of materiality.

Purchase of Shares as Treasury Stock

To illustrate a subsidiary treasury stock purchase, assume the parent, Company P, owned a 70% interest in Company S. On January 1, 20X1, Company S had the following stockholders' equity:

Capital stock ($10 par)	$100,000
Paid-in capital in excess of par	50,000
Retained earnings	90,000
Total stockholders' equity	$240,000

On this date, the subsidiary purchased 2,000 of its 10,000 outstanding shares. The following entry then was recorded by Company S as a result of this purchase from noncontrolling shareholders at a cost of $26 each:

Treasury Stock (at cost)	52,000	
Cash		52,000

As a result of the purchase, Company S had the following stockholders' equity:

Capital stock ($10 par)	$100,000
Paid-in capital in excess of par	50,000
Retained earnings	90,000
Total	$240,000
Less treasury stock (at cost)	52,000
Total stockholders' equity	$188,000

Although the subsidiary views the investment as treasury stock, the consolidated viewpoint treats the investment as an additional interest purchased by the parent. This is the first time an account (Treasury Stock) on the books of the subsidiary should be eliminated against subsidiary equity. Assuming no assets or liabilities had fair values different from book values, the parent's determination and distribution of excess schedule would be prepared as follows:

4 To illustrate the retirement method, consider this example. A subsidiary has 10,000 shares outstanding and has a total stockholders' equity of $240,000. The parent company owns 7,000 shares prior to the purchase of 2,000 noncontrolling shares by the subsidiary for $52,000. The purchase changes the parent's interest to 87.5%. However, as the calculation below shows, the dollar amount of the parent's interest has been reduced due to the large amount paid by the subsidiary for the noncontrolling shares. The parent's change in equity would be calculated as follows:

Parent interest prior to retirement, 70% × $240,000 equity	$168,000
Parent interest after retirement, 87.5% × ($240,000 – $52,000)	164,500
Adjustment	$ 3,500

The adjustment in the investment is accompanied by an adjustment in the parent company paid-in capital in excess of par since the decrease in interest results from a stock transaction in which the parent did not actively participate.

Price paid		$52,000	
Less interest acquired in Company S:			
Common stock ($10 par)	$ 100,000		
Paid-in capital in excess of par	50,000		
Retained earnings, January 1, 20X1	90,000		
Total stockholders' equity	$ 240,000		
Interest acquired	× **20%**	48,000	
Excess of cost over book value attributed to goodwill		$ 4,000	Dr.

The parent's additional 20% investment caused by the subsidiary treasury stock purchase will have the following ramifications on subsequent worksheets:

1. The subsidiary will maintain the investment in treasury stock at cost and would have no reason to make equity adjustments to the cost. This means that a cost-to-equity conversion entry will be required for the investment on the worksheet. The adjustment to the investment account will require an adjustment to the controlling retained earnings.
2. The treasury stock account, which is treated as an additional investment in the subsidiary on the worksheet, will be eliminated against the *subsidiary equity accounts* like any other investment in subsidiary account. The excess will be distributed and amortized (except for goodwill). All previous years' amortizations are, as always, adjustments only to controlling retained earnings.
3. All adjustments of intercompany profits will be based on a 90% (original 70% plus new 20%) interest as of January 1, 20X1.
4. The adjusted internally reported income of the subsidiary now will be distributed 90% to the controlling interest and 10% to the noncontrolling interest.

The above procedures, which treat the subsidiary acquisition of shares as a new block, are a strict interpretation of the *parent company concept.* This concept isolated the excess of cost or book value on each purchase. The 1996 FASB Exposure Draft applies the economic unit concept to subsidiary purchases of its own stock. The change in the parent's interest, as a result of the transaction, is an adjustment to paid-in capital (a negative adjustment could affect retained earnings if there is insufficient paid-in capital).

Resale of Shares Held in Treasury

The purchase and resale of treasury stock by a subsidiary would be handled as two separate events using the previously described methods. There may be alternative procedures which could be used if there is the intent to resell the treasury shares in the near future. When, for example, the treasury stock is purchased and resold within the consolidated company's fiscal period, a shortcut is possible. Since there would be no change in the parent's percentage of ownership by the end of the period, the parent only needs to make an adjustment equal to its ownership interest multiplied by the subsidiary's increase or decrease in equity as a result of the treasury stock transaction. This adjustment should be carried to the additional paid-in capital of the parent and is not viewed as an operating gain or loss since it results from dealings with the company's own shareholders. Using the same reasoning, a decrease in equity reduces parent retained earnings only when no additional paid-in capital is available.

This procedure also might be justified for treasury stock transactions crossing over fiscal periods. It is necessary that only the subsidiary treasury stock account be left on the consolidated worksheet at cost and eliminations be made according to the parent's ownership percentage, unadjusted for the number of treasury shares. When the treasury shares are resold, the parent would adjust its accounts in the same manner as was done for a treasury stock purchase and resale within a fiscal period.

If a parent is using the cost method and did not adjust for subsidiary treasury stock transactions, an adjustment can be made as part of the cost-to-equity conversion process.

REFLECTION

- The repurchase of shares by a subsidiary is considered to be the same as the parent purchasing an additional block. The procedures used in Chapter 7 for block purchases are applied.

4

OBJECTIVE

Demonstrate accounting procedures for multilevel holdings.

INDIRECT HOLDINGS

A parent company may own a controlling interest in a subsidiary which, in turn, owns a controlling interest in another company. For example, Company A may own a 75% interest in Company B which, in turn, owns an 80% interest in Company C. Thus, A has indirect holdings in C. This situation could be diagrammed as follows:

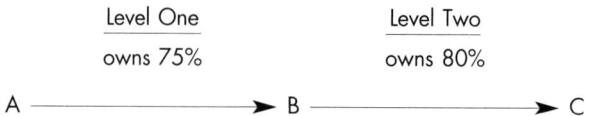

The treatment of the *level one* investment in B and the *level two* investment in C can be mastered with the theory that has been discussed, but the procedures must be applied carefully. The procedures are applied easily to indirect holdings when the level one investment already exists at the time of the level two purchase. Complications arise in preparing the determination and distribution of excess schedule for the new investment when the level two investment exists prior to the time that the parent achieves control over the subsidiary (level one investment). These complications result because the level two investment held by the subsidiary represents one of the subsidiary's assets that may require adjustment to fair value on the determination and distribution of excess schedule prepared at the time of the parent's level one acquisition. The use of separate and distinct determination and distribution of excess schedules for each level of investment should facilitate the maintaining of proper accounting when two or more levels are involved.

	Level One		Level Two	
	owns 75%		owns 80%	
A	→	B	→	C

Level One Holding Acquired First

Assume Company A purchased a 75% interest in Company B on January 1, 20X1, at which time the following determination and distribution of excess schedule was prepared:

Price paid		$400,000	
Less interest acquired in Company B:			
Common stock ($10 par)	$ 200,000		
Retained earnings, January 1, 20X1	100,000		
Total stockholders' equity	$ 300,000		
Interest acquired	× 75%	225,000	
Excess of cost over book value attributed to building and equipment (10-year life)		$175,000	Dr.

On January 1, 20X2, the subsidiary, Company B, purchased an 80% interest in Company C, and the following schedule was prepared:

Price paid		$270,000	
Less Company B's interest acquired in Company C:			
Common stock ($10 par)	$ 100,000		
Retained earnings, January 1, 20X2	120,000		
Total stockholders' equity	$ 220,000		
Interest acquired	× 80%	176,000	
Excess of cost over book value attributed to building and equipment (20-year life)		$ 94,000	Dr.

Equity adjustments must be made carefully. Company A must be sure that Company B has included its equity income from Company C in its net income before Company A records its percentage share of Company B income.

Assume the following internally generated net incomes:

	Company A	Company B	Company C
20X1	$100,000	$100,000	$20,000
20X2	70,000	76,000	30,000
20X3	90,000	100,000	30,000

On this basis, the following simple equity adjustments would be required:

Date	Company B's Books			Company A's Books		
20X1 Dec. 31	None (interest in Company C not yet acquired).			Investment in Company B	75,000	
				Subsidiary Income		75,000
				To adjust for 75% of Company B reported income.		
20X2 Dec. 31	Investment in Company C	24,000		Investment in Company B	75,000	
	Subsidiary Income		24,000	Subsidiary Income		75,000
	To adjust for 80% of Company C reported income.			To adjust for 75% of Company B total income ($76,000 plus $24,000 subsidiary income).		
20X3 Dec. 31	Investment in Company C	24,000		Investment in Company B	93,000	
	Subsidiary Income		24,000	Subsidiary Income		93,000
	To adjust for 80% of Company C reported income.			To adjust for 75% of Company B total income ($100,000 plus $24,000 subsidiary income).		

Worksheet 8-1, pages 482 to 483, is based on the trial balances of the three separate companies on December 31, 20X3. The investment account balances reflect the equity adjustments previously shown. The following additional information for 20X3 is assumed:

Worksheet 8-1: page 482

	Intercompany Sales by B to A	Intercompany Sales by C to B
Selling company goods in buyer's January 1, 20X3, inventory	$8,000	$6,000
Sales during 20X3	$50,000	$40,000
Selling company goods in buyer's December 31, 20X3, inventory	$10,000	$10,000
Gross profit on all sales	25%	30%

The investment accounts must be handled carefully when any eliminations are made in order to ensure that the NCI accounts are available to receive applicable amortizations of excesses. It is suggested that the level one investment be eliminated first, thereby reducing Company B retained earnings to the NCI. Then, it will be possible to allocate the amortizations of excess resulting from the level two (Company C) holding to the controlling interest (Company A) and the Company B NCI. Since Company B owns the interest in Company C, the Company B NCI must share in the amortizations of excess resulting from the investment in Company C.

The eliminations for Worksheet 8-1 in journal entry form are as follows:

Entries to eliminate investment in Company B

	Eliminate current-year equity income:		
(CYB)	Subsidiary Income	93,000	
	Investment in Company B		93,000
	Eliminate subsidiary B equity:		
(ELB)	Common Stock ($10 par), Company B	150,000	
	Retained Earnings, January 1, 20X3, Company B	225,000	
	Investment in Company B		375,000
	Distribute excess to buildings and equipment:		
(DB)	Buildings and Equipment	175,000	
	Investment in Company B		175,000
	Amortize excess:		
(AB)	Retained Earnings, Company A, January 1, 20X3	35,000	
	Expenses	17,500	
	Accumulated Depreciation		52,500

Entries to eliminate investment in Company C

	Eliminate current-year equity income:		
(CYC)	Investment Income	24,000	
	Investment in Company C		24,000
	Eliminate subsidiary C equity:		
(ELC)	Common Stock ($10 par), Company C	80,000	
	Retained Earnings, January 1, 20X3, Company C	120,000	
	Investment in Company C		200,000
	Distribute excess to buildings and equipment:		
(DC)	Buildings and Equipment	94,000	
	Investment in Company C		94,000
	Amortize excess:		
(AC)	Retained Earnings, Company A, January 1, 20X3	3,525	
	Retained Earnings, Company B, January 1, 20X3	1,175	
	Expenses	4,700	
	Accumulated Depreciation		9,400
	Eliminate intercompany sales:		
(IS)	Sales	90,000	
	Cost of Goods Sold		90,000
	Beginning inventory profit, Company B sales:		
(BIB)	Retained Earnings, Company A, January 1, 20X3	1,500	
	Retained Earnings, Company B, January 1, 20X3	500	
	Cost of Goods Sold		2,000

	Ending inventory profit, Company B sales:		
(EIB)	Cost of Goods Sold	2,500	
	Inventory, December 31, 20X3		2,500
	Beginning inventory profit, Company C sales:		
(BIC)	Retained Earnings, Company A, January 1, 20X3	**1,080**	
	Retained Earnings, Company B, January 1, 20X3	**360**	
	Retained Earnings, Company C, January 1, 20X3	**360**	
	Cost of Goods Sold		**1,800**
	Ending inventory profit, Company C sales:		
(EIC)	Cost of Goods Sold	3,000	
	Inventory, December 31, 20X3		3,000

In Worksheet 8-1, the consolidated net income is $196,100, which must be distributed to the two NCIs and to the controlling interest. Distribution must proceed from the lowest level (level two) to ensure proper distribution. Company B adjusted income includes 80% of Company C adjusted income. Thus, the Company C IDS must be completed first, followed by the distribution schedules for Companies B and A. These schedules accompany Worksheet 8-1.

If the cost method was used in the previous example, the investment account balances still would contain the January 1, 20X1, $400,000 cost of the Company B investment and the January 1, 20X2, $270,000 cost of the Company C investment. Conversion entries would be made on the consolidated worksheet to update both investment accounts to their January 1, 20X3, simple equity balances. It is advisable to make equity adjustments at the lowest level of investment first, because the retained earnings of the mid-level firm must be adjusted for its share of investment income before the parent can adjust for the change in its subsidiary's retained earnings. The following simple equity conversion entry would be made first for Company B's investment in Company C:

Investment in Company C	24,000	
Retained Earnings (Company B)		24,000
To record 80% of $30,000 increase in Company C retained earnings between January 1, 20X2, and January 1, 20X3.		

The following conversion entry then would be made for Company A's investment in Company B:

Investment in Company B	150,000	
Retained Earnings (Company A)		150,000
To record 75% of $200,000 increase in Company B retained earnings (including previous equity adjustment for Company B) between January 1, 20X1, and January 1, 20X3.		

Eliminations and adjustments would be made as on Worksheet 8-1, except that there would be no need to eliminate the current year's equity adjustment.

Level Two Holding Exists at Time of Parent's Purchase

When a parent acquires a controlling interest in another parent company, the determination and distribution of excess schedule must be **based on the acquired company's consolidated balance sheet.** For example, assume Company Y purchased an 80% interest in Company Z on January 1, 20X1, and Company X purchased a 70% interest in Company Y on January 1, 20X3. Also assume that on January 1, 20X3, Company Y owns equipment which is undervalued by $40,000 and Company Z (the subsidiary) has equipment which is undervalued by $100,000. Company X would prepare the determination and distribution of excess schedule below based on the controlling interest in Company Y.

Note the following features of the schedule:

1. Company Y consolidated equity is multiplied by the parent's (Company X) ownership interest to arrive at the excess of cost over book value.
2. When a Company Y (level one investment) asset is to be adjusted, it should be adjusted for the parent's ownership portion (70%) of the value discrepancy.
3. When a Company Z (level two investment) asset is to be adjusted, it should be adjusted for only the Company X ownership share of the Company Y share (70% × 80%, or 56%) of the value discrepancy.
4. Resulting goodwill is based on the consolidated asset values for Companies Y and Z.

Price paid		$700,000	
Less interest acquired:			
Company Y common stock	$400,000		
Company Y controlling interest in consolidated retained earnings	320,000		
Total Company Y stockholders' equity	$720,000		
Interest acquired	× 70%	504,000	
Excess of cost over book value (debit balance)		$196,000	
Excess of cost attributable to Company Y equipment: 70% × $40,000 undervaluation		**28,000**	**Dr.**
Excess of cost attributable to Company Z equipment: 70% × 80% × $100,000 undervaluation		**56,000**	**Dr.**
Goodwill		$112,000	Dr.

When the simple equity method is used for the investments, the procedures illustrated in Worksheet 8-1 apply without modification. When the cost method is used, simple equity conversion adjustments again proceed from the lowest level. Be sure to note, however, that in this example Company X would convert to the equity basis for the change in Company Y retained earnings after January 1, 20X3.

Connecting Affiliates

A business combination involving connecting affiliates exists when a parent company has a direct (level one) investment in a company and an indirect (level two) investment in the same company sufficient to result in control. For example, the following diagram illustrates a connecting affiliate structure:

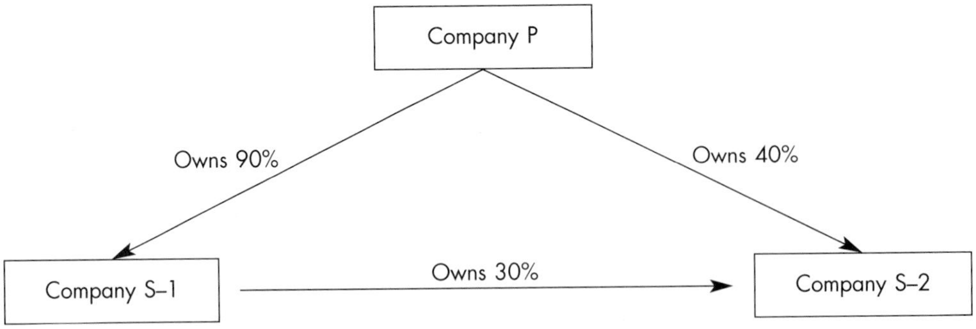

Not only does Company P have a 90% interest in Company S–1, but it also has, in effect, a 67% interest in Company S–2, calculated as follows:

Direct	40%
Indirect (90% × 30%)	27%
Total	67%

This type of structure is consolidated more readily once the determination and distribution of excess schedule has been prepared. Caution must be used in the schedule preparation because of differing dates for each investment. Referring to the diagram, the special concerns in consolidating connecting affiliates are as follows:

1. Company S–2 generally is not included in the consolidation process until the total percentage of S–2 shares held by the parent and its subsidiaries (70% in this example) exceeds 50%. Prior to that time, an investment of 20% or more is treated according to APB Opinion No. 18, and a less-than-20% investment is accounted for under the cost method.
2. Any amortizations of excess resulting from the 30% investment of Company S–1 in Company S–2 are distributed to the controlling and S–1 NCI in retained earnings on a 90/10 basis.
3. Any adjustments to retained earnings caused by Company S–2-generated transactions are distributed 30% to NCI S–2, 3% (10% × 30%) to NCI S–1, and 67% [40% + (90% × 30%)] to the controlling interest.
4. Income distributions would begin with Company S–2: 30% of its income would go to NCI S–2, 30% would flow to the Company S–1 distribution schedule, and 40% would flow to the Company P schedule. Company P will receive 90% of the Company S–1 adjusted income (including the 30% share of Company S–2).
5. When either equity method is used, Companies P and S–1 each must adjust for their interest in Company S–2, even though neither company's interest by itself would merit consolidation techniques.
6. When the cost method is used, each investment is converted to the simple equity method from the purchase date forward. Again, equity conversions must begin at the lowest level. For example, the Company S–1 investment in Company S–2 must be converted first, so that Company S–1 retained earnings are updated before the Company P investment in Company S–1 is converted to the simple equity method.

REFLECTION

- Indirect holdings have three or more ownership tiers and create the ownership of the shares of one subsidiary by another subsidiary.
- Equity adjustments must proceed from the lowest level to the highest to ensure that upper level investments include the effect of income earned by the subsidiary being analyzed.
- Retained earnings and IDS adjustments must be made carefully to assign adjustments to the appropriate ownership group.

MUTUAL HOLDINGS

5 OBJECTIVE

Demonstrate an understanding of the alternatives used for accounting for investments in the parent company by the subsidiary.

A mutual holding structure exists when the subsidiary owns shares of the parent company common stock. The subsidiary's investment in the parent must be eliminated in the consolidation process. When the subsidiary acquires shares of the parent for consideration other than its own common stock shares, the shares are usually viewed as either retired or as treasury stock if there is an intent to resell the shares. In the past, another method called the *reciprocal method* was used. The reciprocal method treated the subsidiary ownership interest in the parent as a separate investment and allocated a portion of the parent income to the NCI. This method, which lacks theoretical support since the parent controls the actions of the subsidiary, is no longer included in this text.

FASB Statement No. 141 reaffirms that where the subsidiary exchanges its shares for those of the parent, the transaction is viewed as the parent company acquiring a portion of the noncontrolling interest. This procedure will be termed the stock swap method and will be demonstrated after the treasury stock method.

Treasury Stock Method

The *treasury stock method* does not view parent shares held by the subsidiary as outstanding. When it is intended that the shares are to be reissued, they are viewed as treasury shares and are recorded at cost. When resold, an excess received over cost is carried to additional paid-in capital. If cost exceeds proceeds on resale, the difference is offset against existing paid-in capital. If there is no paid-in capital, retained earnings are reduced. When it is not intended that the shares be reissued, the stock is retired on the worksheet using the original investment cost as the retirement price. Regardless of the approach used, the resulting capital account adjustments fall entirely upon the parent. The subsidiary is viewed as an agent accomplishing the transaction. An important requirement of either of the treasury stock approaches is that the subsidiary investment in the parent be **maintained at its original cost.** Since the stock is not to be viewed as outstanding, it has no claim on income. If equity adjustments have been made in error, they must be reversed on the consolidated worksheet.

To illustrate the treasury stock method, consider the following example. Suppose Company P acquired an 80% interest in Company S on January 1, 20X1, at which time the following determination and distribution of excess schedule was prepared:

Price paid		$200,000	
Less interest acquired:			
Common stock ($10 par)	$100,000		
Retained earnings	50,000		
Total stockholders' equity	$150,000		
Interest acquired	× 80%	120,000	
Excess of cost over book value attributed to equipment (20-year remaining life)		$ 80,000	Dr.

Further assume that on January 1, 20X3, Company S purchases a 10% interest (1,000 shares) in the parent for $80,000. There would be no need for a determination and distribution of excess schedule for the subsidiary investment, since no excess of cost or book value is acknowledged or distributed. For 20X3, the parent will make the normal simple equity adjustment to acknowledge its 80% interest in subsidiary income of $20,000:

Investment in Company S	16,000	
Subsidiary Income		16,000
To record 80% of subsidiary reported income of $20,000.		

There is no equity adjustment for the Company S investment in the parent since it must remain at cost.

The trial balances of the two companies on December 31, 20X3, are contained in the first two columns of Worksheet 8-2 on pages 486 and 487. The investment in Company S account on Worksheet 8-2 is computed as follows:

worksheet
Worksheet 8-2: page 486

Original cost	$200,000
80% × 20X1 and 20X2 undistributed income of $40,000	32,000
20X3 simple equity adjustment	16,000
Balance, December 31, 20X3	$248,000

The eliminations for Worksheet 8-2 in journal entry form are as follows:

	Eliminate current-year equity income:		
(CY)	Subsidiary Income	16,000	
	Investment in Company S		16,000
	Eliminate subsidiary S equity:		
(EL)	Common Stock, Company S	80,000	
	Retained Earnings, January 1, 20X3, Company S	72,000	
	Investment in Company B		152,000
	Distribute excess to equipment:		
(D)	Equipment	80,000	
	Investment in Company B		80,000
	Amortize excess:		
(A)	Retained Earnings, Company P, January 1, 20X3	8,000	
	Expenses	4,000	
	Accumulated Depreciation		12,000
	Restate investment in Company P as treasury stock:		
(TS)	Treasury Stock (at cost)	**80,000**	
	Investment in Company P (10%), at cost		**80,000**

Examination of the formal statements of the consolidated company reveals that the treasury shares are held by the consolidated company and no income accrues to them. These statements, based on Worksheet 8-2, are as follows:

Company P and Subsidiary Company S
Consolidated Income Statement
For Year Ended December 31, 20X3

Sales	$500,000
Less cost of goods sold	300,000
Gross profit	$200,000
Less expenses	144,000
Consolidated net income	$ 56,000
Noncontrolling interest of Company S	$ 4,000
Controlling interest	$ 52,000

Company P and Subsidiary Company S
Retained Earnings Statement
For Year Ended December 31, 20X3

	Controlling Interest
Balance, January 1, 20X3	$192,000
Net income	52,000
Balance, December 31, 20X3	$244,000

Company P and Subsidiary Company S
Consolidated Balance Sheet
December 31, 20X3

Assets		Stockholders' Equity		
Equipment	$868,000	Noncontrolling interest		$ 42,000
Less accumulated depreciation	162,000	Controlling interest:		
		Common stock	$500,000	
		Retained earnings	244,000	744,000
		Total		$786,000
		Less treasury stock (at cost)		80,000
Total assets	$706,000	Net stockholders' equity		$706,000

Stock Swap

FASB Statement No. 141 reaffirms the use of the *stock swap method*, which was the position of an earlier Accounting Principles Board Interpretation. That interpretation stated that when a subsidiary exchanges its shares for those of the parent, the transaction should be viewed as a stock swap with the parent acquiring shares of the noncontrolling interest.[5] Consider this example:

- Company P already owns 8,000 of the 10,000 shares of subsidiary Company S.
- Company S exchanges 1,000 of its common stock shares for 2,000 shares of Company P.

The transaction is recorded using the market value of the stock with the most determinable market value. In most cases, that would be the parent's stock. Assume that the market value of Company P's stock is $40 per share. That would mean that the value of the shares received from the parent is $40,000. Company S would carry the investment in its parent on its books at $40,000.

When consolidating, the subsidiary's investment in the parent account would be treated as the price paid for an additional interest in a new issuance by the subsidiary and would be eliminated as a new block, as explained in Chapter 7.

To further illustrate this method, assume the same example as used for the treasury stock method above except that instead of paying $80,000 cash for 1,000 parent shares, 3,000 Company S shares were issued in exchange for 1,000 Company P shares with a market value of $80 each. The subsidiary would make the following entry:

Investment in Company P (1,000 shares × $80)	80,000	
Common Stock, $10 Par (3,000 shares × $10)		30,000
Paid-In Capital in Excess of Par ($80,000 – $30,000 par)		50,000

Consolidation procedures require that the $80,000 be viewed as the price paid for a new 3,000-share interest in Company S. The procedures demonstrated in Chapter 7 for a parent increasing its interest by purchasing newly issued subsidiary shares would be applied as follows:

Ownership interest in Company S *after* new issuance:		
Equity prior to sale on January 1, 20X3:		
Common stock, $10 par	$100,000	
Retained earnings	90,000	
Market value of shares issued	80,000	
Total equity after issuance	$270,000	
Ownership interest [(11,000/13,000 shares) × $270,000]		$228,461

5 FASB 141, par. A7.

Ownership interest prior to issuance:		
Equity prior to sale on January 1, 20X3:		
Common stock, $10 par	$100,000	
Retained earnings	90,000	
Total equity prior to issuance	$190,000	
Ownership interest [(8,000/10,000 shares) × $190,000]		152,000
Increase in equity		$ 76,461
Market value of shares issued		80,000
Excess attributed to goodwill		$ 3,539

The excess could be attributed to other subsidiary accounts, but in most cases, it will be attributed to goodwill on the basis of materiality.

The parent and the subsidiary may use the cost or equity method to account for the intercompany investments. In Worksheet 8-3 on pages 488 and 489, both companies are using the simple equity method. Company P has recorded subsidiary income of $16,000 (80% × Company S reported income of $20,000), and Company S has recorded investment income of $800 (1,000/50,000 shares × $40,000 Company P income).

worksheet
Worksheet 8-3: page 488

The eliminations for Worksheet 8-3 in journal entry form are as follows:

	Eliminate current-year equity income recorded by the parent company:		
(CYa)	Subsidiary (Investment) Income	16,000	
	Investment in Company S		16,000
	Eliminate current-year equity income recorded by the subsidiary:		
(CYb)	Subsidiary (Investment) Income	800	
	Investment in Company P		800
	Transfer investment in parent to investment in subsidiary:		
(TR)	Investment in Company S	80,800	
	Investment in Company P		80,800
	Eliminate 11/13 of subsidiary equity against the investment account:		
(EL)	Common Stock, Company S ($10 par)	110,000	
	Paid-In Capital in Excess of Par, Company S	42,308	
	Retained Earnings, January 1, 20X3, Company S	76,153	
	Investment in Company S		228,461
	Distribute excess:		
(D1)	Equipment	80,000	
(D2)	Goodwill	3,539	
(D)	Investment in Company S		83,539
	Amortize excess attributed to equipment for 3 years:		
(A1)	Retained Earnings, January 1, 20X3, Company P	8,000	
	Expenses	4,000	
	Accumulated Depreciation		12,000

The financial statements, based on Worksheet 8-3, are as follows:

Company P and Subsidiary Company S
Consolidated Income Statement
For Year Ended December 31, 20X3

Sales	$500,000
Less cost of goods sold	300,000
Gross profit	$200,000
Less expenses	144,000
Consolidated net income	$ 56,000
Noncontrolling interest of Company S	$ 4,000
Controlling interest	$ 52,000

Company P and Subsidiary Company S
Retained Earnings Statement
For Year Ended December 31, 20X3

Balance, January 1, 20X3	$192,000
Net income	52,000
Balance, December 31, 20X3	$244,000

Company P and Subsidiary Company S
Consolidated Balance Sheet
December 31, 20X3

Assets		Stockholders' Equity		
Current assets	$ 80,000	Noncontrolling interest		$ 45,539
Equipment	868,000			
Accumulated depreciation	(162,000)	Controlling interest:		
		Common stock	$500,000	
Goodwill	3,539	Retained earnings	244,000	744,000
Total assets	$ 789,539	Total equity		$789,539

REFLECTION

- Mutual holdings refer to the ownership of parent common stock by the subsidiary.
- The treasury stock method allows the parent shares, owned by the subsidiary, to remain on the balance sheet as treasury stock. It is the more common and appropriate method.
- The stock swap method is used when subsidiary shares are exchanged for parent shares. It has the effect of creating a new block of subsidiary shares held by the controlling interest.

UNDERSTANDING THE ISSUES

1. Subsidiary Company S had the following stockholders' equity on January 1, 20X4, prior to distributing a 10% stock dividend:

Common stock ($1 par), 100,000 shares issued and outstanding	$ 100,000
Paid-in capital in excess of par	1,900,000
Retained earnings	2,000,000
Total equity	$4,000,000

The fair value of the shares distributed is $60 each. What is the effect of this dividend on the subsidiary equity, the investment account, and the December 31, 20X3, elimination procedures? Assume the parent uses the simple equity method to account for its investment in the subsidiary.

2. Subsidiary Company S had the following stockholders' equity on January 1, 20X4, prior to issuing 20,000 additional new shares to noncontrolling shareholders:

Common stock ($1 par), 100,000 shares issued and outstanding	$ 100,000
Paid-in capital in excess of par	1,900,000
Retained earnings	2,000,000
Total equity	$4,000,000

At that time, the parent company owned 90,000 Company S shares. What is the impact on the parent's investment account of the sale of 20,000 additional shares by the subsidiary for $50 per share?

3. Subsidiary Company S had the following stockholders' equity on January 1, 20X4, prior to issuing 5,000 additional new shares:

Common stock ($1 par), 100,000 shares issued and outstanding	$ 100,000
Paid-in capital in excess of par	1,900,000
Retained earnings	2,000,000
Total equity	$4,000,000

Prior to the sale of additional shares, the parent owned 90,000 shares. Assume that the new shares are sold for $50 each. Describe the general impact (no calculations required) the sale will have on the parent's investment account if:

a. The parent buys less than 90% of the new shares.
b. The parent buys 90% of the new shares.
c. The parent buys all the new shares.

4. Company A owns 60% of Company B. Company B owns 60% of Company C. From a consolidated viewpoint, does A control C? How will $10,000 of Company C income flow to the members of the consolidated firms when it is distributed at year-end?

5. Company P owns 90% of Company S' shares. Assume Company S then purchases 2% of Company P's outstanding shares of common stock. When consolidating, what is the most logical way to disclose the 2% holding in the consolidated financial statements?

Worksheet 8-1

Indirect Holdings; Intercompany Sales
Company A and Subsidiary Companies B and C

Worksheet for Consolidated Financial Statements
For Year Ended December 31, 20X3

	(Credit balance amounts are in parentheses.)	Trial Balance		
		Company A	Company B	Company C
1	Inventory, December 31, 20X3	80,000	20,000	30,000
2				
3	Other Assets	60,000	146,000	130,000
4	Building and Equipment	300,000	200,000	150,000
5				
6	Accumulated Depreciation	(100,000)	(60,000)	(30,000)
7				
8	Investment in Company B	643,000		
9				
10				
11	Investment in Company C		318,000	
12				
13				
14	Common Stock ($10 par), Company A	(300,000)		
15	**Retained Earnings, January 1, 20X3, Company A**	**(500,000)**		
16				
17				
18				
19	Common Stock ($10 par), Company B		(200,000)	
20	**Retained Earnings, January 1, 20X3, Company B**		**(300,000)**	
21				
22				
23				
24	Common Stock ($10 par), Company C			(100,000)
25	**Retained Earnings, January 1, 20X3, Company C**			**(150,000)**
26				
27	Sales	(400,000)	(300,000)	(150,000)
28	Cost of Goods Sold	250,000	160,000	80,000
29				
30				
31	Expenses	60,000	40,000	40,000
32				
33	Subsidiary or Investment Income	(93,000)	(24,000)	
34				
35		0	0	0
36	Consolidated Net Income			
37	To NCI, Company C (see distribution schedule)			
38	To NCI, Company B (see distribution schedule)			
39	To Controlling Interest (see distribution schedule)			
40	Total NCI			
41	Retained Earnings, Controlling Interest, December 31, 20X3			
42				

Worksheet 8-1 (see page 471)

Eliminations & Adjustments				Consolidated Income Statement	NCI	Controlling Retained Earnings	Consolidated Balance Sheet	
Dr.		Cr.						
		(EIB)	2,500				124,500	1
		(EIC)	3,000					2
							336,000	3
(DB)	175,000						919,000	4
(DC)	94,000							5
		(AB)	52,500				(251,900)	6
		(AC)	9,400					7
		(CYB)	93,000					8
		(ELB)	375,000					9
		(DB)	175,000					10
		(CYC)	24,000					11
		(ELC)	200,000					12
		(DC)	94,000					13
							(300,000)	14
(AB)	35,000					(458,895)		15
(AC)	**3,525**							16
(BIB)	1,500							17
(BIC)	**1,080**							18
(ELB)	150,000				(50,000)			19
(ELB)	225,000				(72,965)			20
(AC)	**1,175**							21
(BIB)	500							22
(BIC)	**360**							23
(ELC)	80,000				(20,000)			24
(ELC)	120,000				(29,640)			25
(BIC)	**360**							26
(IS)	90,000			(760,000)				27
(EIB)	2,500	(IS)	90,000	401,700				28
(EIC)	3,000	(BIB)	2,000					29
		(BIC)	**1,800**					30
(AC)	**4,700**							31
(AB)	17,500			162,200				32
(CYB)	93,000							33
(CYC)	24,000							34
	1,122,200		1,122,200					35
				(196,100)				36
				5,760	(5,760)			37
				29,460	(29,460)			38
				160,880		(160,880)		39
					(207,825)		(207,825)	40
						(619,775)	(619,775)	41
							0	42

Eliminations and Adjustments:

(CYB) Eliminate the entry made by Company A to record its share of Company B income. This step returns the investment in the Company B account to its January 1, 20X3, balance to aid the elimination process.
(ELB) Eliminate 75% of the January 1, 20X3, Company B equity balances against the investment in Company B.
(DB) Distribute the $175,000 excess of cost to the building and equipment account according to the determination and distribution of excess schedule applicable to the level one investment.
(AB) Amortize the excess (added depreciation) according to the determination and distribution of excess schedule. This step requires adjustment of Company A retained earnings for 20X1 and 20X2, plus adjustment of 20X3 expenses.
(CYC) Eliminate the entry made by Company B to record its share of Company C income. This returns the investment in Company C account to its January 1, 20X3, balance to aid elimination.
(ELC) Eliminate 80% of the January 1, 20X3, Company C equity balances against the investment in Company C.
(DC) Distribute the $94,000 excess of cost to the building and equipment account according to the determination and distribution of excess schedule applicable to the level two investment.
(AC) Amortize the excess (added depreciation) according to the determination and distribution of excess schedule. Since it is created by actions of subsidiary Company B, the 20X2 amortization must be prorated 25% ($1,175) to the Company B NCI and 75% ($3,525) to the controlling interest. Note that the Company B NCI appears on the worksheet only after the first-level investment has been eliminated, again pointing to the need to eliminate the level one investment first.
(IS) Eliminate intercompany sales to prevent double counting in the consolidated sales and cost of goods sold.
(BIB) Eliminate the Company B profit contained in the beginning inventory. Since Company B generated the sale, the correction of beginning retained earnings is split 75% to the controlling interest and 25% to the noncontrolling interest. The cost of goods sold is decreased since the beginning inventory was overstated.
(EIB) The cost of goods sold is adjusted and the ending inventory is reduced by the $2,500 of Company B profit contained in the ending inventory.
(BIC) Eliminate the Company C profit contained in the beginning inventory. Since Company C generated the retained earnings adjustment, it is apportioned as follows:

To NCI in Company C (20%)	$ 360
To NCI in Company B (25% of 80%)	360
To controlling interest (75% of 80%)	1,080
Total	$1,800

(EIC) The cost of goods sold is adjusted, and the ending inventory is reduced by the $3,000 of Company C profit contained in the ending inventory.

Company C Income Distribution

Ending inventory profit . . . . (EIC)	$ 3,000	Internally generated net income		$30,000
		Beginning inventory profit	**(BIC)**	**1,800**
		Adjusted income		$28,800
		Company B share, 80%		23,040
		Company C NCI, 20%		$ 5,760

Company B Income Distribution

Ending inventory profit . . . . (EIB)	$ 2,500	Internally generated net income		$100,000
Building and equipment depreciation resulting from purchase of investment in Company C. . . . . **(AC)**	**4,700**	Beginning inventory profit	(BIB)	2,000
		80% of Company C adjusted income		23,040
		Adjusted income		$117,840
		Company A share, 75%		88,380
		Company B NCI, 25%		$ 29,460

Company A Income Distribution

Building and equipment depreciation resulting from investment in Company B . . . . (AB)	$17,500	Internally generated income	$ 90,000
		75% of Company B adjusted income	88,380
		Controlling interest	$160,880

Worksheet 8-2

Mutual Holdings, Treasury Stock Method
Company P and Subsidiary Company S
Worksheet for Consolidated Financial Statements
For Year Ended December 31, 20X3

	(Credit balance amounts are in parentheses.)	Trial Balance	
		Company P	Company S
1	Investment in Company S (80%)	248,000	
2			
3			
4	**Investment in Company P (10%, at cost)**		**80,000**
5	Equipment	608,000	180,000
6	Accumulated Depreciation	(100,000)	(50,000)
7	Common Stock, Company P	(500,000)	
8	Retained Earnings, January 1, 20X3, Company P	(200,000)	
9	Common Stock, Company S		(100,000)
10	Retained Earnings, January 1, 20X3, Company S		(90,000)
11	Sales	(300,000)	(200,000)
12	Cost of Goods Sold	180,000	120,000
13	Expenses	80,000	60,000
14	Subsidiary Income	(16,000)	
15	**Treasury Stock (at cost)**		
16		0	0
17	Consolidated Net Income		
18	To NCI (see distribution schedule)		
19	Balance to Controlling Interest (see distribution schedule)		
20	Total NCI		
21	Retained Earnings, Controlling Interest, December 31, 20X3		
22			

Eliminations and Adjustments:

(CY) Eliminate the entry made by the parent during the current year to record its share of Company S income.
(EL) Eliminate 80% of the January 1, 20X3, subsidiary equity balances against the investment in Company S account.
(D) Distribute the excess of cost over book value to the equipment account as specified by the determination and distribution of excess schedule applicable to the level one investment.
(A) Amortize the excess of $80,000 for the past two years and the current year.
(TS) The investment in Company P must be at cost. If any equity adjustments have been made, they must be reversed and the investment in the parent returned to cost. If the shares are to be reissued, as is the case in this example, the investment is then transferred to the treasury stock account, a contra account to total consolidated stockholders' equity.

As an alternative to entry **(TS)**, the cost of the treasury shares could be used to retire them on the worksheet as follows:

Common Stock, Company P	50,000	
Retained Earnings, Company P	30,000	
Investment in Company P		80,000

Worksheet 8-2 (see page 476)

Eliminations & Adjustments				Consolidated Income Statement	NCI	Controlling Retained Earnings	Consolidated Balance Sheet	
Dr.		Cr.						
		(CY)	16,000					1
		(EL)	152,000					2
		(D)	80,000					3
		(TS)	**80,000**					4
(D)	80,000						868,000	5
		(A)	12,000				(162,000)	6
							(500,000)	7
(A)	8,000					(192,000)		8
(EL)	80,000				(20,000)			9
(EL)	72,000				(18,000)			10
				(500,000)				11
				300,000				12
(A)	4,000			144,000				13
(CY)	16,000							14
(TS)	**80,000**						80,000	15
	340,000		340,000					16
				(56,000)				17
				4,000	(4,000)			18
				52,000		(52,000)		19
					(42,000)		(42,000)	20
						(244,000)	(244,000)	21
							0	22

Subsidiary Company S Income Distribution

	Internally generated net income	$ 20,000
	Adjusted income	$ 20,000
	NCI share	× 20%
	NCI	$ 4,000

Parent Company P Income Distribution

Depreciation of excess for current year	(A)	$4,000	Internally generated net income	$40,000
			80% × Company S adjusted income of $20,000	16,000
			Controlling interest	$52,000

Worksheet 8-3

Mutual Holdings, Stock Swap
Company P and Subsidiary Company S
Worksheet for Consolidated Financial Statements
For Year Ended December 31, 20X3

	(Credit balance amounts are in parentheses.)	Trial Balance	
		Company P	Company S
1	Investment in Company S (80%)	248,000	
2			
3			
4			
5	**Investment in Company P (10%)**		**80,800**
6	Current Assets		80,000
7	Equipment	608,000	180,000
8	Accumulated Depreciation	(100,000)	(50,000)
9	Goodwill		
10	**Common Stock, Company P**	(500,000)	
11	**Retained Earnings, January 1, 20X3, Company P**	(200,000)	
12	Common Stock, Company S		(130,000)
13	Paid-In Capital in Excess of Par, Company S		(50,000)
14	Retained Earnings, January 1, 20X3, Company S		(90,000)
15	Sales	(300,000)	(200,000)
16	Cost of Goods Sold	180,000	120,000
17	Expenses	80,000	60,000
18	**Subsidiary (or Investment) Income**	(16,000)	**(800)**
19			
20		0	0
21	Consolidated Net Income		
22	**To NCI**		
23	**Balance to Controlling Interest**		
24	Total NCI		
25	Retained Earnings, Controlling Interest, December 31, 20X3		
26			

Eliminations and Adjustments:

(CYa) Eliminate current-year equity income recorded in Company P's Investment in Company S.
(CYb) Eliminate current-year equity income recorded in Company S's Investment in Company P.
(TR) Transfer Investment in Company P to the parent's investment account.
(EL) Eliminate 11/13 of subsidiary equity against the Company S equity accounts.
(D1) Distribute original $80,000 excess to equipment account.
(D2) Distribute $3,539 excess on investment by Company S to goodwill.
(A) Amortize excess attributed to equipment for 2 prior and the current years.

Worksheet 8-3 (see page 479)

Eliminations & Adjustments				Consolidated Income Statement	NCI	Controlling Retained Earnings	Consolidated Balance Sheet	
Dr.		Cr.						
(TR)	**80,800**	(CYa)	16,000					1
		(CYb)	**800**					2
		(EL)	228,461					3
		(D)	83,539					4
		(TR)	**80,800**					5
							80,000	6
(D1)	80,000						868,000	7
		(A)	12,000				(162,000)	8
(D2)	3,539						3,539	9
							(500,000)	10
(A)	8,000					(192,000)		11
(EL)	110,000				(20,000)			12
(EL)	42,308				(7,692)			13
(EL)	76,153				(13,847)			14
				(500,000)				15
				300,000				16
(A)	4,000			144,000				17
(CYa)	16,000							18
(CYb)	**800**							19
	421,600		421,600					20
				(56,000)				21
				4,000	(4,000)			22
				52,000		(52,000)		23
					(45,539)		(45,539)	24
						(244,000)	(244,000)	25
							0	26

Subsidiary Company S Income Distribution

	Internally generated net income	$20,000
	Adjusted income	$20,000
	NCI share	× 20%
	NCI	$ 4,000

Parent Company P Income Distribution

Depreciation of excess for current year (A)	$4,000	Internally generated net income	$40,000
		80% × Company S adjusted income of $20,000	16,000
		Controlling interest	$52,000

EXERCISES

Exercise 1 *(LO 1)* **Subsidiary stock dividend.** On January 1, 20X1, Tiger Company purchased 90% of the outstanding stock of Lily Company for $800,000. At the time of the acquisition, Lily Company had the following stockholders' equity:

Common stock ($10 par)	$300,000
Paid-in capital in excess of par	150,000
Retained earnings	200,000
Total stockholders' equity	$650,000

It was determined that Lily Company's book values approximated fair values as of the purchase date. Any excess of cost over book value was attributed to goodwill.

On July 1, 20X1, Lily Company distributed a 10% stock dividend when the fair value of its common stock was $35 per share. A cash dividend of $0.50 per share was distributed on December 31, 20X1. Lily Company's net income for 20X1 amounted to $120,000 and was earned evenly throughout the year.

1. Prepare the entry required on Lily Company books to reflect the stock dividend distributed on July 1, 20X1. Prepare the stockholders' equity section of the Lily Company balance sheet as of December 31, 20X1.
2. Prepare the simple equity method entries that Tiger Company would make during 20X1 to record its investment in Lily Company.
3. Prepare the eliminations that would be made on the December 31, 20X1, consolidated worksheet. (Assume the use of the simple equity method.)

Exercise 2 *(LO 2)* **Subsidiary sale of shares to noncontrolling interest.** Track Company owned a 90% interest in Trail Company on January 1, 20X1, when Trail had the following stockholders' equity:

Common stock ($10 par)	$100,000
Paid-in capital in excess of par	250,000
Retained earnings	200,000
Total stockholders' equity	$550,000

On July 1, 20X1, Trail sold 2,000 additional shares to noncontrolling shareholders in a private offering for $80 per share. Trail's net income for 20X1 was $70,000, and the income was earned evenly during the year.

Track uses the simple equity method to record the investment in Trail. Summary entries are made each December 31 to record the year's activity.

Prepare Track's equity adjustments for 20X1 that result from the above activities of Trail Company during 20X1. Assume Track has $500,000 of paid-in capital in excess of par.

Exercise 3 *(LO 2)* **Subsidiary sale of shares, alternative amounts purchased by parent.** On January 1, 20X1, Tom Company purchased an 80% interest in Car Company for $400,000. On the purchase date, Car Company had the following stockholders' equity:

Common stock ($10 par)	$200,000
Paid-in capital in excess of par	100,000
Retained earnings	150,000
Total stockholders' equity	$450,000

Assets and liabilities have fair values equal to book values. Any excess is due to goodwill.

Car Company had net income of $50,000 for 20X1. No dividends were paid or declared during 20X1.

On January 1, 20X2, Car Company sold 10,000 shares of common stock at $40 per share in a public offering.

Assuming the parent uses the simple equity method, prepare all parent company entries required for the issuance of the shares. Also prepare a new determination and distribution of excess schedule for the investment if it is needed. Assume the following alternative situations:

1. Tom Company purchased 8,000 shares.
2. Tom Company purchased 9,000 shares.
3. Tom Company purchased 5,000 shares.

Suggestion: It is helpful to use a 3-column table which, for each case, organizes the changes in ownership interest. See the schedule on page 466.

Exercise 4 *(LO 3)* **Subsidiary treasury stock.** The following comparative statements of stockholders' equity were prepared for Nolte Corporation:

	Jan. 1, 20X1	Jan. 1, 20X3	Jan. 1, 20X5
Common stock ($10 par)	$300,000	$300,000	$300,000
Paid-in capital in excess of par	60,000	60,000	60,000
Retained earnings		42,000	120,000
Total	$360,000	$402,000	$480,000
Less treasury stock (at cost)		(75,000)	(75,000)
Total stockholders' equity	$360,000	$327,000	$405,000

Tarman Corporation purchased 60% of Nolte Corporation common stock for $12 per share on January 1, 20X1, when the latter corporation was formed.

On January 1, 20X3, Nolte Corporation purchased 5,000 shares of its own common stock from noncontrolling interests for $15 per share. These shares were accounted for as treasury stock at cost.

Nolte had $50,000 of net income in 20X5 and has never declared a cash dividend.

Assuming Tarman Corporation uses the cost method to record its investment in Nolte Corporation, prepare the necessary cost-to-simple-equity conversion and the eliminations and adjustments required on the consolidated worksheet as of December 31, 20X5. Include all pertinent supporting calculations in good form. Any excess of cost over book value is considered to be goodwill.

Exercise 5 *(LO 4)* **Three-level purchase.** You have secured the following information for Companies A, B, and C concerning their internally generated net incomes (excluding subsidiary income) and dividends paid:

		A	B	C
20X1	Internally generated net income	$30,000	$20,000	$10,000
	Dividends declared and paid	10,000	5,000	
20X2	Internally generated net income	50,000	30,000	25,000
	Dividends declared and paid	10,000	5,000	5,000
20X3	Internally generated net income	40,000	40,000	30,000
	Dividends declared and paid	10,000	5,000	5,000

1. Assume Company A purchased an 80% interest in Company B on January 1, 20X1, and Company B purchased a 60% interest in Company C on January 1, 20X2. Prepare the simple equity method adjusting entries made by Companies A and B for subsidiary investments for the years 20X1 through 20X3.
2. Assume Company B acquired a 70% interest in Company C on January 1, 20X1, and Company A acquired a 90% interest in Company B on January 1, 20X3. Prepare the simple equity method adjusting entries made by Companies A and B for subsidiary investments for the years 20X1 through 20X3.

Exercise 6 *(LO 4)* **Three-level purchase, intercompany asset sale.** Company SP purchased an 80% interest in the common stock of Company S for $580,000 on January 1, 20X1. Any excess of cost is attributable to a patent with a 10-year life. Company SP maintains its investment in Company S under the cost method.

Company P purchased a 60% interest in the common stock of Company SP on January 1, 20X5, for $2,600,000. Any excess of cost is attributable to Company S equipment, which is understated by $80,000, and a Company SP building, which is understated by $200,000. Any remaining excess is considered goodwill. Relevant stockholders' equities are as follows:

	Company SP	Company S	
	Jan. 1, 20X5	Jan. 1, 20X1	Jan. 1, 20X5
Common stock	$ 400,000	$100,000	$100,000
Paid-in capital in excess of par	1,100,000	150,000	150,000
Retained earnings	2,000,000	300,000	450,000

1. Prepare a determination and distribution of excess schedule for the investment in Company SP.
2. On January 1, 20X6, Company S sold a machine with a net book value of $35,000 to Company P for $50,000. The machine has a 5-year life. Prepare the eliminations and adjustments needed on the December 31, 20X7, trial balance worksheet that relate to this intercompany sale.

Exercise 7 *(LO 4)* **Three-level purchase, inventory and fixed asset sales.** Companies A, B, and C produced the following separate internally generated net incomes during 20X5:

	A	B	C
Sales	$300,000	$400,000	$100,000
Less cost of goods sold	200,000	300,000	60,000
Gross profit	$100,000	$100,000	$ 40,000
Expenses	60,000	30,000	10,000
Internally generated net income	$ 40,000	$ 70,000	$ 30,000

Company A purchased an 80% interest in Company B on January 1, 20X2, and Company B purchased a 60% interest in Company C on January 1, 20X3. Each investment was acquired at a price equal to the book value of the stock purchased.

Additional information:

a. Company A purchased goods billed at $30,000 from Company C during 20X5. The price includes a 40% gross profit. One-half of the goods are held in Company A's year-end inventory.
b. Company B purchased goods billed at $30,000 from Company A during 20X5. Company A always bills Company B at a price that includes a 30% gross profit. Company B had $6,000 of Company A goods in its beginning inventory and $2,400 of Company A goods in its ending inventory.

c. Company C purchased goods billed at $15,000 from Company B during 20X5. Company B bills Company C at a 20% gross profit. At year-end, $7,500 of the goods remain unsold. The goods were inventoried at $5,000, under the lower-of-cost-or-market procedure.
d. Company B sold a machine to Company C on January 1, 20X4, for $50,000. Company B's cost was $70,000, and accumulated depreciation on the date of sale was $40,000. The machine is being depreciated on a straight-line basis over five years.

Prepare the consolidated income statement for 20X5, including the distribution of consolidated net income supported by distribution schedules.

Exercise 8 *(LO 4)* **Purchase of a company with a subsidiary.** On January 1, 20X1, Hartland Company purchased an 80% interest in Fort Company for $120,000. The purchase price represented a $20,000 excess over book value, which was attributed to a patent and given a 10-year life. The investment is recorded under the simple equity method.

On January 1, 20X3, Oconto Company purchased a 60% interest in Hartland Company for $380,000. Oconto Company believes that the patent book value remaining on the investment by Hartland in Fort is stated correctly. Comparative equities of Hartland Company and Fort Company immediately prior to the purchase revealed the following:

Stockholders' Equity	Hartland Company	Fort Company
Common stock ($5 par)	$200,000	
Common stock ($10 par)		$100,000
Paid-in capital in excess of par	100,000	20,000
Retained earnings	150,000	80,000
Total stockholders' equity	$450,000	$200,000

An analysis of the separate accounts of Hartland and Fort on January 1, 20X3, revealed that Fort's inventory was undervalued by $20,000 and that Hartland's equipment with a 5-year future life was undervalued by $30,000. All other book values approximated fair values for Hartland and Fort.

Prepare the determination and distribution of excess schedule for Oconto's purchase of Hartland Company on January 1, 20X3.

Exercise 9 *(LO 4)* **Direct and indirect holdings.** The following diagram depicts the investment affiliations among Companies M, N, and O:

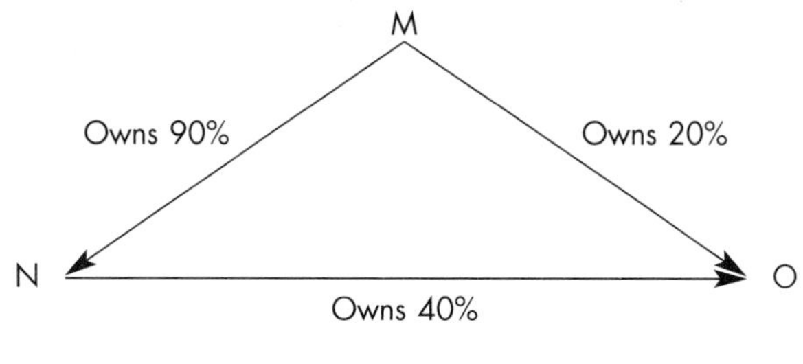

The following facts apply to 20X3 operations:

	M	N	O
Internally generated net income	$200,000	$90,000	$40,000
Dividends declared and paid	40,000	10,000	5,000

All investments were made at a price equal to book value.

1. Prepare the simple equity method adjustments that would be made for the investments owned by Companies M and N during the year 20X3.
2. Intercompany inventory transactions affecting 20X3 were as follows:

	Sold by N to O	Sold by O to M
Profit on sales	25%	30%
Beginning inventory of intercompany goods	$10,000	$15,000
20X3 sales	$50,000	$75,000
Ending inventory of intercompany goods	$12,000	$20,000

Using the facts given, determine the consolidated income of the consolidated company, the noncontrolling interest, and the controlling interest net income. Income distribution schedules may be used for support.

Exercise 10 *(LO 5)* **Treasury stock method.** Myles Corporation and its subsidiary, Dowling Corporation, had the following trial balances as of December 31, 20X3:

	Myles Corporation	Dowling Corporation
Current Assets	400,000	182,000
Investment in Dowling Corporation	398,000	
Investment in Myles Corporation		150,000
Property, Plant, and Equipment (net)	850,00	400,000
Liabilities	(200,000)	(100,000)
Common Stock ($10 par)	(1,000,000)	(500,000)
Retained Earnings, January 1, 20X3	(400,000)	(100,000)
Sales	(800,000)	(350,000)
Dividend Income		(2,000)
Subsidiary Income	(18,000)	
Cost of Goods Sold	600,000	240,000
Expenses	150,000	80,000
Dividends Declared	20,000	
Total	0	0

Myles Corporation purchased its 60% interest in Dowling Corporation for $350,000 on January 1, 20X1. At that time, Dowling's retained earnings balance was $50,000. Any excess of cost over book value was attributed to equipment and given a 20-year life.

Dowling Corporation purchased a 10% interest in Myles Corporation on January 1, 20X3, for $150,000.

No intercompany transactions occurred during 20X3.

1. Prepare determination and distribution of excess schedules for the investment in Dowling.
2. Prepare the 20X3 consolidated income statement, including the consolidated net income distribution, using the treasury stock method for mutual holdings. Prepare the supporting income distribution schedules.

Exercise 11 *(LO 5)* **Mutual Holdings—Stock Swap.** Myles Corporation and its subsidiary, Dowling Corporation, had the following trial balances on December 31, 20X3, just prior to a stock swap:

	Myles Corporation	Dowling Corporation
Current Assets	400,000	332,000
Investment in Dowling Corporation	398,000	
Property, Plant, and Equipment (net)	850,00	400,000
Liabilities	(200,000)	(100,000)
Common Stock ($10 par)	(1,000,000)	(500,000)
Retained Earnings, January 1, 20X3	(400,000)	(100,000)
Sales	(800,000)	(350,000)
Dividend Income		(2,000)
Subsidiary Income	(18,000)	
Cost of Goods Sold	600,000	240,000
Expenses	150,000	80,000
Dividends Declared	20,000	
Total	0	0

Myles Corporation purchased a 60% interest in Dowling Corporation for $350,000 on January 1, 20X1. At that time, Dowling's retained earnings was $50,000. Any excess of cost was attributed to equipment with a 20-year life.

On January 1, 20X3, Dowling issued 10,000 shares of its common stock in exchange for 10,000 shares of the Myles Corporation. Myles shares were trading at $15 per share. Any excess of cost is attributed to goodwill; any excess of book value is attributed to equipment.

No intercompany transactions occurred during 20X3.

1. Prepare a determination and distribution of excess schedule for the Myles Corporation investment in the Dowling Corporation.
2. Calculate any additional excess of cost or book value caused by the stock swap.

PROBLEMS

Problem 8-1 *(LO 1)* **Stock dividend, subsidiary stock sales, equity method.** On January 1, 20X1, Zee Corporation purchased 8,000 shares of Thomas Company stock and 18,000 shares of Sand Company stock for $196,000 and $270,000, respectively. The excess of cost over book value on each investment was attributed to goodwill.

Thomas Company and Sand Company had the following stockholders' equities immediately prior to Zee's purchases:

	Thomas Company	Sand Company
Common stock ($5 par)	$ 50,000	
Common stock ($10 par)		$300,000
Paid-in capital in excess of par	100,000	
Retained earnings	70,000	100,000
Total stockholder's equity	$220,000	$400,000

Additional information:

a. Net income for Thomas Company and Sand Company for 20X1 and 20X2 follows (income is assumed to be earned evenly throughout the year):

	20X1	20X2
Thomas Company	$40,000	$50,000
Sand Company	30,000	40,000

b. No cash dividends were paid or declared by Thomas or Sand during 20X1 and 20X2.
c. Thomas Company distributed a 10% stock dividend on December 31, 20X1. Thomas stock was selling at $25 per share when the stock dividend was declared.
d. On July 1, 20X2, Thomas Company sold 2,750 shares of stock at $32 per share. Zee Corporation purchased none of these shares.
e. Sand Company sold 5,000 shares of stock on July 1, 20X1, at $20 per share. Zee Corporation purchased 3,700 of these shares.
f. On January 1, 20X2, Sand Company purchased 5,000 shares of its common stock from noncontrolling interests at $14 per share.

Required ▶ ▶ ▶ ▶ ▶ Assume Zee Corporation uses the simple equity method. For 20X1 and 20X2, record each of the adjustments to the investment accounts. Provide all supporting calculations in good form.

Problem 8-2 *(LO 1)* **Stock dividend, subsidiary stock sales, cost method.** On January 1, 20X1, Bear Corporation acquired a 60% interest in Keller Company and an 80% interest in Samco Company. The purchase prices were $225,000 and $250,000, respectively. The excess of cost over book value for each investment was considered to be goodwill.

Immediately prior to the purchases, Keller Company and Samco Company had the following stockholders' equities:

	Keller Company	Samco Company
Common stock ($10 par)	$200,000	
Common stock ($20 par)		$200,000
Paid-in capital in excess of par	50,000	
Retained earnings	100,000	100,000
Total stockholder' equity	$350,000	$300,000

Additional information:

a. Keller Company and Samco Company had the following net incomes for 20X1 through 20X3 (incomes were earned evenly throughout the year):

	20X1	20X2	20X3
Keller Company	$50,000	$60,000	$60,000
Samco Company	40,000	30,000	55,000

b. Keller Company had the following equity-related transactions for the first three years after it became a subsidiary of Bear Corporation:

July 1, 20X1	Sold 5,000 shares of its own stock at $20 per share. Bear purchased 3,000 of these shares.
December 31, 20X2	Paid a cash dividend of $1 per share.
July 1, 20X3	Purchased 5,000 shares of NCI-owned stock as treasury shares at $27 per share.

c. Samco Company had the following equity-related transactions for the first three years after it became a subsidiary of Bear Corporation:

December 31, 20X1	Issued a 10% stock dividend. The estimated fair value of Samco common stock was $30 per share on the declaration date.
October 1, 20X2	Sold 4,000 shares of its own stock at $30 per share. Of these shares, 200 were purchased by Bear.

d. Bear Corporation has $200,000 of additional paid-in capital on December 31, 20X3.

◀◀◀◀◀ **Required**

Bear Corporation uses the cost method to account for its investments in subsidiaries. Convert its investments to the simple equity method as of December 31, 20X3, and provide adequate support for the entries. Assume that the 20X3 nominal accounts are closed.

Problem 8-3 *(LO 2)* **Worksheet, subsidiary stock sale, intercompany merchandise.** On January 1, 20X2, Pepka Company purchased 80% of the outstanding common stock of Smart Company for $700,000.

On January 1, 20X4, Smart Company sold 25,000 shares of common stock to the public at $10 per share. Pepka Company did not purchase any of these shares. No entry has been made by the parent. Smart Company had the following stockholders' equity at the end of 20X1 and 20X3:

	December 31	
	20X1	20X3
Common stock ($2 par)	$200,000	$200,000
Paid-in capital in excess of par	400,000	400,000
Retained earnings	100,000	180,000
Total stockholders' equity	$700,000	$780,000

On the January 1, 20X2, acquisition date, Smart Company's book values approximated fair values, except for a building that was undervalued by $60,000. The building had an estimated future life of 20 years. Any additional excess was attributed to goodwill.

Trial balances of the two companies as of December 31, 20X4, are as follows:

	Pepka Company	Smart Company
Cash	179,040	55,000
Accounts Receivable (net)	280,000	190,000
Inventory	325,000	175,000
Investment in Smart Company	700,000	
Property, Plant, and Equipment	2,450,000	1,400,000
Accumulated Depreciation	(1,256,000)	(536,000)
Liabilities	(750,000)	(210,000)
Common Stock ($10 par)	(1,500,000)	
Common Stock ($2 par)		(250,000)
Paid-In Capital in Excess of Par		(600,000)
Retained Earnings, January 1, 20X4	(375,000)	(180,000)
Sales	(1,600,000)	(750,000)
Subsidiary Dividend Income	(23,040)	
Cost of Goods Sold	1,120,000	450,000
Other Expenses	405,000	220,000
Dividends Declared	45,000	36,000
Total	0	0

During 20X4, Smart Company sold $200,000 of merchandise to Pepka Company at a price that includes a 20% gross profit. This was their first intercompany sale. $50,000 of the goods remain in Pepka's ending inventory.

Required ▶ ▶ ▶ ▶ ▶ Prepare the worksheet necessary to produce the consolidated financial statements of Pepka Company and its subsidiary as of December 31, 20X4. Include the determination and distribution of excess and income distribution schedules.

Problem 8-4 *(LO 2)* **Worksheet, subsidiary stock sale with parent purchase, intercompany merchandise.** On January 1, 20X2, Mitta Corporation purchased a 60% interest (12,000 shares) in Trainer Company for $158,000. Trainer stockholders' equity on the purchase date was as follows:

Common stock ($5 par)	$100,000
Paid-in capital in excess of par	50,000
Retained earnings	80,000
Total stockholders' equity	$230,000

At the purchase date, Trainer's book values for assets and liabilities closely approximate fair values. Any excess of cost over book value is attributed to goodwill.

On January 1, 20X3, Trainer Company sold 5,000 shares of common stock in a public offering at $20 per share. Mitta Corporation purchased 4,000 shares. Any excess of cost over book value on the additional interest was attributed to goodwill.

During 20X3, Mitta sold $30,000 of goods to Trainer at a gross profit of 25%. There were $6,000 of Mitta goods in Trainer's beginning inventory and $8,000 of Mitta goods in Trainer's ending inventory.

Merchandise sales by Trainer to Mitta were $20,000 during 20X3 at a gross profit of 30%. There were $6,000 of Trainer goods in Mitta's beginning inventory and $2,000 of Trainer goods in Mitta's ending inventory.

Intercompany gross profit rates have been constant for many years. There are no intercompany payables/receivables.

Mitta's investment in Trainer Company balance was determined as follows:

Original cost	$158,000
60% of Trainer 20X2 income ($40,000 × 60%)	24,000
Subtotal	$182,000
Less 60% of Trainer dividends declared in 20X2 (60% × $8,000)	(4,800)
Subtotal	$177,200
Cost to acquire additional shares (new issue)	80,000
64% of Trainer 20X3 income ($50,000 × 64%)	32,000
Subtotal	$289,200
Less 64% of Trainer dividends declared in 20X3 (64% × $10,000)	(6,400)
Investment balance, December 31, 20X3	$282,800

Trainer has paid a quarterly $0.10 dividend per outstanding common share since the second quarter of 20X1.

The trial balances of the two companies as of December 31, 20X3, are as follows:

	Mitta Corporation	Trainer Company
Cash	104,200	63,500
Accounts Receivable	113,600	60,000

Inventory	350,000	80,000
Investment in Trainer Company	282,800	
Property, Plant, and Equipment	1,800,000	360,000
Accumulated Depreciation	(600,000)	(89,500)
Accounts Payable	(180,000)	(64,000)
Other Current Liabilities	(26,000)	(8,000)
Bonds Payable	(500,000)	
Common Stock ($10 par)	(1,000,000)	
Common Stock ($5 par)		(125,000)
Paid-In Capital in Excess of Par		(125,000)
Retained Earnings, January 1, 20X3	(212,600)	(112,000)
Sales	(1,950,000)	(600,000)
Subsidiary Income	(32,000)	
Cost of Goods Sold	1,170,000	420,000
Other Expenses	630,000	130,000
Dividends Declared	50,000	10,000
Total	0	0

◄◄◄◄◄ **Required**

Prepare the worksheet necessary to produce the consolidated financial statements of Mitta Corporation and its subsidiary as of December 31, 20X3. Include the determination and distribution of excess and income distribution schedules.

Problem 8-5 *(LO 2)* **Worksheet, two subsidiaries, subsidiary stock sales, intercompany merchandise, fixed assets, bonds.** The audit of Barns Company and its subsidiaries for the year ended December 31, 20X2, was completed. The working papers contain the following information:

a. Barns Company acquired 4,000 shares of Webb Company common stock for $320,000 on January 1, 20X1. Webb Company purchased 500 shares of its own stock as treasury shares for $48,000 on January 1, 20X2.
b. Barns Company acquired all 8,000 outstanding shares of Elcho Company stock on January 1, 20X1, for $600,000. On January 1, 20X2, Elcho Company issued through a private sale 2,000 additional shares to new noncontrolling shareholders at $85 per share. Barns has no investments other than the stock of Webb and Elcho.
c. Elcho Company originally issued $200,000 of 10-year, 8% mortgage bonds at 98, due on January 1, 20X5. On January 1, 20X2, Webb Company purchased $150,000 of these bonds in the open market at 98. Interest on the bonds is paid each June 30 and December 31.
d. Condensed balance sheets of Webb and Elcho on January 1, 20X1, and January 1, 20X2, are as follows:

	Webb Company		Elcho Company	
	Jan. 1, 20X1	Jan. 1, 20X2	Jan. 1, 20X1	Jan. 1, 20X2
Current assets	$195,000	$225,000	$280,400	$205,000
Property, plant, and equipment	305,000	350,000	613,000	623,800
Unamortized bond discount			1,600	1,200
Total	$500,000	$575,000	$895,000	$830,000
Current liabilities	$100,000	$125,000	$ 95,000	$105,000
Bonds payable			200,000	200,000
Capital stock ($50 par)	250,000	250,000	400,000	400,000
Retained earnings	150,000	200,000	200,000	125,000
Total	$500,000	$575,000	$895,000	$830,000

e. Total dividends declared and paid during 20X2 were as follows:

Barns Company	$24,000
Webb Company	25,000
Elcho Company	10,000

In addition to the dividend payments, Barns Company and Webb Company each had declared dividends of $1 per share payable in January 20X3.

f. On June 30, 20X2, Barns sold equipment with a book value of $8,000 to Webb for $10,000. Webb depreciates equipment by the straight-line method based on a 10-year life.

g. Barns Company consistently sells to its subsidiaries at prices that realize a gross profit of 25% on sales. Webb and Elcho companies sell to each other and to Barns Company at cost. Prior to 20X2, intercompany sales were negligible, but the following sales were made during 20X2:

	Total Sales	Included in Purchaser's Inventory at December 31, 20X2
Barns Company to Webb Company	$172,000	$20,000
Barns Company to Elcho Company	160,000	40,000
Webb Company to Elcho Company	25,000	5,000
Webb Company to Barns Company	28,000	8,000
	$385,000	$73,000

h. At December 31, 20X2:

Barns Company owed Webb Company	$24,000
Webb Company owed Elcho Company	16,000
Elcho Company owed Barns Company	12,000
Total	$52,000

i. The following trial balances as of December 31, 20X2, were prepared:

	Barns Company	Webb Company	Elcho Company
Cash	110,000	23,500	165,200
Accounts Receivable	85,000	73,500	105,000
Inventories	138,000	163,000	150,000
Investment in Webb Company Stock	320,000		
Investment in Elcho Company Stock	600,000		
Investment in Elcho Company Bonds		148,000	
Property, Plant, and Equipment	700,000	525,000	834,000
Accumulated Depreciation	(402,000)	(325,000)	(240,000)
Accounts Payable	(202,000)	(150,500)	(86,900)
Dividends Payable	(12,000)	(5,000)	
Bonds Payable	(400,000)		(200,000)
Unamortized Bond Discount			800
Capital Stock ($50 par)	(600,000)	(250,000)	(500,000)
Paid-In Capital in Excess of Par			(70,000)
Retained Earnings, January 1, 20X2*	(278,200)	(170,000)	(115,000)
Treasury Stock (at cost)		48,000	
Gain on Sale of Equipment	(2,000)		

Sales	(2,950,000)	(1,550,000)	(1,750,000)
Interest Income on Bonds		(13,000)	
Dividend Income	(28,000)		
Cost of Goods Sold	2,500,000	1,200,000	1,400,000
Operating Expenses	405,000	280,000	290,500
Interest Expense	16,200	2,500	16,400
Total	0	0	0

*Reduced directly for dividends declared.

◄◄◄◄◄ **Required**

Prepare the worksheet necessary to produce the consolidated financial statements of Barns Company and its subsidiaries for the year ended December 31, 20X2. Include the determination and distribution of excess and income distribution schedules. Any excess of cost over book value is attributable to goodwill. All bond discounts are assumed to be amortized on a straight-line basis.

(AICPA adapted)

Suggestion: The treasury stock represents a separate block of stock to be eliminated. The impact of the subsidiary sale of shares should not be reflected as an income statement gain or loss.

Problem 8-6 *(LO 4)* **Worksheet, direct and indirect holding, intercompany merchandise, machine.** The following diagram depicts the relationships among Mary Company, Jack Company, and Jill Company on December 31, 20X4:

template cd

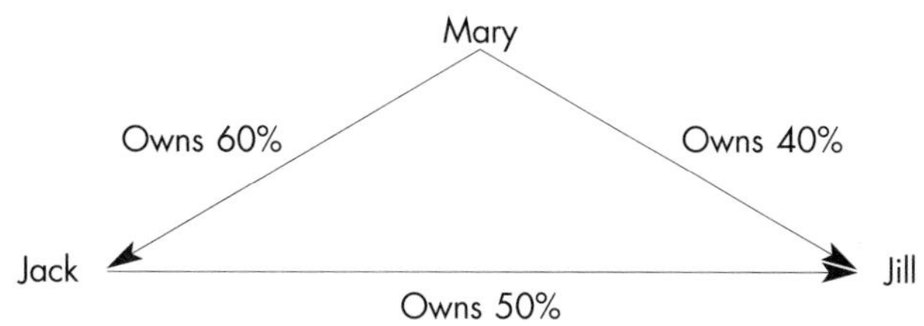

Mary Company purchased its interest in Jack Company on January 1, 20X2, for $200,000. Jack Company purchased its interest in Jill Company on January 1, 20X3, for $75,000. Mary Company purchased its interest in Jill Company on January 1, 20X4, for $72,000.

The following stockholders' equities are available:

	Jack Company	Jill Company	
	December 31, 20X1	December 31, 20X2	20X3
Common stock ($10 par)	$150,000		
Common stock ($20 par)		$100,000	$100,000
Paid-in capital in excess of par	75,000		
Retained earnings	75,000	50,000	80,000
Total equity	$300,000	$150,000	$180,000

On January 2, 20X4, Jill Company sold a machine to Mary Company for $20,000. The machine had a book value of $10,000, with an estimated life of five years and is being depreciated on a straight-line basis.

Jack Company sold $20,000 of merchandise to Jill Company during 20X4 to realize a gross profit of 30%. Of this merchandise, $5,000 remained in Jill Company's December 31, 20X4, inventory. Jill owes Jack $3,000 on December 31, 20X4, for merchandise delivered during 20X4.

Trial balances of the three companies prepared from general ledger account balances on December 31, 20X4, are as follows:

	Mary Company	Jack Company	Jill Company
Cash	66,500	60,000	30,000
Accounts Receivable	200,000	55,000	30,000
Inventory	360,000	80,000	50,000
Investment in Jack Company	266,000		
Investment in Jill Company	86,000	107,500	
Property, Plant, and Equipment	2,250,000	850,000	350,000
Accumulated Depreciation	(938,000)	(377,500)	(121,800)
Intangibles	15,000		
Accounts Payable	(215,500)	(61,000)	(22,000)
Accrued Expenses	(12,000)	(4,000)	(1,200)
Bonds Payable	(500,000)	(300,000)	(100,000)
Common Stock ($5 par)	(500,000)		
Common Stock ($10 par)		(150,000)	
Common Stock ($20 par)			(100,000)
Paid-In Capital in Excess of Par	(700,000)	(75,000)	
Retained Earnings, January 1, 20X4	(290,000)	(130,000)	(80,000)
Sales	(1,800,000)	(500,000)	(300,000)
Gain on Sale of Equipment			(10,000)
Subsidiary Income	(58,000)	(20,000)	
Cost of Goods Sold	1,170,000	350,000	180,000
Other Expenses	525,000	100,000	90,000
Dividends Declared	75,000	15,000	5,000
Total	0	0	0

Required ▶ ▶ ▶ ▶ ▶ Prepare the worksheet necessary to produce the consolidated financial statements of Mary Company and its subsidiaries as of December 31, 20X4. Include the determination and distribution of excess and income distribution schedules. Any excess of cost is assumed to be attributable to goodwill.

Problem 8-7 *(LO 4)* **Worksheet, three-level holding, intercompany merchandise, plant assets.** Shelby Corporation purchased 90% of the outstanding stock of Boehm Company on January 1, 20X1, for $600,000 cash. At that time, Boehm Company had the following stockholders' equity balances: Common Stock, $200,000; Paid-In Capital, $80,000; and Retained Earnings, $300,000.

All book values approximated fair values except for the plant assets (undervalued by $50,000 and with an estimated remaining life of 10 years). Any remaining excess is goodwill.

DeNoma Company acquired a 60% interest in Shelby on January 1, 20X3, for $750,000. At this time, Shelby had consolidated shareholders' equity of Common Stock, $500,000; Paid-In Capital, $150,000; and Controlling Retained Earnings, $500,000 (*not including amortization of excess price applicable to investment in Boehm*).

At that time, it was also determined that Shelby's plant assets were undervalued by $50,000 and had a 10-year remaining life. Boehm's plant assets were undervalued by $18,519. Any remaining excess is goodwill.

Intercompany merchandise sales from Boehm to Shelby for 20X4 were (1) seller's goods in buyer's beginning inventory, $7,500; (2) sales during 20X4, $125,000; (3) seller's goods in buyer's ending inventory, $10,000; and (4) gross profit on intercompany sales, 80%.

On July 1, 20X3, Shelby sold plant assets with a cost of $80,000 and accumulated depreciation of $45,000 to DeNoma for $50,000. Remaining life on the date of sale was estimated to be five years.

Shelby and DeNoma use the simple equity method to account for their investments. The trial balances on December 31, 20X4, were as follows:

	DeNoma Company	Shelby Corporation	Boehm Company
Inventory	75,000	60,000	40,000
Other Current Assets	900,000	5,000	390,000
Plant Assets	1,200,000	800,000	600,000
Accumulated Depreciation	(450,000)	(300,000)	(200,000)
Investment in Shelby Corporation	894,000		
Investment in Boehm Company		825,000	
Common Stock	(1,500,000)	(500,000)	(200,000)
Paid-In Capital in Excess of Par		(150,000)	(80,000)
Retained Earnings	(922,000)	(620,000)	(500,000)
Sales	(900,000)	(700,000)	(600,000)
Cost of Goods Sold	570,000	425,000	400,000
Expenses	205,000	200,000	150,000
Subsidiary Income	(72,000)	(45,000)	
Total	0	0	0

◀◀◀◀◀ **Required**

Prepare the determination and distribution of excess schedule for Shelby's investment in Boehm and DeNoma's investment in Shelby. Prepare the December 31, 20X4, consolidated worksheet and income distribution schedules.

Suggestion: The determination and distribution of excess schedule must show an adjustment to Shelby's retained earnings for the amortization of excess applicable to Shelby's investment in Boehm. (Hint for consolidated balance sheet: The reduced retained earnings in the determination and distribution of excess schedule must be adjusted before eliminating the pro rata share of equity balances.)

Problem 8-8 *(LO 4)* **Worksheet, direct and indirect holdings, preferred stock, intercompany merchandise.** The following diagram depicts the relationships among Ackley Company, Biernat Company, and Cromwell Company on December 31, 20X5:

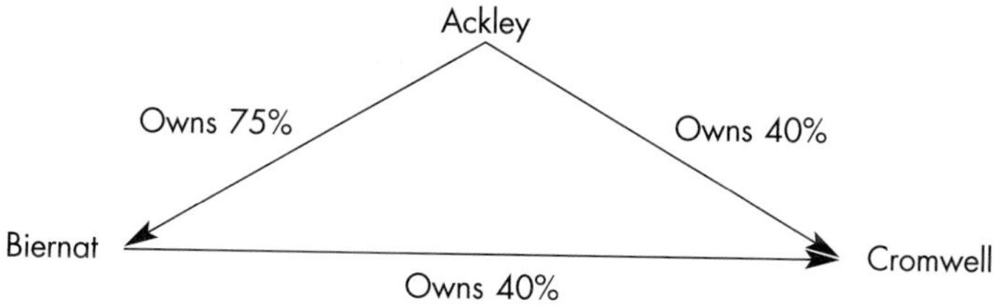

Information regarding the preceding investments follows:

a. Ackley Company purchased its 40% interest in Cromwell Company on December 31, 20X1, for $50,000. On that date, Cromwell Company's book values approximated fair values except for equipment, which is overvalued and has a 10-year life.
b. On January 1, 20X4, Ackley Company purchased a 75% interest in Biernat Company for $400,000. The following determination and distribution of excess schedule was prepared at that time:

Price paid		$400,000
Less interest acquired:		
Common stock ($5 par)	$300,000	
Paid-in capital in excess of par	100,000	
Retained earnings	30,000	
Total stockholders' equity	$430,000	
Interest acquired	× 75%	322,500
Excess of cost over book value		$ 77,500
Excess of cost attributable to building (20-year life), 75% × $40,000		30,000
Patent (10-year life)		$ 47,500

c. On January 1, 20X5, Biernat Company acquired a 40% interest in Cromwell Company for $92,000. Cromwell's book values approximated fair values at this date.

d. The following stockholders' equities have been made available:

	Cromwell Company		Biernat Company
	December 31, 20X1	December 31, 20X4	December 31, 20X3
Noncumulative $6 preferred stock ($100 par and liquidating value)			$ 50,000
Common stock ($5 par)			300,000
Common stock ($10 par)	$200,000	$200,000	
Paid-in capital in excess of par			100,000
Retained earnings (deficit)	(50,000)	30,000	30,000
Total equity	$150,000	$230,000	$480,000

e. The following is information regarding intercompany merchandise sales in 20X5:

	Ackley to Cromwell	Cromwell to Biernat
Seller's merchandise in buyer's December 31, 20X4, inventory	$ 2,000	
20X5 sales	16,000	$5,000
Seller's merchandise in buyer's December 31, 20X5, inventory	1,000	1,000
Intercompany receivable/payable on December 31, 20X5	3,000	500
Gross profit on sales	30%	40%

Trial balances of the three companies as of December 31, 20X5, are as follows:

	Ackley Company	Biernat Company	Cromwell Company
Cash	117,800	49,300	20,000
Accounts Receivable (net)	200,000	100,000	44,000
Inventory	277,000	206,000	58,000
Investment in Cromwell Company	50,000	92,000	
Investment in Biernat Company	400,000		
Property, Plant, and Equipment	2,800,000	1,500,000	220,000
Accumulated Depreciation	(1,120,000)	(593,000)	(90,000)
Accounts Payable	(206,000)	(112,000)	(4,000)
Bonds Payable	(1,000,000)	(700,000)	
Preferred Stock		(50,000)	
Common Stock ($5 par)	(500,000)	(300,000)	

Common Stock ($10 par)			(200,000)
Paid-In Capital in Excess of Par	(700,000)	(100,000)	
Retained Earnings, January 1, 20X5	(270,000)	(61,000)	(30,000)
Sales	(1,500,000)	(850,000)	(400,000)
Subsidiary Dividend Income	(18,800)	(800)	
Cost of Goods Sold	1,050,000	552,500	240,000
Other Expenses	350,000	240,000	140,000
Preferred Dividends Declared		3,000	
Common Dividends Declared	70,000	24,000	2,000
Total	0	0	0

Prepare the worksheet necessary to produce the consolidated financial statements of Ackley Company and its subsidiaries as of December 31, 20X5. Include the determination and distribution of excess and income distribution schedules. ◄◄◄◄◄ **Required**

Problem 8-9 *(LO 5)* **Worksheet, subsidiary owns parent shares, treasury stock method, merchandise.** On January 1, 20X1, Pepe Company purchased 80% of the common stock of Seda Company for $400,000. On this date, Seda had common stock, other paid-in capital, and retained earnings of $50,000, $140,000, and $220,000, respectively.

Any excess of cost over book value is due to goodwill.

In both 20X1 and 20X2, Pepe has accounted for the investment in Seda using the cost method.

On January 1, 20X2, Seda purchased 500 shares (5%) of the common stock of Pepe Company from outside investors for $40,000 cash. It is expected that the shares may be resold later. Seda uses the cost method in accounting for the investment. Any excess is attributed to goodwill.

During the last quarter of 20X2, Pepe sold merchandise to Seda for $40,000, one-fourth of which is still held by Seda on December 31, 20X2. Pepe's usual gross profit on intercompany sales is 40%.

The trial balances for Pepe and Seda on December 31, 20X2, are as follows:

	Pepe Company	Seda Company
Inventory	170,000	120,000
Other Current Assets	216,000	256,000
Investment in Seda Company	400,000	
Investment in Pepe Company		40,000
Land	80,000	70,000
Buildings and Equipment	400,000	280,000
Accumulated Depreciation	(180,000)	(90,000)
Current Liabilities	(98,000)	(74,000)
Long-Term Liabilities	(250,000)	(100,000)
Common Stock—Pepe Company ($10 par)	(100,000)	
Paid-In Capital in Excess of Par—Pepe Company	(200,000)	
Retained Earnings—Pepe Company	(350,000)	
Common Stock—Seda Company ($10 par)		(50,000)
Paid-In Capital in Excess of Par—Seda Company		(140,000)
Retained Earnings—Seda Company		(260,000)
Net Sales	(640,000)	(350,000)
Cost of Goods Sold	360,000	200,000
Operating Expenses	160,000	90,000
Dividend Income	(8,000)	(2,000)
Dividends Declared	40,000	10,000
Total	0	0

Required ▶ ▶ ▶ ▶ ▶

Complete the worksheet for consolidated financial statements for the year ended December 31, 20X2. Use the treasury stock method for the investment in Pepe Company. Round all computations to the nearest dollar. Include a determination and distribution of excess schedule and income distribution schedule.

Problem 8-10 *(LO 5)* **Worksheet, subsidiary owns parent shares through stock swap.** Assume the same facts as Problem 8-9 except that instead of acquiring parent shares for cash, the subsidiary issued 1,000 of its shares for 500 shares of the parent, Pepe Company. The parent shares had a market value of $100,000. Any added excess of cost will be attributed to goodwill.

The trial balances of Pepe and Seda have been revised for this change and are as follows on December 31, 20X2:

	Trial Balance	
	Pepe	Seda
Inventory	170,000	120,000
Other Current Assets	216,000	296,000
Investment in Seda Company	400,000	
Investment in Pepe Company		100,000
Land	80,000	70,000
Buildings and Equipment	400,000	280,000
Accumulated Depreciation	(180,000)	(90,000)
Current Liabilities	(98,000)	(74,000)
Long-Term Liabilities	(250,000)	(100,000)
Common Stock—Pepe Company ($10 par)	(100,000)	
Paid-In Capital in Excess of Par—Pepe Company	(200,000)	
Retained Earnings, January 1—Pepe Company	(350,000)	
Common Stock—Seda Company ($10 par)		(60,000)
Paid-In Capital in Excess of Par—Seda Company		(230,000)
Retained Earnings, January 1—Seda Company		(260,000)
Net Sales	(640,000)	(350,000)
Cost of Goods Sold	360,000	200,000
Operating Expenses	160,000	90,000
Dividend Income	(8,000)	(2,000)
Dividends Declared—Pepe Company	40,000	
Dividends Declared—Seda Company		10,000
Total	0	0

Required ▶ ▶ ▶ ▶ ▶

Prepare the consolidated worksheet necessary to produce consolidated financial statements on December 31, 20X2. Use the stock swap method for the investment in parent company shares. Round all calculations to the nearest dollar. Include determination and distribution of excess schedule, analysis of the effect of the subsidiary purchase of parent shares and income distribution schedules.

Problem 8-11 *(LO 5)* **Worksheet, purchase in blocks, subsidiary stock dividend, subsidiary purchase of parent shares, machinery sale, merchandise.** On January 1, 20X3, Heckert Company purchased a controlling interest in Allen Company. The following information is available:

a. Heckert Company purchased 1,600 shares of Allen Company outstanding stock on January 1, 20X2, for $48,000 and purchased an additional 1,400 shares on January 1, 20X3, for $52,000.

b. An analysis of the stockholders' equity accounts at December 31, 20X2, and 20X1, follows:

	Heckert Company December 31, 20X2	Heckert Company December 31, 20X1	Allen Company December 31, 20X2	Allen Company December 31, 20X1
Common stock ($10 par)	$150,000	$150,000		
Common stock ($5 par)			$ 20,000	$ 20,000
Paid-in capital in excess of par	36,000	36,000	10,000	10,000
Retained earnings	378,000	285,000	112,000	82,000
Total	$564,000	$471,000	$142,000	$112,000

c. Allen Company's marketable securities consist of 1,500 shares of Heckert Company stock purchased on June 15, 20X3, in the open market for $18,000. The securities were purchased as a temporary investment and were sold on January 15, 20X4, for $25,000.

d. On December 10, 20X3, Heckert Company declared a cash dividend of $0.50 per share, payable January 10, 20X4, to stockholders of record on December 20, 20X3. Allen Company paid a cash dividend of $1 per share on June 30, 20X3, and distributed a 10% stock dividend on September 30, 20X3. The stock was selling for $15 per share ex-dividend on September 30, 20X3. Allen Company paid no dividends in 20X2.

e. Allen Company sold machinery, with a book value of $4,000 and a remaining life of five years, to Heckert Company for $4,800 on December 31, 20X3. The gain on the sale was credited to the other income account.

f. Allen Company includes all intercompany receivables and payables in its trade accounts receivable and trade accounts payable accounts.

g. During 20X3, the following intercompany sales were made:

	Net Sales	Included in Purchaser's Inventory at December 31, 20X3
Heckert Company to Allen Company	$ 78,000	$24,300
Allen Company to Heckert Company	104,000	18,000
	$182,000	$42,300

Heckert Company sells merchandise to Allen Company at cost. Allen Company sells merchandise to Heckert at the regular selling price to make a normal profit margin of 30%. There were no intercompany sales in prior years.

The trial balances of the two companies at December 31, 20X3, are as follows:

	Heckert Company	Allen Company
Cash	37,900	29,050
Marketable Securities	33,000	18,000
Trade Accounts Receivable	210,000	88,000
Allowance for Doubtful Accounts	(6,800)	(2,300)
Intercompany Receivables	24,000	
Inventories	275,000	135,000
Machinery and Equipment	514,000	279,000
Accumulated Depreciation	(298,200)	(196,700)

(continued)

	Heckert Company	Allen Company
Investment in Allen Company (at cost)	100,000	
Patents	35,000	
Dividends Payable	(7,500)	
Trade Accounts Payable	(195,500)	(174,050)
Intercompany Payables	(8,000)	
Common Stock ($10 par)	(150,000)	
Common Stock ($5 par)		(22,000)
Paid-In Capital in Excess of Par	(36,000)	(14,000)
Retained Earnings	(370,500)	(102,000)
Sales and Services	(850,000)	(530,000)
Dividend Income	(3,000)	
Other Income	(9,000)	(3,700)
Cost of Goods Sold	510,000	374,000
Depreciation Expense	65,600	11,200
Administrative and Selling Expenses	130,000	110,500
Total	0	0

Required ▶ ▶ ▶ ▶ ▶ Prepare the worksheet necessary to produce the consolidated financial statements of Heckert Company and its subsidiary for the year ended December 31, 20X3. Include the determination and distribution of excess and income distribution schedules. Assume any excess of cost over book value is attributable to goodwill. For any mutual holdings, use the treasury stock method.
(AICPA adapted)

Leveraged Buyouts

SPECIAL APPENDIX

1

Learning Objectives

When you have completed this appendix, you should be able to

1. **Explain the 80% monetary consideration test.**
2. **Record a LBO that meets the 80% monetary consideration test.**
3. **Record LBOs that do not meet the 80% monetary consideration test.**

It has become a common occurrence to form a skeleton corporation for the sole purpose of acquiring a controlling interest in an existing corporation. Frequently, the management of the corporation to be acquired are the instigators of the acquisition. Some leveraged buyouts are financed in part by funds supplied by investment partnerships. A successful example of a leveraged buyout is offered by Harley Davidson Corporation, the only American manufacturer of motorcycles. Once a separate corporation, Harley Davidson was acquired by AMF Corporation. After several years of being a subsidiary, the Harley Davidson division was purchased by new investors, including employees, and again became a separate corporation.

When structured properly, a leveraged buyout follows purchase accounting principles. With only minor exceptions, the fair values of the assets and liabilities of the company subject to the leveraged buyout are recorded. In order to record assets and liabilities at fair value, there must be a change in control. The new control group does not have to be a single individual; it is sufficient to have a group of investors with a common interest act as a control group. The requirements for what constitutes a control group were issued by the Emerging Issues Task Force of the FASB in 1989.[1]

STOCK VALUATION

The most difficult accounting task in a leveraged buyout is to determine the total value available for assignment to the company's assets and liabilities. The total value is the sum of the value assigned to outstanding shares of common stock. Where there may be three blocks of stock, the three blocks are the fair value block, the equity-adjusted cost block, and the book value block. The number of shares included in each block is determined as follows.

Fair Value Block

1 OBJECTIVE

Explain the 80% monetary consideration test.

This block includes the shares owned by shareholders of the new control group *who were not owners* of the shares of the prior company. This block also may include the shares of some shareholders who owned shares of the prior company. In order to include a former shareholder's shares in the fair value block, one of two conditions must be met:

1 Highlights of Financial Reporting Issues, *Leveraged Buyouts: Emerging Issues Task Force Consensus Issue No. 88–16* (Norwalk: Financial Accounting Standards Board, May 1989).

1. The shareholder's new residual ownership interest must be greater than the residual ownership interest in the prior company. The shareholder's new residual ownership interest cannot, however, exceed 5%. The residual ownership interest includes all outstanding common and preferred shares except those shares that have liquidation or redemption features. This is different from the definition of ownership interest that includes only common shares.
2. If the former shareholder's residual interest percentage decreased, all the following requirements must be met to record the shares at fair value.

   a. The shareholder's voting interest in common stock must be under 20%.
   b. The individual must have supplied less than 20% of the new company's total capital including debt.[2]
   c. The shareholder's new residual ownership interest must be less than 5%, and all former owners whose residual ownership interest decreased must have a new residual interest of less than 20%.

There is a limitation on the number of shares included in the fair value block; it is based on the amount of monetary consideration given to owners of the former company. Monetary consideration includes cash, debt, and debt-type securities such as mandatory redeemable preferred stock. If at least 80% of the consideration given to all shareholders (including continuing shareholders) is monetary, there is no limitation on the fair value block. If monetary consideration is under 80% of the total, the fair value block is limited to the monetary consideration percentage times the total common shares outstanding. Thus, for example, if the percentage of shares that would otherwise qualify was 90%, but monetary consideration given for common shares was 70%, the fair value block would be limited to 70% of the outstanding shares. The nonqualifying 20% interest would be assigned book value.

Equity-Adjusted Cost Block

Shares of continuing shareholders who owned shares of the former company are recorded at their simple-equity-adjusted cost unless they meet the above requirements for inclusion in the fair value block. The shareholders whose interest does not qualify for inclusion in the fair value block are termed "continuing shareholders."

Book Value Block

These are the shares that would otherwise be included in the fair value block but are excluded because of the 80% monetary consideration test. Recall the prior example where 90% of the shares otherwise qualified for the fair value block, but only 70% of the consideration was monetary. The excluded 20% of the shares would be valued at current book value.

2

OBJECTIVE

Record a LBO that meets the 80% monetary consideration test.

Acquisition Meeting the 80% Monetary Consideration Test

As an example of a leveraged buyout's meeting the 80% monetary consideration test, assume Former Company had the following balance sheet on the date it is acquired by a new ownership group, New Company:

Assets		Liabilities and Equity	
Current assets	$100,000	Liabilities	$ 80,000
Land and buildings (net)	200,000	Common stock (10,000 shares, $2 par)	20,000
Equipment (net)	50,000	Paid-in capital in excess of par	70,000
		Retained earnings	180,000
Total assets	$350,000	Total liabilities and equity	$350,000

2 This test is applied in steps starting with common stock and proceeding to each lesser risk security. The test may be passed at any level. See Highlights of Financial Reporting Issues, *Leveraged Buyouts: Emerging Issues Task Force Consensus Issue No. 88–16.*

The fair values of Former Company's assets and liabilities equal book value, except for the land and buildings which have a fair value of $300,000. The fair value of Former Company shares is $40 each. 10,000 shares of Former Company are acquired as follows:

1. 2,000 New Company shares are exchanged for 1,000 Former Company shares. These 1,000 shares are owned by continuing shareholders who are members of the new control group. These shares do not meet the tests required to be included in the fair value block and must be recorded at simple-equity-adjusted cost. Their equity-adjusted cost for Former Company shares is $38. The shares originally were purchased for $30 when the retained earnings of Former Company were $100,000.
2. 500 Former Company shares are received in exchange for 1,000 New Company shares from parties that are former owners but are not members of the new control group. The shares do meet the criteria to be included in the fair value block.
3. The remaining 8,500 Former Company shares are purchased for $340,000 cash from shareholders that are not owners of the new company.

Monetary consideration was used to acquire 85% of Former Company shares. Since this exceeds the required 80% level, the entire interest acquired from shareholders who are not considered continuing members is recorded at fair value. The value to be assigned to the net assets is calculated as follows:

Fair Value Block:		
8,500	shares acquired for cash at $40 fair value	$340,000
500	shares acquired in exchange for 1,000 New Company shares from parties that are not continuing members at $40 fair value	20,000
	Total fair value	$360,000
Equity-Adjusted Cost Block:		
1,000	shares acquired in exchange for 2,000 New Company shares from continuing shareholders at $38 simple-equity-adjusted cost	38,000
	Total	$398,000

The determination and distribution of excess schedule would be prepared as follows for the 90% interest acquired from former shareholders that are not continuing members:

Price paid, 9,000 × $40		$360,000
Interest acquired:		
Stockholders' equity	$270,000	
Percentage	× 90%	243,000
Excess of cost over book value		$117,000
Land and buildings, 90% × $100,000		90,000
Goodwill		$ 27,000

The determination and distribution of excess schedule would be prepared as follows for the 10% interest acquired from continuing shareholders:

Simple-equity-adjusted cost, 1,000 × $38		$38,000
Interest acquired:		
Stockholders' equity	$270,000	
Percentage	× 10%	27,000
Excess of cost over book value		$11,000
Land and buildings, 10% × $100,000		10,000
Goodwill		$ 1,000

Separate determination and distribution of excess schedules are recommended for each block since it is possible to have one of the schedules indicate a bargain purchase that would not allow full recognition of fair values for long-term fixed assets. If the two blocks were combined into a single determination and distribution of excess schedule, goodwill from one block could offset a bargain on another.

The entries to record the formation of New Company and to acquire Former Company are as follows:

Formation of New Company		
Cash	40,000	
Common Stock, No Par (2,000 shares × $20)		40,000
Borrowing of $300,000		
Cash	300,000	
Long-Term Debt		300,000
Acquisition of Former Company		
Current Assets	100,000	
Land and Buildings ($200,000 + $90,000 + $10,000)	300,000	
Equipment	50,000	
Goodwill ($27,000 + $1,000)	28,000	
Liabilities		80,000
Cash		340,000
Common Stock, No Par (3,000 shares in exchange for 500 Former shares × $40 and 1,000 Former shares × $38)		58,000

3

OBJECTIVE

Record LBOs that do not meet the 80% monetary consideration test.

Acquisition Not Meeting the 80% Monetary Consideration Test

Let us revise the previous example slightly:

1. Instead of borrowing $300,000, only $240,000 is borrowed.
2. Instead of acquiring 8,500 shares for cash from parties that are not members of the new control group, assume 6,500 shares are acquired for cash at $40 each and a total of 2,500 shares is acquired by exchanging 5,000 shares of New Company common stock; 2,000 New Company shares are still being issued to former shareholders that are part of the new control group in exchange for 1,000 Former Company shares.

Now only 65% (6,500 for cash ÷ 10,000 total shares acquired) of the shares are acquired in exchange for cash and can be recorded at fair value. The remaining 2,000 shares acquired from parties that were not continuing members of Former Company are recorded at book value. The value assigned to the net assets is calculated as follows:

Fair Value Block:		
6,500	shares acquired for cash at $40 market value	$260,000
Equity-Adjusted Cost Block:		
1,000	shares acquired in exchange for 2,000 New Company shares from continuing members of Former Company; at $38 simple-equity-adjusted cost	38,000
Book Value Block:		
2,500	shares acquired in exchange for 5,000 New Company shares from Former Company shareholders who are not a part of the new control group at book value of $27 per share ($270,000 total equity ÷ 10,000 shares)	67,500
	Total	$365,500

A determination and distribution of excess schedule would be prepared for the 65% interest acquired for cash as follows:

Price paid, 6,500 × $40		$260,000
Interest acquired:		
Stockholders' equity	$270,000	
Percentage	× 65%	175,500
Excess of cost over book value		$ 84,500
Land and buildings, 65% × $100,000		65,000
Goodwill		$ 19,500

The determination and distribution of excess schedule for the 1,000 shares acquired from continuing shareholders is unchanged.

Simple-equity-adjusted cost, 1,000 × $38		$38,000
Interest acquired:		
Stockholder's equity	$270,000	
Percentage	× 10%	27,000
Excess of cost over book value		$11,000
Land and buildings, 10% × $100,000		10,000
Goodwill		$ 1,000

There would be no adjustment to fair value for the 2,000 shares acquired from noncontinuing shareholders in exchange for New Company shares.

The entries to record the formation of New Company and acquire Former Company are as follows:

Formation of New Company		
Cash	40,000	
Common Stock, No Par (2,000 shares)		40,000
Borrowing of $240,000		
Cash	240,000	
Long-Term Debt		240,000
Acquisition of Former Company		
Current Assets	100,000	
Land and Buildings ($200,000 + $65,000 + $10,000)	275,000	
Equipment	50,000	
Goodwill ($19,500 + $1,000)	20,500	
Liabilities		80,000
Cash (6,500 × $40)		260,000
Common Stock, No Par (7,000 shares in exchange for 2,500 Former shares × $27 and 1,000 Former shares × $38)		105,500

REFLECTION

- When the 80% monetary consideration test is met, the total price includes stock obtained from noncontinuing members at fair value. Shares of continuing members are at equity-adjusted cost.
- When the 80% monetary consideration test is not met, the total price includes stock obtained from noncontinuing members at book value. Shares of continuing members are at equity-adjusted cost.

SPECIAL APPENDIX UNDERSTANDING THE ISSUES

1. A leveraged buyout that meets the 80% monetary consideration test may not allow the recognition of fair values for the interest acquired from shareholders of the predecessor company. Under what conditions is the interest of former company shareholders recorded at fair value? If fair value is not allowed, at what value are the shares recorded?
2. Some of the interest acquired in a leveraged buyout may have to be recorded at the underlying book value of the former company. Under what conditions does this occur?
3. Lever Company was formed to purchase all of the outstanding shares of Ancient Company in a leveraged buyout. Eighty-five percent of the outstanding Ancient shares were purchased for cash from persons not part of the new control group. The remaining shares were purchased from individuals who would qualify as continuing shareholders who are members of the new control group. What procedures would you follow to assign values to the assets of Ancient Company?

SPECIAL APPENDIX EXERCISES

Exercise SA-1 *(LO 1)* **Examples that do and do not meet the 80% test.** Modum Corporation was formed on January 1, 20X1, by issuing 4,000 shares of $10 par stock for $20 per share. Modum Corporation is going to engage in a leveraged buyout of Antique Company. Antique Company had the following stockholders' equity on January 1, 20X1:

Common stock ($10 par, 10,000 shares outstanding)	$100,000
Paid-in capital in excess of par	150,000
Retained earnings	80,000
Total equity	$330,000

The fair value of Antique Company shares is $40 each. 1,000 Antique shares will be acquired from continuing members of Antique Company's control group in exchange for 2,000 Modum Corporation shares. The equity-adjusted cost of the control group's shares is $25 per share. Calculate the total cost of Antique Company under each of the following assumptions:

1. Modum Corporation borrows $280,000 and purchases for $40 each the remaining 9,000 shares held by parties outside the control group of Antique Company.
2. Modum Corporation borrows $240,000 and purchases 8,000 noncontrol group shares for $40 each. Modum issues 2,000 of its shares in exchange for 1,000 Antique Company shares held by noncontrol group members.
3. Modum Corporation borrows $200,000 and purchases 7,000 noncontrol group shares for $40 each. Modum issues 4,000 of its shares in exchange for 2,000 Antique Company shares held by noncontrol group members.

Exercise SA-2 *(LO 3)* **LBO does not meet 80% test.** Old Time Company has the following balance sheet on January 1, 20X1, when it is the target of a leveraged buyout by Hercules Corporation:

Assets		Stockholders' Equity	
Cash	$ 50,000	Common stock ($5 par, 10,000 shares)	$ 50,000
Inventory	100,000	Paid-in capital in excess of par	160,000
Property and plant	200,000	Retained earnings	140,000
Total assets	$350,000	Total equity	$350,000

The property and plant have a fair value of $230,000.

Hercules Corporation incorporated by issuing 3,000 shares of $10 par common stock for $40 each. The company also borrowed $160,000 from long-term lenders. The leveraged buyout was accomplished as follows:

1,000	shares exchanged on a 1-to-1 basis with continuing members of the old control group. The equity-adjusted cost per share for these shares was $38. These shares do not need the criteria to be included in the fair value block.
2,000	shares exchanged on a 1-to-1 basis with noncontrol group members.
7,000	shares of Old Time purchased from noncontrol group members for $40 per share.

Prepare the balance sheet of Hercules Corporation immediately after the leveraged buyout. Provide supporting calculations in good form.

SPECIAL APPENDIX PROBLEM

Problem SA-1 *(LO 3)* **LBO, 80% test not met.** Newtone Corporation was formed on January 1, 20X5. The shareholder group issued 4,000 shares of $10 par common stock for $25 per share. The company was formed by an employee group to purchase Oldtime (a subsidiary of Gigantic Corporation) which had the following balance sheet on the January 3, 20X5, acquisition date:

Assets		Liabilities and Stockholders' Equity	
Cash	$ 60,000	Bonds payable	$150,000
Inventory	130,000	Common stock ($10 par)	100,000
Accounts receivable	40,000	Paid-in capital in excess of par	120,000
Equipment	75,000	Retained earnings	85,000
Building (net)	120,000		
Land	30,000	Total liabilities and	
Total assets	$455,000	stockholders' equity	$455,000

The fair values differed from book values in the case of the inventory, equipment, and building which were appraised at $150,000, $100,000, and $200,000, respectively.

The fair value of Newtone stock is $25 per share. 2,000 Newtone shares were exchanged for 1,000 Oldtime shares with parties who were continuing members of the control group of Oldtime. These shares do not qualify for inclusion in the fair value block. The equity-adjusted cost of the shares held by Oldtime's control group was $45 per share. These individuals also will be part of the control group of Newtone. The 9,000 remaining shares of Oldtime were acquired from parties that are not part of Newtone's control group.

◀◀◀◀◀ **Required**

1. Assume Newtone borrowed $250,000 on a long-term note. Newtone then paid $50 per share for 7,000 shares of Oldtime and issued 4,000 of its shares in exchange for 2,000 Oldtime shares. Prepare all entries to record the formation of Newtone Corporation, the borrowing, and the buyout of Oldtime. Include a support schedule for the values assigned to the accounts.
2. Assume Newtone borrowed $300,000 on a long-term note. Newtone then paid $50 per share for 8,000 shares of Oldtime and issued 2,000 of its shares in exchange for 1,000 Oldtime shares. Prepare all entries to record the formation of Newtone Corporation, the borrowing, and the buyout of Oldtime. Include a support schedule for the values assigned to the accounts.

Suggestion: Be sure to determine if the 80% test is met in each case before proceeding to assign values to the accounts.

SPECIAL APPENDIX 2

Analysis of FASB Exposure Drafts for Business Combinations by Impact on Chapters 1–8

Learning Objective

When you have completed this appendix, you will understand the changes that are likely to occur for accounting for business combinations.

On June 30, 2005, the FASB issued two exposure drafts that have a major impact on the accounting methods used for business combinations. The Exposure Drafts are:

- Consolidated Financial Statements, Including Accounting and Reporting of Noncontrolling Interests in Subsidiaries – a replacement of ARB No. 51.
- Business Combinations – a replacement of FASB Statement No. 141.

Under the new procedures, all identifiable assets and liabilities will be recorded at full fair value regardless of the price paid for the interest or the size of the controlling interest. A price above the net fair value of the identifiable assets results in goodwill. A lesser price results in a gain.

The accounts of the subsidiary will be adjusted to full fair value only once, the date control is achieved. Any change in the controlling interest that does not cause a loss of control is viewed as an equity transaction with no impact on income.

Consolidated income will be defined as the income of the entire entity, which will then be allocated to the controlling interest and the NCI. The NCI will be displayed on the balance sheet as a portion of stockholders' equity.

SUMMARY OF MAJOR CHANGES

1 OBJECTIVE

Business combinations: Purchase Method Procedures (including Combinations Between Mutual Enterprises) and Certain Issues Related to the Accounting for and Reporting of Noncontrolling (Minority) Interests (as of March 8, 2005)

- Identifiable assets and liabilities of the acquired company will always be recorded at fair value using the guidance of the Exposure Draft on Fair Value Measurements. A price above the sum of the fair values of the net identifiable assets results in goodwill. A price below the sum of the fair values of the net identifiable assets results in a gain (not extraordinary).
- All value measurements are made on the "acquisition date." This is the date that control is transferred to the buyer. This may be a date other than the closing date if there is an agreement to that effect.
- All acquisition costs are expensed; none are included in the price paid.
- Any liability for contingent consideration must be estimated and included in the price paid. Later adjustments affect income of later periods. Goodwill is not adjusted upon the payment of later consideration.
- When there is a less than 100% purchase, all subsidiary accounts are adjusted to 100% of fair value in the consolidation process. The NCI (noncontrolling interest) shares in the fair value adjustments. Goodwill is also attributed to the NCI. It is presumed that the goodwill would be proportional to that recorded on the controlling interest, unless it can be demonstrated that the price reflects a control premium. In that case, the goodwill applicable to the NCI would be separately determined.
- The current text presentation of NCI is affirmed. The NCI portion of equity is included as a single amount in the equity section of the consolidated balance sheet. The income statement must show consolidated net income and then the distribution to the controlling interest and the NCI. The distribution of other comprehensive income to the controlling interest and NCI must also be disclosed. It should be noted that for most companies, the current practice is to treat the NCI as a liability or to locate it in the "mezzanine" between debt and equity.

Currently, the NCI portion of consolidated net income is often shown as an expense and consolidated net income refers to only the controlling share of income.

- Procedures for block purchases are new. When control is achieved and there is a prior noncontrolling interest, that prior interest is adjusted to fair value and is added to the price paid for the later block to form a combined single block. When control exists at the time of the purchase of a new block, the transaction is viewed as an equity transaction, with no impact on income.
- Procedures for the sale of a controlling interest not resulting in a loss of control follow an alternative that is included in the current text. The difference between the sales price and the carrying value is an adjustment to equity and does not create an income statement gain or loss.
- When a portion of the controlling interest is sold and results in a loss of control, there is also a change. The text records a gain or loss on only the shares sold. Now the gain or loss would include the adjustment to fair value of the remaining shares held by the parent.

CHANGES AS THEY IMPACT EACH CHAPTER

Chapter 1

It is presumed that the fair value of the consideration given determines the fair value of the company purchased. If, however, the value of the consideration given is not clear, the fair value of the business acquired must be estimated using fair value measurements. The FASB Exposure Draft on Fair Value Measurement provides guidance in estimating the fair value of the business.

All identifiable assets and liabilities will be recorded at fair value using the new guidance on fair values that will result from the FASB Exposure Draft on Fair Value Measurement.

In-process R&D is to be estimated and included as an asset. The in-process R&D value cannot be increased for expenditures after the acquisition date. The amount assigned to in-process R&D is to be impairment tested in future periods.

Contingent gains and losses of the acquired business, which would otherwise not be recorded, are to be estimated at fair value.

There will be no discounting of assets in a bargain purchase. If the price paid is less than the sum of the fair values of the net identifiable assets, a gain (not extraordinary) is recorded on the purchase. There is to be a close evaluation of fair values before a gain is recorded.

All acquisition costs, including direct acquisition costs (added to cost in the past), are to be expensed. No mention is made of issue costs. Presumably, they would follow the normal practice of reducing the value assigned to the securities issued (current practice).

Where there is contingent consideration, an estimated liability should be recorded for the estimated fair value of the amount to be paid. Any change in that estimate impacts income of later periods. There can be no recording of added goodwill subsequent to the acquisition date. It would appear that the procedure for contingencies based on the share price of the issuer would remain the same since they do not affect the amount paid for the acquired firm.

Application Example. Let us assume that the company to be acquired by Acquisitions Inc. has the following balance sheet.

Johnson Company
Balance Sheet
December 31, 20X1

Cash	$ 40,000	Current liabilities	$ 25,000
Marketable investments	60,000	8%, 5-year bond payable	100,000
Inventory	100,000	Total liabilities	$125,000
Equipment (net)	80,000		
Land	30,000	Common stock, $1 par	$ 10,000
Buildings (net)	150,000	Paid-in capital in excess of par	140,000
		Retained earnings	185,000
		Total equity	$335,000
Total assets	$460,000	Liabilities plus equity	$460,000

Note 1: A customer list with significant value exists.
Note 2: There is an unrecorded warranty liability on prior product sales.

Fair values for all accounts have been established in conformity with the FASB Exposure Draft on Fair Value Measurement as follows:

Account	Method of Estimation	Fair Value
Cash	Book value	$ 40,000
Marketable investment	Level 1—market value	66,000
Inventory	Level 1—market value	110,000
Equipment	Level 1—market value	145,000
Land	Level 2—adjusted market value	72,000
Buildings	Level 2—adjusted market value	288,000
Customer list	Level 3—other estimate, discounted cash flow	123,300
Current liabilities	Book value	(25,000)
Bonds payable		(100,000)
Premium on bonds payable	Level 3—other estimate, discounted cash flow	(4,100)
Warranty liability	Level 3—other estimate, discounted cash flow	(11,912)
Fair value of net identifiable assets		$ 703,288

Recording the Purchase. The price paid for the company being purchased is normally measured as the sum of the consideration (total assets) exchanged for the business. This would be the sum of the cash, other assets, debt securities issued, and any stock issued by the acquiring company. In a rare case, the fair value of the company being purchased may be more determinable than the consideration given. This could be the case where stock is issued which is not publicly traded and the fair value of the business acquired is more measurable.

The basic procedures to record the purchase are:

- **All accounts identified are measured at estimated fair value** as demonstrated above. This is true even if the consideration given for a company is less than the sum of the fair values of the net assets (assets minus liabilities assumed, $703,288 in above example).
- If the total consideration given for a company **exceeds the fair value** of its net identifiable assets ($703,288), the excess price paid is recorded as **Goodwill.**
- In a rare case, where total consideration given for a company **is less than the fair value** of its net identifiable assets ($703,288), the excess of the net assets over the price paid is recorded as a **gain** in the period of the purchase.
- **All acquisition costs are expensed** in the period of the purchase. These costs could include the fees of accountants and lawyers that were necessary to negotiate and consummate the purchase. In the past, these costs were included as part of the price paid for the company purchased.

Examples of Recording a Purchase. Prior to attempting to record a purchase, an analysis should be made comparing the price paid for the company with the fair value of the net assets acquired.

- If the price exceeds the sum of the fair value of the net identifiable assets acquired, the excess price is **goodwill.**
- If the price is less than the sum of the fair value of the net identifiable assets acquired, the price deficiency is a **gain.**

1. Price paid **exceeds fair value** of net identifiable assets acquired.

   Acquisitions Inc. issues 40,000 shares of its $1 par value common stock shares with a market value of $20 each for Johnson Company, illustrated above. Acquisitions Inc. pays related acquisition costs of $35,000.

   Value analysis:

Total price paid (consideration given), 40,000 shares × $20 market value	$ 800,000
Total fair value of net assets acquired from Johnson Company	(703,288)
Goodwill	$ 96,712
Expense acquisition costs	35,000

Entries to record purchase and related costs are as follows:

	Dr.	Cr.
To record purchase of net assets:		
Cash	40,000	
Marketable Investments	66,000	
Inventory	110,000	
Equipment	145,000	
Land	72,000	
Buildings	288,000	
Customer List	123,300	
Goodwill	**96,712**	
Current Liabilities		25,000
Bonds Payable		100,000
Premium on Bonds Payable		4,100
Warranty Liability		11,912
Common Stock, $1 par, 40,000 shares issued		40,000
Paid-In Capital in Excess of Par ($20 per share × 40,000 shares less $40,000 assigned to par)		760,000
Dr. = Cr. Check totals	*941,012*	*941,012*
To record acquisition costs:		
Acquisition Expense	35,000	
Cash		35,000

2. Price paid is **less than fair value** of net identifiable assets acquired.

   Acquisitions Inc. issues 25,000 shares of its $1 par value common stock shares with a market value of $20 each for Johnson Company, illustrated above. Acquisitions Inc. pays related acquisition costs of $35,000.

   Value analysis:

Total price paid (consideration given), 25,000 shares × $20 market value	$ 500,000
Total fair value of net assets acquired from Johnson Company	(703,288)
Gain on purchase of business	$ 203,288
Expense acquisition costs	35,000

Entries to record purchase and related costs are as follows:

	Dr.	Cr.
To record purchase of net assets:		
Cash	40,000	
Marketable Investments	66,000	
Inventory	110,000	
Equipment	145,000	
Land	72,000	
Buildings	288,000	
Customer List	123,300	
Current Liabilities		25,000
Bonds Payable		100,000
Premium on Bonds Payable		4,100
Warranty Liability		11,912
Common Stock, $1 par, 25,000 shares issued		25,000
Paid-In Capital in Excess of Par ($20 per share × 25,000 shares less $25,000 assigned to par		475,000
Gain on Purchase of Business		**203,288**
Dr. = Cr. Check Totals	*844,300*	*844,300*

To record acquisition costs:		
Acquisition Expense	35,000	
Cash		35,000

CHAPTER 1 EXERCISES AND PROBLEMS

Exercise SA1-1 Bargain purchase. Carp Corporation is purchasing the net assets of Bass Company on December 31, 20X6, when Bass Company has the following balance sheet:

Assets		Liabilities and Equity	
Current assets	$100,000	Liabilities	$ 90,000
Land	50,000	Common stock ($10 par)	200,000
Buildings (net)	200,000	Retained earnings	140,000
Equipment (net)	60,000		
Patents	20,000		
Total assets	$430,000	Total liabilities and equity	$430,000

Carp has obtained the following fair values for Bass Company accounts:

Current assets	$120,000
Land	80,000
Buildings	250,000
Equipment	150,000
Patents	20,000
Liabilities	92,000

Direct acquisition costs are $18,000, and indirect acquisition costs are $5,000.

Prepare the entries to record the purchase of Bass Company assuming the cash payment by Carp Corporation to Bass Company is $400,000. Carp Corporation will assume the liabilities of Bass Company. Value analysis is recommended.

Problem SA1-1 Alternate consideration, bargain. Kent Corporation is considering the purchase of Williams Incorporated. Kent has asked you, its accountant, to evaluate the various offers it might make to Williams Incorporated. The December 31, 20X1, balance sheet of Williams is as follows:

Williams Incorporated
Balance Sheet
December 31, 20X1

Assets			Liabilities and Equity		
Current assets:			Accounts payable		$ 40,000
Accounts receivable	$ 50,000				
Inventory	300,000				
		$350,000	Stockholders' equity:		
Noncurrent assets:			Common stock	$ 40,000	
Land	$ 20,000		Paid-in capital in excess of par	110,000	
Building (net)	70,000	90,000	Retained earnings	250,000	400,000
Total assets		$440,000	Total liabilities and equity		$440,000

The following fair values differ from existing book values:

Inventory	$250,000
Land	40,000
Building	120,000

Required ▶ ▶ ▶ ▶ ▶ Record the purchase entry for Kent Corporation that would result under each of the alternative offers. Value analysis is suggested.

1. Kent Corporation issues 20,000 of its $10 par common stock with a fair value of $25 per share for the net assets of Williams Incorporated.
2. Kent Corporation pays $385,000 in cash.

CHAPTER 2

The price paid by the parent company for the controlling interest will no longer include direct acquisition costs, as they are expensed at purchase date.

We will illustrate consolidation procedures using the 80% acquisition of Sample Company by Parental Inc. Presented below are the balance sheet amounts and the fair values of the assets and liabilities of Sample Company as of December 31, 20X1.

Assets	Book Value	Market Value		Book Value	Market Value
Accounts receivable	20,000	20,000	Current liabilities	40,000	40,000
Inventory	50,000	55,000	Bonds payable	100,000	100,000
Land	40,000	70,000	**Total liabilities**	**140,000**	**140,000**
Buildings	200,000	250,000			
Accumulated depreciation	(50,000)		**Stockholders' equity:**		
Equipment	60,000	60,000	Common stock, $1 par	10,000	
Accumulated depreciation	(20,000)		Paid-in excess of par	90,000	
Copyright		50,000	Retained earnings	100,000	
Goodwill	40,000	TBD	Total equity	200,000	
Total assets	**340,000**	**505,000**	**Net assets**	**200,000**	**365,000**

Assume that Parental Inc. issued 16,800 shares of its $1 par value common stock for 80% (8,000 shares) of the outstanding shares of Sample Company. The fair value of a share of Parental Inc. stock is $25. Parental also pays $20,000 in accounting and legal fees to accomplish the purchase. Parental would make the following entry to record the purchase:

	Dr.	Cr.
To record the purchase:		
Investment in Sample Company (16,800 shares issued × $25 fair value)	420,000	
Common Stock, $1 par value (16,800 shares × $1 par)		16,800
Paid-In Capital in Excess of Par ($420,000 – $16,800 par value)		403,200
To record the costs of the acquisition:		
Acquisition Expense (closed to retained earnings since we are examining only balance sheets)	20,000	
Cash		20,000

The separate "zone" and "price" analyses of the current text will be replaced by a single "valuation analysis" for the entire entity. The following "value analysis" would be prepared for the 80% interest:

Value Analysis Schedule

	Parent Price (80%)	NCI Value (20%)	Company Fair Value
1. Company fair value	$420,000	$105,000	$525,000
2. Fair value of net assets **excluding goodwill**	292,000	73,000	365,000
3. Goodwill—Fair value of company exceeds fair value of net assets excluding goodwill	128,000	32,000	160,000
4. Gain—Parent price is less than the parent share of fair value of net assets excluding goodwill	N/A	N/A	N/A

Several assumptions went into the above calculation:

- Line 1, Company fair value—It is assumed that if the parent would pay $420,000 for an 80% interest, then the entire subsidiary company is worth $525,000 ($420,000/80%). We will refer to this as the "implied value" of the subsidiary company. Assuming this to be true, the NCI is worth 20% of the total subsidiary company value (20% × $525,000 = $105,000). This approach assumes that the price the parent would pay is directly proportional to the size of the interest purchased. We will later study the situation where this presumption is defeated.
- Line 2, Fair value of net assets **excluding goodwill**—The fair values of the subsidiary accounts are from the comparison of book and fair values. All identifiable liabilities and all liabilities will be adjusted to 100% of fair value regardless of the size of the controlling interest purchased.
- Line 3, Goodwill—The total goodwill is the excess of the "Company Fair Value" over the fair value of the subsidiary net assets. It is proportionately allocated to the controlling interest and NCI.

Determination and Distribution of Excess Schedule

The D&D schedules in the existing text only analyze, and adjust to fair value, the controlling interest. The D&D must be modified to also revalue the NCI based on the price paid for the controlling interest. The D&D that follows revalues the entire entity, including the NCI.

Determination and Distribution of Excess Schedule

	Implied Company Value	Parent Price	NCI Value	Worksheet Distribution
Fair value of subsidiary	525,000	420,000	105,000	
Less book value interest acquired:				
Common stock, $1 par	10,000			
Paid-in excess of par	90,000			
Retained earnings	100,000			
Total equity	200,000			
Interest acquired		80.00%	20.00%	
Book value		160,000	40,000	
Excess of fair value over book value	325,000	260,000	65,000	

(continued)

	Implied Company Value	Parent Price	NCI Value	Worksheet Distribution
Adjustment of identifiable accounts:				
Inventory ($55,000 fair – $50,000 book value)	**5,000**		—	**debit D1**
Land ($70,000 fair – $40,000 book value)	**30,000**		—	**debit D2**
Buildings ($250,000 – $150,000 net book value)	**100,000**		—	**debit D3**
Equipment ($60,000 fair – $40,000 net book value)	**20,000**		—	**debit D4**
Copyright ($50,000 fair – $0 book value)	**50,000**			**debit D5**
Goodwill ($160,000 fair – $40,000 book value)	**120,000**			**debit D6**
Gain (not applicable)	—	—	—	
Total	**325,000**			

Note the following features of the revised D&D schedule:

- The "fair value of subsidiary" line contains the implied value of the entire company, the parent price paid, and the implied value of the NCI from the above "Value Analysis" schedule.
- The total stockholders' equity of the subsidiary (equal to the net assets of the subsidiary at book value) is allocated 80/20 to the controlling interest and the NCI.
- The excess of fair value over book value is shown for the company, the controlling interest, and the NCI. This line means that the entire adjustment of subsidiary net assets will be $325,000. The controlling interest paid $260,000 more than the underlying book value of subsidiary net assets. This is the excess that will appear on the worksheet when the parent's 80% share of subsidiary stockholders' equity is eliminated against the investment account. Finally, the NCI share of the increase to fair value is $65,000.
- All subsidiary assets and liabilities will be increased to 100% of fair value, just as would be the case for a 100% purchase.
- Goodwill will be adjusted by the $120,000 difference between the new estimated goodwill ($160,000) and that which is already recorded ($40,000).

The D&D provides complete guidance for the worksheet eliminations. Study Worksheet A2-1 on page 531 and note the following:

Worksheet A2-1: page 531

- Elimination "EL" eliminated the subsidiary equity purchased (80% in this example) against the investment account as follows:

(EL)	Common Stock, $1 par, Sample	8,000	
	Paid-In Excess of Par, Sample	72,000	
	Retained Earnings, Sample	80,000	
	Investment in Sample Company		160,000

- The "D" series eliminations distribute the excess applicable to the controlling interest plus the increase in the NCI (labeled "NCI") to the appropriate accounts, as indicated by the D&D schedule. The adjustment of the NCI is carried to subsidiary retained earnings. Recall, however, that only the total NCI will appear on the consolidated balance sheet. Worksheet eliminations are as follows:

(D1)	Inventory	5,000
(D2)	Land	30,000
(D3)	Buildings	100,000
(D4)	Equipment	20,000
(D5)	Copyright	50,000

(D6)	Goodwill ($160,000 total − $40,000 existing goodwill)	120,000	
(D)	Investment in Sample Company (remaining excess after "EL")		260,000
(NCI)	Retained Earnings – Sample (NCI share of fair market adjustment)		65,000
	Check Totals	*325,000*	*325,000*

The amounts that will appear on the consolidated balance sheet are shown in the final column of Worksheet A2-1. The components of the NCI are summed and presented as a single amount in the balance sheet column. Notice that we have consolidated the 100% of the fair values of subsidiary accounts with the existing book values of parent company accounts. The balance sheet columns of the worksheet will show the components of controlling equity (par, paid-in excess, and retained earnings) and the total NCI.

Formal Balance Sheet

The formal consolidated balance sheet resulting from the 80% purchase of Sample Company, in exchange for 16,800 Parental shares, has been taken from the balance sheet column of Worksheet A2-1.

Parental Inc.
Consolidated Balance Sheet
December 31, 20X1

Assets			Liabilities and Equity		
Current assets:			Current liabilities	$120,000	
Cash	$ 84,000		Bonds payable	300,000	
Accounts receivable	92,000		Total liabilities		$ 420,000
Inventory	135,000				
Total		$ 311,000			
Long-term assets:			Stockholders' equity:		
Land	$ 170,000		Common stock, $1 par	$ 36,800	
Buildings	800,000		Paid-in capital in excess of par	603,200	
Accumulated depreciation	(130,000)		Retained earnings	456,000	
Equipment	320,000		Total controlling equity		1,096,000
Accumulated depreciation	(60,000)		Noncontrolling interest	105,000	
Copyright (net)	50,000		Total Equity		1,201,000
Goodwill (net)	160,000				
Total		1,310,000			
Total assets		$1,621,000	Total liabilities and equity		$1,621,000

Adjustment of Goodwill Applicable to NCI

The NCI goodwill value can be reduced below its implied value if there is evidence that the implied value exceeds the real fair value of the NCI's share of goodwill. This could occur when a parent pays a premium to achieve control, which is not dependent on the size of the ownership interest.

The NCI share of goodwill could be reduced to zero, but the NCI share of the fair value of net tangible assets is never reduced. The total NCI can **never be less than the NCI percentage of the fair value of the net assets** (in this case, it cannot be less than 20% × $365,000 = $73,000).

If the fair value of the NCI was estimated to be $90,000 ($15,000 less than the value implied by parent purchase price), the Value Analysis would be modified as follows (changes are boldfaced):

Value Analysis Schedule

	Parent Price (80%)	NCI Value (20%)	Company Fair Value
1. Company fair value	$420,000	**$90,000**	**$510,000**
2. Fair value of net assets **excluding goodwill**	292,000	73,000	365,000
3. Goodwill—Fair value of company exceeds fair value of net assets excluding goodwill	128,000	17,000	**145,000**
4. Gain—Parent price is less than the parent share of fair value of net assets excluding goodwill	N/A		

Several assumptions went into the above calculation:

- Line 1, Company fair value—This is now the sum of the price paid by the parent plus the newly estimated fair value of the NCI.
- Line 2, Fair value of net assets **excluding goodwill**—The fair values of the subsidiary accounts are from the comparison of book and fair values. These values are never less than fair value.
- Line 3, Goodwill—The total goodwill is the excess of the "Company Fair Value" over the fair value of the subsidiary net assets.

The revised D&D schedule with changes (from the previous example) in boldfaced type would be:

Determination and Distribution of Excess Schedule

	Company Value	Parent Price	NCI Value	Worksheet Distribution
Fair value of subsidiary	**510,000**	420,000	**90,000**	
Less book value interest acquired:				
Common stock, $1 par	10,000			
Paid-in excess of par	90,000			
Retained earnings	100,000			
Total equity	200,000			
Interest acquired		80.00%	20.00%	
Book value		160,000	40,000	
Excess of fair value over book value	**310,000**	260,000	**50,000**	
Adjustment of identifiable accounts:				
Inventory ($55,000 fair – $50,000 book value)	5,000		—	debit D1
Land ($70,000 fair – $40,000 book value)	30,000		—	debit D2
Buildings ($250,000 – $150,000 net book value)	100,000		—	debit D3
Equipment ($60,000 fair – $40,000 net book value)	20,000		—	debit D4
Copyright ($50,000 fair – $0 book value)	50,000			debit D5
Goodwill (**$145,000** fair – $40,000 book value)	**105,000**			debit D6
Gain (not applicable)	—	—	—	
Total	**310,000**			

If goodwill becomes impaired in a future period, the impairment charge would be allocated to the controlling interest and the NCI based on the percentage of total goodwill each equity interest received on the D&D. In the original example, where goodwill on the NCI was assumed to be proportional to that recorded on the controlling interest, the impairment charge would be allocated 80/20 to the controlling interest and NCI. In the above example, where goodwill was not proportional, a new percentage would be developed as follows:

	Value	Percentage of Total
Goodwill applicable to parent from Value Analysis schedule.	$128,000	88.28%
Goodwill applicable to NCI from Value Analysis schedule.	17,000	11.72%
Total goodwill	$145,000	

Gain on Purchase of Subsidiary

Let us now study the same example, except that the price paid will be low enough to result in a gain. Assume that Parental Inc. issued 10,000 shares of its $1 par value common stock for 80% of the outstanding shares of Sample Company. The fair value of a share of Parental Inc. stock is $25. Parental also pays $20,000 in accounting and legal fees to complete the purchase. Parental would make the following journal entry to record the purchase:

	Dr.	Cr.
To record the purchase:		
Investment in Sample Company (10,000 shares issued × $25 fair value).	250,000	
Common Stock, $1 par value (10,000 shares × $1 par)		10,000
Paid-In Capital in Excess of Par ($250,000 – $10,000 par value)		240,000
To record the costs of the acquisition:		
Acquisition Expense (closed to retained earnings since we are examining only balance sheets)	20,000	
Cash.		20,000

Refer back to the prior comparison of book and fair values for the subsidiary. The following value analysis would be prepared for the 80% interest:

Value Analysis Schedule

	Parent Price (80%)	NCI Value (20%)	Company Fair Value
1. Company fair value.	$250,000	~~$62,500~~ 73,000	$323,000
2. Fair value of net assets **excluding goodwill**.	292,000	73,000	365,000
3. Goodwill—Fair value of company exceeds fair value of net assets excluding goodwill	N/A	N/A	
4. Gain—Parent price is less than the parent share of fair value of net assets excluding goodwill	42,000		

Several assumptions went into the above calculation:

- Line 1, Company fair value—It is assumed that if the parent would pay $250,000 for an 80% interest, then the entire subsidiary company is worth $312,500 ($250,000/80%). We will refer to this as the "implied value" of the subsidiary company. Assuming this to be true, the NCI is worth 20% of the total subsidiary company value (20% × $312,500 = $62,500). The NCI value, however, can never be less than its share of net identifiable assets ($73,000). Thus, the NCI share of company value is raised to $73,000 (replacing the $62,500).
- Line 2—Fair value of net assets **excluding goodwill**—The fair values of the subsidiary accounts are from the comparison of book and fair values.

- Line 3—There can be no goodwill when the price paid is less than the fair value of the parent's share of the fair value of net identifiable assets. Thus, the line is marked N/A (Not Applicable).
- Line 4—The only gain recognized is that applicable to the controlling interest.

The following D&D would be prepared:

Determination and Distribution of Excess Schedule

	Company Value	Parent Price	NCI Value	Worksheet Distribution
Fair value of subsidiary	323,000	250,000	73,000	
Less book value interest acquired:				
Common stock, $1 par	10,000			
Paid-in excess of par	90,000			
Retained earnings	100,000			
Total equity	200,000			
Interest acquired		80.00%	20.00%	
Book value		160,000	40,000	
Excess of cost over book value (debit)	123,000	90,000	33,000	
Adjustment of identifiable accounts:				
Inventory ($55,000 fair – $50,000 book value)	5,000		—	debit D1
Land ($70,000 fair – $40,000 book value)	30,000		—	debit D2
Buildings ($250,000 – $150,000 net book value)	100,000		—	debit D3
Equipment ($60,000 fair – $40,000 net book value)	20,000		—	debit D4
Copyright ($50,000 fair – $0 book value)	50,000			debit D5
Goodwill ($0 fair value – $40,000 book value)	(40,000)			credit D6
Gain (only applies to the controlling interest)	(42,000)	—	—	credit D7
Total	123,000			

worksheet

Worksheet A2-2: page 532

Worksheet A2-2 on page 532 is the consolidated worksheet for the $250,000 price. The D&D provides complete guidance for the worksheet eliminations:

- Elimination "EL" eliminated the subsidiary equity purchased (80% in this example) against the investment account as follows:

(EL)	Common Stock, $1 par	8,000	
	Paid-In Excess of Par	72,000	
	Retained Earnings	80,000	
	Investment in Sample Company		160,000

- The "D" series eliminations distribute the excess applicable to the controlling interest plus the increase in the NCI (labeled "NCI") to the appropriate accounts as indicated by the D&D schedule. Worksheet eliminations are as follows:

(D1)	Inventory	5,000	
(D2)	Land	30,000	
(D3)	Buildings	100,000	
(D4)	Equipment	20,000	
(D5)	Copyright	50,000	
(D6)	Goodwill (existing goodwill eliminated)		40,000
(D7)	Gain on Purchase of Subsidiary (since we are dealing only with a balance sheet, this would be credited to Controlling Retained Earnings)		42,000
(D)	Investment in Sample Company (remaining excess after "EL")		90,000

(NCI)	Retained Earnings – Sample (NCI share of fair market adjustment)		33,000
	Check Totals	*205,000*	*205,000*

Valuation Schedule Strategy

Here are steps to valuation that will always work if scheduled as shown below:

1. Enter valuable for cell C2 (sum of fair values of company's net identifiable assets), and then enter appropriate percentage of that value into cells A2 and B2. These amounts are fixed regardless of the price paid by the parent. They will never change.

Step 1:

	A 80% Parent	B 20% NCI	C Company
1. Company Fair Value			
2. Fair value of net identifiable assets	**292,000**	**73,000**	**365,000**
3. Goodwill			
4. Gain			—

2. Enter price paid $420,000 for controlling interest by the parent in cell A1.

Step 2:

	A 80% Parent	B 20% NCI	C Company
1. Company Fair Value	**420,000**		
2. Fair value of net identifiable assets	292,000	73,000	365,000
3. Goodwill			
4. Gain			—

3. Compare A1, the price paid by the parent, and A2, the parent's share of the fair value of the company's net identifiable assets:

   a. If A1>A2, enter A3, which is the goodwill applicable to the parent. Then complete cell B1. Normally this amount will be proportional to A1. It can be a lesser amount but never less than cell B2. The proportionate value would be 20%/80% for this example. Calculate values for C1, B2, and B3.

Step 3(a):

	A 80% Parent	B 20% NCI	C Company
1. Company Fair Value	420,000	**90,000***	
2. Fair value of net identifiable assets	292,000	73,000	365,000
3. Goodwill	**128,000**		
4. Gain			—

*Greater than 73,000 and less than 20%/80% × 420,000 = 105,000

Complete remaining cells:

	A 80% Parent	B 20% NCI	C Company
1. Company Fair Value	420,000	90,000*	**510,000**
2. Fair value of net identifiable assets	292,000	73,000	365,000
3. Goodwill	128,000	**17,000**	**145,000**
4. Gain			—

   b. If A2>A1, enter A4, which is the gain applicable to the parent. Then enter cell B1 equal to B2 (the NCI cannot have a gain). Calculate value for C1. Cell C4 = A4.

Try it for Parent price of $250,000:

Step 1:

	A 80% Parent	B 20% NCI	C Company
1. Company Fair Value			
2. Fair value of net identifiable assets	**292,000**	**73,000**	**365,000**
3. Goodwill			
4. Gain			—

Step 2:

	A 80% Parent	B 20% NCI	C Company
1. Company Fair Value	**250,000**		
2. Fair value of net identifiable assets	292,000	73,000	365,000
3. Goodwill			
4. Gain	**42,000**		—

Step 3(b):

	A 80% Parent	B 20% NCI	C Company
1. Company Fair Value	250,000	**73,000**	
2. Fair value of net identifiable assets	292,000	73,000	365,000
3. Goodwill			
4. Gain	42,000		—

Complete remaining cells:

	A 80% Parent	B 20% NCI	C Company
1. Company Fair Value	250,000	73,000	**323,000**
2. Fair value of net identifiable assets	292,000	73,000	365,000
3. Goodwill			
4. Gain	42,000		**42,000**

Gain on Parent Asset Transferred to Subsidiary to Acquire Interest

The parent must bring to fair value any assets, other than cash, that it exchanges for the controlling interest. If those assets are retained and used by the subsidiary company, the gain must be eliminated in the consolidation process.

Assets transferred would be retained by the subsidiary when either:

1. the assets are transferred to the former shareholders of the subsidiary company and the shareholders sell the assets to the subsidiary company, or
2. the assets are transferred directly to the subsidiary company in exchange for newly issued shares or treasury shares.

The gain would be deferred using the procedures demonstrated in Chapter 4 for the parent sale of a fixed asset to the subsidiary.

Worksheet A2-1

80% Interest: Price Exceeds Fair Value of Net Identifiable Assets
Parental Inc. and Subsidiary Sample Company
Worksheet for Consolidated Balance Sheet
December 31, 20X1

(Facts on page 524)

	(Credit balance amounts are in parentheses.)	Balance Sheet		Eliminations & Adjustments		NCI	Consolidated Balance Sheet	
		Parental	Sample	Dr.	Cr.			
1	Cash	84,000	0				84,000	1
2	Accounts Receivable	72,000	20,000				92,000	2
3	Inventory	80,000	50,000	(D1) 5,000			135,000	3
4	Land	100,000	40,000	(D2) 30,000			170,000	4
5	Investment in Sample Company	420,000			(EL) 160,000			5
6					(D) 260,000			6
7	Buildings	500,000	200,000	(D3) 100,000			800,000	7
8	Accumulated Depreciation	(80,000)	(50,000)				(130,000)	8
9	Equipment	240,000	60,000	(D4) 20,000			320,000	9
10	Accumulated Depreciation	(40,000)	(20,000)				(60,000)	10
11	Copyright			(D5) 50,000			50,000	11
12	Goodwill		40,000	(D6) 120,000			160,000	12
13	Current Liabilities	(80,000)	(40,000)				(120,000)	13
14	Bonds Payable	(200,000)	(100,000)				(300,000)	14
15	Common Stock—Sample		(10,000)	(EL) 8,000		(2,000)		15
16	Paid-In Excess—Sample		(90,000)	(EL) 72,000		(18,000)		16
17	Retained Earnings—Sample		(100,000)	(EL) 80,000	(NCI) 65,000	(85,000)		17
18	Common Stock—Parental	(36,800)					(36,800)	18
19	Paid-In Excess—Parental	(603,200)					(603,200)	19
20	Retained Earnings—Parental	(456,000)					(456,000)	20
21	Totals	0	0	485,000	485,000			21
22	NCI					(105,000)	(105,000)	22
23								23
24	Totals						0	24

Eliminations and Adjustments:

(EL) Eliminate 80% subsidiary equity against investment account.
(NCI) Adjust NCI to fair value.
(D) Distribute remaining excess in investment account plus NCI adjustment to:
(D1) Inventory.
(D2) Land.
(D3) Building (recorded cost is increased without removing accumulated depreciation). The alternative is to debit Accumulated Depreciation for $50,000 and the building for $50,000. This would restate the asset at fair value.
(D4) Equipment (recorded cost is increased without removing accumulated depreciation). The alternative is to debit Accumulated Depreciation for $20,000. This would restate the asset at fair value.
(D5) Copyright.
(D6) Goodwill.

Worksheet A2-2

80% Interest: Price Is Less than Fair Value of Net Identifiable Assets
Parental Inc. and Subsidiary Sample Company
Worksheet for Consolidated Balance Sheet
December 31, 20X1

(Facts on page 528)

	(Credit balance amounts are in parentheses.)	Balance Sheet		Eliminations & Adjustments				NCI	Consolidated Balance Sheet	
		Parental	Sample	Dr.		Cr.				
1	Cash	254,000	0						254,000	1
2	Accounts Receivable	72,000	20,000						92,000	2
3	Inventory	80,000	50,000	(D1)	5,000				135,000	3
4	Land	100,000	40,000	(D2)	30,000				170,000	4
5	Investment in Sample Company	250,000				(EL)	160,000			5
6						(D)	90,000			6
7	Buildings	500,000	200,000	(D3)	100,000				800,000	7
8	Accumulated Depreciation	(80,000)	(50,000)						(130,000)	8
9	Equipment	240,000	60,000	(D4)	20,000				320,000	9
10	Accumulated Depreciation	(40,000)	(20,000)						(60,000)	10
11	Copyright			(D5)	50,000				50,000	11
12	Goodwill		40,000			(D6)	40,000			12
13	Current Liabilities	(80,000)	(40,000)						(120,000)	13
14	Bonds Payable	(200,000)	(100,000)						(300,000)	14
15	Common Stock—Sample		(10,000)	(EL)	8,000			(2,000)		15
16	Paid-In Excess—Sample		(90,000)	(EL)	72,000			(18,000)		16
17	Retained Earnings—Sample		(100,000)	(EL)	80,000	(NCI)	33,000	(53,000)		17
18	Common Stock—Parental	(36,800)							(36,800)	18
19	Paid-In Excess—Parental	(603,200)							(603,200)	19
20	Retained Earnings—Parental	(456,000)				(D7)	42,000		(498,000)	20
21	Totals	0	0		365,000		365,000			21
22	NCI							(73,000)	(73,000)	22
23										23
24	Totals								0	24

Eliminations and Adjustments:

(EL) Eliminate 80% subsidiary equity against investment account.
(NCI) Adjust NCI to fair value.
(D) Distribute remaining excess in investment account plus NCI adjustment to:
(D1) Inventory.
(D2) Land.
(D3) Building (recorded cost is increased without removing accumulated depreciation). The alternative is to debit Accumulated Depreciation for $50,000 and the building for $50,000. This would restate the asset at fair value.
(D4) Equipment (recorded cost is increased without removing accumulated depreciation). The alternative is to debit Accumulated Depreciation for $20,000. This would restate the asset at fair value.
(D5) Copyright.
(D6) Goodwill.

CHAPTER 2 EXERCISES AND PROBLEMS

Exercise SA2-1 80% purchase, goodwill. Quincy Company purchased 80% of the common stock of Cooker Company for $720,000 and paid direct acquisition costs of $10,000. At the time of the purchase, Cooker Company had the following balance sheet:

Assets		Liabilities and Equity	
Cash equivalents	$ 120,000	Current liabilities	$ 200,000
Inventory	200,000	Bonds payable	400,000
Land	100,000	Common stock ($5 par)	100,000
Building (net)	450,000	Paid-in capital in excess of par	150,000
Equipment (net)	230,000	Retained earnings	250,000
Total assets	$1,100,000	Total liabilities and equity	$1,100,000

Fair values differ from book values for all assets other than cash equivalents. The fair values are as follows:

Inventory	$300,000
Land	200,000
Building	600,000
Equipment	200,000

Based on the preceding facts, do the following.

1. Prepare a value analysis schedule and a determination and distribution of excess schedule.
2. Prepare the elimination entries that would be made on a consolidated worksheet prepared on the date of purchase.

Exercise SA2-2 80% purchase, alternative prices. Venus Company purchased 8,000 shares of Saturn Company for $82 per share. Just prior to the purchase, Saturn Company had the following balance sheet:

Assets		Liabilities and Equity	
Cash	$ 20,000	Current liabilities	$250,000
Inventory	280,000	Common stock ($5 par)	50,000
Property, plant, and equipment (net)	400,000	Paid-in capital in excess of par	130,000
		Retained earnings	370,000
Goodwill	100,000		
Total assets	$800,000	Total liabilities and equity	$800,000

Venus Company believes that the inventory has a fair value of $400,000 and that the property, plant, and equipment is worth $500,000.

◄◄◄◄◄ **Required**

1. Prepare a value analysis schedule and a determination and distribution of excess schedule.
2. Prepare the elimination entries that would be made on a consolidated worksheet prepared on the date of acquisition.

3. Prepare the value analysis schedule and the determination and distribution of excess schedule and the elimination entries that would be made on a consolidated worksheet prepared on the date of acquisition assuming Venus pays $64 per share.

Problem SA2-1 80% purchase at less than fair value of net identifiable assets, elimination entries only. On March 1, 20X5, Penson Enterprises purchased an 80% interest in Express Corporation for $320,000. Express Corporation had the following balance sheet on February 28, 20X5:

Express Corporation
Balance Sheet
February 28, 20X5

Assets		Liabilities and Equity	
Accounts receivable	$ 60,000	Current liabilities	$ 50,000
Inventory	80,000	Bonds payable	100,000
Land	40,000	Common stock ($10 par)	50,000
Buildings	300,000	Paid-in capital in excess of par	250,000
Accum. depreciation—building	(120,000)	Retained earnings	70,000
Equipment	220,000		
Accum. depreciation—equipment	(60,000)		
Total assets	$ 520,000	Total liabilities and equity	$520,000

Penson Enterprises received an independent appraisal on the fair values of Express Corporation's assets. The controller has reviewed the following figures and accepts them as reasonable.

Accounts receivable	$ 60,000
Inventory	100,000
Land	50,000
Buildings	200,000
Equipment	162,000
Current liabilities	50,000
Bonds payable	95,000

Required ▶ ▶ ▶ ▶ ▶

1. Record the investment in Express Corporation.
2. Prepare a value analysis schedule and a determination and distribution of excess schedule.
3. Prepare the elimination entries that would be made on a consolidated worksheet prepared on the date of acquisition.

Problem SA2-2 80% purchase, goodwill, several adjustments, worksheet. Parton Corporation acquired Soma Corporation on December 31, 20X1. Parton exchanged shares of its $1 par, $50 fair value stock for 80% of the common stock of Soma. Soma had the following balance sheet on the date of acquisition:

Soma Corporation
Balance Sheet
December 31, 20X1

Assets		Liabilities and Equity	
Accounts receivable	$ 50,000	Current liabilities	$ 90,000
Inventory	120,000	Bonds payable	200,000
Land	100,000	Common stock ($1 par)	10,000
Buildings	300,000	Paid-in capital in excess	
Accumulated depreciation	(100,000)	of par	190,000

Equipment	140,000	Retained earnings	140,000
Accumulated depreciation	(50,000)		
Patent	10,000		
Goodwill	60,000		
Total assets	$ 630,000	Total liabilities and equity	$630,000

An appraisal has been performed to determine whether the book values of Soma's net assets reflect their fair values. The appraiser also determined that several intangible assets existed, although they were not recorded. The following assets and liabilities had fair values that differed from their book values:

Accounts receivable	$ 50,000
Inventory	100,000
Land	200,000
Buildings	400,000
Equipment	200,000
Patent	150,000
Computer software	50,000
Current liabilities	90,000
Bonds payable	210,000

Use the preceding information for Parton's purchase of Soma common stock. Assume Parton exchanged 19,000 shares of its own stock for 80% of the common stock of Soma. The stock had a market value of $50 per share and a par value of $1. Parton had the following trial balance immediately after the purchase:

Parton Corporation
Trial Balance
December 31, 20X1 (Parent only)

Cash	170,000
Accounts Receivable	300,000
Inventory	410,000
Land	800,000
Investment in Soma	950,000
Buildings	2,800,000
Accumulated Depreciation	(500,000)
Equipment	600,000
Accumulated Depreciation	(230,000)
Current Liabilities	(150,000)
Bonds Payable	(300,000)
Common Stock ($1 par)	(95,000)
Paid-In Capital in Excess of Par	(3,655,000)
Retained Earnings	(1,100,000)
Total	0

1. Prepare a value analysis schedule and a determination and distribution of excess schedule for the investment in Soma.
2. Complete a consolidated worksheet for Parton Corporation and its subsidiary Soma Corporation as of December 31, 20X1.

CHAPTER 3

The changes to Chapter 3 can be summarized as follows:

- Identifiable assets and liabilities have been adjusted to 100% of fair value regardless of the parent ownership percentage. This means that the entire adjustment to fair value must be amortized in subsequent periods. Since the NCI will share in the amortizations of excess, **all amortizations of excess will now flow through the Subsidiary IDS schedule. Amortizations for prior periods will be allocated to the retained earnings of the controlling interest and NCI.**
- In the period of a bargain purchase (parent price is less than controlling share of fair value of net identifiable assets), the parent will record a gain on the purchase of the subsidiary. The NCI does not share in the gain on the purchase. In later periods, the gain will be credited to only controlling retained earnings.

worksheet

Worksheet A3-1: page 540

Worksheet A3-1 on pages 540 to 541 is an example of an 80% purchase with goodwill. The following table shows book and fair values of Carlos Company on the date of purchase:

	Book Value	Market Value	Life		Book Value	Market Value	Life
Assets:				Current liabilities	50,000	50,000	1
Inventory	75,000	80,000	1	Bonds payable	200,000	186,760	4
Land.	150,000	200,000	—	**Total liabilities**. . . .	**250,000**	**236,760**	
Buildings	600,000	500,000	20	Stockholders' equity:			
Accumulated depreciation .	(300,000)			Common stock.	100,000		
Equipment	150,000	80,000	5	Paid-in excess of par .	150,000		
Accumulated depreciation .	(50,000)			Retained earnings . . .	250,000		
Patent.	125,000	150,000	10				
Existing goodwill.	—			Total equity	500,000		
Total assets . .	**750,000**	**1,010,000**		**Net assets**	**500,000**	**773,260**	

The parent company, Paulos, paid $720,000 for an 80% interest in Carlos Company on January 1, 20X1. It is assumed that the goodwill applicable to the NCI is proportional to that reflected in the parent's purchase price. The following Value Analysis schedule was prepared:

Value Analysis Schedule

	Parent Price (80%)	NCI Value (20%)	Company Fair Value
1. Company fair value.	$720,000	$180,000	$900,000
2. Fair value of net assets **excluding goodwill**.	618,592	154,648	773,240
3. Goodwill—Fair value of company exceeds fair value of net assets excluding goodwill	101,408	25,352	126,760
4. Gain—Parent price is less than the parent share of fair value of net assets excluding goodwill	N/A		

Based on the above information, the following D&D schedule is prepared:

Determination and Distribution of Excess Schedule

	Company Value	Parent Price	NCI Value	Worksheet Distribution	
Fair value of subsidiary	900,000	720,000	180,000		
Less book value interest acquired:					
Common stock	100,000				
Paid-in excess of par	150,000				
Retained earnings	250,000				
Total equity.	500,000				
Interest acquired		80.00%	20.00%		
Book value of interest.		400,000	100,000		
Excess of cost over book value (debit)	400,000	320,000	80,000		
Allocated to:			Life		Amortization per Year
Accounts receivable	—		—		
Inventory	5,000		1	debit D1	
Land.	50,000		—	debit D2	
Buildings	200,000		20	debit D3	10,000
Equipment	(20,000)		5	credit D4	(4,000)
Patent.	25,000		10	debit D5	2,500
Goodwill	126,760			debit D6	
Accounts payable	—				
Discount on bonds payable. . . .	13,240		4	debit D7	3,310
Gain (not applicable)	—				
Total adjustments	400,000				

Worksheet A3-1 is prepared as of December 31, 20X2, the end of the second year.
Eliminations in journal entry form are as follows:

	Eliminate subsidiary income recorded by the parent company:		
(CY1)	Subsidiary Income.	80,000	
	Investment in Carlos.		80,000
	Eliminate dividends paid by Carlos to Paulos:		
(CY2)	Investment in Carlos.	16,000	
	Dividends Declared by Carlos		16,000
	Eliminate 80% of Carlos equity against investment in Carlos:		
(EL)	Common Stock, Carlos	80,000	
	Paid-In Capital in Excess of Par, Carlos.	120,000	
	Retained Earnings, Carlos.	232,000	
	Investment in Carlos.		432,000

	Distribute excess of cost over book value:		
(D1)	Retained Earnings, Paulos (80% of $5,000 prior-year amount)	4,000	
(D1)	Retained Earnings, Carlos (20% of $5,000 prior-year amount)	1,000	
(D2)	Land	50,000	
(D3)	Buildings	200,000	
(D4)	Equipment		20,000
(D5)	Patent	25,000	
(D6)	Goodwill	126,760	
(D7)	Discount on Bonds Payable	13,240	
(D)	Investment in Carlos (noneliminated excess)		320,000
(NCI)	Retained Earnings—Carlos (to adjust NCI to fair value)		80,000
	Amortize excess for current year as shown on schedule following entry:		
(A3)	Depreciation Expense—Building	10,000	
(A4)	Depreciation Expense—Equipment		4,000
(A5)	Other Expenses (patent amortization)	2,500	
(A7)	Interest Expense	3,310	
(A3–A7)	Retained Earnings—Paulos	9,448	
(A3–A7)	Retained Earnings—Carlos	2,362	
(A3)	Accumulated Depreciation—Building		20,000
(A4)	Accumulated Depreciation—Equipment	8,000	
(A5)	Patent		5,000
(A7)	Discount on Bonds Payable		6,620

A summary of depreciation and amortization adjustments follows:

Amortization Adjustments	Life	Annual Amount	Current Year	Prior Years	Total	Key
Buildings	20	$10,000	$10,000	$10,000	$20,000	(A3)
Equipment	5	(4,000)	(4,000)	(4,000)	(8,000)	(A4)
Patent (net)	10	2,500	2,500	2,500	5,000	(A5)
Discount on bonds payable	4	3,310	3,310	3,310	6,620	(A7)
Total		$11,810	$11,810	$11,810	$23,620	
Controlling RE adjustment (80%)				$ 9,448		(A3–A7)
NCI RE adjustment (20%)				$ 2,362		(A3–A7)

Take note of the following issues in Exhibit A3-1:

- The adjustment of the inventory, at the time of the purchase on January 1, 20X1, now goes to parent and NCI retained earnings, since it is a correction of the 20X1 cost of goods sold.
- The amortizations of excess for prior periods and the inventory adjustment are carried to controlling (80%) and NCI (20%) retained earnings. Since the NCI shared in the fair value adjustments as of the purchase date, it must share in current- and prior-year amortizations.
- The controlling and NCI retained earnings balances are adjusted for the above amortizations of excess before they are extended to the Retained Earnings column.

If a worksheet were prepared for December 31, 20X3, the prior years' amortizations of excess would cover two prior years as follows:

Amortization Adjustments	Life	Annual Amount	Current Year	Prior Years	Total	Key
Buildings	20	$10,000	$10,000	$20,000	$ 30,000	(A3)
Equipment	5	(4,000)	(4,000)	(8,000)	(12,000)	(A4)
Patent (net)	10	2,500	2,500	5,000	7,500	(A5)
Discount on bonds payable	4	3,310	3,310	6,620	9,939	(A7)
Total		$11,813	$11,813	$23,620	$ 35,430	
Controlling RE adjustment (80%)				$18,896		(A3–A7)
NCI RE adjustment (20%)				$ 4,724		(A3–A7)

Exhibit A3-1 contains the formal consolidated financial statements for Paulos Company for 20X2. Note the following features of the statements:

- All nominal accounts are merged, as adjusted, for amortizations to arrive at consolidated net income. The consolidated net income is then distributed to the noncontrolling and controlling interests, using the amounts from the income distribution schedules.
- Note that the statement of change in equity includes an analysis of controlling retained earnings and the NCI.
- The consolidated balance sheet shows the NCI as a single line component of stockholders' equity.

Exhibit A3-1

Paulos Company
Consolidated Income Statement
Period Ending December 31, 20X2

Sales revenue		$700,000
Less cost of goods sold		320,000
Gross profit		$380,000
Less operating expenses:		
Depreciation expense (building and equipment)	$101,000	
Patent amortization expense	2,500	
Other operating expenses	123,000	226,500
Operating income		$153,500
Interest expense (rounded down from $15,313 to tie to worksheet income)		15,310
Consolidated net income		$138,190
Distributed to noncontrolling interest		17,638
Distributed to controlling interest		$120,552

Worksheet A3-1

Simple Equity Method, Second Year
Paulos Company and Subsidiary Carlos Company

Worksheet for Consolidated Financial Statements
For the Year Ended December 31, 20X2

	(Credit balance amounts are in parentheses.)	Trial Balance	
		Paulos	Carlos
1	Cash	312,000	160,000
2	Inventory	210,000	120,000
3	Land	200,000	150,000
4	Investment in Carlos	816,000	
5			
6			
7			
8	Buildings	800,000	600,000
9	Accumulated Depreciation	(120,000)	(330,000)
10	Equipment	400,000	150,000
11	Accumulated Depreciation	(90,000)	(90,000)
12	Patent (net)		100,000
13			
14	Goodwill		0
15	Current Liabilities	(150,000)	(40,000)
16	Bond Payable	0	(200,000)
17	Discount (Premium)		
18			
19	Common Stock—Carlos		(100,000)
20	Paid-In Excess—Carlos		(150,000)
21	Retained Earnings, January 1, 20X2—Carlos		(290,000)
22			
23			
24			
25	Common Stock—Paulos	(1,500,000)	
26	Retained Earnings, January 1, 20X2—Paulos	(748,000)	
27			
28			
29			
30			
31	Sales	(400,000)	(300,000)
32	Cost of Goods Sold	200,000	120,000
33	Depreciation Expense—Building	40,000	15,000
34	Depreciation Expense—Equipment	20,000	20,000
35	Patent Amortization Expense		
36	Other Expenses	90,000	33,000
37	Interest Expense		12,000
38			
39	Subsidiary Income	(80,000)	
40	Dividends Declared—Carlos		20,000
41	Totals	0	0
42	Consolidated Net Income		
43	NCI Share		
44	Controlling Share		
45	Total NCI		
46	Retained Earnings—Controlling Interest, December 31, 20X2		
47	Totals		

(Facts on page 536)

Eliminations and Adjustments				Consolidated Income Statement	NCI	Controlling Retained Earnings	Consolidated Balance Sheet	
Dr.		Cr.						
							472,000	1
							330,000	2
(D2)	50,000						400,000	3
		(CY1)	80,000					4
(CY2)	16,000							5
		(EL)	432,000					6
		(D)	320,000					7
(D3)	200,000						1,600,000	8
		(A3)	20,000				(470,000)	9
		(D4)	20,000				530,000	10
(A4)	8,000						(172,000)	11
(D5)	25,000						120,000	12
		(A5)	5,000					13
(D6)	126,760						126,760	14
							(190,000)	15
							(200,000)	16
(D7)	13,240							17
		(A7)	6,620				6,620	18
(EL)	80,000				(20,000)			19
(EL)	120,000				(30,000)			20
(EL)	232,000				(134,638)			21
		(NCI)	80,000					22
(D1)	1,000							23
(A3–A7)	2,362							24
							(1,500,000)	25
								26
(D1)	4,000							27
(A3–A7)	9,448							28
								29
						(734,552)		30
				(700,000)				31
				320,000				32
(A3)	10,000			65,000				33
	0	(A4)	4,000	36,000				34
(A5)	2,500			2,500				35
				123,000				36
(A7)	3,313			15,310				37
								38
(CY1)	80,000							39
		(CY2)	16,000		4,000			40
	983,620		983,620					41
				(138,190)				42
				17,638	(17,638)			43
				120,552		(120,552)		44
					(198,276)		(198,276)	45
						(855,104)	(855,104)	46
							0	47

Eliminations and Adjustments:

(CY1) Eliminate subsidiary income against the investment account.
(CY2) Eliminate dividends paid by subsidiary to parent. After (CY1) and (CY2), the investment account and the subsidiary retained earnings are at the January 1 balances. Then, the investment account can be eliminated.
(EL) Eliminate the controlling share of subsidiary equity balance (as of January 1) against the investment account. The elimination of the controlling share of subsidiary equity leaves only the NCI portion of each subsidiary equity account.
(D) Distribute the $400,000 fair value excess as follows:
(D1) Prior-year inventory is sold, distribute 80/20 to controlling interest and NCI.
(D2) Land.
(D3) Buildings.
(D4) Equipment.
(D5) Patent.
(D6) Goodwill.
(D7) Discount on Bonds Payable.
(A) Amortize distributions as follows:

Account Adjustments	Life	Annual Amount	Current Year	Prior Years	Total	Key
Inventory	1	$ 5,000	$ 0	$ 5,000	$ 5,000	(D1)
Subject to amortization:						
Buildings	20	$10,000	$10,000	$10,000	$20,000	(A3)
Equipment	5	(4,000)	(4,000)	(4,000)	(8,000)	(A4)
Patent	10	2,500	2,500	2,500	5,000	(A5)
Bonds payable	4	3,310	3,310	3,310	6,620	(A7)
Total amortizations		$11,813	$11,813	$11,813	$23,625	
Controlling RE adjustment				$ 9,448		
NCI RE adjustment				$ 2,362		

Income Distribution Schedules

Subsidiary Company S

Current-year amortizations of excess	11,810	Internally generated net income	100,000
		Total	88,190
		NCI share	17,638
		Controlling share	70,552

Parent Company P

		Internally generated net income	50,000
		Controlling share of subsidiary	70,552
		Total	120,552

Paulos Company
Retained Earnings Statement
Period Ending December 31, 20X2

	Controlling Retained Earnings	Noncontrolling Interest
Balance, January 1, 20X2	$734,552	$184,638
Net income	120,552	17,638
Dividends paid		(4,000)
Balance, December 31, 20X2	$855,104	$198,276

Paulos Company
Consolidated Balance Sheet
December 31, 20X2

Assets			Liabilities and Equity		
Current assets:			Current liabilities	$ 190,000	
Cash	$ 472,000		Bonds payable, 6%, due December 31, 20X4	200,000	
Inventory	330,000		Discount on bonds payable	(6,620)	
Total current assets		$ 802,000	Total liabilities		$ 383,380
Long-term assets:					
Land	$ 400,000				
Buildings	1,600,000				
Accumulated depreciation	(470,000)		Stockholders' equity:		
Equipment	530,000		Common stock	$1,500,000	
Accumulated depreciation	(172,000)		Retained earnings	855,104	
Patent (net)	120,000		Controlling interest		2,355,104
Goodwill	126,760		Noncontrolling interest		198,276
Total long-term assets		2,134,760	Total equity		2,553,380
Total assets		$2,936,760	Total liabilities and equity		$2,936,760

CHAPTER 3 PROBLEMS

Problem SA3-1 Equity method adjustments, consolidated worksheet. On January 1, 20X1, Peres Company purchased 80% of the common stock of Soll Company for $308,000. Soll has common stock, other paid-in capital, and retained earnings of $50,000, $100,000, and $150,000, respectively. Net income and dividends for two years for Soll were as follows:

	20X1	20X2
Net income	$60,000	$90,000
Dividends	20,000	30,000

On January 1, 20X1, the only tangible assets of Soll that were undervalued were inventory and the building. Inventory, for which FIFO is used, was worth $10,000 more than cost. The inventory was sold in 20X1. The building, which is worth $25,000 more than book value, has a remaining life of 10 years, and straight-line depreciation is used. The remaining excess of cost over book value is attributed to goodwill.

Required ▶ ▶ ▶ ▶ ▶

1. Using this information and the information in the following trial balances on Dec. 31, 2002, prepare a value analysis and a determination and distribution of excess schedule.

	Peres Company	Soll Company
Inventory, December 31	100,000	50,000
Other Current Assets	148,000	180,000
Investment in Soll Company	388,000	
Land	50,000	50,000
Buildings and Equipment	350,000	320,000
Accumulated Depreciation	(100,000)	(60,000)
Goodwill		
Other Intangibles	20,000	
Current Liabilities	(120,000)	(40,000)
Bonds Payable		(100,000)
Other Long-Term Liabilities	(200,000)	
Common Stock, Peres Company	(200,000)	
Other Paid-In Capital, Peres Company	(100,000)	
Retained Earnings, Peres Company	(214,000)	
Common Stock, Soll Company		(50,000)
Other Paid-In Capital, Soll Company		(100,000)
Retained Earnings, Soll Company		(190,000)
Net Sales	(520,000)	(450,000)
Cost of Goods Sold	300,000	260,000
Operating Expenses	120,000	100,000
Soll Income	(72,000)	
Dividends Declared, Peres Company	50,000	
Dividends Declared, Soll Company		30,000
Totals	0	0

2. Complete a worksheet for consolidated financial statements for 20X2. Include columns for eliminations and adjustments, consolidated income, NCI, controlling retained earnings, and balance sheet.

Problem SA3-2 80%, equity method worksheet, several adjustments, third year. Pcraft Corporation builds powerboats. On January 1, 20X1, Pcraft acquired Sailair Corporation, a company that manufactures sailboats. Pcraft paid cash in exchange for Sailair common stock. Sailair had the following balance sheet on January 1, 20X1:

Sailair Corporation
Balance Sheet
January 1, 20X1

Assets		Liabilities and Equity	
Accounts receivable	$ 32,000	Current liabilities	$ 90,000
Inventory	40,000	Bonds payable	100,000
Land	60,000	Common stock	10,000
Buildings	250,000	Paid-in capital in excess of par	90,000
Accumulated depreciation	(50,000)	Retained earnings	112,000
Equipment	100,000		
Accumulated depreciation	(30,000)		
Total assets	$402,000	Total liabilities and equity	$402,000

An appraisal indicated that the following assets and liabilities had fair values that differed from their book values. Any remaining excess is attributed to goodwill.

Inventory (sold during 20X1)	$ 38,000
Land	150,000
Buildings (20-year life)	300,000
Equipment (5-year life)	100,000
Bonds payable (5-year life)	96,000

Refer to the preceding information for Pcraft's acquisition of Sailair's common stock. Assume that Pcraft paid $300,000 for 80% of Sailair common stock. Pcraft uses the simple equity method to account for its investment in Sailair. Pcraft and Sailair had the following trial balances on December 31, 20X3:

	Pcraft Corp.	Sailair Corp.
Cash	282,000	60,000
Accounts Receivable	90,000	55,000
Inventory	120,000	86,000
Land	100,000	60,000
Investment in Sailair	376,000	
Buildings	800,000	300,000
Accumulated Depreciation	(220,000)	(80,000)
Equipment	150,000	100,000
Accumulated Depreciation	(90,000)	(72,000)
Current Liabilities	(60,000)	(102,000)
Bonds Payable		(100,000)
Common Stock	(100,000)	(10,000)
Paid-In Capital in Excess of Par	(900,000)	(90,000)
Retained Earnings, January 1, 20X3	(375,000)	(182,000)
Sales	(800,000)	(350,000)
Cost of Goods Sold	450,000	210,000
Depreciation Expense—Buildings	30,000	15,000
Depreciation Expense—Equipment	15,000	14,000
Other Expenses	140,000	68,000
Interest Expense		8,000
Subsidiary Income	(28,000)	
Dividends Declared	20,000	10,000
Totals	0	0

1. Prepare a value analysis and a determination and distribution of excess schedule for the investment in Sailair.
2. Complete a consolidated worksheet for Pcraft Corporation and its subsidiary Sailair Corporation as of December 31, 20X3. Prepare supporting amortization and income distribution schedules.

CHAPTER 4

Chapter 4 already eliminates 100% of all intercompany profits regardless of the parent's ownership interest. Thus, none of the existing procedures are changed. Existing worksheets change only with respect to the adjustment of the NCI on the purchase date and the subsequent amortizations which are now allocated to the controlling interest and NCI.

The only addition to Chapter 4 is the possible deferral of a gain that may have existed on parent assets that were transferred to the subsidiary as part of the original purchase (see Chapter 2 portion of this update). The gain would be deferred in the same manner as a gain on the parent sale of a fixed asset to the subsidiary.

CHAPTER 5

Nothing in this chapter is impacted by the Exposure Draft.

CHAPTER 6

Tax Issues. The new issue concerns the added amortization of excess adjustments applicable to the NCI in a taxable exchange. The controlling share of the net identifiable assets has a stepped-up tax basis determined by the fair values on the purchase date. This is equitable from a tax standpoint, because the selling shareholders have paid tax on any gain they had. The NCI shareholders have not been taxed, and the tax basis of their share of net tangible assets remains at book value.

worksheet
Worksheet A6-1: page 548

Consolidated Tax Return. Worksheet A6-1 on pages 548 to 549 is a revision of Worksheet 6-1 in the current text. It has been updated to reflect the increase to fair value of the NCI share of the asset adjustment (patent) at the time of the purchase. Notice the following tax-related complications:

- The subsidiary IDS schedule reflects the tax status of the adjustment to the patent. The subsidiary tax schedule adjusts for the tax status of the patent adjustment. The subsidiary share of taxable income adds back the nondeductible share of the patent adjustment applicable to the NCI. Thus, the NCI share of tax is based on the NCI share of income, $18,000, rather than $16,750.
- The tax entry on the worksheet (T) also adds back the nondeductible NCI share of the patent amortization to the worksheet income figure to calculate the tax provision. It is also the sum of the NCI ($25,500) and controlling share ($46,200) of taxes as shown in the preceding schedules.

worksheet
Worksheet A6-2: page 552

Separate Tax Returns. Worksheet A6-2 on pages 552 to 553 is a revision of Worksheet 6-2 in the current text. It has been updated to reflect the increase to fair value of the NCI share of the asset adjustment (patent) at the time of the purchase. Notice the following tax-related complications:

- The subsidiary IDS schedule reflects the tax status of the adjustment to the patent. A subsidiary tax schedule adjusts for the tax status of the patent adjustment. The subsidiary share of taxable income adds back the nondeductible share of the patent adjustment applicable to the NCI. Thus, the NCI share of tax is based on The NCI share of income, $17,000, rather than $16,500.
- The (T1) tax entry to record the deferred tax asset is based on the support schedule for DTA/DTL adjustments. A DTA is calculated only for the controlling share of the patent amortization resulting from the purchase.
- The (T2) tax entry to record the current-year adjustment of the DTA/DTL is based on the support schedule. Only the parent share of the patent amortization is reflected as creating additional DTA.

Worksheet A6-1

Affiliated File Consolidated Tax Return
Company P and Subsidiary Company S
Worksheet for Consolidated Financial Statements
For Year Ended December 31, 20X3

	(Credit balance amounts are in parentheses.)	Trial Balance	
		Company P	Company S
1	Cash	205,000	380,000
2	Inventory	150,000	120,000
3	Investment in Company S	1,115,000	
4			
5			
6	Patent		
7	Plant and Equipment	900,000	1,100,000
8	Accumulated Depreciation	(440,000)	(150,000)
9			
10	Liabilities		(150,000)
11	Common Stock—Co. S		(500,000)
12	Retained Earnings—Co. S		(700,000)
13			
14			
15			
16	Common Stock—Co. P	(800,000)	
17	Retained Earnings—Co. P	(900,000)	
18			
19			
20	Sales	(600,000)	(400,000)
21	Cost of Goods Sold	350,000	200,000
22			
23	Patent Amortization Expense		
24	Depreciation Expense	25,000	20,000
25	Other Expenses	75,000	80,000
26	Subsidiary Income	(80,000)	
27	Totals	0	0
28	Consolidated Income Before Tax		
29	Consolidated Tax Provision		
30	Income Tax Payable		
31	Consolidated Net Income		
32	NCI Share		
33	Controlling Share		
34	NCI		
35	Controlling Retained Earnings		
36	Totals		

Eliminations and Adjustments:

(CY1) Eliminate the parent's entry recording its share of the current year's subsidiary income. This step returns the investment account to its balance on January 1, 20X3.
(EL) Eliminate 80% of the January 1, 20X3, subsidiary equity balances against the investment in Company S account.
(D) Record the NCI portion of excess of fair value over book value, distribute excess in investment account, and adjust patent to fair value.
(A) Amortize the patent at an amount of $6,250 per year for the current and prior two years. Split retained earnings for prior years 80% controlling retained earnings, 20% NCI.
(IS) Eliminate intercompany merchandise sales of $100,000 to avoid double counting sale and purchase.

(Facts on page 546)

Eliminations and Adjustments				Consolidated		Controlling	Consolidated	
Dr.		Cr.		Net Income	NCI	Retained Earnings	Balance Sheet	
							585,000	1
		(EI)	35,000				235,000	2
		(CY1)	80,000					3
		(EL)	960,000					4
		(D)	75,000					5
(D)	93,750	(A)	18,750				75,000	6
		(F1)	20,000				1,980,000	7
(F1)	4,000							8
(F2)	4,000						(582,000)	9
							(150,000)	10
(EL)	400,000				(100,000)			11
(EL)	560,000	(NCI)	18,750					12
(A)	2,500							13
(F1)								14
(BI)	5,000				(151,250)			15
							(800,000)	16
(A)	10,000							17
(BI)	20,000							18
(F1)	16,000					(854,000)		19
(IS)	100,000			(900,000)				20
		(IS)	100,000					21
(EI)	35,000	(BI)	25,000	460,000				22
(A1)	6,250			6,250				23
		(F2)	4,000	41,000				24
				155,000				25
(CY1)	80,000							26
	1,336,500		1,336,500					27
				(237,750)				28
(T)	71,700			71,700				29
		(T)	71,700				(71,700)	30
				(166,050)				31
				11,350	(11,350)			32
				154,700		(154,700)		33
					(262,600)		(262,600)	34
						(1,008,700)	(1,008,700)	35
							0	36

(BI) Reduce the cost of goods sold by the $25,000 of intercompany profit included in the beginning inventory. Since the sale was made by the subsidiary, the reduction of retained earnings is allocated 20% to the NCI and 80% to the controlling retained earnings.

(EI) Reduce the ending inventory to its cost to the consolidated company by decreasing it $35,000, and increase the cost of goods sold by $35,000.

(F1) Reduce retained earnings for the remaining undepreciated intercompany equipment gain on January 1, 20X3. Since the sale was by the parent, the entire retained earnings adjustment is debited to controlling retained earnings.

(F2) Adjust depreciation expense and accumulated for $4,000 over depreciation of equipment in current year. This is the added depreciation caused by the $20,000 intercompany gain.

(T) Record the provision for taxes ($237,750 + $1,250 adjustment for NCI share of asset adjustments) × 30% = $71,700.

Determination and Distribution of Excess Schedule

	Company	Cont	NCI			
Fair value of subsidiary	993,750	795,000	198,750			
Less book value interest acquired:						
Common stock	500,000					
Paid-in excess of par	—					
Retained earnings	400,000					
Total equity	900,000					
Interest acquired		80,00%	20.00%			
		720,000	180,000		Amortizations	
					Periods	Per year
Excess of cost over book value (debit)	93,750	75,000	18,750			
Patent	93,750			Debit D1	15	6,250

Schedules

Amortization Schedules

Year of Consolidation 3

Account Adjustment To Be Amortized	Life	Annual Amount	Current Year	Prior Years	Total	Key
Patent	15	6,250	6,250	12,500	18,750	A2

Intercompany Inventory Profit Deferral

	Parent Amount	Parent Percent	Parent Profit	Sub Amount	Sub Percent	Sub Profit
Beginning . .	—	0%	—	50,000	50%	25,000
Ending	—	0%	—	70,000	50%	35,000

Intercompany Fixed Asset Profit Deferral

	Parent	Sub
Original profit	20,000	
Year of sale	2	
Realized in prior years	4,000	
Balance, start of year	16,000	
Realized in current Year	4,000	

Subsidiary Income Distribution

Ending inventory profit	35,000	Internally generated net income . . .	100,000
Amortizations	6,250	Ending inventory profit	25,000
		Total	83,750
		Company S share of taxes (see schedule)	(25,500)
		Net income	58,250
		NCI share	11,350
		Controlling share	46,900

Subsidiary Tax Schedule	Controlling	NCI	Total
Total adjusted income	67,000	16,750	83,750
NCI share of asset adjustments		1,250	
Taxable income.........................	67,000	18,000	
Tax..................................	20,100	5,400	25,500
Net of tax share of income................	46,900	11,300	58,250

Parent Income Distribution

	Internally generated net income	150,000
	Realized gain	4,000
	Adjusted income before tax........	154,000
	Company P share of taxes (30% × $154,000)...........	(46,200)
	Company P net income	107,800
	Controlling share of subsidiary	46,900
	Controlling interest	154,700

Worksheet A6-2

Nonaffiliated Group for Tax Purposes
Company P and Subsidiary Company S
Worksheet for Consolidated Financial Statements
For Year Ended December 31, 20X2

	(Credit balance amounts are in parentheses.)	Trial Balance	
		Company P	Company S
1	Cash	19,200	80,000
2	Inventory	170,000	150,000
3	Investment in Company S	504,000	
4			
5			
6	Patent		
7	Plant and Equipment	600,000	550,000
8	Accumulated Depreciation	(410,000)	(120,000)
9			
10	Current Tax Liability	(24,000)	(18,000)
11	**Deferred Tax Liability**	**(13,140)**	
12	Common Stock—Co. S		(250,000)
13	Retained Earnings—Co. S		(350,000)
14			
15			
16			
17	Common Stock—Co. P	(250,000)	
18	Retained Earnings—Co. P	(510,450)	
19			
20			
21	Sales	(430,000)	(240,000)
22	Cost of Goods Sold	280,000	150,000
23			
24	Patent Amortization Expense		
25	Depreciation Expense	20,000	10,000
26	Other Expenses	50,000	20,000
27	**Provision for Tax**	**25,890**	**18,000**
28	Subsidiary Income	(31,500)	
29	Totals	0	0
30	Consolidated Net Income		
31	NCI Share		
32	Controlling Share		
33	NCI		
34	Controlling Retained Earnings		
35	Totals		

Eliminations and Adjustments:

(CY1) Eliminate the parent's entry recording its share of the current year's subsidiary income. This step returns the investment account to its balance on January 1, 20X4.
(EL) Eliminate 75% of the January 1, 20X4, subsidiary equity balances against the investment in Company S account.
(D) Record the NCI portion of excess of fair value over book value, distribute excess in investment account, and adjust patent to fair value.
(A) Amortize the patent at an amount of $2,000 per year for the current and prior three years. Split retained earnings for prior years 75% controlling retained earnings, 25% NCI.
(IS) Eliminate intercompany merchandise sales of $100,000 to avoid double counting sale and purchase.
(BI) Reduce the cost of goods sold by the $24,000 of intercompany profit included in the beginning inventory. Since the sale was made by the parent, the reduction of retained earnings is allocated only to the parent.

(Facts on page 546)

Eliminations and Adjustments				Consolidated Income Statement	NCI	Controlling Retained Earnings	Consolidated Balance Sheet	
Dr.		Cr.						
							99,200	1
		(EI)	16,000				304,000	2
		(CY1)	31,500					3
		(EL)	450,000					4
		(D)	22,500					5
(D)	30,000	(A)	8,000				22,000	6
		(F1)	40,000				1,110,000	7
(F1)	16,000							8
(F2)	8,000						(506,000)	9
							(42,000)	10
(T1)	16,695	(T2)	4,539				(984)	11
(EL)	187,500				(62,500)			12
(EL)	262,500	(NCI)	7,500					13
(A)	1,500	(T1)	1,800					14
(F1)	6,000							15
(BI)	6,000				(83,300)			16
							(250,000)	17
(A)	4,500							18
(BI)	18,000	(T1)	14,895					19
(F1)	18,000					(484,845)		20
(IS)	100,000			(570,000)				21
		(IS)	100,000					22
(EI)	16,000	(BI)	24,000	322,000				23
(A)	2,000			2,000				24
		(F2)	8,000	22,000				25
				70,000				26
(T2)	4,539			48,429				27
(CY1)	31,500							28
	728,734		728,734					29
				(105,571)				30
				11,400	(11,400)			31
				94,171		(94,171)		32
					(157,200)		(157,200)	33
						(579,016)	(579,016)	34
							0	35

(EI) Reduce the ending inventory to its cost to the consolidated company by decreasing it $16,000, and increase the cost of goods sold by $16,000.

(F1) Reduce retained earning for the remaining undepreciated intercompany equipment gain on January 1, 20X4. Since the sale was by the subsidiary, the adjustment is allocated 25% to the NCI and 75% to the controlling retained earnings.

(F2) Adjust depreciation expense and accumulated for $8,000 over depreciation of equipment in current year. This is the added depreciation caused by the $40,000 intercompany gain.

(T1) Prior-year tax adjustment; see accompanying schedule.

(T2) Current-year tax adjustment; see accompanying schedule.

Common Information

Ownership interest	75.00%
Price paid (Including direct acquisition costs)	285,000
Year of consolidation (1 = year of purchase)	4

Price Analysis
Determination and Distribution of Excess Schedule

	Company	Cont	NCI			
Price paid for investment	380,000	285,000	95,000			
Less book value interest acquired:						
Common stock	250,000					
Paid-in excess of par	—					
Retained earnings	100,000					
Total equity	350,000					
Interest acquired		75.00%	25.00%			
		262,500	87,500			
Excess of cost over book value (debit)	30,000	22,500	7,500			
Patent	30,000			**Debit D1**	15	2,000

Schedules

Amortization Schedules

Year of Consolidation 4

Account Adjustments To Be Amortized	**Life**	**Annual Amount**	**Current Year**	**Prior Years**	**Total**	**Key**
Patent	15	2,000	2,000	6,000	8,000	A2

Intercompany Inventory Profit Deferral

	Parent Amount	**Parent Percent**	**Parent Profit**	**Sub Amount**	**Sub Percent**	**Sub Profit**
Beginning	—	0%	—	60,000	40%	24,000
Ending	—	0%	—	40,000	40%	16,000

Intercompany Merchandise Information

	Parent Sales	**Parent Percent**	**Subsidiary Sales**	**Subsidiary Percent**
Current year sales			100,000	
Unpaid account balance, year end			—	
Beginning inventory			80,000	40%
Ending Inventory			40,000	40%

Intercompany Equipment Sales

	By Parent	**By Sub**
Profit amount		40,000
Life of asset		5
Annual depreciation adjustment		8,000
Year of sale (assume beginning of year)		2

Intercompany Fixed Asset Profit Deferral

	Parent	Sub
Origainal profit	40,000	
Year of sale	2	
Realized in prior years	16,000	
Balance, start of year	24,000	
Realized in current year	8,000	

Subsidiary Income Distribution

Ending inventory profit	16,000	Internally generated net income	60,000
Amortizations	2,000	Beginning inventory profit	24,000
		Total	66,000
		Company S share of taxes (30%)	(19,950)
		Net income	46,050
		NCI share	11,400
		Controlling share	34,650

Subsidiary Tax Schedule	Controlling	NCI	Total
Total adjusted income	49,500	16,500	66,000
NCI share of asset adjustments		500	
Taxable income	49,500	17,000	
Tax	14,850	5,100	19,950
Net income	34,650	11,400	

Parent Income Distribution

		Internally generated net income	80,000
		Realized gain	8,000
		Adjusted income before tax	88,000
		Company P share of taxes (30% × $96,000)	(26,400)
		Company P net income	61,600
		Controlling share of subsidiary	34,650
		Second tax on subsidiary income (0.3 × 0.2 × $34,650)	(2,079)
		Controlling interest	94,171

(T1) Adjust beginning retained earnings and create a deferred tax asset (DTA) on consolidated prior period adjustments as follows:

DTA/DTL Adjustments

To beginning retained earnings

Subsidiary Transactions	Total	Parent Share	Subsidiary Share
Remaining fixed asset profit	24,000	18,000	6,000
Amortization of excess (patent, 75% × $6,000)	4,500	4,500	
Total	28,500	22,500	6,000
First tax (30%)	8,550	6,750	1,800
Net income after tax	19,950	15,750	4,200
20% × 30% × $15,750	945	945	
Total tax	9,495	7,695	1,800

Parent Transactions:			
Beginning inventory	24,000	24,000	
First tax (30% × $24,000)	7,200	7,200	
Total increase in DTA and retained earnings	16,695	14,895	1,800

(T2) Adjust current year tax provision and adjust deferred tax asset (DTA) for the effects of current year income adjustments.

Subsidiary Transactions	Total	Parent Share	Subsidiary Share
Realized fixed asset profit	(8,000)	(6,000)	(2,000)
Amortization of excess (patent, 75% × $2,000)	1,500	1,500	
Total	(6,500)	(4,500)	(2,000)
First tax (30%)	(1,950)	(1,350)	(600)
20% × 30 × (4,500 – $1,350) first tax	(189)	(189)	
Total tax	(2,139)	(1,539)	(600)
Parent Transactions:			
Beginning inventory	(24,000)		
Ending inventory	16,000		
Total	(8,000)		
First tax (30% × $8,000)	(2,400)	(2,400)	
Increase (decrease) in DTA	(4,539)	(3,939)	(600)

CHAPTER 6 EXERCISES AND PROBLEMS

Exercise SA6-1 Consolidated taxation, intercompany profits. Deko Company purchased an 80% interest in the common stock of Farelly Company for $850,000 on January 1, 20X7. At the time of the purchase, the total stockholders' equity of Farelly was $968,750. The price paid was $75,000 in excess of the book value of the controlling portion of Farelly equity. The excess was attributed to a patent with a 10-year life.

During 20X9, Deko Company and Farelly Company reported the following internally generated income before taxes:

	Deko Company	Farelly Company
Sales	$ 300,000	$120,000
Cost of goods sold	(200,000)	(90,000)
Gain on machine	5,000	
Expenses	(40,000)	(20,000)
Income before taxes	$ 65,000	$ 10,000

Farelly Company sold goods to Deko Company for $50,000. Deko Company had $20,000 of Farelly Company's goods in its beginning inventory and $6,000 of Farelly's goods in its ending inventory. Farelly Company sells goods to Deko Company at a gross profit of 40%.

Deko Company sold a new machine to Farelly Company on January 1, 20X9, for $30,000. The machine has a 5-year life, and its cost was $25,000. The affiliated group files a consolidated tax return and is taxed at 30%.

Prepare a consolidated income statement for 20X9. Include income distribution schedules for both companies.

Exercise SA6-2 Separate taxation, intercompany transactions. (This is the same as Exercise SA6-1, but with separate taxation.) Decker Company purchased an 80% interest in the common stock of Ferris Company for $850,000 on January 1, 20X7. At the time of the purchase, the total stockholders' equity of Ferris was $968,750. The price paid was

$75,000 in excess of the book value of the controlling portion of Ferris equity. The excess was attributed to a patent with a 10-year life.

During 20X9, Decker Company and Ferris Company reported the following internally generated income before taxes:

	Decker Company	Ferris Company
Sales	$ 300,000	$120,000
Cost of goods sold	(200,000)	(90,000)
Gain on machine	5,000	
Expenses	(40,000)	(20,000)
Income before taxes	$ 65,000	$ 10,000

Ferris Company sold goods to Decker Company for $50,000. Decker Company had $20,000 of Ferris Company's goods in its beginning inventory and $6,000 of Ferris's goods in its ending inventory. Ferris Company sells goods to Decker Company at a gross profit of 40%.

Decker Company sold a new machine to Ferris Company on January 1, 20X9, for $30,000. The machine has a 5-year life, and its cost was $25,000. The companies file separate tax returns. Both are subject to a 30% tax rate. Decker receives an 80% dividend deduction.

Prepare a consolidated income statement for 20X9. Include income distribution for both companies.

Problem SA6-1 Solve problem 6-11 in the current text under the new procedure. Assume that the value of the NCI shares is equal to the price paid per share for the controlling interest.

CHAPTER 7

Step Purchases. A step purchase is a purchase where the parent buys its interest in a subsidiary in stages over time. The simplest case is where the potential parent company has a less than controlling interest (typically under 50%) in voting common stock of another company and then purchases another block of the same company's voting common stock, such that it achieves control of the company. The new procedures require that the prior holding first be adjusted to fair value. Then, the prior holding is added to the newly purchased shares to form a single fair value for the total shares owned. The other situation would be where the parent company purchases enough shares in the first purchase to establish control (and thus to consolidate). If the parent later buys additional shares of the subsidiary, the consolidated viewpoint is that it has retired subsidiary shares. Being a retirement, there is no cause for revaluation of subsidiary accounts or to record a gain or loss. Any impact of the transaction is recorded as an adjustment of paid-in capital in excess of par.

The bottom line in step purchases is that:

- There is only one date upon which control is achieved.
- There is only one revaluation of subsidiary accounts to fair value.
- Only one D&D schedule is ever prepared.

Control Not Achieved upon Initial Investment. The previously owned, noncontrolling investment in voting common stock is adjusted to fair value on the date that the later interest (that creates control) is purchased. This would mean that the prior investment is increased to the share price paid for the later purchase. The exact procedures depend on the category of the prior investment. The procedures are summarized in the following table.

Type of Investment **Sample journal entries assuming an increase in value, where:**
CFV – C = Current fair value (on date control is achieved) – Cost
PPFV – C = Fair value at end of prior period – Cost
CFV – E = Current fair value (on date control is achieved) – Equity adjusted cost (on date control is achieved)

Trading

Note: Trading status would be rare where the intention is to achieve control. The previously owned shares are adjusted to fair value on the date control is achieved. The fair value adjustment, applicable to the shares as of the end of the prior period, is reversed as an adjustment to current-year income.

Investment in S Stock	CFV – C	
Unrealized Gain, Stock Revaluation		CFV – C
Unrealized Gain, Fair Value Adjustment	PPFV – C	
Fair Value Adjustment, Trading Investments		PPFV – C

Available for Sale

The previously owned shares are adjusted to fair value on the date control is achieved. The fair value adjustment, applicable to the shares as of the end of the prior period, is reversed as an adjustment to Other Cumulative Comprehensive Income (a stockholders' equity account).

Investment in S Stock	CFV – C	
Unrealized Gain, Stock Revaluation		CFV – C
Other Cumulative Comprehensive Income	PPFV – C	
Fair Value Adjustment, Available-for-Sale Investments		PPFV – C

Influential (typically over 20%)

The previously owned shares are adjusted form their equity adjusted cost to fair value on the date control is achieved. Prior to this entry, the investment would be equity adjusted up to the date control is achieved.

Investment in S Stock (equity adjusted to date)	CFV – E	
Unrealized Gain, Stock Revaluation		CFV – E

As an example, assume that Company P purchased 10,000 Company S common stock shares on January 1, 20X1, for $400,000 as an available-for-sale investment. Further assume that Company S has 100,000 total shares of common stock outstanding. Assume that on December 31, 20X1, the shares had a value of $45 each. The following accounts would appear on the Company P balance sheet as of December 31, 20X1:

Long-term assets:	
Investment in stock of Company S	$400,000
Adjustment to fair value, available-for-sale investments	50,000
Total investments	$450,000
Stockholders' equity:	
Other cumulative comprehensive income	$50,000

On July 1, 20X2, Company P purchases 60,000 additional shares at $52 per share, a total price of $3,120,000. The entries to record the purchase as a revaluation of the prior investment would be:

To record purchase of 60,000 shares for $52 per share = $3,120,000:		
Investment in Company S	3,120,000	
Cash		3,120,000
To adjust prior 10,000 share investment to current fair value:		
Investment in Company S	520,000	
Unrealized Gain, Fair Value Adjustment CFV – C = [10,000 × ($52 – $40 cost)]		120,000
Available-for-Sale Investment		400,000
To reverse prior fair value adjustment:		
Other Cumulative Comprehensive Income, PPFV – C = [10,000 × ($45 – $40 cost)]	50,000	
Adjustment to Fair Value, Available-for-Sale Investments		50,000

The total investment balance would be calculated as:

Cost of July 1, 20X1, investment of 60,000 shares	$3,120,000
Adjusted fair value of prior January 1, 20X1, purchase ($400,000 + $120,000 fair value adjustment)	520,000
Total fair value of 70% controlling interest	$3,640,000

A D&D schedule would be prepared based on a single value of $3,640,000 for a 70% ownership interest. All revaluations of subsidiary accounts would be based on their values on July 1, 20X2, the date that control is achieved.

Control Achieved upon Initial Investment. When control already exists when a later block of subsidiary shares is purchased, consolidation procedures are already in use. Prior statements have been consolidated based on the D&D schedule prepared on the date control was achieved. The fair value adjustments made on the date control was achieved are binding; the fair value of subsidiary accounts on the date of the later purchase are not acknowledged. The later purchase is viewed, from the consolidated point of view, as a transfer of ownership from the NCI to the controlling interest.

As an example, assume that Company P purchased its original 60% (6,000 shares) controlling interest in Company S on January 1, 20X1, for $126,000. On that date, Company S had the following balance sheet.

Assets		Liabilities and Equity	
Current assets	$ 50,000	Liabilities	$ 40,000
Equipment (net)	150,000	Common stock ($10 par, 10,000 shares)	100,000
		Retained earnings	60,000
Total assets......	$200,000	Total liabilities and equity ...	$200,000

Assume that equipment has a fair value of $180,000 with a 5-year remaining life. Any remaining excess is attributed to goodwill. The following D&D schedule would be prepared for the 6% purchase.

Company P and Subsidiary Company S
Determination and Distribution of Excess Schedule

	Company Value	Parent Price	NCI Value	Amort. Period	Annual Amort.
Fair value of subsidiary	210,000	126,000	84,000		
Less book value of interest acquired:					
Common stock, $10 par	100,000				
Retained earnings	60,000				
Total stockholders' equity....	160,000				
Interest		60%	40%		
Book value of interest.........		96,000	64,000		
Excess of cost over book value....	50,000	30,000	20,000		
Allocated to:					
Equipment	30,000			5	6,000
Goodwill	20,000				

On January 1, 20X3, Company P acquired 2,000 shares from NCI shareholders for $35 each, a total of $70,000. Further assume that the Company S retained earnings on that date was $100,000, a $40,000 increase since the date of the purchase of the original 60% interest. The difference between the $70,000 price paid and the January 1, 20X3, NCI balance is the adjustment of parent paid-in excess caused by the acquisition of the shares. The following modified D&D schedule is prepared for the new 20% interest:

Price paid for 20% interest, 50% of then existing 40% NCI		$70,000
Less book value of NCI interest purchased:		
Common stock, $10 par, 2,000 shares	$ 20,000	
Retained earnings, January 1, 20X3, 20% × $100,000	20,000	
Total book value of interest purchased		40,000
Excess of cost over book value..............................		$30,000

Excess attributed to change in NCI:		
Original excess cost for company	$ 50,000	
Amortizations to date, 2 years × $6,000	(12,000)	
Balance	$ 38,000	
NCI adjustment applicable to shares purchased	× 20%	7,600
Balance, adjustment to parent paid-in capital in excess of par (unless there is none, then adjustment is to parent retained earnings)		$22,400

This $7,600 and $22,400 adjustment becomes much like the distribution of the excess in prior worksheets. This adjustment would be made on each consolidated worksheet in future periods.

Sale of Parent's Investment in Subsidiary

When a parent sells sufficient shares of a subsidiary to lose control, a gain on the sale is recorded. If the parent sells a portion of its investment, but retains a large enough interest to maintain control, no gain or loss can be recorded on the sale. Instead, the consolidated viewpoint holds that the parent has issued additional shares of stock and any resulting adjustment must be recorded in the controlling paid-in excess account.

Sale of Investment Resulting in Loss of Control

There is no change in recording the sale of the parent's entire interest. The investment is adjusted to reflect past amortizations of excess applicable to the controlling interest. A gain or loss is recorded on the sale.

There is a new procedure if the parent retains shares after selling enough shares to lose control. The entire interest must be adjusted to fair value and a gain recorded on all shares owned prior to the sale. For example, if a parent owned an 80% interest in a subsidiary and sold three-fourths (a 60% interest), the entire 80% investment would be adjusted to fair value and a gain would be recorded on the entire interest. The shares still owned by the parent would remain an investment of the parent, restated at fair value.

In making this calculation, it is assumed that the price received for the shares sold would also indicate the fair value of the shares retained.

Partial Sale of Investment with Control Maintained

The current edition of the text does not allow a gain or loss to be recorded on the sale of a partial interest when control is maintained. Instead, any difference between the adjusted cost and the sale price is viewed as an equity transaction that results in an adjustment to paid-in capital. There is no change in the procedures shown for this type of sale.

CHAPTER 7 EXERCISES AND PROBLEMS

Exercise SA7-1 Block purchase, control with first block. Barker Corporation purchased a 60% interest in Hard Knock Company on January 1, 20X1, for $120,000. On that date, Hard Knock Company had the following stockholders' equity:

Common stock ($10 par)	$100,000
Retained earnings	20,000
Total equity	$120,000

Any excess of cost over fair value was due to equipment with a 10-year life.

Barker Corporation purchased another 20% interest for $40,000 on January 1, 20X3, when Hard Knock Company had the following stockholders' equity:

Common stock ($10 par)	$100,000
Retained earnings	50,000
Total equity	$150,000

Prepare the D&D schedule for the 60% interest on January 1, 20X1, and the analysis of the impact of the 20% investment on January 1, 20X3.

Exercise SA7-2 Block purchase, control with second block. Boon Corporation purchased a 10% interest in Doyle Company on January 1, 20X1, as an available-for-sale investment for a price of $40,000.

On January 1, 20X6, Boon Corporation purchased 7,000 additional shares of Doyle Company from existing shareholders for $315,000. This purchase raised Boon's interest to 80%. Doyle Company had the following balance sheet just prior to Boon's second purchase:

Assets		Liabilities and Equity	
Current assets	$165,000	Liabilities	$ 65,000
Buildings (net)	140,000	Common stock, $10 par	100,000
Equipment (net)	100,000	Retained earnings	240,000
Total assets	$405,000	Total liabilities and equity	$405,000

At the time of the second purchase, Boon determined that Doyle's equipment was understated by $50,000 and had a 5-year remaining life. All other book values approximated fair values. Any remaining excess is attributed to goodwill.

1. Prepare a determination and distribution of excess schedule for the second purchase.
2. Record the investment made by Boon on January 1, 20X6, and any required adjustment of the prior 10% interest.

Exercise SA7-3 Block purchase, influence, then control. Cleft Company purchased a 20% interest (10,000 shares) in Key Industries on January 1, 20X2, for $100,000 and another 60% interest on January 1, 20X4, for $360,000. Key had the following stockholders' equity balances immediately prior to each purchase:

Stockholders' Equity	January 1, 20X2	January 1, 20X4
Common stock ($1 par)	$ 50,000	$ 50,000
Paid-in capital in excess of par	400,000	400,000
Retained earnings	20,000	100,000
Total equity	$470,000	$550,000

Cleft's analysis on the two purchase dates revealed the following:

- On January 1, 20X2, Key's equipment was undervalued by $10,000 and had a remaining life of five years.
- On January 1, 20X4, Key's equipment was undervalued by $9,000, with a 3-year remaining life.
- Any excess is attributable to goodwill.

1. Prepare a determination and distribution of excess schedule for each investment.
2. Prepare the entry to record the 60% purchase and to make any adjustments needed for the prior 20% interest.

Exercise SA7-4 Sale of interest, loss of control. Rob Company purchased a 90% interest in Venlo Company for $405,000 on January 1, 20X3. Any excess of cost over book value was attributed to equipment, which is being depreciated over 20 years. Both companies end their reporting periods on December 31. Since the investment in Venlo Company is consolidated, Rob Company has chosen to use the cost method to maintain its investment.

On December 31, 20X6, Rob Company sold 8,000 shares of Venlo Company for $700,000. The remaining shares will be held as an available-for-sale investment. The following stockholders' equity balances of Venlo Company are available:

	January 1, 20X3	January 1, 20X6
Common stock ($10 par)	$100,000	$100,000
Retained earnings	250,000	420,000
Total equity	$350,000	$520,000

Venlo Company earned $70,000 during 20X6.

Prepare a determination and distribution of excess schedule. Record the sale of the shares of Venlo Company and any other adjustments needed to the investment account.

Problem SA7-1 Worksheet, blocks, control with first block. The following information was available on January 1, 20X2, the date on which Parish Company purchased a 60% interest in Sharper Company for $140,000. Sharper Company's equity was as follows:

Common stock ($10 par)	$ 75,000
Retained earnings	60,000
Total stockholders' equity	$135,000

The excess of cost over book value is attributed to equipment with a 10-year life.

On December 31, 20X3, Parish purchased an additional 20% interest in Sharper for $70,000. Sharper's stockholders' equity was determined to be the following at that date:

Common stock	$ 75,000
Retained earnings	85,000
Total stockholders' equity	$160,000

On December 31, 20X5, the following trial balances are available:

	Parish Company	Sharper Company
Current Assets	200,000	55,000
Investment in Sharper Company (60%)	182,000	
Investment in Sharper Company (20%)	79,000	
Property, Plant, and Equipment (net)	450,000	170,000
Current Liabilities	(110,000)	(20,000)
Common Stock ($10 par)	(500,000)	(75,000)
Retained Earnings, January 1, 20X5	(198,000)	(100,000)
Sales	(400,000)	(110,000)
Subsidiary Income	(28,000)	
Cost of Goods Sold	200,000	60,000
Other Expenses	100,000	15,000
Dividends Declared	25,000	5,000
Totals	0	0

Required ▶ ▶ ▶ ▶ ▶

1. Prepare the determination and distribution of excess schedule for the 60% purchase of Sharper stock by Parish Company. Prepare an analysis of the impact of the 20% investment.
2. Prepare the worksheet necessary to produce the consolidated financial statements of Parish Company and its subsidiary as of Dec. 31, 20X5. Include income distribution schedules.

Note: Amortizations of excess are allocated 60% and 40% prior to the purchase of the 20% additional interest, and 75% and 25% after the purchase of the additional 20% interest.

Problem SA7-2 Worksheet, blocks, control with second block. On January 1, 20X4, Madden Company purchased a 20% interest (4,000 shares) in Clayton Company for $100,000. Two years subsequent to this purchase, Madden Company acquired an additional 45% interest (9,000 shares) in Clayton Company for $270,000.

Balance sheets of Clayton Company immediately prior to the purchases were as follows:

Assets	January 1, 20X4	January 1, 20X6
Current assets	$150,000	$120,000
Land	150,000	150,000
Equipment (net)	200,000	300,000
Total assets	$500,000	$570,000
Liabilities and Equity		
Liabilities	$100,000	$110,000
Equity:		
Common stock ($5 par)	$100,000	$100,000
Paid-in capital in excess of par	150,000	150,000
Retained earnings	150,000	210,000
Total equity	$400,000	$460,000
Total liabilities and equity	$500,000	$570,000

On January 1, 20X4, and January 1, 20X6, Clayton's book values approximated fair values, except for the land, which was undervalued by $50,000. Any remaining excess is attributed to a patent with a 10-year life starting January 1, 20X4.

The original 20% investment had been maintained under the sophisticated equity method. Since it now will be necessary to prepare consolidated statements, the simple equity method is in use for 20X6.

On December 31, 20X6, Madden's investment in Clayton was determined as follows:

Original cost of 20% investment	$100,000
20X4–X5 equity adjustment, net of excess amortization	10,000
Original cost of 45% investment	270,000
65% of income, January 1, 20X6–December 31, 20X6	26,000
Investment in Clayton Company	$406,000

The following trial balances were prepared on December 31, 20X6:

	Madden Company	Clayton Company
Current Assets	230,000	225,000
Investment in Clayton Company	406,000	
Land	240,000	150,000
Building (net)	480,000	
Equipment (net)	400,000	220,000
Other Assets	20,000	5,000
Liabilities	(340,000)	(100,000)
Common Stock ($10 par)	(1,000,000)	
Common Stock ($5 par)		(100,000)
Paid-In Capital in Excess of Par		(150,000)
Retained Earnings, January 1, 20X6	(350,000)	(210,000)
Sales	(900,000)	(350,000)
Subsidiary Income	(26,000)	
Cost of Goods Sold	540,000	180,000
Other Expenses	250,000	130,000
Dividends Declared	50,000	
Totals	0	0

1. Correct the investment balance to reflect the fair value of the first 20% investment. Correct the worksheet amounts shown above for the adjustment.
2. Prepare the worksheet necessary to produce the consolidate financial statements of Madden Company and its subsidiary as of December 31, 20X6. Include the determination and distribution of excess and income distribution schedules. Be sure to work from corrected trial balances.

CHAPTER 8

Subsidiary Stock Dividends

No change other than inclusion of NCI in D&D schedules.

Subsidiary Sale of Its Own Shares; Subsidiary Purchase of Its Own Common Stock

Some companies have recorded gains and losses on the effect of subsidiary stock transactions. However, this text treats all transactions as having no impact on income. Any effect is adjusted to controlling paid-in excess (except some negative impacts that are a debit to controlling retained earnings).

The D&D at the time of the original purchase will change to reflect the revaluation of the NCI.

Indirect Holdings; Mutual Holdings

There are no changes in these topics other than the revaluation of the NCI in the original D&D schedule.

CHAPTER 8 EXERCISES

Exercise SA8-1 Subsidiary stock issuance. Star Company had the following stockholders' equity on January 1, 20X1:

Common stock ($1 par, 10,000 shares)	$ 10,000
Paid-in excess of par	190,000
Retained earnings	300,000
Total equity	$500,000

Pardee Company purchased 8,000 shares on January 1, 20X1, for $80 per share. Any excess of cost over book value is attributable to a building with a 10-year life.

On January 1, 20X3, Star's retained earnings had increased by $200,000. On that date, Star sold 2,000 newly issued shares for $120 per share.

Assuming that Pardee uses the simple equity method for its investment in Star, prepare the needed adjusting entry to reflect the impact of the stock scale on its investment.

Exercise SA8-2 Star Company had the following stockholders' equity on January 1, 20X1:

Common stock ($1 par, 10,000 shares)	$ 10,000
Paid-in excess of par	190,000
Retained earnings	300,000
Total equity	$500,000

The Pardee Company purchased 8,000 shares on January 1, 20X1, for $80 per share. Any excess of cost over book value is attributable to a building with a 10-year life.

On January 1, 20X3, Star's retained earnings had increased by $200,000. On that date, Star sold 2,000 newly issued shares for $120 per share.

Assuming that Pardee uses the simple equity method for its investment in Star, prepare the needed adjusting entry to reflect the impact of the stock sale on its investment for each of the following assumptions:

a. Pardee purchases all the newly issued shares.
b. Pardee purchases 1,000 of the newly issued shares. NCI shareholders purchase the remaining shares.

PART

Multinational Accounting and Other Reporting Concerns

2

Chapter 9: *The International Accounting Environment*	**Chapter 11:** *Translation of Foreign Financial Statements*
Module: *Derivatives and Related Accounting Issues*	**Chapter 12:** *Interim Reporting and Disclosures about Segments of an Enterprise*
Chapter 10: *Foreign Currency Transactions*	

In today's evolving global economy, companies buy goods and services from foreign sources, manufacture goods in a number of different countries, and sell their products to customers throughout the world. The complexities of the many international transactions have required accounting to become more international in nature. Efforts are underway to develop accounting principles that are comparable or harmonious between trading nations.

As international trading expands, accounting principles must address how to account for transactions involving different currencies. Since changes in currency exchange rates expose trading parties to potential gains or losses, the economic consequences of such rate changes must be measured. Also, companies often use different strategies to reduce risk. Hedging strategies, including the use of such derivatives as forward contracts, options, and currency swaps, add complexity to accounting for these transactions.

Companies also invest in foreign entities. These investments create a need to translate foreign entity financial statements from one currency into another. Specialized accounting procedures are used for the required translation or remeasurement from the foreign currency into the domestic currency of the investor.

Interim reporting and segmental reporting are designed to provide timely and relevant information for decision making. Both types of reporting involve the application of special accounting principles. Timely reporting of interim information serves as an indicator of annual results. Segmental reports, arising from growing diversification in companies domestically and globally, communicate useful financial information about segmental assets and performance.

The International Accounting Environment

CHAPTER

9

Learning Objectives

When you have completed this chapter, you should be able to

1. **Describe the international business environment.**
2. **Explain why comparable accounting standards are needed.**
3. **Describe major areas of interest involved in international accounting.**
4. **List several factors that influence the development of accounting among nations.**
5. **Identify the major cultural classifications that can be used to categorize accounting systems.**
6. **Explain the goal of harmonization.**
7. **Explain several approaches that characterize attempts to harmonize accounting principles.**
8. **Discuss the role of the International Accounting Standards Board (IASB) and the International Federation of Accountants (IFAC).**
9. **Demonstrate how foreign companies listed on U.S. stock exchanges reconcile their respective accounting principles to U.S. GAAP.**
10. **Describe transfer-pricing issues and differences in tax systems.**

Jacob Corporation (a fictitious company) began with a small facility in central Wisconsin, where it manufactured precision measuring equipment to be used primarily in the food industry. As the company began to grow, its sales extended throughout the continental United States. While attending a trade show in Atlanta, Georgia, company representatives had the opportunity to arrange a sale to a foreign customer in Germany, and that was the beginning of the company's venture into export sales. The sale to the German company was collected in U.S. dollars, and the company began to expand its sales to other foreign customers. However, as these sales increased, a number of customers settled their accounts by payment in foreign currencies rather than U.S. dollars. The company quickly realized that this could be good news or bad news, depending on how the U.S. dollar performed against the respective foreign currencies. For example, if the dollar strengthened against the foreign currency, the foreign currency collected by the company when the other company paid its account was actually worth fewer dollars than its value at the time of sale. To help reduce such risks, Jacob Corporation retained outside consultants.

As the company grew and attempted to increase profit margins, it began to purchase manufacturing parts from a foreign vendor. Years later, the company established a foreign sales office in Frankfurt, Germany, which allowed it to qualify for certain tax benefits associated with such sales offices as provided by the Internal Revenue Service. However, the income associated with the sales office was subject to the tax laws of Germany.

As sales continued to grow, the company decided to open another manufacturing facility in France. This new facility was established as a separate French company subject to the laws of France but owned 90% by the U.S. company. The social, language, legal, taxation, and cultural differences of operating in a foreign country were just a few of the challenges that the company was now dealing with. Shortly after opening the French facility, a national strike resulted in a shutdown of the plant for two months. The French facility has resumed production and ships approximately 40% of its production to a Brazilian company that is a wholly owned subsidiary of the U.S. company. The transfer pricing between the French and Brazilian companies is designed to take advantage of the higher tax rate in France without violating any tax laws that discourage the manipulation of taxable income through transfer-pricing policies.

When developing business policies such as strategic planning, budgeting, inventory control, and internal control, companies must take into consideration the differences between the various parties involved in the operation of domestic and foreign entities. For example, the just-in-time inventory system used in the U.S. manufacturing facility may not work in a foreign manufacturing facility because of less-developed transportation systems or because of instabilities in the countries where major vendors operate.

Today, we find our U.S. company constructing its sixth manufacturing facility—this one in Africa. As part of its agreement with the government of the African country, the U.S. company will be constructing a health clinic and school in the community and guaranteeing a minimum employment level for the next five years. Thus, Jacob Corporation has come a long way from central Wisconsin. It may be a fictitious company, but the scenario described is common in companies today. Welcome to international business and the global economy. All of this is possible when a commercial activity transcends national boundaries or borders.

In this chapter, the derivatives module, and the following two chapters, several issues relating to international accounting will be explored, including the following:

1. Factors influencing international accounting standards,
2. The international standard-setting process,
3. Accounting for transactions denominated or settled in foreign currencies, and
4. The translation and remeasurement of financial statements prepared in a foreign currency.

1

OBJECTIVE

Describe the international business environment.

THE SCOPE OF INTERNATIONAL BUSINESS ACTIVITIES

An entity's involvement in international business can range from export or import activity to that of a multinational or transnational enterprise with a global approach to manufacturing, distribution, and sales. Trade between different nations certainly is not new. It has existed since biblical times and has provided the means by which certain nations have evolved into world powers. England and the Netherlands are just two examples of countries that have been active in international trade for centuries. However, it has been since World War II that international trade has increased significantly, and many more goods and services are becoming part of a global economy.

Dramatic changes occurring in recent times have allowed a global economy to become a reality for an increasing number of entities. The restructuring of Eastern Europe and the former Soviet Union has opened the door for free enterprise. The growth of the European Union has been responsible for reducing the economic barriers between nations by forming a single market with its own common currency, the euro. In 1993, the United States, Mexico, and Canada agreed to a comprehensive free trade agreement known as the North American Free Trade Agreement (NAFTA). The World Trade Organization, formerly the General Agreement on Tariffs and Trade (GATT), is committed to reducing trade barriers through multilateral agreements.

As the barriers to world trade are reduced, the world becomes smaller in a number of ways. For example, modern communications technology makes it much easier to transact business between countries. The credit card purchase you made today may be processed in a center located in Ireland, and tomorrow you will be able to inquire about your account balance which will include your recent purchase. The Internet also is proving to be a significant tool through which entities make their goods and services available to consumers on an international scale.

Not only are goods and services trading in international markets, but the stocks of these companies are also traded internationally. International securities trading has increased rapidly due to a number of forces. As companies expand into different international markets, they need to acquire the factors of production in those markets and, thus, need to raise additional capital. International securities trading also offers investors the opportunity to diversify their portfolios against loss from currency fluctuations, political instabilities, and economic downturns. As of December 31, 2003, over 1,200 foreign companies were registered with and reporting to the U.S. Securities and Exchange Commission, of which over 400 were trading on the New York Stock Exchange.

The Emerging Needs for International Accounting

2

OBJECTIVE

Explain why comparable accounting standards are needed.

Multinational companies, also known as *transnational companies*, must have comparable accounting standards with which to measure the effectiveness and efficiency of their various international subsidiaries, branches, and/or other equity investments. Also, in order to efficiently allocate and regulate the exchange of capital, international capital markets need to evaluate the adequacy of financial statements and disclosures made by those companies seeking to raise capital. Comparable standards of accounting and financial disclosure for companies competing for capital on an international scale are critical to the functioning of such markets. Finally, individual investors exposed to opportunities on an international scale need comparable financial information upon which to base their decisions. Evaluating the profitability or financial position of two competing investment opportunities will have meaning only if comparable accounting standards are in place. The international growth of business and investing naturally creates a need for the international development of accounting. Thus, the development of international accounting standards must be based on an understanding of international business and markets and the factors that affect accounting in various countries.

International accounting standards may also provide a framework that other nations can use to develop their accounting standards. The due process involved in the development of accounting standards is costly and time consuming, and it must consider the positions of a variety of affected parties. An international accounting framework can provide developing nations or nations without a strong accounting profession an important head start.

REFLECTION

- The increasing international business activity includes trading in goods, services, and securities.
- International trade requires comparable financial information and accounting standards.

THE FOCUS OF INTERNATIONAL ACCOUNTING

3

OBJECTIVE

Describe major areas of interest involved in international accounting.

With all of the economic development in the world occurring at such a rapid rate, it is not surprising that international accounting is also rapidly developing. Professional organizations have special interest groups focusing on the area, and a number of organizations concerned with the process of establishing international accounting standards have emerged.

The development of a global economy has drastically changed the environment in which a growing number of entities operate. It is only logical, then, to expect that financial information and accounting systems will evolve to better serve the changing environment. If goods and services are exchanged on an international scale, then financial information will also need to be exchanged on a similar scale. International accounting has developed in response to these changes and is primarily focused on the following major areas of interest:

1. The identification and understanding of principles of financial accounting, managerial accounting, and taxation used in different nations, especially how they differ from nation to nation.
2. The identification of the various organizations and interests involved in the process of establishing international accounting and auditing principles and standards.
3. The special accounting valuation and recognition principles associated with accounting for transactions that are recorded in one nation's currency and denominated or settled in another nation's currency. These transactions are referred to as *foreign currency transactions.*
4. The translation of financial statements that are measured in one nation's currency into another nation's currency. For example, translating a balance sheet measured in euros into a balance sheet measured in dollars.

Due to the expanding nature of international trade and capital markets, today's accounting professional must have some knowledge of international accounting. The balance of this chapter, therefore, will focus on the various environmental factors affecting the development of accounting principles used in certain nations and the establishment of international accounting principles and standards.

The development of accounting principles and standards is an extremely complex process involving a social and cultural environment, various special interest groups, and varying degrees of due process. By studying the standard-setting process in the United States, one realizes how complex the process can be. This complexity holds true in the development of accounting principles and standards in other nations, too. However, it is the factors influencing the process that vary from nation to nation.

4

OBJECTIVE

List several factors that influence the development of accounting among nations.

Factors Influencing the Development of Accounting

Accounting is not defined by nature but, rather, is man-made. It evolves from the environment in which man exists and defines itself in a way which serves the needs of that environment. Given the differences in various environments, it is not surprising that accounting principles may differ between nations. A number of environmental factors such as the following may explain these differences to varying degrees:

1. Social and cultural values
2. Political and legal systems
3. Business activities and economic conditions
4. Standard-setting processes
5. Forms of ownership and capital markets
6. Cooperative efforts between nations

Social and Cultural Values. Social and cultural differences between nations and regions of the world are well documented, and they have had a significant influence on how accounting has developed. For example, if one society places a higher value on privacy than another, it would follow that the financial statement disclosures between the two societies would reflect their respective views toward privacy as well. If a society places emphasis on the individual and his or her immediate family unit over that of a larger group of individuals, it would not be a surprise to see accounting principles being developed in a more independent manner by a professional group rather than a regulatory body. For example, since the United States has emphasized individualism and personal freedoms, the establishment of accounting principles is more the result of private influences rather than regulatory influences.

Political and Legal Systems. A major factor influencing the development of accounting principles has been the political environment in which a nation has developed. For example, nations that previously were ruled or colonized by another country tend to have developed principles similar to those of the ruling nation. Nations such as the United States, Canada, and the Bahamas have accounting principles that historically were patterned after those found in the United Kingdom. Those nations that have more democratic political environments tend to develop principles more through private standard-setting groups than through government decree or regulation. The tax laws and legal requirements of a country also may influence the development of accounting to the extent that differences between accounting income and taxable income are rare or nonexistent.

Business Activities and Economic Conditions. The type and pace of economic development also have influenced the development of accounting. Economies which are more agrarian usually are made up of smaller family-business entities and have not experienced the need for sophisticated accounting practices, such as consolidated financial statements and capitalized lease accounting. On the other hand, those nations which have experienced more rapid economic growth have realized the need for higher-level systems of accounting. Furthermore, as businesses have grown, in most instances in a corporate form, widening investor bases and greater capital needs have led to more emphasis on financial disclosure and the need for audited financial statements.

Standard-Setting Processes. The accounting standard-setting process and the respective views of the standard setters have certainly had an influence on how accounting has developed. The standard-setting process is in response to cultural, political, legal, and other influences. Therefore, it has become a major force through which a number of factors influence accounting. For example, as a country's economy grows, generally the standard-setting process also expands.

Forms of Ownership and Capital Markets. In many countries, most business is still conducted by small, closely held, family businesses. As these economies move toward the corporate form of organization with an increase in equity ownership, the complexity and focus of accounting will change. When a separation of ownership from management occurs, the focus and complexity of accounting also changes. As nations move toward privatization of their infrastructure, encourage free enterprise, and strive to raise the standard of living of their people, their need to attract capital increases. Capital demands, in these instances, are often so great that domestic security markets alone are unable to satisfy them. Providers of capital are fundamentally interested in identifying investment alternatives, evaluating associated risks, and monitoring performance of their investments. Obviously, comparability is a desirable characteristic of accounting information that is sought by providers of capital. As a nation's demand for outside capital increases, there will be pressures to improve the quality of financial measurements and disclosures.

Cooperative Efforts between Nations. As nations engage in cooperative trade efforts, their need for comparable financial information also increases. For example, economic cooperation between the United States, Canada, and Mexico as well as the cooperative efforts of member nations of the European Union have resulted in a need to have common accounting standards to support their common market initiatives. The similarities or differences among accounting principles in various countries may be partially explained by the extent to which cooperative efforts have occurred.

International Accounting Classification Systems

5

OBJECTIVE

Identify the major cultural classifications that can be used to categorize accounting systems.

Once the factors influencing the development of accounting have been identified, it is possible to categorize nations according to one or more of those factors. For example, countries could be categorized as those reflecting more of a macroeconomic or national economic approach to financial reporting compared to those reflecting more of a microeconomic approach with emphasis on the individual entity and maintenance of stakeholder value. The application of these classification systems has resulted in certain countries being grouped together and raises the question of whether social and cultural factors could serve as a useful method of classifying various accounting systems. Using the research performed by S. J. Gray, Radebaugh and Gray have used cultural classification to identify the following categories:[1]

1 Lee H. Radebaugh and Sidney J. Gray, *International Accounting and Multinational Enterprises* (New York: John Wiley & Sons, Inc., 1997), p. 87.

1. Anglo-Saxon accounting
2. Germanic accounting
3. Nordic accounting
4. Latin accounting
5. Asian accounting

Anglo-Saxon accounting is most closely identified with the United States and the United Kingdom. However, it is also easily traceable to countries (Bermuda, Australia, Canada, and Kenya) which were heavily influenced or colonized by major Anglo-Saxon countries. This category is characterized by more independent private standard setting rather than government control and is less constrained by tax laws. The reporting environment is less conservative and less secretive, so there is more disclosure. Germanic accounting has been heavily influenced by a legal system, based on Roman law. As a result, it has a higher level of uniformity in accounting. Differences between accounting income and taxable income are uncommon, thus leading to a conservative approach to accounting measurement. As one might expect, the standard setting at the private level is not significant. Germany, Austria, Switzerland, and Israel are included in this category.

Nordic accounting lies somewhere between Anglo-Saxon and Germanic accounting in that it is less conservative than Germanic and yet more secretive than Anglo-Saxon. The use of replacement-value accounting has been most common within this group. Included in this group are Sweden, Denmark, Norway, the Netherlands, and Finland. Latin accounting is descriptive of the accounting in France, Italy, Belgium, Spain, Portugal, much of South America, Mexico, and certain African nations. Company (corporate) law and taxation are important influences and result in very conservative measurement practices. The high rates of inflation experienced in certain Latin American countries have led to the use of inflation-adjusted financial statements. The accounting profession in these nations does not tend to be well developed. Asian accounting has been influenced by several of the other categories due to the colonial history of the area. For example, accounting in Japan reflects the influences of both the United States and Germany. The accounting in China has been influenced heavily by the former Soviet Union. The government has a major influence over accounting in these countries, and financial reporting adheres to tax law. Accounting tends to be conservative, and yet, in response to the capital markets which have developed, it is becoming more open regarding disclosure.

This system of classification has helped to better understand the factors that have shaped the development of accounting standards within a particular country. Obviously, any progress toward harmonization of accounting systems must begin with an understanding of how various systems differ from each other. Knowledge of these differences and the factors which have influenced them will also help in assessing to what extent harmonization of accounting standards may be achieved. It is very difficult to imagine that differences will not always exist to some extent. Given this observation, comparability can still be achieved indirectly if the differences are well understood.

REFLECTION

- International accounting is primarily focused on the principles employed by various nations, organizations involved in international accounting standard setting, accounting for foreign currency transactions, and translation of foreign financial statements.
- A number of factors may explain why accounting principles between nations differ. Factors include social/cultural values, political/legal systems, types of business activities, economic conditions, the standard-setting process, forms of ownership, the extent of capital markets, and cooperation among nations.
- Through cultural classifications, five major systems of international accounting have been identified as a way to group nations based on their approaches to financial reporting.

HARMONIZATION OF ACCOUNTING SYSTEMS

6
OBJECTIVE
Explain the goal of harmonization.

In a perfect world, identical transactions occurring in different nations should receive identical accounting treatment. Different currencies or languages shouldn't seem to make a difference. Many factors explain why similar transactions receive different accounting treatments. Classification systems, such as the cultural classifications previously discussed, are of further use in understanding and analyzing the differences between countries. Such differences have a significant impact on the measurement and presentation of accounting information. Nevertheless, a number of parties are interested in making accounting information as comparable as possible. Although comparability is their main desire, they may seek it for different reasons. For example, an international labor union may want to have comparable information for collective bargaining and policy decisions. If a governmental body is assessing a multinational enterprise's performance for purposes of determining taxable income, it would be interested in achieving comparability in terms of expense and revenue recognition in each country where the enterprise operates. The government of each country in which it operates would want to know how the enterprise prices goods transferred from one country to another.

Trading partners are interested in evaluating the financial condition and operating results of the respective parties. Obviously, this evaluation would be easier if the parties made accounting measurements based on common accounting standards. Investors seeking to provide capital have a wide range of investment opportunities. In order to achieve the most effective allocation of capital among competing parties, investors are logically seeking as much disclosure of financial information as possible. Furthermore, they are seeking information which is comparable between entities. The International Organization of Securities Commissions (IOSCO) is committed to encouraging international securities trading dependent on providing investors with comparable information which can be used for investment decisions.

Approaches to Harmonization

7
OBJECTIVE
Explain several approaches that characterize attempts to harmonize accounting principles.

The preceding discussion identified a number of parties that would logically be interested in increasing comparability of accounting standards between parties. Harmonization of accounting systems is designed to achieve this goal. Rather than moving toward a strict pattern of uniformity in accounting, harmonization is a flexible approach designed to improve comparability without necessarily requiring a strict system of uniformity in accounting. It is possible to improve comparability through a combination of changes in accounting valuation, presentation, and supplemental disclosures.

International Standard-Setting Process. The harmonization of accounting standards may take several approaches and is a combination of an evolutionary process and a standard-setting process. One approach to the harmonization of accounting standards involves an international standard-setting process on a worldwide basis. The goal is to involve professional accounting organizations from different countries in the development of accounting standards that will be accepted by all countries. This obviously represents a monumental task. The leaders of this movement must be sensitive to the variety of cultural, ethical, and economic differences that exist among countries. This approach to harmonization is gaining recognition, and major forces behind the effort have been the International Accounting Standards Board (IASB) and the International Federation of Accountants (IFAC). The International Accounting Standards Board is concerned with the promulgation and harmonization of international accounting standards. The International Federation of Accountants is concerned with a variety of issues affecting the professional practice of accounting on a worldwide basis, including the harmonization of accounting standards and international auditing standards.

Bilateral Agreements. Another approach to harmonization involves bilateral agreements among two or more countries. This is often a more expedient and efficient method of reducing differences in standards among significant trading partners. The initiatives of the European Union (EU) to harmonize accounting standards among member nations is an example of a bilateral approach to harmonization.

8

OBJECTIVE

Discuss the role of the International Accounting Standards Board (IASB) and the International Federation of Accountants (IFAC).

The International Accounting Standards Board

The International Accounting Standards Board was created in 2001 as a result of a restructuring of its predecessor, the International Accounting Standards Committee (IASC). The IASC was formed in 1973 and had two primary objectives: (1) formulate and publish standards on financial accounting and reporting and promote their worldwide acceptance and (2) work for the harmonization of accounting standards and procedures relating to the presentation of financial statements. Rather than each nation establishing its own accounting standards, the IASC recognized the importance of taking a global approach toward standard setting in order to best serve the global economy. The IASC issued 41 International Accounting Standards (IASs) of which over 30 are still operative.

In the late 1990s, the IASC engaged in a strategy review that resulted in its restructuring. In early 2001, the restructured IASC became the International Accounting Standards Board. The IASB assumed responsibility for establishing a single set of international accounting standards and achieving convergence in or harmonization of accounting standards around the world. The IASC Foundation was formed in 2001 as the parent entity of the IASB, which is based in London. The structure of the IASB consists of the Trustees, the Board, the Standing Interpretations Committee, and the Standards Advisory Council.

Trustees of the IASC Foundation. The Trustees of the IASC Foundation are the ultimate governing body and appoint the members of the Board, the Standing Interpretations Committee, and the Standards Advisory Council. The 19 Trustees come from a variety of countries and have diverse professional backgrounds. Although not responsible for setting international standards, the Trustees are responsible for developing and implementing the strategy and operating policies of the IASB and other committees. The Trustees also appoint members of the IASB and other committees. Decisions are made by simple majority except for amendments to the constitution which require a three-fourths majority.

International Accounting Standards Board. The Board consists of 14 members that are appointed by the Trustees. In order to achieve proper balance, Board membership must consist of the following: a minimum of five with a background as practicing auditors, a minimum of three with a background in the preparation of financial statements, a minimum of three with a background as users of financial statements, and at least one with an academic background. The Trustees are responsible for making sure that the Board is not dominated by a particular constituency and/or geographical area. In order to achieve harmonization of accounting standards and cooperation among standard setters, seven of the Board members have formal liaison responsibilities with national standard setters. The Board has full discretion over the technical agenda and complete responsibility for all technical matters including preparing and issuing International Financial Reporting Standards (IFRSs) and Exposure Drafts and approving Interpretations presented by the International Financial Reporting Interpretations Committee.

The Board has responsibility for establishing a single set of international accounting standards now designated as International Financial Reporting Standards. However, the International Accounting Standards issued by the IASC have been adopted by the IASB and continue to be referred to as IASs. The IASB follows a conceptual accounting framework, "Framework for the Preparation and Presentation of Financial Statements," which was approved in 1989 by the IASC. The framework sets forth the concepts that underlie the preparation and presentation of financial statements for external users and serves as a platform against which future standards are developed and existing standards are reviewed. The Board follows a rigorous due process leading to the issuance of an IFRS. This process includes open meetings, the possible use of an Advisory Committee, and the publication of Discussion Documents and Exposure Drafts for public comment. The Board has the discretion to use field tests and to hold public hearings regarding proposed standards. The publication of a standard, Exposure Draft, or interpretation requires approval by at least eight members of the Board. Other decisions of the Board require a simple majority of the members present at a meeting (at least 60% of the members must be present in person or by telecommunication link). In order to coordinate the standard-setting process of the Board with that of various national standard setters, the Board is proposing a number of procedures that will hopefully lead to an international consensus regarding standards. The Board currently has a number of projects underway that are in various stages of the due process procedure.

International Financial Reporting Interpretations Committee and Standards Advisory Council. The Trustees also appoint 12 individuals to the International Financial Reporting Interpretations Committee. The Committee is responsible for interpreting the application of IFRSs and providing guidance on issues not specifically addressed by an IFRS or IAS. The Committee attempts to identify areas where unsatisfactory or conflicting interpretations have developed and move toward reaching a consensus on an appropriate interpretation. Over 30 interpretations have been issued on a variety of topics of widespread importance. The Trustees also appoint a Standards Advisory Council consisting of 49 members having diverse professional and geographical backgrounds. The council advises the Board on decisions, agenda priorities, implications of proposed standards, and views of other organizations and individuals.

The International Federation of Accountants

Organized in 1977 with headquarters in New York, the International Federation of Accountants (IFAC) is a private body whose membership consists of national professional organizations that represent accountants. Membership is open to such organizations recognized by law or general consensus within their respective countries. The IFAC has over 150 members representing over 100 countries. The IFAC is concerned primarily with aspects of the professional practice of accountancy and represents accountants worldwide in all professional areas including public practice, industry, government, and education. It is involved, not with establishing accounting standards per se, but, rather, with developing the profession and harmonizing its standards worldwide. Therefore, the IFAC is more appropriately compared to the AICPA than the FASB, which is more akin to the IASB.

The IFAC is governed overall by a Council comprised of one representative from each member body. Reporting to the Council is a Board comprised of 22 individuals from various countries. The Board is responsible for setting policy, overseeing operations, implementation of programs, and the work of technical groups. Technical, professional, and ethical publications and guidance are developed by a number of technical committees and task forces. For example, the International Audit and Assurance Standards Board focuses on creating worldwide uniformity in the practice of auditing through the issuance of International Standards on Auditing. The Ethics Committee develops guidance on professional ethics and practices and has developed an IFAC Code of Ethics that serves as a model for national standards of ethical conduct. The Transnational Auditors Committee is the executive committee of the Forum of Firms. Membership in the Forum is open to firms engaged in transnational audits. Member firms commit to quality standards and a global peer review process. The various committees issue statements and guidelines on a variety of topics.

The success of the organizations discussed above is dependent on a variety of factors. Standards generally cannot be imposed; rather, they must be acceptable after appropriate due process. This process must recognize the environmental similarities and, perhaps more important, the dissimilarities between nations. A bridging of the factors separating nations must be accomplished subject to significant time and funding constraints. However, as national economies develop into global economies, the harmonization of accounting standards and the professional practice of accountancy will become more of a natural process.

The European Union: A Bilateral Approach

The European Union is an alliance of nations that have come together to advance their common interests for peace and prosperity. Matters of common interest are made democratically at a group level rather than at a national level. Matters of common interest include, in part, trade and the economy, citizens' rights, the environment, justice and security, and job creation. All decisions are based on treaties and the law of the Union. The European Union (EU) currently consists of 25 nations with additional countries scheduled to become members. The EU has its own floating currency known as the euro which has replaced the old national currency of a number of member nations. Having a single common currency makes it easier for the members to transact business and function on a united basis. The EU consists of five major institutions:

European Parliament, Council of the European Union, European Commission, Court of Justice, and Court of Auditors. In addition, the structure of the EU is supported by other organizations including the European Central Bank and the European Investment Bank.

The European Commission is the primary legislative body of the EU and in that role issues directives and regulations dealing with accounting and financial reporting. In order to reduce the competitive differences which may exist among member nations, Directives on Company Law have been issued which reduce legal differences and promote the comparability of accounting information. The Directives on Company Law include several directives relating to accounting practices among the member nations. In 2000, the European Commission, which is responsible for much of the day-to-day work of the EU, suggested that all listed companies within the EU, including banks and insurance companies, be required to prepare financial statements in accordance with international accounting standards (IASs and IFRSs) after a formal endorsement process by the year 2005. The Council of Ministers of the EU adopted the recommendation as a regulation having the force of law ensuring that financial information serving as a basis for securities trading and business transactions will be more comparable. Some exceptions to the above effective date exist. For example, EU companies that are traded in the United States and use U.S. generally accepted accounting principles (GAAP) will have until 2007 to comply. Furthermore, the Accounting Regulatory Committee, chaired by the Commission, will decide whether to endorse specific international accounting standards. The European Financial Reporting Advisors Group (EFRAG) consisting of private sector accounting experts will provide the expertise needed to assess various international accounting standards. This regulation applies to EU companies that are listed in an EU member securities market. EU member countries have the option as to whether such standards would be required of non-listed companies.

Over 7,000 EU enterprises are expected to be impacted by the regulation requiring the use of IASs and IFRSs. The impact of this regulation is not limited to just EU companies. For example, assume that a U.S. company is wholly owned by an EU-listed company. The U.S. company will have to present financial information on the basis of international accounting standards so that it can be consolidated with the EU parent company. A U.S. parent company of an EU-listed subsidiary will also have to make sure that the EU subsidiary follows international standards. A non-EU-listed company will have to comply with international standards in a number of other instances. The movement toward international accounting standards is so strong that a number of companies have voluntarily adopted such standards knowing that it may not be long before their country requires such use.

Initiatives of the Financial Accounting Standards Board. In addition to the support the IASB has received for its initiatives from the EU, the Financial Accounting Standards Board (FASB) has committed to the support of international accounting standards. The FASB believes that a single set of accounting standards to be used for both domestic and international reporting purposes would be the optimal solution. Clearly, this has not been the case to date. The Securities and Exchange Commission (SEC) allows foreign registrants to use U.S. GAAP, International Accounting Standards, or their own national GAAP. However, if U.S. GAAP are not employed, foreign companies must provide reconciliation to U.S. GAAP. The reconciliation is contained in Form 20-F as set forth in the 1934 SEC Act and highlights differences between U.S. GAAP and the principles used by the registrant.

As of the end of 2003, over 1,200 foreign companies were registered with and reporting to the SEC, of which 480 were Canadian and 115 were from the United Kingdom. A total of 459 companies from 47 countries were listed on the New York Stock Exhange (NYSE) as of October 2004. By way of example, the Imperial Tobacco Group Plc is a U.K. company that prepares its financial statements in accordance with U.K. GAAP. The Company is traded on the NYSE and is required to reconcile its financial statements, measured in pounds, to U.S. GAAP. Excerpts from the Company's Form 20-F filed with the SEC which reconciles to U.S. GAAP are presented in Exhibit 9-1. China Unicom is an integrated provider of telecommunications services in China and prepares its financial statements on the basis of Hong Kong (HK) GAAP. The Company's reconciliation to U.S. GAAP as excerpted from its Form 20-F is also summarized in Exhibit 9-1.

Exhibit 9-1
Reconciliation of Non-U.S. GAAP to U.S. GAAP

Imperial Tobacco Group Plc
Excerpts from Form 20-F

The principal differences between U.K. GAAP and U.S. GAAP as they relate to net income are as follows:

(In millions of pounds)

	2001	2002	2003
Net income under U.K. GAAP	350	272	421
U.S. GAAP adjustments:			
Pensions	45	13	2
Amortization of goodwill	(14)	48	194
Amortization of brands/trademarks/licenses	(8)	(38)	(102)
Deferred taxation	(45)	16	57
Mark to market adjustments on derivatives	106	(10)	(82)
Employee share schemes		(4)	6
Acquisitions inventory step-up	(8)	(42)	
Restructuring costs on acquisition		44	
Net income under U.S. GAAP	426	299	496

China Unicom
Excerpts from Form 20-F

The principal differences between HK GAAP and U.S. GAAP as they relate to net income are as follows:

[In thousands of RBM (renminbi)]*

	2001	2002	2003
Net income under HK GAAP	4,601,859	4,598,213	4,217,097
U.S. GAAP adjustments:			
Related to acquisition of Unicom New Century	433,063	419,906	390,363
Deferral of upfront non-refundable revenue (A)	(1,001,637)	(860,490)	(1,417,474)
Amortization of upfront non-refundable revenue (A)	455,839	526,982	1,223,938
Deferral of direct incremental cost (A)	934,713	776,387	1,417,474
Amortization of direct incremental cost (A)	(358,867)	(435,385)	(1,071,450)
Reversal of depreciation for revalued property, plant, and equipment (B)	7,485	7,485	7,485
Difference in provision for impairment and disposal loss of Paging Business	12,382		55,078
Other adjustments	26,468	(64,245)	(22,070)
Deferred tax effects of U.S. GAAP adjustments	44,190	59,563	(72,018)
Net income under U.S. GAAP	5,155,495	5,028,416	4,728,423

(A) With respect to these items, the Form 20-F states that:
"Under HK GAAP, upfront non-refundable revenue, such as connection fee, is recognized when received upon completion of activation services. Under U.S. GAAP, in accordance with Staff Accounting Bulletin No. 101, 'Revenue Recognition in Financial Statements', upfront non-refundable revenue and the related direct incremental costs incurred are deferred and recognized over the estimated customer service periods. The expected customer service period for the Cellular Business is estimated based on the expected stabilized churn rates. On this basis, the weighted average customer service period based on current estimation considering the prevailing market environment is approximately 4 years (2000: 10 years; 2001 and 2002: 6 years). The effects of the change of accounting estimated were to increase the net income and earnings per share by approximately RMB 70 million and RMB 0.006 respectively for the year ended December 31, 2003 and by approximately RMB 26 million and RMB 0.002 respectively."

(B) With respect to this item, the Form 20-F states that:
"Under HK GAAP, revaluation surplus in relation to buildings is recorded by the Group as part of the property, plant and equipment. Thereafter, depreciation is provided based on the revalued amounts. Under U.S. GAAP, all property, plant and equipment are stated at historical cost less accumulated depreciation, and prepaid land use rights are stated at the unamortized prepaid amount as part of other assets."

*Renminbi (RMB) means "The People's Currency." The yuan is the most common unit of the RMB.

In 2002, the FASB and the IASB signed a memorandum of understanding formalizing their commitment to the convergence of U.S. GAAP and International Accouting Standards. As part of this commitment, the FASB has engaged in a number of intiatives directed to convergence. For example, the FASB and the IASB are conducting a number of joint projects, and a short-term convergence project has already resulted in the issuance of several Exposure Drafts. The short-term convergence project is designed to identify differences between U.S. GAAP and IASs/IFRSs where convergence can likely be achieved promptly. One focus of moving toward a common set of International Accounting Standards is closer communication between the two organizations and consideration of how the development of a new standard can proceed such that convergence rather than divergence is accomplished. In addition to the FASB, the SEC and a number of non-EU nations are also committed to converging to international standards.

9

OBJECTIVE

Demonstrate how foreign companies listed on U.S. stock exchanges reconcile their respective accounting principles to U.S. GAAP.

Demonstrating Differences in Accounting Standards. Even though the initiatives of the IASB, the EU, and the FASB are positive steps toward the harmonization of accounting standards, differences between parties still exist. The very factors that have influenced the development of accounting in the past continue to exist. For example, the accounting treatment surrounding the use of derivatives had been the subject of considerable disagreement between the EU and the IASB. In order to demonstrate some of the continuing differences, Exhibit 9-2 compares the accounting treatment given selected areas by various parties. The accomplishments of the international standard setters have been impressive, and certainly they will meet new challenges in the future. However, as the world gets smaller from a commercial standpoint, the differences between accounting standards among the world's nations also diminish. A significant number of nations outside the EU will either require or allow the use of IASs/IFRSs in the very near future. Examples include Australia, Bolivia, Bulgaria, Egypt, Finland, Jamaica, Peru, and Sweden, and the list goes on. The international standard-setting community is also considering how international standards should be applied to small and medium-sized entities.

Exhibit 9-2
Comparison of Selected Accounting Principles

Factor or Accounting Principle	United States	International Accounting Standard (IAS/IFRS)	China
Approach to standard setting	Principle based	Principle based	Principle based
Member of the European Union	No	IAS/IFRS required of member nations	No
IASs/IFRSs required for domestic listed companies	Not permitted	Yes	No—required for some
Working to achieve convergence between domestic GAAP and IASs/IFRSs	Yes	Yes	Yes
Use of the LIFO inventory method	Permitted	Not permitted (IAS #2)	Not normally permitted
Recognition of deferred taxes	Deferred tax liabilities and assets are recognized	Deferred tax liabilities and assets are recognized (IAS #12)	May elect not to recognize deferred tax accounts

Factor or Accounting Principle	United States	International Accounting Standard (IAS/IFRS)	China
Tax rate used to measure deferred taxes	Measured at the enacted tax rate	Measured at the enacted or "substantially enacted" rate (IAS #12)	Measured at current tax rate or the expected tax rate
Classification as a reportable segment	Based on how management organizes information for decision-making purposes	Based on lines of business and geographical regions (IAS #14)	Based on lines of business and geographical regions
Basis for the valuation of property, plant, and equipment	Historical cost	Historical cost or revalued amount at fair value (IAS #16)	Generally, historical cost
Accounting for research and development (R&D)	Generally, expense all R&D when incurred	Expense research when incurred, development may be capitalized in certain situations (IAS #38)	Generally, expense all R&D when incurred
Valuation of securities classified as trading	Measured at fair value	Measured at fair value (IAS #39)	Measured at lower of cost or market
Disclosure of earnings per share (EPS)	Both basic EPS and diluted EPS are disclosed for all categories of earnings	Both basic EPS and diluted EPS are disclosed for continuing operations and net income (IAS #33)	Two measures of basic EPS are required
Accounting for goodwill	Purchased goodwill is capitalized and tested for impairment	Purchased goodwill is capitalized and tested for impairment (IAS #22)	Purchased goodwill is capitalized and amortized over the investment period stipulated by contract, otherwise amortize over no more than 10 years

REFLECTION

- Users of international financial information need that information to be comparable across entities in order to make the best informed decisions.
- Harmonization may be accomplished through several approaches, including bilateral agreements between nations and an international standard-setting process on a worldwide basis.
- Both the IASB and the IFAC are dedicated to the harmonization of accounting standards. A number of other organizations support the initiatives to harmonize accounting standards.

10

OBJECTIVE

Describe transfer-pricing issues and differences in tax systems.

OTHER ISSUES OF INTERNATIONAL IMPORTANCE

In addition to the identification of differences in accounting standards and the harmonization efforts regarding accounting standards and the practice of accounting, several other issues are of international importance.

Transfer-Pricing Issues

Goods or services transferred or conveyed between units of a multinational enterprise are priced using a variety of methods. These methods of transfer pricing may serve a variety of purposes, many of which relate to taxation and/or the imposition of other trade duties. For example, if the corporate income tax rate is lower in a subsidiary's home country than in the parent's home country, taxes may be minimized by setting a higher transfer price on sales from the subsidiary to the parent. The parent company would then have a resulting higher cost of sales and a lower amount of taxable income. Import duties could be reduced if the value of a foreign company's shipments to its manufacturing facility in another country was determined at a lower transfer price. Furthermore, the savings in duties result in a lower unit cost which may then allow the final product to be sold at lower prices, thereby creating a further competitive advantage. Clearly, the profit measures that are critical to agreements with employees and business partners could be structured in order to achieve a desired goal. At any one time, a multinational enterprise may be confronted with a number of factors that suggest both lower and higher transfer prices. However, in order to address some of the manipulation in transfer-pricing decisions, countries have set out to regulate transfer pricing. The Internal Revenue Code regulates transfer pricing in the United States by encouraging the use of a transfer price that reflects what the prices would have been if the underlying transactions had taken place on an arm's-length basis between unrelated parties. It is important to note that, once again, comparability between multinationals may be affected by differences in transfer-pricing methods.

Differences in Tax Systems

Another issue of international importance relates to the differences in tax systems. These systems vary regarding the definition of allowable revenues and expenses and the type of tax to be imposed. For example, one country may require the use of depreciation methods that are the same for financial reporting and tax reporting purposes, while another country may allow accelerated methods for tax purposes and a different method for financial reporting. Some countries may include only revenue from domestic sources, while others include income from foreign sources as well. Countries obviously establish systems of taxation that best serve their own fiscal, social, and political agendas. Little progress has been made in developing a uniform system of taxation among countries, although the EU recognizes this as a logical part of a common trading environment. Currently, the important issue is to recognize the differences that do exist and understand how they may affect decisions.

The types of taxes imposed also differ among countries, with tax generally being based either on income or some other measure of value. The corporate income tax is common among most major trading nations and may, in some instances, include provisions to reduce the effect of double taxation resulting from distributions to shareholders. Furthermore, many domestic corporate income tax systems also include foreign-source income that already may have been taxed in the foreign country. In order to avoid double taxation, generally, a credit is allowed as a reduction of the domestic tax liability, based on the extent of foreign income taxes incurred. One of the most common methods of taxation is the *value-added tax (VAT)*, which is common throughout Europe. This tax is applied to the amount of value added at each stage or level, from initial production to final sale to the individual consumer. The VAT incurred by a previous level reduces the cost of sales of the current level in order to determine the value added. For example, if a manufacturer produced a good with a value of 100 and a retailer added 70 to the value, the VAT tax would be calculated on the total value added of 170. Assuming the VAT rate is 20%, the tax would be incurred at each level as follows:

	Level		
	Manufacturer	Retailer	Consumer
Input cost of goods	N/A	120	204
VAT included	N/A	20	
Selling price excluding VAT	100	170	
VAT @ 20%	20	34	
Selling price including VAT	120	204	
VAT collected from next level	20	34	
VAT previously remitted to government	0	(20)	
Net VAT due government	20	14	

Certainly, international taxation is very complex and is affected by specific regulations and tax treaties that are beyond the scope of this text.

REFLECTION

- Transfer pricing for goods and services reflects various tax and tariff considerations.
- Tax systems of other nations often differ significantly from that of the United States.

UNDERSTANDING THE ISSUES

1. Identify several environmental factors that may explain why accounting principles differ among countries.
2. What is the goal of harmonization of accounting standards, and what approaches have been used to accomplish this goal?
3. Discuss the steps that the European Union has taken with respect to convergence of domestic accounting standards and international accounting standards.
4. Using accounting for inventory as an example, explain how principles differ among countries and how harmonization may benefit an international investor.

EXERCISES

Exercise 1 *(LO 2, 6, 7)* **Harmonization.** The single market created by the European Union will eliminate trade barriers among its member nations. Most U.S. businesses see the EU as an opportunity for growth.

1. Discuss some of the apparent opportunities presented by the EU.
2. Discuss why harmonization of accounting standards among members of the EU is important to the success of the EU.

Exercise 2 *(LO 4)* **The development of accounting.** The level of a country's technological development is a factor influencing the development of its accounting principles. A small agrarian economy is interested in developing a presence as an exporter of high-technology products.

Discuss how this new focus may affect the development of accounting.

Exercise 3 *(LO 2, 6)* **Harmonization effect.** Harmonization of accounting standards through a private standard-setting process will have both advantages and disadvantages to American investors and businesses.

1. Discuss the advantages of harmonization to American investors.
2. Discuss why differences in accounting principles and disclosure requirements may place American businesses at a competitive disadvantage.
3. Discuss how the U.S. accounting profession can influence the process of harmonization.

Exercise 4 *(LO 8)* **The International Accounting Standards Board.** The International Accounting Standards Board is the primary international organization involved in promulgating International Accounting Standards.

1. Discuss the relationship between the IASB and the International Accounting Standards Committee Foundation.
2. Discuss the relationship between the International Accounting Standards and the International Financial Reporting Standards.
3. Discuss how U.S. GAAP and IASs differ with respect to the use of LIFO and the classification of a reportable segment.

Exercise 5 *(LO 9)* **Differences in accounting standards.** Although efforts are being made to converge U.S. accounting standards with International Accounting Standards, differences still exist. The SEC allows foreign registrants to file financial statements prepared on the basis of either U.S. GAAP, International Accounting Standards, or their own national GAAP. However, if U.S. GAAP are not employed, companies must provide reconciliation to U.S. GAAP.

1. Given the information contained in Exhibit 9-1, discuss how the treatment of upfront nonrefundable revenues by China Unicom differs from U.S. GAAP.
2. Given the information contained in Exhibit 9-1 regarding China Unicom, discuss whether the revaluation of property, plant, and equipment was an upward or downward revaluation. Also, discuss why the adjustment to net income regarding the revaluation is a constant amount per period presented.
3. Using the Securities and Exchange Commission's disclosure data base known as EDGAR (see http://sec.gov), identify a foreign registrant and secure its Form 20-F, which reconciles its financial presentation to U.S. GAAP. Comment on the major differences.

Exercise 6 *(LO 10)* **Value-added tax.** Assuming that a 10% value-added tax is in effect, prepare a schedule to indicate how it would be calculated, assuming also that a manufacturer produces a product which is sold to a wholesaler who, in turn, sells the product to a retailer who then sells the product to a final consumer.

MODULE M

Derivatives and Related Accounting Issues

Learning Objectives

When you have completed this module, you should be able to

1. **State the general characteristics of a derivative instrument, and define *underlying* and *notional amount*.**
2. **Explain the basic features of common derivative instruments, including forward contracts, futures contracts, options, and interest rate swaps.**
3. **Determine and account for the change in value over time of forward and futures contracts.**
4. **Determine and account for the intrinsic and time value components of an option.**
5. **Appreciate the basic objectives of an interest rate swap.**
6. **Explain how a derivative instrument may be used to reduce or avoid the exposure to risk associated with other transactions.**
7. **Demonstrate how a fair value hedge is used, and account for such hedges.**
8. **Demonstrate how a cash flow hedge is used, and account for such hedges.**
9. **Identify the various types of information that should be included in disclosures regarding derivative instruments and hedging activities.**

The use of derivative instruments has increased significantly among both financial and nonfinancial corporations. These instruments derive their value from changes in the price or rate of a related asset or liability. For example, the option or right to buy a share of stock at a fixed price *derives its value* from the price of the related stock. If you could buy the stock at a fixed price of $50 when the stock is trading at $55, the option has value.

Derivative instruments may be held as: (a) investments or (b) part of a strategy to reduce or hedge against exposure to risk associated with some other transaction. The use of derivatives is most common among large corporations and with foreign currency exchange and interest rate exposures. Derivatives received a lot of attention during the mid-1990s due to their use as an investment instrument by large governmental units. These investments were extremely volatile and resulted in huge losses for a number of entities. At that time, derivative instruments were not recorded on the balance sheets. This *off-balance-sheet* treatment made financial analysis even more difficult.

The Financial Accounting Standards Board (FASB) has been moving toward measuring financial instruments at fair value. The emphasis on fair value has also been extended to derivative instruments. After a long, due-process period, the FASB established standards for derivatives that require them to be recorded as assets or liabilities at fair value. These standards are contained

Fischer et al, Advanced Accounting, 9th ed.

in Statement of Financial Accounting Standards No. 133, *Accounting for Derivative Instruments and Hedging Activities,*[1] Statement of Financial Accounting Standards No. 138, *Accounting for Certain Derivative Instruments and Certain Hedging Activities—An amendment to FASB Statement No. 133,*[2] and Statement of Financial Accounting Standards No. 149, *Amendment of Statement 133 on Derivative Instruments and Hedging Activities.*[3] These standards are developed from two critical underpinnings: (1) derivatives represent assets or liabilities, and (2) derivatives are to be measured at fair value.

DERIVATIVES: CHARACTERISTICS AND TYPES

A financial instrument represents a right, through a contractual agreement between two opposite parties called *counterparties,* to receive or deliver cash or another financial instrument on potentially favorable or unfavorable terms. Financial instruments include cash, equity and debt investments, and derivatives. A derivative is a type of financial instrument that has several distinguishing characteristics that have been set forth by the FASB. These characterstics are that a derivative:

1. Derives its value from changes in the rate or price of a related asset or liability. The rate or price is known as an *underlying.*
2. The quantity or number of units specified by a derivative is known as the *notional amount.*
3. Requires little or no initial investment upon inception.
4. Allows for *net settlement* in that the derivative contract can be settled in exchange for cash, without having to actually buy or sell the related asset or liability.

1

OBJECTIVE

State the general characteristics of a derivative instrument, and define *underlying* and *notional amount.*

Characteristics of Derivatives

A critical characteristic of a derivative and the basis for its name is that the instrument derives its value from *changes* in the value of a related asset or liability. The rates or prices that relate to the asset or liability underlying the derivative are referred to as *underlyings.* The underlying may take a variety of forms, including a commodity price, stock price, foreign currency exchange rate, or interest rate. **It is important to note that the underlying is not the asset or liability itself, but rather its price or rate.** For example, the underlying in an option to buy a share of stock at a fixed price of $50 is not the stock itself; it is the $50 price of the stock, and it determines the value of the derivative. Changes in the underlying price or rate cause the value of the derivative to change. For example, if the price of a stock underlies the value of an option to buy that stock, changes in the price of the stock relative to the option price will cause the value of the option to change. If the underlying price of the stock changes from $50 to $52, then the option to buy at $50 has increased in value by $2 (one could buy the stock for $50 when it has a fair value of $52).

In order to fully value a derivative, one must know the number of units (quantity) that is specified in the derivative instrument. This is called the *notional amount,* and it determines the total dollar value of a derivative, traceable to movement or changes in the underlying. For example, if the option to buy stock for $50 increases in value because the underlying price of the stock moves from $50 to $52, the total magnitude of this increase in value depends on how many shares can be purchased under the terms of the option. If the option applies to 1,000 shares, then the total value of the option is $2,000 (a $2 change in the underlying price of $50 to $52 times a notional amount of 1,000 shares). The notional amount of a derivative might refer to so many bushels of a commodity, number of shares, foreign currency units, or principal amount of debt. **Both the underlying price or rate and the notional amount are necessary in order to determine the total value of a derivative at any point in time.**

Typically, a derivative requires little or no initial investment because it is *an investment in a change in value* traceable to an underlying, rather than an investment in the actual asset or liability

1 Statement of Financial Accounting Standards No. 133, *Accounting for Derivative Instruments and Hedging Activities* (Norwalk, CT: Financial Accounting Standards Board, 1998).

2 Statement of Financial Accounting Standards No. 138, *Accounting for Certain Derivative Instruments and Certain Hedging Activities—An amendment to FASB Statement No. 133* (Norwalk, CT: Financial Accounting Standards Board, 2000).

3 Statement of Financial Accounting Standards No. 149, *Amendment of Statement 133 on Derivative Instruments and Hedging Activities* (Norwalk, CT: Financial Accounting Standards Board, 2003).

to which the underlying relates. For example, if the price of a stock increases, the value of an option to buy that stock also increases. If one actually owned the stock, an increase in the price of the stock would also result in increased value. However, the important difference is that in order to experience the increase in value an option holder needs to make little or no initial investment, whereas the owner of the stock has to make a significant investment to acquire the stock in the first place.

Many derivatives do not require the parties to the contract, the counterparties, to actually deliver an asset that is associated with the underlying in order to realize the value of a derivative. For example, the option to buy a share of stock at a fixed price would allow the holder to sell the option rather than requiring the other counterparty to actually transfer stock to them at the option price. Assume that a stock is trading at $52 per share and that one holds an option to buy stock at $50 per share. The holder could sell the option for $2 or require the counterparty to sell them stock at $50. If the stock were purchased for $50, it could readily be converted into cash by selling at $52, thereby realizing a gain of $2. The ability to settle the contract in exchange for cash, without actually buying or selling the related asset or liability, is referred to as *net settlement*.

A derivative may be a separate, distinct financial instrument, or it may be *embedded* in another financial instrument. An embedded derivative has economic characteristics and risks that are not clearly and closely related to those of the host instrument. For example, a convertible bond is a host contract that also contains an embedded derivative. That derivative represents the option to convert the bond into common stock; its underlying is the price of the respective stock. The conversion feature's economic value is more closely related to the underlying stock than the bond. If the embedded derivative meets certain criteria, it should be separated, or *bifurcated*, from the host contract and be accounted for as a separate instrument. The discussion of bifurcation is beyond the scope of this text.

Common Types of Derivatives

2

OBJECTIVE

Explain the basic features of common derivative instruments, including forward contracts, futures contracts, options, and interest rate swaps.

The number of financial instruments that have the characteristics of a derivative has continued to expand, and, in turn, these instruments have become increasingly complex. In spite of the diversity and/or complexity that characterizes them, most derivatives are variations of four basic types, including forwards, futures, options, and swaps. Other more complex derivative instruments are not described here.

Derivatives are often part of a trading portfolio and are held primarily for sale in the short term. As with other trading investments, derivatives are marked-to-market, and the resulting gain or loss is recognized currently in earnings. A specific discussion of each type of derivative follows. In this section, we cover derivatives as investments made for speculative purposes. The use of derivatives as a hedging instrument is discussed in a separate section. Transaction costs (e.g., brokers' fees), which are typically included as part of the original cost or basis of the derivative as with all investments, are ignored for purposes of discussion.

3

OBJECTIVE

Determine and account for the change in value over time of forward and futures contracts.

Forward Contracts. A *forward contract* is an executory contract to buy or sell a specified amount of an asset, such as foreign currency, at a specified fixed price with delivery at a specified future point in time. The party that agrees to sell the asset is said to be in a *short position*, and the party that agrees to buy the asset is said to be in a *long position*. The specified fixed price in the contract is known as a *forward price* or *forward rate*. The current price or rate for the asset is known as the *spot rate*. The specified future point is referred to as the *forward date*. Forward contracts are not formally regulated on an organized exchange, and the parties are exposed to a risk that default of the contract could occur. However, the lack of formal regulation means that such contracts can be customized in response to specialized needs regarding notional amounts and forward dates.

The value of a forward contract is zero at inception and typically does not require an initial cash outlay. However, over time, movement in the price or rate of the underlying results in a change in value of the forward contract. **The total change in the value of a forward contract is measured as the difference between the forward rate and the spot rate "at the forward date."**

For example, on April 1, a party (called the *writer*) writes a contract in which she/he agrees to sell (short position) to another party (called the *holder*) who agrees to buy (long position) 1,000,000 foreign currenices (for example, euros) at a specific price of $0.16 per foreign currency (FC) with delivery in 90 days (June 29). The relationship between the parties is as follows:

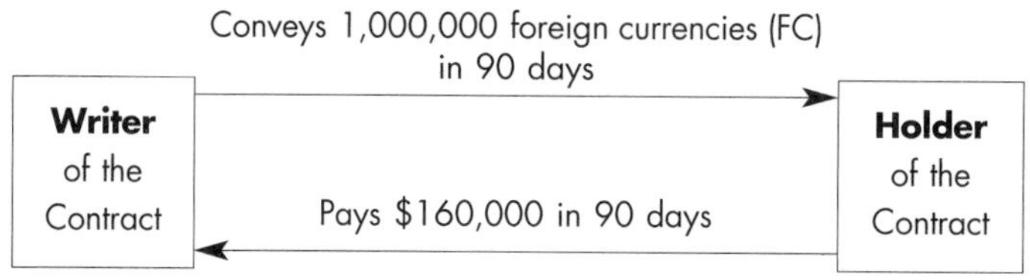

If the spot rate at the end of the forward period is $0.18, the total change in value is determined as follows:

1,000,000 FC at a forward rate (on April 1) of $0.16 (1,000,000 × $0.16)	$160,000
1,000,000 FC at a spot rate (on June 29) of $0.18 (1,000,000 × $0.18)	180,000
Gain in value to holder	$ 20,000

This is a gain because on June 29 the holder received something with a fair value greater than the fair value given up that day. (Conversely, this would be a loss to the writer.) The holder of the forward contract could buy foreign currencies for $160,000 on the forward date compared to the spot value of $180,000 at that time and experience an immediate $20,000 gain. It is important to note that the value of the currency at the final spot rate could have been less than $160,000. In that case, the holder would have experienced a loss and the writer a gain. When the value of a derivative can change in both directions (gain or loss), it is said to have a *symmetric return profile*. It is also important to note that in the case of a forward contract, if the holder of the contact experiences a gain (loss) in value, then the writer of the contract simultaneously experiences a loss (gain) in value.

The forward price or rate is a function of a number of variables, including the length of the forward period and the current spot rate. As these variables change over the life of the contract, the value of the forward contract also changes. Also, because *the forward prices or rates represent values in the future, the current value is represented by the present value of the future rates.* Continuing with the example involving foreign currencies, assume the following forward rates information throughout the 90-day term of the contract:

Remaining Term of Contract	Forward Rate	Notional Amount	Total Forward Value	Cumulative Change in Forward Value
90 days	$0.160	1,000,000	$160,000	
60 days	0.170	1,000,000	170,000	$10,000
30 days	0.170	1,000,000	170,000	10,000
0 days	0.180	1,000,000	180,000	20,000

Assuming a 6% discount rate, the change in value of the forward contract over time is as follows:

	60 Days Remaining	30 Days Remaining	Total Life of Contract
Cumulative change in forward value.	$10,000	$10,000	$20,000
Present value of cumulative change:			
60 days at 6%	$ 9,901		
30 days at 6%		$ 9,950	
0 days at 6%			$20,000
Previously recognized gain or loss	0	(9,901)	(9,950)
Current period gain or loss	$ 9,901	$ 49	$10,050

Note that the total change in the value of the forward contract is $20,000 ($9,901 + $49 + $10,050), which is recognized over the term of the contract as the net present value of changes in the forward rates. Even if the forward rates did not change between two valuation dates (as they barely did between 60 and 30 days here), the value of the contract would change because the remaining term of the forward contract continues to decrease and the present value of the forward value increases. Also, note that *the stated forward rate at the expiration date of the contract is equal to the spot rate at that date.* This is due to the fact that at expiration of the contract the forward date is the same as the current date.

Investors could acquire forward contracts to purchase foreign currencies, even though they have no need for the foreign currencies, hoping that the value of the contract increases and results in investment income. Of course, holding the contract as an investment could also expose them to the risk that the value would decrease over time. As previously stated, the value of a forward contract can move in both directions resulting in a symmetric return profile. Investors in forward contracts would typically settle them by selling prior to the forward date because they do not actually need to buy or sell the foreign currencies. If the above forward contract were held as an investment and settled with 30 days remaining, the entries to account for the contract would be as follows:

Event	Entry		
Initial acquisition.	A memo entry to record acquisition of the contract. At inception, the value of the contract is zero.		
60 days remaining.	Investment in Forward Contract	9,901	
	Gain on Contract		9,901
	To record the change in value of the contract. (This entry is necessary only when financial statements are being prepared.)		
30 days remaining.	Cash	9,950	
	Investment in Forward Contract		9,901
	Gain on Contract		49
	To record the settlement of the contract.		

Futures Contracts. A *futures contract* is exactly like a forward contract in that it too provides for the receipt or payment of a specified amount of an asset at a specified price with delivery at a specified future point in time. However, the futures contract has the following distinguishing characteristics:

- Unlike forward contracts, futures are traded on organized exchanges. The exchanges help ensure that the trading partners honor their obligations. The exchange clearinghouse actually becomes an intermediary between the buyer and seller of the contract. In essence, the clearinghouse becomes the seller for each buyer and the buyer for each seller.
- The formal regulation of futures contracts results in contracts that are standardized in nature versus customized. For example, the exchange specifies the quantity and quality of commodities traded, as well as the delivery place and date.
- A futures contract requires an initial deposit of funds with the transacting broker. This deposit is referred to as a *margin account*; it serves as collateral to help ensure that the parties to the contract are able to perform. Each day the contract is valued and marked-to-market. If the contract loses too much value, the holder will have to contribute additional cash to the margin account. If the margin account balance falls below a minimum balance, called the *maintenance margin*, the investor is required to replenish the account through what is called a *margin call.*
- Forward contracts represent cash amounts settled only at delivery and therefore represent future amounts that must be discounted to yield a current present value. However, future prices are marked-to-market each day. At the close of each trading day, a new futures price or settlement price is established. Therefore, *the futures price represents a current versus future value, and no discounting is necessary.* This new futures price is used to compute the gain or loss on the contract over time.
- The party that has written a futures contract is said to be *short*, and the party that owns the contract is said to be *long*.

For example, assume one buys 50 contracts on the Chicago Board of Trade (CBT) to receive November delivery of corn to a certified warehouse. Each contract is in units of 5,000 bushels at a *futures* price of $2.50 per bushel. Notice that the terms of the contract are standardized. Obviously, a second party must agree to sell corn at a November futures price of $2.50. Acting as an intermediary between the counterparties, the CBT, in essence, writes a contract to sell a corn future to the first party and buys a contract to purchase a corn future from the second party. The relationship between the parties is as follows:

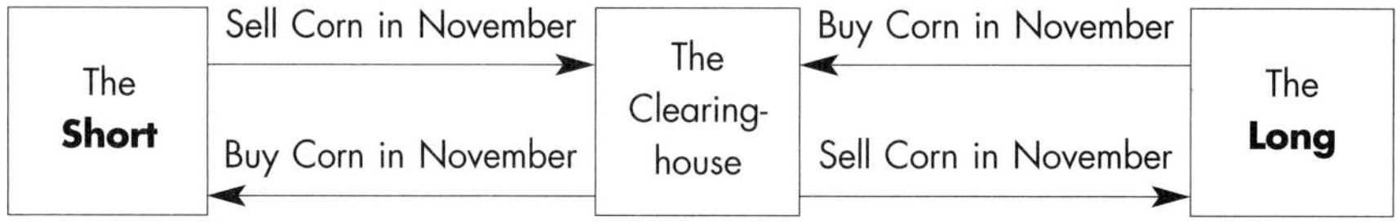

Assume that the initial margin on the above contract is set at $20,000, with a maintenance margin of $15,000, and that future prices are as follows:

Day 1	Day 2	Day 3	Day 4
$2.50	$2.51	$2.49	$2.47

The following entries illustrate the valuation of the futures contracts and the use of a margin account for the long (the owner of the contract).

Day 1	Futures Contract—Margin Account	20,000	
	Cash		20,000
	To record establishment of margin account.		
Day 2	Futures Contract—Margin Account	2,500	
	Gain on Contract		2,500
	To record gain in fair value of contract [50 contracts × 5,000 bushels × ($2.51 vs. $2.50)].		
Day 3	Loss on Contract	5,000	
	Futures Contract—Margin Account		5,000
	To record loss in fair value of contract [50 contracts × 5,000 bushels × ($2.49 vs. $2.51)].		
Day 4	Loss on Contract	5,000	
	Futures Contract—Margin Account		5,000
	To record loss in fair value of contract [50 contracts × 5,000 bushels × ($2.47 vs. $2.49)].		
	Futures Contract—Margin Account	7,500	
	Cash		7,500
	To meet margin call and reestablish initial margin balance of $20,000 (balance before call = $20,000 + $2,500 − $5,000 − $5,000 = $12,500, which is less than $15,000 maintenance margin).		

The value of the futures contract is influenced by either positive or negative movements in the underlying price. Therefore, the risk associated with the contract is symmetrical. Unlike forward contracts, the value of futures contracts, which typically change on a daily basis, can be easily monitored since such contracts are traded on the open market.

4

OBJECTIVE

Determine and account for the intrinsic and time value components of an option.

Option Contracts. An *option* represents a right, rather than an obligation, to either buy or sell some quantity of a particular underlying. Common examples include options to buy or sell stocks, a stock index, an interest rate, foreign currency, oil, metals, and agricultural commodities. The option is valid for a specified period of time and calls for a specified buy or sell price, referred to as the *strike price* or *exercise price*. If an option allows the holder to *buy* an underlying, it is referred to as a *call option*. An option that allows the holder to *sell* an underlying is referred to as a *put option*. Options are actively traded on organized exchanges or may be negotiated on a case-by-case basis between counterparties (over-the-counter contracts). Option contracts require the holder to make an initial nonrefundable cash outlay, known as the *premium*, as represented by the option's current value. The premium is paid, in part, because the writer of the option takes more risk than the holder of the option. The holder can allow the option to expire, while the writer must comply if the holder chooses to exercise it.

During the option period, the strike price of the option on the underlying is generally different from the current value of an underlying. The following terms are used to describe the relationship between the strike price and the current price (note that the premium is not considered in these relationships):

Option Type	Strike Price Is Equal to Current Price	Strike Price Is Greater than Current Price	Strike Price Is Less than Current Price
Call (buy) option	At-the-money	Out-of-the-money	In-the-money
Put (sell) option	At-the-money	In-the-money	Out-of-the-money

As the above table suggests, in-the-money is a favorable condition as compared to being out-of-the-money, which is an unfavorable condition. The original premium is not considered when describing whether an option is or is not in-the-money. However, it is important to note that the original premium certainly is considered when determining whether an investment in an option has experienced an overall profit. The holder of an option has a right, rather than an obligation, and will not exercise the option unless it is in-the-money. In that case, the holder will experience a gain, and the writer will experience a loss. However, if the option is not in-the-money, the option will not be exercised, the holder will limit her/his loss to the amount of the option premium, and the writer will limit her/his gain to the amount of the premium. Therefore, in theory, the opportunities for gain and loss are characterized as follows:

	Potential for	
	Gain	Loss
Holder of option	Unlimited	Limited to amount of premium
Writer of option	Limited to amount of premium	Unlimited

Because the counterparties do not have equal opportunity for both upside and downside changes in value, options are said to have an *asymmetric* or one-sided *return profile.*

Options are traded on an organized exchange and over the counter; therefore, their current value is quoted in terms of present dollars on a frequent basis. The current value of an option depends on forward periods and spot prices. The difference between the strike and spot price, at any point in time, measures the *intrinsic value* of the option, so changes in spot prices will change the intrinsic value of the option. Changes in the length of the remaining forward period will affect the *time value* of the option. The time value is measured as the difference between an option's current value and its intrinsic value as in the following illustration.

- If the option is in-the-money, the option has intrinsic value. For example, if an investor has an April call (buy) option to buy IBM stock at a strike price of $110 and the current stock price is $112, the option is in-the-money and has an intrinsic value of $2. An option that is out-of-the-money or at-the-money has no intrinsic value.
- The difference between the current value of an option and its intrinsic value represents time value. For example, if the IBM April call (buy) option has a current value of $8, the time value component is $6 (the current value of $8, less the intrinsic value of $2). The time value of an option represents a discounting factor and a volatility factor.
- The *discounting factor* relates to the fact that the strike price does not have to be paid currently, but rather at the time of exercise. Therefore, the holder of an option to buy stock could benefit from an appreciation in stock value without actually having to currently pay out the cash to purchase the stock. For example, assume that a 30-day, at-the-money option has a strike price of $100 and that a discount rate of 12% is appropriate. The ability to use the $100 for 30 days at an assumed discount rate of 12%, rather than having to buy the stock at the current price of $100, is worth $1 ($100 × 12% × 1/12 year). Thus, the ability to have the alternative use of the cash equal to the strike price until exercise date of the option has value.
- The *volatility factor* relates to the volatility of the underlying relative to the fixed strike price and reflects the potential for gain on the option. Underlyings with more price volatility

present greater opportunities for gains if the option is in-the-money. Therefore, higher volatility increases the value of an option. Note that volatility could also lead to an out-of-the-money situation. However, this possibility can be disregarded because, unlike forward or futures contracts, the risk for an option is *asymmetric* since the holder can avoid unfavorable outcomes by allowing the option to expire.

To illustrate the value components of an option, assume that a put (sell) option allows for the sale of a share of stock in 60 days at a strike or exercise price of $50 per share. The value of the option would consist of the following:

	Initial Date of Purchase	End of 30 Days	End of 60 Days
Market value of stock	$51	$49	$48
Assumed total value of option	1.30	1.65	2.00
Intrinsic value (never less than zero)	0 (option is out-of-the-money)	1 (in-the-money = $50 – $49)	2 (in-the-money = $51 – $49)
Time value (total value less intrinsic value)	1.30	0.65	0

The value of an option can be realized either through exercise of the option or through cash settlement. If the option can be exercised any time during the specified period, it is referred to as an *American option*; if it is exercisable only at the maturity date/expiration of the contract, it is referred to as a *European option*.

To illustrate the use of an option, assume that a call (buy) option on 10,000 bushels of corn with delivery in April is purchased in February for a premium of $1,000 and has a strike price of $2.20 per bushel. The values of the option at the end of February and March are $1,050 and $700, respectively. It is sold in early April, prior to expiration, for $750. The relationship between the parties is as follows:

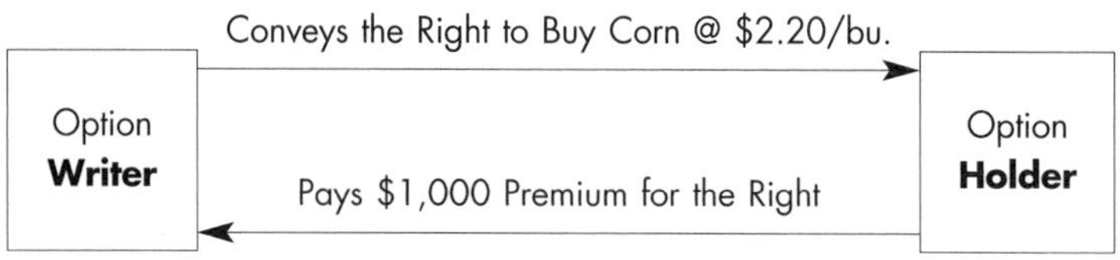

The following entries account for the holder's investment in the option, given various values over time:

Feb. 1	Investment in Call Option	1,000	
	Cash		1,000
	To record purchase of call option.		
28	Investment in Call Option	50	
	Gain on Option		50
	To record change in total value of option ($1,050 – $1,000).		
Mar. 31	Loss on Option	350	
	Investment in Call Option		350
	To record change in total value of option ($700 – $1,050).		
Apr. 2	Cash	750	
	Investment in Call Option (book value)		700
	Gain on Call Option		50
	To record sale of option.		

The basic concepts related to both call (buy) and put (sell) options are set forth in Exhibit M-1.

Exhibit M-1
Basic Concepts Related to Options

Call Options	**Holder**	**Holder**
Rights	Right to buy an underlying asset at a set exercise or strike price.	Obligation to sell an underlying asset at a set exercise or strike price.
Type	European or American—European can be exercised only at maturity date. American can be exercised any time up to and including maturity date.	European or American—European can be exercised only at maturity date. American can be exercised any time up to and including maturity date.
Cost	Pays an initial fixed cost referred to as a premium.	Receives an initial premium.
Value of the call option:		
Net gain	Experienced when the strike price is less than fair value of the underlying asset. In theory, the gain is unlimited. This is referred to as being in-the-money. The value of this difference must exceed the initial premium to produce a net gain.	Experienced when the strike price is more than or equal to the fair value of the underlying asset. The gain is limited to the initial premium.
Net loss	Experienced when the strike price is more than or equal to the fair value of the underlying asset. The loss is limited to the initial premium.	Experienced when the strike price is less than fair value of the underlying asset. In theory, the loss is unlimited. The value of this difference must exceed the initial premium to produce a net loss.
Components of value	The value consists of intrinsic value and time value.	The value consists of intrinsic value and time value.

Put Options	**Holder**	**Writer**
Rights	Right to sell an underlying asset at a set exercise or strike price.	Obligation to buy an underlying asset at a set exercise or strike price.
Type	European or American—European can be exercised only at maturity date. American can be exercised any time up to and including maturity date.	European or American—European can be exercised only at maturity date. American can be exercised any time up to and including maturity date.
Cost	Pays an initial fixed cost referred to as a premium.	Receives an initial premium.
Value of the put option:		
Net gain	Experienced when the strike price is more than fair value of the underlying asset. In theory, the gain is unlimited. This is referred to as being in-the-money. The value of this difference must exceed the initial premium to produce a net gain.	Experienced when the strike price is less than or equal to the fair value of the underlying asset. The gain is limited to the initial premium.
Net loss	Experienced when the strike price is less than or equal to the fair value of the underlying asset. The loss is limited to the initial premium.	Experienced when the strike price is more than fair value of the underlying asset. The value of this difference must exceed the initial premium. The maximum loss is limited to the strike price, less the initial premium.
Components of value	The value consists of intrinsic value and time value.	The value consists of intrinsic value and time value.

5
OBJECTIVE
Appreciate the basic objectives of an interest rate swap.

Swaps. A *swap* is a type of forward contract represented by a contractual obligation, arranged by an intermediary that requires the exchange of cash flows between two parties. Swaps are customized to meet the needs of the specific parties and are not traded on regulated exchanges. Most often swaps are used to hedge against unfavorable outcomes and are explained more fully in the later discussion of hedging. However, it is important to understand the basic format of a swap. Common examples include foreign currency swaps and interest rate swaps. For example, assume a U.S. company has an opportunity to invest in a German joint venture that is expected to last six months. The U.S. company must invest euros in the venture, and its investment will be returned in euros at the end of the 6-month period. Through an intermediary, the U.S. company could contract with a German company that needs U.S. dollars for a similar period of time. Each of the companies would have available or borrow their respective currencies and then swap the currencies, dollars for euros and euros for dollars. At the end of the 6-month investment period, the U.S. company would return euros to the German company, and the German company would return dollars to the U.S. company.

Rather than involving the swap of different currencies, an *interest rate swap* involves exchanging variable or floating (fixed) interest rates for fixed (variable or floating) rates. For example, assume a Company issued $10,000,000 of variable-interest debt when rates were 6% and is now concerned that interest rates will increase. In order to protect against rising rates, the Company contracts with a Bank and agrees to pay a fixed rate of interest of 6.5% to the Bank in exchange for receiving variable rates. The Company is referred to as the *pay fixed* or *receive floating* party, and the Bank is referred to as the *pay floating* or *receive fixed* party. In essence, the Company has converted its floating or variable rate debt into fixed rate debt. The relationship between the parties is as follows:

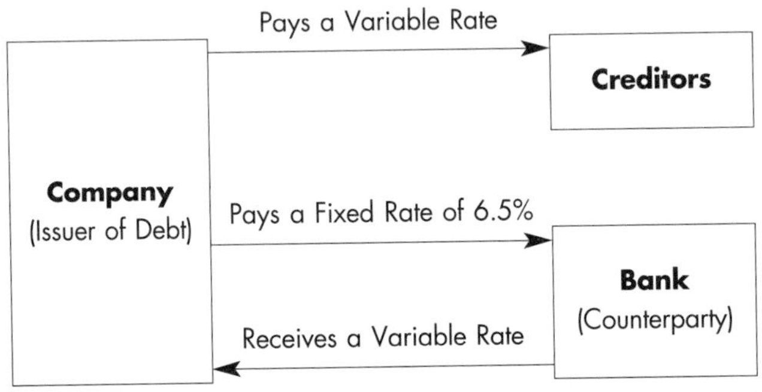

If the variable rate increased to 6.7% on the $10,000,000 of variable interest debt, the Company's semiannual net interest expense would be determined as follows:

Variable interest paid to creditors (6.7% × $10,000,000 × ½ year)	$335,000
Fixed interest paid to the Bank (6.5% ×$10,000,000 × ½ year)	325,000*
Variable interest received from the Bank (6.7% ×$10,000,000×½ year)*	(335,000)
Net interest paid [(−6.7% − 6.5% + 6.7%) × $10,000,000 × ½ year]	$325,000

*Rather than actually paying and receiving, the entities exchange the net difference between the rates (fixed vs. variable) in the amount of $10,000 ($325,000 vs. $335,000). This results in a net interest expense of $325,000 ($335,000 paid to creditors less $10,000 received from the Bank).

The interest swap was entered into because the Company feared that variable rates would increase. In essence, the swap allowed the Company to exchange a variable interest rate for a fixed interest rate as though they had actually issued fixed debt. As the swap continues, new variable rates will be determined and applied to subsequent semiannual interest payments. This process of determining a new rate for the swap is referred to as *resetting* the rate. Generally, the variable interest rate is *reset* at each interest date and is applied to the subsequent period's interest calculations.

In the above example, if the variable rate increased to more than the 6.5% fixed rate paid to the Bank, the Company received a net cash amount from the bank and realized a gain as a result of entering into the swap. Therefore, the value of the swap, represented by the payment of a fixed rate in exchange for a higher variable rate, has increased. If the variable rate had decreased below the 6.5% fixed rate paid to the Bank, the Company would have made a net cash settlement payment to the Bank, and the swap would have lost value. Changes in the variable interest rates expose one party to potential loss and the other party to potential gain. Therefore, swaps, like other forward contracts, are characterized by symmetric risk. In the above example, the Bank is acting as the counterparty and lost value on the swap. However, acting as acounterparty, the Bank will attempt to match the notional amount of the current swap with the notional amount of another swap with a party that is seeking to pay floating/receive fixed. This results in the counterparty Bank having one swap where it pays floating (receive fixed) and another swap where it pays fixed (receive floating). The counterparty will have a spread between the pay and receive floating rate or the pay and receive fixed rate that compensates it for its services. For example, assume a notional amount of $10,000,000. If the counterparty has a pay floating rate of 3.5% and a receive floating rate of 3.7%, then the spread will result in compensation of $20,000 [(−3.5% + 3.7%) × $10,000,000].

The valuation of swaps is complex and dependent on assumptions regarding future rates or prices. For example, if a fixed interest payment is swapped for a variable interest payment, the value of the swap is a function of how future variable rates are expected to compare to the fixed rate. Therefore, an estimate of future variable rates is required. Furthermore, the differences between the future variable rates and the fixed rate represent future differences that need to be discounted in order to produce a present value of the differences.

The above example involved a swap of fixed interest payments to a counterparty in exchange for the receipt of a variable rate of interest. It is also possible to swap a variable interest payment in exchange for a fixed rate of interest. The use of these swaps and the resulting accounting will be discussed in greater detail in a subsequent section of this chapter.

Summary of Derivative Instruments

Exhibit M-2 presents a summary and comparison of the four basic types of derivative instruments discussed in the preceding sections. The most important differences are between options and the other three types of derivatives. Futures, forwards, and swaps each provide symmetric risk to a holder because the value of the derivative can change in both directions (gains or losses) without limits. This symmetric risk profile requires both counterparties to execute the contract whether the effect is favorable or unfavorable. In contrast, the holder of an option is not required or obligated to exercise the option and, in fact, will not do so if the option is at- or out-of-the-money. This provides asymmetric risk for the holder who may want to avoid downside risk. Options also differ from the other derivative instruments described here in the requirement for an initial cash outlay, which represents the initial intrinsic and time values of the option.

Exhibit M-2
Basic Concepts Related to Selected Derivative Instruments

	Forward Contracts	Futures Contracts	Options	Swaps
Basic design	An obligation to buy or sell an asset at a specified forward price/rate with delivery at a specified forward date.	An obligation to buy or sell an asset at a specified forward price/rate with delivery at a specified future date.	A right to buy or sell an asset at a specified strike price. The strike price is valid for a specified period of time.	A contract that exchanges cash flows between two parties. In substance, a type of forward contract.
Trading and regulation	Not traded on an organized exchange. Trading is not formally regulated.	Traded on an organized exchange (e.g., Chicago Board of Trade). Trading is formally regulated.	Traded on an organized exchange (e.g., Chicago Board Options Exchange) and in the over-the-counter (OTC) market. Trading is formally regulated.	Not traded on an organized exchange. Trading is not formally regulated.

(continued)

Exhibit M-2 *(Concluded)*

	Forward Contracts	Futures Contracts	Options	Swaps
Counterparty default risk	Parties are exposed to default risk.	The exchange clearinghouse acts as an intermediary between the counterparties. It helps to ensure that the parties honor their obligations.	Because of the involvement of the exchange, there is no default risk.	Parties are exposed to default risk.
Derivative form	Customized contracts to meet the specialized needs of the counterparties.	The formal regulation of contracts results in standardized contracts.	The formal regulation of options results in standardized contracts.	Swaps are customized to meet the needs of the specific parties.
Initial cash outlay	No initial cash outlay required.	Typically, no initial cash outlay. However, holders of a contract must establish a cash margin account.	Holders are required to make an initial cash outlay known as a premium.	No initial cash outlay required.
Return profile	Symmetric.	Symmetric.	Assymmetric.	Symmetric.

REFLECTION

- An underlying, a notional amount, and the opportunity for net settlement characterize derivatives.
- Major types of derivative instruments include forward contracts, futures contracts, options, and swaps.
- Derivative instruments may be held as an investment and changes in their value should be recognized in current earnings. The value of a derivative is a function of the movement or changes in the underlying and the notional amount.

6

OBJECTIVE

Explain how a derivative instrument may be used to reduce or avoid the exposure to risk associated with other transactions.

ACCOUNTING FOR DERIVATIVES THAT ARE DESIGNATED AS A HEDGE

Changes in the value of a derivative held as an investment are recognized currently in earnings, and the derivative is carried on the balance sheet at its current value. The value of the asset or liability that the underlying related to also changes over time. Furthermore, if the change in the value of the underlying asset or liability is negative, one would want to protect against the adverse effect of the change. One way to protect against such adverse changes is to hedge against the change through the use of a derivative. If the asset or liability (the hedged item) experiences an unfavorable change in value, a properly structured hedge (the hedging instrument) could be effective in providing a change in value in the opposite direction such that there is no adverse effect. If a derivative is properly structured for this purpose, it seems that the change in the value of the derivative (the hedging instrument) should be recognized in the same accounting period as is the change in the value of the related asset or liability (the hedged item). Hedges are generally designated as either *fair value* or *cash flow.* **A fair value** hedge is used to offset changes in the fair value of items with fixed prices or rates. Fair value hedges include hedges against a change in the fair value of

- A recognized asset or liability.
- An unrecognized firm commitment.

A **cash flow hedge** is used to establish fixed prices or rates when future cash flows could vary due to changes in prices or rates. Cash flow hedges include hedges against the change in cash flows associated with

- A forecasted transaction.
- A recognized asset or liability with variable future cash flows.

Derivative instruments are frequently used as hedges with respect to the exposure to risk associated with foreign currency transactions and investments in foreign companies. The use of derivatives in this context is discussed in Chapter 10, which deals with multinational accounting. The following sections deal with the accounting for hedges employed in other contexts.

Special Accounting for Fair Value Hedges

7

OBJECTIVE

Demonstrate how a fair value hedge is used, and account for such hedges.

The hedged item in a fair value hedge is either a recognized asset or liability or a firm commitment. Recognized assets or liabilities in a fair value hedge result from actual past transactions such as a purchase of inventory or a note payable. Commitments relate to transactions that have not yet occurred, such as a contract to purchase inventory or incur debt. A commitment is a binding agreement between two parties that specifies all significant terms related to the prospective transaction. The price of the prospective transaction is fixed or it may involve a specified fixed rate such as a rate of interest. The agreement also includes a large enough disincentive to make performance of the contract probable.

Because the prices or rates are fixed, subsequent changes in prices or rates affect the value of a recognized asset, liability, or commitment. For example, if a company holds an inventory of crude oil, changes in the price of crude oil will affect the fair value of the asset. Similarly, if a company has committed to acquire crude oil for a fixed price, changes in the price of crude oil will affect the value of the commitment. If the price of crude oil increased, the value of the asset or commitment would increase favorably. The existing inventory would be worth more, or the commitment to acquire crude at previously fixed lower prices would have more value. However, if crude oil prices decreased, the resulting effect would be unfavorable.

To avoid the potential unfavorable effect associated with changes in prices or rates on recognized transactions or commitments with fixed terms, an entity could acquire a derivative instrument as a hedge against unfavorable outcomes. For example, in order to hedge against a decrease in the value of crude oil, an entity could acquire a futures contract to sell crude. Many accounting principles do not allow for the *recognition in current earnings* of *both increases and decreases* in the value of recognized assets, liabilities, or firm commitments. However, if the risk of such changes in value is covered by a fair value hedge, special accounting treatment is allowed that provides for the recognition of such changes in earnings. In a qualifying fair value hedge, the gain or loss on the derivative hedging instrument and the offsetting loss or gain on the hedged item are both recognized currently in earnings. For instance, assume an existing liability has a fixed interest rate. A decrease in interest rates will result in a higher fair value of the debt (lower interest rates result in larger present values). If the debt is not hedged, the increase in the value of the debt is not recognized in earnings. However, if the liability is hedged, both the increase in the value of the debt and the change in the value of the derivative instrument used as a hedge are recognized in earnings.

It is important to note that if both increases and decreases in the value of a recognized asset or liability are recognized in current earnings according to existing accounting principles, special hedge accounting is not necessary. For example, if a *trading portfolio* consisted of debt instruments, such investments would be marked-to-market, and both increases and decreases in value would be recognized in current earnings. Therefore, if the portfolio were hedged, special accounting treatment would not be necessary. Changes in the value of both the hedged item and the hedging instrument are already being recognized in earnings. However, if a debt instrument is part of an *available-for-sale portfolio* and the debt is marked-to-market, the resulting changes in value are not recognized in current earnings. Therefore, if the portfolio were hedged, special accounting treatment would be allowed and would result in recognizing in earnings the change in value of the debt instrument.

Qualifying Criteria for Fair Value Hedges. In order to qualify for special fair value hedge accounting, the derivative hedging instrument and the hedged item must satisfy a number of criteria. A critical criterion is that an entity must have formal documentation of the hedging relationship and the entity's risk-management objective and strategy. The entity must indicate the reason for undertaking the designated hedge, identify the hedged item and the derivative hedging instrument, and explain the nature of the risk being hedged. This criterion must be satisfied at inception and cannot be retroactively applied after an entity has determined whether hedging would be appropriate.

Another important criterion is that the hedging relationship must be assessed both at inception and on an ongoing basis to determine if it is highly effective in offsetting the identified risks. Although specific quantitative guidelines are not available to define *highly effective*, the FASB expects a high correlation to exist between changes in the value of the derivative instrument and in the fair value of the hedged item such that the respective changes in value would be substantially offset. Generally speaking, a hedge would be totally effective if the terms (such as notional amount, maturity dates, quality/condition, delivery locations) of the hedging instrument and the hedged item are the same. This approach is known as *critical terms analysis*. It is important to note that in practice the terms of a derivative do not always align with the terms of the related asset or liability. For example, a corn future may call for delivery at a different location than where the related inventory of hedged corn is located.

Another approach to assessing effectiveness is known as *statistical analysis*. This approach statistically measures the correlation between the value of the derivative and the related asset or liability. For example, if you are hedging an inventory of 200 tons of flour with a wheat future for 5,000 bushels of wheat, you would measure the correlation between prices for flour and wheat. You could also examine the relationship between changes in the value of the wheat future derivative and the changes in the value of flour over a period of time. This approach is known as *frequency analysis*, and the ratio between these price changes is known as the *delta ratio*. Although the FASB requires that the hedge be highly effective, it has not set specific quantitative levels of effectiveness that must be satisfied by the hedging relationship. However, practical standards have developed, which suggest target values that must be satisfied in order to be considered highly effective. For example, if the change in the value of a derivative is 80% to 125% of the change in the value of the hedged item, the hedge is considered to be highly effective.

Management must also describe how it will assess hedge effectiveness. Generally, hedge ineffectiveness is the difference between the gains or losses on the derivative and the hedged item. However, the portion of the gain or loss representing time value may be excluded from the assessment of effectiveness and included in current earnings. For example, the hedge of an inventory of corn with an option might only consider changes in the intrinsic value of the option for purposes of assessing effectiveness. The exclusion of a portion of the change in the value of a derivative instrument from the assessment of effectiveness will be illustrated in subsequent discussions.

Although set out in greater detail in the FASB's Statements of Financial Accounting Standards,[4] selected qualifying criteria for fair value hedges are listed in Exhibit M-3.

Accounting for a Fair Value Hedge. If the derivative instrument and the hedged item satisfy the above criteria, then the fair value hedge will qualify for special accounting. The gain or loss on the derivative hedging instrument will be recognized currently in earnings, along with the change in value on the hedged item, and an appropriate adjustment to the basis of the hedged item will be recorded. If the cumulative change in the value of the derivative instrument does not exactly offset the cumulative change in the value of the hedged item, the difference is recognized currently in earnings.

Examples of fair value hedges against inventory, a firm commitment, and a fixed interest notes payable follow. Entries for the transaction/commitment are presented side by side with entries for the hedges. All transaction costs are ignored. The examples include the use of derivatives in the form of a futures contract, forward contract, and swap. Note, however, that other types of derivatives could have been used in some of these examples.

4 Statement of Financial Accounting Standards No. 133, Statement of Financial Accounting Standards No. 138, and Statement of Financial Accounting Standards No. 149.

The special accounting treatment given a fair value hedge should continue unless:

- The criteria necessary for special accounting treatment are no longer satisfied,
- The derivative instrument expires or is sold, terminated, or exercised,
- The entity no longer designates the derivative instrument as a fair value hedge, or
- The hedging relationship is no longer considered highly effective based on management's policies.

Exhibit M-3
Selected Qualifying Criteria for Fair Value Hedges

1. At inception of the hedge, there must be formal documentation of the hedging relationship and the entity's risk-management objective and strategy. Documentation should also identify the hedging instrument, the hedged transaction, the nature of the risk being hedged, and a plan for assessing the effectiveness of the hedge.
2. Both at inception and on an ongoing basis, the hedging relationship must be assessed to determine if it is highly effective in offsetting the risk exposure associated with changes in the hedged item's fair value. The effectiveness of the hedging instrument must be assessed whenever financial statements or earnings are reported and at least every three months.
3. The hedged item is specifically identified as part or all of a recognized asset, recognized liability, or unrecognized firm commitment. The hedged item may be a single asset or liability or a portfolio of similar assets or liabilities.
4. The hedged item has exposure to changes in fair value, due to the hedged risk, that could affect earnings. For example, decreasing prices could affect an existing inventory of materials and result in lower gross profits.
5. The hedged item is not an asset or liability that is being measured at fair value, with changes in fair value, both positive and negative, being currently recognized in earnings. For example, an investment in securities, classified as a trading portfolio, would not qualify for special hedge accounting. The unrealized gains and losses on the portfolio would already be recognized in earnings, and changes in the value of a designated derivative would also be recognized currently in earnings. Therefore, special hedge accounting would only be allowed if generally accepted accounting principles (GAAP) do not already require the hedged item to be measured at fair value.
6. For nonfinancial assets (such as inventory) or liabilities, the risk being hedged against is the change in value of the entire item at its actual location rather than a change in value due to a different location or a component part. Therefore, you could not hedge an inventory of butter by designating price changes of milk as the risk being hedged.
7. Financial assets or liabilities and nonfinancial commitments with a financial component can be designated as hedged items if certain types of risks, such as those related to benchmark interest rate risk, foreign currency exchange rates, and creditworthiness are being hedged. Two or more of the above risks may be hedged simultaneously. Prepayment risk may not be designated as the risk being hedged.

An Example of a Fair Value—Inventory Transaction Hedge Using a Futures Contract

Assume that a Midwest hog producer has an inventory of hogs. On April 1, the producer decides to hedge the fair value of the hog inventory by acquiring two July futures contracts to sell hogs (each contract has a notional amount of 40,000 pounds) at $0.65 per pound. Assume the contracts are settled on July 15. It is assumed that the terms of the futures contracts and the hedged assets match with respect to the delivery location, quantity, and quality of hogs. (Margin amounts and brokers' fees are ignored for purposes of discussion.) On July 20, the producer sells 80,000 pounds of hogs at the current market price of $0.611 per pound and offsets the contract. Assume that the producer's carrying basis (book value) of the hogs is $40,000 before any adjustments related to the hedging transaction. The producer designates the futures contracts as a hedge against changes in the fair value of hogs.

The fair value of the futures contracts will be based on changes in the futures prices over the life of the contract. As previously stated, this difference represents current marked-to-market value, and no discounting is required. Effectiveness of the hedging relationship will be assessed by comparing changes over time in the current spot prices for hogs and changes in the value of the futures contracts attributable to changes in spot prices. The time value of the futures contract will be excluded from the assessment of hedge effectiveness. The time value component of the futures contract is the difference between the original spot rate and the original futures rate and is referred to as the *spot-forward difference.* The time value will periodically be recognized over the life of the contract and is measured in one of two ways. The change in the time value, spot-forward difference, may be calculated as either (1) the difference between the change in fair value of the contract and the change in spot rates or (2) directly as the change in spot-forward rates over time. Relevant values are as follows:

	April 1	May 1	June 1	July 15
Number of lbs.	80,000	80,000	80,000	80,000
Spot price/lb.	$0.640	$0.628	$0.622	$0.610
Futures price/lb.	$0.650	$0.635	$0.624	$0.610
Fair value of contract		$1,200= ($0.650 – $0.635) × 80,000	$2,080= ($0.650 – $0.624) × 80,000	$3,200= ($0.650 – $0.610) × 80,000
(a) Current period change in above fair value of contract – gain (loss)		$1,200 = $1,200 – $0	$880 = $2,080 – $1,200	$1,120 = $3,200 – $2,080
(b) Current period change in intrinsic (spot rates) – gain (loss)		$960 = ($0.640 – $0.628) × 80,000	$480 = ($0.628 – $0.622) × 80,000	$960 = ($0.622 – $0.610) × 80,000
(a) – (b) = Current period change in time value, (spot-forward difference) – gain (loss)		$240 = ($0.650 – $0.640) – ($0.635–$0.628) × 80,000 or $1,200 – $960	$400 = ($0.635 – $0.628) – ($0.624 – $0.622) × 80,000 or $880 – $480	$160 = ($0.624 – $0.622) – ($0.610 – $0.610) × 80,000 or $1,120 – $960

The following entries to record the hedging relationship are on the producer's books:

	Accounting for Hog Inventory			Accounting for Derivative Hedge		
Apr. 1				Memo entry to record the acquisition of the futures contracts.		
May 1	Unrealized Hedging Loss	960		Futures Contract*	960	
	Inventory of Hogs.		960	Unrealized Hedging Gain.		960
	To record the change in the value of the inventory.			To record the change in the value of the contract included in hedge effectiveness.		
				Futures Contract*	240	
				Derivative Gain		240
				To record the change in time value excluded from hedge effectiveness.		

**Note:* The two previous entries regarding the change in the value of the futures contract could be combined into one single entry.

Date	Accounting for Hog Inventory			Accounting for Derivative Hedge		
June 1	Unrealized Hedging Loss	480		Futures Contract	480	
	Inventory of Hogs		480	Unrealized Hedging Gain		480
	To record the change in the value of the inventory.			To record the change in the value of the contract included in hedge effectiveness.		
				Futures Contract	400	
				Derivative Gain		400
				To record the change in time value excluded from hedge effectiveness.		
July 15	Unrealized Hedging Loss	960		Futures Contract	960	
	Inventory of Hogs		960	Unrealized Hedging Gain		960
	To record the change in the value of the inventory.			To record the change in the value of the contract included in hedge effectiveness.		
15				Futures Contract	160	
				Derivative Gain		160
				To record the change in time value excluded from hedge effectiveness.		
20	Cash	48,880		Cash	3,200	
	Sales Revenue		48,880	Futures Contract		3,200
	To record the sale of 80,000 pounds of hogs at $0.611 per pound.			To record settlement of the futures contract.		
	Cost of Sales	37,600				
	Inventory of Hogs		37,600			
	To record the cost of sales consisting of original carrying value of $40,000 less decline in value of $2,400 [($0.640 – $0.610) × 80,000] due to price changes.					

In this example, the hedge totally offsets the adverse effect of price changes on the fair value of the hog inventory. The hedge was highly effective because:

1. The terms of the futures contract and the hedged inventory match regarding quantity, location, and quality.
2. The assessment of the effectiveness of the hedge excludes the time value of the futures contract.

The benefit of the hedge can best be understood by evaluating the fact situation as follows:

	Desired Position	Without the Hedge	With the Hedge
Sales price of hogs	$ 51,200	$ 48,880	$ 48,880
Cost of sales	(40,000)	(40,000)	(37,600)
Gross profit	$ 11,200	$ 8,880	$ 11,280
Hedging gain on derivative ($960 + $480 + $960)			2,400
Hedging loss on inventory ($960 + $480 + $960)			(2,400)
Subtotal	$ 11,200	$ 8,880	$ 11,280
Gain excluded from hedge effectiveness ($240 + $400 + $160)			800
Net effect on earnings	$ 11,200	$ 8,880	$ 12,080

The hedge was highly effective in achieving the desired position which was to maintain the sales value of the inventory at the April 1 spot rate (80,000 pounds × \$0.64 = \$51,200) and realize a gross profit of at least \$11,200. The hedge allowed the producer to avoid the exposure to decreases in the value of the inventory due to adverse price changes (decreasing spot rates). Excluding the \$800 gain from the time value component, the net effect on earnings of \$11,280 (\$12,080 − \$800) resulting from the use of the hedge was basically the same as the desired position of \$11,200. The \$80 difference was due to the increase in the spot rate from the expiration date of the futures contracts (July 15) to the actual sale date (July 20).

An Example of a Fair Value—Firm Commitment Hedge Using a Forward Contract

The special accounting treatment given a fair value hedge is also applicable to a hedge on a firm commitment. By way of example, assume that on April 14, when the current spot rate is \$172, a company makes a firm commitment to sell 3,000 tons of inventories at the end of June for \$172 per ton. It is estimated that the cost of inventory sold under the contract will be \$430,000. Concerned that prices may increase and that the firm commitment will prevent the company from realizing even a higher sales value, on April 14 the company enters into a forward contract to buy 3,000 tons of identical inventory at the current forward rate of \$173 per ton. The forward contract expires on June 30. The forward contract will gain in value if prices increase, because the holder will be able to buy inventory at the lower price of \$173 per ton. Therefore, if prices increase, the loss associated with the firm commitment will be offset by the gain traceable to the forward contract. Changes in the fair value of the contract that are attributable to changes in the time value, that is changes in the spot-forward difference, are excluded from the assessment of hedge effectiveness and reported directly in current earnings.[5]

	April 14	April 30	May 31	June 30
Notional amount in tons	3,000	3,000	3,000	3,000
Spot rate per ton	\$172	\$174	\$174	\$176
Forward rate per ton for remaining time	\$173	\$175	\$174	\$176
Initial forward rate		\$173	\$173	\$173
Change from original forward rate		\$2	\$1	\$3
Fair value of forward contract in future dollars:				
Original forward value		\$ 519,000	\$ 519,000	\$ 519,000
Current forward value		525,000	522,000	528,000
Change – gain (loss) in forward value		\$ 6,000	\$ 3,000	\$ 9,000
Discount rate		6%	6%	6%
Present value of the fair value of the contract:				
FV = \$6,000, n = 2, i = 0.5%		\$ 5,940		
FV = \$3,000, n = 1, i = 0.5%			\$ 2,985	
FV = \$9,000, n = 0, i = 0.5%				\$ 9,000
(a) Change in above fair value of the contract – gain (loss):				
Current present value		\$ 5,940	\$ 2,985	\$ 9,000
Prior present value		0	5,940	2,985
Change in present value		\$ 5,940	\$ (2,955)	\$ 6,015

(continued)

5 Management has the discretion to either include or exclude the time value of the futures contract from the assessment of effectiveness. However, excluding the time value of the contract increases the likelihood that there will be no ineffectiveness in the hedge. Generally speaking, if the terms of the forward contract and the commitment are the same (in terms of notional amount, expiration date, location, etc.) and the time value is excluded, there will be no hedge ineffectiveness.

	April 14	April 30	May 31	June 30
(b) Change in intrinsic value (spot rates) – gain (loss) . . .		$6,000 = ($174 – $172) × 3,000	$0 = ($174 – $174) × 3,000	$6,000 = ($176 – $174) × 3,000
(a) – (b) = Change in time value (spot-forward difference) – gain (loss).		$(60) = $5,940 – $6,000	$(2,955) = $(2,955) – $0	$15 = $6,015 – $6,000

Based on the above relevant information, the entries to record the commitment, hedge, and sales transaction are as follows:

Date	Entry	Debit	Credit
Apr. 30	Loss on Firm Commitment	6,000	
	Firm Commitment.		6,000
	To record change in fair value of firm commitment [3,000 × ($172 – $174)].		
	Forward Contract*	6,000	
	Unrealized Gain on Forward Contract		6,000
	To record the change in value of forward contract included in hedge effectiveness.		
	Unrealized Loss on Forward Contract	60	
	Forward Contract*		60
	To record the change in time value excluded from hedge effectiveness.		

**Note*: The two previous entries regarding the change in the value of the forward contract could be combined into one single entry.

Date	Entry	Debit	Credit
May 31	Derivative Loss	2,955	
	Forward Contract.		2,955
	To record the change in time value exclued from hedge effectiveness.		

Note: There has been no change in the value of the commitment or in the value of the forward contract based on changes in spot rates.

Date	Entry	Debit	Credit
June 30	Loss on Firm Commitment	6,000	
	Firm Commitment.		6,000
	To record change in value of firm commitment [3,000 × ($174– $176)].		
	Cash	516,000	
	Firm Commitment.	12,000	
	Sales		528,000
	To record the sale of inventory covered by the firm commitment (3,000 tons sold at $172).		
	Cost of Sales	430,000	
	Inventory		430,000
	To record the cost of sales.		
	Forward Contract	6,000	
	Unrealized Gain on Forward Contract		6,000
	To record the change in value of forward contract included in hedge effectiveness.		
	Forward Contract	15	
	Unrealized Gain on Forward Contract		15
	To record the change in time value excluded from hedge effectiveness.		
	Cash	9,000	
	Forward Contract.		9,000
	To record the settlement of forward contract.		

The concern with the firm commitment was that prices would increase above the firm sales price and reduce the value of the commitment. A forward contract to buy is an appropriate strategy if prices are expected to increase, because as prices increase, the value of the forward contract would increase. After excluding the time value of the contract, the forward contract was expected to be highly effective as a hedge because the derivative instrument had the same type of inventory, notional amount, and forward rate as the hedged commitment. The effectiveness of the hedge is as follows:

	Desired Position	Without the Forward Contract	With the Forward Contract
Sales value of firm commitment	$ 528,000	$ 516,000	$ 528,000
Cost of sales.	(430,000)	(430,000)	(430,000)
Gross profit	$ 98,000	$ 86,000	$ 98,000
Loss on firm commitment			(12,000)
Gain in value of forward contract			12,000
Net effect on earnings before consideration of time value	$ 98,000	$ 86,000	$ 98,000
Total change in time value			(3,000)
Net effect on earnings	$ 98,000	$ 86,000	$ 98,000

The hedge on the firm commitment was highly effective in that the loss in the value of the firm commitment was totally offset by the gain in the value of the forward contract. This resulted in establishing a sales value that reflected the rate at the actual date of the sale (3,000 tons at $176 = $528,000) rather than the lower value (3,000 tons at $172 = $516,000) that was established at the date of the commitment. Note that the account Firm Commitment serves the purpose of adjusting the sales value of the commitment. In essence, through the use of a hedge, the firm commitment did not prevent the company from realizing even a higher sales value. This was accomplished at a cost of $3,000, representing the time value of the contract.

An Example of a Fair Value—Hedge against a Fixed Interest Notes Payable Using an Interest Rate Swap

If a company has borrowed at a fixed rate of interest, the fair value of the resulting liability will change if benchmark[6] interest rates change. Although the cash flows are fixed, the discount (current interest) rate changes, resulting in a change in present value. For example, if interest rates decrease, the net present value of the cash flows and the liability will increase. Furthermore, if the debtor company anticipates that variable rates will fall below the original fixed rate, it would have preferred to structure the debt with a variable rate rather than a fixed rate of interest. An interest rate swap would allow the company to accomplish this if it paid a variable rate of interest to a counterparty in exchange for the receipt of a fixed rate of interest. In essence, the debt with a fixed rate of interest is converted into debt with a variable rate of interest.

For example, assume that on January 1, 20X1, a company has taken out an 18-month, $20,000,000 note from a bank at a fixed rate of 7% with interest due on a semiannual basis. On January 1, 20X1, believing that interest rates are likely to drop, the company arranged to receive a 7% fixed rate of interest from another financial institution in exchange for the payment of variable rates. Differences between the fixed and variable rates are to be settled on a semiannual basis. The variable rates are based on the LIBOR (London Interbank Offered Rate) rate + 1.25% (125 basis points) and are reset semiannually in order to determine the interest rate to be used for the next semiannual payment. The notional amount of the interest rate swap is $20,000,000, and the expiration date of the swap matches the maturity date of the original bank loan. Relevant values are as follows:

Reset Dates	LIBOR + 1.25% Rates for Next Period	Assumed Fair Value of Swap	Change in Fair Value
Jan. 1, 20X1	7.0%		
June 30, 20X1	6.8	$38,000	$38,000
Dec. 31, 20X1	6.7	29,000	(9,000)

6 Statement of Financial Accounting Standards No. 138 defines the benchmark interest rate as a rate in a financial market that is widely used as a basis for determining interest rates for individual transactions. The benchmark rate is a risk-free rate that, in the United States, is represented by Treasury obligations of the U.S. government and the LIBOR (London Interbank Offered Rate) swap rate.

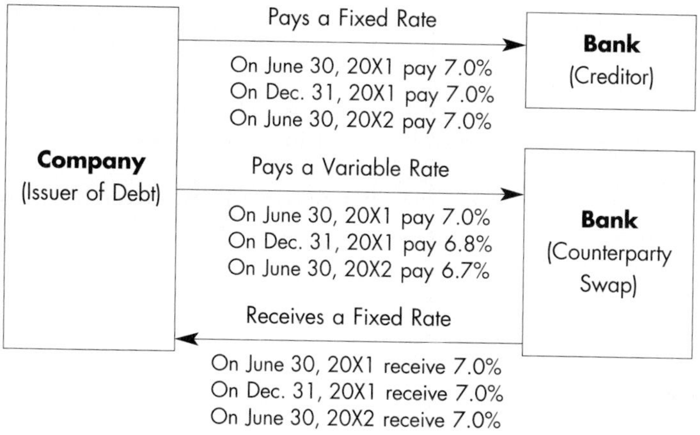

Date	Account	Debit	Credit	Account	Debit	Credit
20X1						
Jan. 1	Cash	20,000,000				
	7% Note Payable.		20,000,000			
	To record receipt of note proceeds.					
June 30	Interest Expense.	700,000				
	Cash		700,000			
	To record semiannual interest payment ($20,000,000 × 7% × ½ year).					
	Unrealized Loss on Swap	38,000		Interest Rate Swap Asset	38,000	
	7% Note Payable.		38,000	Unrealized Gain on Swap. . .		38,000
	To recognize the change in the value of the debt.			To recognize the change in the value of the swap.		
Dec. 31	Interest Expense.	700,000		Cash	20,000	
	Cash		700,000	Interest Expense		20,000
	To record semiannual interest payment ($20,000,000 × 7% × ½ year).			To record settlement of interest rate difference on swap (6.8% vs. 7% on $20,000,000 × ½ year).		
	7% Note Payable	9,000		Unrealized Loss on Swap	9,000	
	Unrealized Gain on Swap. . .		9,000	Interest Rate Swap Asset		9,000
	To recognize the change in the value of the debt.			To recognize the change in the value of the swap.		
20X2						
June 30	Interest Expense.	700,000		Cash	30,000	
	Cash		700,000	Interest Expense		30,000
	To record semiannual interest payment ($20,000,000 × 7% × ½ year).			To record settlement of interest rate difference on swap (6.7% vs. 7% on $20,000,000 × ½ year).		
	7% Note Payable	29,000		Unrealized Loss on Swap	29,000	
	Unrealized Gain on Swap. . .		29,000	Interest Rate Swap Asset		29,000
	To recognize the change in the value of the debt.			To write down swap value to zero at end of contract.		
	7% Note Payable	20,000,000				
	Cash		20,000,000			
	To record repayment of debt.					

During the period covered by the interest rate swap, the carrying amount of the debt was adjusted to reflect changes in the value traceable to movement in benchmark interest rates. In essence, these adjustments represent a discount or premium on the debt. However, while the hedge is in effect, the discount or premium does not have to be amortized. After termination of the swap, any remaining discount or premium must be amortized over the remaining life of the debt.

The interest rate swap was highly effective in replacing a 7.0% fixed rate of interest on the debt with a variable or floating rate of interest equal to LIBOR + 1.25%. The variable rate of interest is derived as follows:

Rate paid on original debt	–7.00%
Receive fixed rate on swap	+7.00%
Pay floating rate on swap	– LIBOR +1.25%
Net pay rate [– 7.00% + 7.00% – (LIBOR +1.25%)]	= LIBOR +1.25%

Given the decreasing pattern of the floating rates, the company experienced a reduction is interest expense and cash outflows as follows:

Total interest expense at fixed rate	$2,100,000
Total interest expense at floating rate	2,050,000
Reduction in interest expense and cash flows	$ 50,000

The change in the value of the swap offsets the change in the value of the debt. The fair value hedge was expected to be highly effective (in this case perfectly effective) in offsetting changes in the fair value of the debt due to the fact that:

- The notional amount of the swap matches that of the debt.
- The maturity date of the swap matches that of the debt.
- The fair value of the swap at inception is zero.
- The fixed rate is the same over the life of the note, and the variable rate is based on the same index (LIBOR) over the life of the note.
- The debt is not prepayable.
- There is no floor or ceiling on the variable interest rate.
- The intervals between reset dates are frequent enough to justify an assumption that the settlement amounts are based on market rates.

8

OBJECTIVE

Demonstrate how a cash flow hedge is used, and account for such hedges.

Special Accounting for Cash Flow Hedges

The hedged item in a cash flow hedge is an existing asset or liability with variable future cash flows (e.g., variable rate debt) or a forecasted transaction. A forecasted transaction is one that is expected to occur in the future at a market price that will be in existence at the time of the transaction. This is in contrast to a commitment, which involves market prices that have been previously determined at the time of the commitment. Unlike a commitment, a forecasted transaction does not provide an entity with any present rights or obligations and therefore does not have any fixed prices or rates. Because fixed prices or rates are not present in a forecasted transaction, an entity is exposed to the risk that future cash flows may vary due to changes in prices/rates. In order to reduce the risk associated with unfavorable cash flow variability, a strategy is developed to hedge the variable cash flows. These hedges are known as cash flow hedges. For example, assume that a food processor forecasts that it will need to purchase corn in 60 days. Absent a fixed commitment, the producer is exposed to the risk that corn prices may increase and more cash will be needed to acquire the inventory. In order to reduce the risk associated with uncertain variable cash flows, the producer could acquire a futures contract to buy corn or perhaps a call option to buy corn. The objective of the hedge is to allow the entity to fix the price or rate and reduce the variability of cash flows.

Qualifying Criteria for Cash Flow Hedges. As is the case with a fair value hedge, special hedge accounting is not available for a cash flow hedge unless a number of criteria are satisfied. Cash flow hedges must also meet the criteria regarding documentation and assessment of effectiveness. Although set forth in greater detail in the FASB's Statements of Financial Accounting Standards,[7] selected qualifying criteria for a cash flow hedge are set forth in Exhibit M-4.

Accounting for a Cash Flow Hedge. If the derivative instrument and the hedged item satisfy the criteria, then the cash flow hedge will qualify for special accounting. The gain or loss on the derivative instrument will be reported in **other comprehensive income (OCI)**,[8] and the ineffective portion, if any, will be recognized currently in earnings. As with fair value hedges, a portion of the derivative instrument's gain or loss may be excluded from the assessment of effectiveness. That portion of the gain or loss will be recognized currently in earnings rather than as a component of other comprehensive income.

The gain or loss on a cash flow hedge is reported as OCI, rather than recognized currently in earnings, because the hedged forecasted cash flows have not yet occurred or been recognized in the financial statements. The hedge is intended to establish the values that will be recognized once the forecasted transaction occurs and is recognized. Once the forecasted transaction has actually occurred, the OCI gain or loss will be reclassified into earnings in the same period(s) as the forecasted transaction affects earnings. For example, assume that a forecasted sale of inventory is hedged. Once the inventory is sold and recognized in earnings, the applicable amount, the OCI gain or loss, will also be recognized in earnings. If the forecasted transaction were a purchase of a depreciable asset, the applicable portion of the OCI would be recognized in earnings when the asset's depreciation expense is recognized.

Exhibit M-4
Selected Qualifying Criteria for Cash Flow Hedges

1. At inception of the hedge, there must be formal documentation of the hedging relationship and the entity's risk-management objective and strategy. Documentation should also identify the hedging instrument, the hedged transaction, the nature of the risk being hedged, and a plan for assessing the effectiveness of the hedge.
2. Both at inception and on an ongoing basis, the hedging relationship must be assessed to determine if it is highly effective in achieving offsetting cash flows attributable to the hedged item's fair value. The effectiveness of the hedging instrument must be assessed whenever financial statements or earnings are reported and at least every three months.
3. If a hedging instrument is used to modify variable interest rates on a recognized asset or liability to another variable interest rate (such instruments are known as basis swaps), the hedging instrument must be a *link* between a recognized asset with variable rates and a recognized liability with variable rates. For example, an entity with a variable rate loan receivable (e.g., prime rate + 1%) and a variable rate loan payable (e.g., LIBOR) may use a hedging instrument (e.g., swap prime rate + 1% for LIBOR) to link the two variable rate instruments.
4. The forecasted transaction is specifically identified as a single transaction or a group of individual transactions.
5. The forecasted transaction is with an external party, probably will occur, and presents exposure to variability in cash flows that could affect earnings.
6. The forecasted transaction is not the acquisition of an asset or incurrence of a liability that will subsequently be measured at fair value with changes in fair value being currently recognized in earnings. If the forecasted transaction relates to a recognized asset or liability, such asset or liability is not remeasured with changes in fair value being reported in current earnings.

7 Statement of Financial Accounting Standards No. 133, Statement of Financial Accounting Standards No. 138, and Statement of Financial Accounting Standards No. 149.

8 Other comprehensive income is not included in the income statement; it bypasses the traditional income statement but is shown as a component of equity.

7. For the forecasted purchase or sale of a nonfinancial item (such as inventory), the risk being hedged against is the change in cash flows due to price/rate changes rather than a change in cash flows due to a different location or a component part.
8. The forecasted purchase or sale of a financial asset or liability (or the interest payments on that asset or liability) or the variable cash flows associated with an existing financial asset or liability can be designated as a hedged item if certain types of risks, such as those related to changes in cash flows, benchmark interest rates, foreign currency exchange rates, and creditworthiness are being hedged. Two or more of the above risks may be hedged simultaneously. Prepayment risk may not be designated as the risk being hedged.

The deferral of a loss on a cash flow hedge as a component of OCI is not appropriate if it is likely to result in a combined basis/cost that exceeds the fair value of the resulting asset or liability. For example, assume a derivative loss associated with a forecasted purchase of equipment will, when combined with the expected cost of the equipment, result in a total cost in excess of the item's fair value. If this is expected, the derivative's loss should be recognized immediately in earnings, to the extent that it exceeds the equipment's fair value.

The change in the value of a derivative instrument that equals the change in the value of the forecasted cash flows is recognized as OCI. If the change in the value of the derivative is less than the change in forecasted cash flows, only the lesser amount is recorded. However, if the change in the value of the derivative exceeds the change in forecasted cash flows, the excess (ineffective portion of the derivative) is recognized in current earnings. For example, if a derivative instrument increases $1,000 in value and the forecasted cash flows decrease in value by $900, a $900 gain will be shown as OCI, and a $100 gain will be recognized in current earnings.

If the change in value of a derivative instrument is less than the change in value of the forecasted transaction, all of the change in value of the derivative instrument is recognized as a component of other comprehensive income. However, the excess change in value of the forecasted transaction is not recognized. To do so would allow partial recognition of a transaction that has not yet occurred. For example, assume a derivative instrument changes $1,000 in value and the forecasted cash flows change in value by $1,200. Only $1,000 of the change in value is recognized as a component of other comprehensive income and the $200 difference is not accounted for.

If all or part of a transaction is still forecasted, there may be some gain or loss on a corresponding derivative that is still being classified as a component of OCI. On an ongoing basis, it is important to make sure that the gain (loss) on a derivative that remains as a component of OCI does not more than offset the cumulative loss (gain) in the value of the remaining forecasted transaction. If excessive amounts are classified as OCI, such excess amounts must be reclassified as a component of current earnings. By way of illustration, consider the following independent cases:

	Case A	Case B	Case C
Amount of gain (loss) on derivative that is still being classified as OCI.	$ 10,000	$10,000	$(10,000)
Cumulative gain (loss) on remaining forecasted transaction.	(12,000)	(8,000)	8,000
Extent to which OCI gain (loss) more than offsets the cumulative loss (gain) in the value of the remaining forecasted transaction	Not applicable	2,000	(2,000)
Amount of OCI to be reclassified as a component of current earnings	Not applicable	2,000	(2,000)

The accounting treatment given a cash flow hedge should continue unless:

- The criteria identified above are no longer satisfied,
- The derivative instrument expires or is sold, terminated, or exercised,
- The entity no longer designates the derivative instrument as a cash flow hedge, or
- The hedging relationship is no longer considered highly effective based on management's policies.

If any of the above conditions occur, the cumulative balance remaining in other comprehensive income should be reclassified into earnings in the same period or periods as the forecasted transaction affects earnings. Furthermore, if it is probable that a forecasted transaction will not occur by the end of the original anticipated time or within an additional two-month period thereafter, the cumulative balance remaining in other comprehensive income should generally be immediately reclassified into earnings.

Examples of cash flow hedges against a forecasted transaction and a variable interest notes payable follow. Entries for the transactions are presented side-by-side with entries for the hedges for clarity. All transaction costs are ignored. The examples include the use of derivatives in the form of an option and a swap.

An Example of a Cash Flow—Hedge against a Forecasted Transaction Using an Option

Assume that in March, a processor of cereals and other food forecasts a purchase of 300 tons of soybean meal for June delivery. Concerned that prices may increase, the processor purchases three at-the-money, June call options on March 10. On the Chicago Board of Trade (CBT), the options are trading at $800 per option with a strike price of $165 per ton. Note that the option was trading at-the-money, which means that the strike price ($165) and current spot price ($165) are equal and that the option has no intrinsic value. The $800 paid for the option reflects time value. Each option is for a 100-ton unit with delivery at a warehouse specified by the (CBT) and a settlement date of June 25. Effectiveness of the hedge is measured by comparing changes in the option's intrinsic value, with changes in the forecasted cash flows based on spot rates for soybean meal. Therefore, the change in time value of the option is excluded from the assessment of hedge effectiveness. In addition to the information given above, the following data are relevant to the hedging strategy:

Given:	March 10	March 31	April 30	May 31	June 25
Spot price per ton	$165	$167	$164	$172	$178
Strike price	$165	$165	$165	$165	$165
Number of tons per option	100	100	100	100	100
Fair value per option (given)	$800	$920	$700	$1,100	$ 1,300
Calculations per Option:					
Intrinsic value (Spot minus strike × number of tons)[a]	$ 0	$ 200	$ 0	$ 700	$ 1,300
Time value	800	720	700	400	0
Total (intrinsic + time)	$800	$ 920	$700	$1,100	$ 1,300
Value of expected cash flows [change in spot rates – gain (loss)]		$ (200)[b]	$100[c]	$ (700)[d]	$(1,300)[e]
OCI balance after adjustments Dr (Cr) (lesser of intrinsic value or expected cash flows		(200)	0	(700)	(1,300)
Adjustment to OCI – Dr (Cr) (change in OCI balance)		(200)	200	(700)	(600)
Adjustment to income – Dr (Cr) (change in time value)		80	20	300	400

[a]The intrinsic value is never less than zero because the holder does not have to exercise the option if it is not in-the-money.
[b]($165 – $167) × 100 = $(200)
[c]($165 – $164) × 100 = $100
[d]($165 – $172) × 100 = $(700)
[e]($165 – $178) × 100 = $(1,300)

The following entries relate only to the hedge because no transaction has yet occurred. The recorded amounts are based on the above calculations:

Mar. 10	Investment in Call Option	2,400	
	Cash		2,400
	To record purchase of three options at $800 each.		
31	Investment in Call Option [($920 – $800) × 3]	360	
	Unrealized Loss on Hedge ($80 × 3)	240	
	Other Comprehensive Income ($200 × 3)		600
	To record the change in the value of the option. The change in time value is excluded from the assessment of hedge effectiveness.		
Apr. 30	Unrealized Loss on Hedge ($20 × 3)	60	
	Other Comprehensive Income ($0 – $200 ×3)	600	
	Investment in Call Option [($700 – $920) × 3]		660
	To record the change in the value of the option (note the absence of intrinsic value).		
May 31	Investment in Call Option [($1,100 – $700) × 3]	1,200	
	Unrealized Loss on Hedge ($300 × 3)	900	
	Other Comprehensive Income [($700 – $0) × 3]		2,100
	To record the change in the value of the option.		
June 25	Investment in Call Option [($1,300 – $1,100) × 3]	600	
	Unrealized Loss on Hedge ($400 × 3)	1,200	
	Other Comprehensive Income [($1,300 – $700) × 3]		1,800
	To record the change in the value of the option.		
	Cash ($1,300 × 3)	3,900	
	Investment in Call Option		3,900
	To record settlement of option.		
	Inventory—Soybean Meal	53,400	
	Cash		53,400
	To record purchase of 300 tons at the spot rate of $178 per ton.		

When the inventory of soybean meal is recognized as a component of cost of sales and thereby affects earnings, the applicable amount of other comprehensive income will also be recognized in earnings. Entries to reflect this are as follows:

Cost of Sales—Soybean Meal	53,400	
Inventory—Soybean Meal		53,400
To recognize cost of sales.		
Other Comprehensive Income	3,900	
Cost of Sales—Soybean Meal		3,900
To adjust cost of sales by the gain accumulated in other comprehensive income.		

There are several important points to note about the above entries regarding the cash flow hedge.

- Changes in the time value of the option are recognized currently in earnings, not OCI, as an unrealized loss of $2,400 ($240 + $60 + $900 + $1,200) on the hedge.
- At the end of April, the cumulative change in the value of the expected cash flows associated with the forecasted purchase of inventory was a $300 gain ($100 × 3), but the intrinsic

value of the derivative hedge was $0. Therefore, the balance in OCI must be the lesser of the *absolute value* of these two values. At the end of April, the OCI balance is zero even though there is a cumulative loss due to changes in the spot rates.

- The cumulative balance in OCI will be reclassified into earnings in the same periods(s) in which the inventory of soybean meal affects earnings (as cost of sales). As shown above, this occurred through the entry that reduced the cost of goods sold by the OCI balance amount.

Note that this example contained no hedge ineffectiveness because of the following:

1. The terms of the derivative option and the forecasted transaction match in terms of comodity, quantities, qualities, location, and timing.
2. The time value of the option was excluded from an assessment of the hedge effectiveness.
3. The call option was in-the-money, and, therefore, the changes in intrinsic value could offset the changes in the forcasted cash flows based on spot rates. If an option is out-of-the-money, it has no intrinsic value and cannot offset the changes in the forecasted cash flows.

The hedge was effective against adverse effects of increases in the spot price. By entering into the hedging relationship, the cost of the inventory, and ultimately the resulting cost of sales, was fixed at the strike price of $49,500 (300 tons at the strike price of $165 per ton). This was accomplished by incurring a cost of $2,400, represented by the initial premium on the three options (3 × $800 = $2,400). The effect the cash flow hedge had on the forecasted transaction is summarized as follows:

	Without the Call Option	With the Call Option
Cost of inventory to be included in cost of sales based on spot prices (300 tons @ $178 per ton)	$53,400	$53,400
Gain included in other comprehensive income and reclassified as an adjustment to cost of sales [300 tons × ($165 – $178)]		(3,900)
Adjusted basis of inventory to be included in cost of sales	$53,400	$49,500
Time value of the option recognized as a loss on hedge equal to the premium (3 options @ $800)		2,400
Net cost to be recognized in income statement	$53,400	$51,900

Although this hedge was effective, it is important to note that if the spot rate on June 25 had been less than the strike price, the hedge would not have been effective.

An Example of a Cash Flow—Hedge against a Variable Interest Notes Payable Using an Interest Rate Swap

If an entity has a note receivable or payable that is based on a variable rate of interest, the entity may hedge the variable interest cash flows. Note that a hedge of an asset or liability involving a fixed rate of interest would be a fair value hedge, but if the interest rate is variable, it is a cash flow hedge. The purpose of the cash flow hedge is to offset the risk associated with uncertain variable cash flows by establishing a fixed interest rate.

For example, assume that on January 1, 20X1, an entity has loaned $10,000,000 for two years with semiannual interest due based on a variable rate of LIBOR + 1% (100 basis points). On June 30, 20X1, concerned that variable interest rates will decline, the entity enters into a swap to receive a fixed rate of 7% in return for payment of a variable LIBOR + 1.25% (125 basis points) rate. The notional amount of the swap is $10,000,000. At each semiannual period, the swap is settled, and the variable rate is reset for the following semiannual interest payment. Relevant values are as follows:

Reset Dates	Receive LIBOR + 1% for Next Period	Pay LIBOR + 1.25% for Next Period	Fair Value of Swap	Change in Fair Value
June 30, 20X1	6.75%	7.0%		
Dec. 31, 20X1	6.65%	6.9	$ 9,505	$9,505
June 30, 20X2	6.35%	6.6	19,361	9,856*

*Note that the loan is for two years and matured on December 31, 20X2. Therefore, the swap does not exist after that point in time.

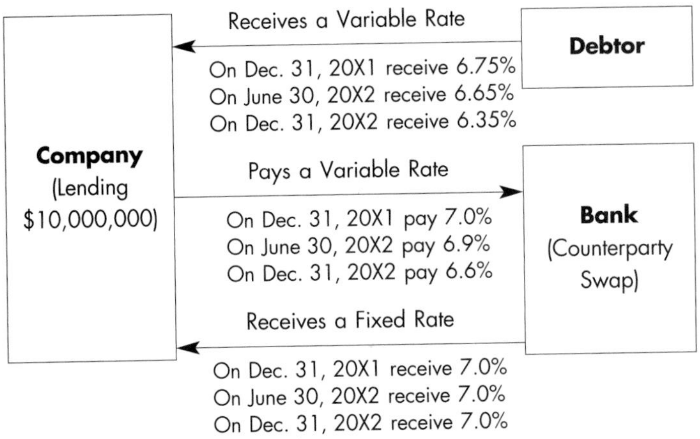

The entries to record the interest rate swap are as follows:

20X1			
Dec. 31	Cash	337,500	
	Interest Income		337,500
	To record interest income at the variable rate ($10,000,000 × 6.75% × ½ year).		
	Interest Rate Swap Asset	9,505	
	Other Comprehensive Income*		9,505
	To record settlement of the swap [$10,000,000 × (7% – 7.0%) × ½ year] and the change in the value of the swap.		
20X2			
June 30	Cash	332,500	
	Interest Income		332,500
	To record interest income at the variable rate ($10,000,000 × 6.65% × ½ year).		
	Cash	5,000	
	Interest Rate Swap Asset	9,856	
	Other Comprehensive Income		14,856
	To record settlement of the swap [$10,000,000 × (7% – 6.9%) × ½ year] and the change in the value of the swap.		
	Other Comprehensive Income*	5,000	
	Interest Income		5,000
	To reclassify other comprehensive income to earnings (equal to the cash settlement associated with interest currently being recognized in earnings).		

Dec. 31	Cash	317,500	
	Interest Income		317,500
	To record interest income at the variable rate ($10,000,000 × 6.35% × ½ year).		
	Cash	20,000	
	Interest Rate Swap Asset		19,361
	Other Comprehensive Income		639
	To record settlement of the swap [$10,000,000 × (7% − 6.6%) × ½ year] and the change in the value of the swap.		
	Other Comprehensive Income	20,000	
	Interest Income		20,000
	To reclassify other comprehensive income to earnings.		

* *Note: The two previous entries could be combined into one entry. However, it is important to note that other comprehensive income is reclassified into earnings only in the period in which the forecasted transaction affects earnings (i.e., interest income is recognized).*

The swap was not a hedge against changing values of the debt but rather a hedge against the changing cash values of the variable interest payments. The interest rate swap was highly effective in replacing a LIBOR + 1.00% variable or floating rate of interest on the note receivable with a fixed rate of interest equal to 6.75%. The fixed rate of interest is derived as follows:

Rate received on original debt	LIBOR + 1.00%
Pay floating rate on swap	− LIBOR + 1.25%
Receive fixed rate on swap	+ 7.00%
Net receive rate [(LIBOR + 1.00%) − (LIBOR + 1.25%) + 7.00%]	= 6.75%

Given the decreasing pattern of the floating rates, the company experienced an increase in interest income and cash inflows with a swap to pay floating for receive fixed as follows:

Total interest income from receive fixed rate swap (net rate of 6.75% × $10,000,000 × 1.5 years)	$1,012,500
Total interest income at floating rate	987,500
Increase in interest income and cash inflows	$ 25,000

The $25,000 increase in interest income was initially recorded in OCI and was then reclassified into earnings when interest on the loan receivable affected earnings.

REFLECTION

- Fair value hedges apply to recognized assets and liabilities or firm commitments. The terms, prices, and/or rates for these items are fixed. Therefore, changes in the prices or rates affect the fair value of the recognized item or commitment.
- Cash flow hedges apply to existing assets or liabilities with variable future cash flows and to forecasted transactions. The prices or rates for these items are not fixed, and, therefore, future cash flows may vary due to changes in prices or rates.
- In a fair value hedge, both the derivative instrument and the hedged item are measured at fair value. Changes in the fair value of the respective items are recognized currently in earnings.

- In a cash flow hedge, the derivative instrument is measured at fair value with changes in value being recognized in other comprehensive income. The amounts in other comprehensive income are recognized in current earnings in the same period(s) as are the gains or losses on the hedged cash flow.

9

OBJECTIVE

Identify the various types of information that should be included in disclosures regarding derivative instruments and hedging activities.

DISCLOSURES REGARDING DERIVATIVE INSTRUMENTS AND HEDGING ACTIVITIES

The FASB requires entities that hold or issue derivative instruments to disclose the purpose for holding or issuing such instruments, the context needed to understand the objectives, and strategies for achieving the objectives. With respect to derivative instruments that are designated as hedges, the FASB calls for the following disclosures:

1. The objective of using hedging instruments and the strategies for achieving the objective.
2. Descriptions of the various types of hedges, such as fair value hedges and cash flow hedges.
3. A description of the entity's risk-management policy for hedging types, along with a description of the types of transactions that are hedged.

In addition, specific disclosures for fair value hedges include the following:

1. The current period effect on earnings traceable to hedge ineffectiveness, the portion of gain or loss excluded from the assessment of hedge effectiveness, and where net gains or losses are reported on the income statement.
2. The amount of gain or loss recognized in earnings when a firm commitment no longer qualifies as a fair value hedge.

For a cash flow hedge, specific additional disclosures include the following:

1. The current period effect on earnings traceable to hedge ineffectiveness, the portion of gain or loss excluded from the assessment of hedge effectiveness, and where net gains or losses are reported on the income statement.
2. The transactions or events that will result in reclassification of OCI to earnings and the amount to be reclassified within the next 12 months.
3. For other than variable interest rate hedges, the maximum length of time over which forecasted transactions are being hedged.
4. The amount of gains or losses reclassified as earnings, because it is probable that a forecasted transaction will not occur.

Certain other disclosures are required for hedges relating to an investment in a foreign operation. These disclosures will be discussed in Chapter 11.

Exhibit M-5 summarizes excerpts from the footnotes of Johnson Controls, Inc.'s 2004 annual report that provide insight into the company's use of derivative instruments and the accounting given them.

Exhibit M-5
Footnote Excerpts Regarding Derivative Instruments—Johnson Controls, Inc.

Summary of significant accounting policies

Derivative Financial Instruments The Company has written policies and procedures that place all financial instruments under the direction of corporate treasury and restrict all derivative transactions to those intended for hedging purposes. The use of financial instruments for trading purposes is strictly prohibited. The Company uses financial instruments to manage the market risk from changes in foreign exchange rates and interest rates.

The fair values of all derivatives are recorded in the Consolidated Statement of Financial Position. The change in a derivative's fair value is recorded each period in current earnings or accumulated other comprehensive income (OCI), depending on whether the derivative is designated as part of a hedge transaction and if so, the type of hedge transaction.

The Company hedges 70 to 90 percent of its known foreign exchange transactional exposures. The Company primarily enters into forward exchange contracts to reduce the earnings and cash flow impact of non-functional currency denominated receivables and payables. Gains and losses resulting from these contracts offset the foreign exchange gains or losses on the underlying assets and liabilities being hedged. The maturities of the forward exchange contracts generally coincide with the settlement dates of the related transactions. Gains and losses on these contracts are recorded in Miscellaneous – net in the Consolidated Statement of Income and are recognized in the same period as gains and losses on the hedged items.

Cash Flow Hedges The Company selectively hedges anticipated transactions that are subject to foreign exchange exposure, primarily using foreign currency exchange contracts. These instruments are designated as cash flow hedges in accordance with SFAS No. 133. "Accounting for Derivative Instruments and Hedging Activities," as amended by SFAS No. 137, No. 138 and No. 149 and are recorded in the Consolidated Statement of Financial Position at fair value. The effective portion of the contracts' gains or losses due to changes in fair value are initially recorded as a component of accumulated OCI and are subsequently reclassified into earnings when the hedged transactions, typically sales and costs related to sales, occur and affect earnings. These contracts are highly effective in hedging the variability in future cash flows attributable to changes in currency exchange rates. The Company also selectively uses interest rate swaps to modify its exposure to interest rate movements. These swaps also qualify as cash flow hedges, with changes in fair values recorded as a component of accumulated OCI. Interest expense is recorded in earnings at the fixed rate set forth in the swap agreement. At September 30, 2003, the Company had one interest rate swap outstanding designated as a cash flow hedge related to the Company's $250 million variable rate note associated with an October 2001 acquisition (see Note 11). There were no interest rate swaps outstanding designated as cash flow hedges at September 30, 2004.

For the years ended September 30, 2004 and 2003, the net amounts recognized in earnings due to ineffectiveness and amounts excluded from the assessment of hedge effectiveness were not material. The amount reported as realized and unrealized gains/losses on derivatives in the accumulated OCI account within shareholders' equity represents the net gain/loss on derivatives designated as cash flow hedges.

Fair Value Hedges The Company had two interest rate swaps outstanding at September 30, 2004 designated as a hedge of the fair value of a portion of fixed-rate bonds (see Note 11). Both the swap and the hedged portion of the debt are recorded in the Consolidated Statement of Financial Position. The change in fair value of the swaps exactly offsets the change in fair value of the hedged debt, with no net impact on earnings.

Net Investment Hedges The Company has cross-currency interest rate swaps and foreign currency-denominated debt obligations that are designated as hedges of the foreign currency exposure associated with its net investments in foreign operations. The currency effects of the debt obligations are reflected in the accumulated OCI account where they offset translation gains and losses recorded on the Company's net investments in Europe and Japan. The cross-currency interest rate swaps are recorded in the Consolidated Statement of Financial Position at fair value, with changes in value attributable to changes in foreign exchange rates recorded in the foreign currency translation adjustments component of accumulated OCI. Net interest payments or receipts from the interest rate swaps are recorded as adjustments to interest expense in earnings on a current basis. Net losses of approximately $86 million and $70 million associated with hedges of net investments in foreign operations were recorded in the accumulated OCI account for the periods ended September 30, 2004 and 2003, respectively.

Financial Instruments

The Company selectively uses derivative instruments to reduce market risk associated with changes in foreign currency and interest rates. The use of derivatives is restricted to those intended for hedging purposes: the use of any derivative instrument for trading purposes is strictly prohibited. See the Summary of significant accounting policies for additional information regarding the Company's objectives for holding certain derivative instruments, its strategies for achieving those objectives, and its risk management and accounting policies applicable to these instruments.

(continued)

The Company has global operations and participates in the foreign exchange markets to minimize its risk of loss from fluctuations in currency exchange rates. The Company primarily uses foreign currency exchange contracts to hedge certain of its foreign currency exposure.

The Company selectively uses interest rate swaps to reduce market risk associated with changes in interest rates (cash flow or fair value hedges). In May 2002, the Company entered into a four-and-a-half-year interest rate swap to hedge a portion of the Company's 5% notes maturing in November 2006. Under the swap, the Company receives interest based on a fixed U.S. dollar rate of 5% and pays interest based on a floating three-month U.S. dollar LIBOR rate plus 14.75 basis points. Terms of the four-and-a-half-year swap were modified since inception of the swap resulting in a decrease of notional amount of $100 million from the original $250 million. In October 2003, the Company entered into a four-year and three-month interest rate swap to hedge the Company's 6.3% notes maturing in February 2008. Under the swap, the Company receives interest based on a fixed U.S. dollar rate of 6.3% and pays interest based on a floating three-month U.S. dollar LIBOR rate plus 283.5 basis points.

The Company also selectively uses cross-currency interest rate swaps to hedge the foreign currency exposure associated with its net investment in certain foreign operations (net investment hedges). Under the swap, the Company receives interest based on a variable U.S. dollar rate and pays interest based on variable yen and euro rates on the outstanding notional principal amounts in dollars, yen and euro, respectively.

In addition, the Company selectively uses equity swaps to reduce market risk associated with its stock-based compensation plans, such as its deferred compensation plans and stock appreciation rights. In March 2004, the Company entered into an equity swap agreement. In connection with the swap agreement, a third party may purchase shares of the Company's stock in the market or in privately negotiated transactions up to an amount equal to $135 million in aggregate.

The Company's derivative instruments are recorded at fair value in the Consolidated Statement of Financial Position as follows:

In millions / September 30,	2004		2003	
(U.S. dollar equivalents)	Notional Amount	Fair Value Asset (Liability)	Notional Amount	Fair Value Asset (Liability)
Other noncurrent assets				
Interest rate swaps	**$325**	**$9**	**$150**	**$14**
Other current liabilities				
Foreign currency exchange contracts.	**1,219**	**1**	**1,681**	**1**
Other noncurrent liabilities				
Interest rate swaps	—	—	**250**	**(4)**
Cross-currency interest rate swaps. . .	**816**	**(24)**	**734**	**(106)**

It is important to note that the Company's derivative instruments are hedges protecting against underlying changes in foreign currency and interest rates. Accordingly, the implied gains/losses associated with the fair values of foreign currency exchange contracts and cross-currency interest rate swaps would be offset by gains/losses on underlying payables, receivables and net investments in foreign subsidiaries. Similarly, implied gains/losses associated with interest rate swaps offset changes in interest rates and the fair value of long-term debt.

The fair values of interest rate and cross-currency interest rate swaps were determined using dealer quotes and market interest rates. The fair values of foreign currency exchange contracts were determined using market exchange rates.

REFLECTION

- The FASB requires general and specific financial statement disclosures by companies holding or issuing derivative instruments.

UNDERSTANDING THE ISSUES

1. Explain how both the intrinsic value and the time value are measured for a forward contract to sell and for a put option.
2. What is the exposure to risk associated with a firm commitment to sell inventory that a fair value hedge is intended to reduce?
3. Describe the type of item that a cash flow hedge relates to, and tell how a hedge of a forecasted purchase of raw materials affects earnings of a manufacturer.
4. Why might an option be preferred over a futures contract?
5. Using an example, explain how an interest swap works.

EXERCISES

Exercise 1 *(LO 1, 2)* **Terminology and valuation relating to a call option.** A Milwaukee manufacturer uses copper in its manufacturing operations and anticipates that copper prices will increase over the next several months. On February 1, the company purchased an at-the-money May call (buy) option for $800. The option has a notional amount of 25,000 pounds and a strike price of $0.80 per pound. Copper spot rates and option values at selected dates are as follows:

	Spot Rate per Pound	Option Value
February 28	$0.79	$ 700
March 31	0.81	800
April 30	0.85	1,400
May 15	0.87	1,750

1. For each of the above dates, calculate the intrinsic value and the time value of the option.
2. If the call option were designated as a hedge of a forecasted purchase of copper, explain how the changing value of the option would be recognized in the income statement over time.
3. If the price of copper remained below $0.80 per pound subsequent to February 1, calculate the effect on earnings traceable to the hedge.
4. Explain why the pure time value of the option would be expected to decrease over time.

Exercise 2 *(LO 3, 7)* **Futures contracts for forecasted inventory needs.** Precision Flow Engineering, Inc. is a manufacturer of precision valves and pumps used for the movement of fluids. Copper is used as a raw material in the manufacturing process, and the company typically purchases copper futures to hedge against price changes.

In early June 20X4, the company purchased a futures contract to buy 10,000,000 pounds of copper with a July delivery and 8,000,000 pounds with an August delivery at futures prices of $0.7590 per pound and $0.7595 per pound, respectively. At the time of purchase, the futures contracts had a spot price per pound of $0.7585. On June 30, the company settled the July contract, and early in the next month purchased 10,000,000 pounds of copper. On July 31, the company settled the August contract, and early in the next month purchased 8,000,000 pounds of copper.

During July, a total of 10,000,000 pounds of copper purchased in early July were introduced into production. Of this production, 80% of the items were sold in July, and the balance were sold in August. All of the copper purchased in August was used in products sold that month.

Selected spot and future prices are as follows:

	Spot Price per Pound		Futures Price per Pound
June 30	$0.7600	July delivery	$0.7610
		August delivery	0.7613
July 31	0.7620	August delivery	0.7621

It is assumed that the terms of futures contracts match with respect to delivery location, quantity, and quality. The time value of the futures contracts will be excluded from the assessment of hedge effectiveness and will be reported directly in earnings.

Calculate the effect the above contracts would have on Cost of Sales—Copper during the months of June, July, and August.

Exercise 3 *(LO 3, 7)* **Fair value hedge—an interest rate swap's effect on interest and the carrying value of a note.** On July 1, 20X2, the Hargrove Corporation issued a 2-year note with a face value of $4,000,000 and a fixed interest rate of 9%, payable on a semiannual basis. On January 15, 20X3, the company entered into an interest rate swap with a financial institution in anticipation of lower variable rates. At the initial date of the swap, the company paid a premium of $9,200. The swap had a notional amount of $4,000,000 and called for the payment of a variable rate of interest in exchange for a 9% fixed rate. The variable rates are reset semiannually beginning with January 1, 20X3, in order to determine the next interest payment. Differences between rates on the swap will be settled on a semiannual basis. Variable interest rates and the value of the swap on selected dates are as follows:

Reset Date	Variable Interest Rate	Value of the Swap
January 1, 20X3	8.75%	
June 30, 20X3	8.50	$14,000
December 31, 20X3	8.85	3,500

For each of the above dates, determine:

1. The net interest expense.
2. The carrying value of the note payable.
3. The net unrealized gain or loss on the swap.

Exercise 4 *(LO 6, 7)* **Evaluating a hedge of a firm commitment with a put option.** A major cattle feeding operation has entered into a firm commitment to buy 100,000 bushels of corn to be delivered to its feed lot in Kansas. The corn is expected to be delivered in 90 days. The company is committed to pay $1.50 per bushel. If corn yields are greater than expected, the price of corn could decline and the company would experience higher operating costs than necessary as a result of the commitment.

In order to protect itself against falling corn prices, the company purchased an option to sell corn in 90 days at a strike price of $1.51 per bushel delivered to a facility in Nebraska.

1. Assuming that the company designated the swap as a fair value hedge, identify several critical criteria that would need to be satisfied in order to justify this classification.
2. Identify several factors that would suggest that the company's hedge would qualify as being highly effective in reducing the risk associated with the firm's commitment to buy 100,000 bushels of corn.
3. Explain why an option to sell corn rather than a corn futures may provide the company with more flexibility.

4. Assume that at the time of acquiring the put option, the price of corn was less than $1.51. Explain why the option had a value at inception of more than zero.
5. Assume that one of your colleagues made the following comment: "An option can never have a negative value; therefore, you can never lose money on an option." Discuss whether or not you agree with your colleague.
6. Assuming that only the intrinsic value is used to assess effectiveness, explain how the option's time value affects earnings prior to the end of the commitment.

Exercise 5 *(LO 4)* **Entries to record a hedge of a firm commitment with an option.** The Glasner Candy Corporation has a firm commitment dated April 1 to purchase cocoa with delivery on June 15. The commitment is for 1,000 metric tons of cocoa at $700 per ton. In order to hedge against decreases in the spot prices of cocoa, the company designated an option as a hedge against changes in the fair value of the commitment. The put (sell) option was acquired on April 1 for a premium of $1,000 and has a strike price of $700 per ton. The option has a notional amount of 1,000 tons and an expiration date of June 15. Spot prices per ton and the value of the option at selected dates are as follows:

	April 1	April 30	May 31	June 15
Spot price per ton	$ 701	$ 696	$ 697	$ 695
Fair value of option	1,000	4,300	3,500	5,000

The change in the option's time value will be excluded from an assessment of hedge effectiveness.

1. Prepare all entries to record this hedging relationship.
2. If the option's strike price would have been $698, would the hedge have been totally effective?

Exercise 6 *(LO 4, 8)* **Entries to record a hedge of a forecasted purchase with an option.** A Midwest food processor forecasts purchasing 300,000 pounds of soybean oil in May. On February 20, the company acquires an option to buy 300,000 pounds of soybean oil in May at a strike price of $1.60 per pound. Information regarding spot prices and option values at selected dates is as follows:

	February 20	February 28	March 31	April 20
Spot price per pound.	$ 1.61	$ 1.59	$ 1.62	$ 1.64
Fair value of option	3,800	1,200	6,800	12,500

The company settled the option on April 20 and purchased 300,000 pounds of soybean oil on May 3 at a spot price of $1.63 per pound. During May, the soybean oil was used to produce food. One-half of the resulting food was sold in June. The change in the option's time value is excluded from the assessment of hedge effectiveness.

1. Prepare all necessary journal entries through June to reflect the above activity.
2. What would the effect on earnings have been had the forecasted purchase not been hedged?

Exercise 7 *(LO 8)* **Cash flow hedge of a variable rate note.** Doral Enterprises has an opportunity to borrow $150 million for expansion purposes. The loan will be amortized over 20 quarters. Quarterly payments will consist of principal of $3,750,000 plus applicable interest. Doral has two options available regarding interest. The first option provides for a fixed rate of interest of 4.5% over the term of the loan. The other option calls for variable or floating rates over the term of the loan. Variable rates will be reset at the beginning of each quarter at the rate of LIBOR plus 0.5%. LIBOR is currently at 4.3%.

After considering its options, Doral elected to borrow the funds at the fixed interest rate. The company made eight quarterly payments on the loan and began to think that maybe a variable interest rate would have been a better option. The Federal Reserve Bank was indicating that interest rates might be cut even further. With this in mind, the company engaged in an interest rate swap where it would pay floating and receive fixed. The fixed rate was 4.2%, and the floating rate was LIBOR plus 0.75%. Assume that LIBOR is as follows during the first year of the swap:

	Beginning of Quarters During First Year of the Swap			
	1st Quarter	2nd Quarter	3rd Quarter	4th Quarter
LIBOR.	3.5%	3.6%	3.1%	2.9%

All interest rates are stated as annual rates.

1. Prepare a schedule for the first year of the swap that summarizes by quarter:
   a. The interest paid on the original loan.
   b. The interest received from the counterparty.
   c. The interest paid to the counterparty.
2. Assume that LIBOR at the beginning of the first quarter of the second year of the swap is 2.8% and is expected to remain at that rate over the remaining duration of the swap. Prepare a schedule for the second year of the swap that summarizes by quarter:
   a. The interest paid to the counterparty.
   b. The interest received from the counterparty.
   c. The net payment.
3. Once again assume that LIBOR at the beginning of the first quarter of the second year of the swap is 2.8% and is expected to remain at that rate over the remaining duration of the swap. Using this LIBOR rate, calculate the net present value of the net payment determined in item (2) above.
4. Discuss what the calculation in item (3) above tells you about the value of the swap and what the value of the swap would be if LIBOR rates were expected to increase rather than remain constant over time.

PROBLEMS

Problem M-1 *(LO 4, 7)* **Entries to record fixed for variable interest rate swap.** Several years ago, the Traker Corporation borrowed $5,000,000 from the New West Bank of Albuquerque at a fixed rate of 8.5%. The loan becomes due on December 31, 20X3, and has interest due dates of June 30 and December 31. Prior to 20X2, variable interest rates were typically higher than the 8.5% fixed rate. However, Traker feels that variable interest rates are likely to decline. Therefore, on January 1, 20X2, Traker entered into an interest rate swap with the First National Bank of Denver. The swap has a notional amount of $5,000,000 and requires Traker to receive a fixed rate of 8.5% and pay a variable rate. The variable interest rate is a LIBOR rate and reset dates are January 1 and July 1. Settlement payments are made on June 30 and December 31. Relevant information regarding rates and values is as follows:

Reset Date	LIBOR Rate	Value of Swap
January 1, 20X2	8.1%	
July 1, 20X2	7.6	$62,677
January 1, 20X3	7.3	56,868
July 1, 20X3	7.9	14,430

Required ▶ ▶ ▶ ▶ ▶ Prepare all entries to record the transactions involving the loan payable and the interest rate swap through December 31, 20X3.

Problem M-2 *(LO 3, 8)* **Cash flow hedge of a forecasted purchase of wheat.** Custom Brand Bakeries, Inc. (CBBI) located in Erie, Pennsylvania, bakes a variety of products for various parties on a contract basis. For example, a food company may contract with CBBI to make energy bars that are then sold under the food company's private lable. Contracts are typically signed several months in advance of actual production and set forth a fixed sales price. Because sales prices are fixed by contact, CBBI is concerned that materials costs do not increase and further reduce profits. However, CBBI does not want to guard against increasing costs by purchasing materials in advance of their scheduled production. Corn and wheat flour are two major ingredients used in the production process where increasing costs are of concern. CBBI wants to hedge against these costs increasing but cannot buy flour futures. However, buying corn and wheat futures can provide an effective hedge against changing flour prices. Changes in the price of corn flour and wheat flour often correlate highly with changes in the price of corn and wheat.

On September 1, 20X5, the company purchased, on the Chicago Board of Trade (CBT), futures for delivery of the commodities in November. The CBT required a deposit of $70,000 toward a margin account.

Corn Futures

Date	Spot Price per Bushel	Futures Price per Bushel	Notional Amount
September 1	$2.5000	$2.5100	1,000,000 bushels
September 30	2.5380	2.5420	1,000,000
October 31	2.5680	2.5700	1,000,000
November 5	2.5685	2.5710	1,000,000

Wheat Futures

Date	Spot Price per Bushel	Futures Price per Bushel	Notional Amount
September 1	$3.5150	$3.5210	2,000,000 bushels
September 30	3.5480	3.5520	2,000,000
October 31	3.5700	3.5710	2,000,000
November 5	3.5700	3.5705	2,000,000

CBBI properly documents the hedging relationship, and all critieria for special accounting as a hedge are satisfied. The hedging instruments are determined to be highly effective as a hedge against changing flour prices. The changes in the time value of the futures contracts are to be excluded from the assessment of hedge effectiveness.

In early November, CBBI actually purchased both corn flour and wheat flour used in products sold to contracting parties on November 21. The futures contracts are settled net on November 5.

◄◄◄◄◄ **Required**

1. Prepare all monthly enteries to record hedging activity.
2. Identify and discuss several factors that might cause the futures contracts to not be perfectly effective as a hedge against changes in the price of flour used by CBBI.

Problem M-3 *(LO 3, 6)* **Essay and schedules focusing on how to assess hedge effectiveness.** Richland Agricultural Enterprises, Inc., is a large corporate farming operation located in Sioux Falls, Iowa. The company has farming and ranching operations in Iowa, Kansas, Nebraska, and North Dakota. The company has 500,000 bushels of wheat in inventory at its Fargo, North Dakota, warehouse. The wheat has a cost of $3.20 a bushel.

template cd

Relevant spot prices and futures prices per bushel are as follows:

	Spot Price— Fargo Delivery	Spot Price— Minneapolis Delivery	July 10 Futures Price— Minneapolis Delivery
May 1	$3.410	$3.400	$3.395
May 31	3.430	3.420	3.410
June 30	3.410	3.410	3.400
July 10	3.380	3.375	3.375

◄◄◄◄◄ **Required**

1. In order for a futures contract to be *perfectly* effective as a hedge against changing prices of the company's inventory of wheat, what conditions would be necessary?

2. If the company hedged its inventory in Fargo with a futures contract calling for delivery in Minneapolis, would the hedge likely be perfectly effective or highly effective?
3. Assume that on May 1, the company acquires a futures contract to sell 500,000 bushels of wheat in July with delivery in Minneapolis. Furthermore, assume that the contract is settled on July 10 and that the inventory of wheat is subsequently sold for $3.380 per bushel. Prepare a schedule to illustrate the effect on current earnings with and without the hedge for each of the months May through July. Assume that changes in the time value of the contract are excluded from the assessment of hedge effectiveness.
4. Given the hedge in requirement (3) above, explain why the company did not achieve its desired position.

Problem M-4 *(LO 5)* **Hedging both fixed and floating interest rates.** Pasu International purchased a plant in Louisiana on December 31, 20X5, and financed $20,000,000 of the purchase price with a 5-year note. The note bears interest at the fixed rate of 5%, and payments on the note are made quarterly in the amount of $1,136,408. At the beginning of 20X8, Pasu became concerned that variable or floating interest rates would be less than its fixed rate on the above note. Given this concern, Pasu arranged an interest rate swap on a notional amount equal to the outstanding balance of the note at the beginning of each quarter beginning with the January 1, 20X8, balance of the note. The swap calls for the payment of a variable or floating interest rate on the principal balance of the note to a counterparty in exchange for a fixed rate of 4.75%. The floating rate is LIBOR plus 1.5% and is reset at the beginning of each quarter for that quarter's calculations.

In an unrelated transaction, on June 30, 20X8, Pasu sold its plant in Europe and as part of the transaction received an 18-month $10,000,000 note receivable from the buyer. The note bears interest at a rate of LIBOR plus 2.0%, and interest-only payments are made each quarter during 20X8. The floating rate is reset at the beginning of each quarter. Concerned that declining floating interest rates will decrease the value of the note, Pasu has arranged an interest rate swap with a counterparty effective July 1, 20X8. The swap calls for the payment by Pasu of floating rate of LIBOR plus 1.7% in exchange for a fixed rate of 4.5%.

LIBOR rates at the beginning of each calendar quarter of 20X8 are as follows:

January 1	3.25%
April 1	3.15
July 1	2.90
October 1	2.65

Required ▶ ▶ ▶ ▶ ▶

All interest rates are stated as annual interest rates. As of December 31, 20X8, calculate each of the following:

1. Annual fixed interest paid on the note resulting from the purchase of the Louisiana plant.
2. Annual floating interest paid to the counterparty on the note resulting from the sale of the European plant.
3. Annual net interest expense on the note resulting from the purchase of the Louisiana plant.
4. Annual net interest income on the note receivable.
5. Assuming that the LIBOR rate at October 1, 20X8, will continue into the future, determine the December 31, 20X8, value of the interest rate swap associated with the note receivable. (*Hint:* Compare the year-end present value of paying a floating rate on the notional amount with the year-end present value of receiving a fixed rate on the notional amount.)
6. If the note receivable had been denominated in euros versus U.S. dollars, determine what additional risks Pasu would have been exposed to.

Problem M-5 *(LO 8)* **Prepare entries to account for a cash flow hedge involving an option.** The Industrial Plating Corporation coats manufactured parts with a variety of coatings such as Teflon, gold, and silver. The company intends to purchase 100,000 troy ounces of silver in September. The purchase is highly probable, and the company has become concerned that the prices of silver may increase, and, therefore, the forecasted purchase will become even more expensive. In order to reduce the exposure to rising silver prices, on July 10 the company purchased 20 September call (buy) options on silver. Each option is for 5,000 troy ounces and has a strike price of $5.00 per troy ounce. The company excludes from hedge effectiveness changes in the time value of the option. Spot prices and option value per troy ounce of silver are as follows:

	July 10	July 31	August 31	September 10
Spot price	$5.10	$5.14	$5.35	$5.32
Option value	0.20	0.23	0.37	0.33

On September 10, the company settled the option and on September 15 purchased 100,000 troy ounces of silver on account at $5.33 per ounce. The silver was used in the company's production process over the next three months. In September and October, plating services were provided as follows:

	September	October
Units of silver used	15,000	50,000
Other costs.	$105,000	$350,000
Plating revenues	$225,000	$750,000

Prepare all necessary entries to account for the above activities through October. Assume that the hedge satisfies all necessary criteria for special hedge accounting. ◄◄◄◄◄ **Required**

Problem M-6 *(LO 4)* **Prepare a schedule to determine the earnings effect of various hedging relationships.** During the third quarter of the current year, the Beamer Manufacturing Company had invested in derivative instruments for a variety of reasons. The various investments and hedging relationships are as follows:

a. Call Option A—This option was purchased on July 10 and provided for the purchase of 10,000 units of commodity A in October at a strike price of $45 per unit. The company designated the option as a hedge of a commitment to sell 10,000 units of commodity A in October at a fixed price of $45 per unit. Information regarding the option and commodity A is as follows:

	July 10	July 31	August 31	September 30
Spot price	$ 45	$ 46	$ 44	$ 46.50
Value of option	2,000	12,400	1,000	16,000

b. Call Option B—This option provided for the purchase of 10,000 units of commodity B in October at a strike price of $30 per unit. The company designated the option as a hedge of a forecasted purchase of commodity B in October. Information regarding the option and commodity B is as follows:

	July 1	July 31	August 31	September 30
Spot price	$ 29	$29.50	$ 29	$28.75
Value of option	1,100	900	600	200

c. Put Option C—This option provided for the sale of 10,000 units of commodity C in September at a strike price of $30 per unit. The company designated the option as a hedge of a forecasted sale of 10,000 units of commodity C on September 10. Information regarding the option and commodity C is as follows:

	July 1	July 31	August 31	September 10
Spot price	$ 30	$29.50	$ 29	$ 28.75
Value of option	500	5,600	10,200	12,600

The company settled the option on September 10 and sold 10,000 units of commodity C at the spot price. The manufacturing cost of the units sold was $20 per unit.

d. Futures Contract D—The contract calls for the sale of 10,000 units of commodity D in October at a future price of $10 per unit. The company designated the contract as a hedge on a forecasted sale of commodity D in October. Information regarding the contract and commodity D is as follows:

	July 1	July 31	August 31	September 30
Spot price	$9.95	$9.92	$9.89	$9.85
Futures price	9.94	9.90	9.87	9.84

e. Interest Rate Swap—The company has a 12-month note receivable with a face value of $10,000,000 that matures on June 30 of next year. The note calls for interest to be paid at the end of each month based on the LIBOR variable interest rate at the beginning of each month. On July 31, the company entered into an agreement to receive a 7% fixed rate of interest beginning in August in exchange for payment of a variable rate based on LIBOR. The reset date is at the beginning of each month, and net settlement occurs at the end of each month. LIBOR rates and swap values are as follows:

	July	August	September
LIBOR for month.................	6.8%	6.8%	6.7%
Swap value at end of month	$17,729	$24,249	$21,884

In all of the above cases, the change in the time value of the derivative instrument is excluded from the assessment of hedge effectiveness. Furthermore, the company assesses hedge effectiveness on a continuing basis. Such an assessment at the end of June concluded that call option B was not effective.

Required ▶ ▶ ▶ ▶ ▶ Prepare a schedule to reflect the effect on current earnings of the above hedging relationships. The schedule should show relevant amounts for each month from July through September.

Problem M-7 *(LO 4)* **Prepare entries to record a variable for fixed interest rate swap.** The Hauser Corporation has $20,000,000 of outstanding debt that bears interest at a variable rate and matures on June 30, 20X4. At inception of the debt, the company had a lower credit rating, and most available financing carried a variable rate. The company's variable rate is the LIBOR rate plus 1%. However, the company's credit rating has improved, and the company feels that a fixed, lower rate of interest would be most appropriate. Furthermore, the company is of the opinion that variable rates will increase over the next 24 months. In May 20X2, the company negotiated with First Bank of Boston an interest rate swap that would allow the company to pay a fixed rate of 7% in exchange for receiving interest based on the LIBOR rate. The terms of the swap call for settlement at the end of June and December, which coincides with the company's interest payment dates. The variable rates are reset at the end of each 6-month period for the following 6-month period. The terms of the swap are effective for the 6-month period beginning July 20X2.

The hedging relationship has been properly documented, and management has concluded that the hedge will be highly effective in offsetting changes in the cash flows due to changes in interest rates. The criteria for special accounting have been satisfied.

Relevant LIBOR rates and swap values are as follows:

	June 30, 20X2	Dec. 31, 20X2	June 30, 20X2	Dec. 31, 20X2
LIBOR rate	7.0%	7.1%	6.9%	6.8%
Swap value		$27,990	$(19,011)	$(19,342)

Required ▶ ▶ ▶ ▶ ▶

1. Prepare the necessary entries to record the activities related to the debt and the hedge from July 1, 20X2, through June 30, 20X4.
2. Prepare a schedule to evaluate the positive or negative impact the hedge had on each 6-month period of earnings.
3. What would the LIBOR rate on December 31, 20X3, have had to be in order for the interest expense to be the same whether or not there was a cash flow hedge?

Foreign Currency Transactions

CHAPTER 10

Learning Objectives

When you have completed this chapter, you should be able to

1. **Explain the floating international monetary system, and identify factors that influence rates of exchange between currencies.**
2. **Define the various terms associated with exchange rates, including spot rates, forward rates, premiums, and discounts.**
3. **Account for a foreign currency transaction, including the measurement of exchange gain or loss.**
4. **Identify the contexts in which a company may be exposed to foreign currency exchange risk.**
5. **Explain the accounting treatment given various types of foreign currency hedges.**

As discussed in the previous chapter, modern businesses often find themselves affected by a global economy that presents a variety of challenges and opportunities. This chapter focuses on how a domestic entity should account for transactions which are denominated or settled in a foreign currency. For example, a U.S. company may purchase raw materials from a French vendor and pay for the goods with euros. Such transactions may expose the U.S. entity to risks or opportunities depending on how exchange rates change over time. Strategies to manage the exposure to exchange rate fluctuations are also presented in this chapter. Chapter 11 will describe the issues associated with a domestic entity having an investment interest in a foreign entity. The primary focus is on the translation and/or remeasurement of foreign financial statements so that they may be consolidated with the domestic parent's financial statements.

The global economy has increased the level of trade between nations to levels previously thought unimaginable. For example, total export trade in goods for the United States had reached $746 billion in the first 11 months of 2004. U.S. import of goods had reached $1,342 billion in the same time frame. During this period of time, trading levels with the top five trading nations were as follows:

	Exports			Imports	
Nation	(in billions)	% of Total	Nation	(in billions)	% of Total
Canada	$172.8	23.2	Canada	$ 235.1	17.5
Mexico	101.6	13.6	China	179.2	13.3
Japan	49.9	6.7	Mexico	143.2	10.7
United Kingdom	32.9	4.4	Japan	118.3	8.8
China	31.5	4.2	Germany	70.2	5.3
Total all nations	745.9	100.0	Total all nations	1,342.2	100.0

Fischer, Taylor + Cheng, Adv. Acctg (2006).

Companies in the United States and throughout the world are expanding their markets into a number of countries as evidenced by the following disclosures (to be discussed more fully in Chapter 12) regarding international sales:

Company	Nike, Inc.	Ford Motor	IBM	Sony
Year-End				
Allocation of Net Revenue	May 31, 2004 (in millions)	December 31, 2003 (in billions)	December 31, 2003 (in millions)	March 31, 2004 (in millions)
United States	$ 4,793.7	$ 83.6	$33,762.0	$20,395.0
Europe	3,834.4	22.2		16,972.0
Asia Pacific	1,613.4	5.8		
Japan		26.8	11,694.0	21,353.0
Others	2,011.6		43,675.0	13,361.0
Total	$12,253.1	$138.4	$89,131.0	$72,081.0

When parties from two different nations transact business, each would normally like to use its own national currency. Since it is impossible to use more than one currency as the medium of exchange, a currency must be selected, and rates of exchange must be established between the two competing currencies.

For example, if a U.S. footwear manufacturer purchases leather from a German supplier, the transaction must be settled in either U.S. dollars or euros. If euros are chosen, a rate of exchange between the U.S. dollar and the euro must be determined in order to record the transaction on the American company's books in dollars. Given that rates of exchange vary, the number of U.S. dollars needed to acquire the necessary euros also could change between the time the order is placed and the goods are paid for. If, during this time, more dollars are needed to acquire the necessary euros to pay for the leather, the U.S. purchaser is exposed to an additional business risk. The more volatility there is in exchange rates, the more risk to which the party is exposed. Similarly, if the dollar is used as the medium of exchange, this risk would still exist, but it would be transferred to the German vendor.

It becomes readily apparent that the currency decision becomes an important factor in negotiating such transactions. Due to the volatility of currency exchange rates, companies transacting business in foreign markets should aggressively control and measure exchange risk. Management should develop a model that enables them to forecast the direction, magnitude, and timing of exchange rate changes. This model, in turn, can be used to develop a strategy to minimize foreign exchange losses and maximize foreign exchange gains.

Business transactions that are settled in a currency other than that of the domestic (home country) currency are referred to, in this text, as *foreign currency transactions* and require the use of special terminology. One of the transacting parties will settle the transaction in its own domestic currency and also measure the transaction in its domestic currency. For example, a German company may sell inventory to a U.S. company and require payment in euros. The currency used to settle the transaction is referred to as the *denominated currency* and would be the euro in this case. The other transacting party will settle the transaction in a foreign currency but will need to measure the transaction in its domestic currency. For example, a U.S. company that purchases inventory from a German company must settle the resulting accounts payable in euros and yet must measure the purchase of inventory and the accounts payable in terms of U.S. dollars. The currency used to measure or record the transaction is referred to as the *measurement currency* and would be the U.S. dollar in this case. Whenever a transaction is denominated in a currency different than the measurement currency, exchange rate risk exists, and exchange rates must be used for measurement purposes. The process of expressing a transaction in the measurement currency when it is denominated in a different currency is referred to as a *foreign currency translation.*

THE INTERNATIONAL MONETARY SYSTEM

1

OBJECTIVE

Explain the floating international monetary system, and identify factors that influence rates of exchange between currencies.

Denominating a transaction in a currency other than the entity's domestic currency requires the establishment of a rate of exchange between the currencies. The international monetary system establishes rates of exchanges between currencies through the use of a variety of systems. The selection of a particular monetary system and the resulting exchange rates have a significant effect on international business and the risk associated with such business.

Alternative International Monetary Systems

Several major international monetary systems have been employed over time, and previous systems have occasionally been reestablished. Prior to 1944, the *gold system* provided a strict apolitical system based on gold. The currencies of nations were backed by or equivalent to some physical measure of gold. To illustrate, suppose Nation A has 1 million currency units backed by 1,000 ounces of gold and Nation B has 2 million currency units also backed by 1,000 ounces of gold. With gold as the common denominator, exchange rates between currencies could be established. In the above example, one unit of Nation A's currency could be exchanged for two units of Nation B's currency. A nation's supply of gold, therefore, influenced its money supply, rates of exchange, prices, and international trading levels (imports and exports).

In 1944, the *Bretton Woods Agreement*, which created the International Monetary Fund (IMF) and a *fixed rate exchange system*, was signed. The fixed rate system required each nation to set a par value for its currency in terms of gold or the U.S. dollar. In turn, the U.S. dollar's value was defined in terms of gold. Modest variations from a currency's par value were allowed, and each nation could adjust its money supply in order to maintain its par value. The IMF could provide support to a nation in order to maintain its par value. Changes in a currency's par value were referred to as *devaluations* and *revaluations*.

As pressures to maintain the par values established by the fixed rate system increased, pressure was placed on the U.S. dollar. The ability of the dollar to support the system became questionable, and fears arose that countries with dollar surpluses might seek to convert these dollars into gold. In 1971, the U.S. government, for all practical purposes, terminated the Bretton Woods Agreement by suspending the convertibility of the dollar into gold.

Currencies temporarily became part of a *floating system* where rates of exchange were in response to the supply and demand factors affecting a currency. Shortly thereafter, the IMF accepted the *Smithsonian Agreement* which devaluated the U.S. dollar and did not allow for the convertibility of the dollar into gold. Par values of currencies were established along with a wider margin of acceptable values around the par value. The Smithsonian Agreement was short-lived, and in response to increasing pressures on the U.S. dollar, the fixed rate system was abandoned in 1973.

Today, the international monetary system is a floating system whereby the factors of supply and demand primarily define currency exchange rates. Each nation's central bank may intervene in order to move its currency toward a target rate of exchange. This intervention results in a managed, or "dirty" float, versus an unmanaged, or "clean" float. Supply and demand factors along with possible central bank intervention result in much more uncertainty and risk than that experienced in a fixed rate system. Unfortunately, a myriad of factors beyond supply and demand affect exchange rates in a floating system including the following:[1]

- The speed of recovery from a recession.
- A nation's vulnerability to an energy crisis.
- A nation's trade and payment balances.
- The supply of and growth in the domestic money supply.
- Stability in the national economy, including a stable inflation rate, political stability, national prosperity, labor costs, and unemployment rates.

1 Thomas G. Evans, Martin E. Taylor, and Oscar Holzmann, *International Accounting and Reporting* (Boston: PWS-Kent Publishing Company, 1988), pp. 134–135.

- A currency's vulnerability to rumors.
- Domestic interest rates and changes in these rates. (If interest rates are relatively high, others will want to obtain that currency and invest it in the securities of that nation and earn high yields.)
- The strength or weakness of the domestic GNP as a major gauge of a nation's underlying economic strength.
- Confidence and expectations, especially during uncertainty and crisis.
- In a dirty float, the amount of governmental intervention in the market.

Although the present international monetary system is best described as a floating system, there are a number of special variations within the system. Some nations still maintain a fixed system whereby the rate of exchange is established by their central bank. However, because these fixed rates are changed frequently, sometimes daily, they may be viewed as a controlled or "dirty" float. A currency that is frequently adjusted downward, such as those in less developed nations, is referred to as a "crawling peg" currency. Tiered systems also exist whereby special rates are established for certain types of transactions, such as import and export sales and dividend payments, to accomplish desired political and economic objectives. For example, to encourage exports and to discourage capital withdrawal, a foreign government may establish favorable official rates for export sales and less favorable exchange rates for the payment of dividends to investors in other countries. The forces of supply and demand, however, occasionally make it difficult for a government to maintain an official exchange rate. In response, the government either devalues or revalues its currency.

2

OBJECTIVE

Define the various terms associated with exchange rates, including spot rates, forward rates, premiums, and discounts.

The Mechanics of Exchange Rates

An exchange rate is a measure of how much of one currency may be exchanged for another currency. These rates may be in the form of either *direct* or *indirect quotes* made by a foreign currency trader who is usually employed by a large commercial bank. A direct quote measures how much of the domestic currency must be exchanged to receive one unit of the foreign currency (1 FC). Direct quotes allow the party using the quote to understand the price of the foreign currency in terms of its own "base" or domestic currency. This method is frequently used in the United States, and direct quotes are published daily in financial papers such as *The Wall Street Journal.* Indirect quotes, also known as European terms, measure how many units of foreign currency will be received for one unit of the domestic currency. Thus, if the direct quote for a foreign currency (FC) is $0.25, then one FC would cost $0.25. The indirect quote would be the reciprocal of the direct quote, or 4 FC per dollar ($1.00 divided by $0.25).

Exchange Rate Quotes

Direct Quote	Indirect Quote
1 FC = $0.25	$1 = 4 FC

Foreign currency exchange rate quotes are reported in *The Wall Street Journal* and are also available on selected Web sites. Using Canada as an example, as of January 18, 2005, the direct quote is $0.8169, and the indirect quote is $1 = 1.2241 Canadian dollars.

The business news often reports that a currency has strengthened (gained) or weakened (lost) relative to another currency. Assuming a direct quote system, such changes measure the difference between the new rate and the old rate, as a percentage of the old rate. For example, if the dollar strengthened or gained 20% against a foreign currency (FC) from its previous rate of $0.25, the dollar would now command more FC (i.e., the FC would be cheaper to buy). To be exact, the new exchange rate would be $0.20 [$0.25 − (20% × 0.25)]. Therefore, *the strengthening currency would be evidenced by a reduction in the directly quoted amount and an increase in the indirectly quoted amount.* The opposite would be true for a weakening of the domestic currency. The reaction to a strengthening or weakening of a currency depends on what type of transaction is contemplated. For example, an American exporter would want a weaker dollar because the foreign importer would need fewer of its currency units to acquire a dollar's worth of U.S. goods. Thus, U.S. goods would cost less in terms of the foreign currency. If the dollar strengthened so that one could acquire more foreign currency units for a dollar, importers would benefit. Therefore, U.S. companies and citizens would have to spend fewer U.S. dollars to buy the imported goods.

Changes Relative to Another Currency

A Strengthening U.S Currency		A Weakening U.S. Currency	
Before:	1 FC = \$0.25	Before:	1 FC = \$0.25
After:	1 FC = \$0.20	After:	1 FC = \$0.30
Result:	The dollar gained 20%. (\$0.25 − \$0.20 = \$0.05; \$0.05 ÷ \$0.25 = 20%)	Result:	The dollar lost 20%. (\$0.25 − \$0.30 = −\$0.05; −\$0.05 ÷ 0.25 = −20%)

Exchange rates often are quoted in terms of a buying rate (the bid price) and a selling rate (the offered price). The buying and selling rates represent what the currency broker (normally a large commercial bank) is willing to pay to acquire or sell a currency. The difference or spread between these two rates represents the broker's commission and is often referred to as the points. The spread is influenced by several factors, including the supply of and demand for the currency, the number of transactions taking place, currency risk, and the overall volatility of the market. For example, assume a currency broker agrees to pay \$0.20 to a holder of a foreign currency and agrees to sell that currency to a buyer of foreign currency for \$0.22. In this case, the broker will receive a commission of \$0.02 (\$0.22 − \$0.20). In the United States, rates generally are quoted between the U.S. dollar and a foreign currency. However, rates between two foreign currencies are also quoted and are referred to as cross rates.

Exchange rates fall into two primary groups. A *spot rate* is the rate of exchange for a currency with delivery, selling, or buying of the currency normally occurring within two business days. In addition to exchange rates governing the immediate delivery of currency, *forward rates* apply to the exchange of different currencies at a future point in time, such as in 30 or 180 days. Although not all currencies are quoted in forward rates, virtually all major trading nations have forward rates.

Types of Exchange Rates

	Buying Rate		Selling Rate	
	Spot Rate	Forward Rate	Spot Rate	Forward Rate
Exchange:	Within 2 days	In the future (e.g., 30 days)	Within 2 days	In the future (e.g., 30 days)

An agreement to exchange currencies at a specified price with delivery at a specified future point in time is a forward contract. As more fully discussed in the derivatives module, a forward contract is a derivative instrument whose underlying is a foreign currency exchange rate. Forward exchange contracts may be held as an investment or held as part of a strategy to reduce or hedge against exchange rate risk associated with another transaction. A forward contract, used to hedge against the risk associated with changing exchange rates, specifies the future exchange date and the forward rate of exchange. Although future exchange dates typically are quoted in 30-day intervals, contracts can be written to cover any number of days. To illustrate a forward contract, assume the forward rate to buy a FC to be delivered in 90 days is \$1.650. This means that, after the specified time from the inception of the contract date (90 days), one FC will be exchanged for \$1.650, regardless of what the spot rate is at that time.

Inception of Contract ◄——	90 Days	——► Settlement of Contract
Forward Rate		**Exchange Rate**
1 FC = $1.650		1 FC = $1.650 (Regardless of what the spot rate is on that day.)
Spot Rate		**Spot Rate**
1 FC = $1.640		1 FC = $1.655

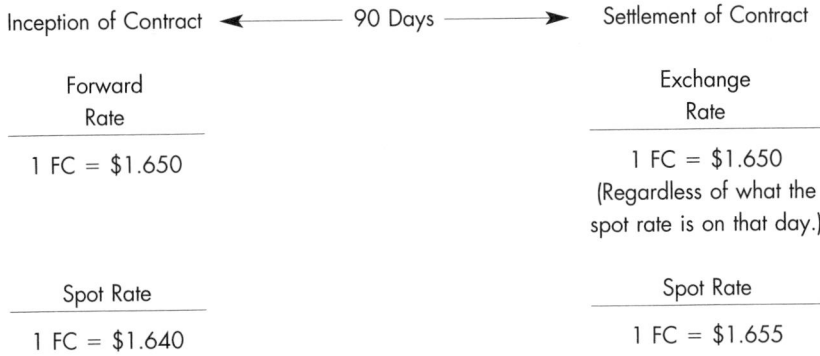

Several aspects of spot rates and forward rates are noteworthy. First, typically both rates are constantly changing. Spot rates are revised daily; as they change, forward rates for the *remaining time* covered by a given forward contract also change even though the forward rate at inception is fixed. When there is no more remaining time, the current forward rate becomes the spot rate. Therefore, the value of a forward contract changes over the forward period. For instance, in the above example, if the forward rate is 1 FC = $1.652 with 30 days remaining, the right to *buy* FC at the original fixed forward rate of 1 FC = $1.650 suggests that the value of the forward contract has increased. Rather than paying a forward rate of $1.652 to acquire FC in 30 days, the holder of the original forward contract must only pay the fixed rate of $1.650. Second, the ultimate value of the forward contract must be assessed by comparing the fixed forward rate against the spot rate at the settlement date. In the above example, at the settlement date, the holder of the contract will pay the fixed rate of 1 FC = $1.650 to buy an FC rather than the spot rate of 1 FC = $1.655. The total change in value is represented by the difference between the original fixed forward rate and the spot rate at settlement date. Finally, the difference between a forward rate and a spot rate represents a premium or discount which is traceable to a number of factors. This difference between the spot and forward rate represents the time value of the forward contract.

If the forward rate is greater than the spot rate at inception of the contract, the contract is said to be at a *premium* (as in the above example). The opposite situation results in a discount. Quoting premiums or discounts (known as forward differentials), rather than forward rates, is common industry practice.

Forward Rates Employ a Forward Exchange Contract	
At a Premium	**At a Discount**
Forward Rate > Spot Rate (At inception of contract)	Forward Rate < Spot Rate (At inception of contract)

At inception, the difference between the forward and spot rates represents a contract expense or income to the purchaser of the forward contract. A number of factors influence forward rates and, thus, account for the difference between a forward rate and a spot rate. A primary factor is the interest rate differential between holding an investment in foreign currency and holding an investment in domestic currency over a period of time. It is for this reason that the difference between a forward rate is referred to as the *time value* of the forward contract. For example, if a broker sold a contract to deliver foreign currency in 30 days, the interest differential would be the difference between

1. The interest earned on investing foreign currency for the 30 days prior to delivery date and
2. The 30 days of interest lost on the domestic currency that was not invested but was used to acquire the foreign currency needed for delivery.

Assume that the spot rate is 1 FC = $0.60 and that you want to determine a 6-month forward rate. Further, assume that the dollar could be invested at 4.5% and the FC could be invested at 7.25%. The forward rate would be calculated as follows:

	U.S. Dollars	Foreign Currency (FC)
Value today	$600.00	1,000 FC
Interest rate	4.5%	7.25 %
Six months of interest	$13.50	36.25 FC
Value in six months	$613.50	1036.25 FC

6-month forward rate = $613.50 ÷ 1036.25 FC = 1 FC = $0.592

The forward rate for a currency can also be derived by the following formula:

$$\text{Forward rate} = \text{Direct spot rate at the beginning of period } t \times \frac{1 + \text{Interest rate for domestic investment during period } t}{1 + \text{Interest rate for foreign country investment during period } t}$$

Using the formula to solve the previous example results in the following, based on 6-month interest rates:

$$\text{Forward rate of } \$0.592 = \$0.60 \times \frac{1 + 0.0225}{1 + 0.03625}$$

If the interest yield on the FC is greater than the yield on the U.S. dollar, the forward rate will be less than the spot rate (contract sells at a discount). The forward contract will sell at a premium if the opposite is true. The forward rate based on interest differentials will be slightly different than the quoted forward rate because the quoted rate includes a commission to the foreign currency broker. Furthermore, other factors in addition to interest differentials could be incorporated into the forward rate. These other factors include the volatility of the spot rates, the time period covered by the contract, expectations of future exchange rate changes, and the political and economic environments of a given country.

The student of international accounting should have an understanding of the international monetary system and exchange rates. As previously mentioned, changes in exchange rates represent an additional business risk when transactions are denominated in a foreign currency. The accounting for foreign currency transactions measures this risk and demonstrates the use of both spot and forward rates.

REFLECTION

- **The current international monetary system is a floating system in which rates of exchange between currencies change in response to a variety of factors including trade balances, interest rates, money supply, and other economic factors.**
- **Spot rates represent the current rate of exchange between two currencies. A forward rate represents a future rate of exchange at a future point in time. If the forward rate exceeds the spot rate, the contract is at a premium rather than a discount.**

3

OBJECTIVE

Account for a foreign currency transaction, including the measurement of exchange gain or loss.

ACCOUNTING FOR FOREIGN CURRENCY TRANSACTIONS

Assume a U.S. company sells mining equipment to a foreign company and the equipment must be paid for in 30 days with U.S. dollars. This transaction is denominated in dollars and will be measured by the U.S. company in dollars. Changes in the exchange rate between the U.S. dollar and the foreign currency from the transaction date to the settlement date will not expose the U.S. company to any risk of gain or loss from exchange rate changes. Now assume that the same transaction occurs except that the transaction is to be settled in the foreign currency. Because this transaction is denominated in the foreign currency and will be measured by the U.S. company in dollars, changes in the exchange rate subsequent to the transaction date expose the U.S. company to the risk of an exchange rate loss or gain. If the U.S. dollar strengthens, relative to the foreign currency, the U.S. company will experience a loss because it is holding an asset (a receivable of foreign currency) whose price and value have declined. If the dollar weakens, the opposite effect would be experienced. Whether a transaction is settled in dollars versus a foreign currency is a matter that is negotiated between the transacting parties and is influenced by a number of factors. For one of the parties, the currency will be a foreign currency; for the other party, the currency will be its domestic currency. A bank wire transfer is generally used to transfer currency between parties in different countries. When a bank wire transfer is used, the owing party instructs its bank to reduce its bank account by the appropriate amount. Its bank in turn notifies the receiving party's bank to add a corresponding translated amount to the receiving party's bank account. Therefore, the bank wire transfer, through the use of electronic means, eliminates the need to physically transfer currencies between transacting parties.

To summarize, *changes in exchange rates do not affect transactions that are both denominated and measured in the reporting entity's currency.* Therefore, these transactions require no special accounting treatment. However, *if a transaction is denominated in a foreign currency and measured in the reporting entity's currency, changes in the exchange rate between the transaction date and settlement date result in a gain or loss to the reporting entity.* These gains or losses are referred to as exchange gains or losses, and their recognition requires special accounting treatment.

Effect of Rate Changes	
No Exchange Gain or Loss	Exchange Gain or Loss
Transactions are denominated and measured in the reporting entity's currency.	Transactions are denominated in the foreign currency and measured in the reporting entity's currency.

Originally, two methods were proposed for the treatment of exchange gains or losses arising from foreign currency transactions. After considering the merits of these two methods, the FASB adopted the *two-transactions method* which views the initial foreign currency transaction as one transaction. The effect of any subsequent changes in the exchange rates and the resulting exchange gain or loss are viewed as a second transaction. Therefore, the initial transaction is recorded independently of the settlement transaction. This method is consistent with accepted accounting techniques, which normally account for the financing of a transaction as a separate and distinct event. (The required two-transactions method is used in all instances with one exception. The exception relates to a hedge on a foreign currency commitment that is discussed later in this chapter. Therefore, unless otherwise stated, the two-transactions method will be used throughout the chapter.)

In order to illustrate the two-transactions method, assume that a U.S. company sells mining equipment on June 1, 20X4, to a foreign company, with the corresponding receivable to be paid or settled on July 1, 20X4. The equipment has a selling price of $306,000 and a cost of $250,000. On June 1, 20X4, the foreign currency is worth $1.70, and on July 1, 20X4, the foreign currency is worth $1.60. Illustrations 10-1 and 10-2 present the entries to record the sale of the mining equipment, assuming that the transaction is denominated in dollars ($306,000) and then in foreign currency (180,000). Note that, when the transaction is denominated in dollars (in Illustration 10-1), the U.S. company does not experience an exchange gain or loss. However, because the foreign company measures the transaction in foreign currency but denominates the transaction in dollars, it experiences an exchange loss. In substance, the value of the foreign company's accounts payable changed because it was denominated in a foreign currency (dollars, in this case), that is, in a currency other than its own. In order to emphasize that the value of certain asset or liability balances is not fixed and will change over time, these changing accounts are identified in boldface type throughout the text.

When the transaction is denominated in foreign currency, as in Illustration 10-2, the U.S. company experiences an exchange loss (or gain). The exchange loss (or gain) is accounted for separately from the sales transaction and does not affect the U.S. company's gross profit on the sale. This separately recognized exchange gain or loss is not viewed as an extraordinary item, but should be included in determining income from continuing operations for the period and, if material, should be disclosed in the financial statements or in a note to the statements. Finally, it is important to note in Illustration 10-2 that the foreign company does not experience an exchange gain or loss. This is because the foreign company both measured and denominated the transaction in foreign currency.

Unsettled Foreign Currency Transactions

If a foreign currency transaction is unsettled at year-end, an unrealized gain or loss should be recognized to reflect the change in the exchange rate occurring between the transaction date and the end of the reporting period (e.g., year-end). This treatment focuses on accrual accounting and the fact that exchange gains and losses occur over time rather than only at the date of settlement or payment. Therefore, at any given time the asset or liability arising from a foreign currency transaction that is denominated in a foreign currency *should be measured at its fair value* as suggested by current spot rates. The changes in fair value, both positive and negative, are recognized in current earnings. In essence, the asset or liability is *marked-to-market.*

Illustration 10-1
Transaction Denominated in **Dollars:** Two-Transactions Method

U.S. Company (dollars)			Foreign Company (foreign currency—FC)		
June 1, 20X4					
Accounts Receivable	306,000		Equipment	180,000*	
Sales Revenue		306,000	**Accounts Payable—FC** . . .		**180,000**
Cost of Goods Sold	250,000				
Inventory		250,000			
July 1, 20X4					
Cash	306,000		**Accounts Payable—FC**	**180,000**	
Accounts Receivable		306,000	Exchange Loss	11,250	
			Cash		191,250**

Note: The U.S. company experienced no exchange gain or loss because its transaction was both denominated and measured in dollars. However, under the two-transactions method, the foreign company did experience an exchange loss since its transaction was measured in foreign currency and denominated in dollars. The decrease in the value of the foreign currency relative to the U.S. dollar means more foreign currency must be paid to cover the liability.

*($306,000 ÷ $1.70 = 180,000 FC)
**($306,000 ÷ $1.60 = 191,250 FC)

Illustration 10-2
Transaction Denominated in **Foreign Currency (FC):** Two-Transactions Method

U.S. Company (dollars)			Foreign Company (foreign currency)		
June 1, 20X4					
Accounts Receivable—FC	**306,000**		Equipment	180,000	
Sales Revenue		306,000	Accounts Payable		180,000
Cost of Goods Sold	250,000				
Inventory		250,000			
July 1, 20X4					
Cash	288,000*		Accounts Payable	180,000	
Exchange Loss	18,000**		Cash		180,000
Accounts Receivable—FC		**306,000**			

Note: The loss is considered to be part of a separate financing decision and unrelated to the original sales transaction.

*The company received 180,000 FC when the exchange rate was 1 FC = $1.60 (180,000 FC × $1.60 = $288,000). Normally, the company would not physically receive FC but would have the dollar equivalent wired to its bank account. Through the use of a bank wire transfer, the foreign company's account would be debited for the number of FC, and the U.S. company's bank account would be credited for the applicable number of dollars, given the exchange rate.

**The decrease in the value of the FC from $1.70 to $1.60 results in an exchange loss to the U.S. company since the FC it received is less valuable than it was at the transaction date [180,000 × ($1.60 – $1.70) = –$18,000].

To illustrate the accounting for unsettled transactions, assume a U.S. company purchases goods from a foreign company on November 1, 20X1. The purchase in the amount of 1,000 foreign currencies (FC) is to be paid for on February 1, 20X2, in foreign currency. To record or measure the transaction, the domestic company would make the following entry, assuming an exchange rate of 1 FC = $0.50:

Inventory	500	
Accounts Payable—FC		500
Purchase of inventory for 1,000 FC when the exchange rate is 1 FC = $0.50.		

Assuming the exchange rate on the December 31, 20X1, year-end is 1 FC = $0.52, the following entry would be necessary:

Exchange Loss [1,000 × ($0.52 – $0.50)]*	20	
Accounts Payable—FC		20
To accrue the exchange loss on the unperformed portion of the foreign currency transaction when 1 FC = $0.52.		

*The increase in the value of each FC from $0.50 to $0.52 results in a loss to the domestic company since, as of year-end, the company would have to pay out more dollars than originally recorded in order to eliminate the liability.

If the transaction had been settled at year-end, the domestic company would have had to expend $520 to acquire 1,000 FC. Therefore, a loss of $20 is traceable to the unperformed portion of the transaction. Some theorists have suggested that an exchange gain or loss should not be recognized prior to settlement because the gain or loss has not been "realized" through settlement. This position fails to recognize the merits of accrual accounting and is in conflict with the position of the FASB, which requires that the assets or liabilities that are denominated in a foreign currency be measured at fair value with the recognition of resulting unrealized gains or losses being recognized in current earnings.

Finally, assuming an exchange rate of 1 FC = \$0.55 on the settlement date (February 1, 20X2), the domestic entity would make the following entry to record the settlement:

Accounts Payable—FC (\$500 + \$20)	520	
Exchange Loss [1,000 × (\$0.55 − \$0.52)]	30	
Cash		550
To record payment of liability for 1,000 FC, when 1 FC = \$0.55.		

Note that the company experiences a \$50 loss due to changes in the exchange rate. This is allocated between 20X1 and 20X2 in accordance with accrual accounting.

REFLECTION

- If a transaction is denominated in a foreign currency, there is exposure to risk associated with exchange rate changes.
- Assets or liabilities that are denominated in foreign currency are to be measured at fair value using spot exchange rates at the date of measurement. In essence, such accounts are marked-to-market. Exchange gains and losses are recorded in current earnings even if not yet realized.

HEDGING THE EXPOSURE TO FOREIGN CURRENCY EXCHANGE RISK

4 OBJECTIVE

Identify the contexts in which a company may be exposed to foreign currency exchange risk.

When business is conducted between parties with different currencies, one of the transacting parties will be exposed to the exchange rate risk associated with having a transaction denominated in a foreign currency. Companies may be exposed to foreign currency exchange risk in several contexts including the following:

1. *An actual existing foreign currency transaction that results in the recognition of assets or liabilities.* As previously illustrated, the risk to be hedged against is the risk that exchange rates may change between the transaction date and the settlement date.
2. *A firm commitment to enter into a foreign currency transaction.* Such a commitment is an agreement between two parties that specifies all significant terms related to the prospective transaction including prices or amounts of consideration stated in foreign currency units. Beginning at the date of the commitment, the risk to be hedged against is the risk that the value of the commitment which is fixed in a foreign currency amount could be adversely affected by subsequent changes in exchange rates. Such a hedge is known as a *fair value hedge*. For example, a commitment to purchase inventory for a fixed amount of foreign currency could have a value of \$10,000 at the commitment date but, due to exchange rate changes, have a value of \$11,000 at the transaction date thus resulting in a higher inventory cost than anticipated.
3. *A forecasted foreign currency transaction that has a high probability of occurrence.* Such a forecasted transaction, unlike a commitment or an existing transaction, does not provide an entity with any present rights or obligations and does not have any fixed prices or rates. Because fixed prices or rates are not present, an entity is exposed to the risk that future cash flows may vary due to changes in prices and exchange rates. The risk being hedged against is the risk associated with exchange rate changes. Such a hedge is known as a *cash flow hedge*. For example, if a manufacturer forecasted needing raw materials to meet future production, even if material prices to be paid in foreign currency did not change in the future, the dollar equivalent cash flows associated with the forecasted purchase could change over time due to changes in exchange rates.

4. *An investment in a foreign subsidiary.* Translating the financial statements of a foreign subsidiary expressed in foreign currency into the domestic currency of the investor entity can affect the equity of the investor entity. The risk being hedged against is the risk that the translation will reduce the investor's equity due to adverse changes in exchange rates. Such a hedge is known as a *hedge of a net investment.*

With the exception of item (4) above, which will be discussed in Chapter 11, the special accounting for the hedges associated with the other items will be discussed in the balance of this chapter.

As previously illustrated, an existing transaction that is denominated in foreign currency exposes an entity to the risk that exchange rates may change between the date of the transaction and the settlement date. A commitment to enter into a foreign currency transaction is an agreement between two parties that specifies all significant terms related to the prospective transaction including the price in FC units. A forecasted foreign currency transaction, unlike a commitment or existing transaction, does not provide an entity with any present rights or obligations and does not have any fixed prices or rates. Because fixed prices or rates are not present, an entity is exposed to the risk that future cash flows may vary due to changes in prices and exchange rates.

The foreign currency exchange rate risk associated with either an existing transaction, a commitment to transact, or a forecasted transaction may be reduced through a hedging strategy. Hedging is a form of risk-reduction management in response to fluctuating currency exchange rates. The extent and conditions under which exchange risk is hedged are a function of management policy and perceived risks. Obviously, a company would like to reduce exchange rate risk and will often do so if negative changes are anticipated. However, some companies, as a matter of policy, hedge all foreign currency denominated activity over a specific amount. This approach recognizes the uncertainties regarding whether exchange rate changes will affect a company in a positive or negative manner.

Hedging strategies often employ the use of derivative instruments, as discussed earlier in the derivatives module. Companies may use forward contracts, options, or swaps.

- A forward contract obligates the holder to buy or sell FC at a future date at a fixed forward rate.
- An option gives the holder the right, but not the obligation, to buy (a call option) or sell (a put option) FC at a fixed exercise or strike rate of exchange.
- The swap is a contractual obligation, arranged by an intermediary, between two parties to deliver a sum of money in one currency in exchange for a sum of money in another currency.

The following sections describe accounting for hedges against existing transactions, firm commitments, and forecasted transactions in FC using forward contracts and options. See the derivatives module for an example of a swap.

5

OBJECTIVE

Explain the accounting treatment given various types of foreign currency hedges.

Hedging an Existing Foreign Currency Transaction Using a Forward Contract

Management could eliminate the risk associated with exchange rate fluctuations by settling the related transaction immediately. However, this would deprive the company of the opportunity to use the required cash amounts for other purposes. Furthermore, no discounts for prompt payment may be offered as a necessary condition of the transaction. Obviously, opportunity costs must be evaluated against the potential exposure to exchange rate changes for such transactions. If an existing transaction is not settled immediately, management may elect to hedge against the exposure associated with exchange rate changes.

The gain or loss associated with the foreign currency exposure of a recognized, foreign currency-denominated asset or liability as measured by changes in the spot rate is generally recognized in earnings. However, this recognition does not prevent such exposed positions from being hedged with a fair value hedge or a cash flow hedge.[2] Therefore, recognized foreign

2 Statement of Financial Accounting Standards No. 138, *Accounting for Certain Derivative Instruments and Certain Hedging Activities* (Norwalk, CT: Financial Accounting Standards Board, 2000), par. 4j.

currency denominated assets or liablities may be the subject of a fair value or cash flow hedge and receive special hedge accounting treatment if all necessary qualifying criteria for such accounting are satisfied.[3]

As previously illustrated, the asset or liability (account receivable or account payable) resulting from an unsettled foreign currency transaction will be remeasured as a result of accruing exchange gains or losses due to exchange rate changes. The exchange gains or losses are reported currently in earnings; obviously, one would prefer to avoid exchange losses. The goal of a hedge is to offset the exchange loss associated with the existing foreign currency transaction (the hedged item) with a gain traceable to the change in the value of the hedging instrument. It is impossible to know with certainty whether an exchange gain or loss will be associated with the hedged item. However, it is possible that a gain on the hedged item could be offset by a loss on the hedging instrument. As stated earlier, many companies as a matter of policy hedge against both gains and losses associated with the hedged item.

The hedge of an existing foreign currency transaction generally is not designated as a hedge of a foreign currency commitment or forecasted foreign currency transaction. Therefore, this "undesignated" hedge does not receive the special accounting treatment accorded other types of hedges. The accounting for the undesignated hedge of a foreign currency transaction is characterized as follows:

1. The accounting for the hedge (the hedging instrument) is separate from the accounting for the foreign currency transaction (the hedged item).
2. The hedging instrument will be carried at fair value, and changes in value over time will be recognized as an unrealized gain or loss and be reported in earnings.
3. The change in value of the hedging instrument consists of a change in the instrument's intrinsic value and its time value. These changes in value can be recognized separately or combined. Regardless of how it is recognized, the total change in value is reported currently in earnings.
4. Changes in the value of the hedging instrument should be accrued at the end of a reporting period.
5. The gains (losses) on the hedging instrument will offset or net against the losses (gains) on the foreign currency transaction (the hedged item).
6. A hedge would be fully effective or "perfect" if the critical terms (nature of the underlying, notional amount, delivery dates, settlement date, type of currency, etc.) of the hedging instrument matched the terms of the hedged item. In a perfect hedge, the net offset amount will merely equal the change in the time value of the hedging instrument.
7. That portion of the hedging instrument which exceeds the exposed position is considered to be a speculative hedge and is accounted for accordingly.

Hedging Illustrated. Assume that a U.S. company purchases inventory from a foreign vendor with subsequent payment due in FC and that the company acquires a forward contract to buy FC. If prior to settlement, the dollar weakens relative to the FC, the accounts payable will increase in value resulting in an exchange loss. However, the forward contract to buy FC (an asset) will increase in value if the dollar weakens.

Additional information supporting this illustration is as follows:

1. On November 1, 20X1, the company bought inventory from a foreign vendor with payment due on February 1, 20X2, in the amount of 100,000 FC.
2. On November 1, 20X1, the company purchased a forward contract to buy 100,000 FC on February 1, 20X2, at a forward rate of 1 FC = \$0.506.
3. Selected spot and forward rates are as follows:

3 The necessary criteria are discussed in the derivatives module of this text.

Date	Spot Rate	Forward Rate for Remaining Term of Contract
November 1,20X1	1 FC = $0.50	1 FC = $0.506
December 31, 20X1	1 FC = 0.52	1 FC = 0.530
February 1, 20X2	1 FC = 0.55	1 FC = 0.550

4. Changes in the value of the forward contract are to be discounted at a 6% rate.
5. Changes in the value of the forward contract over time are as follows:

	November 1— 90 days remaining	December 31— 30 days remaining	Transaction Date
Number of FC	100,000	100,000	100,000
Spot rate 1 FC	$0.500	$0.520	$0.550
Forward rate for remaining time – 1 FC	$0.506	$0.530	$0.550
Initial forward rate – 1 FC		$0.506	$0.506
Fair value of forward contract:			
Original forward value		$50,600	$50,600
Current forward value		53,000	55,000
Change—gain (loss)—in forward value		$ 2,400	$ 4,400
Present value of change:			
n = 1, i = 6%/12		$ 2,388	
n = 0, i = 6%/12			$ 4,400
Change in value from prior period:			
Current present value		$ 2,388	$ 4,400
Prior present value		0	2,388
(a) Change in present value		$ 2,388	$ 2,012
(b) Change in intrinsic value (spot rates)—gain (loss)		2,000	3,000
		[100,000 × ($0.50 – $0.52)]	[100,000 × ($0.52 – $0.55)]
(a) – (b) = Change in time value (spot-forward difference)		$ 388	$ (988)
		($2,388 – $2,000)	($2,012 – $3,000)

Illustration 10-3 presents the entries to record the foreign currency transaction and the related forward contract. Once again, in order to emphasize that the value of certain account balances is not fixed and will change over time, these accounts are identified in boldface type.

Illustration 10-3
Hedging a Foreign Currency Transaction—Exposed Liability Position

Relating to the Purchase of Inventory			Relating to the Forward Contract		
November 1, 20X1					
Inventory	50,000		**Forward Contract Receivable—FC**	50,600	
Accounts Payable—FC		50,000	Forward Contract Payable—$		50,600
Purchase of inventory for 100,000 FC when 1 FC = $0.50.			Purchase of contract to buy 100,000 FC at a forward rate of 1 FC = $0.506.[a]		
December 31, 20X1					
Exchange Loss	2,000		**Forward Contract Receivable—FC**	2,000	
Accounts Payable—FC		2,000	Unrealized Gain on Contract		2,000
To accrue the exchange loss on the FC denominated payable when the spot rate is $0.52.			To record change in intrinsic value due to spot rate changes.		
			Forward Contract Receivable—FC	388	
			Unrealized Gain on Contract		388
			To record change in time value.		
			Note that the above entries to recognize the change in the value of the forward contract can be combined into a single entry.		
February 1, 20X2					
Accounts Payable—FC	52,000		**Forward Contract Receivable—FC**	3,000	
Exchange Loss	3,000		Unrealized Gain on Contract		3,000
Foreign Currency		55,000			
To record settlement of the liability when 1 FC = $0.55.			To record change in intrinsic value due to spot rate changes.		
			Unrealized Loss on Contract	988	
			Forward Contract Receivable—FC		988
			To record change in time value.		
			Foreign Currency[b]	55,000	
			Forward Contract Payable—$	50,600	
			Forward Contract Receivable—FC		55,000
			Cash		50,600
			To record settlement of contract.[c]		

[a]Noting the offsetting nature of the two accounts, an alternative for this entry would be a memo entry to describe the commitment resulting from the contract. Such treatment emphasizes the executory nature of the contract and is most common in practice. However, recognizing the forward contract with entries helps in understanding the relationships in using forward contracts. If no entry were made at inception, subsequent changes in the value of the hedging instrument would still be recognized by either debiting or crediting a "forward contract" in the case of an unrealized gain or loss, respectively. It should be noted that no separate accounting is given to the contract.

[b]Generally, the company would not physically receive the foreign currency. Instead, a bank wire transfer would be used to settle the transaction. The currency broker would debit the domestic company's bank account for the necessary number of dollars and credit the foreign company's bank account for the necessary number of foreign currencies. If a bank wire transfer were used, the entry would be as follows:

Cash	4,400	
Forward Contract Payable — $	50,600	
Forward Contract Receivable — FC		55,000

[c]If a memo entry was initially used to account for the forward contract, the settlement of the contract would be recorded as follows:

Foreign Currency	55,000	
Forward Contract—FC		4,400
Cash		50,600

The entries have been separated between those relating to the purchase of inventory and those relating to the forward contract. This emphasizes that the company is entering into two separate, but related, transactions. One relates to a transaction with a foreign party that is denominated in foreign currency (an FC transaction) and is exposed to risk resulting from exchange rate changes. The other transaction accounts for a forward contract between the company and a broker and is designed to hedge against the exchange risk related to the FC transaction. Remember that either the asset or liability arising from a foreign currency transaction and the hedging instrument are to be measured at fair value with resulting gains or losses recognized currently in earnings. In an effective hedge, the respective gains and losses should offset each other except to the extent of the original premium or discount (time value component) on the forward contract.

Because a forward contract is an executory contract, technically there is no need to record the contract at inception. In reality, most companies follow this nonrecording practice but do keep supporting schedules detailing contracts. Even if this practice is followed, the forward contract is marked to market in order to reflect changes in the value of the underlying foreign currency. These changes in fair value are recorded by the company. For instructional purposes, forward contracts will be recorded at inception. Note, however, that the forward contract receivable and forward contract payable accounts will be netted against each other for presentation purposes. This netting results in balance sheet amounts equal to those that would have existed if no entry had been made at inceptions to record the hedging instrument.

The hedge accounted for in Illustration 10-3 was effective in that the losses associated with the changing value of the FC denominated account payable were offset by the positive changes in the value of the forward contract. Instead of a $5,000 exchange loss, the company incurred only a $600 loss, which represents the premium on the forward rate of 0.506 versus the spot rate of 0.50 on the inception date of the forward contract. If financial statements were presented on December 31, 20X1, the purchase and hedge would be reported as follows:

Income Statement		Balance Sheet	
		Assets:	
Exchange loss	$(2,000)	Inventory	$ 50,000
Unrealized gain on contract	2,388	Forward contract receivable—FC	$ 52,988
Net gain	$ 388	Forward contract payable—$	(50,600)
		Net contract	$ 2,388
		Liabilities:	
		Accounts payable—FC	$ 52,000

The exchange loss on the transaction is offset against the gain on the hedge, netting a $388 gain. Further, the forward contract receivable and the forward contract payable accounts are netted, which results in a net contract receivable of $2,388.

The overall effect of the hedge presented in Illustration 10-3 is summarized as follows:

	Without the Hedge	With the Hedge
Exchange gain (loss) on foreign currency transaction [100,000 FC × ($0.55 – $0.50)]	$(5,000)	$(5,000)
Gain on forward contract due to changes in spot rates (intrinsic value)		5,000
Subtotal	$(5,000)	$ 0
Loss on forward contract due to changes in time value		(600)
Net income effect	$(5,000)	$ (600)

The net effect on income represents the original premium on the forward contract of $600 [100,000 × (forward rate of $0.506 versus original spot rate of $0.500)].

It is important to note that a hedge may also eliminate exchange gains associated with a foreign currency transaction. For instance, when a forward contract establishes a forward rate, it is possible that changes in the spot rate may not move in the same direction or may not move as much as had been expected. Considering the previous transactions, assume the same facts except that the spot rates are as follows:

Date	Spot Rate
November 1, 20X1	1 FC = $0.50
December 31, 20X1	1 FC = $0.49
February 1, 20X2	1 FC = $0.48

In effect, the hedge eliminated potential exchange gains, and the company paid the same $600 premium for the forward contract:

	Without the Hedge	With the Hedge
Exchange gain (loss) on foreign currency transaction [100,000 FC × ($0.48 – $0.50)]	$2,000	$ 2,000
Loss on forward contract due to changes in spot rates (intrinsic value)		(2,000)
Subtotal	$2,000	$ 0
Loss on forward contract due to changes in time value		(600)
Net income effect	$2,000	$ (600)

Although this hedge had a negative impact on earnings, it did eliminate the uncertainty associated with exchange rate risk. By entering into a forward contract on the date of the transaction, the company established a known purchase price of $50,600. It is important to recognize that the use of a forward contract, unlike an option, results in the gain (loss) on the foreign currency transaction being offset or reduced by the loss (gain) on the hedging instrument. In a perfect hedge, this counterbalancing effect results in a net gain/loss equal to the original discount/premium on the forward contract.

Illustration 10-3 involved the use of a forward contract to buy FC in order to settle the FC denominated accounts payable. A forward contract may also be used to sell FC when an FC denominated receivable is settled. For example, if a U.S. company sold inventory to a foreign customer and the resulting account receivable was denominated in FC, the company would receive FC. The company could acquire a forward contract to sell FC upon receipt from the foreign customer. If the dollar strengthened relative to the FC, the U.S. company's receivable would decrease in value. However, a forward contract to sell FC in this scenario would increase in value and serve as a hedge against the losses on the receivable.

HW

Special Hedging Complications

The previous examples assumed that a forward contract covered the same period of time as the settlement period, which is defined as the period of time between the transaction date and the settlement date. However, it is possible that a forward contract could cover a period of time different from the settlement period. The previous examples also assumed that the forward contract was for the same number of foreign currency units as required by the foreign currency transaction. It also is possible that a forward contract could be for a number of foreign currency units different from the number of units required by the transaction.

Forward Contract Expires Before Settlement Date. Prior to the expiration date of a forward contract, it is possible for the holder of the contract to settle the contract in exchange for cash. Net settlement is a characteristic of all derivatives such as a forward contract. However, if the contract expires before the settlement date of the underlying hedged transaction, the holder of the contract has several alternatives for dealing with the contract. For example, assuming that a contract to sell foreign currency expires before the customer remits the foreign currency, the seller may: (a) roll over the forward contract, (b) purchase the necessary foreign currency to satisfy the contract and acquire a new forward contract to sell the foreign currency when the customer pays, or (c) simply purchase the necessary foreign currency to satisfy the contract and deal with the foreign currency when it is received.

Transactions and forward contracts are commonly settled on different dates. Some currency brokers will extend a forward contract for a short time at the original forward rate as a courtesy to their clients. However, if settlement is not expected soon, the original contract may be rolled over into a new contract to settle on the anticipated date of payment. Rather than rolling over a forward contract, the needed FC can be purchased to settle the forward contract. When the hedged transaction is ultimately settled, the FC received could then be sold at the spot rate. Obviously, this route creates exposure to the risk that spot rates will change between the time of purchasing FC and receiving FC from the customer. In order to avoid this exposure, a new forward contract to sell FC could be employed.

Forward Contract Expires After Settlement Date. Forward contracts can also expire after the settlement date. For example, suppose a customer paying in foreign currency accelerates the payment date in order to improve his/her current ratio. The seller once again has several options: (a) hold the foreign currency until the date of the original forward contract, (b) roll the contract back and sell the foreign currency immediately, (c) sell the foreign currency immediately and sell the forward contract to another party, and (d) sell the foreign currency immediately and acquire FC at the spot rate when the forward contract is settled. Alternative (d) results in a speculative position. (There is no hedged transaction, and it is discouraged by many company policy statements.) If a forward contract expires after the settlement date, any gain or loss that accrues on the forward contract after the transaction settlement date is recognized as a component of current operating income.

Forward Contract Amount Different from Transaction Amount. If a forward contract is for a smaller number of foreign currency units than the foreign currency transaction, the contract gain or loss is recognized as a partial hedge on the exposed position. However, if the forward contract is for a greater number of foreign currency units than the exposed asset or liability position, special treatment is required. That portion of the hedging instrument which exceeds the exposed position is considered to be a speculative hedge and is accounted for as an investment. The gain or loss on that portion of the contract which exceeds the exposed position is accordingly accounted for as an investment gain or loss.

Hedging an Identifiable Foreign Currency Commitment Using a Forward Contract

An identifiable commitment is a binding agreement between two parties that specifies all significant terms related to a yet-to-be-executed transaction. If the commitment requires ultimate settlement in a fixed amount of FC, then exposure to exchange rate risk exists. Because the terms and prices of the commitment in FC are fixed, changes in FC exchange rates affect the value of the commitment. In order to avoid the unfavorable effect of exchange rate changes on the fixed prices, an entity could designate a derivative instrument as a hedge against unfavorable outcomes. This type of hedge is referred to as a *fair value hedge*, as discussed in the derivatives module, and if certain criteria are satisfied, it will qualify for special accounting treatment. The special accounting for a fair value hedge of a firm foreign currency commitment is characterized as follows:

1. The accounting for the hedge (the hedging instrument) is separate from the accounting for the foreign currency commitment (the hedged item). If the commitment were not hedged, no special accounting treatment would be given the commitment.
2. The hedging instrument will be carried at fair value, and changes in value over time will be recognized as an unrealized gain or loss and be reported currently in earnings.

3. The change in the value of the hedging instrument consists of a change in the instrument's intrinsic value and its time value. The change in the time value may be excluded from the assessment of hedge effectiveness if so elected at inception of the hedge. However, changes in both the intrinsic and time values are reported currently in earnings.
4. Changes in the value of the hedging instrument should be accrued at the end of a reporting period.
5. The gain or loss in the value of the firm commitment is measured by changes in the spot rate over time and is reported currently in earnings. The change in the value of the firm commitment from the time of the commitment to the transaction date is recognized as a firm commitment asset or liability. This recognized change in value will result in an adjustment to the basis of the committed item. The gains (losses) on the hedging instrument will offset or net against the losses (gains) on the commitment (the hedged item).
6. A hedge would be fully effective or "perfect" if the critical terms (nature of the underlying, notional amount, delivery dates, settlement date, type of currency, etc.) of the hedging instrument matched the terms of the hedged item. In a perfect hedge, the net offset amount will merely equal the change in the time value of the hedging instrument.
7. If the hedge is perfectly effective, the change in the value of the firm commitment will result in an adjustment, at the date of the transaction, to the basis of the committed item so that the effect of exchange rate changes on fixed prices can be offset. The result is that the dollar basis of the transaction is established at the commitment date rather than the later transaction date, and the targeted values at the date of the commitment can be realized.
8. That portion of the hedging instrument which exceeds the notional amount of the commitment is considered to be a speculative hedge and is accounted for accordingly. Therefore, the special accounting treatment given a fair value hedge is not extended to the portion of the hedge which is deemed to be ineffective.

To illustrate, assume that on March 31, a U.S. company commits to selling specialty equipment to a foreign customer with delivery and payment in 90 days. The firm commitment calls for a selling price of 100,000 FC, and it is estimated that the cost to manufacture the equipment will be $55,000. Assume that the spot rate at the date of the commitment is 1 FC = $0.85. If the spot rate were to remain constant over time, management would be able to realize a target gross profit on the sale of $30,000 [(100,000 FC × $0.85) – $55,000]. However, management fears that the FC could weaken relative to the dollar and the target gross profit margin could be reduced. For example, if the rate of exchange at the transaction date were 1 FC = $0.80, the gross profit would be reduced to $25,000 [(100,000 FC × $0.80) – $55,000]. Recognizing that it may be desirable to establish the dollar basis of a transaction at the commitment date rather than the later transaction date, management could enter into a hedge.

To continue the above example, assume that at the date of the commitment, management decides to hedge the commitment by acquiring a forward contract to sell FC in 90 days. Management has elected to exclude from the assessment of effectiveness the time value of the forward contract as measured by the difference between the forward rate and the spot rate at inception of the forward contract. Assume that a 6% discount rate is to be used. Selected rates and changes in value are presented in the following table. It is important to note the following:

1. The forward contract calls for the sale of FC. Therefore, as remaining forward rates fall below the original forward rate (FC can be sold forward for fewer dollars) the contract increases in value and gains are experienced.
2. The difference between the initial spot and forward rate, referred to as the spot-forward difference, represents the time value of the contract and is either a premium or discount. In the present case, the spot-forward difference is a loss. The initial forward rate to sell is less than the initial spot value of the FC. This loss is recognized over the life of the contract and is to be excluded from the assessment of hedge effectiveness as so elected at inception of the hedge. The hedge is expected to be fully effective because the critical terms (nature of the underlying, notional amount, delivery dates, settlement date, type of currency, etc.) of the hedging instrument match the terms of the hedged item.
3. Changes in the value of the firm commitment are measured as changes in the spot rate over time. As the spot rates decrease over time the commitment to sell becomes less valuable. For

example, if the commitment to sell for 100,000 FC had a dollar value of $85,000 (100,000 FC × Spot rate of 1 FC, which is $0.85) at the commitment date, then the dollar value of the commitment would be less than $85,000 if the spot rate subsequently decreased to 1 FC = $0.84.

	March 31—90 Days Remaining	60 Days Remaining	30 Days Remaining	Transaction Date
Number of FC	100,000	100,000	100,000	100,000
Spot rate 1 FC	$0.850	$0.840	$0.820	$0.800
Forward rate for remaining time – 1 FC	$0.845	$0.838	$0.814	$0.800
Initial forward rate – 1 FC		$0.845	$0.845	$0.845
Fair value of forward contract:				
Original forward value		$84,500	$84,500	$84,500
Current forward value		83,800	81,400	80,000
Change—gain (loss)—in forward value		$ 700	$ 3,100	$ 4,500
Present value of change:				
n = 2, i = 6%/12		$ 693		
n = 1, i = 6%/12			$ 3,085	
n = 0, i = 6%/12				$ 4,500
Change in value from prior period:				
Current present value		$ 693	$ 3,085	$ 4,500
Prior present value		0	693	3,085
(a) Change in present value		$ 693	$ 2,392	$ 1,415
(b) Change in intrinsic (spot rates) – gain (loss)		1,000[a]	2,000[b]	2,000[c]
[a][100,000 × ($0.85 – $0.84)]				
[b][100,000 × ($0.84 – $0.82)]				
[c][100,000 × ($0.82 – $0.80)]				
(a) – (b) = Change in time value (spot-forward difference)		$ (307)	$ 392	$ (585)

Entries by the U.S. company to record the fair value hedge are set forth in Illustration 10-4.

An analysis of the entries in Illustration 10-4 reveals that the fair value hedge was effective in accomplishing the concerns of the U.S. company. At the commitment date, the commitment to receive FC had a value of $85,000 represented by 100,000 FC at a then spot rate of 1 FC = $0.85. Nevertheless, the company was concerned that the FC would weaken resulting in a reduction of the targeted gross profit. In fact the value of the commitment to receive FC did lose value over time as evidenced by a declining spot rate. However, by hedging the commitment the company was able to ultimately adjust the basis of the sales transaction and attain the targeted gross profit. Note that the account "Firm Commitment" serves the purpose of fixing the basis of the

Illustration 10-4
Hedge of an Identifiable Foreign Currency Commitment

Relating to the Commitment and Sale of Equipment			Relating to the Forward Contract		
March 31					
Memo: Company commits to sell equipment.			Forward Contract Receivable—$	84,500	
			Forward Contract Payable—FC		84,500
			Purchase of contract to sell 100,000 at a forward rate of 1 FC = $0.845.		
60 days remaining					
Loss on Firm Commitment	1,000		**Forward Contract Payable—FC**	1,000	
Firm Commitment		1,000	Unrealized Gain on Contract		1,000
To record the loss on commitment (100,000 FC at $0.84 now vs. $0.85).			To record change in value due to spot rate changes.		
			Unrealized Loss on Contract	307	
			Forward Contract Payable—FC		307
			To record change in time value excluded from hedge effectiveness.		
30 days remaining					
Loss on Firm Commitment	2,000		**Forward Contract Payable—FC**	2,000	
Firm Commitment		2,000	Unrealized Gain on Contract		2,000
To record the loss on commitment (100,000 FC at $0.82 now vs. $0.84).			To record change in value due to spot rate changes.		
			Forward Contract Payable—FC	392	
			Unrealized Gain on Contract		392
			To record change in time value excluded from hedge effectiveness.		
0 days remaining					
Loss on Firm Commitment	2,000		**Forward Contract Payable—FC**	2,000	
Firm Commitment		2,000	Unrealized Gain on Contract		2,000
To record the loss on commitment (100,000 FC at $0.80 now vs. $0.82).			To record change in value due to spot rate changes.		
			Unrealized Loss on Contract	585	
			Forward Contract Payable—FC		585
			To record change in time value excluded from hedge effectiveness.		
Foreign Currency	80,000		**Forward Contract Payable—FC**	80,000	
Firm Commitment	5,000		**Foreign Currency**		80,000
Sales Revenue		85,000	To record settlement of forward contract.		
To record sale and adjustment to basis of sale.					
Cost of Sales	55,000		Cash	84,500	
Equipment Inventory		55,000	**Forward Contract Receivable—$**		84,500
To record cost of sales.			To record receipt of cash from broker.		

sales by the amount of the loss on firm commitment recognized during the commitment period. The effect of the above fair value hedge on reported income can be summarized as follows:

	Targeted Position	Without the Hedge	With the Hedge
Sales price	$85,000	$80,000	$85,000
Cost of sales	55,000	55,000	55,000
Gross profit	$30,000	$25,000	$30,000
Loss on commitment			(5,000)
Gain on forward contract			5,000
Subtotal	$30,000	$25,000	$30,000
Derivative loss excluded from assessment of effectiveness (the time value)			(500)
Net income effect	$30,000	$25,000	$29,500

If the commitment had not been hedged, the actual gross profit on the sale would have been reduced from the targeted gross profit of $30,000 to $25,000. However, the fair value hedge was effective in maintaining the targeted gross profit. This was accomplished at a cost of $500, which represents the time value (the original discount – a forward rate less than the spot rate) on the forward contract [($0.845 – $0.850) × 100,000 FC]. Although this hedge was highly effective in offsetting losses on the commitment, it is important to remember that spot rates could have increased over time, and the hedge would have effectively eliminated gains on the commitment.

If financial statements were presented on April 30, with 60 days remaining on the hedge, the sale and hedge would be reported as follows:

Income Statement		Balance Sheet	
		Assets:	
Loss on firm commitment	$(1,000)	Forward contract receivable—$	$84,500
Unrealized gain on contract	1,000	Forward contract payable—FC	83,807
Unrealized loss on contract	(307)	Net contract	$ 693
Net loss	$ (307)	Liabilities:	
		Firm commitment	$ 1,000

The gains and losses on the firm commitment and forward contract are offset, netting a $307 loss on the firm commitment (or forward contract). On the balance sheet, the forward contract payable—FC and receivable—$ also are offset to net a receivable balance of $693.

The special accounting treatment given a fair value hedge of a firm commitment continues during the commitment period unless

- The necessary criteria to qualify as a fair value hedge are no longer satisfied,
- The derivative instrument expires or is sold, terminated, or exercised,
- The entity no longer designates the derivative as a fair value hedge, or
- The hedging relationship is no longer considered highly effective based on management's policies. (See the derivatives module for discussion.)

Furthermore, note that the treatment given a fair value hedge does not continue beyond the point in time where the commitment actually becomes a transaction. If the term of the derivative instrument extends beyond the transaction date, any exchange gains or losses after the transaction date are treated as shown in Illustration 10-3.

Foreign currency commitments are frequently hedged through the use of forward contracts. However, other forms of derivative and nonderivative instruments may be effective. For example, in the above illustration, management could have acquired a put option to sell foreign currency at the transaction date. Alternatively, management could have borrowed dollars for a short term with a promise to repay the loan with a fixed number of FC. The FC received from the sales transaction could have been used to settle the loan denominated in FC. Regardless of the instrument used, the goal of a fair value hedge of a commitment is to reduce the exposure that exchange rate changes may have on the value or amount of the U.S. (domestic) currency to be received or paid. Although the above illustration focused on a commitment involving the receipt of FC in connection with a sale, it is also possible that a commitment might involve the payment of FC. For example, if a company was committed to acquire inventory to be paid for in FC, changes in exchange rates could result in the inventory costing more than anticipated. Such increases in the cost of inventory could reduce gross profits associated with the subsequent sale of the inventory.

Hedging a Forecasted Transaction Using an Option

A forecasted transaction is one that is expected to occur in the future at market prices that will be in existence at the time of the transaction. This is in contrast to a foreign currency commitment, which typically involves market prices that have been previously determined at the time of the commitment. Unlike a firm commitment, a forecasted transaction does not provide an entity with any present rights or obligations and therefore does not have any fixed prices or rates. Because no terms are fixed, an entity is exposed to the risk that future cash flows associated with the forecasted transaction could change. For example, if a company forecasted a purchase of inventory, the cost of the inventory could change. Furthermore, if the forecasted transaction were denominated in FC, not only could the FC price change, but the number of dollars needed to acquire the necessary FC could also change. To illustrate, assume that a company forecasts purchasing inventory for 100,000 FC and that the current spot rate is 1 FC = \$1.10. The entity is exposed to the risk that the actual cost of the inventory could exceed 100,000 FC and that the FC could strengthen relative to the dollar. For example, if it turned out that the inventory actually cost 105,000 FC and that 1 FC = \$1.14, then the transaction that was forecasted to cost \$110,000 (100,000 FC × \$1.10) would actually cost \$119,700 (105,000 FC × \$1.14).

The impact that foreign currency exchange rate changes might have on the cash flows associated with a forecasted transaction can be hedged with a derivative instrument. The objective of the hedge is to reduce the variability of cash flows associated with the forecasted transaction by fixing exchange rates. Such hedges are referred to as *cash flow hedges* and were discussed in greater detail in the earlier derivatives module. If the hedge meets certain criteria, it will qualify for special accounting treatment. The special accounting for a cash flow hedge of a forecasted foreign currency transaction is characterized as follows:

1. The accounting for the hedge (the hedging instrument) is separate from the accounting for the forecasted foreign currency transaction (the hedged item). Furthermore, since the hedged item is a forecasted transaction, which obviously has not yet occurred or been firmly committed to, no accounting is necessary until the forecasted transaction actually takes place. Unlike in the case of a foreign currency transaction and/or firm commitment, there are no recognized gains or losses in the value of the forecasted transaction being concurrently recognized along with changes in the value of the hedging instrument.
2. The change in the value of the hedging instrument consists of a change in the instrument's intrinsic value and its time value. The change in the time value may be excluded from the assessment of hedge effectiveness if so elected at inception of the hedge.
3. If the change in the time value is excluded from the assessment of hedge effectiveness, the change in the time value is reported currently in earnings. Changes in the instrument's intrinsic value are reported as a component of other comprehensive income (OCI) rather than being currently recognized in earnings subject to the constraint addressed in item (4) below.
4. The cumulative amount of OCI represented by the change in the instrument's intrinsic value cannot exceed the cumulative change in the value of expected/forecasted cash flows as measured by changes in spot rates over time. If the cumulative amount of OCI exceeds the

cumulative change in the value of expected/forecasted cash flows, the difference is removed from OCI and recognized currently as earnings. In essence, if the hedge is over effective, that amount will be taken to earnings rather than OCI. If the hedge is under effective, then all of the change in intrinsic value will be recorded as a component of OCI.

5. Changes in the value of the hedging instrument should be accrued at the end of a reporting period.
6. When the forecasted transaction actually affects earnings (versus occurs), the change in the hedging instrument's intrinsic value recognized as a component of OCI is reclassified into current earnings.
7. If the hedge is perfectly effective, the variability of forecasted cash flows due to changes in exchange rates will be reduced. The component of OCI that is reclassified into current earnings when the forecasted transaction actually affects earnings will reduce the effect that changes in exchange rates have had on the underlying cash flows. The result of the hedge is that resulting cash flows are fixed at an exchange rate rather that being allowed to vary as would be the case without a hedge.

To illustrate the special accounting for a cash flow hedge, assume the following:

1. On June 1, a company forecasted the purchase of 5,000 units of inventory from a foreign vendor. The purchase would probably occur on September 1 and require the payment of 100,000 FC.
2. It is anticipated that the inventory could be further processed and delivered to customers by early October.
3. On June 1, the company purchased an out-of-the-money call option to buy 100,000 FC at a strike price of 1 FC = $0.55 during September. An option premium of $900 was paid.
4. Effectiveness of the hedge is measured by comparing changes in the option's intrinsic value with changes in the forecasted cash flows based on changes in the spot rates for FC. Changes in the time value of the option will be excluded from the assessment of hedge effectiveness. The hedge is expected to be fully effective because the critical terms (nature of underlying, notional amounts, delivery dates, settlement date, type of currency, etc.) of the hedging instrument match the terms of the hedged item.
5. Spot rates, option values, and changes in value over time are as follows:

	June 1	June 30	July 31	September 1
Strike price 1 FC	$0.55	$0.55	$0.55	$0.55
Spot rate 1 FC	$0.53	$0.552	$0.57	$0.575
Fair value of options	$ 900	$1,350	$2,400	$2,600
Intrinsic value of option	0	200	2,000	2,500
Time value of option	$900	$1,150	$ 400	$ 100
Cumulative change – gain/(loss) in:				
Intrinsic value		$200	$2,000	$2,500
Value of expected cash flows (change in spot rates over time)		$(2,200)	$(4,000)	$(4,500)
Lesser (in absolute amount) of derivative's cumulative gain (loss) or loss (gain) in value of expected/forecasted cash flows		$200	$2,000	$2,500

6. On September 1, the company purchased 5,000 units of inventory at a cost of 103,000 FC. The option was settled/sold on September 1 at its fair value of $2,600.
7. After incurring further processing costs of $20,000, the inventory was sold for $95,000 on October 5.

Illustration 10-5 presents the necessary entries to account for the cash flow hedge of the above forecasted transaction and the subsequent actual transactions.

Illustration 10-5
Cash Flow Hedge of a Forecasted Transaction

The following entries relate to the hedge. There is no corresponding transaction.

June 1		
Investment in Call Option	900	
Cash		900
To record purchase of option.		
June 30		
Investment in Call Option ($1,350 – $900)	450	
Unrealized Gain on Option		250
OCI [($0.552 – $0.55) × 100,000 FC]		200
To record change in the value of the option.		

The change in the time value is excluded from the assessment of hedge effectiveness. The portion of the gain recorded in OCI equals the change in the option's intrinsic value, which was zero on June 1 because the strike price of $0.55 was greater than the spot rate of $0.53.

July 31		
Investment in Call Option ($2,400 – $1,350)	1,050	
Unrealized Loss on Option	750	
OCI [($0.57 – $0.552) × 100,000 FC]		1,800
To record change in the value of the option.		
September 1		
Investment in Call Option	200	
Unrealized Loss on Option	300	
OCI		500
To record change in the value of the option.		
Cash	2,600	
Investment in Call Option		2,600
To record net settlement of option.		

The remaining entries relate to the inventory purchase and subsequent sale. There is no hedge outstanding.

Inventory	59,225	
Cash		59,225
To record payment of 103,000 FC × $0.575.		
Inventory	20,000	
Cash		20,000
To record additional processing costs.		
October 5		
Cash	95,000	
Sales Revenue		95,000
To record sale of inventory.		
Cost of Sales ($59,225 + $20,000)	79,225	
Inventory		79,225
To recognize cost of sales.		
OCI (balance)	2,500	
Cost of Sales		2,500
To adjust cost of sales by the gain accumulated in OCI.		

An analysis of the entries in Illustration 10-5 reveals that the cash flow hedge was effective in accomplishing the concerns of the U.S. company. At the time of the forecasted transaction, the company anticipated purchasing inventory for 100,000 FC. At a current spot rate of 1 FC = $0.53, the cash outflow would have been $53,000. However, as the spot rate began to increase, the cost of the inventory would increase, and the potential gross profit on its eventual sale would decrease. At the date of the transaction, the spot rate was 1 FC = $0.575. If the price of the inventory had remained at 100,000 FC, the cost of the inventory would have been $57,500. Acquiring an option to buy FC allowed the company to reduce the variability of cash flows and acquire FC at a fixed strike price of 1 FC = $0.550. The effect of the cash flow hedge of the forecasted transaction can be summarized as follows:

	Without the Call Option	With the Call Option
Sales price of inventory	$ 95,000	$ 95,000
Cost of sales – Raw materials	(59,225)	(59,225)
Cost of sales – Processing costs	(20,000)	(20,000)
Gross profit	$ 15,775	$ 15,775
Adjustment to cost of sales due to change in the intrinsic value of the option		2,500
Adjusted gross profit	$ 15,775	$ 18,275
Unrealized loss on hedge excluded from assessment of hedge effectiveness		(800)
Net income effect	$ 15,775	$ 17,475

The adjusted gross profit resulting from the use of a hedge results from the following:

Sales revenue	$ 95,000
Locked in cost of sales on 100,000 FC at the strike price of $0.550	(55,000)
No hedge on the additional cost of 3,000 FC at the transaction date spot rate of $0.575	(1,725)
Processing costs	(20,000)
Adjusted gross profit	$ 18,275

FC price ↑

An analysis of the entries also shows that the balance in OCI at any point in time never exceeded the lesser (in absolute amounts) of the derivative's cumulative gain (loss) in intrinsic value or the loss (gain) in the value of the expected/forecasted cash flows (as measured by changes in spot rates).

The cash flow hedge was effective in reducing the variability of cash flows and was accomplished at a cost of $800, which represents the change in the time value of the option over the holding period ($900 – $100). Once again, remember that the variability of cash flows may also produce a positive effect. For example, if the spot rate had decreased, the purchase of inventory would have required even less cash flow than originally forecasted, and additional gross profit may have resulted. However, an option is a useful derivative to employ in such situations. Remember that the option represents a right, rather than an obligation, to buy FC. If spot rates had declined below the strike price, the holder of the out-of-the-money option could have elected not to exercise and merely recognized the option premium of $900 as a loss. If a forward contract to buy FC had been employed, the holder would have been obligated to exercise or settle the contract. In that case, the hedging instrument would have had an unfavorable effect, offseting the positive effects associated with variable cash flows.

If financial statements were presented at June 30, the hedge would be reported as follows:

Income Statement		Balance Sheet	
		Assets:	
Unrealized gain on option.	$250	Investment in options	$1,350
		Stockholders' Equity:	
		Other comprehensive income—Gain on option . . .	$ 200

The special accounting treatment given a cash flow hedge of a forecasted transaction continues unless

- The necessary criteria to qualify as a cash flow hedge are no longer satisfied,
- The derivative instrument expires or is sold, terminated, or exercised,
- The derivative instrument is no longer designated as a hedge on a forecasted transaction, or
- The hedging relationship is no longer highly effective based on management's policies.

Once a forecasted transaction actually occurs, it is possible at that time to designate the original derivative, if not expired, or a new derivative as a hedge on any exposed asset or liability resulting from the actual transaction. However, if the forecasted transaction is no longer probable, the gain or loss accumulated in OCI should be recognized immediately in earnings.

Summary of Hedging Transactions

When transactions are denominated in one currency and measured in another, changes in currency exchange rates can expose the transacting party to potential exchange gains or losses. In order to reduce the uncertainty associated with exchange rate changes, forward contracts and other derivatives are often used to hedge against the exposure associated with:

- A forecasted foreign currency transaction,
- A foreign currency commitment, or
- An actual existing foreign currency transaction.

The following table summarizes some of the details relating to these risk-management techniques.

	Transaction Is Forecasted	Commit to Transaction	Transaction Occurs
	Hedge of a Forecasted Transaction	Hedge of an Identifiable Firm Commitment	Hedge of an Existing FC Transaction
1. Type of hedge.	Cash flow hedge.	Fair value hedge.	Hedge of an exposed position. (This could be either a cash flow or a fair value hedge.)
2. Basic purpose of hedge.	Hedge against changes in the cash flows due to exchange rate risk occurring between the time of the probable forecasted transaction and the resulting actual transaction.	Hedge against exchange rate risk occurring between the commitment date and the transaction date.	Hedge the exchange rate risk between the transaction date and the payment date.

(continued)

	Transaction Is Forecasted Hedge of a Forecasted Transaction	Commit to Transaction Hedge of an Identifiable Firm Commitment	Transaction Occurs Hedge of an Existing FC Transaction
3. Effect on the basis of the resulting transaction.	Fixes the dollar basis of the actual transaction.	Fixes the dollar basis of the actual transaction.	None.
4. Measurement of the value of a forward contract at a point in time.	Measured as the net present value of the difference between the notional amount at the forward rate at inception and the notional amount at the now current forward rate.	Measured as the net present value of the difference between the notional amount at the forward rate at inception and the notional amount at the now current forward rate.	Measured as the net present value of the difference between the notional amount at the forward rate at inception and the notional amount at the now current forward rate.
5. Measurement of the value of an option at a point in time.	Measured as the quoted option value.	Measured as the quoted option value.	Measured as the quoted option value.
6. Portion of the change in value of a derivative that is excluded from assessment of hedge effectiveness.	May exclude that portion traceable to the time value of the derivative.	May exclude that portion traceable to the time value of the derivative.	May exclude that portion traceable to the time value of the derivative.
7. Measurement of the time value of a derivative.	For a forward contract, the difference between the initial forward rate and the initial spot rate times the notional amount. For an option, the total value of the option at inception less the intrinsic value at inception.	For a forward contract, the difference between the initial forward rate and the initial spot rate times the notional amount. For an option, the total value of the option at inception less the intrinsic value at inception.	For a forward contract, the difference between the initial forward rate and the initial spot rate times the notional amount. For an option, the total value of the option at inception less the intrinsic value at inception.
8. Recognition of the change in time value, gain or loss, that may be excluded from the assessment of effectiveness.	Recognized currently in earnings.	Recognized currently in earnings.	Recognized currently in earnings.
9. Recognition of the change in value, gain or loss, on hedging instrument included in assessment of effectiveness (assuming time value is excluded).	The gain or loss from changes in intrinsic value is recognized as a component of other comprehensive income (OCI). When the resulting transaction affects earnings, the amount in OCI is recognized currently in earnings.	The gain or loss from changes in intrinsic value is recognized currently in earnings.	The gain or loss from changes in intrinsic value is recognized currently in earnings.
10. Measurement of the gain or loss on the hedged item.	No gain or loss is recognized.	Measured as the difference in spot rates between the date of the commitment and the transaction date.	Measured as the difference in spot rates between the date of the transaction and the settlement date.
11. Recognition of the gain or loss on the hedged item.	No gain or loss is recognized.	Recognized currently in earnings and results in an adjustment to the basis of the hedged transaction.	Recognized currently in earnings.

Disclosures Regarding Hedges of Foreign Currency Exposure

Disclosures regarding foreign currency hedges are required by the FASB as part of its broader disclosure requirements for derivative instruments and hedging activity.[4] More specific disclosure requirements also exist for fair value and cash flow hedges. The derivatives module sets forth the disclosure requirements that apply to the hedging relationship discussed in this chapter.

REFLECTION

- A company may be exposed to foreign currency exchange risk in several contexts including foreign currency transactions, commitments, and/or forecasted transactions.
- In a hedge of an existing foreign currency transaction, both the hedging instrument and the hedged transaction are measured at fair value with resulting gains or losses being recognized currently in earnings.
- A hedge of a foreign currency commitment is a fair value hedge that is given special accounting treatment. Changes in the fair value of both the hedging instrument and the commitment are recognized currently in earnings. When the transaction occurs, the hedged item is adjusted for the accumulated gain or loss on the commitment.
- A hedge of a forecasted foreign currency transaction is a cash flow hedge that is given special accounting treatment. Changes in the fair value of the hedging instrument are recognized as a component of other comprehensive income (OCI). Components of OCI are subsequently recognized in earnings in the same period(s) as the actual transaction affects earnings.

UNDERSTANDING THE ISSUES

1. If the U.S. dollar was expected to strengthen relative to a foreign currency (FC), what effect might this have on a U.S. exporter?
2. A U.S. company purchases inventory from a foreign vendor, and purchases are denominated in the foreign currency (FC). The U.S. dollar is expected to weaken against the FC. Explain how a forward contract might be employed as a hedge against exchange rate risk.
3. Explain how a U.S. company's commitment to purchase inventory with settlement in foreign currency (FC) might become less attractive over time and how adverse effects on earnings could be reduced.
4. If a forecasted purchase of equipment were to be denominated in foreign currency (FC), how would the change in value of a cash flow hedge of the forecasted transaction be accounted for?

EXERCISES

Exercise 1 *(LO 3)* **Purchase and sale denominated in euros.** Frankfurt Engineering, Inc., a U.S. company, reconditions and sells injection molding equipment. Reconditioning

4 Statement of Financial Accounting Standards No. 133, *Accounting for Derivative Instruments and Hedging Activities* (Norwalk, CT: Financial Accounting Standards Board, 1998).

facilities exist in the United States, Germany, and South Korea. The German facility had the following transactions:

a. Purchased used equipment from a French equipment broker for 200,000 euros to be paid for in 30 days on June 1, 20X5.
b. Incurred reconditioning costs of 80,000 euros uniformly throughout June 20X5.
c. Paid the French equipment broker on June 28, 20X5.
d. Sold the reconditioned equipment for 350,000 euros with terms of net 30 on July 15, 20X5.
e. Collected 350,000 euros in connection with the above sale on August 10, 20X5.

Relevant spot rates are as follows:

	1 euro =
June 1, 20X5	$1.1705
June 20X5 average	1.1707
June 28, 20X5	1.1709
July 15, 20X5	1.1710
August 10, 20X5	1.1712

Prepare the entries to record the above transactions on the books of the U.S. company.

Exercise 2 *(LO 2)* **Spot rates and forward rates.** On January 1, 20X5, one U.S. dollar can be exchanged for eight foreign currencies (FC). The dollar can be invested short term at a rate of 4%, and the FC can be invested at a rate of 5%.

1. Calculate the direct and indirect spot exchange rates as of January 1, 20X5.
2. Calculate the 180-day forward rate to buy FC (assume 365 days per year).
3. If the spot rate is 1 CA$ = $0.740 and the 90-day forward rate is $0.752, what does this suggest about interest rates in the two countries?
4. Explain why a weak dollar relative to the FC would likely increase U.S. exports.
5. Discuss what would happen to the forward rate if the dollar strengthened relative to the FC.

Exercise 3 *(LO 3, 5)* **Measuring changes in value of FC transaction and a forward contract.** Dettner Corporation purchased inventory from a foreign vendor in the amount of 75,000 FC on December 1 of the current year. On this same date, Dettner entered into a 90-day forward contract to buy FC. Dettner has a calendar year-end, and payment is due to the vendor on March 1 of the next year. When measuring changes in the current value of the forward contract, Dettner uses the present values of changes in the forward value of contracts. The discount rate is 6%.

Various spot and forward rates are as follows:

	December 1	December 31	March 1
Spot rate	$1.40	$1.43	$1.48
Forward rate	1.45	1.47	1.48

Prepare a schedule that calculates the value of accounts payable, the cumulative gain/loss on the transaction, and the forward contract for all relevant dates.

Exercise 4 *(LO 3, 5)* **Hedge with forward contract.** Stark Inc. placed an order for inventory costing 500,000 FC with a foreign vendor on April 15 when the spot rate was 1 FC = $0.683. Stark received the goods on May 1 when the spot rate was 1 FC = $0.687. Also on May 1, Stark entered into a 90-day forward contract to purchase 500,000 FC at a forward rate of 1 FC = $0.693. Payment was made to the foreign vendor on August 1 when the spot rate was 1 FC = $0.696. Stark has a June 30 year-end. On that date, the spot rate was 1 FC = $0.691, and the forward rate on the contract was 1 FC = $0.695. Changes in the current value of the forward contract are measured as the present value of the changes in the forward rates over time. The relevant discount rate is 6%.

1. Prepare all relevant journal entries suggested by the above facts.
2. Prepare a partial income statement and balance sheet as of the company's June 30 year-end that reflect the above facts.

Exercise 5 *(LO 4, 5)* **Hedge with forward contract or loan with FC payoff.** Cortez Electronics buys subassemblies from a foreign vendor. On June 1, 20X9, the company committed to acquire subassemblies costing 400,000 foreign currency units (FC). The parts will be shipped, f.o.b. shipping point, on June 15, 20X9, with payment due on July 31, 20X9. Cortez is considering two alternative forms of hedging its exposed liability position. One alternative would involve acquiring a forward contract on June 1 to buy 400,000 FC for delivery on July 31, 20X9. The forward rate would be 1 FC = $0.62, and the spot rate on June 1 is 1 FC = $0.60. As an alternative, the company has an opportunity to lend $240,000 to another party with payment due in FC and interest at the rate of 8%. The loan would be dated June 1, 20X9, and would be due on July 31, 20X9.

Determine under what conditions the company would favor one alternative over the other.

Exercise 6 *(LO 4, 5)* **Hedging a commitment; forecasted transaction—forward contract vs. option.** Jackson, a U.S. company, acquires a variety of raw materials from foreign vendors with amounts payable in foreign currency (FC). The company needs to acquire 20,000 units of raw material, and the goods are expected to have a price of 100,000 FC. Assume that the inventory can be subsequently sold to U.S. customers for $160,000.

Jackson is contemplating committing to the purchase of the inventory on September 1 with delivery on November 1. However, rather than making a commitment, the company could forecast a probable purchase of inventory with delivery on November 1. In either case, assume that on September 1 the company would either (a) acquire a forward contract to buy 100,000 FC with a forward date of November 1 or (b) acquire an option to buy FC in November at a strike price of $1.25. The option premium is expected to cost $2,100.

Various spot rates, forward rates, and option values are as follows:

	Spot Rate	Forward Rate for November 1	Value of Option
September 1	1 FC = $1.25	1 FC = $1.27	$2,100
October 1	1 FC = $1.30	1 FC = $1.31	$1,100
November 1	1 FC = $1.32	1 FC = $1.32	$1,000

1. Prepare a schedule that would compare the effect on current earnings of the two alternatives (commit or forecast), given the alternative hedging instruments.
2. Show the income statement effect for the period prior to the transaction date separately from the effect after the transaction date. The time value component of the hedging instruments is excluded from the assessment of hedge effectiveness. Discuss your conclusion, and explain to Jackson why one alternative might be preferable over the other.

Exercise 7 *(LO 5)* **Hedging existing FC transaction; forecasted transaction.** The Berger Corporation received delivery of equipment purchased from a foreign manufacturer on June 1. The cost of the equipment was 1,200,000 FC with payment due on July 31. On June 1, the company also forecasted the need to purchase raw materials to be processed with the equipment. The forecasted purchase would occur on July 31 and have a cost of 200,000 FC. In order to hedge the purchases of the equipment and raw materials, on June 1 the company bought a forward contract to buy 1,400,000 FC on July 31. The forward contract was designated as a hedge on the purchase of equipment to the extent of 1,200,000 FC and as a hedge on the forecasted purchase of inventory to the extent of 200,000 FC. The time value of the forward contract is to be excluded from the assessment of hedge effectiveness.

On July 31, the company purchased the raw materials at a cost of 200,000 FC. The materials were processed for an additional cost of $100,000 and were sold in September for $500,000. Selected spot and forward rates are as follows:

	Spot Rate	Forward Rate for July 31
June 1	1 FC = $1.10	1 FC = $1.108
June 30	1 FC = $1.15	1 FC = $1.146
July 31	1 FC = $1.14	1 FC = $1.140

Assuming that the company has a June 30 year-end, prepare the necessary journal entries to record the above transactions. Changes in the forward rates are to be discounted at a 6% rate.

Exercise 8 *(LO 4, 5)* **Income statement effects with and without hedging.** In the past, Baxter Manufacturing has engaged in a number of foreign currency transactions but has never before attempted to hedge these transactions. Baxter has given you three past events and asked you to illustrate how hedging could have been employed. The events are as follows:

Event A: Purchased raw materials from a foreign supplier for 100,000 FC when 1 FC = $1.10. The supplier was paid 60 days later when 1 FC = $1.15. When the goods were purchased, a 60-day forward contract to buy FC had a forward rate of 1 FC = $1.11.

Event B: Committed to sell inventory (with a cost of $120,000) to a foreign buyer for 200,000 FC when 1 FC = $1.13. Sixty days later, when the inventory was shipped, 1 FC = $1.17, and 90 days later, when the customer paid, 1 FC = $1.18. At the date of the commitment, the 90-day forward rate to sell was 1 FC = $1.15, and at the date of shipment, a 30-day forward rate was 1 FC = $1.172.

Event C: Forecasted needing to buy inventory with a cost of 60,000 FC in 60 days in order to meet a sale in the amount of $100,000. When the inventory was actually purchased, it had a cost of 68,000 FC. At the time of the forecast, the spot rate was 1 FC = $1.16, and a 60-day forward contract to buy FC was 1 FC = $1.15. At the time the goods were actually purchased, the spot rate was 1 FC = $1.17.

For each of the above events, indicate how income would have been affected with and without the accompanying hedge.

PROBLEMS

Problem 10-1 *(LO 5)* **FC transactions, commitments, forcasted transactions—earnings impact.** Jarvis Corporation transacts business with a number of foreign vendors and customers. These transactions are denominated in FC, and the company uses a number of hedging strategies to reduce the exposure to exchange rate risk. Several such transactions are as follows:

Transaction A: On November 30, the company purchased inventory from a vendor in the amount of 100,000 FC with payment due in 60 days. Also on November 30, the company purchased a forward contract to buy FC in 60 days.

Transaction B: On November 1, the company committed to provide services to a foreign customer in the amount of 100,000 FC. The services will be provided in 30 days. On November 1, the company also purchased a forward contract to sell 100,000 FC in 30 days.

Transaction C: On November 1, the company forecasted a purchase of equipment in 30 days. The forecasted cost is 100,000 FC, and the equipment is to be depreciated over five years using the straight-line method of depreciation. On November 1, the company acquired a forward contract to buy 100,000 FC in 30 days.

Transaction D: On November 30, the company purchased an option to sell 100,000 FC in 60 days to hedge a forecasted sale to a customer in 60 days. The option sold for a premium of $1,200 and had a strike price of $1.155. The value of the option on December 31 was $2,000.

The time value of all hedging instruments is excluded from the assessment of hedge effectiveness. Relevant spot and forward rates are as follows:

	Spot Rate	Forward Rate for 30 Days from November 1	Forward Rate for 60 Days from November 30
November 1	1 FC = $1.12	1 FC = $1.132	
November 15	1 FC = $1.13		
November 30	1 FC = $1.15		1 FC = $1.146
December 31.	1 FC = $1.14		1 FC = $1.138

◄◄◄◄◄ **Required**

Assuming that the company's year-end is December 31, for each of the above transactions determine the current-year effect on earnings. All necessary discounting should be determined by using a 6% discount rate.

Problem 10-2 *(LO 5)* **Hedge forecasted transactions, forward contracts.** Riker International is building a water purification system in Mexico which will sell for $1,200,000. Although most of the costs incurred will be paid for in U.S. dollars, the company is forecasting that several necessary purchases of project components will be denominated in foreign currency (FC). The forecasted costs are as follows:

May 31: Purchase of fluid movement equipment—cost of 200,000 FC with payment due June 30.
June 30: Purchase of standby generators—cost of 100,000 FC with payment due June 30.

On May 15, Riker acquired a forward contract to buy 300,000 FC for delivery on June 30 in order to hedge the above forecasted transactions. The time value of the forward contract will be excluded from the assessment of hedge effectiveness.

Other construction costs related to the project include $300,000 in May, $200,000 in June, and $250,000 in July. The project was completed in late July, and the company was paid the selling price. The completed contract method is used to account for the project.

Selected spot and forward rates are as follows:

	Spot Rate	Forward Rate for June 30
May 15	1 FC = $1.100	1 FC = $1.108
May 31	1 FC = $1.110	1 FC = $1.112
June 10	1 FC = $1.095	1 FC = $1.100
June 30	1 FC = $1.120	1 FC = $1.120

◄◄◄◄◄ **Required**

1. Prepare all necessary entries for the months April through June. Use a 6% discount rate for all necessary discounting.
2. Compute the gross profit to be recognized on the above project.

Problem 10-3 *(LO 3, 5)* **Income statement effects of transactions, commitments, and hedging.** Clayton Industries sells medical equipment worldwide. On March 1 of the current year, the company sold equipment, with a cost of $160,000, to a foreign customer for 200,000 euros payable in 60 days. At the same time, the company purchased a forward contract to sell 200,000 euros in 60 days. In another transaction, the company committed, on March 15, to deliver equipment in May to a foreign customer in exchange for 300,000 euros. This equipment is anticipated to have a completed cost of $210,000. On March 15, the company hedged the commitment by acquiring a forward contract to sell 300,000 in 90 days. The time value of the forward contracts is excluded from the assessment of hedge effectiveness, and all discounting is based on a 6% discount rate.

Various spot and forward rates for the euro are as follows:

	Spot Rate	Forward Rate for 60 Days from March 1	Forward Rate for 90 Days from March 15
March 1	$1.180	$1.181	
March 15	1.181	1.180	$1.179
March 31	1.179	1.178	1.177
April 30	1.175		1.174

Required ▶ ▶ ▶ ▶ ▶ For March and April, calculate the income statement effect of:

1. The foreign currency transaction.
2. The hedge on the foreign currency transaction.
3. The foreign currency commitment.
4. The hedge on the foreign currency commitment.

Problem 10-4 *(LO 3, 5)* **Hedging foreign currency transactions and commitments.** Medical Distributors, Inc., is a U.S. company that buys and sells used medical equipment throughout the United States and Canada. During the month of June, the company had the following transactions with Canadian parties.

1. Purchased used equipment on June 1 from a hospital located in Toronto for 220,000 Canadian dollars (CA$) payable in 45 days. On the same day, the company paid $1,000 for a call option to buy 220,000 Canadian dollars during July at a strike price of 1 CA$ = $0.726. The option had a fair value of $3,200 on June 30.
2. Sold equipment on June 1 for 300,000 Canadian dollars to be paid in 30 days. At the same time, the company purchased a forward contract to sell the Canadian dollars in 30 days.
3. Committed to buy equipment on June 15 from a Montreal health care provider for 400,000 Canadian dollars in 45 days. At the same time, the company purchased a forward contract to buy 400,000 Canadian dollars in 45 days.
4. Paid 30,000 Canadian dollars on June 20 to refurbish the equipment purchased on June 1.
5. Sold the equipment purchased on June 1 on June 20 for 310,000 Canadian dollars to be received in 30 days.
6. Collected the 300,000 Canadian dollars on June 30 from the sale on June 1.

Selected spot and forward rates are as follows:

	Spot Rate 1 CA$ =	Forward Rate 1 CA$ =
June 1	$0.720	30-day sell rate = $0.729
June 15	0.729	45-day buy rate = $0.731
June 20	0.732	
June 30	0.735	30-day buy rate = $0.737

Required ▶ ▶ ▶ ▶ ▶ Prepare all of the necessary journal entries to record the above activities during the month of June. The time value of forward contracts is excluded from the assessment of hedge effectiveness, and all necessary discounting should be determined using a 6% discount rate.

Problem 10-5 *(LO 3, 5)* **FC bank loan, hedge of forecasted inventory purchase, impact on earnings.** Wagner Corporation transacts business in a number of foreign currencies and had the following activities during the current year. On July 1, the company signed a 60-day, 400,000 foreign currency A (FCA) note with a foreign bank. The note is to be repaid in FCA and bears simple interest at the rate of 7.2%. The company used the proceeds of the note to purchase manufacturing equipment. The equipment will be depreciated by the straight-line method over a useful life of 15 years (salvage value is to be ignored).

On July 15, the company committed to purchase inventory from a foreign vendor with a delivery date of August 31. Payment of 250,000 foreign currency B (FCB) is due on

September 30. In order to limit its exposure on this transaction, on July 15, the company hedged the commitment by acquiring a contract to buy 250,000 FCB for delivery on September 30. Forward rates for a contract to buy FCB on September 30 are as follows:

On July 15	$1.060
On July 31	1.061
On August 31	1.068

On September 1, the company shipped (f.o.b. shipping point) inventory to a foreign customer with payment due on October 15. These items were the inventory that the company ordered on July 15, as discussed above. The sales price was $336,000.

Selected spot rates are as follows:

	1 FCA =	1 FCB =
July 1	$0.62	
July 15		$1.04
July 31	0.66	1.05
August 1	0.65	
August 31	0.64	1.05
September 1		1.06
September 30	0.67	1.07

◀◀◀◀◀ **Required**

1. Prepare a schedule by month that details the effect on net income of the above transactions for the months of July, August, and September. The time value of the forward contracts is excluded from the assessment of hedge effectiveness. Use a 6% discount rate for all necessary discounting.
2. Prepare all necessary entries through the end of July.

Problem 10-6 *(LO 5)* **Comparison of strategies: no hedge, hedge commitment, hedge transaction.** Boyd Enterprises has begun to purchase certain component parts from a foreign vendor. These purchases will be denominated in foreign currency units (FC), and the company is trying to evaluate various alternative methods of paying for the purchases. The company does not expect to order from the foreign vendor more than twice a year and with the following terms:

Commitment (order date)	30 days before delivery
Delivery	f.o.b. destination
Payment date	60 days after receipt

Various alternative methods of payment are as follows:

Option A Do not hedge the exposed liability position.
Option B Hedge the commitment with a forward contract due on payment date.
Option C Hedge the transaction at delivery date versus commitment date.

The company wants to evaluate the options under two alternative assumptions regarding spot and forward rates. The assumptions are as follows:

	Assumption 1	Assumption 2
Spot rate at commitment date	$1.200	$1.20
Spot rate at delivery date	1.224	1.17
Spot rate on payment date	1.289	1.12

(continued)

#
vs Ex 6?
Consider options –
No hedge
Hedge @ 2 alt dates
Diff assmp. re: spot rates

	Assumption 1	Assumption 2
Spot rate 30 days after payment date	$1.320	$1.10
90-day forward rate at commitment date	1.210	1.18
120-day forward rate at commitment date	1.220	1.17
60-day forward rate at delivery date.	1.230	1.19

Required ▶ ▶ ▶ ▶ ▶ Prepare a schedule that shows the effect on net income for each of the payment options, given the assumptions regarding exchange rates. Assume that the average purchase is for 100,000 FC. The time value of the forward contracts is excluded from the assessment of hedge effectiveness.

Problem 10-7 *(LO 5)* **Hedge a commitment to sell.** On February 1, Pettit Corporation committed to sell inventory with a cost of $75,000 to a foreign company for 100,000 FC. Payment for this transaction is to be settled on May 1. In anticipation of this sale, Pettit entered into a 90-day forward contract to sell 100,000 FC on May 1. In assessing the effectiveness of this hedge, Pettit has chosen to exclude the change in the time value of the forward contract from the assessment of hedge effectiveness.

Relevant spot and forward rates are as follows:

	February 1	March 1	April 1	May 1
Spot rate	$0.90	$0.87	$0.85	$0.81
Forward rate	0.91	0.87	0.83	0.81

Required ▶ ▶ ▶ ▶ ▶ Prepare all relevant journal entries to record this commitment and forward contract.

Translation of Foreign Financial Statements

CHAPTER 11

Learning Objectives

When you have completed this chapter, you should be able to

1. **Define the functional currency, and identify factors suggesting the functional currency.**
2. **Explain the objectives of the translation process.**
3. **Apply the functional currency translation process to a trial balance, and calculate the translation adjustment.**
4. **Explain how the translation adjustment is accounted for and how a hedge may be employed.**
5. **Describe the consolidation process and the sophisticated equity method, giving particular attention to modifications due to translation.**
6. **Apply the remeasurement process to a trial balance, and explain how to account for the remeasurement gain or loss.**
7. **Differentiate between the two methods for converting functional currency to the parent/investor's currency, and explain the circumstances under which each should be used.**

The magnitude of U.S. investment abroad has increased significantly in response to a more global economy, a reduction in trade barriers, and the growth of international capital markets. Similarly, these same factors have encouraged an increase in foreign investment in the United States. The size and growth of these investment patterns are suggested by the following statistics.

U.S. Direct Investment Abroad: Position and Balance of Payment Flows
(in millions of dollars)

	1999	2000	2001	2002	2003
Direct investment position* at historical cost	$1,215,960	$1,316,247	$1,460,352	$1,601,441	$1,788,911
Direct investment position at market value	2,839,639	2,694,014	2,314,934	2,039,780	2,730,289
Capital outflows (inflows):					
Equity capital	$ 98,929	$ 78,041	$ 60,942	$ 24,558	$ 24,595
Reinvested earnings	48,708	77,018	52,307	74,973	119,192
Intercompany debt	61,756	(12,341)	11,624	15,809	8,096
Total	$ 209,393	$ 142,718	$ 124,873	$ 115,340	$ 151,883
Income**	$ 114,348	$ 133,692	$ 110,029	$ 126,694	$ 164,712

*Direct investment position is the value of U.S. direct investors' equity in, and net outstanding loans to, their foreign affiliates. The equity includes reinvested earnings.

**Income is the return on the direct investment position abroad. It consists of the parent's share of the foreign affiliates net income and the net interest received by the parent on outstanding debt with the affiliate.

Source: U.S. Department of Commerce—Bureau of Economic Analysis.

The previous chapter identified a variety of transactions that may occur between a domestic (U.S.) company and a foreign entity. These transactions were not dependent on the domestic company's having any type of ownership interest in the foreign entity. However, as the preceding statistics suggest, many domestic companies do have an ownership interest in or control of foreign companies, and accounting for these interests presents special problems. The accounting treatments of domestic and foreign entity relationships that involve some degree of control are summarized as follows.

Domestic Entity	Foreign Entity	Accounting Treatment
Home office	Branch	Branch accounting
Parent	Subsidiary	Consolidated financial statements or separate financial statements
Investor	Investee	Investment in foreign entity at market or equity

The above relationships suggest the need to combine or consolidate the foreign entity financial statements with those of the domestic entity. The financial statements of a foreign entity typically are measured in the currency of that foreign country. This currency usually is different from the reporting currency of the domestic entity. Therefore, a methodology must be developed to express the foreign entity's financial statements in the reporting currency of the domestic entity. The process of expressing amounts denominated or measured in foreign currencies into amounts measured in the reporting currency (dollars) of the domestic entity (U.S.) is referred to as *foreign currency translation*.

In addition to establishing a methodology for translation, the process is complicated by the reality that the foreign financial statements may have been prepared using accounting principles that are different from those of the domestic reporting entity. As discussed in Chapter 9, there are a number of differences between generally accepted accounting principles (GAAP) employed in the United States and principles employed in financial statements of certain foreign entities. Therefore, prior to translation, the statements of a foreign entity must be adjusted to reflect the principles (GAAP) employed by the domestic reporting entity. For example, a foreign subsidiary may not be required to capitalize leases although the lease would be capitalized if GAAP followed by the parent company were employed. Before proceeding with translation, the accounting for these leases must be adjusted to conform with the principles employed by the reporting entity.The international efforts to harmonize accounting principles are eliminating the need for such adjustments.

STATEMENT OF FINANCIAL ACCOUNTING STANDARDS NO. 52

1

OBJECTIVE

Define the functional currency, and identify factors suggesting the functional currency.

In late 1981, after considering two Exposure Drafts, the FASB issued Statement of Financial Accounting Standards No. 52, *Foreign Currency Translation*. FASB Statement No. 52 adopted a *functional currency* approach which focuses on whether the domestic reporting entity's cash flows will be indirectly or directly affected by changes in the exchange rates of the foreign entity's currency. Assume a foreign entity operates exclusively in its own country using only its currency (see Illustration 11-1a). It is questionable whether changes in the exchange rate between its currency and that of the parent entity would directly affect the parent's cash flows. After all, how could changes in the rate of exchange between the foreign currency and the dollar affect you if your transactions were primarily denominated in the foreign currency? However, if a foreign entity operates or functions in a currency other than its own currency, exchange rate changes between these currencies presumably will directly affect cash flows of the foreign entity and ultimately the cash flows of the parent (see Illustration 11-1b). For example, if the foreign subsidiary has to convert one foreign currency into another type of foreign currency (FC-A) in order to pay a foreign supplier, this additional use of cash will ultimately affect cash flows of the parent. If the foreign subsidiary has less cash, then the parent would, in turn, expect to receive less cash from its investment in the subsidiary. In this instance, the resulting effect should be the same as if transactions were denominated in a foreign currency.

Illustration 11-1a—Exchange Rate Changes Do Not Affect Parent

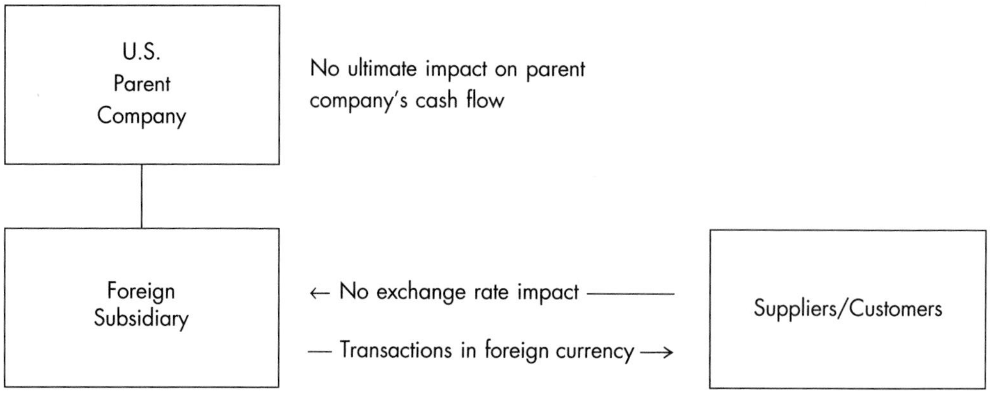

Illustration 11-1b—Exchange Rate Changes Affect Parent

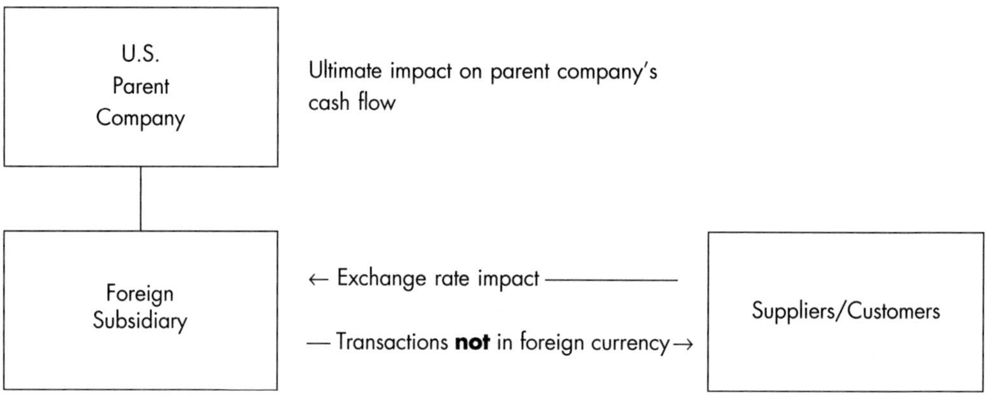

Functional Currency Identification

In order to achieve the objectives of the translation process, it is critical to identify the foreign entity's functional currency. The functional currency is the currency of the primary economic environment in which the entity generates and expends cash. For example, assume a French company that is a subsidiary of a U.S. company purchases labor and materials and pays for these items with euros (see Illustration 11-2a). The finished product of the company is sold, and payment is received in euros. In this situation, changes in the exchange rate between the euro and the dollar of the U.S. parent do not generally have an economic impact on the French company or its U.S. parent. Because of this, the French company's day-to-day operations are not dependent on the economic environment of the U.S. parent's currency (dollars). Therefore, the euro would be considered the functional currency of the French company.

The functional currency of an entity is not always that of its own country. Assume the French company discussed above received most of its debt capital in the form of dollars from an American bank and that its products were sold primarily in the United States with payment being received in dollars (see Illustration 11-2b). In this case, changes in the exchange rate between the euro and the dollar would have an impact on the French company's cash flows and ultimately those of the parent. The French company's day-to-day operations are dependent on the economic environment of the U.S. parent's currency (dollars). Changes in the foreign entity's assets and liabilities will, or will have the potential to, immediately impact the cash flows of the U.S. parent. In this case, the functional currency is that of the parent (U.S. dollars). It is important to note that a foreign entity may have a functional currency which is not its domestic currency or that of the parent entity. Thus, the French company could have the Japanese yen as its functional currency, rather than the euro or the dollar, if the yen is the currency that primarily influences the company's cash flows (see Illustration 11-2c). This might be the case if the French company's financing, sales, and purchases of goods and services are denominated in yen.

Illustration 11-2a—Foreign Subsidiary Functions in Its Own Currency (euros)

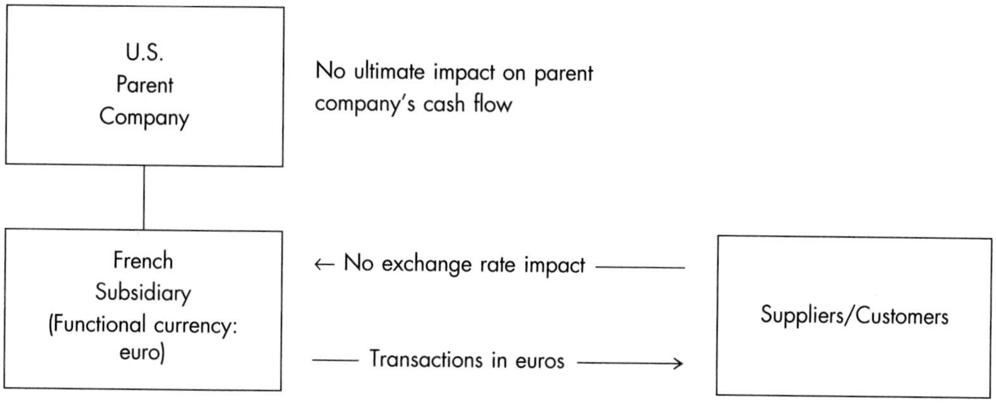

Illustration 11-2b—Foreign Subsidiary Functions in Parent's Currency (U.S. dollars)

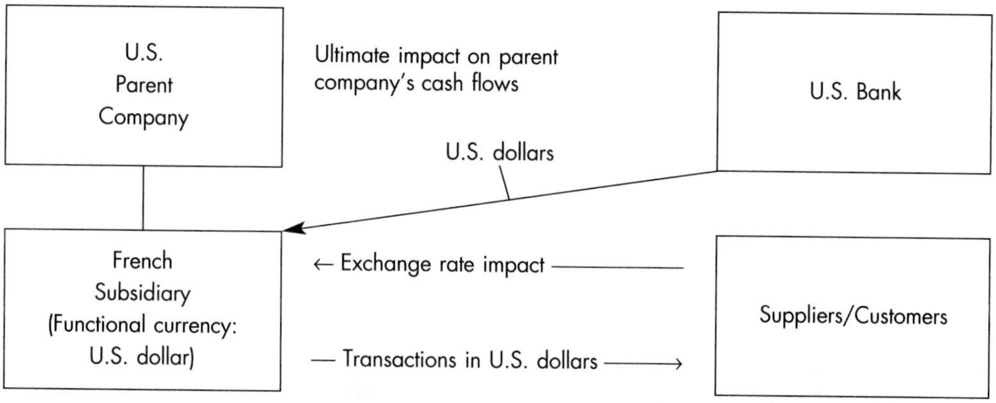

Illustration 11-2c—Foreign Subsidiary Functions in Currency Other than Its Own or Parent's (Japanese yen)

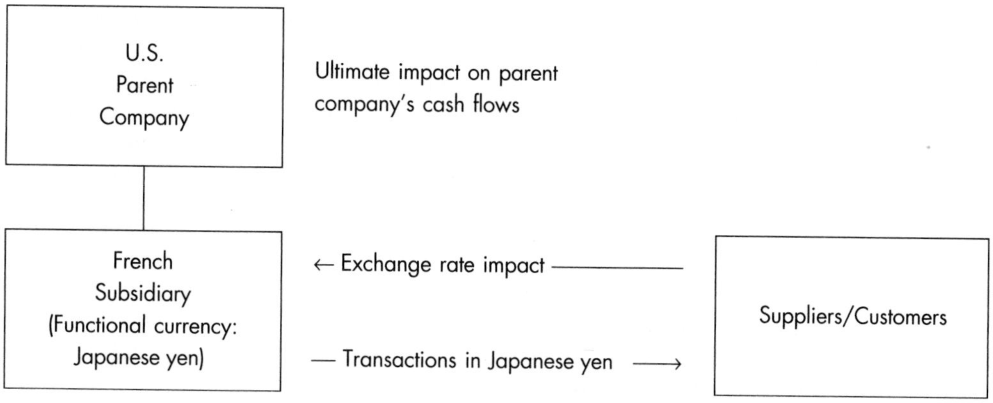

Identification of the functional currency is not subject to definitive criteria. However, certain basic economic factors should be considered in making this identification.[1] Some of these factors are summarized in Exhibit 11-1.

Exhibit 11-1
Factors Suggesting the Functional Currency

Indicator	Foreign Entity's Currency Is the Functional Currency	Parent's Currency Is the Functional Currency
Cash flows	Cash flows are primarily in the currency of the foreign entity. Such flows do not impact the parent's cash flows	Cash flows directly impact the parent's cash flows and are readily available to the parent.
Sales price	Sales prices are influenced by local factors rather than exchange rates.	Sales prices are influenced by international factors and exchange rate changes.
Sales market	There is an active and primarily local market.	The sales market is primarily in the parent's country.
Expenses	Goods and services are acquired locally and denominated in local currencies.	Goods and services are acquired from the parent's country.
Financing	Financing is secured locally and denominated in local currencies. Debt is serviced through local operations.	Financing is secured primarily from the parent or is denominated in the parent's currency.
Intercompany transaction and arrangements	Intercompany transaction volume is low. Major interrelationships between foreign and parent operations do not exist.	Intercompany transaction volume is high. There are major interrelationships between entities. A foreign entity holds major assets and obligations of the parent.

These factors should be considered both individually and collectively in order to identify the functional currency. The selection of a functional currency should be applied consistently over time, unless significant changes suggest that the functional currency has changed. Changes should not be accounted for on a retroactive basis or as a cumulative effect.

Although these factors focus on the parent's currency as a possible functional currency, remember that the functional currency may be one other than that of the foreign entity or the parent.

2

OBJECTIVE

Explain the objectives of the translation process.

Objectives of the Translation Process

The focus of FASB Statement No. 52 is critical to achieving the objectives of translation. The compatibility resulting from translating various financial statements into a common reporting currency is a practical necessity. However, this process should not alter the significance of the results and relationships experienced by the individual consolidated entity. Consistent with this underlying concern, the translation process should accomplish the following objectives. The first objective is explained in this section. The second objective is explained later in the chapter.

1. Provide information that is generally compatible with the expected economic effects of a rate change on an enterprise's cash flows and equity.

1 Statement of Financial Accounting Standards No. 52, *Foreign Currency Translation* (Stamford: Financial Accounting Standards Board, 1981), par. 42.

2. Reflect in consolidated statements the financial results and relationships of the individual consolidated entities as measured in their functional currencies in conformity with U.S. generally accepted accounting principles.[2]

The first objective recognizes that exchange rate changes may or may not have any substantial or direct effect on the cash flows and economic well-being of the related entities. If the foreign entity conducts business in its own currency, exchange rate changes relative to the parent would not affect the cash flow or economic well-being of the foreign entity. Thus, translation should not impact reported income. For example, assume that a foreign subsidiary borrows 1,000 foreign currencies (FC) from a bank in order to purchase a tract of land for 1,000 FC when the rate of exchange is 1 FC = $1 (see Illustration 11-3a). If the land were to be sold for 1,000 FC when the rate of exchange is 1 FC = $0.80, 1,000 FC would be available to repay the loan. Neither the foreign entity's nor the parent's cash flows, or their economic well-being, would have been adversely affected by the change in exchange rates.

However, if the foreign entity conducts business primarily in another currency (i.e., the parent's), changes in the exchange rate would affect the cash flow or economic well-being of the foreign entity. Therefore, the effect of translation should be included in reported income. To illustrate, assume the same facts as in the above example except that the funds necessary to purchase the land were borrowed from a U.S. bank in dollars and then converted to FC with ultimate repayment of the loan due in dollars (see Illustration 11-3b). If the land were to be sold for 1,000 FC and the proceeds converted to U.S. dollars when 1 FC = $0.80, only $800 would be available to repay the loan. The French subsidiary would then need to use more cash in order to pay off the remaining $200 of debt. This would have a negative impact on the cash flows of the subsidiary and ultimately on those of the U.S. parent. Therefore, the change in exchange rates would have an effect on both the potential cash flows available to the parent and the parent's economic well-being. This adverse effect of the exchange rate changes should be reflected in the current-period net income.

Illustration 11-3a—Exchange Rate Changes Do Not Impact Enterprise's Cash Flows and Equity

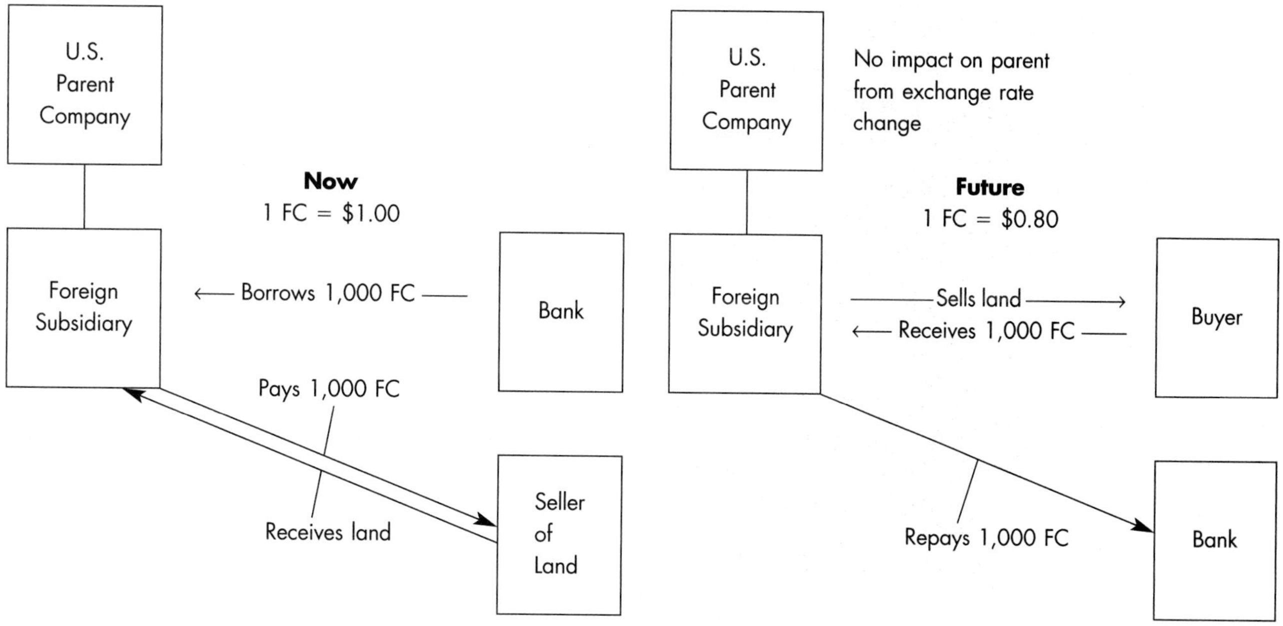

Note: Parent's net cash flow is not affected, so parent's economic well-being is not affected.

2 *Ibid.*, par. 4.

Illustration 11-3b—Exchange Rate Changes Do Impact Enterprise's Cash Flows and Equity

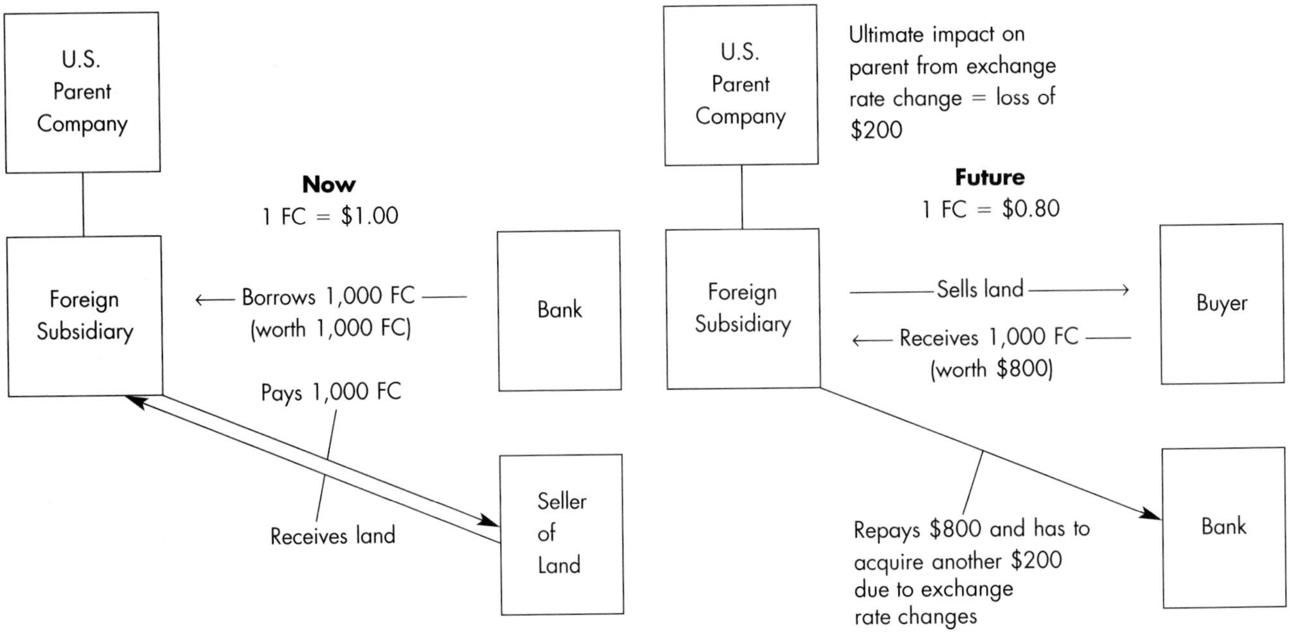

Note: Parent's net cash flow is adversely affected, so parent's economic well-being is affected.

The expected economic effects of rate changes must be properly reflected in financial statements and may be analyzed as follows:

Expected Economic Effect of Rate Changes	Accounting Response to Effect of Rate Changes
Cash inflows increase, and/or cash outflows decrease. Economic well-being is affected.	Translation gains should be included in net income.
Cash inflows decrease, and/or cash outflows increase. Economic well-being is affected.	Translation losses should be included in net income.
Cash inflows and/or outflows are not affected. Economic well-being is not affected.	No translation gain or loss should be included in net income. The effect of rate changes will not be realized until the parent's investment in the foreign entity is disposed of or liquidated. Therefore, the effect of translation does not affect current net income and is shown as a separate component of other comprehensive income.

Expected Economic Effects of Rate Changes when the Functional Currency Is Not the Foreign Currency. The first objective of translation seeks to provide accounting information that is consistent or compatible with the expected economic effects of rate changes. This objective is satisfied by focusing on the functional currency and may be demonstrated by consideration of the following example. Assume that a foreign subsidiary is formed on January 1, Year 1, when the rate of exchange is 1 foreign currency (FC) = $1.50. At the date of formation, the subsidiary

1. Received a $30,000 equity investment in dollars from the parent company's sale of stock;
2. Received a $120,000 loan in dollars from a U.S. bank; and
3. Purchased a parcel of land for 100,000 FC payable in dollars.

At the end of Year 1 when the rate of exchange is 1 FC = $2.00, the parcel of land is sold for 100,000 FC collectible in dollars. Shortly thereafter, dollars will be remitted to the U.S. bank and the parent.

When evaluating the factors used to identify the functional currency, it would appear that the dollar, not the foreign currency, is the functional currency, because financing is denominated in dollars, acquisitions of goods and services are paid for in dollars, and sales are receivable in dollars. Furthermore, the substance of these transactions suggests that the foreign subsidiary is merely a conduit through which the U.S. parent conducts business and experiences dollar cash flows. Therefore, if the translation process is sound, it should provide information that is compatible with the expected economic effects of rate changes. In this particular example, the translated dollar amounts for the subsidiary should be identical to the dollar balances that would have resulted had the U.S. parent engaged in these transactions without the foreign subsidiary serving as a conduit. In that case, entries in column A would have been appropriate.

Entries if the parent records the transactions—measured in U.S. dollars are as follows:

		Column A	
Jan. 1	Cash	150,000	
	Owners' Equity		30,000
	Loans Payable		120,000
	To record receipt of $30,000 from stock sale and $120,000 from loan proceeds.		
	Land	150,000	
	Cash		150,000
	To record purchase of land (100,000 × $1.50 direct rate).		
Dec. 31	Cash	200,000	
	Land		150,000
	Gain on Sale		50,000
	To record sale of land (100,000 × $2.00 direct rate).		

Resulting financial statements at year-end—measured in U.S. dollars are as follows:

Balance Sheet

Cash	$200,000
Loan payable	$120,000
Owners' equity:	
Original amount	30,000
Net income	50,000
	$200,000

Income Statement

Gain on sale	$50,000

Ratios

Debt-to-equity	1.50 to 1	(120/80)
Current ratio*	1.67 to 1	(200/120)
Return on equity	167%	(50/30)

*Assumes loan is a current liability.

If the U.S. parent engaged in the transactions through a foreign subsidiary, the entries in column B would be appropriate.

Entries if the foreign subsidiary records the transactions—measured in FC are as follows:

		Column B	
Jan. 1	Cash	100,000	
	Owners' Equity		20,000
	Loans Payable		80,000
	To record receipt of $30,000 equity investment ($30,000 ÷ 1.5) and $120,000 loan ($120,000 ÷ 1.5) when the exchange rate was 1FC = $1.50.		
	Land	100,000	
	Cash		100,000
	To record purchase of land for 100,000 FC.		
Dec. 31	Loan Payable	20,000	
	Exchange Gain on Loan		20,000
	To adjust $120,000 loan payable, which is denominated in dollars, to an equivalent amount of FC due to change in rate from 1 FC = $1.50 to 1 FC = $2.00 [($120,000 ÷ 2.0) – ($120,000 ÷ 1.5)].		
	Cash	100,000	
	Land		100,000
	To record sale of land for 100,000 FC.		

Resulting financial statements at year-end—measured in FC and translated into U.S. dollars are as follows:

Balance Sheet

	Foreign Currency	Relevant Exchange Rate	U.S. Dollars
Cash	100,000 FC	2.00	$200,000
Loan payable	60,000 FC	2.00	$120,000
Owners' equity:			
Original amount	20,000	1.50	30,000
Net income	20,000	(see below)	50,000
	100,000 FC		$200,000

Income Statement

	Foreign Currency	Relevant Exchange Rate	U.S. Dollars
Exchange gain on loan	20,000 FC	2.00	$ 40,000
Translation adjustment		**(to balance)**	**10,000**
	20,000 FC		$ 50,000

Ratios

Debt-to-equity	1.50 to 1	(60/40)	1.50 to 1	(120/80)
Current ratio	1.67 to 1	(100/60)	1.67 to 1	(200/120)
Return on equity	100%	(20/20)	167%	(50/30)

The goal of translating the FC statements was to produce identical values to those that would have resulted if the U.S. parent had engaged in the same transactions. A comparison of the above financial statements compared to those that would have resulted had the U.S. parent recorded the transactions reveals that the values are identical. The relevant exchange rates necessary to accomplish this goal are dependent upon a proper identification of the functional currency. The first objective of the translation process has been satisfied, and the results confirm the following:

1. The foreign subsidiary merely acted as a conduit through which the U.S. parent operated.
2. The foreign subsidiary's translated financial statements are identical to those statements that would have resulted had the transactions been originally recorded in the dollar functional currency.
3. The transactions of the foreign entity had an immediate or potentially immediate impact on the dollar cash flows and equity; therefore, the impact was included in net income.

If the proceeds from the sale of the land were subsequently remitted to the U.S. bank and the parent, the proceeds of 100,000 FC collectible in dollars would result in $200,000 being available. The U.S. bank would receive $120,000 (ignoring interest for purposes of discussion). The remaining $80,000 would be distributed to the parent, which is $50,000 more than its original investment of $30,000. Therefore, the exchange rate change did have a potentially immediate effect on the cash flows and economic well-being of the parent and should be included in net income of the period in which exchange rates change. (This example parallels the one in Illustration 11-2b on page 663). Furthermore, if the rate had not changed, the proceeds of 100,000 FC collectible in dollars would have resulted in $150,000 (the rate remains at 1 FC = $1.50), of which $120,000 would have been remitted to the U.S. bank. The remaining $30,000 is the same as the parent's original investment, and clearly the absence of an exchange rate change had no effect on the parent's potentially immediate cash flows and/or economic well-being.

Expected Economic Effects of Rate Changes when the Functional Currency Is the Foreign Currency. If the foreign currency (FC) is the functional currency, rate changes are not expected to have an immediate impact on the parent's cash flows (as shown in Illustration 11-3a on page 665. Therefore, in response to rate changes, the accounting information should not include any translation adjustment in the determination of current net income. Instead, translation adjustments should be classified as a separate component of other comprehensive income. This component would be recognized as a component of net income when realized through the liquidation or disposition of the foreign entity. In order to demonstrate these concepts, consider the following example.

Assume a foreign subsidiary is formed on January 1, Year 1, when the rate of exchange is 1 FC = $1.50. At the date of formation, the subsidiary

1. Received 20,000 FC from the U.S. parent;
2. Received an 80,000 FC loan from a local bank; and
3. Purchased a parcel of land from a local party for 100,000 FC.

At the end of Year 1 when the rate of exchange is 1 FC = $2.00, the parcel of land is sold to a local party for 100,000 FC.

When evaluating the factors used to identify a functional currency, it would appear that the FC is the functional currency because financing is denominated in FC, acquisitions of goods and services are paid for in FC, and sales prices are based on local economics and are collected in FC. Furthermore, the substance of these transactions suggests that the foreign subsidiary operates independently of the U.S. parent, and its day-to-day operations are not dependent on the economic environment of the U.S. parent's currency but on that of the foreign country. Consider the following analysis of the foreign entity's activities.

Entries if the foreign subsidiary records the transactions—measured in FC are as follows:

Jan. 1	Cash	100,000	
	Owners' Equity		20,000
	Loans Payable		80,000
	To record receipt of 20,000 FC from equity investment and 80,000 FC from loan proceeds.		
	Land	100,000	
	Cash		100,000
	To record purchase of land for 100,000 FC.		
Dec. 31	Cash	100,000	
	Land		100,000
	To record sale of land for 100,000 FC.		

Resulting financial statements at year-end—measured in FC and translated into U.S. dollars (using the functional method) are as follows:

Balance Sheet

	Foreign Currency	Relevant Exchange Rate	U.S. Dollars
Cash	100,000 FC	2.00	$200,000
Loan payable	80,000 FC	2.00	$160,000
Owners' equity			
Original amount	20,000	1.50	30,000
Net income	0		0
Translation adjustment—other comprehensive income		**(to balance)**	10,000
	100,000 FC		$200,000

Ratios

Debt-to-equity	4.00 to 1	(80/20)	4.00 to 1	(160/40)
Current ratio	1.25 to 1	(100/80)	1.25 to 1	(200/160)
Return on equity	0%	(0/20)	0%	(0/30)

In comparing the results of the above example to that of the prior example, where the foreign entity was merely a conduit and the functional currency was the dollar, several important differences surface:

- The exchange rate change required an adjustment to the loan payable when the dollar was the functional currency but not when the foreign currency was the functional currency.
- When the FC is the functional currency, changes in the exchange rate did not produce a gain with respect to the loan because the loan is denominated in FC and rate changes have no impact on the settlement value of the loan.

- There is no indication that the exchange rate changes will immediately impact the parent's cash flows or equity. Therefore, to include the translation adjustment as a component of net income would not be compatible with the economic effects of the rate change. It is quite likely that the foreign entity will redeploy available cash by buying more goods and services and/or by repaying the loan. In either case, cash flows are not being remitted to the parent. Because the impact on the parent's cash flows is unclear, the translation adjustment is included as a separate component of other comprehensive income rather than as net income.

It is important to note that the translation adjustment amount may be temporary and, in fact, either increase or decrease over time. For example, if the trial balance of the subsidiary at the end of Year 2 is the same as it was at the end of Year 1 and the rate of exchange returns to 1 FC = $1.50, then the balance of the cumulative translation adjustment will be zero. However, if the exchange rate increases to 1 FC = $2.20, the balance of the cumulative translation adjustment will increase.

If there is a balance in the cumulative translation adjustment included as a component of other comprehensive income, its impact on the parent's cash flows and/or economic well-being is normally not considered to be immediate or potentially immediate unless the parent liquidates or disposes of its investment in the foreign subsidiary. At that time, the separate component of other comprehensive income should be transferred to the income statement and recognized as a component of net income. To illustrate, assume that in the above example the foreign subsidiary is liquidated after having sold the land. Keeping in mind that the FC is the functional currency, 80,000 FC of cash would be used to repay the loan (ignoring interest for purposes of discussion), and this would leave 20,000 FC of cash. In the final liquidation transaction, the 20,000 FC of cash is remitted to the parent in exchange for its equity investment. The 20,000 FC received by the parent has a value of $40,000 (assuming the exchange rate remains at 1 FC = $2.00). When compared to the historical basis of the parent's original $30,000 investment in the equity of the subsidiary, the current equity of $40,000 represents a $10,000 realized gain which may now be recognized in net income.

As a second objective of the translation process, the FASB stated that the translation process should produce (consolidated) financial statements that reflect the financial results and relationships of the individual entities as measured in their functional currency. In both of the above examples, this objective was evident by the following ratio analysis:

	First Example: U.S. Dollar = Functional Currency			Second Example: FC = Functional Currency	
	If Parent Records Statements in U.S. Dollars	If Subsidiary Records Statements in FC	Translated Statements	Statements in FC	Translated Statements
Debt-to-equity	1.50 to 1	1.50 to 1	1.50 to 1	4.00 to 1	4.00 to 1
Current ratio*	1.67 to 1	1.67 to 1	1.67 to 1	1.25 to 1	1.25 to 1
Return on equity	167%	100%	167%	0%	0%

*Assumes loan is a current liability.

The above illustrations emphasize the importance of properly identifying the functional currency. The expected economic effects of rate changes vary, and the foreign subsidiary's financial statements differ significantly, depending upon the identification of the functional currency. The translation process set forth by the FASB achieves its objectives when the functional currency is properly identified.

Relative to a parent/subsidiary relationship, a summary of the critical implications associated with the identification of the functional currency is as follows:

	When the Functional Currency	
	Is Not the Foreign Currency	Is the Foreign Currency
Nature of the subsidiary entity.	Operates as a conduit through which transactions occur in the parent's functional currency.	Operates as an independent entity through which transactions occur in the subsidiary's functional currency.
Exchange rate changes.	Affect the economic well-being of the parent.	Do not affect the economic well-being of the parent.
Effect of exchange rate changes on net income.	The effect is a gain or loss which is recognized as a component of net income.	The effect is not currently recognized as a component of net income but rather as a component of other comprehensive income.
Effect of exchange rate changes on the parent's cash flows.	Changes have an immediate or potentially immediate impact on cash flows.	Changes do not have an immediate or potentially immediate impact on cash flows. The impact on cash flows is currently unclear.
Financial relationships between accounts.	Relationships subsequent to translation are different than they were prior to translation, therefore reflecting the economic effect of exchange rate changes.	Relationships subsequent to translation retain the same values as they had prior to translation. Exchange rate changes do not have an economic effect on the parent.

Adoption of a translation method that fails to properly reflect the economic effects of rate changes may produce misleading results. Prior to FASB Statement No. 52, financial statements were subject to the major criticism that they resulted in the recognition of major translation gains and losses that distorted earnings and had no effect on cash flows. The functional currency approach adopted in FASB Statement No. 52 does not remeasure foreign operations as though they originally had been conducted in the domestic reporting currency. Rather, this approach retains the financial results and relationships that were influenced by the economic environment in which the foreign entity operates.

REFLECTION

- The functional currency is the primary currency in which an entity experiences cash inflows and outflows. Evaluating cash flows, marketing practices, financing arrangements, and procurement of necessary factors of production may identify this currency.
- Given a functional currency, the objectives of translation are to provide information that is reflective of the economic effects of exchange rate changes. Translation should also reflect the financial results and relationships of entities consistent with their functional currency and U.S. GAAP.

3

OBJECTIVE

Apply the functional currency translation process to a trial balance, and calculate the translation adjustment.

BASIC TRANSLATION PROCESS: FUNCTIONAL CURRENCY TO REPORTING CURRENCY

Before beginning the translation process, **the financial statements of the foreign entity must be adjusted to conform with generally accepted accounting principles.** Although this is a very important step in the accounting process, the specifics are not covered in this text. It is assumed that all of the adjustments to GAAP have already been made. The next step in the translation process is to identify the functional currency of the foreign entity.

- If the functional currency is determined to be the foreign entity's local currency, the *current rate method* is used to translate. This is also called the *functional* or *translation method.*

- If the foreign entity's local currency is not the functional currency, the *historical rate method* is used to translate. This is also called the *temporal* or *remeasurement method.*

If the foreign entity's currency is the functional currency, then the current rate method would be used for translation. The **current rate/functional method requires** that:

1. All assets and liabilities are translated at the current exchange rate at the date of translation.
2. Elements of income are translated at the current exchange rates that existed at the time the revenues and expense were recognized. As a practical consideration, income elements normally are translated at a weighted-average exchange rate for the period.
3. Equity accounts other than retained earnings are translated at the historical exchange rate on the date of investment in the subsidiary.
4. Retained earnings are translated in layers:
   a. Retained earnings that exist on the date of investment are translated at the historical rate on the date of investment.
   b. Income additions to retained earnings since the initial acquisition are included as translated in item (2).
   c. Reductions for dividends are translated at the historical exchange rates at the date of declaration.
5. Components of the statement of cash flows are translated at the exchange rates in effect at the time of the cash flows. Operations are translated at the rate used for income elements [see item (2) above]. The reconciliation of the change in cash and cash equivalents during the period should include the effect of exchange rate changes on cash balances.

If the foreign entity's currency is not the functional currency, then the historical rate method is used for translation. The **historical rate/temporal method requires** that:

1. Monetary assets and all liabilities are translated at the current exchange rate at the date of translation. All other assets are translated at the historical exchange rate on the date the assets were acquired. (Use the historical rate on the date of the investment if assets were acquired before the investment was made in the foreign entity.)
2. Elements of income are translated at the weighted-average exchange rate for the period except for items that can be specifically identified with a date of acquisition. For example, use the historical rate on the date inventory and fixed assets were acquired for translating cost of goods sold and depreciation expense, respectively.
3. Equity accounts are translated as they were for the current method.
   a. Equity and retained earnings balances on the date of investment are translated at the historical exchange rate on that date.
   b. Income additions to retained earnings are included as translated in item (2).
   c. Dividend deductions to retained earnings are translated at the historical exchange rates at the date of declaration.

The basic translation process is applied to a foreign subsidiary's trial balance prior to its inclusion in consolidated financial statements, home and branch combined statements, or the computation of equity income for influential foreign investments.

With respect to consolidated financial statements, recall that one of the primary criteria to determine if consolidation is appropriate deals with the extent of control the parent entity exercises over the subsidiary. For foreign subsidiaries, effective control is determined, in part, by currency restrictions and the possibility of nationalization of the operations by foreign governments. Assuming consolidation is appropriate, the financial statements of the foreign entity must be translated into dollars according to the principles expressed in FASB Statement No. 52. Then intercompany eliminations are made, and the statements are consolidated according to the principles of consolidation discussed earlier in this text.

Demonstrating the Current Rate/Functional Method

Illustration 11-4 demonstrates the translation of a subsidiary's financial statements for the purpose of preparing consolidated financial statements and is based on the following facts:

1. Sori Corporation began operations on January 1, 20X0. On January 1, 20X1, when net assets totaled 100,000 foreign currency units (FC), 90% of Sori stock was acquired by Pome Corporation. Sori's functional currency is the foreign currency, and it maintains its records in the functional currency.
2. Sales to Pome are billed in the foreign currency, and all receivables from Pome have been collected except for the amount shown in the account Due from Pome. All other sales are billed in the foreign currency as well. The level of sales and purchases was constant over the year. None of the inventory purchased from Sori remains in Pome's ending inventory.
3. Selected exchange rates between the functional currency and the dollar are as follows:

Date	Rate
January 1, 20X0	1 FC = $0.98
January 1, 20X1	1 FC = 1.00
December 31, 20X1	1 FC = 1.05
20X1 average	1 FC = 1.03

Illustration 11-4
Sori Corporation
Trial Balance Translation
December 31, 20X1

Account	Balance in Functional Currency	Relevant Exchange Rate (Dollars/FC)	Balance in Dollars
Cash	10,000 FC	1.05	$ 10,500
Accounts Receivable	21,000	1.05	22,050
Allowance for Doubtful Accounts	(1,000)	1.05	(1,050)
Due from Pome	14,000	1.05	14,700
Inventory (at Market, Cost = 32,000)	30,000	1.05	31,500
Prepaid Insurance	3,000	1.05	3,150
Land	18,000	1.05	18,900
Depreciable Assets	120,000	1.05	126,000
Accumulated Depreciation	(15,000)	1.05	(15,750)
Cost of Goods Sold	180,000	1.03	185,400
Depreciation Expense	10,000	1.03	10,300
Income Tax Expense	30,000	1.03	30,900
Other Expenses	23,000	1.03	23,690
Total (Note B)	443,000 FC		$460,290
Accounts Payable	20,000 FC	1.05	$ 21,000
Taxes Payable	30,000	1.05	31,500
Accrued Interest Payable	1,000	1.05	1,050
Mortgage Payable—Land	10,000	1.05	10,500
Common Stock	80,000	1.00	80,000
Retained Earnings (January 1, 20X1)	20,000	Note A	20,000
Sales—Pome	80,000	1.03	82,400

Account	Balance in Functional Currency	Relevant Exchange Rate (Dollars/FC)	Balance in Dollars
Sales—Other....................	200,000	1.03	206,000
Gain on Sale of Depreciable Assets....	2,000	1.03	2,060
Cumulative Translation Adjustment (to balance).......			**5,780**
Total (Note B)...................	443,000 FC		$460,290

Note A: The beginning balance of retained earnings normally is equal to the translated value of the previous period's ending retained earnings. However, since 20X1 is the first year Pome has owned Sori, the beginning balance is set equal to the January 1, 20X1 (acquisition date), balance of retained earnings in foreign currency translated at the January 1, 20X1, spot rate (in this case, 1.00). The balance sheet for 20X1 would show a translated value for retained earnings equal to the translated beginning balance of retained earnings plus the translated value of net income less dividends translated at the rate existing on the declaration date.

Note B: If the accounts in this trial balance were arranged in balance sheet and income statement order, the following totals would be calculated:

Total revenues and gains.................	282,000 FC	$290,460
Total expenses.........................	243,000	250,290
Net income	39,000 FC	$ 40,170
Total assets	200,000 FC	$210,000
Total liabilities	61,000 FC	$ 64,050
Total equity (including NI)	139,000	140,170
Total liabilities and equity (including NI).....	200,000 FC	$204,220
Cumulative translation adjustment to balance.		5,780
Total liabilities and equity (December 31, 20X1)............................	200,000 FC	$210,000

4

OBJECTIVE

Explain how the translation adjustment is accounted for and how a hedge may be employed.

Accounting for the Cumulative Translation Adjustment. Translation adjustments result from the process of translating foreign financial statements *from their functional currency into the domestic entity's reporting currency.* Because various exchange rates (current, historical, and weighted-average) are used in the translation process, the basic equality of the balance sheet equation is not preserved. Therefore, from a mechanical viewpoint, the translation adjustment is an amount necessary to balance a translated entity's trial balance. Translation adjustments do not exist in terms of the functional currency and have no immediate effect on the cash flows of the foreign or domestic entity. At the time of the translation, exchange rate fluctuations do not have an economic impact on the foreign entity or its domestic parent. Furthermore, any potential impact on the reporting (parent) entity is uncertain and remote. Therefore, as discussed above, it would be improper to include the translation adjustment in current reported net income. However, the translation adjustment must be reported somewhere. Rather than being included as a component of reported earnings, the translation should be included as a component of other comprehensive income. It is important to remember that the translation adjustment on the trial balance is a cumulative amount which changes from period to period.

Direct Calculation of the Current Period Translation Adjustment. Although the translation adjustment is a balancing amount necessary to satisfy the balance sheet equation, the current period's (not cumulative) adjustment may be calculated directly as follows:

1. The change in exchange rates during the period multiplied by the amount of net assets (i.e., owners' equity) held by the domestic investor at the beginning of the period; plus
2. The difference between the weighted-average exchange rate used in translating income elements and the end-of-period exchange rate multiplied by the increase or decrease in net assets for the period traceable to net income, excluding capital transactions; plus (minus)

3. The increase (decrease) in net assets as a result of capital transactions, including investments by the domestic investor during the period (e.g., stock issuances, retirements, and dividends), multiplied by the difference between the end-of-period exchange rate and the exchange rate at the time of the transaction.

Based on the information given in Illustration 11-4, the direct calculation of the translation adjustment is as follows:

Reconciliation of Annual Translation Adjustment

Net assets at beginning of period multiplied by the change in exchange rates during the period [0[a] × ($1.05 − $1.00)]	$ 0
Increase in net assets (excluding capital transactions) multiplied by the difference between the current rate and the average rate used to translate income [39,000 FC[b] × ($1.05 − $1.03)]	780
Increase in net assets due to capital transactions (including investments by the domestic investor) multiplied by the difference between the current rate and the rate at the time of the capital transaction [100,000 FC[c] × ($1.05 − $1.00)]	5,000
Translation adjustment	$5,780

[a]Although Sori Corporation began operations in 20X0, the parent company, Pome Corporation, had not acquired an interest until 20X1. Therefore, Pome had no investment in Sori as of the beginning of 20X1.
[b]This is the net income for the period (see Illustration 11-4, Note B on page 674).
[c]This is the original capital balance as of the date of the parent's acquisition.

The above reconciliation is not a required disclosure but may help in understanding the factors which contribute to the translation adjustment. Note that the reconciliation explains only the $5,780 translation adjustment traceable to 20X1. After the first year of operation, the annual translation adjustments will be accumulated and presented as a component of other comprehensive income. For example, if Sori Corporation has a translation adjustment of $4,400 traceable to 20X2, the accumulated other comprehensive income portion of equity on the balance sheet at the end of 20X2 will show a cumulative translation adjustment of $10,180 ($5,780 + $4,400).

Accomplishing the Objectives of Translation. The translation demonstrated in Illustration 11-4 (see page 674) has accomplished the objectives of translation as presented in FASB Statement No. 52. The economic effect of the exchange rate change (i.e., translation adjustment) has been presented as an increase in stockholders' equity. The spot rate had increased from a beginning-of-the-year rate of 1 FC + $1.00 to an end-of-period rate of 1 FC = $1.05. This change indicates that the foreign currency strengthened relative to the dollar. Therefore, the domestic company's investment in the net assets of the foreign subsidiary has increased as evidenced by the increase in stockholders' equity. However, because the foreign entity's currency is the functional currency, exchange rate changes do not have an immediate effect on the cash flows of the foreign or domestic entity. Thus, the translation adjustment is not reported as a component of current net income but rather as a component of other comprehensive income. Therefore, the presentation is compatible with the expected economic effects of exchange rate changes. In addition, the translated financial statements reflect the same financial results and relationships of the foreign company as originally measured in its functional currency. For instance, the following ratios indicate that the original relationships have been preserved after translation.

Ratio	Before Translation	After Translation
Current	1.51 (77,000 ÷ 51,000)	1.51 (80,850 ÷ 53,550)
Debt-to-equity	0.44 (61,000 ÷ 139,000)*	0.44 (64,050 ÷ 145,950)**
Gross profit percent	36% (100,000 ÷ 280,000)	36% (103,000 ÷ 288,400)

*See Illustration 11-4, Note B on page 674.
**After translation equity includes the cumulative translation adjustment ($140,170 + $5,780).

Subsequent Recognition of the Translation Adjustment. Although translation adjustments have no immediate effect on reported earnings, they may ultimately affect income when there is a *partial or complete sale or complete or substantially complete liquidation of the investment in the foreign entity.*[3] Unfortunately, the FASB has not defined what constitutes a substantially complete liquidation. Given such a sale or liquidation, some or all of the accumulated translation adjustment included in equity would be removed and included as part of the gain or loss on disposition of the investment. For example, assume a company owns 100% of a foreign entity, its investment account has a balance of $4,200,000, and its owners' equity includes accumulated other comprehensive income containing a debit of $320,000 representing the accumulated translation adjustment. If the entire investment in the subsidiary is sold for $4,750,000, the translation adjustment does affect the gain on sale as follows:

Proceeds from sale of investment	$ 4,750,000
Basis of investment account	(4,200,000)
	$ 550,000
Balance in cumulative translation adjustment	(320,000)
Gain on sale of investment	$ 230,000

It is important to note that if only a portion of the investment in the subsidiary were sold, then only a pro rata portion of the translation adjustment would have been allocated to the sale.

Consolidating the Foreign Subsidiary

5 OBJECTIVE

Describe the consolidation process and the sophisticated equity method, giving particular attention to modifications due to translation.

Once a foreign subsidiary's financial statements have been translated into the reporting currency, certain eliminations and adjustments due to intercompany transactions generally will be required. With regard to the exchange rate that should be used to translate such transactions, the FASB concluded that **all intercompany balances, except for intercompany profits and losses, should be translated at the rates used for all other accounts. Intercompany profits and losses should be translated using the exchange rate that existed at the date of the sale or transfer.** As a practical matter, however, *average rates or approximations may be used* to translate such profits and losses.

The facts of Illustration 11-4 are used here to demonstrate the consolidation process. Assume Pome Corporation paid 105,000 FC for its 90% interest in Sori Corporation. Recall that at the time of acquisition (January 1, 20X1), Sori equity consisted of 80,000 FC of common stock and 20,000 FC of retained earnings. Upon acquisition of Sori, Pome recorded its investment as follows:

Investment in Sori	105,000	
Cash (105,000 × $1.00)		105,000

Assuming that any excess is traceable to patents with a 10-year useful life, the excess of cost over book value is determined as follows:

Price paid		105,000 FC
Equity purchased:		
Common stock	80,000 FC	
Retained earnings	20,000	
Total	100,000 FC	
90% Interest acquired		90,000
Excess cost traceable to patents		15,000 FC

3 See FASB Interpretation No. 37, *Accounting for Translation Adjustments upon Sale of Part of an Investment in a Foreign Entity* (Norwalk, CT: Financial Accounting Standards Board, 1983) and Statement of Financial Accounting Standards No. 52, *op. cit.*, pars. 110 and 119.

Notice that the determination of excess is calculated in the foreign currency (FC). The excess will be translated into the parent's currency separately. Assume that Pome used the simple equity method to account for its investment in Sori. The following translation would be required to determine the subsidiary income recorded by Pome. Note that under the current rate method the weighted-average exchange rate for the year is used to translate income items.

Account	Balance in Functional Currency	Relevant Exchange Rate (Dollars/FC)	Balance in Dollars
Sales—Pome	80,000 FC	1.03	$ 82,400
Sales—Other	200,000	1.03	206,000
Gain on Sale of Depreciable Assets	2,000	1.03	2,060
Cost of Goods Sold	(180,000)	1.03	(185,400)
Depreciation Expense	(10,000)	1.03	(10,300)
Income Tax Expense	(30,000)	1.03	(30,900)
Other Expenses (including interest)	(23,000)	1.03	(23,690)
Net Income	39,000 FC		$ 40,170
Pome's share			× 90%
Pome's interest in Sori net income (in dollars)			$ 36,153

The parent's entry to record its interest in the foreign subsidiary's undistributed income would be as follows:

Investment in Sori	36,153	
Subsidiary Income		36,153

Worksheet 11-1: page 698

Worksheet 11-1, pages 698 to 699, shows the consolidated financial statements of the Pome and Sori corporations. The trial balance amounts for Pome are assumed, and Sori's balances are based on Illustration 11-4. Entries (CY1) and (EL) in the worksheet follow the usual procedures of eliminating the current-period entry recording the parent's share of the subsidiary net income and its share of the subsidiary equity accounts as of the beginning of the period. Entry **(CT)** allocates 90% of Sori's cumulative adjustment to the controlling interest. These entries do not require any translating because the balances being eliminated have already been translated into U.S. dollars.

Entries (D) and (A) for the distribution of asset markups and their amortizations, however, do require translation. The calculations for entry (D) are as follows:

Distribution of Asset Markup	FC	Exchange Rate	U.S. Dollars
Accounts:			
Depreciable Assets and Patents	15,000	1.05*	$15,750 DR
Investment in Sori Corporation	15,000	1.00**	15,000 CR
Cumulative Translation Adjustment—Pome (to balance)			750 CR

*Use the current exchange rate for asset markup as used in the current rate method for all asset accounts.
**Use the date of investment exchange rate for crediting the investment account because the objective of the entry is to eliminate this balance, and it was initially recorded at a 1.00 exchange rate.

Calculations for entry (A) are as follows:

Amortization of Asset Markups	FC	Exchange Rate	U.S.Dollars
Accounts:			
Accumulated Depreciation and Amortization (15,000/10). . .	1,500	1.05*	$1,575 CR
Depreciation and Amortization Expense.	1,500	1.03**	1,545 DR
Cumulative Translation Adjustment—Pome (to balance).			30 DR

*Use the current exchange rate for accumulated depreciation and amortization as used in the current rate method for all asset accounts.

**Use the weighted-average exchange rate for expenses as used in the current rate method for all income items.

Entries (IA) and (IS) follow the usual worksheet eliminations and adjustments for intercompany transactions and require no additional translation.

The consolidation procedures just discussed also are applicable to periods subsequent to the first year of acquisition. Although the methodology is the same, the following should be noted:

1. The parent must continue to recognize its interest in the amortization of any original excess of cost over book value.
2. Any additional cumulative adjustment traceable to the excess of cost over book value should continue to be recognized.

When consolidating a foreign subsidiary, special attention must be paid to the elimination of intercompany profits. This is true only when the foreign entity's currency is the functional currency. The problem arises because the exchange rates used to translate receivables and payables resulting from intercompany transactions are different from the rates which existed at the date of the intercompany transaction. In order to illustrate this point, assume that a U.S. parent sold inventory to a foreign subsidiary and that none of the inventory had been sold by the subsidiary as of the end of the period. In the consolidation process, it would be appropriate to eliminate the parent's receivable and the subsidiary's corresponding payable. Furthermore, the unrealized intercompany profit on the unsold inventory must also be eliminated. For purposes of discussion, assume that the intercompany transaction is denominated in foreign currencies (FC) in the amount of 1,000 FC and that relevant exchange rates are as follows:

Date of sale	1 FC = $1.00	End of period	1 FC = $1.20

Relevant balances at the end of the period would be as follows:

	Value in FC	Exchange Rate	Value in U.S. Dollars
Parent's Accounts (recorded as in Ch. 10):			
Accounts Receivable	1,000	1.20	$1,200
Sales Revenue	1,000	1.00	1,000
Cost of Sales (assume 80%).			800
Subsidiary's Accounts (translated using current rate method):			
Accounts Payable	1,000	1.20	$1,200
Inventory	1,000	1.20	1,200

It is clear from the preceding schedule of account balances that the dollar values of the parent's accounts receivable and the subsidiary's accounts payable are equal and could be eliminated against each other. However, the problem arises with the elimination of the unrealized intercompany profit included in the ending inventory of the subsidiary. If the profit of 20% were eliminated using the translated value of the inventory, then $240 (20% × $1,200) of profit would be eliminated, which does not agree with the $200 of intercompany profit which actually existed at the date of the transaction. However, if the intercompany profit is eliminated using the rate of exchange which existed at the date of the transaction, no inconsistency exists. At the date of the transaction, the inventory had a dollar equivalent of $1,000 (1,000 FC × $1), and the 20% unrealized profit of $200 (20% × $1,000) would be the appropriate amount of profit to eliminate against the parent's gross profit of $200 (sales revenue of $1,000 versus the cost of sales of $800). Therefore, the exchange rate at the date of the original transaction must *always* be used to determine the amount of unrealized profit to be eliminated. Once again, this complication will be encountered only when translating from the functional currency into the parent's reporting currency.

Gains and Losses Excluded from Income

The other comprehensive income section of equity in which cumulative translation adjustments are reported also should include gains and losses attributable to:

1. Foreign currency transactions that are designated and effective as economic hedges of a net investment in a foreign entity, beginning with the designation date.
2. Intercompany foreign currency transactions that are long-term investments in nature (i.e., settlement is not planned or anticipated in the foreseeable future) when the entities involved in the transaction are consolidated, combined, or accounted for by the equity method in the reporting enterprise's financial statements.[4]

Foreign Currency Transactions as Hedges of a Net Investment in a Foreign Entity. When translating foreign financial statements from their functional currency into dollars, a translation adjustment is produced and classified as a component of other comprehensive income (OCI). Noting that OCI is a component of owners' equity, the translation adjustment has the effect of either increasing or decreasing the parent company's equity as a result of its net investment in the foreign subsidiary. A parent company would certainly want to minimize any adverse impact on equity and may decide to hedge against such impacts. This is referred to as a hedge of a net investment in a foreign entity. Not knowing whether the impact of translation on equity will be positive or negative, some companies hedge net investments as a matter of policy. Such hedges may be accomplished through the use of a nonderivative or derivative instrument. The purpose of the hedging strategy is to offset the negative (positive) effect of the translation adjustment on the net investment with the gain (loss) on the hedging instrument. Such a hedge would be subject to the same criteria and disclosures discussed in Chapter 10.

In order to demonstrate a hedge of a net investment in a foreign entity, recall the facts surrounding Illustration 11-4 and Worksheet 11-1. The facts supporting Illustration 11-4 were based on a parent company (Pome Corporation) acquiring a 90% interest in a subsidiary company (Sori Corporation) when the subsidiary's net equity was 100,000 foreign currency units (FC). Initially not knowing whether the translation adjustment would have a positive or negative impact on equity, assume that the parent company, as a matter of policy, hedged its net investment in the foreign subsidiary. Assume that in order to hedge its investment on January 1, 20X1, the parent company secured a foreign bank loan denominated in the foreign currency when the spot rate was 1 FC = $1.00. The bank loan has a principal amount of 90,000 FC (90% of the subsidiary's equity). Interest calculations are ignored for purposes of this example. The bank loan is designated as a hedge of the net investment and is considered to have satisfied all necessary criteria. Because exchange rates have changed, the value of the hedging instrument has also changed as follows:

Value of loan payable at December 31, 20X1 (90,000 FC × $1.050) . . .	$94,500
Value of loan payable at inception (90,000 FC × $1.000)	90,000
Change in value of loan payable	$ 4,500

4 Statement of Financial Accounting Standards No. 52, *op. cit.*, par. 20.

The entry to record the change in value of the payable is as follows:

Translation Adjustment (OCI) . . .	4,500	
Loan Payable . . .		4,500

Illustration 11-4 presented the translation of a foreign subsidiary's (Sori Corporation) financial statements into dollars. The translation resulted in a current-year translation adjustment of $5,780. The net amount of the translation adjustment that impacts the parent company's (Pome Corporation) other comprehensive income (OCI) is determined as follows based on Worksheet 11-1:

Current-year translation adjustment (from Illustration 11-4) . . .	$5,780
Portion allocated to noncontrolling interest (Worksheet 11-1) . . .	(578)
Subtotal . . .	$5,202
Increase due to distribution of excess and amortization [Worksheet 11-1 entry (D)] . . .	750
Decrease due to amortization of excess [Worksheet 11-1 entry (A)] . . .	(30)
Current-year translation adjustment allocated to parent company . . .	$5,922

The above $5,922 translation adjustment would be shown as a component of the parent's OCI. Offset against this amount would be the $4,500 traceable to the hedge of the net investment. Therefore, the hedge was considered to be effective.

Note that the effectiveness of the hedging instrument (the FC denominated bank loan) against the net investment in the subsidiary is as follows:

Effect on parent's OCI of translation . . .	$5,922 credit
Effect on OCI of hedge on net investment . . .	4,500 debit
Net effect on OCI. . .	$1,422 credit

If the change in the value of the hedging instrument exceeds the related translation adjustment recognized during the period of the hedge, the excess is ineffective and recognized in earnings. In the above example, none of the hedge was ineffective. However, if the hedge had involved a loan for 130,000 FC, the change in the value of the loan payable would have been $6,500 [130,000 FC × ($1.05 − $1.00)] which would have exceeded the related translation adjustment. Therefore, the excess change in value that does not offset the translation adjustment would be recognized in current earnings.

The foreign currency strengthened against the dollar resulting in an increase in equity due to the translation adjustment. In retrospect, the parent should not have hedged its investment even though the hedge was effective in offsetting the effect on OCI of the translation. Once again, we are reminded that exchange rates may not actually change as one had hoped or anticipated.

The above example involved the hedge of a net investment with a nonderivative instrument. However, it is also possible to employ a derivative instrument such as a forward contract and be accorded the same accounting treatment.

Intercompany Foreign Currency Transactions of a Long-Term Nature. The second example of an exchange gain or loss that may be excluded from income and be included as a component of equity relates to certain long-term investment transactions between a domestic company and its foreign subsidiary. For example, assume a U.S. parent borrows funds from a French subsidiary with the loan being denominated in euros. If the settlement of the loan is not planned or anticipated in the foreseeable future, the effect of rate changes on the loan also would not have a foreseeable effect on the income of the U.S. parent. Therefore, the effect of rate changes on long-term investment transactions should be reflected in owners' equity as other comprehensive income, not current net income.

Unconsolidated Investments: Translation for the Cost or Equity Method

Unconsolidated foreign investments are accounted for by either the cost method or the sophisticated equity method. Under the cost method, a complete translation of the foreign financial statements is not necessary. The parent company must record the cost basis of its investment in dollars. If the cost is incurred in foreign currency, the exchange rate at the date of acquisition should be used. Investment income is translated at the exchange rate at the date dividends are declared.

If the parent's interest in the foreign subsidiary is considered influential, the subsidiary will not be consolidated and the sophisticated equity method should be employed. This method requires the adjustment of subsidiary income or loss for the amortization of differences between book and market values of the investment and any intercompany profits or losses. Application of this method to an investment in a foreign entity will be demonstrated using the facts of Illustration 11-4 (see page 674).

Assume Pome Corporation paid 35,000 FC ($35,000) for a 30% interest in Sori Corporation on January 1, 20X1. Furthermore, assuming that any excess is traceable to patents with a 10-year useful life, the excess of cost over book value is determined as follows:

Price paid		35,000 FC
Equity purchased:		
Common stock	80,000 FC	
Retained earnings	20,000	
Total	100,000 FC	
30% Interest acquired		30,000
Excess cost traceable to patents		5,000 FC

Pome's interest in the adjusted net income of Sori is calculated as follows:

Sori net income translated into dollars	$40,170
Pome's share	× 30%
Pome's interest in Sori net income	$12,051
Amortization of excess related to the patents (5,000 FC ÷ 10 years × $1.03 average rate)	(515)
Pome's equity share of Sori net income adjusted for amortization of excess	$11,536

The investor also must recognize its interest in the cumulative translation adjustment for 20X1, calculated as follows:

Cumulative translation adjustment (from Illustration 11-4)	$5,780
Pome's share	× 30%
Pome's interest in the cumulative translation adjustment	$1,734

The following entries are to record Pome's interest in the foreign entity under the sophisticated equity method:

20X1			
Jan. 1	Investment in Sori Corporation	35,000	
	Cash		35,000
	To record the initial investment of 35,000 FC when the spot rate was 1 FC = $ 1.00.		

Dec. 31	Investment in Sori Corporation	13,270	
	Subsidiary Income		11,536
	Cumulative Translation Adjustment		1,734
	To record share of net income adjusted for the amortization of excess and share of cumulative translation adjustment.		

Notice that under the sophisticated equity method the investor recorded both the amortization of the excess of cost over book value and its share of the current year's translation adjustment.

REFLECTION

- If the foreign entity's currency is the functional currency, the current rate method is used and the translation process is as follows: all assets and liabilities are translated at current rates, net income at weighted-average rates, and equity accounts (excluding retained earnings) at historical rates.
- The translation adjustment is classified as a component of other comprehensive income and generally is not recognized in current earnings until there is a sale or liquidation of the foreign subsidiary.
- The net investment in a foreign entity may be hedged and the change in value of the hedging instrument will be recognized as a component of other comprehensive income.
- The consolidation of a parent and a foreign subsidiary involves special adjustments involving the excess over cost and the elimination of intercompany profits. Under the sophisticated equity method, the parent must recognize its proportional interest in the translation adjustment.

REMEASURED FINANCIAL STATEMENTS: FOREIGN CURRENCY TO FUNCTIONAL CURRENCY

6 OBJECTIVE

Apply the remeasurement process to a trial balance, and explain how to account for the remeasurement gain or loss.

The previous illustrations of the translation process assumed that the currency of the foreign entity was the functional currency. However, there are certain instances when the functional currency is not the currency of the foreign entity. In these instances, the financial statements of the foreign entity must be remeasured into the functional currency before the financial statements can be translated into the parent's domestic currency. The remeasurement process is intended to produce financial statements that are the same as if the foreign entity's transactions had been originally recorded in the functional currency. Generally speaking, the remeasurement process is based on the historical rate or *temporal method*. The temporal method was originally adopted by FASB Statement No. 8, which has been superseded by Statement No. 52. In essence, *the historical exchange rates between the functional currency and the foreign currency are used to remeasure certain accounts*. The adjustment resulting from the remeasurement process is referred to as a *remeasurement gain or loss* and is included as a component of net income. The remeasurement process is encountered in two situations. One situation arises when the entity's financial statements are prepared in a currency that is not the functional currency. Another situation arises when the foreign entity is in a highly inflationary economy. In that case, the functional currency is the domestic entity's reporting currency (dollars for U.S. parent companies).

Books of Record Not Maintained in Functional Currency

Perhaps one of the most common situations in which the books of record are not maintained in the functional currency is when the functional currency is the parent/investor's currency. For example, assume that a U.S. company has a Mexican subsidiary. That parent invested dollars in that subsidiary, and dollar-denominated loans were arranged on behalf of the subsidiary. As shown in Illustration 11-5, the Mexican company acquires raw materials from Japanese suppliers that are paid in U.S. dollars and sells the manufactured products throughout Central and North America. The subsidiary's sales are denominated in dollars, and distributions of earnings are remitted to the parent in dollars. Based on the above information, it is clear that the Mexican company's functional currency (FC) is the U.S. dollar even though it maintains its books of record (BR) in Mexican pesos.

Illustration 11-5
Subsidiary Using Parent/Investor's Currency as Functional Currency

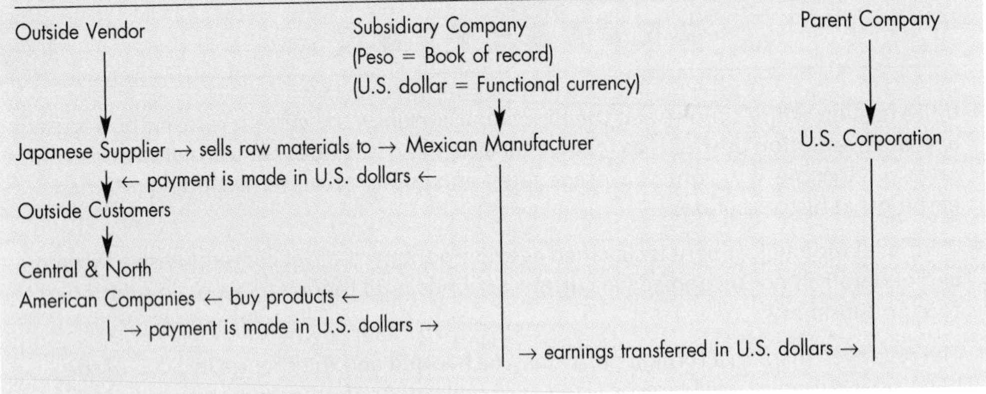

It is also possible that a foreign entity that maintains its books of record in its domestic currency may have a functional currency that is not the parent/investor's currency. For instance, as shown in Illustration 11-6, assume a Mexican subsidiary of an American company purchases materials from Belgian vendors with amounts due payable in euros. The materials are assembled in Mexico and then returned to the Belgium for resale. Sales revenues are collected in euros. Considering the factors used to identify the functional currency, the euro would be the Mexican company's functional currency. However, the Mexican company maintains its books of record (accounting records) in pesos although its functional currency is the euro. In this example, a two-step process is involved. First, the financial statements prepared in pesos would have to be remeasured into euros, the functional currency. Second, the remeasured financial statements would have to be translated into dollars.

Illustration 11-6
Subsidiary Using Functional Currency that Is Not the Parent/Investor's Currency

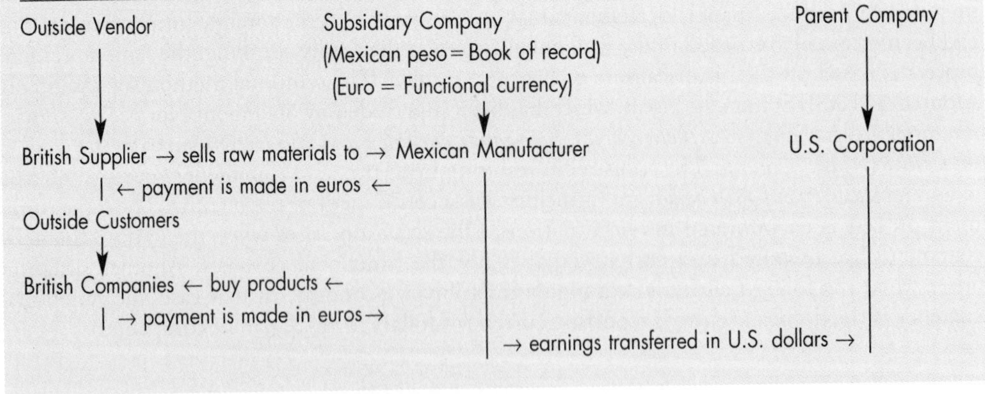

If the books of record are not maintained in the functional currency, a remeasurement process, which differs significantly from the functional currency approach of FASB Statement No. 52, is employed in order to express trial balance amounts in the functional currency.

Furthermore, *the adjustment resulting from the remeasurement is included as a component of net income rather than as a component of other comprehensive income.* It is important to remember that once the trial balance is remeasured into the functional currency, further translation may or may not be necessary. Possible scenarios are as follows:

1. Books of record currency (not U.S. dollars) remeasured to U.S. dollar functional currency. Therefore, no further translation is necessary. This is demonstrated in Illustration 11-7 on pages 686 through 689.
2. Books of record currency (not U.S. currency) remeasured into functional currency (not U.S. dollars). Therefore, further translation is necessary in order to translate the functional currency (not U.S. dollars) into U.S. dollars. This is demonstrated in Illustration 11-8 on pages 690 through 692.

Remeasurement when Functional Currency Is the Same as the Parent/Investor's Currency

7

OBJECTIVE

Differentiate between the two methods for converting functional currency to the parent/investor's currency, and explain the circumstances under which each should be used.

Illustration 11-7 demonstrates the remeasurement process and is based on the same facts as Illustration 11-4 (see page 674) with the following additional information:

1. The U.S. dollar, rather than the books of record (BR), is determined to be the functional currency.
2. Inventory is recorded at its market value of 30,000 FC even though its historical cost is 32,000 FC. The historical cost of sales is based on the FIFO method of costing. Ending inventory consists of the following:

    10,000 FC acquired October 1, 20X1
    22,000 FC acquired November 1, 20X1

3. The prepaid insurance represents amounts that were incurred on October 1, 20X1.
4. The depreciable assets, with 10-year lives, were acquired as follows:

    80,000 FC acquired on January 1, 20X0*
    60,000 FC acquired on July 1, 20X1

    *20,000 FC of these assets were sold on July 1, 20X1, for $19,760 U.S.

5. The cost of sales consists of the following purchases:

    20,000 FC acquired December 1, 20X0
    60,000 FC acquired March 1, 20X1
    80,000 FC acquired July 1, 20X1
    20,000 FC acquired October 1, 20X1

6. The other expenses include 3,000 FC of insurance expense that was originally prepaid on October 1, 20X1. The balance of other expenses was incurred uniformly throughout the year.
7. The land and the related mortgage were acquired on March 1, 20X1.
8. Selected exchange rates between the FC and the U.S. dollar functional currency are as follows:

Jan. 1, 20X0	1 FC = $0.98	July 1, 20X1	1 FC = $1.04
July 1, 20X0	1 FC = 1.01	Oct. 1, 20X1	1 FC = 1.045
Dec. 1, 20X0	1 FC = 0.99	Nov. 1, 20X1	1 FC = 1.043
Jan. 1, 20X1	1 FC = 1.00	Dec. 31, 20X1	1 FC = 1.05
Mar. 1, 20X1	1 FC = 1.015	20X1 average	1 FC = 1.03

A special remeasurement rule is necessary for inventory when the rule of cost or market value, whichever is lower, is applied. Before the rule is applied, the inventory cost and market values must be expressed in the functional currency. A possible result is for an inventory write-down to occur in the functional currency, even if no write-down is suggested in the books of record currency. It also is possible for a write-down in the books of record currency to no longer be appropriate in the functional currency. This special rule is demonstrated in Illustration 11-7.

In reviewing Illustration 11-7, it is important to note the following:

1. If amounts are to be remeasured at historical exchange rates that are traceable to transactions occurring prior to the parent's date of acquisition, they should be remeasured at the *historical exchange rate existing at the parent's date of acquisition.* This special treatment is appropriate if the acquisition is accounted for as a purchase.
2. The remeasurement gain or loss is recognized as a component of income rather than as a component of other comprehensive income. Remeasurement gains or losses from prior years would be included in the remeasured amount of retained earnings at the beginning of the current year.
3. Because the functional currency is the U.S. dollar in this example, only the remeasurement process was necessary. If the functional currency had been in a different currency than that of the parent, it would have been necessary to first remeasure into the functional currency and then translate into the currency of the parent/investor. For example, if the book of record currency (BR) is the Japanese yen, the functional currency (FC) is the euro, and the currency of the parent/investor is the U.S. dollar, it would be necessary to remeasure the Japanese yen into euros and then translate the euros to U.S. dollars.
4. The remeasurement process resulted in a gain that favorably affects net income. This is because the FC strengthened against the dollar and made the parent's net investment in the subsidiary more valuable. If the FC had weakened, a remeasurement loss would have likely occurred. If the parent's management felt a remeasurement loss might occur, it might employ some type of financial instrument to hedge against the loss.
5. If the investor is using the equity method of accounting for its investment in the investee, income from the investment should include the investor's share of the remeasurement gain or loss. Therefore, the investment account must be adjusted to reflect the investor's interest in the remeasurement gain or loss. For example, if an investor has a 30% interest in an investee and there is a current remeasurement gain of $50,000, the following entry would be made under the equity method:

Investment in Investee	15,000	
Investment Income		15,000

Illustration 11-7
Sori Corporation
Trial Balance Remeasurement
December 31, 20X1

Account	Balance in Books of Record (BR) Currency	Relevant Exchange Rate (Dollars/FC)	Balance in Functional Currency (Dollars)
Cash	10,000 BR	1.050	$ 10,500
Accounts Receivable	21,000	1.050	22,050
Allowance for Doubtful Accounts	(1,000)	1.050	(1,050)
Due from Pome	14,000	1.050	14,700
Inventory (at Market, Cost = 32,000)	30,000	Note A	31,500
Prepaid Insurance	3,000	1.045	3,135

Land	18,000	1.015	18,270
Depreciable Assets	120,000	Note B	122,400
Accumulated Depreciation	(15,000)	Note C	(15,120)
Cost of Goods Sold	180,000	Note D	185,000
Depreciation Expense	10,000	Note E	10,120
Income Tax Expense	30,000	1.030	30,900
Other Expenses	23,000	Note F	23,735
Total	443,000 BR		$456,140
Accounts Payable	20,000 BR	1.050	$ 21,000
Taxes Payable	30,000	1.050	31,500
Accrued Interest Payable	1,000	1.050	1,050
Mortgage Payable—Land	10,000	1.050	10,500
Common Stock	80,000	1.000	80,000
Retained Earnings	20,000	Note G	20,000
Sales—Pome	80,000	1.030	82,400
Sales—Other	200,000	1.030	206,000
Gain on Sale of Depreciable Assets	2,000	Note H	2,760
Remeasurement Gain (to balance)			**930**
Total	443,000 BR		$456,140

Note A—Inventory:

The historical cost and fair value of the ending inventory must be remeasured into the functional currency before the rule of cost or market, whichever is lower, may be applied.

	FC × Exchange Rate		U.S. Dollars
Historical cost	(10,000 × 1.045)		$10,450
	(22,000 × 1.043)		22,946
			$33,396
Fair value	(30,000 × 1.05)		$31,500

Because the fair value in functional currency is still less than the historical cost in functional currency, fair value will be the carrying basis.

Note B—Depreciable Assets:

	Balance in BR	Exchange Rate (Dollars/FC)	Remeasured Functional Currency (Dollars)
January 1, 20X0, acquisition	80,000 BR	1.00	$ 80,000
July 1, 20X1, acquisition	60,000	1.04	62,400
July 1, 20X1, disposition	(20,000)	1.00	(20,000)
	120,000 BR		$122,400

(continued)

Note C—Accumulated Depreciation:

	Balance in BR	Exchange Rate (Dollars/FC)	Remeasured Functional Currency (Dollars)
January 1, 20X0, acquisition (60,000 BR ÷ 10 × 2)	12,000 BR	1.00	$12,000
July 1, 20X1, acquisition (60,000 BR ÷ 10 × ½) . . .	3,000	1.04	3,120
	15,000 BR		$15,120

Note D—Cost of sales is remeasured as follows:

	Balance in BR	Exchange Rate (Dollars/FC)	Remeasured Functional Currency(Dollars)
December 1, 20X1, acquisition	20,000 BR	1.000*	$ 20,000
March 1, 20X1	60,000	1.015	60,900
July 1, 20X1	80,000	1.040	83,200
October 1, 20X1	20,000	1.045	20,900
Total	180,000 BR		$185,000

*Note that the exchange rate on the parent's date of acquisition is used rather than any earlier historical exchange rates.

Note E—Depreciation Expense:

	Balance in BR	Exchange Rate (Dollars/FC)	Remeasured Functional Currency (Dollars)
January 1, 20X0, acquisition (60,000 BR ÷ 10) . .	6,000 BR	1.00	$ 6,000
July 1, 20X1, disposal (20,000 BR ÷ 10 × ½) . . .	1,000	1.00	1,000
July 1, 20X1, acquisition (60,000 BR ÷ 10 × ½) .	3,000	1.04	3,120
	10,000 BR		$10,120

Note F—Other expenses are remeasured as follows:

	Balance in BR	Exchange Rate (Dollars/FC)	Remeasured Functional Currency (Dollars)
Insurance expense	3,000 BR	1.045	$ 3,135
Balance of expense	20,000	1.030	20,600
			$23,735

Note G—Retained Earnings:

	Balance in BR	Exchange Rate (Dollars/FC)	Remeasured Functional Currency (Dollars)
January 1, 20X1, balance (date of investment)	20,000 BR	1.00	$20,000

The beginning balance of retained earnings normally is equal to the remeasured value of the previous period's ending retained earnings. However, since 20X1 is the first year Pome has owned Sori, the beginning balance is set equal to the January 1, 20X1 (acquisition date), balance of retained earnings in foreign currency remeasured at the January 1, 20X1, spot rate. The balance sheet for 20X1 would show a remeasured value for retained earnings equal to the remeasured beginning balance of retained earnings plus the remeasured value of net income less dividends remeasured at the rate existing on the declaration date.

Note H—Gain on Sale of Depreciable Assets:

	Balance in BR	Exchange Rate (Dollars/FC)	Remeasured Functional Currency (Dollars)
Cost	20,000 BR		
Accumulated depreciation	(3,000)		
Book value	17,000 BR	1.00	$ 17,000
Selling price in U.S. dollars			(19,760)
Gain			$ 2,760

Worksheet 11-2, pages 702 to 703, shows the consolidated financial statements of the Pome and Sori corporations. The trial balance for Sori has been remeasured into dollars based on Illustration 11-7 (see page 686). Note that the remeasurement gain is included in the subsidiary income distribution schedule.

worksheet
Worksheet 11-2: page 702

Remeasurement and Subsequent Translation when Functional Currency Is Not the Same as the Parent/Investor's Currency

Illustration 11-8, on pages 690 to 692, demonstrates the remeasurement of a subsidiary's trial balance into the functional currency and the subsequent translation into the parent's reporting currency. This might be the case if, by way of example, the subsidiary records in Japanese yen, functions in euros, and has a U.S. parent. Illustration 11-8 is based on the following information:

1. Chen Corporation began operations on January 1, 20X1, as a wholly owned foreign subsidiary of Drake Inc., a U.S. company. Chen maintains its financial statements in the books of record currency (BR), and its functional currency is the FC.
2. Inventory in the books of record currency (BR) is carried at fair value even though its historical cost is 16,000 BR. Inventory was acquired uniformly throughout the year. The weighted-average cost method is used to determine the cost of sales.
3. Depreciable assets were acquired (sold) on the following dates:

Date	Cost
January 1, 20X1	10,000 BR
	90,000
May 1, 20X1	30,000
July 1, 20X1	(10,000)

   The asset sold was acquired on January 1, 20X1. The selling price of this asset was 11,000 BR.
4. Depreciation is based on the straight-line method and a 10-year useful life.

5. Relevant direct exchange rates are as follows:

Date	FC/BR	Dollars/FC
January 1, 20X1	1 BR = 2.0 FC	1 FC = $1.40
May 1, 20X1	1 BR = 2.1 FC	1 FC = 1.30
July 1, 20X1	1 BR = 2.4 FC	1 FC = 1.10
December 31, 20X1	1 BR = 2.8 FC	1 FC = 1.00
20X1 average	1 BR = 2.5 FC	1 FC = 1.25

Highly Inflationary Economies. When a foreign entity's financial statements are expressed in the functional currency, the statements are translated directly into the parent's reporting currency. However, this procedure is not followed for a foreign entity in a country that has a highly inflationary economy. The FASB defines such an economy as one that has a cumulative inflation rate of approximately 100% or more over a 3-year period. Other factors, such as the trend of inflation, also may suggest a highly inflationary economy.[5]

If a foreign entity's currency has lost its utility as a measure of value and lacks stability, its use as a functional currency is likely to produce misleading results. The translation of noncurrent assets of a foreign company in a highly inflationary economy at current rates of exchange produces curious results. The translated amounts may not represent reasonable dollar-equivalent measures of those assets' historical costs.

Suppose a foreign company acquires a fixed asset for a cost of 100,000 FC when the exchange rate is 1 FC = $1.00. Since that time, the foreign country has experienced a cumulative rate of inflation of 270%, and the current rate of exchange is 1 FC = $0.40. If the fixed asset was translated using the current-rate method, the translated value of the asset would be $40,000 versus its original translated cost of $100,000. One proposed solution to this curious result would be to adjust the foreign financial statements for inflation rates since acquisition and then apply the current-rate method. The inflation-adjusted value of the fixed asset would be 270,000 FC (100,000 FC × 270%), and its translated value at current rates would be $108,000 (270,000 FC × $0.40). This translated amount is more meaningful than the $40,000 value previously determined. The FASB decided against adjusting foreign amounts for inflationary effects and instead decided that the domestic currency (dollars) should serve as the foreign entity's functional currency. Thus, the foreign entity's statements should be remeasured into the functional currency (U.S. dollars). Applying this to the fixed asset example would require the use of the original historical rate of exchange and result in a remeasured value of $100,000 (100,000 FC × $1.00). This value is more meaningful than the $40,000 value previously determined, and it does not commingle historical and inflation-adjusted values into the same set of financial statements. It is important to note that (1) this will result in the remeasurement of the statements into dollars, making any further translation unnecessary, and (2) the remeasurement gain or loss should be included in the net income for the period.

Illustration 11-8
Chen Corporation
Trial Balance Translation
December 31, 20X1

Account	Balance in BR	Relevant Exchange Rate (FC/BR)	Balance in FC	Relevant Exchange Rate (Dollars/FC)	Balance in Dollars
Cash	10,000 BR	2.80	28,000 FC	1.00	$ 28,000
Accounts Receivable	28,000	2.80	78,400	1.00	78,400

5 *Ibid.*, par. 11.

Inventory (at fair value)*	15,000	Note A	40,000	1.00	40,000
Prepaid Expenses	5,000	2.50	12,500	1.00	12,500
Depreciable Assets	120,000	Note B	243,000	1.00	243,000
Cost of Goods Sold	145,000	2.50	362,500	1.25	453,125
Depreciation Expense	11,500	Note C	23,200	1.25	29,000
Other Expenses	27,000	2.50	67,500	1.25	84,375
Income Tax Expense	16,500	2.50	41,250	1.25	51,562
Remeasurement Loss			**58,650**	**1.25**	**73,313**
Total Debits	378,000 BR		955,000 FC		$1,093,275
Accounts Payable	7,500 BR	2.80	21,000 FC	1.00	$ 21,000
Accrued Expenses	12,000	2.80	33,600	1.00	33,600
Notes Payable	84,000	2.80	235,200	1.00	235,200
Common Stock	40,000	2.00	80,000	1.40	112,000
Cumulative Transaction Adjustment	0		0		(33,075)
Retained Earnings	0	Note D	0		0
Sales	220,000	2.50	550,000	1.25	687,500
Gain on Sale of Depreciable Assets	1,500	Note E	7,400	1.25	9,250
Allowance for Doubtful Accounts	2,000	2.80	5,600	1.00	5,600
Accumulated Depreciation	11,000	Note F	22,200	1.00	22,200
Total Credits	378,000 BR		955,000 FC		$1,093,275

*In more complex instances, the remeasurement of ending inventory and cost of sales will depend on the inventory valuation method used. LIFO ending inventory will consist of the (1) beginning inventory multiplied by the applicable exchange rate(s) plus (2) unsold current purchases multiplied by the applicable exchange rate(s).

Note A—Inventory:

The historical cost and fair value of the ending inventory must be remeasured into the functional currency before the rule of cost or market, whichever is lower, may be applied.

BR × Exchange Rate	FC
Historical cost (16,000 BR × 2.50)	40,000
Fair value (15,000 BR × 2.80)	42,000

Because the historical cost in functional currency is less than the fair value in functional currency, historical cost will be the carrying basis.

Note B—Depreciable Assets:

	Balance in BR	Exchange Rate (FC/BR)	Remeasured Functional Currency (FC)
January 1, 20X1, acquisition	90,000 BR	2.00	180,000 FC
January 1, 20X1, acquisition	10,000	2.00	20,000
May 1, 20X1, acquisition	30,000	2.10	63,000
July 1, 20X1, disposition	(10,000)	2.00	(20,000)
	120,000 BR		243,000 FC

(continued)

Cash (11,000 BR × 2.40)	26,400	
Accumulated Depreciation (500 BR × 2.00)	1,000	
Depreciable Assets (10,000 BR × 2.00)		20,000
Gain on Sale of Depreciable Assets		7,400

	Balance in BR	Exchange Rate (FC/BR)	Remeasured Functional Currency (FC)
Cost (see Note B)	10,000 BR	2.00	20,000 FC
Accumulated depreciation (see Note F)	(500)	2.00	(1,000)
Book value	9,500 BR		19,000 FC
Selling price	11,000 BR	2.40	(26,400)
Gain			7,400 FC

Note F—Accumulated Depreciation:

	Balance in BR	Exchange Rate (FC/BR)	Remeasured Functional Currency (FC)
Annual expense	11,500 BR	see Note C	23,200 FC
Asset disposed	(500)	2.00	(1,000)
	11,000 BR		22,200 FC

Summary of Translation and Remeasurement Methodologies

This chapter has discussed the translation and/or remeasurement of foreign financial statements into the reporting currency (dollars) of the domestic parent/investor entity. The situations requiring the use of a particular translation and/or remeasurement methodology are summarized in Exhibit 11-2 and the flowchart in Exhibit 11-3, on page 695.

Exhibit 11-2 compares the methodologies applicable to the remeasurement and translation processes. The following factors regarding Exhibit 11-2 should be noted:

1. When remeasuring, the exchange rates represent the relationship between the books of record currency and the functional currency. When translating, the exchange rates represent the relationship between the functional currency and the parent/investor currency.
2. Examples of accounts that should be remeasured (versus translated) at historical rates include the following:

    - Marketable securities carried at cost
    - Inventories carried at cost
    - Prepaid expenses such as insurance, advertising, and rent
    - Property, plant, and equipment
    - Accumulated depreciation on property, plant, and equipment
    - Patents, trademarks, licenses, and formulas
    - Goodwill
    - Other intangible assets
    - Deferred charges and credits except deferred income taxes and policy acquisition costs for life insurance companies
    - Deferred income
    - Common stock
    - Preferred stock carried at issuance price
    - Examples of revenues and expenses related to nonmonetary items:

      Cost of goods sold
      Depreciation of property, plant, and equipment
      Amortization of intangible items such as patents and licenses
      Amortization of deferred charges or credits except deferred income taxes and policy acquisition costs for life insurance companies[6]

3. If amounts to be remeasured at historical exchange rates are traceable to transactions occurring prior to the parent's date of acquisition, the historical exchange rate existing at the date of acquisition should be used.
4. The remeasurement gain or loss is included as a component of net income expressed in the functional currency, whereas the translation adjustment is not included as a component of net income but rather as a component of other comprehensive income.

The accounting policies footnote (Exhibit 11-4 , on page 696) to the financial statements of Ford Motor Company illustrates how both translation and remeasurement are applied to the foreign subsidiaries of the company.

Tax Allocation and Disclosure Requirements

Interperiod tax allocation is appropriate when temporary differences exist due to differences in the timing or recognition of items for financial statement purposes and for tax purposes. To the extent that remeasurement gains or losses and/or translation adjustments are recognized in different periods for financial and tax purposes, tax allocation is required. In addition, the principles of intraperiod tax allocation require that the income taxes related to items recorded as components of other comprehensive income should also be allocated to equity. Therefore, this would be applicable to translation adjustments and certain gains or losses excluded from income that are recorded as other comprehensive income.

---

6 *Ibid.*, par. 48.

	books of record (local) currency or when the functional currency is highly inflationary	of record (local) currency or when the functional currency is *not* highly inflationary
Assets and Liabilities:		
Monetary items* or measured at current values	Remeasure using current exchange rate	Translate using current exchange rate
Not monetary items or not measured at current values	Remeasure using historical exchange rates	Translate using current exchange rate
Equity Accounts:		
Equity accounts (excluding retained earnings)	Remeasure using historical exchange rates**	Translate using historical exchange rates**
Retained earnings	Beginning remeasured balance plus (minus) remeasured net income (loss) less dividends (remeasured using historical exchange rates)	Beginning translated balance plus (minus) translated net income (loss) less dividends (translated using historical exchange rates)
Revenues and Expenses:		
Representing amortization of historical amounts	Remeasure using historical exchange rates	Translate using weighted-average exchange rate for the period
Other income and expense items	Remeasure using weighted-average exchange rate for the period	Translate using weighted-average exchange rate for the period
Accounting for remeasurement gain or loss and transition adjustment	Remeasurement gain or loss recorded as a component of net income	Cumulative translation adjustment recorded as a component of other comprehensive income

*Monetary items represent rights to receive or pay an amount of money which is (1) fixed in amount or (2) determinable without reference to future prices of specific goods/services; that is, its value does not change according to changes in price levels.

**If amounts are to be remeasured or translated at historical exchange rates which are traceable to transactions occurring prior to the parent's date of acquisition, they should be remeasured/translated at the historical exchange rate existing at the parent's date of acquisition.

Exhibit 11-3 Translation/Remeasurement Flowchart

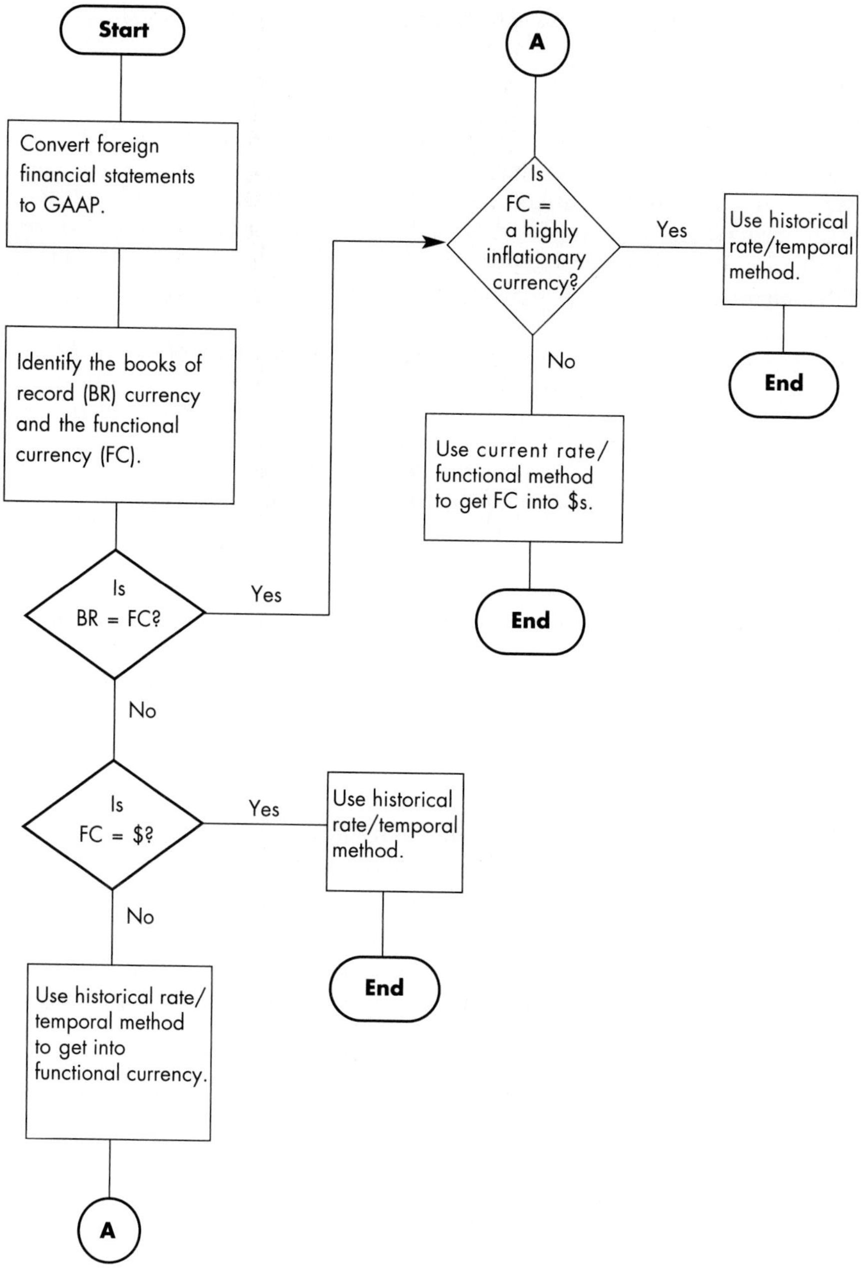

Exhibit 11-4
Ford Motor Company

Foreign Currency Translation

Results of operations and cash flows of foreign subsidiaries are, in most cases, translated to U.S. dollars at average-period currency rates. Assets and liabilities are translated at end-of-period exchange rates.

Included in the statement of income are the impact of remeasuring assets and liabilities of foreign subsidiaries using U.S. dollars as the functional currency, gains and losses arising from transactions denominated in a currency other than the functional currency, and the results of foreign currency hedging activities (Note 16). The net income effects of these adjustments were gains of $454 million and losses of $19 million and $315 million in 2003, 2002, and 2001, respectively.

Translation adjustments related to foreign subsidiaries using the local currency as the functional currency are generally included in accumulated other comprehensive income (loss), a component of stockholders' equity. Translation adjustments were a $2.9 billion increase in 2003, a $2.9 billion increase in 2002, and a $1.1 billion decrease in 2001.

Source: Ford Motor Company, 2003 Annual Report, Note 1. Accounting Policies.

FASB Statement No. 52 requires that foreign currency transaction and hedging gains or losses included in the determination of net income be disclosed in the financial statements or the accompanying notes. An analysis of the separate component of other comprehensive income affected by certain foreign currency transactions and hedges and translation adjustments should be presented. The analysis may be in a separate statement, in a note to the financial statements, or as part of the statement of changes in equity. At a minimum, the analysis should disclose the following:

1. Beginning and ending amount of cumulative translation adjustments.
2. The aggregate adjustment for the period resulting from translation adjustments and gains and losses from certain hedges and intercompany balances.
3. The amount of income taxes for the period allocated to translation adjustments.
4. The amounts transferred from cumulative translation adjustments and included in determining net income for the period as a result of the sale or complete or substantially complete liquidation of an investment in a foreign entity.[7]

Although the various effects of rate changes subsequent to the end of the period normally are not disclosed, their effects on unsettled balances arising from foreign currency transactions should be disclosed if significant.

REFLECTION

- If the foreign entity's functional currency is not its books of record (local) or reporting currency, the historical rate or temporal method is applied in order to remeasure the financial statements into the functional currency. This method is based on the premise that changes in the exchange rate between the books of record currency and the functional currency affect the cash flows and economic well-being of the foreign entity and parent/investor.

7 *Op. cit.*, par. 31.

- The remeasurement process follows the historical rate/temporal method that remeasures foreign financial statements from their reporting currency into the functional currency. This method remeasures balances representing historical amounts using historical exchange rates.
- The remeasurement gain or loss is recognized as a component of current period earnings.
- If the foreign entity's books of record (local) currency is the functional currency (FC), the current-rate or functional method is used to translate the financial statements into the parent/investor's currency. It is based on the premise that changes in exchange rates will have no effect on the cash flows or economic well-being of the foreign entity or parent/investor.

Worksheet 11-1

Consolidating the Foreign Subsidiary
Pome Corporation and Subsidiary Sori Corporation
Worksheet for Consolidated Financial Statements (in dollars)
For Year Ended December 31, 20X1

	(Credit balance amounts are in parentheses.) In U.S. dollars	Trial Balance	
		Pome Corporation	Sori Corporation
1	Cash	56,800	10,500
2	Accounts Receivable	112,000	22,050
3	Allowance for Doubtful Accounts	(5,600)	(1,050)
4	Due from Pome		14,700
5	Inventory, December 31, 20X1	154,700	31,500
6	Prepaid Insurance	9,050	3,150
7	Investment in Sori Corporation	141,153	
8			
9			
10	Land	125,000	18,900
11	Depreciable Assets and Patents	500,000	126,000
12	Accumulated Depreciation and Amortization	(100,000)	(15,750)
13	Accounts Payable	(112,000)	(21,000)
14	Taxes Payable	(150,000)	(31,500)
15	Accrued Interest Payable	(16,000)	(1,050)
16	Mortgage Payable—Land	(105,000)	(10,500)
17	Common Stock	(350,000)	(80,000)
18	Paid-In Capital in Excess of Par	(100,000)	
19	Retained Earnings, January 1, 20X1	(116,000)	(20,000)
20	**Cumulative Translation Adjustment—Sori**		(5,780)
21	**Cumulative Translation Adjustment—Pome**		
22			
23	Sales—Pome		(82,400)
24	Sales—Other	(908,600)	(206,000)
25	Gain on Sale of Depreciable Assets	(8,600)	(2,060)
26	Cost of Goods Sold	703,850	185,400
27	Depreciation and Amortization Expense	45,600	10,300
28	Income Tax Expense	108,000	30,900
29	Other Expenses (including interest)	51,800	23,690
30	Subsidiary Income	(36,153)	
31		0	0
32	Consolidated Net Income		
33	To Noncontrolling Interest		
34	Balance to Controlling Interest		
35	Total Noncontrolling Interest		
36	Retained Earnings, Controlling Interest, December 31, 20X1		
37			

Worksheet 11-1 (see page 678)

Eliminations & Adjustments Dr.	Eliminations & Adjustments Cr.	Consolidated Income Statement	Minority Interest	Controlling Retained Earnings	Consolidated Balance Sheet	
					67,300	1
					134,050	2
					(6,650)	3
	(IA) 14,700					4
					186,200	5
					12,200	6
	(CY1) 36,153					7
	(EL) 90,000					8
	(D) 15,000					9
					143,900	10
(D) 15,750					641,750	11
	(A) 1,575				(117,325)	12
(IA) 14,700					(118,300)	13
					(181,500)	14
					(17,050)	15
					(115,500)	16
(EL) 72,000			(8,000)		(350,000)	17
					(100,000)	18
(EL) 18,000			(2,000)	(116,000)		19
(CT) 5,202			(578)			20
	(CT) 5,202				(5,922)	21
(A) 30	**(D) 750**					22
(IS) 82,400						23
		(1,114,600)				24
		(10,660)				25
	(IS) 82,400	806,850				26
(A) 1,545		57,445				27
		138,900				28
		75,490				29
(CY1) 36,153						30
245,780	245,780					31
		(46,575)				32
		4,017	(4,017)			33
		42,558		(42,558)		34
			(14,595)		(14,595)	35
				(158,558)	(158,558)	36
					0	37

Eliminations and Adjustments:

(CY1) Eliminate the entries in the subsidiary income account against the investment in Sori account to record the parent's 90% controlling interest in the subsidiary.

(EL) Eliminate 90% of the subsidiary's January 1, 20X1, equity balances against the balance of the investment account.

(CT) Distribute the cumulative translation adjustment between controlling interest and NCI.

(D) Distribute the excess of cost over book value of 15,000 FC to patent.

(A) Record appropriate patent amortization.

(IA) Eliminate the intercompany trade balances.

(IS) Eliminate the intercompany sales assuming that none of the goods purchased from Sori remain in Pome's ending inventory.

Subsidiary Sori Corporation Income Distribution

		Internally generated net income	$40,170
		Adjusted income	$40,170
		Noncontrolling share	× 10%
		NCI	$ 4,017

Parent Pome Corporation Income Distribution

Patent amortization . . . **(A)**	$1,545	Internally generated net income	$ 7,950
		Share of subsidiary income (90% × $40,170)	36,153
		Controlling interest	$42,558

Worksheet 11-2

Consolidating the Foreign Subsidiary
Pome Corporation and Subsidiary Sori Corporation
Worksheet for Consolidated Financial Statements (in dollars)
For Year Ended December 31, 20X1

	(Credit balance amounts are in parentheses.) **In U.S. dollars**	Trial Balance	
		Pome Corporation	Sori Corporation
1	Cash	56,800	10,500
2	Accounts Receivable	112,000	22,050
3	Allowance for Doubtful Accounts	(5,600)	(1,050)
4	Due from Pome		14,700
5	Inventory, December 31, 20X1	154,700	31,500
6	Prepaid Insurance	9,050	3,135
7	Investment in Sori Corporation	143,101	
8			
9			
10	Land	125,000	18,270
11	Depreciable Assets and Patents	500,000	122,400
12	Accumulated Depreciation and Amortization	(100,000)	(15,120)
13	Accounts Payable	(112,000)	(21,000)
14	Taxes Payable	(150,000)	(31,500)
15	Accrued Interest Payable	(16,000)	(1,050)
16	Mortgage Payable—Land	(105,000)	(10,500)
17	Common Stock	(350,000)	(80,000)
18	Paid-In Capital in Excess of Par	(100,000)	
19	Retained Earnings, January 1, 20X1	(116,000)	(20,000)
20	**Remeasurement Gain**		(930)
21			
22			
23	Sales—Pome		(82,400)
24	Sales—Other	(908,600)	(206,000)
25	Gain on Sale of Depreciable Assets	(8,600)	(2,760)
26	Cost of Goods Sold	703,850	185,000
27	Depreciation and Amortization Expense	45,600	10,120
28	Income Tax Expense	108,000	30,900
29	Other Expenses (including interest)	51,800	23,735
30	Subsidiary Income	(38,101)	
31		0	0
32	Consolidated Net Income		
33	To Noncontrolling Interest		
34	Balance to Controlling Interest		
35	Total Noncontrolling Interest		
36	Retained Earnings, Controlling Interest, December 31, 20X1		
37			

Worksheet 11-2 (see page 689)

Eliminations & Adjustments Dr.		Eliminations & Adjustments Cr.		Consolidated Income Statement	Minority Interest	Controlling Retained Earnings	Consolidated Balance Sheet	
							67,300	1
							134,050	2
							(6,650)	3
		(IA)	14,700					4
							186,200	5
							12,185	6
		(CY1)	38,101					7
		(EL)	90,000					8
		(D)	15,000					9
							143,270	10
(D)	15,000						637,400	11
		(A)	1,500				(116,620)	12
(IA)	14,700						(118,300)	13
							(181,500)	14
							(17,050)	15
							(115,500)	16
(EL)	72,000				(8,000)		(350,000)	17
							(100,000)	18
(EL)	18,000				(2,000)	(116,000)		19
				(930)				20
								21
								22
(IS)	82,400							23
				(1,114,600)				24
				(11,360)				25
		(IS)	82,400	806,450				26
(A)	1,500			57,220				27
				138,900				28
				75,535				29
(CY1)	38,101							30
	241,701		241,701					31
				(48,785)				32
				4,234	(4,234)			33
				44,551		(44,551)		34
					(14,234)		(14,234)	35
						(160,551)	(160,551)	36
							0	37

Eliminations and Adjustments:

(CY1) Eliminate the entries in the subsidiary income account against the investment in the Sori account to record the parent's 90% controlling interest in the subsidiary.

(EL) Eliminate 90% of the subsidiary's January 1, 20X1, equity balances against the balance of the investment account.

(D) Distribute the excess of cost over book value of 15,000 FC.

(A) Record appropriate amortization of patent.

(IA) Eliminate the intercompany trade balances.

(IS) Eliminate the intercompany sales assuming that none of the goods purchased from Sori remain in Pome's ending inventory.

Subsidiary Sori Corporation Income Distribution

		Internally generated net income	$42,335*
		Adjusted income	$42,335
		Noncontrolling share	× 10%
		NCI	$ 4,234

Parent Pome Corporation Income Distribution

Patent amortization (A)	$1,500	Internally generated net income	$ 7,950
		Share of subsidiary income (90% × $42,335)	38,101
		Controlling interest	$44,551

*This amount includes the remeasurement gain of $930.

UNDERSTANDING THE ISSUES

1. A foreign company maintains its books and records in its domestic currency. Identify several factors that might suggest that the domestic currency is not the entity's functional currency.
2. Assume that a U.S. company has a French subsidiary whose functional currency is the euro. Explain why the translation adjustment is not included as a component of net income on the consolidated income statement.
3. Explain how a German subsidiary's year-end balance in retained earnings is expressed in dollars assuming that the euro is the functional currency.
4. Assume that a U.S. company has a foreign subsidiary whose functional currency is the U.S. dollar. Explain how exchange rates between the foreign currency and the dollar would have to change in order to result in a current-year remeasurement loss and how the company could use a foreign currency loan receivable or payable to hedge against its net investment in the foreign subsidiary.
5. Explain why functional currency should be remeasured, rather than translated, when a foreign entity's functional currency is highly inflationary.

EXERCISES

Exercise 1 *(LO 3, 4)* **Direct calculation of a translation adjustment and hedging strategies.** At the beginning of 20X5, the rate of exchange between the foreign currency (FC) and the U.S. dollar was 1 FC = $1.20. A foreign company had net assets at the beginning of 20X5 in the amount of 150,000 FC and was wholly owned by a U.S. company. During 20X5, the foreign company had net income of 75,000 FC and sold additional common stock to the parent company. The common stock had a par value of 50,000 FC and was sold for 60,000 FC when the exchange rate was 1 FC = $1.15. The average exchange rate during 20X5 was 1 FC = $1.13, and at the end of 20X5, the rate was 1 FC = $1.10.

1. Calculate the amount of the translation adjustment which would be traceable to 20X5.
2. Explain how the company could hedge to reduce the effect of the reduction in other comprehensive income.
3. Discuss how to account for a hedge of the net investment in the above foreign operation.

Exercise 2 *(LO 2)* **The effect on a parent of alternative functional currencies.** Luxor Corporation has a 100% interest in a foreign subsidiary known as Luminaire. The foreign subsidiary was created for the primary purpose of distributing electronic components throughout a number of foreign countries. The parent initially invested 3,000,000 FC to finance equipment purchases, and it is anticipated that a dividend equivalent to $1,110,000 will be paid to the parent company at the end of each year. Luxor is trying to determine whether to structure the subsidiary with the foreign currency (FC) or the U.S. dollar ($) as Luminaire's functional currency. Projections for the subsidiary's first year of operations are as follows: sales of 10,000,000 FC; cost of sales (excluding depreciation) of 3,700,000 FC; and selling, general, and administrative expenses (excluding depreciation) of 1,200,000 FC. It is anticipated that the company will purchase 2,000,000 FC of equipment at the beginning of the year and another 1,000,000 FC of equipment at midyear. All equipment is depreciated over 10 years using the straight-line method.

It is anticipated that the exchange rate between the FC and the $ are as follows:

Beginning of year	1 FC = $1.00
Average for year	1 FC = 1.06
Midyear...............	1 FC = 1.05
End of year	1 FC = 1.11

For the first year, prepare a schedule to determine the effect on the parent company's translated net income, balance sheet, and cash flows assuming the functional currency is: (a) the dollar and (b) the FC. (*Hint:* Assume that all sales revenues increase cash and that all cost of sales and selling, general, and administrative expenses decrease cash.)

Exercise 3 *(LO 5)* **Net investment under the sophisticated equity method.** On June 30, 20X5, Fabinet's, a foreign corporation, shareholders' equity was 10,500,000 FC (foreign currencies). At that time, Newcore, a U.S. corporation, acquired 40% in Fabinet paying $3,120,000 when 1 FC was equal to $0.60. Equipment, with a fair market value that exceeded cost by $240,000, accounted for a portion of the cost in excess of book value. The equipment was expected to have a remaining useful life of 10 years and be depreciated using the straight-line method. The balance of the cost in excess of book value was traceable to goodwill.

During the balance of 20X5, Fabinet reported net income of 1,260,000 FC of which 126,000 FC was declared and paid as a dividend. At the end of 20X5, Newcore tested the goodwill for impairment and recognized an impairment loss of $100,000. Additional exchange rates are as follows:

Weighted average for last six months of 20X5	1 FC = $0.64
Date of dividend declaration	1 FC = 0.66
December 31, 20X5	1 FC = 0.68

Prepare all relevant entries to record Newcore's interest in Fabinet under the sophisticated equity method.

Exercise 4 *(LO 5)* **Measurement of net investment under the sophisticated equity method.** On June 1, 20X8, the Auburn Company (a U.S. company) acquired a 30% interest in a foreign company which was formed on November 1, 20X7. Auburn accounted for the investment using the sophisticated equity method. At the date of acquisition, the net assets of the foreign company were 800,000 foreign currencies (FC), and Auburn paid $600,000 for its interest. Appreciated land accounted for approximately 20% of the excess paid by Auburn, and the balance was traceable to depreciable assets. On average, depreciable assets have a remaining useful life of 12 years and are depreciated using the straight-line method of depreciation. The foreign company's net income for the last seven months of 20X8 was 140,000 FC. The functional currency is the FC, and the translation adjustment at year-end is a credit of $13,000. Selected exchange rates are as follows:

November 1, 20X7	1 FC = $2.10
Weighted-average (June 1 to December 31, 20X8)	1 FC = 2.24
June 1, 20X8	1 FC = 2.20
December 31, 20X8	1 FC = 2.27

Determine the U.S. dollar balance of Auburn's investment in the foreign company as of December 31, 20X8.

Exercise 5 *(LO 4)* **Hedging a net investment in a foreign subsidiary.** Crosswell, Inc. has a 100% interest in a foreign subsidiary whose functional currency is the FC. The interest was acquired when 1 FC = $1.45. As of September 30, 20X4, the pre-closing trial balance as of December 31, 20X4, is forecasted to be as follows:

	Debit (Credit)
Cash	40,000 FC
Accounts Receivable	220,000
Inventory	320,000
Equipment (net of depreciation)	825,000
Accounts Payable	(360,000)

6% Note Payable	(400,000) FC
Accrued Interest Payable	(4,000)
Common Stock	(200,000)
Contributed Capital in Excess of Par Value	(200,000)
Beginning Retained Earnings	(140,000)
Sales	(600,000)
Cost of Sales	366,000
Selling Expenses	55,000
Administrative Expenses	48,000
Interest Expense	30,000
Total	0 FC

Actual exchange rates between the FC and the dollar are 1 FC = $1.40 as of January 1, 20X4, and $1.24 as of September 30, 20X4. It is estimated that the year-end 20X4 rate will be 1 FC = $1.20 and that the 20X4 weighted-average rate will be 1 FC = $1.28.

Crosswell is considering hedging its investment in the foreign subsidiary by borrowing or lending FC as of September 30, 20X4. The annual interest rate will be 6% with interest-only payments due at the end of each calendar quarter. At year-end 20X3, the cumulative translation adjustment was a $120,000 debit balance.

Determine the amount of the FC hedge that would be necessary to offset the 20X4 change in the translation adjustment. Assume that the translated value of retained earnings at December 31, 20X3, was $200,000.

Exercise 6 *(LO 6)* **Remeasuring selected balances with various functional currencies.** For each of the following independent cases, determine the translated value of the relevant accounts.

Case A: A foreign subsidiary has inventory accounted for by the lower-of-cost-or-market rule. The 20X7 ending inventory, with a cost of 180,000 FC, was written down to a fair value of 176,000 FC. The cost of the inventory is traceable to an October 1, 20X7, purchase of 150,000 FC and a December 15, 20X7, purchase of 30,000 FC. The foreign company's functional currency is the U.S. dollar. Relevant exchange rates on October 1, 20X7, December 15, 20X7, and December 31, 20X7, are 1 FC = $1.76, 1 FC = $1.72, and 1 FC = $1.82, respectively. Calculate the translated value of the December 31, 20X7, ending inventory.

Case B: A foreign subsidiary purchased inventory for 380,000 FC from its U.S. parent on November 1, 20X7. The parent's cost of the inventory sold was $500,000. As of December 31, 20X7, the subsidiary has 60% of the inventory on hand. The subsidiary's functional currency is the foreign currency. Relevant exchange rates on November 1, 20X7, and December 31, 20X7, are 1 FC = $2.00 and 1 FC = $2.10, respectively. Calculate the translated value of the subsidiary's December 31, 20X7, inventory after eliminating the intercompany profit.

Case C: A foreign subsidiary acquired depreciable assets measured in foreign currency A (FCA) over several years. The subsidiary's functional currency is foreign currency B (FCB). All assets are depreciable on a straight-line basis over a 10-year useful life. Relevant asset costs and exchange rates are as follows:

	Asset Cost	1 FCA =	1 FCB =
January 1, 20X6	380,000	2.10 FCB	$1.10
March 1, 20X6	710,000	1.98	1.08
July 1, 20X6	216,000	1.92	1.06
December 1, 20X6	30,000	2.01	1.04
20X6 average		2.03	1.05

Calculate the translated value of the 20X6 depreciation expense.

Exercise 7 *(LO 3)* **Translation of equity accounts and direct calculation of translation adjustment.** Paco Industries is a foreign corporation which was formed in 20X5. An analysis of activity affecting equity accounts reveals the following through December 31, 20X7:

Date	Activity/Event	Amount in Foreign Currency (FC)	Exchange Rate 1 FC =
Mar. 1, 20X5	Initial sale of common stock (1,400,000 par value)	2,000,000	$1.20
Mar. 1—Dec. 31, 20X5	Net income	200,000	1.25 weighted ave.
Mar. 1, 20X6	Dividend declared	30,000	1.27
Oct. 1, 20X6	Second offering of common stock (1,500,000 par value)	3,000,000	1.32
20X6	Net income	450,000	1.30 weighted ave.
Apr. 1, 20X7	Acquisition of treasury stock (210,000 par value)	300,000	1.28
July 1, 20X7	Dividend declared	90,000	1.25
20X7	Net income	550,000	1.22 weighted ave.

1. Assuming that the foreign currency is the functional currency, prepare the translated equity section for Paco as of December 31, 20X7, noting that the year-end exchange rates were as follows: 20X5, 1 FC = $1.29; 20X6, 1 FC = $1.32; 20X7, 1 FC = $1.21.
2. Calculate what amount of the December 31, 20X7, translation adjustment balance was traceable to 20X7.

PROBLEMS

template cd

Problem 11-1 *(LO 2, 3)* **Adjust to U.S. GAAP and translate trial balance.** On January 1, 20X8, Richter Corporation acquired an 80% interest in Morgan Company, a foreign company, for 9,000,000 FC. On the date of acquisition, Morgan's equity consisted of common stock of 3,000,000 FC and retained earnings of 5,500,000 FC. Any excess of cost over book value is attributable to additional depreciable assets, which have a useful life of 20 years. The unadjusted trial balances for Richter and Morgan as of December 31, 20X9, are as follows:

	Richter Corporation	Morgan Company
Cash	4,630,000	3,850,000 FC
Short-Term Investments	1,250,000	1,100,000
Accounts Receivable	3,790,000	4,620,000
Inventory	4,800,000	2,950,000
Investment in Morgan	6,930,000	
Depreciable Assets	27,400,000	17,700,000
Accumulated Depreciation	(12,120,000)	(7,250,000)
Depreciable Assets—Leased	4,540,000	
Accumulated Depreciation—Leased Assets	(1,900,000)	
Capitalized Research and Development		980,000
Accounts Payable	(2,860,000)	(1,200,000)
Interest Payable	(150,000)	

Obligation Under Capital Lease	(3,170,000)	
Common Stock	(10,000,000)	(3,000,000)
Retained Earnings, January 1, 20X9	(18,460,000)	(15,656,000)
Sales	(25,000,000)	(18,000,000)
Cost of Goods Sold	16,500,000	11,600,000
Depreciation Expense	2,875,000	1,550,000
Interest Expense	150,000	
Research and Development Expense	740,000	
Rent Expense		8,000
Other Expenses	955,000	748,000
OCI—Unrealized Holding Gain—AFS	(900,000)	
Total	0	0 FC

Morgan's trial balance is based, in part, on certain national accounting principles that are accepted in the country in which Morgan operates. However, these principles do not conform to U.S. GAAP. These differences include the following:

Short-Term Investments—All of these available-for-sale investments, acquired on January 1, 20X9, have been recorded at cost, without consideration of fair value. As of December 31, 20X9, fair value is 1,500,000 FC for these investments.

Research and Development—Research and development costs have been capitalized, although GAAP require these costs to be expensed in the period incurred. Morgan has no prior R&D costs. Therefore, all capitalized R&D costs were incurred uniformly during 20X9.

Leases—On January 1, 20X9, Morgan entered into a contract to lease machinery from an outside company. Morgan treated the lease as operating; however, GAAP require that it be capitalized. The lease contract requires an 8,000 FC payment at the start of each year for four years. At the end of the lease term, title to the asset is transferred to Morgan. The machinery has a fair value of 27,215 FC and is depreciated using the straight-line method over its remaining 5-year life. The implicit interest rate is 12%.

Morgan employs the FIFO inventory method. The most recent purchases of inventory occurred on August 1, 20X9, and November 15, 20X9, in the amounts of 1,000,000 FC and 2,000,000 FC, respectively. Morgan acquired additional equipment costing 5,000,000 FC on July 1, 20X9. Equipment is depreciated over 10 years, using the straight-line method. No other equipment has been acquired or disposed of since January 1, 20X9.

The cost of sales is traceable to goods purchased during 20X9 as follows:

Acquired in the 4th quarter of 20X8	2,400,000 FC
Acquired uniformly over the first six months of 20X9	9,150,000 FC
Acquired August 1, 20X9	50,000 FC

No dividends are paid. Morgan's 20X8 remeasured income (excluding any remeasurement gain or loss) was $8,370,000.

Relevant exchange rates are as follows:

	1FC =		1FC =
January 1, 20X7	$0.78	1st Quarter, 20X9 Average	$0.81
20X7 Average	0.76	1st Six months, 20X9 Average	0.83
January 1, 20X8	0.77	July 1, 20X9	0.84

(continued)

	1 FC =		1 FC =
December 31, 20X8	0.80	August 1, 20X9	0.83
4th Quarter, 20X8 Average	0.78	November 15, 20X9	0.86
20X8 Average	0.79	December 31, 20X9	0.89
January 1, 20X9	0.82	20X9 Average	0.88

Required ▶ ▶ ▶ ▶ ▶

1. Prepare all relevant journal entries to adjust Morgan's trial balance to U.S. GAAP.
2. Assuming Morgan's functional currency is the U.S. dollar, prepare a consolidated worksheet through the "Eliminations and Adjustments" column.

Problem 11-2 *(LO 3, 5)* **Translate a trial balance and prepare a consolidation worksheet with amortization of patents.** Keltner Enterprises has acquired an 80% interest in Jacklandia (a foreign company). The acquisition was accounted for as a purchase and occurred on January 1, 20X6, as follows:

Purchase price of 7,200,000 FC for net assets with a book value of $5,600,000 FC (7,000,000 FC × 80%)	
Allocation of excess paid:	
Patents (10-year remaining life, straight-line amortization)	1,600,000 FC

A condensed trial balance for both Keltner and Jacklandia as of December 31, 20X8, is as follows:

	Keltner (in dollars)	Jacklandia (in FC)
Working Capital	32,120,800	9,550,000
Due from Jacklandia	800,000	
Investment in Jacklandia	14,221,200	
Land	5,120,000	1,000,000
Depreciable Assets	54,000,000	6,000,000
Accumulated Depreciation	(27,000,000)	(2,000,000)
Other Assets	5,978,800	1,500,000
Due to Keltner		(620,155)
Other Long-Term Debt	(31,320,800)	(4,679,845)
Common Stock (issued July 1, 20X5)	(30,000,000)	(5,000,000)
Paid-In Capital in Excess of Par	(6,000,000)	(1,000,000)
Retained Earnings	(15,000,000)	(3,450,000)
20X8 Net Income	(2,920,000)	(1,300,000)

Jacklandia had net income expressed in foreign currency (FC) in the following amounts for 20X6 and 20X7 of 1,400,000 FC and 2,250,000 FC, respectively. Furthermore, Jacklandia declared a dividend of 1,200,000 FC on February 1, 20X8.

The FC is Jacklandia's functional currency, and various exchange rates are as follows:

July 1, 20X5	1 FC = $1.39	December 31, 20X7	1 FC = $1.32
January 1, 20X6	1 FC = 1.40	20X8 Average	1 FC = 1.27
20X6 Average	1 FC = 1.42	February 1, 20X8	1 FC = 1.25
20X7 Average	1 FC = 1.35	December 31, 20X8	1 FC = 1.29

Required ▶ ▶ ▶ ▶ ▶

Prepare a columnar worksheet to present the combined income statement and balance sheet of Keltner and its foreign subsidiary, Jacklandia, with all amounts stated in U.S. dollars. Key and explain worksheet eliminations and adjustments, and show supporting computations in good form. Ignore income taxes, and assume use of the simple equity method. (You may want to prepare a translated trial balance for Jacklandia first and then prepare a consolidated worksheet.)

Problem 11-3 *(LO 3, 5)* **Translate a trial balance and prepare a consolidation worksheet with excess of cost over book value traceable to equipment.** Due to increasing pressures to expand globally, Pueblo Corporation acquired a 100% interest in Sorenson Company, a foreign company, on January 1, 20X6. Pueblo paid 12,000,000 foreign currency (FC), and Sorenson's equity consisted of the following:

template cd

Common stock	3,000,000 FC
Paid-in capital in excess of par	2,000,000
Retained earnings	4,200,000
Total	9,200,000 FC

On the date of acquisition, equipment which has a 10-year life was undervalued by 500,000 FC. Any remaining excess of cost over book value is attributable to additional equipment, which has a 20-year life. The trial balances for Pueblo and Sorenson as of December 31, 20X8, are as follows:

	Pueblo Corporation	Sorenson Company
Cash	4,050,000	2,840,000 FC
Accounts Receivable	5,270,000	3,990,000
Inventory	5,540,000	5,800,000
Investment in Sorenson	20,969,000	
Fixed Assets	21,000,000	15,000,000
Accumulated Depreciation	(12,560,000)	(6,800,000)
Accounts Payable	(3,450,000)	(1,580,000)
Long-Term Debt	(10,000,000)	(5,000,000)
Common Stock	(4,000,000)	(3,000,000)
Paid-In Capital in Excess of Par	(6,500,000)	(2,000,000)
Retained Earnings, January 1, 20X8	(12,180,000)	(7,950,000)
Sales	(26,000,000)	(10,000,000)
Cost of Goods Sold	16,380,000	7,500,000
Operating Expenses	3,210,000	1,200,000
Subsidiary Income	(1,729,000)	
Total	0	0 FC

The investment in Sorenson consists of the following:

Initial investment (12,000,000 FC × $1.20)	$14,400,000
20X6 Income (1,750,000 FC × $1.28)	2,240,000
20X7 Income (2,000,000 FC × $1.30)	2,600,000
20X8 Income	1,729,000
Total	$20,969,000

Relevant exchange rates are as follows:

	1 FC =
January 1, 20X6	$1.20
20X6 Average	1.28
January 1, 20X7	1.25
20X7 Average	1.30
December 31, 20X8	1.31
20X8 Average	1.33

Assuming the FC is Sorenson's functional currency, prepare a consolidated worksheet. ◀◀◀◀◀ **Required**

Problem 11-4 *(LO 2, 5)* **Adjust to U.S. GAAP and translate trial balance.** Potter Corporation purchased a 100% interest in Stone Corporation, a foreign subsidiary, on January 1, 20X5, for 9,000,000 foreign currency (FC). On this date, Stone had common stock of 5,000,000 FC, paid-in capital in excess of par of 1,600,000 FC, and retained earnings of 2,000,000 FC. Bonds payable, which have a 5-year life, were overvalued by 50,000 FC. Any remaining excess of cost over book value is attributable to goodwill. The December 31, 20X8, unadjusted trial balances for Stone and Potter are as follows:

	Stone Corporation	Potter Corporation
Cash	2,253,000 FC	4,862,000
Net Accounts Receivable	5,580,000	15,500,000
Inventory	6,400,000	11,138,000
Investment in Stone		14,664,900
Depreciable Assets	25,750,000	44,600,000
Accumulated Depreciation	(8,200,000)	(17,400,000)
Accounts Payable	(3,290,000)	(5,230,000)
Unearned Revenue	(2,437,000)	
Bonds Payable	(10,200,000)	(11,300,000)
Accrued Expenses	(2,180,000)	(3,961,100)
Common Stock	(5,000,000)	(20,000,000)
Paid-In Capital in Excess of Par	(1,600,000)	(4,750,000)
Retained Earnings, January 1, 20X8	(5,870,000)	(14,872,400)
Sales	(24,000,000)	(55,000,000)
Cost of Goods Sold	18,460,000	32,180,000
Operating Expenses	5,184,000	11,340,000
Interest Income		(146,000)
Subsidiary Income		(1,625,400)
Gain on Appreciation of Inventory	(650,000)	
Gain on Appreciation of Equipment	(200,000)	
Total	0 FC	0

Stone's trial balance contains amounts that reflect national accounting principles that are accepted in the country in which Stone operates, but do not conform to U.S. GAAP. These differences include the following:

Inventory—Stone records its inventory at fair value when goods are purchased and when they are sold. It has been determined that inventory would be valued at a lower amount had FIFO been used. Inventory is overvalued by 200,000 FC, and the related cost of goods sold is overvalued by 450,000 FC.

Depreciable Assets—Beginning in 20X7, appreciation was recognized on certain depreciable assets and included in net income. As of the beginning of 20X8, property, plant, and equipment and accumulated depreciation are overstated by 900,000 FC and 180,000 FC, respectively. During the current year, another 200,0000 FC of appreciation was recognized, and current-year depreciation expense was overstated by 55,000 FC.

Depreciable Assets—In 20X7, the company incurred 1,000,000 FC of research and development costs that were capitalized. These costs were amortized/depreciated over the life span of the resulting products. Annual amortization amounts were 400,000 FC and 300,000 FC for years 20X7 and 20X8, respectively.

The investment in Stone, expressed in dollars, consists of the following as measured by the simple equity method:

Initial investment (9,000,000 FC × $1.10)	$ 9,900,000
20X5 Income (1,000,000 FC × $1.15)	1,150,000
20X6 Income (1,200,000 FC × $1.27)	1,524,000
20X7 Income (350,000 FC × $1.33)	465,500
20X8 Income	1,625,400
Total	$14,664,900

Relevant exchange rates (dollars/FC) are as follows:

January 1, 20X5	$1.10
20X5 Average	1.15
20X6 Average	1.27
20X7 Average	1.33
December 31, 20X8	1.42
20X8 Average	1.40

Assuming the FC is Stone's functional currency, prepare all necessary adjustments to U.S. GAAP, and translate Stone's trial balance. ◄◄◄◄◄ **Required**

Problem 11-5 *(LO 3, 6, 7)* **Analyzing the effect of alternative functional currencies.** Patterson Distributors, Inc. purchases various electronic components from a variety of manufacturers and then distributes the products to end users. In the past, both domestic and foreign manufacturers of the components shipped the product to Patterson's two U.S. distribution warehouses. In order to reduce costs and serve its customers on a more timely basis, Patterson is considering opening two international distribution centers. The company will form a 100%-owned foreign subsidiary to own the centers. The foreign subsidiary will need to secure financing and build and furnish a distribution warehouse in each location. Projections, in the respective country's foreign currency (FCA), for the first 12 months of operations are as follows:

	Company A (FCA)
Investment of parent company	1,000,000 FCA
Debt financing:	
Principal balance at beginning of year	4,000,000 FCA
Interest rate	6%
Repayment frequency	quarterly
Amortization period	20 quarters
Periodic payment	232,983 FCA
Year-end principal balance	3,292,344 FCA
Sales revenue	2,200,000 FCA
Inventory:	
Purchases	1,460,000 FCA
Frequency of purchases	equal amounts at end of each quarter
Ending inventory per LIFO	140,000 FCA
Other expenses (excluding interest and depreciation)	158,068 FCA
Cost of distribution center:	
Land	1,600,000 FCA
Building	2,200,000 FCA
Furnishings	720,000 FCA

(continued)

	Company A (FCA)
Useful life based on straight-line depreciation:	
Building	40 years
Furnishings	12 years
End of year:	
Accounts receivable	210,000 FCA
Accounts payable	130,000 FCA
Other current assets	50,000 FCA

Various projected exchange rates throughout the forecast period are as follows:

	1 FCA =
At beginning of year	$1.000
At end of first quarter	1.020
At end of second quarter	1.030
At end of third quarter	1.050
At end of fourth quarter	1.040
Average for the year	1.025

Although Patterson has prepared the projections in the respective foreign currencies, the company has the ability to structure transactions in such a way that either the foreign currency or the U.S. dollar is the functional currency.

Required ▶ ▶ ▶ ▶ ▶

1. Construct a year-end trial balance for the foreign subsidiary. Based on the information provided, calculate the translation adjustment and remeasurement gain or loss for the subsidiary assuming that the functional currency is the FCA and the dollar, respectively.
2. Discuss, in retrospect, whether the parent company would want to hedge its investment and, if so, how that might be accomplished.
3. Assume that the parent did hedge its investment in the subsidiary. This was accomplished by borrowing 600,000 FCA at the end of the first quarter. No principal payments were made during the year. How much of the gain or loss on this hedge would have been considered ineffective against the translation adjustment? The remeasurement gain?

Problem 11-6 *(LO 6)* **Prepare a remeasured trial balance and entries to eliminate excess of cost over book value.** On July 1, 20X6, Spencer International acquired an 80% interest in the net assets of Quatro Corporation, which is a foreign company, for $6,260,000. At that time, the net assets of Quatro in foreign currency (FC) were as follows:

Common stock	8,000,000 FC
Paid-in capital in excess of par	1,000,000
Retained earnings	3,000,000

Any excess paid over book value was attributed to the fair value of certain licensing agreements which were held by Quatro. The agreements had an original useful life of 10 years, have a remaining life of five years, and are amortized using the straight-line method.

Spencer's investment in Quatro was designed to provide Spencer with additional manufacturing capacity for its product line and a distribution system which would allow for expanded sales in foreign markets. In order to implement these goals, Spencer loaned Quatro $5,940,000 in 20X6 for the purpose of improving the manufacturing capacity. For the next five years, only interest payments at the rate of 8% would be made on a monthly basis. The loan originated on October 1, 20X6, and the proceeds were disbursed at that time as follows:

Purchase of additional machinery	$3,410,000
Purchase of additional tooling	992,000
Purchase of additional inventory	1,538,000

On July 1, 20X6, depreciable asset balances were as follows:

Machinery and Equipment	17,450,000 FC
Accumulated Depreciation—Machinery and Equipment	2,617,500
Tooling	4,400,000
Accumulated Depreciation—Tooling	660,000

All depreciable assets are depreciated using the straight-line method, and salvage values are ignored. Machinery is depreciated over a 10-year useful life, and tooling is depreciated over 10 years. No other additions or dispositions of depreciable assets have occurred since Spencer's acquisition of Quatro.

The manufacturing lead time for Quatro's products is such that the inventory typically turns over approximately four times a year; however, production costs are incurred fairly uniformly throughout the year. Virtually all material costs are denominated in U.S. dollars, although labor costs are denominated in FCs. The company employs the FIFO inventory method, and 20X7 ending inventory and cost of sales details are as follows:

Ending Inventory	
2,200,000 FC acquired in the last quarter of 20X7 when on average	1 FC = $0.55
1,500,000 FC acquired in the third quarter of 20X7 when on average	1 FC = 0.56

Cost of Sales	
800,000 FC acquired in the third quarter of 20X6 when on average	1 FC = $0.61
1,200,000 FC acquired in the fourth quarter of 20X6 when on average	1 FC = 0.62
3,200,000 FC acquired in the first quarter of 20X7 when on average	1 FC = 0.60
4,100,000 FC acquired in the second quarter of 20X7 when on average	1 FC = 0.57
3,400,000 FC acquired in the third quarter of 20X7 when on average	1 FC = 0.56

The December 31, 20X7, trial balance for Quatro is as follows:

	Debit	Credit
Cash and Receivables	2,200,000 FC	
Inventory	3,700,000	
Machinery and Equipment	22,950,000	
Accumulated Depreciation—Machinery and Equipment		5,922,500 FC
Tooling	6,000,000	
Accumulated Depreciation—Tooling		1,520,000
Licensing Agreements	500,000	
Accumulated Amortization—Licensing Agreements		325,000
Accounts and Notes Payable		2,000,000
Due to Spencer		11,000,000
Common Stock		8,000,000
Paid-In Capital in Excess of Par		1,000,000
Retained Earnings		3,700,000
Sales Revenue		20,527,500
Cost of Sales (excluding depreciation)	12,700,000	
Depreciation Expense	2,895,000	
Amortization Expense	50,000	
Other Expenses	3,000,000	
Total	53,995,000 FC	53,995,000 FC

The retained earnings balance as of December 31, 20X7, reflects net income for the last half of 20X6 of 1,300,000 FC (which had a translated value of $806,000) and dividend declarations in the amount of 300,000 FC each on both August 1, 20X6, and August 1, 20X7.

Additional exchange rates are as follows:

July 1, 20X6	1 FC = $0.60	20X7 Average	1 FC = $0.57
October 1, 20X6	1 FC = 0.62	August 1, 20X7	1 FC = 0.55
August 1, 20X6	1 FC = 0.61	December 31, 20X7	1 FC = 0.54
Last half of 20X6 Average	1 FC = 0.62		

Required ▶ ▶ ▶ ▶ ▶

1. Prepare a remeasured trial balance in dollars as of December 31, 20X7, assuming that Quatro's functional currency is the dollar.
2. Prepare all of the necessary elimination entries to account for the acquisition price being in excess of the book value of net assets.

Problem 11-7 *(LO 6)* **Remeasurement: books of record (euro) and functional currency (FC) differ.** Husky Industries, Inc. is a U.S. company that manufactures and distributes specialized emission control devices. In the past, approximately 5% of the company's sales came from export sales primarily in Western Europe. In 20X4, the company committed to an aggressive plan to expand export sales by acquiring a controlling interest in a British company that distributed specialized equipment throughout Western Europe and Asia. At the time of the acquisition, on September 1, 20X4, the British company's trial balance in euros was as follows:

	Debit (Credit)
Working Capital Excluding Inventory	(1,900,000) €
Inventory (per FIFO)	2,300,000
Licensing Agreements	840,000
Accumulated Amortization—Licensing Agreements	(400,000)
Equipment	840,000
Accumulated Depreciation—Equipment	(600,000)
Buildings	2,160,000
Accumulated Depreciation —Buildings	(880,000)
Land	500,000
Note Payable	(1,000,000)
Common Stock	(400,000)
Paid-In Capital in Excess of Par	(860,000)
Retained Earnings	(600,000)
Total	0 €

The British company's accounting policies regarding straight-line amortization and depreciation are as follows: licensing agreements, 5-year useful life; equipment, 10-year useful life; and buildings, 40-year useful life.

Since September 1, 20X4, the British company reported the following transactions:

1. Earned net income from operations, excluding cost of inventory sold, amortization, and depreciation, of 650,000 euros in the last four months of 20X4 and 14,520,000 euros in 20X5.
2. Purchased inventory as follows: 3,000,000 euros evenly throughout the first quarter of 20X5, 4,000,000 euros on June 1, 20X5, and 5,400,000 euros on September 1, 20X5. Ending inventory on December 31 of 20X4 and 20X5 was 2,000,000 euros and 2,200,000 euros, respectively.
3. Made principal payments of 150,000 FC on the September 1, 20X4, note payable at the end of each calendar quarter. Borrowed 500,000 FC on October 31, 20X5, with principal and interest payments beginning in 20X6.
4. Acquired a licensing agreement of March 31, 20X5, for 286,000 FC.

5. Sold land on March 31, 20X5, with a book value on September 1, 20X4, of 100,000 euros for 200,000 euros. The gain on the sale was reported as other income, not operating income.
6. Declared and paid annual dividends of 143,000 FC on March 31, 20X5.

Although the British company records its transactions in euros, it has been determined that its functional currency is the FC. Various exchange rates are as follows:

	Direct Quote Euro to FC	Direct Quote FC to Dollar
September 1, 20X4	1.40	1.17
September 30, 20X4	1.42	1.18
September 1–December 31, 20X4, average	1.44	1.19
December 31, 20X4	1.46	1.21
20X5 average	1.37	1.24
1st quarter, 20X5 average	1.45	1.24
March 31, 20X5	1.43	1.25
June 1, 20X5	1.40	1.27
June 30, 20X5	1.39	1.26
September 1, 20X5	1.38	1.22
September 30, 20X5	1.35	1.21
October 31, 20X5	1.34	1.23
Last quarter, 20X5 average	1.32	1.24
December 31, 20X5	1.30	1.25

◄◄◄◄◄ **Required**

1. Prepare a trial balance for the British company as of December 31, 20X5, expressed in its functional currency (FC). All supporting schedules should be in good form.
2. Compute the translated (in dollars) value of cost of sales for the 4-month period ending December 31, 20X4, and the year ended December 31, 20X5.

Problem 11-8 *(LO 3, 5)* **Translate a trial balance and prepare a consolidation worksheet. Useful comparison with Problem 11-9.** Balfour Corporation acquired 100% of Tobac, Inc., a foreign corporation, for 33,000,000 foreign currency units (FC). The acquisition, which was accounted for as a purchase, occurred on July 1, 20X5, when Tobac's equity, in foreign currency units, was as follows:

Common stock	19,000,000 FC
Paid-in capital in excess of par	8,480,000
Retained earnings	2,520,000

Any excess of cost over book value is traceable to equipment which is to be depreciated over 10 years. Balfour uses the simple equity method to account for its investment in Tobac.

On April 1, 20X7, Tobac acquired additional equipment costing 4,000,000 FC. Equipment is depreciated by the straight-line method over 10 years. No other equipment had been acquired or disposed of since 20X4. Tobac employs the LIFO inventory method. Ending inventory on December 31, 20X7, consists of the following:

Acquired in the 1st quarter of 20X4	1,000,000 FC
Acquired in the 1st quarter of 20X5	500,000
Acquired in the 1st quarter of 20X7	6,500,000

The cost of sales is traceable to goods purchased during 20X7 as follows:

Acquired uniformly over the last nine months	23,400,000 FC
Acquired in the 1st quarter	4,200,000

Other expenses were incurred evenly over the year.

On April 1, 20X7, Tobac borrowed $1,280,000 from the parent company in order to help finance the purchase of equipment. The note is due in one year and bears interest at the rate of 8%. Principal and interest amounts are due to the parent in dollars.

Various spot rates are as follows:

	1 FC =		1 FC =
1st Quarter, 20X4 Average	$0.46	December 31, 20X6	$0.60
20X4 Average	0.49	1st Quarter, 20X7 Average	0.62
January 1, 20X5	0.51	April 1, 20X7	0.64
1st Quarter, 20X5 Average	0.53	20X7 Average	0.67
July 1, 20X5	0.55	Last nine months, 20X7 Average	0.66
December 31, 20X5	0.58	December 31, 20X7	0.65
Last six months, 20X5 Average	0.57		
20X6 Average	0.58		

The December 31, 20X7, trial balances for Tobac and Balfour are as follows:

	Tobac, Inc.	Balfour Corporation
Cash	3,087,385 FC	$ 4,463,200
Net Accounts Receivable	12,000,000	15,350,000
Inventory	8,000,000	16,300,000
Due from Tobac		1,356,800
Investment in Tobac—See Note A		23,712,363
Depreciable Assets	34,000,000	68,000,000
Accumulated Depreciation	(12,300,000)	(42,000,000)
Due to Balfour	(2,087,385)	
Other Liabilities	(3,700,000)	(27,000,000)
Common Stock	(19,000,000)	(35,000,000)
Paid-In Capital in Excess of Par	(8,480,000)	(2,000,000)
Retained Earnings, January 1, 20X7	(7,520,000)	(4,500,000)
Sales	(40,000,000)	(98,000,000)
Cost of Sales	27,600,000	64,000,000
Depreciation Expense	3,300,000	8,076,800
Interest Expense on Balfour Loan (accrued on December 31, 20X7)—See Note B	118,154	
Exchange Gain on Balfour Loan—See Note B	(30,769)	
Other Expenses	5,012,615	10,000,000
Interest Income		(76,800)
Subsidiary Income		(2,682,363)
Total	0 FC	$ 0

Note A—Balfour's investment in Tobac consists of the following:

Initial investment (33,000,000 FC × $0.55)	$18,150,000
Last six months, 20X5 income (2,000,000 FC × $0.57)	1,140,000
20X6 income (3,000,000 FC × $0.58)	1,740,000
20X7 income	2,682,363
Balance	$23,712,363

Note B—The original loan from Balfour was 2,000,000 FC, or $1,280,000 (2,000,000 FC × $0.64). On December 31, 20X7, it would require 1,969,231 FC ($1,280,000 ÷ $0.65) to settle the loan. This represents an exchange gain of 30,769 FC (2,000,000 FC − 1,969,231 FC).

The year-end balance due to Balfour is determined as follows:

Principal balance.	1,969,231 FC
Accrued interest ($1,280,000 × 8% × 9/12 ÷ $0.65)	118,154
Balance	2,087,385 FC

The interest is accrued at year-end; therefore, interest expense should be translated at the year-end rate.

Assuming the FC is Tobac's functional currency, translate Tobac's trial balance, and prepare a consolidating worksheet. ◄◄◄◄◄ **Required**

Problem 11-9 *(LO 5, 6)* **Same facts as Problem 11-8 except involve remeasurement. Useful comparison with Problem 11-8.** Assume the same facts as Problem 11-8 with the following exceptions:

a. Tobac's functional currency is the U.S. dollar.
b. Balfour's investment in Tobac consists of the following:

Initial investment (33,000,000 FC × $0.55)	$18,150,000
Last six months, 20X5 income (including the remeasurement gain or loss) .	1,610,000
20X6 income (including the remeasurement gain or loss)	1,860,000
20X7 income (excluding the remeasurement gain or loss)	3,495,363
Balance	$25,115,363

Note that the balance has not yet been adjusted for the 20X7 remeasurement gain or loss.

c. The trial balances for Tobac and Balfour are the same as in Problem 11-8 with the following exceptions:

Balfour	
Investment in Tobac.	$25,115,363
Retained earnings, January 1, 20X7	(5,090,000)
Subsidiary income	(3,495,363)

Remembering that Tobac's functional currency is the U.S. dollar, translate Tobac's trial balance and prepare a consolidating worksheet. ◄◄◄◄◄ **Required**

Remember that transactions traceable to pre-July 1, 20X5, should be remeasured at the rate in effect on July 1, 20X5. This is because on July 1, 20X5, Balfour acquired its interest in Tobac and established the dollar basis of net assets existing at that time.

Problem 11-10 *(LO 3, 5)* **Translation and consolidation with excess of cost over book value.** On July 1, 20X4, Troutman International acquired a 90% interest in Korbel Manufacturing when Korbel's shareholders' equity was 20,000,000 FC (foreign currencies) including retained earnings with a balance of 5,000,000 FC. Troutman paid 21,000,000 FC for their interest, when 1 FC equaled $1.10, and the excess of cost over book value was allocated as follows:

Licensing agreement	900,000 FC
Goodwill	2,100,000

The licensing agreement expired at the end of 20X8 and was to be amortized using a straight-line pattern. At year-end 20X5, Troutman recognized that the goodwill of 2,100,000 FC was impaired by 20%, or 420,000 FC.

Troutman records its investment in Korbel under the simple equity method, and Korbel's functional currency is the FC. Since the acquisition, Korbel has reported net income and dividends as follows:

	Last 6 Months of 20X4	20X5	20X6
Net income	900,000 FC	800,000 FC	1,100,000 FC
Dividends declared	240,000 FC	0 FC	200,000 FC
Average exchange rate (for 1 FC)	$1.12	$1.20	$1.17
Exchange rate at year-end (for 1 FC)	$1.14	$1.23	$1.15
Exchange rate when dividends were declared (for 1 FC)	$1.13		$1.20

A condensed trial balance for Troutman and Korbel as of December 31, 20X6, is as follows:

	Troutman (in dollars)	Korbel (in FC)
Working Capital	7,418,580	5,200,000
Depreciable Assets	34,000,000	22,500,000
Accumulated Depreciation	(11,560,000)	(6,740,000)
Due from Korbel	92,000	
Investment in Korbel	25,569,420	
Other Assets	2,070,000	3,080,000
Due to Troutman		(80,000)
Notes Payable	(4,000,000)	(1,600,000)
Common Stock at Par Value	(16,000,000)	(5,000,000)
Paid-In Capital in Excess of Par	(26,000,000)	(10,000,000)
Retained Earnings	(8,000,000)	(6,260,000)
20X6 Net Income	(3,590,000)	(1,100,000)
Total	0	0

Required ▶ ▶ ▶ ▶ ▶ Prepare a columnar worksheet to present the 20X6 consolidated income statement and balance sheet for the parent company and its subsidiary with all amounts stated in U.S. dollars. Key and schedule worksheet eliminations and adjustments.

Interim Reporting and Disclosures about Segments of an Enterprise

CHAPTER 12

Learning Objectives

When you have completed this chapter, you should be able to

1. **Explain the goal of interim reporting and how the interim period is viewed relative to an annual period.**
2. **Demonstrate how principles of revenue and expense recognition may be modified for interim reporting purposes.**
3. **Show how income tax expense or benefits tied to income from continuing operations are determined for an interim period.**
4. **Determine the income tax expense or benefit for nonordinary items of income and loss reported for interim periods.**
5. **Explain why segmental reporting is important, and define an operating segment.**
6. **Apply the criteria used to determine which segment is reportable.**
7. **Describe the information about a reportable segment that must be disclosed.**
8. **State which enterprise-wide disclosures must be provided.**

This chapter focuses on two areas of significance to most large, publicly held enterprises: interim reporting and segmental disclosure. The relevance of financial information is enhanced if the information is provided on a timely basis. Interim financial reporting addresses the need for timely information and provides users with relevant data which may be used to evaluate the present and help to project future results. The division of an annual reporting period into shorter interim periods results in some unique accounting problems which are addressed in this chapter. Disclosure about segments of an enterprise is designed to provide relevant information about the various business activities in which an enterprise is involved. Such disclosures also provide information about the economic environments in which enterprises operate. Many enterprises consist of operating segments that differ significantly from each other in terms of products, economic environments, markets served, and manufacturing methods. The disclosure of segmental information follows a management approach which emphasizes how management organizes the segments of the enterprise for decision-making purposes and evaluation of performance. This approach will allow users of such information to better understand the activities and environments which affect an enterprise's performance, cash flows, and business risks. The disclosures called for by this approach for both annual and interim reporting purposes are discussed in this chapter.

1 OBJECTIVE

Explain the goal of interim reporting and how the interim period is viewed relative to an annual period.

INTERIM REPORTING

To satisfy the need for timely financial information, many business enterprises have developed interim reporting models that provide financial information on a monthly or quarterly basis or at other defined intervals. These interim data may consist of statements of financial position and retained earnings, income statements, and statements of cash flows. However, primary emphasis is placed on the public disclosure of interim income data.

A substantial amount of empirical research has been devoted to an examination of the utility of publicly disclosed interim financial reports. This research has identified significant stock market reaction to the issuance of interim reports and has noted the influence of interim reports on actual investment decisions. Interim reports provide such an important basis for the prediction of annual income that the demand for these reports nearly parallels the demand for annual reports.

The established utility of interim data emphasizes the importance of applying generally accepted accounting principles, including the principle of adequate disclosure, to interim reports. Therefore, the American Institute of Certified Public Accountants, the National Association of Accountants, the Financial Executives Institute, the Financial Analysts Federation, the Financial Accounting Standards Board, the Securities and Exchange Commission, and the principal stock exchanges have directed efforts toward the development and improvement of interim financial reporting.

Approaches to Reporting Interim Data

Earlier forms of interim reporting provided the user of such data with various disclosures other than the computation of net income. However, as the importance of interim income statements became more apparent, different views of the interim period developed. One view of the interim period is that it represents a distinct, independent accounting period, separate from the annual accounting period. Therefore, interim net income should be determined by using the same principles and estimations as would be used if the interim period were an annual accounting period. For example, annual research and development incurred during the interim period should be expensed in that period rather than deferred to future interim periods.

Another view of the interim period is that it is an integral part of the annual period and does not stand as a distinct, independent period. Therefore, interim data should include appropriate adjustments and estimates so that they can be used to predict annual amounts. For example, assume annual income normally includes a year-end accrual for executive bonuses in the amount of $120,000. If the interim statements are to serve as a predictor of annual values, it would seem appropriate that quarterly income statements should include a proportionate amount of this year-end adjustment. Including a $30,000 adjustment for bonuses in the quarterly income statement would allow one to predict annual bonuses in the amount of $120,000. If this interim adjustment were not made, bonuses would be reflected only in the fourth quarter, and previous quarters would not have provided the user with a basis for predicting this annual amount. From this example, one can see that an interim period is viewed as an integral part of a larger annual period. This view of the interim period has been adopted as the underlying theory used to formulate interim accounting principles and practices.

2

OBJECTIVE

Demonstrate how principles of revenue and expense recognition may be modified for interim reporting purposes.

Accounting Principles Board Opinion No. 28

In 1973, the Accounting Principles Board issued APB Opinion No. 28, *Interim Financial Reporting*, which applies to both internally and externally issued reports. This Opinion was in response to the growing interest in the credibility of interim data and to the apparent need for an authoritative statement from the accounting profession regarding generally accepted accounting principles for such data. The Opinion also may have been influenced by the interim reporting requirements of the SEC.

APB Opinion No. 28 is based on the conclusion that an interim period should be viewed as an *integral part of the annual period*, not as a distinct, independent period. The Opinion reflects the APB's concern for the consistent application of principles by stating that financial statements for each interim period should be based on the *same accounting principles and practices* that are used for the preparation of annual financial statements. However, certain modifications of these principles and practices that relate to costs and expenses may be necessary so that the reported results of an interim period are more indicative of anticipated annual income statement amounts. Modifications of accounting principles and practices also are necessary in order to provide timely information.

Modifications for Costs and Expenses. Those costs that are directly related or allocated to products sold or to services rendered for annual reporting purposes should be given similar treatment for interim reporting purposes. However, the following modifications are acceptable in the area of inventory costing:

1. The gross profit method or other estimation methods that are not acceptable for annual purposes may be used for interim purposes in those instances where taking an interim physical inventory would be too costly or where perpetual inventory records are lacking or unreliable. Furthermore, use of the gross profit method provides a timely measurement which may not be the case if other methods of inventory accounting were employed. The inventory method used for interim purposes should be disclosed. Significant differences between estimates of the perpetual annual inventory and the annual physical inventory also should be recorded in interim statements on a proportionate basis.
2. Use of the LIFO method for interim purposes may result in inventory liquidations that will be replaced by year-end. To compensate for these interim liquidations, the interim cost of goods sold should include the *replacement cost* of temporarily liquidated inventory rather than its historical cost.
3. The use of lower of cost or market may suggest inventory losses for the interim period. Recoveries of these losses in subsequent periods should be recognized as gains to the extent of the losses previously recognized in interim periods within the same fiscal year. An exception to this rule is that temporary market declines that can reasonably be expected to be restored in the fiscal year need not be recognized for the interim period.
4. The use of standard costs for determining inventory generally should be applied on the same basis as is required for annual purposes. Price and volume variances that are planned and expected to be absorbed by year-end should be deferred at interim reporting dates.[1] However, unplanned or unanticipated variances should be reported at the end of an interim period.

Illustration of an Interim Liquidation of Inventory. In order to illustrate the special treatment given interim liquidations, assume a company's LIFO inventory available for sale during the third quarter consisted of beginning inventory of 1,200 units at a cost of $20 each and current purchases of 2,000 units at a cost of $30 each. Assume 2,500 units were sold during the quarter with the expectation that they would be replaced for $32 a unit. Management anticipates that the annual ending inventory will be 1,100 units. Therefore, although the beginning inventory has been liquidated by 500 units, management expects to replenish 400 of these units by year-end. Assuming the company anticipates paying $32 each to replenish the inventory, the third-quarter cost of sales would be calculated as follows:

Current purchases (2,000 units @ $30)	$60,000
Prior inventory (500 units @ $20 original cost)	10,000
Excess replacement cost (400 units @ $12)	4,800
	$74,800

The entry to record the third-quarter cost of sales would be as follows:

Cost of Sales	74,800	
Inventory		70,000
Excess of Replacement Cost for Temporary Liquidation		4,800
To record cost of sales with a historical cost of $70,000 and an excess of additional replacement cost equal to $4,800 ($12 × 400 units).		

1 Accounting Principles Board Opinion No. 28, *Interim Financial Reporting* (New York: American Institute of Certified Public Accountants, 1973), par. 14.

The Excess of Replacement Cost for Temporary Liquidation is classified as a current liability on the interim financial statements. When the 400 units are replenished in the fourth quarter at an assumed cost of $32, the following entry is made:

Inventory	8,000	
Excess of Replacement Cost for Temporary Liquidation	4,800	
Accounts Payable (cash)		12,800
To record replenishment of inventory previously liquidated.		

Notice that the 400 units replenish the inventory account at a cost of $20 each as though no liquidation had occurred. That is, the inventory now consists of 1,100 units (700 at the end of the third quarter plus the 400 replenished) at a cost of $20 each.

Illustration of Cost or Market for Interim Inventory. Assume at the end of the second quarter, ending inventory has a cost of $380,000 and a fair value of $350,000. The use of lower of cost or market would require a $30,000 loss due to market declines to be recognized in the second quarter. At the end of the third quarter, the company has ending inventory with a cost of $520,000 and a fair value of $560,000. Of the $40,000 excess of fair value over cost, the company can recognize $30,000 of this amount as a recovery of the second-quarter loss. Therefore, the third-quarter financial statements would include a $30,000 gain due to market recoveries.

Reporting of Costs Unrelated to Inventory. In reporting costs and expenses that are not allocated to products sold or to services rendered but are charged against income in the interim period, the following standards apply:

a. Costs and expenses other than product costs should be charged to income in interim periods as incurred or be allocated among interim periods based on an estimate of time expired, benefit received, or activity associated with the periods. Procedures adopted for assigning specific cost and expense items to an interim period should be consistent with the bases followed by the company in reporting results of operations at annual reporting dates. However, when a specific cost or expense item charged to expense for annual reporting purposes benefits more than one interim period, the cost or expense item may be allocated to those interim periods.
b. Some costs and expenses incurred in an interim period, however, cannot be readily identified with the activities or benefits of other interim periods and should be charged to the interim period in which they were incurred. Disclosure should be made as to the nature and amount of such costs unless items of a comparable nature are included in both the current interim period and in the corresponding interim period of the preceding year.
c. Arbitrary assignment of the amount of such costs to an interim period should not be made.
d. Gains and losses that arise in any interim period similar to those that would not be deferred at year-end should not be deferred to later interim periods within the same fiscal year.[2]

To illustrate the above concepts, assume the following expenditures have occurred at the beginning of the second quarter:

1. A 12-month insurance premium was paid in the amount of $1,200.
2. Research costs in the amount of $18,000 were paid and are expected to benefit the company over the next 18 months.
3. A contribution in the amount of $1,000 was made, although the benefits to subsequent quarters are uncertain.

The expenses to be recognized in the second quarter are as follows:

Insurance expense ($1,200 ÷ 12 × 3 months)	$ 300
Research costs ($18,000 ÷ 3 quarters—not to be deferred beyond year-end)	6,000
Contribution expense	1,000
	$7,300

2 *Ibid.*, par. 15.

Certain costs and expenses of an entity are subject to year-end adjustments, such as inventory shrinkage, allowance for uncollectible accounts, and year-end bonuses. These adjustments should not be recognized totally in the final interim period if they relate to activities of other interim periods. Therefore, to generate interim financial reports that contain a reasonable portion of annual expenses, a portion of estimated year-end adjustments should be allocated to each interim period on the basis of a revenue or a cost relationship. For example, a company that estimates an expected material year-end adjustment to its perpetual inventory, based on a physical inventory, should allocate a portion of that estimated adjustment to each interim period. In this case, a portion of the annual estimated inventory shrinkage could be allocated to the quarter using a ratio of current quarter cost of sales to annual estimated cost of sales. Changes in earlier quarters' estimates should be accounted for in the current quarter.

The costs and expenses as well as revenues of some businesses are subject to seasonal variations. Since interim reports for such businesses must be considered as representative of the annual period, APB Opinion No. 28 states that

> *... such businesses should disclose the seasonal nature of their activities, and consider supplementing their interim reports with information for twelve-month periods ended at the interim date for the current and preceding years.*[3]

Adjustments Related to Prior Interim Periods. By the definitions set forth in FASB Statement No. 16, *Prior Period Adjustments*, many items that were viewed previously as prior-period adjustments became elements of current operating income. However, certain items are treated as adjustments related to prior interim periods of the current fiscal year. These items include an adjustment or settlement of: litigation or similar claims, income taxes, renegotiation proceedings, or utility revenue under rate-making processes. Treating these items as prior-period adjustments is appropriate if all of the following criteria are met:

a. The effect of the adjustment or settlement is material in relation to income from continuing operations of the current fiscal year or in relation to the trend of income from continuing operations or is material by other appropriate criteria, and
b. All or part of the adjustment or settlement can be specifically identified with and is directly related to business activities of specific prior interim periods of the current fiscal year, and
c. The amount of the adjustment or settlement could not be reasonably estimated prior to the current interim period but becomes reasonably estimable in the current interim period.[4]

If such an item occurs in other than the first interim period of the current fiscal year and if all or part of the item is an adjustment related to prior interim periods of the current fiscal year, it should be reported as follows:

a. The portion of the item that is directly related to business activities of the enterprise during the current interim period, if any, shall be included in the determination of net income for that period.
b. Prior interim periods of the current fiscal year shall be restated to include the portion of the item that is directly related to business activities of the enterprise during each prior interim period in the determination of net income for that period.
c. The portion of the item that is directly related to business activities of the enterprise during prior fiscal years, if any, shall be included in the determination of net income of the first interim period of the current fiscal year.[5]

Disclosure also is required regarding adjustments related to prior interim periods of the current year in the period in which the adjustment occurs. Disclosures should be made for each prior period of the current year setting forth both the effect on and actual adjusted amount of income from continuing operations, net income, and related per-share amounts.

---

3 *Ibid.*, par. 13.
4 Statement of Financial Accounting Standards No. 16, *Prior Period Adjustments* (Stamford: Financial Accounting Standards Board, 1977), par. 13.
5 *Ibid.*, par. 14.

Finally, it is important to note that those adjustments that are related to prior interim periods do not include normal recurring corrections and adjustments that result from the use of estimates. For example, in the current interim period, the revision of estimates used to measure uncollectible accounts is not accounted for as an adjustment related to prior interim periods. Instead, this correction is accounted for in the current interim period and prospectively, as is the case with other changes in estimates.

3

OBJECTIVE

Show how income tax expense or benefits tied to income from continuing operations are determined for an interim period.

Accounting for Income Taxes in Interim Statements

Keeping in mind that the interim period is viewed as an integral part of a larger annual period, interim financial statements should reflect a proportionate amount of the estimated annual income taxes. Each interim period will not be viewed as a separate tax period; therefore, estimates of annual tax amounts and rates become critical. The basic objective of accounting for income taxes in interim periods is to estimate the annual effective tax rate and apply that rate to the interim periods' pretax net incomes.

Accounting for income taxes in interim financial statements is based on the application of principles established in APB Opinion Nos. 23 and 24, FASB Interpretation No. 18, and FASB Statement No. 109. In addition, the following guidelines are applicable to the determination of an effective tax rate for interim purposes that is representative of the estimated annual effective tax rate:

1. The effective tax rate for the annual fiscal period must be estimated at the end of each interim period and applied to year-to-date interim income from ordinary continuing operations. The current interim period's tax expense or benefit is the difference between (a) the year-to-date tax expense or benefit and (b) the amounts of tax reported in previous interim periods of the current year.
2. The estimated effective tax rate should reflect tax planning alternatives, such as capital gains rates, permanent differences, and tax credits.
3. Nonordinary items of income or loss (unusual or infrequently occurring items, extraordinary items, discontinued operations, and the cumulative effect of changes in accounting principles) are not included in the computation of the estimated annual effective tax rate, nor are these items prorated over the balance of the fiscal period. The tax effect on these items is determined incrementally.
4. Changes in tax legislation are to be accounted for in interim periods subsequent to the effective date of the legislation.[6]

The first guideline is designed to ensure that the interim income tax rate is representative of the tax rate applicable to the entire fiscal period. For example, if income from continuing operations during the first interim period is $25,000, under a graduated taxing system the effective tax rate at this level of income might be 15%. However, if the annual ordinary income is expected to be $335,000, the effective annual tax rate might be approximately 34%. Therefore, the latter rate should be used as the interim tax rate. If this estimated annual effective tax rate were not used, a reader of the first interim period's financial statements might conclude that income is taxed at only 15%.

Mechanically speaking, the first guideline also provides a simple way of accounting for changes in the estimated annual effective tax rate. As mentioned earlier, normal recurring corrections and adjustments that result from the use of estimates are accounted for in the current interim period. Applying the estimated annual effective tax rate to the year-to-date income and then subtracting (adding) the tax expenses (benefits) traceable to prior interim periods of the current year results in a difference that represents

1. The tax on the current interim period's pretax income at the present estimated annual effective tax rate, and
2. Corrections of previous interim periods' tax expenses or benefits resulting from a change in the estimated annual effective tax rate.

---

6 Accounting Principles Board Opinion No. 28, *op. cit.*, pars. 19–20.

To illustrate, assume that the first quarter's pretax income of $40,000 was taxed at a 30% rate, resulting in a $12,000 tax expense. At the end of the second quarter, the estimated annual effective tax rate is 32%, and the second quarter's pretax income is $50,000. The tax on the year-to-date pretax income of $90,000 ($40,000 + $50,000) is $28,800 (32% × $90,000). Subtracting from this year-to-date amount the first-quarter tax expense of $12,000 results in a current second-quarter tax expense of $16,800. The $16,800 consists of

1. The tax on the second quarter's pretax income at the present estimated annual effective tax rate (50,000 × 32%)	$16,000
2. Corrections of prior interim period's tax expense resulting from a change in the estimated annual effective tax rate [$40,000 × (32% – 30%)]	800
	$16,800

If necessary, the estimated effective annual tax rate should be revised each interim period in order to reflect changed expectations. The guidelines indirectly emphasize that changes in the estimated annual effective tax rate should be accounted for as a change in estimate. Therefore, such changes in the tax rate from period to period should be reflected in the tax expense or benefit of the current period in which the change occurs. The second guideline emphasizes that tax planning alternatives should be reflected in the determination of the estimated effective annual tax rate. For example, if it is estimated that pretax operating income will include some tax-exempt income (a permanent difference), this should be reflected in a lower estimated tax rate. Tax credits and/or lower capital gains tax rates will also have the effect of lowering the estimated rate. Tax allocation principles resulting from the existence of timing differences would be factored into the calculation of the estimated effective annual tax rate as well.

The third guideline recognizes that nonordinary items of income or loss may have a distortive effect on estimated annual effective tax rates; therefore, they are excluded from such calculations. This guideline also recognizes that such items are not allocated to other interim periods of the current year. Thus, such items are accounted for entirely in the interim period in which they occur, and the resulting tax impact must be separately determined. The separate determination of the tax employs an incremental approach which is demonstrated in a later section of this chapter.

The fourth guideline echoes the underlying theory of the first guideline in that changes in estimated tax rates are to be accounted for currently and prospectively. Changes in tax legislation are just one possible explanation for a change in estimated annual effective tax rates.

The computation of the estimated effective tax rate is presented in Cases 1 and 2 on page 728. Case 3, on page 729, demonstrates the determination of the tax expense traceable to interim income and the handling of a change in the estimated effective tax rate.

Year-to-Date Operating Losses. In some instances, an interim year-to-date (YTD) operating loss may be present. Given this loss, a question arises as to the potential tax benefit associated with the loss. The potential tax benefit is a function of several factors.

The YTD loss first must be combined with the projected income or loss for the remaining interim periods of the current fiscal year. If the YTD loss is offset by the projected income, a tax benefit traceable to the YTD loss may be recognized. However, if it is more likely than not that some portion of the projected income will not be recognized, then the recognized tax benefit traceable to the loss will be reduced accordingly. The concept of "more likely than not" means a level of likelihood at least more than 50% and requires the consideration of many sources of evidence, both positive and negative.[7] For example, a backlog of unfilled orders and/or a strong earnings history exclusive of the YTD loss would suggest that, more likely than not, losses may be offset by projected income. A history of operating losses or unsettled circumstances or economic conditions may suggest that, more likely than not, losses will not be offset totally by projected income.

7 Further discussion of the phrase "more likely than not" can be found in Statement of Financial Accounting Standards No. 109, *Accounting for Income Taxes* (Norwalk, CT: Financial Accounting Standards Board, 1992).

Case 1
Income in All Interim Periods—Tax Credit; No Permanent Differences

Year-to-date (YTD) pretax income is $170,000, and projected pretax income for the balance of the fiscal year is $30,000. No permanent differences exist, and it is anticipated that an annual tax credit of $13,250 will be available. Corporate income is taxed as follows: first $50,000 at 15%, next $25,000 at 25%, next $25,000 at 34%, amounts over $100,000 up to $335,000 at 39%. The effective tax rate is computed as follows:

	Pretax Income (Pretax Loss)	
YTD income	$170,000	
Projected income	30,000	
Estimated annual income	$200,000	
Permanent differences	0	
Estimated adjusted income	$200,000	
Tax on estimated adjusted income	$ 61,250*	
Tax credits	(13,250)	
Net tax (Note A)	$ 48,000	
Effective tax rate	(24%)	($48,000 ÷ $200,000)

*[($50,000 × 15%) + ($25,000 × 25%) + ($25,000 × 34%) + ($100,000 × 39%)]

Note A: A general business tax credit that cannot be used in the current period may be carried back to the prior year. If tax credits still remain after the carryback, they may be carried forward 20 years.

Case 2
Income in All Interim Periods—Tax Credit; Permanent Difference; No Tax Credit

Year-to-date (YTD) pretax income is $30,000, and projected pretax income for the balance of the fiscal year is $90,000. Annual income includes $10,000 of expense which is never deductible for tax purposes (i.e., a permanent difference). Assume that corporate income is taxed at the rates set forth in Case 1 above. The effective tax rate is computed as follows:

	Pretax Income (Pretax Loss)	
YTD income	$ 30,000	
Projected income	90,000	
Estimated annual income	$120,000	
Permanent differences	10,000	
Estimated adjusted income	$130,000	
Tax on estimated adjusted income	$ 33,950*	
Tax credits	0	
Net tax	$ 33,950	
Effective tax rate	(28%)	($33,950 ÷ $120,000)**

*[($50,000 × 15%) + ($25,000 × 25%) + ($25,000 × 34%) + ($30,000 × 39%)]

**Note that the rate always is based on estimated annual pretax income versus adjusted income.

Case 3
Income in All Interim Periods—Change in Effective Tax Rate

In the third quarter, a change in the estimated annual income results in a change in the effective tax rate.

Interim Period (Quarter)	Ordinary Pretax Income (Loss) Current Period	Year-to-Date	Effective Tax Rate	Tax Expense (Benefit) Year-to-Date	Previously Reported	Current Period
First	$30,000	$ 30,000	28%	$ 8,400	—	$ 8,400
Second	40,000	70,000	28	19,600	$ 8,400	11,200
Third	20,000	90,000	32	28,800	19,600	9,200
Fourth	50,000	140,000	32	44,800	28,800	16,000

After considering the projected income or loss for the balance of the current year, an estimated annual operating loss may exist. The potential tax benefit traceable to this estimated annual operating loss is a function of the following factors:

1. The extent to which the operating loss may be offset by income of the prior two fiscal years included in the carryback period and/or
2. The extent to which the operating loss may be offset by subsequent years' annual income which is more likely than not to be recognized in the 20-year carryforward period.

The basic concern addressed by these factors is whether the operating loss is able to be offset against operating income and, therefore, result in a tax benefit. If the facts suggest that such a benefit is more likely than not, the benefit should be recognized in the calculation of the effective annual tax rate.

Offsetting YTD Operating Losses against Subsequent Interim Income. The benefit associated with a YTD operating loss should be recognized if the loss will be offset against income in later interim periods of the fiscal year. This offset against income may be recognized if it is more likely than not that such income will be recognized. Although "more likely than not" is a subjective concept, knowledge of a company's past performance, existing commitments relating to the future, and seasonal patterns must be considered. APB Opinion No. 28 states that

> *An established seasonal pattern of loss in early interim periods offset by income in later interim periods should constitute evidence that realization is assured beyond reasonable doubt, unless other evidence indicates the established seasonal pattern will not prevail. The tax effects of losses incurred in early interim periods may be recognized in a later interim period of a fiscal year if their realization, although initially uncertain, later becomes assured beyond reasonable doubt. When the tax effects of losses that arise in the early portions of a fiscal year are not recognized in that interim period, no tax provision should be made for income that arises in later interim periods until the tax effects of the previous interim losses are utilized.*[8]

The offset of an established seasonal loss by subsequent interim income is demonstrated in Case 1[9] that follows. Case 2 demonstrates a YTD loss whose tax benefit is not initially certain but later becomes recognizable. It is important to note that, in both Cases 1 and 2 on page 730, it is assumed that no pretax income is available in prior and/or subsequent years to absorb the current year's operating losses.

8 Accounting Principles Board Opinion No. 28, *op. cit.*, par. 20.

9 Note that throughout this chapter the effective tax rates used in the illustrative examples are not based on the actual corporate tax rates but, rather, are only for illustrative purposes.

Case 1
Seasonal YTD Loss Offset by Subsequent Interim Income which Is "More Likely Than Not" and No Pretax Income Available in Other Years

	Ordinary Pretax Income (Loss)			Tax Expense (Benefit)		
Interim Period (Quarter)	Current Period	Year-to-Date	Effective Tax Rate	Year-to-Date	Previously Reported	Current Period
First	$(30,000)	$(30,000)	40%	$(12,000)		$(12,000)
Second	20,000	(10,000)	40	(4,000)	$(12,000)	8,000
Third	40,000	30,000	40	12,000	(4,000)	16,000
Fourth	40,000	70,000	40	28,000	12,000	16,000

Case 2
YTD Loss where Tax Benefit Is Initially Uncertain and No Pretax Income Available in Other Years

	Ordinary Pretax Income (Loss)			Tax Expense (Benefit)		
Interim Period (Quarter)	Current Period	Year-to-Date	Effective Tax Rate	Year-to-Date	Previously Reported	Current Period
First	$(30,000)	$(30,000)	0%			
Second	20,000	(10,000)	0			
Third	40,000	30,000	40	$12,000		$12,000
Fourth	40,000	70,000	40	28,000	$12,000	16,000

Offsetting YTD or Annual Operating Losses against Income of Prior Fiscal Years. In certain instances, a current YTD interim loss may not be offset entirely by income in later interim periods of the current fiscal year. However, as suggested by the first factor discussed above, the tax benefit of the YTD loss should be recognized to the extent that the loss may be carried back against the prior two years of income. Loss carrybacks must begin with the earliest of the prior two years and then proceed to the next earlier year. The tax benefit traceable to the loss, therefore, is a function of the tax rate applied to a prior year's income. Case 3 involves the carryback of a YTD loss. Note that, in this case, the loss is not offset completely against prior income. However, the tax benefit is recognized to whatever extent possible.

The same carryback principles apply if an annual loss is anticipated. For example, if a company has a YTD loss of $40,000 and an anticipated annual loss of $100,000, the amount of tax benefit would be dependent upon the extent to which the $100,000 loss may be carried back. If a company has a year-to-date income of $60,000 and an anticipated annual loss of $20,000, the estimated annual effective tax rate would be dependent upon the tax benefit associated with the annual loss of $20,000. These principles are demonstrated in Case 4.

Case 3
YTD Loss with No Assurance of Subsequent Interim Income;
$30,000 of Prior Two Years' Income Taxed at 50%

Interim Period (Quarter)	Ordinary Pretax Income (Loss) Current Period	Year-to-Date	Effective Tax Rate	Tax Expense (Benefit) Year-to-Date	Previously Reported	Current Period
First	$(40,000)	$(40,000)	37.5%	$(15,000)*		$(15,000)
Second	10,000	(30,000)	50	(15,000)	$(15,000)	
Third	35,000	5,000	40**	2,000	(15,000)	17,000
Fourth	30,000	35,000	40	14,000	2,000	12,000

*Only $30,000 of the $40,000 loss can be offset against the prior years' income, resulting in a tax benefit of $15,000; $15,000 ÷ $40,000 = 37.5%.
**The current-year statutory tax rate is assumed to be 40%.

Case 4
YTD and Anticipated Annual Loss (of $100,000) with $60,000 of Prior Two Years' Income Taxed at 50%

Interim Period (Quarter)	Ordinary Pretax Income (Loss) Current Period	Year-to-Date	Effective Tax Rate	Tax Expense (Benefit) Year-to-Date	Previously Reported	Current Period
First	$(40,000)	$ (40,000)	30%*	$(12,000)		$(12,000)
Second	(30,000)	(70,000)	30	(21,000)	$(12,000)	(9,000)
Third	5,000	(65,000)	30	(19,500)	(21,000)	1,500
Fourth	(35,000)	(100,000)	30	(30,000)	(19,500)	(10,500)

*The effective tax rate of 30% is based on a $30,000 tax benefit of ($60,000 × 50%) expressed as a percentage of the $100,000 anticipated annual loss.

Offsetting Annual Operating Losses against Future Annual Income. To the extent that losses are not absorbed by income in later interim periods of the current fiscal year and/or the prior two years of income, tax benefits still may be recognized currently. Losses not already offset may be carried forward against future annual income which more likely than not will be recognized in the 20-year carryforward period. Estimating whether future annual income will more likely than not be recognized is one of the most difficult aspects of determining the estimated annual effective tax rate associated with operating losses. Certain amounts of future annual income may have a low level of likelihood that they will be recognized. For example, if an entity has a history of operating losses and is in an industry experiencing a significant number of bankruptcies, a low level of likelihood would seem reasonable. Alternatively, certain amounts of future annual income have a high level of likelihood. For example, the future taxable amounts represented by deferred tax liabilities are considered to have a very high level of likelihood. Therefore, such future taxable amounts will more likely than not be recognized and serve as a basis for offsetting a current annual operating loss. The principles of offsetting current annual operating losses against likely future annual income are demonstrated in Case 5, on page 732.

Case 5
YTD and Anticipated Annual Loss (of $80,000) with Carrybacks and Carryforwards Available

	Ordinary Pretax Income (Loss)			Tax Expense (Benefit)		
Interim Period (Quarter)	Current Period	Year-to-Date	Effective Tax Rate	Year-to-Date	Previously Reported	Current Period
First	$(20,000)	$(20,000)	30%*	$ (6,000)		$ (6,000)
Second	15,000	(5,000)	30	(1,500)	$ (6,000)	4,500
Third	(35,000)	(40,000)	30	(12,000)	(1,500)	(10,500)
Fourth	(40,000)	(80,000)	30	(24,000)	(12,000)	(12,000)

*The calculation of the effective tax rate is based on the following:

Prior 2 years' total income of $10,000 taxed at a prior rate of 40% . . .	$ 4,000
Deferred tax liability reversing the next 20 years based on the current tax rate of 40% ($50,000 of temporary differences). . .	20,000
Total tax benefit. . .	$24,000

$24,000 ÷ $80,000 anticipated annual loss = 30%

Note: In Case 5, the likely future income for offsetting the loss is $50,000, resulting from temporary timing differences. However, if likely future income in the carryforward period had been at least $70,000, a tax benefit would have been recognized on the entire current operating loss of $80,000. The $80,000 of loss would have been carried back in the amount of $10,000 and carried forward in the amount of $70,000.

Operating Losses that Are Not Offset. If present net operating losses cannot be offset totally by any of the options discussed (subsequent interim income of the current fiscal year, carrybacks, or carryforwards), the potential tax benefit is reduced accordingly. However, those losses that are not offset may be offset subsequently against future years' recognized income or additional deferred tax liabilities which may arise in the carryforward period. When the tax benefit associated with these remaining losses is recognized, it is classified the same as the item against which the losses were offset. For example, if the remaining losses were offset against subsequent income from continuing operations, the benefit would become a component of income from continuing operations. However, if the remaining losses were offset against a subsequent extraordinary item, the tax benefit would be classified as extraordinary. To demonstrate these principles, consider the facts of Case 5. In this instance, the annual anticipated loss of $80,000 was used to offset $10,000 of prior years' income and $50,000 of likely future income in the carryforward period taxed at 40%. Therefore, the equivalent of $60,000 ($10,000 + $50,000) of the loss was offset in order to generate the $24,000 tax benefit. The remaining loss of $20,000 (original $80,000 − $60,000 offset) may offset future income or deferred tax liabilities arising in the 20-year carryforward period. Assuming the subsequent year has a recognized pretax income from continuing operations of $25,000 which would be taxed at 40%, a tax benefit of $8,000 ($20,000 × 40%), representing the offsetting of the remaining $20,000 loss against the income from continuing operations, would be recognized. The subsequent year's net tax expense on the continuing income would be $2,000 [($25,000 − $20,000) × 40%], for an effective tax rate of 8% ($2,000 ÷ $25,000). The net tax expense results from the tax expense of $10,000 on the $25,000 of income reduced by the $8,000 tax benefit.

Case 6 demonstrates a special limitation of the tax benefits associated with operating losses. This special limitation arises when a YTD operating loss exceeds the annual operating loss.

Case 6
YTD and Anticipated Annual Loss (of $48,000) with a $40,000 Carryback at 30% Available

Interim Period (Quarter)	Ordinary Pretax Income (Loss) Current Period	Year-to-Date	Effective Tax Rate	Tax Expense (Benefit) Year-to-Date	Previously Reported	Current Period
First	$(10,000)	$(10,000)	25%*	$ (2,500)		$(2,500)
Second	(20,000)	(30,000)	25	(7,500)	$ (2,500)	(5,000)
Third	(30,000)	(60,000)	Note	(12,000)	(7,500)	(4,500)
Fourth	12,000	(48,000)	25	(12,000)	(12,000)	

*The calculation of the effective tax rate is based on the following:

Prior 2 years' total income of $40,000 taxed at a prior rate of 30% $12,000

The effective tax rate of 25% is based on the $12,000 total tax benefit expressed as a percentage of the $48,000 anticipated annual pretax loss ($12,000 ÷ $48,000).

Note: If the rate of 25% were used, a YTD tax benefit of $15,000 would be suggested. However, a YTD loss of $60,000 could receive a benefit of only $12,000 (30% × $40,000 prior year's income). Therefore, the YTD benefit is limited to $12,000. This special rule arises when a YTD operating loss exceeds the annual anticipated operating loss. Notice that both YTD and annual amounts must be losses. In this case, the YTD tax benefit is limited to the amount ($12,000) that would be recognized if the YTD loss were the expected loss for the entire fiscal year ($48,000).

4

OBJECTIVE

Determine the income tax expense or benefit for nonordinary items of income and loss reported for interim periods.

Nonordinary Items of Income or Loss. Certain elements making up an entity's net income are reported separately and/or shown net of tax. These elements include unusual or infrequently occurring items, discontinued operations, extraordinary items, and cumulative effects of changes in accounting principles. For purposes of discussion, these items are referred to as nonordinary items. There also are interim gains or losses that are directly accounted for as a component of owners' equity. The tax impact on these items should be determined by the same methodology as is used for nonordinary items. As previously stated, these items are not included in the determination of the estimated effective tax rate applied to ordinary income. The estimated effective tax rate applied to ordinary income may not be appropriate for nonordinary items of income for a variety of reasons, including the following:

1. Nonordinary items may be taxed at different statutory tax rates, such as capital gains tax rates, than ordinary items.
2. Nonordinary items, when combined with ordinary items, may cause the total income to increase (decrease), and a higher (lower) progressive tax rate will then become applicable.
3. Nonordinary items may, in total, represent a loss whose tax benefit is limited because there are not adequate sources of other income which can be offset by the loss.
4. Nonordinary items may, in total, represent income that provides a source against which ordinary losses may find tax benefit.

Therefore, the tax effect of these nonordinary items must be determined independently on an incremental basis.

If *one* nonordinary item exists, the incremental income tax is the *difference* between

1. The income tax expense (benefit) traceable to the estimated annual pretax *ordinary* income (loss), and
2. The income tax expense (benefit) traceable to the *total pretax income* (loss) [the sum of the estimated annual pretax ordinary income or loss and the nonordinary income or loss].

When several nonordinary items exist, the calculation of their individual tax impact becomes more complex. This complexity usually occurs because of differences in tax rates for nonordinary items, surtax charges, and tax credit limitations. If several nonordinary items exist, the incremental tax traceable to each nonordinary item or category is determined as follows:

1. The incremental income tax expense (benefit) traceable to *all* nonordinary categories is the difference between
   a. *The income tax expense (benefit) traceable to the estimated annual pretax ordinary income (loss) and*
   b. *The income tax expense (benefit) traceable to the* total *of all sources of pretax income (loss).*
2. The incremental income tax benefit traceable to *all* nonordinary *loss* categories is the difference between
   a. *The income tax expense (benefit) traceable to the* total *of all sources of pretax income (loss) (step 1b) and*
   b. *The income tax expense (benefit) traceable to the* total *of all sources of pretax income (loss) excluding all nonordinary losses.*
3. The incremental income tax expense traceable to *all* nonordinary *gain* categories is the difference between
   a. *The incremental income tax expense (benefit) traceable to* all *nonordinary items (step 1) and*
   b. *The incremental income tax benefit traceable to* all *nonordinary loss categories (step 2).*

   Note that the incremental tax expense or benefit traceable to all nonordinary items from step 1 has been allocated between nonordinary losses (step 2) and nonordinary gains (step 3).
4. Next, the incremental income tax benefit traceable to each *individual* nonordinary *loss* category is the difference between
   a. *The income tax expense (benefit) traceable to the* total *of all sources of pretax income (loss) (step 1b) and*
   b. *The income tax expense (benefit) traceable to the total of all sources of pretax income (loss), excluding the* individual *nonordinary* loss *category.*

   Note that this step is repeated for each nonordinary loss category. Furthermore, it is likely that the sum of each of the incremental tax benefits will not equal the total tax benefit associated with all nonordinary losses, as calculated in step 2 above.
5. Then, the incremental income tax benefit traceable to *all* nonordinary *loss* categories (step 2) is *apportioned ratably* to each individual loss category based on the incremental income tax benefit of each *individual* nonordinary *loss* category (step 4).
6. The incremental income tax expense traceable to each *individual* nonordinary *gain* category is the difference between
   a. *The income tax expense (benefit) traceable to the* total *of all sources of pretax income (loss) (step 1b) and*
   b. *The income tax expense (benefit) traceable to the total of all sources of pretax income (loss), excluding the* individual *nonordinary gain category.*

   Note that this step is repeated for *each* nonordinary gain category. Furthermore, it is likely that the sum of each of the incremental tax expenses will not equal the total tax expense associated with all nonordinary gains, as calculated in step 3 above.
7. Finally, the incremental income tax expense traceable to *all* nonordinary *gain* categories (step 3) is *apportioned ratably* to each individual gain category based on the incremental income tax expense traceable to each *individual* nonordinary *gain* category (step 6).

The tax impact of nonordinary gains and losses based on the above steps is demonstrated in Illustration 12-1. It is important to remember that the principles discussed earlier regarding offsetting YTD losses also are applicable to nonordinary loss categories. This particular illustration assumes the nonordinary gains and losses are separated into four categories.

Illustration 12-1
Tax Impact on Nonordinary Gains and Losses (Assuming Four Different Categories)

Facts:

Ordinary income of		$180,000
Nonordinary losses consist of:		
Loss (Category #1)	$(30,000)	
Loss (Category #2)	(20,000)	(50,000)
Nonordinary gains consist of:		
Gain (Category #3)	$ 20,000	
Gain (Category #4)	10,000	30,000
Total pretax income of		$160,000
Tax information:		
Tax rate on income	30%	
Surtax on income between $100,000 and $170,000[a]	5%	
Tax credit	$10,000	
Tax rate on gain (Category #3) which is also exempt from the surtax	20%	

[a]This surtax effectively means income between $100,000 and $170,000 is taxed at a 35% (30% + 5%) rate.

Calculation of Total Incremental Tax Impact (steps 1, 2, and 3):

	Ordinary Income	Total Income	Total Income Excluding Nonordinary Losses	Total Income Excluding Nonordinary Gains
Pretax income	$180,000	$160,000[b]	$210,000 ($160,000 + $50,000)	$130,000 ($160,000 – $30,000)
Tax expense (benefit)[c]	**A** 47,500 (step 1a)	**B** 38,000 (step 1b)	**C** 54,500 (step 2b)	

[b]Includes the $20,000 Category #3 gain.

[c]

Tax on income: $180,000 × 30% = $54,000	$160,000	$140,000 × 30% = $42,000	$210,000	$190,000 × 30% = $57,000
		20,000 × 20% = 4,000		20,000 × 20% = 4,000
Surtax: 70,000 × 5% = 3,500		40,000 × 5% = 2,000		70,000 × 5% = 3,500
Tax credit: (10,000)		(10,000)		(10,000)
Tax expense: **A** $47,500		**B** $38,000		**C** $54,500

Incremental tax expense (benefit) traceable to:

D	All nonordinary items	($38,000 – $47,500) (step 1: **B** – **A**)	$ (9,500)
E	All nonordinary losses	($38,000 – $54,500) (step 2: **B** – **C**)	(16,500)
F	All nonordinary gains	[($9,500) – ($16,500)] (step 3: **D** – **E**)	7,000[d]

[d]If the incremental tax associated with all nonordinary items is a $9,500 benefit and the incremental tax associated with all nonordinary losses is a benefit of $16,500, the incremental tax expense associated with all nonordinary gains must be $7,000 [($9,500) = ($16,500) + $7,000]. That is, the incremental tax associated with all nonordinary items must be allocated to either nonordinary losses or gains. Furthermore, the amounts allocated to nonordinary losses and gains must equal the amount traceable to all nonordinary items.

(continued)

Calculation of Incremental Tax Benefit Traceable to Each Individual Loss Category (step 4):

	Total Income	Total Income Excluding All Nonordinary Losses	Total Income Excluding Loss (Category #1)	Total Income Excluding Loss (Category #2)
Pretax income	$160,000	$210,000	$190,000	$180,000
Tax expense (benefit)[e]	**B** 38,000	**C** 54,500	**G** 48,500 (step 4b)	**H** 45,000 (step 4b)

[e]Tax on income	$190,000	$170,000 × 30% = $ 51,000	$180,000	$160,000 × 30% = $ 48,000
		20,000 × 20% = 4,000		20,000 × 20% = 4,000
Surtax:		70,000 × 5% = 3,500		60,000 × 5% = 3,000
Tax credit:		(10,000)		(10,000)
Tax expense:		**G** $ 48,500		**H** $ 45,000

Incremental tax expense (benefit) traceable to:

E	All nonordinary losses	($38,000 – $54,500) (step 2: **B** – **C**)	$(16,500)
I	Nonordinary loss (Category #1)	($38,000 – $48,500) (step 4, first loss category: **B** – **G**)	(10,500)
J	Nonordinary loss (Category #2)	($38,000 – $45,000) (step 4: second loss category: **B** – **H**)	(7,000)[f]

[f]Notice that the sum of the incremental tax benefit on categories 1 and 2 of $17,500 [($10,500) + ($7,000)] does not equal the incremental tax benefit of $16,500 on all losses. It is for this very reason that an apportionment of the tax impact of individual categories is necessary.

Apportionment of Tax Benefit Traceable to Nonordinary Losses (step 5):

The $16,500 incremental tax benefit traceable to all nonordinary losses is ratably apportioned to each individual loss category as follows:

	Each Loss Category: Incremental Benefit	Each Loss Category: Percent	Apportioned Amount	
Loss (Category #1) **I**	$(10,500)	60%	$ (9,900)	= (60% × $16,500)
Loss (Category #2) **J**	(7,000)	40	$ (6,600)	= (40% × $16,500)
	$(17,500)	100%	**E** $(16,500)	

Calculation of Incremental Tax Expense Traceable to Each Individual Gain Category (step 6):

	Total Income	Total Income Excluding Gain (Category #3)	Total Income Excluding Gain (Category #4)
Pretax income	$160,000	$140,000	$150,000
Tax expense (benefit)[g]	**B** 38,000	**K** 34,000 (step 6b)	**L** 34,500 (step 6b)

[g]Tax on income	$140,000 × 30% = $42,000	$150,000	$130,000 × 30% = $39,000
			20,000 × 20% = 4,000
Surtax:	40,000 × 5% = 2,000		30,000 × 5% = 1,500
Tax credit:	(10,000)		(10,000)
Tax expense:	**K** $34,000		**L** $34,500

Incremental tax expense (benefit) traceable to:

F	All nonordinary gains	[($9,500) – ($16,500)] .... (step 3: **D** – **E**)	$7,000
M	Nonordinary gain (Category #3)	($38,000 – $34,000) .... (step 6, first gain category: **B** – **K**)	4,000
N	Nonordinary gain (Category #4)	($38,000 – $34,500) .... (step 6, second gain category: **B** – **L**)	3,500

Apportionment of Tax Expense Traceable to Nonordinary Gains (step 7):

The $7,000 incremental tax expense traceable to all nonordinary gains is ratably apportioned to each individual gain category as follows:

	Each Gain Category Incremental Benefit	Percent	Apportioned Amount
Gain (Category #3)................................**M**	$4,000	53%	$3,710 = (53% × $7,000)
Gain (Category #4)................................**N**	3,500	47	3,290 = (47% × $7,000)
	$7,500	100%	**F** $7,000

Summary of Tax Impact Associated with Ordinary and Nonordinary Items:

	Pretax Income (Loss)	Tax Expense (Benefit)
Ordinary Income..........................	$180,000	**A** $47,500
Loss (Category #1)	(30,000)	(9,900)
Loss (Category #2)	(20,000)	(6,600)
Gain (Category #3)........................	20,000	3,710
Gain (Category #4)........................	10,000	3,290
Totals....................................	$160,000	**B** $38,000

If there is a nonordinary loss, the tax benefit of the loss should be recognized if it can be offset by other existing YTD elements of income and projected income for the balance of the year, which is likely. If the nonordinary loss category cannot be offset by elements of income in the current fiscal year, the principles discussed previously regarding carrybacks against prior years' income and carryforwards against likely future income would be applicable. Illustration 12-2, on page 738, demonstrates the offsetting of a nonordinary (an extraordinary item) loss under various situations.

Illustration 12-2

Case A: Offsetting a Nonordinary Loss Against Sufficient Current-Year Ordinary Income

Interim Period (Quarter)	Type of Income	Pretax Income (Loss) Current Period	Pretax Income (Loss) Year-to-Date	Effective Tax Rate	Tax Expense (Benefit) Year-to-Date	Tax Expense (Benefit) Previously Reported	Tax Expense (Benefit) Current Period
First	Continuing Op.	$ 40,000	$ 40,000	26%	$ 10,400		$ 10,400
Second	Continuing Op.	30,000	70,000	28	19,600	$ 10,400	9,200
Third	Continuing Op.	20,000	90,000	28	25,200	19,600	5,600
Third	Extraordinary	(50,000)	(50,000)	Note A	(14,000)		(14,000)
Fourth	Continuing Op.	40,000	130,000	30	39,000	25,200	13,800
Fourth	Extraordinary		(50,000)	Note B	(15,000)	(14,000)	(1,000)

Note A: The entire extraordinary loss can be offset against ordinary income which has an effective tax rate of 28%.

Note B: Due to a change in the estimated effective tax rate from 28% to 30%, the benefit associated with the extraordinary loss has increased.

Case B: Offsetting a Nonordinary Loss—Assuming Future Interim Income Is *Not* "More Likely Than Not" and Carrybacks and Carryforwards Are *Not* Available

Interim Period (Quarter)	Type of Income	Pretax Income (Loss) Current Period	Pretax Income (Loss) Year-to-Date	Effective Tax Rate	Tax Expense (Benefit) Year-to-Date	Tax Expense (Benefit) Previously Reported	Tax Expense (Benefit) Current Period
First	Continuing Op.	$ 40,000	$ 40,000	26%	$ 10,400		$ 10,400
Second	Continuing Op.	30,000	70,000	28	19,600	$ 10,400	9,200
Third	Continuing Op.	20,000	90,000	28	25,200	19,600	5,600
Third	Extraordinary	(110,000)	(110,000)	Note C	(25,200)		(25,200)
Fourth	Continuing Op.	40,000	130,000	30	39,000	25,200	13,800
Fourth	Extraordinary		(110,000)	Note D	(33,000)	(25,200)	(7,800)

Note C: Because future income is not "more likely than not," and carrybacks/carryforwards are not available, the extraordinary loss can be offset only against YTD income of $90,000.

Note D: Because additional income is available in the fourth quarter, an additional amount of tax benefit traceable to the extraordinary loss can be recognized. Additional benefit also is recognized because of the change in the effective tax rate from 28% to 30%.

Case C: Offsetting a Nonordinary Loss—Assuming Future Interim Income of $40,000 Is "More Likely Than Not" and a Carryback Is Available Against Prior Income of $30,000, Taxed at 30%

Interim Period (Quarter)	Type of Income	Pretax Income (Loss) Current Period	Pretax Income (Loss) Year-to-Date	Effective Tax Rate	Tax Expense (Benefit) Year-to-Date	Tax Expense (Benefit) Previously Reported	Tax Expense (Benefit) Current Period
First	Continuing Op.	$ 40,000	$ 40,000	26%	$ 10,400		$ 10,400
Second	Continuing Op.	30,000	70,000	28	19,600	$ 10,400	9,200
Third	Continuing Op.	20,000	90,000	28	25,200	19,600	5,600
Third	Extraordinary	(180,000)	(180,000)	Note E	(45,400)		(45,400)
Fourth	Continuing Op.	40,000	130,000	28	36,400	25,200	11,200
Fourth	Extraordinary		(180,000)	Note F	(45,400)	(45,400)	

Note E: Because future income of $40,000 is assured, the extraordinary loss can be offset against $130,000 ($90,000 + $40,000) of current-year income at an estimated effective tax rate of 28%. This results in a tax benefit of $36,400. In addition, another $30,000 of the extraordinary loss can be offset against prior income of $30,000. This results in an additional tax benefit of $9,000 for a total benefit of $45,400 ($36,400 + $9,000). If future interim income had not been more likely than not, the total benefit would have consisted of $25,200 resulting from an offset of YTD income plus the $9,000 resulting from the carryback against prior years' income.

Note F: Of the $180,000 extraordinary loss, $160,000 has been offset ($130,000 against current income and $30,000 against prior years'). The tax benefit on the remaining $20,000 of loss not offset may be recognized in the future, as subsequent annual income becomes recognized. If $20,000 of future income was more likely than not to be recognized in the carryforward period, the tax benefit on the entire extraordinary loss could have been recognized in the current year.

Accounting for Discontinued Operations

Discontinued operations consist of the operating results of a component of an entity that either has been disposed of or is being held for sale. A component is defined by operations and cash flows that can be clearly distinguished from the rest of the entity both operationally and for financial reporting purposes. In order for the component to be reported as discontinued, both of the following conditions must be met:

1. The operations and cash flows of the component have been (or will be) eliminated from the ongoing operations of the entity as a result of the disposal transaction, and
2. The entity will not have any significant continuing involvement in the operations of the component after the disposal transaction.[10]

If a component qualifies as a discontinued operation, the income statement will report the results of the discontinued operations, less applicable taxes, as a separate component of income before extraordinary items and the cumulative effect of accounting changes. The reported results for a period will include the results of operations and disposals including any initial or subsequently recognized impairment losses (or revisions of earlier recognized impairment losses).

When interim statements are prepared, a problem arises in that income or losses traceable to the discontinued operation would have been classified in previous interim periods as part of continuing operations. Furthermore, these amounts would have influenced the determination of the estimated annual effective tax rate for those previous periods. Once a decision to dispose of a component has been made, known as the measurement date, the pretax measures of income (loss) and the related taxes for prior interim periods must be restated. The restatement involves allocating prior interim period amounts between income (loss) traceable to continuing operations and income (loss) traceable to the now-discontinued operations. This allocation of previously reported information is necessary in order to achieve comparability between prior and subsequent interim periods. Not only is this allocation applied to prior interim periods presented, but prior annual periods presented must also be restated to reflect the allocation between continuing and discontinued operations. The restatement of pretax income (loss) and related taxes for each of the prior interim periods presented involves the following steps:

1. The original YTD and balance-of-the-year projections used to calculate the estimated effective tax rate are allocated between the now presently defined continuing and discontinued operations.
2. The original tax planning alternatives, permanent differences, and tax credits used to calculate the tax rate are allocated between the continuing and discontinued operations.
3. The projected items being allocated in (1) and (2) are the originally reported amounts. That is, the projections relating to the balance of the year are not changed or revised but remain the same as in the prior interim periods. To permit the revision of an earlier projection would have the effect of accounting for a change in estimate on a retroactive basis, which is not acceptable.
4. The amounts now allocated to continuing operations are used to calculate a new effective tax rate traceable to continuing operations. The tax on the continuing operations of the prior interim period(s) also is recalculated.
5. The new tax on the continuing operations of the prior interim period(s) is compared to the originally reported tax (which included both the continuing and discontinued operations), with the difference representing the tax traceable to the discontinued operations.

From the measurement date forward, the discontinued operations will not be commingled with the continuing operations. Thus, the tax effect of the discontinued operations is calculated on an incremental basis, as is the case with other nonordinary items of income. The interim effect of a discontinued operation is demonstrated in Illustration 12-3.

10 Statement of Financial Accounting Standards No. 144, *Accounting for the Impairment or Disposal of Long-Lived Assets* (Norwalk, CT: Financial Accounting Standards Board, 2001), par. 42.

Illustration 12-3
Discontinued Operation

Facts:

After issuing first-quarter interim data, the company adopted in the second quarter a formal plan calling for the disposal of one of its operations. Ordinary income reported in the first quarter included a $10,000 loss traceable to the operation being discontinued. It is assumed that any loss traceable to the discontinued operation will have tax benefits and that the estimated effective tax rate of 40% on income from continuing operations, used in the first quarter, is to be revised to 45% and applied to the remaining continuing operations.

Analysis:

The following schedule illustrates the retroactive restatement of previously issued interim data in order to disclose separately both continuing and discontinued operations.

		Pretax Income (Loss)			Tax Expense (Benefit)		
Interim Period (Quarter)	Type of Income	Current Period	Year-to-Date	Effective Tax Rate	Year-to-Date	Previously Reported	Current Period
First	Continuing Op.	$ 40,000	$ 40,000	40%	$ 16,000	$ —	$ 16,000
First—Restated	Continuing Op.	50,000	50,000	45	22,500	—	22,500
First—Restated	Discontinued Op.*	(10,000)	(10,000)	Note A	(6,500)	—	(6,500)
Second	Continuing Op.	30,000	80,000	45	36,000	22,500	13,500
Second	Discontinued Op.	(55,000)	(65,000)	Note B	(29,250)	(6,500)	(22,750)
Third	Continuing Op.	50,000	130,000	45	58,500	36,000	22,500
Third	Discontinued Op.	—	(65,000)	Note B	(29,250)	(29,250)	—
Fourth	Continuing Op.	55,000	185,000	45	83,250	58,500	24,750
Fourth	Discontinued Op.	(10,000)	(75,000)	Note C	(33,750)	(29,250)	(4,500)

*This amount is entirely traceable to premeasurement-date operations of the discontinued operation. None of this amount is traceable to the gain or loss on disposal of the discontinued operation.

Note A: The $6,500 tax benefit traceable to the discontinued operation is the result of comparing the tax of $22,500 traceable to continuing operations with the $16,000 of tax previously recognized on the continuing operations. Therefore, the difference between the two tax amounts relates to the exclusion and inclusion, respectively, of the results traceable to the discontinued operation. Notice that the total tax expense presented for the first period, restated, totals $16,000, which is the tax originally reported for the first quarter.

Note B: The YTD tax benefit of $29,250 traceable to the discontinued operation is the assumed incremental tax benefit associated with the component's YTD results of operations and disposals/impairments totaling a $65,000 pretax loss.

Note C: The fourth-quarter current-period loss of $10,000 is traceable to results of operations and disposals/impairments. The $33,750 YTD tax benefit is the assumed incremental tax benefit traceable to the discontinued operation.

Accounting for a Change in Accounting Principle

APB Opinion No. 28 indicates that, in general, a change in accounting principle during an interim period should be accounted for in accordance with APB Opinion No. 20, *Accounting Changes.* To simplify the accounting for such changes, the APB encouraged management to adopt accounting changes in the first interim period of the current fiscal year. Nevertheless, the APB recognized that changes would continue to be made in other than the first interim period and, therefore, prescribed special procedures. However, these procedures were amended in 1974 by FASB Statement No. 3, *Reporting Accounting Changes in Interim Financial Statements.* When interim reports are prepared, the proper accounting for a change in an accounting principle depends on (a) whether the change requires the determination of a cumulative effect or retroactive restatement and (b) whether the change takes place in the first interim period of the fiscal year.

A Change Requiring Retroactive Restatement. A change requiring retroactive restatement of previously issued annual financial statements, rather than the determination of the cumulative effect, will require the restatement of previously issued interim financial information. If such a change occurs in other than the first interim period, such restatement will also involve the restatement of taxes to reflect the estimated effective tax rate, which is based on annual income (or loss) from continuing operations as determined in accordance with the newly adopted accounting principle. The restatement of the previous tax rate is affected by only the change in principle and, therefore, does not allow for any revisions of projected data that were used to calculate the earlier tax rate. This treatment is consistent with the principle that changes in estimates should not be accounted for on a retroactive basis.

A Change Requiring a Cumulative Effect. If a cumulative-effect-type change takes place in the first interim period of the fiscal year, the cumulative effect of the change on retained earnings as of the beginning of the year should be included in net income of the first interim period. However, if the cumulative-effect-type change is made in other than the first interim period, it is assumed for accounting purposes that it took place in the first interim period. Therefore, the change should be accounted for as follows:

1. Financial statements for all interim periods in the current fiscal year should be restated to reflect the adoption of the new principle, and
2. The cumulative effect of the change on retained earnings as of the beginning of the current fiscal year should be included in the restated net income of the first interim period rather than in the interim period in which the change was adopted.[11]

Accounting for the cumulative effect of a change in principle may result in a restated tax rate for the interim periods prior to the change. As is the case with all other restatements of earlier tax rates, only the effect of the *nonordinary* income items should be considered. Therefore, the tax on the cumulative effect should be computed on an *incremental* basis, as previously illustrated for nonordinary items of income or loss, and the tax previously reported for ordinary income of the prechange interim periods should be restated as follows:

> *The restated tax (or benefit) shall reflect the year-to-date amounts and annual estimates originally used for the prechange interim periods, modified only for the effect of the change in accounting principle on those year-to-date and estimated annual amounts.*[12]

The principle described above for a cumulative-effect-type change is demonstrated in Illustration 12-4.

Illustration 12-4
Change in Accounting Principle: Cumulative Effect

Facts:

During the third quarter, management decided to change depreciation methods. The effect of the change is to decrease the pretax income of quarters one and two by $30,000 and $20,000, respectively. The effect on prior years is to decrease pretax income by $40,000.

(continued)

11 Statement of Financial Accounting Standards No. 3, *Reporting Accounting Changes in Interim Financial Statements* (Norwalk, CT: Financial Standards Board, 1974), par. 10.

12 FASB Interpretation No. 18, *Accounting for Income Taxes in Interim Periods* (Stamford: Financial Accounting Standards Board, 1977), par. 64.

Analysis:

The following schedule illustrates the restatement of previously issued interim data in order to reflect the cumulative effect of the change.

		Pretax Income (Loss)			Tax Expense (Benefit)		
Interim Period (Quarter)	Type of Income	Current Period	Year-to-Date	Effective Tax Rate	Year-to-Date	Previously Reported	Current Period
First	Continuing Op.	$ 80,000	$ 80,000	40%	$ 32,000	—	$ 32,000
Second	Continuing Op.	50,000	130,000	40	52,000	$ 32,000	20,000
First—Restated	Continuing Op.	50,000	50,000	42*	21,000	—	21,000
First—Restated	Cumulative Effect	(40,000)	(40,000)	Note A	(16,800)	—	(16,800)
Second—Restated	Continuing Op.	30,000	80,000	42	33,600	21,000	12,600
Second—Restated	Cumulative Effect	—	(40,000)	Note A	(16,800)	(16,800)	—
Third & Fourth	Continuing Op.	70,000	150,000	42	63,000	33,600	29,400
Third & Fourth	Cumulative Effect	—	(40,000)	Note A	(16,800)	(16,800)	—

*Note that a new effective tax rate of 42% has been calculated as a result of modifications relating to only the change in accounting principle.

Note A: It is assumed that the cumulative effect of a $40,000 loss will offset annual income taxed at an effective rate of 42%. This results in a tax benefit of $16,800 ($40,000 × 42%).

A cumulative-effect-type change in principle also requires the following disclosures:

1. For the interim period in which the new accounting principle is adopted:
   a. *income from continuing operations, net income, and related per share amounts computed on a pro forma basis for (i) the interim period in which the change is made and (ii) any interim periods of prior fiscal years for which financial information is being presented;*
   b. *the nature of and justification for the change and the effect of the change on income from continuing operations, net income, and related per share amounts for that interim period;*
   c. *when that period occurs after the first period (i) the effect of the change on income from continuing operations, net income, and related per share amounts for each current fiscal year interim period prior to the change and (ii) income from continuing operations, net income, and related per share amounts for each restated current-fiscal-year interim period prior to the change.*
2. In the period of change, if no financial information for interim periods of prior fiscal years is being presented:
   a. *the actual and pro forma amounts of income from continuing operations, net income, and related per share amounts for the interim period of the immediately preceding fiscal year that corresponds to the interim period of change.*
3. For year-to-date and last-12-months-to-date financial reports through the interim period of the adoption:
   a. *the effect of the change on income from continuing operations, net income, and related per share amounts and their pro forma bases.*
4. For a subsequent (post-change) interim period of the fiscal year in which the new accounting principle is adopted:
   a. *the effect of the change on income from continuing operations, net income, and related per share amounts for that post-change interim period.*[13]

In a change to the LIFO inventory method, the disclosures for a cumulative-effect-type change are required except that the cumulative effect of the change on retained earnings and pro forma amounts should not be determined. If the change is made in other than the first

13 Statement of Financial Accounting Standards No. 3, *op. cit.*, par. 11.

interim period, all prechange interim statements must be restated to reflect the adoption of the new accounting principle. The beginning inventory computed by the previous inventory method is assumed to be the beginning measure of base stock for purposes of applying LIFO.

Disclosures of Summarized Interim Data

To maintain the timeliness of interim data, companies frequently report summarized interim data rather than complete financial statements. When publicly traded companies report summarized interim data, the following disclosures are required, at a minimum:

1. Sales or gross revenues, provision for income taxes, extraordinary items (including related income tax effects), cumulative effect of a change in accounting principles or practices, and net income.
2. Basic and diluted earnings-per-share data for each period presented, determined in accordance with the provisions of FASB Statement No. 128, *Earnings per Share.*
3. Seasonal revenue, costs, or expenses.
4. Significant changes in estimates or provisions for income taxes.
5. Disposal of a segment of a business and extraordinary, unusual, or infrequently occurring items.
6. Contingent items.
7. Changes in accounting principles or estimates.
8. Significant changes in financial position.
9. Information about reportable operating segments determined according to the provisions of FASB Statement No. 131, *Disclosures about Segments of an Enterprise and Related Information,* including provisions related to restatement of segment information in previously issued financial statements.[14]

The information in (9) above is more fully discussed in the following section of this chapter dealing with disclosures about segments of an enterprise.

In addition to providing this data for the current quarter, such data should be provided for the current year to date or the last 12 months to date, plus comparable data for the preceding year.

Frequently, companies do not issue separate fourth-quarter reports or provide fourth-quarter disclosure of summarized data because annual audited statements will be forthcoming. In such cases, a note to the annual financial statements should disclose the effect of the following items for the fourth quarter: disposals of a segment, extraordinary items, unusual or infrequently occurring items, and changes in accounting principles. Disclosure in the annual financial statements should also include the aggregate effect of year-end adjustments that are material to the fourth-quarter results.

REFLECTION

- Interim reporting generates timely and useful information that may provide insight into annual results.
- Since interim periods are treated as integral parts of a larger annual period, the results of one interim period can significantly affect other interim periods in the same fiscal year.
- While revenue recognition principles do not change, some expense recognition principles are modified for interim reporting purposes in order to provide more timely information.
- The income tax expense or benefits traceable to an interim period should reflect the estimated effective tax rate to be experienced for the entire annual period.
- The tax expense or benefit traceable to nonordinary items of income or loss is determined on an incremental basis.

14 Accounting Principles Board Opinion No. 28, *op. cit.,* par. 30 (as amended).

5

OBJECTIVE

Explain why segmental reporting is important, and define an operating segment.

DISCLOSURES ABOUT SEGMENTS OF AN ENTERPRISE

For various reasons, enterprises may develop a strategy which allows them to become involved in a variety of activities, some of which may be similar or related. For example, an enterprise in the entertainment/recreation industry may have business activities in film, theme parks, hotels, and restaurants. Enterprises with such activities are referred to as being *horizontally integrated*. In other instances, the activities may be *vertically integrated*, which suggests that they relate to the sales and distribution of a final good or service. For example, a manufacturer of modular housing may also be involved in activities such as the growing and harvesting of timber, the manufacture of windows, and the development of land for housing subdivisions. Enterprises may also become involved in activities which do not necessarily have a close relationship to their original core business but, rather, allow them to diversify their business. Such businesses are referred to as *conglomerates* or *diversified companies*. For example, a single enterprise may be involved in such diverse activities as radio and television broadcasting, managed care facilities, development of software for engineering applications, and the manufacture of fluid metering devices.

The traditional consolidated financial statements of a truly diversified enterprise would provide the user of these statements with limited information regarding the diversity of the enterprise's activities and the economic environments in which those activities function. For example, unless separate disclosures were present, it would not be possible to tell what portion of consolidated sales was traceable to various business activities. Certainly, the uncertainties affecting potential cash flows can be better understood if information related to an enterprise's products and services, as well as geographical areas of operation, is provided. Fortunately, special disclosures regarding the segments or activities of an enterprise are required and provide users with fundamental information through which they can better understand operating performance and prospects for future cash flows for both individual segments and the enterprise as a whole. Furthermore, such information will provide users with an improved basis for making comparisons between enterprises that are not diversified with those that are.

There is a strong body of empirical research that supports the position that segmental data have utility. This research and the prominence of diversified companies have effectively established the importance of segmental data for maintaining an efficient capital market. For example, studies have suggested that segmental data can lead to more accurate predictions of enterprise earnings and changes in earnings levels. In addition, surveys have shown that sophisticated users, such as financial analysts, find the use of segmental data to be a significant factor in the area of security valuation.

A number of professional groups, including the American Institute of Certified Public Accountants, the Financial Executives Institute, the Financial Analysts Federation, the International Accounting Standards Committee, the Association for Investment Management and Research, and the FASB, have consistently emphasized the importance of segmental disclosures. In 1976, the FASB had issued Statement of Financial Accounting Standards No. 14, which also dealt with the topic of segmental disclosures. However, that statement had come under criticism from both reporting enterprises and users of the information. A major criticism was that the definition of a segment resulted in the reporting of information which did not necessarily represent the information that the top management of an enterprise actually used for making internal operating decisions and assessing performance. It became obvious that an external reporting requirement that did not align with internal reporting, which was used for decision-making purposes, was not serving the needs of external users of segmental information. Why provide external users information that they will use to make assessments of an enterprise if the information is not what is being used by enterprise management to make decisions? Furthermore, the segmental disclosures called for were not consistent with how management discussed and analyzed segmental data in other sections of annual reports. Segmental reporting standards were also criticized for not requiring more information about a greater number of segments. **Aligning external reporting of segmental information with internal reporting helps users view an enterprise in a way that will allow them to better anticipate and understand the actions of management.**

The importance of segmental reporting, coupled with the criticisms directed toward earlier authoritative pronouncements, has resulted in a renewed interest, both nationally and globally, in establishing standards for segmental reporting. Of recent importance is the joint effort of the FASB and the Accounting Standards Board of the Canadian Institute of Chartered Accountants (CICA). This cooperative effort to develop disclosure standards for segmental reporting is an excellent example of the emphasis which is being placed on the harmonization of accounting principles both regionally and globally. The FASB and the CICA reached the same conclusions regarding appropriate standards and have each issued new authoritative standards regarding segmental disclosures. In the case of the FASB, the authoritative standard is Statement of Financial Accounting Standards No. 131, *Disclosures about Segments of an Enterprise and Related Information.*[15]

Statement of Financial Accounting Standards No. 131

FASB Statement No. 131, which replaces the earlier Statement No. 14, is applicable to public business enterprises. A company is considered to be a public enterprise if it (a) has issued debt or equity securities that are traded in a public market, (b) is required to file financial statements with the Securities and Exchange Commission (SEC), or (c) provides financial statements for the purpose of issuing securities in a public market. Although the statement does not apply to nonpublic enterprises or not-for-profit organizations, such enterprises or organizations are encouraged to adopt the requirements of the standard.

Definition of an Operating Segment. The FASB chose to define operating segments by emphasizing a "management approach" which focuses on how management organizes information for purposes of making operating decisions and assessing performance. For example, assume that a public company, which manufactures circuit boards for a variety of applications, organizes information by sales-market area for decision-making purposes. Therefore, the segments of the company might logically be defined as sales-market areas such as North America, South America, etc. Also, consider a public company that is involved in a number of diverse industries such as banking, retail brokerage services, and real estate development. If this company organizes information for decision-making purposes according to the types of products or services it offers, such as life insurance, then its segments would be defined accordingly. The segments should be evident from the structure of the organization in terms of how information is organized for internal decision-making purposes. Furthermore, if this information is already being generated internally, then management should be able to disclose certain relevant portions of this information to external users without incurring significant incremental costs.

The segments which emerge from an analysis of how management organizes information for decision-making purposes are called *operating segments* and are defined as a component of an enterprise

1. That engages in business activities from which it may earn revenues and incur expenses (including revenues and expenses relating to transactions with other components of the same enterprise),
2. Whose operating results are regularly reviewed by the enterprise's chief operating decision maker to make decisions about resources to be allocated to the segment and assess its performance, and
3. For which discrete financial information is available.[16]

It is important to note that not all parts of an enterprise will necessarily qualify as an operating segment. For example, some parts may not earn revenues of an operating nature, such as is the case with corporate headquarters. The chief operating decision maker who reviews a segment is one who assesses performance and allocates resources. This is a function which could be held by one individual, such as a chief executive officer (CEO) or chief operating officer (COO)

15 Statement of Financial Accounting Standards No. 131, *Disclosures about Segments of an Enterprise and Related Information* (Stamford, CT: Financial Accounting Standards Board, 1997).

16 *Ibid.*, par. 10.

or a group of individuals. One or more individuals typically have responsibility to account and report to the chief operating decision maker. This function is carried out by segment managers whose identification may also help identify operating segments.

Once operating segments have been identified, it is possible that some of the segments will appear to be similar due to similar economic characteristics. These segments may have virtually the same future prospects, and separate reporting of them may provide users with additional data of limited utility. Therefore, it may be possible to combine two or more of these segments into a single segment, if they are similar in each of the following areas:

- The nature of the products or services.
- The nature of the production processes.
- The type or class of customer for their products and services.
- The methods used to distribute their products or provide their services.
- The nature of the regulatory environment (if applicable); for example, banking, insurance, or public utilities.[17]

6

OBJECTIVE

Apply the criteria used to determine which segment is reportable.

Once segments have been identified and aggregated, if necessary, information should be disclosed about those segments which are deemed to be reportable. That is, even though there may be an operating segment, it may not be significant enough to require disclosure. A *reportable segment* is one which is deemed to be significant because of any of the following:

- Its reported revenue, including both sales to external customers and intersegment sales or transfers, is 10% or more of the combined revenue, internal and external, of all reported operating segments.
- The absolute amount of its reported profit or loss is 10% or more of the greater, in absolute amount, of (a) the combined profit of all operating segments that did not report a loss, or (b) the combined reported loss of all operating segments that did report a loss.
- Its assets are 10% or more of the combined assets of all operating segments.[18]

It is important to note that, even if a segment does not satisfy the above criteria, management may report information about that individual segment if they believe it to be material.

For those operating segments which do not meet the above criteria, they will constitute a separate "all other" category for reporting purposes. It is possible that those segments which qualify as reportable do not represent a significant enough portion of the enterprise's operating activities. The total of **external revenues** for reportable segments must constitute at least 75% of the total consolidated revenue. If this is not the case, then additional operating segments must be designated as reportable even though they did not initially qualify as such. The goal of these guidelines is to reach a balance between providing users with information about a reasonable number of segments and yet not be excessive. In the latter regard, if the number of reportable segments exceeds 10 in number, consideration should be given to whether this number should be reduced by aggregating certain segments. The above criteria used to identify reportable segments and analyze the appropriate number of reportable segments are shown in Illustration 12-5.

17 *Ibid.*, par. 17.
18 *Ibid.*, par. 18.

Illustration 12-5
Reportable Segments: Demonstration of Criteria

Facts:

Whalen Corporation has classified its operations into segments and has provided the following data for each segment:

	Revenues				
Segment	Unaffiliated Customers	Intersegment Sales	Total	Operating Profit (Loss)	Assets
A	$100,000	$15,000	$115,000	$ 45,000	$ 280,000
B	20,000		20,000	(10,000)	80,000
C	230,000	40,000	270,000	130,000	1,100,000
D	45,000	5,000	50,000	(60,000)	320,000
E	37,000	8,000	45,000	25,000	295,000
F	140,000	14,000	154,000	85,000	760,000
	$572,000	$82,000	$654,000	$215,000	$2,835,000
Corporate level	60,000		60,000	20,000	705,000
Total	$632,000	$82,000	$714,000	$235,000	$3,540,000

Analysis:

The determination of which segments are reportable requires the following evaluation, in which only combined data relating to the segments (not including corporate-level activity) are employed:

1. Total sales to unaffiliated customers	$572,000
Total intersegment sales	82,000
Combined revenue	$654,000

Segment revenue required to satisfy criterion (a): $654,000 × 10% = $65,400

2. Segment	Operating Profit	Operating Loss
A	$ 45,000	$ —
B	—	10,000
C	130,000	—
D	—	60,000
E	25,000	—
F	85,000	—
Total	$285,000	$70,000

Portion of absolute amount of the greater of the operating profit or the operating loss to satisfy criterion (b): $285,000 × 10% = $28,500

3. Segment assets required to satisfy criterion (c): $2,835,000 × 10% = $283,500

(continued)

Whether the criteria are satisfied is summarized as follows:

Segment	Criterion Satisfied Revenue		Operating Profit (Loss)		Identifiable Assets		Segment Reportable
A	Yes	($115,000 > $65,400)	Yes	($ 45,000 > $28,500)	No	($ 280,000 < $283,500)	Yes
B	No	($ 20,000 < $65,400)	No	($ 10,000 < $28,500)	No	($ 80,000 < $283,500)	No
C	Yes	($270,000 > $65,400)	Yes	($130,000 > $28,500)	Yes	($1,100,000 > $283,500)	Yes
D	No	($ 50,000 < $65,400)	Yes	($ 60,000 > $28,500)	Yes	($ 320,000 > $283,500)	Yes
E	No	($ 45,000 < $65,400)	No	($ 25,000 < $28,500)	Yes	($ 295,000 > $283,500)	Yes
F	Yes	($154,000 > $65,400)	Yes	($ 85,000 > $28,500)	Yes	($ 760,000 > $283,500)	Yes

All of the segments are reportable except for Segment B.

4. Significance of the reportable segments:

Consolidated revenue	$632,000
Percentage requirement	× 75%
Dollar requirement	$474,000
External revenue of reportable segments (all segments except Segment B)	$552,000

The reportable segments represent a significant portion of the enterprise.

5. Reasonableness of the number of reportable segments:

The five reportable segments do not exceed the guideline number of 10.

Comparability of Segmental Information. Another issue that arises deals with comparability of segmental information over time. For example, it is possible for a segment to meet the criteria as being reportable in one fiscal period and not in another, resulting, therefore, in a lack of compatibility. In order to ensure comparability, the following guidelines are appropriate for both interim and annual periods:

1. If a segment is deemed to be reportable in the current period, prior-period segmental data should also include the segment for comparative purposes.
2. If a segment was deemed to be reportable in prior-period segmental data presented, the segment should continue to be deemed reportable if it is considered to be of continuing significance.
3. If an enterprise's structure changes such that the composition or makeup of segments changes, then prior-period segmental data presented should be restated, if practical, to reflect the new composition of segments. It should be disclosed as to whether or not prior-period information has been restated. If such information has not been restated, segment information for the current period should be presented on both the current and previous basis of segmentation. This dual presentation is appropriate only in the current period of change and if practical.

7

OBJECTIVE

Describe the information about a reportable segment that must be disclosed.

Content of Segmental Disclosures. Once the identification of reportable segments and the proper guidelines regarding the number of segments have been satisfied, various general and financial information regarding segments is required to be disclosed as part of a complete set of financial statements. The factors used to identify reportable segments must be disclosed along with a discussion of how the segments are organized. For example, segments could be organized around products or services, geographical areas, marketing areas, or products within geographical areas. For each reportable segment, the type of products and/or services from which they derive their revenues should be disclosed. Certain information about profit or loss and assets must also be disclosed for each reportable segment, and then these amounts must be reconciled to corresponding enterprise consolidated amounts.

Information about Profit or Loss and Assets. The measure of profit or loss which is disclosed is a function of what information is reviewed by the chief operating decision maker of the enterprise. For example, the measure could exclude items relating to the cost of capital, or the measure could include an allocation of general corporate overhead. It is important to note that the measure of profit or loss follows a management approach focusing on internal decision making rather than any strict definition of profit used by the enterprise for general purpose external reporting. Therefore, it is possible that segmental profit or loss may not necessarily incorporate the same generally accepted accounting principles (GAAP) as are employed at the consolidated level. For example, segment profit or loss may not include the effects of tax allocation or pension expense. The following items regarding profit or loss should be disclosed **only if** the items are included in the values reviewed by the chief operating decision maker: revenues from external customers, revenues from other operating segments, interest revenue, interest expense, depreciation, depletion, amortization expense, unusual items, equity in net income of investees accounted for under the equity method, income tax expense/benefit, extraordinary items, and other significant noncash items such as deferred tax expense. If a majority of a segment's revenues are from interest, such as those of a financial segment, and the decision-making process focuses on net interest (interest revenue less interest expense), then interest revenue may be reported net of interest expense.

In order to better evaluate a segment, it would be useful to disclose the assets which were employed to generate the profit or loss traceable to that segment. Therefore, those segment assets which are evaluated by the chief operating decision maker are also to be disclosed. The following items regarding assets should be disclosed **only if** the items are included in the values reviewed by the chief operating decision maker: the carrying basis of investments in investees measured under the equity method and total expenditures for additions to long-lived assets (other than financial instruments, long-term customer relationships of a financial institution, mortgage and other servicing rights, deferred policy acquisition costs, and deferred tax assets).

Because the measurement of segment profit or loss and assets follows a management approach, additional disclosures are necessary in order to assist users in understanding how these values are measured. For example, segment profit may not include the allocation of certain corporate-level expenses, or it may measure cost of sales using a method different from that used for consolidated purposes. Therefore, an enterprise should disclose, at a minimum, the following:

1. The basis of accounting for any transactions between reportable segments.
2. The nature of any differences between the measurements of the reportable segments' profits or losses and the enterprise's consolidated income before income taxes, extraordinary items, discontinued operations, and the cumulative effect of changes in accounting principles (if not apparent from the reconciliations). Those differences could include accounting policies and policies for allocation of centrally incurred costs that are necessary for an understanding of the reported segment information.
3. The nature of any differences between the measurements of the reportable segments' assets and the enterprise's consolidated assets (if not apparent from the reconciliations). Those differences could include accounting policies and policies for allocation of jointly used assets that are necessary for an understanding of the reported segment information.
4. The nature of any changes from prior periods in the measurement methods used to determine reported segment profit or loss and the effect, if any, of those changes on the measure of segment profit or loss.
5. The nature and effect of any asymmetrical allocations to segments. For example, an enterprise might allocate depreciation expense to a segment without allocating the related depreciable assets to that segment.[19]

19 *Ibid.*, par. 31.

The various dollar amounts disclosed for reportable segments represent a significant portion of the respective consolidated dollar amounts. For example, the sum of profit or loss for all reportable segments will naturally represent a significant portion of consolidated profit or loss. However, all of the consolidated profit or loss will not be traceable to the reportable segments. The difference between the sum of the reportable segment values and the respective consolidated value is most often due to the following:

1. Not all segments are considered to be reportable. Therefore, some values are allocated to the category of segments known as "all other."
2. Segment revenues, profits, and assets include the effect of intersegment transactions that are eliminated from consolidated amounts. Note that intersegment transactions that have *not been realized* through an exchange with an outside entity must be eliminated from consolidated amounts.
3. Certain values are not allocated to segments because they are not part of the information that is used by the chief operating decision maker as a basis for evaluating performance and allocating resources.
4. Certain values cannot be allocated to segments on a reasonable basis.
5. The accounting methods used to determine values for a reportable segment may be different from those used to prepare consolidated values. This is due to the focus on the management approach and the information used for internal rather than external reporting purposes.

A requirement of segmental reporting is that the revenue, profit or loss, and asset amounts presented for reportable segments must be reconciled to the respective consolidated amounts for the enterprise as a whole. A reconciliation must also be made for other significant items presented by reportable segments. The reconciliation should be described in sufficient detail. Illustration 12-6 contains an example of the required segmental disclosures and the reconciliation to consolidated enterprise values.

Illustration 12-6
Presentation of Segmental Values

	Auto Parts	Motor Vessels	Software	Electronics	Finance	All Other	Totals
Revenues from external customers	$3,000	$5,000	$9,500	$12,000	$ 5,000	$1,000*	$35,500
Intersegment revenues	—	—	3,000	1,500	—	—	4,500
Interest revenue	450	800	1,000	1,500	—	—	3,750
Interest expense	350	600	700	1,100	—	—	2,750
Net interest revenue**	—	—	—	—	1,000	—	1,000
Depreciation and amortization	200	100	50	1,500	1,100	—	2,950
Segment profit	200	70	900	2,300	500	100	4,070
Other significant noncash items:							
Cost in excess of billings on long-term contracts	—	200	—	—	—	—	200
Segment assets	2,000	5,000	3,000	12,000	57,000	2,000	81,000
Expenditures for segment assets	300	700	500	800	600	—	2,900

*Revenue from segments below the quantitative thresholds are attributable to four operating segments of Diversified Company. Those segments include a small real estate business, an electronics equipment rental business, a software consulting practice, and a warehouse leasing operation. None of those segments has ever met any of the quantitative thresholds for determining reportable segments.

**The finance segment derives a majority of its revenue from interest. In addition, management relies primarily on net interest revenue, not the gross revenue and expense amounts, in managing that segment. Therefore, only the net amount is disclosed.

(continued)

Reconciliation of Segmental Values to Enterprise Consolidated Values

Revenues	
Total revenues for reportable segments	$34,500
Other revenues	1,000
Elimination of intersegment revenues	(4,500)
Total consolidated revenues	$31,000

Profit or Loss	
Total profit or loss for reportable segments	$ 3,970
Other profit or loss	100
Elimination of intersegment profits	(500)
Unallocated amounts:	
Litigation settlement received	500
Other corporate expenses	(750)
Adjustment to pension expense in consolidation	(250)
Income before income taxes and extraordinary items	$ 3,070

Assets	
Total assets for reportable segments	$79,000
Other assets	2,000
Elimination of receivables from corporate headquarters	(1,000)
Goodwill not allocated to segments	4,000
Other unallocated amounts	1,000
Consolidated total	$85,000

Other Significant Items

	Segment Totals	Adjustments	Consolidated Totals
Interest revenue	$3,750	$ 75	$3,825
Interest expense	2,750	(50)	2,700
Net interest revenue (finance segment only)	1,000	—	1,000
Expenditures for assets	2,900	1,000	3,900
Depreciation and amortization	2,950	—	2,950
Cost in excess of billing on long-term contracts	200	—	200

The reconciling item to adjust expenditures for assets is the amount of expenses incurred for the corporate headquarters building, which is not included in segment information. None of the other adjustments are significant.

Source: Statement of Financial Accounting Standards No. 131, *Disclosures about Segments of an Enterprise and Related Information.*

Interim Period Disclosures. The current standard on segmental reporting addresses a criticism of the previous standard regarding interim reporting disclosures. The previous standard was criticized for not requiring segmental disclosures in interim reports. Interim information has become increasingly important, and users would find it even more useful if it included information regarding segments. Therefore, the new standard requires that *condensed* financial statements for interim periods include the following for each reportable segment: revenues from both external customers and intersegment sales, profit or loss, a reconciliation of reportable segments' profit or loss to enterprise pretax net income from continuing operations, total assets which have materially changed from the values reported in the most recent annual report, and disclosure of any differences from the last annual report in terms of whether the basis for segmentation and/or measurement of segment profit or loss have changed. It is important to note that these disclosures are appropriate for only condensed financial statements of an interim period. If a complete set of financial statements is presented, then the more comprehensive disclosures discussed earlier would be appropriate.

8

OBJECTIVE

State which enterprise-wide disclosures must be provided.

Enterprise-Wide Disclosures. Because of the use of the management approach to defining segments, it is possible that segments may not necessarily be defined around product/service groups or geographical areas. For example, a segment may consist of several unrelated products because that is how information is structured for decision-making purposes. A company which produces beverages, produces snack foods, operates a chain of restaurants, and operates amusement parks may decide to include all but the amusement parks in a single segment. Segments may also be defined in such a way that a given segment includes activities which are occurring in more than one foreign geographical area. If information regarding product/service groups and/or geographical areas is not provided as part of the segmental disclosures, such information must be provided as an additional disclosure. These additional disclosures must be presented if practical; if it is not practical, that fact must be disclosed. These additional disclosures are presented on an enterprise-wide basis, not on a segmental basis. Furthermore, the disclosures are required even if there is only one reportable segment. The enterprise is required to[20]

1. Report revenues from **external** customers for each product or service or each group of related products or services. The revenues are based on the information used for general purpose financial statements.
2. Report revenues from **external** customers for the enterprise's country of domicile and all foreign countries in total. The revenues are based on the information used for general purpose financial statements. If material, revenues from separate foreign countries should be disclosed. Subtotals of revenue may also be disclosed by groups of foreign countries (e.g., South America). The basis used to allocate revenues to separate foreign countries must be disclosed. For example, revenues may be allocated based on where products are shipped or based on the location of customers.
3. Report **long-lived** assets located in the enterprise's country of domicile and all foreign countries in total. The measurement of assets is based on the information used for general purpose financial statements. If material, assets traceable to separate foreign countries should be disclosed. Subtotals of assets may also be disclosed by groups of foreign countries (e.g., South America).

Disclosures Regarding Major Customers. Enterprises are also required to disclose information about major customers if revenues traceable to a single customer represent 10% or more of total enterprise revenues. For each such customer, the enterprise must disclose the total amount of revenues and identify the segment or segments to which the revenues are traceable. The specific identity by name of the major customer need not be disclosed. For purposes of this disclosure, a group of entities under common control is considered to be a single customer. Federal, state, local, and foreign governments or agencies should each be considered as a single customer.

20 *Ibid.*, pars. 37–39.

REFLECTION

- A management approach is used to define what constitutes an operating segment.
- Operating segments are deemed to be reportable if a number of criteria involving segmental revenues, profits/losses, or assets are satisfied.
- A number of disclosures must be made for each reportable segment and the total of nonreportable segments. Furthermore, the financial disclosures are to be reconciled to the respective consolidated amounts.
- Given the management approach to defining an operating segment, information regarding product groups and/or foreign business activities may not otherwise be disclosed. Therefore, special enterprise-wide disclosures containing such information should be disclosed.

UNDERSTANDING THE ISSUES

1. What are the benefits of viewing an interim period as an integral part of a larger annual period rather than as a separate distinct period?
2. What factors are necessary for determining the estimated annual effective income tax rate?
3. Why must the tax expense or benefit traceable to nonordinary items of income be computed on an incremental basis, and why does it involve a process of ratable allocation?
4. Why isn't the total operating profit of all reportable segments normally equal to the consolidated operating profit?

EXERCISES

Exercise 1 *(LO 1, 2)* **Cost of goods sold, interim income statement.** Wert Company has sought assistance in preparing its second-quarter income statement for 20X2. Figures for sales revenue, selling expenses, and general and administrative expenses are $860,000, $68,000, and $117,000, respectively.

For each of the following situations, determine the cost of goods sold and prepare an interim income statement in good form for the three months ended June 30, 20X2.

1. Wert uses a standard cost accounting system for inventory and product costs. Net unfavorable cost variances for the second quarter total $2,600 and represent the difference between actual and standard production costs. Management considers such variances as a manufacturing cost and includes them in the income statement above the gross profit line. It is expected that an unfavorable purchase price variance of $900 will be absorbed by December 31, 20X2. Production for the second quarter at standard cost was $600,000. Beginning and ending finished goods inventories (standard cost) were $71,000 and $98,000, respectively.
2. The LIFO cost of goods sold was $596,000 and includes sales of 15,000 units costed out at their 20X1 base layer cost of $7 per unit. The current replacement cost of these units is $11 per unit. It is expected that the 20X2 year-end inventory will be 2,000 units less than the 20X1 year-end inventory.
3. Beginning inventory of $52,000 reflects a first-quarter write-down of $2,200 due to the application of the lower-of-cost-or-market rule. Through a market price recovery in the second quarter, inventory increased in value by $3,750. Wert purchased 18,000 units of inventory ($28 per unit) in the second quarter. Ending inventory (FIFO basis) was $60,500.

Exercise 2 *(LO 1, 2)* **Accounting for R&D, tax rate differences.** Your client is seeking advice on each of the following interim reporting issues related to the current year:

1. In the first quarter of the current year, the client incurred $130,000 of research and development (R&D) costs which will hopefully generate additional revenues in the current and next four years. He is aware of the fact that the R&D will have to be expensed in its entirety in the current year. However, he is not sure how to report the item in the first-quarter financials. What advice would you give?
2. In the second quarter of the current year, your client revised his estimated effective annual tax rate on pretax net income from continuing operations (NICO). The second-quarter tax expense expressed as a percentage of the second-quarter pretax NICO income is greater than the statutory rate of tax. This confuses your client. What is the logical explanation for this?

Exercise 3 *(LO 2, 3)* **Cost of goods sold and tax expense in interim periods.** Granger Supply, Inc., has two main areas of inventory, industrial supplies and industrial cleaning equipment. The FIFO inventory method is used for industrial supplies, and the LIFO method is used for the cleaning equipment. Prior to considering special interim reporting modifications for LIFO liquidations and lower of cost or market, the company reported the following results for the first two quarters of 20X7:

	Quarter 1	Quarter 2
Net sales	$12,000,000	$9,000,000
Cost of sales—industrial supplies	4,300,000	4,700,000
Cost of sales—cleaning equipment	3,000,000	3,200,000
Gross profit	$ 4,700,000	$1,100,000
Selling, general, and administrative	2,100,000	1,800,000
Net income before taxes	$ 2,600,000	$ (700,000)

During the first quarter of 20X7, the company experienced unprecedented demand for its cleaning equipment and as a result liquidated a significant portion of its beginning inventory of equipment. The cost of sales—cleaning equipment is based on the historical cost of the liquidated layers. Management anticipates that 400 units of beginning inventory that were included in cost of sales at $1,500 per unit will be replaced during the year and remain in ending inventory at a cost of $2,700 per unit. The cost of sales—industrial supplies does not reflect the fact that the ending inventory of supplies has a fair value of $120,000 less than FIFO cost.

During the second quarter of 20X7, the market for industrial supplies strengthened and the inventory of industrial supplies at the end of the second quarter had a fair value of only $25,000 less than FIFO cost.

Interim income tax expense is based on the following estimates:

	At End of Quarter 1	At End of Quarter 2
Statutory tax rate	35%	35%
Projected net income before taxes for the balance of the year	$5,100,000	$4,000,000
Annual deductions permanently disallowed for tax purposes	$60,000	$35,000
Estimated annual tax credits	$18,000	$30,000

Prepare an income statement for each of the first two quarters of 20X7. All supporting schedules should be in good form.

template cd

Exercise 4 *(LO 3, 4)* **Tax expense/benefit traceable to nonordinary items of income.** Your client has no permanent or temporary differences between accounting and tax measures of income. However, the client has a tax credit **carryforward** from last year in the amount of $6,000. The benefit of this credit was recognized last year to the extent of $4,000 because at that time it was anticipated that, more likely than not, there would be future income resulting in some tax liability. The client incurs income taxes at the following rates: 15% on the first $50,000, 20% on the next $25,000, 30% on the next $25,000, and 40% on all additional income. Your client has year-to-date (YTD) pretax net income from continuing operations (NICO) of $24,000 and is projecting another $36,000 of such income for the balance of the year. Furthermore, your client has the following additional YTD *pretax* components of income:

Extraordinary gain	$ 40,000
Loss from discontinued operation	(20,000)
Cumulative effect of a change in accounting method	30,000

Calculate the amount of tax expense traceable to the extraordinary gain.

Exercise 5 *(LO 3, 4)* **Estimated effective annual tax rate for various fact situations.** The following data represent the accounting results for the year ended December 31, 20X3, for four different manufacturing corporations. The effective tax rates were as follows: 30% for 20X1, 32% for 20X2, and 40% for 20X3 and thereafter.

	Corporation A	Corporation B	Corporation C	Corporation D
YTD operating income (loss)	$95,000	$ 5,000	$ (80,000)	$ 20,000
Projected interim income (loss)	30,000	(70,000)	(50,000)	(35,000)
Tax exempt municipal income		15,000		
Deductions not allowed for tax purposes		8,000	2,000	
Annual tax credit available	2,000	3,500		1,000
Carryback income:				
For 20X1		32,000	105,000	
For 20X2		15,000	35,000	
Projected future income for carryforward period:				
More likely than not				12,500
Not more likely than not		40,000		

Calculate the estimated effective annual tax rate for each company.

Exercise 6 *(LO 3, 4)* **Restating prior periods due to a discontinued operation.** Baxter Holdings reported pretax net income from continuing operations of $800,000 in the first quarter of 20X4. At the end of that quarter, the company estimated an effective annual tax rate of 29.5% based on a statutory tax rate of 30% on the first $1,500,000 of pretax income and 35% thereafter, projected pretax income for the balance of the year of $1,100,000, and tax credits of $29,500.

During the second quarter of 20X4, the company decided to discontinue a component of its business that manufactured custom cabinetry. At the end of the first quarter of 20X4, the cabinetry component had reported pretax losses of $220,000, projected losses of $320,000 for the balance of the year, and no estimated tax credits for the year. During the second quarter of the year, the discontinued component reported pretax losses of $80,000 prior to being shut down. Pretax impairment losses of $400,000 were also reported for the component during the second quarter of 20X4.

Excluding the discontinued component, the company reported pretax income in the second quarter of 20X4 of $525,000 and projected pretax income for the balance of the year of $1,050,000. Annual tax credits of $15,000 traceable to the continuing operations are projected for the year.

For quarter 1 restated and quarter 2 of 20X4 prepare a schedule that shows pretax income, tax expense or benefit, and net income for both continuing operations and the discontinued operation.

Exercise 7 *(LO 4)* **Restatement of prior interim income statements, change in accounting principle.** Tripper Industries, Inc., decided to change accounting principles in the third quarter of the current year. Originally, the first six months had a YTD pretax income of $40,000, a projected pretax income for the balance of the year of $60,000, and an estimated annual effective tax rate of 20%. The rate is based on statutory rates of 15% on the first

$50,000 of income, 25% on the next $50,000 of income, and 35% on amounts in excess of $100,000. Had the new principle been adopted at the beginning of the year, the first six months' pretax income would have been $30,000, and projected pretax income for the balance of the year would have been $30,000. The effect of the change in principle on prior years is to decrease net income by $50,000.

The third-quarter pretax income, based on the new accounting principle, is $50,000, and the projected pretax income for the balance of the year is $40,000.

Calculate the pretax income and related tax expense (benefit) for the first three quarters of the current year.

Exercise 8 *(LO 4)* **Tax on nonordinary items.** For the first nine months of 20X5, Walton Corporation is reporting the following pretax amounts of income (loss): net income from continuing operations of $100,000, loss on discontinued operations of ($20,000), extraordinary gain of $70,000, and cumulative effect of a change in accounting method of $30,000. The statutory tax rates are as follows: 20% on the first $50,000 of pretax income, 25% on the next $50,000 of pretax income, 30% on the next $50,000 of pretax income, and 40% on all additional pretax income.

Determine the amount of tax expense to be allocated to the nonordinary items. Note that annual pretax net income from continuing operations is estimated to be $90,000.

Exercise 9 *(LO 5)* **Defining an operating segment.** Norfo International is a large company with extremely diversified activities. These activities include the following:

a. Food-processing operations in California, Spain, and Italy. Processed foods are sold throughout Europe, South America, and the United States. Cans and containers for the processed foods are manufactured by Canco Industries, a wholly owned subsidiary of Norfo. Canco has manufacturing facilities in Arizona, Germany, and Spain.
b. Seven citrus groves in central Florida. Approximately 70% of a harvest is trucked to the company's Louisville food-processing operation; the balance of the harvest is processed, on location, into frozen juice concentrates.
c. A Chicago operation that manufactures packaging for perishable food products and cardboard packaging for transporting equipment components, such as engines and transmissions.
d. Four large resort hotels, three of which are located along the eastern seaboard, and one of which is located in the Bahamas.
e. A chain of travel agencies in the New York and Boston areas.
f. A paper products division located in Maine that manufactures napkins, paper plates, paper towels, and greeting cards. These products are sold to grocery stores and variety stores.

Given the management approach, discuss various ways in which the segments of Norfo might be structured.

Exercise 10 *(LO 6)* **Determination of reportable segments.** The chief operating decision maker of a publicly traded company has defined segments around four product/service groups. Various revenues, profits or losses, and assets associated with the segments are as follows:

	Film Studios	Software Development	Leisure Clothing	Office Design Group	Total Enterprise Values
Revenues:					
External	$82,000,000	$12,000,000	$45,000,000	$22,000,000	$177,000,000
Intersegment	0	3,400,000	0	2,700,000	0
Expenses	93,000,000	18,000,000	22,000,000	18,000,000	166,000,000
Assets	38,000,000	5,400,000	13,000,000	5,000,000	70,000,000

Determine which segments are considered to be reportable and whether the reportable segments represent a significant portion of enterprise consolidated revenues.

Exercise 11 *(LO 6)* **Determination of reportable segments, reconciliation to consolidated totals.** A large diversified company divides its operations into several operating segments.

Determine which of the following segments are reportable, and reconcile the reportable segments to the consolidated revenue and profit.

template cd

	Publishing	Talent Agency	Cable Networks	Radio Stations	Film Production	Consolidated Totals
Revenues:						
External	$1,200,000	$ 850,000	$3,771,500	$ 810,700	$1,090,000	$9,074,000
Intersegment	110,000	0	672,000	0	57,800	0
Expenses	385,000	1,299,000	1,257,700	1,048,700	727,800	4,634,500
Assets.	970,000	670,000	3,893,500	770,000	720,500	8,276,000

Assume that there is no intercompany profit included in ending inventory.

Exercise 12 *(LO 6)* **Determination of reportable segments, analysis, disclosure.** The following information is given for the seven segments of Staven Supplies:

Segment	Revenues	Operating Profit (Loss)	Assets
1	$1,540,000	$ 602,000	$1,600,000
2	805,000	(208,000)	870,000
3	1,948,000	530,000	1,250,000
4	1,070,000	375,000	1,800,000
5	760,000	220,000	965,000
6	980,000	402,000	1,400,000
7	1,071,000	(106,000)	1,380,000
Corporate-level items.	820,000	170,000	560,000
	$8,994,000	$1,985,000	$9,825,000
Intercompany adjustments and eliminations.	(278,300)	(75,000)	(305,000)
Consolidated total	$8,715,700	$1,910,000	$9,520,000

Ten percent of the revenues of segments 2, 4, and 5 are traceable to intersegment sales.

1. Determine which segments are reportable.
2. Determine whether a substantial portion of Staven's total operations is represented by reportable segments.
3. Discuss how information traceable to nonreportable segments should be presented.
4. Assume that segment 3 has revenues in the amount of $1,230,000 which result from sales to the U.S. government. Prepare the necessary disclosure which is required due to this assumption.

PROBLEMS

Problem 12-1 *(LO 2)* **Interim income statement, accounting for various items.** Mikelson Company, a California corporation listed on the Pacific Coast Stock Exchange, budgeted activities for 20X5 as follows:

	Amount	Units
Net sales	$6,000,000	1,000,000
Cost of goods sold	3,600,000	1,000,000
Gross profit	$2,400,000	
Selling, general, and administrative expenses	1,400,000	
Operating income	$1,000,000	
Nonoperating revenue and expenses	0	
Income before income taxes	$1,000,000	
Estimated income taxes (current and deferred)	550,000	
Net income	$ 450,000	
Earnings per share of common stock	$ 4.50	

Mikelson has operated profitably for many years and has experienced a seasonal pattern of sales volume and production. For 20X5, sales volume is expected to follow a quarterly pattern of 10%, 20%, 35%, and 35%, respectively, because of the seasonality of the industry. Also, due to production and storage capacity limitations, it is expected that production will follow a pattern of 20%, 25%, 30%, and 25% per quarter, respectively.

At the end of the first quarter of 20X5, the controller of Mikelson prepared and issued the following interim report for public release:

	Amount	Units
Net sales	$ 600,000	100,000
Cost of goods sold	360,000	100,000
Gross profit	$ 240,000	
Selling, general, and administrative expenses	275,000	
Operating loss	$ (35,000)	
Loss from warehouse fire	(175,000)	
Loss before income taxes	$(210,000)	
Estimated income taxes	0	
Net loss	$(210,000)	
Loss per share of common stock	$ (2.10)	

The following additional information is available for the first quarter but was not included in the public information released:

a. The company uses a standard cost system in which standards are set at currently attainable levels on an annual basis. At the end of the first quarter, there was an underapplied fixed factory overhead (volume variance) of $50,000 that was treated as an asset at the end of the quarter. Production during the quarter was 200,000 units, of which 100,000 were sold.
b. The selling, general, and administrative expenses were budgeted on a basis of $900,000 fixed expenses for the year plus $0.50 variable expenses per unit of sales.
c. Assume the warehouse fire loss met the conditions of an extraordinary loss. The warehouse had an undepreciated cost of $320,000; $145,000 was recovered from insurance on the warehouse. No other gains or losses are anticipated this year from similar events or transactions, nor has Mikelson had any similar losses in preceding years; thus, the full loss will be deductible as an ordinary loss for income tax.
d. The effective income tax rate, for federal and state taxes combined, is expected to average 55% of income before income taxes during 20X5. There are no permanent differences between pretax accounting income and taxable income.

Required ▶ ▶ ▶ ▶ ▶

1. Without reference to the specific situations described in this problem, what are the standards of disclosure for interim financial data (published interim financial reports) for publicly traded companies? Explain.

2. Identify the weakness in form and content of Mikelson's interim report without reference to the additional information.
3. For each of the four items of additional information, indicate the preferable treatment for interim reporting purposes and explain why that treatment is preferable.

Problem 12-2 *(LO 3, 4)* **Determining the tax expense traceable to various components of income.** McClure Manufacturing reported a pretax loss from operations of $45,000 for the first quarter of 20X3. The estimated effective annual tax rate at that time was based on the following information:

1. A statutory tax rate of 32% and annual estimated tax credits of $7,000.
2. Projected annual pretax loss of $70,000.
3. Taxable income of $12,000 and $10,000, respectively, for 20X1 and 20X2.
4. Statutory tax rates in 20X1 and 20X2 of 30% and 28%, respectively.
5. No recognized tax benefit associated with net operating loss carryforwards.

During the second quarter of 20X3, McClure decided to discontinue an operation that had reported pretax losses of $15,000 in the first quarter. At the end of the first quarter of 20X3, the discontinued operation had accounted for $2,000 of the annual estimated tax credit and $55,000 of the annual pretax loss. In the second quarter, the discontinued operation reported pretax operating losses of $15,000 and pretax impairment losses of $42,000. Continuing operations reported second-quarter pretax income of $58,000, projected annual pretax income of $90,000, and annual estimated tax credits of $5,000.

During the third quarter of 20X3, continuing operations reported pretax income of $40,000, projected annual pretax income of $110,000, and annual estimated tax credits of $8,000. Also during the third quarter, the discontinued operation reported operating losses of $30,000, and gains from the disposal of assets of $25,000, revised the earlier impairment losses from $42,000 to $34,000, and recorded additional impairment losses of $16,000.

◄◄◄◄◄ **Required**

Given the 20X3 statutory tax rate of 32%, calculate the pretax income (loss) and related tax expense (benefit) for the first three quarters of 20X3 for continuing and discontinued operations.

Problem 12-3 *(LO 3, 4)* **Tax expense/benefit, nonordinary items of gain/loss.** During 20X8, Midway Corporation reported first six months' pretax income of $120,000 from continuing operations and a year-to-date tax expense of $37,668. The tax expense reflects projected pretax income for the balance of the year of $100,000 and the following statutory tax rates:

Tax on first $50,000	15%
Tax on next $25,000	25%
Tax on next $25,000	34%
Tax on next $235,000	39%
Tax on remaining income	34%

The first six months also included the following nonordinary items:

A.	Extraordinary gain	$ 10,000
B.	Loss on noncurrent marketable securities recorded as a component of owners' equity	(85,000)
C.	Loss on discontinued operations	(80,000)

◄◄◄◄◄ **Required**

Calculate the incremental tax impact traceable to each of the nonordinary items directly affecting income or owners' equity.

Problem 12-4 *(LO 3, 4)* **Tax expense/benefit, ordinary and nonordinary income.** Prior to the second quarter of 20X9, Portico, Inc., had depreciated its assets by the straight-line method. However, during the second quarter of 20X9, the company changed to an accelerated method of depreciation. The effect of the change on the first quarter of 20X9 was an increase in pretax income of $5,000. The effect of the change in prior years was to decrease pretax income by $84,000. The first quarter of 20X9 had originally reported a pretax income of $30,000 and a tax expense of $5,832. The projected income for the balance of the year was originally estimated to be $60,000 at the end of the first quarter. However, due to the change in depreciation methods, the projection should have been $75,000. Pretax income, based on the new depreciation method for the second quarter of 20X9 and the balance of the year, is $25,000 and $80,000, respectively. At this time, anticipated annual tax credits were $4,000.

During the third quarter of 20X9, the company experienced a pretax income of $40,000 and a projected $20,000 of pretax income for the balance of the year. Annual tax credits were anticipated to be $3,000. Also during the quarter, the company experienced an extraordinary gain of $20,000, which is taxed at 20%.

The statutory tax rate is 15% on the first $50,000 of income, 25% on the next $50,000, and 35% on all additional income.

Required ▶▶▶▶▶ Calculate the pretax income and related tax expense for the first three quarters of 20X9.

Problem 12-5 *(LO 3, 4)* **Tax expense/benefit, ordinary and nonordinary income.** The following information relates to three independent cases:

template cd

	Case A	Case B	Case C
Pretax net income (loss) from continuing operations:			
Year-to-date	$(80,000)	$ 30,000	$20,000
Projected	60,000	20,000	40,000
Tax-exempt income included in above net income:			
Year-to-date	0	3,000	0
Projected	3,000	3,000	0
Statutory tax rate	30%	30%	30%
Tax credits:			
Year-to-date	0	4,000	2,000
Projected	2,000	2,200	2,000
Information regarding prior two years:			
Taxable income	50,000	100,000	20,000*
Effective tax rate	30%	40%	25%

*The $20,000 is equally divided between the two prior years.

Required ▶▶▶▶▶

1. For Case A, calculate the year-to-date tax expense or benefit.
2. Assume that the YTD tax expense was originally calculated using the facts of Case B. Furthermore, assume that the original amounts are to be restated because of a subsequent decision to discontinue an operation. Calculate the year-to-date restated tax expense or benefit traceable to the discontinued operation assuming the following allocation of year-to-date and projected amounts.

	Total	Continuing Operations	Discontinued Operations
Pretax income (loss):			
Year-to-date	$30,000	$50,000	$(20,000)
Projected	20,000	90,000	(70,000)
Tax-exempt income included in above net income:			
Year-to-date	3,000	3,000	0
Projected	3,000	2,000	1,000
Tax credits:			
Year-to-date	4,000	3,500	500
Projected	2,200	2,000	200

3. For Case C, calculate the year-to-date tax expense or benefit associated with, in addition to the continuing income, a $50,000 extraordinary loss and a $20,000 loss due to a change in accounting principle.

Problem 12-6 *(LO 3, 4)* **Interim income statement, expense recognition, non-ordinary income items.** The Treetop Corporation is a manufacturer of specialty equipment used in the film editing industry. The company needs an income statement for the second quarter of its fiscal year and has requested that you prepare such a statement. Management of the company has provided you with the following information that may be relevant to your engagement:

1. Revenues for the quarter were $510,000. The revenues are traceable to the sale of 2,100 units.
2. The company employs the LIFO inventory method for the following items: beginning inventory of 900 units at a cost of $100 per unit and purchases of 1,500 units at a cost of $120 per unit. It is anticipated that ending inventory for the fiscal year will exceed the beginning levels of inventory. Furthermore, management anticipates that inventory acquired in the next quarter will cost approximately $124 per unit.
3. Selling, general, and administrative expenses, excluding the items in (4) through (5) below, totaled $110,000 for the quarter.
4. During the quarter, management expended $75,000 for research and development costs which are expected to provide for new technologies in the coming fiscal year.
5. Management bonuses for the current fiscal year will be approximately $160,000.
6. Based on prior experiences, it is estimated that a year-end physical inventory will reveal that the perpetual inventory is overstated. The adjustment is estimated to be in the range of $30,000.
7. During the second quarter, the company experienced two unrelated extraordinary gains (A and B) in the amount of $20,000 and $15,000, respectively.

The company's income tax rates are as follows: 15% on the first $50,000 of taxable income, 25% on the next $25,000, 34% on the next $25,000, 39% on the next $230,000, and 34% thereafter. In the first quarter of the fiscal year, the company reported net income before taxes (NIBT) of $20,000 and tax expense of $1,000. The company expects that for the last six months of the fiscal year there will be a pretax loss of $40,000 traceable to continuing operations. Annual tax credits will likely amount to $7,000.

Prepare an income statement for the second quarter of the current fiscal year. All supporting schedules should be presented in good form. ◀◀◀◀◀ **Required**

Problem 12-7 *(LO 7, 8)* **Analysis of segmental disclosures.** The following table contains selected information from the annual report of Snap-On Incorporated.

For fiscal years ended in December (in millions)	2003	2002
Company-wide data:		
Operating income	$ 150.1	$ 198.3
Net sales	2,233.2	2,109.1
Assets	2,138.5	1,994.1
Segmental data:		
Net sales:		
Snap-On Dealer group	$1,073.2	$1,039.7

(continued)

For fiscal years ended in December (in millions)	2003	2002
Commercial and industrial group	$1,133.9	$1,045.7
Diagnostics and information group	309.0	334.4
Total	$2,516.1	$2,419.8
Operating income:		
Snap-On Dealer group	$ 70.2	$ 89.6
Commercial and industrial group	13.1	46.0
Diagnostics and information group	23.0	25.0
Total	$ 106.3	$ 160.6
Assets:		
Snap-On Dealer group	$ 779.9	$ 759.7
Commercial and industrial group	1,101.9	1,010.7
Diagnostics and information group	189.9	198.5
Total	$2,071.7	$1,968.9
Depreciation/Amortization:		
Snap-On Dealer group	$ 27.1	$ 24.3
Commercial and industrial group	25.8	22.9
Diagnostics and information group	7.4	4.5
Total	$ 60.3	$ 51.7
Capital expenditures:		
Snap-On Dealer group	$ 9.7	$ 15.0
Commercial and industrial group	15.2	23.9
Diagnostics and information group	4.5	6.9
Total	$ 29.4	$ 45.8

Required ▶ ▶ ▶ ▶ ▶

1. Calculate the company's operating income as a percentage of average assets and net sales for the most current year, and comment on how each segment relates or contributes to these ratios.
2. Explain why the total of segmental net sales exceeds the net sales for the entire company.
3. Explain why the total of segmental operating income may not equal the operating income for the entire company.
4. Free cash flow is often defined as cash flows from operations less net capital expenditures to maintain productive capacity. For the most current year, calculate the free cash flow as a percentage of average assets for each segment.
5. Using the segmental data, comment on the growth of the segments over time.

template cd

Problem 12-8 *(LO 6, 7, 8)* **Determination of reportable segments, disclosures, ratio analysis.** A U.S. multinational corporation has divided its operations into several operating segments and has provided the following data for each segment:

	Semiconductors	Control Devices	Educational and Productivity Solutions	Financing Activities	Corporate	Consolidated Totals
Revenues:						
External	$19,920,000	$61,700,000	$5,360,000	$3,300,000	$ 8,288,000	$ 98,568,000
Intersegment	3,970,000	11,411,000	0	964,000	0	0
Expenses	23,800,000	28,422,000	5,467,000	7,962,000	7,020,000	0
Total assets	28,220,000	36,320,000	6,750,000	6,015,000	23,000,000	100,305,000
Long-lived assets	18,230,000	24,000,000	5,540,000	3,760,000	15,434,000	66,964,000

It is important to note that all purchases of goods or services from other segments have been sold to outside parties except one. Control devices with a cost of $1,000,000 were sold to the Semiconductors segment for $1,700,000. These items remain in inventory at year-end.

	United States	Japan	Germany	Other International	Total of All Countries
Semiconductors:					
Revenues (excluding intersegment)	$12,967,000	$ 3,240,000	$1,880,000	$ 1,833,000	$19,920,000
Long-lived assets	13,440,000	2,100,000	1,200,000	1,490,000	18,230,000
Control devices:					
Revenues (excluding intersegment)	16,467,000	31,000,000	4,432,300	9,800,700	61,700,000
Long-lived assets	4,011,000	15,020,000	1,419,000	3,550,000	24,000,000
Educational and productivity solutions:					
Revenues (excluding intersegment)	3,007,000	807,000	526,000	1,020,000	5,360,000
Long-lived assets	2,900,000	1,020,000	550,000	1,070,000	5,540,000
Financing activities:					
Revenues (excluding intersegment)	1,902,000	303,300	770,900	323,800	3,300,000
Long-lived assets	2,000,000	192,900	893,000	674,100	3,760,000
Corporate:					
Revenues (excluding intersegment)	6,607,000	807,000	474,000	400,000	8,288,000
Long-lived assets	11,026,000	2,000,000	1,504,000	904,000	15,434,000
Total revenues	$40,950,000	$36,157,300	$8,083,200	$13,377,500	$98,568,000
Total long-lived assets	$33,377,000	$20,332,900	$5,566,000	$ 7,688,100	$66,964,000

◄◄◄◄◄ **Required**

1. Determine which segments are reportable.
2. Given the available information, prepare all of the necessary schedules and disclosures regarding the enterprise's segments, geographical areas, and reconciliations to consolidated amounts.
3. Identify and determine the value of several ratios which may be helpful in analyzing the above information.

Problem 12-9 *(LO 7, 8)* **Schedule of reportable segments and reconciliation to the consolidated company.** Tress Corporation is a rapidly growing company that has diversified into a number of different segments. The following partial trial balance, which includes the effect of intercompany transactions, is for the year ended December 31, 20X9:

Net Sales..	$(14,332,250)
Cost of Goods Sold	7,180,000
General and Administrative Expenses..................	1,620,000
Gain on Sale of Fixed Asset..........................	(100,000)
Investment Income	(315,000)
Interest Income....................................	(162,000)

Tress Corporation has five distinct segments (A through E), in addition to corporate operations. Net sales are allocated to the segments as follows:

Segment	Net Sales
A	$ 4,023,500
B..	2,749,000
C	574,500
D	6,185,250
E..	800,000
Total..	$14,332,250

Ten percent of D's sales are made to A, and 7% of B's sales are made to C. The cost of the goods sold to A by D is $200,000, and the cost of the goods sold to C by B is $144,000. The total cost of goods sold is allocated to the segments by the following percentages: A—30%, B—29%, C—6%, D—24%, and E—11%. Of the items C purchased from B, 25% are included in C's ending inventory.

Of general and administrative expenses, 20% are traceable to corporate operations. The balance is allocated in proportion to the segment revenues, including interest income and the gain on the sale of the fixed asset.

Investment income is traceable to corporate operations.

Interest income is traceable directly to the segments and the corporate level as follows:

Segment A	$48,000
Segment B	10,000
Segment C	0
Segment D	60,000
Segment E	12,000
Corporate level	32,000

Unconsolidated assets are identifiable as follows:

	A	B	C	D	E	Corporate
Current assets	$ 912,000	$ 681,000	$ 305,000	$ 309,000	$ 389,000	$ 115,000
Property, plant, and equipment (net)	7,136,000	4,643,000	1,480,000	4,181,000	1,543,000	1,737,000

Included in B's property, plant, and equipment is a machine that B purchased at the beginning of the year from A for $300,000. Segment A originally purchased the machine for $250,000, two years prior to the sale. Accumulated depreciation (straight-line method) on the machine was $50,000 at the time of the sale. Segment B recorded $30,000 of depreciation on the machine for the year based on the straight-line method. The gain on the sale of equipment is included in A's revenue.

Required ▶ ▶ ▶ ▶ ▶

1. Assuming that segments A, B, and D are reportable, prepare a schedule that discloses the revenues, operating profits or losses, and assets for each of the reportable segments and the "all other" segments.
2. Prepare a schedule which reconciles the above amounts to the respective enterprise consolidated amounts.

Problem 12-10 *(LO 6, 7, 8)* **Determination of reportable segments, disclosures, reconciliation to consolidated amounts.** Autoplus International is a publicly traded company which manufactures and distributes a number of products for use within the automobile industry. Major products are categorized as follows:

A. Automobile collision repair equipment
B. Automobile battery and starter parts
C. Automobile seating and safety belts
D. Automobile paints and trim parts
E. Automobile tire retreading equipment
F. Miscellaneous automobile products

The chief operating decision maker for the enterprise uses information organized by product groups for purposes of evaluating performance and allocating resources. Intersegment transactions can be summarized as follows:

Selling Segment	Buying Segment	Cost of Sales	Selling Price	Amount Included in Ending Inventory of Buying Segment
Miscellaneous Products	Battery and Starter Parts	$2,540,000	$3,556,000	$420,000
Paint and Trim Parts	Collision Repair Equipment	4,500,000	5,400,000	720,000
Seating and Safety	Collision Repair Equipment	1,650,000	2,200,000	440,000

For the year ended December 31, 20X7, amounts allocated to the segments are as follows:

Segment	Revenues (Including Intersegment Activity)	Cost of Sales	General and Administrative Expenses	Total Assets	Long-Lived Assets
A	$24,840,000	$17,560,000	$ 2,480,000	$ 45,720,000	$ 34,250,000
B	6,470,000	4,250,000	1,120,000	14,780,000	10,100,000
C	13,850,000	7,560,000	1,840,000	37,500,000	21,500,000
D	25,500,000	18,650,000	4,570,000	47,800,000	32,000,000
E	4,780,000	3,100,000	980,000	13,950,000	8,540,000
F	8,650,000	4,320,000	2,130,000	16,570,000	9,870,000
Corporate	6,750,000	0	4,730,000	29,860,000	15,500,000
	$90,840,000	$55,440,000	$17,850,000	$206,180,000	$131,760,000

The products of the enterprise are sold throughout the world. The percentage of revenues from external customers (excluding corporate revenues) and long-lived assets (including corporate assets) traceable to various geographic areas are as follows:

Percentage of	United States	United Kingdom	Italy	Germany	Mexico	All Other Foreign
External sales traceable to:	51%	20%	10%	5%	9%	5%
Long-lived assets traceable to:	54	21	8	4	10	3

◄◄◄◄◄ **Required**

1. Determine which of the segments are considered to be reportable and whether the guidelines regarding the number of reportable segments have been satisfied.
2. Given the available information, prepare all of the necessary schedules and disclosures regarding the enterprise's segments, geographical areas, and reconciliations to consolidated amounts.

PART

3 Partnerships

Chapter 13: *Partnerships: Characteristics, Formation, and Accounting for Activities*

Chapter 14: *Partnerships: Ownership Changes and Liquidations*

A business may be organized in a variety of ways: as a sole proprietorship, a commercial corporation, a limited liability company, a limited liability partnership, or a regular partnership. Partnerships continue to be a common form of organization, and even the recent limited liability entities have many of the characteristics of a partnership. Assisting business owners in the proper selection of an organizational form is a necessary, yet complex, part of serving the needs of a business. A partnership is governed by a partnership agreement or, in some instances, by the Uniform Partnership Act. The partnership agreement must be carefully drafted to cover a variety of topics, including the purpose of the partnership, the responsibilities of the partners, the allocation of profits and losses, the admission or withdrawal of a partner, and the valuation of the partnership given changes in the ownership structure. Changes in the ownership structure provide insight into some of the basic factors which must be considered in valuing a business, whether it be a partnership or not. In addition to special financial accounting principles governing partnerships, such entities are also required to follow different rules for determining income and basis for tax purposes. If a decision is made to terminate a partnership, several legal doctrines and special accounting procedures must be applied in order to produce an equitable distribution of partnership assets.

Partnerships: Characteristics, Formation, and Accounting for Activities

CHAPTER

13

Learning Objectives

When you have completed this chapter, you should be able to

1. **Explain the basic characteristics of a partnership.**
2. **Identify basic components that should be included in a partnership agreement.**
3. **Describe the relationship between a partner's drawing and capital accounts.**
4. **Demonstrate an understanding of the various bases that could be used to allocate profits or losses among partners.**
5. **(Appendix) Describe how a partner's tax basis in a partnership is different from the book basis, and be able to calculate the tax basis.**
6. **(Appendix) Explain the concept of double taxation, and discuss how it may be minimized.**

A partnership is an association of two or more people for the purpose of carrying on a trade or business as co-owners. Partnerships continue to be a popular form of organization for many smaller businesses as well as certain larger businesses. Common examples of partnerships include professional services, such as the practice of accounting or law, real estate investment/development companies, and a variety of smaller manufacturing concerns.

In a majority of states, the legal nature and functioning of a partnership is governed by the *Uniform Partnership Act (UPA)*. The UPA deals with such topics as the rights of partners, relations with persons dealing with the partnership, and the dissolution and termination of a partnership.

CHARACTERISTICS OF A PARTNERSHIP

1 OBJECTIVE

Explain the basic characteristics of a partnership.

Practicing accountants frequently are asked to advise clients regarding the formation of a business and the accounting for the business activities. Often, a choice must be made between a partnership and a corporate form of organization. Therefore, it is important for accounting students to understand the basic characteristics of a partnership and the related accounting implications.

Relationship of Partners

A partnership represents a voluntary association of individuals carrying out a business purpose. In this association, a *fiduciary relationship* exists among the partners, requiring them to exercise good faith, loyalty to the partnership, and sound business judgment in conducting the partnership's business. An individual partner is viewed as a co-owner of partnership property, creating a *tenancy in partnership*. When specific assets are contributed by a partner, they lose their identity as to source and become the shared property of the partnership. Without the consent of all partners, such property cannot be utilized by any partner for personal purposes.

The relationship between partners also is characterized as one of *mutual agency*, which means that each partner is an agent for the other partners and the partnership when transacting partnership business. Therefore, in carrying on the business of the partnership, the acts of every partner bind the partnership itself, even when a partner commits a wrongful act or a breach of trust. However, if a partner has no authority to act for the partnership and the party with whom the partner is dealing knows this, the partnership is not bound by the partner's actions.

Legal Liability of a Partnership

Partnerships are classified as either general or limited regarding liability of the partners. In a *general partnership*, the partners act publicly on behalf of the partnership and are personally liable, jointly and severally, for the unsatisfied obligations of the partnership. This unlimited liability is in sharp contrast to the limited liability of a corporation and its shareholders. Thus, if a partnership were insolvent, the unsatisfied creditors could seek to recover against the net personal assets of individual partners. Newly admitted partners, who are personally liable for partnership debts incurred subsequent to this admission, are liable for debts of the previous partnership only to the extent of their capital interest in the partnership.

In contrast, a *limited partnership* consists of one or more general partners and one or more limited partners who contribute capital but do not participate in the management of the company. The one or more general partners have unlimited liability as in the case of a general partnership. However, the limited partners' liability for partnership obligations is restricted to a stated amount, usually equal to their capital interest in the partnership.

The legal liability of partners is obviously a serious factor to consider when assessing whether a partnership is the appropriate form of organization. One could argue that unlimited liability, as a matter of social policy, is a good thing. Society has a right to be protected from the consequences of serious errors in judgment whether they be unintentional or intentional. However, without proper limits, such exposure to liability may also impair an entity's ability to provide useful goods or services. Virtually every product or service industry, from cigarette manufacturers to the medical profession, has been affected by liability issues. For example, the public accounting profession has had to operate in such a litigious environment that major initiatives have been undertaken in response to the legal liability crisis.

In response to this growing concern, two new forms of organization have been created, a *limited liability company* (LLC) and a *limited liability partnership* (LLP). The LLC is a hybrid form of organization which has many of the advantages of both a partnership and a corporation but few of the disadvantages of either. Similar to a corporation, shareholders of an LLC do not have personal legal liability for actions undertaken by the entity. This limited liability does not necessarily protect an individual shareholder from personal liability for his/her own wrongs. This is consistent with common law doctrine which views each individual as being responsible for the consequences of his/her own negligence and the ability of courts to "pierce the corporate veil" in order to seek recovery for wrongdoings.

An LLP is a subcategory of general partnerships. The LLP compares favorably to limited or general partnerships with respect to liability. All partners in an LLP may participate in management (unlike limited partners) and still have limited liability. Partners in an LLP are **not personally** jointly and/or severally liable for obligations of the partnership arising from the omissions, negligence, wrongful acts, misconduct, or malpractice of other partners. However, a partner does remain personally responsible for liabilities arising from his/her own actions and the actions of those who are acting under the partner's actual supervision and control in the specific activity in which the action occurred.

Underlying Equity Theories

Equity theories relate to how an entity is viewed from an accounting and legal viewpoint. These theories deal with the question of who is the entity. For example, an entity may be viewed as being providers of capital, individual owners (partners/shareholders), management, or a separate, distinct legal entity. Partnerships have been primarily affected by the *proprietary theory*, which looks at the entity through the eyes of the owners. Characteristics of a partnership that emphasize that the entity is viewed as the individual owners include the following:

- Salaries to partners are viewed as distribution of income rather than a component of income.
- Unlimited liability of general partners extends beyond the entity to the individual partners.
- Income of the partnership is not taxed at the partnership level but, rather, is included as part of the partners' individual taxable income.
- An original partnership is dissolved upon the admission or withdrawal of a partner.

Partnerships also have been influenced by the *entity theory* which views the business unit as a separate and distinct entity possessing its own existence apart from the individual partners. This theory is characteristic of corporations; yet, it is the basis for certain partnership characteristics. For example, a partnership may enter into contracts in its own name. Also, property contributed to a partnership by individual partners becomes the property of the partnership, and the contributing partner no longer retains a claim to the specific assets contributed.

Formation and Agreements

2

OBJECTIVE

Identify basic components that should be included in a partnership agreement.

A partnership may come into existence without having to receive formal, legal, or state approval and may result simply from the actions of the parties involved. This lack of formality may be viewed as an advantage of a partnership. However, it is still necessary to carefully plan and evaluate various factors affecting the partnership. Forward and formal thinking when organizing a partnership will benefit both the business and its partners.

In order to properly capture the intent of the partners involved, it is advisable to develop a written partnership agreement. Critical issues that must be addressed include: admission of partners, withdrawal of partners, and the allocation of profits and losses. Such an agreement is referred to as the *articles of partnership* and, at minimum, should include the following provisions:

1. Partnership name and address.
2. Partners' names and addresses.
3. Effective date of partnership.
4. A description of the general business purpose and the limited duration of such purpose, if applicable.
5. Powers and duties of partners.
6. Procedures governing the valuation of assets invested.
7. Procedures governing the admission of a new partner(s).
8. Procedures governing the distribution of profits and losses.
9. Procedures governing the payment of receipt of interest on loans (versus capital contributions) among partners.
10. Salaries to be accrued to partners.
11. Withdrawals of capital to be allowed each partner and the determination of what constitutes excess withdrawals.
12. Procedures governing the voluntary withdrawal, disability, death, or divorce of a partner and the determination of the procedures for valuing the partner's interest in the partnership.
13. Matters requiring the consent of all partners.
14. The date when the profits and losses are divided and the partnership books are closed.
15. The basis of accounting (e.g., accrual or cash).

As the accounting for a partnership is developed more fully in this text, it will become apparent that the articles of partnership provide crucial guidance. Even though the UPA covers certain topics found in the articles of partnership, it is important to note that **many sections of the UPA are applicable only in the absence of a partnership agreement**. Legal and accounting issues affecting a partnership are often best resolved by evaluating the intent of the partners as set forth in a partnership agreement, rather than looking to the UPA.

Acceptable Accounting Principles

There is a general presumption that an entity's financial position and results of operations should be accounted for in conformity with generally accepted accounting principles (GAAP). As GAAP have developed and become more complex, many have questioned the applicability of such principles to smaller business organizations, a large number of which are organized as partnerships. In response to this concern, it is recognized that, in some circumstances, a basis or method of accounting other than GAAP may be appropriate and may not adversely affect the fairness of the financial statements.

The Auditing Standards Board of the American Institute of Certified Public Accountants (AICPA) recognizes several *other comprehensive bases of accounting (OCBOA)* other than GAAP, including the following:

- The cash (receipts and disbursements) basis of accounting and modifications of the basis, such as a modified accrual basis.
- The tax basis of accounting based on taxation principles that are used to file an income tax return.

Tax-basis accounting generally consists of a cash-basis format or an accrual-basis format with certain exceptions primarily resulting from tax regulations differing from GAAP. The tax basis of accounting is a frequent choice of many partnerships. Depreciation accounting can be used to illustrate the focus of tax-basis accounting. Assume a depreciable asset has an economic useful life of six years and is consumed uniformly over its life. If accrual accounting were used, it would seem that the asset should be depreciated over six years using the straight-line method of depreciation. However, adoption of the tax basis of accounting could involve the use of a shorter life and an accelerated depreciation method. Furthermore, in some instances tax-basis accounting would allow the immediate expensing of depreciable assets even though such treatment would not be justified by accrual accounting.

The recognition of these other comprehensive bases provides many smaller and more specialized entities, many of which may be partnerships, with an acceptable alternative to GAAP. The use of OCBOA will not impair the fairness of their financial statements as evaluated by outside independent accountants. In practice, it is very common to find partnerships using a comprehensive basis of accounting other than GAAP. Due to the special tax aspects of a partnership, many such entities use the tax basis of accounting rather than GAAP.

Partnership Dissolution

Although a partnership is easily formed and does not need state approval, its life is limited and it may be dissolved much more easily than a corporation. *Dissolution* is defined in Section 29 of the UPA as "the change in the relation of the partners caused by any partner ceasing to be associated in the carrying on as distinguished from the winding up of the business." Generally, a partnership is dissolved upon the death, withdrawal, or bankruptcy of an individual partner (owner). The admission of a new partner also results in the dissolution of the former partnership. Thus, any change in the association of the individual partners is termed a dissolution.

Although dissolution occurs when there is a change in a partner's association with the other partners, it does not necessarily result in the termination of the basic business function. Therefore, a change in the ownership structure dissolves the former partnership, but often this change results in the formation of a new partnership to carry on the business purpose of the original partnership. The dissolution of a partnership resulting from the admission or withdrawal of a partner is more fully discussed in Chapter 14 of this text.

Tax Considerations

Unlike corporations, a partnership is not a separate taxable entity but a conduit through which taxable income or operating losses pass to the tax returns of the individual partners. The partnership must file an information return (Federal Form 1065) detailing the partnership revenues and expenses which pass through to the individual partners.

Even though a partnership is not a taxable entity, accounting for partnerships for tax-reporting purposes can become extremely complex. **The tax code does not view a partnership as a separate, distinct entity but focuses, rather, on the individual partners.** Therefore, activities of the partnership must be evaluated from a tax standpoint based on their impact on individual partners. This viewpoint results in special rules which must be understood by practicing accountants. Furthermore, the unique tax-related aspects of a partnership must be understood in order to advise clients as to whether the partnership form of organization is appropriate. The appendix to this chapter discusses in greater detail the tax-related aspects of a partnership.

REFLECTION

- Partnerships have a number of characteristics of a legal, tax, and accounting nature that distinguish them from other forms of organization.
- A number of factors must be considered before forming a partnership, and a partnership agreement is a critical document that will help guide and manage the partnership.

ACCOUNTING FOR PARTNERSHIP ACTIVITIES

The activities of a partnership consist of several phases, including the initial contribution of capital to the partnership. This initial phase provides the capital necessary to begin operating activities. The remainder of this chapter discusses accounting for the partners' capital investments and the allocation of operating profits and losses among the partners. Although partners' capital investments may be subsequently influenced by partners entering or exiting the partnership and the liquidation of a partnership, these topics are discussed in the next chapter.

Contributions and Distributions of Capital

3

OBJECTIVE

Describe the relationship between a partner's drawing and capital accounts.

The capital contributed by shareholders to a corporation is accounted for in several accounts, including Capital Stock, Paid-In Capital in Excess of Par, and Retained Earnings. Unlike a corporation, the capital investment in a partnership generally is accounted for through two accounts for each partner, a temporary account referred to as the *drawing account* and a permanent account referred to as the *capital account*.

It is not unusual for a partner to withdraw available assets (typically cash) from a partnership throughout the year. Preferably, the amount and timing of a partner's withdrawal of assets should be addressed in the articles of partnership. Practically speaking, however, withdrawals are often informal and are not easily projected due to cash flow constraints. In some instances, withdrawals in excess of some amount are considered to be direct reductions of a partner's capital account rather than a withdrawal. Some partnerships view any withdrawal as a direct reduction of a capital account. However, in some partnerships a separate account referred to as a drawing account is used to record a partner's withdrawal of capital. Withdrawals of assets, regardless of how accounted for, reduce the overall net capital of individual partners and the partnership.

A partner's withdrawals also include payments that are made by the partnership on behalf of an individual partner. For example, if a partnership pays off an individual partner's automobile loan, this is no different than if the partner had withdrawn the cash from the partnership and then paid off the loan personally.

The drawing account is a temporary account and is periodically closed to the partner's capital accounts. The balance sheet of a partnership, therefore, will present only the capital account balances of the partners. To summarize, the drawing account established for each partner is debited and credited for the following transactions:

Drawing Account

Debit	Credit
Periodic withdrawals of partnership assets up to a specified amount	Closing of balance to partner's capital account

Each partner's interest in the net assets of the partnership is measured at book value in the capital account established for that partner. This account indicates the destination of capital (claims to net assets) upon dissolution of the partnership. It is important to note that the capital balance does not normally reflect the fair value or tax basis of the partner's interest in the net assets of the partnership.

To summarize, the partner's capital account is debited and credited for the following transactions:

Capital Account

Debit	Credit
Withdrawals in excess of a specified amount	Initial and subsequent investments of capital
Closing of a net debit balance in the partner's drawing account	Partner's share of partnership profits
Partner's share of partnership losses	

As is the case with all entities, the investment of capital in a partnership should initially be measured at the fair value of all tangible and intangible assets contributed. An individual partner's liabilities that have been assumed by the partnership also should be recorded at fair value.

The exception to this would be in the case where a partnership has adopted the tax basis of accounting. The appendix to this chapter discusses how a partner's interest in capital is measured for tax purposes. The proper valuation of each partner's net investment of capital is extremely important. For example, if an asset invested by a partner is initially undervalued by the partnership and is sold immediately for a gain, all the partners share in the realized gain, which properly should have accrued to the original investing partner.

The post-closing balances in the capital accounts of the various partners represent each partner's interest in the net assets of the partnership at a point in time. A partner's interest in the partnership is different from the partner's interest in the profits and losses of the partnership. To illustrate, assume Partners A and B have capital balances of $8,000 and $32,000, respectively. Also assume that profits and losses are allocated to Partners A and B in the amount of 40% and 60%, respectively. These profit and loss ratios should not be confused with the partners' capital ratios which are 20% ($8,000 divided by $40,000) and 80% ($32,000 divided by $40,000) for A and B, respectively.

Occasionally, partners will loan assets to the partnership, or the partnership will loan assets to partners. It is important from a legal standpoint to differentiate between a loan and an additional investment of capital, especially when the liquidation of a partnership occurs. The nature of such transactions should be made clear by examining the intent of the individual partner or the partnership. If the contribution by a partner is really an additional investment of capital, it should be accounted for in the partner's capital account. However, if the transaction is truly a loan, it should be accounted for in a separate loan account for the partner, and provision for the payment of interest on the loan should be made.

Illustration 13-1 demonstrates the use of various partnership accounts in order to record partnership activity.

Illustration 13-1
Examples of Accounting for Partnership Activity

Event	Entry		
Partner A contributes cash to the partnership. Partner B contributes inventory and office equipment, and the partnership assumes the liability associated with the equipment. The equipment was recorded by B at a book value of $6,000. However, the equipment's fair value is $4,000.	Cash	10,000	
	Inventory	5,000	
	Office Equipment	4,000	
	Note Payable		2,000
	Partner A, Capital		10,000
	Partner B, Capital		7,000
Partner B loans the partnership $3,000 to be repaid in one year at a stated annual interest rate of 6%.	Cash	3,000	
	Partner B, Loan		3,000
A personal debt owed by Partner A is paid by the partnership.	Partner A, Drawing	500	
	Cash		500
Partners A and B withdraw cash of $500 and $1,200, respectively. Drawings in excess of $1,000 are viewed as excessive withdrawals and are charged against capital.	Partner A, Drawing	500	
	Partner B, Drawing	1,000	
	Partner B, Capital	200	
	Cash		1,700
The net income of the partnership is divided equally between the partners.	Income Summary	10,000	
	Partner A, Capital		5,000
	Partner B, Capital		5,000
The partners' drawing accounts are closed to their respective capital accounts.	Partner A, Capital	1,000	
	Partner B, Capital	1,000	
	Partner A, Drawing		1,000
	Partner B, Drawing		1,000

The Allocation or Division of Profits and Losses

4
OBJECTIVE

Demonstrate an understanding of the various bases that could be used to allocate profits or losses among partners.

An important process to be outlined in the articles of partnership is the manner in which profits and losses are to be divided among the partners. There are several alternative methods of allocating profits and losses. However, if the articles of partnership are silent on this point, Section 18 of the UPA states that profits and losses are to be divided equally among the partners. The division of partnership income should be based on an analysis of the correlation between the capital and labor committed to the firm by individual partners and the income that subsequently is generated. As a result, profits might be divided in one or more of the following ways:

1. According to a ratio.
2. According to the capital investments of the partners.
3. According to the labor (or service) rendered by the partners.

Profit and Loss Ratios. Partnership agreements frequently call for the allocation or division of profits and losses according to some ratio. Normally, the ratio set forth for the division of profits also is used for the division of losses, unless a specific provision to the contrary exists. This method obviously provides a simplified way of dividing profits and, if approached properly, may provide an equitable division as well. Theoretically, the ratio should attempt to combine into one base the capital and service contributions made by the respective partners. Again, it is important to note that a partner's interest in profits and losses is often different from the partner's interest in total partnership capital (net assets).

To illustrate this method, assume the articles of partnership state that partnership profits and losses should be divided between Partners A and B in the ratio of 60:40. Partnership income of $20,000 would be divided as follows:

	Partner A	Partner B
Income to partners:		
A: $20,000 × 60%	$12,000	
B: $20,000 × 40%		$8,000

Capital Investment of Partners. The capital investments of the partners, represented by the balances in their respective capital accounts, may be employed as a basis for dividing a portion of the profits. The division is accomplished by imputing interest on the invested capital at some specified rate. This interest is not viewed as a partnership expense but, rather, as a means of allocating profits and losses among the partners. Typically, the balance of profits not allocated on the basis of invested capital is allocated according to some profit and loss ratio.

When the partners' capital investments are to be used as the basis for allocating profits, the partnership agreement should specify the following:

1. Whether the respective partners' capital balances are to be determined before or after the partners' year-to-date withdrawals recorded in their drawing accounts are offset against their capital accounts.
2. Whether the amount of capital investment for allocation purposes is to be:
   a. Capital at the beginning of the accounting period,
   b. Capital at the end of the accounting period, or
   c. Weighted-average capital during the accounting period.
3. The rate of interest to be imputed on the invested capital.

With respect to the first point, it is important that the partnership agreement clearly establish how invested capital is to be determined. Since each partner's equity is really a combination of capital and drawing account balances, partners' drawings may be offset against the balances in their respective capital accounts for purposes of allocating income based on invested capital. However, a partnership agreement may state that only withdrawals above a certain limit are to be viewed as offsets against capital balances. It is possible for a partnership agreement to call for interest to be imputed only if the amount of invested capital exceeds some prescribed limit or average amount.

To illustrate the use of invested capital as a basis for allocating partnership profits, assume the following:

1. Partnership profit is $20,000.
2. Interest on invested capital is to be imputed at the rate of 10%. (Capital is determined before considering withdrawals.)
3. Profits not allocated on the basis of invested capital are to be allocated equally among the partners.
4. The capital accounts of Partners A and B, just prior to the closing of their drawing accounts, are as follows:

Partner A, Capital

Oct. 1, 20X1	30,000	Jan. 1, 20X1	100,000
		July 1, 20X1	10,000

Partner B, Capital

Apr. 1, 20X1	10,000	Jan. 1, 20X1	60,000

If interest is to be imputed on the partners' invested capital at the beginning of the period (January 1, 20X1), the partnership profit of $20,000 would be allocated as follows:

	Partner A	Partner B	Total
Interest on beginning capital:			
A: 10% × $100,000	$10,000		$10,000
B: 10% × $60,000		$6,000	6,000
			$16,000
Balance per ratio (equally)	2,000	2,000	4,000
Allocation of profit	$12,000	$8,000	$20,000

If interest is to be imputed on the partners' invested capital at the end of the period (December 31, 20X1), the partnership profit of $20,000 would be allocated as follows:

	Partner A	Partner B	Total
Interest on ending capital:			
A: 10% × $80,000	$ 8,000		$ 8,000
B: 10% × $50,000		$5,000	5,000
			$13,000
Balance per ratio (equally)	3,500	3,500	7,000
Allocation of profit	$11,500	$8,500	$20,000

If interest is to be imputed on the partners' weighted-average invested capital during the period, the partnership profit of $20,000 would be allocated as follows:

	Partner A	Partner B	Total
Interest on weighted-average capital:			
A: 10% × $97,500 (Schedule A)	$ 9,750		$ 9,750
B: 10% × $52,500 (Schedule B)		$5,250	5,250
			$15,000
Balance per ratio (equally)	2,500	2,500	5,000
Allocation of profit	$12,250	$7,750	$20,000

Schedule A
Weighted-Average Capital of Partner A

(1) Amount Invested	(2) Number of Months Invested	(1 × 2) Weighted Dollars
$100,000	6	$ 600,000
110,000	3	330,000
80,000	3	240,000
	12	$1,170,000

Weighted-average capital: $1,170,000 ÷ 12 = $ 97,500

Schedule B
Weighted-Average Capital of Partner B

(1) Amount Invested	(2) Number of Months Invested	(1 × 2) Weighted Dollars
$60,000	3	$180,000
50,000	9	450,000
	12	$630,000

Weighted-average capital: $630,000 ÷ 12 = $ 52,500

Services Rendered by Partners. A partner's labor or service to the partnership may be a primary force in the generation of revenue. Normally, the profit and loss agreement recognizes variations in effort by calling for a portion of income to be allocated to partners as salary. Such salaries, like interest on capital investments, are viewed as a means of allocating income rather than as an expense. It is important to note that this treatment of partners' salaries differs from the treatment of employee/shareholder salaries in a corporation, and the difference should be considered when the performance of a partnership is compared with that of a competing corporation.

When dealing with a profit and loss agreement that employs salaries as a means of allocating income, it is important not to confuse such salaries with partners' drawings. For example, a partner's withdrawal of $1,000 a month from the partnership may suggest that $12,000 of partnership income is being distributed to the partner as an annual salary or that these withdrawals may be ignored for purposes of dividing profits. Generally, a partner's drawing is not viewed as a salary but as a withdrawal of assets that reduces the partner's equity. For clarification purposes, the partnership agreement should state whether regular withdrawals of specific amounts should be viewed as salary for purposes of allocating income among the partners.

Bonuses to partners also may be used as a means of recognizing a partner's service to the partnership. Such bonuses are most often stated as a percentage of partnership income either before or after certain other components of the allocation process. Bonuses may be stated in reference to a variety of variables such as sales, gross profit, or a particular component of net income. In its most simple form, the bonus is a percentage of net income. However, if the bonus is to reward service beyond that already recognized by salaries and/or interest, the bonus may be expressed as a percentage of partnership net income after salaries and interest. In some instances, the bonus may be expressed as a percentage of net income after the bonus. To illustrate the calculation of a bonus, assume a partnership has net income of $120,000 of which $60,000 and $5,000 have already been allocated as salaries and interest, respectively. The bonus is defined in the partnership agreement as 10% of partnership net income after salaries and interest. The bonus is calculated as follows:

Bonus = X% (Net Income − Salaries − Interest)
Bonus = 10% ($ 120,000 − $60,000 − $5,000)
Bonus = 10% ($ 55,000)
Bonus = $5,500

If the agreement had stated that the bonus would be calculated based on net income after salaries, interest, and bonus, the calculation would be as follows:

Bonus = X% (Net Income − Salaries − Interest − Bonus)
Bonus = 10% ($ 120,000 − $60,000 − $5,000 − Bonus)
110% Bonus = 10% ($ 120,000 − $60,000 − $5,000)
110% Bonus = 10% ($ 55,000)
110% Bonus = $5,500
Bonus = $5,000

Multiple Bases of Allocation. In many cases, income is allocated to the respective partners by combining several allocation techniques. To illustrate, assume a profit and loss agreement of the ABC Partnership contains the following provisions:

1. Interest of 6% is to be allocated on that portion of a partner's ending capital balance in excess of $100,000.
2. Partner C is to be allocated a bonus equal to 10% of partnership income after the bonus.
3. Salaries of $13,000 and $12,000 are to be allocated to Partners A and C, respectively.
4. The balance of income is to be allocated in the ratio of 2:1:1 to A, B, and C, respectively.

Notice that these provisions govern the allocation of profit and not the actual distribution of assets.

Assuming a partnership income of $33,000 and ending capital balances of $80,000, $150,000, and $110,000 for Partners A, B, and C, respectively, income is allocated to the partners as shown in Illustration 13-2.

Illustration 13-2
Profit Allocation: Multiple Bases

	Partner A	Partner B	Partner C	Total
Interest on excess capital balance.....		$3,000	$ 600	$ 3,600
Bonus..........................			3,000*	3,000
Salaries........................	$13,000		12,000	25,000
Subtotal.......................	$13,000	$3,000	$15,600	$31,600
Remaining profit..................	700	350	350	1,400
Income allocation...............	$13,700	$3,350	$15,950	$33,000

*Bonus = 10% (Net Income − Bonus)
Bonus = 10% ($33,000 − Bonus)
(110%) Bonus = $3,300
Bonus = $3,000

Allocation of Profit Deficiencies and Losses. In the previous examples of profit allocations, the partnership income was large enough to satisfy all of the provisions of the profit and loss agreement. However, if the income is not sufficient or an operating loss exists, one of the two following alternatives may be employed assuming that the agreement governs both the allocation of profits or losses:

1. Completely satisfy all provisions of the profit and loss agreement and use the profit and loss ratios to absorb any deficiency or additional loss caused by such action.
2. Satisfy each of the provisions to whatever extent is possible. For example, the allocation of salaries would be satisfied to whatever extent possible before the allocation of interest is begun.

To illustrate these alternatives, assume the same information used in Illustration 13-2 for the ABC Partnership, except that the partnership income is $22,000. In Illustration 13-3, the income of $22,000 is divided by using the first alternative. When studying Illustration 13-3, it is important to note that the allocation of interest, bonus, and salaries results in an excessive allocation or deficiency of $8,600 (subtotal of $30,600 less the income of $22,000), which must be subtracted from the partners' previously allocated amounts. This deficiency is allocated among the partners according to their profit and loss ratios just like a remaining profit, except that the deficiency is subtracted rather than added.

Illustration 13-3
Profit Allocation: Deficiency Allocated in Profit and Loss Ratio

	Partner A	Partner B	Partner C	Total
Interest on excess capital balance		$ 3,000	$ 600	$ 3,600
Bonus.			2,000*	2,000
Salaries	$13,000		12,000	25,000
Subtotal	$13,000	$ 3,000	$14,600	$30,600
Deficiency	(4,300)	(2,150)	(2,150)	(8,600)
Income allocation	$ 8,700	$ 850	$12,450	$22,000

*Bonus = 10% (Net Income – Bonus)
Bonus = 10% ($22,000 – Bonus)
(110%) Bonus = $2,200
Bonus = $2,000

Normally, the first method also is used when the partnership has an overall loss. For example, given a partnership loss of $2,400, the methodology in Illustration 13-3 would be employed, except that a bonus would not be recognized.

However, it is possible that a separate provision governs those situations in which a net loss exists. The allocation of the assumed loss of $2,400 is shown in Illustration 13-4. In this case, the allocation of the interest and salaries results in allocating $28,600 of income even though there is a loss of $2,400. This results in a deficiency of $31,000 (subtotal of $28,600 plus the loss of $2,400) which must be allocated among the partners according to their profit and loss ratios.

Illustration 13-4
Loss Allocation: Deficiency Allocated in Profit and Loss Ratio

	Partner A	Partner B	Partner C	Total
Interest on excess capital balance		$ 3,000	$ 600	$ 3,600
Bonus (not applicable)				
Salaries	$ 13,000		12,000	25,000
Subtotal	$ 13,000	$ 3,000	$12,600	$ 28,600
Deficiency	(15,500)	(7,750)	(7,750)	(31,000)
Loss allocation	$ (2,500)	$(4,750)	$ (4,850)	$ (2,400)

The second alternative, which is used less frequently, requires that the provisions of the profit and loss agreement be ranked by order of priority. Assuming the components listed in Illustration 13-3 are already in order of priority, a partnership income of $22,000 would be distributed as shown in Illustration 13-5.

Illustration 13-5
Profit Allocation: Deficiency Allocated by Order of Priority

	Partner A	Partner B	Partner C	Total
Interest on excess capital balance.		$3,000	$ 600	$ 3,600
Bonus.			2,000*	2,000
Salaries	$8,528		7,872	16,400
Income allocation	$8,528	$3,000	$10,472	$22,000

*Bonus = 10% (Net Income – Bonus)
Bonus = 10% ($22,000 – Bonus)
(110%) Bonus = $2,200
Bonus = $2,000

The salaries of $16,400 would be allocated to Partners A and C according to the ratio suggested by their normal salaries of $13,000 and $12,000, respectively. Therefore, A would receive 13/25 of the $16,400, or $8,528, while C would receive 12/25, or $7,872.

Special Allocation Procedures. A partnership profit and loss agreement may include special provisions for handling items that represent (1) corrections of prior years' income or (2) current-period, nonoperating gains or losses. Even though a correction of prior years' income may not satisfy the criteria for a prior-period adjustment, as defined by the Financial Accounting Standards Board, it may be more equitable to allocate the item among the partners according to the profit and loss agreement for the relevant prior period rather than the current period. For example, assume that Partners A, B, and C, who previously shared profits equally, currently share profits in the ratio of 2:2:1. Also assume that, in the current year, the partnership incurs a loss of $10,000 due to the settlement of litigation involving a matter arising in a prior period. Rather than allocating the loss according to the current profit ratios, it may be more equitable to base the allocation on the prior ratios.

A similar procedure may be adopted for the current-period recognition of nonoperating gains or losses. Rather than allocating a gain on the sale of a plant asset according to the partners' current profit-sharing ratios, it may be more equitable to use the ratios that existed during the period when unrealized appreciation actually took place.

To illustrate, assume that land with a basis of $40,000 has been held for three years and is sold for $60,000 in the current period. Based on the assumed profit-sharing ratios of prior periods and amounts of annual appreciation, the $20,000 gain would be allocated to Partners A, B, and C as follows:

			Profit Allocation		
Year	Profit Ratio	Appreciation	A	B	C
1	1:1:2	$ 4,000	$1,000	$1,000	$2,000
2	2:1:2	10,000	4,000	2,000	4,000
3	2:2:2	6,000	2,000	2,000	2,000
		$20,000	$7,000	$5,000	$8,000

If the partnership had not established special provisions for handling such items, the gain of $20,000 would have been allocated equally among the partners according to their current profit ratio of 2:2:2.

REFLECTION

- The balance in a partner's drawing account, along with the share of profits or losses, is closed out to the partner's capital account.
- The nature of the business a partnership is engaged in should suggest the various bases that might be appropriate for an allocation of profits or losses.
- The allocation of profits or losses may be based on salaries, bonuses, interest on invested capital, and/or a profit/loss percentage.

5

OBJECTIVE

Describe how a partner's tax basis in a partnership is different from the book basis, and be able to calculate the tax basis.

APPENDIX: TAX-RELATED ASPECTS OF A PARTNERSHIP

As pointed out earlier in this chapter, a partnership is not a separate taxable entity. However, the tax impact of partnership activities must be allocated to the partners and reported by them on their individual tax returns. This process is referred to as the *flowthrough of tax items.* Because the partnership is a conduit for tax purposes, certain elements of revenue and expense maintain their identity on the individual partner's tax return. For example, a partner's share of partnership investment income also will be classified as investment income on the individual return. It is important that certain items maintain their identity on the individual return because they are subject to special limitations and rules. Therefore, accounting for partnership income requires that certain items of revenue and expense be separately reported on the partnership informational tax return.

Tax Basis of a Partner's Interest

Because the partnership is not viewed for tax purposes as a separate distinct entity but, rather, as consisting of separate distinct individuals, the individual partner's interest in the partnership must be measured for tax purposes. This individual interest is referred to as the *partner's tax basis.* The tax basis is primarily used to measure the tax gain or loss resulting from a partner's sale of his/her interest in the partnership. In the most simple of cases, the partner's tax basis is equal to cash contributed plus his/her personal tax basis in other property transferred to the partnership. This personal tax basis would represent the tax basis of the asset before transfer to the partnership.

To illustrate, assume a partner contributes $10,000 cash and equipment with a fair value of $70,000. The original cost of the equipment less depreciation taken for tax purposes resulted in a personal tax basis of $50,000. The tax and GAAP (book) basis of the partner's interest is calculated as follows:

	Tax Basis	GAAP (Book) Basis
Cash contributed	$10,000	$10,000
Equipment	50,000	70,000
Basis for partner's interest	$60,000	$80,000

Notice that the partner's tax basis in assets prior to transfer is not changed subsequent to transfer. In other words, the individual partner receives no increase (step-up) or decrease (step-down) in basis.

The calculation of a partner's tax basis becomes more complex when personal liabilities are transferred to and assumed by the partnership. A partner's tax basis is decreased by the value of the liabilities assumed by other partners. When the other partners assume a portion of the debt, it is as though that amount of debt has been forgiven. Forgiveness of debt represents income to a taxpayer. This income is eventually recognized upon the sale of a partnership interest because the tax basis has been reduced by this amount; therefore, the gain on the sale is increased by this amount. Alternatively, a partner's tax basis is increased by the value of other partners' liabilities assumed by them. The allocation among partners of liabilities transferred to a partnership is based on the partners' respective profit and loss ratios.

To illustrate, assume Partners A and B contribute assets with personal tax bases of $80,000 and $110,000, respectively. Liabilities associated with these assets are $30,000 and $60,000, respectively for A and B. Profits and losses are allocated 40% to Partner A and 60% to Partner B. The tax basis of the partners is determined as follows:

	Partner A	Partner B
Tax basis of assets contributed	$ 80,000	$110,000
Tax basis of other partner's liabilities assumed (40% of $60,000 for A and 60% of $30,000 for B)	24,000	18,000
Tax basis of liabilities assumed by other partners (60% of $30,000 for A and 40% of $60,000 for B)	(18,000)	(24,000)
Tax basis of partner's interest	$ 86,000	$104,000

It is important to note that the sum of the tax bases of partners' interests ($86,000 plus $104,000 in the above example) must always equal the sum of the tax basis of assets contributed by the partners ($80,000 plus $110,000 in the above example).

The initial tax basis of a partner subsequently changes due to the ongoing activities of the partnership. The basis will be increased by the following:

1. Additional contributions of individual assets.
2. The partner's share (based on profit and loss ratios) of increases in partnership liabilities resulting from:
   a. Assuming partners' personal liabilities.
   b. Direct liabilities of the partnership.
3. The partner's share of partnership income measured on a tax basis.
4. The partner's share of separately identified items of income not included in tax income (loss).

A partner's basis will be decreased by the following:

1. Distributions of partnership assets.
2. The portion of the partner's additional personal liabilities assumed by the other partners.
3. The partner's share of partnership losses measured on a tax basis.
4. The partner's share of separately identified items of loss not included in taxable income (loss).

A partner's tax basis may not be decreased below zero. If operating losses would decrease the basis below zero, they are carried forward by the partners and used to offset subsequent increases in basis.

Avoidance of Double Taxation

6

OBJECTIVE

Explain the concept of double taxation, and discuss how it may be minimized.

Major differences exist between partnerships and corporations in the area of taxation. These differences result from the fact that corporations, unlike partnerships, are viewed as separate and distinct taxable entities. The primary result of this difference is that a corporation is taxed when the income is earned (assuming an accrual tax basis), and the individual shareholders are taxed when the income is distributed as dividends. This characteristic is referred to as *double taxation,* and its significance depends on the extent to which dividends are distributed and on the tax rates to which the shareholders are subject. The effect of double taxation may be minimized if employee-shareholders do not receive dividends but are rewarded in the form of salaries, which are deductible expenses. However, the Internal Revenue Service must be satisfied that the amount of such salaries is reasonable. A corporation also may attempt to avoid double taxation by accumulating earnings or by electing to be taxed as a partnership through a Subchapter S selection.

Rather than distributing taxable dividends, the corporation may retain income so that the shareholders are not currently taxed on that income. However, if the shareholders sell their stock in the corporation and if the stock sells at a price that exceeds its tax basis, the gain on the sale would be taxed at the rate applied to capital gains. In effect, the accumulated earnings then become taxed.

It should be noted, however, that the retention of income may not be practical because of the accumulated earnings tax. This tax is a penalty imposed on a corporation that accumulates its earnings to avoid the income tax that would have been incurred by the shareholders if dividends had been distributed. The intent to avoid taxes may be established by demonstrating that the corporation has accumulated earnings in excess of the reasonable needs of the business. Reasonable needs of the business would include such items as plant expansion, asset replacement, debt retirement, stock retirement, customer-supplier loans, and working capital.

The disadvantage associated with double taxation may be eliminated if a corporation elects to be taxed as a *Subchapter S corporation*. Under this election, the corporation is treated as a partnership for tax purposes. The corporate entity itself pays no tax, and the shareholders pay tax on their share of corporate income, whether or not it is distributed to them. This special treatment is based on the view that certain corporations, in substance, are the same as a partnership. This analogy is appropriate for nonpublic corporations, in which major shareholders act in the same capacity as partners in a partnership.

The corporation electing to be taxed as a Subchapter S corporation must meet certain requirements. For example, the corporation must have only one class of stock owned by 75 or fewer stockholders. Certain technical procedures also are employed with respect to the determination and classification of taxable income.

A limited liability company (LLC), if properly structured, will be treated as a partnership for federal tax purposes. Most LLCs are formed with the intent of being classified as a partnership for tax purposes and therefore must avoid having a majority of their attributes or characteristics suggest a corporate form of organization. The tax code will classify an entity as a corporation rather than a partnership if it has more corporate, versus noncorporate, characteristics or attributes. These characteristics are associates, an objective to carry on business and divide the gains, continuity of life, centralization of management, limited liability, and free transferability of interests. Most LLC agreements are structured to avoid the attributes of continuity of life and free transferability of interests in order to receive tax treatment as a partnership rather than a corporation.

Some of the more significant tax-related differences between a partnership and a corporation are summarized in Exhibit 13-1.

Exhibit 13-1
Significant Tax-Related Differences Between a Partnership and a Corporation

	Partnership	Corporation
Level(s) of Taxation	Not a separate taxable entity but, rather, a conduit through which taxable items are passed on to the owners (partners). The individual partners are taxed on their shares of partnership income, whether distributed or not, at the progressive tax rates applicable to individuals.	A separate, distinct taxable entity apart from the shareholder. Therefore, income is taxed once at the corporate level and again at the shareholder level when such income is distributed (i.e., double taxation).
Maintaining the Identity of Various Elements of Taxable Income	Elements making up a partnership's income maintain their special tax status on the returns of the individual partners; e.g., if a partnership has tax-exempt income, it retains its identity in the preparation of the individual partners' tax returns as tax-exempt income.	Elements making up corporate income do not maintain their special status when distributed to shareholders in the form of a dividend; e.g., if corporate income includes some tax-exempt income, that income will be taxed to the shareholders when distributed in the form of a dividend.
Other Tax	The tax advantages associated with certain fringe benefits are much greater for employee-shareholders than they would be if the employees were partners in a partnership. Such fringe benefits may involve profit-sharing plans, pension plans, medical reimbursement and insurance plans, group life insurance, and death benefits.	

REFLECTION

- Their capital contribution and the extent to which individual partners assume their liabilities and those of other partners influence the tax basis of a partner.
- A partnership is a common form of organization that allows for the avoidance of double taxation. Subchapter S corporations, limited liability partnerships, and limited liability corporations are also able to avoid double taxation.

UNDERSTANDING THE ISSUES

1. A major issue faced by people who are starting their own business is the form of organization they should select. What are some major characteristics of a partnership that might influence their decision?
2. Under what circumstances might a salary or bonus be more appropriate than interest on capital balances as a means of allocating profits?
3. When an individual partner contributes assets to a partnership, the partnership's tax basis of the assets is generally not the fair value at the date of transfer. What is the logic underlying this treatment?
4. Assume there are two identical business entities; one is organized as a partnership and the other is organized as a corporation. How would the financial statements of the two entities differ with respect to income taxes and how would such differences affect the owners of the entity?

EXERCISES

Exercise 1 *(LO 1)* **Partnership versus corporate balance sheets and income statements.** In 20X1, a new partnership purchased land on the edge of the town of Otisville. The partners erected a building and opened a furniture and appliance store under the name of Otisville Furniture Fair. The partnership agreement specified that profits or losses should be shared equally after the allocation of partners' salary allowances and interest on average capital balances.

Otisville has grown considerably, and the store is now one of the most prominent stores in a fashionable suburban area. Good management, imaginative merchandising, and the general growth in the economy have made Otisville Furniture Fair the leading and most profitable company of its type in the Otisville trade area.

Now, the partners wish to admit another investor and incorporate the business. The original partners will purchase at par an amount of preferred stock equal to the book value of their interest in the partnership and common stock equal to that portion of fair value that exceeds their book value. The new investor will purchase, at a 10% premium over par value, common and preferred stock equal to one-third of the total number of shares purchased by the original partners. The corporation will then purchase the Otisville Furniture Fair partnership at its fair value from the partners. After the consummation of the partners' plan, the corporation will acquire the partnership assets, assume the liabilities, and employ the partners to manage the corporation.

1. List and explain the differences in terms and valuations that would be expected in comparing the assets that appear on the balance sheet of the proposed corporation and the assets that appear on the partnership balance sheet.
2. List and explain the differences that would be expected in a comparison of an income statement prepared for the proposed corporation and an income statement prepared for the partnership.

(AICPA adapted)

Exercise 2 *(LO 2)* **Partnership agreement.** Grandey, Feldman, and O'Connor (G, F, and O) have decided to form a partnership for the purpose of operating an environmental consulting firm. The partners will have to invest enough capital in order to acquire necessary working capital, diagnostic software, and a variety of other capital assets. Grandey and Feldman both have experience as environmental consultants and will be active in the firm. However, O'Connor has a marketing background and will not be active in the firm on a daily basis. O'Connor will be a major contributor of capital and provide advice as necessary.

The three partners have sketched out a preliminary agreement that contains the following components:

1. Normal income will be allocated among all three partners as follows: all partners will receive a salary, Feldman will receive a bonus equal to 10% of normal income, and all partners will receive interest on capital in excess of $50,000.
2. Nonnormal income will be allocated among all three partners according to their respective capital balances.
3. Upon withdrawal, a partner must first offer her or his partnership interest to the partnership for an amount equal to 120% of book value.
4. Capital balances will be measured according to generally accepted accounting principles.
5. No partner may withdraw more than 80% of his or her respective share of income.

The partners recognize that an independent party should review the preliminary agreement and provide appropriate advice. Identify potential problems and concerns with the agreement.

Exercise 3 *(LO 4)* **Evaluating a change to the partnership agreement.** Kennedy, Walker, and O'Brien are partners in an environmental engineering firm. The firm was originally started by Kennedy and Walker. O'Brien joined the firm in 20X4. The current partnership agreement calls for the allocation of profits as follows:

1. Salaries of $80,000, $80,000, and $60,000 for Kennedy, Walker, and O'Brien, respectively.
2. Interest on average capital of 5%. Measures of average capital exclude the first $30,000 of individual partner's annual withdrawals.
3. Annual allowance for charitable contributions of $4,000 per partner.
4. A bonus of 12% of net income after the bonus allocated equally between Kennedy and Walker.
5. All remaining profits are allocated 35%, 35%, and 30% to Kennedy, Walker, and O'Brien, respectively.

Net income for the year 20X6 was $420,000 after expensing charitable contributions of $63,000. The contributions made on behalf of Kennedy, Walker, and O'Brien were $30,000, $30,000, and $3,000, respectively. January 1, 20X6, capital balances and 20X6 withdrawals are as follows:

	Kennedy	Walker	O'Brien
January 1, 20X6, capital balances	$100,000	$120,000	$70,000
March 31 withdrawal	60,000	60,000	
July 1 withdrawal	20,000	20,000	30,000
November 30 withdrawal			30,000

During 20X6, O'Brien has become increasingly bothered by the profit-sharing agreement and feels that the partners have been especially harmed by the provisions related to interest on capital and charitable contributions. O'Brien is suggesting that the profit-sharing agreement be amended as follows: (a) net income excludes charitable contributions, (b) charitable contributions made by the partnership on behalf of partners are considered withdrawals, and (c) no amount of profit is allocated for a contribution allowance. All other previous profit allocation provisions are to remain the same. Furthermore, O'Brien is requesting that the three partners be allocated a one-time bonus of $30,000 in 20X7 representing a retroactive application of the proposal to the 20X6 net income.

O'Brien has been instrumental in securing a significant amount of new business and has indicated that he is considering leaving the partnership if things do not change. The possible loss of business is of concern to the senior partners, and they need to respond to O'Brien's concerns.

Kennedy and Walker are inclined to accept O'Brien's offer, except they think that the bonus in 20X7 is overstated.

Prepare a schedule that would provide Kennedy and Walker with a more reasonable measure of the effect of retroactively applying O'Brien's proposal.

Exercise 4 *(LO 4)* **Approaches to the allocation of profits and losses.** Medina, Harris, and Anderson are partners in Entertainment Systems. The partnership earned a modest profit of $30,000 in 20X3. The partnership agreement includes the following regarding the allocation of profits or losses:

1. Interest of 8% is to be paid on the portion of a partner's ending capital balance in excess of $75,000.
2. Medina and Harris receive salaries of $20,000 and $30,000, respectively. Both individuals are actively involved with day-to-day operations.
3. The balance of income is to be distributed in the ratio of 2:1:1 to Medina, Harris, and Anderson, respectively.

Assume ending capital balances of $60,000, $80,000, and $100,000 for partners Medina, Harris, and Anderson, respectively.

1. Allocate the profit among the partners, assuming the following:
   a. The profit and loss ratios are used to absorb any deficiency or additional loss.
   b. Each of the provisions of the profit and loss agreement is satisfied to whatever extent possible. The priority order is interest, salaries, and then remaining amounts per the profit and loss ratios.
2. Discuss which method would be best suited for this partnership.

Exercise 5 *(LO 4)* **Approaches to the allocation of profits and losses.** Collins, Baker, and Lebo are partners in a business that distributes various electronic components used to control machinery in the printing industry. The partners have a lucrative business and have allocated profits according to the following agreement:

1. Salaries of $50,000 to each of the partners.
2. A bonus to Baker of 5% of sales to International Printers, Inc., in excess of $1,000,000.
3. A bonus to Collins of 10% of net income after this bonus.
4. Interest of 10% on each partner's average annual invested capital in excess of $100,000.
5. Remaining profits to be allocated in the ratio of 5:3:2 for Collins, Baker, and Lebo, respectively.

In a typical year, the above agreement is applied under the following conditions: net income of $880,000, sales to International Printers, Inc., of $1,500,000, and average annual invested capital of $50,000, $120,000, and $250,000 for Collins, Baker, and Lebo, respectively.

Gordon, who is seeking to be admitted to the partnership, has approached the partners. Gordon has an exclusive licensing agreement with a manufacturer of control devices that can significantly reduce the amount of electricity used by machinery. Gordon is confident that these products will be extremely successful, but they lack an established customer base. Therefore, Gordon is most interested in pursuing discussions with the existing partnership. Gordon has proposed contributing $50,000 cash and the exclusive licensing agreement to the partnership in exchange for an interest in capital and profits. Furthermore, Gordon proposes that a new profit agreement be established with the following terms:

1. Salaries of $50,000 to each of the partners.
2. A bonus to Baker of 5% of sales to International Printers, Inc., in excess of $1,000,000 traceable to products not covered by the exclusive licensing agreement.
3. A bonus to Gordon of 15% of sales in excess of $2,000,000 traceable to those products covered by the exclusive licensing agreement. Gordon estimates that total sales associated with these products will be approximately $4,200,000.

4. Interest of 10% on each partner's average annual invested capital in excess of $100,000.
5. Remaining profits to be allocated in the ratio of 3:3:2:2 for Collins, Baker, Lebo, and Gordon, respectively.

Collins is your personal tax client and comes to you for advice. Baker and Lebo are very excited about the Gordon proposal. However, Collins feels that Gordon may be unrealistic regarding the success of this new product line. Collins is concerned about giving Gordon a voice in the management of the partnership; but more importantly, she feels that her interest in profits may be less under the Gordon proposal. You understand your client's concern and try to be positive by saying that the Gordon proposal may be worth it. Collins responds by saying, "Maybe it is worth it if I can make another $60,000 before taxes." Prepare a quantitative analysis that your client Collins may use to better assess the implications associated with the Gordon proposal.

Exercise 6 *(LO 3)* **Assessing the impact of withdrawals on the allocation of profits.** Cramer, Larson, and Hughes have allocated profits of the partnership as follows:

1. Salaries of $80,000, $60,000, and $60,000 to Cramer, Larson, and Hughes, respectively.
2. All remaining profit is allocated equally among the partners.

In the past, the partners had not formalized policies regarding withdrawals of capital, and operating cash levels were adequate. Due to a changing business environment, the partnership has begun to experience liquidity problems and has had to increase its outside borrowings. The partners acknowledge that all partners bear the burden of increased interest expense and debt service. However, the partners do not equitably bear the impact of partner withdrawals.

As of January 1, 20X8, the partners have agreed to reallocate 20X6 and 20X7 profits among the partners. The reallocation of profits will follow the existing profit-sharing agreement with the addition of a provision that interest will be allocated to the partners based on 10% of the weighted-average capital balance including the withdrawals but excluding current-year profits. Net income for 20X6 and 20X7 was $500,000 and $410,000, respectively.

Capital balances and withdrawals are as follows:

	Cramer	Larson	Hughes
Capital balance as of December 31, 20X5	$180,000	$250,000	$ 60,000
March 31, 20X6, withdrawal	150,000	170,000	
September 30, 20X6, withdrawal	20,000	50,000	50,000
January 31, 20X7, withdrawal	170,000	190,000	150,000

Prepare the January 1, 20X8, entry to reallocate profits among the partners.

Exercise 7 *(LO 3, 4)* **Profit allocation based on several factors; weighted-average interest.** Gabriel and Hall are partners in a manufacturing business located in Portland, Oregon. Their profit and loss agreement contains the following provisions:

1. Salaries of $35,000 and $40,000 for Gabriel and Hall, respectively.
2. A bonus to Gabriel equal to 10% of net income after the bonus.
3. Interest on weighted-average capital at the rate of 8%. Annual drawings in excess of $20,000 are considered to be a reduction of capital for purposes of this calculation.
4. Profit and loss percentages of 40% and 60% for Gabriel and Hall, respectively.

Capital and drawing activity of the partners for the year 20X5 are as follows:

	Gabriel Capital	Gabriel Drawing	Hall Capital	Hall Drawing
Beginning balance	$120,000	$ 0	$ 60,000	$ 0
April 1	20,000			
June 1		15,000		20,000
September 1	30,000			
November 1		15,000	40,000	
Ending balance	$170,000	$30,000	$100,000	$20,000

Assuming net income for 20X5 of $132,000, determine how much profit should be allocated to each partner.

Exercise 8 *(LO 3, 4)* **Interest calculation; determination of capital account balances.** Xavier, Yates, and Zale are partners in a dry-cleaning business. Their partnership agreement provides that the partners shall receive interest on their respective average yearly capital balances at the rate of 8%. Any residual profits or losses shall be divided equally among the partners. The following information is available for the second year of operations:

a. Partners' capital balances as of January 1, 20X2:

Xavier	$24,000
Yates	17,500
Zale	13,000

b. Additional investments were made during the year as follows:

Xavier	$4,500 on April 1, 20X2
Zale	$2,000 on July 1, 20X2
	$15,000 on September 1, 20X2

c. The drawing accounts of the partners have the following debit balances at the end of 20X2:

Xavier	$1,000
Yates	1,000
Zale	500

d. Partnership income for the year is $21,100.

1. Discuss the advantages and disadvantages of using the weighted-average capital balance as the base for determining interest on capital contributed.
2. Determine the interest on weighted-average capital balances that partners Xavier, Yates, and Zale should receive for the year 20X2. Assume that the partners' withdrawals are not to influence the capital balances for purposes of computing interest.
3. Determine the capital account balances for Xavier, Yates, and Zale after all closing entries have been journalized and posted at the end of 20X2. Supporting schedules should be in good form.

Exercise 9 *(LO 4)* **Evaluating alternative profit-sharing arrangements.** Patton is considering joining Microtech Enterprises as a partner. The company provides data imaging for a variety of end users. Patton will have to contribute $100,000 of capital upon admission as a partner and will need to decide on a profit-sharing arrangement. Three alternatives are being proposed as follows:

Alternative A—Patton will be allocated a salary of $120,000, 10% of average capital after considering withdrawals, and 10% of net income. At the end of each calendar quarter, $30,000 will be distributed to Patton. No additional profits will be allocated to Patton.

Alternative B—Patton will be allocated a salary of $96,000, 10% of average capital after considering withdrawals in excess of $60,000, and a bonus of 10% of net income. At the end of the second, third, and fourth calendar quarters, Patton will receive a distribution of $24,000. At the end of the first quarter of the following year, Patton will receive a distribution of $60,000. No additional profits will be allocated to Patton.

Alternative C—Patton will be allocated a salary of $80,000 and 20% of net income. Patton will receive a distribution of $20,000 at the end of calendar quarters 1 through 3 and $80,000 at the end of quarter 4.

Patton has retained you to assist in evaluating the above alternatives and has asked you to assume that cash distributions could be reinvested at 6%. Furthermore, Patton believes that the probability of various levels of partnership income are as follows: a 30% probability of $500,000 of income, a 50% probability of $560,000 of income, and a 20% probability of $600,000 of income.

1. Prepare a schedule that evaluates the alternatives in terms of profitability and the present value of cash flows for the first year of the partnership.
2. Discuss which alternative you consider to be the most attractive.

APPENDIX EXERCISES

Exercise 13A-1 *(LO 5)* **Calculation of book and tax basis.** Thomas is considering joining Baker and Nap in a partnership. Baker and Nap will each contribute cash of $39,000 to the new partnership. The partners will share profits and losses equally, and all partners have individual tax rates of 30%. Thomas is considering contributing to the partnership a parcel of land that has a fair value of $99,000 and an individual tax basis of $39,000. If the parcel is contributed to the partnership, the partnership would sell the parcel and distribute $6,000 to each partner in order to pay the resulting individual taxes on the sale. Thomas wants to know if he or she would be better off to personally sell the parcel and contribute the after-tax proceeds to the partnership. How would you advise Thomas?

Exercise 13A-2 *(LO 5)* **Calculation of book and tax basis; change in interest over time.** Berkshire Investments is a partnership consisting of three partners: Pearson, Ellis, and Parker. Pearson and Ellis each have a 40% interest in capital prior to withdrawals and the allocation of profits. Ellis and Parker are considering selling their interest in the partnership and want to estimate the personal tax impact of this sale. The activity of the partnership is summarized as follows:

	Fair Value/GAAP Basis	Tax Basis
Contributions of cash:		
Pearson	$ 80,000	$80,000
Ellis	25,000	25,000
Contributions of noncash assets:		
Ellis	100,000	70,000
Parker	60,000	68,000
Liabilities transferred to the partnership:		
Ellis	45,000	45,000
Parker	20,000	20,000
Withdrawals of cash:		
Pearson	30,000	30,000
Ellis	20,000	20,000
Parker	15,000	15,000
Allocation of profits:		
Pearson	30,000	28,000
Ellis	30,000	28,000
Parker	30,000	28,000

1. Calculate the book and tax basis of Ellis's and Parker's interest in the partnership.
2. Discuss why a partner's percentage interest in capital may change over time.

PROBLEMS

Problem 13-1 *(LO 1)* **Characteristics of a partnership and proper organization form.** A client is seeking your advice on how to organize a new business. The client is proposing to acquire several single-story residences and convert them into group homes for the elderly. Each home would house eight elderly individuals, and the homes would be staffed 24 hours a day. Residents would receive housing, food, and daily-planned activities for a monthly fee. Group homes are licensed by the state and are closely monitored. Such homes do not provide any direct health care to the residents. The client plans to have an active role in the organization and management of the homes and is seeking another individual or two to provide necessary capital as passive investors. It is anticipated that the homes will operate at a loss for the first 12 to 18 months. The client hopes to open two group homes for each of the next four years and then sell his interest in the business. Your client is interested in organizing the company as a partnership and wants to know how that might affect him and other potential partners.

Identify and discuss some of the characteristics of a partnership of which your client should be aware. ◄◄◄◄◄ **Required**

Problem 13-2 *(LO 3, 4)* **Allocation of profits and determination of withdrawals.** Sandburg and Williams are the owners of a partnership that manufactures commercial lighting fixtures. Profits are allocated among the partners as follows:

	Sandburg	Williams
Salaries	$100,000	$125,000
Bonus as a percentage of net income after the bonus	10%	0%
Interest on weighted-average capital including withdrawals and excluding current-year profits	5%	5%

Sandburg was divorced as of the beginning of 20X5 and as part of the divorce stipulation agreed to the following:

1. The spouse is to receive annual distributions traceable to years 20X5 and 20X6. The annual distribution is to be the greater of $100,000 or 25% of base earnings.
2. Base earnings are defined as net income of the partnership less: (a) salaries traceable to Sandburg and Williams of $75,000 and $125,000, respectively and (b) bonus to Sandburg as stated subject to the limitation that it not exceed $50,000.
3. Sandburg's spouse would receive a distribution from the partnership on August 31 of each current year and on February 28 of each subsequent year. The August 31 target distribution is $50,000. If the August distribution is less than $50,000, Sandburg's spouse will receive one-half year's interest on the deficiency at the rate of 10% per year. The following distribution on February 28 must be of an amount such that the two distributions equal the required distribution traceable to the calendar year just ended plus any interest associated with the August distribution.
4. All distributions to Sandburg's spouse are to be considered as a withdrawal of capital by Sandburg.
5. Aside from distributions to Sandburg's spouse, Sandburg's annual withdrawals cannot exceed $125,000.
6. Upon sale or dissolution of the partnership prior to February 28, 20X6, Sandburg's spouse would receive 50% of the net realizable value of Sandburg's partnership capital.
7. On February 28, 20X7, Sandburg's spouse will receive an additional final distribution equal to 50% of Sandburg's capital balance as of December 31, 20X6.

Capital balances at the beginning of 20X5 were $180,000 and $125,000, respectively, for Sandburg and Williams. Activity related to the partnership during 20X5 and 20X6 is as follows:

	20X5	20X6
Partnership net income	$750,000	$700,000
Distribution to Sandburg's spouse on August 31	40,000	50,000
Distributions to Sandburg:		
June 30	60,000	125,000
September 30	65,000	0
Distributions to Williams:		
June 30	30,000	300,000
September 30	90,000	20,000

Required ▶▶▶▶▶ Prepare a schedule to determine the total amount of the distributions due Sandburg's spouse as of February 28, 20X7.

Problem 13-3 *(LO 4)* **Decision to admit a new partner, profit allocation.** Thomas and Purnell are general partners in a partnership along with four limited partners. Ten percent of partnership profit is allocated to each of the limited partners, and the balance of the profits is allocated to Thomas and Purnell as follows:

1. Salaries of $40,000 and $60,000 to Thomas and Purnell, respectively.
2. A bonus to Thomas of 10% of sales in excess of $1,200,000.
3. A bonus to Purnell of 5% of net income after the bonus.
4. Remaining profits to be allocated 60% and 40%, respectively, to Thomas and Purnell.

The general partners have been approached by Wiggins, who has significant experience in the area of foreign sales and is seeking admission to the partnership. Wiggins is confident that she can generate significant increases in sales and that any capital needed to finance the expansion will be raised and guaranteed by her. Furthermore, Wiggins is proposing that the existing profit agreement be modified as follows:

1. Wiggins will be allocated a salary of $40,000.
2. A bonus to Wiggins of 15% of all international sales in excess of $500,000.
3. Thomas's bonus will be limited to domestic sales only.
4. Remaining profits to be allocated 40%, 40%, and 20% to Thomas, Purnell, and Wiggins, respectively.

The limited partners are in favor of admitting Wiggins, noting that their opportunities for increased profits would be improved. However, Thomas and Purnell are concerned that unless sales and profits grow significantly, they will receive a smaller allocation of profits than they did before Wiggins. Without Wiggins, the partnership is projecting domestic sales and profits of $1,450,000 and $280,000, respectively, for the next year. Thomas and Purnell feel that if their interest in profits increases by $16,000 and $24,000, respectively, they will be inclined to admit Wiggins as a partner.

Required ▶▶▶▶▶ Assume that Wiggins is able to generate $700,000 of additional foreign sales which include a 40% gross profit margin and that the general and administrative expenses associated with this increase are 15% of such sales. Prepare an analysis for Thomas and Purnell that summarizes their profit allocation with and without Wiggins.

Problem 13-4 *(LO 4)* **Expert witness, economic loss measurement.** A law firm that specializes in personal injury work has engaged you to assist in some litigation. The firm represents a Mr. Lawson, who was injured in an automobile accident and is alleging that he was totally disabled as a result of the accident. Lawson is seeking damages that in part reflect the loss of income from his interest in a partnership known as L & S Contractors (L & S). L & S is in the business of contracting to do residential remodeling jobs and has three partners: Lawson, Schmidt, and Jacobsen.

Sales and related income of the partnership have grown over the years although the residential construction industry is cyclical in nature. The law firm has provided you with copies of various partnership documents that may be relevant to this matter. A review of the partnership agreement reveals the following regarding the allocation of annual profits:

1. Salaries for Lawson, Schmidt, and Jacobsen of $60,000, $60,000, and $40,000, respectively.
2. Bonuses of 10% and 5% of net income after the bonuses for Lawson and Schmidt, respectively.
3. Profit and loss percentages of 30%, 30%, and 40% for Lawson, Schmidt, and Jacobsen, respectively.

Other relevant components of the partnership agreement are as follows:

1. Partners receive a draw on July 1 and December 1 of each year. Each partner's draw is equal to one-third of 40% of the net income from the preceding year. Partners will receive draws for all years in which they were active in the business.
2. Unless modified by a majority of the partners, no more than 80% of annual income may be distributed to the partners.
3. Upon total disability, death, or retirement of a partner (referred to as a triggering event), the partnership will acquire such partner's capital interest in the partnership. The amount paid will be equal to three times such partner's average share of annual partnership income for the two years prior to the year of the triggering event. The acquisition price will be paid out in four equal semiannual payments beginning six months after the triggering event.

The automobile accident involving Mr. Lawson occurred on December 31, 20X3. At his deposition, Mr. Lawson indicated the following:

1. He anticipated retiring at the end of 20X8.
2. Net income of the partnership for years 20X1, 20X2, and 20X3 was $161,000, $207,000, and $210,000, respectively.
3. Based on past and projected factors, he anticipated net income for years 20X4 through 20X8 to be $230,000 per year.

◄◄◄◄◄ Required

Prepare a tentative measure of the economic loss suffered by Mr. Lawson as a result of the alleged total disability. Your measure of loss should be expressed as of the date of the accident and include appropriate present-value considerations.

Problem 13-5 *(LO 3, 4)* **Investment decision, capital retention decision.** Rodriquez is one of your tax clients and has come to you seeking your input about a potential investment opportunity. Your client has the opportunity to acquire a 30% interest in the capital of a partnership. However, this would require him to give up his current job. The partnership will consist of Rodriquez, Monroe, and Zito, and the partners will allocate profits and losses as follows:

1. Salaries to Rodriquez and Monroe of $40,000 and $50,000, respectively.
2. Interest at the rate of 9% on weighted-average net capital in excess of $20,000. All partners are required to maintain $20,000 in their net capital accounts throughout the year. Net capital is defined in the partnership agreement as capital balances less drawing account balances. It is estimated that in all cases, Monroe and Zito will maintain weighted-average net capital balances of $40,000 and $150,000, respectively. Unless otherwise stated, it is assumed that Rodriquez will maintain the minimum balance of net capital.
3. Bonus to Monroe of 5% of sales in excess of $500,000. It is estimated that sales for the year will be $650,000.
4. Profit and loss percentages of 40%, 40%, and 20% for partners Rodriquez, Monroe, and Zito, respectively.

Rodriquez is very interested in the opportunities that the partnership presents. However, he is concerned that his allocation of profits may not justify changing jobs.

◄◄◄◄◄ Required

1. Determine how much partnership profit would have to be realized in order for Rodriquez's allocated portion to equal his current job salary of $60,000.
2. Determine whether Rodriquez is best advised to withdraw available capital in excess of the minimum balance or retain capital in the partnership.

3. Assume that annual sales were less than $500,000 and that Rodriquez maintained the minimum net capital balance during the year. The other partners are assumed to maintain capital balances as stated. Furthermore, assume that all allocated profits are withdrawn. What is the minimum amount of partnership income that would be necessary in order for Rodriquez not to have to make an additional investment of capital?

Problem 13-6 *(LO 3, 4)* **Correction of previously misstated capital and drawing accounts.** Lewis, Clark, and Jefferson are partners in a company that manufactures store fixtures. The partnership agreement calls for the following provisions regarding the allocation of profits:

1. Lewis and Clark will be allocated a quarterly salary of $20,000 each. Jefferson will be allocated a quarterly salary of $15,000.
2. Clark and Jefferson, both being responsible for sales, will share a bonus of 20% of net income after the bonus. Of the 20%, 40% is allocated to Clark, and the balance is allocated to Jefferson. Bonus amounts are to be determined semiannually.
3. Interest of 8% per year will be allocated to each partner's weighted-average annual capital balance.
4. Any remaining profits will be allocated to Lewis, Clark, and Jefferson in the amounts of 35%, 35%, and 30%, respectively.
5. In the case that net income is not adequate to satisfy the above requirements, any deficiency will be allocated to the partners in the percentages set forth in item (4) above.

The partnership agreement also contains the following provisions regarding capital and drawing balances:

1. For purposes of calculating interest on capital balances, drawing account balances and allocations of current-year profits are to be ignored. However, the beginning-of-a-year capital balance should include the effect of closing drawings and profits traceable to a given partner.
2. All partners are required to maintain a minimum capital balance of $50,000 at all times.
3. At the end of each quarter, the partners will receive a draw equal to 80% of their allocated quarterly salary.
4. Any draws beyond those provided by item (3) above must be approved by at least two of the partners and will be considered a direct reduction of capital for purposes of item (1) above.
5. Upon withdrawal of a partner, the existing partner will first offer their partnership interest to the partnership in exchange for consideration equal to 125% of their net capital and drawing account balances as of the end of the quarter prior to withdrawal.

The partnership began operations July 1, 20X5, with each partner contributing $50,000 of capital. The partnership has reported annual net income of $120,000, $300,000, and $420,000 for years 20X5 through 20X7, respectively. During this entire time, Jefferson assumed responsibility for overseeing the partnership's accounting function. Early in 20X7, Jefferson began to have some personal financial problems, and on March 31, 20X7, the partners unanimously approved an immediate draw by Jefferson of an additional $50,000. During the latter half of 20X7, Jefferson appeared to be extremely stressed out and began to miss a lot of work. Lewis and Clark became concerned; their concern was heightened in January of 20X8 when Jefferson indicated that he would be withdrawing immediately from the partnership. Furthermore, Jefferson became irate when the partners indicated that it would take at least a month to secure the $200,000 necessary to buy Jefferson out.

Due to the strange way in which Jefferson was acting, Lewis and Clark began to think that Jefferson might be involved in some type of impropriety. You have been retained to determine if the provisions of the partnership agreement relating to accounting and balances have been properly complied with. You have been provided with the post-closing capital account balances as of the end of 20X7 of $139,000, $176,000, and $185,000 for Lewis, Clark, and Jefferson, respectively, as determined by Jefferson. Upon further investigation, it appears that net income in 20X7 has been overstated by $90,000. The overstatement was achieved by a $65,000 overstatement of credit sales and a $25,000 overstatement in ending inventory.

Prepare a schedule to determine the proper equity balances of the partners as of December 31, 20X7, and also prepare the entry to correct the financial statements assuming 20X7 drawing account balances have been closed. ◀◀◀◀◀ **Required**

Problem 13-7 *(LO 3, 4)* **Error effect on capital balances.** Carson, Dowman, and Evans own an office automation and consulting business organized as a partnership. Evans is considering retirement from the partnership. In order to more fairly measure Evans' interest in capital, an audit of the company's first two years of operations was performed in early 20X9. The original partnership agreement called for Carson to receive a 10% bonus on income after the bonus, with the remaining profits or losses to be divided as follows: Carson, 30%; Dowman, 30%; and Evans, 40%. Reported income for 20X7 was $44,000. In the second year of operations, the agreement was modified to reflect Evans' decision to become less involved in the business. The new agreement called for Carson still to receive a 10% bonus on income after the bonus, but it altered the allocation of remaining amounts as follows: Carson, 35%; Dowman, 35%; and Evans, 30%. Reported income for 20X8 was $42,000. The partners had always agreed that any adjustment to reported amounts would be allocated based on the profit and loss agreement in effect during the period to which the adjustment relates. The audit indicated that the following items were not properly accounted for:

1. 20X7:
   a. Failed to amortize (in 20X8 as well) the business name contributed by Carson. The fair value of the intangible was $50,000 and should have been amortized over a 10-year life using straight-line amortization.
   b. Failed to defer prepaid 20X8 insurance premiums of $3,000.
   c. A capital withdrawal of $5,000 made by Carson on July 1, 20X7, was classified incorrectly as a note receivable.
   d. Failed to accrue $2,000 of employee wages on December 31, 20X7.
   e. Failed to record consulting fees of $8,400 earned in 20X7 but billed in 20X8.
2. 20X8:
   a. Purchases of inventory included a computer invoiced on December 31, 20X8, for $4,000 but not yet received. Terms were f.o.b. destination. The item was not included in the year-end physical inventory.
   b. Failed to accrue $8,600 of rent expense on December 31, 20X8.
   c. Failed to reverse $3,000 of interest income properly accrued at the end of 20X7, resulting in income recognition in both years.

Assume the following unadjusted December 31, 20X8, capital account balances: Carson, $25,000; Dowman, $30,000; and Evans, $28,000. Prepare a schedule to reflect the adjusted capital balances as of December 31, 20X8. Supporting calculations should be in good form. ◀◀◀◀◀ **Required**

Problem 13-8 *(LO 3, 4)* **Determination of capital balances over time.** At the beginning of 20X5, Harris, Piano, and Tyler each contributed $80,000 of assets to begin a partnership. The partnership agreement provided for the following with respect to the allocation of profits and losses:

1. Salaries to Harris, Piano, and Tyler of $76,000, $76,000, and $48,000, respectively. Salaries are to be distributed to the individual partners in equal amounts at the end of each calendar quarter.
2. A bonus to Tyler of 5% of annual net sales.
3. Interest on average capital of 6%. During a given year, drawings, to the extent they exceed salaries, are to be offset against capital balances for purposes of this calculation. Beginning-of-the-year capital balances should reflect all appropriate closing entries.
4. Profit and loss percentages of 35%, 35%, and 30% for Harris, Piano, and Tyler, respectively.
5. Each of the provisions of the profit and loss agreement is satisfied to whatever extent possible. The priority order is salaries, bonus, interest, and then remaining amounts per the profit and loss percentages.

In addition to the distribution of salaries, withdrawals are as follows:

	Harris	Piano	Tyler
January 31, 20X6, withdrawal	$50,000		$ 30,000
February 28, 20X6, withdrawal	20,000	$48,000	
June 30, 20X7, withdrawal.	10,000	20,000	100,000

Early in April of 20X8, Piano was permanently disabled. The partnership agreement addresses the potential of a permanent disability of a partner and provides the following:

1. The affected partner will receive an immediate distribution equal to 20% of their annual salary.
2. The affected partner's capital balance will be credited for their profit and loss percentage of current partnership net income from the beginning of the current year to the end of the month preceding the determination of disability. This is in lieu of the normal agreement regarding the allocation of profits.
3. 125% of the affected partner's capital balance as of the end of the month preceding the determination is disability will be distributed to the partner in equal payments over each of the next six quarters including interest on the unpaid balance at the rate of 6%.

Income statement data for the partnership are as follows:

	20X5	20X6	20X7	Jan. 1–Mar. 31, 20X8
Sales	$800,000	$950,000	$1,400,000	$320,000
Sales returns and allowances	40,000	70,000	80,000	10,000
Net income	220,000	260,000	270,000	80,000

Required ▶ ▶ ▶ ▶ ▶

1. Prepare a schedule to Piano's capital balance as of March 31, 20X8.
2. Prepare a schedule that shows the payments to be received by Piano subsequent to the determination of their disability.

APPENDIX PROBLEMS

template cd

Problem 13A-1 *(LO 4, 5)* **Profit allocation; book and tax basis calculation.** Nichols, James, and Wilson are environmental consultants who agree to consolidate their individual practices into a partnership as of January 1, 20X4. Each partner is contributing the following assets and related liabilities:

	Nichols	James	Wilson
Fair value of:			
Cash	$ 20,000	$ 5,000	$ 20,000
Accounts receivable.	24,000	15,000	35,000
Supplies.	5,000	2,000	3,000
Equipment	28,000	24,200	34,000
Equipment notes payable	(18,000)	(10,000)	(24,000)
	$ 59,000	$ 36,200	$ 68,000
Tax basis of equipment	$ 20,000	$ 24,000	$ 22,000

The partnership agreement provides for the allocation of profits as follows:

1. All partners will receive 6% interest on their weighted-average capital balances as defined. Capital balances will be reduced by amounts withdrawn in excess of partners' salaries. The resulting weighted average will then be reduced by salaries. Partners with deficit balances will have their profits reduced by the interest on such amounts.

2. Salaries for Nichols, James, and Wilson are $40,000, $32,000, and $50,000, respectively. All salaries are withdrawn during the year.
3. Each partner will receive a bonus equal to 20% of individual gross billings in excess of $100,000.
4. James will receive an extra 10% bonus of net income reduced by the value of items (1) to (3) above.
5. Remaining profits will be allocated equally among partners.

During the year 20X4, the partnership recognized the following net income components:

Gross billings:	
Nichols	$120,000
James	80,000
Wilson	180,000
Depreciation expenses:	
Book amount	6,120
Tax return amount	20,144
Other operating expenses	203,880

During the year, the partners had the following drawings in excess of their salaries:

	Nichols	James	Wilson
March 1	$10,000		
June 1		$ 4,000	
September 1		12,000	$20,000

Required

1. Determine how the 20X4 accounting income of $170,000 would be allocated among the partners.
2. Determine the net capital balances for each partner as of December 31, 20X4.
3. Perform the same requirements as for items (1) and (2), but assume the calculations are being made for tax purposes.

Problem 13A-2 *(LO 5)* **Reconciliation of GAAP-to-tax-basis income, tax basis calculation.** Fandek and Franklin formed a partnership on January 1, 20X7, and contributed assets and liabilities to the partnership as follows:

	Fandek		Franklin	
	Fair Value	Tax Basis	Fair Value	Tax Basis
Net assets contributed:				
Cash	$60,000	$60,000	$ 10,000	$ 10,000
Securities			15,000	10,000
Goodwill	12,000	0		
Equipment			65,000	40,000
Equipment loan			(42,000)	(42,000)

Fandek and Franklin will have initial interests in capital of 60% and 40%, respectively, and will equally share profits and losses. The partners also agreed that they would receive monthly withdrawals in the amounts of $2,000 and $3,000, respectively. During the year, the company recognized sales of $240,000 and a corresponding cost of sales equal to $144,000 (60% of sales). Of the total sales, $60,000 is uncollected at year-end. These sales are being recognized for tax purposes by the installment method. For accounting purposes only, the goodwill is being amortized over a 3-year period on a straight-line basis. Equipment also is being amortized on a straight-line basis, assuming a 10-year useful life and a $5,000 residual value. For tax purposes, the equipment is depreciated by the modified accelerated cost recovery system (MACRS) and has a 20X7 depreciation rate of 25%. Of the original securities contributed, securities with a book value and tax basis of $6,000 and $2,000, respectively, were sold for $8,000. The remaining securities have a fair value of $5,000.

Required ▶ ▶ ▶ ▶ ▶

1. Assuming the partnership reports 20X7 net income of $54,000 in conformity with GAAP, prepare a schedule to reconcile this amount to the tax-basis measure of net income.
2. Calculate the tax basis for each of the partners at the end of 20X7.

Partnerships: Ownership Changes and Liquidations

CHAPTER

14

Learning Objectives

When you have completed this chapter, you should be able to

1. **Define partnership dissolution, and explain what accounting issues should be addressed upon dissolution.**
2. **Account for the partners' capital balances under the bonus method.**
3. **Account for the partners' capital balances under the goodwill method.**
4. **Describe the conceptual differences between the bonus and goodwill methods.**
5. **Account for the admission of a new partner through direct contribution to an existing partner.**
6. **Explain the impact of a partner's withdrawal from the partnership.**
7. **Describe the order in which assets must be distributed upon liquidation of a partnership, and explain the right-of-offset concept.**
8. **Explain the doctrine of marshaling of assets.**
9. **Calculate the assets to be distributed to a given partner in a lump-sum or installment liquidation.**
10. **Prepare an installment liquidation statement, a schedule of safe payments, and a predistribution plan.**

In theory, a partnership may be viewed as a conduit or entity through which individual partners carry on a common business purpose. It is natural that the circumstances surrounding the individual partners' lives may change and affect their involvement in the partnership. Individual partners may increase or decrease their interest in the partnership or withdraw entirely from the partnership. In turn, new partners may become involved in the partnership. Such ownership changes are common in a partnership just as they are in other forms of organizations, such as a corporation. However, unlike a corporation, which is recognized as a separate and distinct entity having an infinite life, changes in the ownership structure of a partnership result in the dissolution of the previous partnership.

The Uniform Partnership Act (UPA) defines *dissolution* as "the change in the relation of the partners caused by any partner ceasing to be associated in the carrying on as distinguished from the winding up of the business." Sections 31 and 32 of the UPA identify the various causes of dissolution and suggest that the admission or withdrawal of a partner results in dissolution. Although dissolution ends the association of partners for their original purpose, it does not result necessarily in the termination of the partnership's basic business function. The remaining partners may continue to operate the business, or they may decide to terminate, or *liquidate*, the business.

The previous chapter stressed the importance of a well-conceived partnership agreement. Changes in the ownership structure of a partnership are one of the most important areas that should be addressed. Often, the initial concerns of a new partnership are such that the partners overlook the certain reality that, someday, there will be a change in the ownership. Accountants can be of significant help to their clients in advising them in the structuring of buy/sell agreements for the partnership. Proper planning for such changes will help to ensure smooth and equitable transitions.

In certain instances, a partnership may elect not to continue but, rather, liquidate and distribute its net assets to the partners. For example, a partnership may be organized to develop and manage a real estate investment for a designated period of time. At the end of the designated period of time, the partnership will be liquidated. It is important to note that, unlike a dissolution where the partnership purpose continues, a liquidation results in the termination or winding up of the business purpose.

1

OBJECTIVE

Define partnership dissolution, and explain what accounting issues should be addressed upon dissolution.

OWNERSHIP CHANGES

Changes in the ownership structure of a corporation are everyday occurrences, as evidenced by the activity of security exchanges. These changes typically involve transactions between existing and prospective shareholders and, therefore, create no special accounting problems for the corporate entity other than updating its listings of stockholders. In the case of a partnership, however, changes in ownership structure are events that require special accounting treatment.

Accounting for changes in the ownership of a partnership is influenced heavily by the legal concept of dissolution. When there is a change in the ownership structure, the original partnership is dissolved and, most often, a new partnership is created. This dissolution and subsequent creation of a partnership indicate that a new legal entity has been created, and accounting should properly measure the initial contributions of capital being made to the new partnership.

Accounting for a partnership is influenced by the *propriety theory*, which views a partnership not as a distinct entity but, rather, as a group of individual investors. Measuring changes in the equity of the individual partners is a major aspect of partnership accounting. Because ownership changes result in the dissolution of the partnership, this provides an excellent opportunity for accounting to measure the current wealth or equity of the partners. Changes in the ownership structure of the partnership are presumed to be arm's-length transactions which reflect the current value of the partnership. Therefore, such changes may indicate that

1. The existing assets of the original partnership should be revalued;
2. Previously unrecorded intangible assets exist that are traceable to the original partnership; *and/or*
3. Intangible assets, such as goodwill, exist that are traceable to a new partner.

In practice, a change in ownership normally suggests the need to both revalue net assets and recognize intangible assets.

Admission of a New Partner

The admission of a new partner requires the approval of the existing partners, although a partner's interest may be assigned to someone outside the partnership without the consent of the other partners. However, **assigning an interest does not dissolve the partnership,** and it does not allow the assignee to participate in the management of the partnership or to review transactions and records of the partnership. The assignee receives only the agreed-upon portion of the assigning partner's profit or loss.

Assuming a new partner has been approved by the existing partners, the new partner, normally, will experience the same general risks and rights of ownership as do the other existing partners. However, creditors presenting claims against the partnership that were incurred prior to admission of the new partner cannot attach the personal assets of the new partner for settlement of their claims. Therefore, the level of liability of a new partner is less than that of an existing partner. Section 17 of the UPA states:

> *A person admitted as a partner into an existing partnership is liable for all the obligations of the partnership arising before his admission as though he had been a partner when such obligations were incurred, except that this liability shall be satisfied only out of partnership property.*

Contribution of Assets to Existing Partnership. One method of gaining admission to an existing partnership involves contributing assets directly to the partnership entity itself. In this case, the exchange represents an arm's-length transaction between the entity and the incoming partner. If the book value of the original partnership's net assets approximates fair value, the incoming partner's contribution would be expected to be equal to his/her percentage interest in the capital of the new partnership. For example, if an incoming partner is to acquire a one-fourth interest in a partnership that has a book value and a fair value of $60,000, the original $60,000 would now represent a three-fourths interest in the new partnership. Therefore, the total partnership capital must be $80,000, of which $60,000 is traceable to the original partners and $20,000 is traceable to the assets contributed by the new partner.

An incoming partner may acquire an interest in the partnership for a price **in excess of** that indicated by the book value of the original partnership's net assets. This situation would suggest the existence of

1. Unrecognized appreciation on the recorded net assets of the original partnership, and/or
2. Unrecognized goodwill that also is traceable to the original partnership.

However, it is possible that an incoming partner may acquire an interest in the partnership at a price *less than* that indicated by the book value. This situation would suggest the existence of

1. Unrecognized depreciation or write-downs on the recorded net assets of the original partnership, and/or
2. A contribution by the incoming partner of some intangible asset (goodwill) in addition to a measured contribution.

When an incoming partner's contribution is different from that indicated by the book values of the original partnership, the admission of the partner, typically, is recorded by either the *bonus method* or *the goodwill method.* These two methods are mutually exclusive of each other. Both methods comprehend the possibility of adjusting the value of existing assets and/or the existence of goodwill. However, they differ in how these conditions are recognized.

2

OBJECTIVE

Account for the partners' capital balances under the bonus method.

Bonus Method. The bonus method generally follows a *book-value approach.* That is, existing book values should not be adjusted to current values unless such adjustments would have otherwise been allowed by generally accepted accounting principles (GAAP). More specifically, increases in the value of assets as suggested by the admission of a new partner should not be recognized until they are realized through an actual subsequent exchange transaction. However, following the principle of conservatism, decreases or write-downs in the value of assets, which are suggested by the admission of a new partner, may be recognized even though they are not realized. Recognition of unrealized losses is not unique to partnership accounting and is not in conflict with GAAP. Even if no new partner were being admitted, unrealized losses suggested by economic events should be recognized. For example, if inventory has a cost in excess of market, or if long-lived assets are impaired, these losses should be recognized regardless of whether a new partner is being admitted. Therefore, use of the bonus method should not preclude a partnership from recognizing losses which would otherwise be recognized through the application of GAAP. However, the bonus method does preclude the recognition of asset appreciation which would otherwise not be allowed per GAAP.

Therefore, when a new partner is admitted to an existing partnership, the total capital of the new partnership consists of the following:

1. The book value of the previous partnership *less*
2. Any write-downs in the value of the previous partnership's assets as recognized by GAAP *plus*
3. The value of the consideration paid to the partnership by the incoming partner.

The book-value approach of the bonus method does not directly recognize increases in asset values suggested by the consideration that the incoming partner pays. However, the method does indirectly recognize such increases by reallocating or adjusting the capital balances of the partners. For example, if increases in net asset values are suggested as being traceable to the original partners, this suggests that their equity or capital has increased. This increase in capital, or *bonus*, is accomplished by increasing their capital balances. If increases in asset values are not directly recognized, the indirect recognition through the capital balances of original partners must be offset by decreasing the capital of the incoming partner. Therefore, **the incoming partner's new capital balance is equal to the value of the consideration paid by the incoming partner less the bonus or increase in capital recorded for the original partners.** These adjustments result in the new incoming partner's capital balance always being equal to

1. The book value (BV) of the new partnership [book value of the previous partnership less asset write-downs plus the fair value (FV) of consideration received from the incoming partner] times
2. The interest in capital being acquired by the incoming partner.

$$\begin{bmatrix} \text{BV of Original} \\ \text{Partnership} - \text{Asset} \\ \text{Write-Downs} \\ + \\ \text{FV of New Partnership} \\ \text{Contribution} \end{bmatrix} \times \begin{matrix} \text{New Partner's} \\ \text{Interest \%} \end{matrix} = \begin{matrix} \text{New Partner's} \\ \text{Capital Balance} \end{matrix}$$

The difference between the value of the consideration received from the incoming partner and his/her capital balance represents the bonus traceable to the original partners. This bonus is allocated to the original partners according to their profit and loss ratios in existence prior to the new partner's admission.

It is important to note that the profit and loss ratios of the original partners are used for this allocation rather than their percentage interest in capital. If the increases in the value of assets, as suggested by the admission of a new partner(s), are traceable to the original partners, such increases could have been alternatively realized by a sale of appreciated assets to an outside party. If this were the case, the realized gains would have become a component of net income. This net income would have, in turn, been allocated to the original partners according to their profit and loss ratios.

If the gain on such appreciated assets were realized subsequent to the admission of a new partner(s), a portion of this gain would be allocated to the new partner based on his/her profit ratio. Keeping in mind that this original appreciation in value should not accrue to the benefit of the new partner, the reduction of his/her capital balance (equal to the bonus granted to the original partners) compensates for any subsequent allocation of gains resulting from the realization of such appreciated assets.

Bonus to the Original Partners. When an incoming partner's contribution indicates the existence of unrecorded asset appreciation and/or unrecorded goodwill, the bonus method does not record these previously unrecorded items but, rather, grants a "bonus" to the original partners. The bonus, which increases the capital accounts of the original partners and reduces the capital balance of the new partner(s), is made possible by recording in the new partner's capital account only a portion of the actual contribution to the partnership.

To illustrate this method, assume the following:

		Percentage Interest in	
Existing Partners	Capital Balance	Capital	Profit
Partner A	$30,000	40%	50%
Partner B	45,000	60	50

Then assume that C invests $27,000 in the partnership in exchange for a 20% interest in capital and a 20% interest in profits. The $27,000 of consideration invested by Partner C in exchange for a 20% interest in capital suggests that the total value of the new partnership is $135,000 ($27,000 ÷ 20%). The $135,000 of value is comprised of the following:

Book value of original partners	$ 75,000
Investment of new partner	27,000
	$102,000
Asset appreciation traceable to original partners	33,000
Total suggested value	$135,000

Partners A and B will each have a 40% interest in the profits of the new partnership. Since the total capital of the new partnership equals $102,000 ($30,000 + $45,000 + $27,000) and the new partner is acquiring a 20% interest in capital, it seems reasonable that the incoming partner's capital account initially should reflect 20% of the total capital, or $20,400. The $6,600 difference between C's contribution and the interest recorded for C indicates the existence of unrecorded intangibles (goodwill) or unrecorded appreciation on existing assets. Regardless of the identity of the $6,600, the value must be allocated to the appropriate parties. If the unrecorded value had been realized through a sale, the resulting profit would have been divided between the original partners in accordance with their profit and loss agreement. Therefore, assuming the $6,600 is identified as a bonus to the original partners and is divided between them according to their profit and loss ratio prior to admission of the new partner, the entry to record C's investment is as follows:

Assets	27,000	
A, Capital		3,300
B, Capital		3,300
C, Capital		20,400

If the suggested appreciation in value of $33,000 were subsequently realized, it would be allocated among Partners A, B, and C according to their profit and loss percentages of 40%, 40%, and 20%, respectively. Therefore, Partner C will be allocated $6,600 (20% × $33,000) of the gain. The $6,600 reduction in Partner C's initial capital balance, represented by the bonus to the original partners, compensates for or negates the subsequent allocation of the realized gain to Partner C. In substance, none of the $33,000 gain should accrue to the benefit of the new partner. The bonus of $6,600 to the original partners is, in substance, the reallocation to them of the subsequently realized gain which would be allocated to Partner C.

Bonus to the New Partner. When the new partner invests some intangible asset, such as business acumen or an established clientele, it is possible to have a bonus credited to the new partner. For example, given the same basic facts as in the previous illustration, assume that C invests $10,000 for a 20% interest in capital and a 20% interest in profits. Total capital of the partnership would be $85,000 ($30,000 + $45,000 + $10,000), and C's share of the total capital would be 20%, or $17,000. Partner C is acquiring a $17,000 interest in capital in exchange for an investment of $10,000, and the original partners are transferring $7,000 of their capital to C in exchange for unrecorded intangible assets invested by C. Partner C's admission is recorded by the following entry:

Assets	10,000	
A, Capital	3,500	
B, Capital	3,500	
C, Capital		17,000

Partner C's bonus may be viewed as a cost incurred to acquire C's goodwill. Since all costs to acquire assets eventually affect income and are allocated among the partners, C's bonus is allocated to A and B according to their profit and loss ratio.

Overvaluation of the Original Partnership. The recording of a bonus traceable to the incoming partner was based on the assumption that the new partner was contributing an intangible asset in addition to other assets valued at $10,000. However, the substance of the transaction may indicate that no intangibles are being contributed and the existing assets of the old partnership are overvalued. For example, in the previous illustration, C invested $10,000 in return for a 20% interest in the new partnership's total capital. Therefore, the total capital of the new partnership may be interpreted from C's investment to be equal to $50,000 ($10,000 ÷ 20%). Of this total, $10,000 is traceable to the new partner, and the balance of $40,000 represents the fair value of the original partners' capital. Assuming this is a proper interpretation of the substance of the transaction between the new partner and the partnership, it suggests that the assets of the original partnership are overvalued by $35,000 ($75,000 less $40,000). C's admission to the partnership is recorded as follows:

A, Capital	17,500	
B, Capital	17,500	
Assets		35,000
To record the write-down of the original partners' capital from a book value of $75,000 ($30,000 + $45,000) to its implied fair value of $40,000.		
Assets	10,000	
C, Capital		10,000
To record C's contribution of assets to the partnership.		

After these entries are posted, the total capital of the new partnership is $50,000 ($30,000 + $45,000 − $35,000 + $10,000), of which C's share is $10,000 (20% × $50,000), as initially represented by the balance in C's capital account.

3

OBJECTIVE

Account for the partners' capital balances under the goodwill method.

Goodwill Method. The goodwill method emphasizes the legal significance of a change in the ownership structure of a partnership. From a legal viewpoint, the entrance of a new partner results in the dissolution of the previous partnership and the creation of a new legal entity. Since a new entity has resulted, the assets transferred to this entity should be recorded at their **current fair value.** After a complete analysis, both tangible and intangible assets acquired by the new entity, including goodwill created by the previous partnership, should be recorded. Therefore, the total capital of the new partnership will consist of the following values:

1. The book value of the net assets of the previous partnership *plus*
2. Unrecognized appreciation or less unrecognized depreciation on the recorded net assets of the previous partnership *plus*
3. Unrecognized goodwill (GW) traceable to the previous partnership *plus*
4. The value of the consideration, both tangible and intangible, received from the new incoming partner.

BV of Original Partnership	+	Unrecognized Appreciation (or − Unrecognized Depreciation)	+	Unrecognized GW of Original Partnership	+	FV of New Partner's Contribution Including GW	=	Total Capital of New Partnership

When the bonus method is used to account for the admission of a new partner, the total capital of the new entity equals the book value of the previous partners' capital adjusted for asset write-downs, if appropriate, plus the incoming partner's investment. When the goodwill method is employed, however, the total capital of the new partnership must approximate the fair value of the entity.

To illustrate the goodwill method, assume the following:

		Percentage Interest in	
Existing Partners	Capital Balance	Capital	Profit
Partner A	$30,000	40%	50%
Partner B	45,000	60	50

If C invests $27,000 in the partnership in exchange for a 20% interest in capital and a 20% interest in profit, such an investment implies that the entity has a fair value of $135,000 ($27,000 ÷ 20%). However, the book value of the new partnership equals only $102,000 when the former partners' capital balances of $75,000 are added to C's $27,000 investment. Thus, $33,000 must be added to the existing book value.

Another interpretation of the transaction would be that, given the $102,000 book value of the new partnership, a 20% interest should have cost $20,400 ($102,000 × 20%). The new partner paid an extra $6,600 ($27,000 − $20,400) for a 20% interest in the difference between the implied fair value and the book value of the new entity. Therefore, the total difference must be $33,000 ($6,600 ÷ 20%).

Asset Appreciation. The difference between the higher fair value and the book value of the new entity, as previously discussed, may be traceable to unrecognized appreciation and/or unrecognized goodwill. Each of these possible explanations should be thoroughly analyzed to properly account for a change in the ownership structure of a partnership. If differences between the fair value and the book value of recorded assets are identifiable, appropriate adjustments to asset balances should be considered. Since a change in ownership structure creates a new, distinct legal entity, every attempt should be made to identify differences between fair and book values, whether such differences represent appreciation or write-downs in value. However, the absence of objective and independent valuations often prevents such an analysis. For example, fair values are not readily available for certain specialized assets, and the alternative of engaging an independent appraiser could become an expensive option. Furthermore, estimating fair values with the use of specific price-level indexes is often difficult because of the absence of relevant indexes. Another reason for not recording changes in fair values is that the resulting differences between the bases for tax purposes and the bases for book purposes would require more complex records.

Assuming objective measures of unrecorded appreciation are available, the appreciation would be recognized and allocated to the previous partners according to their old profit and loss ratios. To illustrate, assume that the $33,000 difference in values from our previous example is entirely traceable to the unrecognized net appreciation of the recorded net assets of the previous partnership as follows:

Land appreciation	$ 43,000
Inventory write-down	(10,000)
Net appreciation	$ 33,000

This appreciation and the investment by C would be recorded as follows:

Assets (from C)	27,000	
Land	43,000	
Inventory		10,000
A, Capital		16,500
B, Capital		16,500
C, Capital		27,000

Goodwill Traceable to the Original Partners. Unrecorded goodwill also may be identifiable. In the previous example, assuming there are no differences between the fair value and book value of recorded assets, the new partner's willingness to pay more than the proportionate book value of the new entity indicates that goodwill existed prior to the new partner's admission. If this intangible asset could have been sold prior to the admission of the partner, the realized profit would have been allocated to the original partners. Therefore, the goodwill is recorded and allocated to the original partners according to their profit and loss ratio. The investment by C is recorded under the goodwill method as follows:

Assets (from C)	27,000	
Goodwill	33,000	
A, Capital		16,500
B, Capital		16,500
C, Capital		27,000

It is important to note that the new partner's capital account balance represents a 20% interest in the total capital of the new partnership, as verified by the following computation:

Original capital	$ 75,000
C's investment	27,000
Goodwill	33,000
	$ 135,000
C's interest	× 20%
C's capital balance	$ 27,000

In comparing the assumption that the $33,000 difference was traceable to net appreciation of assets versus goodwill, it should be noted that

1. In one case, the net appreciation is allocated to specific assets versus goodwill, yet the amount is the same.
2. Some combination of appreciated assets and goodwill could account for the $33,000 difference.
3. The adjusted capital balances of the partners are the same regardless of whether asset appreciation and/or goodwill is recognized.

The recognition of goodwill traceable to the previous partners is criticized by some accountants. If the concept of a new legal entity is cast aside, some would argue that the goodwill is self-created and, therefore, should not be recognized. APB Opinion No. 17, *Intangible Assets*, prohibits the recognition of goodwill unless it has been purchased from another entity. To argue that the new partnership is, in substance, a continuation of the previous partnership would prevent the recognition of goodwill traceable to the original partnership. Furthermore, viewing the new partnership as a continuation of the previous partnership would prevent the recognition of appreciation on other assets as well.

It also may be argued that the difficulties associated with the measurement of the fair value of existing assets unjustifiably forces the recognition of goodwill for lack of a more precise analysis. However, the argument that the fair value of a new partnership, as indicated by the new partner's investment, is not objectively or independently determined overlooks the basic nature of the transaction. Negotiations between previous partners and a new partner would be described as arm's length, since both parties involved are independently seeking a fair price.

Asset Write-Downs. Given the same basic facts as in the previous illustrations, assume that C invests $10,000 to acquire a 20% interest in the partnership of A and B. C's investment implies a fair value of the new entity equal to $50,000 ($10,000 ÷ 20%). However, the book value of the new partnership equals $85,000, consisting of the original partners' capital balances of $75,000 plus C's investment of $10,000. This difference between the fair value and the higher book value indicates the existence of unrecorded net write-downs and/or goodwill contributed by the incoming partner.

If objective evidence supports the write-down of existing assets, the previous partners' capital balances would be reduced accordingly in proportion to their profit and loss ratios. The amount of the suggested write-down is calculated by comparing the implied fair value of $50,000 to the $85,000 representing the book value of the previous partnership plus the new partner's investment. Therefore, the difference of $35,000 is equal to the necessary net write-down. Assuming the net write-down is represented by land appreciation of $20,000 and a write-down of $55,000 to inventory, the net write-down would be recorded as follows:

A, Capital	17,500	
B, Capital	17,500	
Land	20,000	
Inventory		55,000

This reduces the net assets of the previous partnership to $40,000, and the new partner's investment of $10,000 would then represent 20% of the new partnership's total capital of $50,000 ($40,000 + $10,000).

Goodwill Traceable to the New Partner. Assuming net assets of the original partnership are properly valued and should not be written down, it is possible that goodwill may be traceable to the incoming partner. The amount of this contributed goodwill may be computed as the difference between

1. The amount that should have been paid by the new partner, as indicated by the book value of the previous partnership (calculated by dividing the original book value of the partnership by the total percentage interest of the original partners in the new partnership, and subtracting the original book value),

$$\left[\begin{array}{c}\text{Book Value of}\\ \text{Original}\\ \text{Partnership}\end{array} \div \begin{array}{c}\text{Original Partners'}\\ \text{Interest in } \textbf{New}\\ \text{Partnership}\end{array}\right] - \begin{array}{c}\text{Book Value}\\ \text{of Original}\\ \text{Partnership}\end{array} = \begin{array}{c}\text{New Partner's}\\ \text{Capital Balance}\end{array}$$

and

2. The amount of consideration, excluding any goodwill, contributed by the new partner.

Using the previous example, the $75,000 original book value would represent 80% of the new partnership capital, or $93,750 ($75,000 ÷ 80%). Therefore, it appears that the new partner should have paid $18,750 ($93,750 less the original $75,000 book value) for a 20% interest in the partnership; however, the partner actually paid only $10,000 cash. The difference between what should have been paid ($18,750) and the amount actually paid ($10,000) represents the goodwill traceable to the incoming partner. The investment by C would be recorded under the goodwill method as follows:

Assets	10,000	
Goodwill	8,750	
C, Capital		18,750

Note that the new partner's capital account balance represents a 20% interest in the total capital of the new partnership, as shown by the following computation:

Original capital	$75,000
C's investment of cash	10,000
Goodwill	8,750
	$93,750
C's interest	× 20%
C's capital balance	$18,750

The fact that a new legal entity is created supports the recognition of goodwill and other contributed assets at their fair value. If the concept of a new entity is set aside, the goodwill may be viewed as being purchased by the previous partnership in exchange for partnership equity. Accounting theory and current practice support the recording of goodwill acquired or purchased from other entities.

Revaluation of Assets and Goodwill. The previous examples of accounting for a new partner's investment assumed that either asset revaluations or goodwill recognition were appropriate as mutually exclusive choices. In reality, some combination of the two may be appropriate. Continuing with the previous example, assume that the $75,000 book value of the previous partnership has a fair value of $64,000 and new partner C's investment remains at $10,000. The first step to be taken is to recognize the write-down of the previous partnership's net assets as follows:

A, Capital	5,500	
B, Capital	5,500	
Assets.		11,000

The adjusted value of the previous partnership, then, is used to determine the goodwill traceable to the new partner. In this example, the $64,000 fair value of the previous partnership would represent 80% of the new partnership capital, or $80,000 ($64,000 ÷ 80%). Therefore, it appears that the new partner should have paid $16,000 ($80,000 less the fair value of the previous partnership) for a 20% interest in the partnership. The difference between what should have been paid ($16,000) and the amount actually paid ($10,000) represents the goodwill traceable to the incoming partner. The entry to record C's investment is as follows:

Assets.	10,000	
Goodwill	6,000	
C, Capital		16,000

Methodology for Determining Goodwill. An analysis of the previous examples reveals that goodwill may be traceable to either the original partners or the incoming partner. To properly apply the goodwill method, the following methodology may be helpful in identifying the origin of the goodwill and its amount:

1. Determine the entity's fair value, as indicated by the new partner's investment (new partner's investment divided by the percentage interest acquired in the partnership).
2. If the fair value determined is
   a. Greater than the book value of the new partnership adjusted for net appreciation or net write-downs, implied goodwill is traceable to the original partners and is allocated among them according to their original profit ratios. The amount of goodwill is equal to the difference between (1) the fair value indicated by the new partner's investment and (2) the adjusted book value of the new partnership.
   b. Less than the adjusted book value of the new partnership, implied goodwill is traceable to the new partner. The amount of goodwill is equal to the difference between (1) the amount that should have been paid by the new partner to acquire an interest in the adjusted book value of the previous partnership and (2) the actual amount paid.
3. The initial capital balance of the new partner always is equal to the new partner's interest in the total capital of the new partnership after goodwill is recognized.

4

OBJECTIVE

Describe the conceptual differences between the bonus and goodwill methods.

Comparison of Bonus and Goodwill Methods. The bonus method adheres to the historical cost concept and is often used in accounting practice. It is objective in that it establishes total capital of the new partnership at an amount based on actual consideration received from the new partner. The bonus method indirectly acknowledges the existence of appreciation of assets and/or goodwill by giving a bonus to either original or new partners.

The goodwill method results in the recognition of an asset implied by a transaction rather than recognizing an asset actually purchased. Historically, goodwill has been recognized only when purchased so that a more objective measure of its value is established. Therefore, opponents of the goodwill method contend that goodwill is not determined objectively and other factors may have influenced the amount of investment required from the new partner. Also, certain recipients of partnership financial statements may question the valuation of goodwill, since increasing total assets may result in an understatement of the return on total assets or equity. However, in defense of the goodwill method, the current value of net assets, whether tangible or intangible, is reflected on the financial statements resulting in a more relevant measure of invested capital.

Use of the goodwill method could produce inequitable results if either of the following conditions exist:

1. The new partner's interest in profits does not equal the new partner's initial interest in capital.
2. After the formation of the new partnership, the former partners do not share profits and losses in the same relationship to each other as they did before the admission of a new partner.

The importance of these concepts can be illustrated using the following facts:

	Original Partners		New Partner
	A	B	C
Original capital	$30,000	$45,000	
Original profit and loss percentage	50%	50%	
New partner's capital			$27,000
New profit and loss percentage	33⅓%	33⅓%	33⅓%
New partner's interest in capital			20%

The new capital balances that result from using the goodwill method and the bonus method are as follows:

	Original Partners		New Partner
	A	B	C
Goodwill method:			
Goodwill allocation	$16,500	$16,500	
New capital balances	46,500	61,500	$27,000
Bonus method:			
Bonus allocation	3,300	3,300	
New capital balances	33,300	48,300	20,400

Assuming the recorded goodwill proves to be worthless (or assuming that goodwill is amortized in total), the decline in asset value would reduce the partners' capital balances according to their profit and loss ratio as follows:

	Partners			
	A	B	C	Total
Capital balances if goodwill method is used	$ 46,500	$ 61,500	$ 27,000	$135,000
Goodwill write-off (amortization)	(11,000)	(11,000)	(11,000)	(33,000)
Capital balances after write-off	$ 35,500	$ 50,500	$ 16,000	$102,000
Capital balances if bonus method is used	33,300	48,300	20,400	102,000
Differences	$ 2,200	$ 2,200	$ (4,400)	$ 0

The capital balances that result from using the two methods are different because the new partner's interest in profits and interest in capital are not equal. In this illustration, C acquired a 20% capital interest and a 33⅓% interest in profits. Therefore, C paid for 20% of the implied goodwill but had to absorb 33⅓% of the goodwill amortization.

To further illustrate these concepts, assume the same facts, except that the new profit and loss percentages are 50%, 30%, and 20% for Partners A, B, and C, respectively. If the recorded goodwill proves to be worthless, the decline in asset value would affect the partners' capital balances as follows:

	Partners			
	A	B	C	Total
Capital balances if goodwill method is used	$ 46,500	$61,500	$27,000	$135,000
Goodwill write-off (amortization)	(16,500)	(9,900)	(6,600)	(33,000)
Capital balances after write-off	$ 30,000	$51,600	$20,400	$102,000
Capital balances if bonus method is used	33,300	48,300	20,400	102,000
Differences	$ (3,300)	$ 3,300	$ 0	$ 0

In this case, Partners A and B shared equally in the initial recording of goodwill but unequally in the subsequent amortization of goodwill.

Now, assume the same facts, except that the new profit and loss percentages are 40%, 40%, and 20% for Partners A, B, and C, respectively. After the amortization of goodwill, the capital balances would be identical to those achieved under the bonus method, as indicated in the following table:

	Partners			
	A	B	C	Total
Capital balances if goodwill method is used	$ 46,500	$ 61,500	$27,000	$135,000
Goodwill write-off (amortization)	(13,200)	(13,200)	(6,600)	(33,000)
Capital balances after write-off	$ 33,300	$ 48,300	$20,400	$102,000
Capital balances if bonus method is used	33,300	48,300	20,400	102,000
Differences	$ 0	$ 0	$ 0	$ 0

The equality between the capital balances is achieved because neither of the two conditions that produce inequities exists. If these conditions do exist, preference is given, typically, to the bonus method because of the possible inequities that may result from the write-off of goodwill.

5

OBJECTIVE

Account for the admission of a new partner through direct contribution to an existing partner.

Contribution of Assets to Existing Partners. A new partner also may be admitted to the partnership by acquiring all or part of the capital interest of one or more existing partners in exchange for some consideration (assets). In this case, **the new partner deals directly with an existing partner or partners** rather than with the partnership entity. Therefore, the acquisition price is paid to the selling partner(s) and not to the partnership itself. The partnership records the redistribution of capital interests by transferring all or a portion of the seller's capital to the new partner's capital account but does not record the transfer of any assets.

To illustrate, assume the following facts:

		Percentage Interest in	
Existing Partners	Capital Balance	Capital	Profit
Partner A	$30,000	40%	50%
Partner B	45,000	60	50

Now, assume new Partner C purchased 50% of A's interest in capital and 50% of B's interest in capital in exchange for $50,000. This purchase resulted in C's having a 50% interest in the total partnership capital.

There are several alternative ways of recording the contribution of assets by C to the existing partners. If the consideration paid by the incoming partner is not used to impute the fair value of the partnership, the transaction would be recorded by the partnership entity as follows:

A, Capital (50% × $30,000)	15,000	
B, Capital (50% × $45,000)	22,500	
C, Capital		37,500

The $50,000 actually paid by C was not used as a basis for the entry because it represents consideration paid to the individual partners personally rather than to the partnership entity. This accounting treatment frequently is compared to that of a corporation when a stockholder sells shares or an interest in corporate capital to another investor in the corporation. The corporation does not record the transaction or use it as a basis for revaluing corporate assets but merely acknowledges the changing identity of its shareholders. The preceding entry would also be appropriate if the existing partners had sold their interests for less than book value. Even though depreciation of existing assets is suggested, such depreciation is not recorded because the transaction did not involve the partnership entity itself.

An alternative but less frequently used method of recording this transaction would be to impute the fair value of the partnership entity from the consideration paid by the new partner. For example, if C paid $50,000 to acquire a 50% interest in the capital of the partnership vis-à-vis the individual partners, the total implied current value of the original partnership would be $100,000 ($50,000 ÷ 50%). The difference between the imputed value of $100,000 and the partnership's previous book value of $75,000 ($30,000 + $45,000) is interpreted to represent undervalued existing assets and/or goodwill traceable to the original partnership. This alternative interpretation would result in recording the transaction as follows:

Assets and/or Goodwill	25,000	
A, Capital		12,500
B, Capital.............................		12,500
To record the previously unrecognized increase in value of the partnership.		
A, Capital [50% × ($30,000 + $12,500)]	21,250	
B, Capital [50% × ($45,000 + $12,500)]	28,750	
C, Capital		50,000
To record the transfer of the original partners' adjusted capital to incoming Partner C.		

Normally, this alternative method is not employed because (a) the transaction was not between the partnership and the incoming partner but, rather, between individual partners and (b) the consideration paid by the incoming partner may not provide a reliable indicator of the partnership entity's current value. However, the method may provide useful information for deciding how to allocate the acquisition price between the selling partners. The selling partners' original capital plus their share of any imputed value increments may indicate the current values for which the incoming partner was paying. For example, the purchase price of $50,000 may be allocated to Partners A and B as follows:

	Partners		
	A	B	Total
Original capital	$30,000	$45,000	$ 75,000
Share of value increment	12,500	12,500	25,000
Total imputed value	$42,500	$57,500	$100,000
Percentage acquired by new partner	× 50%	× 50%	× 50%
Total purchase price	$21,250	$28,750	$ 50,000

6

OBJECTIVE

Explain the impact of a partner's withdrawal from the partnership.

Withdrawal of a Partner

When a partner withdraws, the partnership agreement should be consulted to determine whether any guidelines have been established that would influence the procedure. The withdrawal of a partner requires a determination of the fair value of the partnership entity and a measurement of partnership income to the date of withdrawal. Also, in many cases, the equity of the retiring partner may not be equal to the partner's capital balance as a result of (a) the existence of accounting errors, (b) differences between the fair value and the recorded book value of assets, and/or (c) unrecorded assets such as goodwill.

If accounting errors are discovered, they should be treated as prior-period adjustments and corrected by adjusting the capital balances of the partners. Theoretically, an error should be allocated to partners' capital balances according to the profit and loss ratio that existed when the error was committed. Therefore, it is necessary to identify the period to which the error is traceable. This practice can become complicated, and a well-designed partnership agreement should include procedures for dealing with the correction of errors.

Recognizing differences between book value and fair value may be as appropriate when an individual withdraws from the partnership as when an individual is admitted. If accounting recognition of such differences is not desired, however, these differences nevertheless should influence the amount to be paid to the withdrawing partner.

The Selling of an Interest to Existing Partners. As is the case with the admission of a partner, the withdrawal of a partner may involve (a) a transaction with existing partners or a new partner or (b) a transaction with the partnership entity itself. In the first case, the equity of the withdrawing partner will be purchased with the personal assets of existing or new partners rather than with the assets of the partnership.

To illustrate, assume the following:

	Partners		
	A	B	C
Capital balance	$30,000	$50,000	$20,000
Profit and loss percentage	40%	40%	20%
Percentage interest in capital	30%	50%	20%

Now assume Partner A withdraws from the partnership and C uses personal funds to purchase A's interest at its current value of $36,000. If the price paid by C is not used to impute the value of the entity, the transaction would be recorded as follows:

A, Capital	30,000	
C, Capital		30,000

The above entry also may be appropriate if the existing partners sold their interests for less than book value. Even though depreciation of existing assets is suggested, such depreciation is not recorded because the transaction did not involve the partnership entity itself. As previously discussed, an alternative treatment would be to recognize any suggested appreciation or write-downs indicated by the transaction and then transfer the adjusted capital balances.

The Selling of an Interest to the Partnership. When a withdrawing partner sells an interest to the partnership rather than to an individual partner, the bonus or goodwill methods may be employed. The bonus method is used most frequently, but the choice between methods should be based on a thorough analysis of the transaction. Using the same facts as in the previous illustration and assuming the use of the bonus method, the purchase of A's equity by the partnership would be recorded as follows:

A, Capital	30,000	
B, Capital	4,000	
C, Capital	2,000	
Cash		36,000

The entry indicates that the remaining partners granted a bonus to A, measured by the difference between the recorded capital and the fair value of A's equity. The bonus is charged to the remaining partners according to their proportionate profit and loss ratio.

The goodwill method focuses on the payment to the withdrawing partner as an indication of the fair value of the partnership. If the imputed goodwill or undervalued assets were disposed of, the partners would divide the gain according to their profit and loss ratio. Assuming existing assets are properly valued, the $36,000 payment to A consists of A's capital balance of $30,000 plus a $6,000 share of the unrecorded goodwill. Therefore, the $6,000 represents A's 40% interest in total goodwill of $15,000 ($6,000 ÷ 40%). Notice that the $6,000 represents A's interest in the gain which would be realized if the unrecorded goodwill were sold. Therefore, A's profit percentage is used to suggest the total value of the goodwill.

Two alternatives are now available: (a) recognize only the goodwill that is traceable to the retiring partner or (b) recognize the amount of goodwill traceable to the entire entity. The first alternative stresses the importance of recognizing only the amount of goodwill that actually is purchased from the withdrawing partner. Using this alternative, A's withdrawal would be recorded as follows:

Goodwill	6,000	
A, Capital		6,000
A, Capital	36,000	
Cash		36,000

If the amount of goodwill traceable to the entire entity is recognized, the goodwill would be allocated to the partners according to their profit and loss ratio, as reflected in the following entries to record A's withdrawal:

Goodwill	15,000	
A, Capital		6,000
B, Capital		6,000
C, Capital		3,000
A, Capital	36,000	
Cash		36,000

Whether part or all of the goodwill is recognized, opponents of this procedure contend that transactions between partners should not be viewed as arm's length; therefore, the measure of goodwill may not be determined objectively. Also, inequitable results may be produced if the remaining partners subsequently change their profit and loss ratio.

It is important to note that a withdrawing partner could sell his/her interest in a partnership for less than book value. If that interest is sold to the partnership, the following recognition would take place depending on whether the bonus or goodwill method is employed:

1. Bonus method: A bonus traceable to the remaining partners would be recognized. The bonus would be measured as the difference between the withdrawing partner's capital balance and the consideration paid for the partner's interest.
2. Goodwill method: Paying less than the withholding partner's capital balance (book value) would suggest that existing assets are overvalued. A write-down of existing assets would be recognized as the difference between the withdrawing partner's capital balance and the consideration paid for the partner's interest. As an alternative, the asset write-down traceable to the entire entity could be recognized based on the amount suggested by the transaction with the withholding partner. The write-down traceable to the withdrawing partner represents his/her percentage interest (based on profit and loss ratios) in the asset write-down traceable to the entire entity.

Effects of a Partner's Withdrawal. When the interest of a withdrawing partner is acquired by the remaining partners or the partnership, serious demands upon the liquidity of the partners and the partnership may result. If withdrawal is due to the death of the partner, funds may be provided from the proceeds of life insurance policies taken out by the partnership itself or by individual partners. For example, if Partner A takes out a life insurance policy on Partner B, and B subsequently dies, the proceeds payable to A may be used to acquire B's interest.

The UPA, in Section 42, states that a retiring or deceased partner's estate may receive interest as an ordinary creditor on that portion of the withdrawing partner's capital interest that remains in the partnership (i.e., has not yet been disbursed). In lieu of interest, the UPA states that the profits attributable to the use of the withdrawing partner's capital still retained in the partnership may be received. Once again, a partnership agreement that addresses the valuation of a withdrawing partner's interest and the means of payment is a valuable aid in properly accounting for the withdrawal of a partner.

REFLECTION

- A change in the ownership structure of a partnership results in the dissolution of the prior partnership and provides an opportunity to properly recognize and value the net assets of the partnership.
- The bonus and goodwill methods are alternative methods of accounting for the change in ownership of a partnership when a new partner acquires an interest from the partnership entity itself.
- The more conservative bonus method only recognizes declines in the value of net assets suggested by a change in ownership.
- The goodwill method recognizes both increases and decreases in the value of net assets.
- If a new partner acquires an interest in the partnership directly from a partner(s) as compared to from the partnership entity itself, neither the bonus or goodwill methods are employed.
- When a partner withdraws by selling an interest to the partnership, a bonus or goodwill payment may be made to the exiting partner.

PARTNERSHIP LIQUIDATION

Unlike a dissolution where the partnership continues its business purpose, a liquidation results in the partnership's ending or terminating its business. The process of liquidation consists of the conversion of partnership assets into a distributable form and the distribution of these assets to creditors and owners. To achieve an orderly and legally sound liquidation, some fundamental guidelines need to be identified.

Liquidation Guidelines

7

OBJECTIVE

Describe the order in which assets must be distributed upon liquidation of a partnership, and explain the right-of-offset concept.

The underlying theme in accounting for partnership liquidation is the equitable distribution of the assets. To be equitable, a distribution should recognize the legal rights of the partnership creditors and individual partners. All liquidation expenses and gains or losses from conversion of partnership assets also must be allocated to the partners before assets actually are distributed to the individual partners. Failure to consider these factors may result in the premature or incorrect distribution of assets to a partner. If a premature or incorrect distribution of assets cannot be recovered, the partnership fiduciary who authorized the distribution may be held liable.

The Ranking of Partnership Liabilities. The UPA establishes rules governing the priority in which partnership assets are distributed to creditors and partners. Subject to any agreement to the contrary, the following sequence of payments should be observed:

1. Amounts owed to creditors other than partners.
2. Amounts owed to partners other than for capital and profits (i.e., partners' loans to the partnership).
3. Amounts owed to partners as capital.
4. Amounts owed to partners as profits not currently closed to partners' capital accounts.

Although loans from partners have a higher legal priority than amounts owed as capital and profits, the doctrine of *right of offset* sets aside this ranking in favor of procedural and economic considerations that facilitate the actual liquidation process. The effect of this doctrine is that loans due to partners, which have a credit balance, are combined with the respective partners' capital balances. Without the right of offset, it would be possible to distribute assets to a partner in payment of the loan balance while at the same time the partner has a debit capital account balance. In order to eliminate the debit capital balance, the partnership would have to recover personal assets from the partner. Therefore, it is possible for the partnership to distribute assets to the partner and then try to recover assets from the partner, hoping that such assets are still available. The doctrine of right of offset eliminates this problem by combining the loan and capital balances.

Amounts owed to partners as capital and profits are typically viewed as one element rather than two separate priority levels. Therefore, items (2), (3), and (4) may be combined without destroying the fairness of a distribution.

Liability for Debit Capital Balances. The UPA, in Section 40, states that partners should contribute assets to the partnership to the extent of their debit balances. However, if such a contribution is not possible because of special personal or legal considerations, the debit balance will be viewed as a realization loss and allocated according to the remaining partners' profit and loss ratio. For example, assume Partners A, B, and C share in profits and losses in the ratio of 1:2:1, respectively. If C is unable to contribute any asset to eliminate a debit capital balance, that balance would be allocated to A and B in the ratio of 1:2. Partners who absorb other partners' debit capital balances have a legal claim against the deficient partners. However, the collectibility of such a claim depends on the personal wealth of the deficient partners.

8

OBJECTIVE

Explain the doctrine of marshaling of assets.

The Marshaling of Assets. The provisions that call for the contribution of personal assets to a liquidating partnership illustrate the characteristics of unlimited liability discussed in the previous chapter. However, such personal liability depends on the legal doctrine of *marshaling of assets*. This doctrine, which is applied when the partnership and/or one or more of the partners are insolvent, states that

1. Partnership assets are first available for the payment of partnership debts. Any excess assets are available for payment of the individual partner's debts, but only to the extent of the partner's interest in the capital of the partnership.
2. Personal assets of a partner are applied against personal debts, ranked in order of priority as follows:
   a. Amounts owed to personal creditors.
   b. Amounts owed to partnership creditors.
   c. Amounts owed to partners by way of contribution.

"Amounts owed to partners by way of contribution" refers to amounts owed the partnership as represented by the partner's debit capital balance. This amount is viewed by the UPA as separate from the amounts owed to personal creditors. For example, if a partner has personal assets of $12,000, personal liabilities of $8,000, and a debit capital balance of $16,000, personal assets would be distributed as follows:

Payable to personal creditors	$ 8,000
Payable to partnership for debit capital balance	4,000
Total personal assets	$12,000

Under common law and federal bankruptcy law, which may be applicable when the UPA has not been adopted, amounts owed to partners by way of contribution are on an equal basis (*pari passu*) with personal creditors of the partner. According to this rule, the $12,000 of personal assets would be distributed as follows:

Payable to personal liabilities [($8,000 ÷ $24,000) × $12,000]	$ 4,000
Payable to partnership for debit capital balance [($16,000 ÷ $24,000) × $12,000]	8,000
Total personal assets	$12,000

The legal doctrine of marshaling of assets is demonstrated by the following cases:

Case 1
Insolvent Partners

The partnership is solvent, with total assets of $16,000 and total liabilities of $9,000. Information relating to the individual partners is as follows:

	Partner A	Partner B
Total personal assets	$10,000	$15,000
Total personal liabilities	13,000	18,000
Partnership capital balances	5,000	2,000

Analysis: Unsatisfied personal creditors may attach a partner's interest in the solvent partnership but only to the extent of the partner's capital balance. Thus, unsatisfied personal creditors could seek recourse as follows:

	Partner A	Partner B
Unsatisfied personal creditors	$ 3,000	$ 3,000
Interest in partnership capital available to personal creditors	(3,000)	(2,000)
Personal liabilities not satisfied	$ 0	$ 1,000

Case 2
Insolvent Partnership

The partnership is insolvent, with total assets of $23,000 and total liabilities of $25,000. Information relating to individual partners is as follows:

	Partner A	Partner B
Total personal assets	$10,000	$ 8,000
Total personal liabilities	6,000	7,000
Partnership capital balances	500	(2,500)

Analysis: Unsatisfied partnership creditors may seek recourse from the individual partners in accordance with a proper marshaling of assets, as reflected in Illustration 14-1.

Illustration 14-1
Distribution of Assets—Insolvent Partnership

	Partner A		Partner B		AB Partnership			
	Assets	Liab.	Assets	Liab.	Assets	Liab.	A, Capital	B, Capital
Beginning balances[a]	$10,000	$ 6,000	$ 8,000	$ 7,000	$ 23,000	$ 25,000	$ 500	$(2,500)
Payment of liabilities	(6,000)	(6,000)	(7,000)	(7,000)	(23,000)	(23,000)		
	$ 4,000	$ 0	$ 1,000	$ 0	$ 0	$ 2,000	$ 500	$(2,500)
Payment of partnership creditors[b]	(2,000)					(2,000)	2,000	
	$ 2,000	$ 0	$ 1,000	$ 0	$ 0	$ 0	$ 2,500	$(2,500)
Payment toward debit capital balance[c]			(1,000)		1,000			1,000
	$ 2,000	$ 0	$ 0	$ 0	$ 1,000	$ 0	$ 2,500	$(1,500)
Capital distribution to A	1,000				(1,000)		(1,000)	
Balances[d]	$ 3,000	$ 0	$ 0	$ 0	$ 0	$ 0	$ 1,500	$(1,500)

[a]Beginning asset balances represent realizable values.

[b]Unsatisfied partnership creditors may claim the net personal assets of any solvent partner, regardless of the amount of the partner's interest in the capital of the partnership. A's capital interest is increased by the payment of partnership liabilities.

[c]If the payment toward the debit capital balance had preceded B's payment of personal liabilities, a proper marshaling of assets would not have been achieved and B's personal creditors would not have been satisfied.

[d]If B later pays the debit capital balance, the funds would be distributed to A. However, if B cannot pay, the loss will be borne by A.

Case 3
Insolvent Partner and Partnership

The partnership is insolvent, with total assets of $20,000 and total liabilities of $25,000. Information relating to individual partners is as follows:

	Partner A	Partner B
Total personal assets	$13,000	$12,000
Total personal liabilities.	10,000	15,000
Partnership capital balances	(7,000)	2,000

Analysis: Partner B is insolvent, and the recourse B's personal creditors have against the partnership depends upon A's future contribution to the partnership. Illustration 14-2 reflects the distribution of assets in accordance with the marshaling concept.

Illustration 14-2
Distribution of Assets—Insolvent Partner and Partnership

	Partner A		Partner B		AB Partnership			
	Assets	Liab.	Assets	Liab.	Assets	Liab.	A, Capital	B, Capital
Beginning balances[a]	$ 13,000	$ 10,000	$ 12,000	$ 15,000	$ 20,000	$ 25,000	$(7,000)	$2,000
Payment of liabilities	(10,000)	(10,000)	(12,000)	(12,000)	(20,000)	(20,000)		
	$ 3,000	$ 0	$ 0	$ 3,000	$ 0	$ 5,000	$(7,000)	$2,000
Payment of partnership creditors.	(3,000)					(3,000)	3,000	
Balances[b]	$ 0	$ 0	$ 0	$ 3,000[c]	$ 0	$ 2,000	$(4,000)	$2,000

[a]Beginning asset balances represent realizable values.

[b]If A later pays $4,000 to the partnership to eliminate the debit capital balance, the payment will be allocated first to the partnership liabilities and then to B. However, if A is not able to make a payment, claims against the partnership by the creditors and B will be totally uncollectible.

[c]The unsatisfied personal creditors of B are unable to seek recovery against the credit capital balance of B because the partnership itself is not solvent.

9

OBJECTIVE

Calculate the assets to be distributed to a given partner in a lump-sum or installment liquidation.

Lump-Sum Liquidations

The guidelines discussed in the preceding section are important factors influencing the procedural and legal aspects of a partnership liquidation. Upon liquidation of a partnership, the amount of assets ultimately to be distributed to the individual partners is determined through the use of either a lump-sum liquidation schedule or an installment liquidation schedule. A *lump-sum liquidation* requires that all assets be realized before a distribution is made to partners, thus avoiding the possibility of a premature distribution. To illustrate a lump-sum liquidation, assume the following:

1. Asset, liability, loan, and capital balances are as shown in Illustration 14-3, after books for the final operational period are closed.
2. Profit and loss percentages for Partners A, B, and C are 40%, 40%, and 20%, respectively.
3. Personal assets and debts of the partners are as follows:

	A	B	C
Total personal assets	$30,000	$40,000	$20,000
Total personal liabilities	10,000	37,200	24,000

4. Sales of assets are as follows:

Date	Book Value	Selling Price	Gain (Loss)
February 15	$50,000	$60,000	$ 10,000
March 2	30,000	10,000	(20,000)
March 7	40,000	20,000	(20,000)

5. Total liquidation expenses of $2,000 are paid on March 4.

Illustration 14-3
Lump-Sum Liquidation Statement

					Capital Balances		
	Cash	Noncash Assets	Liabilities	Loan from A	A	B	C
Beginning balances	$ 10,000	$120,000	$ 80,000	$ 9,000	$ 25,000	$10,000	$ 6,000
February 15, sale of assets at a gain	60,000	(50,000)			4,000	4,000	2,000
March 2, sale of assets at a loss	10,000	(30,000)			(8,000)	(8,000)	(4,000)
Payment of liquidation expenses	(2,000)				(800)	(800)	(400)
March 7, sale of assets at a loss	20,000	(40,000)			(8,000)	(8,000)	(4,000)
Balances	$ 98,000	$ 0	$ 80,000	$ 9,000	$ 12,200	$ (2,800)	$ (400)
Payment of liabilities	(80,000)		(80,000)				
Balances	$ 18,000	$ 0	$ 0	$ 9,000	$ 12,200	$ (2,800)	$ (400)
B's contribution	2,800					2,800	
Balances	$ 20,800	$ 0	$ 0	$ 9,000	$ 12,200	$ 0	$ (400)
Absorption of C's balance					(400)		400
Balances	$ 20,800	$ 0	$ 0	$ 9,000	$ 11,800	$ 0	$ 0
Payment to A	(20,800)			(9,000)	(11,800)		
Final balances	$ 0	$ 0	$ 0	$ 0	$ 0	$ 0	$ 0

Illustration 14-3 presents the lump-sum distribution and demonstrates the following concepts that were discussed previously:

1. Gains and losses on realization are allocated according to the partners' profit and loss ratio.
2. Claims against the partnership are paid in the proper order.
3. The marshaling of assets doctrine is followed to determine the disposition of B's and C's debit balances in their capital accounts. That is, a partner's personal assets first are used to satisfy personal liabilities. Then, to the extent possible, remaining assets are contributed to the partnership to eliminate debit capital balances.

4. C's debit capital balance is charged against A, the only personally solvent partner.
5. Partner A will have a claim against C's future personal assets for the debit balance that was absorbed.

10

OBJECTIVE

Prepare an installment liquidation statement, a schedule of safe payments, and a predistribution plan.

Installment Liquidations

The complete liquidation process might extend over several months or longer, and it may not be possible to postpone payments to creditors and partners until all assets have been realized. Therefore, payments may be made on an installment basis to creditors and partners during the liquidation process. To avoid the problem associated with premature payments, installment payments may be made to partners only after anticipating all liabilities, possible losses, and liquidation expenses. To provide a proper solution to installment liquidations, either a *schedule of safe payments* is prepared as amounts become available for distribution or a *predistribution plan* is used to direct the distribution of any available sum.

Schedule of Safe Payments. The possibility of premature payments to partners is reduced by using a schedule of safe payments, which reflects a conservative approach to liquidation. The schedule indicates how available funds should be distributed to partners. It is based on the anticipation of all possible liabilities and expenses, including those expected to be incurred in the process of liquidation. The effect of these items on partnership capital is allocated among the partners according to their profit and loss agreement.

In keeping with the conservative approach, the schedule also is based on the assumption that all noncash assets will be worthless; therefore, the assumed loss is allocated among the partners according to their profit and loss ratio. The allocation of the assumed loss could produce debit balances in partners' capital accounts, and these balances are treated as being uncollectible. Therefore, the assumed debit capital balances are allocated to those partners with credit balances according to their profit and loss ratio. When the allocation of estimated liabilities, expenses, liquidation losses, and debit balances is completed, assets may be distributed safely to the partners in amounts equal to the resulting credit capital balances.

A new schedule of safe payments is prepared each time a distribution to partners is scheduled. These schedules support an installment liquidation statement, which summarizes changes in real account balances as the liquidation proceeds. When the partners' capital balances are in the profit and loss ratio, all partners will share in a given distribution. All future distributions to partners will be allocated automatically according to their profit ratio, thus eliminating the need for another schedule of safe payments.

To illustrate the use of schedules of safe payments in conjunction with an installment liquidation, assume the following:

1. Asset, liability, loan, and capital balances are shown, in Illustration 14-4, after books for the final operational period are closed.
2. Profit and loss percentages for Partners A, B, and C are 40%, 40%, and 20%, respectively.
3. Sales of assets are as follows:

Date	Book Value	Selling Price	Gain (Loss)
February 15	$60,000	$40,000	$(20,000)
March 2	30,000	15,000	(15,000)
March 17	10,000	20,000	10,000
April 1	20,000	24,000	4,000

4. Liquidation expenses are estimated to be $10,000. Cash is to be restricted in that amount until expenses are paid.
5. Installment distributions of unrestricted cash are made on February 17, March 5, March 18, and April 2.
6. Total liquidation expenses of $8,000 are paid on March 4.

Illustration 14-4
Installment Liquidation Statement

	Cash	Noncash Assets	Liabilities	Loan from A	Capital Balances A	B	C
Beginning balances	$ 10,000	$120,000	$ 30,000	$ 5,000	$25,000	$ 55,000	$15,000
February 15, sale of assets	40,000	(60,000)			(8,000)	(8,000)	(4,000)
Balances	$ 50,000	$ 60,000	$ 30,000	$ 5,000	$17,000	$ 47,000	$11,000
Payment of liabilities	(30,000)		(30,000)				
February 17, distribution (Schedule A)	(10,000)					(10,000)	
Balances	$ 10,000	$ 60,000	$ 0	$ 5,000	$17,000	$ 37,000	$11,000
March 2, sale of assets	15,000	(30,000)			(6,000)	(6,000)	(3,000)
Payment of liquidation expenses	(8,000)				(3,200)	(3,200)	(1,600)
Balances	$ 17,000	$ 30,000	$ 0	$ 5,000	$ 7,800	$ 27,800	$ 6,400
March 5, distribution (Schedule A)	(17,000)			(800)		(15,800)	(400)
Balances	$ 0	$ 30,000	$ 0	$ 4,200	$ 7,800	$ 12,000	$ 6,000
March 17, sale of assets	20,000	(10,000)			4,000	4,000	2,000
Balances	$ 20,000	$ 20,000	$ 0	$ 4,200	$11,800	$ 16,000	$ 8,000
March 18, distribution (Schedule A)	(20,000)			(4,200)	(3,800)	(8,000)	(4,000)
Balances	$ 0	$ 20,000	$ 0	$ 0	$ 8,000	$ 8,000	$ 4,000
April 1, sale of assets	24,000	(20,000)	0	0	1,600	1,600	800
Balances	$ 24,000	$ 0	$ 0	$ 0	$ 9,600	$ 9,600	$ 4,800
Final distribution	(24,000)				(9,600)	(9,600)	(4,800)
Balances	$ 0	$ 0	$ 0	$ 0	$ 0	$ 0	$ 0

Schedule A—Schedule of Safe Payments

	A	B	C	Total
Profit and loss percentage	40%	40%	20%	100%
February 17 Distribution:				
Combined capital and loan balances before distribution	$ 22,000	$ 47,000	$ 11,000	$ 80,000
Estimated liquidation expenses	(4,000)	(4,000)	(2,000)	(10,000)
Balances	$ 18,000	$ 43,000	$ 9,000	$ 70,000
Maximum loss possible	(24,000)	(24,000)	(12,000)	(60,000)
Balances	$ (6,000)	$ 19,000	$ (3,000)	$ 10,000
Allocation of debit capital balances	6,000	(9,000)	3,000	0
Safe payment	$ 0	$ 10,000	$ 0	$ 10,000
March 5 Distribution:				
Combined capital and loan balances before distribution	$ 12,800	$ 27,800	$ 6,400	$ 47,000
Maximum loss possible	(12,000)	(12,000)	(6,000)	(30,000)
Safe payments	$ 800	$ 15,800	$ 400	$ 17,000
March 18 Distribution (schedule not required):				
Combined capital and loan balances before distribution	$ 16,000	$ 16,000	$ 8,000	$ 40,000
Maximum loss possible	(8,000)	(8,000)	(4,000)	(20,000)
Safe payments	$ 8,000	$ 8,000	$ 4,000	$ 20,000

Illustration 14-4 is based on these facts and demonstrates the following concepts:

1. Gains and losses on realization are allocated according to the partners' profit and loss ratio.
2. Unsold noncash assets are assumed to be worthless for purposes of determining the safe payments to partners.
3. Loan balances are combined with capital balances according to the right-of-offset doctrine. This offset can result in partners receiving distributions of capital before other partners' loan accounts have been paid (as in the February 17 distribution in Illustration 14-4). However, such distributions may be placed in escrow until it is certain that debit balances will not develop in these partners' capital accounts.
4. Distributions are applied to a partner's loan balance before they are applied to the partner's capital balance.
5. Typically, the doctrine of marshaling of assets is ignored until all assets have been realized, at which time debit balances in partners' capital accounts may be satisfied through contributions of personal assets.
6. A schedule of safe payments is an iterative process that will cease when the schedule indicates that a given distribution will be shared among all partners. Further distributions will be allocated among the partners according to their profit and loss ratio. For example, when the March 5 distribution in Schedule A indicates that all partners will receive a portion of the distribution, the distribution on March 18 would be made in the profit and loss ratio, with results identical to those that would be indicated by continuing the schedule of safe payments:

Partner	(1) Total Distribution to All Partners	(2) Partners' Profit and Loss Percentage	(1) × (2) Amount to Be Distributed	Amount to Be Distributed per Schedule of Safe Payments
A	$20,000	40%	$ 8,000	$ 8,000
B	20,000	40	8,000	8,000
C	20,000	20	4,000	4,000
			$20,000	$20,000

7. The partner with the greatest ability to absorb anticipated losses (i.e., to preserve a credit capital balance after allocating anticipated losses) will be the first to receive a safe payment.

Predistribution Plan. Schedules of safe payments provide a means of guaranteeing the propriety of installment distributions to partners, especially in complex situations. However, a predistribution plan provides a less tedious means of determining distributions to partners. The predistribution plan is prepared in advance of actual distributions and provides the user with information regarding the order and amount of all future distributions. As was the case with schedules of safe payments, the predistribution plan (a) combines partners' loan balances with their capital balances, (b) anticipates all possible liabilities, losses on realization, and liquidation expenses, and (c) recognizes that the partner with the greatest ability to absorb anticipated losses will be the first partner to receive safe payments.

To prepare the predistribution plan, all anticipated but unrecorded liabilities and liquidation expenses are allocated to the various partners' capital balances according to their profit and loss ratio. The resulting capital balances then are evaluated to determine the maximum loss from realization that could be absorbed by the partners before a debit balance is created in each of their capital accounts. As suggested by the schedule of safe payments, the partner who maintains a credit capital balance after assuming that all noncash assets are worthless is the partner with the greatest ability to absorb realization losses. Therefore, that partner will be the first to receive an actual distribution of assets.

The maximum loss a partner could absorb *(maximum loss absorbable)*, before a debit balance in the partner's capital account is created, is determined by the following calculation:

$$\text{Maximum Loss Absorbable (MLA)} = \frac{\text{Partner's Capital Balance}}{\text{Partner's Profit and Loss Percentage}}$$

Since the partner with the largest MLA will be the first to receive an actual distribution, the MLAs are used to indicate the order in which partners will receive distributions. However, it should be noted that the MLAs do not indicate the amounts of the distributions. To illustrate, assume a partnership consists of three partners (A, B, and C) who have capital balances, before the realization of noncash assets, of $70,000, $60,000, and $40,000, respectively, and profit and loss percentages of 35%, 25%, and 40%, respectively. The maximum losses absorbable by Partners A, B, and C are determined as follows:

Partner	(1) Capital Balance	(2) Profit and Loss Percentage	(1) ÷ (2) Maximum Loss Absorbable	Rank
A	$70,000	35%	$200,000	Second
B	60,000	25	240,000	First
C	40,000	40	100,000	Third

If all partners had identical MLAs, all partners would share in any given distribution. Therefore, the amount of any distribution to be paid to a particular partner can be determined by calculating the distributions needed ultimately to give all partners the same MLA. In the present example, Partner B should receive distributions first, until his/her MLA is equal to the next highest MLA of $200,000. If B's capital balance was reduced to $50,000 (next highest MLA multiplied by the partner's profit and loss percentage, $200,000 × 25%) as the result of an actual distribution of $10,000, B's new MLA would be equal to A's original MLA as follows:

Partner	(1) Capital Balance	(2) Profit and Loss Percentage	(1) ÷ (2) Maximum Loss Absorbable
A	$70,000	35%	$200,000
B	50,000	25	200,000
C	40,000	40	100,000

Therefore, the first $10,000, or any portion thereof, that is available for distribution to partners should be paid entirely to Partner B.

Partners A and B should now receive distributions until their MLAs of $200,000 are reduced to the next highest MLA of $100,000, traceable to Partner C. If A's capital balance was reduced to $35,000 ($100,000 × 35%) and B's capital balance was reduced to $25,000 ($100,000 × 25%) as the result of actual distributions of $35,000 and $25,000, respectively, to these partners, all partners would then have equivalent MLAs. Thus, the predistribution plan suggests that the next $60,000 ($35,000 + $25,000), or any portion thereof, that is available for distribution to partners should be paid to Partners A and B according to the profit ratio of 35:25 and all further distributions should be divided among all partners according to their respective profit ratio.

The process of preparing the predistribution plan is summarized as follows:

1. Calculate each partner's MLA.
2. Rank partners in descending order according to the amounts of their MLAs.
3. Determine what amount must be paid to the partner ranked first to achieve equality between the MLAs of that partner and the second-ranked partner. This amount represents the safe payment that can be paid to the first-ranked partner.
4. Determine what amount must be paid in total to those partners having equivalent MLAs so that their new MLAs would be equal to those of the next-highest-ranked partner.

This amount would be divided among the partners receiving the distribution according to the relationship that their profit percentages have to each other.

5. Continue step (4) until all partners have equivalent MLAs.
6. When all partners have equal MLAs, distributions would be allocated according to the partners' profit ratio.

To demonstrate this entire process, the following facts are used as the basis for the predistribution plan in Illustration 14-5.

	Partners		
	A	B	C
Profit and loss percentage	30%	50%	20%
Combined capital and loan balance.	$33,000	$45,000	$14,000
Total liabilities of the partnership equal $20,000.			
Total liquidation expenses are expected to be $10,000.			

To relate the predistribution plan in Illustration 14-5 to an actual distribution, assume that distributions are made as follows:

Date	Amount	Purpose
February 15	$20,000	Pay liabilities
March 1	5,000	Pay partners
March 15	8,000	Pay liquidation expenses
March 27	9,000	Pay partners
April 4	30,000	Pay partners

Rather than constructing numerous schedules of safe payments to determine the recipients of these distributions, the predistribution plan indicates the following distribution:

Date	Amount	Liabilities	Liquidation Expenses	A	B	C	Level per Plan (Illustration 14-5)
February 15	$20,000	$20,000					I
March 1	5,000			$ 5,000			III
March 15	8,000		$8,000				II
March 27	9,000			1,000			III
				3,000	$ 5,000		IV
April 4	30,000			3,000	5,000		IV
				6,600	11,000	$4,400	V
	$72,000	$20,000	$8,000	$18,600	$21,000	$4,400	

Several aspects of this distribution need to be emphasized. First, notice that actual payments to partners precede the payment of the liquidation expenses. This action is acceptable because the computations in Illustration 14-5 had already allowed for liquidation expenses of $10,000. However, if liquidation expenses exceed the estimated amount of $10,000, previous payments to partners could prove to be premature and, ultimately, could require repayments from partners to the partnership. Another important feature is that all payments required by a specific level of the plan shown in Illustration 14-5 must be satisfied before another level of the plan is entered. Finally, when a particular distribution is divided among several partners, the amount is allocated to the sharing partners according to their respective proportionate profit ratios.

Illustration 14-5
Predistribution Plan
Computation of Payments to Partners

		Capital Balances			Maximum Loss Absorbable		
		A	B	C	A	B	C
(1)	Profit and loss percentage	30%	50%	20%			
	Capital and loan balance	$33,000	$ 45,000	$14,000			
	Allocate expected liquidation expenses	(3,000)	(5,000)	(2,000)			
(2)	Balances	$30,000	$ 40,000	$12,000			
	Maximum loss absorbable (MLA) [(2) ÷ (1)]				$100,000	$ 80,000	$60,000
(3)	Amount needed to reduce highest-ranked MLA to next-highest-ranked MLA				(20,000)		
	New MLAs				$ 80,000	$ 80,000	$60,000
(4)	Reduction in capital (payment) needed to achieve reduction in MLA [(3) × (1)]	(6,000)					
(5)	New capital balance [(2) − (4)]	$24,000	$ 40,000	$12,000			
(6)	Amount needed to reduce highest-ranked MLAs to next-highest-ranked MLA				(20,000)	(20,000)	
	New MLAs				$ 60,000	$ 60,000	$60,000
(7)	Reduction in capital (payment) needed to achieve reduction in MLA [(6) × (1)]	(6,000)	(10,000)				
(8)	New capital balance [(5) − (7)]	$18,000	$ 30,000	$12,000			

When MLAs are equal, future distributions are allocated to all partners according to their profit and loss percentages.

		Payable to				
Level	Amount	Liabilities	Estimated Liquidation Expenses	A	B	C
I	First $20,000	$20,000				
II	Next $10,000		$10,000			
III	Next $6,000			100%		
IV	Next $16,000			37.5% (3/8)	62.5% (5/8)	
V	Any additional payments			30%	50%	20%

REFLECTION

- Upon liquidation of a partnership, the distribution of available assets must follow a prescribed order. The claims of outside creditors should always be satisfied before those of individual partners.
- The right-of-offset doctrine is important in a liquidation in order to make sure that partners with the potential for debit capital balances do not receive premature distributions of assets.
- The doctrine of marshaling of assets comes into play when either a partnership is insolvent and/or individual partners are personally insolvent.
- The actual liquidation of a partnership may follow several approaches, including a lump-sum liquidation or an installment liquidation supported by a schedule of safe payments or a predistribution plan. In all cases, the goal is to convert assets into a distributable form, respect the rights of those with claims against the partnership, and not make premature distributions.

UNDERSTANDING THE ISSUES

1. If consideration paid to acquire an interest in a partnership is based on the fair value of the net assets, why doesn't the bonus method recognize all of the suggested values?
2. If an individual were to acquire an interest in a partnership from the partnership entity itself, how would one calculate the suggested value of the acquired interest?
3. The liquidation of a partnership can be a complex and time-consuming process. What basic guidelines should be followed in order to ensure that the process is proper?
4. What does a partner's maximum loss absorbable (MLA) suggest in terms of the order in which liquidating distributions will be made available to partners?

EXERCISES

Exercise 1 *(LO 2, 3, 4)* **Entry of a new partner under the bonus and goodwill methods.** Pearson and Murphy have partner capital balances, at book value, of $45,000 and $65,000 as of December 31, 20X5. Pearson is allocated 60% of profits or losses, and Murphy is allocated the balance. The partners believe that tangible net assets have a market value in excess of book value in the amount of $30,000 net. The $30,000 is allocated as follows:

	Book Value	Market Value
Accounts receivable	$120,000	$102,000
Inventory	200,000	258,000
Warranty obligations	20,000	30,000

They are considering admitting Warner to the partnership in exchange for total consideration of $84,000 cash. In exchange for the consideration, Warner will receive a 30% interest in capital and a 35% interest in profits.

1. Prepare the entries associated with the admission of Warner to the partnership.
2. If the goodwill suggested by the admission of Warner proved to be worthless, determine by how much Warner would be harmed.

Exercise 2 *(LO 2, 3)* **Entries for addition of new partner, bonus, goodwill.** Baxter and Murphy are partners whose profit and loss percentages are 60% and 40%, respectively. The book values of the partners' capital balances are $78,000 and $52,000 for Baxter and Murphy, respectively. The partners have agreed to admit Tuttle as a partner in exchange for a contribution to the partnership of cash, equipment, and land with fair values of $25,000, $30,000, and $35,000, respectively. In exchange for her investment, Tuttle will receive a 30% interest in capital and a 20% interest in profits and losses. Baxter and Murphy have agreed to revise their profit and loss percentages to 48% and 32%, respectively. An analysis of existing assets held by the original partnership indicates the following book values and current values:

	Book Value	Current Value
Accounts receivable	$120,000	$110,000
Inventory	200,000	240,000
Equipment	354,000	374,000

Prepare the entries to record the admission of Tuttle under both the bonus and goodwill methods.

Exercise 3 *(LO 4)* **Comparison of the bonus and goodwill methods.** Your client Kennedy is considering an investment in an existing partnership and is interested in knowing how her investment will be accounted for. You have explained to your client that an investment in a partnership may be accounted for by either the bonus method or the goodwill method. Your client has posed the following questions regarding these methods:

1. How do the methods differ with respect to how asset write-downs are accounted for?
2. How is goodwill traceable to the original partnership accounted for under the bonus method?
3. How is it possible that a new partner's initial capital balance may be more than the value of the net assets that the partner contributed to the partnership?
4. Which method would be most appropriate if the allocation of profits is based in part on interest on capital balances?
5. Assume that the goodwill method was used to recognize appreciated assets traceable to the original partners. If the value of these assets were erroneously overstated and subsequently restated, how would the end result differ from that which would have existed had the bonus method been used?

Provide a response to your client's questions.

Exercise 4 *(LO 2, 3, 5)* **Acquisition of a partnership interest from a partner versus the partnership.** Rainbow Properties is a partnership consisting of three partners: Ross, Gilmore, and Bates. The partnership's primary business is the acquisition and development of land into homesites. Projects require a significant amount of capital, which often is borrowed from area banks. The three partners share profits and losses equally and have the following capital balances: $160,000 for Ross, $120,000 for Gilmore, and $200,000 for Bates. Recently, Ross was approached to sell her personal interest in the partnership to William Lane for $210,000.

1. What advantages would there be to the partnership if Lane acquired an interest directly from the partnership rather than directly from Ross?
2. What amount would Lane have to contribute to the partnership in order to have the same interest in capital as would have been acquired had Lane purchased an interest directly from Ross?
3. Assume Lane purchased a one-fourth interest in the partnership by contributing $210,000 to the partnership. Prepare the entry to record the contribution noting that existing land has a fair value of $330,000 and a book value of $300,000 and goodwill is recognized.

Exercise 5 *(LO 3, 6)* **Withdrawal and admission of a partner using the goodwill method.** As of December 31, 20X5, Stegnitz, Hipki, and Ergos have capital balances of $70,000, $50,000, and $80,000, respectively. Profits and losses are shared equally among the partners. During the fourth quarter of 20X5, Ergos decided to withdraw from the partnership effective at the end of the year. The partnership agreed to distribute $105,000 to Ergos in exchange for his partnership interest. The amount paid to Ergos reflects the fact that accounts receivable are overstated by $21,000 and that unrecorded goodwill exists. Effective at the beginning of 20X6, Olsen will join the partnership with a 20% interest in capital and profits. In exchange for admission, Olsen will contribute $30,000 of cash plus intangibles.

Prepare the entries to record the withdrawal of Ergos and the admission of Olsen. The goodwill method is to be used to fully account for all goodwill suggested by the above transactions.

Exercise 6 *(LO 7)* **Liquidation, doctrine of right of offset.** The following information relates to Pfarr and Williams, who are partners in a business being liquidated:

	Pfarr	Williams
Partnership balances:		
Loan payable—Williams		$ 5,000
Capital balance (deficit)	$20,000	(14,000)
Personal assets (including partnership loan payable)	30,000	22,000
Personal liabilities	15,000	21,000
Profit and loss percentage	70%	30%

1. After applying the right-of-offset doctrine, indicate how each partner's personal assets would be distributed, assuming the Uniform Partnership Act is applicable.
2. Determine the effect on the calculations in item (1) if the right-of-offset doctrine were ignored.
3. After applying the right-of-offset doctrine, indicate how each partner's personal assets would be distributed assuming common law is applicable.

Exercise 7 *(LO 9)* **Adjustment of capital balances and lump-sum liquidation.** Palmyra Tooling is a partnership owned by Crawford, Meyer, and Jensen. Capital balances (deficits) and profit/loss percentages are as follows:

	Crawford	Meyer	Jensen
Capital balances at December 31, 20X5	$55,000	$115,000	$60,000
Profit and loss percentage	50%	30%	20%

The partnership agreement grants each of the partners a single vote and requires a majority vote to approve certain partnership actions including the liquidation of the partnership. Crawford and Meyer, as founders of Palmyra Tooling, have seen the company experience significant growth and then lose significant market share in the past five years due to local and foreign competition. Given the near term prospects of continuing difficulties and the further erosion of their capital balances, Crawford and Meyer have voted to liquidate the business. As of December 31, 20X5, book values differ from net realizable values as follows (all other assets/liabilities can be disposed of at book value):

	Book Value	Net Realizable Value
Accounts receivable	$130,000	$ 90,000
Inventory	35,000	15,000
Equipment (net)	725,000	645,000

Unlike his partners, Jensen feels that the company can restructure itself and that liquidation is not appropriate. Jensen is unable to persuade his partners and has offered to personally acquire Crawford's and Meyer's interests for $10,000 and $70,000, respectively. Unsure about the net personal assets of the individual partners, Meyer seeks your advice regarding whether it should accept Jensen's offer.

How would you advise Meyer?

Exercise 8 *(LO 1, 9)* **Admission of a new partner with determination of contribute vs. liquidation.** Arnold (A), Bower (B), and Chambers (C) are partners in a small manufacturing firm whose net assets are as follows:

	Book Value	Fair Value		Book Value	Fair Value
Current assets	$285,000	$210,000	Loan payable to Bower	$ 40,000	$ 40,000
Equipment (net of depreciation)	320,000	225,000	Other liabilities	430,000	434,000
			Arnold, capital	50,000	
Vacant land	60,000	85,000	Bower, capital	100,000	
Other assets	15,000	10,000	Chambers, capital	60,000	
Total assets	$680,000	$530,000	Total liabilities	$680,000	$474,000

The partnership agreement calls for the allocation of profits and losses as follows:

1. Salaries to A, B, and C of $30,000, $30,000, and $40,000, respectively.
2. Bonus to A of 10% of net income after the bonus.
3. Remaining amounts are allocated according to profit/loss percentages of 50%, 20%, and 30% for A, B, and C, respectively.

Unfortunately, the business finds itself in difficult times: annual profits remain flat at approximately $132,000, additional capital is needed to finance equipment which is necessary to stay competitive, and all of the partners realize that they could make more money working for someone else, with a lot fewer headaches.

Chambers has identified Dawson (D) as an individual who might be willing to acquire an interest in the partnership. Dawson is proposing to acquire a 30% interest in the capital of the partnership and a revised partnership agreement which calls for the allocation of profits as follows:

1. Salaries to A, B, C, and D of $30,000, $30,000, $40,000, and $30,000, respectively.
2. Bonus to D of $20,000 if net income exceeds $250,000.
3. Remaining amounts are allocated according to profit/loss percentages of 30%, 10%, 30%, and 30% for A, B, C, and D, respectively.

An alternative to admitting a new partner is to liquidate the partnership. Net personal assets of the partners are as follows:

	Arnold	Bower	Chambers
Personal assets	$240,000	$530,000	$300,000
Personal liabilities	228,000	150,000	200,000

Assuming that you are Bower's personal CPA, you have been asked to provide your client with your opinions regarding the alternatives facing the partnership.

1. Bower does not believe it would be worth it to him to admit a new partner unless his allocation of income increased by at least $10,000 over that which existed under the original partnership agreement. What would the average annual profit of the new partnership have to be in order for Bower to accept the idea of admitting a new partner?
2. Given the net assets of the original partnership, what is the suggested purchase price that Dawson should pay for a 30% interest in the partnership?

3. Assume that the original partnership was liquidated and Bower received a business vehicle, with a fair value of $15,000 and a net book value of $20,000, as part of his liquidation proceeds. How much additional cash would Bower receive if the partnership were liquidated?

Exercise 9 *(LO 8, 9)* **Installment liquidation with insolvent partners, the doctrine of marshaling of assets.** Coleman, Moore, and Ramsey are partners in a business being liquidated. The partnership has cash of $8,000, noncash assets with a book value of $96,000, and liabilities of $63,000. The following information relates to the individual partners as of June 1, 20X7.

	Coleman	Moore	Ramsey
Loan payable to partners		$ 5,000	
Capital balance (deficit)	$47,000	(14,000)	$ 3,000
Personal assets	10,000	15,000	25,000
Personal liabilities	5,000	6,000	15,000
Profit and loss percentage	60%	20%	20%

On June 15, 20X7, assets with a book value of $30,000 were sold for $20,000 cash. The proceeds were used to pay off liabilities of the partnership. During the balance of June, no additional assets were liquidated, and outside creditors began to pressure the partnership for payment. On July 1, the partners agreed to contribute personal assets, to whatever extent possible, in order to eliminate their respective capital deficits. Shortly thereafter, assets with a book value of $20,000 and a fair value of $23,000 were distributed to Coleman.

Assuming additional noncash assets with a book value of $40,000 are sold in July for $54,000, determine how available cash would be distributed.

Exercise 10 *(LO 10)* **Installment liquidation, schedule of safe payments.** A real estate partnership had the following condensed balance sheet prior to liquidation:

Assets		Liabilities and Capital	
Cash	$ 12,000	Liabilities (to outsiders)	$ 35,000
Noncash assets	180,000	Loan payable to A	15,000
		A, capital (50%)	45,000
		B, capital (30%)	70,000
		C, capital (20%)	27,000
Total assets	$192,000	Total liabilities and capital	$192,000

The percentages in parentheses after the partners' capital balances represent their respective interests in profits and losses. The following situations are independent of each other unless otherwise stated:

1. If assets with a book value of $30,000 were sold for $20,000, how much of the available cash could be distributed to Partner A?
2. If assets with a book value of $60,000 were sold for $70,000, how much of the available cash could be distributed to Partner A?
3. Assume assets with a book value of $70,000 were sold for $50,000 and that all available cash was distributed. For what amount would the remaining assets have to be sold in order for Partner B to receive a *total* of $79,000 cash from all liquidation activities?

Exercise 11 *(LO 10)* **Predistribution plan, possible liquidation.** Delaney, Gray, and Sullivan are considering the liquidation of their partnership, which has assets of $110,000 and liabilities, including a $10,000 loan from Sullivan, of $30,000. Delaney and Gray each have capital balances of $33,000. Profits and losses are shared 30%, 30%, and 40% for Delaney, Gray, and Sullivan, respectively.

Prepare a predistribution plan to govern the possible liquidation, assuming liquidation expenses of $10,000.

PROBLEMS

Problem 14-1 *(LO 2, 3, 5, 6)* **Admission and departure of partners under the goodwill method.** Carlton, Weber, and Stansbury share profits equally and have capital balances of $120,000, $70,000, and $80,000, respectively, as of December 31, 20X4. Effective January 1, 20X5, Stansbury has transferred his interest in the partnership to Laidlaw for total consideration of $100,000. As part of agreeing to admit Laidlaw to the partnership, the profit- and loss-sharing agreement was modified as follows:

1. Carlton, Weber, and Laidlaw would receive annual salaries of $120,000, $90,000, and $90,000, respectively, to be withdrawn in equal amounts at the end of each calendar quarter.
2. A bonus of 20% of net income after the bonus will be allocated between Weber and Laidlaw in the ratio of 1 to 3. The bonus would be distributed at the end of the first quarter subsequent to year-end.
3. Profit and loss percentages of 40%, 30%, and 30%, respectively, for Carlton, Weber, and Laidlaw.
4. If income is not sufficient or an operating loss exists, all provisions of the profit-sharing agreement are to be satisfied, and the profit and loss percentages are used to absorb any deficiency or additional losses.

The original partners were excited about the new arrangement because Laidlaw had indicated that they would be able to attract a number of customers from his previous place of employment. Weber was willing to shift some salary to a bonus status in order to capture more of the upside potential being presented by Laidlaw. As expected, over the first six months of 20X5, a number of Laidlaw's previous customers transferred their business to the partnership. However, the next 12 months were very disappointing. Not only did very few additional Laidlaw customers transfer their business, but it became clear that Laidlaw was not compatible with the other partners. Furthermore, a number of long-standing customers ceased doing business with the company due to issues with Laidlaw. Income for the year 20X5 was $300,000, and income for the first six months of 20X6 was only $120,000.

On July 1, 20X6, Carlton and Weber agreed to acquire Laidlaw's interest in the partnership. The transaction would be recorded as a purchase of Laidlaw's interest by the partnership under the bonus method. Laidlaw was paid $79,000 for their capital balance as of June 30, 20X6, and no other distributions were made to him.

After Laidlaw left the partnership, Carlton and Weber went back to sharing profits and losses equally with quarterly withdrawals of $10,000 per partner at the end of each calendar quarter. Weber agreed not to receive an additional distribution traceable to the bonus earned during the first six months of 20X6. Income in the second half of 20X6 was $73,000. However, the partners realized that they needed to expand operations if the company was to be saved. On January 1, 20X7, the partnership admitted Wilson. Wilson contributed tangible assets of $70,000 and intangibles to the partnership in exchange for a 40% interest in capital and one-third interest in profits. The admission of Wilson was recorded using the goodwill method. Carlton, Weber, and Wilson continue to share profits equally, and the partnership experienced net income of $420,000 in 20X7. Quarterly withdrawals of $30,000 were paid to each of the partners beginning in 20X7.

During the first six months of 20X8, the partnership had net income of $255,000 in spite of Carlton's reduced involvement due to health problems. On July 1, 20X8, Carlton sold his interest to the partnership for $160,000. The sale was recorded by recognizing the goodwill traceable to the entire partnership.

Prepare a schedule analyzing the changes in partners' capital accounts since December 31, 20X4. Supporting calculations should be in good form. ◄◄◄◄◄ **Required**

Problem 14-2 *(LO 1, 2, 3, 5)* **New partner, asset and capital balance determination, bonus, goodwill, tax basis.** Kravitz and Rowe are partners in an excavating business known as K & R Excavating. The partners are considering a number of options regarding the partnership, including the admission of a new partner and a potential sale of the partnership. The following information has been prepared as a basis for evaluating various alternatives:

Item	Book Value	Fair Value	Tax Basis
Cash and cash equivalents	$ 20,000	$ 20,000	$ 20,000
Accounts receivable	85,000	72,000	92,000
Inventory	42,000	30,000	50,000
Prepaid and other current assets	18,000	15,000	18,000
Property, plant, and equipment (net)	358,000	300,000	320,000
Total assets	$523,000	$437,000	$500,000
Accounts payable	$ 54,000	$ 54,000	$ 54,000
Other current liabilities	29,000	35,000	29,000
Notes/loans payable	240,000	240,000	240,000
Kravitz, capital	120,000		
Rowe, capital	80,000		
Total liabilities and capital	$523,000		

The partners currently share profits and losses 60% and 40%, respectively, for Kravitz and Rowe.

Required ▶ ▶ ▶ ▶ ▶ Given the preceding information, respond to each of the following items:

1. Given the stated fair values, if Rowe were to sell one-half of her interest in capital to someone outside the partnership, what would be a suggested asking price?
2. Given the stated fair values, if a third party were to convey assets to the partnership in exchange for a 40% interest in the partnership, what would the value of those assets have to be?
3. Assume a new partner was admitted to the partnership with a 40% interest in capital in exchange for a cash contribution of $60,000. What would Rowe's capital balance be as a result of this transaction, assuming use of the bonus method?
4. Given the facts of (3) above, what would Rowe's capital balance be, assuming use of the goodwill method?
5. Assume a new partner was admitted to the partnership with a 30% interest in capital in exchange for a contribution of $55,000 of net tangible assets. What would the new partner's capital balance be as a result of this transaction, assuming use of the bonus method?
6. Assume a new partner was admitted to the partnership with a 30% interest in capital and a 40% interest in profits in exchange for net assets with the following tax bases: Inventory, $20,000; Equipment, $120,000; and Equipment Loan, $70,000. As a result of this transaction, what would be the tax basis in the partnership for the new partner? (*Note:* This ties to the Chapter 13 appendix.)

Problem 14-3 *(LO 3)* **Determination of new partner contribution, evaluation of risks under the goodwill method.** Andrews and Block are partners in an engineering consulting company sharing profits and losses 40% and 60%, respectively, and their capital balances are $110,000 and $150,000, respectively. The recorded net assets of the company are as follows:

	Book Value	Fair Value
Working capital	$240,000	$220,000
Net property and equipment	80,000	108,000
Noncurrent liabilities	60,000	60,000

In addition to the recorded assets, the partners feel that the company has goodwill valued at $40,000 because the company enjoys a strong client base and has earnings that are consistently above industry averages.

Carver is interested in merging his environmental consulting company with Andrews and Block. Carver's net assets to be conveyed to the partnership include the following:

	Book Value	Fair Value
Working capital	$50,000	$40,000
Net equipment	60,000	50,000

In addition to the above recorded net assets, Carver feels that his business contacts and expertise will add value to the existing partnership. Carver has valued these intangibles at $20,000.

◄◄◄◄◄ **Required**

1. If Carver were to acquire a 30% interest in the new partnership, how much additional cash would Carver have to contribute to the partnership?
2. If Carver were admitted to the partnership, all partners would share equally in profits and losses. All parties are somewhat uncertain about the values placed on intangible assets. Andrews and Block favor using the goodwill method to record Carver's investment in the partnership. Calculate the amount of risk to all partners this method would entail should the intangible assets not have value.
3. Discuss how a profit and loss agreement might be used to reward a new partner for intangible assets while not recording the intangibles on the financial statements.

Problem 14-4 *(LO 2, 10)* **Exiting partners under the bonus method and liquidation.** Midway Construction was a partnership owned by Davis, Murray, and Clay with year-end 20X3 capital balances of $50,000, 80,000, and $70,000, respectively. Davis and Murray each received an annual salary of $100,000. Clay was primarily involved in sales and received a salary of $70,000 and a bonus of 20% of net income after salaries. All remaining profits were allocated equally among the partners. In the event of insufficient income or operating losses, each provision of the agreement would be satisfied to whatever extent possible given the order of salaries, interest, bonus, and percentages. Salaries are distributed at the end of each calendar quarter, and Clay's bonus is distributed at the end of the first month subsequent to year-end. Eighty percent of all other allocated income (income other than salary and bonus) is distributed to the partners at the end of the first quarter subsequent to year-end. During 20X3, the partnership had net income of $450,000 and proceeded to construct a number of spec homes during 20X4.

Unfortunately, during 20X4, interest rates increased, and the economy experienced a significant slowdown resulting in partnership income of only $300,000. In order to improve cash flows, on January 1, 20X5, Rayburn made a capital contribution to the partnership of $59,000 cash and received a 50% interest in capital. Rayburn would receive a profit allocation equal to interest on average capital of 10% and a 10% profit percentage. The previous partners' profit and loss agreement was modified to provide for salaries at one-half of previous levels, none of which were to be distributed, and profit percentages of 30% each. All other aspects of the previous profit-sharing agreement remained in effect. During the year 20X5, conditions worsened, and the partnership reported income of $142,000. At year-end 20X5, Davis sold its capital interest to the partnership in exchange for $49,400 and received no further distributions. At the beginning of 20X6, Murray loaned the partnership $50,000 with the necessary loan documents providing for interest at the rate of 6%. The profit-sharing agreement for 20X6 was completely changed to simply provide for interest on capital to Rayburn as previously set forth and all remaining profits to be allocated 40%, 40%, and 20% for Murray, Clay, and Rayburn, respectively. The only withdrawal to take place during 20X6 was the distribution of Clay's 20X5 bonus.

The partnership could no longer sustain the economic downturn, and the decision was made to liquidate the partnership after having reported net income of $110,000 during the first six months of 20X6. At the beginning of the liquidation process, the partnership had $15,000 in cash and liabilities, excluding loans from partners, of $84,000. Noncash assets of the partnership were liquidated as follows:

1. On August 1, 20X6, assets with a book value of $220,000 were sold for $180,000.

2. On September 1, 20X6, assets with a book value of $70,000 were sold for $82,000.

Prior to any further liquidation of assets, all available cash other than $10,000 held for future expenses was to be distributed to the partners on September 15, 20X6.

Required ▶ ▶ ▶ ▶ ▶

1. Prepare a schedule analyzing the partners' capital prior to liquidation of the partnership. Assume use of the bonus method to record all changes in the ownership structure of the partnership.
2. Prepare a schedule of cash payments on September 15, 20X6, of the liquidation, showing how the available cash was distributed. Supporting calculations should be in good form.

Problem 14-5 *(LO 2, 3, 6)* **Entries, new partner, old partner, alternative methods.** Buckner and Pressey are partners in a dry-cleaning business in which profits and losses are shared equally. Buckner and Pressey have capital balances of $40,000 and $60,000, respectively.

Required ▶ ▶ ▶ ▶ ▶

For each of the six situations presented, prepare the necessary journal entries for the partnership records.

	Situations		
	(1)	(2)	(3)
Admission of new partner:			
Entering partner	Nelson	Nelson	Nelson
Purchase price	$60,000	$30,000	$40,000
Interest in capital acquired	30%	20%	30%
Paid to	Partnership	Partnership	Pressey
Method used	Bonus	Goodwill	N/A

	Situations		
	(4)	(5)	(6)
Withdrawal of previous partner:			
Exiting partner	Buckner	Buckner	Buckner
Selling price	$48,000	$25,000	$39,000
Interest in capital sold	40%	20%	30%
Paid by	Partnership	Partnership	Partnership
Method used	Bonus	Goodwill traceable to exiting partner	Goodwill traceable to all partners

template cd

Problem 14-6 *(LO 10)* **Liquidation, predistribution schedule, schedule of safe payments.** Part I: The partnership of Aikens, Barnes, and Clinton is winding up its affairs. The following information has been gathered:

a. The trial balance of the partnership at June 30, 20X7, is as follows:

	Debit	Credit
Cash	6,000	
Accounts Receivable	22,000	
Inventory	14,000	
Property, Plant, and Equipment (net)	99,000	
Aikens, Loan	12,000	
Clinton, Loan	7,500	
Accounts Payable		17,000

Aikens, Capital		67,000
Barnes, Capital		45,000
Clinton, Capital		31,500
Total	160,500	160,500

b. The partners share profits and losses as follows: Aikens, 50%; Barnes, 30%; and Clinton, 20%.
c. The partners are considering an offer of $100,000 for the accounts receivable, inventory, and plant assets as of June 30. The $100,000 would be paid to the partners in installments, but the number and amounts are to be negotiated.

◄◄◄◄◄ **Required**

Prepare a predistribution plan schedule as of June 30, 20X7, showing how the $100,000 would be distributed as it becomes available.

Part II: Assume the same facts as in Part I, except that the partners have decided to liquidate their partnership instead of accepting the offer of $100,000. Cash is distributed to the partners at the end of each month. A summary of liquidation transactions follows:

July:

$16,500—collected on accounts receivable; balance is uncollectible.
$10,000—received from sale of entire inventory.
$1,000—liquidation expenses paid.
$8,000—cash retained in the business at the end of month.

August:

$1,500—liquidation expenses paid. Clinton's capital was reduced when Clinton accepted a piece of special equipment that had a book value of $4,000. The partners agreed that a value of $10,000 should be placed on the machine for liquidation purposes.
$2,500—cash retained in the business at the end of the month.

September:

$75,000—received on sale of remaining plant assets.
$1,000—liquidation expenses paid.
No cash was retained in the business.

◄◄◄◄◄ **Required**

Prepare a schedule of cash payments as of September 30, 20X7, showing how the cash actually was distributed. Supporting calculations should be in good form.

(AICPA adapted)

Problem 14-7 *(LO 10)* **Predistribution plan.** Baker, Tubbs, and Knapp have decided to liquidate their partnership due to competitive pressures. At this time, the partnership has cash of $21,000, noncash assets of $140,000, and liabilities of $130,000. The partners' capital balances, loan balances, and profit/loss percentages are as follows:

	Baker	Tubbs	Knapp
Capital balances	$12,000		$10,000
Loan balances	2,000	$3,000	4,000
Profit and loss percentage	60%	20%	20%

Liquidation expenses are estimated to be $4,000.

◄◄◄◄◄ **Required**

1. Prepare a predistribution plan that may be used to determine how liquidation proceeds would be distributed to the partners.
2. Given the predistribution plan, indicate the order in which the following alternative distributions would be allocated: Distribution A: Cash of $175,000. Distribution B: Cash of

$156,500 and equipment with a value of $17,000 given to Baker.

3. Assume that the noncash assets of the partnership are liquidated as follows:

	Book Value	Proceeds
First sale.	$40,000	$60,000
Second sale	70,000	82,000
Third sale	30,000	12,000

Determine how the cash available after each sale would be distributed using an installment liquidation schedule.

4. Compare the result of required part (2) Distribution A to required part (3), and comment on the comparison.

Problem 14-8 *(LO 10)* **Liquidation.** In light of major downturns in the economy, Barker Manufacturing experienced declining profits and defaults on several loans. In a recent meeting, the three partners in the business agreed to continue operations another six months if the partners would make personal loans to the company. These loans were made; yet no significant favorable changes occurred, and the partners agreed to liquidate the partnership. The trial balance prior to liquidation is as follows:

	Debit	Credit
Cash		2,000
Other Assets	141,000	
Loans from Barker		50,000
Loans from Dunton.		24,000
Other Liabilities		82,000
Capital, Barker		16,000
Capital, Dunton.	18,000	
Capital, Jacoby	15,000	
Total.	174,000	174,000

Following the decision to liquidate, the partners agreed that available funds will be distributed at the end of each month. Furthermore, if necessary, the partners will contribute available personal assets to satisfy capital deficits. However, they agreed that the right of offset, with respect to partnership loans, would be observed.

During the first month of liquidation, assets with a book value of $32,000 were sold for $26,000. Actual liquidation expenses of $4,000 occurred, and future liquidation expenses of $3,000 were estimated. Personal assets and liabilities were as follows:

	Barker	Dunton	Jacoby
Personal assets (including loans to partnership)	$160,000	$48,000	$50,000
Personal liabilities	100,000	30,000	21,000

During the second month of liquidation, assets with a book value of $68,000 were sold for $30,000. Actual liquidation expenses of $5,000 were incurred during the month, and no future liquidation expenses were anticipated. Personal assets and liabilities were as follows:

	Barker	Dunton	Jacoby
Personal assets (including loans to partnership)	$130,000	$40,000	$28,000
Personal liabilities	110,000	20,000	24,000

During the third and final month of liquidation, the balance of the other assets was sold for $11,000. Personal assets and liabilities were as follows:

	Barker	Dunton	Jacoby
Personal assets (including loans to partnership)	$108,000	$36,000	$20,000
Personal liabilities	90,000	18,000	26,000

Required

Assume the profit and loss percentages are 50%, 30%, and 20% for Barker, Dunton, and Jacoby, respectively. Prepare a schedule that details monthly cash distributions for the liquidation.

Problem 14-9 *(LO 10)* **Installment liquidation, premature distributions, insolvent partners.** Green Acres Enterprises is a partnership that constructed and sold assisted living facilities for the elderly. The firm has been in existence for seven years, and the partners have decided that the market for such facilities has become saturated and that the partnership should be liquidated. The partners Dvorak, Kelsen, and Morgan share profits and losses 30%, 30%, and 40%, respectively. The following information, presented in chronological order, is relevant to the liquidation of the partnership.

template cd

1. The following balances existed prior to the commencement of the liquidation:

Assets		Liabilities and Capital	
Cash	$ 15,000	Accounts payable	$ 80,000
Accounts receivable	60,000	Note payable—mortgage	450,000
Inventory	90,000	Note payable—Kelsen	40,000
Prepaid assets	12,000	Contingent liability	83,000
Furniture and fixtures (net)	150,000	Dvorak, capital	20,000
Office equipment (net)	30,000	Kelsen, capital	47,000
Vehicles (net)	30,000	Morgan, capital	17,000
Assisted living home (net)	350,000		
Total assets	$737,000	Total liabilities and capital	$737,000

2. Accounts receivable with a book value of $40,000 were collected in the amount of $30,000. The inventory was sold for $60,000.
3. All the prepaid amounts were refunded to the company with the exception of $2,000 that was forfeited.
4. The partners agreed that any additional available cash should be used to pay off the accounts payable rather than the contingent liability.
5. Office equipment with a book value of $15,000 and a fair value of $12,000 was distributed to Morgan. A vehicle with a book value of $10,000 and a fair value of $8,000 was distributed to Dvorak.
6. The balance of the office equipment and vehicles were sold for 80% of their book value.
7. The contingent liability was settled for $43,000.
8. The partners agreed that 90% of any available cash should be distributed to the partners.
9. The furniture and fixtures were consigned to a broker who sold them for net proceeds of $120,000.
10. The balance of the accounts receivable had been turned over to a collection agency, and the partnership received $5,000 upon final settlement of all accounts.

11. The assisted living home proved difficult to dispose of and was finally sold for $400,000. Furthermore, legal fees and brokers' commissions totaling $25,000 were incurred in connection with the sale. The note payable—mortgage was paid off in full in addition to previously unrecorded interest in the amount of $5,000.
12. Prior to distributing the remaining cash, partners with deficit balances were required to make the necessary contribution from net personal assets. At that time, the net assets (liabilities) of the partners were as follows: Dvorak, ($8,000); Kelsen, $140,000; and Morgan, $10,000.
13. All available cash was distributed to the partners.

Required ▶ ▶ ▶ ▶ ▶

1. Prepare a liquidation schedule for the above partnership.
2. Determine whether the distributions of office equipment and vehicles to the individual partners were, in fact, "safe" distributions.
3. What is the nature of the claim solvent partners have against a partner who is not able to satisfy a deficit capital balance?

Problem 14-10 *(LO 10)* **Liquidate now or later.** Skeeba, Tank, and King are considering whether or not to liquidate their partnership due to worsening economic conditions. As of December 31, 20X4, the partnership had total assets and liabilities (excluding loans from partners) of $360,000 and $110,000, respectively. The following relates to the partners:

	Skeeba	Tank	King
Capital balance	$80,000	$90,000	$40,000
Loan to partner balance	$20,000		$20,000
Profit and loss percentage	40%	30%	30%

In 20X5, it is anticipated that the partnership could recognize $30,000 of normal operating income. Furthermore, if the partners were willing to contribute another $30,000, it appears that an additional $40,000 of nonrecurring income could be recognized. However, it is unlikely that the partnership could continue to operate beyond 20X5 without a significant change in its capital structure and the economic climate.

Each of the partners has been asked to contribute $10,000 of additional capital in order to continue operations into 20X5. However, King is not sure that this is a good decision. Alternatively, Tank has offered to purchase King's interest in the partnership as of year-end 20X4 for $60,000. It is also possible that King could convince the partnership to liquidate as of year-end 20X4. King is seriously considering selling its interest to Tank. However, it needs to consider whether liquidation at year-end 20X4 or 20X5 would be more advantageous.

Required ▶ ▶ ▶ ▶ ▶

Assuming you have been retained by King to evaluate its alternatives, prepare an analysis that would be useful to its decision process. Assume that net assets, excluding partnership loans, could be liquidated for an amount equal to 80% and 85% of book value at the end of 20X4 and 20X5, respectively.

Problem 14-11 *(LO 6, 10)* **Decision to buy out other partners or to liquidate.** Partners Schmidt, Janis, and Glomski operate a fuel oil business serving both residential and commercial customers. Due to existing soil contamination and new federal environmental laws, the operation is being required to spend approximately $90,000 to correct present conditions and acquire new equipment. Rather than incur this expense, the partners are considering liquidating the company.

A summary of the net assets of the operation is as follows:

Net Assets	Book Value	Current Value
Cash	$ 25,000	$ 25,000
Receivables and prepaids	42,000	35,000
Inventory	27,000	22,000
Equipment	125,000	75,000

Real estate	210,000	140,000
Accounts payable	(40,000)	(40,000)
Mortgage payable	(54,000)	(54,000)
Note payable to previous partner	(100,000)	(90,000)
Equipment note	(80,000)	(80,000)
Total	$ 155,000	$ 33,000

It is estimated that, in order to realize the above current values, approximately $10,000 in expenses will have to be incurred for brokerage fees, commissions, and other liquidation costs.

Partnership and personal information relating to the partners is as follows:

	Schmidt	Janis	Glomski
Partnership capital balance	$ 85,000	$ 47,000	$ 23,000
Partnership profit and loss percentage	30%	35%	35%
Personal assets	225,000	167,000	140,000
Personal creditors	165,000	170,000	130,000

Schmidt had hoped to retire in three to five years and would welcome the opportunity to retire early. However, he is concerned that with the low liquidating values for the net assets of the company, it is possible that some of his net personal assets may have to be contributed to the partnership as part of the liquidation. Schmidt is also uncomfortable because he believes that his partners, especially Glomski, may not have adequate net personal assets to meet their partnership responsibilities. Schmidt's nephew has just returned from an extended stay in the Navy and had worked for the fuel company prior to his Navy career. The nephew has some net assets, is energetic, and is not adverse to working in the fuel business. Even though the cost to comply with the new federal standards is high, Schmidt feels that he could secure the necessary capital and persuade his nephew to join the business with an opportunity to ultimately own the company.

◄◄◄◄◄ Required

Schmidt has come to you seeking your advice. He is considering purchasing each of his partners' interests in the partnership rather than liquidating the company. Prepare an analysis which would suggest what Schmidt might offer to pay each of his partners, and summarize your findings in a memo to Schmidt.

Problem 14-12 *(LO 8, 10)* **Installment liquidation, schedule of safe payments, doctrine of marshaling of assets.** Ziegler, Nolan, and Petersen are partners in a residential construction business which has operated for the last 32 years in the Los Angeles area. The partners have decided to leave the business and focus on other pursuits. Initially, they had hoped to sell the business to an employee or other construction company. However, the weak housing market in the area has made liquidation of the company a more likely scenario.

You have been retained to account for the liquidation and to advise the partners as to how available assets of the company should be distributed. Events surrounding the liquidation during 20X8 are as follows:

1. On June 1, the company's balance sheet reflected the following: cash—$12,000; noncash assets—$228,000; liabilities to nonpartners—$120,000; loan payable to Nolan—$15,000; Ziegler, capital—$20,000; Nolan, capital—$35,000; and Petersen, capital—$50,000. Ziegler, Nolan, and Petersen share profits and losses of 30%, 30%, and 40%, respectively.
2. A review of the financial statements reveals that additional adjustments may be in order. The company has a contingent liability associated with a previous building contract dispute. It is probable that the company will incur $13,000 of cost in connection with this matter. Final wages and related payroll tax liabilities totaling $4,400 have not been accrued.
3. On June 15, vehicles with a current value of $23,000 and a book value of $14,000 were conveyed to Ziegler. Other assets with a book value of $90,000 were sold for $70,000 to a competing contractor. All available cash was distributed.

4. On June 30, inventory, tools, and other equipment were sold to various employees for a total of $92,000. The items had a book value of $80,000.
5. On July 10, a subcontractor was paid $15,000 to complete work on a final construction project which had not been finished prior to the liquidation. The customer was billed $20,000 for the work performed, and final payment was expected by late July.
6. On July 15, available cash was distributed. However, in addition to the $13,000 of cash retained to satisfy the contingent liability, another $5,000 of cash was retained as a precaution.
7. On July 25, title to a vehicle with a fair value of $12,000 and a book value of $8,000 was transferred to Petersen.
8. At the end of July, the contingent liability was settled for $10,000, and $20,000 was received from the last customer in payment for services performed in July.
9. On August 1, all available cash was distributed.
10. At mid-August, all the remaining assets were disposed of for $24,000. Associated attorney and accounting fees of $6,000 were paid. All available cash was distributed.

After all of the above events, the personal financial statements of the partners reveal the following:

	Ziegler	Nolan	Petersen
Personal assets	$185,000	$187,000	$240,000
Personal creditors	165,000	140,000	120,000

Required ▶ ▶ ▶ ▶ ▶

Prepare an installment liquidation schedule with all necessary supporting schedules. The schedule should also reflect the marshaling-of-assets doctrine where appropriate.

Problem 14-13 *(LO 5, 8, 10)* **Decision to sell interest or liquidate a troubled partnership, doctrine of marshaling of assets.** Your client Baker is in a partnership that has encountered significant business difficulties. Baker has become increasingly disenchanted with the business and is suggesting that it be liquidated over the next six months. However, one of Baker's partners has offered to acquire Baker's interest in the partnership, including loans due Baker, for $200,000, payable in four equal semiannual payments. The first payment would be due upon transfer of the partnership interest. Your client is not convinced that this would be a more attractive alternative than liquidation. A detailed inventory of the partnership net assets is as follows:

Item	Book Value	Fair Value
Cash and cash equivalents	$ 10,000	$ 10,000
Accounts receivable	240,000	200,000
Inventory	320,000	280,000
Equipment (net)	480,000	400,000
Land	80,000	200,000
Goodwill	60,000	0
Total assets	$1,190,000	$1,090,000
Accounts payable	$ 330,000	$ 330,000
Notes payable—bank	590,000	570,000
Notes payable—Baker	160,000	160,000
Baker, capital	60,000	
Meyer, capital	30,000	
Paulsen, capital	20,000	
Total liabilities and capital	$1,190,000	

If a partner has a deficit balance, the doctrine of marshaling of assets should be employed. It is estimated that the net assets of individual partners are as follows:

Partner	Assets	Liabilities
Baker	$400,000	$220,000
Meyer	180,000	140,000
Paulsen	122,000	107,000

Profits and losses are allocated among the partners as follows: Baker, 30%; Meyer, 50%; and Paulsen, 20%. It is estimated that liquidation/transaction costs associated with realizing the fair value of assets will be 8%.

Prepare a schedule that compares the options of selling or liquidating the partnership. ◄◄◄◄◄ **Required**

PART 4

Governmental and Not-for-Profit Accounting

Government and not-for-profit organizations are a major force in our society, comprising one-third of the United States expenditures and employing a substantial work force.

There are approximately 87,000 local governments in the United States. These include villages, towns, cities, counties, states, school districts, universities, public authorities, or special districts. There are over one million not-for-profits in the United States. These include schools; hospitals; social service, advocacy, cultural, and civic organizations; churches, synagogues, and mosques; and foundations.

The primary objective of external financial reporting for governmental units and not-for-profit organizations is accountability. However, there is no "bottom-line" amount or earnings per share figure to judge success. Instead, there is the elusive factor of service. To control activities and measure service, variations in the accounting and reporting process are introduced. Budgets have far greater power for control, particularly when they are entered formally into the accounting records in order to provide close comparisons with actual results. With financial resources being derived from many different sources, some with specific restrictions as to their consumption, fund accounting has traditionally been used to display proper use for intended purposes. More recently, standards setters have moved away from fund accounting for private not-for-profit organizations to an organization-wide reporting of unrestricted and donor-restricted assets and liabilities. Similarly, new government standards include entity-wide financial statements.

Governmental Accounting: The General Fund and the Account Groups

CHAPTER

15

Learning Objectives

When you have completed this chapter, you should be able to

1. **Differentiate between the financial reporting needs of governmental entities and those of profit-seeking business enterprises.**
2. **Identify the role of the various authoritative bodies for state and local government accounting and financial reporting.**
3. **State the difference between the financial resources measurement focus and the economic resources measurement focus, and indicate where each is reported under GASB Statement No. 34.**
4. **Identify the types of funds and account groups in state and local government.**
5. **Show how to account for transactions in governmental funds.**
6. **Explain the purpose of budgets and how governments account for appropriations.**
7. **Prepare journal entries for the general fund.**
8. **Demonstrate how to account for encumbrances.**
9. **Prepare fund financial statements for the general fund.**
10. **Complete schedules for general capital assets and long-term liabilities.**
11. **(Appendix) Demonstrate an understanding of the 13 basic governmental accounting principles.**

This chapter, the first of two that address accounting procedures used by governmental bodies, deals with the general fund. This fund accounts for most of the ordinary transactions of a governmental body. Also explained are the unique methods used to record fixed assets and long-term debt in separate accounting records called *groups*. The presentation is applicable to state and local governments. The governmental accounting procedures used in Chapters 15–17 provide a general understanding of *fund* accounting and current governmental accounting standards issued by the Governmental Accounting Standards Board (GASB). Also included is a discussion of the significant recent changes to the existing government financial reporting model. The presentation in Chapters 18 and 19 incorporates Financial Accounting Standards Board (FASB) standards issued specifically for not-for-profits.

Accounting and financial reporting for governmental and not-for-profit (also called nonprofit) entities have become more important because an increasing portion of our national economy has been devoted to this sector. Decision makers, such as legislators, citizens, managers, and contributors, need better information about governmental and not-for-profit organizations if they are to make optimal resource allocations to those entities and manage them efficiently and effectively. In addition, many accounting students will hold governmental and not-for-profit accounting jobs, perform audits on such organizations, and take the CPA examination, which contains questions on governmental and not-for-profit accounting.

1 OBJECTIVE

Differentiate between the financial reporting needs of governmental entities and those of profit-seeking business enterprises.

COMMERCIAL AND GOVERNMENTAL ACCOUNTING: A COMPARISON

Exhibit 15-1A summarizes the flow of resources in a profit-seeking business enterprise. Demand for goods and services made by customers in the commercial sector of the economy is satisfied by business enterprises. Assets of a business enterprise are supplied voluntarily by proprietors, stockholders, bondholders, and other creditors. The assets are consumed during operating processes which produce goods and services sold to customers who choose to deal with the company. The sales generate revenue for the company. The objective of the entity is to generate net income. The income statement measures the attainment of this goal by matching revenues earned with expenses incurred using accrual accounting.

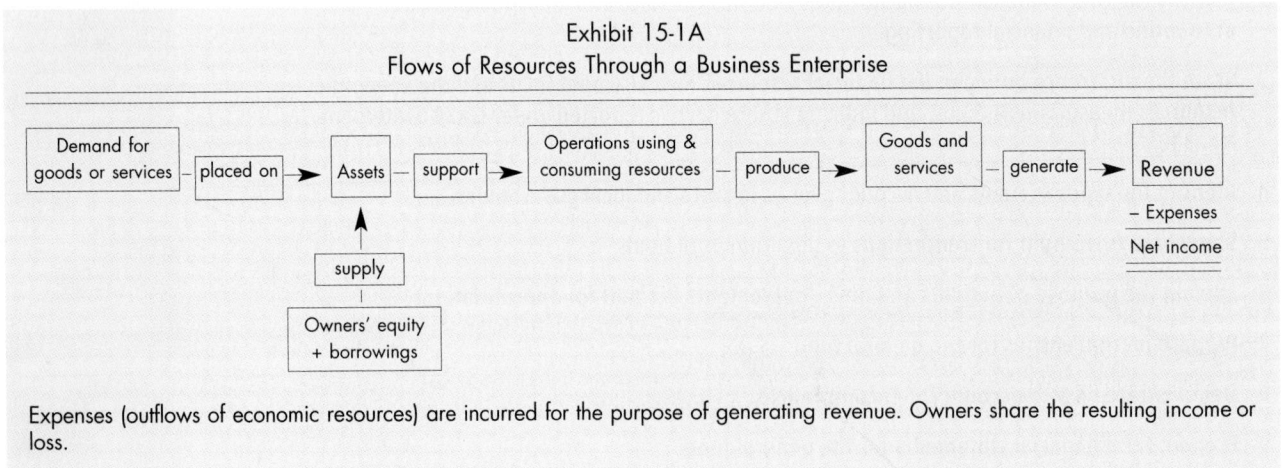

Exhibit 15-1A
Flows of Resources Through a Business Enterprise

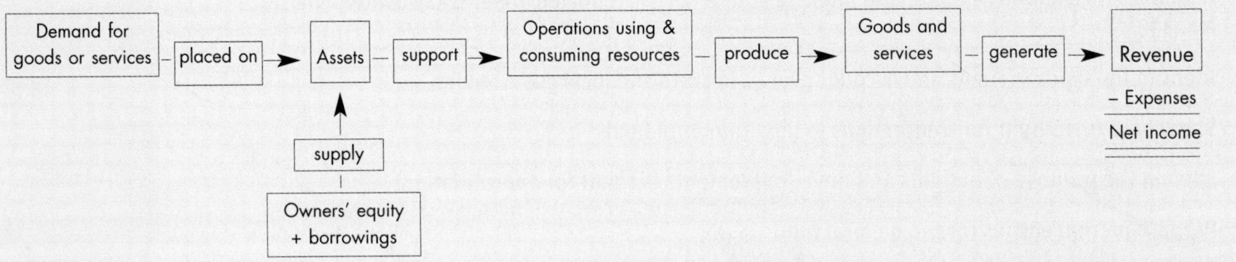

Expenses (outflows of economic resources) are incurred for the purpose of generating revenue. Owners share the resulting income or loss.

A separate cash flow statement is prepared to show the cash consequences of the period's operating, financing, and investing activities.

Exhibit 15-1B is a summary of the flow of resources for a governmental entity. Residents and businesses within a government's jurisdiction demand goods and services from that governmental unit. Assets of a government are supplied primarily through the involuntary payment of taxes by taxpayers. Typical taxes are those levied on property, income, and sales of goods and services. Creditors may also provide some financing. The assets are consumed during operating processes, which produce goods and services dispensed to those who are legally entitled to receive them. The operations performed to provide services are not intended to generate a profit. Leftover resources at the end of a fiscal period merely lessen the need for revenue in the next period. The results of operations for an accounting period are summarized in a statement called the Statement of Revenues, Expenditures, and Changes in the Fund Balance.

To finance general governmental activities, revenues are raised according to laws and are increases in financial resources that flow from outside the governmental unit—for example, taxes based on incomes or property values. Expenditures, such as salary payments, debt principal and interest payments, and fixed assets purchases, follow from budget appropriations and are decreases in financial resources that flow to entities outside the governmental unit. The expenditures usually are not related to the amount of taxes people pay. For example, a 7-year-old child who pays no taxes may receive a public education. Other increases in financial resources for general governmental purposes are termed *other financing sources*. These include transfers from other funds within the same governmental unit and resources from several other

Exhibit 15-1B
Flows of Resources Through a Governmental Entity

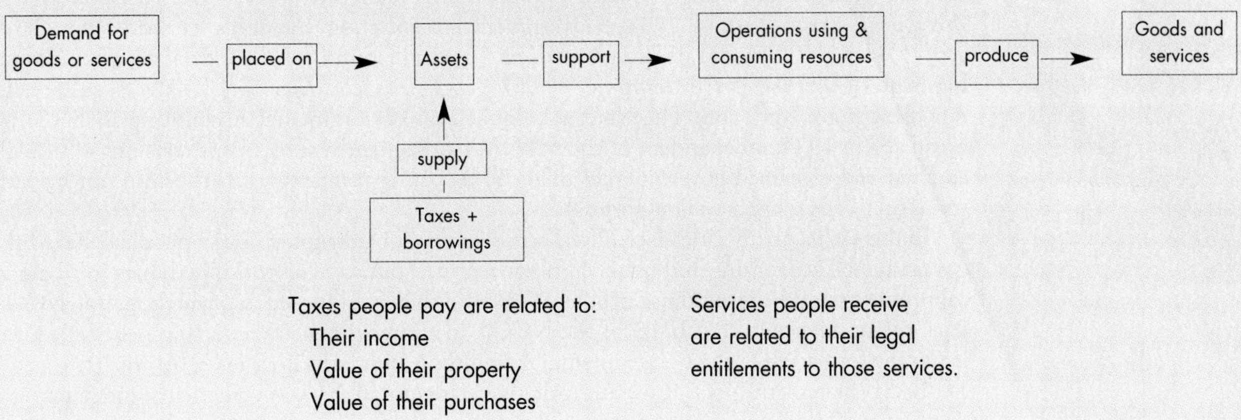

sources including proceeds from bond issues and resources from the sale of fixed assets. Other decreases in financial resources for general governmental activities come from *other financing uses,* which are typified by a transfer of financial resources to another fund within the same governmental unit. In addition, many governments engage in business activities that provide goods or services to users and finance these activities through user charges.

An important focus of governmental financial reporting is demonstrating fiscal compliance. Operating statements report whether or not financial resources received during a period are sufficient to cover the expenditures of that period. Furthermore, in addition to total expenditures, whether or not spending in particular areas was in compliance with approved budgets is reported. Consequently, division of resources into funds, each of which is a self-balancing set of accounts, is used to keep track of the flows of financial resources dedicated to specific activities. Financial reporting on fund activities should reveal whether uses of financial resources were within restrictions imposed by law or by third parties.

A further environmental distinction between business enterprises and governmental units is ownership versus jurisdiction. The balance sheet residual of a business enterprise is owners' equity, denoting the ownership interest in the company. The balance sheet residual of a governmental unit, however, is fund balance, merely denoting the difference between assets and liabilities.

REFLECTION

- **Because the decision-making environment for governments is not profit seeking, the accounting and financial reporting needs are different from those in the business environment.**

HISTORY OF GOVERNMENTAL FINANCIAL REPORTING

2
OBJECTIVE

Identify the role of the various authoritative bodies for state and local government accounting and financial reporting.

Three prominent periods of development in modern governmental financial reporting followed crises. In the late 1800s, large cities were rocked by misuses of funds, and accounting and financial reporting recommendations developed by the National Municipal League were adopted by some cities. In 1904, the state of New York was first to require standardized financial reporting by cities.

In the 1930s, new demands were being placed on governments while available resources were reduced by the Great Depression. The Municipal Finance Officers of America (MFOA)[1] formed its National Committee on Municipal Accounting (NCMA)[2] to promulgate accounting and financial reporting standards. The NCMA Bulletin No. 1, *Principles of Municipal Accounting*, was issued in 1934. Governmental accounting standards evolved through the actions of the NCMA and its successors. The National Committee on Governmental Accounting issued *Governmental Accounting, Auditing, and Financial Reporting* (GAAFR), also called the "Blue Book," in 1968. The National Council on Governmental Accounting (NCGA) was organized in 1974, independent of the MFOA. Consequently, subsequent revisions of GAAFR codified and explained governmental financial reporting principles, but they did not have the status of *authoritative pronouncements*.

In the 1970s, many cities faced fiscal stress and near bankruptcy. Many people believed that governmental accounting and financial reporting methods were responsible in part for these fiscal problems and believed those problems were not being addressed adequately by the NCGA. Lack of confidence in the ability of the NCGA to address financial reporting issues effectively led to the formation of the Governmental Accounting Standards Board (GASB) in 1984.

GASB Statement No. 1 gave authoritative status to all NCGA statements and interpretations, as well as accounting and financial reporting guidance contained in the Industry Audit Guide, *Audits of State and Local Governmental Units*, issued by the American Institute of Certified Public Accountants (AICPA) until superseded by subsequent GASB pronouncements.[3] A summary of the basic governmental accounting principles included in GASB Statement No. 1 is provided in the appendix to this chapter.

Financial reporting standard setting for governmental units has a long history and has been a focus of numerous standard-setting boards. Exhibit 15-2 presents an abridged history of financial reporting standards applicable to governments issued by major standard setters.

Organization and Processes of the FASB and the GASB

The GASB is a sister board to the Financial Accounting Standards Board (FASB). The Financial Accounting Foundation (FAF), which appoints both boards, is responsible for their funding and the determination of their respective jurisdictions, as well as the resolution of any disputes which may arise between the boards.

Both the FASB and the GASB subscribe to a due process of standard setting to ensure that preparers, attestors, and users of financial statements affected by standards have a voice in the establishment of those standards. Due process includes (a) issuing discussion memoranda setting forth financial reporting issues and arguments for and against possible alternative standards; (b) issuing exposure drafts proposing financial reporting standards regarding issues; and (c) issuing standards after considering written comments, testimony from public hearings, and research conducted by FASB and GASB staff and others throughout the due process period.

Jurisdictions of the FASB and the GASB

The authority to set external financial reporting standards for business and nonbusiness organizations rests with several standard-setting bodies. The identity of an entity's primary standard setter depends upon the nature of the operating activities of the entity issuing financial reports. Exhibit 15-3, on page 850, shows the primary standard setters for commercial, governmental, and not-for-profit entities.

Accountants and auditors often rely on financial reporting standards issued by bodies of expert accountants, such as AICPA committees, that are not the entity's primary financial reporting standard setter. In addition, accountants sometimes rely on widely recognized industry practices and other relevant accounting literature, such as accounting textbooks and AICPA issues papers, in preparing financial reports in accordance with generally accepted accounting

1 Now, the Government Finance Officers Association (GFOA).

2 Renamed National Committee on Governmental Accounting in 1951 and reorganized as the National Council on Governmental Accounting (NCGA) in 1974. The NCGA was superseded by the GASB in 1984.

3 GASB Statement No. 1, *Authoritative Status of NCGA Pronouncements and AICPA Industry Audit Guide* (Norwalk, CT: Governmental Accounting Standards Board, July 1984).

Exhibit 15-2
Major Contributions of Governmental Accounting Standard Setters

Year	MFOA/GFOA Committees	AICPA	GASB
1934 to 1941	NCMA—Principles of Municipal Accounting and twelve later standards		
1951 to 1968	NCGA—four publications including 1968 *Governmental Accounting, Auditing, and Financial Reporting* (GAAFR)		
1974		*Audits of State and Local Governmental Units*	
1979 to 1982	NCGA—Four statements including the 1980 GAAFR, six interpretations and one Concepts Statement, *Objectives of Accounting and Financial Reporting for Governmental Units*		
1980		Statement of Position 80–2 declared that financial statements presented in accordance with NCGA Statement No. 1 are in conformity with generally accepted accounting principles.	
1984 to 1994			GASB, organized in 1984, has issued 38 standards and two concepts statements, *Objectives of Financial Reporting and Accounting for Service Efforts and Accomplishment Reporting*. A recent standard, GASB Statement No. 34, requires sweeping changes in the way financial reports are reported. *Codification of Governmental Accounting and Financial Reporting Standards* contains generally accepted accounting principles for governmental units and is issued annually.

principles (GAAP). In order for accountants to know which financial reporting standards have primacy when there are multiple possibilities, the AICPA has published a hierarchy of applicable accounting principles referred to as the "GAAP hierarchy."[4] The GAAP hierarchy is directed at nongovernmental entities that look primarily to the FASB for financial reporting standards and at governmental entities that look primarily to the GASB for financial reporting standards. Generally, nongovernmental entities follow FASB pronouncements, APB Opinions, and AICPA Accounting Research Bulletins, while state and local governments follow GASB pronouncements and AICPA and FASB pronouncements if they are made applicable to state and local governments by GASB action.

4 Statement on Auditing Standards No. 69, *The Meaning of "Present Fairly in Conformity with Generally Accepted Accounting Principles" in the Independent Auditor's Report* (New York: American Institute of Certified Public Accountants, January 1992).

Exhibit 15-3
Authorities for Commercial, Governmental, and Not-for-Profit Accounting Reporting Standards

Type of Entity	Primary Financial Reporting Standard Setter(s)
Business enterprises	Financial Accounting Standards Board (FASB) and Securities and Exchange Commission (SEC)
Federal government	General Accounting Office (GAO), Comptroller General, Department of the Treasury, Office of Management and Budget (OMB), and Federal Accounting Standards Advisory Board (FASAB)
State/local governments	Governmental Accounting Standards Board (GASB)
Colleges and universities	Public—GASB Private—FASB
Heathcare organizations	Public—GASB Private—FASB
Voluntary health and welfare organizations	FASB
Other not-for-profit organizations	FASB

GASB Objectives of Financial Reporting

Differences in environments and purposes of financial reporting between business enterprises and governmental entities have led to the creation of separate financial reporting standard-setting boards for business enterprises and governments, and each board has examined and defined the objectives of financial reporting by its respective constituency. *Objectives of Financial Reporting by Business Enterprises*, Concept Statement No. 1, was issued by the FASB in 1978. *Objectives of Financial Reporting*, Concept Statement No. 1, was issued by the GASB in 1987.

In its Concept Statement No. 1, the GASB stated that "**accountability** is the cornerstone of all financial reporting in government."[5] A closely related concept referred to by the GASB in the concept statement is **interperiod equity**. Both concepts are described below.

The GASB believes that financial reporting helps a government fulfill its duty to be publicly accountable to its citizenry. They believe that taxpayers have a "right to know;" that is, a right to receive information about government activities that may lead to public debates. At a minimum, *accountability* through financial reporting means "providing information to assist in evaluating whether the government was operated within the legal constraints imposed by the citizenry."[6]

A significant part of accountability is *interperiod equity*, which may be demonstrated by showing "whether current-year revenues are sufficient to pay for current-year services or whether future taxpayers will be required to assume burdens for services previously provided."[7] As with business financial reports, state and local government financial reports should possess the characteristics of understandability, reliability, relevance, timeliness, consistency, and comparability.

5 GASB Concept Statement No. 1, *Objectives of Financial Reporting* (Norwalk, CT: Governmental Accounting Standards Board, 1987), par. 58.
6 *Ibid.*
7 *Ibid.*, par. 61.

Measurement Focus and Basis of Accounting

3

OBJECTIVE

State the difference between the financial resources measurement focus and the economic resources measurement focus, and indicate where each is reported under GASB Statement No. 34.

Measurement focus refers to which resources are being measured. *Basis of accounting* refers to when the effects of transactions or events should be recognized for financial reporting purposes. The traditional measurement focus for state and local governments has been *financial resources.* In June 1999, the GASB issued Statement No. 34 after nearly 15 years of deliberation and dialogue with its constituents. Statement No. 34, *Basic Financial Statements—and Management's Discussion and Analysis—for State and Local Governments*, is a significant change from current practice. Large governments were required to implement the standards in fiscal years beginning after June 15, 2001, and medium-size and smaller governments adopted the standard in fiscal years beginning after June 15, 2002, and 2003, respectively.[8]

The new model requires governments to prepare two separate, but related, sets of financial statements. The first set, the fund financial statements, is similar to the current reporting model and focuses on reporting activity as a collection of separate funds. Governmental and business-type funds are reported on separate statements. And, rather than follow the reporting of traditional fund-types (as described in the following section), these statements will report major funds and combine all the nonmajor funds into one column.

The second set of financial statements are government-wide statements that concentrate on the government as a whole. These statements adopt an *economic resources measurement focus* and consolidate all of a government's operations on *a full accrual basis* similar to that found in the business world.

The sections that follow present an overview of the main funds maintained by governments and describe the accounting for activities in the general fund. A discussion of accounting for long-term assets and liabilities also follows. Chapter 16 discusses accounting for activities in the remaining funds, while Chapter 17 describes the fund financial statements and the more recently required government-wide statements as well as the articulation from one to the other.

REFLECTION

- Governmental accounting and financial reporting standards for state and local governments are established by the GASB.
- GASB Statement No. 34 requires governments to modify their accounting systems and reporting procedures. Both fund financial statements and government-wide statements are now required.

GOVERNMENTAL ACCOUNTING STRUCTURE OF FUNDS

4

OBJECTIVE

Identify the types of funds and account groups in state and local government.

Governmental units create individual funds to account for financial resources used for specific purposes. Each fund is an accounting entity containing a self-balancing set of accounts for which financial statements can be prepared. Business enterprises, on the other hand, report all of their profit-making activity on a single income statement and summarize their financial position on a single balance sheet.

Historically, general purpose financial statements for governments aggregated financial information by fund type. The combined balance sheet is not subjected to the rules of consolidation for the purpose of eliminating the effects of interfund transactions and interfund balances. With the adoption of GASB Statement No. 34, governments are now required to prepare consolidated financial statements restricted to summarizing the effects of transactions between a governmental unit and external parties as presented in Chapter 17. Since many argue that governmental activity does not reduce well to a single statement about profit or loss, fund-based

8 GASB Statement No. 34, *Basic Financial Statements—and Management's Discussion and Analysis—for State and Local Governments* (Norwalk, CT: Governmental Accounting Standards Board, June 1999).

financial statements are also required under Statement No. 34, helping to demonstrate accountability (i.e., compliance with laws governing numerous activities). Government-wide and fund financial statements for the city of Milwaukee are found in the student companion book.

Three fund types and two account groups are used in government financial reporting:

1. **Governmental funds** account for activities that provide citizens with services financed primarily by taxes and intergovernmental grants. These funds have a *working capital* focus and include only current assets and current liabilities.
2. **Proprietary funds** account for business-type activities that derive their revenue from charges to users for goods or services. They follow the commercial accounting model in measuring net income. An example would be a publicly owned utility.
3. **Fiduciary funds** account for resources for which the governmental unit acts as a trustee or agent.
4. **Account groups** account for and serve as a record of general capital assets and general long-term liabilities. Account groups are no longer required under GASB Statement No. 34, but many governments may continue to use them as a convenient means of keeping track of these items. Alternatively, some governments are changing their account systems to allow for the generation of lists of capital assets and long-term liabilities without using account groups.

The GASB specifies different methods of applying the accrual concept in accounting for governmental funds and proprietary funds. The *modified accrual basis,* a hybrid system that includes some aspects of both accrual and cash-basis accounting, is used for recognition of revenues and expenditures of governmental funds. The accrual basis refers to recognition of revenues and expenses of proprietary funds and fiduciary funds as in business accounting.

Governmental Funds

All governments have a general fund and may have other governmental funds as well, depending on their types of activities. The five governmental funds are as follows:

1. The **general fund** accounts for resources that have no specific restrictions and are available for operational expenditures not relegated to one of the other governmental funds. Since it accounts for general operations, it is the most essential fund. Every governmental unit has a general fund.
2. **Special revenue funds** account for resources that legally are restricted to expenditure for specific operational purposes, such as a toll tax levied for road maintenance expenses.
3. **Capital projects funds** account for resources to be used for the construction or acquisition of major capital facilities.
4. **Debt service funds** account for resources to be used for payment of general long-term debt and interest.
5. **Permanent funds** account for resources that are legally restricted so that only their earnings, not the principal, may be used to finance operations.

5

OBJECTIVE

Show how to account for transactions in governmental funds.

Accounting for Transactions of Governmental Funds

The modified accrual method of accounting is used for governmental funds to measure the flow of working capital. Under modified accrual, revenue is recorded in the accounting period in which it is both measurable and available to finance expenditures made during the current fiscal period (this includes resources expected to be available shortly after year-end). Expenditures are recognized in the period in which the liabilities are both measurable and incurred.

Revenues. Increases in financial resources from transactions with external parties that do not have to be repaid are called **revenues.** Revenues may come from nonexchange or exchange transactions. Nonexchange transactions are those in which people and companies pay amounts to governments but governments give nothing directly to the payors in return. Exchange transactions are those in which the government provides goods or services for fees. Under modified accrual, some revenues are recognized on the accrual basis and some revenues are recognized on the cash basis. Revenue from property taxes, intergovernmental grants, entitlements, and shared revenues; interest on investments and delinquent taxes; and billed charges for services are normally recognized under the modified accrual basis if funds will be "collectible within the current period or soon enough thereafter to be used to pay liabilities of the current period."[9]

Property taxes, fines, and other *imposed* tax revenues are recorded as revenue at the time taxes are levied on property owners and others provided the taxes will be collected during the current period or soon enough after year-end to pay the liabilities of the current period. Taxes levied in one year but not available until the following year are recognized as deferred revenue. Governments are conservative in recognizing property tax revenue. Only the net amount estimated to be collected is recognized.

Resources to be received from federal, state, or local governmental units (intergovernmental grants, entitlements, and shared revenues for operational purposes) should be recognized as revenue in the year for which all eligibility requirements, including time restrictions, have been met and the resources are available to finance expenditures. If resources are received prior to the time period in which they may be used, or if the receivable is not expected to be collected soon enough to be used for the current fiscal period, Deferred Revenues is credited. Some grants to a governmental unit may carry strong restrictions on their use. For example, the federal government may be willing to give a locality a grant providing it builds a bridge over a river and connects its main road to the federal highway. In this case, the restricted grant should be recognized as revenue only to the extent that expenditures have been made, with the remainder of the grant recorded as deferred revenue. This type of restricted grant is sometimes called an *expenditure-driven* grant.

Revenues from voluntary nonexchange transactions, such as donations and certain grants, should be recognized in governmental funds when the assets are received. Donations of capital assets are not recognized in governmental funds. Rather, donated capital assets are recorded in the general fixed assets account group discussed later in this chapter.

Revenue for services charges should be recognized when billed if it is expected to be received within the current period or soon enough thereafter to be used to pay liabilities of the current period. Such revenues may be from goods or services provided for fees, such as golf course fees, garbage removal fees, inspection fees, and sales of maps and other publications.

Interest and dividend revenue from investments should be recognized when earned. Investment gains and losses should be recognized when an investment is sold.

Revenues normally recognized under the cash-basis method include fees for licenses and permits, fines and forfeits, and parking meter receipts. These resources are recognized when received in cash because the amount is usually not known prior to collection. In addition, these items are often not an important source of a governmental unit's income.

Taxes levied directly on taxpayers are accounted for in the same modified accrual basis of accounting that already applies to most other revenue sources.[10] Examples are taxes on income, inheritance, gasoline, general sales, and tobacco. Revenue from these taxpayer-assessed or *derived* taxes, net of estimated refunds, is recognized in the accounting period in which they become susceptible to accrual [e.g., when the underlying transaction (sale or earning of income) occurs and the amounts are measurable and will be collected within the current period or soon enough after year-end to finance expenditures for the period]. A lag often occurs from the time of the underlying transaction to the reporting of such events, so, in practice, revenue is recorded when either the merchant or the employer submits the required reports to the governmental unit.

Other Financing Sources. These inflows of financial resources arise from issuing general long-term debt, recording the present value of capital lease obligations, selling capital assets, and receiving of interfund operating transfers from other governmental funds. Use of the **other**

9 GASB Statement No. 33, *Accounting and Financial Reporting for Nonexchange Transactions* (Norwalk, CT: Governmental Accounting Standards Board, December 1998) identifies four classes of nonexchange transactions: *derived tax revenues*, such as income taxes and sales taxes; *imposed nonexchange revenues*, such as property taxes and fines; *government-mandated nonexchange transactions*, such as federal programs that state and local governments are required to perform; and *voluntary nonexchange transactions*, such as grants and private donations.

10 *Ibid.*

financing sources classification avoids multiple countings of inflows as revenues. Proceeds from issuing general long-term debt represent inflows of financial resources that must be repaid to lenders from later tax revenues. Tax revenue recorded in the general fund would be counted as revenue twice if amounts transferred to another governmental fund were recorded in the second fund as revenue rather than as other financing sources. The same is true for proceeds from the sale of a fixed asset. Financial resources raised by tax revenues are used to purchase fixed assets. Their later sale is a conversion of fixed assets into financial resources, not a raising of new financial resources from entities outside the governmental unit.

Expenditures. Most **expenditures** are decreases in financial resources as a result of transactions with external parties. Some expenditures, however, result from consumption of previously purchased financial resources, such as inventories and prepaid items. Expenditures are recognized in the period the fund liability is both measurable and incurred.[11] This usually means that an expenditure is recognized if the related liability is expected to be liquidated through the use of current-year expendable and available financial resources. Expenditures result from operating activities, acquiring capital assets, and payment of debt principal and interest. In many cases, expenditures will be recorded simultaneously with cash payments. Consider the following examples:

Expenditures	50,000	
Cash		50,000
The payment of current maintenance expenses.		
Expenditures	100,000	
Cash		100,000
Acquisition of a new capital asset for cash.		

Expenditures for interest and principal on general long-term debt are recorded on a cash basis when they are due to match them with the tax revenue raised for the interest and principal payment.

Expenditures	42,000	
Cash		42,000
Payment of $12,000 of interest and $30,000 principal on existing general obligation debt.		

Other expenditures will be recorded if the amount is to be paid with existing resources. Consider the following entries to record wages:

Expenditures	16,500	
Cash		10,500
Liability for State and Federal Withholdings		6,000

While the liability for withholdings is current, another common payroll liability for future payment of compensated absences (such as for vacations and holidays) is considered to be long term. Under the *modified accrual basis* of governmental accounting, such long-term liabilities would not be recorded in the general fund, but would appear in the government-wide statements. The traditional means of keeping track of long-term obligations has been through the use of account groups. The concept of using accounts groups for internal control and support for financial reporting will be described in detail later in this chapter. Long-term vacation and sick leave liabilities are recorded in the general long-term debt account group as follows:

11 GASB Exposure Draft, *Recognition and Measurement of Certain Liabilities and Expenditures in Governmental Fund Financial Statements* (Norwalk, CT: Governmental Accounting Standards Board, June 1999).

Amount to Be Provided in Future Periods	1,500	
Liability for Compensated Absences		1,500

Only the expenditure and related current liability for compensated absences reasonably expected to be paid from the current governmental fund financial resources are included in the fund. All long-term liabilities are recorded separately.

GASB standards for recording pension expenditures require a calculation of the "actuarial required contribution" (ARC).[12] This calculation can be made using acceptable actuarial methods and assumptions. As in the preceding example for compensated absences, the portion of the ARC that will be paid from current resources will be recorded as an expenditure in the fund.

Expenditures	5,000	
Current Pension Liability		5,000

The portion to be funded from future resources is recorded as general long-term debt in the account group as follows:

Amount to Be Provided in Future Periods	2,000	
Unfunded Pension Liability		2,000

Governments are also required to measure and report on postretirement benefits such as health care and life insurance in a manner similar to the illustration for pension benefits above.[13]

The GASB requires a liability for claims and judgments outstanding to be recognized in the accounts if it is probable that the liability has been incurred and the amount can be reasonably estimated. During the year, the government will record the amounts paid or vouchered as payable as expenditures in the fund. The noncurrent liability for claims and judgments is recorded directly in the general long-term debt account group.

In many cases, cash will be paid or a liability recorded to purchase goods and services in advance of their use. These items are recorded in the fund as financial resources (assets) as follows:

Prepaid Rent	12,000	
Prepaid Insurance	18,000	
Supplies Inventory	40,000	
Cash		70,000
Acquiring goods and services to be consumed in the future.		

Expenditures are recorded in the fund as follows when the financial resources are consumed:

Expenditures	45,000	
Prepaid Rent		10,000
Prepaid Insurance		15,000
Supplies Inventory		20,000
Receiving services and consuming supplies acquired previously.		

Note that the expenditure examples in this section show the consumption of only those assets defined as financial resources. This is a narrower definition than expenses reported in the new government-wide statements where the measurement focus is flows of economic resources. Expenses are the expirations of economic resources that include not only the use of current

12 GASB Statement No. 27, *Accounting for Pensions by State and Local Governmental Employers* (Norwalk, CT: Governmental Accounting Standards Board, November 1994).

13 GASB Statement No. 45, *Accounting and Financial Reporting by Employers for Postemployment Benefits Other than Pensions* (Norwalk, CT: Governmental Accounting Standards Board, June 2004).

assets but also the amortization of long-term assets such as buildings and equipment. Examples of the differences between recording expenditures and expenses are as follows:

A Governmental Fund Using the Flows of Financial Resources Measurement Focus			Government-Wide Statements Using the Flows of Economic Resources Measurement Focus		
Expenditures	10,000		Salary Expense	10,000	
Cash		10,000	Cash		10,000
Payment of salaries; expiration of financial resource.			Payment of salaries; expiration of economic resource.		
Expenditures	90,000		Equipment	90,000	
Cash		90,000	Cash		90,000
Purchase of truck; expiration of financial resource.			Purchase of truck.		
			Depreciation Expense	15,000	
			Accumulated Depreciation		15,000
			Expiration of economic resource.		

Other Financing Uses. The greatest use of the **other financing uses** classification is for interfund operating transfers-out to other governmental funds. Using this classification for such fund outflows prevents double counting of expenditures. For example, if an amount transferred from the general fund to the debt service fund were debited to expenditures and then debited to expenditures again in the debt service fund when interest and long-term debt principal were liquidated, a double counting of expenditures would occur. Also classified as other financing uses are payments made from financial resources of refunding general long-term debt (using proceeds from issuing new debt to pay old debt).

The following summary shows the debit and credit effects of flows of financial resources through a governmental fund.

Governmental Fund Actual Transactions

Debits	Credits
Expenditures	Revenues
Other Financing Uses	Other Financing Sources

Operating Debt. Governments may issue short- and long-term debt to finance their operating activities. Such financing is treated as **operating debt** when the debt is not incurred to acquire capital assets or other long-term economic benefits for the government. Examples of short-term operating debt include accounts payable to vendors and tax anticipation notes. Examples of long-term operating debt include certain bonds or notes payable and long-term vendor financing. Also recognized as long-term operating debt are those obligations described above that a government incurs but does not pay for in a particular year (e.g., liabilities for compensated absences, claims and judgments, and unfunded pensions).

Short-term debt is recorded in the fund as a liability if it is "normally expected to be liquidated with expendable available financial resources." Hence, governmental fund liabilities (and a corresponding expenditure) are recorded if they are normally paid in a timely manner from current financial resources. Examples are salaries, professional services, supplies, utilities, and travel. Long-term operating debt is reported as a liability in the general long-term debt account group. As this debt matures and becomes due and payable, it will become a fund liability.

Tax anticipation notes are an example of short-term operating debt. Cash inflows from property tax or income tax collections peak near the due dates for payment. Prior to their receipt, a governmental unit may have obligations that must be paid. Local banks usually provide short-term financing, using as security the taxing power of the government, which is required to sign an instrument referred to as a tax anticipation note. Receipt of cash from such notes would be recorded in the general fund with the following entry:

Cash	150,000	
Tax Anticipation Notes Payable		150,000

Later, as cash inflows from taxes provide resources, the following entry would record the payment of the notes and the interest:

Tax Anticipation Notes Payable	150,000	
Expenditures (for interest)	1,875	
Cash		151,875

Interest associated with short-term operating debt is accrued. Interest associated with long-term operating debt is not accrued.

General Long-Term Capital Debt. Debt financing incurred to acquire capital assets or other long-term economic benefits through governmental funds is termed **general long-term capital debt.** The majority of the proceeds acquired from issuing this debt is accounted for in capital projects funds, as an other financing source. Capital project funds are discussed in Chapter 16. The face amount of capital debt is accounted for in the general long-term debt account group discussed later in this chapter. Debt service (principal and interest payments) expenditures on all general long-term debt are accounted for in the debt service funds discussed in Chapter 16.

Special and Extraordinary Items. Statement No. 34 requires separate reporting of both **special items** and **extraordinary items** in both the governmental and proprietary fund financial statements. Extraordinary items are those which are both unusual in nature and infrequent in occurrence. Special items arise from significant transactions or other events that are (1) within the control of management and (2) either unusual in nature or infrequent in occurrence. Special items are to be reported separately in the financial statements below nonoperating revenue and before extraordinary items. The recognition of special items and extraordinary items follows the revenue, expenditure, other financing source, and use criteria described above. An example of an extraordinary item is a natural disaster. An example of a special item is the sale of a significant governmental asset or a loss incurred as a result of a civil riot. Separate reporting of such items serves to inform the citizens and other users of the financial statements when governments engage in unusual practices such as selling assets in order to balance the budget. Items that are either unusual or infrequent but not within the control of management should be disclosed in the notes to the financial statements.

REFLECTION

- Three fund types—governmental, proprietary, and fiduciary—are used to account for activities. Each fund type has a different measurement focus and basis of accounting.
- There are two types of account groups: general capital asset and general long-term liabilities.
- Governmental funds have a measurement focus of current financial resources and use a modified accrual basis of accounting.
- Revenues are recognized when they are measurable and available.
- Expenditures are recognized when current financial resources will be used.

USE OF BUDGETARY ACCOUNTING

6

OBJECTIVE

Explain the purpose of budgets and how governments account for appropriations.

Generally, finance personnel work with operating department personnel to develop a proposed expenditures budget for a fiscal year. The governmental unit's legislative body deliberates and acts on the budget which authorizes a certain level of expenditures for operating activities, capital acquisitions, and debt service. Authorized expenditures are termed **appropriations.** An authorization to raise revenue and, perhaps, long-term debt is approved. Estimates for other financing sources and other financing uses are also budgeted. An executive head, such as a governor or mayor, may be responsible for approving the budget or sending it back to the legislative body for further action. The budget, as finally approved, is recorded in the general ledger in summarized control accounts and in the subsidiary ledgers in detail accounts.

General Ledger Entries

Budgetary totals for appropriations (which are authorized expenditures), estimated revenues, other financing sources, and other financing uses are recorded in the general ledger as control accounts over more detailed budgetary entries in subsidiary ledgers. The following summary shows the debit and credit effects of budgetary entries:

Governmental Fund Budgetary Entries

Debit	Credit
Estimated Revenues	Appropriations
Estimated Other Financing Sources	Estimated Other Financing Uses

If estimated inflows do not equal estimated outflows, the difference is either a debit or credit to Budgetary Fund Balance—Unreserved. A budgetary entry is made to the appropriate fund as follows:

Estimated Revenues	10,000,000	
Estimated Other Financing Sources	1,000,000	
Appropriations		9,300,000
Estimated Other Financing Uses		1,500,000
Budgetary Fund Balance—Unreserved		200,000
To record an approved annual budget.		

Actual transactions occurring during the budget year are recorded in separate general ledger accounts. This simplifies the closing process. To close the budgetary accounts, merely reverse the entry made to record the budget. Amounts may include amendments to the original budget recorded during the year. The closing entry must be entered in the same fund as follows:

Appropriations	9,300,000	
Estimated Other Financing Uses	1,500,000	
Budgetary Fund Balance—Unreserved	200,000	
Estimated Revenues		10,000,000
Estimated Other Financing Sources		1,000,000
To close an annual budget as amended.		

Subsidiary Ledger Entries

Illustration 15-1, on page 860, details the relationship between the general ledger control accounts and the subsidiary ledger detail accounts. Usually, budgets are prepared according to object of expenditure. These are, for example, salaries, employee benefits, utilities, and supplies. Each object of expenditure is a line item in the budget or a classification of authorized spending by a department or function of the government. The appropriation for each line item is recorded in an expenditures subsidiary ledger account as a credit. During the accounting period, such credits will be offset by debits recording actual expenditure transactions. The credit balance in the subsidiary ledger account tells managers how much money they have remaining to spend for that line item purpose. Budgetary amounts of estimated other financing uses and actual other financing uses are recorded in the same manner. The detailed information recorded in the subsidiary ledgers is a key mechanism of budgetary control. That is, the accounting records should show whether spending for a line item meets or exceeds the authorization.

A subsidiary ledger for revenues is also maintained. The budgetary amount of each revenue source is recorded in a revenues subsidiary ledger account as a debit. During the accounting period, such debits will be offset by credits recording actual revenue recognition. Budgetary amounts of estimated other financing sources and actual other financing sources are recorded in the same manner.

To emphasize accounting techniques and to conserve space, this text will use only general ledger control accounts in its examples for budgetary and actual accounts.

REFLECTION

- Governments use budgets and funds because of the need to demonstrate accountability.

OVERVIEW OF GENERAL FUND PROCEDURES

7 OBJECTIVE

Prepare journal entries for the general fund.

Illustration 15-1 is designed to be a simple example of general fund procedures that is not burdened by the complexities that follow in this chapter. It is meant to acquaint you with the mechanics of governmental accounting. The accounting and financial reporting procedures shown for the general fund are similar to those used by the special revenue, capital projects, debt service, and permanent funds, which are illustrated in Chapter 16.

You should understand three important features of this example:

1. The general ledger includes three types of accounts. **Permanent balance sheet accounts** contain financial resources, liabilities, and fund balances. **Budgetary accounts** are used to record the budget. Budget amounts are entered at the start of the period, possibly amended during the period, and closed at the end of the period. There are no actual transactions recorded in these accounts during the period. **Operating accounts** contain the actual expenditures, other financing uses, revenues, and other financing sources that occur during the period.
2. Three types of journal entries are made during the accounting period. The **budgetary entry** enters the budget into the accounting records. The **operating entries** record actual events. The **closing entries** close the budgetary accounts in one entry and the actual accounts in a second closing entry.
3. For every entry in the general ledger, there are detailed entries in the subsidiary ledgers.

Each entry in Illustration 15-1 is explained as follows:

1. The budget is entered into the general ledger budgetary accounts. An excess of estimated revenues, estimated other financing sources over appropriations, and estimated other financing uses would create a credit to the budgetary fund balance. In this case, appropriations (there are no estimated other financing uses) exceed revenues and estimated other financing sources; thus, there is a debit to the budgetary fund balance. The debit entry to the budgetary fund balance anticipates a decrease in the fund balance during the period. Budgetary amounts may be amended during the year by legislative action but are otherwise left unchanged during the period and are reversed at the end of the period as part of the closing

Illustration 15-1
Simple Example of Governmental Accounts—General Ledger and Subsidiary Ledger Entries

GENERAL LEDGER ACCOUNTS:

Permanent Balance Sheet Accounts:

Cash

Jan. 1, 20X2, Balance	8,000	(7) Pay vouchers	110,000
(5) Tax collection	90,500		
(3) Cash revenues	14,500		
(4) Asset sale	4,800		
Dec. 31, 20X2, Balance	7,800		

Property Taxes Receivable

Jan. 1, 20X2, Balance	12,000	(5) Tax collection	90,500
(2) Tax levy	85,000		
Dec. 31, 20X2, Balance	6,500		

Vouchers Payable

(7) Vouchers paid	110,000	Jan. 1, 20X2, Balance	13,000
		(6) Expenditures	106,800
		Dec. 31, 20X2, Balance	9,800

Fund Balance

(9) Close 20X2	2,500	Jan. 1, 20X2, Balance	7,000
		Dec. 31, 20X2	4,500

Budgetary Accounts:

Estimated Revenues

(1) Budget entry	97,000	(8) Close budget	97,000

Estimated Other Financing Sources

(1) Budget entry	5,000	(8) Close budget	5,000

Appropriations

(8) Close budget	105,000	(1) Budget entry	105,000

Budgetary Fund Balance

(1) Budget entry	3,000	(8) Close budget	3,000

Operating Accounts:

Revenues

(9) Close actual	99,500	(2) Tax levy	85,000
		(3) Cash revenues	14,500

Other Financing Sources

(9) Close actual	4,800	(4) Asset sale	4,800

Expenditures

(6) Expenditures	106,800	(9) Close actual	106,800

procedure, so they never actually impact the fund balance.[14] The budgetary entry is as follows:

Estimated Revenues	97,000	
Estimated Other Financing Sources	5,000	
Budgetary Fund Balance	3,000	
Appropriations		105,000

14 Some governments do not maintain separate budgetary accounts. These governments enter the budget into the actual accounts. Since the budget is reversed at year-end, the net effect is to increase or decrease the fund balance by the difference between actual revenues and expenditures—the same impact as would have been recorded had the budgetary entries not been made.

SUBSIDIARY LEDGER ACCOUNTS:

Expenditures—Salary

(6) Expenditures	57,000	(1) Enter budget	55,000
Balance	2,000		

Revenues—Property Tax

(1) Enter budget	82,000	(2) Tax levy	85,000
		Balance	3,000

Expenditures—Supplies

(6) Expenditures	22,000	(1) Enter budget	23,000
		Balance	1,000

Revenues—Fines

(1) Enter budget	12,000	(3) Cash collected	11,500
Balance	500		

Expenditures—Repairs

(6) Expenditures	9,600	(1) Enter budget	9,000
Balance	600		

Revenues—Licenses

(1) Enter budget	3,000	(3) Cash collected	3,000

Expenditures—Capital

(6) Expenditures	11,500	(1) Enter budget	11,000
Balance	500		

Other Financing Sources—Asset Sale

(1) Enter budget	5,000	(4) Cash collected	4,800
Balance	200		

Expenditures—Miscellaneous

(6) Expenditures	6,700	(1) Enter budget	7,000
Balance	300		

This entry is supported by detailed entries in subsidiary ledger revenue accounts, other financing sources accounts, and expenditure accounts. See entries marked "1" in the subsidiary ledger accounts. The real control feature of the budget entry is found in the subsidiary ledgers. Consider the subsidiary ledger revenue and other financing sources accounts. Budgeted amounts are entered in the accounts as debits so that they can be compared to the actual credits as they actually occur. At any time during the year, a fast comparison of budget versus year-to-date actual is possible. At the end of the year, actual amounts are compared to budgeted amounts to arrive at a variance. Appropriations (budgeted expenditures) are entered as credits so that they can be compared to actual debits as they occur. Again, there can be a comparison of budget versus year-to-date actual for variance analysis at the end of the period.

2. Property taxes are recorded as receivables at the time taxes are levied on property owners. Revenue is credited in the period for which the taxes are levied (that is, in the period the money will be spent) provided the taxes are due by the end of the period. Not shown are the individual receivables for each property recorded in a receivables subsidiary ledger.

Property Taxes Receivable	85,000	
Revenues		85,000

3. Revenues from fines and licenses are recorded when cash is received because these amounts cannot be predicted accurately. The detailed source of each revenue is recorded in the subsidiary ledger.

Cash	14,500	
Revenues		14,500

4. Proceeds from the sale of used fixed assets are recorded in the general and subsidiary ledgers.

Cash	4,800	
Other Financing Sources		4,800

5. Property taxes are collected, including amounts from previous periods.

Cash	90,500	
Property Taxes Receivable		90,500

6. Expenditures are recorded when the liability is incurred and formal vouchers are prepared. Vouchers are documents attached to vendor invoices that contain information about the payables. They must be signed to authorize payments of the liabilities. Details of the expenditures are recorded in the subsidiary ledger.

Expenditures	106,800	
Vouchers Payable		106,800

7. Vouchers are paid.

Vouchers Payable	110,000	
Cash		110,000

8. The budgetary entry is closed by reversing the original budgetary entry. This "zeros out" the budgetary accounts.

Appropriations	105,000	
Estimated Revenues		97,000
Estimated Other Financing Sources		5,000
Budgetary Fund Balance		3,000

This entry is made only in the general ledger. The amounts in the subsidiary ledgers are not removed but remain so that the budget can be compared to actual amounts.

9. Actual revenues and actual other financing sources are closed against actual expenditures to arrive at the change in the actual fund balance for the year. Again, this entry is made only in the general ledger. Detailed amounts are left in the subsidiary ledger so that variance analysis may be performed.

Revenues	99,500	
Other Financing Sources	4,800	
Fund Balance	2,500	
Expenditures		106,800

Each subsidiary ledger revenue, other financing sources, and expenditures account now may be analyzed as to the cause of variances from budgeted amounts. Once the budgetary comparisons are done, the balances are closed to allow for the recording of the next period's activity.

Accounting for the General Fund—An Expanded Example

To visualize the accounting process of the general fund and the flow of information that produces the financial reports, the activities of the city of Middletown are examined for the fiscal year ended September 30, 20X7. The general fund trial balance on September 30, 20X6, appears in Illustration 15-2.

Illustration 15-2
City of Middletown
General Fund Trial Balance
September 30, 20X6

	Debit	Credit
Cash	82,000	
Investments	153,000	
Taxes Receivable—Delinquent	30,000	
Allowance for Uncollectible Delinquent Taxes		20,000
Tax Liens Receivable	24,000	
Allowance for Uncollectible Tax Liens		8,000
Supplies Inventory	10,000	
Vouchers Payable		170,000
Fund Balance—Reserved for Inventory		10,000
Fund Balance—Unreserved, Designated for Public Safety		16,000
Fund Balance—Unreserved, Undesignated		75,000
Total	299,000	299,000

The city has $271,000 in financial resources (cash, net receivables, and inventory). The liability Vouchers Payable offsets $170,000 of the resources with the fund balances offsetting the remaining $101,000. The fund balance may be *reserved* to show obligations of a fund or legal restrictions on financial resources. The fund balance also may be reserved if amounts are committed and not available as cash, such as outstanding purchase orders, petty cash, receivables that are long-term advances to other funds, or supplies inventory. The reserves are adjusted at year-end.

The second classification of fund balances is *unreserved*, which may be divided between *designated* and *undesignated*. The $16,000 designated for equipment may show the city council's intent to purchase a new police car. Only the $75,000 is unreserved and undesignated and, thus, available for unrestricted use in 20X7.

Uncollected property taxes may appear in three accounts. Taxes Receivable—Current is debited when property taxes are levied, and Revenue is credited. When uncollected property taxes are past due and interest revenue begins to accrue, the account balance is transferred to Taxes Receivable—Delinquent. When tax liens (a claim to take property for unpaid taxes) are placed on properties for uncollected taxes, the remaining amount of uncollected property taxes is transferred to Tax Liens Receivable. In the Middletown September 30, 20X6, general fund trial balance, all property taxes receivable are past due. An allowance account for estimated uncollectibles is established for each receivable.

Recording the Budget. The city council and the mayor have approved the budget for the following fiscal year, with estimated revenues of $1,350,000, appropriations of $1,300,000, and an estimated transfer of $30,000 to be made during the year to the debt service fund. Again, transfers to other funds are not expenditures and are segregated in the budgetary entry into a budgetary account labeled Estimated Other Financing Uses. The October 1, 20X6, entry to record Middletown's fiscal year 20X7 budget for its general fund is as follows:

B1.	Estimated Revenues	1,350,000	
	Appropriations		1,300,000
	Estimated Other Financing Uses		30,000
	Budgetary Fund Balance—Unreserved		20,000

To support total estimated revenues of $1,350,000, a breakdown of sources should be provided in the explanation of the budget entry or in a separate schedule. In practice, there could be as many as 100 or more revenue items. As an example, however, the number of revenue items is condensed, as shown in the schedule of estimated revenues (Illustration 15-3).

Illustration 15-3
City of Middletown
General Fund Estimated Revenues
For Year Ended September 30, 20X7

General property taxes	$ 882,500
Fines	75,500
Licenses and permits	50,000
Revenue from federal grants	200,000
Other revenues	142,000
Total estimated revenues	$1,350,000

Just as the total projected income is debited to Estimated Revenues in the general ledger, so each of the detailed estimated sources is debited to its own account in the subsidiary revenue ledger. The following subsidiary account for general property taxes illustrates the procedure of posting to subsidiary records:

Revenue Ledger

ACCOUNT General Property Taxes				ACCOUNT NO.
DATE	ITEM	DEBIT (Estimate)	CREDIT (Actual)	BALANCE (DR.) CR.
Oct. 1	Budget estimate	**882,500**		(882,500)

Not only must the accounting system provide for control of revenues, but it also must accommodate expenditures. To provide a basis for comparison between expected and actual expenditures, budgetary as well as actual expenditures accounts are an integral part of the accounting system. In the entry to record Middletown's budget for its general fund, the credit to Appropriations represents the estimate of the expenditures of $1,300,000 for the coming year. In support of the appropriations total, a summary of approved estimated expenditures by departments or activities might appear as shown in Illustration 15-4.

Illustration 15-4
City of Middletown
Department or Activity Appropriations
For Year Ended September 30, 20X7

General government: legislative, judicial, and executive	$ 129,000
Public safety	277,300
Education	591,450
Highways and streets	94,500
Sanitation and health	97,750
Welfare	51,000
Culture and recreation	59,000
Total appropriations	$1,300,000

Each of these departments or activities must submit detailed appropriation requests on the basis of subfunctions and object of expenditure. The Education Division, for example, might present the estimate of expenditures shown in Illustration 15-5.

Illustration 15-5
City of Middletown
Education Division
Request for Appropriation
For Year Ended September 30, 20X7

Supplies	$160,000
Salaries	350,000
Equipment	60,000
Professional fees	21,450
Total	$591,450

A further modification to controlling expenditures is to establish subsidiary accounts by division or department. If this approach is followed by the city of Middletown, each of the expenditure items for the Education Division would have its own subsidiary account, such as the one that follows for supplies. Each expenditure account would be designed to show the original appropriation, the encumbrances (amounts committed), the expenditures (amounts spent), and the remaining unobligated (i.e., neither encumbered nor expended) balance.

Education Division Expenditure Ledger

ACCOUNT Supplies							ACCOUNT NO.
		ENCUMBRANCES			EXPENDITURES		UNOBLIGATED
DATE	ITEM	DEBIT	CREDIT	BALANCE	ITEM	TOTAL	BALANCE
Oct. 1	Budget appropriation						**160,000**

Recording Actual Revenues and Transfers. Property taxes are a major source of revenue for Middletown's general fund and should be recognized in the fiscal period for which the taxes are levied. The property tax roll provides information about property owners, legal descriptions, and amounts of gross tax levies. The following journal entry shows that the total tax levy against property owners is debited to Taxes Receivable—Current in a general ledger entry. The amount of allowance for uncollectible taxes is credited in the same journal entry, and the net amount (the amount the government expects to receive) is credited to Revenues:

1. Taxes Receivable—Current	919,000	
Revenues		881,300
Allowance for Uncollectible Current Taxes		37,700

Recording the revenue for the expected amount to be received is different from the accounting we would see for a business enterprise. A business enterprise would credit revenue for the entire amount of sales. In a separate entry, bad debt expense would be debited for the amount of receivables expected to be uncollectible. In a business enterprise, bad debt expense is viewed as a cost of doing business. The costs of doing business for a period (expenses) are matched on the income statement with revenues for the same period to determine net income. In governmental funds, however, property tax revenues are generated by levying taxes rather than by earning them through the production and sale of goods and services. Consequently, uncollected taxes are viewed as reductions of revenue, not as costs of doing business. If allowance amounts eventually prove to be overstated, they are written down with an offsetting credit entry to Revenues. If understated, they are increased with an offsetting debit to Revenues.

The general property taxes account in the subsidiary revenue ledger is credited for the actual revenue. After the preceding entry is posted, General Property Taxes appears as follows:

Revenue Ledger

ACCOUNT General Property Taxes				ACCOUNT NO.
DATE	ITEM	DEBIT (Estimate)	CREDIT (Actual)	BALANCE (DR.) CR.
Oct. 1	Budget estimate	882,500		(882,500)
1	Tax levy		**881,300**	(1,200)

During the fiscal period, a debit balance in a subsidiary revenue account usually represents additional revenue expected in the future. At the end of the fiscal period, a debit balance indicates a deficiency of actual revenue as compared to estimated revenue, while a credit balance shows an excess of actual over estimated revenues.

During the year, the following additional events related to revenue are recorded in the general fund of Middletown, whose beginning trial balance is shown on page 863.

Event	Entry in the General Fund		
2. Of the total delinquent taxes of $30,000 carried over from the prior period, $14,000 is collected. The balance is uncollectible.	Cash	14,000	
	Allowance for Uncollectible Delinquent Taxes	16,000	
	Taxes Receivable—Delinquent		30,000
3. The excess allowance for uncollectible delinquent taxes is transferred to Revenues. This transaction is viewed as a change in an accounting estimate made in a prior period.	Allowance for Uncollectible Delinquent Taxes	4,000	
	Revenues		4,000
4. Of $24,000 total tax liens carried over from the prior period, $11,000 is collected. The balance is uncollectible.	Cash	11,000	
	Allowance for Uncollectible Tax Liens	8,000	
	Tax Liens Receivable		19,000
5. The remaining Tax Liens Receivable are charged against Revenues. This transaction is viewed as a change in an accounting estimate made in a prior period.	Revenues	5,000	
	Tax Liens Receivable		5,000
6. Of current taxes receivable (due on or before the end of the fiscal period), $850,000 is collected during the year and $12,700 is written off as uncollectible.	Cash	850,000	
	Allowance for Uncollectible Current Taxes	12,700	
	Taxes Receivable—Current		862,700
7. A 1% sales tax on restaurant food and beverages beginning on the first day of the last quarter is adopted by Middletown. The annual budget is amended to reflect the impact of this new legislation.	Estimated Revenues	9,000	
	Budgetary Fund Balance		9,000
8. Restaurant food and beverage sales for the last quarter of the year are estimated at $950,000.	Sales Taxes Receivable	9,500	
	Revenues		9,500

Event	Entry in the General Fund		
9. Police fines of $79,000 are imposed and collected during the year.	Cash	79,000	
	Revenues		79,000
10. Pet licenses are sold for 2-year periods. Half of the pet license fees collected during the current year apply to the current year. The other half apply to next year. None of the fees are refundable.	Cash	12,000	
	Revenues		6,000
	Deferred Revenues		6,000
11. Revenues from other licenses and permits apply only to the current period and are not refundable.	Cash	35,000	
	Revenues		35,000
12. Interest revenue earned on investment of idle cash during the year.	Cash	17,000	
	Revenues		17,000
13. A contribution by a business to entice the city to extend a storm sewer to its property along a city street.	Cash	130,000	
	Revenues		130,000
14. City council decided that the city's Fund Balance—Unreserved, Undesignated was too lean and rescinded its plan to buy a new police car.	Fund Balance—Unreserved, Designated for Public Safety	16,000	
	Fund Balance—Unreserved, Undesignated		16,000
15. At year-end, property taxes not collected are classified as delinquent, as are the estimated uncollectible allowances.	Taxes Receivable—Delinquent	56,300	
	Taxes Receivable—Current ($919,000 – $862,700)		56,300
	Allowance for Uncollectible Current Taxes	25,000	
	Allowance for Uncollectible Delinquent Taxes ($37,700 – $12,700)		25,000
16. Middletown receives a $150,000 check from the federal government for the current fiscal year to assist in the operation of its child-care program and documentation promising an additional $50,000, half of which is for the current fiscal year and half for the next fiscal year.	Cash	150,000	
	Due from Federal Government	50,000	
	Revenues		175,000
	Deferred Revenue		25,000

As indicated in the second and fourth entries, a revision of the estimated amount of uncollectible current and delinquent taxes and tax liens is treated as a change in accounting estimate through Revenues. Adjustments of confirmed errors of prior periods and adjustments from a change in accounting principle are recorded directly in the Fund Balance—Unreserved, Undesignated.

8

OBJECTIVE

Demonstrate how to account for encumbrances.

Recording Encumbrances and Actual Expenditures. To prevent overexpenditure, the Middletown general fund uses an encumbrance system. An encumbrance can be viewed as an *expected expenditure* and assists the administration to avoid overspending and to plan for payment of the *expected liability* on a timely basis. It can also be viewed as a contra account to the fund balance to reflect the ultimate decrease that will occur. Under this system, whenever a purchase order or other commitment is approved, an entry is made to record the estimated cost of the commitment. For example, an approved purchase order for school supplies, estimated to cost $10,000, is recorded as follows:

17.	Encumbrances	10,000	
	Fund Balance—Reserved for Encumbrances		10,000

The entry is posted to the general ledger, where Encumbrances is a quasi expenditure account and where Fund Balance—Reserved for Encumbrances is a form of restriction of the fund balance. The entry also is entered in the encumbrances section of the supplies account of the subsidiary expenditure ledger for the Education Division, reducing the unobligated balance, as follows:

Education Division Expenditure Ledger

ACCOUNT Supplies							ACCOUNT NO.
		ENCUMBRANCES			EXPENDITURES		UNOBLIGATED
DATE	ITEM	DEBIT	CREDIT	BALANCE	ITEM	TOTAL	BALANCE
Oct. 1	Budget appropriation						160,000
4	Purchase order	**10,000**		10,000			150,000

When the invoice is received for the purchase of items or services, the encumbrance entry is reversed. The contra account to the fund balance is no longer needed since the expenditure recorded will directly reduce the fund balance in the closing procedure. Note that it is always the amount of the original estimate and not the actual cost that is used in the reversing entry. Assuming that the invoice for supplies amounts to $10,200, the two entries to record the receipt of the supplies invoice are as follows:

18.	Fund Balance—Reserved for Encumbrances	10,000	
	Encumbrances		10,000
	To reverse entry for encumbrance at estimated cost.		
19.	Expenditures	10,200	
	Vouchers Payable		10,200
	To record invoice at actual cost.		

The supplies account in the subsidiary expenditure ledger appears as follows:

Education Division Expenditure Ledger

ACCOUNT Supplies							ACCOUNT NO.
		ENCUMBRANCES			EXPENDITURES		UNOBLIGATED
DATE	ITEM	DEBIT	CREDIT	BALANCE	ITEM	TOTAL	BALANCE
Oct. 1	Budget appropriation						160,000
4	Purchase order	**10,000**		10,000			150,000
Nov. 7	Invoice received		**10,000**	0	**10,200**	10,200	149,800

When the encumbrance and the actual amount are identical, the unobligated balance is not changed. However, when the amounts are not identical, the net effect is an adjustment of the unobligated balance to reflect the amount of the actual expenditure. Thus, at any time, the subsidiary ledgers provide a continuing record of the unobligated balances and of how closely the actual expenditures match encumbrances. The following equation is derived from an examination of the supplies account:

Unobligated Balance = Appropriations − Expenditures Total − Encumbrances Balance

The encumbrances account can appear as a contra to the Fund Balance—Unreserved, Undesignated at year-end as shown in the following example:

Fund balances:		
Reserved for Encumbrances		XXX
Unreserved, Undesignated	XXX	
Less Encumbrances	XXX	XXX
Total Fund Balance		XXX

It is, however, preferable to close it against the fund balance at year-end to clarify what amount of the fund balance is available for the future. At year-end, the remaining balance in the encumbrance account is closed against Fund Balance—Unreserved, Undesignated as follows:

Fund Balance—Unreserved, Undesignated	XXX	
Encumbrances		XXX

This will leave the amount of the outstanding encumbrances in Fund Balance—Reserved for Encumbrances, which is reported in the fund balances section of the balance sheet. Such treatment demonstrates the commitment of the government to provide for outstanding purchase orders and serves to reduce the amount of expendable available financial resources for new expenditures indicated in Fund Balance—Unreserved, Undesignated. Encumbrances are not reported in the Statement of Revenues, Expenditures, and Changes in Fund Balances since the actual transaction with outside parties has not yet occurred.

For expenditures such as salaries, which are subject to little variation and to additional internal controls, it is not customary to involve the encumbrance accounts. When salaries are paid, they are recorded directly as expenditures, and they reduce the unobligated balance of the salaries account in the subsidiary expenditure ledger.

Encumbrances of a Prior Period. When encumbrances are carried over from the prior year to the current year, the encumbrance closing entry of the prior year is reversed in order to reinstate the past commitments that will be honored in the current year.

Encumbrances	XXX	
Fund Balance—Unreserved, Undesignated		XXX

Included in the current-year budgetary entry for appropriations should be an amount equal to that prior year-end encumbrance. The encumbrances will be disposed of in the manner described earlier. The unreserved fund balance will ultimately be reduced by the current year's actual expenditures.

The following events relate to Middletown's expenditures and transfers during the year.

Event		Entry in the General Fund		
20. Throughout the year, encumbrances totaling $738,000 were recorded; there were no prior-year encumbrances.		Encumbrances	738,000	
		Fund Balance—Reserved for Encumbrances		738,000
21. Vouchers were approved, liquidating $700,000 of encumbrances for:		Fund Balance—Reserved for Encumbrances	700,000	
		Encumbrances		700,000
Supplies	$300,000			
Building	200,000*	Inventory of Supplies	300,000	
Other expenditures	272,000	Expenditures	472,000	
Total	$772,000	Vouchers Payable		772,000

*This also requires an entry in the general fixed asset account group.

(continued)

Event		Entry in the General Fund		
22. Vouchers were approved for the following nonencumbered items:		Expenditures	518,000	
		Vouchers Payable		518,000
Salaries	$490,000			
Other expenditures	28,000			
Total	$518,000			
23. Vouchers totaling $1,300,000 were paid.		Vouchers Payable	1,300,000	
		Cash		1,300,000
24. Transfer of $30,000 is made to the debt service fund.		Other Financing Uses	30,000	
		Cash		30,000
25. Supplies totaling $260,000 were consumed.		Expenditures	260,000	
		Inventory of Supplies		260,000
26. Adjust Fund Balance—Reserved for Inventory of Supplies to equal inventory. (See following discussion.)		Fund Balance—Unreserved, Undesignated	40,000	
		Fund Balance—Reserved for Inventory of Supplies		40,000

Fund Balance Reserves. The amount of unreserved fund balance represents expendable, available financial resources. Any resources not available to finance expenditures of the current or future years must be removed from the unreserved fund balance. The reserve for encumbrances has already been discussed. An asset not available to finance expenditures for Middletown is the inventory of supplies, which will not be converted into cash and will not be available to meet future commitments. Therefore, the unreserved fund balance must be restricted by an amount equal to the inventory on the financial statement date. In this case, the amount of the inventory at year-end is $50,000 ($10,000 + $300,000 − $260,000). The account Fund Balance—Reserved for Inventory of Supplies is kept equal to the inventory amount by periodic adjustment through the unreserved fund balance account. Similarly, fund balance reserves may be established for petty cash and advances to other funds that will not be converted to cash in the current period.

Corrections of Prior Years' Errors. Corrections of previous years' errors are made directly through the account Fund Balance—Unreserved, Undesignated. For example, Middletown failed to record invoiced expenditures for last year of $30,600 that were not encumbered. Of this amount, $10,100 was paid this year and incorrectly debited to Expenditures. The unpaid portion of $20,500 is vouchered. The entry is as follows:

27. Fund Balance—Unreserved, Undesignated	30,600	
Expenditures		10,100
Vouchers Payable		20,500
To correct error for failure to record expenditures chargeable to last year.		

Reimbursement for Expenditure. When expenditures are made from the general fund on behalf of other funds, a transfer is made to reimburse the general fund. The reimbursement is recorded as an expenditure by the reimbursing fund and as a reduction in expenditures by the recipient (general) fund. For example, $3,000 is received from the special revenue fund to reimburse the general fund for payroll expenditures. The entry in the general fund is recorded as follows:

28. Cash	3,000	
Expenditures		3,000

Investments in Marketable Securities and Other Financial Instruments. Governmental entities frequently have cash available for short-, intermediate-, and long-term investment. For example, the general fund may have cash available for short periods of time pending disbursement for operating needs, the capital projects funds may have bond proceeds available for intermediate-term investment pending disbursement for construction costs, and fiduciary funds may have cash available for long-term investment. Investment pools used by several funds within a single government or by several governments may have cash available for investment for varying terms.

Governments usually make deposits with financial institutions (such as demand deposit accounts and certificates of deposit) and direct investments in U.S. government obligations. Governmental entities also invest in commercial paper, bankers' acceptances, mutual funds, pooled investment funds managed by a state treasurer, and repurchase agreements with broker-dealers. All investments, except for money market investments and participating interest-earning investment contracts with a remaining maturity of one year or less, are to be reported at *fair value* on the balance sheet. Fair value is defined as the amount at which an investment could be exchanged in a current transaction between willing parties, other than in a forced or liquidation sale.[15] The change in fair value of investments is reported as a *net increase (decrease) in the fair value of investments* and recognized as revenue in the operating statement. For example, if general fund investments increased in value during the period, the following entry would be made to reflect the change in fair value:

29. Investments	4,500	
Net Increase in the Fair Value of Investments		4,500

To meet cash flow requirements for operating or capital purposes, or to earn a higher return on investment, many governments enter into *reverse repurchase agreements* and/or *securities lending transactions*. In a reverse repurchase agreement, the government temporarily converts securities in their portfolios to cash by selling securities to a broker-dealer for cash, with a promise to repay cash plus interest in exchange for the return of the same securities.[16] In securities lending transactions, governments lend out their portfolio securities in return for collateral—which may be cash, securities, or letters of credit—and simultaneously agree to return the collateral for the same securities in the future.[17]

The investments must remain on the balance sheet of the government in both cases—whether selling securities with a promise to repurchase or lending them for a period of time. The agreements to repurchase (or return) are reported as fund liabilities. Any cash received (including cash received as collateral) is reported as an asset. Interest costs and broker fees are reported as expenditures and are not netted with any interest earned.

Extensive note disclosures on all investments and deposits with banks and other financial institutions are required. Governments must disclose their relevant accounting policies as to investments. They must also disclose credit risk, market risk, and legal risk for all investments, including derivatives.

The preclosing year-end trial balance for Middletown is presented in Illustration 15-6.

---

15 GASB Statement No. 31, *Accounting and Financial Reporting for Certain Investments and for External Investment Pools* (Norwalk, CT: Governmental Accounting Standards Board, March 1997).

16 GASB Statement No. 3, *Deposits with Financial Institutions, Investments (including Repurchase Agreements, and Reverse Repurchase Agreements)* (Norwalk, CT: Governmental Accounting Standards Board, April 1986).

17 GASB Technical Bulletin No. 94-1, *Disclosure about Derivatives and Similar Debt and Investment Transactions* (Norwalk, CT: Governmental Accounting Standards Board, December 1994).

Illustration 15-6
City of Middletown
General Fund Trial Balance
September 30, 20X7

	Debit	Credit
Cash	50,000	
Investments	157,500	
Property Taxes Receivable—Delinquent	56,300	
Allowance for Uncollectible Delinquent Taxes		25,000
Deferred Revenue		31,000
Inventory of Supplies	50,000	
Vouchers Payable		190,700
Sales Taxes Receivable	9,500	
Due from Federal Government	50,000	
Fund Balance—Reserved for Inventory of Supplies		50,000
Fund Balance—Unreserved, Undesignated		20,400
Revenues		1,336,300
Expenditures	1,250,100	
Other Financing Uses	30,000	
Encumbrances	38,000	
Fund Balance—Reserved for Encumbrances		38,000
Estimated Revenues	1,359,000	
Appropriations		1,300,000
Estimated Other Financing Uses		30,000
Budgetary Fund Balance—Unreserved		29,000
Total	3,050,400	3,050,400

Closing the General Fund

The simplest closing process is, first, to reverse the budgetary entries and then to close the actual revenue and expenditure accounts, including the other financing sources and uses accounts, into the fund balance—unreserved, undesignated account. The outstanding balance in the encumbrances account is also temporarily closed. Budgetary closing entries for Middletown would appear as follows:

		Debit	Credit
B2.	Appropriations	1,300,000	
	Estimated Other Financing Uses	30,000	
	Budgetary Fund Balance—Unreserved	29,000	
	Estimated Revenues		1,359,000
	To reverse entry recording budget (including amendment).		

The actual closing entries are as follows:

		Debit	Credit
30.	Revenues	1,336,300	
	Expenditures		1,250,100
	Other Financing Uses		30,000
	Fund Balance—Unreserved, Undesignated		56,200
	To close the actual accounts.		

31.	Fund Balance—Unreserved, Undesignated	38,000	
	Encumbrances		38,000
	To close outstanding encumbrances.		

REFLECTION

- The general ledger contains permanent balance sheet, budgetary, and operating accounts.
- Budgetary, operating, and closing entries are used in accounting for the general ledger accounts.
- Understanding the accounting and reporting procedures of the general fund will help in understanding accounting for other funds.

FINANCIAL REPORTS OF THE GENERAL FUND

9

OBJECTIVE

Prepare fund financial statements for the general fund.

Financial statements covering all funds of state and local governments are presented in Chapter 17. The required financial statements include fund-based and consolidated government-wide statements. Greater detail, including comparative data, may be provided by supplemental reports for individual funds and account groups and will be illustrated when appropriate.

To illustrate the recommended form of the financial statements, the year-end reports of Middletown's general fund are developed from the year-end trial balance shown on page 872. These reports consist of a balance sheet and a statement of revenues, expenditures, and changes in fund balances.

Balance Sheet

The general fund year-end balance sheet for the city of Middletown, shown in Illustration 15-7 on page 874, differs substantially from its private business counterpart. First, it deals primarily with current assets and current liabilities, and the difference between these two amounts appears as the fund balance—either reserved (committed) or unreserved. Second, the long-term classifications of assets and liabilities are excluded, since the general fixed assets are included in the general fixed assets account group, and the general long-term debt is carried in the general long-term debt account group.

Statement of Revenues, Expenditures, and Changes in Fund Balances

The **statement of revenues, expenditures, and changes in fund balances** is prepared on an all-inclusive basis, disclosing all elements that contribute to the change in fund balances. This operating statement contains details on the major revenue sources and on expenditures by function or program. Other financing sources or uses and any corrections that altered the fund balance are also presented. The detailed source of each revenue and purpose for each expenditure is obtained from the subsidiary ledger, not the control entries of the previous example.

For governmental funds for which an annual budget legally is adopted, a comparison of actual results to both the original and amended budget is required. The comparison can be accomplished either as a schedule provided as required supplementary information (RSI) immediately following the financial statements or as a separate statement. Both original and final budget amounts are compared with actual amounts, and a variance column showing the difference between budgeted and actual amounts is encouraged. In order for the comparisons to

Illustration 15-7
City of Middletown
General Fund Balance Sheet
September 30, 20X7

Assets		
Cash		$ 50,000
Investments		157,500
Property taxes receivable—delinquent	$ 56,300	
Less allowance for uncollectible delinquent taxes	25,000	31,300
Sales taxes receivable		9,500
Due from federal government		50,000
Inventory of supplies		50,000
Total assets		$348,300
Liabilities and Fund Equity		
Liabilities:		
Vouchers payable	$190,700	
Deferred revenue	31,000	
Total liabilities		$221,700
Fund balances:		
Reserved for encumbrances	$ 38,000	
Reserved for inventory of supplies	50,000	
Unreserved, undesignated	38,600	
Total fund balance		126,600
Total liabilities and fund balance		$348,300

be meaningful, GASB Statement No. 34 requires that the actual amounts in the schedule be reported on a budgetary basis. Further, a reconciliation from the budgetary basis to GAAP is required either on the face of the budgetary comparison statement or on a separate schedule.

The budgetary comparison schedule for the general fund of Middletown is shown in Illustration 15-8. Estimated and actual amounts of revenues, expenditures, and other changes are reported on a budgetary basis. The beginning and ending fund balances are reported. The final actual fund balances amount ($126,600) must agree with the total fund balance shown on the balance sheet.

REFLECTION

- The two year-end statements of the general fund are the balance sheet and the statement of revenues, expenditures, and changes in fund balances.
- Budgetary comparison schedules or statements are also required for the general fund and other funds for which a budget is adopted.
- Both annual statements differ significantly from those in the private sector.

Illustration 15-8
City of Middletown
Budgetary Comparison Schedule
General Fund
For Year Ended September 30, 20X7
(budgetary basis)

	Original Budget	Amended Budget	Actual Results	Variance Favorable (Unfavorable)
Revenues:				
General property taxes	$ 881,000	$ 882,500	$ 880,300	$ (2,200)
Fines	75,000	75,500	79,000	3,500
Licenses and permits	50,000	50,000	41,000	(9,000)
Intergovernmental revenues	200,000	200,000	175,000	(25,000)
Sales taxes	10,000	9,000	9,500	500
Other revenues	145,000	142,000	151,500	9,500
Total revenues	$1,361,000	$1,359,000	$1,336,300	$(22,700)
Expenditures:				
General government	$ 130,000	$ 129,000	$ 120,305	$ 8,695
Public safety	275,000	277,300	252,795	24,505
Highways and streets	95,000	94,500	86,100	8,400
Sanitation and health	98,000	97,750	87,750	10,000
Welfare	50,000	51,000	46,000	5,000
Culture and recreation	60,000	59,000	53,400	5,600
Education	590,000	591,450	603,750	(12,300)
Total expenditures	$1,298,000	$1,300,000	$1,250,100	$ 49,900
Excess of revenues over expenditures	$ 63,000	$ 59,000	$ 86,200	$ 27,200
Other financing sources (uses)	(30,000)	(30,000)	(30,000)	0
Excess of revenues and other sources over expenditures and other uses	$ 33,000	$ 29,000	$ 56,200	$ 27,200
Fund balances, October 1, 20X6	101,000	101,000	101,000	0
Correction of prior year's expenditures	0	0	(30,600)	(30,600)
Fund balances, September 30, 20X7	$ 134,000	$ 130,000	$ 126,600	$ (3,400)

ACCOUNTING FOR GENERAL CAPITAL ASSETS AND GENERAL LONG-TERM OBLIGATIONS

10
OBJECTIVE

Complete schedules for general capital assets and long-term liabilities.

Accounting control over general capital assets and general long-term obligations (including capital debt) has traditionally been maintained in the general fixed assets account group (GFAAG) and the general long-term debt account group (GLTDAG). The account groups are used only to keep accounting control of general capital assets and general long-term debt of the governmental unit. Under GASB Statement No. 34, account groups are not reported on the fund financial statements, but detailed information about general capital assets and long-term obligations is required in the notes and in the government-wide statements. The presentation in this text assumes that governments will continue to maintain account groups as convenient means of keeping track of such long-term items and for internal control. It is expected, however, that some governments may find alternative types of records, including simple listings, to be more convenient or less costly.

Accounting and Financial Reporting for General Capital Assets

Fixed assets of a proprietary fund or a fiduciary fund are accounted for within those funds and often are referred to as **fund capital assets.** All other fixed assets are considered **general capital assets** and are accounted for in the general fixed assets account group. This account group, which was created to report capital assets that are not resources of any specific fund, may be thought of as an inventory record of fixed assets for the purpose of assigning responsibility for custody and proper use. Typical capital asset categories include: land, buildings, improvements other than buildings, machinery and equipment, and construction in progress. Each category should be substantiated by supporting detailed records. Major infrastructure assets, such as sidewalks, streets, curbs, and bridges acquired after 1980, must also be recorded. Major general infrastructure assets are networks or subsystems that comprise at least 10% of the total cost of all general capital assets. Governments are encouraged, but not required, to capitalize their art and similar assets as long as they are (a) held for public exhibition, education, or research, (b) protected and cared for, and (c) subject to an organizational policy that requires proceeds from sales to be used for acquiring other items for the collection.

The general fixed asset account group is little more than a list of government-owned assets in double-entry form. The acquisition of a general capital asset is recorded in the general fixed assets account group by a debit to one of the six specific asset accounts. The offsetting credit indicates the original funding source of the asset, selected from the following recommended titles:

Investment in General Fixed Assets	
—Capital Projects Funds	—Special Revenue Funds
—General Fund Revenues	—Donations

To illustrate this procedure, a building acquired with general fund revenues would require the following entries:

Fund or Group in which Entry Is Recorded	Entry		
32. General fund	Expenditures	200,000	
	Vouchers Payable		200,000
	(This entry is part of the entry on page 869, which records vouchers of $772,000.)		
33. General fixed assets account group	Buildings	200,000	
	Investment in General Fixed Assets— General Fund Revenues		200,000
	To record the fixed asset.		

The typical basis of a general capital asset is cost or, if the asset is donated, estimated fair value at time of receipt. Subsequent to the acquisition of a capital asset, capital outlay and maintenance expenditures must be accounted for separately, as they are in commercial accounting, since maintenance expenditures should not increase the book values of fixed assets.

As will be explained in Chapter 17, depreciation expense is reported in the government-wide statements. Depreciation expense, however, is not reported in the governmental funds.

> *To record depreciation expense in governmental funds would inappropriately mix two fundamentally different measurements, expenses and expenditures. General fixed asset acquisitions require the use of governmental fund financial resources and are recorded as expenditures. General fixed asset sale proceeds provide governmental fund financial resources. Depreciation expense is neither a source nor a use of governmental fund financial resources, and thus is not properly recorded in the accounts of such funds.*[18]

18 Statement 1, *Government Accounting and Financial Reporting Principles* (Chicago: Municipal Finance Officers Association of the United States and Canada, March 1979), p. 10.

Governments must record accumulated depreciation of general capital assets in the government-wide statements. An entry is made in the general fixed assets account group by debiting the appropriate investment in the general fixed asset account and crediting the accumulated depreciation account.

When a governmental unit disposes of a general capital asset, the original cost (less accumulated depreciation) of the asset is removed from the general fixed assets account group. In the general fund, proceeds from the sale are recorded with a credit to Other Financing Sources. For example, if a governmental unit sells equipment for $90,000, carried in the general fixed assets account group at $100,000, the following entries would be made:

Fund or Group in which Entry Is Recorded	Entry		
34. General fund	Cash	90,000	
	Other Financing Sources		90,000
	To record the proceeds from the sale.		
35. General fixed assets account group	Investment in General Fixed Assets—		
	General Fund Revenues	100,000	
	Machinery and Equipment		100,000
	To remove the fixed asset.		

Instead of selling the equipment, assume the governmental unit traded it for a larger model costing $235,000, with an allowance of $90,000 for the smaller unit. The new asset is recorded at its total cost, with the trade-in value merely functioning as a reduction in the amount to be paid. The entries then would be as follows:

Fund or Group in which Entry Is Recorded	Entry		
36. General fund	Expenditures	145,000	
	Vouchers Payable		145,000
	To record the outflow of cash.		
37. General fixed assets account group	Investment in General Fixed Assets—		
	General Fund Revenues	100,000	
	Machinery and Equipment		100,000
	To remove the old asset.		
	Machinery and Equipment	235,000	
	Investment in General Fixed Assets—		
	General Fund Revenues		235,000
	To record the new fixed asset.		

GASB Statement No. 34 allows governments to avoid charging depreciation on infrastructure assets if they can demonstrate that they have incurred costs to preserve these assets at or above a conditional level established by the government. Under this *modified preservation approach*, all costs to maintain the assets are expensed, and no depreciation is recorded. If a government elects to follow the modified approach, it must assess periodically and disclose in the notes to the financial statements the condition of its infrastructure assets (usually an engineering report) and estimate the annual amount necessary to maintain and preserve the specified assets at or above the condition level. It must also disclose actual amounts spent compared to these estimates. A change from the depreciation method to the modified approach should be accounted for as a change in accounting estimate.

Governments are required to monitor and determine if impairment of a capital asset has occurred. A capital asset is considered impaired if *both* (a) the decline in service utility of the capital asset is large in magnitude *and* (b) the event or change in circumstance is outside the normal life cycle of the capital asset. Impaired capital assets that will no longer be used by the government should be reported at the lower of carrying value or fair value. Impairment losses on capital assets that will continue to be used by the government should be measured using a method that best reflects the diminished service utility of the capital asset, such as cost to restore, percentage of service units provided before and after the impairment, and deflated depreciated replacement cost.[19]

Disclosures about capital assets are required in the notes to the financial statements. Capital assets that are not being depreciated are disclosed separately from those assets that are being depreciated. In addition, beginning-year and end-of-year balances are shown along with capital acquisitions, sales, or other dispositions. A schedule of capital assets that will be included in the notes for Middletown is shown in Illustration 15-9.

Illustration 15-9
City of Middletown
Schedule of Capital Assets

	Beginning Balance	Additions	Retirements	Ending Balance
Governmental activities:				
Land	$ 8,595,000	$4,000,000		$ 12,595,000
Buildings	28,555,000		$ (200,000)	28,355,000
Improvements other than buildings	10,367,500			10,367,500
Machinery and equipment	4,390,000	135,000		4,525,000
Construction in progress	17,222,500			17,222,500
Infrastructure	120,000,000		(2,000,000)	118,000,000
Totals (at historical cost)	$189,130,000	$4,135,000	$(2,200,000)	$191,065,000
Less accumulated depreciation:				
Buildings	$ (850,000)	$ (85,000)	$ 40,000	$ (895,000)
Improvements other than buildings	(150,000)	(20,000)		(170,000)
Machinery and equipment	(215,000)	(50,000)		(265,000)
Infrastructure	(15,000,000)	(350,000)	1,000,000	(14,350,000)
Total depreciation	$ (16,215,000)	$ (505,000)	$ 1,040,000	$ (15,680,000)
Governmental activities capital assets (net)	$172,915,000	$3,630,000	$(1,160,000)	$175,385,000

Accounting and Financial Reporting for General Long-Term Debt

When long-term debt is related to and will be paid from proprietary or fiduciary funds, it is accounted for in those funds and is termed a specific fund liability. When long-term debt is related to and will be paid from governmental funds, the liability is recorded in the general long-term debt account group.

The general long-term debt account group, which was designed to monitor long-term debt that is not the responsibility of any particular fund, furnishes a record of the unmatured principal of all general long-term obligations of the governmental unit. Referring to a long-term obligation as *general* indicates that the community can use its taxing power to pay debt principal and interest. The general long-term debt account group is not limited to liabilities arising from debt issuance and may include numerous types of unmatured general government liabilities; for example, claims and judgments, accumulated sick leave and other compensated absences, underfunded pension contributions, unfunded postretirement benefits other than pensions, and capital lease obligations, as well as unmatured bonds and notes. Interest is not accounted for in the general long-term debt account group. To maintain the self-balancing nature of the account group, the incurrence of long-term obligations is recorded by debiting Amount to Be Provided for Payment of (properly identified) Debt and crediting a liability account. As emphasized in the previous section, the use of account groups is a convenient mechanism for keeping track of long-term liabilities that may eventually be replaced by other means, such as simple ledgers.

19 GASB Statement No. 42, *Accounting and Financial Reporting for Impairment of Capital Assets and for Insurance Recoveries* (Norwalk, CT: Governmental Accounting Standards Board, November 2003).

To illustrate the entries for the general long-term debt account group, assume that a unit incurs a general long-term obligation in the form of term bonds of $1,000,000 to acquire property.[20] Regardless of whether the bonds are issued at a premium or discount, the bond issue is recorded at its face amount in the general long-term debt account group. As shown in the following entry, the bonds are recorded in the general long-term debt account group at the face value to be redeemed at maturity.

38.	Amount to Be Provided for Payment of Term Bonds	1,000,000	
	Term Bonds Payable		1,000,000

Payment of both principal and interest is handled by the debt service fund, where *service* is synonymous with *payment*, but the general long-term debt account group records only amounts that become available in the debt service fund for retirement of general long-term debt principal. Assuming the debt service fund receives an annual appropriation of $80,000 to provide for the eventual retirement of the term bonds, the following entry is recorded in the general long-term debt account group.

39.	Amount Available in Debt Service Funds—Term Bonds	80,000	
	Amount to Be Provided for Payment of Term Bonds		80,000

If sound actuarial practices have been employed, the debt service fund will retire the obligation at the appropriate time and the general long-term debt account group will make the following entry:

40.	Term Bonds Payable	1,000,000	
	Amount Available in Debt Service Funds—Term Bonds.		1,000,000

A schedule of general long-term liabilities for Middletown appears in Illustration 15-10. The schedule includes the example transactions in this section. With the adoption of GASB Statement No. 34, governments report long-term obligations on a full-accrued basis in the government-wide statements. A discussion of the adjusting entries needed to reflect amortization of premium or discount and interest accruals is found in Chapter 17.

Information about long-term debt, significant contingent liabilities, pension plan obligations, accumulated sick leave and other compensated absences, debt service requirements to maturity, commitments under noncapitalized leases, and changes in general long-term debt are required note disclosures.

Illustration 15-10
City of Middletown
Schedule of Long-Term Liabilities

	Beginning Balance	Additions	Retirements	Ending Balance
General long-term debt payable:				
General obligation debt	$21,962,000	$2,000,000	$999,950	$22,962,050
Special assessment debt	2,000,000			2,000,000
Unfunded pension costs.	139,000	2,123		141,123
Capital lease payable	99,950	35,944		135,894
Unfunded compensated absences.	160,325	3,433		163,758
Unfunded claims and judgment.	412,222	179,923		592,145
Total general long-term debt payable	$24,773,497	$2,221,423	$999,950	$25,994,970

20 A term bond is one in which the entire principal is due on one date; a serial bond issue is redeemed in periodic payments. Term bonds are rare, but they better illustrate entries in the general long-term debt account group.

Leasing of equipment has become common practice among governments. When leases qualify as operating, the rent expenditures are recorded in the fund, and no entry is made in the account group. However, if a lease qualifies as a capital lease (using the criteria of FASB No. 13), then the substance of the transaction is similar to the purchase of a fixed asset with long-term debt proceeds. Therefore, entries are as follows:

Event and Fund or Group in which Entry Is Recorded		Entry		
41. At inception of the lease, the present value of the lease payments is recorded in the fund as expenditures and other financing sources.	General fund	Expenditures Other Financing Sources	50,000	 50,000
42. In the account group, the leased asset is recorded at its present value.	General fixed assets account group	Leased Asset Investment in GFA—General Funds	50,000	 50,000
43. In the account group, the long-term lease obligation is recorded.	General long-term debt account group	Amount to Be Provided Lease Obligation	50,000	 50,000

Subsequent lease payments are made from the Debt Service Fund as will be presented in Chapter 16.

REFLECTION

- Account groups have traditionally been used to keep track of capital assets and long-term debt.
- Under GASB Statement No. 34, account groups will not be reported on the financial statements. Rather, schedules of capital assets and long-term liabilities will be presented in the notes to the financial statements. Capital assets and long-term debt will also be reported in the government-wide statements.
- Many governments continue to use the account groups as a convenient means of recording additions and deductions from capital assets and long-term debt.
- Governments are required to record infrastructure assets and depreciation.

REVIEW OF ENTRIES FOR THE GENERAL FUND AND ACCOUNT GROUPS

The following example will provide a comprehensive review of the general fund, the general fixed assets account group, and the general long-term debt account group. The general fund balance sheet for Junction City, as of December 31, 20X6, is shown in Illustration 15-11.

Illustration 15-11
Junction City
General Fund Balance Sheet
December 31, 20X6

Assets		
Cash		$100,000
Taxes receivable, delinquent, 20X6	$50,000	
Less allowance for uncollectible delinquent taxes, 20X6	20,000	30,000
Tax liens receivable, 20X5	$25,000	
Less allowance for uncollectible tax liens, 20X5	5,000	20,000
Inventory of supplies		20,000
Total assets		$170,000
Liabilities and Fund Equity		
Liabilities:		
Vouchers payable		$ 30,000
Fund balances:		
Reserved for encumbrances	$40,000	
Reserved for inventory of supplies	20,000	
Unreserved, undesignated	80,000	
Total fund balance		140,000
Total liabilities and fund balance		$170,000

During 20X7, the following entries are recorded in the general fund of Junction City. If an event also requires that an entry be made in one of the account groups, the necessary entry is indicated as part of the event.

Event		Entry in the General Fund		
The budget is approved.		Estimated Revenues	600,000	
Estimated inflows are from:		Estimated Other Financing Sources	284,000	
Revenues	$ 600,000	Budgetary Fund Balance—Unreserved	26,000	
General long-term debt issuance	200,000	Appropriations		860,000
Transfers from other funds	60,000	Estimated Other Financing Uses		50,000
Sales of fixed assets carried at $100,000	24,000			
Estimated outflows are for:				
Expenditures [Includes 20X6 holdover encumbrances ($40,000) and use of supplies ($20,000)]	860,000			
Transfers to other funds	50,000			
The amount of the Fund Balance—Reserved for Encumbrances was reinstated in Encumbrances.		Encumbrances	40,000	
		Fund Balance—Unreserved, Undesignated		40,000
Property taxes of $500,000 are levied, of which $30,000 is estimated to be uncollectible.		Taxes Receivable—Current	500,000	
		Allowance for Uncollectible Current Taxes		30,000
		Revenues		470,000

(continued)

Event	Entry in the General Fund		
Cash obtained from local banks to finance government operations in advance of collection of first property tax installment.	Cash	200,000	
	Tax Anticipation Note Payable		200,000
Collection of taxes and related interest for the year:	Cash	495,000	
Current taxes . . . $ 450,000	Taxes Receivable—Current		450,000
Delinquent taxes, 20X6 . . . 32,000	Taxes Receivable—Delinquent, 20X6		32,000
Interest on delinquent taxes . . . 2,000	Tax Liens Receivable, 20X5		10,000
Tax liens, 20X5 . . . 10,000	Revenues		3,000
Interest on tax liens, 20X5 . . . 1,000			
Total . . . $ 495,000			
Repayment of tax anticipation note payable plus interest upon collection of property taxes.	Tax Anticipation Notes Payable	200,000	
	Expenditures	3,000	
	Cash		203,000
Property against which there are unpaid tax liens for 20X5 is sold for $7,000. (The loss is an adjustment of current revenue, since it represents a change in estimate.)	Cash	7,000	
	Allowance for Uncollectible Tax Liens, 20X5	5,000	
	Revenues	3,000	
	Tax Liens Receivable, 20X5		15,000
Tax liens totaling $18,000 are issued against 20X6 delinquent taxpayers.	Tax Liens Receivable, 20X6	18,000	
	Taxes Receivable—Delinquent, 20X6		18,000
Allowance for Uncollectible Delinquent Taxes is reclassified and reduced, so as not to exceed the related receivable of $18,000. As a change in estimate, the credit is made to Revenues.	Allowance for Uncollectible Delinquent Taxes, 20X6	20,000	
	Allowance for Uncollectible Tax Liens, 20X6		18,000
	Revenues		2,000
Uncollected current taxes are declared delinquent, and the related allowance is reclassified.	Taxes Receivable—Delinquent, 20X7	50,000	
	Taxes Receivable—Current		50,000
	Allowance for Uncollectible Current Taxes	30,000	
	Allowance for Uncollectible Delinquent Taxes, 20X7		30,000
Revenue for licenses, fees, and fines is recognized.	Fines Receivable	3,000	
	Cash	67,000	
	Revenues		70,000
To acquire land, a general long-term $200,000 serial bond issue is sold for 102.	Cash	204,000	
	Other Financing Sources		204,000
The premium is transferred to the debt service fund.	Other Financing Uses	4,000	
	Cash		4,000

This event requires an entry in the general long-term debt account group:

Amount to Be Provided for Payment of Serial Bonds	200,000	
Serial Bonds Payable		200,000

Event	Entry in the General Fund		
Other funds transfer $60,000 to the general fund.	Cash	60,000	
	Other Financing Sources		60,000
Additional amount encumbered for approved purchase orders was $600,000.	Encumbrances	600,000	
	Fund Balance—Reserved for Encumbrances		600,000

Event		Entry in the General Fund		
Compensated absences earned by employees amounted to $75,000.		No entry in the General Fund		
This event requires an entry in the general long-term debt account group: Amount to Be Provided for Payment of Compensated Absences ... 75,000 Unfunded Compensated Absences .. 75,000				
The actuarial required contribution (ARC) of the government was calculated by the actuary to be $50,000. $20,000 was paid. The remaining $30,000 will not be funded this year.		Expenditures	20,000	
		Cash		20,000
This event requires an entry in the general long-term debt account group: Amount to Be Provided for Payment of Pension Obligation .... 30,000 Unfunded Pension Obligation 30,000				
The following vouchers were approved:		Expenditures	800,000	
General expenditures	$760,000	Inventory of Supplies	70,000	
Purchase of equipment	40,000	Vouchers Payable		870,000
Purchase of supplies (a perpetual inventory system is used)	70,000			
Total	$870,000			
Of this total, $630,000 was encumbered.		Fund Balance—Reserved for Encumbrances	630,000	
		Encumbrances		630,000
The following entry is required in the general fixed assets account group: Machinery and Equipment .... 40,000 Investment in General Fixed Assets—General Fund 40,000				
A lease agreement was signed for equipment. The present value of the lease payments is $30,000.		Expenditures	30,000	
		Other Financing Sources		30,000
This event requires an entry in the general long-term debt account group: Amount to Be Provided ... 30,000 Lease Payable .... 30,000 This event also requires an entry in the general fixed asset account group: Leased Asset .... 30,000 Investment in General Fixed Asset—Capital Lease 30,000				

(continued)

Event	Entry in the General Fund		
$50,000 was transferred from the general fund to other funds.	Other Financing Uses	50,000	
	Cash		50,000
Vouchers totaling $880,000 were paid.	Vouchers Payable	880,000	
	Cash		880,000
The year-end supplies inventory amounted to $26,000.	Expenditures	64,000	
	Inventory of Supplies ($20,000 + $70,000 – $26,000)		64,000
Fund Balance—Reserved for Inventory of Supplies is adjusted to agree with the inventory of supplies.	Fund Balance—Unreserved, Undesignated	6,000	
	Fund Balance—Reserved for Inventory of Supplies ($26,000 – $20,000)		6,000
Equipment carried at $100,000 in the general fixed assets account group is sold for $24,000.			
The following entry is required in the general fixed assets account group: Investment in General Fixed Assets—General Fund ...... 100,000 Machinery and Equipment 100,000	Cash	24,000	
	Other Financing Sources		24,000
Closing entries.	Appropriations	860,000	
	Estimated Other Financing Uses	50,000	
	Estimated Revenues		600,000
	Estimated Other Financing Sources		284,000
	Budgetary Fund Balance—Unreserved		26,000
	Revenues	542,000	
	Other Financing Sources	318,000	
	Fund Balance—Unreserved, Undesignated	111,000	
	Expenditures		917,000
	Other Financing Uses		54,000
	Fund Balance—Unreserved, Undesignated	10,000	
	Encumbrances		10,000

REFLECTION

- It is important to analyze each event to determine whether the entry is made to the general fund or to one of the account groups. Some events will require an entry in the fund and an entry in an account group.

11

OBJECTIVE

Demonstrate an understanding of the 13 basic governmental accounting principles.

APPENDIX: SUMMARY OF ACCOUNTING PRINCIPLES

There are 13 basic governmental accounting principles included in GASB Statement No. 1 and in *Codification of Governmental Accounting and Financial Reporting Standards.* These principles form a model of fund accounting theory and are summarized on the following pages.

Principle 1—Accounting and Reporting Capabilities

A governmental accounting system must make it possible both (a) to present fairly and with full disclosure the financial position and results of financial operation of the funds and account groups of the governmental unit in conformity with generally accepted accounting principles and (b) to determine and demonstrate compliance with finance-related legal and contractual provisions.

Principle 2—Fund Accounting System

Governmental accounting systems should be organized and operated on a fund basis. A fund is defined as a fiscal and accounting entity with a self-balancing set of accounts recording cash and other financial resources, together with all related liabilities and residual equities or balances, and changes therein, which are segregated for the purpose of carrying on specific activities or attaining certain objectives in accordance with special regulations, restrictions, or limitations. Fund financial statements should be used to report detailed information about the primary government, including its blended component units. The focus of governmental and proprietary fund financial statements is on major funds.

Principle 3—Types of Funds

The following types of funds should be used by state and local governments:

Governmental Funds:

1. The General Fund—to account for all financial resources except those required to be accounted for in another fund.
2. Special Revenue Funds—to account for the proceeds of specific revenue sources (other than expendable trusts or for major capital projects) that are legally restricted to expenditure for specified purposes.
3. Capital Projects Funds—to account for financial resources to be used for the acquisition or construction of major capital facilities (other than those financed by proprietary funds and trust funds).
4. Debt Service Funds—to account for the accumulation of resources for, and the payment of, general long-term debt principal and interest.
5. Permanent Funds—to account for legally restricted resources provided by trust in which the earnings, but not the principal, may be used for purposes that support the primary government's programs (those that benefit the government or its citizenry).

Proprietary Funds:

6. Enterprise Funds—to account for operations that are (a) financed and operated in a manner similar to private business enterprises where the intent of the governing body is that the costs (expenses, including depreciation) of providing goods or services to the general public on a continuing basis be financed or recovered primarily through user charges or (b) where the governing body has decided that periodic determination of revenues earned, expenses incurred, and/or net income is appropriate for capital maintenance, public policy, management control, accountability, or other purposes.
7. Internal Service Funds—to account for financing of goods or services provided by one department or agency to other departments or agencies of the governmental unit, or to other governmental units, on a cost-reimbursement basis.

Fiduciary Funds:

These are trust and agency funds used to account for assets held by a governmental unit in a trustee capacity or as an agent for individuals, private organizations, other governmental units, and/or other funds. These include the following:

8. Private-Purpose Trust Funds.
9. Investment Trust Funds.
10. Pension (and other employee benefit) Trust Funds.
11. Agency Funds.

Principle 4—Number of Funds

Governmental units should establish and maintain those funds required by law and sound financial administration. Only the minimum number of funds consistent with legal and operating requirements should be established, however, because unnecessary funds result in inflexibility, undue complexity, and inefficient financial administration.

Principle 5—Reporting Capital Assets

A clear distinction should be made between general capital assets and capital assets of proprietary and fiduciary funds. Capital assets of proprietary funds should be reported in both government-wide and fund financial statements. Capital assets of fiduciary funds should be reported in only the statement of fiduciary net assets. All other capital assets of the governmental unit are general capital assets. They should not be reported as assets in governmental funds but rather in the governmental activities column in the governmental-wide statements of net assets.

Principle 6—Valuation of Capital Assets

Capital assets should be accounted for at historical cost. The cost of a capital asset should include ancillary charges necessary to place the asset into its intended location and condition for use. Donated capital assets should be recorded at their estimated fair value at the time of the acquisition plus ancillary charges, if any.

Principle 7—Depreciation of Capital Assets

Capital assets should be depreciated over their estimated useful lives unless they are either inexhaustible or are infrastructure assets using the modified approach as set forth in GASB Statement No. 34, pars. 23–26. A change from the depreciation method to the modified approach should be reported as a change in accounting estimate. Inexhaustible assets such as land and land improvements should not be depreciated. Depreciation expense should be reported in the government-wide statement of activities; the proprietary fund statement of revenues, expenses, and changes in fund net assets; and the statement of changes in fiduciary net assets.

Principle 8—Reporting Long-Term Liabilities

A clear distinction should be made between fund long-term liabilities and general long-term liabilities. Long-term liabilities directly related to and expected to be paid from proprietary funds should be reported in the proprietary fund statement of net assets and in the government-wide statement of net assets. Long-term liabilities directly related to and expected to be paid from fiduciary funds should be reported in the statement of fiduciary net assets. All other unmatured general long-term liabilities should be reported in the governmental activities column in the government-wide statement of net assets.

Principle 9—Measurement Focus and Basis of Accounting in the Basic Financial Statements

The government-wide financial statement of net assets and statement of activities should be prepared using the economic resources measurement focus and the accrual basis of accounting. Revenues, expenses, gains, losses, assets, and liabilities resulting from the exchange and exchange-like transactions should be recognized when the exchange takes place. Revenues, expenses, assets, and liabilities resulting from nonexchange transactions should be recognized in accordance with GASB Statement No. 33.

In fund financial statements, the modified accrual or accrual basis of accounting, as appropriate, should be used in measuring financial position and operating results.

1. Financial statements for governmental funds should be presented using the current financial resources measurement focus and the modified accrual basis of accounting. Revenues should be recognized in the accounting period in which they become available and measurable. Expenditures should be recognized in the accounting period in which the fund liability is incurred, if measurable, except for unmatured interest on general long-term liabilities, which should be recognized when due.

2. Proprietary fund statements of net assets and revenues, expenses, and changes in fund net assets should be presented using the economic resources measurement focus and the accrual basis of accounting.
3. Financial statements of fiduciary funds should be reported using the economic resources measurement focus and the accrual basis of accounting, except for the recognition of certain liabilities of defined benefit pension plans and certain postemployment healthcare plans.
4. Transfers between funds should be reported in the accounting period in which the interfund receivable and payable arise.

Principle 10—Budgeting, Budgetary Control, and Budgetary Reporting

An annual budget(s) should be adopted by every governmental unit. The accounting system should provide the basis for appropriate budgetary control. Budgetary comparison schedules should be presented as required supplementary information (RSI) for the general fund and each major special revenue fund that has a legally adopted annual budget. The budgetary comparison schedule should present both the original and the final appropriated budgets for the reporting period, as well as actual inflows, outflows, and balances, as stated on the government's budgetary basis.

Principle 11—Transfer, Revenue, Expenditure, and Expense Account Classification

Transfers and proceeds of general long-term debt issues should be classified separately from fund revenues and expenditures or expenses. Governmental fund revenues should be classified by fund and source. Expenditures should be classified by fund, function (or program), organization unit, activity, character, and principal classes of objects. Proprietary fund revenues and expenses should be classified in essentially the same manner as those of similar business organizations, functions, or activities. The statement of activities should present governmental activities at least at the level of detail required in the governmental fund statement of revenues, expenditures, and changes in fund balances—and, at a minimum, by function. Governments should present business-type activities at least by segment.

Principle 12—Common Terminology and Classification

A common terminology and classification should be used consistently throughout the budget, accounts, and financial reports of each fund.

Principle 13—Annual Financial Reports

A comprehensive annual financial report (CAFR) should be prepared and published, covering all funds and account groups of the primary government (including its blended component units) and providing an overview of all discreetly presented component units of the reporting entity—including the introductory section, management's discussion and analysis (MD&A), basic financial statements, required supplementary information other than MD&A, combining and individual fund statements, schedules, narrative explanation, and statistical section. The reporting entity is the primary government (including blended component units) and all discretely presented component units presented in accordance with GASB Statement No. 14.

The basic financial statements should include:

a. Government-wide financial statements.
b. Fund financial statements.
c. Notes to the financial statements.

The financial reporting entity consists of (a) the primary government, (b) organizations for which the primary government is financially accountable, and (c) other organizations for which the nature and significance of their relationship with the primary government are such that exclusion would cause the reporting entity's financial statements to be misleading or incomplete. The reporting entity's government-wide financial statements should display information about the reporting government as a whole, distinguishing between the total primary government and its discretely presented component units, as well as between the primary government's governmental and business-type activities. The reporting entity's fund financial statements should present the primary government's (including its blended component units, which are, in substance, part of the primary government) major funds individually and its nonmajor funds in the aggregate. Funds and components units that are fiduciary in nature should be reported only in the statements of fiduciary net assets and changes in fiduciary net assets.

The nucleus of a financial reporting entity usually is a primary government. However, a governmental organization other than a primary government (such as a component unit, joint venture, jointly governed organization, or other stand-alone government) serves as the nucleus for its own reporting entity when it issues separate financial statements. For all of these entities, the GASB financial reporting entity provisions should be applied in layers *from the bottom up*. At each layer, the definition and display provisions should be applied before the layer is included in the financial statements of the next level of the reporting government.

REFLECTION

- The 13 basic governmental accounting principles form a model of fund accounting theory.

UNDERSTANDING THE ISSUES

1. GASB Statement No. 34 requires reporting using both the financial resources measurement focus and the economic resources measurement focus. How do these two focuses differ, and what impact do they have on the presentation of financial information? Why would the addition of reporting under the economic resources focus provide added value to the understanding of the governmental operations? Identify two accounts that would be accounted for differently under the two focuses.
2. Name three advantages gained by government reporting through the use of the three different fund types and the account groups. Explain why this method of reporting is advantageous.
3. Why are budgets crucial in accounting for governmental entities? If appropriations were not included in fund accounting, what impact would this exclusion have on the financial statements?
4. What advantage is gained by categorizing unreserved fund balances as designated and undesignated?
5. How does the use of an encumbrance system aid in accounting for governmental entities?
6. Why do some transactions require an entry in a fund and another in an account group? What impact would there be if a journal entry were made only in the fund or only in the account group?
7. (Appendix) What is the source of the 13 basic governmental accounting principles, and what benefit is there to studying these principles?

EXERCISES

Exercise 1 *(LO 3, 4, 5)* **Accounting for transactions.** Select the best answer for each of the following multiple-choice questions. (Nos. 3, 5, 8, and 9–11 are AICPA adapted.)

1. In a governmental fund, which one of the following constitutes revenue?
   a. Cash received from another fund of the same unit
   b. Bond proceeds
   c. Property taxes
   d. Refund on an invoice for fuel
2. In a governmental fund, which of the following is considered an expenditure?
   a. The purchase of a capital asset
   b. The consumption of supplies
   c. Salaries earned by employees
   d. All of the above
3. Fixed assets donated to a governmental unit should be recorded
   a. at estimated fair value when received.
   b. at the lower of donor's carrying amount or estimated fair value when received.
   c. at the donor's carrying amount.
   d. as a memorandum entry only.
4. In the recording of a city's budget, which one of the following accounts is debited?
   a. Appropriations
   b. Estimated Revenues
   c. Estimated Other Financing Uses
   d. Encumbrances
5. Which of the following accounts of a governmental unit is usually credited when taxpayers are billed for property taxes?
   a. Appropriations
   b. Taxes Receivable—Current
   c. Estimated Revenues
   d. Revenues
6. When a portion of property tax proceeds recorded in the general fund is transferred to another fund, the account to be debited in the general fund is
   a. Expenditures.
   b. Revenues.
   c. Estimated Revenues.
   d. Other Financing Uses.
7. The general long-term debt account group includes
   a. all long-term debt of a governmental unit.
   b. general long-term capital debt applicable to governmental funds.
   c. long-term capital debt and all long-term operating debt applicable to governmental funds.
   d. all general long-term capital debt plus accrued interest thereon.

8. When equipment was purchased with general fund resources, an appropriate entry was made in the general fixed asset account group. What account would have been debited in the general fund?

   a. Due from Other Funds
   b. Expenditures
   c. Appropriations
   d. No entry should be made in the general fund.

9. Which of the following accounts should Moon City close at the end of its fiscal year?

   a. Vouchers Payable
   b. Expenditures
   c. Fund Balance
   d. Fund Balance—Reserved for Encumbrances

10. Which of the following accounts of a governmental unit is debited when a purchase order is approved?

    a. Appropriations
    b. Vouchers Payable
    c. Fund Balance—Reserved for Encumbrances
    d. Encumbrances

11. Elgar City recorded a 20-year building rental agreement as a capital lease. An asset for the building lease was recorded in the general fixed assets account group. Where should the lease liability be reported?

    a. In the general long-term debt account group
    b. In the debt service fund
    c. In the general fund
    d. A lease liability should not be reported.

12. The Amount Available in the Debt Service Fund is an account of a government unit that is included

    a. in the general long-term debt account group.
    b. in the debt service fund.
    c. in neither the general long-term debt account group nor the long-term debt account group.
    d. in both the debt service fund and the general long-term debt account group.

Exercise 2 *(LO 5, 7, 9)* **Accounting and reporting.** Indicate the part of the general fund statement of revenues, expenditures, and changes in fund balance affected by the following transactions:

a. Revenues.
b. Expenditures.
c. Other financing sources and uses.
d. Residual equity transfers.
e. Statement of revenues, expenditures, and changes in fund balance is not affected.

1. An unrestricted state grant is received.
2. The general fund paid pension fund contributions that were recoverable (reimbursed) from an internal service fund.
3. The general fund paid $60,000 for electricity supplied by the electric utility enterprise fund.
4. General fund resources were used to subsidize the swimming pool enterprise fund.
5. $90,000 of general fund resources were loaned to an internal service fund.

6. A motor pool internal service fund was established by a transfer of $80,000 from the general fund. This amount will not be repaid unless the motor pool is disbanded.
7. General fund resources were used to pay amounts due on an operating lease.

(AICPA adapted)

Exercise 3 *(LO 5, 6)* **Budgetary accounting.** Given the following information, you have been asked to record the budget for the general fund of the city of Monroe.

1. Inflows for 20X4 are expected to total $552,000 and include property tax revenue of $355,000, fines of $7,000, state grants of $90,000, and bond issue proceeds of $100,000.
2. Expenditures for general operations and equipment purchases for the year are estimated to be $500,000.
3. Authorized transfers include $30,000 to the debt service fund to pay interest on bond indebtedness and $15,000 to the capital projects fund to pay for cost overruns on construction of a new civic center.
4. Additional estimated receipts include a $15,000 operating transfer from the special revenue fund and a $50,000 payment from the Electric Utility Enterprise Fund for property taxes.

Exercise 4 *(LO 3, 5, 7)* **Accounting for revenues.** The following information concerns tax revenues for the city of Cedar Crest. The balances concerning property taxes on January 1, 20X3, were as follows:

Delinquent property taxes receivable	$135,000
Allowance for uncollectible delinquent taxes	(40,000)
Tax liens receivable	45,000
Allowance for uncollectible tax liens	(23,000)

Prepare entries in the general fund for the following 20X3 events:

Jan.	Since current property taxes would not be collected for several months, $275,000 was borrowed using tax anticipation notes.
Feb.	Tax liens of $12,000 were collected; in addition, $2,000 of interest was collected that had not been accrued. The balance of tax liens was settled by receiving $16,000 for the property subject to the tax liens.
Apr.	Collections on delinquent property taxes were $100,000, and interest of $4,500 was collected. The interest had not been accrued. The balance of the account was converted into tax liens.
July	Current property taxes were levied for $422,000 with a 5% allowance for uncollectible amounts.
Sept.	Collection of current property taxes totaled $365,000. The tax anticipation notes were paid off with interest of $18,000.

Exercise 5 *(LO 3, 5, 7)* **Accounting for revenues and other inflows.** Prepare journal entries in the general fund for the following 20X4 transactions that represent inflows of financial resources to Bork City:

1. To pay the wages of part-time city maintenance employees, the Cemetery Expendable Trust Fund transfers $45,000 to the general fund.
2. A resident donates land worth $75,000 for a park.
3. The city is notified by the state that it will receive $30,000 in road assistance grants this year.
4. A fire truck with an original cost of $36,000 is sold for $9,000.
5. Sales of license stickers for park use total $5,000. The fees cover this year and next year. Patrolmen are paid from these fees to check for cars in the park without stickers.

Exercise 6 *(LO 3, 5, 7)* **Accounting for expenditures.** Prepare entries in the general fund for the following transactions that represent outflows of financial resources to the city of Greene in 20X4:

1. Vouchers are prepared for the following items and amounts:

Salaries	$120,000
Repairs and maintenance	60,000
Inventory of supplies	45,000
Capital equipment	125,000
Tax anticipation notes:	
Principal	200,000
Interest	13,000

2. A transfer of $57,000 is made to the debt service fund.
3. There was no inventory of supplies at the start of the year. The inventory of supplies at year-end is $2,500.

Exercise 7 *(LO 3, 7, 8, 9)* **Accounting for expenditures and encumbrances.** Laster City had the following balance sheet accounts and amounts as of January 1, 20X4:

Inventory of supplies	$ 31,000
Fund balance, reserved for inventory	(31,000)
Fund balance, reserved for encumbrances	(18,000)
Fund balance, unreserved, undesignated	(40,000)

Prepare general fund journal entries for the following 20X4 transactions:

1. Prior-period supplies encumbrances are reinstated in 20X4. These are included in the 20X4 budget.
2. Orders are placed for supplies inventory at an estimated cost of $70,000.
3. All inventory ordered (including amounts encumbered last year) is received; actual invoices are for $87,000.
4. The physical inventory of supplies at year-end is $35,000.

Exercise 8 *(LO 5, 7, 8, 9)* **Accounting for expenditures and encumbrances.** You are maintaining a subsidiary ledger account for Police-Training Expenditures for 20X3. The following columns are used:

Date	Item	Encumbrances			Expenditures	Unobligated Balance
		Dr.	Cr.	Bal.		

Inventory purchases are initially recorded as expenditures.

Record the following 20X3 transactions in the police-training expenditures subsidiary ledger account:

Jan.	1	The budget includes $23,000 for police-training expenditures.
	15	Equipment and supplies, estimated at $14,000 cost, are ordered.
Feb.	1	Vouchers for $5,000 are approved for items not encumbered.
	15	Items encumbered for $12,000 on January 15 are received with invoices totaling $12,300. Supplies are expended when purchased; however, an inventory is taken at year-end, and expenditures are adjusted at that time.
June	3	The remaining encumbered expenditures arrive. The invoice totals $4,300, including items not included in the encumbered amount.
Dec.	31	An inventory of training supplies is taken and recorded at $1,500.

Exercise 9 *(LO 5, 7)* **Account for transactions.** Prepare the entries to record the following general fund transactions for the village of Spring Valley for the year ended September 30, 20X4:

a. Revenues are estimated at $520,000; expenditures are estimated at $515,000.
b. A tax levy is set at $378,788, of which 1% will likely be uncollectible.
c. Purchase orders amounting to $240,000 are authorized.
d. Tax receipts total $280,000.
e. Invoices totaling $225,000 are received and vouchered for orders originally estimated at $223,000.
f. Salaries amounting to $135,000 are approved for payment.
g. A state grant-in-aid of $100,000 is received.
h. Fines and penalties of $10,000 are collected.
i. Property for a village park is purchased, costing $120,000. No encumbrance had been made for this item.
j. Additional recreational property valued at $88,000 is donated.
k. Amounts of $12,000 due to other village funds are approved for payment. (*Note:* To establish the liability to other funds, credit Due to Other Funds.)
l. The village's share of sales tax due from the state is $30,000. Payment will be received in 30 days.
m. Vouchers totaling $175,000 are paid.
n. Accounts are closed at year-end.

Exercise 10 *(LO 9)* **Budgetary comparison schedule.** The preclosing trial balance of the general fund of Marshal Village for fiscal year ended June 30, 20X5, is as follows:

	Debit	Credit
Cash	210,000	
Receivables (net)	134,000	
Vouchers Payable		125,000
Fund Balance—Reserved for Encumbrances		60,000
Fund Balance—Unreserved, Undesignated		92,000
Budgetary Fund Balance		50,000
Estimated Revenues	600,000	
Estimated Other Financing Sources	150,000	
Appropriations		650,000
Estimated Other Financing Uses		50,000
Expenditures	598,000	
Encumbrances	60,000	
Revenues		605,000
Other Financing Sources		166,500
Other Financing Uses	46,500	
Total	1,798,500	1,798,500

1. Prepare closing entries.
2. Prepare a budget to actual comparison schedule. (Assume there are no differences between the original and final budgets.)
3. Prepare a balance sheet as of June 30, 20X5.

Exercise 11 *(LO 4, 7)* **Journal entries, identify funds.** A city purchased land costing $75,000 for park development. The amount had been encumbered at $80,000. Ten years later, because of a population shift, the park is no longer practical. The city sells the land for $117,000. Prepare journal entries to record the purchase and subsequent sale of the land, indicating in what fund or group each entry would be made. Use this format:

Event	Fund or Group	Entry

Exercise 12 *(LO 4, 7, 10)* **Journal entries, capital assets.** For the following transactions, prepare the entries that would be recorded in the general fixed assets account group for the city of Evert.

a. The city purchased property costing $1,300,000, with three-fourths of the cost allocated to a building.
b. A mansion belonging to the great-granddaughter of the city's founder was donated to the city. The land cost the original owner $600, and the house was built for an additional $50,000. At the time of donation, the property had an estimated fair value of $550,000, of which $330,000 was allocable to the land. The property was accepted and is to be used as a park and a museum.
c. A central fire station, financed by general obligation bonds, was two-thirds complete at year-end with costs to date of $800,000 that were recorded in the capital project fund.
d. A new fire engine was purchased for $165,000. The city traded a used fire engine originally purchased for $100,000. The trade-in value was $25,000. Both engines were purchased from general property tax revenues.
e. A new street was completed at a cost of $250,000, which is to be charged, through the capital projects fund's special assessments, against property owners in the vicinity. The city follows GASB recommendations and records infrastructure assets.

Exercise 13 *(LO 4, 7)* **Journal entries, general long-term debt.** The following transactions directly affected Rose City's general fund and other governmental funds. Prepare journal entries to reflect their impact upon the general long-term debt account group.

1. Rose City employees earned $8.8 million in vacation pay during the year, of which they took only $6.6 million. They may take the balance in the following three years.
2. The employees took $0.4 million of vacation pay that they had earned in previous years.
3. Rose City settled a claim brought against it during the year by a building contractor. The city agreed to pay $7.5 million immediately and $11 million at the end of the following year.
4. Rose City issued $100 million in general obligation bonds at a price of $99.8 million—i.e., a discount of $0.2 million.
5. Rose City transferred $5 million from the general fund to the debt service fund. Of this, $4 million was for the first payment of interest; the balance was for repayment of principal.
6. Rose City earned $0.3 million in interest on investments held in the debt service fund. These investments have a fair value $4.5 million greater than at the end of last period. The funds are available for the repayment of debt principal.

Exercise 14 *(LO 4, 7)* **Journal entries, general long-term debt.** Prepare the entries that would be made in the general long-term debt account group for the following events:

a. To finance the construction of an art center, $13,000,000 of general obligation term bonds were sold for $12,500,000.
b. The general fund allocated $1,300,000 to a debt service fund to begin providing for retirement of the bonds in item (a) at maturity.
c. To help finance an addition to the community health center, $6,000,000 of 6%, 10-year serial bonds were sold at 101. $960,000 was transferred from the general fund to the debt service fund to cover the annual interest and the first serial redemption.
d. Serial bonds of $600,000 matured and were retired through the debt service fund.

Exercise 15 *(LO 1, 2, 3)* **Understanding state and local government financial statements.** Go to the GASB Web site at http://www.gasb.org. Write a brief description of the mission of the GASB, its relation to the FASB, and the current project agenda of the GASB board. Are there any exposure drafts, discussion memoranda, and/or invitations to comment documents outstanding to which you could respond? What is the purpose of the Governmental Accounting Standards Advisory Council?

PROBLEMS

Problem 15-1 *(LO 1, 2, 3)* **Measurement focus and basis of accounting.** Select the best answer for each of the following multiple-choice questions. (Nos. 5 and 6 are AICPA adapted.)

1. The measurement focus for governmental funds is the
   a. flow of cash.
   b. flow of financial resources.
   c. amount of gross revenue.
   d. matching of revenues and expenditures.
2. Interperiod equity measurement for governmental funds determines whether
   a. there is a positive cash flow.
   b. there is a profit.
   c. current-year revenues are sufficient to pay for current-year services.
   d. actual amounts exceed budgeted amounts.
3. The proceeds of a long-term bond issue were used by a county to acquire general fixed assets. The long-term liability is recorded
   a. only in the general long-term debt account group.
   b. only in the general fund.
   c. both in the general fund and in the general long-term debt account group.
   d. in the appropriate governmental fund, depending on the nature of the asset involved.
4. What is the underlying reason a governmental unit uses separate funds to account for its transactions?
   a. Governmental units are so large that it would be unduly cumbersome to account for all transactions as a single unit.
   b. Because of the diverse nature of the services offered and legal provisions regarding activities of a governmental unit, it is necessary to segregate activities by functional nature.
   c. Generally accepted accounting principles require that not-for-profit entities report on a funds basis.
   d. Many activities carried on by governmental units are short lived, and their inclusion in a general set of accounts could cause undue probability of error and omission.
5. The primary authoritative body for determining the measurement focus and basis of accounting standards for governmental fund operating statements is the
   a. Governmental Accounting Standards Board (GASB).
   b. National Council on Governmental Accounting (NCGA).
   c. Government Accounting and Auditing Committee of the AICPA (GAAC).
   d. Financial Accounting Standards Board (FASB).
6. Encumbrances outstanding at year-end in a state's general fund should be reported as a
   a. liability in the general fund.
   b. fund balance reserve in the general fund.
   c. liability in the general long-term debt account group.
   d. fund balance designation in the general fund.

7. An expenditure for general obligation long-term debt is always recorded at year-end in the governmental funds for

    a. accrued interest and accrued principal.
    b. accrued principal but not accrued interest.
    c. accrued interest but not accrued principal.
    d. neither accrued interest nor accrued principal.

Problem 15-2 *(LO 1, 2, 3)* **Measurement focus and basis of accounting.** Select the best answer for each of the following multiple-choice questions. (Nos. 3 and 6–10 are AICPA adapted.)

1. Lacking sufficient cash for operations, a city borrows money from a bank, using as collateral the expected receipts from levied property taxes. Upon receipt of cash from the bank, the general fund would credit

    a. Revenues.
    b. Other Financing Sources.
    c. Tax Anticipation Notes Payable.
    d. Taxes Receivable—Delinquent.

2. The recorded amount for uncollectible taxes was overstated. To revise the estimate during the same fiscal period, the journal entry would credit

    a. Expenditures.
    b. Revenues.
    c. Allowance for Uncollectible Delinquent Taxes.
    d. Fund Balance—Unreserved, Undesignated.

3. The encumbrances control account of a governmental unit is increased when a voucher payable is

    a. not recorded and the budgetary accounts are not closed.
    b. not recorded but the budgetary accounts are closed.
    c. recorded and the budgetary accounts are closed.
    d. recorded but the budgetary accounts are not closed.

4. If not expenditure driven, a grant approved by the federal government to assist in a city's welfare program during the current year should be credited to

    a. Revenues.
    b. Fund Balance—Reserved for Welfare Programs.
    c. Fund Balance—Unreserved, Undesignated.
    d. Other Financing Sources.

5. Which one of the following equations will yield the available balance in an expenditure subsidiary ledger account?

    a. Appropriations − Expenditures Total
    b. Appropriations − Encumbrances Balance
    c. Appropriations − Expenditures Total − Encumbrances Balance
    d. Appropriations − Expenditures Total + Encumbrances Balance

6. Elm City issued a purchase order for supplies with an estimated cost of $5,000. When the supplies were received, the accompanying invoice indicated an actual price of $4,950. What amount should Elm debit (credit) to the reserve for encumbrances after the supplies and invoice were received?

    a. ($50)
    b. $50
    c. $4,950
    d. $5,000

7. Boa City had the following fixed assets:

Fixed assets used in proprietary fund activities	$1,000,000
Fixed assets used in general government activities	9,000,000

What aggregate amount should Boa account for in the general fixed assets account group?

a. $9,000,000
b. $10,000,000
c. $10,800,000
d. $11,800,000

8. Power City's year-end is June 30. Power levies property taxes in January of each year for the calendar year. One-half of the levy is due in May, and one-half is due in October. Property tax revenue is budgeted for the period in which payment is due. The following information pertains to Power's property taxes for the period from July 1, 20X0, to June 30, 20X1:

	Calendar Year	
	20X0	20X1
Levy	$2,000,000	$2,400,000
Collected in:		
May	950,000	1,100,000
July	50,000	60,000
October	920,000	
December	80,000	

The $40,000 balance due for the May 20X1 installments was expected to be collected in August 20X1. What amount should Power recognize for property tax revenue for the year ended June 30, 20X1?

a. $2,160,000
b. $2,200,000
c. $2,360,000
d. $2,400,000

9. Dodd Village received a gift of a new fire engine from a local civic group. The fair value of this fire engine was $400,000. Which of the following is the correct entry to be made in the general fixed assets account group for this gift?

	Debit	Credit
a. Memorandum entry only		
b. General Fund Assets	400,000	
Private Gifts		400,000
c. Investment in General Fixed Assets	400,000	
Gift Revenue		400,000
d. Machinery and Equipment	400,000	
Investment in General Fixed Assets from Private Gifts		400,000

10. The following information pertains to Spruce City's liability for claims and judgments:

Current liability at January 1, 20X2	$100,000
Claims paid during 20X2	800,000
Current liability at December 31, 20X2	140,000
Noncurrent liability at December 31, 20X2	200,000

What amount should Spruce report for 20X2 claims and judgment expenditures?

a. $1,040,000
b. $940,000
c. $840,000
d. $800,000

Required ▶ ▶ ▶ ▶ ▶

Problem 15-3 *(LO 7)* **Journal entries.** Omitting amounts, prepare journal entries in the general fund to record the following selected events:

a. The budget is approved. The city will float a bond issue to finance fixed assets. Inflows of resources are expected to exceed outflows.
b. Property taxes are levied, of which some percentage will be uncollectible.
c. Some of the delinquent property taxes from last year are collected. Others are written off as uncollectible, using the available allowance account.
d. Purchase orders are approved.
e. Payroll for the month is vouchered. Ignore payroll deductions.
f. An invoice is vouchered for an amount less than its encumbrance.
g. Bonds are sold at face value to finance the acquisition of new fixed assets.
h. Fixed assets are purchased.
i. Short-term tax anticipation notes are issued.

Problem 15-4 *(LO 4, 7)* **Journal entries, identify funds.** Sauk City leases a fleet of garbage trucks. The term of the lease is 10 years, approximately the useful life of the equipment. Based on a sales price of $800,000 and an interest rate of 6%, the city agrees to make annual payments of $108,694. Upon the expiration of the lease, the trucks will revert to the city.

Required ▶ ▶ ▶ ▶ ▶

1. Prepare appropriate journal entries in the general fund, the general fixed assets account group, and the general long-term debt account group to record the signing of the lease.
2. Prepare appropriate journal entries in the same funds and account groups to record the first payment on the lease. The city records depreciation on garbage trucks using the straight-line method.

Problem 15-5 *(LO 4, 7, 9)* **Journal entries, statement of revenue expenditures, and change in fund balance.** On July 1, 20X0, the beginning of its fiscal year, the trial balance of the general fund of the city of Elsworth was as follows:

	Debit	Credit
Cash	20,000	
Taxes Receivable—Delinquent	120,000	
Allowance for Uncollectible Delinquent Taxes		12,000
Interest and Penalties Receivable on Taxes	8,000	
Allowance for Uncollectible Interest and Penalties		800
Due from Other Funds	28,000	
Vouchers Payable		87,200
Fund Balance Reserved for Encumbrances		16,000
Fund Balance—Unreserved, Undesignated		60,000
Total	176,000	176,000

The following events occurred:

a. The budget shows estimated general fund revenues of $450,000 and estimated expenditures (including $16,000 encumbered in the prior year) of $392,000.
b. In July, the item ordered in the previous year was received at an invoice cost of $16,400. A voucher is prepared.
c. Property taxes amounting to $300,000 were levied, with 4% estimated to be uncollectible.

d. Cash collections during the year were as follows:

Current taxes	$270,000
Delinquent taxes (in full settlement)	104,000
Interest and penalties on last year's taxes (in full settlement)	7,600
Due from other funds	28,000
Total	$409,600

The controller wishes variations in estimates to be recorded in the appropriate revenue or expenditure account.

e. Purchase orders totaling $276,000 were placed. Later, invoices for $260,000 were received and vouchered; supplies inventory purchases were $16,000 of the total. The purchase covered $254,000 of the encumbrances.
f. Payrolls of $50,000 were paid. (Ignore payroll taxes and other deductions.) In addition, vouchers totaling $280,000 were paid.
g. An automobile was purchased for the fire department. It cost $16,000 and was not previously encumbered. The invoice is vouchered.
h. At year-end, $6,000 in supplies was on hand. There were no supplies on hand a year ago. The city wishes to show the inventory and to establish a proper reserve.

◀◀◀◀◀ **Required**

1. Prepare journal entries that would be made in the general fund for the above events.
2. Prepare closing entries.
3. Prepare a statement of revenues, expenditures, and changes in fund balance.

Problem 15-6 *(LO 4, 7, 9)* **Journal entries, budgetary comparison schedule.** A summary of the general fund transactions for the city of Wautoma for the year ended December 31, 20X7, is as follows:

a. A budget was approved, showing estimated revenues of $900,000, appropriations of $875,000, transfers-in of $27,000 from other funds, and required transfers of $20,000 to other funds.
b. The reserve for encumbrance at the end of 20X6 was $15,000. Amounts encumbered in the prior period are included in appropriations for 20X7.
c. Property taxes for $650,000 were levied. In past years, 1% of the property taxes levied proved uncollectible.
d. Encumbrances for $25,000 had not been liquidated by the end of 20X6. Invoices for all these items were received in 20X7 and totaled $24,000.
e. Collections from property taxes totaled $644,000, of which $20,000 represented collections on delinquent taxes. Delinquent taxes of $8,000 remain uncollected, on which a $3,000 allowance is carried. Remaining taxes receivable—current and taxes receivable—delinquent were converted into taxes receivable—delinquent and tax liens receivable, respectively.
f. Purchase orders totaling $700,000 were issued. Subsequently, invoices were received amounting to $685,000 for items estimated to cost $680,000. Included were supplies for $10,000.
g. An ending inventory of supplies amounted to $2,000, for which the fund balance should be reserved.
h. A tract of land was purchased for $250,000. Payment was made from the general fund, in whose appropriations the item had been included. The amount had not been encumbered. The purchase was made with the intent of reselling the land to a suitable developer.
i. Wautoma received $300,000 as its part of federal revenue-sharing programs. Grants-in-aid of $60,000 due from the state government are recorded. None of the grants is expenditure driven.
j. Required transfers of $20,000 are made to other funds.
k. A $50,000 payment is made on a mortgage payable. The payment includes $21,000 of interest and a principal payment of $29,000.

l. An offer was received from a land developer who will pay $380,000 for the land acquired by the city in item (h). The sale is approved. The developer remits $100,000 with a note due in 90 days, bearing 8% interest. Any gain is to be considered revenue.
m. Transfers received from other funds amount to $23,000.
n. The developer in item (l) remits payment for the note plus interest.

Required ▶ ▶ ▶ ▶ ▶

1. Prepare journal entries to record the general fund transactions.
2. Prepare closing entries for the general fund.
3. Prepare a budgetary comparison schedule. On January 1, 20X7, the unreserved fund balance showed a debit balance (deficit) of $180,000.

Problem 15-7 *(LO 3, 5, 7)* **Journal entries, pensions.** Harth City maintains a defined benefit pension plan for its employees. In a recent year, the city contributed $4 million to its pension fund. However, its annual required contribution as calculated by its actuary was $6 million. The city accounts for the pension contributions in the general fund.

Required ▶ ▶ ▶ ▶ ▶

1. Record the pension expenditure and related liability in the general fund and account group.
2. Suppose that in the following year the city contributed $6 million to its pension fund, but its annual required contribution per its actuary was only $5 million. Prepare the appropriate journal entries.

Problem 15-8 *(LO 5, 7)* **Journal entries, general fund.** The general fund trial balance of the city of Oakwood at December 31, 20X3, was as follows:

	Debit	Credit
Cash	62,000	
Taxes Receivable—Delinquent	46,000	
Allowance for Uncollectible Delinquent Taxes		8,000
Inventory	18,000	
Vouchers Payable		28,000
Fund Balance—Reserved for Stores		18,000
Fund Balance—Reserved for Encumbrances		12,000
Fund Balance—Unreserved, Undesignated		60,000
Total	126,000	126,000

The following data pertain to 20X4 general fund operations:

a. Budget adopted:

Revenues and other financing sources:	
Taxes	$220,000
Fines, forfeits, and penalties	80,000
Miscellaneous revenues	100,000
Share of bond issue proceeds	200,000
	$600,000
Expenditures and other financing uses:	
Program operations	$300,000
General administration	120,000
Supplies	60,000
Capital outlay	80,000
Transfer to debt service fund	20,000
	$580,000

Encumbrances from 20X3 are included in the budget.

b. Taxes were assessed at an amount that would result in revenues of $220,800, after a deduction of 4% of the tax levy as uncollectible.

c. Orders placed for:

Program operations	$176,000
General administration	80,000
Capital outlay	60,000
	$316,000

d. The city council designated $20,000 of the unreserved fund balance for possible appropriation for capital outlay.

e. Cash collections and transfer:

Delinquent taxes (balance is uncollectible)	$ 38,000
Current taxes	226,000
Refund of overpayment on equipment invoice in 20X3	4,000
Fines, forfeits, and penalties	88,000
Miscellaneous revenues	90,000
Share of bond issue proceeds	200,000
Operating transfer from capital projects fund	18,000
	$664,000

f. Vouchers approved for payment (all previously encumbered):

	Estimated	Actual
Applicable to prior year but rebudgeted	$ 12,000	$ 12,000
Program operations	144,000	154,000
General administration	84,000	80,000
Capital outlay	62,000	62,000
	$302,000	$308,000

g. Additional vouchers approved (not previously encumbered):

Program operations	$148,000
Supplies	40,000
General administration	38,000
Capital outlay	18,000
Transfer to debt service fund	20,000
	$264,000

h. A taxpayer overpaid 20X4 taxes by $2,000. (The taxes were credited to miscellaneous revenue upon receipt.) The taxpayer applied for a $2,000 credit against 20X5 taxes. The city council granted the request. The council instructed the city controller to adjust the estimated uncollectible current taxes to cover the remaining uncollected balance.

i. Vouchers paid amounted to $580,000.

j. Inventory on December 31, 20X4, amounted to $12,000.

◀◀◀◀◀ Required

Using control accounts, prepare journal entries to record the foregoing data. Omit explanations.

(AICPA adapted)

Problem 15-9 *(LO 5, 7)* **Journal entries, leases.** Brock County has acquired equipment through a noncancelable lease-purchase agreement dated December 31, 20X7. This agreement requires no down payment and the following minimum lease payments:

December	Principal	Interest	Total
20X8	$50,000	$15,000	$65,000
20X9	50,000	10,000	60,000
20Y0	50,000	5,000	55,000

Required ▶ ▶ ▶ ▶ ▶

1. What account should be debited for $150,000 in the general fund at inception of the lease if the equipment is a general fixed asset and Brock does not use a capital projects fund?
2. What account should be credited for $150,000 in the general fixed assets account group at inception of the lease if the equipment is a general fixed asset?
3. What journal entry is required for $150,000 in the general long-term debt account group at inception of the lease if the lease payments are to be financed with general government resources?

(AICPA adapted)

Required ▶ ▶ ▶ ▶ ▶

Problem 15-10 *(LO 5, 7)* **Journal entries, capital assets.** Prepare journal entries to record the following events using the general fund and the general fixed assets account group:

a. The general fund vouchered the purchase of trucks for $75,000. The purchase had been encumbered earlier in the year at $70,000.
b. Several years ago, equipment costing $15,000 was acquired with general fund revenues. It was sold for $5,000, with proceeds belonging to the general fund.
c. Early in the year, a citizen donated to the city land appraised at $100,000. She submitted plans for a new library and agreed to cover the total cost of construction, paying the company directly as work proceeded. At year-end, the building was two-thirds finished, with costs to date of $300,000. The expenditures are recorded in a capital projects fund.
d. A snow plow was purchased with general fund cash for $68,000, which represented a cost of $80,000 less trade-in of $12,000 for an old snow plow originally purchased for $35,000 from special revenue funds. As an emergency purchase, the acquisition of the new snow plow had not been encumbered.

Required ▶ ▶ ▶ ▶ ▶

Problem 15-11 *(LO 4, 5, 7)* **Journal entries, general fund.** Prepare the necessary journal entries to record the following transaction for the city of Maineville during 20X7 in the general fund and account groups, and specify the account group used. Entries in the Debt Service Fund and Capital Projects Fund should be ignored.

a. General obligation term bonds with a face value of $2,700,000 were sold for $2,705,000. The proceeds from the bond issue were to be used to construct a new library and were received by the capital projects fund.
b. $200,000 was transferred from the general fund to the debt service fund to begin saving for the retirement of the bonds in transaction (a) at maturity.
c. $135,000 was transferred from the general fund to the debt service fund to retire a portion of a serial bond due in 20X9.
d. A police car was purchased for $22,000 plus the trade-in of an old police car with a fair value of $3,000, originally purchased for $15,000 from the general fund.
e. The serial bonds funded in transaction (c) were retired on their maturity date.
f. By year-end, $450,000 of the work had been completed on the new library.

Problem 15-12 *(LO 5, 7, 9, 10)* **Journal entries, schedule of capital assets.** The following schedule of capital assets was obtained from the records of the city of Elmwood:

City of Elmwood
Schedule of General Fixed Assets
December 31, 20X6

Governmental activities:	
Land	$1,000,000
Buildings	2,150,000
Machinery and equipment	800,000
Construction in progress	250,000
Infrastructure assets	1,400,000
Total general fixed assets	$5,600,000
Less accumulated depreciation:	
Buildings	$ 400,000
Construction in progress	0
Machinery and equipment	300,000
Infrastructure	500,000
Total investment in governmental capital assets	$4,400,000

A summary of fixed asset transactions for 20X7 follows:

a. Construction on the new school, a capital project started during 20X6, was completed at a total cost of $850,000, which was financed by a serial bond issue. No other construction was in progress at the beginning of 20X7.
b. A citizen donated 400 acres of land to the city to be used as a park. The land had a fair value of $140,000 when donated.
c. The municipal waterworks constructed a new pumping plant at a cost of $120,000. The plant was financed from the water utility revenues. The water utility is accounted for in a proprietary fund.
d. The fire department traded in an old fire engine and $105,000 cash for a new model. The old equipment originally had cost $65,000, and $15,000 was allowed on the trade-in.
e. The city hall was refurbished at a cost of $40,000, which was paid from general fund revenues. The refurbishing constituted a capital improvement.
f. Road-use taxes of $30,000 were collected by a special revenue fund, of which $20,000 has been used for improvements other than buildings.
g. Depreciation of $100,000 on buildings, $50,000 on machinery and equipment, and $25,000 on infrastructure were recorded.

◄◄◄◄◄ **Required**

1. Prepare journal entries only for those transactions that are to be accounted for in the general fixed assets account group. Use the city's account titles.
2. Prepare a schedule of capital assets as of December 31, 20X7.

Problem 15-13 *(LO 5, 7, 9, 10)* **Journal entries, schedule of long-term debt.** The city of Chester was incorporated on January 1, 20X2. On December 31, 20X7, a careful study of the city's records revealed the following information regarding long-term debt:

a. General obligation bonds in the amount of $1,500,000 were authorized and issued at face value on July 1, 20X2, to finance the construction of a school. The 6% bonds pay interest semiannually on January 1 and July 1, and they mature 10 years from the issuance date.
b. Serial bonds of $1,000,000 were sold at 99 on January 1, 20X4, to help finance a new city hall and cultural center. An additional $750,000 was received from an anonymous benefactor. The 5% serial bonds were to be redeemed in annual amounts of $100,000, beginning on January 1, 20X7. A sinking fund was established on January 2, 20X4, to provide for the retirement of the serial bonds. Deposits of $70,000 were to be made on January 2 of each year, beginning in 20X4. All amounts deposited were invested immediately at a net yield of 8%.
c. Property owners were assessed $750,000, to be paid in five equal annual installments, to finance construction of a storm sewer system and repaving of the affected roadways. To have

cash when needed to pay for the construction, $600,000 of 5%, 5-year bonds were issued at face value by the Storm Sewer Proprietary Fund.

d. Term bonds totaling $400,000 were sold at face value on January 1, 20X5, to finance construction. The 5%, 10-year bonds pay interest semiannually on January 1 and July 1. Each year, starting with January 1, 20X5, $40,000 was to be set aside in a sinking fund to provide for retirement of the bonds at maturity. Any income earned by the sinking fund was to be applied to the semiannual interest payments.

Required ▶▶▶▶▶

1. Prepare only the journal entries for the transactions that would be recorded in the general long-term debt account group through December 31, 20X7.
2. Prepare a schedule of long-term liabilities for the city of Chester as of December 31, 20X7.

Problem 15-14 *(LO 5, 8, 9)* **Financial statements.** The following selected information was taken from Sun City's general fund statement of revenues, expenditures, and changes in fund balance for the year ended December 31, 20X7:

Revenues:	
Property taxes—20X7	$ 825,000
Expenditures:	
Current services:	
Public safety	350,000
Capital outlay (police vehicles)	100,000
Debt service	74,000
Expenditures—20X7	$1,349,000
Expenditures—20X6	56,000
Expenditures	$1,405,000
Excess of revenues over expenditures	$ 153,000
Other financing uses	(125,000)
Excess of revenues over expenditures and other financing uses	$ 28,000
Decrease in reserve for encumbrances during 20X7	15,000
Residual equity transfers-out	(190,000)
Decrease in unreserved fund balance during 20X7	$ (147,000)
Unreserved fund balance, January 1, 20X7	304,000
Unreserved fund balance, December 31, 20X7	$ 157,000

The following information was taken from Sun's December 31, 20X7, general fund balance sheet:

Property taxes receivable—delinquent—20X7	$ 34,000
Less: Allowances for estimated uncollectible taxes—delinquent	20,000
Vouchers payable	89,000
Fund balance:	
Reserved for encumbrances—20X7	43,000
Reserved for supplies inventory	38,000
Unreserved	157,000

Additional information is as follows:

a. Debt service was for bonds used to finance a library building and included interest of $22,000.
b. $8,000 of 20X7 property taxes receivable was written off; otherwise, the allowance for uncollectible taxes balance is unchanged from the initial entry at the time of the original tax levy at the beginning of the year.
c. Sun reported supplies inventory of $21,000 at December 31, 20X6.

Provide the best answer to the following questions: ◀◀◀◀◀ **Required**

1. What recording method did Sun use for its general fund supplies inventory?
2. What was the reserved fund balance of the 20X6 general fund?
3. What amount was collected from 20X7 tax assessments?
4. What amount is Sun's liability to general fund vendors and contractors at December 31, 20X7?
5. What amount should be included in the general fixed assets account group for the cost of assets acquired in 20X7 through the general fund?
6. What amount arising from 20X7 transactions decreased liabilities reported in the general long-term debt account group?
7. What amount of total actual expenditures should Sun report in its 20X7 general fund statement of revenues, expenditures, and changes in fund balance—budget and actual?

(AICPA adapted)

Problem 15-15 *(LO 5, 9)* **Journal entries, balance sheet.** The January 2, 20X8, trial balance of Croix Township follows:

template cd

	Debit	Credit
Cash	45,000	
Taxes Receivable—Delinquent	20,000	
Allowance for Uncollectible Delinquent Taxes		2,000
Tax Liens Receivable	4,000	
Allowance for Uncollectible Tax Liens		1,000
Due from Parks Fund	12,000	
Inventory of Supplies	5,000	
Vouchers Payable		43,000
Due to Utility Fund		4,000
Fund Balance—Reserved for Supplies Inventory		5,000
Fund Balance—Unreserved, Undesignated		31,000
Total	86,000	86,000

The following events occurred during the first six months of 20X8:

a. The adopted budget showed the following:

Estimated expenditures	$620,000
Transfers to other funds	27,000
Estimated revenues	655,000

b. Six-month tax anticipation notes were issued in the amount of $120,000.
c. Property taxes of $430,000 were levied, with 2% of the gross levy considered uncollectible.
d. Tax liens proved uncollectible. The property was foreclosed and sold for $4,000.
e. Amounts encumbered totaled $250,000.
f. Cash collected:

All delinquent property taxes	$ 20,000
Current taxes	290,000
Due from Parks Fund	11,000
Fines and penalties	23,000
	$344,000

Items vouchered totaled $186,000, representing $183,000 of encumbrances. Included in both were $26,000 for supplies, for which a perpetual inventory system is maintained.

Cash payments:

Vouchered items	$151,000
Nonvouchered items that were not encumbered	49,000
Due to Utility Fund	4,000
	$204,000

Supplies inventory on June 30 was $21,000.

Required ▶ ▶ ▶ ▶ ▶

1. Using the format below, complete the general fund worksheet for the six months ended June 30, 20X8. Ignore entries for any other fund or group. Label entries on the worksheet according to their corresponding events. Formal journal entries are not required.
2. Prepare a balance sheet as of June 30, 20X8.

	Trial Balance		Operating Entries		Revenues and Expenditures		Balance Sheet	
Accounts	Dr.	Cr.	Dr.	Cr.	Dr.	Cr.	Dr.	Cr.

Problem 15-16 *(LO 3, 4, 5, 7, 9, 10)* **Journal entries, error correction.** You have been engaged by the town of Rock Elm to examine its June 30, 20X8, balance sheet. You are the first CPA to be engaged by the town, and you find that acceptable methods of municipal accounting have not been employed. The town clerk stated that the books had not been closed and presented the following trial balance of the general fund as of June 30, 20X8:

	Debit	Credit
Cash	150,000	
Taxes Receivable—Current Year	59,200	
Allowance for Uncollectible Current Taxes		18,000
Taxes Receivable—Delinquent	8,000	
Allowance for Uncollectible Delinquent Taxes		10,200
Estimated Revenues	310,000	
Appropriations		348,000
Donated Land	27,000	
Expenditures—Building Addition Constructed	50,000	
Expenditures—Serial Bonds Paid	16,000	
Other Expenditures	280,000	
Revenues		354,000
Accounts Payable		126,000
Fund Balance—Unreserved, Undesignated		82,000
Budgetary Fund Balance	38,000	
Total	938,200	938,200

Additional information is as follows:

a. The estimated uncollectible taxes of $18,000 for Taxes Receivable—Current Year were determined to be reasonably estimated, but for the prior year they should not exceed 100% of Taxes Receivable Delinquent.
b. Included in the revenues account is a credit of $27,000 representing the value of land donated by the state for construction of a municipal park.
c. The Expenditures—Building Addition Constructed balance is the cost of an addition to the town hall building. This addition was constructed and completed in June 20X8. The general fund recorded the payment as authorized.

d. The Expenditures—Serial Bonds Paid balance reflects the transfer to the debt service fund for serial bond retirement. A transfer of $7,000 for interest payments on this bond issue is included in Other Expenditures.
e. Operating supplies ordered in the prior fiscal year and chargeable to that year were received and consumed in June 20X7. The vendors' invoices amounting to $8,800 for these supplies were incorrectly charged to Other Expenditures when paid in July 20X7.
f. Outstanding purchase orders at June 30, 20X8, for operating supplies totaled $2,100. These purchase orders were not recorded on the books.
g. The balance in Revenues includes credits for $20,000 from a note issued to a bank to obtain cash in anticipation of tax collections and for $1,000 from the sale of scrap iron from the town's water plant. The note was still outstanding at June 30, 20X8. Operations of the water plant are accounted for in the Water Fund (a proprietary fund), which is to receive the proceeds from the scrap sale.
h. At year-end, current taxes are to be reclassified as delinquent.

◀◀◀◀◀ **Required**

1. Prepare the adjusting entries for the general fund for the fiscal year ended June 30, 20X8. Account titles should be respected if acceptable, even though different. Closing entries are not required.
2. Prepare formal adjusting journal entries for the general fixed assets account group and for the general long-term debt account group.

(AICPA adapted)

Governmental Accounting: Other Governmental Funds, Proprietary Funds, and Fiduciary Funds

CHAPTER 16

Learning Objectives

When you have completed this chapter, you should be able to

1. **Tell why governments use special revenue, permanent, capital projects, and debt service funds, and demonstrate how transactions are accounted for and reported using those funds.**
2. **Account for and prepare financial statements of proprietary funds.**
3. **Explain the usefulness of and the accounting process for fiduciary funds and how these funds are reported.**
4. **Identify and account for transactions that affect different funds and/or account groups.**

A variety of funds may be used to record events and to exhibit results for a specific area of responsibility. In a small town, there may not be enough activity to warrant more than a general fund, but the larger the governmental unit and the more diverse the activities with which it is involved, the greater the necessity to introduce special funds. While the Governmental Accounting Standards Board (GASB) recognizes the need for funds to manage and demonstrate accountability, it cautions against too many funds that unnecessarily fragment financial reporting. GASB Statement No. 1 suggests that a governmental unit establish only the *minimum* number of funds consistent with legal and operating requirements.

OTHER GOVERNMENTAL FUNDS

1 OBJECTIVE

Tell why governments use special revenue, permanent, capital projects, and debt service funds, and demonstrate how transactions are accounted for and reported using those funds.

Typical funds used by state and local governments include special revenue funds, permanent funds, capital project funds, and debt service funds. A special revenue fund would be used when revenues are collected for a specific purpose, such as road repair or education. Permanent funds are used to account for trusts that are set up to accomplish a specific, *public* purpose. The principal of a permanent fund must not be expended. When a major, general capital asset, such as a building, is being acquired, the governmental entity uses a capital project fund to account for related transactions. Once the government has borrowed money for a capital project or for other reasons, the debt principal is recorded and tracked in the long-term debt account group (see Chapter 15), and the accounting for that debt is recorded in a debt service fund.

Special Revenue Funds

When revenue obtained from specified sources is restricted by law or donor for a specified current operating purpose or to the acquisition of a relatively minor fixed asset, accounting is accomplished through a *special revenue fund.* Although the government will have only one general fund, it could have many special revenue funds, or none at all. Examples of activities that are accounted for in special revenue funds are nonexchange transactions, such as the hotel room taxes restricted for expenditures that promote tourism, federal and state grant proceeds restricted to financing community development expenditures, gasoline tax revenues for highway maintenance, specific federal and/or state funds for education, resources for food stamp programs administered by state governments, other pass-through grants and on-behalf payment programs for fringe benefits and salaries,[1] and exchange transactions such as golf fees charged at a city golf course to cover a portion of the cost of course maintenance.[2] A new use of special revenue funds as a result of GASB Statement No. 34 is to account for activities of an expendable public-purpose trust fund; that is, both the principal and earnings can be spent for the benefit of the government's programs. These revenues are recognized under the modified accrual method of accounting. The following are examples of revenues recorded in the special revenue funds.

Event	Entry in the Special Revenue Funds		
1. During the year, local hotels/motels paid to the city a room tax totaling $98,000. The remittance included $6,000 payable from last year and $92,000 expected to be available in the current year.	Cash	98,000	
	Taxes Receivable		6,000
	Revenues		92,000
2. In addition, the city estimates a $9,000 receivable from December rentals. In this city, the hotels/motels are allowed a 1-month administrative lead time and are not required to pay the December tax until January 31 of the following year.	Taxes Receivable	9,000	
	Revenues		9,000
3. Federal food stamp coupons of $10,000 are received by the state government.	Food Stamp Coupons	10,000	
	Deferred Revenues		10,000
4. $9,000 of coupons are distributed.	Expenditures	9,000	
	Food Stamp Coupons		9,000
	Deferred Revenues	9,000	
	Revenues		9,000
5. Charges for services from exchange transactions for the year are as follows:	Cash	370,000	
	Accounts Receivable	10,000	
	Revenues		360,000
	Deferred Revenues		20,000

	Earned	Collected
Golf fees (collected at time of use)	$ 35,000	$ 35,000
Garbage fees (collected in advance of providing service)	240,000	260,000
Snow removal fees (collected after service is provided)	85,000	75,000
Total	$360,000	$370,000

Event	Entry in the Special Revenue Funds		
6. A $100,000 federal grant is received for economic development. An additional $50,000 is due prior to year-end. Revenue is recognized when expenditures are incurred for the grant program.	Cash	100,000	
	Due from Federal Government	50,000	
	Deferred Revenues		150,000

1 GASB Statement No. 24, *Accounting and Financial Reporting for Certain Grants and Other Financial Assistance* (Norwalk, CT: Governmental Accounting Standards Board, June 1994). Pass-through grants are defined in GASB No. 24 as grants received by a government to transfer to or spend on behalf of a secondary recipient. Generally, these transactions are to be accounted for in a special revenue fund or a general fund if the government has discretion over the distribution of these funds.

2 When revenue raised for activities is on a fee basis for goods or services provided and the operations are intended to be self-supporting, the flows of resources are accounted for in proprietary funds discussed later in this chapter.

In a special revenue fund, the accounting must be designed to permit close scrutiny of activities. If resources are greater than anticipated, the project is not permitted to expand beyond the original authorization, nor is money permitted to accumulate beyond reasonable needs. However, sufficient resources should be generated to permit the activity. The desired control may be accomplished by using the same accounting procedures as those used by the general fund. Annual budgets are prepared for each special revenue fund and are required to be integrated into the accounting system by using the appropriate budgetary control accounts and their related subsidiary records. Commitments are recorded by using an encumbrance and expenditure system. Since both the accounting procedures and the financial statements for special revenue funds are so similar to those of the general fund, they will not be illustrated beyond the preceding revenue recognition examples.

When a governmental unit has more than one special revenue fund, major funds are identified and nonmajor individual funds are presented in *combining* balance sheets and revenue and expenditure statements. Combining statements provide information on each special revenue fund plus a total column of all the nonmajor special revenue funds. Illustration 16-1 presents a combining balance sheet, and Illustration 16-2 presents a combining statement of revenues, expenditures, and changes in fund balances.

Illustration 16-1
City of Berryville—Special Revenue Funds
Combining Balance Sheet
December 31, 20X7

Assets	Federal Food Stamp Program	Community Development Block Grant	Tourism Promotion Projects	Charges for City Golf Course	Total
Cash		$100,000	$ 98,000	$370,000	$568,000
Taxes receivable			9,000	10,000	19,000
Due from other governmental agencies		50,000	40,000		90,000
Food stamp coupons	$1,000				1,000
Total assets	$1,000	$150,000	$147,000	$380,000	$678,000
Liabilities and Fund Balances					
Liabilities:					
Vouchers payable			$ 15,000	$105,000	$120,000
Due to other funds			10,000	55,000	65,000
Deferred revenues	$1,000	$150,000		20,000	171,000
Total liabilities	$1,000	$150,000	$ 25,000	$180,000	$356,000
Fund balances:					
Reserved for encumbrances			$ 95,000	$175,000	$270,000
Unreserved, designated			27,000	25,000	52,000
Total fund balances	$ 0	$ 0	$122,000	$200,000	$322,000
Total liabilities and fund balances	$1,000	$150,000	$147,000	$380,000	$678,000

Illustration 16-2
City of Berryville
Special Revenue Funds
Combining Statement of Revenues, Expenditures, and Changes in Fund Balances
For Year Ended December 31, 20X7

	Federal Food Stamp Program	Community Development Block Grant	Tourism Promotion Projects	Charges for City Golf Course	Total
Revenues	$9,000	$40,000	$101,000	$360,000	$510,000
Expenditures	9,000	40,000	40,000	200,000	289,000
Excess of revenues over (under) expenditures	$ 0	$ 0	$ 61,000	$160,000	$221,000
Other financing sources (uses):					
Operating transfers-out	$ 0	$ 0	$ (10,000)	$ (55,000)	$ (65,000)
Total other financing sources (uses)	$ 0	$ 0	$ (10,000)	$ (55,000)	$ (65,000)
Excess of revenues and other financing sources over (under) expenditures and other financing uses	$ 0	$ 0	$ 51,000	$105,000	$156,000
Fund balances—January 1			71,000	95,000	166,000
Fund balances—December 31	$ 0	$ 0	$122,000	$200,000	$322,000

In addition, a government is required to present budgetary comparison information for any "major" special revenue fund that has a legally adopted budget. The purpose of the schedule is to compare the original and final amended budget information to actual amounts. The selection of major funds will be described in Chapter 17. A columnar format like the following will be presented for these special revenue funds.

Special Revenue Fund A				Special Revenue Fund B			
Original	Final	Actual	Variance	Original	Final	Actual	Variance
Budget	Budget		Favorable (Unfavorable)	Budget	Budget		Favorable (Unfavorable)

Permanent Funds

Permanent funds are established to account for public-purpose trusts for which the earnings are expendable for a specified purpose, but the principal amount is not expendable. These funds are often referred to as endowments. As described in the previous section, public-purpose trusts for which both principal and earnings can be spent for a specified purpose are accounted for in special revenue funds. Further, private-purpose trusts are accounted for in fiduciary funds as will be described later in this chapter. Permanent funds will capture much of the current trust activity in local governments. These trusts have been established to benefit a government program or function, or the citizens, rather than an external individual, organization, or government. For example, resources received to be invested of which only the income, not the principal, is expended to support a park, cemetery, library, or some other government program, are now accounted for in permanent funds.

The following are examples of transactions recorded in permanent funds:

Event	Entry in the Permanent Fund		
7. During the year, securities were received to initiate a trust fund to support the operations of the town cemetery. The donors stipulated that the earnings, not the principal, be spent. The fair value of the securities at the date of donation is $750,000.	Investment in Stocks................ Revenues......................	750,000	 750,000
8. Dividends are received on the investments, totaling $15,000.	Cash .... Revenues......................	15,000	 15,000
9. The earnings are transferred out to the Cemetery Operating Fund. Cemetery operations are accounted for in a Special Revenue Fund.	Other Financing Uses .... Cash	15,000	 15,000

The entry in the Special Revenue Fund to record the transfer-in is as follows:

Cash	15,000	
Other Financing Sources......		15,000

When a governmental unit has more than one permanent fund, major funds are identified and nonmajor individual funds are presented in *combining* balance sheets and revenue and expenditure statements. Combining statements provide information on each permanent fund plus a total column of all the permanent funds. These statements are similar in content and form to those presented in the previous section for special revenue funds and are not illustrated here.

Capital Projects Funds

Capital projects funds account for the purchase, construction, or capital lease of major, *general* capital assets, which excludes construction of capital facilities by proprietary funds that account for their own construction activities. Each project should be accounted for separately in subsidiary records to demonstrate compliance with legal and contractual provisions.

Resources for capital projects result from transfers received from the general fund or some other fund, proceeds of general obligation bonds, grants from another governmental unit, or special assessments levied against property owners who benefit from the project. Grants from another governmental unit and special assessments levied are recorded as revenues. Bond proceeds (because they must be repaid) and transfers from other funds (because they were previously recognized as revenue) are accounted for as other financing sources.

When the capital projects are expected to take several years to complete and will involve large amounts of money, budgetary control is advisable. The operating budget is prepared on an *annual* basis; therefore, it includes the expected revenues, estimated other financing sources, and estimated expenditures for only the current fiscal year. Adopting annual reporting permits the accounting for project events to be the same as for the general fund and the special revenue funds. The budget entry is as follows:

Estimated Other Financing Sources[a]	XXX	
Estimated Revenues[b]	XXX	
Appropriations[c]		XXX
Budgetary Fund Balance—Unreserved (either debited or credited)		XXX

[a]Resources from the general fund or other funds and the sale of general obligation bonds.
[b]Resources from county, state, or federal grants and interest income on temporary investments and from special assessments.
[c]Estimated expenditures for current year.

The full amount of the bond issue proceed is recorded as an other financing source in the fund that will use the resources. Bond premiums and discounts are recorded separately as other financing sources or uses, respectively. Bond issuance costs are recorded as expenditures. Since bond premiums and discounts arise because of adjustments to the interest rate, the premium and any payment received for accrued interest are transferred to the debt service fund to cover future *interest* payments. If bonds are sold at a discount, a project authorization must be reduced by the bond discount amount and/or issuance costs unless additional resources are transferred from the general fund or other funds.

Governments sometimes issue short-term *bond anticipation* notes after obtaining necessary voter and legislative authorization to issue long-term bonds. Since these short-term notes are expected to be replaced by long-term bonds, they are, in essence, long term and are accounted for in the General Long-Term Debt Account Group (GLTDAG), which was explained in Chapter 15. Proceeds of the bond anticipation notes are recorded in the governmental funds (often a Capital Project Fund) as other financing sources—proceeds from bond anticipation notes.[3]

Proceeds of bond issues not immediately needed for project expenditures are often temporarily invested to earn interest. These temporary investments are limited to securities whose yield does not exceed the interest rate of the tax-exempt borrowing. Interest earned on temporary investments is recognized as revenue in the capital projects fund. These earnings are often required to be transferred to the debt service fund to help finance bond interest expenditures.[4]

Capital projects funds have the authority through annually approved budgets to continue expenditures within prescribed limits until a project is completed. Although a project may not be completed at the end of a fiscal period, typical closing entries are recorded. Annual closing permits the actual activity to be compared with the legally adopted annual operating budget. Also, in the closing process, the credit to Expenditures provides the amount of capitalizable expenditures to be recorded in the general fixed assets account group as construction in progress.

The actual cost of a capital project probably will differ from its estimated cost. A deficiency usually is covered by a transfer from the general fund. If an excess of resources exists upon completion of the project, it generally is returned to the general fund or to the debt service fund. Such a transfer is reported as an other financing use on the statement of revenues, expenditures, and changes in fund balance. Upon completion of the project, it is customary to withhold part of the payment until final inspection and approval. The liability is recorded in contracts payable—retained percentage.

To illustrate accounting for capital projects funds, assume the city of Berryville plans to build a $300,000 addition to its municipal auditorium. The project will begin in 20X7 and is to be completed in 20X8. The following entries record the events that occur during construction:

Event	Entry in the Capital Projects Fund		
20X7			
10. The project budget is $300,000, to be financed by a general bond issue. The 20X7 operating budget is based on one-third of the work's being completed that year.	Estimated Other Financing Sources	300,000	
	Appropriations		100,000
	Budgetary Fund Balance—Unreserved		200,000
11. A $300,000, 8% general obligation bond issue is floated at 101.	Cash	303,000	
	Other Financing Sources		300,000
An entry also is made in the general long-term debt account group as follows:	Other Financing Sources—Premium		3,000
Amount to Be Provided 300,000			
Serial Bonds Payable 300,000			

3 The GASB states that a government may recognize bond anticipation notes as long-term obligations if, by the date the financial statements are issued, "all legal steps have been taken to refinance the bond anticipation notes and the intent is supported by an ability to consummate refinancing of the short-term note on a long-term basis." *Codification of Government Accounting and Reporting Standards* (Norwalk, CT: Governmental Accounting Standards Board, 1996, Section B50.101).

4 Governments are not required to capitalize construction-period interest for governmental activities.

Event	Entry in the Capital Projects Fund		
12. The bond premium is transferred to the debt service fund to be used for interest.	Other Financing Uses	3,000	
	Cash		3,000
An entry also is made in the debt service fund as follows: Cash . . . 3,000 Other Financing Sources . . . 3,000 (*Note:* Since bond premium is assumed to be used for interest payments, no entry is made in the account group.)			
13. A contract is signed for the auditorium construction at an estimated cost of $270,000.	Encumbrances	270,000	
	Fund Balance—Reserved for Encumbrances		270,000
14. The architect's bill for $10,650 is received, of which $7,650 is paid. Upon final building approval, the balance is due. The item was not encumbered.	Expenditures	10,650	
	Cash		7,650
	Contracts Payable—Retained Percentage		3,000
15. A partial billing is received from the contractor for $60,000, equal to the amount encumbered for these items. The contracts payable account is credited for the liability to the principal contractor. (If the amount of equivalent encumbrance is not specified, the encumbrance entry is reversed for the amount of the billing.)	Fund Balance—Reserved for Encumbrances	60,000	
	Encumbrances		60,000
	Expenditures	60,000	
	Contracts Payable		60,000
16. The contractor is paid $60,000.	Contracts Payable	60,000	
	Cash		60,000
17. Books for 20X7 are closed.	Budgetary Fund Balance—Unreserved	200,000	
	Appropriations	100,000	
	Estimated Other Financing Sources		300,000
18. The credit to Expenditures is the basis for the following entry in the general fixed assets account group: Construction in Progress . . . 70,650 Investment in General Fixed Assets—Capital Project Funds . . . 70,650	Other Financing Sources	303,000	
	Expenditures		70,650
	Other Financing Uses		3,000
	Fund Balance—Unreserved, Undesignated		229,350
19. Encumbrances are closed at year-end.	Fund Balance—Unreserved, Undesignated	210,000	
	Encumbrances		210,000
20X8			
20. The operating budget for 20X8 is recorded; completion is estimated to cost an additional $215,000, including the amount encumbered in the previous year.	Budgetary Fund Balance—Unreserved	215,000	
	Appropriations		215,000
21. The encumbrances are reinstated at the beginning of 20X8.	Encumbrances	210,000	
	Fund Balance—Unreserved, Undesignated		210,000
	Fund Balance—Reserved for Encumbrances	210,000	
	Encumbrances		210,000
22. The contract is completed in 20X8. Additional cost is $227,000, of which $10,000 is withheld in a separate account until final inspection and approval.	Expenditures	227,000	
	Contracts Payable		217,000
	Contracts Payable—Retained Percentage		10,000

(continued)

Event	Entry in the Capital Projects Fund		
23. The construction is accepted, and the contractor and architect are paid.	Contracts Payable	217,000	
	Contracts Payable—Retained Percentage. . . .	13,000	
	Cash		230,000
24. Books for 20X8 are closed.	Appropriations	215,000	
	Budgetary Fund Balance—Unreserved		215,000
25. The credit to Expenditures is the basis for the following entry in the general fixed assets account group: Buildings . . . . . . 297,650 Construction in Progress . . . . 70,650 Investment in General Fixed Assets—Capital Projects Funds . 227,000	Fund Balance—Unreserved, Undesignated . .	227,000	
	Expenditures		227,000
26. The residual balance is transferred to the debt service fund.	Other Financing Uses	2,350	
	Cash		2,350
An entry also is made in the debt service fund as follows: Cash . . . . . . 2,350 Other Financing Sources . . . . 2,350 Other Financing Sources. . . . . . 2,350 Fund Balance—Reserved for Debt Service. . . . . 2,350 (*Note:* Since the project was financed with general obligation debt, an additional entry in the general long-term debt account group indicating availability of funds to repay the debt is required.) Amount Available in the Debt Service Fund . . . . 2,350 Amount to Be Provided. . . . 2,350			
27. The Municipal Auditorium Capital Project Fund is closed.	Fund Balance—Unreserved, Undesignated . .	2,350	
	Other Financing Uses		2,350

When a governmental unit has more than one capital project, major funds are identified and nonmajor funds are presented in combining financial statements. Illustration 16-3 presents a combining balance sheet for the city of Berryville's capital projects funds. The 20X7 year-end balance sheet for the auditorium project, for which the accounting entries are shown, and the 20X7 year-end balance sheet for a bridge construction capital project, for which the accounting entries are *not* shown, are included in the combining balance sheet.

The combining statement of revenues, expenditures, and changes in fund balances (shown in Illustration 16-4) will show as revenues those resources obtained by special assessment, by grant, or from some other governmental unit. Transfers from other funds within the same governmental unit or proceeds of a bond issue are presented as other financing sources.

Debt Service Funds

As discussed in Chapter 15, the function of the general long-term debt account group is to provide a record of the unredeemed principal of long-term liabilities incurred to acquire general fixed assets. Closely related to this account group are *debt service funds*, whose primary function is to account for financial resources accumulated to cover the payment of principal and interest on general government obligations.

As in other governmental funds, the modified accrual basis is used for recognizing revenues, other financing sources, and expenditures in debt service funds. Interest and principal on

Illustration 16-3
City of Berryville
Capital Projects Funds
Combining Balance Sheet
December 31, 20X7

Assets	Municipal Auditorium	Bridge Construction Project	Total
Cash	$232,350	$102,000	$334,350
Special assessments receivable		160,000	160,000
Investments		40,000	40,000
Total assets	$232,350	$302,000	$534,350
Liabilities and Fund Balance			
Vouchers payable		$157,000	$157,000
Contracts payable—retained percentage	$ 3,000	50,000	53,000
Total liabilities	$ 3,000	$207,000	$210,000
Fund balances:			
Reserved for encumbrances	$210,000	$ 90,000	$300,000
Unreserved, undesignated	19,350	5,000	24,350
Total fund balances	$229,350	$ 95,000	$324,350
Total liabilities and fund balances	$232,350	$302,000	$534,350

Illustration 16-4
City of Berryville
Capital Projects Funds
Combining Statement of Revenues, Expenditures, and Changes in Fund Balances
For Year Ended December 31, 20X7

	Municipal Auditorium	Bridge Construction Project	Total
Revenues		$118,000	$ 118,000
Expenditures	$ 70,650	157,000	227,650
Excess (deficiency) of revenues over expenditures	$ (70,650)	$ (39,000)	$(109,650)
Other financing sources (uses):			
Proceeds of bonds	$303,000	$196,000	$ 499,000
Payments to debt service	(3,000)	(62,000)	(65,000)
Total other financing sources (uses)	$300,000	$134,000	$ 434,000
Excess (deficiency) of revenues and other sources over expenditures and other uses	$229,350	$ 95,000	$ 324,350
Fund balances at beginning of year	0	0	0
Fund balances at end of year	$229,350	$ 95,000	$ 324,350

general long-term debt are items for which the accrual basis is modified. For example, assume a governmental unit has a fiscal year ending June 30, with interest and principal on long-term debt to be paid on July 31. Since expenditures are authorized by appropriations, it is essential that expenditures be recorded in the same period as the appropriations. Thus, the interest and principal will not be accrued on June 30, because the appropriation to cover the principal and interest will not be provided until the budget for the next period is recorded on July 1. This method recognizes expenditures for interest and principal when they are *due*.

The most popular method of raising long-term resources is by the issuance of serial bonds, which are redeemed in a series of installments. Term bonds, whose total face value becomes due at one time, are now extremely rare. When serial bonds are issued, there is no substantial accumulation of cash in a sinking fund. Instead, the budget for the year of payment provides for interest and principal redemption. In debt service funds, an entry to record the budget is seldom used because expenditures for principal and interest are known and there is no need to compare them with budgetary amounts.

Resources to cover expenditures may come from several sources. A portion of a property tax levy may be authorized to be recorded directly into a debt service fund. The entries would be similar to those made in the general fund to record a tax levy. The net amount of taxes estimated to be collected is credited to Revenues since the resources are received from outsiders. Transfers received by the debt service fund from funds that have already recorded the resources as revenues are credited to Other Financing Sources. As discussed in Chapter 15, this procedure prevents revenues from being credited in two funds for the same resources—once in the originating fund (in this case, the general fund) and again in the recipient fund (in this case, a debt service fund).

Prior to redemption, the bond liability for unmatured general obligation debt is not recorded in a debt service fund but is recorded in the general long-term debt account group or similar listing. However, when a serial bond matures and payment of interest is due, the following entry is recorded in a debt service fund:

Expenditures	XXX	
Matured Bonds Payable		XXX
Matured Interest Payable		XXX

An entry to record payment of these matured items would then be made. Simultaneously, an entry to record reduction of the bond principal is made in the general long-term debt account group. Many governmental units employ the services of financial institutions to conduct actual payments for interest and serial redemptions. When cash is released to such a fiscal agent, the account debited is Cash with Fiscal Agent. Upon notification by the agent that actual payments have been made, the debt service fund entry is as follows:

Matured Bonds Payable	XXX	
Matured Interest Payable	XXX	
Cash with Fiscal Agent		XXX

The following entries would be made in a debt service fund for the indicated events that relate to a serial bond issue. As demonstrated by these entries, the interaction between funds and groups is especially prevalent in accounting for general obligation bond issues.

Event	Entry in the Debt Service Fund		
28. An 8%, $300,000 general obligation serial bond issue for bridge construction is sold at 101. The premium is transferred from the capital projects fund to the debt service fund.	Cash	3,000	
	Other Financing Sources		3,000

Event	Entry in the Debt Service Fund

Entries are also made in the capital projects fund as follows:
Cash 303,000
  Other Financing Sources 300,000
  Other Financing Sources—Premium 3,000
Other Financing Uses 3,000
  Cash 3,000
Entries are also made in the general long-term debt account group:
Amount to Be Provided 300,000
  Serial Bonds Payable 300,000	

29. Of the property taxes, $50,000 is levied specifically to cover debt service on these bonds; the levy, less 1% of the taxes estimated to be uncollectible, is recorded in the debt service fund.	Taxes Receivable—Current 50,000
	  Allowance for Uncollectible Current Taxes . 500
	  Revenues 49,500

30. All property taxes are collected except for $400 that is written off. The difference between estimated and actual uncollectible taxes is recorded in Revenues.	Cash 49,600
	Allowance for Uncollectible Current Taxes ... 400
	  Taxes Receivable—Current 50,000
	
	Allowance for Uncollectible Current Taxes ... 100
	  Revenues 100

31. Assuming $30,000 is to be used toward the first installment on the principal payment, an additional entry is made in the general long-term debt account group as follows:
Amount Available in the Debt
  Service Fund 30,000
    Amount to Be Provided 30,000	

32. The fund receives $7,000 of its $9,000 share of state gasoline taxes. The city is not entitled to the balance until the next fiscal period.	Cash 7,000
	Due from State 2,000
	  Revenues 7,000
	  Deferred Revenues 2,000

33. A transfer of $30,000 is received from the general fund.	Cash .... 30,000 Other Financing Sources 30,000

Since the $30,000 is for payment of principal, an additional entry is made in the general long-term account group debt:
Amount Available in the Debt Service
  Fund 30,000
    Amount to Be Provided 30,000	

34. Cash is transmitted to a fiscal agent for payment of the first $60,000 of maturing bonds and $24,000 of interest due on the last day of the fiscal period.	Cash with Fiscal Agent .... 84,000 Cash 84,000

35. The matured bonds and interest are recorded.	Expenditures 84,000
	  Matured Bonds Payable 60,000
	  Matured Interest Payable 24,000

Principal of $60,000 is matured and no longer long term. The entry to reclassify the debt in the general long-term account group debt is as follows:
Serial Bonds Payable 60,000
  Amount Available in the Debt
    Service Fund 60,000	

(continued)

Event	Entry in the Debt Service Fund		
36. The fiscal agent reports that all payments have been made except for $1,000 of interest.	Matured Bonds Payable	60,000	
	Matured Interest Payable	23,000	
	Cash with Fiscal Agent		83,000
37. Books are closed at year-end.	Revenues	56,600	
	Other Financing Sources	33,000	
	Expenditures		84,000
	Fund Balance—Reserved for Debt Service		5,600

Assets transferred to a debt service fund must be used to redeem bonds or to pay interest. There are no unreserved assets. Any excess of assets over liabilities is reserved for debt service. Therefore, at year-end, the accounts are closed to fund balance—reserved for debt service rather than to an unreserved fund balance.

In addition to term bonds and serial bonds, debt service funds may be used to service debt arising from notes or warrants having a maturity of more than one year after date of issue and to make periodic payments on capital leases. Although each issue of long-term debt is a separate obligation with unique legal restrictions and servicing requirements, GASB standards provide that, if legally permissible, a single debt service fund may be used to account for the service of all issues of tax-supported and special-assessment debt. If legal restrictions do not allow the servicing of all issues to be accounted for by a single debt service fund, the number of debt service funds should be held to a minimum.

Sometimes, governments will defease existing debt accounted for in the general long-term debt account group. Through advanced refunding, new debt is issued to provide resources to pay interest on old, outstanding debt as it becomes due and to pay the principal on the old debt either as it matures or for an earlier call date. As demonstrated by the following entries, when advanced refunding results in defeasance of debt (either legally or in substance), the proceeds of the new debt are reported as *other financing sources—proceeds of refunding bonds* in the debt service fund.[5] Subsequent payments from resources provided by the new debt to actually retire the old debt or to transfer funds to an escrow agent are other financing uses, not expenditures. In either case, the old debt is removed from the general long-term debt account group, and the new debt is reported as a long-term liability.

Event	Entry in the Debt Service Fund		
38. A $100,000 bond was issued, proceeds from which are to be used to pay principal and interest of an $85,000 old bond issue. The criteria for in-substance defeasance is met.	Cash	100,000	
	Other Financing Sources—Proceeds of Refunding Bonds		100,000
39. Cash is transmitted to an escrow agent to administer the payment of principal and interest on the old debt. If the debt was actually retired, the debit would be to Other Financing Uses—Retirement of Old Bonds.	Other Financing Uses—Payment to Escrow Agent	100,000	
	Cash		100,000

The entries in the general long-term debt account group to record the new debt are as follows:

Bonds Payable	85,000	
Amount to Be Provided		85,000

The entries in the general long-term debt account group to record the new debt are as follows:

Amount to Be Provided	100,000	
Bonds Payable		100,000

5 GASB Statement No. 7, *Advanced Refunding Resulting in Defeasance of Debt* (Norwalk, CT: Governmental Accounting Standards Board, March 1987).

Debt service funds employ two financial statements for reporting purposes: a balance sheet and a statement of revenues, expenditures, and changes in fund balances. If two or more debt service funds are used, major funds are identified and nonmajor funds are presented in combining statements. Illustration 16-5 is a combining balance sheet for Vernon Town. This balance sheet has a column for general obligation debt, for which the entries were shown, and a column for special assessment debt explained later in this chapter, for which the entries were not shown.

Illustration 16-5
Vernon Town
Debt Service Funds
Combining Balance Sheet
December 31, 20X7

Assets	General Obligation Debt	Special Assessment Debt	Total
Cash	$5,600	$ 20,000	$ 25,600
Cash with fiscal agents	1,000		1,000
Due from state	2,000		2,000
Special assessment receivable		20,000	20,000
Special assessment receivable—deferred		160,000	160,000
Total assets	$8,600	$200,000	$208,600
Liabilities and Fund Balance			
Liabilities:			
Matured interest payable	$1,000		$ 1,000
Deferred revenues	2,000	$160,000	162,000
Fund balance:			
Reserved for debt service	5,600	40,000	45,600
Total liabilities and fund balance	$8,600	$200,000	$208,600

The combining statement of revenues, expenditures, and changes in fund balances for Vernon Town's debt service funds is shown in Illustration 16-6. This statement itemizes revenues by source and expenditures by function, and it summarizes the causes of changes in fund balances during the period.

Special Assessments. Local governments may provide capital improvements and services for the primary benefit of particular groups of property owners, which are paid partially or totally by the same property owners. Such arrangements are called *special assessment projects* and are accounted for through the local government.

Service-type special assessments cover operating activities, such as snow plowing, that do not result in increases in fixed assets. Payment for service special assessments seldom is arranged on an installment basis. A single charge is added to the property tax bill. Service assessments are accounted for in the fund type (usually the general fund, a special revenue fund, or an enterprise fund) that best reflects the nature of the transaction.

Capital-improvement special assessments result in additions or improvements to a government's fixed assets. If an improvement provides capital assets that become part of an enterprise activity, such as water main construction for a utility, accounting would be done in an enterprise fund. If the improvement results in a general fixed asset, such as streets, gutters, or sidewalks, the asset would be recorded in the general fixed asset account group (if the government records infrastructure assets), in which case the accounting is divided into two phases.

Illustration 16-6
Vernon Town
Debt Service Funds
Combining Statement of Revenues, Expenditures, and Changes in Fund Balances
For Year Ended December 31, 20X7

	General Obligation Debt	Special Assessment Debt	Total
Revenues:			
Taxes	$ 49,600	$20,000	$ 69,600
Intergovernmental	7,000		7,000
Total revenues	$ 56,600	$20,000	$ 76,600
Expenditures:			
Principal retirement	$ 60,000		$ 60,000
Interest charges	24,000		24,000
Total expenditures	$ 84,000	$ 0	$ 84,000
Excess (deficiency) of revenues over expenditures	$ (27,400)	$20,000	$ (7,400)
Other financing sources (uses):			
Proceeds of refunding bonds	$ 100,000		$ 100,000
Operating transfers-in	33,000		33,000
Payment to escrow agent	(100,000)		(100,000)
Total other finance sources (uses)	$ 33,000	$ 0	$ 33,000
Excess (deficiency) of revenues and other financing sources over expenditures	$ 5,600	$20,000	$ 25,600
Fund balances at beginning of year	0	20,000	20,000
Fund balances at end of year	$ 5,600	$40,000	$ 45,600

The *first phase* consists of financing and constructing the project and usually is accounted for through a capital projects fund. The initiative for such projects is often taken by the property owners who request the improvement. However, authorization must be approved through appropriate channels. Special assessment projects typically are financed through issues of long-term debt but may be financed with existing government resources. Once the project is approved, the estimates for the budget period (not the total project budget) are recorded in a capital projects fund.

Proper recordings of inflows of financial resources into the capital projects fund depend upon the source of financing. Illustration 16-7 presents proper recording of inflows under three possible sources of financing. When the capital improvements are financed by special-assessment-related debt for which the government is obligated in some manner, such as accounting for resources raised and for the expenditure of funds during construction, accounting procedures are the same as for other capital projects, assuming secondary liability in the event of default by property owners.[6]

When the capital improvements are financed by debt for which the government is not obligated in any manner, proceeds from issuing the debt are credited by the governmental unit to contributions from property owners, in the capital projects fund.

6 GASB Statement No. 6, *Accounting and Financial Reporting for Special Assessments* (Norwalk, CT: Governmental Accounting Standards Board, January 1987), states that a government is obligated in some manner if (a) it is legally obligated to assume all or part of the debt in the event of default or (b) the government may take certain actions to assume secondary liability for all or part of the debt—and the government takes, or has given indications that it will take, these actions.

When the capital improvements are financed by existing governmental resources and debt is not issued, transfers from other funds are credited as other financing sources, in the capital projects fund.

Expenditures are recorded in the capital projects fund as costs are incurred for the special assessment project. At year-end, the capitalizable costs of an unfinished special assessment project are entered in the general fixed assets account group.

40. Capital Projects Fund	Expenditures	80,000	
	Cash		80,000
41. General Fixed Assets Account Group	Construction in Progress	80,000	
	Investment in General Fixed Assets—Capital Projects Funds (special assessments)		80,000

Completion of the special assessment project in the second year is recorded with the following entries:

42. Capital Projects Fund	Expenditures	120,000	
	Cash		120,000
43. General Fixed Assets Account Group (This entry is also shown in Illustration 16-7.)	Capital Asset Account	200,000	
	Construction in Progress		80,000
	Investment in General Fixed Assets—Capital Projects Funds (special assessments)		120,000

The *second phase* of accounting for special assessment projects consists of collecting the special assessments on an installment basis from benefited property owners and repaying the cost of financing the project. When the project is financed with special assessment debt and the government is obligated in some manner for this debt, the liability should be recorded in the general long-term debt account group, as shown in this entry:

44. Amount to Be Provided for Payment of Special Assessment Debt	200,000	
Special Assessment Debt with Governmental Commitment		200,000

In some cases, the governmental unit has the primary responsibility for repayment of the bonds. In these situations, they are recorded, as follows, in the general long-term debt account group with the same type of entry used to record any other general obligation debt.

45. Amount to Be Provided for Payment of Special Assessment Debt	200,000	
Special Assessment Bonds Payable		200,000
(This entry is also used as an example in Illustration 16-7.)		

The special assessment receivable and special assessment revenue are divided between current and deferred portions in the debt service fund. Amounts levied and demanded to service-related debt in the current period are credited to Revenues as shown on the following page. The remainder to be collected and used for debt service in future periods is credited to Deferred Revenues.

Illustration 16-7
Accounting for Special Assessment Projects under Three Methods of Financing*

Debt Issued	Flows of Financial Resources through the Capital Projects Fund		
Government obligated in some manner	Cash	200,000	
	Other Financing Sources—Bond Proceeds		200,000
Government not obligated in any manner	Cash	200,000	
	Contributions from Property Owners		200,000
Debt not issued	Cash	200,000	
	Other Financing Sources—Transfers from Other Funds		200,000
	Expenditures incurred during construction are recorded in the same manner as expenditures recorded for other capital projects.		

*Note that budgetary entries have been omitted from this illustration.

46. Special Assessments Receivable—Current	20,000	
Special Assessments Receivable—Deferred	180,000	
Revenues		20,000
Deferred Revenues		180,000

Through the term of the debt, the amount to be collected from property owners for a period is levied and demanded by the governmental unit; consequently, that portion of deferred revenue should be recognized as revenue in that period. Recognition of the receivable from the levy and the revenue are shown below. Details of the assessments are entered in a subsidiary ledger, where the levy against each property owner and collections from the owner are indicated.

47. Special Assessments Receivable—Current	20,000	
Special Assessments Receivable—Deferred		20,000
48. Deferred Revenues	20,000	
Revenues		20,000

The general long-term debt account group is updated to reflect the amount available in the debt service fund. The debt is liquidated in the same manner as other governmental-fund debt.

When the government is not obligated in any manner, collection of the special assessment and debt service payments should be accounted for through an agency fund (discussed on pages 939 through 941 in the Agency Funds section) since the government is acting merely as an agent for the property owners and bondholders. In that case, the debt is not shown in the general long-term debt account group; it should appear, however, in the notes to the financial statements.

When no debt is issued, Revenues is credited in the general fund for the current levy of the special assessment. Amounts to be levied and collected in future periods are credited to Deferred Revenues. These special tax assessments will serve as installments to pay back the original amount transferred from the general fund to the capital projects fund for the project costs.

Eventual Recording of Constructed Asset in the General Fixed Assets Account Group			Recording of Special Assessment Debt in the General Long-Term Debt Account Group		
Fixed Assets	200,000		Amount to Be Provided for Payment of Special Assessment Debt	200,000	
Construction in Progress		80,000	Special Assessment Bonds Payable		200,000
Investment in General Fixed Assets		120,000			
Fixed Assets	200,000		Long-term debt is not recorded because the government is not obligated for the debt. Debt service is accounted for through an agency fund.		
Construction in Progress		80,000			
Investment in General Fixed Assets		120,000			
Fixed Assets	200,000		Long-term debt is not issued.		
Construction in Progress		80,000			
Investment in General Fixed Assets		120,000			
			Liquidation of the special assessment debt is as described for all other general government debt.		

REFLECTION

- Accounting and financial reporting for other governmental funds follow the modified accrual basis of accounting.
- GASB Statement No. 34 introduces a new fund—the permanent fund—that accounts for nonexpendable trust funds established for the sole purpose of supporting governmental activities or programs.
- Also commonly used are special revenue funds, capital project funds, and debt service funds.
- When more than one fund of each type exists, major funds are identified and combining funds is necessary to total the amount of the nonmajor funds in each fund type. These totals are used on the financial statements.

PROPRIETARY FUNDS

2
OBJECTIVE

Account for and prepare financial statements of proprietary funds.

The funds discussed to this point have been governmental funds. The second category of funds—*proprietary funds*—will now be discussed. By definition, the term "proprietary" means pertaining to a proprietor and implies that users of goods or services will be charged on the basis of consumption, similar to the practice in private industries. Usually, charges are set to recover as much as possible of the total cost, including depreciation. Whatever is not recovered must be subsidized.

Governments account for their business-type activities in two types of proprietary funds. Enterprise funds account for operations in which goods or services are provided to the general public.

Internal service funds account for operations in which goods or services are provided by one government department to other departments within the same government or to other governments.

Proprietary funds focus on capital maintenance to measure whether revenues are sufficient to cover expenses (including the amortization of noncurrent items) of the fiscal period. This is consistent with an economic resources measurement focus and the full accrual basis of accounting. Financial reporting for proprietary funds is similar to financial reporting for business enterprises in that income statements show revenues, expenses, and net income for a fiscal period, and balance sheets include both current and noncurrent assets and liabilities. The proprietary fund balance sheet residual is its net assets.

The GASB requires proprietary funds to follow all accounting standards set forth by the FASB prior to November 30, 1989, unless they have been specifically overridden by a GASB pronouncement. In addition, an enterprise fund (but not internal service funds) *may* apply all FASB pronouncements developed for business enterprises issued after that date unless they conflict with or contradict GASB standards.[7] Enterprise funds may also apply FASB standards and interpretations limited to not-for-profit organizations (such as FASB Statement Nos. 116, 117, 124, and 136 described in Chapters 18 and 19). This option is designed to increase comparability between similar government enterprises and the private sector.

When proprietary funds furnish goods or services to other funds, for example, a computer center accounted for in an internal service fund provides service to departments accounted for in the general fund. This transaction is considered to be an "interfund service provided and used" and is *reported as if it were an external transaction.* Therefore, the billing represents revenue to the internal service fund and an expenditure to the general fund. Entries in each fund are as follows:

49. Internal Service Fund	Due from the General Fund	XXX	
	Revenues		XXX
50. General Fund	Expenditures	XXX	
	Due to the Internal Service Fund..............		XXX

Conversely, if a proprietary fund pays the general fund for services, the proprietary fund records expenses, and the general fund records revenue. For example, the general government may bill an enterprise fund for payments in lieu of property taxes. Entries in each fund are as follows:

51. General Fund	Due from the Enterprise Fund..................	XXX	
	Revenues		XXX
52. Enterprise Fund	Expenses	XXX	
	Due to the General Fund		XXX

Enterprise Funds

Enterprise funds account for goods or services provided by a governmental unit to the general public. The user is charged for these goods or services, based on consumption. For example, the operations of utilities, public housing, public parking, municipal solid waste landfills, economic development corporations, cultural activities, and airports would be covered by enterprise funds. These funds continue indefinitely and are self-supporting, depending upon the amounts charged to cover part or all of the costs of operation, debt service, and maintenance of capital facilities.

Governments *may* account for any activity in an enterprise fund as long as it charges a fee to external users. Government *must* use an enterprise fund if one of the following criteria is met: (1) the activity is financed solely with revenue debt secured merely by the revenues from a specific activity, (2) laws or regulations require that the activity's costs of providing services

7 GASB Statement No. 20, *Accounting and Financial Reporting for Proprietary Funds and Other Governmental Entities that Use Proprietary Fund Accounting* (Norwalk, CT: Governmental Accounting Standards Board, September 1993).

(including capital costs) be recovered by fees and charges rather than general taxes, or (3) the pricing policies of the activity establish fees and charges designed to recover its costs, including capital costs (such as depreciation or debt service).

At the inception of an enterprise fund (or internal service fund), capital must be provided either by issuance of long-term debt or by transfer from some other source, such as a municipality's general fund. In the latter case, the contribution received is credited to an account labeled *interfund transfer in* from the general fund. These interfund transfers are reported below nonoperating revenues as in Illustration 16-9. As a measure of original asset sources, the contribution remains in the fund indefinitely or until the fund is terminated. If operations are profitable and arrangements specify that profits shall be shared with the general fund, an amount is reported as an interfund transfer out—classified with expenses. Financing may also be provided from loans or advances by the municipality. In such cases, the loans or advances are recorded as interfund payables in the proprietary funds and as interfund receivables in the general fund.

Enterprise funds, in particular, receive capital contributions both from internal (other funds) and external (customers, developers, other governments) sources. Whatever the source, these contributions are recognized as revenues on a line below income from operations.

An enterprise fund's operational efficiency may be monitored in part by the net income or net loss figure. As in commercial operations, budgets are prepared. However, budgets are not recorded formally in the accounts, perhaps because the fund's self-supporting nature requires a high degree of operational freedom, but more likely because fixed budgetary amounts would be of much less value when there is a variable demand by the public for goods and services.

Control accounts for revenues and expenses commonly are used, with details in supporting records. In accounting for revenues, two control accounts are used: operating revenues for charges for services and nonoperating revenues for grants and interfund transfers received, interest and rent earned, or other miscellaneous financial revenues. A similar breakdown is used to account for expenses: operating expenses for expenses directly related to goods or services produced, such as salaries, depreciation, heat, light, materials, and taxes and nonoperating expenses for financial expenses, such as bond interest. Recording of revenues and expenses, including adjustments, is much the same as in private enterprise accounting.

One of the unusual features of accounting for enterprise funds is the introduction of restricted assets and the current liabilities to be paid with restricted assets. *Restricted assets* are assets (cash and investments) upon which some limitation has been imposed that makes them available only for designated purposes. Examples of restricted assets are amounts of customer deposits subject to refund, proceeds from long-term debt for construction, and monies set aside for bond interest or principal redemption.

Restricted assets and their related current liabilities are recorded in specially designated accounts so that the segregation of these items is ensured. For example, if a water utility receives deposits covering meter installations for customers and these deposits are refundable, they would be recorded as follows:

53. Restricted Assets—Customers' Deposits Cash	XXX	
Customers' Deposits Payable from Restricted Assets		XXX

If the deposits are invested, the entry to record the investment would be as follows:

54. Restricted Assets—Customers' Deposits Investments	XXX	
Restricted Assets—Customers' Deposits Cash		XXX

The existence of restricted assets and their related current liabilities is especially common when an enterprise fund is used to account for a public utility. A major source of funding for utilities is the sale of revenue bonds, which are issued to permit the construction of, or an addition to, a facility. Since payments for these bonds depend on the existence of operating income, the bond indenture usually includes several restrictions. For example, it may require that the bond proceeds be expended only for construction, making the proceeds a restricted asset. The following entry would be required:

55. Restricted Assets—Revenue Bond Construction Cash	XXX	
Revenue Bonds Payable		XXX

As amounts are committed, the liability would be identified as payable from a restricted asset.

56. Construction in Progress	XXX	
Construction Contracts Payable from Restricted Assets		XXX

Payment of the liability would be recorded with the following entry:

57. Construction Contracts Payable from Restricted Assets	XXX	
Restricted Assets—Revenue Bond Construction Cash		XXX

If a municipality received approval to expand its utility facilities by issuing a combination of special assessment bonds and revenue bonds, the following entry would be required in an enterprise fund:

58. Restricted Assets—Construction Cash	XXX	
Special Assessment Bonds Payable		XXX
Revenue Bonds Payable		XXX

Note that the redemption and servicing of both the revenue bonds and the special assessment bonds are the financial responsibility of the utility enterprise fund. Therefore, the liability appears in the enterprise fund balance sheet rather than in the general long-term debt account group.[8]

The balance sheet for the Clermont County Water and Sewer Fund, shown in Illustration 16-8, reports restricted assets following the regular current assets and preceding the capital assets. Note also that current liabilities are segregated to show amounts payable from regular current assets and amounts payable from restricted assets.

Most revenue bonds for enterprise funds are serial bonds that require the earmarking of monies for the payment of interest and for the establishment of a fund for principal redemption. These resources are labeled restricted assets. The current interest and serial installment payables are recorded as current liabilities payable from restricted assets. To further protect the bondholder, at least psychologically, many serial revenue bonds require that unreserved retained earnings be restricted in an amount equal to the excess of restricted assets related to debt service of the bond issue over the current liability for interest and principal. If the amounts in the Water and Sewer Fund balance sheet are compared with assumed amounts at the end of the previous year, the additional amount to be reserved would be determined as follows:

	Dec. 31, 20X7	Dec. 31, 20X6 (assumed)
Restricted assets related to revenue bonds:		
Cash with fiscal agent for bond service	$ 80,444	$ 87,200
Revenue bond debt service cash	5,000	3,000
Revenue bond fund	124,155	93,975
Total	$209,599	$184,175
Current liabilities related to revenue bonds:		
Accrued revenue bond interest payable	$ 32,444	$ 37,200
Matured revenue bonds payable	48,000	50,000
Total	$ 80,444	$ 87,200
Excess of bond-related restricted assets over bond-related current liabilities	$129,155	$ 96,975

8 Governments are also required to capitalize construction-period interest for business-type activities.

Illustration 16-8
Clermont County
Water and Sewer Fund
Balance Sheet
December 31, 20X7

Assets

Current assets:			
Cash		$ 257,036	
Receivables (net)		33,480	
Inventories and prepaid expenses		24,230	
Total current assets			$ 314,746
Restricted assets:			
Cash with fiscal agent for bond service		$ 80,444	
Revenue bond construction cash		17,760	
Revenue bond debt service cash		5,000	
Revenue bond fund:			
Cash	$ 10,355		
Investments	113,800	124,155	
Customers' deposits:			
Investments	$ 63,000		
Interest receivable on investments	650	63,650	
Total restricted assets			291,009
Property, plant, and equipment:			
Land		$ 211,100	
Buildings	$ 447,700		
Less accumulated depreciation	90,718	356,982	
Improvements other than buildings	$3,887,901		
Less accumulated depreciation	348,944	3,538,957	
Machinery and equipment	$1,841,145		
Less accumulated depreciation	201,138	1,640,007	
Construction in progress		22,713	
Total property, plant, and equipment			5,769,759
Total assets			$6,375,514

Liabilities and Fund Equity

Liabilities:		
Current liabilities (payable from current assets):		
Vouchers payable	$195,071	
Accrued wages and taxes payable	2,870	
Construction contracts payable	8,347	$ 206,288
Current liabilities (payable from restricted assets):		
Construction contracts payable	$ 17,760	
Accrued revenue bond interest payable	32,444	
Matured revenue bonds payable	48,000	
Customer deposits	63,000	161,204
Total current liabilities		$ 367,492
Long-term liabilities:		
Revenue bonds payable		2,448,000
Total liabilities		$2,815,492
Net assets:		
Invested in capital assets, net of related debt		$3,232,968
Restricted		3,961
Unrestricted		323,093
Total net assets		$3,560,022

If the bond indenture requires that the reserves be increased to equal the bond-related restricted assets that are not offset by bond-related current liabilities, the following entry becomes necessary:

59. Net Assets—Unrestricted ($129,155 – $96,975)	32,180	
Net Assets—Restricted for Bond Debt Service ($5,000 – $3,000)		2,000
Net Assets—Restricted for Bond Retirement ($124,155 – $93,975)		30,180

The statement of revenues, expenses (not expenditures), and changes in net assets for an enterprise fund, as shown in the GASB *Codification of Governmental Accounting and Financial Reporting,* focuses on total net assets, both restricted and unrestricted. Such a statement for the Clermont County Water and Sewer Fund is shown in Illustration 16-9.

Illustration 16-9
Enterprise Fund
Clermont County
Water and Sewer Fund
Statement of Revenues, Expenses, and Changes in Net Assets
For Year Ended December 31, 20X7

Operating revenues:		
Charges for services		$ 727,150
Operating expenses:		
Personnel services (salaries and fees)	$306,100	
Materials and supplies	106,580	
Depreciation	103,600	
Heat, light, power, and taxes	47,900	
Total operating expenses		564,180
Operating income		$ 162,970
Nonoperating revenues (expenses):		
Operating grants	$ 5,000	
Interest revenue	2,830	
Rental income	1,000	
Interest expense	(92,988)	
Total nonoperating revenues (expenses)		(84,158)
Interfund transfers in—Contributions from municipality		1,000,000
Change in net assets		$1,078,812
Total net assets at beginning of year		2,481,210
Total net assets at end of year		$3,560,022

GASB Statement No. 9, *Reporting Cash Flows of Proprietary and Nonexpendable Trust Funds and Governmental Entities that Use Proprietary Fund Accounting,* stipulates that a statement of cash flows for such funds shows movements of combined unrestricted and restricted cash and cash equivalents for the reported period, segregated into four categories:

1. Cash flows from *operating activities,* which would include cash received from sales of goods or services and cash paid to suppliers, employees, and providers of services.

2. Cash flows from *noncapital financing activities*, which would include proceeds from borrowings not related to capital asset acquisition and repayments thereon, as well as operating grants or transfers not related to capital asset acquisition.
3. Cash flows from *capital and related financing activities* to acquire or dispose of capital assets, which would include grants or transfers related to capital asset acquisition.
4. Cash flows from *investing activities*.

Government enterprises classify interest paid as financing activity and interest earned as investing activity rather than as operating activities. Whether interest paid is classified as capital or noncapital depends on the purpose of the underlying debt.

The statement of cash flows reports net cash provided or used for each of the four categories. With the adoption of GASB Statement No. 34, governments are required to use the direct method, as shown in Illustration 16-10A for a hypothetical electric utility. In addition, a reconciliation of net operating income to net cash flow from operating activities (Category 1) must be provided in a separate schedule to accompany the cash flows statement or in the notes to the financial statements. Such a reconciliation is presented in Illustration 16-10B on page 932.

Illustration 16-10A
Zenith City
Electric Utility Fund
Statement of Cash Flows
Increase (Decrease) in Cash and Cash Equivalents
For Year Ended June 30, 20X7

Cash flows from operating activities:		
Cash received from customers	$ 456,000	
Cash paid to suppliers and employees	(400,300)	
Other operating revenues	7,500	
Net cash provided by operating activities		$ 63,200
Cash flows from noncapital financing activities:		
Net repayments under revolving loan arrangement	$ (10,700)	
Operating grants received	50,000	
Operating transfers-out to other funds	(37,500)	
Net cash provided by noncapital financing activities		1,800
Cash flows from capital and related financing activities:		
Proceeds from sale of capital bonds	$ 125,000	
Principal and interest paid on capital bonds	(100,000)	
Acquisition and construction of capital assets	(75,000)	
Proceeds from sale of equipment	70,000	
Net cash provided by capital and related financing activities		20,000
Cash flows from investing activities:		
Purchases of investment securities	$ (62,500)	
Proceeds from sale and maturities of securities	36,500	
Interest and dividends received on investments	3,000	
Net cash used in investing activities		(23,000)
Net increase in cash and cash equivalents		$ 62,000
Cash and cash equivalents at beginning of year		100,000
Cash and cash equivalents at end of year		$162,000

Illustration 16-10B
Zenith City
Electric Utility Fund
Reconciliation of Net Operating Income to
Net Cash Provided by Operating Activities
For Year Ended June 30, 20X7

Net operating income (loss)		$ (49,800)
Adjustments to reconcile net operating income to net cash provided by operating activities:		
Depreciation	$122,000	
Provision for uncollectible accounts	1,000	
Changes in assets and liabilities:		
Increase in accounts receivable	(15,000)	
Decrease in inventory	2,000	
Decrease in prepaid expenses	500	
Increase in accounts payable	2,500	
Total adjustments		113,000
Net cash provided by operating activities		$ 63,200

Many governments account for landfill operations in enterprise funds. GASB standards require closure and post-closure costs to be recognized in the years in which the landfill is in operation rather than when they are to be paid.[9] Therefore, in each year of the landfill's useful life, the government recognizes, as both an expense and an increase in a liability, a portion of the estimated costs for closure and post-closure care. The estimated total cost of landfill closure and post-closure care include:

1. The cost of equipment expected to be installed and facilities expected to be constructed (e.g., ground-water monitoring wells, storm-water management systems, gas monitoring systems, etc.) near or after the date that the landfill stops accepting waste.
2. The cost of final cover.
3. The cost of monitoring and maintaining the landfill during the post-closure period.

The current expense (and liability) is based on the percentage of the landfill actually used up during the current period multiplied by the total estimated cost of closure and post-closure care. For example, suppose a government uses 90,000 cubic feet of a landfill in one year. Total landfill capacity is estimated at 4.5 million cubic feet. If closure and post-closure care costs are estimated at $18,000,000, the entry to record the expense and liability for the year [based on $18,000,000 × (90,000 ÷ 4,500,000)] is as follows:

60. Landfill Expense	360,000	
Liability for Landfill Costs		360,000

In year 2, closure and post-closure cost estimates are adjusted to $18,500,000. Landfill used during the year totaled 210,000 cubic feet. Landfill capacity has decreased to 4,250,000. The entry to record the expense and liability for year 2 [$18,500,000 × (300,000 ÷ 4,250,000)], less $360,000 already recognized in year 1, is as follows:

9 GASB Statement No. 18, *Accounting for Municipal Solid Waste Landfill Closure and Post-Closure Care Costs* (Norwalk, CT: Governmental Accounting Standards Board, August 1993). Landfills accounted for in governmental funds will calculate the accrued liability the same as in the given example. These landfills will recognize expenditures and fund liabilities using the modified accrual basis of accounting. The long-term portion of the liability will be reported in the general long-term debt account group.

61. Landfill Expense	945,882	
Liability for Landfill Costs		945,882

These standards allow for all expenses to be recognized by the date of the landfill closing. Any landfill capital assets excluded from the calculation of the estimated total cost of landfill closure and post-closure care should be fully depreciated by the date that the landfill stops accepting solid waste.

If a municipality operates more than one enterprise fund, combining statements are required in order to disclose the details of each nonmajor fund. GASB standards also require that *different, identifiable activities* for major nonhomogeneous enterprise funds be presented to prevent misleading financial statements. Presentation of information about these activities in the notes to the financial statements is also required. An activity within an enterprise fund is *identifiable* if it has specific revenue stream and related expenses. An activity is *different* if the product, program, or services are generated from or provided by different activities. Examples of different, identifiable activities are natural gas, water, and electricity utility services that may be accounted for in one utility enterprise fund.

Internal Service Funds

Internal service funds are similar to enterprise funds in that they are self-sustaining, depend on amounts charged for services rendered, and receive start-up resources. The difference is that users of their services are other departments of the same governmental unit or other governmental units. A computer center, a printing department, a central purchasing department, a central garage, and risk financing and self-insurance activities are accounted for in internal service funds.

GASB Statement No. 34 permits governments to establish internal service funds "to report any activity that provides goods or services to other funds, departments, or agencies of the primary government and its component units, or to other governments, on a cost-reimbursement basis."

Since internal service funds do not deal with the general public and usually do not issue bonds that result in restrictions, they do not have restricted assets. Their accounting procedures resemble those for a commercial business. Internal service funds must recover their costs, including depreciation, or be subsidized. Therefore, they maintain records of capital assets and use the accrual basis of accounting. Budgetary accounts are not used, although budget forecasts facilitate the calculation of overhead rates to be applied in determining charges. Billing rates of internal service funds have received much attention because of the impact on expenditures of other funds. Most experts agree that the amount of net income for any internal service fund should be sufficient to allow for replacement of capital assets or payment of risk-related losses but not so large as to accumulate large balances that could otherwise have stayed in the other funds.

As discussed for enterprise funds, the establishment of an internal service fund may be by a contribution or an advance from the municipality. Charges to customer departments are considered interfund services and appear as expenditures in the governmental funds, expenses in the other proprietary funds, and revenue to the internal service fund.[10]

The financial statements of internal service funds consist of the balance sheet, the statement of revenues, expenses, and changes in retained earnings, and the statement of cash flows. When more than one internal service fund exists, combining statements are prepared. Major internal services funds are not highlighted. These statements closely resemble commercial financial statements and will not be illustrated.

10 GASB Statement No. 10, *Accounting and Financial Reporting for Risk Financing and Related Insurance Issues* (Norwalk, CT: Governmental Accounting Standards Board, November 1989), allows governments to use either the general fund or internal service fund for all risk financing and self-insurance activities. Many governments choose an internal service fund to charge other funds of the government entity for claims liabilities, including future catastrophe losses based on actuarial estimates.

REFLECTION

- Proprietary funds have a measurement focus of economic resources and use full accrual basis accounting.
- The two proprietary funds are enterprise funds and internal service funds.
- Interfund activities between the proprietary funds and governmental funds are either reciprocal transactions for the provision of goods or services (accounted for as revenue and expenditures) or nonreciprocal (accounted for as interfund transfers).

3

OBJECTIVE

Explain the usefulness of and the accounting process for fiduciary funds and how these funds are reported.

FIDUCIARY FUNDS: TRUST AND AGENCY FUNDS

As mentioned in Chapter 15, fiduciary funds account for resources for which a governmental unit is acting as a trustee or agent for an external individual, organization, or government. This category of funds includes private-purpose trust funds, investment trust funds, pension trust funds, and agency funds.

Private-Purpose Trust Funds

GASB Statement No. 34 significantly changes the accounting for trusts. As shown in the previous sections, accounting for these assets and the operation of the trust fund depend on the document that created the fund. Public-purpose trusts are accounted for as special revenue funds if both the assets contributed (the principal) and the earnings may be expended (these were formally called *expendable trust funds*). Other public-purpose trusts where only the earnings are spent are accounted for as permanent funds. This section will describe the accounting for private-purpose, investment, and pension trusts, whose primary beneficiaries are external individuals, organizations, or other governments. Examples of private-purpose funds are those established for holding performance deposits of licenses, the establishment of scholarship funds to benefit external individuals, endowments held to benefit needy employees or their families, Internal Revenue Code Section 457 deferred compensation plans,[11] and funds used to account for escheat property per GASB Statement No. 21. *Escheat property* is defined by the GASB as "the reversion of property to a government entity in the absence of legal claimants or heirs."[12] Since the rightful owner or heir can reclaim escheat property at any time, the receipt of escheat property is recorded in the governmental or proprietary fund in which the property ultimately will be used and is offset with a liability representing the best estimate of the amount ultimately expected to be reclaimed and paid. Revenue is recognized for the amount not expected to be reclaimed. Escheat property held for others is reported in a private-purpose trust or agency fund (depending on the length of time the assets are expected to be held). Agency funds are described later in this chapter.

Private-purpose trust funds are accounted for in much the same manner as proprietary funds. The establishment of these trusts results from the acceptance of assets that are invested to produce earnings for a designated external purpose. Depreciation on real property included in the principal of the trust would be recognized in order to protect that principal. It also would be essential to differentiate between principal items and revenue items. One common way to segregate the principal from revenues is to establish two funds—one to record principal items and another to account for the earnings. This procedure becomes especially useful if bonds are purchased at a premium as part of the trust fund. Cash flows and available revenue are not identical

11 GASB Statement No. 32, *Accounting and Financial Reporting Internal Revenue Code Section 457, Deferred Compensation Plans* (Norwalk, CT: Governmental Accounting Standards Board, October 1997).

12 GASB Statement No. 21, *Accounting for Escheat Property* (Norwalk, CT: Governmental Accounting Standards Board, October 1993) as amended by GASB Statement No. 37, *Basic Financial Statements—and Management's Discussion and Analysis—for State and Local Governments: Omnibus* (Norwalk, CT: Governmental Accounting Standards Board, June 2001).

because of the amortization of the premium. The segregation process protects the principal. When donors establish a private-purpose trust, the assets donated are credited to Additions-Contributions in the endowment principal fund. Later, revenues earned are credited to Additions-Revenues. A liability to the endowment earnings fund for the period's interest earnings is established, and a debit is made to recognize the interfund operating transfer.

The only source of assets for the endowment earnings fund is the net earnings transferred from the private-purpose principal fund. These earnings are credited to Additions-Interfund Operating Transfers. Distributions of such revenues are recorded as deductions. In the year-end closing process of the private-purpose earnings fund, any difference between the amounts received from the principal fund and total deductions is closed to Net Assets Held in Trust, which indicates that the undistributed assets are restricted.

The procedures for both the private-purpose endowment principal trust fund and the endowment earnings fund for Cedar City are shown by the events and entries in Illustration 16-12 on pages 936 and 937.

Two financial statements are required for private-purpose trust funds: a statement of fiduciary net assets and a statement of changes in fiduciary net assets. The statements of fiduciary net assets for Cedar City's Governmental Accounts Scholarship Fund are shown in Illustration 16-11.

Illustration 16-11
Cedar City
Governmental Accounts Scholarship Fund
Statement of Fiduciary Net Assets
For Period Ended December 31, 20X7

Assets	
Cash	$10,640
Investments	40,000
Unamortized premiums on investments	360
	$51,000
Liabilities	
Due to governmental accounts scholarship earnings fund	1,000
Net assets held in trust for benefit of scholarship recipients	$50,000

Cedar City
Governmental Accounts Scholarship Fund
Statement of Fiduciary Net Assets
For Period Ended December 31, 20X7

Assets	
Cash	$ 560
Due from governmental accounting scholarship principal fund	1,000
	$1,560
Net assets held in trust for benefit of scholarship recipients	$1,560

Illustration 16-12

Event
Cedar City receives an endowment of $50,000 to establish a nonexpendable trust fund whose revenue is to be used to encourage students to study governmental accounting.
9% bonds with a face value of $40,000 are purchased at 101, maturing in 10 years. The premium will be amortized using the straight-line method.
Bond interest of $3,600 is received.
The liability to endowment revenues fund for net revenue is recorded.
Cash due is remitted.
A grant of $3,000 is given to a student.
Books are closed at year-end.

Investment Trust Funds

An *investment trust fund* is used to account for the assets, liabilities, net assets, and changes in net assets of external participants in an investment pool managed by the government for other governments and not-for-profit organizations. Because the accounting and financial reporting requirements are very similar to the private-purpose trust fund, already illustrated, no journal entries or financial statements are provided in this chapter. As in the examples of private-purpose trusts, proper accounting for gains and losses, whether realized through the sale of investments or unrealized through the appreciation or depreciation of fair value, is an important topic to the preservation of the trust. Thus, the economic measurement focus and full accrual basis of accounting are used in these funds.

Pension Trust Funds

Public employees retirement system funds are accounted for in *pension trust funds*. In no other area of accounting is actuarial assistance so vital. Abiding by the requirements of the retirement plan and considering the employee population as to age, gender, marital status, and the myriad of other variables that affect working lives and retirement, actuaries must estimate the amount of resources necessary as of a given date to meet retirement commitments. To protect the employees' interests, pension trust funds use a full accrual basis of accounting.

Contributions to a retirement plan may be from both the employer and employees (a contributory plan) or from the employer only (a noncontributory plan). Employees who resign usually have the option to withdraw their own contributions (but not the employer's

Entries in Endowment Principal Trust Fund (Nonexpendable Trust)			Entries in Endowment Earnings Trust Fund (Expendable Trust)		
Cash	50,000		No entry.		
Fund Balance		50,000			
Investments	40,000		No entry.		
Unamortized Premium	400				
Cash		40,400			
Cash	3,600		No entry.		
Unamortized Premium		40			
Revenues		3,560			
Operating Transfers-Out	3,560		Due from Endowment Principal Fund	3,560	
Due to Endowment Earning Fund		3,560	Other Financing Sources		3,560
Due to Endowment Revenues Fund	3,560		Cash	3,560	
Cash		3,560	Due from Endowment Principal Fund		3,560
No entry.			Expenditures	3,000	
			Cash		3,000
Revenues	3,560		Other Financing Sources	3,560	
Operating Transfers-Out		3,560	Expenditures		3,000
			Fund Balance—Reserved for Endowments		560

contributions) or to leave them in the plan as vested amounts, providing certain requirements are met. The amounts belong to the employee, who will have access to them upon meeting prescribed retirement conditions.

Increases in the resources of pension trust funds result from employee and employer contributions, investment earnings, and net appreciation (depreciation) in plan assets. Decreases in resources result from payments to retired employees, refunds to contributors, and administrative costs.

All assets of a pension trust belong to the employees, and claims against these assets are reflected in either the liabilities or the restricted net asset balance.

A statement of changes in plan net assets[13] is shown in Illustration 16-13 on page 938. The statement of changes in plan net assets reports *additions* to net assets rather than revenues, and *deductions* from net assets rather than expenses. The statement of plan net assets for Desert City's retirement plan as of June 30, 20X7, is shown in Illustration 16-14 on page 939. The fund has been operating for several years and has significant investments.

The liability shown on the statement of plan net assets (see Illustration 16-14) is the current benefits payable. The long-term, actuarially determined, projected benefit obligation is disclosed in the footnotes.

13 GASB Statement No. 25, *Financial Reporting for Defined Benefit Pension Plans and Note Disclosures for Defined Contribution Plans* (Norwalk, CT: Governmental Accounting Standards Board, November 1994).

Illustration 16-13
Desert City's Retirement Plan
Statement of Changes in Plan Net Assets
For Year Ended June 30, 20X7

Additions:	
Contributions:	
Employer	$ 137,000
Plan member	90,000
Total contributions	$ 227,000
Investment income:	
Net appreciation (depreciation) in fair value	$ (241,400)
Interest	157,000
Dividends	123,900
Real estate operating income, net	10,700
Less investment expense	(54,000)
Net investment income	$ (3,800)
Total additions	$ 223,200
Deductions:	
Benefits	$ 170,434
Refunds of contributions	15,750
Administrative expense	5,000
Total deductions	$ 191,184
Net increase	$ 32,016
Net assets held in trust for pension benefits:	
Beginning of year	3,651,964
End of year	$3,683,980

The statement of plan net assets adheres to the all-inclusive approach, whereby the net increase (decrease) is added to the total of plan assets at the beginning of the period to yield their total at the end of the period. A statement of cash flows is not required. Governments must also include in the notes to the financial statements as Required Supplementary Information (1) a schedule of funding progress, (2) a schedule of employer contributions for at least six plan years, and (3) information on actuarial methods and assumptions.

Issued in 2004, GASB Statement No. 43 establishes accounting and financial reporting standard for plans that provide other postemployment benefits (OPEB), such as health care benefits and life insurance. The financial report of the participating employer plan sponsor, public employee retirement system, or other entity that administers the plan should include (1) a statement of postemployment plan net assets, (2) a statement of changes in postemployment plan net assets, and (3) notes to the financial statements, all prepared in accordance with the pension plan reporting standards.[14]

14 GASB Statement No. 43, *Financial Reporting for Postemployment Benefit Plans Other than Pension Plans* (Norwalk, CT: Governmental Accounting Standards Board, April 2004).

Illustration 16-14
Desert City's Retirement Plan
Statement of Plan Net Assets
As of June 30, 20X7

Assets	
Cash and short-term investments	$ 66,000
Receivables:	
Employer	$ 16,500
Interest and dividends	33,500
Total receivables	$ 50,000
Investments, at fair value:	
U.S. government obligations	$ 541,300
Municipal bonds	33,585
Domestic corporate bonds	892,300
Domestic stocks	1,276,500
International stocks	461,350
Mortgages	149,100
Real estate	184,900
Venture capital	26,795
Total investments	$3,565,830
Properties, at cost, net of accumulated depreciation	$ 6,350
Total assets	$3,688,180
Liabilities	
Refunds payable	4,200
Net assets held in trust for pension benefits	$3,683,980

Agency Funds

An *agency fund* is required when money collected or withheld, such as deductions from government employees' salaries for social security or for hospitalization premiums, must be forwarded to the proper destination. Agency funds frequently have no end-of-period balances because money is transferred prior to the end of the period. When the money has not been forwarded, a liability to the ultimate recipient is shown. There is no fund equity, and the only financial statement would be a balance sheet listing the assets held and the related liabilities. If the agency fund is to receive a fee for its services, the amount usually is recorded as a liability to the general fund of the governmental unit. The general fund records a receivable and revenue if the amount is to be collected within the current period. For example, state law may give a county the responsibility for collecting property taxes levied within its boundaries, with the county receiving a fee to cover its administration of the plan. The county, as well as each political subdivision, would record its share of taxes receivable in its general fund. The tax agency fund of Zee County would make the following series of entries for the events described:

Event			Entry in Tax Agency Fund		
62. Gross taxes receivable to be collected for all units are as follows:			Taxes Receivable for All Units	1,000,000	
			Due to Other Governmental Funds and Units		1,000,000
Zee County	$ 300,000				
X City	600,000				
T Town	100,000				
Total	$1,000,000				
Entry in Zee County general fund:					
Taxes Receivable	300,000				
Revenues		300,000			
63. Taxes are collected.			Cash	1,000,000	
			Taxes Receivable for All Units		1,000,000
64. The liability to each unit is recorded, net of a 2% fee earned by the county for collection and processing for other units. (The county would not charge itself a fee.) The fee is to be remitted to the county general fund.			Due to Other Governmental Funds and Units	1,000,000	
			Due to Zee County General Fund. .		314,000
			Due to X City.		588,000
			Due to T Town.		98,000
Entry in Zee County general fund:					
Due from Agency Fund	314,000				
Taxes Receivable		300,000			
Revenue		14,000			
65. Cash is released to each governmental unit.			Due to Zee County General Fund	314,000	
			Due to X City	588,000	
Entry in Zee County general fund:			Due to T Town	98,000	
			Cash		1,000,000
Cash	314,000				
Due from Agency Fund		314,000			

The general fund of X City records the receipt of cash from the tax agency fund, net of the fee, as follows:

66. Cash (for net proceeds)	588,000	
Expenditures (for fee charged)	12,000	
Taxes Receivable—Current		600,000

Agency funds also are used in the case of a capital project undertaken by a government in which special assessment bonds were issued but for which it has no financial responsibility in case of nonpayment. The government functions as an agent or a financial conduit between the bondholders and the owners of the assessed property. When property owners are assessed, an entry is recorded in the agency fund as follows:

67. Special Assessments Receivable—Current	XXX	
Special Assessments Receivable—Deferred	XXX	
Due to Special Assessment Bond Creditors		XXX

When collections from assessed property owners are received by the agency fund, this entry is made:

68. Cash	XXX	
Special Assessments Receivable—Current	XXX	
Due to Special Assessment Bond Creditors (interest)		XXX

Upon payment to the bondholders, the entry is as follows:

69. Due to Special Assessment Bond Creditors	XXX	
Due to Special Assessment Bond Creditors (interest)	XXX	
Cash		XXX

Neither the liability for principal repayment nor the debt service expenditures are recorded in any other fund or group because the governmental unit was not obligated in any manner.

Finally, a government may account for the proceeds and disbursement of "pass-through" grants, entitlements, or shared revenues from federal or state governments in an agency fund only when it serves as a cash conduit, e.g., merely transmitting funds to the secondary recipient without having any administrative or direct financial involvement in the grant.[15]

REFLECTION

- **Fiduciary funds include private-purpose trust funds, investment trust funds, pension trust funds, and agency funds.**
- **Fiduciary funds use full accrual basis accounting.**
- **Financial statements of fiduciary funds include a statement of net assets and a statement of changes in net assets.**

GOVERNMENTAL ACCOUNTING—INTERACTIONS AMONG FUNDS

4 OBJECTIVE

Identify and account for transactions that affect different funds and/or account groups.

In governmental accounting, each fund or group is a separate accounting entity, entrusted to record only a limited phase of an event. Complete recording, as shown in Chapters 15 and 16, often involves more than one fund or group. In addition, transactions among funds are frequent. Throughout this and the previous chapter, interfund transactions have been defined. They include:

1. interfund operating transfers between governmental funds for services provided and used—recorded as other financing sources/uses;
2. interfund operating transfers between governmental and proprietary funds for services provided and used—recorded as revenues and expenditures/expenses;
3. interfund nonreciprocal transfers (where no expectation or requirement of repayment exists as in the case of contributions and payments in lieu of taxes)—recorded as other financing sources/uses if between governmental funds, and as interfund transfers that appear after nonoperating revenues if between governmental and proprietary funds; and
4. interfund loans—classified into two categories—as either due to/from other funds for short-term amounts or advances to/from other funds for amounts that will be repaid over several years.

15 GASB Statement No. 24, *Accounting and Financial Reporting for Certain Grants and Other Financial Assistance* (Norwalk, CT: Governmental Accounting Standards Board, June 1994).

A final interfund transaction is a reimbursement where one fund may reimburse another for supplies or other items paid on its behalf. For example, the general fund might pay the entire rental of a facility even though the facility is to be used for both the general government and activities of a special revenue fund. When the expenditure is made by the general fund, the entry is as follows:

70. Expenditures	XXX	
Cash		XXX

When the reimbursement is received from the special revenue fund for its share of the rent, the entries in each fund are as follows:

Illustration 16-15
Matrix of Selected Events Requiring Entry in More than One Fund or Account Group

Events to Be Recorded

1. Purchase of equipment with general fund resources for $40,000.
2. Issuance of $500,000 of general obligation serial bonds at an $8,000 premium for city hall construction.
3. Transfer by general fund to meet $100,000 matured serial bonds and $50,000 interest payments.
4. Payment of $50,000 bond interest and $100,000 matured serial bonds. Fiscal agent is used for payment.
5. Completion of special assessment construction project. $150,000 paid to date; $50,000 final payment.
6. Levy of $5,000 property taxes by general fund against city's utility (quasi-external).
7. Billing of general and special revenue funds for central computer service ($12,000 and $20,000) (quasi-external).
8. Contribution made by city to establish a nonexpendable trust fund of $98,500. Income will be used for library operations.
9. Remittance of the city's $16,000 share of self-insurance costs for current period to an internal service fund.
10. Reimbursement of $15,000 by the special revenue fund to the general fund for general government supplies expenditures initially made in the general fund properly charged to a community development project.
11. Recording of depreciation, $6,000 enterprise fund, $13,000 internal service fund.
12. Redemption of final $100,000 serial of general obligation bonds, with $3,000 deficiency covered by general fund. Fiscal agent is used for payment.
13. Closing entry for capital projects fund involving a partially completed project. Cost to date is $130,000; revenues during the period are $300,000.
14. Payroll expenditures totaled $5,000 and included $1,000 payroll withholdings for taxes and insurance plus employer's share of these costs. $1,000 is transferred to an agency fund for remittance as follows: Private insurance company, $200; federal government, $600; and state government, $150. The agency fund makes the remittances.
15. A 5-year lease agreement was signed for equipment. The present value of the lease payments is $50,000.
16. The actuarial required contribution for pensions was $4,500. Of this amount, $3,000 was transferred to the pension trust and $1,500 will be transferred in the future.
17. Claims and judgments against the city were estimated at $15,000. The city attorney determined that it was probable that the claims would be settled against the city. Of the $15,000, $3,000 was estimated to be paid out this fiscal year.
18. Closure and post-closure costs of local landfill were estimated at $600,000. Landfill used this period was estimated at 1,000 cubic yards, and total landfill is 100,000 cubic yards. Landfill operations are accounted for in enterprise funds.
19. Debt was refunded. The refunding met the criteria for in-substance defeasance. Proceeds of the new debt issue were placed in trust with an escrow agent.
20. Investments carried at $5,500 have a fair value of $5,750 in the general fund. Pension investments carried at $102,000 have a fair value of $101,000.

71. General fund:	Cash		XXX	
	Expenditures			XXX
Special revenue fund:	Expenditures		XXX	
	Cash			XXX

To serve as a reference and to review governmental accounting, Illustration 16-15 provides a matrix of selected events that are recorded in more than one fund or group. Used in the matrix are the five governmental funds (general, special revenue, debt service, capital projects, and permanent funds), the two types of proprietary funds (enterprise and internal service), trust and agency funds, and the two account groups for general fixed assets and general long-term debt.[16]

The entries to record the events related to the 20 events in the matrix are as follows:

Governmental Funds					Proprietary Funds		Fiduciary Fund	Account Groups		
General	Special Revenue	Debt Service	Capital Projects	Permanent	Enterprise	Internal Service	Trust and Agency	General Fixed Assets	General Long-Term Debt	
X	—	—	—	—	—	—	—	X	—	1.
—	—	X	X	—	—	—	—	—	X	2.
X	—	X	—	—	—	—	—	—	X	3.
—	—	X	—	—	—	—	—	—	X	4.
—	—	—	X	—	—	—	—	X	—	5.
X	—	—	—	—	X	—	—	—	—	6.
X	X	—	—	—	—	X	—	—	—	7.
X	—	—	—	X	—	—	—	—	—	8.
X	—	—	—	—	—	X	—	—	—	9.
X	X	—	—	—	—	—	—	—	—	10.
—	—	—	—	—	X	X	—	—	—	11.
X	—	X	—	—	—	—	—	—	X	12.
—	—	—	X	—	—	—	—	X	—	13.
X	—	—	—	—	—	—	X	—	—	14.
X	—	—	—	—	—	—	—	X	X	15.
X	—	—	—	—	—	—	X	—	X	16.
X	—	—	—	—	—	—	—	—	X	17.
—	—	—	—	—	X	—	—	—	—	18.
—	—	X	—	—	—	—	—	—	X	19.
X	—	—	—	—	—	—	X	—	—	20.

16 GASB Statement No. 38, *Certain Financial Statement Note Disclosures* (Norwalk, CT: Governmental Accounting Standards Board, June 2001), requires that details about interfund transfers and balances are reported in the notes to the financial statements. These details should include the purpose of the transfer, the provider and recipient funds, and a description and amount of significant nonroutine transfers.

Journal Entries for Transactions Affecting More than One Fund

Event	Funds	Accounts		
1. Purchase of equipment with general fund resources for $40,000.	General Fund	Expenditures	40,000	
		Vouchers Payable		40,000
	General Fixed Assets Account Group	Equipment	40,000	
		Investment in General Fixed Assets—General Fund Revenues		40,000
2. Issuance of $500,000 of general obligation serial bonds at an $8,000 premium for city hall construction.	Capital Projects Fund	Cash	508,000	
		Other Financing Sources		500,000
		Other Financing Sources—Premium		8,000
		Other Financing Uses	8,000	
		Cash		8,000
	Debt Service Fund	Cash	8,000	
		Other Financing Sources		8,000
	General Long-Term Debt Account Group	Amount to Be Provided for Payment of Serial Bonds	500,000	
		Serial Bonds Payable		500,000
3. Transfer by general fund to meet $100,000 matured serial bonds and $50,000 interest payment.	General Fund	Other Financing Uses	150,000	
		Cash		150,000
	Debt Service Fund	Cash	150,000	
		Other Financing Sources		150,000
	General Long-Term Debt Account Group	Amount Available in Debt Service Fund—Serial Bonds	100,000	
		Amount to Be Provided for Payment of Serial Bonds		100,000
4. Payment of $50,000 bond interest and $100,000 matured serial bonds. Fiscal agent is used for payment.	Debt Service Fund	Expenditures	150,000	
		Matured Bonds Payable		100,000
		Matured Interest Payable		50,000
		Cash with Fiscal Agent	150,000	
		Cash		150,000
	Debt Service Fund	Matured Bonds Payable	100,000	
		Matured Interest Payable	50,000	
		Cash with Fiscal Agent		150,000
	General Long-Term Debt Account Group	Serial Bonds Payable	100,000	
		Amount Available in Debt Service Fund—Serial Bonds		100,000
5. Completion of special assessment construction project. $150,000 paid to date; $50,000 final payment.	Capital Projects Fund	Expenditures	50,000	
		Cash		50,000
	General Fixed Assets Account Group	Improvements Other than Buildings	200,000	
		Construction in Progress		150,000
		Investments in General Fixed Assets—Capital Projects Funds (special assessments)		50,000
6. Levy of $5,000 property taxes by general fund against city's utility.	General Fund	Due from Enterprise Fund	5,000	
		Revenues		5,000
	Enterprise Fund	Property Tax Expense	5,000	
		Due to General Fund		5,000

Event	Funds	Accounts		
7. Billing of general and special revenue funds for central computer service ($12,000 and $20,000, respectively).	Internal Service Fund	Due from General Fund	12,000	
		Due from Special Revenue Fund	20,000	
		Revenues		32,000
	General Fund	Expenditures	12,000	
		Due to Internal Service Fund		12,000
	Special Revenue Fund	Expenditures	20,000	
		Due to Internal Service Fund		20,000
8. Contribution made by city to establish a nonexpendable trust fund of $98,500. Income from this fund will be used for library operations.	General Fund	Other Financing Uses—Transfer to Trust Fund	98,500	
		Cash		98,500
	Permanent Fund	Cash	98,500	
		Other Financing Sources—Transfer from General Fund		98,500
9. Remittance of the city's $16,000 share of self-insurance costs for current period to an internal service fund.	General Fund	Expenditures	16,000	
		Cash		16,000
	Internal Service Fund	Cash	16,000	
		Revenues		16,000
10. Reimbursement of $15,000 by the special revenue fund to the general fund for general government supplies expenditures initially made in the general fund and properly charged to a community development project.	Special Revenue Fund	Expenditures	15,000	
		Cash		15,000
	General Fund	Cash	15,000	
		Expenditures		15,000
11. Recording of depreciation, $6,000 enterprise fund, $13,000 internal service fund.	Enterprise Fund	Depreciation Expense	6,000	
		Accumulated Depreciation		6,000
	Internal Service Fund	Depreciation Expense	13,000	
		Accumulated Depreciation		13,000
12. Redemption of final $100,000 serial of general obligation bonds, with $3,000 deficiency covered by general fund. Fiscal agent is used for payment.	General Fund	Other Financing Uses	3,000	
		Cash		3,000
	Debt Service Fund	Cash	3,000	
		Other Financing Sources		3,000
		Cash with Fiscal Agent	100,000	
		Cash		100,000
		Expenditures	100,000	
		Matured Bonds Payable		100,000
		Matured Bonds Payable	100,000	
		Cash with Fiscal Agent		100,000
	General Long-Term Debt Account Group	Amounts Available in Debt Service Fund	100,000	
		Amount to Be Provided for Payment of Serial Bonds		100,000
		Serial Bonds Payable	100,000	
		Amounts Available in Debt Service Fund		100,000
13. Closing entry for capital projects fund involving a partially completed project. Cost to date is $130,000; revenues during the period are $300,000.	Capital Projects Fund	Revenues	300,000	
		Expenditures		130,000
		Fund Balance—Unreserved, Undesignated		170,000

(continued)

Event	Funds	Accounts		
13. (continued)	General Fixed Assets Account Group	Construction in Progress	130,000	
		Investment in General Fixed Assets—Capital Projects Fund		130,000
14. Payroll expenditures totaled \$5,000 and included \$1,000 payroll withholdings for taxes and insurance plus employer's share of these costs. \$1,000 is transferred to an agency fund for remittance as follows: private insurance company, \$200; federal government, \$650; and state government, \$150. The agency fund makes the remittances.	General Fund	Expenditures	5,000	
		Due to Agency Fund		1,000
		Cash		4,000
	Agency Fund	Due from General Fund	1,000	
		Due to Insurance Company		200
		Due to Federal Government		650
		Due to State		150
	General Fund	Due to Agency Fund	1,000	
		Cash		1,000
	Agency Fund	Cash	1,000	
		Due from General Fund		1,000
		Due to Insurance Company	200	
		Due to Federal Government	650	
		Due to State	150	
		Cash		1,000
15. A 5-year lease agreement was signed for equipment. The present value of the lease payments is \$50,000.	General Fund	Expenditures	50,000	
		Other Financing Sources		50,000
	General Long-Term Debt Account Group	Amount to Be Provided	50,000	
		Lease Payable		50,000
	General Fixed Assets Account Group	Leased Asset	50,000	
		Investment in General Fixed Assets—Capital Lease		50,000
16. The actuarial required contribution for pensions was \$4,500. Of this amount, \$3,000 was transferred to the pension trust. \$1,500 will be transferred in the future.	General Fund	Expenditures	3,000	
		Cash		3,000
	General Long-Term Debt Account Group	Amount to Be Provided	1,500	
		Unfunded Pension Obligation		1,500
	Pension Trust Fund	Cash	3,000	
		Receivable from Employer	1,500	
		Contributions—Employer		4,500
17. Claims and judgments against the city were estimated at \$15,000. The city attorney determined that it was probable that the claims would be settled against the city. Of the \$15,000, \$3,000 was estimated to be paid out this fiscal year.	General Fund	Expenditures	3,000	
		Claims and Judgments Payable		3,000
	General Long-Term Debt Account Group	Amount to Be Provided	12,000	
		Claims and Judgments Payable		12,000
18. Closure and post-closure costs of local landfill were estimated at \$600,000. Landfill used this period was estimated at 1,000 cubic yards, and total landfill is 100,000 cubic yards. Landfill operations are accounted for in enterprise funds.	Enterprise Fund	Landfill Expense	6,000	
		Liability for Landfill Costs		6,000

Event	Funds	Accounts		
19. Debt was refunded. The refunding met the criteria for in-substance defeasance. Proceeds of the new debt issue were placed in trust with an escrow agent.	Debt Service Fund	Cash	100,000	
		Other Financing Sources		100,000
		Other Financing Uses	100,000	
		Cash		100,000
	General Long-Term Debt Account Group	Bonds Payable	100,000	
		Amount to Be Provided		100,000
		Amount to Be Provided	100,000	
		Bonds Payable		100,000
20. Investments carried at $5,500 have a fair value of $5,750 in the general fund. Pension investments carried at $102,000 have a fair value of $101,000.	General Fund	Investments	250	
		Net Appreciation in Fair Value of Investments		250
	Pension Trust Fund	Net Depreciation in Fair Value of Investments	1,000	
		Investments		1,000

REFLECTION

- Each fund or group is a separate accounting entity.
- One transaction often affects more than one fund or group.

UNDERSTANDING THE ISSUES

1. Why are fixed assets, acquired with proceeds from general obligation bond issues, not permanently accounted for in a capital projects fund?
2. If a capital projects fund has authority to continue operations over several fiscal periods, why is it desirable to close its records at the end of each period?
3. Explain the necessity to introduce a deferred revenues account in the levy of capital special assessments.
4. The debt service fund does not use budgetary accounts. What is the logic for not doing so?
5. When a debt service fund receives resources, it might credit Revenues or Other Financing Sources. Under what circumstances would each of these credits be used?
6. What characteristic determines whether an activity should be accounted for in a special revenue fund or in a permanent fund?
7. Describe two major types of interfund transfers. Under what circumstances is each used?
8. What is the difference between an agency fund and a trust fund?
9. What is the difference between an enterprise fund and an internal service fund?
10. Explain the difference between expenses and expenditures in a state and a local government.
11. Describe the difference between accounting for governmental funds and proprietary funds.
12. What is the difference between a permanent fund and a private-purpose trust fund?

EXERCISES

Exercise 1 *(LO 1, 2)* **Other governmental funds, proprietary funds.** Select the best answer for each of the following multiple-choice items. (Numbers 1, 3, 5, 6, 8, and 9 are AICPA adapted.)

1. Revenues that are legally restricted to expenditures for specified purposes should be accounted for in special revenue funds, including
   a. accumulation of resources for payment of general long-term debt principal and interest.
   b. pension trust fund revenues.
   c. gasoline taxes to finance road repairs.
   d. proprietary fund revenues.

2. Bonds are issued at a premium by a capital projects fund. The premium should be
   a. retained in the capital projects fund.
   b. credited directly to the unreserved fund balance of the capital projects fund.
   c. transferred to the debt service funds.
   d. used to reduce the net cost of the project involved.

3. Which of the following funds of a governmental unit recognizes revenues in the accounting period in which they become available and measurable?

	General Fund	Enterprise Fund
a.	Yes	No
b.	No	Yes
c.	Yes	Yes
d.	No	No

4. At the beginning of a fiscal period, encumbrances that remained at the previous year-end relating to an incomplete project in the capital projects funds generally are reinstated by crediting
   a. Fund Balance—Unreserved, Undesignated.
   b. Fund Balance—Reserved for Encumbrances.
   c. Encumbrances.
   d. Expenditures.

5. Which of the following statements is *correct* concerning a governmental entity's statement of cash flows?
   a. Cash flows from capital financing activities and cash flows from noncapital financing activities are reported separately.
   b. The statement format is the same as that of a business enterprise's statement of cash flows.
   c. Cash flows from operating activities may not be reported using the indirect method.
   d. The statement format includes columns for the general, governmental, and proprietary fund types.

6. The billings for transportation services provided to other governmental units are recorded by the internal service fund as
   a. other financing sources.
   b. intergovernmental transfers.
   c. transportation appropriations.
   d. operating revenues.

7. Resources for a capital improvement are provided by special assessments. At the start of the second year of the project, a reclassification entry in the debt service fund that debits Deferred Revenues would credit

a. Special Assessments Receivable—Deferred.
b. Revenues.
c. Unreserved Fund Balance.
d. Fund Balance Reserved for Special Assessments.

8. Gaffney City's serial bonds are serviced through a debt service fund with cash provided by the general fund. In a debt service fund's statements, how are cash receipts and cash payments reported?

Cash Receipts	Cash Payments
a. Revenues	Expenditures
b. Revenues	Operating transfers
c. Operating transfers	Expenditures
d. Operating transfers	Operating transfers

9. Eureka City should issue a statement of cash flows for which of the following funds?

	Eureka City Hall Capital Projects Fund	Eureka Water Enterprise Fund
a.	No	Yes
b.	No	No
c.	Yes	No
d.	Yes	Yes

10. If an internal service fund is intended to operate on a cost-reimbursement basis, then user charges should
    a. cover the full costs, both direct and indirect, of operating the fund.
    b. cover the full costs of operating the fund and provide for future expansion and replacement of capital assets.
    c. cover at a minimum the direct costs of operating the fund.
    d. do all of the above.

Exercise 2 *(LO 3, 4)* **Trust funds, various funds, and account groups.** Select the best answer for each of the following multiple-choice items. (Numbers 3, 6, and 8 are AICPA adapted.)

1. Accounting for permanent funds closely resembles the accounting for
    a. general funds.
    b. capital projects funds.
    c. enterprise funds.
    d. agency funds.

2. In which of the following fund types of a city government are revenues and expenditures recognized on the same basis of accounting as the general fund?
    a. Private-purpose trust funds
    b. Internal service
    c. Enterprise
    d. Debt service

3. On June 28, 20X1, Gus City's debt service fund received funds for the future repayment of bond principal. As a consequence, the general long-term debt account group reported
    a. an increase in the amount available in debt service funds and an increase in the fund balance.
    b. an increase in the amount available in debt service funds and an increase in the amount to be provided for bonds.
    c. an increase in the amount available in debt service funds and a decrease in the amount to be provided for bonds.
    d. no changes in any amount until the bond principal is actually paid.

4. A debt service fund should be used to account for the payment of interest and principal on
   a. debt recorded in the general long-term debt account group or similar list.
   b. debt secured by the revenues of an enterprise fund.
   c. debt recorded as a liability in the general fund.
   d. all of the above.
5. If a governmental unit makes no guarantees regarding repayment of a capital improvement special assessment bond issue, the liability for the bonds would
   a. not appear in the financial statements or in their notes.
   b. not appear in the financial statements but would appear in the notes to the financial statements.
   c. appear in the capital projects fund.
   d. appear in the general long-term debt account group.
6. Taxes collected and held by Dunne County for a school district would be accounted for in which of the following funds?
   a. Trust
   b. Agency
   c. Special revenue
   d. Internal service
7. The following is a correct entry:

Construction in Progress	XXX	
Investment in General Fixed Assets—Capital Projects Funds.		XXX

   The entry would be found in the
   a. capital projects fund.
   b. enterprise fund.
   c. general fund.
   d. general fixed assets account group.
8. In what fund type should the proceeds from special assessment bonds issued to finance construction of sidewalks in a new subdivision be reported?
   a. Agency fund
   b. Special revenue fund
   c. Enterprise fund
   d. Capital projects fund
9. When establishing an investment pool, Eureka City will account for all of the pooled investments in
   a. an investment trust fund at fair value at the date the pool is created.
   b. an agency fund at fair value as of the last balance sheet date.
   c. the general fund at fair value as of the last balance sheet date.
   d. the general fund at fair value at the date the pool is created.
10. Which of the following is not a fiduciary fund?
    a. Permanent fund
    b. Agency fund
    c. Investment trust fund
    d. Pension trust fund

Exercise 3 *(LO 1)* **General obligation bonds, fixed asset construction.** Select the best response for each of the following multiple-choice questions which refer to the transactions of Finch City. (Number 4 is AICPA adapted.)

On March 2, 20X1, Finch City issued 10-year general obligation bonds at face amount, with interest payable on March 1 and September 1. The proceeds were to be used to finance the construction of a civic center over the period of April 1, 20X1, to March 31, 20X2. During the fiscal year ended June 30, 20X1, no resources had been provided to the debt service fund for the payment of principal and interest.

1. On June 30, 20X1, Finch's debt service fund should include interest payable on the general obligation bonds for
   a. zero months.
   b. three months.
   c. four months.
   d. six months.
2. Proceeds from the general obligation bonds should be recorded in the
   a. general fund.
   b. capital projects fund.
   c. general long-term debt account group.
   d. debt service fund.
3. The liability for the general obligation bonds should be recorded in the
   a. general fund.
   b. capital projects fund.
   c. general long-term debt account group.
   d. debt service fund.
4. On June 30, 20X1, the balance sheet part of Finch's fund financial statements should report the construction in progress for the civic center in the

	Capital Projects Fund	General Fixed Assets Account Group
a.	Yes	Yes
b.	Yes	No
c.	No	No
d.	No	Yes

Exercise 4 *(LO 1)* **General obligation bonds, fixed asset construction.** Prepare journal entries to record the following events. Identify every fund(s) or group of accounts in which an entry is made.

a. The city authorized the construction of a city hall to be financed by a $400,000 contribution of the general fund and the proceeds of a $2,000,000 general obligation serial bond issue. Both amounts are budgeted to be received in the current year. Expenditures during the current year are estimated to be $850,000. Budgetary accounts are used.
b. The general fund remits the $400,000.
c. The bonds are sold for 99; issue costs totalled $5,000.
d. A contract is signed with Rollins Construction Company for the construction of the city hall for an estimated contract cost of $2,300,000.
e. By year-end, $1,000,000 is paid against the contract with Rollins Construction Company.

Exercise 5 *(LO 1)* **Special assessments levy, capital projects fund.** In 20X7, the town of Waterview authorized the construction of two concrete roadways. The public works department estimates the project cost at $400,000, $40,000 of which is transferred from the general fund to the capital projects fund. The balance will be paid for through a special assessments levy on benefiting property owners. On January 1, 20X7, $360,000, 4-year, 10% special assessment bonds are issued at face value to finance the property owners' portion. Payments of $45,000 plus interest are made each June 30 and December 31. The bonds were issued. The town guarantees payment of the debt.

Purchase orders totaling $80,000 are issued, and a contract is signed for the estimated $320,000 additional cost of the project. Invoices for all purchase orders total $74,000. The actual contract cost is $325,000. Liabilities for these amounts are entered. Except for $30,000 withheld on the contract until final approval, all liabilities related to the completed construction are paid. Waterview does not use budgetary accounts for these projects. Prepare entries in the capital projects fund for these events.

Exercise 6 *(LO 1, 4)* **Special assessments levy, serial bonds, debt service fund, long-term debt account group.** This exercise is based on the facts of Exercise 5 for the town of Waterview's special assessment project. Assume special assessment property owners make the required payments to the debt service fund, and the debt service fund, in turn, makes the payments required by the serial bonds. Record all entries in the debt service fund and in the general long-term debt account group for 20X7.

Exercise 7 *(LO 1)* **Debt service fund, serial bonds.** Prepare journal entries required by a debt service fund to record the following transactions:

a. On January 2, a $5,000,000, 6%, 10-year general obligation serial bond issue is sold at 99. Interest is payable annually on December 31, along with one-tenth of the original principal.
b. At year-end, the first serial bond matures, along with interest on the bond issue.
c. The general fund transfers cash to meet the matured items.
d. A check for the matured items is sent to First Bank, the agent handling the payments.
e. Later, the bank reports that the first serial bond has been redeemed. One check for interest of $9,000 was returned by the post office because the bond owner had moved. The bank will search for the new address.

Exercise 8 *(LO 2)* **Enterprise fund.** Prepare journal entries to record the following events in the city of Rosewood's Water Commission enterprise fund:

a. From its general fund revenues, the city transferred $300,000, which is restricted for the drilling of additional wells.
b. Billings for water consumption for the month totaled $287,000, including $67,000 billed to other funds within the city.
c. The Water Commission collected $42,000 from other funds and $190,000 from other users on billings in item (b).
d. To raise additional funds, the utility issued $700,000 of 5%, 10-year revenue bonds at face value. Proceeds are restricted to the development of wells.
e. The contract with the well driller showed an estimated cost of $930,000.
f. The well driller bills $360,000 at year-end.
g. The utility pays a $300,000 bill from the well driller.

Exercise 9 *(LO 1, 3, 4)* **Endowment trust fund, special revenue fund.** On January 1, 20X8, Jack Kinn donated $100,000 to the city of Larkin to be set aside as a trust fund for water quality improvements made by the city. The funds were fully invested in bonds purchased at a premium with a face value of $94,000. During the year, cash received on investments was $7,500. Premiums on the bonds purchased were amortized at $600 per year. All income earned is transferred to the endowment revenue fund. A total of $6,000 was transferred to a special revenue fund to carry out the purpose of the trust. Prepare the journal entries to record these transactions in the permanent fund and closing entries. Prepare the balance sheet of the permanent fund as of December 31, 20X8.

Exercise 10 *(LO 4)* **Impact of transactions on different funds.** Indicate into which fund a city would record each of the following transactions. (You need not make any entries.)

a. Fixed assets are purchased with general fund cash.
b. Long-term serial bonds are issued to finance the construction of a new art museum. The bonds are sold at a premium.
c. The general fund transfers a sufficient amount of money to cover principal and interest requirements of a debt issue.
d. The fund receiving the payment in item (c) makes the scheduled payment of principal and interest.
e. A special assessment project is one-half completed at year-end.
f. Income is earned by an endowment fund and is transferred to a recipient fund, which is restricted as to its expenditures by the trust agreement specified for a government program.
g. Possible depreciation entries on assets are recorded.
h. The government-owned water utility issues debt to purchase new equipment.

i. The new city prison is completed, and leftover funds are transferred to the fund responsible for repaying the debt used to finance the project.

Use the following symbols and funds for your responses:

GF	General Fund	PF	Permanent Fund
SRF	Special Revenue Fund	PPT	Private-Purpose Trust Fund
DSF	Debt Service Fund	GFAAG	General Fixed Assets Account Group
CPF	Capital Projects Fund		
ENT	Enterprise Fund	GLTDAG	General Long-Term Debt Account Group
INT	Internal Service Fund		

Exercise 11 *(LO 4)* **Selection of appropriate debit or credit entry, various funds.** Match the appropriate letter indicating the recording of the following transactions:

1. General obligation bonds were issued at par.
2. Approved purchase orders were issued for supplies.
3. The above-mentioned supplies were received, and the related invoices were approved.
4. General fund salaries and wages were incurred.
5. The internal service fund had interfund billings.
6. Revenues were earned from a previously awarded grant.
7. Property taxes were collected in advance.
8. Appropriations were recorded on adoption of the budget.
9. Short-term financing was received from a bank and secured by the city's taxing power.
10. There was an excess of estimated inflows over estimated outflows.

Recording of transactions:

a. Credit Appropriations.
b. Credit Budgetary Fund Balance—Unreserved.
c. Credit Expenditures.
d. Credit Deferred Revenues.
e. Credit Interfund Revenues.
f. Credit Tax Anticipation Notes Payable.
g. Credit Other Financing Sources.
h. Credit Other Financing Uses.
i. Debit Appropriations.
j. Debit Deferred Revenues.
k. Debit Encumbrances.
l. Debit Expenditures.

(AICPA adapted)

Exercise 12 *(LO 4)* **Identification of fund type.** Identify the letter that *best* describes the accounting and reporting by the following funds and account groups:

1. Enterprise fund fixed assets.
2. Capital projects fund.
3. General fixed assets.
4. Infrastructure fixed assets.
5. Enterprise fund cash.
6. General fund.
7. Agency fund cash.
8. General long-term debt.
9. Special revenue fund.
10. Debt service fund.

a. Accounted for in a fiduciary fund.
b. Accounted for in a proprietary fund.
c. Accounted for in a quasi-endowment fund.
d. Accounted for in a self-balancing account group and included in financial statements.

e. Accounted for in a special assessment fund.
f. Accounts for major construction activities.
g. Accounts for property tax revenues.
h. Accounts for payment of interest and principal on tax-supported debt.
i. Accounts for revenues from earmarked sources to finance designated activities.
j. Reporting is optional.

(AICPA adapted)

PROBLEMS

Problem 16-1 *(LO 4)* **Various funds and account groups.** Select the *best* response for each of the following multiple-choice questions. (Numbers 1-8 are AICPA adapted.)

1. Maple Township issued the following bonds during the year ended June 30, 20X7:

Bonds issued for the Garbage Collection Enterprise Fund that will service the debt	$500,000
Revenue bonds to be repaid from admission fees collected by the Township Zoo Enterprise Fund	350,000

What amount of these bonds should be accounted for in Maple's general long-term debt account group?

a. $0
b. $350,000
c. $500,000
d. $850,000

2. On December 31, 20X9, Elm Village paid a contractor $4,500,000 for the total cost of a new Village Hall built in 20X9 on Elm-owned land. Financing for the capital project was provided by a $3,000,000 general obligation bond issue sold at face amount on December 31, 20X9, with the remaining $1,500,000 transferred from the general fund. What account and amount should be reported in Elm's 20X9 fund financial statements for the general fund?

a. Other Financing Sources	$4,500,000
b. Expenditures	$4,500,000
c. Other Financing Sources	$3,000,000
d. Other Financing Uses	$1,500,000

3. During 20X9, Spruce City reported the following receipts from self-sustaining activities paid for by users of the services rendered:

Operation of water supply plant	$5,000,000
Operation of bus system	900,000

What amount should be accounted for in Spruce's enterprise funds?

a. $0
b. $900,000
c. $5,000,000
d. $5,900,000

4. Through an internal service fund, Wood County operates a centralized data-processing center to provide services to Wood's other governmental units. In 20X9, this internal service fund billed Wood's Parks and Recreation Fund $75,000 for data-processing services.

What account should Wood's internal service fund credit to record this $75,000 billing to the Parks and Recreation Fund?

a. Operating Revenues
b. Interfund Exchanges
c. Intergovernmental Transfers
d. Data-Processing Department Expenses

5. The following information pertains to Pine City's special revenue fund in 20X9:

Appropriations	$6,500,000
Expenditures	5,000,000
Other financing sources	1,500,000
Other financing uses	2,000,000
Revenues	8,000,000

After Pine's general fund accounts were closed at the end of 20X9, the fund balance increased by

a. $3,000,000.
b. $2,500,000.
c. $1,500,000.
d. $1,000,000.

6. Kew City received a $15,000,000 federal grant to finance the construction of a center for rehabilitation of drug addicts. The proceeds of this grant should be accounted for in the

a. special revenue funds.
b. general fund.
c. capital projects funds.
d. trust funds.

7. Lisa County issued $5,000,000 of general obligation bonds at 101 to finance a capital project. The $50,000 premium was to be used for payment of interest. The transactions involving the premium should be accounted for in the

a. capital projects funds, debt service funds, and the general long-term debt account group.
b. capital projects funds and debt service funds only.
c. debt service funds and the general long-term debt account group only.
d. debt service funds only.

8. In 20X9, a state government collected income taxes of $8,000,000 for the benefit of one of its cities that imposes an income tax on its residents. The state periodically remitted these collections to the city. The state should account for the $8,000,000 in the

a. general fund.
b. agency funds.
c. internal service funds.
d. special assessment funds.

Problem 16-2 *(LO 4)* **Various funds and account groups.** (Numbers 5–7 are AICPA adapted.)

1. The following revenues were among those reported by Ariba Township in 20X4:

Net rental revenue (after depreciation) from a parking garage owned by Ariba	$ 40,000
Interest earned on investments held for employees' retirement benefits	100,000
Property taxes	6,000,000

What amount of the foregoing revenues should be accounted for in Ariba's governmental funds?

a. $6,140,000
b. $6,100,000
c. $6,040,000
d. $6,000,000

Items 2 and 3 are based on the following information:

The events relating to the city of Albury's debt service funds that occurred during the year ended December 31, 20X5, are as follows:

Debt principal matured	$2,000,000
Unmatured (accrued) interest on outstanding debt at January 1, 20X5	50,000
Interest on matured debt	900,000
Unmatured (accrued) interest on outstanding debt at December 31, 20X5	100,000
Interest revenue from investments	600,000
Cash transferred from the general fund for retirement of debt principal	1,000,000
Cash transferred from the general fund for payment of matured interest	900,000

All principal and interest due in 20X5 were paid on time.

2. What is the total amount of expenditures that Albury's debt service funds should record for the year ended December 31, 20X5?

   a. $940,000
   b. $950,000
   c. $2,900,000
   d. $2,500,000

3. How much revenue should Albury's debt service funds record for the year ended December 31, 20X5?

   a. $600,000
   b. $1,600,000
   c. $1,900,000
   d. $2,500,000

4. The following assets are among those owned by the city of Foster:

City hall	$ 800,000
Three fire stations	1,000,000
City streets and sidewalks	5,000,000

   What amount should be included in Foster's general fixed assets account group?

   a. Either $1,800,000 or $6,800,000
   b. Either $1,000,000 or $6,000,000
   c. Either $6,800,000 or $6,000,000
   d. $6,800,000

5. Financing for the renovation of Fir City's municipal park, begun and completed during 20X6, came from the following sources:

Grant from state government	$400,000
Proceeds from general obligation bond	500,000
Transfer from Fir's general fund	100,000

   What amounts should be recorded as revenue and other financing sources?

	Revenues	Other Financing Sources
a.	$1,000,000	$0
b.	$900,000	$100,000
c.	$400,000	$600,000
d.	$0	$1,000,000

6. On April 1, 20X6, Oak County incurred the following expenditures in issuing long-term bonds:

Issue costs	$400,000
Debt insurance	90,000

When Oak establishes the accounting for operating debt service, what amount should be deferred and amortized over the life of the bonds?

a. $0
b. $900,000
c. $400,000
d. $490,000

7. Lake County received the following proceeds that are legally restricted to expenditure for specified purposes:

Levies on affected property owners to install sidewalks	$500,000
Gasoline taxes to finance road repairs	900,000

What amount would be accounted for in Lake's special revenue funds?

a. $1,400,000
b. $900,000
c. $500,000
d. $0

8. The initial contribution of cash from the general fund in order to establish an internal service fund would require the general fund to credit Cash and debit

a. Accounts Receivable.
b. Interfund Transfers-Out.
c. Interfund Loans Receivable.
d. Expenditures.
e. Residual Equity Transfers-Out.

Problem 16-3 *(LO 4)* **Bonds, various funds/groups.** Tyler City formally integrates budgetary accounts into its general fund. During the year ended December 31, 20X7, Tyler received a state grant to buy a bus and an additional grant for bus operation in 20X7. In 20X7, only 90% of the capital grant was used for the bus purchase, but 100% of the operating grant was disbursed. Tyler has incurred the following long-term obligations:

a. General obligation bonds issued for the water and sewer fund which will service the debt.
b. Revenue bonds to be repaid from admission fees collected from users of the municipal recreation center.

These bonds are expected to be paid from enterprise funds and are secured by Tyler's full faith, credit, and taxing power as further assurance that the obligations will be paid. Tyler's 20X7 expenditures from the general fund include payments for structural alterations to a firehouse and furniture for the mayor's office.

1. In reporting the state grants for the bus purchase and operation, what should Tyler include as grant revenues for the year ended December 31, 20X7?

	90% of the Capital Grant	100% of the Capital Grant	Operating Grant
a.	Yes	No	No
b.	No	Yes	No
c.	No	Yes	Yes
d.	Yes	No	Yes

2. Which of Tyler's long-term obligations should be accounted for in the general long-term debt account group?

	General Obligation Bonds	Revenue Bonds
a.	Yes	Yes
b.	Yes	No
c.	No	Yes
d.	No	No

3. When Tyler records its annual budget, which of the following accounts indicates the amount of authorized spending limitation for the year ending December 31, 20X7?

    a. Reserved for Appropriations
    b. Appropriations
    c. Reserved for Encumbrances
    d. Encumbrances

4. In Tyler's general fund balance sheet presentation at December 31, 20X7, which of the following expenditures should be classified as capital assets?

	Purchase of Vehicles	Purchase of City Park
a.	No	No
b.	No	Yes
c.	Yes	No
d.	Yes	Yes

(AICPA adapted)

Problem 16-4 *(LO 1)* **Capital projects fund, financial statements.** The pre-closing, year-end trial balance for a capital projects fund of the city of Craig as of December 31, 20X7, follows:

	Debit	Credit
Cash	75,000	
Investments	200,000	
Contracts Payable—Retained Percentage		60,000
Revenues		16,600
Other Financing Sources		900,000
Expenditures	686,600	
Other Financing Uses	15,000	
Encumbrances	80,000	
Fund Balance—Reserved for Encumbrances		80,000
Estimated Revenues	20,000	
Estimated Other Financing Sources	950,000	
Appropriations		640,000
Estimated Other Financing Uses		25,000
Budgetary Fund Balance—Unreserved		305,000
Total	2,026,600	2,026,600

Required ▶ ▶ ▶ ▶ ▶

1. Prepare closing entries as of December 31, 20X7.
2. Prepare the year-end statement of revenues, expenditures, and changes in fund balance for this project that began on January 2, 20X7.
3. Prepare the balance sheet for this project as of December 31, 20X7.

Problem 16-5 *(LO 1, 4)* **Capital projects fund, effect on other funds/groups.** The following information pertains to Arnold Township's construction and financing of a new administration center:

Estimated total cost of project	$9,000,000
Project financing:	
State entitlement grant	$3,000,000
General obligation bonds:	
Face amount	$6,000,000
Stated interest rate	6%
Issue date	December 1, 20X8
Maturity date	November 30, 20Y8

Arnold's fiscal year ended on June 30, 20X8. The following events occurred that affected the capital projects fund established to account for this project:

July 1, 20X8—	The capital projects fund borrowed $250,000 from the general fund for preliminary expenses.
July 9, 20X8—	Engineering and planning costs of $200,000, for which no encumbrance had been recorded, were paid to Krew Associates.
December 1, 20X8—	The bonds were sold at 101. The premium is transferred to the debt service fund.
December 1, 20X8—	The entitlement grant was formally approved by the state.
April 30, 20X9—	A $7,000,000 contract was executed with Kimmel Construction Corporation, the general contractors for the major portion of the project. The contract provides that Arnold will withhold 4% of all billings pending satisfactory completion of the project.
May 9, 20X9—	$1,000,000 of the state grant was received.
June 10, 20X9—	The $250,000 borrowed from the general fund was repaid.
June 30, 20X9—	Progress billing of $1,200,000 was received from Kimmel.

Arnold uses encumbrance accounting for budgetary control. Unencumbered appropriations lapse at the end of the year.

Required

1. Prepare journal entries in the administration center capital projects fund to record the foregoing transactions.
2. Prepare the June 30, 20X9, closing entries for the administration center capital projects fund.
3. Prepare the Administration Center Capital Projects Fund balance sheet at June 30, 20X9.
4. Prepare entries needed in other funds and groups.

(AICPA adapted)

Problem 16-6 *(LO 1, 4)* **Special assessments, capital projects fund, debt service fund, effect on other funds/groups.** You are given the following post-closing trial balance for the Special Assessment Capital Projects Fund of the city of Stone Bank as of January 1, 20X2. The project was started last year and should be completed in June of 20X2.

	Debit	Credit
Cash	290,000	
Contracts Payable—Retained Percentage		60,000
Fund Balance—Reserved for Encumbrances		80,000
Fund Balance—Unreserved, Undesignated		150,000
Total	290,000	290,000

The special assessments are collected by the debt service fund, which also makes payments of principal and interest. The city has guaranteed payment of the debt in the event of nonpayment by the special assessment property owners. The debt service fund has the following balances on January 1, 20X2:

	Debit	Credit
Cash	20,000	
Special Assessments Receivable—Current	250,000	
Special Assessments Receivable—Deferred	250,000	
Revenues		250,000
Deferred Revenues		250,000
Fund Balance—Reserved for Debt Service		20,000
Total	520,000	520,000

The following events occurred during 20X2:

January 2—	The city adopted an operating budget for 20X2 construction activities. Expenditures are estimated at $223,400, including amounts encumbered in the prior year. Budgetary accounts are used.
January 5—	Prior-year encumbrances are restored, and new encumbrances of $138,000 are recorded.
February 1—	$220,000 of special assessments are collected, along with interest of $17,600. Interest of $2,400 was billed on the uncollected current assessments, which were classified as delinquent.
February 28—	$115,000 was paid on outstanding special assessment bonds, including interest of $15,000.
March 14—	Delinquent special assessments and interest thereon of $2,650 were collected.
May 1—	Expenditures of $220,000 were vouchered to Contracts Payable. The usual 5% retained percentage was entered. The project is now complete at a total cost of $896,000.
May 10—	A check for $100,000 was issued to the contractor.

Required ▶ ▶ ▶ ▶ ▶ Prepare journal entries to record each of the preceding events in the proper funds and groups of accounts using the following format:

Date	Fund or Account Group	Entry

Problem 16-7 *(LO 2, 4)* **Internal service fund, effect on other funds/groups.** Allioto County elects not to purchase commercial insurance. Instead, it sets aside resources for potential claims in an internal service "self-insurance" fund. During the year, the fund recognized $1.5 million for claims filed during the year. Of this amount, it paid $1.3 million. Based on the calculations of an independent actuary, the insurance fund billed and collected $2.0 million in premiums from the other county departments insured by the fund. Of this amount, $1.2 million was billed to the funds accounted for in the general fund and $0.8 million to the county utility fund. The total charge for premiums was based on historical experience and included a reasonable provision for future catastrophe losses.

Required ▶ ▶ ▶ ▶ ▶

1. Prepare the journal entries in the internal service fund to record the claims recognized and paid and the premiums billed and collected.
2. Prepare the journal entries in the other funds affected by the above.
3. If the county accounted for its self-insurance within its general fund, how would the above entries differ?

Problem 16-8 *(LO 4)* **Bonds, various funds/groups.** During 20X1, Krona City issued bonds for financing the construction of a civic center and bonds for financing improvements in the environmental controls for its water and sewer enterprise. The latter bonds require a sinking fund for their retirement. Items (1)–(4) represent items Krona should report in its 20X1 financial statements. Determine whether each item would be included in the following funds and account groups.

Required ▶ ▶ ▶ ▶ ▶

a. General fund.
b. Enterprise funds.
c. Capital projects funds.
d. Debt service funds.
e. General fixed assets account group.
f. General long-term debt account group.

1. Bonds payable.
2. Accumulated depreciation.
3. Amounts identified for the repayment of the two bond issues.
4. Reserved for encumbrances.

(AICPA adapted)

Problem 16-9 *(LO 4)* **Various funds and account groups.** Which fund or account group should be used to record the following?

◄◄◄◄◄ **Required**

1. A primary government's general fund equity interest in a joint venture.
2. Fixed assets of a governmental unit, other than those accounted for in a proprietary fund.
3. A governmental unit's unmatured general obligation bonds payable.
4. Cost of maintenance for a municipal motor pool that maintains all city-owned vehicles and charges the various departments for the cost of rendering those services.
5. General long-term debt of a governmental unit.
6. Deferred compensation plans, for other than proprietary fund employees, adopted under IRC 457.
7. Debt service transactions of a special assessment issue for which the government is not obligated in any manner.
8. Taxes collected and held for a separate school district.
9. Investments donated to the city, income from which is to be used to acquire art for the city's museum.
10. Receipts from the federal government for the food stamp program.

Problem 16-10 *(LO 1, 4)* **Capital projects fund, special assessments, debt service fund, effect on other funds/groups.** In response to a petition signed by the property owners of River Hills Subdivision, the city of Pierce will oversee the installation of sidewalks, curbs, and gutters in the subdivision, to be accounted for in the city's capital projects fund. Pierce reports on a calendar-year basis. Construction is estimated to cost $900,000 and will be financed by a $100,000 county grant, a $50,000 transfer from the city's general fund, and special assessments of $750,000 to be levied against subdivision property owners. One-third of the levy is to be due on February 1 of each year, starting with 20X8. The first $250,000 installment will be received by the capital projects fund directly. The remaining installments will be collected by the debt service fund and will be used to service the related bond debt. The project is to begin on January 15, 20X8, and is to take 18 months to complete. It is estimated that 70% of the work will be completed during 20X8.

To cover construction costs, a 6%, $500,000 special assessment serial bond issue will be floated on March 1, 20X8. Interest is to be paid semiannually on September 1 and March 1 by the debt service fund. One-fifth of the principal will be redeemed on March 1 of each year, starting with 20X9. Since interest earned on special assessments will offset bond interest cost, the city will not accrue interest.

Although the special assessments will provide cash to redeem the bond principal and pay the bond interest, Pierce has pledged its full faith and credit as security for the bond obligation. The following events happen during 20X8:

January 2—	The city council adopted the annual budget for the River Hills project in the capital projects fund.
January 2—	The receivables from the general fund and the county were recorded.
January 5—	Special assessments were levied in accordance with the plan, with one-third due on February 1.
January 9—	Amounts due from the general fund and the county were received.
January 10—	Encumbrances for the year were recorded at $675,000.
February 1—	The first special assessment installment was collected.
March 1—	Bonds with a $500,000 face value were sold at 101. Except for the price, other conditions remained in accordance with the bond plan. The premium was to be transferred to the debt service fund for interest payments.
March 1—	$600,000 was invested in a 5% money market account by the capital projects fund.

August 31—	$10,000 for interest payment was transferred by the capital projects fund to the debt service fund.
September 1—	The semiannual bond interest was paid by the debt service fund.
December 15—	The contractor submitted an invoice for $600,000 that was approved for payment, except for a 10% amount to be paid on completion and acceptance of the project. Related encumbrances totaled $595,000.
December 29—	$400,000 was withdrawn from the money market investment. Interest of $16,600 was received.
December 30—	The contractor was mailed a check for $540,000. In addition, vouchers for $76,600 were prepared and paid for items on the project that were not encumbered.
In addition—	The next assessment installment was reclassified upon special direction of the city council, and an amount equal to project expenditures-to-date was capitalized.

Required ▶ ▶ ▶ ▶ ▶

For each of the preceding events, prepare the journal entries for all of the funds and groups of accounts involved, using the following format:

Date	Fund or Account Group	Entry

Required ▶ ▶ ▶ ▶ ▶

template cd

Problem 16-11 *(LO 2)* **Internal service fund, statement of cash flows.** Prepare a statement of cash flows for the internal service fund of the city of Cleveville from the following information:

Cash on hand at the beginning of the year	$ 122
Interest from investments	45
Wages and salaries paid	(3,470)
Purchases of supplies	(1,650)
Collections (for services) from other funds	6,380
Interest on long-term debt	(150)
Repayment of loans to other funds	(880)
Purchase of fixed assets	(900)
Proceeds of revenue bonds	800
Purchases of investments	(440)
Proceeds from sale of fixed assets	23
Proceeds from sale of investments	33
Loans from other funds	600

Problem 16-12 *(LO 2)* **Internal service fund.** The city of Danbury operates a central computer center through an internal service fund. The Computer Internal Service Fund was established by a contribution of $1,000,000 from the general fund on July 1, 20X2, at which time a building was acquired at a cost of $300,000 cash. A used computer was purchased for $600,000. The post-closing trial balance of the fund at June 30, 20X3, was as follows:

	Debit	Credit
Cash	120,000	
Due from General Fund	140,000	
Inventory of Materials and Supplies	80,000	
Land	60,000	
Building	300,000	
Allowance for Depreciation—Building		15,000
Computer Equipment	660,000	
Allowance for Depreciation—Computer Equipment		264,000
Vouchers Payable (to outsiders)		41,000
Contributions from General Fund		1,000,000
Retained Earnings—Unreserved		40,000
Total	1,360,000	1,360,000

The following information applies to the year ended June 30, 20X4:

a. Materials and supplies were purchased on account for $72,000.
b. The inventory of materials and supplies at June 30, 20X4, was $65,000.
c. Salaries paid totaled $235,000, including related costs.
d. A billing from the Utility Enterprise Fund for $40,000 was received and paid.
e. Depreciation on the building and on the equipment was $6,500 and $133,000, respectively.
f. Billings to other departments for service were as follows:

General Fund	$392,000
Water and Sewer Fund	84,000
Special Revenue Fund	42,000

g. Unpaid interfund receivable balances at June 30, 20X4, were as follows:

General Fund	$136,000
Special Revenue Fund	16,000

h. Vouchers payable at June 30, 20X4, were $19,000.

◄◄◄◄◄ **Required**

1. For the period July 1, 20X3, through June 30, 20X4, prepare journal entries to record the transactions in the Computer Internal Service Fund. The city uses control accounts for revenues and expenses.
2. Prepare closing entries at June 30, 20X4.

Problem 16-13 *(LO 2, 4)* **Enterprise fund, general fund.** In 20X8, a city opens a municipal landfill, which it will account for in an enterprise fund. It estimates capacity to be 6 million cubic feet and usable life to be 20 years. To close the landfill, the municipality expects to incur labor, material, and equipment costs of $4 million. Thereafter, it expects to incur an additional $6 million of cost to monitor and maintain the site.

◄◄◄◄◄ **Required**

1. In 20X8, the city uses 300,000 cubic feet of the landfill. Prepare the journal entry to record the expense for closure and post-closure care.
2. In 20X9, it again uses 300,000 cubic feet of the landfill. It revises its estimate of available volume to 5.8 million cubic feet and closure and post-closure costs to $10.2 million. Prepare the journal entry to record the expense for closure and post-closure care.
3. Suppose the city accounts for the landfill in the general fund. How would the above entries for 20X8 and 20X9 differ?

Problem 16-14 *(LO 3)* **Trust fund, financial statements.** The following trial balance of the Employee's Retirement System Fund for Redford City was prepared by a clerk who used only balance sheet accounts in recording the events for the fiscal year ended June 30, 20X8:

template cd

Cash	$ 38,000
Due from the city	4,000
Interest receivable	5,000
Investments, at fair value	497,000
Due to resigned employees	(1,000)
Annuities payable	(3,000)
Net plan assets	(540,000)
	$ 0

(continued)

Balance on June 30, 20X7	$ 464,000
Events during 20X8:	
Amounts received from employees	32,000
Amounts received from employer	16,000
Amount due from city at year-end	4,000
Annuities paid during the year	13,000
Refunds made during the year	2,500
Annuities payable at year-end	3,000
Due to resigned employees at year-end	1,000
Investment earnings received	30,000
Accrued earnings at year-end	5,000
Difference between carrying value and fair value of the investments	13,500
Administrative expenses	5,000
Balance on June 30, 20X8	$ 540,000

Required ▶ ▶ ▶ ▶ ▶ Prepare a statement of net assets and a statement of changes in net assets of the Employees' Retirement System Fund for the fiscal year ended June 30, 20X8.

Problem 16-15 *(LO 3, 4)* **Agency fund, effect on various funds/groups.** In compliance with a newly enacted state law, Hayward County assumed the responsibility of collecting all property taxes levied within its boundaries as of July 1, 20X3. The following composite property tax rate per $100 of net assessed valuation was developed for the fiscal year ending June 30, 20X4:

Hayward County General Fund	$ 6.00
Reed City General Fund	3.00
Newbury Township General Fund	1.00
	$10.00

All property taxes are due in quarterly installments and, after being collected, are distributed to the governmental units represented in the composite rate. To administer the collection and distribution of such taxes, Hayward County has established a tax agency fund.

Additional information:

a. To reimburse itself for estimated administrative expenses of operating the tax agency fund, the county is to deduct 2% from the tax collections for Reed City and Newbury Township. The total amount deducted is to be remitted to the Hayward County general fund.
b. Current-year tax levies to be collected by the tax agency fund are as follows:

	Gross Levy	Estimated Amount to Be Collected
Hayward County	$3,600,000	$3,500,000
Reed City	1,800,000	1,740,000
Newbury Township	600,000	560,000
Totals	$6,000,000	$5,800,000

c. In its original computation of the gross levy, Newbury Township made an error that will reduce both the gross and estimated amounts to be collected by $10,000.
d. As of September 30, 20X3, the tax agency fund has received $1,440,000 in first-quarter payments. On October 1, the agency fund made a distribution to the three governmental units on the basis of the composite property tax rate.

For the period July 1, 20X3, through October 1, 20X3, prepare journal entries to record the preceding transactions, using the following format: ◀◀◀◀◀ **Required**

	Hayward County Tax Agency Fund		Hayward County General Fund		Reed City General Fund		Newbury Township General Fund	
Accounts	Debit	Credit	Debit	Credit	Debit	Credit	Debit	Credit

(AICPA adapted)

Problem 16-16 *(LO 4)* **Various funds and account groups.** A selected list of transactions for the city of Butler for the fiscal year ending June 30, 20X8, follows:

1. The city government authorized a budget with estimated revenues of $2,500,000 and appropriations of $2,450,000.
2. The city's share of state gasoline taxes is estimated to be $264,500. These taxes are to be used only for highway maintenance. Appropriations are authorized in the amount of $250,000.
3. Property taxes of $1,400,000 are levied by the city. In the past, uncollectible taxes have averaged 2% of the gross levy.
4. A $1,000,000 term bond issue for construction of a school is authorized and sold at 99. Bond issue costs were $5,000.
5. Contracts are signed for the construction of the school at an estimated cost of $1,000,000.
6. The school is constructed at a cost of $990,000.
7. A transfer of $100,000 is made by the general fund to the debt service fund.
8. Land with a fair value of $100,000 is donated to the city.
9. The city received $205,000 in partial payment of its share of state gasoline taxes, with an additional $60,000 due from the state government in 60 days.
10. Vouchers totaling $210,000, which represent highway labor maintenance costs, are approved for payment by the special revenue fund.

For each event, prepare the journal entries for all of the funds and groups of accounts involved, using the following format: ◀◀◀◀◀ **Required**

Fund or Account Group	Journal Entry

Problem 16-17 *(LO 4)* **Various funds and account groups.** The village of Dexter was recently incorporated and began financial operations on July 1, 20X8, the beginning of its fiscal year.

The following transactions occurred during this first fiscal year from July 1, 20X8, to June 30, 20X9:

1. The village council adopted a budget for general operations during the fiscal year ending June 30, 20X9. Revenues were estimated at $400,000. Legal authorizations for expenditures were $394,000.
2. Property taxes were levied for $390,000. It was estimated that 2% of this amount would prove to be uncollectible. These taxes were available on the date of the levy to finance current expenditures.
3. During the year, a resident of the village donated marketable securities, valued at $50,000, to the village under the terms of a trust agreement. The agreement stipulated that the principal is to be kept intact. The use of revenue generated by the securities is to be restricted to financing college scholarships for needy students. Revenue earned and received on these marketable securities amounted to $5,500 through June 30, 20X9.

4. A general fund transfer of $5,000 was made to establish an Intragovernmental Service Fund to provide for a permanent investment in inventory.
5. The village decided to install lighting in the village park. A special assessment project was authorized to install the lighting at a cost of $75,000. The appropriation was formally recorded. To finance the project, $3,000 is to be transferred from the general fund, and the balance is from special assessments.
6. Assessments were levied for $72,000, with the village contributing $3,000 from the general fund. All assessments and the village contributions were collected during the year.
7. A contract for $75,000 was let for the installation of lighting. At June 30, 20X9, the contract was completed for $75,000. The contractor was paid all but 5%, which was retained to ensure compliance with the terms of the contract. Encumbrances and other budgetary accounts are maintained.
8. During the year, the internal service fund purchased various supplies at a cost of $1,900.
9. Cash collections recorded by the general fund during the year were as follows:

Property taxes	$386,000
Licenses and permits	7,000

10. The village council decided to build a village hall, at an estimated cost of $500,000, to replace space occupied in rented facilities. The village does not record project authorizations. It was decided that general obligation bonds bearing interest at 6% would be issued. On June 30, 20X9, the bonds were issued at their face value of $500,000, payable in 20 years. No contracts have been signed for this project, and no expenditures have been made.
11. A fire truck was purchased for $150,000, and the voucher was approved. Payment was made through the general fund. This expenditure was previously encumbered for $145,000.

Required ▶ ▶ ▶ ▶ ▶ Prepare journal entries to properly record each of the preceding transactions in the appropriate fund(s) or group of accounts of Dexter for the fiscal year ended June 30, 20X9. Use the following funds and groups of accounts:

a. General fund
b. Capital projects fund
c. Internal service fund
d. Private-purpose principal fund
e. Private-purpose earnings fund
f. General long-term debt account group
g. General fixed assets account group

Journal entries should be numbered to correspond with the appropriate transactions. Do not prepare closing entries for any fund.

Your answer sheet should be organized as follows:

Transaction No.	Fund or Account Group	Account Title and Explanation	Amount Debit	Amount Credit

(AICPA adapted)

Problem 16-18 *(LO 4)* **Various funds and account groups.** The following information relates to Dane City during its fiscal year ended December 31, 20X7:

a. On October 31, 20X7, to finance the construction of a city hall annex, Dane issued 8%, 10-year general obligation bonds at their face value of $600,000. Construction expenditures during the period equaled $364,000.
b. Dane reported $109,000 from hotel room taxes, restricted for tourist promotion, in a special revenue fund. The fund paid $81,000 for general promotions and $22,000 for a motor vehicle.
c. 20X7 general fund revenues of $104,500 were transferred to a debt service fund and used to repay $100,000 of 9%, 15-year term bonds and $4,500 of interest. The bonds were used to acquire a citizens' center.

d. At December 31, 20X7, as a consequence of past services, city firefighters had accumulated entitlements to compensated absences valued at $86,000. General fund resources available at December 31, 20X7, are expected to be used to settle $17,000 of this amount, and $69,000 is expected to be paid out of future general fund resources.
e. At December 31, 20X7, Dane was responsible for $83,000 of outstanding general fund encumbrances, including $8,000 for the following supplies.
f. Dane uses the purchases method to account for supplies. The following information relates to supplies:

Inventory:	
January 1, 20X7	$ 39,000
December 31, 20X7	42,000
Encumbrances outstanding:	
January 1, 20X7	6,000
December 31, 20X7	8,000
Purchase orders during 20X7	190,000
Amounts credited to vouchers payable during 20X7	181,000

◄◄◄◄◄ **Required**

1. The amount of 20X7 general fund operating transfers-out is ___________.
2. The 20X7 general fund liabilities from entitlements for compensated absences are ___________.
3. The 20X7 reserved amount of the general fund balance is ___________.
4. The 20X7 capital projects fund balance is ___________.
5. The 20X7 fund balance on the special revenue fund for tourist promotion is ___________.
6. The amount of 20X7 debt service fund expenditures is ___________.
7. The amount to be included in the general fixed assets account group for the cost of assets acquired in 20X7 is ___________.
8. The amount by which 20X7 transactions and events decreased the general long-term debt account group is ___________.
9. The amount of 20X7 supplies expenditures using the purchases method is ___________.
10. The total amount of 20X7 supplies encumbrances is ___________.

(AICPA adapted)

Problem 16-19 *(LO 4)* **Various funds and account groups.** The following information relates to Bel City, whose first fiscal year ended December 31, 20X7. Assume Bel has only the long-term debt as specified below and only the funds necessitated by the following information.

1. General fund:

	Budget	Actual
Property taxes	$5,000,000	$4,700,000
Other revenues	1,000,000	1,050,000
Total revenues	$6,000,000	$5,750,000
Total expenditures	$5,600,000	$5,700,000
Property taxes receivable—delinquent		$ 420,000
Less allowance for estimated uncollectible taxes—delinquent		50,000
		$ 370,000

a. There were no amendments to the budget as originally adopted.
b. No property taxes receivable have been written off, and the allowance for uncollectibles balance is unchanged from the initial entry at the time of the original tax levy.
c. There were no encumbrances outstanding at December 31, 20X7.

2. Capital projects fund:
   a. Finances for Bel's new civic center were provided by a combination of general fund transfers, a state grant, and an issue of general obligation bonds. Any bond premium on issuance is to be used for the repayment of the bonds at their $1,200,000 par value. At December 31, 20X7, the capital projects fund for the civic center had the following closing entries:

Revenues	800,000	
Other Financing Sources—Bond Proceeds	1,230,000	
Other Financing Sources—Operating Transfers-In	500,000	
Expenditures		1,080,000
Other Financing Uses—Operating Transfers-Out		30,000
Unreserved Fund Balance		1,420,000

   b. Also, at December 31, 20X7, capital projects fund entries reflected Bel's intention to honor the $1,300,000 purchase orders and commitments outstanding for the center.
   c. During 20X7, total capital projects fund encumbrances exceeded the corresponding expenditures by $42,000. All expenditures were previously encumbered.
   d. During 20X8, the capital projects fund received no revenues and no other financing sources. The civic center building was completed in early 20X8, and the capital projects fund was closed by a transfer of $27,000 to the general fund.

3. Water utility enterprise fund:
   a. Bel issued $4,000,000 revenue bonds at par. These bonds, together with a $700,000 transfer from the general fund, were used to acquire a water utility. Water utility revenues are to be the sole source of funds to retire these bonds beginning in the year 20Y2.

Required ▶ ▶ ▶ ▶ ▶ Answer questions 1–15 with a yes (Y) or no (N) in the space provided. Answer questions 16–20 with the correct amount in the space provided.

1. Did recording budgetary accounts at the beginning of 20X7 increase the fund balance by $50,000? ____________
2. Should the budgetary accounts for 20X7 include an entry for the expected transfer of funds from the general fund to the capital projects fund? ____________
3. Should the $700,000 payment from the general fund, which was used to help establish the water utility fund, be reported as "other financing uses—operating transfers-out"? ____________
4. Did the general fund receive the $30,000 bond premium from the capital projects fund? ____________
5. Should a payment from the general fund for water received for normal civic center operations be reported as "other financing uses—operating transfers-out"? ____________
6. Does the net property taxes receivable of $370,000 include amounts expected to be collected after March 15, 20X8? ____________
7. Would closing budgetary accounts cause the fund balance to increase by $400,000? ____________
8. Would the interaction between budgetary and actual amounts cause the fund balance to decrease by $350,000? ____________
9. In the general fixed assets account group, should a credit amount be recorded for 20X7 in "Investment in General Fixed Assets—Capital Projects Fund"? ____________

10. In the general fixed assets account group, should Bel record depreciation on water utility equipment? ___________
11. Should the capital projects fund be included in Bel's combined statement of revenues, expenditures, and changes in fund balances? ___________
12. Should the water utility enterprise fund be included in Bel's combined governmental funds balance sheet? ___________
13. Should Bel report capital and related financing activities in its statement of cash flows in its debt service fund? ___________
14. Should Bel report capital and related financing activities in its statement of cash flows in its capital projects fund? ___________
15. Should Bel report capital and related financing activities in its statement of cash flows in its water utility enterprise fund? ___________
16. What amount was recorded in the opening entry for appropriations? ___________
17. What was the total amount debited to Property Taxes Receivable? ___________
18. In the general long-term debt account group, what amount should be reported for bonds payable at December 31, 20X7? ___________
19. In the general fixed assets account group, what amount should be recorded for "Investment in General Fixed Assets—Capital Projects Fund" at December 31, 20X7? ___________
20. What was the completed cost of the civic center? ___________
21. How much was the state capital grant for the civic center? ___________
22. In the capital projects fund, what was the amount of the total encumbrances recorded during 20X7? ___________
23. In the capital projects fund, what was the unreserved fund balance reported at December 31, 20X7? ___________

(AICPA adapted)

Problem 16-20 *(LO 2, 4)* **Various funds and account groups, capital projects fund financial statement.** Port Washington's citizens authorized the construction of a new library. As a result of this project, the city had the following transactions during 20X8:

a. On January 3, 20X8, a $600,000 serial bond issue having a stated interest rate of 8% was authorized for the acquisition of land and the construction of a library building. The bonds are to be redeemed in 10 equal annual installments beginning February 1, 20X9.
b. On January 10, 20X8, the city made a $50,000 down payment deposit on the purchase of land, which is to be the site of the library. The contracted price for the land is $150,000, which is $40,000 below what the city estimated it would have to spend to acquire a site.
c. On March 1, 20X8, the city issued serial bonds having a $450,000 face value at 102. The bond indenture requires any premium to be set aside for servicing bond interest.
d. On March 10, 20X8, the city paid the remaining amount on the land contract and took title to the land.
e. On March 17, 20X8, the city signed a $400,000 construction contract with Rower Construction Company.
f. On July 10, 20X8, the contractor was paid $200,000 based on work completed to date.
g. On September 1, 20X8, a semiannual interest payment was made on the outstanding bonds. [The general fund transferred funds to supplement the cash received from the premium in item (c).]
h. On December 1, 20X8, the city issued serial bonds having a $100,000 face value at par.
i. On December 2, 20X8, the contractor completed the library and submitted a final billing of $210,000, which includes $10,000 of additional work authorized by the city in October 20X8. The $210,000 was paid to the contractor on December 12, 20X8.
j. Through December 10, 20X8, the city had invested excess cash (from the bond offering) in short-term certificates of deposit. The amount collected on these investments totaled $12,000.

Required ▶ ▶ ▶ ▶ ▶

1. Prepare the journal entries in all fund/account groups.
2. Prepare any appropriate year-end adjusting and closing entries for the capital projects fund and the general fixed assets account group.
3. Prepare a statement of revenues, expenditures, and changes in fund balance for 20X8 for the capital projects fund.

Financial Reporting Issues

CHAPTER

17

Learning Objectives

When you have completed this chapter, you should be able to

1. **Identify the basic components of a comprehensive annual financial report (CAFR).**
2. **Explain which governmental entities are required to report financial information.**
3. **Demonstrate an understanding of the new financial reporting model required by GASB Statement No. 34.**
4. **Tell when GASB Statement No. 34 took effect, list the requirements of the Single Audit Act, and describe what other reporting efforts the GASB has been encouraging.**

As discussed in the previous chapters, in June 1999 the Governmental Accounting Standards Board (GASB) issued Statement No. 34, *Basic Financial Statements—and Management's Discussion and Analysis—for State and Local Governments*. Statement No. 34 significantly changed the financial reporting requirements for all state and local governments, including special purpose governments such as school districts, special taxing authorities, and districts. The GASB No. 34 requirements are the most significant change in the history of government financial reporting. This chapter is intended to highlight the requirements of the standard that were not addressed in Chapters 15 and 16 and to provide a complete discussion of financial reporting for state and local governments.

GASB Statement No. 34 requires a "new reporting model." It mandates several financial statements to include (1) government-wide financial statements, (2) funds-based financial statements, and (3) a management's discussion and analysis (MD&A) report. In addition, certain information must be presented in the footnotes or in separate statements or schedules. This information is considered required supplementary information (RSI). The reporting model builds from the accounting standards described in Chapters 15 and 16. Many users of financial statements are confident that these rules will provide important information for decision makers. Indeed, for the first time, information about the government as a whole is presented along with more detailed information about the funds. The student companion book includes a complete set of financial statements from the city of Milwaukee.

ANNUAL FINANCIAL REPORTING

1

OBJECTIVE

Identify the basic components of a comprehensive annual financial report (CAFR).

The principal role of financial reporting is to provide information. A *comprehensive annual financial report (CAFR)* should be prepared by every governmental unit in order to demonstrate that it has complied with the provisions of the law. The CAFR includes at least two sets of financial statements, along with their notes and any additional data that may be considered necessary. These two sets are (a) the general purpose financial statements (GPFS) and (b) combining statements for nonmajor funds by fund type.

A complete set of GPFS includes the following information:

1. Management's discussion and analysis statement (MD&A).
2. Separate fund financial statements for governmental, proprietary, and fiduciary funds.
3. Government-wide financial statements presenting the entire government.
4. Notes to the financial statements, including descriptions of the activities accounted for in the major funds, internal service fund type, and fiduciary fund types; length of time used to define "available" for purposes of revenue recognition in the governmental fund financial statements; actions taken to address significant violations of finance-related legal or contractual provisions; debt service requirements to maturity, separately identifying principal and interest for each of the subsequent five years and in 5-year increments thereafter; obligations under leases for each of the five subsequent years and in 5-year increments thereafter; a schedule of changes in short-term debt and the purpose for which short-term debt was issued; amounts due from other funds by individual major fund, nonmajor governmental funds in the aggregate, nonmajor enterprise funds in the aggregate, internal service funds in the aggregate, and fiduciary fund type, the purpose for those balances, and amounts that are not expected to be repaid within one year; interest requirements for variable-rate debt computed using the rate effective at year-end; terms of interest rate changes for variable-rate debt; details about major components of receivable and payable balances and identification of receivable balances not expected to be collected within one year; and amounts transferred from other funds by individual major fund, nonmajor governmental funds in the aggregate, nonmajor enterprise funds in the aggregate, internal service funds in the aggregate, and fiduciary fund type, a general description of the principal purposes of interfund transfers, and purposes for and amounts of certain transfers.
5. *Required supplementary information (RSI)* which includes a budgetary comparison statement or schedule, information about the condition of infrastructure assets, pension-related information, risk-financing and self-insurance activity. Although RSI contains information similar to the notes, it is not considered part of the basic financial statements and therefore may be subject to a lower level of audit scrutiny.

The general purpose financial statements provide the minimum financial reporting necessary for a fair presentation according to generally accepted accounting principles. The GPFS are part of the *financial section* of a comprehensive annual financial report along with the auditor's report and combining and individual funds statements that provide more detailed financial information than the combined statements. Chapter 16 illustrates several combining statements for nonmajor special revenue, permanent, capital project, and debt service funds. Combined statements are an aggregation of the individual fund financial statements. Combining statements are used to add together funds of the same type in order to present summary data in the combined statements as follows:

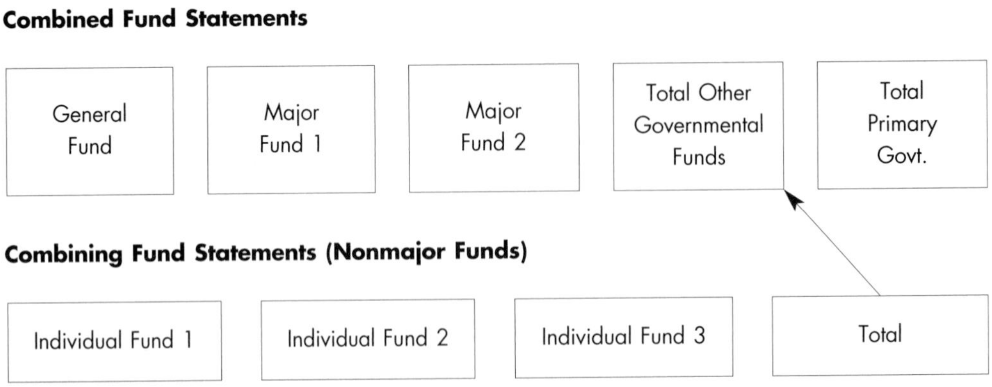

Two additional sections of the CAFR, not part of the financial section, are the *introductory section* and the *statistical section*. The introductory section includes a table of contents, a letter of transmittal from the chief executive or finance officer to the mayor (or the mayor and legislative body), and other information. The letter of transmittal tells about the contents of the CAFR,

Illustration 17-1
The Financial Reporting "Pyramid"

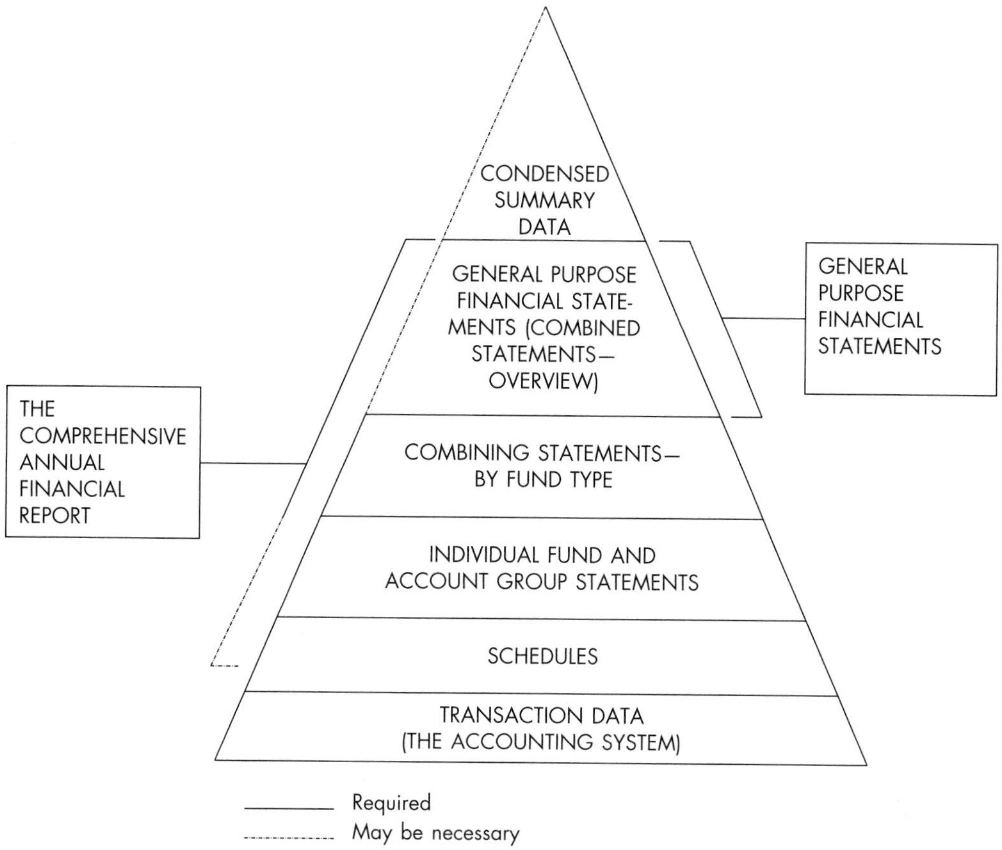

Source: Codification of Governmental Accounting and Reporting Standards as of June 30, 2000. *The Financial Reports Pyramid,* Section 1900.117.

management's view of the economic condition of the governmental unit, and the community and management's summary of governmental operating activity. The statistical section includes data, often in chart or graph form, about the governmental unit and the community such as general governmental expenditures by function and community demographic statistics.

The GASB Codification of Governmental Accounting and Financial Reporting provides a pyramid of financial reporting, as shown in Illustration 17-1. The top of the pyramid represents highly aggregated consolidated financial statements, while the bottom represents details of transactions. With the adoption of GASB Statement No. 34, governments are, for the first time, reporting entity-wide summarized information at the top of the pyramid. This chapter will give students information on both government-wide and funds-based financial statements.

REPORTING ENTITY

2
OBJECTIVE
Explain which governmental entities are required to report financial information.

GASB Statement No. 14, issued in June 1991, defines the criteria a government must use to determine whether its reporting entity should be limited to the primary government or whether one or more of the associated organizations (referred to as component units) are also part of the government's reporting entity. A primary government can be a state government, a general purpose local government such as a city or county, or a legally separate special purpose government that has a separately elected governing body and is fiscally independent of other state and local governments. A component unit is a legally separate organization for which the elected officials of the primary government are financially accountable or for which the nature and significance of the relationship with the primary government is such that exclusion would cause the financial statements of the primary government to be misleading or incomplete. Examples of component units are authorities, commissions, boards, pension plans, development corporations, hospitals, and school districts.

As indicated, the definition of the reporting entity is based primarily on the notion of *financial accountability.* Financial accountability is measured by (a) fiscal dependence or (b) the ability of a primary government to appoint a voting majority of an organization's governing body and either be able to impose its will on the potential component unit or have the potential to receive specific financial benefit or burden. Most component units should be included in the financial report by discrete presentation (i.e., in one or more columns that are separate from the financial data of the primary government) as shown below:

Total Primary Government	Total Component Units

Other component units are so intertwined with the primary government that they are blended or included with the primary government and only footnote disclosure can inform the reader of their existence. This usually happens either when the component unit is established to serve the primary government or the two boards are essentially the same. When a primary government blends one or more component units into its own financial statements, it reports the funds of the component unit as if they were its own funds. Thus, the primary government adds the component unit special revenue funds to its own. The only exception to this blending is that the general fund of a component unit should be blended into the primary government's special revenue fund. This is done so the primary government's very important general fund information is presented. The flowchart in Illustration 17-2 highlights the decision process for determining a component unit and its presentation in the financial statements.

Governments sometimes enter into joint ventures with other governments, whereby they agree to share both the risks and rewards of a common activity. If a government has an equity interest in the joint venture, it should account for the investment as a long-term asset in the general long-term debt account group (or in a proprietary fund if the investment was made with proprietary resources).

The GASB also requires affiliated organizations for which the government is not financially accountable, e.g., booster clubs, fund-raising organizations, and foundations, to be discretely presented as component units if (1) the economic resources are entirely, or almost entirely, for the benefit of the government, *and* (2) the government is entitled to the majority of these resources, *and* (3) these resources are significant to that government.[1]

3

OBJECTIVE

Demonstrate an understanding of the new financial reporting model required by GASB Statement No. 34.

HIGHLIGHTS AND ILLUSTRATIVE EXAMPLES OF THE NEW REPORTING MODEL

Statement No. 34 represents a dramatic shift in the way state and local governments present financial information to the public. The new statements will have more and easier to understand information about the government. The new reporting standard also reaffirms the importance of information that governments already include in their annual reports. Major innovations of Statement No. 34 can be summarized as follows:

- An introductory narrative section highlighting and analyzing the governments' financial performance.
- A refinement of the current funds-based information.
- An overall view of the government in new government-wide statements.
- Comprehensive information about the cost of delivering services to citizens.
- Information about infrastructure assets—such as bridges, roads, and storm sewers.

1 GASB Statement No. 39, *Determining Whether Certain Organizations Are Component Units—an amendment to GASB 14,* (Norwalk, CT: Governmental Accounting Standards Board, May 2002).

Illustration 17-2
The Financial Reporting Entity

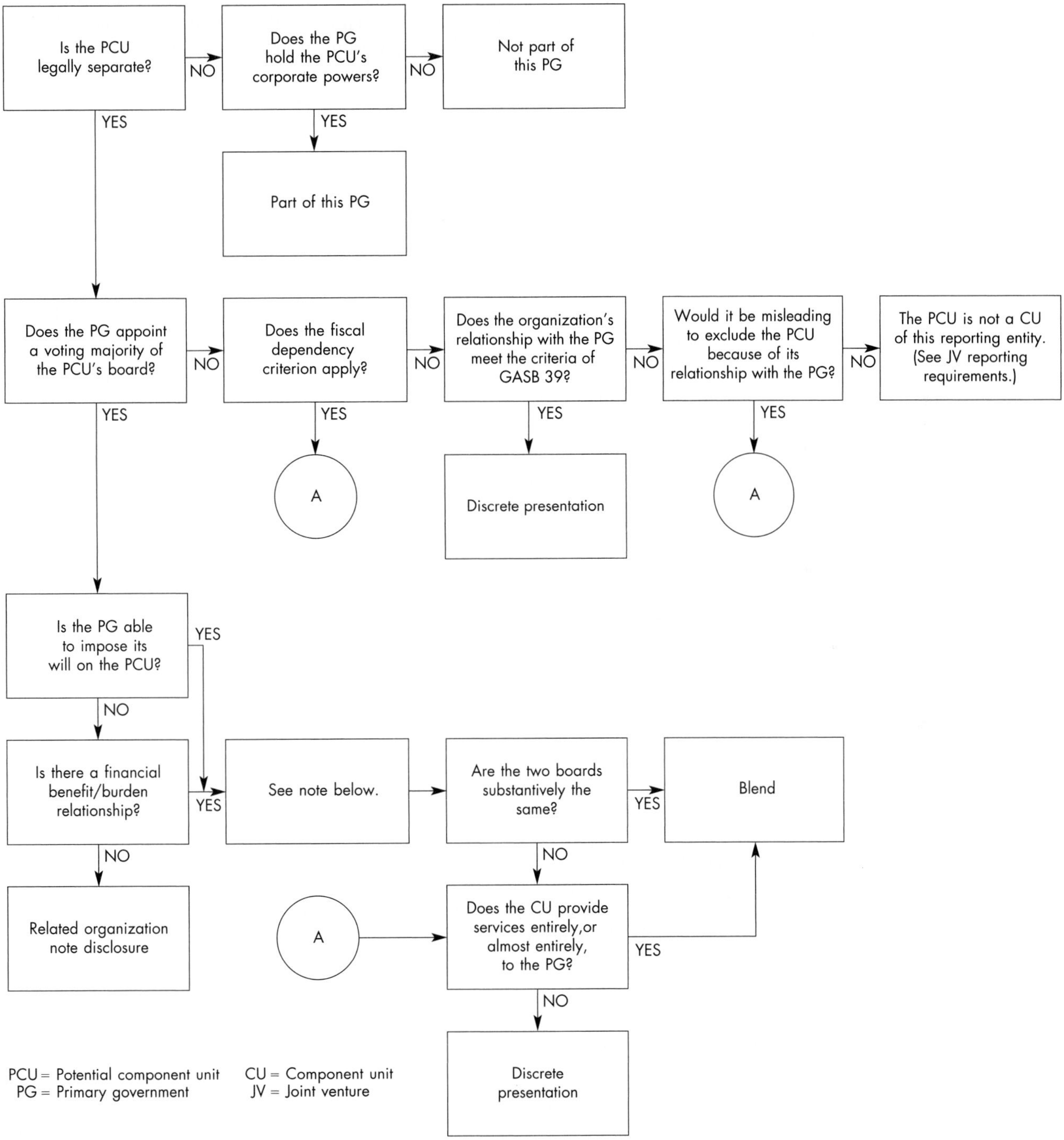

Source: GASB Statement No. 39, *Determining Whether Certain Organizations Are Component Units*—an amendment to GASB 14, *The Financial Reporting Entity*, May 2002.

Management's Discussion and Analysis

The statement requires the inclusion of a management's discussion and analysis (MD&A) as supplementary information before the basic financial statements. The purpose of the MD&A is to give a concise overview and analysis of the information in the government's financial statements. This analysis is focused on the primary government and is based on currently known facts, decisions, or conditions. It is not a forecast. Its purpose it to help users (citizens, the media, bond raters, creditors, legislators, and others) assess whether the government's financial position has improved or deteriorated during the year. Governments must limit the topics discussed in the MD&A to the following:[2]

- A brief discussion of the basic financial statements, including how they relate to each other and the significant differences in the information they provide.
- Condensed current- and prior-year financial information from the government-wide financial statement.
- An analysis of the government's overall financial position and results of operations including impact of important economic factors.
- An analysis of individual fund financial information, including the reasons for significant changes in fund balances (or net assets) and whether limitations significantly affect the future use of the resources.
- An analysis of significant variations between original and final budget amounts and between final budget amounts and actual budget results for the general fund.
- A description of changes in capital assets and long-term liabilities during the year.
- A discussion of the condition of infrastructure assets.
- A description of currently known facts, decisions, or conditions that have, or are expected to have, a material effect on the financial position or results of operations.

Excerpts from a sample MD&A provided by the GASB in Statement No. 34 are shown in Illustration 17-3.[3]

Illustration 17-3
Management's Discussion and Analysis

Our discussion and analysis of Berryville's financial performance provides an overview of the City's financial activities for the fiscal year ended December 31, 20X2.

Financial Highlights

- The City's net assets remained virtually unchanged as a result of this year's operations. While net assets of our business-type activities increased by $3.2 million, or nearly 4%, net assets of our governmental activities decreased by $3.1 million, or nearly 2.5%.
- During the year, the City had expenses that were $6.3 million more than the $99.5 million generated in tax and other revenues for governmental programs (before special items). This compares to last year, however, when expenses exceeded revenues by $8.9 million.
- In the City's business-type activities, revenues increased to $15 million (or 5.6%) while expenses decreased by 1.7%.
- Total cost of all of the City's programs was virtually unchanged (increasing by $800,000, or less than 1%) with no new programs being added this year.
- The general fund reported a deficit this year of $1.3 million despite the one-time proceeds of $3.5 million from the sale of some of our park land.

(continued)

2 GASB Statement No. 37, *Basic Financial Statements—and Management's Discussion and Analysis—for State and Local Governments: Omnibus* (Norwalk, CT: Governmental Accounting Standards Board, June 2001) requires governments to confine topics in the MD&A.

3 The source for Illustrations 17-3 through 17-14 can be found in GASB Statement No. 34, *Basic Financial Statements—and Management's Discussion and Analysis—for State and Local Governments*, pp. 151, 201, 210–211, 220–224, 228–231, 235–236, 254–255, 258–261, and 269.

Illustration 17-3 *(continued)*

- The resources available for appropriation were $1.1 million less than budgeted for the general fund. However, we kept expenditures within spending limits primarily through a mid-year hiring and overtime freeze and our continuing staff restructuring efforts.

Using this Annual Report

This annual report consists of a series of financial statements. The statement of net assets and the statement of activities [on page 991 (Illustration 17-13) and pages 994 and 995 (Illustration 17-14)] provide information about the activities of the City as a whole and present a longer-term view of the City's finances. Fund financial statements start on page 980 (Illustration 17-4). For governmental activities, these statements tell how these services were financed in the short term as well as what remains for future spending. Fund financial statements also report the City's operations in more detail than the government-wide statements by providing information about the City's most significant funds. The remaining statements provide financial information about activities for which the City acts solely as a trustee or agent for the benefit of those outside the government.

Reporting the City as a Whole

The Statement of Net Assets and the Statement of Activities

Our analysis of the City as a whole begins on page 978 (Table 1). One of the most important questions asked about the City's finances would be, "Is the City as a whole better or worse off as a result of the year's activities?" The statement of net assets and the statement of activities report information about the City as a whole and about its activities in a way that helps answer this question. These statements include *all* assets and liabilities using *the accrual basis of accounting*, which is similar to the accounting used by most private-sector companies. All of the current year's revenues and expenses are taken into account regardless of when cash is received or paid.

These two statements report the City's net assets and changes in them. You can think of the City's net assets—the difference between assets and liabilities—as one way to measure the City's financial health, or *financial position*. Over time, *increases* or *decreases* in the City's net assets are one indicator of whether its *financial health* is improving or deteriorating. You will need to consider other nonfinancial factors, however, such as changes in the City's property tax base and the condition of the City's roads, to assess the *overall health* of the City.

In the statement of net assets and the statement of activities, we divide the City into three kinds of activities:

- Governmental activities—Most of the City's basic services are reported here, including the police, fire, public works, and parks departments, and general administration. Property taxes, franchise fees, and state and federal grants finance most of these activities.
- Business-type activities—The City charges a fee to customers to help it cover all or most of the cost of certain services it provides. The City's water and sewer system and parking facilities are reported here.
- Component units—The City includes two separate legal entities in its report: the City School District and the City Landfill Authority. Although legally separate, these "component units" are important because the City is financially accountable for them.

Reporting the City's Most Significant Funds

Fund Financial Statements

Our analysis of the City's major funds begins on 979. The fund financial statements begin on page 980 (Illustration 17-4) and provide detailed information about the most significant funds—not the City as a whole. Some funds are required to be established by state law and by bond covenants. However, the city council establishes many other funds to help it control and manage money for particular purposes (like the Route 7 reconstruction project) or to show that it is meeting legal responsibilities for using certain taxes, grants, and other money (such as grants received from the U.S. Department of Housing and Urban Development). The City's two kinds of funds—*governmental and proprietary*—use different accounting approaches.

- Governmental funds—Most of the City's basic services are reported in governmental funds, which focus on how money flows into and out of those funds and the balances left at year-end that are available for spending. These funds are reported using an accounting method called modified accrual accounting, which measures cash and all other financial assets that can readily be converted to cash. The

Illustration 17-3 *(continued)*

governmental fund statements provide a detailed short-term view of the City's general government operations and the basic services it provides. Governmental fund information helps you determine whether there are more or fewer financial resources that can be spent in the near future to finance the City's programs. We describe the relationship (or differences) between governmental activities (reported in the statement of net assets and the statement of activities) and governmental funds in a reconciliation at the bottom of the fund financial statements.

- Proprietary funds—When the City charges customers for the services it provides—whether to outside customers or to other units of the City—these services are generally reported in proprietary funds. Proprietary funds are reported in the same way that all activities are reported in the statement of net assets and the statement of activities. In fact, the City's enterprise funds (a component of proprietary funds) are the same as the business-type activities we report in the government-wide statements but provide more detail and additional information, such as cash flows, for proprietary funds. We use internal service funds (the other component of proprietary funds) to report activities that provide supplies and services for the City's other programs and activities—such as the City's Telecommunications Fund.

The City as Trustee

Reporting the City's Fiduciary Responsibilities

The City is the trustee, or fiduciary, for its employees' pension plans. It is also responsible for other assets that—because of a trust arrangement—can be used only for the trust beneficiaries. All of the City's fiduciary activities are reported in separate statements of fiduciary net assets and changes in fiduciary net assets on pages 987 and 988 (Illustrations 17-9 and 17-10). We exclude these activities from the City's other financial statements because the City cannot use these assets to finance its operations. The City is responsible for ensuring that the assets reported in these funds are used for their intended purposes.

The City as a Whole

The City's combined net assets were virtually unchanged from a year ago—increasing from $209.0 million to $209.1 million. In contrast, last year net assets decreased by $6.2 million. Looking at the net assets and net expenses of governmental and business-type activities separately, however, reveals two very different stories. Our analysis below focuses on the net assets (Table 1) of the City's governmental and business-type activities.

Table 1
Net Assets
(in millions)

	Governmental Activities		Business-Type Activities		Total Primary Government	
	20X2	20X1	20X2	20X1	20X2	20X1
Current and other assets	$ 54.3	$ 49.0	$ 13.8	$ 15.7	$ 68.1	$ 64.7
Capital assets	170.0	162.1	151.4	147.6	321.4	309.7
Total assets	$ 224.3	$211.1	$165.2	$163.3	$ 389.5	$ 374.4
Long-term debt outstanding	$ (79.3)	$ (61.8)	$ (78.3)	$ (77.3)	$(157.6)	$(139.1)
Other liabilities	(21.4)	(22.6)	(1.4)	(3.7)	(22.8)	(26.3)
Total liabilities	$(100.7)	$ (84.4)	$ (79.7)	$ (81.0)	$(180.4)	$(165.4)
Net assets:						
Invested in capital assets, net of debt	$ 103.7	$100.3	$ 73.1	$ 71.6	$ 176.8	$ 171.9
Restricted	22.8	27.1	1.4	2.8	24.2	29.9
Unrestricted (deficit)	(2.9)	(0.7)	11.0	7.9	8.1	7.2
Total net assets	$ 123.6	$126.7	$ 85.5	$ 82.3	$ 209.1	$ 209.0

Illustration 17-3 *(concluded)*

Net assets of the City's governmental activities decreased by 2.5% ($123.6 million compared to $126.7 million). Unrestricted net assets—the part of net assets that can be used to finance day-to-day operations without constraints established by debt covenants, enabling legislation, or other legal requirements—changed from a $700,000 deficit at December 31, 20X1, to a $2.9 million deficit at the end of this year.

This deficit in unrestricted governmental net assets arose primarily because of three factors. First, the City did not include in past annual budgets the amounts needed to fully finance liabilities arising from property and casualty claims. The City does not purchase commercial insurance to cover these claims. The City also did not include in past budgets amounts needed to pay for unused employee vacation and sick days. The City will need to include these amounts in future years' budgets as they come due. Second, during the past two years, tax revenues and state grants have fallen short of amounts originally anticipated. Finally, the city council decided to draw down accumulated cash balances to delay the need to approve new tax increases.

The net assets of our business-type activities increased by 3.9% ($85.5 million compared to $82.3 million) in 20X2. This increase, however, cannot be used to make up for the decrease reported in governmental activities. The City generally can only use these net assets to finance the continuing operations of the water and sewer and parking operations.

Source: Government Accounting Standards Board Statement No. 34, *Basic Financial Statements—and Management's Discussion and Analysis—for State and Local Government*, June 1999, Appendix C.

Funds-Based Statements

The focus in the funds-based statements is to provide detailed information about short-term spending and fiscal compliance by major funds. Separate funds-based statements for governmental, proprietary, and fiduciary funds are required. The statements highlight *major* funds and aggregate nonmajor funds into one column. The general fund is always considered a major fund. Other major funds are defined as those in which assets, liabilities, revenues, or expenditures/expenses are at least 10% of all funds in that category or type (i.e., all governmental *or* all enterprise funds, respectively), *and* the same element is also at least 5% of all government and enterprise funds combined. In addition, a government may designate as major any other governmental or enterprise fund it believes is important to the users of its financial statements. This gives government officials great latitude in deciding how data are presented in the statements to promote better understanding of its activities and financial health.

Illustrations 17-4 and 17-5 (shown on pages 980 to 982) show examples of a governmental funds balance sheet and a governmental funds statement of revenues, expenditures, and changes in fund balances. Following a separate column for the general fund and each major fund, the remaining nonmajor funds are added together into one column, and the final column presents a total of all governmental funds. Note that the nonmajor funds are included in the column titled *Other Governmental Funds* and that the fund balance includes special revenue, debt service, capital project, and permanent fund information, as described in Chapter 16 after adjusting out the major fund balances.

Proprietary funds statements will include enterprise funds and internal service funds. Enterprise funds that meet the percentage test described previously will be presented individually. A column that summarizes all nonmajor enterprise funds is included, and a total for all enterprise funds is provided. The enterprise funds are labeled as *business-type activities*. A major change in GASB Statement No. 34 is to classify internal service funds as proprietary funds in the funds-based statements but report them in a separate column because their services usually are provided predominantly to general government activities. Also, internal service funds are not presented as major funds; hence, there will only be one column totaling all internal service fund activity. All internal service funds will also be labeled *governmental activities*.

Illustrations 17-6 and 17-7 (shown on pages 982 to 984) present the proprietary funds balance sheet and the statement of revenues, expenses, and changes in fund net assets, respectively.

Illustration 17-4
City of Berryville
Balance Sheet
Governmental Funds
December 31, 20X2

	General Fund	Housing Program	Community Block Grants	Highway Fund	Other Governmental Funds	Total Governmental Funds
Assets:						
Cash and cash equivalents	$ 40,000	$12,400			$ 55,000	$107,400
Investments	—	—	$13,500	$ 75,000	35,000	123,500
Receivables, net	37,400	29,500	35,500	51,000	1,500	154,900
Due from other funds	15,900		—	—		15,900
Receivables from other governments		12,000	—	—	16,000	28,000
Liens receivable	79,000	32,000	—	—	—	111,000
Inventories	18,500	—	—	—	—	18,500
Total assets	$190,800	$85,900	$49,000	$126,000	$107,500	$559,200
Liabilities and fund balances:						
Liabilities:						
Accounts payable	$ 32,400	$13,000	$ 9,000	$ 11,000	$ 12,000	$ 77,400
Due to other funds	—	2,400	—	—	—	2,400
Payable to other governments	9,400	—	—	—	—	9,400
Deferred revenue	41,000	6,300	15,000	51,000	—	113,300
Total liabilities	$ 82,800	$21,700	$24,000	$ 62,000	$ 12,000	$202,500
Fund balances:						
Reserved for:						
Inventories	$ 18,500		$ —	$ —	$ —	$ 18,500
Liens receivable	79,000		—	—	—	79,000
Encumbrances	4,100	$ 4,200	12,000	38,000	18,000	76,300
Debt services			—	—	38,000	38,000
Other purposes			—	—	14,000	14,000
Unreserved, reported in:			—	—	—	—
General fund	6,400		—	—	—	6,400
Special revenue funds		60,000	—	—	13,000	73,000
Capital projects funds	—	—	13,000	26,000	12,500	51,500
Total fund balances	$108,000	$64,200	$25,000	$ 64,000	$ 95,500	$356,700
Total liabilities and fund balances	$190,800	$85,900	$49,000	$126,000	$107,500	$559,200

Total fund balances—Governmental funds	$ 356,700
Amounts reported for governmental funds in statement of net assets are different because:	
Capital assets used in governmental activities are not financial resources and are not reported in the funds.	235,000
Other long-term assets not available to pay for current-period expenditures are deferred in the funds.	102,800
Internal service funds assets and liabilities are included in governmental activities in the statement of net assets. (Illustrations 17-13 and 17-15)	10,100*
Long-term liabilities, including bonds payable, are not reported in the funds.	(135,600)
Net assets of governmental activities	$ 569,000

*See Illustration 17-7 (Internal service funds, Total net assets—ending)

Source: Adapted from GASB 34, Appendix C.

Illustration 17-5
City of Berryville
Statement of Revenues, Expenditures, and Changes in Fund Balances
Governmental Funds
For Year Ended December 31, 20X2

	General Fund	Housing Program	Community Block Grants	Highway Fund	Other Governmental Funds	Total Governmental Funds
Revenues:						
Property taxes	$ 52,000	$ —	$ —	$ —	$ 47,000	$ 99,000
Franchise taxes	40,000	—	—	—		40,000
Public service taxes	90,000	—	—	—	—	90,000
Fees and fines	41,000	—	—	—	—	41,000
Licenses and permits	12,000	—	—	—	—	12,000
Intergovernmental	52,000	24,900	—	—	28,000	104,900
Charges for services	9,000	—	—	—	103,100	112,100
Investment earnings	55,000	37,000	35,000	27,200	36,500	190,700
Miscellaneous	88,000	52,000	—	3,000	100	143,100
Total revenues	$439,000	$113,900	$ 35,000	$30,200	$214,700	$ 832,800
Expenditures:						
Current:						
General government	$ 85,000	$ —	$ 22,500	$16,700	$ 11,500	$ 135,700
Public safety	42,000	—	—			42,000
Public works	49,000	—	—		37,500	86,500
Engineering services	13,000	—	—	—	—	13,000
Health and sanitation	61,000	—	—	—	—	61,000
Cemetery	70,000	—	—	—	—	70,000
Culture and recreation	11,000	—	—	—	—	11,000
Community development	—	29,500	—	—	—	29,500
Education—payment to school district	22,000	—	—	—	—	22,000
Debt service			—			
Principal	—	—	—	—	34,500	34,500
Interest and other charges	—	—	—	—	52,700	52,700
Capital outlay	—	—	22,500	11,500	32,000	66,000
Total expenditures	$353,000	$ 29,500	$ 45,000	$28,200	$168,200	$ 623,900
Excess (deficiency) of revenues over expenditure	$ 86,000	$ 84,400	$(10,000)	$ 2,000	$ 46,500	$ 208,900
Other financing sources (uses):						
Proceeds of refunding bonds	$ —	$ —	$ —	$ —	$ 38,000	$ 38,000
Proceeds of long-term capital-related debt	—	—	37,500	—	15,000	52,500
Payment to bond refunding escrow	—	—	—	—	(38,000)	(38,000)
Transfer-in	53,000	—	—	—	78,000	131,000
Transfer-out	(71,000)	(35,000)	(22,500)	—	(22,000)	(150,500)
Total other financing sources and uses	$ (18,000)	$ (35,000)	$ 15,000	$ —	$ 71,000	$ 33,000
Special item:						
Proceeds from sales in park	$ 34,750	$ —	$ —	$ —	$ —	$ 34,750
Net change in fund balances	$102,750	$ 49,400	$ 5,000	$ 2,000	$117,500	$ 276,650
Fund balances—beginning	5,250	14,800	20,000	62,000	(22,000)	80,050
Fund balances—ending	$108,000	$ 64,200	$ 25,000	$64,000	$ 95,500	$ 356,700

Source: Adapted from GASB 34, Appendix C.

(continued)

Illustration 17-5 *(continued)*
City of Berryville
Reconcilation of the Statement of Revenues, Expenditures, and
Changes in Fund Balances of Governmental Funds to the Statement of Activities
For Year Ended December 31, 20X2

Net change in fund balances—total governmental funds	$ 276,650
Amounts reported for governmental activities in the statement of activities are different because:	
In governmental funds, capital outlays are expenditures.	
However, in the statement of activities, depreciation expense is recorded. Necessary adjustment—the amount by which capital outlay exceeds depreciation.	36,000
In the statement of activities, only the gain on the sale of the park land is reported.	
In governmental funds, the proceeds from the sale increase financial resources. Necessary adjustment—the cost of the land sold.	7,750
Revenues in the statement of activities that do not provide current financial resources are not reported as revenues in the funds.	125,000
Bond proceeds provide current financial resources to governmental funds, but issuing debt increases long-term liabilities in the statement of net assets. Repayment of bond principal is an expenditure in the governmental funds, but the repayment reduces long-term liabilities in the statement of net assets. Necessary adjustment—amount of proceeds less repayments.	56,000
Some expenses reported in the statement of activities do not require the use of current financial resources and therefore are not reported as expenditures in governmental funds.	(116,300)
The net revenue (expense) of the internal service funds is reported with governmental activities.	(122,500)
Change in net assets of governmental activities (see Illustration 17-14)	$ 262,600

Source: Adapted from GASB 34, Appendix C.

Illustration 17-6
City of Berryville
Balance Sheet
Proprietary Funds
December 31, 20X2

	Business-Type Activities Enterprise Funds			Governmental Activities
	Electric Utility	City Bus	Totals	Internal Service Funds
Assets:				
Current assets:				
Cash	$ 94,000	$ 57,000	$151,000	$ 24,000
Investments	—	—	—	15,000
Receivables, net	46,000	2,500	48,500	16,000
Due from other governments	4,000	—	4,000	—
Inventories	13,000	—	13,000	14,000
Total current assets	$157,000	$ 59,500	$216,500	$ 69,000

(continued)

Illustration 17-6 *(continued)*

	Business-Type Activities Enterprise Funds			Governmental Activities
	Electric Utility	City Bus	Totals	Internal Service Funds
Assets *(continued)*:				
Noncurrent assets:				
Restricted cash and cash equivalents	$ —	$ 25,000	$ 25,000	$ —
Capital assets:			—	
Land	81,000	100,000	181,000	—
Distribution and collection systems	49,500	—	49,500	—
Buildings and equipment	14,500	40,000	54,500	87,800
Less accumulated depreciation	(15,500)	(30,000)	(45,500)	(27,800)
Total noncurrent assets	$129,500	$135,000	$264,500	$ 60,000
Total assets	$286,500	$194,500	$481,000	$129,000
Liabilities:				
Current liabilities:				
Accounts payable	$ 35,000	$ 1,000	$ 36,000	$ 8,000
Due to other funds	17,500	—	17,500	—
Compensated absences	11,500	4,500	16,000	13,500
Claims and judgments	—	—	—	8,000
Bonds, notes, and loans payable	39,000	16,000	55,000	25,000
Total current liabilities	$103,000	$ 21,500	$124,500	$ 54,500
Noncurrent liabilities:				
Compensated absences	$ 45,000	$ 15,000	$ 60,000	$ 10,000
Claims and judgments	—	8,000	8,000	14,400
Bonds, notes, and loans payable	54,500	29,500	84,000	40,000
Total noncurrent liabilities	$ 99,500	$ 52,500	$152,000	$ 64,400
Total liabilities	$202,500	$ 74,000	$276,500	$118,900
Net assets:				
Invested in capital assets, net of related debt	$ 73,000	$ 95,000	$168,000	$ 47,000
Restricted for debt service	—	15,000	15,000	—
Unrestricted	11,000	10,500	21,500	(36,900)
Total net assets	$ 84,000	$120,500	$204,500[a]	$ 10,100[b]
Total liabilities and net assets	$286,500	$194,500	$481,000	$129,000

[a]Although internal service funds are classified as proprietary funds, they account for governmental activities and are reported separately from the proprietary funds that account for business-type activities. Information in the Totals column on this statement flows directly to the Business-Type Activities column on the statement of net assets (see Illustration 17-13).
[b]Information in the Internal Service Funds column is combined with other governmental activities in Illustration 17-13.

Source: Adapted from GASB 34, Appendix C.

Illustration 17-7
City of Berryville
Statement of Revenues, Expenses, and Changes in Fund Net Assets
Proprietary Fund
For Year Ended December 31, 20X2

	Business-Type Activities Enterprise Funds			Governmental Activities
	Electric Utility	City Bus	Totals	Internal Service Funds
Operating revenues:				
Charges for services	$110,500	$ 53,000	$163,500	$ 15,000
Miscellaneous	—	3,800	3,800	11,000
Total operating revenues	$110,500	$ 56,800	$167,300	$ 26,000
Operating expenses:				
Personal services	$ 24,000	$ 7,500	$ 31,500	$ 42,000
Contractual services	25,000	9,500	34,500	58,000
Utilities	—	10,000	10,000	21,500
Repairs and maintenance	14,000	6,500	20,500	19,500
Other supplies and expenses	50,000	1,500	51,500	23,000
Insurance claims and expenses	—	—	—	8,000
Depreciation	11,500	5,400	16,900	17,000
Total operating expenses	$124,500	$ 40,400	$164,900	$ 189,000
Operating income (loss)	$ (14,000)	$ 16,400	$ 2,400	$(163,000)
Nonoperating revenues (expenses):				
Interest and investment revenue	$ 45,000	$ 15,000	$ 60,000	$ 13,500
Miscellaneous revenue	—	10,000	10,000	2,000
Interest expense	(16,000)	(11,000)	(27,000)	(4,000)
Miscellaneous expense	—	(8,500)	(8,500)	(17,500)
Total nonoperating revenue (expenses)	$ 29,000	$ 5,500	$ 34,500	$ (6,000)
Income (loss) before contributions and transfers	$ 15,000	$ 21,900	$ 36,900	$(169,000)
Capital contributions	$ 16,500	$ —	$ 16,500	$ 18,000
Transfers-out	(12,500)	(1,000)	(13,500)	(17,500)
Change in net assets	$ 19,000	$ 20,900	$ 39,900	$(168,500)
Total net assets—beginning	65,000	99,600	164,600	158,400
Total net assets—ending	$ 84,000	$120,500	$204,500	$ (10,100)

Source: Adapted from GASB 34, Appendix C.

Note that in the net assets section of the balance sheet, there is a significant change in the classification of proprietary fund equity. Under the new standards, equity (or net assets) of a proprietary fund will be classified into three broad components:

1. *Invested in capital (fixed) assets, net of related debt*—This amount includes the fixed assets of the fund less all fixed asset-related debt (both current and long-term).
2. *Restricted*—This amount includes the difference between assets externally restricted by creditors, grantors, donors, or laws and regulations of other governments or internally restricted by constitutional provisions or enabling legislation and any liabilities payable from these restricted assets.

3. *Unrestricted*—This amount includes the difference between the remaining assets and liabilities in the fund as well as reclassified restricted assets when the government has satisfied the restriction.

In order to determine if the government's business-type activities have met their cash needs during the year and show how they have been met, a statement of cash flows is also required (see Illustration 17-8 on pages 985 and 986). All governments report their cash flows in four categories. *Operating cash flows* from basic operating purposes are reported first. Most of these cash flows are related to the provision of services and the production and sale of goods. *Cash flows from financing activities* are broken down into (a) *cash flows from noncapital financing* which relate to borrowing for purposes other than buying or constructing capital assets and to certain grants and subsidies to and from other governments and (b) *capital and related financing cash flows* from borrowing and repaying funds for the purposes of purchasing, building, or reconstructing capital assets and selling capital assets and aid received from other levels of government to finance capital. Finally, *investing cash flows* relate to the acquisition and sale of investments, loan of money, and collection on loans. Almost all of the receipts in this category are interest and dividends from investments. All enterprise and internal service fund activities report cash flows. The *direct method* of presentation of cash flows from operations is *required*. In addition, major enterprise funds are reported in separate columns.

Fiduciary funds are presented using a format similar to the guidance in the pension standards (see Chapter 16, pages 938 and 939). Fiduciary funds are used to account for resources the government holds while acting as the trustee or agent for an outside individual or organization as defined in Chapter 16. The two required statements for the fiduciary funds, the statement of fiduciary net assets and the statement of changes in fiduciary net assets, are shown in Illustrations 17-9 and 17-10.

Illustration 17-8
City of Berryville
Statement of Cash Flows
Proprietary Fund
For Year Ended December 31, 20X2

	Business-Type Activities Enterprise Funds			Governmental Activities
	Electric Utility	City Bus	Totals	Internal Service Funds
Cash flows from operating activities:				
Receipts from customers	$ 50,000	$ 43,000	$ 93,000	$ 13,000
Payments to suppliers	(27,000)	(26,000)	(53,000)	(10,000)
Payments to employees	(33,000)	(50,000)	(83,000)	(15,000)
Internal activity—payments	(12,000)	—	(12,000)	—
Claims paid	—	—	—	(35,000)
Other receipts (payments)	30,000	—	30,000	15,000
Net cash provided by operating activities	$ 8,000	$(33,000)	$ (25,000)	$ (32,000)
Cash flows from noncapital and related financing activities:				
Operating subsidies and transfers to other funds	$(12,500)	$ (1,000)	$ (13,500)	$ (15,000)

(continued)

Illustration 17-8 *(continued)*

	Business-Type Activities Enterprise Funds			Governmental Activities
	Electric Utility	City Bus	Totals	Internal Service Funds
Cash flows from capital and related financing activities:				
Proceeds from capital debt	$ 40,000	$ 85,000	$125,000	$ 25,000
Capital contributions	16,500	—	16,500	14,000
Purchases of capital assets	(30,000)	(14,000)	(44,000)	(20,000)
Principal paid on capital debt	(20,000)	(50,000)	(70,000)	(20,000)
Interest paid on capital debt	(15,000)	(10,000)	(25,000)	(4,000)
Other receipts (payments)	—	2,000	2,000	34,000
Net cash (used) by capital and related financing activities	$ (8,500)	$ 13,000	$ 4,500	$ 29,000
Cash flows from investing activities:				
Proceeds from sales and maturates of investments	$ 25,000	$ 15,000	$ 40,000	$ 2,000
Net cash provided by investing activities	$ 25,000	$ 15,000	$ 40,000	$ 2,000
Net (decrease) in cash and cash equivalents	$ 12,000	$ (6,000)	$ 6,000	$ (16,000)
Balances—beginning of the year	82,000	63,000	145,000	40,000
Balances—end of the year	$ 94,000	$ 57,000	$151,000	$ 24,000
Reconciliation of operating income (loss) to net cash provided (used) by operating activities:				
Operating income (loss)	$ 9,000	$ 27,200	$ 36,200	$(163,000)
Adjustments to reconcile operating income to net cash provided (used) by operating activities:				
Depreciation expense	9,000	5,000	14,000	17,000
Change in assets and liabilities:		2,000	2,000	
Receivables, net	64,500	800	65,300	58,000
Inventories	500	—	500	60,000
Accounts and other payables	(30,000)	(55,000)	(85,000)	(2,000)
Accrued expenses	(45,000)	(13,000)	(58,000)	(2,000)
Net cash provided by operating activities	$ 8,000	$(33,000)	$ (25,000)	$ (32,000)

Source: Adapted from GASB 34, Appendix C.

Illustration 17-11 summarizes the measurement focus and basis of accounting and financial statement requirements for each fund type.

The most notable features of the funds statements are in the format (column titles) being given by major fund rather than by fund type; the use of separate statements for governmental, proprietary, and fiduciary funds; and the presentation of equity in the proprietary fund balance sheet. Other highlights include:

- As detailed in Chapter 16, permanent funds account for assets legally restricted so that the earnings, but not the principal, may be used to finance governmental programs.
- General fixed assets, including infrastructure assets, and general long-term debt are included only in the government-wide financial statements. A schedule is required for general fixed assets detailing the beginning balances—followed by additions, deductions,

Illustration 17-9
City of Berryville
Statement of Fiduciary Net Assets
Fiduciary Funds
December 31, 20X2

	Employee Retirement Plan	Private-Purpose Trust	Agency Funds
Assets:			
Cash and cash equivalents	$ 2,000	$ 1,250	$ 4,500
Receivables:			
Interest and dividends	$ 51,000	$ 700	$ —
Other receivables	7,000	—	18,000
Total receivables	$ 58,000	$ 700	$18,000
Investments, at fair value:			
U.S. government obligations	$ 13,000	$80,000	$ —
Municipal bonds	65,000	—	—
Corporate bonds	16,000	—	—
Corporate stocks	26,000	—	—
Other investments	32,000	—	—
Total investments	$152,000	$80,000	$ —
Total assets	$212,000	$81,950	$22,500
Liabilities:			
Accounts payable	$ —	$ 1,950	$ —
Refunds payable and others	1,000	—	22,500
Total liabilities	$ 1,000	$ 1,950	$22,500
Net assets:			
Held in trust for pension benefits and other purposes	$211,000	$80,000	

Source: Adapted from GASB 34, Appendix C.

and depreciation charged in the current period—to reconcile to the ending balance. A schedule is also required for general long-term debt to give information on beginning balances, new debt issued, debt principal retired, and ending balances.

- As indicated in Chapter 16, all interfund activity is classified as either reciprocal or nonreciprocal. Reciprocal interfund activities include (1) interfund loans, which are treated as due to/from (short-term) or advances to/from (long-term), and (2) interfund services between governmental and proprietary funds that are reported as revenue and expenditures/expenses. Nonreciprocal interfund activities include (1) interfund transfers and (2) interfund reimbursements. All transfers are reported in the government funds as "other financing sources or uses." And, in the proprietary funds, all transfers are reported simply as "transfers." Payments in lieu of taxes are classified as transfers. Extensive footnotes are required to provide users of the financial statements detailed information about the purpose and nature of these transfers and the funds affected.
- Special and extraordinary items are reported separately in both the governmental and proprietary fund financial statements. *Extraordinary items* are defined as in business accounting—both unusual in nature and infrequent in occurrence. *Special items* are defined as arising from significant transactions or other events that are (1) within the control of

Illustration 17-10
City of Berryville
Statement of Changes in Fiduciary Net Assets
Fiduciary Funds
December 31, 20X2

	Employee Retirement Plan	Private-Purpose Trust
Additions:		
Contributions:		
Employer	$ 47,000	$ —
Plan members	44,000	—
Total contributions	$ 91,000	$ —
Investment earnings:		
Net (decreased) in fair value of investments	$ (11,500)	$ —
Interest	95,000	4,500
Dividends	70,000	—
Total investment earnings	$153,500	$ 4,500
Less investment expense	15,000	—
Net investment earnings	$138,500	$ 4,500
Total additions	$229,500	$ 4,500
Deductions:		
Benefits	$ 24,500	$ 3,800
Refunds of contribution	46,000	—
Administrative expenses	9,000	700
Total deductions	$ 79,500	$ 4,500
Change in net assets	$150,000	$ —
Net assets—beginning of the year	61,000	80,000
Net assets—end of the year	$211,000	$80,000

Source: Adapted from GASB 34, Appendix C.

management and (2) either unusual in nature or infrequent in occurrence. Special items are reported separately and before extraordinary items. Footnote disclosure is required for any significant transactions or other events that are either unusual or infrequent but not within the control of management.

- Budgetary comparisons are required in either a separate statement or schedule as part of the integrated set of basic financial statements or as required supplementary information (RSI). Further, a column for the original budget as well as the final revised budget column must be included. The final budget is compared with actual amounts using the government's budgetary basis to determine compliance with the legally adopted budget. Budgetary comparisons are required for the general fund and for each annually budgeted major special revenue fund. Illustration 17-12 shows a budgetary comparison schedule for the city of Berryville general fund. No budgetary comparisons are required in the basic financial statements or RSI for any capital project, debt service, or permanent funds.

Illustration 17-11
Basic Financial Statements by Fund Category

Fund Category	Measurement Focus and Basis of Accounting	Basic Financial Statements
Governmental	Current financial resources, modified accrual	Balance sheet Statement of revenues, expenditures, and changes in fund balances
Proprietary	Economic resources, accrual	Balance sheet/statement of net assets Statement of revenues, expenses, and changes in fund net assets/fund equity Statement of cash flows
Fiduciary	Economic resources, accrual	Statement of fiduciary net assets Statement of changes in fiduciary net assets*

*Does not apply to agency funds.

Source: GASB Statement No. 34, *Basic Financial Statements—and Management's Discussion and Analysis—for State and Local Governments*, p. 151.

Illustration 17-12
City of Berryville
Budgetary Comparison Schedule
General Fund
For Year Ended December 31, 20X2

	Budgeted Amounts		Actual Amounts	Variance with Final Budget
	Original	Final	(Budgetary Basis)	Positive (Negative)
Budgetary fund balance, January 1	$ 5,250	$ 5,250	$ 5,250	$ —
Resources (inflows):				
Property taxes	52,000	51,800	52,000	(200)
Franchise taxes	45,000	42,000	40,000	2,000
Public service taxes	90,000	90,000	90,000	—
Licenses and permits	12,000	12,300	12,000	300
Fines and forfeitures	42,300	40,000	41,000	(1,000)
Charges for services	12,000	11,200	9,000	2,200
Grants	55,000	55,000	52,000	3,000
Sale of land	33,500	35,000	34,750	250
Miscellaneous	95,000	90,000	88,000	2,000
Interest received	48,000	50,000	55,000	(5,000)
Transfers from other funds	50,000	50,000	53,000	(3,000)
Amounts available for appropriation	$540,050	$532,550	$532,000	$ 550

(continued)

Illustration 17-12 (*continued*)

	Budgeted Amounts Original	Budgeted Amounts Final	Actual Amounts (Budgetary Basis)	Variance with Final Budget Positive (Negative)
Charges to appropriations (outflows)				
General government:				
Legal	$ 26,000	$ 26,000	$ 25,500	$ 500
Mayor, legislative, city manager	25,000	25,000	24,000	1,000
Finance and accounting	9,000	9,500	8,000	1,500
City clerk and elections	5,000	3,500	3,000	500
Employee relations	7,000	10,000	11,300	(1,300)
Planning and economic development	14,000	14,000	14,200	(200)
Public safety:				—
Police	11,000	10,000	10,500	(500)
Fire department	17,000	16,000	15,500	500
Emergency medical services	12,000	12,000	12,000	—
Inspections	5,000	5,000	5,000	—
Public works:				—
Public works administration	18,500	19,000	18,750	250
Street maintenance	11,500	11,000	11,250	(250)
Street lighting	7,000	7,200	7,500	(300)
Traffic operations	8,000	8,000	8,000	—
Mechanical maintenance	5,000	5,000	4,500	. 500
Engineering services:				
Engineering administration	5,700	5,500	6,000	(500)
Geographical information system	7,500	7,500	7,100	400
Health and sanitation:				—
Garbage pickup	60,000	61,000	61,500	(500)
Cemetery:				—
Personal services	41,500	41,000	41,000	—
Purchase of goods and services	29,950	30,000	29,500	500
Culture and recreations:				—
Library	2,800	3,000	2,750	250
Parks and recreation	5,200	5,000	5,250	(250)
Community communications	3,000	3,000	3,000	—
Nondepartmental:				—
Transfers to other funds	71,000	71,000	71,000	—
Funding for school district	22,000	22,000	22,000	—
Total charges to appropriation	$429,650	$430,200	$428,100	$ 2,100
Budgetary fund balance, December 31	$110,400	$102,350	$103,900	$(1,550)

Source: Adapted from GASB 34, Appendix C.

Government-Wide Financial Statements

The requirement for a government-wide set of financial statements prepared on an accrual basis has received much attention and resulted in a great deal of controversy. The required statements—a statement of net assets and a statement of activities—are shown in Illustrations 17-13 and 17-14. These statements have one column for governmental activities and one column for proprietary (business-type) activities. In addition, there is a total for the government as a whole. Discretely presented component units are also presented in a separate column.

The Statement of Net Assets

The statement of net assets in Illustration 17-13 includes all assets, such as infrastructure assets, and all liabilities of the government. The net assets (equity) are divided into three categories: unrestricted, restricted, and capital-related. The first column reports all assets and liabilities of general government activities, essentially on a consolidated basis and adjusted to reflect full accrual accounting.[4]

Illustration 17-13
City of Berryville
Statement of Net Assets
December 31, 20X2

	Primary Government			
	Governmental Activities	Business-Type Activities	Total	Component Units
Assets:				
Cash and cash equivalents	$131,400	$176,000	$ 307,400	$ 25,000
Investments	138,500	—	138,500	55,000
Receivable, net	255,000	48,500	303,500	30,000
Internal balances	13,500	(13,500)	—	—
Inventories	32,500	13,000	45,500	9,000
Capital assets, net	295,000	239,500	534,500	40,000
Total assets	$865,900	$463,500	$1,329,400	$159,000
Liabilities:				
Accounts payable	$ 85,400	$ 36,000	$ 121,400	$ 18,000
Deferred revenue	10,500	—	10,500	4,000
Noncurrent liabilities:				
Due within one year	58,000	55,000	113,000	15,000
Due in more than one year	143,000	168,000	311,000	28,000
Total liabilities	$296,900	$259,000	$ 555,900	$ 65,000
Net assets:				
Invested in capital assets, net of related debt	$198,000	$168,000	$ 366,000	$ 16,000
Restricted for:				
Capital projects	150,000	—	150,000	50,000
Debt service	100,000	15,000	115,000	—
Community development projects	85,000	—	85,000	—
Other purposes	65,000	—	65,000	—
Unrestricted (deficit)	(29,000)	21,500	(7,500)	28,000
Total net assets	$569,000*	$204,500	$ 773,500	$ 94,000

*As reported in Illustration 17-4 (Net assets of governmental activities) and Illustration 17-15. This includes the internal service funds.

Source: Adapted from GASB 34, Appendix C.

4 All FASB standards (and other business guidance) issued on or before November 30, 1989, that do not contradict GASB and predecessor body standards are to be applied to both governmental and business-type activities in the government-wide statements. FASB standards issued after 1989 are applied only to business-type activities if a government chooses the option to apply all subsequent FASB standards that do not conflict with GASB standards per GASB Statement No. 20.

The statement of net assets has several key characteristics, including the following:

- All capital assets are listed, including infrastructure assets.
- All capital assets are required to be depreciated. An exception for infrastructure assets is allowed if they are maintained in a condition that will result in an extended useful life. (See Chapter 16 for further discussion of the new requirements for infrastructure asset reporting.)
- General long-term liabilities are not recorded at face value but rather adjusted to reflect application of the effective interest method of accounting.
- Current and noncurrent liabilities are distinguished on the statement of net assets.
- Interfund payables and receivables between governmental funds are eliminated.
- Interfund payables and receivables between enterprise funds are eliminated.
- Net payables and receivables between governmental activities and business-type activities are shown separately as internal balances.

The Statement of Activities

The statement of activities shown in Illustration 17-14, on pages 994 to 995, is a very unique statement that begins with a reporting of expenses by program. Direct expenses and allocated indirect expenses are reported in the first two columns. Then, revenue, generated from grants, fees, fines, forfeitures, and appropriations that are specifically connected to a program, is reported. The balance in each program after subtracting the program revenue is then the amount of expenses that must be paid for by general governmental revenues (e.g., from taxes, unrestricted grants and appropriations, and other financing sources).

In the statement of activities, program revenues are reported in three classifications: *charges for services, program-specific operating and capital grants, and contributions.* These revenues are deducted from the expenses of the related function or program. All revenues that are not program revenues are classified as general revenues.

Expenses, not expenditures, are reported for governmental activities in the government-wide statement of activities. Expenses include depreciation of general fixed assets, such as infrastructure assets, interest measured using the effective interest method, compensated absences, claims and judgments, pension accruals, and other changes in long-term liabilities. Expenses do not include capital outlay expenditures and debt principal retirement expenditures.

As discussed in Chapter 16 (page 933), internal service funds provide goods or services to other departments or agencies of the government. The charges to the user departments are set to reimburse for actual costs of running the internal service operation. Thus, internal service funds may be thought of as a cost allocation mechanism used by a government to allocate common costs to various activities or functions. Recognizing this relationship, the assets, liabilities, and net assets of an internal service fund are included in the governmental activities column in the government-wide statements. Further, in developing the government-wide financial statements, internal service fund revenues and expenses are eliminated (similar to a business parent company and subsidiary consolidation). Any differential between revenues and expenses (e.g., profit) is eliminated by reducing the expenses for internal service fund services that are charged to the various functions in the government-wide statements.

A controversial and challenging aspect of GASB Statement No. 34 for many governments is the requirement to report infrastructure assets. Most governments do not currently record or report their general infrastructure fixed assets. Most governments will also have difficulty implementing the necessary record-keeping involved in applying traditional fixed asset accounting and reporting of infrastructure assets such as streets, roads, sidewalks, curbs, storm sewers, and bridges. In recognition of this difficulty, the GASB included several special provisions in Statement No. 34 for infrastructure assets. They include the following:

1. Delaying by four years the effective date for retroactive reporting (for years beginning after June 15, 2005) to allow governments time to inventory and assign costs to their infrastructure fixed assets.
2. Allowing various approaches to estimating infrastructure cost, including using price-level adjusted current replacement costs to estimate historical costs at implementation.

3. Allowing prospective-only application for small governments.
4. Limiting the requirement to major infrastructure fixed assets (defined as a network or subsystem) acquired after 1981 so that all larger governments have to include 25 years of data.
5. Permitting a *modified approach* to measuring the cost of using infrastructure assets that allows governments to avoid reporting depreciation expense. As indicated in Chapter 16, a government is permitted to use a modified approach if it can demonstrate that the eligible infrastructure assets are being preserved at or above a condition level established by the government. Under the modified "preservation" approach, all costs to maintain the assets are expensed and no depreciation is recorded. However, if a government stops maintaining the infrastructure at the target condition level, the government must depreciate those assets. A change from the depreciation method to the modified approach should be reported as a change in accounting estimate, i.e., similar to a change in service life from finite to infinite.

Converting Funds-Based Statements to Government-Wide Statements

Since the information necessary to prepare the fund financial statements and the government-wide statements is different, a reconciliation from the funds-based to the government-wide statements is required on the face of the funds-based statements. This reconciliation is necessary to convert from the modified accrual basis of accounting and the detail of fund accounting to the full accrual and summarized government-wide statements. It is quite easy to convert the business-type activities from the total enterprise funds column of the fund financial statements to the government-wide statements. The most common difference is that the government-wide statement of activities must present operating data by function (or program) and use a format that differs considerably from the proprietary funds statement of revenues, expenses, and changes in fund equity. Also, interfund payables and receivables must be eliminated, and internal balances from nonenterprise funds must be identified. In addition, the assets and liabilities of internal service funds whose primary customers are enterprise funds are aggregated with the enterprise fund data in the business-type activity column. The expenses reported in the statement of activities for business-type activities must also be adjusted to eliminate the net increase or decrease in internal service net assets.

Conversion from the funds-based governmental funds statements to the aggregated governmental activities in the government-wide statements is much more complex. Steps in this conversion include the following:

1. To convert the governmental fund balance sheet to the government-wide statement of net assets:

   - Add general fixed assets, including infrastructure fixed assets, net of accumulated depreciation.
   - Add general long-term debt, measured at the appropriate carrying amount, using the effective interest method.
   - Add the assets and liabilities of most internal service funds (those whose primary customer is the general government).
   - Adjust assets and liabilities from the current financial resources measurement focus to an economic resources measurement focus.
   - Eliminate the fund balance and classify net assets as invested in capital assets, restricted net assets, and unrestricted net assets.

Assuming a government continues to use the account groups to track capital assets and long-term liabilities, a schedule such as the one in Illustration 17-15 will assist in the conversion.

2. To convert the governmental fund statement of revenues, expenditures, and changes in fund balances to the government-wide statement of activities:

   - Eliminate other financing sources for general long-term debt proceeds.
   - Eliminate capital outlay expenditures.
   - Eliminate expenditures or other financing uses for debt principal retirement.
   - Record depreciation expense or maintenance/preservation costs and allocate the expenses to functions or programs.
   - Convert revenues from the flow of current financial resources modified accrual basis to the flow of economic resources accrual basis.

Illustration 17-14
City of Berryville
Statement of Activities
For Year Ended December 31, 20X2

			Program Revenues			Net (Expense) Revenue Changes in Net Assets			
						Primary Government			
	Expenses	Indirect Expenses Allocation	Charges for Services	Operating Grants and Contributions	Capital Grants and Contributions	Governmental Activities	Business-Type Activities	Total	Component Units
Functions/programs:									
Governmental activities:									
General government	$175,000	$(56,000)	$ 3,000	$24,000	$ —	$ (92,000)	$ —	$ —	$ —
Public safety	35,000	40,500	12,000	13,000	6,000	(44,500)	—	(44,500)	—
Public works	90,000	33,000	25,000	—	22,500	(75,500)	—	(75,500)	—
Engineering services	22,000	11,200	20,000	—	—	(13,200)	—	(13,200)	—
Health and sanitation	68,000	56,000	26,000	27,500	—	(70,500)	—	(70,500)	—
Cemetery	73,000		22,000	—	—	(51,000)	—	(51,000)	—
Culture and recreation	11,500	18,500	10,000	14,500	—	(5,500)	—	(5,500)	—
Community development	30,000	17,500	—		25,800	(21,700)	—	(21,700)	—
Education (payment to school district)	22,000		—	—	—	(22,000)	—	(22,000)	—
Interest on long-term debt	61,000	(61,000)	—	—	—	—	—	—	—
Total governmental activities	$ 587,500	$ 59,700	$118,000	$79,000	$54,300	$(395,900)	$ —	$(303,900)	$ —
Business-type activities:									
Electric utility	$ 117,500		$110,500	$ —	$16,500	$ —	$ 9,500	$ 9,500	$ —
City bus	49,100		53,000	—	—	—	3,900	3,900	—
Total business-type activities	$ 166,600		$163,500	$ —	$16,500	$ —	$ 13,400	$ 13,400	$ —
Total primary government	$ 754,100		$281,500	$79,000	$70,800	$(395,900)	$ 13,400	$(290,500)	$ —
Component units:									
Landfill	$ 33,000		$ 28,000	$ —	$11,000	$ —	$ —	$ —	$ 6,000
Public school system	110,000		25,000	39,000	—	—	—	—	(46,000)
Total component	$ 143,000		$ 53,000	$39,000	$11,000	$ —	$ —	$ —	$(40,000)

(continued below)

General revenues:				
Taxes:				
Property taxes, levied for general purposes	$ 52,000	$ —	$ 52,000	$ —
Property taxes, levied for debt service	47,000	—	47,000	—
Franchise taxes	40,000	—	40,000	—
Public service taxes	90,000	—	90,000	—
Payment from city of Berryville	—	—	—	22,000
Grant and contributions not restricted to specific programs	14,600	—	14,600	25,000
Investment earnings	231,200	13,800	245,000	38,000
Miscellaneous	143,200	60,000	203,200	2,000
Special item—gain on sale of park land	27,000	—	27,000	—
Transfers	13,500	(13,500)	—	—
Total general revenues, special items, and transers	$ 658,500	$ 60,300	$ 718,800	$ 87,000
Change in net assets	$ 262,600[a]	$ 73,700	$ 336,300	$ 47,000
Net assets—beginning	306,400	130,800	437,200	47,000
Net assets—ending	$ 569,000	$204,500[b]	$ 773,500	$ 94,000

[a]As reported in the Illustration 17-5 reconciliation.
[b]As reported in Illustration 17-6 (Total business-type activities, totals column, total net assets).

Source: Adapted from GASB 34, Appendix C.

Illustration 17-15—Explanation of Differences between Governmental Funds Balance Sheet and the Statement of Net Assets

Total fund balances of the City's governmental fund ($356,700) differ from "net assets" of governmental activities ($569,000) reported in the statement of net assets. This difference primarily results from the long-term economic focus of the statement of net assets versus the current financial resources focus of the governmental fund balance sheets.

Balance Sheet/Statement of Net Assets

	Total Governmental Funds	Total Account Group Balances[a]	Reclassifications & Eliminations Debit	Reclassifications & Eliminations Credit	Internal Services Funds[b]	Statement of Net Assets Total
Assets:						
Cash and cash equivalents	$107,400		$ —		$ 24,000	$131,400
Investments	123,500	$ —	—		15,000	138,500
Receivables, net	154,900	—	84,100		16,000	255,000
Due from other funds	15,900	—	—	$ 2,400	—	13,500
Due from other governments	28,000	—	—	28,000	—	—
Liens receivable	111,000	—	—	111,000	—	—
Inventories	18,500	—	—	—	14,000	32,500
Capital assets, net of accumulated depreciation		235,000	—	—		235,000
Amount to be provided		100,000	—	100,000		—
Amount available	—	35,600	—	35,600	60,000	60,000
Total assets	$559,200	$370,600			$129,000	$865,900
Liabilities:						
Accounts payable	$ 77,400		—		$ 8,000	$ 85,400
Due to other funds	2,400		2,400		—	—
Due to the governments	9,400		9,400			—
Deferred revenue	113,300		102,800		—	10,500
Long-term liabilities		$135,600	45,500		110,900	201,000
Total liabilities	$202,500	$135,600			$118,900	$296,900
Fund balances/net assets:						
Investment in general fixed assets		$235,000	235,000			$ —
Total fund balance	$356,700		356,700	—	$ —	—
Net assets						
Capital assets, net of related debt			90,100	235,000		144,900
Restricted				56,700		56,700
Unrestricted			—	357,300	10,100	367,400
Total net assets			$926,000	$926,000	$ 10,100	$569,000

[a]Capital assets and capital long-term debt are recorded in account groups. These balances need to be added to the other assets and liabilities in the government-wide statement of net assets. The net of these balances is termed "capital assets, net of related debt." Several receivables are offset by deferred revenue in the governmental funds and are not included in the fund balance. A conversion to full accrual accounting will increase the amount recognized as revenue in the statement of activities and increase the net assets, usually unrestricted, in the statement of net assets. Adjustments are also necessary to report all liabilities—both current and long-term—in the statement of net assets.

Source: Adapted from GASB 34, Appendix C.

[b]Internal service funds are included in governmental activities in the statement of net assets.

- Reclassify revenues as either program revenues or general revenues.
- Convert interest expenditures to interest expense by adjusting for interest accruals, amortization of premium/discount, bond issue costs, and deferred interest adjustments.
- Record bad debts expense.
- Convert other expenditures to expenses, i.e., compensated absences, pension, claims and judgments, landfill closure and postclosure care, and postretirement benefits other than pensions.
- Convert special items and extraordinary items to the economic resources measurement focus and accrual basis of accounting.

An example of a schedule to convert from the statement of revenues, expenditures, and changes in fund balances to the statement of activities is shown in Illustration 17-16.

REPORTING AND AUDITING IMPLEMENTATION AND ISSUES

4

OBJECTIVE

Tell when GASB Statement No. 34 took effect, list the requirements of the Single Audit Act, and describe what other reporting efforts the GASB has been encouraging.

Statement No. 34 represents a dramatic shift in the way state and local governments present financial information to the public. In a June 10, 1999, news release, GASB Chairman Tom L. Allen called Statement No. 34 "the most significant change to occur in the history of governmental accounting."[5] Allen went on to state that "never before has the public been able to get a comprehensive overview of a state or local government's finances in one place. This new financial reporting system will give citizens a clearer picture of what a government is doing with the taxes it collects: Are current revenues paying for current services, or will the services be paid for by the next generations? How much is invested in roads and bridges? Are taxes subsidizing the local public pool, or are swimmers' fees covering operating costs? The new financial statements could help to answer those questions."

As this edition goes to press, all governments have prepared GASB 34 financial statements at least once. Many continue to work on issues relating to reporting of their infrastructure assets. The relatively new standard took effect for larger governments (those with $100 million or more in revenues) in fiscal years beginning after June 15, 2001, medium-sized governments (those with between $10 and $100 million in revenue) in fiscal years beginning after June 15, 2002, and smaller governments (those with $10 million or less in revenue) in fiscal years beginning after June 15, 2003. As previously indicated, prospective (forward-looking) recognition of infrastructure assets was required at the same time as the other provisions of GASB Statement No. 34. Large and medium-sized governments have three additional years to apply the 25-year retroactive implementation (back to 1981). Smaller governments are exempt from retroactive infrastructure reporting.

Audits of State and Local Governments

In order for users of the financial statements to have assurance that the statements are prepared in conformity with GASB accounting and reporting standards, the statements are accompanied by an audit report. Most governments are audited annually because of state or federal requirements or because long-term creditors demand audited statements as part of the debt agreements. The audits of governmental units are broader than audits of a business and include both a financial audit and a performance audit. The *financial audit*, which is the primary audit, deals with compliance with fiscal requirements including applicable accounting standards and federal and state laws. As in business, the primary purpose of the financial audit is to render a report expressing an opinion about whether the financial statements present fairly the financial position, results of operation, and where appropriate, the cash flows of the government in accordance with generally accepted accounting principles (GAAP) or other financial related criteria. *Performance audits* emphasize economy, efficiency, program results, and managerial effectiveness. Performance audits are intended to provide an independent report, but not an opinion, about the extent to which government officials are carrying out their responsibilities in an efficient and economic way and also whether their programs are producing desired results.

---

5 Governmental Accounting Standards Board, *Action Report* (Norwalk, CT: Governmental Accounting Standards Board, July 1999).

Illustration 17-16
Explanation of Differences between Governmental Fund Operating Statements and the Statement of Activities

The "net change in fund balances" for governmental funds (−$106,657) differs from the "change in net assets" for governmental activities (−$3,114,286) reported in the statement of activities. The differences arise primarily from the long-term economic focus of the statement of activities versus the current financial resources focus of the governmental funds. The effect of the differences is illustrated below.

Statement of Revenues, Expenditures, and Changes in Fund Balances/Statement of Activities

	Total Governmental Funds	Long-Term Revenues, Expenses[a]	Capital Related Items[b]	Internal Service Funds[c]	Long-Term Debt Transactions[d]	Statement of Activities Totals
Revenues and other sources:						
Taxes	$229,000		$ —	$ —	$ —	$229,000
Fees and fines	41,000		—	—	—	41,000
Licenses and permits	12,000	$ 1,500	—	—	—	13,500
Intergovernmental	104,900	1,500	—	28,000	—	134,400
Charges for services	112,100	(35,100)	—		—	77,000
Interest	190,700	27,000	—	13,500	—	231,200
Miscellaneous	143,100	100	—		—	143,200
Other sources:						
Bond proceeds	90,500	—	—		(90,500)	—
Sale of park land	34,750	—	(7,750)	—	—	27,000
Total revenue and other sources	$958,050	$ (5,000)	$ (7,750)	$ 41,500	$ (90,500)	$896,300
Expenditures/expenses:						
Current:						
General government	$135,700		$ (58,700)	$ 42,000	$ —	$119,000
Public safety	42,000	$ 500	(25,000)	58,000	—	75,500
Public works	86,500	(200)	15,200	21,500	—	123,000
Engineering services	13,000	700	—	19,500	—	33,200
Health and sanitation	61,000	—	23,000	40,000	—	124,000
Cemetery	70,000	600	2,400	—	—	73,000
Culture and recreation	11,000	(100)	1,600	17,500	—	30,000
Community development	29,500	—	10,000	8,000	—	47,500
Education—payment to school district	22,000	—	—	—	—	22,000

(continued below)

Debt service:						
Principal	34,500	—	—	—	(34,500)	—
Interest and other charges	52,700	100	(56,800)	4,000	—	—
Capital outlay	66,000	—	(66,000)	—	—	—
Total expenditures/expenses	$623,900	$ 1,600	$(154,300)	$ 210,500	$ (34,500)	$647,200
Other financing uses/changes net assets:						
Net transfers to (from) other funds	19,500	—	—	(500)	(32,500)	(13,500)
Debt refunding	38,000	—	—	—	(38,000)	—
Total	$681,400	$ 1,600	$(154,300)	$ 210,000	$(105,000)	$633,700
Net change for the year	$276,650	$ (6,600)	$ 146,550	$(168,500)	$ 14,500	$262,600

[a]Because some property taxes will not be collected for several months after the fiscal year ends, they are not considered as "available" revenues in the governmental funds. Similarly, certain license and permit revenues not currently available at year-end are not reported as revenue in the governmental funds.

Some expenses reported in the statement of activities do not require the use of current financial resources and therefore are not reported as expenditures in governmental funds.

Interest expense in the statement of activities differs from the amount reported in governmental funds.

[b]The proceeds from the sale of land are reported as revenue (as a special item) in the governmental funds. However, the cost of the land sold is removed from the capital assets account in the statement of net assets and offset against the sale proceeds resulting in a "gain on sale of land" in the statement of activities. Thus, more revenue is reported in the governmental fund than gain in the statement of activities.

[c]Internal services funds are used by management to charge the costs of certain activities, such as insurance and telecommunications, to individual funds. In the government-wide statements, they are included in governmental activities.

Bond proceeds are reported as financing sources in governmental funds. In the government-wide statements, however, issuing debt increases long-term liabilities in the statement of net assets and does not affect the statement of activities.

[d]Bond principal is reported as an expenditure in the governmental funds. However, the repayment reduces the liabilities in the statement of net assets and does not result in an expense in the statement of activities.

Source: Adapted from GASB 34, Appendix C.

Government auditing standards have been developed by the U.S. General Accounting Office (GAO) in its Yellow Book entitled *Government Auditing Standards*. The American Institute of Certified Public Accountants (AICPA) publishes the AICPA audit guide, *Audits of State and Local Governmental Units*, which incorporates the Yellow Book standards. In 1984, the federal government passed the *Single Audit Act* requiring audits of all entities receiving federal grants and contracts. The Single Audit Act, revised in 1996, requires state and local governments that receive $500,000 or more of federal financial assistance to have a single audit for that fiscal year. The act exempts governments receiving less than $500,000 of federal assistance. A single audit has two main components: an audit or the financial statements conducted under generally accepted government auditing standards and an audit of federal financial awards. Not all federal award programs are audited in a single audit. Larger programs (those with more than $300,000 or 3% of all federal assistance expenditures) must be audited unless they are considered low risk. In addition, certain high risk smaller programs (less than $300,000 or 3% of federal assistance expenditures) are audited until at least 50% of the total federal awards expended are audited. A higher level of auditing is required of major federal award programs as defined by size and risk. This includes more testing and reporting on compliance with laws and regulations, internal control, and inherent risk. Audit reports prepared under the Single Audit Act include (a) an opinion on the fairness of financial statement presentation, (b) a report on the study and evaluation of internal control systems' ability to provide reasonable assurance that federal programs are being managed in compliance with laws and regulations, (c) a report on compliance with laws and regulations that may have a material effect on specific programs, and (d) a schedule of findings and questioned costs. Detailed guidance for administering and conducting single audits is provided in OMB Circular A-133, *Audits of State and Local Governments and Nonprofit Organizations*.

The Statistical Section

The statistical section information should focus on the primary government, rather than on the financial reporting entity, and include the following five categories:[6]

- *Financial trends information*—to help users understand and assess how a government's financial position has changed over time.
- *Revenue capacity information*—to help users understand and assess factors affecting a government's ability to generate its own source revenues.
- *Debt capacity information*—to help users understand and assess a government's debt burden and its ability to issue additional debt.
- *Demographic and economic information*—to help users understand the socioeconomic environment within which a government operates and compare financial statement information over time and among governments.
- *Operating information*—to provide contextual information about a government's operations and resources to help the user understand and assess a government's economic condition.

Ten-year trend information is required for government employment levels, operating statistics, captial assets, net assets, and changes in net assets. Trend information is also required for governmental fund balances and principal employers. All sources of information and assumptions used to produce information must be clearly idetified and narrative explanations are to be used as appropriate.

Other Financial Reporting Issues

The GASB continues to encourage governments to experiment with developing and reporting *nonfinancial* measures of efficiency and effectiveness through its service efforts and accomplishments (SEA) projects. In 1994, the GASB issued Concepts Statement No. 2, *Service Efforts and*

6 GASB Statement No. 44, *Economic Condition Reporting: The Statistical Section—an amendment of NCGA Statement 1*, May 2004.

Accomplishments Reporting, which identified three broad categories of SEA measures to include service efforts and service accomplishments and measures that relate the two. Extensive research has been conducted on appropriate SEA measures for schools, hospitals, police and fire departments, mass transit, sanitation departments, and others. Many advocate the use of these nonfinancial measures in the financial statements or in separate performance reports in order to improve financial statement users' ability to assess the service efforts, costs, and accomplishments of a government.

Another effort by the GASB to encourage more effective communication of financial statement information is through the publication of popular reports. A growing number of governments prepare and distribute popular reports that provide condensed financial and budget information (and sometimes SEA measures). These reports often include graphs and charts to facilitate better understanding and decision making by those who use the financial statements. Popular reports do not replace the CAFR, but may serve to supplement it. Currently, this supplemental information is not audited.

Other organizations continue to participate in the efforts to improve financial reporting for governments. Two examples are the Government Finance Officers Association and Standard & Poor's Corporation. The Government Finance Officers Association (GFOA) recognizes excellence in financial reporting through its Certificate of Achievment for Excellence in Financial Reporting award program. Certificates are awarded to governments who publish financial reports (CAFRs) that demonstrate efficient, organized, full disclosure in accordance with generally accepted accounting principles (GAAP). Standard & Poor's (S&P) has also taken an active role in government financial reporting by requiring that governments follow GAAP. Because of the impact of the S&P bond rating on borrowing costs, the S&P requirement has significantly improved the quality of government financial reports. Other financial institutions and professional organizations continue to work with the GASB on issues of accounting and financial reporting in state and local governments.

UNDERSTANDING THE ISSUES

1. Compare the basis of accounting that is used to report governmental activities vs. business-type activities.
2. Describe the purpose of each of the financial statements required under Statement No. 34.
3. What are major funds? Describe major fund reporting.
4. What benefits are derived from including the management's discussion and analysis (MD&A) in state and local governmental financial reports? What information is required to be included in the MD&A?
5. Explain budgetary reporting requirements.
6. How are interfund transactions reported?

EXERCISES

Exercise 1 *(LO 2)* **Determining a major fund.** Based on the information presented in the 2003 city of Milwaukee, Wisconsin, financial statements in the student companion book, list the major funds disclosed by the city. How were these funds determined? Likewise, what minimum amounts of which statement items were used to determine whether a specific enterprise fund was a major fund?

Exercise 2 *(LO 3)* **New standards.** Go to the GASB Web site, and review the list of current projects and recently released standards. What are the most pressing issues facing the Board? In your opinion, is the Board effectively communicating these issues to the public on its Web site?

Exercise 3 *(LO 2, 3)* **Reporting major funds.** Assume Elmwood City has the following fund structure:

General fund
Special revenue fund (4)
Capital projects fund (2)
Debt service fund (2)
Expendable trust funds (5)
Internal service funds (3)
Enterprise funds (6)
General fixed assets account group
General long-term debt account group

Elmwood City determined that Special Revenue Fund B, capital projects funds, Enterprise Fund D, and Enterprise Fund E are the only major funds.

a. Present the column headings that Elmwood City must use in its governmental fund statement of revenues, expenditures, and changes in fund balance.
b. Present the column headings that Elmwood City must use in its governmental fund statement of revenues, expenses, and changes in net assets.

Exercise 4 *(LO 3)* **Government-wide financial statements.** Select the best answer to the following multiple-choice questions.

1. Which of the following adjustments is necessary to move from governmental fund financial statements to government-wide financial statements?
   a. Eliminate expenditures for debt principal
   b. Eliminate expenditures for capital outlay and add depreciation expense
   c. Both of the above
   d. Neither of the above
2. Which of the following is *true* regarding government-wide financial statements?
   a. Internal service funds are normally included with governmental-type activities.
   b. Component units and fiduciary funds are not included.
   c. Both of the above
   d. Neither of the above
3. Which of the following would be considered a program revenue in the statement of activities for a governmental unit?
   a. A grant from the state restricted for an after-school child care program
   b. Hotel taxes restricted for tourist development
   c. Both of the above
   d. Neither of the above
4. Which of the following is *true* regarding the incorporation of internal service funds into government-wide financial statements?
   a. Internal service funds are not included in the government-wide financial statements.
   b. Internal service funds are incorporated into the business-type activities section of the government-wide financial statements.
   c. Both of the above
   d. Neither of the above
5. Which of the following adjustments would likely be made when moving from governmental funds financial statements to government-wide financial statements?
   a. Recording an additional expense for compensated absences
   b. Recording an additional expense related to salaries earned at year-end
   c. Both of the above
   d. Neither of the above

6. Which of the following must exist in order for a government to use the modified approach for recording infrastructure?

   a. An up-to-date inventory of eligible infrastructure assets must be maintained.
   b. A condition assessment must be performed at least every three years.
   c. Both of the above
   d. Neither of the above

7. Which of the following is *true* regarding government-wide financial statements?

   a. Internal service funds are not included with governmental-type activities.
   b. Component units and fiduciary funds are not included.
   c. Both of the above
   d. Neither of the above

8. Which of the following is *true* regarding government-wide financial statements?

   a. All capital assets, including infrastructure, are required to be reported.
   b. Internal service funds are not included.
   c. Both of the above
   d. Neither of the above

9. Which of the following is *true* about the reconciliation from governmental fund changes in fund balances to governmental activities changes in net assets?

   a. Reconciliation is required to be presented either on the face of the fund financial statement or as a separate statement.
   b. The reconciliation converts from modified accrual to full accrual.
   c. Both of the above
   d. Neither of the above

10. Which of the following is *true* regarding government-wide financial statements?

   a. The government-wide statements include a statement of net assets, a statement of activities, and a statement of cash flows.
   b. The government-wide statements include a statement of net assets and a statement of activities, but not a statement of cash flows.
   c. The government-wide statements include a balance sheet, an income statement, and a statement of cash flows.
   d. None of the above

Exercise 5 *(LO 3)* **Converting to government-wide statements.** List some of the major adjustments required when converting from fund financial statements to government-wide statements. Why are these adjustments necessary?

Exercise 6 *(LO 1, 3)* **CAFR.** Select the best answer to the following multiple-choice questions.

1. Which of the following statements is correct concerning a governmental entity's combined statement of cash flows?

   a. Cash flows from capital financing activities are reported separately from cash flows from noncapital financing activities.
   b. The statement format is the same as that of a business enterprise's statement of cash flows.
   c. Cash flows from operating activities may be reported using the indirect method.
   d. The statement format includes columns for the general, governmental, and proprietary fund types.

2. In a government's comprehensive annual financial report (CAFR), proprietary fund types are included in which of the following combined financial statements?

	Statement of Revenues, Expenditures, and Changes in Fund Balances	Statement of Net Assets
a.	Yes	Yes
b.	No	No
c.	No	Yes
d.	Yes	No

3. In a government's comprehensive annual financial report, account groups are included in which of the following combined financial statements?

	Net Assets	Statement of Activities
a.	Yes	No
b.	No	Yes
c.	Yes	Yes
d.	No	No

4. Clover City's comprehensive annual financial report contains both combining and combined financial statements. Total columns are

   a. required for both combining and combined financial statements.
   b. optional, but commonly shown, for combining financial statements and required for combined financial statements.
   c. required for combining financial statements and optional, but commonly shown, for combined financial statements.
   d. optional, but commonly shown, for both combining and combined financial statements.

5. Eureka City should issue a statement of cash flows for which of the following funds?

	Eureka City Hall Capital Projects Fund	Eureka Water Enterprise Fund
a.	No	Yes
b.	No	No
c.	Yes	No
d.	Yes	Yes

6. On March 2, 20X1, Finch City issued 10-year general obligation bonds at face amount, with interest payable on March 1 and September 1. The proceeds were to be used to finance the construction of a civic center over the period from April 1, 20X1, to March 31, 20X2. During the fiscal year ended June 30, 20X1, no resources had been provided to the debt service fund for the payment of principal and interest. On June 30, 20X1, in which statements should Finch report the construction in progress for the civic center?

	Capital Projects Fund Balance Sheet	Government-Wide Statement of Net Assets
a.	Yes	Yes
b.	Yes	No
c.	No	No
d.	No	Yes

Exercise 7 *(LO 3)* **Infrastructure reporting.** What are the rules for recording infrastructure under the new GASB reporting model? When are these rules effective? What conditions must exist in order to use one method versus another? What are the advantages and disadvantages of each approach?

PROBLEMS

Problem 17-1 *(LO 1, 3)* **Reporting under GASB Statement No. 34.** Select the best answer to the following multiple-choice questions.

1. Which of the following is *not* part of the basic financial statements?
   a. Government-wide statement of net assets
   b. Proprietary funds statement of revenues, expenses, and changes in fund net assets
   c. Combining balance sheet—nonmajor governmental funds
   d. Notes to the financial statements
2. Which of the following is *true* regarding the government-wide financial statements?
   a. The government-wide financial statements include the statement of net assets and the statement of activities.
   b. The government-wide financial statements are to be prepared using the economic resources measurement focus and the accrual basis of accounting.
   c. The government-wide financial statements include information for governmental activities, business-type activities, the total primary government, and its component units.
   d. All of the above are true.
3. In the statement of activities,
   a. all expenses are subtracted from all revenues to get net income.
   b. it is possible to determine the net program expense (revenue) for major functions and programs of the primary government and its component units.
   c. some tax revenues are considered program revenues, and others are considered general revenues.
   d. extraordinary items are those that are either unusual in nature or infrequent in occurrence.
4. Which of the following is *true* regarding financial reporting under GASB Statement No. 34?
   a. A comparison of budget and actual revenues and expenditures for the general fund is required as part of the basic financial statements.
   b. Infrastructure must be recorded and depreciated as part of the statement of activities in the basic financial statements.
   c. Public colleges and universities are to report in exactly the same manner as private colleges and universities.
   d. Special purpose governments that have only business-type activities are permitted to report only the financial statements required for enterprise funds.
5. Which of the following is *not* part of the basic financial statements?
   a. Governmental funds statement of revenues, expenditures, and changes in fund balances
   b. Budgetary comparison schedules—general and special revenue funds
   c. Government-wide statement of activities
   d. Notes to the financial statements
6. Which of the following is *true* regarding the organization of the comprehensive annual financial report (CAFR)?
   a. The three major sections are introductory, financial, and statistical.
   b. The management's discussion and analysis (MD&A) is considered to be part of the introductory section.
   c. The auditor's report is considered to be part of the statistical section.
   d. Basic financial statements include the government-wide statements, the budgetary statement, and the notes to the financial statements.

7. Which of the following is *true* regarding the government-wide financial statements?

   a. The government-wide financial statements include the statement of net assets and the statement of activities.
   b. The government-wide financial statements are prepared on the financial resources measurement focus for governmental activities and the economic resources measurement focus for business-type activities.
   c. Prior-year data must be presented.
   d. Works of art, historical treasures, and similar assets must be capitalized.

8. Under GASB Statement No. 34, which of the following are *true* of infrastructure?

   a. Infrastructure must be recorded and depreciated unless a modified approach is used, in which case, depreciation is not required.
   b. Infrastructure must be recorded and depreciated in all cases.
   c. Infrastructure is not to be recorded and depreciated.
   d. The state and local governments have the option, but are not required, to record and depreciate infrastructure.

9. Which statement is *true* regarding the "major" funds?

   a. The general fund is always considered major.
   b. Other funds are considered major if both of the following conditions exist: (1) total assets, liabilities, revenues, or expenditures/expenses of that individual governmental or enterprise fund constitute 10% of the governmental or enterprise categories, and (2) total assets, liabilities, revenues, or expenditures/expenses are 5% of the total of the governmental and enterprise categories.
   c. A government may choose to reflect a fund as major even if it does not meet the criteria for major funds.
   d. All of the above are true.

10. Which of the following groups sets *standards* for audits of federal financial assistance recipients?

    a. U.S. General Accounting Office
    b. U.S. Office of Management and Budget
    c. Governmental Accounting Standards Board
    d. Financial Accounting Standards Board

11. OMB Circular A-133 applies

    a. only to state and local governmental units.
    b. only to not-for-profit organizations.
    c. to both state and local governments and not-for-profit organizations.
    d. to neither state and local governments nor not-for-profit organizations.

12. The total amount of grant expenditures that must be covered in the audit of major programs is

    a. $500,000.
    b. 50% of federal expenditures.
    c. 25% of federal expenditures.
    d. 50% of federal expenditures generally but only 25% if the government is considered to be a low-risk auditee.

Required ▶ ▶ ▶ ▶ ▶

Problem 17-2 *(LO 1, 2)* **Usefulness of reported information.** Search the Internet for a popular report of a state or city government. Evaluate the usefulness of the popular reports from the perspective of the citizen. In particular, focus on financial accounting information provided in the report. Do you think this information is adequate? Does the state or city report nonfinancial measures of efficiency and effectiveness (service efforts and accomplishments) information? If so, evaluate its usefulness in determining the financial position and overall condition of the government.

Problem 17-3 *(LO 2)* **Reporting entities.** Based on the following very limited information, indicate whether and how the city should report its related entity. ◀◀◀◀◀ **Required**

1. Its school district, although not a legally separate government, is managed by a school board elected by city residents. The system is financed with general tax revenues of the city, and its budget is incorporated into that of the city at large (and thereby is subject to the same approval and appropriation process as other city expenditures).
2. Its fixed asset financing authority is a legally separate government that leases equipment to the city. To finance the equipment, the authority issues bonds that are guaranteed by the city and expected to be paid from the rents received from the city. The authority leases equipment exclusively to the city.
3. Its housing authority, which provides loans to low-income families within the city, is governed by a 5-person board appointed by the city's mayor.
4. Its hospital is owned by the city but managed under contract by a private hospital management firm.
5. Its water purification plant is owned in equal shares by the city and two neighboring counties. The city's interest in the plant was acquired with resources from its water utility (enterprise) fund.
6. Its community college, a separate legal entity, is governed by a board of governors elected by city residents and has its own taxing and budgetary authority.

Problem 17-4 *(LO 2)* **Reporting entity.** A city's urban development authority is a legally constituted government entity. It has a 10-person board, of which six members are appointed by the city's common council and four others are selected by the other members of the board. The board members serve staggered terms of three years. Once appointed, the members can be removed from office only for illegal activities. The city provides 80% of the urban development authority's resources and thereby can control the total amount spent by the system. However, the governing board adopts the authority's budget, and the budget need not be approved by the city. The board also controls the day-to-day operations of the authority.

Using the flowchart shown in Illustration 17-2, indicate whether or not the city should incorporate the authority into its own financial statements. If so, how would the city accomplish this? ◀◀◀◀◀ **Required**

Problem 17-5 *(LO 2)* **Reporting entity.** Define a financial reporting entity. Give an example of a primary government. Define and give an example of a component unit. Explain the two methods of reporting the primary government and component units in the financial reporting entity and when each is required. ◀◀◀◀◀ **Required**

Problem 17-6 *(LO 3)* **Fund-based statements.** The preclosing, year-end trial balance for a capital projects fund of the city of Craig as of December 31, 20X7, follows:

	Debit	Credit
Cash	75,000	
Investments	200,000	
Contracts Payable—Retained Percentage		60,000
Revenues		16,600
Other Financing Sources		900,000
Expenditures	686,600	
Other Financing Uses	15,000	
Encumbrances	80,000	
Fund Balance—Reserved for Encumbrances		80,000
Estimated Revenues	20,000	
Estimated Other Financing Sources	950,000	
Appropriations		640,000
Estimated Other Financing Uses		25,000
Budgetary Fund Balance—Unreserved		305,000
	2,026,600	2,026,600

Required ▶▶▶▶▶

1. Prepare closing entries as of December 31, 20X7.
2. Prepare the year-end statement of revenues, expenditures, and changes in fund balance for this project that began on January 2, 20X7.
3. Prepare the fund balance sheet as of December 31, 20X7.

Required ▶▶▶▶▶

Problem 17-7 *(LO 3)* **Converting to a government-wide statement of activities.** Using the information from Problem 17-6, illustrate and explain the adjustments necessary to convert to a government-wide statement of activities, assuming all expenditures are for capital assets and other finance sources are the result of issuance of general long-term obligations.

Required ▶▶▶▶▶

Problem 17-8 *(LO 3)* **Statement of net assets.** From the following information, prepare a statement of net assets for the city of Lester as of June 30, 20X8.

Cash and cash equivalents, governmental activities	$ 280,000
Cash and cash equivalents, business-type activities	75,000
Receivables, governmental activities	36,000
Receivables, business-type activities	145,000
Inventories, business-type activities	56,000
Capital assets, net, governmental activities	1,500,000
Capital assets, net, business-type activities	1,100,000
Accounts payable, governmental activities	65,000
Accounts payable, business-type activities	56,000
Noncurrent liabilities, governmental activities	500,000
Noncurrent liabilities, business-type activities	300,000
Net assets, invested in capital assets, net, governmental activities	1,000,000
Net assets, invested in capital assets, net, business-type activities	800,000
Net assets, restricted for debt service, governmental activities	65,000
Net assets, restricted for debt service, business-type activities	36,000

Required ▶▶▶▶▶

Problem 17-9 *(LO 3)* **Statement of activities.** From the following information, prepare a statement of activities for the city of Rose as of June 30, 20X8.

Expenses:	
General government	$1,300,000
Public safety	240,000
Public works	1,000,000
Health and sanitation	650,000
Culture and recreation	450,000
Interest on long-term debt, governmental type	60,000
Water and sewer system	1,500,000
Parking system	45,000
Revenues:	
Charges for services, general government	100,000
Charges for services, public safety	25,000
Operating grant, public safety	70,000
Charges for services, health and sanitation	250,000
Operating grant, health and sanitation	150,000
Charges for services, culture and recreation	200,000
Charges for services, water and sewer	1,800,000
Charges for services, parking system	40,000
Property taxes	2,500,000
Sales taxes	2,000,000
Investment earnings, business-type	30,000
Special item—gain on sale of unused land, governmental type	140,000
Transfer from governmental activities to business-type activities	70,000

Net assets, July 1, 20X7, governmental activities	1,400,000
Net assets, July 1, 20X7, business-type activities	2,500,000

Problem 17-10 *(LO 3)* **Reporting under GASB Statement No. 34.** Go to the Web site featuring the financial statements of Corona, California, at http://www.ci.corona.ca.us/depts/finance/cafr04/financial.cfm.

Provide brief answers to the following: ◀◀◀◀◀ **Required**

1. The financial section includes the basic financial statements, notes to the financial statements, required supplementary information, and supplementary information. Describe key features of each of these components of the financial statements. What key information do you see that was not included in the text? Compare the Corona statements with those of the city of Milwaukee found in the student companion book and on the text's Web site.
2. Compare the information found in the letter of transmittal (in the Introductory Section) with that found in the newly required management's discussion and analysis (in the Financial Section).
3. Where do you find budgetary comparison information?
4. List the major governmental funds. How does Corona determine major funds? List the non-major governmental funds.
5. How is Corona handling the new requirements for reporting and depreciating infrastructure assets?

Problem 17-11 *(LO 4)* **Measurement focus: comparing statements.** Under the reporting model required by GASB Statement No. 34, fund statements are required for governmental, proprietary, and fiduciary funds. Government-wide statements include the statement of net assets and the statement of activities.

◀◀◀◀◀ **Required**

1. Explain the measurement focus and basis of accounting for (a) governmental fund statements, (b) proprietary fund statements, (c) fiduciary fund statements, and (d) government-wide statements.
2. Explain some differences between fund financial statements and government-wide statements with regard to (a) component units, (b) fiduciary funds, and (c) location of internal service funds.
3. What should be included in the statement of net assets categories (a) invested in capital assets, net of related debt, (b) restricted, and (c) unrestricted?

Problem 17-12 *(LO 4)* **Audit concerns.** The city of Cedar expended federal awards from the following programs during 20X3.

Program	Amount Expended
1. Cedar Community Block Grant	$ 400,000
2. Hazardous Waste Management.	300,000
3. Law Enforcement	250,000
4. Energy Assistance	200,000
5. Economic Development.	150,000
6. Clean Water Program	50,000
	$1,350,000

Assume the auditor has given an unqualified opinion on the financial statements and reports no material weaknesses or reportable conditions in internal control at the financial statement level. Also, assume the auditor has given an unqualified opinion on the schedule of expenditures of federal awards. Programs 2 and 4 are classified as low risk, and Program 6 was not assessed for risk due to its small size.

◀◀◀◀◀ **Required**

1. Which programs should the auditor audit as major programs for the purpose of internal control evaluation and compliance testing for the year 20X3?
2. How would your answer differ if Program 2 was classified as high risk?

Accounting for Private Not-for-Profit Organizations

CHAPTER

18

Learning Objectives

When you have completed this chapter, you should be able to

1. **Distinguish not-for-profit organizations from other entities.**
2. **Explain the jurisdictions of the GASB and the FASB with regard to not-for-profit organizations.**
3. **Explain how financial accounting and reporting for private not-for-profit organizations differs from that of state and local governments.**
4. **Demonstrate an understanding of the accounting for unrestricted and restricted contributions.**
5. **Demonstrate an understanding of the accounting for expenses in a private not-for-profit organization.**
6. **Identify and describe the financial statements and notes disclosure required of not-for-profit organizations.**
7. **State the requirements an organization must meet to be classified as voluntary health and welfare, and describe the accounting for public support.**
8. **Explain how to account for revenues and costs in a VHWO.**
9. **Prepare financial statements for not-for-profit organizations.**
10. **Prepare journal entries related to typical events of a not-for-profit organization.**
11. **(Appendix) Describe the typical funds used to account for VHWO transactions, and prepare optional VHWO fund-based financial statements.**

This chapter and the next detail accounting for the four major not-for-profit organizations. These organizations include: (1) colleges and universities, (2) hospitals, (3) voluntary health and welfare organizations, and (4) other organizations such as museums, country clubs, and religious organizations. Chapter 18 outlines the unique characteristics of not-for-profit organizations and the accounting and reporting standard-setting activities in this sector. The accounting and reporting guidance for all not-for-profits with specific illustration for voluntary health and welfare organizations is also described. Chapter 19 includes a discussion of the accounting and financial reporting for public (governmental) and private colleges and universities and health care organizations.

1

OBJECTIVE

Distinguish not-for-profit organizations from other entities.

NOT-FOR-PROFIT ORGANIZATIONS

Not-for-profit activities make up a significant portion of the U.S. economy. All not-for-profit organizations provide services without the intention of realizing a profit. Such organizations are generally financed by contributions, earnings from endowments or other investments, charges for services, and government grants. The AICPA defines a **not-for-profit organization** as an entity that (1) has significant contributions from resource providers who do not expect to get anything in return, (2) has an operating purpose other than to make a profit, and (3) has no owners. Examples of not-for-profits include voluntary health and welfare organizations (VHWO) or human service organizations such as the American Cancer Society, American Red Cross, Girl Scouts, and Boy Scouts. Other not-for-profits have charitable, educational, or scientific purposes and can be classified as mutual not-for-profits. Examples are libraries and museums, performing arts and other cultural organizations, private elementary and secondary schools, private colleges and universities, not-for-profit health care organizations, public broadcasting stations, religious organizations, research and scientific organizations, cemetery organizations, civic and fraternal organizations, labor unions, political parties, private and community foundations, professional associations, social and country clubs, trade associations, and zoological and botanical societies. External users of a not-for-profit organization's financial statements have common interests in assessing (1) its services and ability to continue those services, (2) its creditworthiness, and (3) how its managers discharge their stewardship responsibilities and perform in other aspects.[1]

2

OBJECTIVE

Explain the jurisdictions of the GASB and the FASB with regard to not-for-profit organizations.

Development of Accounting Principles

Accounting principles for not-for-profit organizations were originally developed by not-for-profit industry groups, such as the National Association of College and University Business Officers (NACUBO), the Health Care Financial Management Association (HFMA), and the National Health Council. These industry groups, representing colleges and universities, hospitals, voluntary health and welfare organizations, and other organizations such as museums, country clubs, and religious organizations, developed manuals with accounting guidance. In response to an increasing awareness of the not-for-profit sector, the American Institute of Certified Public Accountants (AICPA) worked in conjunction with these industry groups to develop and issue accounting and audit guides in the early 1970s. These guides have been updated and amended over the years. As a result of the separate evolution of standards by each not-for-profit industry group, significant differences have existed for the four types of not-for-profits in terms of fund classifications, measurement criteria, account classifications, and financial statement disclosures. Over the last decade, a considerable effort has been made by the AICPA, the Financial Accounting Standards Board (FASB), and the Government Accounting Standards Board (GASB) to standardize the accounting and financial reporting for the diverse set of not-for-profit organizations in this sector and to reduce the inconsistencies in and across organizations in the not-for-profit sector. Two current applicable AICPA accounting and audit guides also reflect standardization for private and governmental not-for-profit organizations: The Audit and Accounting Guide, *Not-for-Profit Organizations* (May 1, 2004), includes guidance for voluntary health and welfare organizations and other not-for-profits, and the Audit and Accounting Guide, *Health Care Organizations* (May 1, 2004), includes guidance for both private and governmental health care organizations.

Jurisdiction for accounting and financial reporting for not-for-profit organizations is shared by the FASB and the GASB. The GASB has jurisdiction over accounting and financial reporting of governmental not-for-profits (public colleges and universities and government hospitals). The FASB has jurisdiction over accounting and financial reporting of all private not-for-profit organizations including voluntary health and welfare organizations, private colleges and universities, private health care providers, and other private not-for-profits. The accounting and financial reporting for voluntary health and welfare organizations is described in this chapter. Chapter 19 will cover private and governmental health care organizations and college and universities.

1 FASB Statement No. 117, *Financial Statements of Not-for-Profit Organizations* (Norwalk, CT: Financial Accounting Standards Board, 1993), par. 4.

REFLECTION

- The FASB sets standards for all private not-for-profit organizations.

ACCOUNTING FOR PRIVATE NOT-FOR-PROFIT ORGANIZATIONS

3 OBJECTIVE

Explain how financial accounting and reporting for private not-for-profit organizations differs from that of state and local governments.

The full accrual basis of accounting is used in accounting and reporting for all not-for-profits. Financial reporting for private not-for-profits emphasizes the organization as a whole. FASB Statement No. 117 requires not-for-profit organizations to provide financial statements with organization-wide totals of assets, liabilities, and net assets as well as information concerning organization-wide changes in net assets and organization-wide cash flows. There has been a shift away from fund accounting, which has traditionally been used by not-for-profits to organize and manage resources for various purposes in accordance with regulations, restrictions, or limitations imposed by parties outside the organization, or with directions issued by the governing board. Under FASB Statement No. 117, *three net asset classes—unrestricted, temporarily restricted, and permanently restricted—are used instead of fund balances.* These net asset classes provide a clear distinction between resources that are externally restricted and those that are internally designated by action of the governing board. Because of a shift away from a fund group focus toward an organization-wide focus, external financial statements are not required to include fund group reporting. However, even though both the FASB and GASB have in recent years set standards that emphasize organization-wide financial reporting, not-for-profit organizations are expected to continue to use funds for *internal management.* To aid in understanding the relationship between traditional funds and the new reporting requirements, a discussion of the voluntary health and welfare fund structure and illustrative financial statements reporting fund detail are included in the chapter appendix.

Accounting for Revenues, Gains, and Contributions

4 OBJECTIVE

Demonstrate an understanding of the accounting for unrestricted and restricted contributions.

Not-for-profit organizations record all events as either exchange transactions, contributions, agency transactions, capital acquisitions, or expenses. Contributions are distinguished from exchange transactions or agency relationships. Only contributions with donor-imposed restrictions affect the restricted assets. All other transactions, such as charges for services and government and other awards funding research or programs, are now considered exchange transactions, and they affect unrestricted net assets. Government or private-sponsored flow-through awards to individuals or other organizations are accounted for as agency transactions, rather than as restricted asset activities.

FASB Statement No. 116 requires private not-for-profits to recognize both contributions received and unconditional promises (pledges) to give as *revenues or gains* in the period the gift or promise is received. *Contributions* are defined by FASB Statement No. 116 as "unconditional transfers of cash or other assets to an entity or a settlement or cancellation of its liabilities in a voluntary nonreciprocal transfer."[2] These nonexchange transactions may include cash, securities, land, and buildings. They may also include noncash items or gifts in kind such as free or discounted use of facilities or utilities, donated materials and supplies, intangible assets, and services of unpaid workers. All of these items are recorded at the *fair value* at the date of the gift. In the case of noncash gifts, a corresponding asset or expense is recorded.

Exceptions to the general recognition provision are made for contributions of services and works of art. Donated services, typically relied on to supplement the efforts of paid employees,

2 FASB Statement No. 116, *Accounting for Contributions Received and Contributions Made* (Norwalk, CT: Financial Accounting Standards Board, 1993), par. 5. The FASB defines a nonreciprocal transfer as a transaction in which an organization receives an asset or cancellation of a liability without directly gaining value in exchange.

are recognized only if they (a) create or enhance nonfinancial assets or (b) require specialized skills, are provided by individuals possessing those abilities, and typically would have to be purchased if not provided by donation. Additionally, not-for-profit organizations need not recognize contributed works of art, historical treasures, and similar assets as contributions "if the donated items are added to collections that are (a) held for public exhibition, education, or research rather than financial gain, (b) protected and preserved, or (c) subject to an organization policy that requires the proceeds from sales of collection items to be used to acquire other items for collections."[3] Although organizations can choose whether or not to capitalize their collections, the choice must be applied to all collections. Capitalization may be done retroactively or prospectively.

Pledges (promises to give) are divided into unconditional pledges and conditional pledges. *Unconditional pledges* depend only on the passage of time or the demand by the not-for-profit to be collected and are recognized as a receivable and revenue or support in the year made. *Conditional pledges* depend on the occurrence of uncertain future events and should be recognized as revenue when the conditions are substantially met (i.e., the pledge becomes unconditional). An example of a conditional pledge might be a donation restricted for construction of a new building given only if the organization can raise the remaining funds through additional contributions. Pledges or other assets received subject to such conditions are recorded as refundable advances until the conditions have been substantially met, at which time revenue is recorded.

Unconditional pledges payable in the future, or multiyear pledges, are treated as temporarily restricted revenue or support and then reclassified to the unrestricted net asset class when the period of the donor stipulation is met. FASB Statement No. 116 states that "the present value of estimated future cash flows using a discount rate commensurate with the risks involved is an appropriate measure of the fair value of unconditional promises to give cash." Promises receivable within one year need not be discounted. An allowance for doubtful contributions should be established based on historical experience and other factors to cover any uncertainties concerning collectibility. An unconditional pledge with no donor restriction is recognized as follows:

Contributions Receivable	XXX	
Revenues—Unrestricted Contributions		XXX
Provision for Uncollectible Contributions	XXX	
Allowance for Uncollectible Contributions		XXX

Donor-Imposed Restrictions and Reclassifications. All contributions received (or unconditional promises to give) are classified into one of three categories: unrestricted, temporarily restricted, or permanently restricted resources. *Donor-imposed restrictions* do not affect the timing of when contributions are recognized. Rather, these donor restrictions affect the manner of reporting contributions and related assets. If a donor does not stipulate how the asset should be used, then the gift is classified as unrestricted. If the donor does impose a restriction, such as identifying a particular program, capital asset, or time period that the donated asset may be used, the contribution is classified as temporarily restricted. Other assets may be donated as permanently restricted endowments.

A temporary restriction expires when (a) the stipulated time has elapsed, (b) the stipulated purpose has been fulfilled, or (c) the useful life of the donated asset has ended. Expenditure or time restrictions require a reclassification entry to release the restriction. Gifts of long-lived assets (or long-lived assets acquired with restricted gifts of cash) with donor stipulations specifying the use of the donated asset are initially reported as temporarily restricted. The expiration (or release) of the time restriction is recorded over the useful life of the asset. Organizations have an option to record long-lived assets acquired with donor-restricted cash as either temporarily restricted or unrestricted. If the asset is recorded as temporarily restricted, the organization reclassifies a portion of the temporarily restricted amount each year as depreciation is recorded. This *releasing of donor-imposed restrictions (reclassification)* simultaneously decreases temporarily restricted net assets and increases unrestricted net assets in order to *match* the expenses they support (operating expenses, depreciation, etc., which decrease unrestricted net assets).

3 *Ibid.*, par. 11.

Not-for-profits also have the option to record contributions whose restrictions are met in the same reporting period as increases in unrestricted net assets, instead of increases in temporarily restricted net assets with subsequent reclassifications from temporarily restricted net assets to unrestricted net assets.

Furthermore, if an expense is incurred for a purpose for which both unrestricted and temporarily restricted net assets are available, a donor-imposed restriction is fulfilled to the extent of the expense incurred, unless the expense is for a purpose that is directly attributable to another specific external source of revenue. This provision to use restricted resources first to fund expenses does not allow institutions to choose either restricted or unrestricted sources of funding.

A cash contribution restricted by the donor for a specific expenditure is recorded when received.	Cash	XXX	
	Revenues—Temporarily Restricted Contributions		XXX
Expenses made in compliance with donor restrictions are funded by the restricted resources. Temporarily restricted net assets are released with a reclassification entry.	Expense	XXX	
	Cash		XXX
	Reclassification Out—Temporarily Restricted—Satisfaction of Donor Restrictions	XXX	
	Reclassification In—Unrestricted—Satisfaction of Donor Restrictions		XXX

A key part of FASB Statement No. 116 is the distinction between accounting for exchange transactions, agency transactions, and contributions. Exchange transactions, that is, reciprocal transfers in which each party receives and sacrifices approximately equal value, are not considered restricted. Many transactions that traditionally are thought of as contributions, for example, grants, awards, sponsorships, and appropriations, may be categorized as exchange transactions rather than contributions and accounted for as increases in unrestricted assets. Government grants that require performance by the not-for-profit organization are accounted for as refundable deposits (liabilities) until earned. Unrestricted revenue is earned when expenses are made in conjunction with the provisions of the grant. Other grants that just specify for support research or community work and do not have specific performance or rights to patents or products may be reported as contributions. And, government grants, which are essentially pass-through financial aid to students, are accounted for as agency transactions. FASB Statement No. 136 requires the recording of assets received on behalf of another individual or organization to be offset with a payable to the alternative beneficiary unless: (1) the donor has granted variance power to the not-for-profit organization (i.e., the right to redirect the use of the assets), or (2) the recipient organization and beneficiary are financially interrelated. In both cases, the not-for-profit organization recognizes the contribution as revenue.[4]

Grant monies received.	Cash	XXX	
	U.S. Government Grants Refundable		XXX
Expenses incurred in conjunction with provisions of grant.	Expenses	XXX	
	Cash		XXX
Revenue is recognized as the amount earned above expenses.	U.S. Government Grants Refundable	XXX	
	Revenues—Unrestricted		XXX

Investments. Permanently restricted contributions are called *endowments.* Earnings on endowment investments are reported in the period earned as a credit to either unrestricted revenue or temporarily restricted revenue depending on donor specification as to the use of the earnings. FASB Statement No. 124 requires not-for-profits organizations to mark all investments in equity securities that have readily determinable values and all debt securities to fair value. Reporting at original cost, amortized cost, or lower-of-cost-or market is not allowed. Unlike

4 FASB Statement No. 136, *Transfers of Assets to a Not-for-Profit Organization or Charitable Trust that Raises or Holds Contributions for Others* (Norwalk, CT: Financial Accounting Standards Board, 1999).

businesses, there is no requirement for not-for-profits to classify their investments into trading, available-for-sale, and held-to-maturity categories. Realized and unrealized gains on endowment investments are reported as increases or decreases in unrestricted net assets unless their use is temporarily or permanently restricted by explicit donor stipulations or by law. Losses on endowment investments reduce temporarily restricted net assets to the extent that donor-imposed restrictions on net appreciation have been met before the loss occurs. Any remaining loss would reduce unrestricted net assets.[5]

5

OBJECTIVE

Demonstrate an understanding of the accounting for expenses in a private not-for-profit organization.

Accounting for Expenses

Private not-for-profit organizations recognize expenses on an accrual basis rather than as expenditures. Furthermore, all expenses are reported as decreases in unrestricted net assets. Whereas expenditures denote outlays of resources, expenses denote *using up* of resources. Therefore, flows of resources involving outlays of cash to purchase other assets are not presented in the statement of activities but instead in the statement of cash flows. Depreciation of capital assets, including contributed capital assets, is also recorded as an expense per FASB Statement No. 93, *Recognition of Depreciation by Not-for-Profit Organizations.*[6] Land and individual works of art or historical treasures that have an extraordinarily long life are not depreciated.

Not-for-profit organizations segregate expenses between program functions and those functions supporting the programs. Program expenses include the direct and indirect cost of providing or conducting a particular mission or part of the organizational mission. Supporting expenses include management and general expenses and fund-raising activity. Natural or object classifications, e.g., supplies, salaries, and telephone, are allocated to the functions. Depreciation expenses are allocated to programs as well as to support function expenses.

Not-for-profits often conduct activities that combine program and fund raising. In the past, the cost of the joint activity often was reported entirely as a functional program expense with no allocation to the functional support expense of fund raising. In response to concerns about fund-raising costs being *hidden* within the program and management activities, the AICPA issued Statement of Position 98-2 making it more difficult to allocate *educating the public* or *advocacy* costs to programs. SOP 98-2 sets forth the following requirements:

1. Costs of all materials and activities that include a fund-raising appeal should be reported as fund-raising costs . . . unless a bona fide program or management function has been conducted in conjunction with the appeal.
2. Criteria of purpose, audience, and content must be met in order to conclude that a bona fide program or management and general function has been conducted in conjunction with the appeal of funds.
3. If a bona fide program or management function has been conducted, the joint costs should be allocated using an equitable allocation base.
4. Certain information must be disclosed if joint costs are allocated.[7]

6

OBJECTIVE

Identify and describe the financial statements and notes disclosure required of not-for-profit organizations.

Financial Statements

Financial statements prepared in accordance with FASB Statement No. 117 emphasize the organization as a whole. Classification of the organization's net assets is based on the existence or absence of donor-imposed restrictions. The financial statements must display three classes of net assets: unrestricted, temporarily restricted, and permanently restricted. Changes in each of

5 FASB Statement No.124, *Accounting for Certain Investments Held by Not-for-Profit Organizations* (Norwalk, CT: Financial Accounting Standards Board,1995) standardizes not-for-profit reporting of investments. It requires that investments in equity securities with readily determinable fair values and all investments in debt securities shall be measured at fair value. It does not apply to investments in equity securities accounted for under the equity method or to investments in consolidated subsidiaries.

6 FASB Statement No. 93, *Recognition of Depreciation by Not-for-Profit Organizations* (Norwalk, CT: Financial Accounting Standards Board, 1987), par. 5.

7 AICPA, SOP 98-2, *Accounting for Costs of Materials and Activities of Not-for-Profit Organizations and State and Local Government Entities that Include Fund-Raising* (New York: American Institute of Certified Public Accountants, 1998).

these three classes of net assets must also be reported. Reclassifications that simultaneously decrease temporarily restricted net assets and increase unrestricted net assets are reported separately.

Required external financial statements include the following:

1. *Statement of Financial Position* (balance sheet) which will report organization-wide totals for assets, liabilities, and net assets, and net assets identified as unrestricted, temporarily restricted, and permanently restricted.
2. *Statement of Activities* which reports revenues, expenses, gains, losses, and reclassifications (between classes of net assets). Minimum requirements include organization-wide totals, changes in net assets for each class of assets, and all expenses recognized only in the unrestricted classification. A display of a measure of operations in the statement of activities is permitted.
3. *Statement of Cash Flows* with categories (operating, financing, investing, etc.) similar to business organizations.
4. *Statement of Functional Expenses* which reports detailed program, fund-raising, and management and general expenses (required only for voluntary health and welfare organizations).

In addition, information about liquidity is provided. Liquidity is commonly reported through sequencing assets and liabilities according to nearness of conversion to or use of cash on the statement of financial position. Such sequencing requires cash and contributions receivable restricted by donors to investment in land, building, and equipment to be included in "assets restricted to investment in land, building, and equipment" rather than cash and contributions. Cash and equivalents of permanent endowment funds held temporarily until suitable long-term investment opportunities are identified must be included in the classification "long-term investments." Other organizations provide liquidity information in the notes to the financial statements.

Not-for-profit organizations are encouraged to develop the format for their financial statements that is most meaningful to their users. Models, suggested by the FASB and included in this chapter, are (1) a single-column, *corporate* format and (2) disaggregation by net asset class. Organizations appear to prefer the former model for the statement of financial position and the latter for the statement of activities. Illustration 18-2 (shown on page 1029) presents the statement of activities. Illustration 18-4 (shown on page 1030) presents the statement of financial position. A cash flow statement is included in Illustration 18-5 (shown on page 1031).

Required note disclosures include a description of the fund accounting groups and their relationship to the classes of net assets, classification of revenues, expenses, gains, losses, classification and valuation of contributions, description of accounting policies for release of donor restrictions, anticipated collection period of contributions receivables, description of collections, and detail on contributed services not meeting the reporting criteria. Disclosure of expenses by natural classification is suggested but not required.

Proper recording of both reciprocal exchange transactions, agency transactions, and nonreciprocal contributions is essential to providing organization-wide financial statements of assets, liabilities, net assets, changes in net assets, and cash flows. Managers of not-for-profit organizations will have to carefully analyze the nature of each transaction to properly identify contributions and exchange transactions.

REFLECTION

- Private not-for-profits use full accrual accounting.
- All transactions of a not-for-profit organization may be classified as exchange, nonexchange, or agency. Accounting for exchange transactions follows full accrual accounting. Agency transactions are accounted for in the same way as in governments.
- Nonexchange transactions, or contributions, are accounted for in the period received or made. Contributions may be classified as unrestricted, temporarily restricted, or permanently restricted by the donor.

- A reclassification (release of restriction) is made when the donor-imposed restriction is met. This may be a result of satisfying a program, equipment, or time restriction.
- The financial statements of all not-for-profits include a statement of financial position, statement of activities, and statement of cash flows. Each of the three net assets (unrestricted, temporarily restricted, and permanently restricted) and any changes to these asset categories are shown on the financial statements.

7

OBJECTIVE

State the requirements an organization must meet to be classified as voluntary health and welfare, and describe the accounting for public support.

ACCOUNTING FOR VOLUNTARY HEALTH AND WELFARE ORGANIZATIONS

To qualify as a *voluntary health and welfare organization (VHWO)*, two criteria must be met. First, a primary source of revenue should be contributions from donors who do not themselves directly benefit from the organization's programs. Second, the program must be in the area of health, welfare, or community service, such as care for the elderly, the indigent, or the handicapped, or projects to protect the environment.

Accounting Principles and Procedures

The dependence upon public support for the majority of its resources influences the accounting for a VHWO. Two major categories are used to record and communicate inflows of resources: public support and revenues. Public support is the inflow of resources from voluntary donors who receive no direct, personal benefit from the organization's usual programs in exchange for their contributions. Revenues are inflows of resources resulting from a charge for service from financial activities or from other exchange transactions.

A significant aspect of accounting and reporting for VHWOs is that financial reports must show expenses on a program basis. As a result of this requirement, the costs of each program and supporting service are available, and the effectiveness with which the organization's resources have been managed can be measured.

Public Support

The following accounts are used to record receipts of assets in the public support category:

1. Contributions,
2. Special Events Support,
3. Legacies and Bequests, and
4. Received from Federated and Nonfederated Campaigns.

Contributions. Contributions are recognized as public support in the period received and as assets, decreases of liabilities, or expenses depending on the form of the benefits received.[8] Although most contributions to VHWOs are made with no restrictions attached, some donations specify the purpose for which they must be expended. Contributions also include unconditional promises to give (pledges). Therefore, unconditional promises to give must also be recognized as support in the period received. Contributions may be unrestricted or restricted for a specific purpose. Contributions that have no donor-imposed restrictions attached to them are reported as unrestricted. Contributions that have donor-imposed restrictions attached to them must be classified as temporarily or permanently restricted based on the nature of the restriction.

8 A contribution is defined as an "unconditional transfer of cash or other assets to an entity or a settlement or cancellation of its liabilities in a voluntary nonreciprocal transfer by another entity acting other than as an owner" (FASB Statement No. 116, par. 5).

Cash collections that do not involve a previous promise to give are credited to the account Contributions. VHWOs also receive pledges for contributions, which are recorded at the gross amount as Contributions Receivable, with a credit to Contributions. A provision and an allowance for estimated uncollectible pledges are established, based on historical collection experience. The provision for uncollectible pledges is an expense account, while the allowance is a contra account to Pledges Receivable.

Expiration of donor restrictions must be recognized in the period in which the restriction expires. The expiration of a restriction may be based on the lapse of time, the fulfillment of a stipulated purpose, or both. Recognition of an expiration of donor restrictions is done with a reclassification entry. Reclassifications result in an increase in the unrestricted class of net assets and a decrease in temporarily restricted net assets class. Such a reclassification increases unrestricted net assets to *match* the decrease resulting from the stipulated expense.

Temporarily restricted unconditional promises to give (pledges) are reclassified to unrestricted in the period in which the unconditional promise is received or the restriction lapses. A gift or promise to give that involves a condition is not considered a contribution until the condition is met and is therefore not recognized as an increase in net assets in the period in which it is received but is disclosed in the footnotes.

Securities and other property received should be recorded at fair value at the time of receipt. These assets are most likely to be received as temporarily or permanently restricted contributions. The donor may restrict not only the purpose but also the timing of use. If the donation is not available for use until some future fiscal period, it is recorded as Contributions—Temporarily Restricted. The amount is released from restriction (unclassified) in the period when it becomes available.

Common to VHWOs is the donation of materials to be used in providing service or to be processed for subsequent sale. These materials should be recorded as inventory, with a credit to Unrestricted Contributions at their fair value when received, provided that they are substantial in amount and a measurable value for them can be established, either by sale shortly thereafter or by appraisal. An example would be the donation of clothing or household goods to Goodwill Industries.

Occasionally, a VHWO will be permitted to use building facilities rent free. In this situation, both the contribution and the rent expense should be recorded at fair rental value, usually equivalent to the amount that normally would be charged for rent. Donated fixed assets for which title is received, such as equipment, land, and buildings, should be entered as an unrestricted, temporarily restricted, or permanently restricted contribution at fair value depending upon the donor's stipulations. Expiration of donor restrictions will occur either at the time the asset is placed in service or over the asset's useful life. Permanent restrictions do not expire.

Although the range of personal services that volunteers donate varies between VHWOs, these services should be recorded if they are significant and if the following criteria are met:

1. The services received create or enhance nonfinancial assets, or
2. The services received require specialized skills, are provided by individuals possessing those skills, and would typically need to be purchased if not provided by donation. (Usually the individuals performing such services are treated in a similar fashion to employees; they have schedules, assigned duties, are supervised, etc.)

Promises to give services are also included. Recognizing contributed services that are specialized and would need to be purchased indicates to readers of the financial statements the impact these contributions have on the organization. It also indicates the need for future cash outflows in the event these services are no longer contributed.

If the criteria are met, donated services are recorded with a debit to an expense account, such as Salary Expense, and a credit to Contributions. Contributed services received that are not required to be recognized as revenues are disclosed at their fair value in the footnotes to the financial statements.

Special Events Support. Another subdivision of the public support category covers an organization's special fund-raising events in which the participant has the opportunity to receive something of value in exchange for a contribution. Raffles, dinners, bingo games, and bake sales are examples of special events. The gross inflow of resources is credited to Special Events Support in the fund that it is to benefit. Direct costs of the event, excluding promotional costs, are charged to Cost of Special Events. Comparing these two balances permits one to judge the effectiveness of the event. It also determines that portion of the proceeds that is a contribution to the organization. If such *special events* are peripheral or incidental, they may be disclosed net of costs (which used to be the general practice), but if they are ongoing and major activities, then gross revenue is recorded and direct costs of those activities are considered fund-raising expenses. Promotional costs, such as advertising or the salaries of employees involved in the event, are charged against fund-raising expense. The portion of the budget consumed by fund-raising expenses must also be revealed.

Legacies and Bequests. Every VHWO hopes that its programs will be so deserving that they will encourage donors to make major contributions of personal property or real property through their wills. Since these items tend to be more substantial in amount, the audit guide recommends that such contributions be shown as a separate item of public support under Legacies and Bequests. They are entered as a credit to that account when the organization is reasonably certain of the amount to be received. Such contributions are classified as unrestricted, temporarily restricted, or permanently restricted based on donor stipulations.

Received from Federated and Nonfederated Campaigns. The final item considered as public support is the amount received from federated (associated) and nonfederated organizations. This amount is credited to Received from Federated and Nonfederated Campaigns. An amount allocated by United Way to a health and welfare organization would be an example of support received from a federated organization. An amount raised by independent, professional fund-raising groups would be an illustration of resources received from nonfederated campaigns. Usually, contributions received from federated and nonfederated campaigns are unrestricted.

8

OBJECTIVE

Explain how to account for revenues and costs in a VHWO.

Revenues

In addition to public support, resources may be received from exchange transactions that are classified as unrestricted revenue. These resources would include the following accounts:

1. Membership Dues Revenue for dues charged members to join and use facilities or receive publications.
2. Program Services Fees for amounts charged clients for services of the organization, such as consulting, testing, or advising.
3. Sales of Publications and Supplies for proceeds from the sales of these items.

Investment transaction revenue, classified as unrestricted or restricted, could include the following accounts:

1. Investment Revenue for interest, dividends, and other earnings.
2. Realized Gain on Investment Transactions for gains from the sale or exchange of investments.
3. Net Increase (or Decrease) in Carrying Value of Investments for the unrealized appreciation (or depreciation) of investments if they are carried at fair value.

Each of the items of investment transactions revenue would be recorded as unrestricted or restricted depending on donor stipulations. Thus, the unrestricted revenue from an endowment would be recorded with a credit to Investment Revenue—Unrestricted. Restricted investment revenue is reported as temporarily or permanently restricted in compliance with the donor's wishes.

VHWOs are required to carry their investments at fair value.[9] Cost includes not only the total cost of purchased investments but also the fair value at the date of receipt of donated investments. When a relatively permanent reduction in fair value occurs, the impairment to cost

9 FASB Statement No. 124, *Investments of Not-for-Profit Organizations* (Norwalk, CT: Financial Accounting Standards Board, 1995).

should be recorded. The unrealized appreciation (or depreciation) is shown separately in Net Increase (or Decrease) in Carrying Value of Investments. Realized and unrealized gains and losses on all investments are considered increases or decreases in unrestricted net assets unless restricted by donor or law.

Program and Supporting Services Costs

VHWOs exist to render service or to conduct programs. Their operating statements will not show typical expenses, such as salaries or rent, but will show the cost of each program or service the organization provides—the costs in which the general public, the contributors, and the controlling agencies are primarily interested. For example, the operating statement of an environmental protection association might show the cost of conducting a program to reduce river pollution or to provide an animal and bird sanctuary. These projects fall in an expense grouping called Program Services. The other expense grouping shown on an operating statement is referred to as Supporting Services, which includes fund-raising costs, management and general costs, and membership development activities for the overall direction of the organization. Management and general activities include all management, financing, and administrative activities, except for direct activities of programs or fund raising. Fund-raising activities include publicizing and conducting fund-raising campaigns, maintaining donor mailing lists, conducting special fund-raising events, preparing and distributing fund-raising materials, and other activities involved with soliciting contributions. Membership development activities include soliciting for prospective members and membership dues, membership relations, and similar activities.

Individual expenses, such as salaries or rent, are recorded in the respective natural expense accounts in much the same way that they would be recorded in the accounts of profit entities. All expenses are considered reductions in unrestricted net assets. Therefore, when expenses are recorded for purposes stipulated by donors, a reclassification of temporarily restricted to unrestricted net assets is recorded. At the end of the fiscal year, the expenses are allocated to the individual programs conducted and to the supporting services of management, fund raising, and membership development. Allocation of joint costs should be on some rational basis, such as assigning salaries on the basis of time expended, allotting rental charges on the basis of floor space, or apportioning supplies expense on the basis of consumption. However, it is not always simple to allocate costs.

The public has been deluged with informational materials that attempt to educate the reader about proper health habits to avoid disease or infection, birth control and other family planning issues, and the need to protect endangered species or the environment. Included in much of this material is a fund-raising appeal. A question arises as to whether the total cost of sending such literature should be charged to the program publicized or to fund raising, or whether it should be allocated between them. Since board members, donors, and the general public pay particular attention to the percentages of revenue consumed by administrative and fund-raising purposes, the desire to keep those percentages at a minimum is understandable. AICPA guidance on joint-cost allocation described in the previous section must be followed by all VHWOs.

Closing Entries

After all expenses have been assigned, an entry is made to close the expense accounts and charge each of the expenses to the individual programs and supporting services. For the environmental protection association used earlier as an example, the following entry might be recorded:

River Pollution Program Expense	XXX	
Animal and Bird Sanctuary Program Expense	XXX	
Management and General Services Expense	XXX	
Fund-Raising Services Expense	XXX	
Salary Expense, Supplies Expense, etc.		XXX

The final closing entries close support and revenue accounts, as well as the program and services accounts, to the appropriate net asset classification. The closing entry for the Unrestricted Net Assets of the environmental protection association might be as follows:

Contributions—Unrestricted	XXX	
Legacies and Bequests—Unrestricted	XXX	
Membership Dues Revenue	XXX	
Investment Revenue—Unrestricted	XXX	
Reclassification In—Unrestricted—Satisfaction of Donor Restrictions	XXX	
River Pollution Program Expense		XXX
Animal and Bird Sanctuary Program Expense		XXX
Management and General Services Expense		XXX
Fund-Raising Services Expense		XXX
Unrestricted Net Assets		XXX

If the board of directors should decide to designate a specified sum of the Unrestricted Net Assets for a future program to reduce air pollution, the following entries are recorded:

Unrestricted Net Assets	XXX	
Unrestricted Net Assets—Designated for Air Pollution Program		XXX

Similar entries to close temporarily restricted and permanently restricted accounts include the following:

Contributions—Temporarily Restricted	XXX	
Legacies and Bequests—Temporarily Restricted	XXX	
Investment Revenue—Temporarily Restricted	XXX	
Reclassifications Out—Temporarily Restricted—Satisfaction of Donor Restrictions		XXX
Temporarily Restricted Net Assets		XXX

Contributions—Permanently Restricted	XXX	
Legacies and Bequests—Permanently Restricted	XXX	
Permanently Restricted Net Assets		XXX

9

OBJECTIVE

Prepare financial statements for not-for-profit organizations.

Financial Statements

Consistent with other not-for-profits, the financial statements for VHWOs are a statement of financial position, a statement of activities, and a statement of cash flows. In addition, VHWOs must provide a statement of functional expenses. A statement of financial position is prepared either in single-column form or with a column for each asset class. Organization-wide totals of assets, liabilities, and net assets are presented. An activities statement can be prepared after the expense allocation entry has been recorded. It is structured with a column for each asset class and shows how effectively the organization operated during the period. Since program costs and not the typical expenses, such as salaries, are shown in an operating statement, a summary of expenses by object-of-expense classification is provided in a separate statement. This statement of functional expenses supplements the operating statement. It presents the total of each functional expense to programs and supporting services.

Day Star Activity and Respite Center serves older adults afflicted with Alzheimer's disease or other memory impairment and their families. Day Star operates an adult day care center, which provides a respite from constant caregiving for primary caregivers. Day Star also provides limited home care for clients. The expenses that were incurred by Day Star are as follows:

Expense	Amount
Salaries and payroll taxes	$17,000
Crafts and activities	4,000
Meals on Wheels	4,000
Office expenses	2,000
Repairs and maintenance	1,500
Depreciation expense	5,000
Total expenses	$33,500

Day Star management has estimated the allocation of financial resources to organization activities and prepared the following allocation scheme:

	Day Care	Home Care	Management
Operating expenses	40%	35%	25%
Capital-related expenses	90	10	0

Expenses are allocated to programs and supporting services in the following manner. Then, they are presented in the statement of activities.

	Total	Day Care	Home Care	Management and General
Operating expenses	$28,500	$11,400	$9,975	$7,125
Capital-related expenses	5,000	4,500	500	

Expenses also are allocated to programs and supporting services using the allocation matrix for presentation in the statement of functional expenses. The following example shows this procedure for three object-of-expense categories:

Object of Expense	Total	Day Care	Home Care	Management and General
Salaries and payroll taxes	$17,000	$ 6,800	$ 5,950	$4,250
Crafts and activities	4,000	1,600	1,400	1,000
Meals on Wheels	4,000	1,600	1,400	1,000
Office expenses	2,000	800	700	500
Repairs and maintenance	1,500	600	525	375
Depreciation	5,000	4,500	500	
Total expenses	$33,500	$15,900	$10,475	$7,125

Illustrative Transactions for a Voluntary Health and Welfare Organization

10
OBJECTIVE
Prepare journal entries related to typical events of a not-for-profit organization.

To illustrate the recording of events and the preparation of financial reports for a VHWO, assume the People's Environmental Protection (PEP) Association, a voluntary community organization, has three programs: Valley Air Project, Fish in the Lakes, and Flood Control. The statement of financial position of PEP on December 31, 20X6, is shown in Illustration 18-1.

Illustration 18-1
People's Environmental Protection (PEP) Association
Statement of Financial Position
As of December 31, 20X6

Assets:	
Cash and cash equivalents	$ 253,500
Contributions receivable (net of $3,100 allowance)	21,500
Inventories	10,000
Short-term investments	152,000
Property, plant, and equipment (net of $16,700 accumulated depreciation)	676,000
Long-term endowment investments	253,000
Total assets	**$1,366,000**
Liabilities and net assets:	
Accounts payable	$ 37,000
Notes payable	100,000
Total liabilities	**$ 137,000**
Net assets:	
Unrestricted	**$ 289,000**
Temporarily restricted	**687,000**
Permanently restricted	**253,000**
Total net assets	**$1,229,000**
Total liabilities and net assets	$ 1,366,000

The following events occur during the calendar year 20X7. They are summarized to conserve space and minimize duplication. Entries are shown following each transaction. Although no fund designations are recorded, VHWOs may choose to use fund accounting for donor-restricted resources, plant, and permanently restricted endowments. Fund-based financial statements for VHWOs are illustrated in the appendix to this chapter.

Event	Entry		
1. As a result of its fund-raising program, cash contributions of $325,000 were received. $315,000 was unrestricted, and $10,000 was restricted for Valley Air Project operating costs. In addition, unconditional promises to give totaled $100,000, of which $80,000 was unrestricted and $20,000 restricted for acquisition of equipment.	Cash	325,000	
	Contributions—Unrestricted		315,000
	Contributions—Temporarily Restricted		10,000
	Contributions Receivable	100,000	
	Contributions—Unrestricted		80,000
	Contributions—Temporarily Restricted		20,000
2. Based on past experience, 5% of the promises to give was estimated to be uncollectible.	Provision for Uncollectible Contributions	5,000	
	Allowance for Uncollectible Contributions		5,000
3. During the year, cash was collected from some unconditional promises to give, while others were written off as uncollectible.	Cash	95,500	
	Allowance for Uncollectible Contributions	5,600	
	Contributions Receivable		101,100

Event	Entry		
4. A cash donation of $40,000 was received, with the donor stipulation that it be used to acquire equipment for water quality improvement.	Cash	40,000	
	Contributions—Temporarily Restricted		40,000
5. With the donor's approval, the $40,000 served as a partial payment on the purchase of a filter system costing $50,000. A note was signed for the unpaid balance. PEP chooses to release the donor restriction over the life of the asset.	Land, Building, and Equipment	50,000	
	Cash		40,000
	Notes Payable on Equipment		10,000
6. PEP received $5,000 from an individual who restricted its use to a special project within a Fish in the Lakes program. If that special project is not accomplished within six months, the individual requested that the money be returned. PEP has not yet undertaken the project. Two months remain in the time period specified by the donor.	Cash	5,000	
	Refundable Advances		5,000
7. The following bequests were received: $100,000 unrestricted and $20,000 to be invested in an endowment whose earnings are to be unrestricted.	Cash	120,000	
	Legacies and Bequests—Unrestricted		100,000
	Legacies and Bequests—Permanently Restricted		20,000
8. PEP received donated goods with a fair value of $2,350. Of those donated goods, $750 is restricted by the donor for use in the Fish in the Lakes program; the remaining gifts can be used at management's discretion.	Inventories	2,350	
	Contributions—Unrestricted		1,600
	Contributions—Temporarily Restricted		750
9. PEP held a special summer event to promote its activities, the net proceeds of which were unrestricted. Gross revenues totaled $9,000, with direct costs for the event amounting to $2,000.	Cash	9,000	
	Special Events Support—Unrestricted		9,000
	Costs of Special Events	2,000	
	Cash		2,000
10. PEP uses volunteers to distribute brochures about its operations, to assist the staff with routine office work, and to make phone calls during the annual fund-raising appeal. The volunteers provided 1,000 hours of service this year. If the volunteers were not available, the tasks would either be performed by staff at a later date or not done at all.			
11. Members were assessed and all paid membership dues of $118,000.	Cash	118,000	
	Membership Dues Revenues		118,000
12. The local PEP unit receives unrestricted cash of $16,000 as its share of a campaign run by its national affiliate.	Cash	16,000	
	Received from Federated and Nonfederated Campaigns—Unrestricted		16,000
13. Earnings on endowment investments total $28,000, of which $21,000 is not restricted and $7,000 is restricted to investment in equipment for flood control.	Cash	28,000	
	Investment Revenue—Unrestricted		21,000
	Investment Revenue—Temporarily Restricted		7,000

(continued)

Event	Entry		
14. PEP carries its investments in all funds at fair value. Endowment investments are sold for $27,000. They had a cost of $20,000 and a carrying value of $25,000 in the investment account. All endowment gains are to be permanently restricted according to donor specifications.	Cash	27,000	
	Investment (at fair)		25,000
	Gain on Sale of Investments—Permanently Restricted		2,000
15. An additional $46,000 of investments are purchased from endowment funds.	Investments—Permanently Restricted	46,000	
	Cash		46,000
16. Unrestricted investments have shown no material change in fair value over the year. At year-end, the fair value of permanently restricted endowment investments has increased from $265,000 to $294,000. All endowment gains are to be permanently restricted according to the donor specification.	Investments	29,000	
	Net Increase in Carrying Value of Investments—Permanently Restricted		29,000
17. A lawyer provided five hours of service to PEP to draw up an endowment agreement. She did not charge for her services. She normally would charge a client $500 for consultation on a similar type of agreement. In the absence of the donated professional services, PEP would have hired a lawyer to draft the agreement.	Professional Services	500	
	Contributions—Unrestricted		500
18. A special recreational building and dock costing $96,000 were purchased with unrestricted cash.	Land, Building, and Equipment	96,000	
	Cash		96,000
19. Contributions received in the prior period with the stipulation that they be used for expenses of this period are now available.	Reclassification Out—Temporarily Restricted—Satisfaction of Time Requirements	10,000	
	Reclassification In—Unrestricted—Satisfaction of Time Requirements		10,000
20. Accounts payable and expenses were paid or established. Operating expenses related to donor-specific programs totaled $103,000.	Accounts Payable (January 1)	37,000	
	Salaries Expense	200,000	
	Payroll Taxes	30,000	
	Mailing and Postage Expense	50,000	
	Rent Expense	28,000	
	Telephone Expense	6,000	
	Research Expense	215,000	
	Professional Services: Legal and Audit	34,000	
	Supplies Expense	13,000	
	Miscellaneous Expense	5,000	
	Accounts Payable		32,000
	Cash		586,000
	Reclassification Out—Temporarily Restricted—Satisfaction of Program Requirements	103,000	
	Reclassification In—Unrestricted—Satisfaction of Program Requirements		103,000

Event	Entry		
21. Contributed goods of $1,450 were used during the year for the Fish in the Lakes program. This amount includes the $750 donor-restricted contribution in item (8).	Supplies Expense	1,450	
	Inventories		1,450
	Reclassification Out—Temporarily Restricted—Satisfaction of Program Requirements	750	
	Reclassification In—Unrestricted—Satisfaction of Program Requirements		750
22. Depreciation on equipment purchased with donor-restricted contributions amounted to $22,000 for the year. (Valley Air Project—$2,000; Fish in the Lakes program—$3,000; Flood Control program—$16,000; management and general services—$1,000). An equivalent amount of temporarily unspecified net assets is released from restrictions.	Depreciation Expense	22,000	
	Accumulated Depreciation		22,000
	Reclassification Out—Temporarily Restricted—Satisfaction of Equipment Acquisition Requirements	22,000	
	Reclassification In—Unrestricted—Satisfaction of Equipment Acquisition Requirements		22,000
23. Early in the year, cash contributions for current operations were received, but they cannot be used until late in the following year.	Cash	2,000	
	Contributions—Temporarily Restricted		2,000
24. At year-end, the expenses were allocated to the various programs and supporting services. The direct cost of a special event is not included in the allocation process because it is subtracted from the gross proceeds of that event. The special event is considered an incidental activity and reported "net" in the statement of activities.	Valley Air Project	132,000	
	Fish in the Lakes Program	184,450	
	Flood Control Program	251,000	
	Management and General Services	29,500	
	Fund-Raising Services	11,000	
	Membership Development	2,000	
	Salaries Expense		200,000
	Payroll Taxes		30,000
	Mailing and Postage Expense		50,000
	Rent Expense		28,000
	Telephone Expense		6,000
	Research Expense		215,000
	Professional Services: Legal and Audit		34,500
	Supplies Expense		14,450
	Miscellaneous Expense		5,000
	Provision for Uncollectible Contributions		5,000
	Depreciation Expense		22,000
25. Closing entries. Each class of asset is closed separately.	Contributions—Unrestricted	397,100	
	Special Events Support	9,000	
	Legacies and Bequests—Unrestricted	100,000	
	Received from Federated and Nonfederated Campaigns	16,000	
	Membership Dues Revenue	118,000	
	Investment Revenue	21,000	
	Reclassifications In—Unrestricted—Satisfaction of Program Restrictions	103,750	
	Reclassifications In—Unrestricted—Satisfaction of Equipment Acquisition Restrictions	22,000	

(continued)

Entry		
Reclassifications In—Unrestricted—Satisfaction of Time Restrictions	10,000	
Valley Air Project		132,000
Fish in the Lakes Program		184,450
Flood Control Program		251,000
Management and General Services		29,500
Fund-Raising Services		11,000
Membership Development		2,000
Cost of Special Events		2,000
Unrestricted Net Assets		**184,900**
Contributions—Temporarily Restricted	72,750	
Investment Revenue—Temporarily Restricted	7,000	
Temporarily Restricted Net Assets	**56,000**	
Reclassifications Out—Unrestricted—Satisfaction of Program Restrictions		103,750
Reclassifications Out—Unrestricted—Satisfaction of Equipment Acquisition Restrictions		22,000
Reclassifications Out—Unrestricted—Satisfaction of Time Restrictions		10,000
Legacies and Bequests—Endowment—Permanently Restricted	20,000	
Net Increase in Carrying Value of Endowment Investments—Permanently Restricted	29,000	
Gain on Sale of Endowment Investments—Permanently Restricted	2,000	
Permanently Restricted Net Assets		**51,000**

The final entry at year-end closes the support and revenue accounts, as well as the program and supporting services expenses, into the appropriate net asset accounts. With expenses allocated to programs and supporting services, it is now possible to prepare the statement of activities (see Illustration 18-2 on page 1029). The sequence of items is suggested by the title. Inflows of resources from public support, revenues, and reclassification are listed first, followed by the expense totals for each program and supporting service, taken directly from the closing and allocation entries. The beginning net asset balance for each class is added, resulting in the net asset balance at the end of the period.

Since the investments account is carried at fair value, it is entirely possible that the carrying value may decrease. If this situation occurs, the account Net Decrease in Carrying Value of Investments is debited, and the investments account is credited. The closing entry would credit Net Decrease in Carrying Value of Investments and debit unrestricted or permanently restricted net assets depending on donor specifications or law.

The statement of activities of a VHWO provides valuable data on the total cost per period of each program and of supporting services. To provide the reader of its financial statements with additional information, a statement of functional expenses is included in the reports. This statement shows the allocation of each expense (salaries, rent, etc.) and reveals the cost by function of carrying on the organization's activities. The statement of functional expenses for PEP is shown in Illustration 18-3 on page 1030.

The statement of financial position for PEP on December 31, 20X7, is given in Illustration 18-4. The statement of cash flows shown in Illustration 18-5 includes, under *financing activities*, all cash inflows from contributions and investment income restricted by donor for long-term investments (or endowments) or for acquisition of fixed assets.

As is true in reporting for-profit enterprises, financial statements of VHWOs would be prepared with comparative figures for the preceding year. The statements also should be accompanied by notes that would summarize significant accounting policies.

Illustration 18-2
People's Environmental Protection (PEP) Association
Statement of Activities
For Year Ended December 31, 20X7

	Unrestricted	Temporarily Restricted	Permanently Restricted	Total
Public support:				
Contributions	$ 397,100	$ 72,750		$ 469,850
Special events (net of $2,000 direct costs)	7,000			7,000
Legacies and bequests	100,000		$ 20,000	120,000
Received from federated and nonfederated campaigns	16,000			16,000
Total public support	$ 520,100	$ 72,750	$ 20,000	$ 612,850
Revenue:				
Membership dues	$ 118,000			$ 118,000
Investment revenue	21,000	$ 7,000		28,000
Net increase in carrying value of investments			$ 29,000	29,000
Realized gain on investments			2,000	2,000
Total revenue	$ 139,000	$ 7,000	$ 31,000	$ 177,000
Net assets released from restrictions:				
Satisfaction of program requirements	$ 103,750	$ (103,750)		
Satisfaction of equipment acquisition requirements	22,000	(22,000)		
Expiration of time restrictions	10,000	(10,000)		
Total net assets released from restrictions	$ 135,750	$ (135,750)		
Total public support and revenue	$ 794,850	$ (56,000)	$ 51,000	$ 789,850
Expenses:				
Valley Air Project	$ 132,000			$ 132,000
Fish in the Lakes program	184,450			184,450
Flood Control program	251,000			251,000
Management and general	29,500			29,500
Fund raising	11,000			11,000
Membership development	2,000			2,000
Total expenses	$ 609,950			$ 609,950
Change in net assets	**$184,900**	**$ (56,000)**	**$ 51,000**	**$ 179,900**
Net assets beginning of year	**289,000**	**687,000**	**253,000**	**1,229,000**
Net assets end of year	**$473,900**	**$631,000**	**$304,000**	**$1,408,900**

Illustration 18-3
People's Environmental Protection (PEP) Association
Statement of Functional Expenses
For Year Ended December 31, 20X7

		Program Services				Supporting Services			
	Total All Services	Valley Air Project	Fish in the Lakes	Flood Control	Total Programs	Management and General	Fund Raising	Membership Development	Total Supporting
Salaries	$200,000	$ 36,000	$ 60,000	$ 80,000	$176,000	$19,000	$ 4,500	$ 500	$24,000
Payroll taxes	30,000	5,400	9,000	12,000	26,400	3,000	500	100	3,600
Mailing and postage	50,000	10,000	20,000	19,700	49,700		200	100	300
Rent	28,000	8,000	5,000	11,600	24,600	2,000	400	1,000	3,400
Telephone	6,000	1,500	1,300	2,500	5,300		400	300	700
Research	215,000	35,000	80,000	100,000	215,000				
Professional: legal and audit	34,500	24,000	2,000	4,000	30,000	4,500			4,500
Supplies	14,450	10,100	1,450	2,900	14,450				
Provision for uncollectible contributions	5,000						5,000		5,000
Miscellaneous	5,000		2,700	2,300	5,000				
Total expenses before depreciation	$587,950	$130,000	$181,450	$235,000	$546,450	$28,500	$11,000	$2,000	$41,500
Depreciation of building and equipment	22,000	2,000	3,000	16,000	21,000	1,000			1,000
Total expenses	$609,950	$132,000	$184,450	$251,000	$567,450	$29,500	$11,000	$2,000	$42,500

Illustration 18-4
People's Environmental Protection (PEP) Association
Statement of Financial Position
As of December 31, 20X7

Assets:	
Cash and cash equivalents	$ 268,000
Contributions receivable (net of $2,500 allowance)	21,000
Inventories	10,900
Short-term investments	152,000
Property, plant, and equipment (net of $38,700 accumulated depreciation)	800,000
Long-term endowment investments	304,000
Total assets	**$1,555,900**
Liabilities and net assets:	
Accounts payable	$ 32,000
Refundable advances	5,000
Notes payable	110,000
Total liabilities	**$ 147,000**
Net assets:	
Unrestricted	**$ 473,900**
Temporarily restricted	**631,000**
Permanently restricted	**304,000**
Total net assets	**$1,408,900**
Total liabilities and net assets	$ 1,555,900

Illustration 18-5
People's Environmental Protection (PEP) Association
Statement of Cash Flows
For Year Ended December 31, 20X7

Cash flows from operating activities:	
Cash received from members	$ 118,000
Cash received from contributions	402,500
Cash received from special events	7,000
Cash received from federated and nonfederated campaigns	16,000
Cash received from legacies and bequests	100,000
Cash received on a refundable advance	5,000
Interest and dividends received	21,000
Cash paid to employees and suppliers	(586,000)
Net cash provided by (used for) operating activities	**$ 83,500**
Cash flows from investing activities:	
Proceeds from sales and maturities of investments	$ 27,000
Purchases of investments	(46,000)
Purchase of land, building, and equipment	(146,000)
Net cash provided by (used for) investing activities	**$(165,000)**
Cash flow from financing activities:	
Proceeds from issuance of notes payable	$ 10,000
Receipts of interest and dividends restricted for reinvestment	7,000*
Contributions received restricted for long-term investment	20,000
Contributions received restricted for investment in plant	60,000
Net cash provided by (used for) financing activities	**$ 97,000**
Net increase (decrease) in cash and cash equivalents	**$ 15,500**
Cash and cash equivalents at beginning of year	**252,500**
Cash and cash equivalents at end of year	**$ 268,000**
Reconciliation of change in net assets to net cash provided by operating activities:	
Change in net assets	$ 179,900
Depreciation	22,000
Decrease in contributions receivable	500
Increase in inventories	(900)
Increase in notes payable	10,000
Increase in refundable advances	(5,000)
Decrease in accounts payable	(5,000)
Increase in net carrying value of investments	(29,000)
Gain on sale of investments	(2,000)
Interest restricted for long-term investment	(7,000)
Contributions restricted for long-term investment	(20,000)
Contributions restricted for plant	(60,000)
Net cash provided by operating activities	$ 83,500

*$4,000 of cash at beginning of year and $5,000 of cash at year-end are included in the classification "long-term endowment investments" on the statement of financial position.

REFLECTION

- Voluntary health and welfare organizations account for public support and revenues.
- Public support categories include contributions, special events, legacies and bequests, and federated and nonfederated campaigns.
- Expenditures are separated into program and supporting services. Joint cost allocation rules are followed for the allocation of fund-raising costs.
- A fourth financial statement is required of all VHWOs (but not of other not-for-profits)—the statement of functional expenses—which provides detailed information on the expenses for each program and support service.

The Budget

Budgets are also prepared in not-for-profit organizations. As in a commercial enterprise, the budgeting process involves the establishment of goals, the measurement of actual performance, and the comparison of actual with projected performance to evaluate results. This process requires the input of persons who can determine what resources will become available, what the organization desires to achieve with those resources, and how the resources should be applied to yield the greatest benefit. If the organization or program is well established, a useful starting point is the previous year's budget and its variances, adjusted for any changes in objectives. If the group or program is new, the preparation of an effective operating budget requires careful research to produce realistic estimates of both revenues and expenditures. Expenditures should be planned to maximize service output without producing either a surplus or a deficit. A sizable excess of revenues over expenditures implies that more or better service could be provided. A deficit may indicate the need to curtail future services, since future funds may have to be committed to cover past deficits.[10]

SUMMARY

FASB Statement Nos. 116 and 117 serve to enhance the information provided to readers of the financial statements about financial viability, financial flexibility, liquidity, cash flows, and service efforts. Use of financial statements based on net asset classifications is a much different concept from traditional fund group reporting. While the detailed examples in this chapter focused on a VHWO, these same standards apply to all not-for-profits, including those in the arts, health care, and education. An example of optional funds-based financial statements is presented in the appendix.

10 In accounting for not-for-profit organizations, it is not as common to find budgetary amounts formally entered into principal ledger accounts as it is in governmental accounting. If a budgetary entry is recorded, it would be similar to the one used in governmental accounting, and it would be reversed at year-end. Assuming estimated revenues exceed estimated expenditures and allocations, the budgetary journal entry for a governmental college or university would be as follows:

Estimated Revenues	XXX	
Estimated Expenditures (or Budget Allocations for Expenditures)		XXX
Unallocated Balance		XXX

APPENDIX: OPTIONAL FUND ACCOUNTING FOR VOLUNTARY HEALTH AND WELFARE ORGANIZATIONS

11

OBJECTIVE

Describe the typical funds used to account for VHWO transactions, and prepare optional VHWO fund-based financial statements.

To segregate resources and demonstrate compliance with restrictions, fund accounting is sometimes used by voluntary health and welfare organizations. As described in the text, voluntary health and welfare organizations have two current funds consisting primarily of current assets and current liabilities, a separate plant fund, and an endowment fund. Unlike health care organizations, where donor-restricted funds act as feeders to the general funds, all funds of voluntary health and welfare organizations record expenses. As a result, there are few interfund transactions compared with other not-for-profit organizations.

VHWO Funds

The following table lists the funds used by most VHWOs with the three *net asset* categories.

Funds	Unrestricted Net Assets	Temporarily Restricted Net Assets	Permanently Restricted Net Assets
Current Unrestricted	X		
Current Restricted	X	X	
Land, Building, and Equipment (Plant Fund)	X	X	X
Endowment Fund		X	X
Agency (Custodial) Fund			

Current Unrestricted Fund. The current unrestricted fund accounts are for resources that have no external restrictions and are available for current operations at the discretion of the governing board. The board, however, may place its own limitations on the fund unrestricted net assets. In the same manner that industry appropriates retained earnings, the board of directors of a health and welfare organization may designate a portion of its unrestricted net assets for a special project. To reflect such an action, a subset of unrestricted net assets, Unrestricted Net Assets—Designated, may be displayed, provided the total amount of Unrestricted Net Assets is shown.

Current Restricted Fund. The current restricted fund accounts for assets received from outside sources for a current operating purpose specified by the donor. The distinguishing feature between unrestricted and restricted funds is whether or not an externally imposed restriction exists. A contribution received by a health agency to conduct nutrition classes is an example of a restricted resource. When donor-restricted contributions are expensed, the restriction is released or reclassified to offset the expense. Specifically excluded from this fund are contributions of endowments or contributions restricted to the acquisition of plant assets, which are recorded in other appropriate funds.

Some net assets of this fund may be unrestricted; for example, grants, awards, sponsorships, and appropriations have traditionally been recorded in the restricted current fund. These may now be defined as exchange transactions in which the grantor or sponsor expects to receive something of value in return for the grant. All exchange transactions are unrestricted per FASB Statement No. 116.

Land, Building, and Equipment Fund (or Plant Fund). The plant fund accounts for the activity related to fixed assets, including the accumulation of resources to acquire or replace them and the liabilities related to them, as well as their acquisition, disposal, and depreciation. To determine the total cost of rendering service, depreciation of assets employed in providing that service must be recorded in the plant fund, with the typical depreciation entry debiting Depreciation Expense and crediting Accumulated Depreciation.

The plant fund of a VHWO may have all three net asset classes: unrestricted, temporarily restricted, and permanently restricted. Unrestricted net assets may be transfers from current funds at the discretion of the governing board. Assets acquired with unrestricted funds are unrestricted. Donor-restricted contributions specified for property and equipment are temporarily restricted. As with other not-for-profits, a VHWO may choose to release the restriction of these assets upon acquisition or over the useful life. Contributions of land are considered permanently restricted if the land cannot be sold. If no restriction exists, donated land is an unrestricted contribution.

Endowment Fund. The endowment fund accounts for gifts or bequests with the legal restriction that the principal be maintained in perpetuity (permanently restricted) or until the occurrence of a specified event (temporarily restricted). Various conditions are possible, depending upon the desires of the contributor. Unless otherwise specified, net gains or losses on the sale of endowment fund assets are increases or decreases of the fund principal.

Endowment fund investment revenue may be restricted or unrestricted. Income is recorded directly in the fund that is to receive it. Such income not subject to any restrictions by the principal donor may be recorded directly in the current unrestricted fund as unrestricted investment revenue. If the revenue is subject to a restriction, it would be recorded as temporarily or permanently restricted in the appropriate restricted fund.

Agency (Custodian) Fund. Agency funds of not-for-profit organizations account for assets that do not belong to the organization holding them. They are often established for payroll withholding. Custodian funds are established to account for assets received by an organization to be held or disbursed only on instructions of the person or organization from whom they were received. Flow-through government grants are examples of this latter use of agency funds. Assets are recorded when received, along with a related liability. Only when the assets are released by the contributor will they be recognized as revenue in the appropriate fund.

Pooling of Investments. If an organization accumulates substantial investments in its various funds, pooling may be advisable. Pooling of investments is the process of combining the investments of various funds into one group or pool to provide greater flexibility at lower cost and to provide diversification to spread the risk. Once pooled, individual investments lose their identity as to fund. Each contributing fund merely maintains in its investment account an amount representing its portion of the pool. Before any additions or withdrawals may be made, the fair value of the total portfolio must be determined. Realized gains and losses (and unrealized, if investments are carried at fair value rather than cost) are allocated to each participating fund on the basis of its share of the total fair value at the previous valuation date. The proportion of each fund's fair value may be expressed in terms of units or in terms of percentages of the total. The latter method is more flexible and is used in Illustration 18A-1, which shows changes in pooled investments over a period of time.

Illustration 18A-1
Pooling of Investments

	(1)	(2)	(3)	(4)	(5)	(6)	(7)	(8)
	Cash and/or	Original	Total Pool		Fair Value	Revised	After	New
	FV of	Equity	December 31, 20X0		Including	Equity	Withdrawal	Equity
Fund	Securities	Percent	Cost	Fair	$50,000	Percent	of $25,000	Percent
Unrestricted . . .	$ 36,000	20%	$ 40,000	$ 50,000	$ 50,000	16.67%	$ 25,000	9.09%
Plant.	54,000	30	60,000	75,000	75,000	25.00	75,000	27.27
Endowment . . .	90,000	50	100,000	125,000	175,000	58.33	175,000	63.64
Total.	$180,000	100%	$200,000	$250,000	$300,000	100.00%	$275,000	100.00%

Illustrative Funds-Based Financial Statements for Voluntary Health and Welfare Organizations

Statements reflect information from the entries in the text for the People's Environmental Protection (PEP) Association within the existing funds structure for voluntary health and welfare organizations as described below.

Note that in Illustration 18A-2, all the funds—total public support and revenue (A), total expenses (B), change in net assets (F = C + D + E), net assets beginning of year (G), and net assets end of year (H)—match up with the related disclosures in Illustration 18-2 (page 1029). Similarly, the fund totals shown in Illustration 18A-3 present the same disclosures required in Illustration 18-4 (page 1030). In addition, the net assets end of year (H) disclosure on both the statement of financial position and the statement of activities ties these two reports together.

Illustration 18A-2
People's Environmental Protection (PEP) Association
Statement of Activities
For Year Ended December 31, 20X7

	Unrestricted Current Fund	Restricted Current Fund	Plant Fund	Endowment Fund	Total	
Public support:						
Contributions	$397,100				$ 397,100	
Special events (net of $2,000 direct costs)	7,000				7,000	
Legacies and bequests	100,000				100,000	
Received from federated and nonfederated campaigns	16,000				16,000	
Total public support	$520,100				$ 520,100	
Revenue:						
Membership dues	$118,000				$ 118,000	
Investment revenue	21,000				21,000	
Total revenue	$139,000				$ 139,000	
Net assets released from restrictions:						
Satisfaction of program restrictions		$ 103,750			$ 103,750	
Satisfaction of equipment acquisition restrictions			$ 22,000		22,000	
Expiration of time restrictions		10,000			10,000	
Total net assets released from restrictions		$ 113,750	$ 22,000		$ 135,750	
Total public support and revenue	$659,100	$ 113,750	$ 22,000		$ 794,850	A
Expenses:						
Valley Air Project	$117,000	$ 13,000	$ 2,000		$ 132,000	
Fish in the Lakes program	131,700	49,750	3,000		184,450	
Flood Control program	204,000	31,000	16,000		251,000	
Management and general	20,500	8,000	1,000		29,500	
Fund raising	8,000	2,000	1,000		11,000	
Membership development	2,000				2,000	
Total expenses	$483,200	$ 103,750	$ 23,000		$ 609,950	B
Increase (decrease) in unrestricted net assets	$175,900	$ 10,000	$ (1,000)		**$ 184,900**	C
Transfers among funds	$ (96,000)		$ (96,000)		—	

(continued)

	Unrestricted Current Fund	Restricted Current Fund	Plant Fund	Endowment Fund	Total	
Changes in temporarily restricted net assets:						
Contributions		$ 12,750	$ 60,000		$ 72,750	
Investment income on endowment			7,000		7,000	
Net assets released from restrictions		(113,750)	(22,000)		(135,750)	
Increase (decrease) in temporarily restricted net assets		$(101,000)	$ 45,000		**$ (56,000)**	D
Changes in permanently restricted net assets:						
Legacies and bequests				$ 20,000	$ 20,000	
Net increase in carrying value of investments				29,000	29,000	
Gain on sale of investments				2,000	2,000	
Increase (decrease) in permanently restricted net assets				$ 51,000	**$ 51,000**	E
Change in net assets	$ 79,900	$ (91,000)	$140,000	$ 51,000	**$ 179,900**	F
Net assets beginning of year	184,000	132,000	660,000	253,000	**1,229,000**	G
Net assets end of year	$263,900	$ 41,000	$800,000	$304,000	**$1,408,900**	H

Illustration 18A-3
People's Environmental Protection (PEP) Association
Statement of Financial Position
As of December 31, 20X7

	Unrestricted Current Fund	Restricted Current Fund	Plant Fund	Endowment Fund	Total	
Assets:						
Cash and cash equivalents	$193,000	$40,000	$ 35,000		$ 268,000	
Contributions receivable (net of $2,500 allowance)	21,000				21,000	
Inventories	10,900				10,900	
Short-term investments	70,000	7,000	75,000		152,000	
Property, plant, and equipment (net of $38,700 accumulated depreciation)			800,000		800,000	
Long-term endowment investments				$304,000	304,000	
Total assets	$294,900	$47,000	$910,000	$304,000	$ 1,555,900	
Liabilities and net assets:						
Accounts payable	$ 31,000	$ 1,000			$ 32,000	
Refundable advances		5,000			5,000	
Notes payable			$110,000		110,000	
Total liabilities	$ 31,000	$ 6,000	$110,000		**$ 147,000**	
Net assets:						
Unrestricted	$263,900	$10,000	$200,000		**$ 473,900**	
Temporarily restricted		31,000	600,000		**631,000**	
Permanently restricted				$304,000	**304,000**	
Total net assets	$263,900	$41,000	$800,000	$304,000	**$1,408,900**	H
Total liabilities and net assets	$294,900	$47,000	$910,000	$304,000	$ 1,555,900	

REFLECTION

- For external purposes, VHWOs may choose to prepare reports of the results of fund activities and the fund balances at period-end. These statements also reflect the organization-wide disclosures required.
- Most VHWOs use five different funds.
- Investments accounted for by different funds may be pooled together. Any net realized (or unrealized) gain or loss is allocated proportionately to the funds involved.

UNDERSTANDING THE ISSUES

1. How is it helpful for a private not-for-profit organization to account for current funds as restricted or unrestricted?
2. The FASB requires for-profit entities to classify their investments as trading, available-for-sale, or held-to-maturity. However, it does not require not-for-profit entities to do the same. What might be the reasoning for this difference in requirements? Which approach is more beneficial to the readers of the financial statements of a not-for-profit organization? Why?
3. Differentiate between public support and revenues as sources of assets for private not-for-profit organizations. What benefit is there in accounting for these differently?
4. Explain the accounting for funds received by an organization acting as an agent, trustee, or intermediary, rather than as a donor or donee. What might be the reasoning for the differences?
5. A voluntary health and welfare organization is required to present an additional financial statement that is not required of other private not-for-profit entities. Why is this an important statement?
6. (Appendix) Why would a VHWO wish to present its financial information on a fund basis rather than simply on an organization-wide basis? What benefits are there in fund-basis reporting?

EXERCISES

Exercise 1 *(LO 1, 2, 6)* **Understanding not-for-profit financial statements.** Go to the Web site of a not-for-profit organization. Are audited financial statements provided on the Web site? Is other financial information made available? Assuming you are a potential donor, evaluate its performance compared with similar organizations. What benchmarks (or industry averages) for this type of not-for-profit did you use in your evaluation? Were they financial or nonfinancial indicators of performance? [*Hint:* Goodwill Industries is a not-for-profit organization (http://www.goodwill.org). The BBB Wise Giving Alliance (http://www.give.org) and the Council of Better Business Bureau (CBBB) Philanthropic Advisory Service (http://www.bbb.org) have comparison data on not-for-profit organizations.]

Exercise 2 *(LO 4, 6)* **Contributions, statement of activities.** Early in 20X8, a not-for-profit organization received a $4,000,000 gift from a wealthy benefactor. This benefactor specified that the gift be invested in perpetuity with income restricted to provide speaker fees for a lecture series named for the benefactor. The not-for-profit is permitted to choose suitable investments and is responsible for all other costs associated with initiating and administering this series. Neither the donor's stipulation nor the law addresses gains and losses on this permanent endowment. In 20X8, the investments purchased with the gift earned $100,000 in dividend income. The fair value of the investments increased by $240,000.

Three presentations in the lecture series were held in 20X8. The speaker fees for the three presentations amounted to $140,000. The not-for-profit organization used the $100,000 dividend income to cover part of the total fees. Because the board of directors did not wish to sell part of the investments, the organization used $40,000 in unrestricted resources to pay the remainder of the speaker fees.

For items (1) through (5), determine whether the transaction should be recorded in the 20X8 statement of activities as an increase in:

A. Unrestricted net assets.
B. Temporarily restricted net assets.
C. Permanently restricted net assets.
D. Either unrestricted or temporarily restricted net assets.

1. The receipt of the $4,000,000 gift
2. The $100,000 in dividend income assuming the not-for-profit's accounting policy is to record increases in net assets, for which a donor-imposed restriction is met in the same accounting period as gains and investment income are recognized, as increases in unrestricted net assets
3. The $240,000 unrealized gain
4. The $100,000 in dividend income, assuming the lecture series is not to begin until 20X9
5. The $240,000 unrealized gain, assuming the lecture series is not to begin until 20X9

Exercise 3 *(LO 1, 3, 8, 9)* **Comparison of accounting for VHWO and governmental organizations.** Distinguish between accounting and financial reporting for state and local governments and VHWOs for the following issues:

a. Measurement focus and basis of accounting
b. Revenue recognition
c. Expenses or expenditures
d. Capital assets

Exercise 4 *(LO 9)* **VHWO, statement of activities.** The Better Life Clinic is a VHWO that has three main programs:

Drug rehabilitation
Alcohol recovery
Weight control

Unrestricted public support received during the period was $35,000; revenues from membership services were $12,000. The following expenses and allocations to program and supporting services are shown for 20X0. Better Life elects to release donor restrictions for property, plant, and equipment over the useful life of the asset.

Item	Amount	Distribution				
		Drug Rehab.	Alcohol Recovery	Weight Control	Fund Raising	Gen. & Adm.
Secretarial salary	$ 5,000					100%
Office supplies	6,000	20%	10%	10%	10%	50
Printing	8,000	10	10	20	50	10
Depreciation (All depreciation is on assets acquired with donor-restricted contributions.)	4,000	20	20	20		40
Instruction	9,000	30	25	35	10	
Rent	10,000	30	20	30		20

Temporarily restricted net assets totaled $30,000 on January 1; the unrestricted net asset balance was $12,000. Prepare a statement of activities for the year.

Exercise 5 *(LO 10)* **VHWO, journal entries.** Record the following events of the Chemical Dependency Clinic, a VHWO:

1. Membership dues of $9,000 were collected.
2. Cash contributions of $22,000 and pledges for $32,000 were received.
3. It is estimated that 10% of the above pledges will prove uncollectible.
4. A fund-raising dinner grossed $12,000 from the sale of 480 tickets. The catered dinner cost $15 each for the 420 people who attended, plus $200 for the rental of the dining room. Payment for these costs was made.
5. A classic car was donated to the organization. The car has an estimated fair value of $75,000. It will be the main attraction of an auction to be held in the next accounting period. The proceeds of the auction are part of the budget for activities in the next period.
6. To expand the services of the clinic, a professional fund-raising group was hired to undertake a 6-month campaign. At the end of the six months, the group submitted the following report:

Cash collected	$ 70,000
Pledges (estimated to be 95% collectible)	30,000
Total proceeds	$100,000
Less 20% fund-raising fee (regardless of collections)	20,000
Net proceeds from drive	$ 80,000

Exercise 6 *(LO 10)* **VHWO, journal entries.** Record the following events of the Mental Health Clinic, a VHWO:

1. A contribution of $10,000 was received and is to be used for the purchase of equipment, but not until an addition to the building is constructed. Construction has begun on the building.
2. Equipment costing $17,000, with a book value of $8,000, was sold for $10,000. The gain is unrestricted.
3. Depreciation of $9,000 is recorded on various plant items.
4. Equipment was purchased for $12,000, with payment due in 30 days from donor-restricted resources. Mental Health Clinic elects to release the donor restriction upon acquisition of the equipment.
5. The liability for the equipment purchased in item (4) was paid.

Exercise 7 *(LO 10)* **VHWO, journal entries.** Record the following events of Mercy Health Clinic, a VHWO:

1. In her will, a leading citizen left a bequest of $200,000 to the clinic. Stipulations were that the amount was to become the corpus of a permanent endowment. Any income received would be used first to cover any loss of principal, with the remaining revenue to be used for an educational program on mental problems. The total amount was received and invested in 8% municipal bonds purchased at face value on an interest date.

2. Three months later, half of the bond investment was sold at 101, plus $2,500 of accrued interest.
3. The remaining endowment bond investments earned $6,000. The amount is not subject to any limitations.
4. At year-end, the remaining endowment bond investments have a fair value of $103,500.

APPENDIX EXERCISES

Exercise 18A-1 *(LO 4, 8, 11)* **VHWO, funds, contributions.** The Health Awareness Club is a not-for-profit organization that conducts meetings and special programs dedicated to promoting better health for members of the community. Members participate in regularly scheduled classes and exercise programs. There are also a variety of community services available to the general population. During the year, various funds flow to the organization. A list of receipts follows. For each item, indicate which of the following funds records the item, and indicate the category within which the item is recorded in that fund.

Name of Fund	Category
Current unrestricted fund	Revenue—Unrestricted
Current restricted fund	Public Support—Unrestricted
Plant fund	Deferred Revenue
Endowment fund	Public Support—Temporarily Restricted
	Public Support—Permanently Restricted
	Revenue—Temporarily Restricted

The transactions were as follows:

1. General membership dues.
2. Receipts for pancake breakfast open to public.
3. Donation of equipment to be used in exercise room. Restrictions are released when assets are placed in service.
4. Donation of equipment to be sold; proceeds are to be used to support education program.
5. Share of federated national fund drive.
6. Sale of educational books produced by the organization.
7. Auction of donated services to be used to acquire additional land for expansion.
8. Receipt of endowment from former president of organization.
9. Income on endowment that supports youth health program.
10. Pledge of $5,000 from local corporation for youth health program. The pledge is conditional, in that the organization must match the grant with funds raised from other corporate sponsors.

Exercise 18A-2 *(LO 5, 8, 11)* **VHWO, funds, expenses.** For the Health Awareness Club of above, various expenditures are recorded during the year. For each item listed, indicate the fund in which the entry would be made and the nature of the transaction. The available funds and transaction types are as follows:

Name of Fund	Nature of Transaction
Current unrestricted fund	Fund-raising expense
Current restricted fund	General and administrative expense
Plant fund	Program expense
Endowment fund	Offset to public support

The transactions were as follows:

1. Cost of brochures asking for donations.
2. Accounting services received.
3. Office supplies consumed.
4. Repair and maintenance of exercise room equipment.
5. Depreciation on exercise room equipment.
6. Costs associated with pancake breakfast.
7. Costs of cancer awareness program paid from donations that are restricted to this use.

Exercise 18A-3 *(LO 11)* **VHWO, funds.** On January 2, 20X9, the available cash in the following funds was placed into an investment pool:

Fund	Cash Pooled
Current unrestricted	$ 40,000
Current restricted	30,000
Plant	10,000
Endowment	20,000
Total	$100,000

During the next year, no additional cash was placed into the pool, nor was any amount withdrawn. At the end of the year, the pooled investments had a basis of $120,000, representing original contributions plus $20,000 of realized gains that remained in the investment pool. At year-end, the fair value of the pool amounted to $130,000. Prepare a schedule reflecting pooling activities for the year 20X9.

PROBLEMS

Problem 18-1 *(LO 3, 4, 6)* **FASB Nos. 116 and 117, contributions.** Select the best answer for each of the following multiple-choice items dealing with not-for-profit organizations.

1. Under FASB No. 117, which of the following statements is *true?*

   a. All not-for-profit organizations must include a statement of functional expenses.
   b. Donor-restricted contributions whose restrictions have been met in the reporting period may be reported as unrestricted support.
   c. Statements should focus on the individual unrestricted and restricted funds of the organization.
   d. FASB No. 117 contains requirements that are generally more stringent than those relating to for-profit organizations.

2. Which of the following factors, if present, would indicate that a transaction is *not* a contribution under FASB No. 116?

   a. The resource provider entered into the transaction voluntarily.
   b. The resource provider received value in exchange.
   c. The transfer of assets was unconditional.
   d. The organization has discretion in the use of the assets received.

3. Securities donated to voluntary health and welfare organizations should be recorded

   a. at the donor's recorded amount.
   b. at fair value at the date of the gift.
   c. at fair value at the date of the gift or the donor's recorded amount, whichever is lower.
   d. at fair value at the date of the gift or the donor's recorded amount, whichever is higher.

4. Which of the following is *not* a criterion that must be met under FASB No. 116 for contributed services?
   a. They are provided by persons possessing required skills.
   b. They are provided by licensed professionals.
   c. They create or enhance nonfinancial assets.
   d. They would typically have to be purchased if not provided by the donors/volunteers.
5. Which of the following criteria would suggest that a not-for-profit capitalize its works of art, historical treasures, or similar assets?
   a. They are held for public inspection, education, or research in furtherance of public service rather than financial gain.
   b. They are protected, kept unencumbered, cared for, and preserved.
   c. They are subject to be used in the acquisition of other items for the collection.
   d. They are held primarily to be resold for financial gain.

Problem 18-2 *(LO 8, 9)* **VHWO, accounting and reporting.** Select the best answer for each of the following multiple-choice items. Items (1) through (3) are based on the following:

The Bay Ridge Humane Society, a VHWO caring for lost animals, had the following financial inflows and outflows for the year ended December 31, 20X5:

Inflows:	
Cash received from federated campaign	$680,000
Cash received that is designated for 20X6 operations	30,000
Contributions pledged for 20X5, not yet received	90,000
Contributions pledged for 20X6, not yet received	25,000
Sales of pet supplies	10,000
Pet adoption fees	50,000
Outflows:	
Kennel operations	$350,000
Pet health care	100,000
Advertising pets for adoption	50,000
Fund raising	70,000
Administrative and general	200,000

1. In the humane society's statement of activities for the year ended December 31, 20X5, what amount should be reported under the classification of public support—unrestricted?
   a. $740,000
   b. $762,000
   c. $770,000
   d. $825,000
2. In the humane society's statement of activities for the year ended December 31, 20X5, what amount should be reported under the classification of program services expense?
   a. $770,000
   b. $450,000
   c. $550,000
   d. $500,000
3. In the humane society's balance sheet as of December 31, 20X5, what amount should be reported under the classification of public support—temporarily restricted?
   a. $55,000
   b. $30,000
   c. $25,000
   d. $0

4. Arbor Haven, a voluntary welfare organization funded by contributions from the general public, received unrestricted pledges of $500,000 during 20X6. It was estimated that 12% of these pledges would be uncollectible. By the end of 20X6, $400,000 of the pledges had been collected, and it was expected that $40,000 more would be collected in 20X7, with the balance of $60,000 to be written off as uncollectible. Donors did not specify any periods during which the donations were to be used. What amount should Arbor Haven include under public support in 20X6 for contributions?

   a. $500,000
   b. $452,000
   c. $440,000
   d. $400,000

5. The following expenditures were among those incurred by a voluntary welfare organization during 20X7:

Printing of annual report	$10,000
Unsolicited merchandise sent to encourage contributions.	20,000

   What amount should be classified as fund-raising costs in the society's statement of activities?

   a. $0
   b. $10,000
   c. $20,000
   d. $30,000

6. Apex Inc. donated a computer to Bird Shelter, a voluntary welfare organization. The computer cost Apex $40,000. On the date of donation, it had a book value of $25,000 and a fair value of $20,000. Bird Shelter's depreciation expense should be based on

   a. $40,000.
   b. $25,000.
   c. $20,000.
   d. $15,000.

Problem 18-3 *(LO 5, 7, 8, 9)* **Expenses.** Select the best answer for each of the following multiple-choice items. (No. 1 is AICPA adapted.)

1. In the statement of activities of a not-for-profit, depreciation expense should

   a. be included as an element of expense.
   b. be included as an element of other changes in fund balances.
   c. be included as an element of support.
   d. not be included.

2. Environs, a community foundation, incurred $10,000 in management and general expenses during 20X1. In Environs' statement of activities for the year ended December 31, 20X1, the $10,000 should be reported as

   a. a direct reduction of unrestricted net assets.
   b. part of supporting services expense.
   c. part of program services expense.
   d. a contra account to offset revenue and support.

3. Super Seniors is a not-for-profit organization that provides services to senior citizens. Super employs a full-time staff of 10 people at an annual cost of $150,000. In addition, two volunteers work as part-time secretaries replacing last year's full-time secretary who earned $10,000. Services performed by other volunteers for special events had an estimated value of $15,000. These volunteers were employees of local businesses, and they received small-value

items for their participation. What amount should Super report for salary and wage expenses related to the above items?

a. $150,000
b. $160,000
c. $165,000
d. $175,000

4. The League, a not-for-profit organization, received the following pledges:

Unrestricted	$200,000
Restricted for capital additions	150,000

All pledges are legally enforceable; however, the League's experience indicates that 10% of all pledges prove to be uncollectible. What amount should the League report as pledges receivable net of any required allowance account?

a. $135,000
b. $180,000
c. $315,000
d. $350,000

5. When a nonprofit organization combines fund-raising efforts with bona fide educational efforts or program services, the total combined costs incurred are

a. reported as program services expenses.
b. allocated between fund-raising and program services expenses using an appropriate allocation basis.
c. reported as fund-raising costs.
d. reported as management and general expenses.

Problem 18-4 *(LO 3, 4, 7, 8, 9, 11)* **Assets.** Select the best answer for each of the following multiple-choice questions.

1. A VHWO receives a donation that is restricted to its endowment and another donation that is restricted to use in acquiring a child care center. How should these donations be reported in the year received, assuming neither donation is expended in that year?

	Donation for Endowment	Donation for Child Care Center
a.	Contributions—Temporarily Restricted	Contributions—Temporarily Restricted
b.	Deferred Capital Additions	Capital Additions
c.	Contributions—Unrestricted	Contributions—Unrestricted
d.	Capital Additions Deferred	Capital Additions
e.	Contributions—Permanently Restricted	Contributions—Temporarily Restricted

2. Donor-restricted contributions that have been given to a VHWO for the purpose of purchasing fixed assets should be recorded as increases to

a. Unrestricted Net Assets.
b. Temporarily Restricted Net Assets.
c. Permanently Restricted Net Assets.
d. Fund Balance—Restricted.

3. The following correct entry is found on the books of a VHWO:

Unrestricted Net Assets—Undesignated	XXX	
Unrestricted Net Assets—Designated for AIDS Research		XXX

From the entry, one should conclude that the board of directors has

a. designated a portion of the unrestricted net assets for a future AIDS research program.
b. designated a portion of the restricted net assets for a future AIDS research program.
c. transferred resources to an AIDS research program.
d. directed that unused resources previously assigned to an AIDS research program be returned to unrestricted net asset classification.

4. Friends of the Forest received a donation of marketable equity securities from a member. The securities had appreciated in value after they were purchased by the donor, and they continued to appreciate through the end of Friends of the Forest's fiscal year. At what amount should Friends of the Forest report its investment in marketable equity securities in its year-end balance sheet?

    a. Donor's cost
    b. Fair value at the date of receipt
    c. Fair value at the balance sheet date
    d. Fair value at either the date of receipt or the balance sheet date

5. The investments of a VHWO are carried at fair value. At the end of the period, there is a decrease in total fair value. The fair value decrease should

    a. not be recorded until the loss is realized.
    b. be debited to Realized Loss on Pooled Investments.
    c. be debited to Endowment Fund Balance.
    d. be debited to Net Decrease in Carrying Value of Investments.

6. (Appendix) Mapleton Volunteers (MV) has cash available for investments in several different accounting funds. The organization's policy is to maximize its financial resources. How may MV pool its investments?

    a. MV may not pool its investments.
    b. MV may pool all investments but must equitably allocate realized and unrealized gains and losses among participating funds.
    c. MV may pool only unrestricted investments but must equitably allocate realized and unrealized gains and losses among participating funds.
    d. MV may pool only restricted investments but must equitably allocate realized and unrealized gains and losses among participating funds.

7. (Appendix) Which of the following VHWO funds does *not* have a counterpart in governmental accounting?

    a. Land, Building, and Equipment
    b. Current Unrestricted
    c. Custodian
    d. Endowment

(AICPA adapted)

Problem 18-5 *(LO 9, 10)* **Journal entries, statement of activities.** The following selected events relate to the 20X7 activities of Aires Nursing Home, Inc., a not-for-profit agency:

a. Gross patient service revenue totaled $2,200,000. The provision for uncollectible accounts was estimated at $92,000. The allowance for contractual adjustments was increased by $120,000.
b. After a conference with representatives of Gold Star Insurance Company, differences between the amounts accrued and subsequent settlements reduced receivables by $60,000.
c. A grateful patient donated securities with a cost of $20,000 and a fair value at date of donation of $75,000. The donation was restricted to expenditure for modernization of equipment. The donation was accepted.

(continued)

d. Cash of $37,000 that had been restricted by a donor for the purchase of furniture was used this year. Aires chose to release the donor restriction over the useful life of the asset.
e. The board voluntarily transferred $50,000 of cash to add to the resources held for capital improvements.
f. Pledges of $60,000 and cash of $20,000 were received to defer operating expenses. Of the pledges, 10% are considered uncollectible. Term endowments of $10,000 matured and were released to cover operations.
g. Equipment costing $250,000 was purchased on account. Restricted resources held for that purpose will be released from restriction over the useful life of the asset.
h. The nursing home uses functional operating expense control accounts. Expenses for the year were as follows:

Nursing services	$1,120,000
Dietary services	230,000
Maintenance services	115,000
Administrative services	285,000
Interest	160,000
Subtotal (of which $253,000 is unpaid)	$1,910,000
Depreciation [$20,000 from assets purchased with resources in items (d) and (g) above]	60,000
Total	$1,970,000

Required ▶ ▶ ▶ ▶ ▶

1. Omitting explanations, prepare journal entries for the foregoing events.
2. Prepare a statement of activities for the year ended December 31, 20X7.

Problem 18-6 *(LO 10)* **Journal entries.** The Super Senior Agency is a VHWO. The following events occurred during the year. The agency uses one control account for its fixed assets, with supporting subsidiary records.

a. Property was purchased for $200,000. A down payment of $40,000 was made from unrestricted cash, and a 14% mortgage was signed for the remainder.
b. Office furniture was purchased for $9,000 on open account.
c. A local corporation donated and installed room partitions. The value of the donated items and services was $4,000. Super Senior's policy is to release donor restrictions over the useful life of the assets to match depreciation expense.
d. At year-end, a payment was made covering mortgage interest for one year, plus a $10,000 payment on the principal.
e. Office equipment costing $3,000, with a book value of $1,000, was sold for $1,800 cash. The gain is unrestricted.
f. Fully depreciated equipment costing $7,000 was written off. There was no scrap value.
g. A depreciation schedule was prepared, showing annual depreciation expense of $46,000, which was recorded. Depreciation of $20,000 was for equipment donated or purchased with donated cash.
h. Two years ago, the will of an agency volunteer granted $50,000 for the acquisition and installation of theater equipment, providing the organization acquired a new building. The amount now was expended in accordance with the stipulations of the will, and payment of $50,000 was made.
i. The account payable of $9,000 mentioned in item (b) was paid.

Required ▶ ▶ ▶ ▶ ▶

Prepare journal entries to record the preceding events.

Problem 18-7 *(LO 10)* **Journal entries.** Carleton Agency, a VHWO, conducts two programs: Medical Services and Community Information Services. It had the following transactions during the year ended June 30, 20X9:

1. Received the following contributions:

Unrestricted pledges	$800,000
Restricted cash	95,000
Building fund pledges	50,000
Endowment fund cash	1,000

2. Collected the following pledges:

Unrestricted	$450,000
Building fund	20,000

3. Received the following unrestricted cash flows from:

Theater party (net of direct costs)	$ 12,000
Bequests	10,000
Membership dues	8,000
Interest and dividends	5,000

4. Program expenses incurred (processed through vouchers payable):

Medical services	$ 60,000
Community information services	15,000

5. Services expenses incurred (processed through vouchers payable):

General administration	$150,000
Fund raising	200,000

6. Purchased fixed assets:

Fixed assets purchased with donor-restricted cash	$ 18,000

   Carleton's policy is to release donor restrictions when assets are placed in service.

7. Depreciation of all buildings and equipment in the land, buildings, and equipment fund was allocated as follows:

Medical services program	$ 4,000
Community information services program	3,000
General administration	6,000
Fund raising	2,000

8. Vouchers paid:

Paid vouchers payable	$330,000

(AICPA adapted)

Record journal entries for the preceding transactions. Number your journal entries to coincide with the preceding transaction numbers.

Problem 18-8 ***(LO 9, 10)*** **Journal entries, statement of activities.** Thirty years ago, a group of civic-minded merchants in Mayfair organized the "Committee of 100" for the purpose of establishing the Mayfair Sports Club, a not-for-profit sports organization for local youth. Each of the Committee's 100 members contributed $1,000 toward the Club's capital. In addition, each participant agreed to pay dues of $200 a year for the Club's operations. All dues have been collected in full by the end of each fiscal year, which ends on March 31. Members who have discontinued their participation have been replaced by an equal number of new members by transferring the participation certificates from the former members to the new ones. Following are the Club's trial balances at April 1, 20X6:

	Debit	Credit
Cash	29,000	
Investments (at market value, equal to cost)	88,000	
Inventories	5,000	
Land	10,000	
Building	164,000	
Accumulated Depreciation—Building		130,000
Furniture and Equipment	54,000	
Accumulated Depreciation—Furniture and Equipment		46,000
Endowment Investments	400,000	
Accounts Payable		10,000
Participation Certificates (100 @ $1,000 each)		100,000
Unrestricted Net Assets		12,000
Temporarily Restricted Net Assets		52,000
Permanently Restricted Net Assets		400,000
Totals	750,000	750,000

Transactions and adjustment data for the year ended March 31, 20X7, are as follows:

a. Collections from participants for dues totaled $20,000.
b. Snack bar and soda fountain sales amounted to $31,000.
c. Interest and dividends totaling $6,000 were received. This investment income is unrestricted.
d. The following additions were made to the voucher register:

House expense	$17,000
Snack bar and soda fountain	26,000
General and administrative	11,000

e. Vouchers totaling $55,000 were paid.
f. Assessments for capital improvements not yet incurred totaled $10,000. The assessments were made on May 20, 20X5, and were to be collected during the year ending March 31, 20X7.
g. An unrestricted bequest of $5,000 was received.
h. Investments are valued at fair value, which amounted to $95,000 at March 31, 20X5. There were no investment transactions during the year.
i. Depreciation for the year is as follows:

Building	$4,000
Furniture and equipment	8,000

Depreciation is allocated to

House expense	$9,000
Snack bar and soda fountain	2,000
General and administrative	1,000

j. The actual physical inventory, which was $1,000 at March 31, 20X7, pertains to the snack bar and fountain.

k. A donor contributed $10,000 to be used to acquire land for expansion.
l. An unconditional pledge of $100,000 to be permanently restricted is received. Income is to be used to maintain the building.

◀◀◀◀◀ **Required**

1. Prepare entries for each of the above transactions.
2. Prepare the statement of activities for the year ended March 31, 20X7.

(AICPA adapted)

Problem 18-9 *(LO 8, 9, 10)* **Allocation of expenses, journal entries.** The Caring Clinic, a VHWO, conducts two programs: Alcohol and Drug Abuse and Outreach to Teens. It has the typical supporting services of management and fund raising. Expense accounts from the preallocation trial balances as of December 31, 20X7, are as follows:

	Funded by Unrestricted Resources	Funded by Donor-Restricted Resources	Total
Salaries and Payroll Taxes	63,000	23,000	86,000
Telephone and Miscellaneous Expenses	10,000	2,000	12,000
Nursing and Medical Fees	70,000	50,000	120,000
Educational Seminars Expense	46,000	20,000	66,000
Research Expense	137,000	16,000	153,000
Medical Supplies Expense	65,000	22,000	87,000
Rent Expense		10,000	10,000
Interest Expense on Equipment Mortgage	4,000		4,000
Depreciation Expense		20,000	20,000
Provision for Uncollectible Pledges	26,000		26,000
Totals	421,000	163,000	584,000

In preparation for the allocation of expenses to programs and supporting services, a study was conducted to determine an equitable manner for assigning each expense. The study resulted in the following table for percentage allocations.

Percentage of Allocations

	Programs		Supporting Services	
Expenses to Be Allocated	Alcohol and Drug Abuse	Outreach to Teens	Management	Fund Raising
All expenses (other than depreciation) financed by donor-restricted contributions	60%	40%		
Expenses financed by unrestricted resources:				
Salaries and payroll taxes	30	20	30%	20%
Telephone and miscellaneous	20	20	15	45
Nursing and medical fees	70	30		
Educational seminars	30	60		10
Research	60	40		
Medical supplies	90	10		
Equipment-related expenses:				
Interest	50	10	30	10
Depreciation	50	10	30	10

◀◀◀◀◀ **Required**

1. Using a total of allocable expenses financed by donor-restricted resources, prepare a journal entry to assign those expenses to the programs.

2. With the following format, prepare a schedule to show the assignment of the allocable expenses financed by unrestricted resources to the various programs and supporting services, using the percentages provided by the problem.

Caring Clinic Allocation of Expenses
For Year Ended December 31, 20X7

		Programs		Supporting Services	
Expense Allocated	Total Amount	Alcohol and Drug Abuse	Outreach to Teens	Management	Fund Raising

3. Using the schedule from requirement 2, prepare a journal entry to record the allocation and closing of expenses financed by unrestricted resources.
4. Prepare a journal entry to assign plant-related expenses to programs and support services.

Problem 18-10 *(LO 8, 9)* **Statement of activities, closing entries.** The Caring Clinic, a VHWO, conducts two programs: Alcohol and Drug Abuse and Outreach to Teens. It has the typical supporting services of management and fund raising. The condensed trial balances after allocable expenses have been assigned are presented as follows:

Caring Clinic
Condensed Post-Allocation Trial Balances
December 31, 20X7

Debits	
Assets	716,000
Endowment Assets	256,000
Alcohol and Drug Abuse Program	322,200
Outreach to Teens Program	184,100
Management and General Services	27,600
Fund-Raising Services	50,100
Cost of Special Events	18,000
Reclassification Out—Temporarily Restricted—Satisfaction of Program Restrictions	143,000
Reclassification Out—Temporarily Restricted—Satisfaction of Equipment Acquisition Restrictions	20,000
Totals	1,737,000

Credits	
Liabilities	179,000
Unrestricted Net Assets	202,000
Temporarily Restricted Net Assets	196,000
Permanently Restricted Net Assets	201,000
Contributions—Unrestricted	407,000
Contributions—Temporarily Restricted	254,000
Special Events Support—Temporarily Restricted	48,000
Legacies and Bequests—Permanently Restricted	30,000
Investment Revenue—Unrestricted	13,000
Investment Revenue—Temporarily Restricted	11,000
Gain on Sale of Investments—Temporarily Restricted	8,000
Gain on Sale of Investments—Permanently Restricted	25,000
Reclassification In—Unrestricted—Satisfaction of Program Restrictions	143,000
Reclassification In—Unrestricted—Satisfaction of Equipment Acquisition Restrictions	20,000
Totals	1,737,000

◄◄◄◄◄ Required

1. Prepare a statement of activities in the format shown in Illustration 18-2 on page 1029.
2. Prepare closing entries for each net asset classification.

Problem 18-11 *(LO 9)* **Statement of functional expenses.** From the expense accounts information and allocation schedule shown in Problem 18-9, prepare a statement of functional expenses for the Caring Clinic for the year ended December 31, 20X7.

template cd

APPENDIX PROBLEMS

Problem 18A-1 *(LO 10, 11)* **Funds, journal entries.** Listed are five independent transactions or events that relate to a local government and to a VHWO:

a. $30,000 was disbursed from the general fund (or its equivalent) for the cash purchase of new equipment.
b. An unrestricted cash gift of $100,000 was received from a donor.
c. A cash gift of $40,000 was received. The use of the funds was restricted to purchase life saving equipment. To purchase qualifying equipment, $15,000 was used.
d. Listed common stocks with a total carrying value of $50,000 were sold by an endowment fund for $55,000 before any dividends were earned on these stocks.
e. $1,000,000 (face amount) of general obligation bonds payable were sold at par, with the proceeds required to be used solely for construction of a new building. This building was completed at a total cost of $1,000,000, and the total amount of bond issue proceeds was disbursed in payment.

◄◄◄◄◄ Required

1. For each of the listed transactions or events, prepare journal entries, without explanations, specifying the affected funds and account groups and showing how these transactions or events should be recorded by a local government whose debt is serviced by general tax revenues.
2. For each of the listed transactions or events, prepare journal entries, without explanations, specifying the affected funds and showing how these transactions or events should be recorded by a VHWO that maintains a separate plant fund.

(AICPA adapted)

Problem 18A-2 *(LO 10, 11)* **Funds, journal entries.** The Caring Clinic, a VHWO, conducts two programs: Alcohol and Drug Abuse and Outreach to Teens. It has the typical supporting services of management and fund raising. The trial balances of its various funds as of January 1, 20X7, are as shown.

Debits	Unrestricted Current Fund	Restricted Current Fund	Plant Fund	Endowment Fund	Total
Cash	$ 31,000	$ 5,000	$ 12,000	$ 1,000	$ 49,000
Investments	120,000	23,000	45,000	200,000	388,000
Accrued Investment Revenue	6,000				6,000
Pledges Receivable	45,000				45,000
Grants Receivable	16,000				16,000
Inventories of Educational Materials	11,000				11,000
Inventories of Medical Supplies	12,000				12,000
Land, Building, and Equipment			173,000		173,000
Total	$241,000	$28,000	$230,000	$201,000	$700,000

Credits	Unrestricted Current Fund	Restricted Current Fund	Plant Fund	Endowment Fund	Total
Allowance for Uncollectible Pledges	$ 9,000				$ 9,000
Accumulated Depreciation			$ 22,000		22,000
Accounts Payable	14,000				14,000
State Grants Refundable	16,000				16,000
10% Mortgage Payable			40,000		40,000
Unrestricted Net Assets—Undesignated	112,000		70,000		182,000
Unrestricted Net Assets—Designated for Research	50,000				50,000
Temporarily Restricted Net Assets	40,000	$28,000	98,000		166,000
Permanently Restricted Net Assets				$201,000	201,000
Total	$241,000	$28,000	$230,000	$201,000	$700,000

During 20X7, the following events related to the clinic occurred. To minimize repetition, similar events for the year are combined.

	Unrestricted	Restricted
a. Contribution pledges received	$396,000	$162,000
b. Estimated uncollectible pledges	20,000	6,000
c. Cash collected on pledges	380,000	148,000
Pledges written off as uncollectible	18,000	5,000
d. Investment revenue received (including accrued)	9,000	1,000
e. Items paid:		
Accounts payable as of January 1, 20X7	14,000	
Salaries and payroll taxes	60,000	23,000
Rent expense		10,000
Telephone and miscellaneous expenses	10,000	2,000
Nursing and medical fees	70,000	50,000
Educational seminars expense	38,000	20,000
Research expense	137,000	16,000
Medical supplies (perpetual inventory is used)	71,000	29,000

f. The residence of a leading citizen was bequeathed in a will to the clinic. After the person's death, it was found that the building was not suitable for clinical use, and it would be sold as soon as possible. The residence was appraised at $92,000. The will stipulated that proceeds from the sale must be used to expand the clinic building. The will also provided $30,000 in cash to create a fund, the revenue from which must be devoted to an alcohol-abuse program.

g. During the year, a dinner was held to raise additional funds for the clinic building. Gross cash proceeds were $48,000, of which $18,000 was paid for direct costs.

h. Bids for construction of a wing for the clinic building were sought. The contract was let at a cost of $250,000. The residence received from the citizen was sold for $100,000, which was used as a partial payment on the contract, along with the net proceeds from the dinner mentioned in item (g). The wing was completed. A 12%, 20-year mortgage was signed for the remaining $120,000. Caring's policy is to release donor restrictions over the life of the fixed asset to match depreciation.

i. A grant of $16,000 from the state government, awarded last year for a special drug-abuse program, was received. The item originally was recorded as a grant receivable.

j. At year-end, a physical inventory shows $3,000 of educational materials and $18,000 of medical supplies in the unrestricted fund and $7,000 of medical supplies in the restricted fund.

k. Annual depreciation amounts to $20,000. $10,000 depreciation was for temporarily restricted assets.

l. A payment of $5,000 was made against the 10% mortgage payable, and a payment of $4,000 for interest was made.

m. Plant fund investment revenue was $4,000, of which $3,000 was received. Revenue must be used for plant purposes.
n. Endowment fund investment revenue received amounted to $16,000. There is no restriction on $10,000 of the revenue. The remaining $6,000 must be devoted to alcohol-abuse programs. Items are entered directly in recipient funds.
o. $11,000 of the contributions restricted for future periods in the Restricted Current Fund became available.
p. The board of directors has decided to increase the Fund Balance Designated for Research from $50,000 to $90,000.
q. Unpaid and unrecorded items in the unrestricted fund on December 31, 20X7, consist of $3,000 for accrued salaries and $10,000 for previously distributed educational brochures.
r. Endowment fund investments costing $40,000 were sold for $65,000. The gain is unrestricted.

◄◄◄◄◄ **Required**

1. Prepare journal entries to record the events, using the following format:

Event	Fund	Journal Entry	Unrestricted	Restricted
(a)				

2. Prepare preallocation trial balances, reflecting balances immediately after the preceding entries are posted, in the same format as the trial balances at the beginning of the problem.

Accounting for Not-for-Profit Colleges and Universities and Health Care Organizations

CHAPTER

19

Learning Objectives

When you have completed this chapter, you should be able to

1. **Explain how fund accounting is used by not-for-profit colleges and universities, and differentiate among those funds.**
2. **Demonstrate an understanding of the accounting for revenues and expenses for not-for-profit colleges and universities.**
3. **Demonstrate an understanding of the accounting for unrestricted and restricted contributions to not-for-profit colleges and universities.**
4. **Account for transactions of not-for-profit colleges or universities using funds.**
5. **Prepare financial statements for not-for-profit colleges and universities.**
6. **Explain GAAP and fund accounting as applied to governmental and private health care service providers.**
7. **Demonstrate an understanding of how revenues and expenses are calculated and accounted for by governmental and private health care service providers.**
8. **Demonstrate an understanding of the accounting for unrestricted and restricted contributions to governmental and private health care service providers.**
9. **Explain the financial impact of medical malpractice claims on governmental and private health care service providers.**
10. **Account for transactions of governmental and private health care service providers.**
11. **Prepare financial statements for governmental and private health care service providers.**

Both colleges and universities and health care organizations are complex entities that cross public and private sectors. As a result, statements of the Financial Accounting Standards Board (FASB) and the Governmental Accounting Standards Board (GASB) directly impact accounting and financial reporting for these organizations. This chapter illustrates financial accounting and reporting for colleges and universities and not-for-profit health care organizations. Differences between generally accepted accounting principles for public and private institutions are noted where applicable.

1

OBJECTIVE

Explain how fund accounting is used by not-for-profit colleges and universities, and differentiate among those funds.

ACCOUNTING FOR COLLEGES AND UNIVERSITIES (PUBLIC AND PRIVATE)

The responsibilities of a not-for-profit university may be classified as academic, financial, student services, and public relations. Academic functions include instruction, research, and public service. The financial sphere covers the management and reporting of business and financial affairs as well as auxiliary enterprises, such as housing, food service, and student union operation. Student services includes all student activities not directly classified as academic or financial, such as admissions, records, health, counseling, and publications. Public relations involves the communication and establishment of goodwill with academic and administrative staff, alumni, and the community.

The effectiveness with which a university accomplishes its objectives in these four areas depends in part upon the resources at its disposal. A university levies tuition fees, but these fees do not cover total operational costs. Therefore, other sources of revenue are essential. These sources include gifts, income from endowment funds, and grants from governmental units or foundations, and for public universities, appropriations from state legislatures.

Previous editions of this book have presented the accounting and financial statements for public colleges and universities following the guidance set forth in the AICPA *Audits of Colleges and Universities* (1994).[1] But, with the issuance of GASB Statement No. 35 in 1999, public colleges and universities are required to use the guidance for special-purpose governments engaged in business-type activities, engaged only in governmental activities, or engaged in both. Most colleges and universities are expected to follow the model for public institutions engaged only in business-type activities. Thus, *the basic financial statements are those required of an enterprise fund* (see Chapter 16). And, most probably, these institutions will be included as enterprise funds or component units of another government entity. Prior to the issuance of GASB Statement No. 35, there was much divergence in the financial reporting of public and private colleges and universities. But, as colleges and universities begin to implement GASB Statement Nos. 34 and 35, the wide differences will narrow. The financial statements of both public and private colleges and universities *emphasize the organization as a whole.* The financial statements present organization-wide totals of assets, liabilities, and net assets as well as information concerning organization-wide changes in net assets and organization-wide cash flows. Because of a shift away from a fund group focus to an organization-wide focus, there is no requirement for external financial statements to include fund group reporting. But, *most colleges and universities continue to use fund accounting for internal purposes.* And, since both the FASB and GASB standards prescribe minimum reporting standards, many colleges and universities may choose to include additional fund information in the annual report. Because of the use internally of fund accounting, a presentation for colleges and universities following pronouncements set forth by the FASB and GASB using the fund structure in the 1994 Audit Guide is used in this chapter.[2]

Funds

College and university funds include three broad categories: current funds, plant funds, and trust and agency funds. The day-to-day activities of a public university are recorded in its current funds, which consist of two self-balancing subfunds. The *unrestricted current fund* represents amounts that are available for any current activity commensurate with the university's

1 GASB Statement No. 15, *Governmental College and University Accounting and Financial Reporting Models,* requires public colleges and universities to use either the governmental model as outlined in Chapter 16 or the 1993 AICPA Audit Guide model which will be described in this chapter.

2 The divergence arising in financial accounting and reporting standards under the current two-board structure is most pronounced in colleges and universities. Recent GASB statements suggest sharp differences of opinion between the two boards on many issues. For example, GASB Statement No. 8 (issued in 1988) does not require depreciation by governmental universities; Statement No. 15 (issued in 1991) allows governmental colleges and universities to follow either the governmental model or the AICPA Audit Guide (as amended in 1993); Statement No. 19 (issued in 1993) requires governmental colleges and universities to account for federally sponsored student financial aid in a current restricted fund; Statement No. 29 (issued in 1996) prohibits governmental colleges and universities from applying the provisions of FASB Statement Nos. 116 and 117; and GASB Statement No. 31 states that public colleges and universities that elect to follow the AICPA Audit Guide model should assign investment income, including changes in the fair value of investments, to funds.

objectives. The *restricted current fund* accounts for those resources available only for an externally specified purpose. The segregation of unrestricted current funds from restricted current funds substantiates that the limitations placed on restricted funds by outside sources have been observed. Plant funds account for capital assets and for resources to be used to acquire additional capital assets or to retire indebtedness related to capital assets. *Plant funds* consist of several subgroups, each of which is designed to record a certain phase of activity related to fixed assets. *Endowment and similar funds* account for endowments received. In addition, a university may employ *loan funds, annuity funds, life income funds, and agency funds.*

Accounting for Revenues

2

OBJECTIVE

Demonstrate an understanding of the accounting for revenues and expenses for not-for-profit colleges and universities.

Colleges and universities recognize revenues in all funds on the accrual basis. A university might establish one master control account for unrestricted revenues, with details as to major sources recorded in subsidiary records. More commonly, separate revenue accounts are established, using the following three major groups of revenues:

Educational and general revenues group, with accounts for:
- Student tuition and fees (recognized when due or billed, net of an appropriate allowance for uncollectibles)
- Governmental appropriations (detailed as to federal, state, and local)
- Governmental grants and contracts (detailed as to federal, state, and local)
- Gifts and private grants
- Endowment income
- Other sources

Auxiliary enterprises revenues

Expired term endowment revenues

Operating revenues and nonoperating revenues are recorded in these accounts. Student tuition and fees, federal appropriations, and governmental grants are classified as operating revenues. All appropriations from the state government, gifts, investment income, endowment income, and interest are recorded as nonoperating revenues. Auxiliary enterprises revenues are segregated to permit the evaluation of performance and the degree of self-support. Expired term endowment income represents dollar amounts of term endowments on which the restriction has lapsed, freeing them to become unrestricted resources.

Accounting for Expenses

Expenses are recognized in all funds on the accrual basis and may be classified on a natural basis or by function. The most common classification is by function for two major groupings, which are the same as the first two used to classify revenues.

Educational and general expenses group, with accounts for:
- Instruction (expenses for credit and noncredit courses)
- Research (expenses to produce research results)
- Public support (expenses for noninstructional services, including conferences, seminars, and consulting)
- Academic support (expenses supporting instruction and public services, such as libraries, galleries, audiovisual services, and academic deans)
- Student services (expenses for student admission and registration and cultural and athletic activities)
- Institutional support (expenses for central administration)
- Operation and maintenance of plant (expenses for capital repairs and depreciation)
- Student aid (expenses for scholarships, fellowships, tuition remissions, and outright grants)

Auxiliary enterprises expenses

3

OBJECTIVE

Demonstrate an understanding of the accounting for unrestricted and restricted contributions to not-for-profit colleges and universities.

Accounting for Contributions

Contributions are defined by FASB Statement No. 116, as noted in Chapter 18, as "unconditional transfers of cash or other assets to an entity or a settlement or cancellation of its liabilities in a voluntary nonreciprocal transfer. . ."[3] and in GASB Statement No. 33 as voluntary nonexchange transactions with private parties. Other donated assets may include securities, land, buildings, use of facilities or utilities, materials and supplies, intangible assets, services, and unconditional promises to give those items in the future. *Private colleges and universities recognize contributions and unconditional promises to give as revenues or gains in the period received. Public colleges and universities recognize contributions as revenue when any eligibility requirements and time requirements have been met.* Exceptions to the general recognition provision are made for contributions of services and works of art. Contributions other than services are recognized in the period received and are measured at their fair value. Services would be recognized only if they (a) create or enhance nonfinancial assets or (b) require specialized skills, are provided by individuals possessing those abilities, and typically would have to be purchased if not provided by donation. Private colleges and universities are not required to recognize contributions of works of art, historical treasures, and similar assets if the donated items are added to collections, held for public exhibition, and preserved, cared for, and protected. Currently, GASB standards are silent on the issue of reporting revenue and expenses for services.

Conditional pledges depend on the occurrence of uncertain future events and are only recognized as revenue in both public and private colleges and universities when the conditions are substantially met (i.e., the pledge becomes unconditional). An example of a conditional pledge might be a donation restricted for construction of a new building given only if the organization can raise the remaining funds through additional contributions. Pledges or other assets received subject to such conditions are recorded as refundable advances until the conditions have been substantially met, at which time revenue is recorded.

When contributions extend over a long period of time, the college or university should report the "present value of estimated future cash flows using a discount rate commensurate with the risks involved." Promises receivable within one year need not be discounted. An allowance for doubtful contributions should be established based on historical experience and other factors to cover any uncertainties concerning collectibility. An unconditional pledge with no donor restriction is recognized as follows:

Contributions Receivable	XXX	
Revenues—Unrestricted Contributions		XXX
Provision for Uncollectible Contributions	XXX	
Allowance for Uncollectible Contributions		XXX

Donor-Imposed Restrictions and Reclassifications

Private universities following FASB Statement No. 116 are required to reclassify the net assets (a) when the donor's stipulated time has elapsed, (b) when the donor's stipulated purpose has been fulfilled, or (c) over the useful life of donated asset. Gifts of assets with no donor restrictions are classified as unrestricted. Public colleges and universities under GASB Statement No. 34 must maintain separate unrestricted and restricted net assets. Therefore, any expenses made in compliance with donor restrictions are funded directly out of restricted resources.

A cash contribution restricted by the donor for a specific expenditure is recorded when received.

Cash	XXX	
Revenues—Temporarily Restricted Contributions		XXX

3 FASB Statement No. 116, *Accounting for Contributions Received and Contributions Made* (Norwalk, CT: Financial Accounting Standards Board, 1993), par. 5. The FASB defines a nonreciprocal transfer as a transaction in which an organization receives an asset or cancellation of a liability without directly gaining value in exchange.

Expenses made in compliance with donor restrictions are funded by the restricted resources. Temporarily restricted net assets are released with a reclassification entry.	Expenses	XXX	
	Cash		XXX
	Reclassification Out—Temporarily Restricted—Satisfaction of Donor Restrictions	XXX	
	Reclassification In—Unrestricted—Satisfaction of Donor Restrictions		XXX

GASB Statement No. 33, FASB No. 116, and the AICPA Audit and Accounting Guide Not-for-Profit Organizations distinguish between accounting for exchange transactions, agency transactions, and contributions. *Exchange transactions,* that is, reciprocal transfers in which each party receives and sacrifices approximately equal value, are not considered restricted. In private universities, many transactions that traditionally had been accounted for in much the same way as contributions, such as grants, awards, sponsorships, and appropriations, are now categorized as exchange transactions rather than contributions and accounted for as increases in unrestricted assets. Government grants that require performance by the not-for-profit organization will be accounted for as refundable deposits (liabilities) until earned. Unrestricted revenue will be earned when expenses are made in conjunction with the provisions of the grant. Other government grants, which are essentially pass-through financial aid to students, will now be accounted for as *agency transactions.*

In public universities, GASB Statement No. 34 requires receipts that are externally imposed by creditors (such as through debt covenants), grantors, contributors, or laws and regulations of other governments, and those imposed by law must be recorded as restricted revenue.

Grant monies received.	Cash	XXX	
	U.S. Government Grants Refundable		XXX
Expenses incurred in conjunction with provisions of grant.	Expenses	XXX	
	Cash		XXX
Revenue is recognized up to the amount earned by incurring above expenses.	U.S. Government Grants Refundable	XXX	
	Revenues—Unrestricted		XXX

Permanently restricted contributions are called *endowments.* Earnings on endowment investments are reported in the period earned as a credit to unrestricted revenue or temporarily restricted revenue depending on donor specification as to the use of the earnings. Realized and unrealized gains on endowment investments are reported as increases or decreases in unrestricted net assets unless their use is temporarily or permanently restricted by explicit donor stipulations or by law. Losses on endowment investments reduce temporarily restricted net assets to the extent that donor-imposed restrictions on net appreciation have been met before the loss occurs. Any remaining loss would reduce unrestricted net assets.[4]

University Accounting and Financial Reporting within Existing Fund Structure

4

OBJECTIVE

Account for transactions of not-for-profit colleges or universities using funds.

The following transactions are for private colleges and universities. Events are marked with an asterisk when public and private entries differ. The asterisk is followed by the appropriate *public college or university* entry.

Current Unrestricted Fund. The unrestricted current fund of a university is similar to the general fund of a state or local government in that it accounts for current assets available to cover current operational costs and resulting expenses for private colleges and universities.

4 FASB Statement No. 124, *Accounting for Certain Investments Held by Not-for-Profit Organizations* (Norwalk, CT: Financial Accounting Standards Board, 1995), standardizes not-for-profit reporting of investments. It requires that investments in equity securities with readily determinable fair values and all investments in debt securities shall be measured at fair value. It does not apply to investments in equity securities accounted for under the equity method or to investments in consolidated subsidiaries.

	Event		Entry		
1.	Educational and general revenue is earned or billed:				
	Student tuition and fees (of which $20,000 is considered uncollectible)	$1,700,000	Accounts Receivable	2,750,000	
	Government appropriations	750,000	Revenues—Student Tuition and Fees		1,700,000
	Endowment income	50,000	Revenues—Governmental Appropriations		750,000
	Other investment income	250,000	Revenues—Unrestricted Endowment Income		50,000
			Revenues—Unrestricted Other Investment Income		250,000
	The provision for uncollectible student accounts receivable is considered an expense and is allocated to institutional support.		Expenses—Institutional Support (provision for uncollectible student accounts receivable)	20,000	
			Allowance for Uncollectible Student Accounts Receivable		20,000
	Unrestricted contributions (the other investment income) are pledged in the amount of $250,000. 10% of these pledges are assumed uncollectible.		Contributions Receivable	250,000	
			Revenues—Unrestricted Contributions		250,000
			Expenses—Institutional Support (provision for uncollectible contributions)	25,000	
			Allowance for Uncollectible Contributions		25,000
2.	Of the total revenues, $2,800,000 is collected, including $200,000 of pledges.		Cash	2,800,000	
			Accounts Receivable		2,600,000
			Contributions Receivable		200,000
3.	Revenue billed for dormitories (an auxiliary enterprise) is $400,000, of which $20,000 is not yet received.		Cash	380,000	
			Accounts Receivable	20,000	
			Revenues—Sales and Services of Auxiliary Enterprises		400,000
4.	Purchase of materials and supplies totaling $400,000, of which $25,000 is not yet paid.		Inventory of Supplies	400,000	
			Cash		375,000
			Accounts Payable		25,000
5.	Expenses are paid and assigned to:				
	Instruction	$1,050,000	Expenses—Instruction	1,050,000	
	Research	100,000	Expenses—Research	100,000	
	Academic support	150,000	Expenses—Academic Support	150,000	
	Student services	200,000	Expenses—Student Services	200,000	
	Institutional support	200,000	Expenses—Institutional Support	200,000	
	Operation and maintenance of plant	400,000	Expenses—Operation and Maintenance of Plant	400,000	
	Scholarships and fellowships	40,000	Expenses—Student Aid	40,000	
	Sales and services of auxiliary enterprises	260,000	Expenses—Sales and Services of Auxiliary Enterprises	260,000	
			Cash		2,400,000
6.	Materials and supplies used:				
	Instruction	$268,000	Expenses—Instruction	268,000	
	Student services	22,000	Expenses—Student Services	22,000	
	Auxiliary enterprises	90,000	Expenses—Sales and Services of Auxiliary Enterprises	90,000	
			Inventory of Supplies		380,000
7.	Aid is granted to students:				
	Remission of tuition	$140,000	Expenses—Student Aid	175,000	
	Cash scholarships	35,000	Accounts Receivable		140,000
			Cash		35,000

Event	Entry		
8. *Services that meet the criteria of (1) creating or enhancing nonfinancial assets or (2) requiring specialized skills and are provided by individuals possessing those abilities are typically purchased if not donated. The fair value of the services is $35,000. Currently, GASB Statement No. 35 is silent on the reporting of services.	Expenses—Instruction	35,000	
	Revenues—Unrestricted Contributions		35,000
9. Cash contributions are given without donor restriction.	Cash	100,000	
	Revenues—Unrestricted Contributions		100,000
10. *Closing entries are prepared for the unrestricted net assets. Public universities will close to unrestricted net assets.	Revenues—Student Tuition and Fees	1,700,000	
	Revenues—Governmental Appropriations	750,000	
	Revenues—Unrestricted Contributions	385,000	
	Revenues—Unrestricted Endowment Income	50,000	
	Revenues—Unrestricted Other Investment Income	250,000	
	Expenses—Instructional		1,353,000
	Expenses—Research		100,000
	Expenses—Academic Support		150,000
	Expenses—Student Services		222,000
	Expenses—Institutional Support		245,000
	Expenses—Operations and Maintenance of Plant		400,000
	Expenses—Student Aid		215,000
	Unrestricted Net Assets		**450,000**
	Revenues—Sales and Services of Auxiliary Enterprises	400,000	
	Expenses—Sales and Services of Auxiliary Enterprises		350,000
	Unrestricted Net Assets		**50,000**

Current Restricted Fund. For an activity to enter the restricted current fund of a university, some limitation must exist on the resources received from an external entity. The same revenue and expense accounts used in the unrestricted current fund are available, but restricted current fund revenues arise primarily from governmental grants and contracts, private gifts, and endowment income. Expenses generally are relegated to instruction, research, and student aid.

Unless the restriction placed upon contributed resources or governmental grants is respected, these resources may have to be returned to the donor. Until they are expended properly, they should not be considered as revenue. As a consequence, expenditures govern the recognition of revenue. These resources are expenditure driven, similar to such items in governmental accounting. The current restricted fund will have both donor-restricted contributions and resources from exchange transactions, including government grants. A difficult decision for many universities will be to differentiate donor-restricted contributions as defined by FASB No. 116 from exchange transactions.

Event	Entry		
11. A donor-restricted cash contribution is received to assist in library operations.	Cash	70,000	
	Revenues—Temporarily Restricted Contributions		70,000
12. Endowment income of $8,000 is restricted to student aid activities.	Cash	8,000	
	Revenues—Temporarily Restricted Endowment Income		8,000

(continued)

Event	Entry		
13. Of the following expenses, all but $4,000 are paid.			
For library operations $67,000	Expenses—Academic Support	67,000	
For student aid 6,000	Expenses—Student Aid	6,000	
	Accounts Payable		4,000
	Cash		69,000
14. *Temporarily restricted revenues of $73,000 are reclassified as unrestricted when donor specifications are met. Public colleges and universities will not record the reclassification entry but will close expenses to restricted net assets.	Reclassifications Out—Temporarily Restricted—Satisfaction of Program Restrictions	73,000	
	Reclassifications In—Unrestricted—Satisfaction of Program Restrictions		73,000
15. Federal grants for student awards are through the Pell Grant. See Agency Fund events and entries. Program funds are received in the amounts of $75,000. All $75,000 is distributed to qualified students.			
16. A federal grant was awarded for research.	Cash	100,000	
	U.S. Government Grants Refundable ..		100,000
17. Expenses for the research project totaled $45,000 to date. All expenses have been paid. Revenue is recognized to the extent that resources have been properly spent.	Expenses—Research	45,000	
	Cash		45,000
	U.S. Government Grants Refundable.....	45,000	
	Revenues—Government Grants and Contracts		45,000
18. *Closing entries are prepared for the unrestricted net assets. Public universities will close to unrestricted net assets.	Revenues—Unrestricted Government Grants and Contracts	45,000	
	Reclassifications In—Unrestricted—Satisfaction of Program Restrictions....	73,000	
	Expenses—Academic Support......		67,000
	Expenses—Student Aid		6,000
	Expenses—Research		45,000
	Unrestricted Net Assets		**0**
19. *Closing entries are prepared for the temporarily restricted net assets. Public universities will close to restricted net assets.	Revenues—Temporarily Restricted Contributions	70,000	
	Revenues—Temporarily Restricted Endowment Income	8,000	
	Reclassifications Out—Temporarily Restricted—Satisfaction of Program Restrictions		73,000
	Temporarily Restricted Net Assets		**5,000**

Loan Funds. Loan funds are established to account for resources that are available for loans primarily to students and possibly to faculty and staff. A separate fund is used because of the large amounts of federal and state resources made available to universities for student loans. In addition, donor-restricted contributions may also specify use of the contributed resources for student loan purposes. Loan funds are revolving (self-perpetuating), with repayments of principal and the excess of interest collected over costs incurred becoming the base for additional loans. Both principal and earnings must be available for loan purposes. If only the income from a gift or grant may be used for loan purposes, the principal should not be in the loan fund but in the endowment fund.

The resources of loan funds consist mainly of gifts restricted for loan purposes and unrestricted current fund resources transferred by authorization of the governing board. Although assets are not segregated by restriction, the net assets must reveal their restricted and unrestricted portions.

Event	Entry		
20. A contribution of $25,000 is received from an alumnus for student loan purposes.	Cash	25,000	
	Revenues—Temporarily Restricted Contributions		25,000
21. Investments costing $5,000 are sold for $5,500. Gain is restricted.	Cash	5,500	
	Investments		5,000
	Revenues—Temporarily Restricted—Net Realized Gains on Investments		500
22. Loans totaling $24,000 are made to students. Collections from other loans made to students total $20,000 plus $1,000 of interest. (FASB No. 116 assumes that restricted resources are used first.)	Loans Receivable	24,000	
	Cash		24,000
	Reclassifications Out—Temporarily Restricted—Satisfaction of Program Restrictions	24,000	
	Reclassifications In—Unrestricted—Satisfaction of Program Restrictions		24,000
	Cash	21,000	
	Loans Receivable		20,000
	Revenues—Unrestricted Other Investment Income		1,000
23. Federal government monies of $30,000 restricted for student loans are received.	Cash	30,000	
	U.S. Government Grants Refundable		30,000
24. A $500 student loan is uncollectible.	Expenses—Institutional Support (Loan Cancellations/Write-Offs)	500	
	Loans Receivable		500
25. *Closing entries are prepared for the unrestricted net assets. Public universities will close to unrestricted net assets.	Revenues—Unrestricted Interest Income	1,000	
	Reclassifications In—Unrestricted—Satisfaction of Program Restrictions	24,000	
	Expenses—Institutional Support		500
	Unrestricted Net Assets		**24,500**
26. *Closing entries are prepared for the temporarily restricted net assets. Public universities will close to restricted net assets.	Revenues—Temporarily Restricted Contributions	25,000	
	Revenues—Temporarily Restricted Net Realized Gains on Investments	500	
	Reclassifications Out—Temporarily Restricted—Satisfaction of Program Restrictions		24,000
	Temporarily Restricted Net Assets		**1,500**

Endowment and Similar Funds. Colleges and universities traditionally account for permanent endowments, term endowments, and board-designated (quasi-) endowment resources in separate funds. This practice is common because external users of financial data, such as the debt market, consider all three categories of endowments important in the lending decision. Each of these endowment funds has a unique purpose:

1. *Regular or pure endowments* are funds whose principal has been specified by the donor as nonexpendable. The resources are invested, and the earnings are available for expenditure, usually by the unrestricted current fund.
2. *Term endowments* are funds whose principal is expendable after a specified time period or after a designated event, at which point the resources are added to the unrestricted current fund, unless the original donor has specified some other application.

3. *Quasi-endowments* are funds set aside by the board or controlling body, usually from unrestricted current funds. Restricted current funds also may be set aside if the donor's limitations are not violated. Since these funds are discretionary, technically they do not belong to the endowment category; hence, the addition to the title of "and Similar Funds."

The resources for endowment funds often are pooled for investment purposes, with the various fund balances sharing proportionately in the outcome based on the fair values of investments at the time of pooling or at specified future dates. Procedures for investment pooling are discussed in Chapter 18. Income earned on restricted endowment resources should be transferred immediately to and recorded directly in the restricted current fund, the loan fund, the endowment fund, or a plant fund, depending upon which fund the donor has specified should reap the benefits. Income on which there is no restriction should be transferred to and recorded directly in the unrestricted current fund, where it is credited to Endowment Income. If for some reason there is a delay in making the transfer, the income received should be recorded in the endowment fund, with a credit to a liability to the proper fund. The costs of managing endowment funds should be borne by the university's unrestricted current fund.

GASB Statement No. 31, *Accounting and Financial Reporting for Certain Investments and External Investment,* and FASB Statement No. 124, *Accounting for Certain Investments Held by Not-for-Profit Organizations,* require all investments to be reported at fair value in the statement of net assets. All investment income, including changes in the fair value of investments, should be recognized as revenue in the operating statement. Realized gains are not displayed separately from unrealized gains and losses.[5]

Event	Entry		
27. Common stock with a fair value of $60,000 and $60,000 cash are received as pure endowment contributions.	Cash	60,000	
	Endowment Investments	60,000	
	Revenues—Permanently Restricted Contributions		120,000
28. *Term endowments expire, making $20,000 cash available.	Reclassifications Out—Temporarily Restricted—Expiration of Time Restrictions	20,000	
	Reclassifications In—Unrestricted—Expiration of Time Restrictions		20,000
29. Endowment fund investments carried at $200,000 are sold for $260,000 and investment earnings are $40,000, of which $20,000 is temporarily restricted for research projects and $20,000 is unrestricted.	Cash	300,000	
	Endowment Investments		200,000
	Revenues—Unrestricted Net Realized Gains on Endowment		60,000
	Revenues—Temporarily Restricted Endowment Income		20,000
	Revenues—Unrestricted Endowment Income		20,000
30. Investments are purchased with fund cash.	Endowment Investments	360,000	
	Cash		360,000
31. *Closing entries are prepared for the unrestricted net assets. Public universities will close to unrestricted net assets.	Reclassifications In—Unrestricted—Expiration of Time Restrictions	20,000	
	Revenues—Unrestricted Income on Endowments	20,000	
	Revenues—Unrestricted Net Realized Gains on Endowment	60,000	
	Unrestricted Net Assets		**100,000**

5 GASB Statement No. 31, *Accounting and Financial Reporting for Certain Investments and External Investment* (1997), is effective for years beginning after June 15, 1997.

Event	Entry		
32. *Closing entries are prepared for the temporarily restricted net assets. Public universities will close to restricted net assets.	Revenues—Temporarily Restricted Endowment Income	20,000	
	Reclassifications Out—Temporarily Restricted—Expiration of Time Restriction.		20,000
	Temporarily Restricted Net Assets.		**0**
33. *Closing entries are prepared for the permanently restricted net assets. Public universities will close to restricted net assets.	Revenues—Permanently Restricted Endowment Contributions	120,000	
	Permanently Restricted Net Assets.		**120,000**

Annuity and Life Income Funds. Resources may be accepted by a university under the stipulation that periodic payments are to continue as an annuity to the donor or other designated beneficiary for an indicated time period. Often referred to as *split interest trusts*, these resources should be accounted for in an annuity fund at their fair value on the date of receipt. A liability for the actuarially computed present value of expected total annuity payments is recorded, with the excess credited to revenue from contributions. As each payment is made, a debit is charged directly to the Annuity Payable each period, and the liability is adjusted to bring it to an amount equal to the present value. For example, assume a retired administrator donated $50,000 to a university. The administrator is to receive annuity payments of $3,000 per year for life; thereafter, the principal is to be used for student aid. Assuming an estimated life of 15 years and an 8% interest rate, the present value of the annuity is actuarially computed to be $25,678. The entry to record receipt of the donation is as follows:

Cash—Annuity	50,000	
Annuities Payable		25,678
Revenues—Temporarily Restricted Contribution		24,322

During the year, interest earned on annuity investments is added to the fund balance. At the end of the first year, the present value of the liability is adjusted by adding interest of $2,054 (8% × $25,678). The administrator is mailed a check for $3,000. Entries to record the adjustment of the liability to present value and payment to the annuitant are as follows:

Annuity Interest Expense	2,054	
Annuities Payable		2,054
Annuities Payable	3,000	
Cash		3,000

A life income fund is used if all income received on contributed assets is to be paid to the donor or other specified recipient for life. When the original contributed assets are recorded at fair value, the corresponding credit is to Life Income revenues from contributions. As income is received, a liability for its payment is established immediately.

When the annuity payments or the life income payments cease, the principal is transferred to the donor-specified fund or to the unrestricted current fund if no donor restriction exists. Also, unless otherwise specified, gains or losses on the sale of investments are treated as changes in principal and are recorded directly in the appropriate fund net asset account.

Event	Entry		
34. Cash of $12,000 from life income fund investments and $18,000 from annuity fund investments are received.	Cash	12,000	
	Revenues—Temporarily Restricted Income on Investments		12,000
	Cash	18,000	
	Revenues—Temporarily Restricted Income on Investments		18,000

(continued)

Event		Entry		
35. A retired professor donated $100,000. The professor is to receive $6,000 per year for an estimated life of 10 years. Thereafter, the principal is to be used for student aid. The present value of the annuity at 8% is actuarially computed to be $40,260.		Cash	100,000	
		Annuities Payable		40,260
		Revenues—Temporarily Restricted Contributions		59,740
36. Interest on the annuity is recorded for the year (8% × $40,260 = $3,221).		Actuarial Adjustment of Annuities Payable	3,221	
		Annuities Payable		3,221
37. Payments are made to:				
Annuitant	$ 6,000	Annuities Payable	6,000	
Life income beneficiaries	12,000	Cash		6,000
		Life Income Beneficiaries	12,000	
		Cash		12,000
38. Annuity fund investments with a book value of $50,000 are sold for $59,500.		Cash	59,500	
		Annuity Investments		50,000
		Revenues—Temporarily Restricted Net Realized Gains on Investments		9,500
39. *Closing entries are prepared for temporarily restricted net assets. Public universities will close to restricted net assets.		Revenues—Temporarily Restricted Contributions	59,740	
		Revenues—Temporarily Restricted Net Realized Gains on Investments	9,500	
		Revenues—Temporarily Restricted Income on Annuity and Life Income Investments	30,000	
		Payment to Life Income Beneficiaries		12,000
		Loss on Actuarial Adjustment of Annuities—Payable		3,221
		Temporarily Restricted Net Assets		**84,019**

Plant Funds. The plant funds of public universities include four separate, self-balancing subgroups:

1. *Unexpended plant fund* accounts for resources that are to be used to acquire properties.
2. *Plant fund for renewals and replacements* accounts for resources that are available to keep the physical plant in operating condition.
3. *Plant fund for retirement of indebtedness* accounts for the resources accumulated for the payment of interest and principal of plant fund indebtedness.
4. The *investment in plant* subgroup controls all plant assets and related long-term debt.

GASB Statement No. 35 requires public colleges and universities to record all capital assets, including infrastructure, and to include a *provision for depreciation* of all plant fund assets. The only exceptions are works of art and historical treasures that meet the provisions outlined in the standard.

Cost computations that include depreciation expenses are useful in establishing charges for auxiliary enterprise services, which include dormitories, bookstores, cafeterias and restaurants, medical service, and the student union. Especially for services provided to the general public, amounts charged should include depreciation considerations. Part of the amount that a university receives from grants reimburses it for overhead, which also should include depreciation.

FASB Statement No. 93, *Recognition of Depreciation by Not-for-Profit Organizations*, requires colleges and universities to disclose "depreciation expense for the period." Land and individual works of art or historical treasures that have an extraordinarily long life were excluded from these reporting requirements. The following entries assume one plant fund, although the subgroups described above could be retained.

Event	Entry		
40. Stock with a fair value of $90,000 is received from an art patron to finance an art gallery addition.	Investments	90,000	
	Revenue—Temporarily Restricted Contributions		90,000
41. A collection of first editions appraised at $30,000 is donated to the university. The university adopts a policy of recording contributed collections.	Library Books	30,000	
	Revenue—Unrestricted Contributions		30,000
42. An $800,000 bond issue is sold at face value to finance a business school wing.	Cash	800,000	
	Bonds Payable		800,000
43. Earnings received on investments are restricted for building acquisition.	Cash	45,000	
	Revenues—Temporarily Restricted Other Investment Income		45,000
44. Construction of the business school wing is one-fourth completed.	Construction in Progress	200,000	
	Contracts Payable		200,000
45. Business school wing contract is completed at additional cost of $640,000 and is paid in full.	Construction in Progress	640,000	
	Contracts Payable	200,000	
	Cash		840,000
46. Completed building costs are transferred to the building account.	Building	840,000	
	Construction in Progress		840,000
47. Payment of $100,000 is made on mortgage related to the completed project.	Mortgage Payable	100,000	
	Cash		100,000
48. The cost of constructing an art gallery addition totals $250,000 and is financed with donor-restricted cash. University policy is to release restrictions when assets are placed in service.	Building	250,000	
	Cash		250,000
	Reclassifications Out—Temporarily Restricted—Satisfaction of Plant Restrictions	250,000	
	Reclassifications In—Unrestricted—Satisfaction of Plant Acquisition Restrictions		250,000
49. Land valued at $160,000 is donated by an alumnus.	Land	160,000	
	Revenues—Unrestricted Property Contribution		160,000
50. Building repairs of $50,000 are paid, of which $5,000 is from restricted resources.	Expenses	50,000	
	Cash		50,000
	Reclassifications Out—Temporarily Restricted—Satisfaction of Program Restrictions	5,000	
	Reclassifications In—Unrestricted—Satisfaction of Program Restrictions		5,000
51. *Depreciation expense for the current period is $150,000. Depreciation expenses are allocated to operation and maintenance of plant expenses. Public universities will have new depreciation expense.	Expenses—Operation and Maintenance of Plant (provision for depreciation)	150,000	
	Accumulated Depreciation		150,000
52. *Closing entries are prepared for the unrestricted net assets. Public universities will close to unrestricted net assets.	Reclassifications In—Unrestricted—Satisfaction of Plant Acquisition Restrictions	250,000	
	Reclassifications In—Unrestricted—Satisfaction of Program Restrictions	5,000	
	Revenues—Unrestricted Property Contributions	190,000	
	Expenses—Operation and Maintenance of Plant		200,000
	Unrestricted Net Assets		**245,000**

(continued)

Event	Entry		
53. *Closing entries are prepared for the temporarily restricted net assets. Public universities will close to restricted net assets.	**Temporarily Restricted Net Assets**	**120,000**	
	Revenues—Temporarily Restricted Contributions	90,000	
	Revenues—Temporarily Restricted Other Investment Income	45,000	
	Reclassifications Out—Temporarily Restricted—Satisfaction of Plant Acquisition		250,000
	Reclassifications Out—Temporarily Restricted—Satisfaction of Program Restrictions		5,000

Agency Funds. Agency funds account for resources that are not the property of the university but are held in the university's custody. An example of such resources is assets belonging to student organizations. The total amount of these resources represents a liability. As a result, there are no net assets. FASB Statement No. 116 specifically includes federal monies that pass through the university to student recipients (Pell Grants) as agency transactions. In public universities, the GASB requires that agency funds be used if no program administration responsibility or oversight is determined.

Event	Entry		
54. Federal grants for student awards through the Pell Grant Program are received in the amount of $75,000. All $75,000 is distributed to qualified students.	Cash	75,000	
	Amounts Held on Behalf of Others		75,000
	Amounts Held on Behalf of Others	75,000	
	Cash		75,000

5

OBJECTIVE

Prepare financial statements for not-for-profit colleges and universities.

Financial Statements

The financial statements of public and private colleges and universities will become more alike with the adoption of GASB Statement No. 35. Under the new governmental standards, *public* colleges and universities are required to report the following financial statements:

1. *Statement of New Assets* (balance sheet) which will report organization-wide totals for assets, liabilities, net assets, and net assets identified as invested in capital [net of related debt, restricted (nonexpendable and expendable), and unrestricted (see Illustration 19-1 on page 1069)].
2. *Statement of Revenues, Expenses, and Changes in Net Assets* which reports operating revenues and expenses and nonoperating activities, including gifts, grants, and additions to endowments (see Illustration 19-2 on page 1070).
3. *Statement of Cash Flows* with categories (operating, noncapital financing, capital and related financing, and investing activities) prescribed for all governments (see Illustration 19-3 on page 1071).

Private colleges and universities have the following required financial statements:

1. *Statement of Financial Position* (balance sheet) which will report organization-wide totals for assets, liabilities, net assets, and net assets identified as unrestricted, temporarily restricted, and permanently restricted (see Illustration 19-4 on page 1072).
2. *Statement of Activities* which reports revenues, expenses, gains, losses, and reclassifications (between classes of net assets). Minimum requirements are organization-wide totals, changes in net assets for each class of assets, and all expenses recognized only in the unrestricted classification. A display of a measure of operations in the statement of activities is permitted (see Illustration 19-5 on page 1073).
3. *Statement of Cash Flows* with categories (operating, financing, investing) similar to business organizations (see Illustration 19-6 on page 1074).

Illustration 19-1
Public University
Statement of Net Assets
June 30, 20X7

Assets:	
Current assets:	
Cash and cash equivalents	$ 1,470,100
Short-term investments	673,000
Accounts receivables, net	130,000
Contributions receivable	335,481
Inventories of supplies	20,000
Prepaid expenses	28,000
Total current assets	$ 2,656,581
Noncurrent assets:	
Restricted cash and cash equivalents	$ 24,200
Student loans receivable	55,500
Endowment investments	954,000
Other long-term investments	1,118,700
Assets restricted to investment in capital	1,350,000
Capital assets, net of accumulated depreciation of $150,000	41,450,000
Total noncurrent assets	$44,952,400
Total assets	$47,608,981
Liabilities:	
Current liabilities:	
Accounts payable and accrued liabilities	$ 1,039,000
Deferred revenues	85,000
Other current liabilities	1,500
Total current liabilities	$ 1,125,500
Noncurrent liabilities:	
Assets held on behalf of others	$ 110,000
Annuities payable	237,481
Long-term debt (capital related)	3,000,000
Total noncurrent liabilities	$ 3,347,481
Total liabilities	$ 4,472,981
Net assets:	
Invested in capital assets, net of related debt	$38,450,000
Restricted for:	
Nonexpendable:	
Instruction	525,000
Research	429,000
Expendable:	
Scholarships and fellowships	45,000
Research	150,000
Instructional department uses	50,000
Loans	82,500
Capital projects	1,350,000
Other	336,000
Unrestricted	1,718,500
Total net assets	$43,136,000

Illustration 19-2
Public University
Statement of Revenues, Expenses, and Changes in Net Assets
For Year Ended June 30, 20X7

Operating revenues:	
Student tuition and fees	$ 1,700,000
Contributions	575,000
Government appropriations, grants, and contracts	275,000
Sales and services of auxiliary enterprises	400,000
Total operating revenues	$ 2,950,000
Operating expenses:	
Salaries	$ 1,592,000
Benefits	582,500
Scholarships and fellowships	221,000
Utilities	50,000
Repairs and maintenance	400,000
Auxiliary enterprises expenses	350,000
Depreciation	150,000
Total operating expenses	$ 3,345,500
Operating income (loss)	$ (395,500)
Nonoperating revenues (expenses):	
Contributions	$ 164,740
Investment income	424,000
Interest on capital asset—related debt	(20,000)
Net nonoperating revenues	$ 568,740
Income before other revenues, expenses, gains, or losses	$ 173,240
Capital appropriations	520,000
Capital grants and gifts	200,000
Realized gains on investments	10,000
Adjustment on annuity obligations	(3,221)
Additions to permanent endowments	60,000
Increase in net assets	$ 960,019
Net assets—beginning of year	$42,175,981
Net assets—end of year	$43,136,000

Illustration 19-3
Public University
Statement of Cash Flows
For Year Ended June 30, 20X7

Cash flows from operating activities:	
Student tuition and auxiliary fees	$ 2,030,000
Governmental appropriations	275,000
Research activities receipts	100,000
Contributions received	150,000
Payments to vendors for goods and services	(958,000)
Salaries and wages paid to faculty and staff	(1,935,000)
Disbursements to students for financial aid	(105,000)
Repayments of loans from students and faculty	20,000
Payments to life income beneficiaries and annuitants	(18,000)
Other receipts (payments)	105,000
Net cash provided (used) by operating activities	$ (336,000)
Cash flows from noncapital financing activities:	
Governmental appropriations	$ 180,000
Gifts and grants received for other than capital purposes:	
Private gifts for long-term investment	245,000
Net cash flows provided by noncapital financing activities	$ 425,000
Cash flows from capital and related financing activities:	
Proceeds from capital debt	$ 800,000
Capital appropriations	195,000
Capital grants and gifts received	200,000
Purchases of capital assets	(840,000)
Principal and interest paid on capital debt and lease	(100,000)
Net cash used by capital and related financing activities	$ 255,000
Cash flows from investing activities:	
Proceeds from sales and maturities of investments	$ 325,000
Interest and dividends received	383,000
Purchase of investments	(360,000)
Net cash provided (used) by investing activities	$ 348,000
Net increase in cash	$ 692,000
Cash—beginning of year	802,300
Cash—end of year	$ 1,494,300*

*Cash and cash equivalents ($1,470,100) + restricted cash and cash equivalents ($24,200) = $1,494,300.

Illustration 19-4
Private University
Statement of Financial Position
For Period Ended June 30, 20X7

Assets:	
Cash	$ 1,494,300
Short-term investments	673,000
Accounts receivable (net of $20,000 allowance)	130,000
Contributions receivable (net of $25,000 allowance)	335,481
Inventories of supplies	20,000
Prepaid expenses	28,000
Student loans receivable	55,500
Assets restricted to investment in land, buildings, and equipment	1,350,000
Land, buildings, and equipment (net of accumulated depreciation of $150,000)	41,450,000
Long-term investments	1,118,700
Endowment investments	954,000
Total assets	**$47,608,981**
Liabilities:	
Accounts payable and accrued liabilities	$ 1,039,000
Other liabilities	1,500
Amounts held on behalf of others	110,000
U.S. government grants refundable	85,000
Annuities payable	237,481
Long-term debt	3,000,000
Total liabilities	**$ 4,472,981**
Net assets:	
Unrestricted	**$40,168,500**
Temporarily restricted	**2,013,500**
Permanently restricted	**954,000**
Total net assets	**$43,136,000**
Total liabilities and net assets	**$47,608,981**

REFLECTION

- Private colleges and universities follow FASB standards.
- Public colleges and universities will report as special purpose governments engaged in business-type activities and, as such, follow FASB standards per GASB Statement No. 35.
- Student aid is considered an expense; Pell Grants are agency transactions.
- Universities use fund accounting for internal control and decision making, but funds are not required in the external financial reports.

Illustration 19-5
Private University
Statement of Activities
For Year Ended June 30, 20X7

	Unrestricted	Temporarily Restricted	Permanently Restricted	Total
Changes in net assets:				
Revenues and gains:				
Tuition and fees	$ 1,700,000			$ 1,700,000
Contributions	575,000	$ 244,740	$ 120,000	939,740
Governmental appropriations, grants, and contracts	795,000			795,000
Investment income on endowment	70,000	28,000		98,000
Other investment income	251,000	45,000		296,000
Sales and services of auxiliary enterprises	400,000			400,000
Investment income on life income and annuity agreements		30,000		30,000
Net realized gains on other investments		10,000		10,000
Net realized gains on endowment	60,000			60,000
Total revenues and gains	$ 3,851,000	$ 357,740	$ 120,000	$ 4,328,740
Net assets released from restrictions:				
Satisfaction of program restrictions	$ 102,000	$ (102,000)		$ 0
Satisfaction of plant acquisitions restrictions	250,000	(250,000)		0
Satisfaction of time restrictions	20,000	(20,000)		0
Total net assets released from restriction	$ 372,000	$ (372,000)		$ 0
Total revenues and gains and other support	$ 4,223,000	$ (14,260)	$ 120,000	$ 4,328,740
Expenses and losses:				
Educational and general:				
Instruction	$ 1,353,000			$ 1,353,000
Research	145,000			145,000
Academic support	217,000			217,000
Student services	222,000			222,000
Institutional support	245,500			245,500
Operation and maintenance of plant	600,000			600,000
Student aid	221,000			221,000
Total educational and general expenses	$ 3,003,500			$ 3,003,500
Auxiliary enterprises	350,000			350,000
Total expenses	$ 3,353,500	$ 0	$ 0	$ 3,353,500
Actuarial adjustment on annuity obligations		3,221		3,221
Payments to life income beneficiaries		12,000		12,000
Total expenses and losses	$ 3,353,500	$ 15,221	$ 0	$ 3,368,721
Increase (decrease) in net assets	**$ 869,500**	**$ (29,481)**	**$120,000**	**$ 960,019**
Net assets at beginning of year	**39,299,000**	**2,042,981**	**834,000**	**42,175,981**
Net assets at end of year	**$40,168,500**	**$2,013,500**	**$954,000**	**$43,136,000**

Illustration 19-6
Private University
Statement of Cash Flows
For Period Ended June 30, 20X7

Cash flows from operating activities:	
Student tuition and auxiliary fees	$ 2,030,000
Governmental appropriations	650,000
Research activities receipts	100,000
Interest and dividends received	308,000
Contributions received	395,000
Other receipts	75,000
Salaries and wages paid to faculty and staff	(1,935,000)
Payments to vendors for goods and services	(958,000)
Disbursements to students for financial aid	(81,000)
Payments to life income beneficiaries	(12,000)
Net cash provided by (used for) operating activities	**$ 572,000**
Cash flows from investing activities:	
Proceeds from sales and maturities of investments	$ 325,000
Purchases of investments	(360,000)
Purchases of land, buildings, and equipment	(840,000)
Disbursements of loans to students and faculty	(24,000)
Repayments of loans from students and faculty	20,000
Net cash provided by (used for) investing activities	**$ (879,000)**
Cash flows from financing activities:	
Proceeds from issuance of notes payable	$ 800,000
Payments on long-term debt	(100,000)
Receipts of interest and dividends restricted for reinvestment	75,000
Contributions received restricted for long-term investment	200,000
Payments to annuitants	(6,000)
Receipts of refundable government loans funds	30,000
Net cash provided by (used for) financing activities	**$ 999,000**
Net increase (decrease) in cash and cash equivalents	**$ 692,000**
Cash and cash equivalents at beginning of year	**802,300**
Cash and cash equivalents at end of year	**$1,494,300**

6

OBJECTIVE

Explain GAAP and fund accounting as applied to governmental and private health care service providers.

ACCOUNTING FOR PROVIDERS OF HEALTH CARE SERVICES—GOVERNMENTAL AND PRIVATE

Advancement in medical practice and increased demand for access to health care services have led to significant growth in the health care industry. Expenditures for medical care now equal more than 10% of the gross national product. Health care entities include hospitals, clinics, continuing care retirement communities, health maintenance organizations, home health agencies, and nursing homes. Classified by sponsorship or equity structure, health care units fall into three categories:

1. Investor-owned health care entities (or proprietary entities), which are privately owned and operated for a profit.

2. Governmental health care entities (or public entities), which are operated by a governmental unit and accounted for as an enterprise fund, such as a veterans' hospital.
3. Voluntary not-for-profit health care entities, including those with a religious affiliation, which are organized and sustained by members of a community.

A modern health care provider may be a complex entity with medical, surgical, research, teaching, and public service aspects. One very unusual element about health care operations is the manner of payment for services. A significant portion of the fees for health care service is paid by a third party, such as Medicare, Medicaid, Blue Cross, or some other insurance provider. Health care entities are reimbursed not on the basis of listed prices but on the basis of the cost of providing services, as that cost is defined by the third-party payor. A cost determination must be made according to formulas agreed upon in the law (Medicare and Medicaid) or in the contract (other insurance providers). Cost determination requires allocation of overhead, including depreciation. Thus, not-for-profit health care organizations follow the accrual basis of accounting, permitting comparison of results with profit-oriented health care units.

Generally Accepted Accounting Principles

Generally accepted accounting principles (GAAP) for hospitals and other health care organizations have evolved through the efforts of two industry professional associations, the American Hospital Association (AHA) and the Health Care Financial Management Association (HFMA), and the American Institute of Certified Public Accountants (AICPA). The AICPA Accounting and Audit Guide, *Health Care Organizations*, updated in May 2000, incorporates FASB Statement Nos. 116 and 117 that were described in the previous chapter. This guide is currently the principal source of accounting guidelines for private and governmental health care entities that choose to follow FASB standards.[6]

Governmental hospitals or health care providers are considered special purpose governments engaged in business-type activities for purposes of applying GASB Statement No. 34. As such, *health care entities will report as enterprise funds.* And, they may elect to apply all FASB statements and interpretations issued after November 30, 1989, except those that conflict with or contradict GASB pronouncements.

Funds

With the many restrictions resulting from donations, endowments, insurance company contracts, and government regulations for reimbursement, the activities of a health care provider have traditionally been accounted for using fund accounting.[7] Health care entities employ two classes of funds:

1. *General funds*, which account for resources available for general operations, with no restrictions placed upon those resources by an outsider, and other exchange transactions including resources from government grants and subsidies, tax support, and reimbursements from insurance contracts.
2. *Donor-restricted funds*, which account for temporarily and permanently restricted resources. This class is subdivided into:

   a. *Specific purpose funds*, which account for donor-restricted resources temporarily restricted for current but specified operations.

6 FASB Statement Nos. 116 and 117 are applicable to governmental health care organizations under GASB Statement No. 20, *Accounting and Financial Reporting for Proprietary Funds and Other Governmental Entities that Use Proprietary Fund Accounting* (Norwalk, CT: Governmental Accounting Standards Board, 1993), par. 7.

7 Most hospitals have traditionally used the fund structure described in this chapter. However, other health care entities, such as health maintenance organizations, nursing homes, and home health care agencies may find it unnecessary to use fund accounting.

b. *Plant replacement and expansion funds*, which account for resources temporarily restricted by the donor for the acquisition, construction, or improvement of property, plant, and equipment.
c. *Endowment funds*, which account for resources that are received to create permanently restricted endowments (whose income only may be expended) and temporarily restricted term endowments (whose principal eventually will become available for expenditure).
d. Other donor-restricted funds such as annuities, life income funds, or loan funds.

Each fund consists of a set of self-balancing accounts designed to reflect activities within its domain. Although the new FASB guidance on accounting and financial reporting represents a shift away from fund accounting to an organization-wide perspective, health care organizations are expected to continue some form of fund accounting for internal management and reporting. Some may even choose to continue to include information on funds in the external financial reports. To demonstrate the organization-wide emphasis on accounting and financial reporting and to simplify the presentation, the following discussion assumes no fund structure.

Classification of Assets and Liabilities

Assets of a health care provider comprise three distinct segments: current assets, assets whose use is limited, and property and equipment. Assets and liabilities are sequenced by liquidity and are classified as current or noncurrent according to GAAP.

Assets whose use is limited include assets set aside by the governing board for a specific purpose, sometimes referred to as board-designated assets. For example, the board may authorize that $10,000 be set aside for capital improvements, which would be recorded as follows:

Cash—Limited in Use for Capital Expansion	10,000	
Cash		10,000

The limitation is internal and, therefore, assets remain unrestricted since "restrictions" can only be created by outside sources. This segment also includes assets resulting from an operational agreement entered into by the board, such as the proceeds of a bond issue limited in use as stipulated by the bond indenture. Assets set aside to provide for self-insurance or to meet depreciation fund requirements with third-party payors belong to this segment as well.

Property and equipment include the physical properties used in operations, along with their accumulated depreciation. Current liabilities may include accounts and notes payable, deposits from patients, and advances from and amounts payable to third-party payors. Long-term liabilities may include notes, mortgages, capital leases, bond payables, and estimated malpractice costs. The net assets of the entire health care organization (which represents the difference between assets and liabilities) are divided into three classes—permanently restricted net assets, temporarily restricted net assets, and unrestricted net assets—based on the existence or absence of donor-imposed restrictions.

Classification of Revenues, Expenses, Gains, and Losses

7
OBJECTIVE
Demonstrate an understanding of how revenues and expenses are calculated and accounted for by governmental and private health care service providers.

Revenues, expenses, gains, and losses increase or decrease the net assets of a health care entity. Other events, such as expirations of donor-imposed restrictions, that simultaneously increase one class of net assets and decrease another (reclassifications) are reported as separate items. Revenues and gains may increase unrestricted net assets, temporarily restricted net assets, or permanently restricted net assets. Expenses reduce unrestricted net assets.

Revenues and expenses are considered operating if they relate to the principal activity of providing health care services. Revenues, expenses, gains, or losses from activities that are incidental to the providing of health care services or from events beyond the entity's control are classified as nonoperating.

Hospital payment systems have changed significantly in recent years. The systems include fees based on *diagnosis-related groups (DRGs), capitation premiums* (paid per member, per month), *fees based on negotiated bids*, and *cost-reimbursement methods.* Some payments are established prospectively (in advance of service delivery) at fixed amounts. Other payment rates may be based on interim billing amounts, subject to retrospective (after the accounting period ends) adjustment. Medicare generally pays hospitals prospectively, based on DRGs. Under the DRG system, all potential diagnoses are classified into a number of medically meaningful groups, each of which has a different value. Each hospital in a specific geographical region receives the same amount for each DRG, depending on whether the hospital is classified as urban or rural, and teaching or nonteaching. The thinking behind the DRG system is that a hospital that is more efficient will benefit because it may keep any reimbursement in excess of cost.

Under capitation agreements with HMOs, hospitals generally receive agreed-upon monthly premiums based on the number of participants in the HMO. In exchange, the hospitals agree to provide all medical services to the HMO's subscribers. The hospitals will receive the capitation payment regardless of the actual services they perform. The hospitals may also receive fees from the HMO for certain services. Other payment methods include prospectively determined rates per discharge, prospectively determined daily rates, and discounts from established charges. When rates are determined retrospectively, the hospital is generally required to submit audited cost reports with detail on allowable costs. Retrospective adjustment can result in either an increase or decrease to the rates allowed for interim billing purposes.

The following operating revenue classifications are used in health care:

1. *Patient Service Revenue*, the major revenue account for a hospital, in which the gross revenues earned are recorded on an accrual basis at established rates for:
   a. Routine services (room and board, general nursing, and home health care).
   b. Other nursing services (in operating, recovery, and delivery rooms).
   c. Professional services (physician's care, lab work, pharmacy, blood bank, radiology, dialysis, and physical therapy).
2. *Premium Revenue*, based on fees from agreements under which a hospital or HMO has agreed to provide any necessary patient services for a specific fee, e.g., a capitation agreement whereby the HMO receives an agreed-upon payment from another HMO for a specific number of members per month regardless of actual services.
3. *Resident Service Revenue*, the major revenue account for a nursing home or continuing care retirement community. It records rental fees earned from residents or amortization of their advance payment of fees.
4. *Other Operating Revenue*, which records revenue from services other than health care provided to patients and residents. Also recorded is revenue from sales or services to persons other than patients. Thus, Other Operating Revenue would include:
   a. Revenue from educational programs, such as nursing school tuition.
   b. Revenue from specific-purpose contributions.
   c. Revenue from government grants to the extent that the related expenditures are included in operations. Grants that may be refundable if provisions that are not met are recorded as a liability. As expenses are incurred, a matching portion of the grant is recorded from liabilities and recognized as current-period revenue.
   d. Revenue from sales of medical or pharmacy supplies to employees or physicians.
   e. Revenue from sale of cafeteria meals to employees, medical staff, and visitors.
   f. Revenue from snack bars, gift shops, parking lots, and other service facilities.

The control account *Nonoperating Revenue* records revenue not related directly to an entity's principal operations. These items are primarily financial in nature and include unrestricted and donor-restricted pledges, gifts, or grants, unrestricted income from endowment funds, maturing of term endowment funds, income and gains from investments, and gains on sales of hospital property. Investments are reported at fair value with both realized and unrealized gains included as part of nonoperating revenue.

Patient Service Revenue is initially recorded at the hospital's gross (established) rates. A third-party payor, such as Blue Cross, HMOs, Medicare, or Medicaid, may reimburse a hospital on the basis of predetermined amounts that are less than the original gross charges for described services. The difference between the gross revenue and the amount expected to be collected from the third-party payors is referred to as the *contractual adjustment.* It is deducted from the gross patient service revenue prior to preparing the financial statements. A credit is made to an allowance account in order to reduce the receivables to net expected. Also deducted from gross revenue are adjustments for services provided as courtesy allowances granted to hospital employees. Not-for-profit hospitals also provide care without charge (charitable services) to persons who have demonstrated an inability to pay. Each hospital is required to establish criteria for charity care consistent with its mission statement and financial ability. Charity services are not reported as revenues or as receivables in the financial statements. Hospitals may, however, initially record the patient services charges because of an initial lack of knowledge that an account qualifies as charity service and the need to disclose the level of charity service. Under these circumstances, the charity care amount is recorded as contra revenue with a credit to an allowance account to reduce the receivable similar to the contractual adjustment. Since charity care represents health care services that are provided but are never expected to result in cash flows, it is distinguished from bad debts. Other uncollectible amounts are reported as bad debt expense. The objective of grouping these items is to be able to show accurate net patient service revenue, an expense for uncollectibles, and net receivables on the financial statements. Illustrative entries are as follows:

Patient Accounts Receivable	XXX	
Patient Service Revenues		XXX
Contractual Adjustments	XXX	
Allowance for Uncollectible Third-Party Contracts and Charity		XXX
Provision for Bad Debts	XXX	
Allowance for Uncollectible Third-Party Contracts and Charity		XXX
Charity Services	XXX	
Accounts Receivable		XXX

Payments made to a health care unit by third parties include reimbursement for depreciation. Often this portion of the payment is limited in use to replacing or adding to property, plant, or equipment. Total billings are included in revenue of the general funds to permit matching of total revenues and expenses. When collected, the specified portion is transferred to a special account with the following entry:

Cash—Assets Whose Use Is Limited by Agreement with Third-Party Payors for Funded Depreciation	XXX	
Cash		XXX

Titles given to operating expenses of a health care facility may differ, depending upon the nature of the facility's activities. Expenses may be reported on the face of the financial statements using either a natural classification or a functional presentation. Functional allocations are to be based on full cost allocations. The following functional expense categories are common to many health care organizations:

1. Nursing Services Expense, for the cost of nursing services directly related to the patient or resident.
2. Other Professional Services Expense, for professional services indirectly related to the patient or resident, such as lab fees or pharmacy costs. Note that some hospitals combine the two accounts Nursing Services Expense and Other Professional Services Expense into one account labeled Professional Care of Patients Expense.
3. General Services Expense, for costs of the cafeteria, food service, and housekeeping. Where food services constitute a major cost, some hospitals prefer to segregate them into the account Dietary Services Expense.
4. Fiscal Services Expense, for admitting, data processing, billing, and accounting costs.
5. Administrative Services Expense, for purchasing, public relations, insurance, taxes, and personnel costs.
6. Other Services.
7. Malpractice Insurance Expense, if not already allocated.

8. Depreciation Expense, if not already allocated.
9. Interest Expense, if not already allocated.
10. Provision for Bad Debts, if not already allocated.

For example, salaries expense is often recorded and allocated to the first six functional expense accounts at year-end. The statement of activities (operating statement) would show the total for each service, such as Nursing Services Expense, but not the nature of that total (salaries, supplies, etc.). The footnotes to the financial statements provide detail on the natural classifications of the expense, such as salaries, supplies, etc.

Accounting for Donations/Contributions Received

8

OBJECTIVE

Demonstrate an understanding of the accounting for unrestricted and restricted contributions to governmental and private health care service providers.

Health care entities may receive gifts or donations that meet the definition of an unconditional contribution. These contributions may be unrestricted as to use or may be limited to a specific use. Unrestricted contributions are recognized at fair value with a credit to Other Operating Revenue—Unrestricted, or Nonoperating Revenue—Unrestricted, depending on whether these contributions are deemed to be ongoing major or central activities, or peripheral or incidental transactions.

Bequests and gifts restricted by the donor to be used for (1) specific operating purposes, (2) additions to plant, (3) endowments, or (4) annuities or life incomes are recorded when received at their fair value with a credit to Revenues (other operating or nonoperating)—Temporarily Restricted or Revenues (other operating or nonoperating)—Permanently Restricted.[8] When expenditures are made consistent with the donor's stipulation, or when term endowments become available, a reclassification is made from the temporarily restricted net asset category to an unrestricted net asset category. Should resources from expired term endowments be restricted further, for example, to purchase equipment, they will remain in the temporarily restricted net asset category. Resources temporarily restricted for the purchase or construction of property, plant, and equipment may be released from restriction either in the period the asset is placed into service or over its useful life. Donor-restricted contributions in which the restriction will be met in the current period may be classified as unrestricted revenues. Some promises to give are conditional and will not be recognized until the condition is met.

Activities of health care providers are enhanced by volunteers who donate their time and abilities. Donated services must be recognized if the services received (1) create or enhance nonfinancial assets or (2) require specialized skills, are provided by individuals possessing those skills who are scheduled and supervised in much the same way as employees, and would typically need to be purchased if not contributed. Services provided by doctors, nurses, and other professionals in a health care entity may meet the above criteria. Incidental services provided by other volunteers for such things as fund raising or other activities that would not otherwise be staffed by employees would not meet the criteria. For example, most voluntary service by senior citizens, candy stripers, and others is not recorded. When an institution is operated by a religious group whose members receive token payment or no payment at all, the value of donated services should be charged to the proper expense account and credited to other operating revenue or nonoperating revenue depending on the nature of the donated services.

Professional Care of Patients Expense	XXX	
Other Revenue—Donated Services		XXX

Donated items may also be unrestricted or restricted. Examples of donated items in a health care entity are laboratory and pharmaceutical supplies donated by drug companies or associa-

8 Prior to FASB Statement No. 116, health care organizations credited the appropriate temporarily restricted or permanently restricted fund balance account. When donor-restricted assets were used for their intended purpose, they were recorded as a transfer or, more commonly, as a direct debit to the appropriate fund balance. The transfer was recorded in the general fund as a credit to Other Operating Revenue or Nonoperating Revenue as appropriate. Revenue recognition was delayed until expenditures were incurred. Transfers for capital purchases were not recorded as revenue but as increases in the fund balance account of the general funds.

tions of doctors; donated property, plant, and equipment; and contributed use of facilities. Donated items are recognized at fair value with a credit to Other Operating Revenue—Unrestricted or Nonoperating Revenue—Unrestricted, depending on whether the donations constitute the entity's ongoing major or central operations or are peripheral or incidental transactions. If donated items have a donor-specified use, they may be temporarily restricted until they are used for their intended purpose. Unrestricted donations of property are recognized as Nonoperating Revenue—Unrestricted. If donations of property are donor restricted, the same entry is made but with a credit to temporarily or permanently restricted revenues.

9

OBJECTIVE

Explain the financial impact of medical malpractice claims on governmental and private health care service providers.

Medical Malpractice Claims

Settlements and judgments on medical malpractice claims constitute a potential major expense for hospitals. The current environment in relation to medical malpractice claims has caused insurance companies to raise premiums to health care providers dramatically or to limit the amount of risk they are willing to insure. To find a health care provider that is fully insured against medical malpractice losses is a rarity. Many have dropped their malpractice insurance or have adopted other approaches for protection. Some pay losses as they occur. Others establish trust funds with a trustee.

Whether expenses and liabilities need to be recognized on malpractice claims depends on whether risk has been transferred by the hospital to the third-party insurance company or to public entity risk pools. An AICPA statement stipulates that:

> *The ultimate costs of malpractice claims, which include costs associated with litigating or settling claims, should be accrued when the incidents occur that give rise to the claims, if it can be determined that it is probable that liabilities have been incurred and if the amounts of the losses can be reasonably estimated.*[9]

The basic rule applies whether or not claims for incidents occurring before the balance sheet date [incurred but not reported (IBNR)] have been asserted. An estimate must be made for losses on IBNR claims if it is probable that incidents have occurred and that losses will result. Historical experience of both the hospital and the health care industry are often used in estimating the probability of IBNR claims. If the health care provider is covered by insurance, the premiums applicable to the reporting period are expensed. The entry to record payment of insurance premums is as follows:

Medical Malpractice Costs (or administrative services expense)	XXX	
Cash		XXX

The entry to record an amount for estimated claim costs for the reporting period not covered by the insurance arrangement is as follows:

Medical Malpractice Costs (or administrative services expense)	XXX	
Estimated Additional Malpractice Liability		XXX

Although hospitals report expenses on a functional basis by major program area, the medical malpractice costs are sometimes segregated from the other administrative services costs to emphasize their critical nature.

As a result of the large settlements granted in malpractice cases, some health care organizations became self-insured, establishing a trust account with an outside trustee who determines funding requirements. Two entries are necessary. The first establishes the estimated claim costs and liability as follows:

9 Statement of Position 87-1, *Accounting for Asserted and Unasserted Medical Malpractice Claims of Health Care Providers and Related Issues* (New York: American Institute of Certified Public Accountants, March 16, 1987), par. 21.

Medical Malpractice Costs (or administrative services expense)	XXX	
Estimated Malpractice Liability		XXX

The second entry records the contribution to the trustee:

Cash—Limited in Use Under Malpractice Funding Arrangement	XXX	
Cash		XXX

The amount in the trust account is reported in the balance sheet as an asset whose use is limited. Claims expected to be paid during the next operating cycle are classified as current liabilities, while the remainder of the liability balance is shown as noncurrent.

Whether the health care provider is covered by insurance, pays losses as they occur, or has a trust fund arrangement, the amount of the expense should reflect the best estimate of ultimate costs of malpractice claims related to incidents that occurred during the reporting period.

Illustrative Entries

10

OBJECTIVE

Account for transactions of governmental and private health care service providers.

To illustrate the recording of events for a hospital, the year's affairs of Columbia Hospital are summarized next. The illustrative entries employ broad categories of control accounts and natural expense classification which are allocated to the functional categories at year-end.

	Event		Entry		
1.	Gross charges to patients are for:		Accounts Receivable	5,200,000	
			Patient Service Revenue		5,000,000
	Daily patient services	$3,200,000	Other Operating Revenue—Unrestricted		200,000
	Other nursing services	500,000			
	Professional services	1,300,000			
	Other nonmedical services	200,000			
	Total	$5,200,000			
2.	Estimates are made for:		Provision for Bad Debts	22,000	
			Contractual Adjustments	380,000	
	Contractual adjustments	$ 380,000	Allowance for Uncollectible Receivables		
	Uncollectibles	22,000	and Third-Party Contractual		
	Total	$ 402,000	Adjustments		402,000
3.	An analysis of accounts receivable shows:		Cash	3,800,000	
			Allowance for Uncollectible		
	Cash collected	$3,800,000	Receivables and Third-Party		
	Contractual adjustments with third-party		Contractual Adjustments	290,000	
	payors	200,000	Accounts Receivable		4,090,000
	Uncollectible	90,000			
	Total	$4,090,000			
4.	The hospital determined that $200,000 of the services were to patients who met hospital criteria for charity care.		Charity Services	200,000	
			Accounts Receivable		200,000
5.	Inventory purchases amounted to $700,000; payments totaled $690,000.		Inventories	700,000	
			Cash		690,000
			Accounts Payable		10,000

(continued)

Event	Entry		
6. Drugs and supplies costing $720,000 are requisitioned.	Drugs and Supplies Used	720,000	
	Inventories		720,000
7. Salaries earned (ignore payroll deductions) amounted to $3,000,000, of which $2,950,000 is paid.	Wages, Salaries, and Benefits	3,000,000	
	Cash		2,950,000
	Accrued Expenses		50,000
8. Outside professional fees of $300,000 are paid.	Purchased Services	300,000	
	Cash		300,000
9. Jacob Pharmaceutical Co. donated $2,000 of medicines to Columbia Hospital. Such contributions constitute a major ongoing activity of the hospital. If not donated, these medicines would have to be purchased.	Inventories	2,000	
	Other Operating Revenues—Unrestricted (contributions)		2,000
10. Unrestricted earnings from long-term investments totaled $540,000.	Cash	540,000	
	Nonoperating Revenues—Unrestricted (investment earnings)		540,000
11. Payments are made on: Current installment of long-term debt $ 80,000 Notes payable 200,000 Interest expense 66,000 Total $ 346,000	Current Installment of Long-Term Debt	80,000	
	Notes Payable	200,000	
	Interest Expense	66,000	
	Cash		346,000
12. A donor promised to give Columbia $50,000 annually for each of the next four years (recorded at present value).	Contributions Receivable	165,606	
	Nonoperating Revenues—Unrestricted (contributions)		165,606
13. The hospital was recently served with a malpractice lawsuit. A prominent local trial attorney decided to assist in the defense of the hospital. Normal fees are $150 per hour. A total of 100 hours were devoted to the case.	Purchased Services	15,000	
	Nonoperating Revenues—Unrestricted (contributions)		15,000
14. Equipment costing $110,000 is purchased for cash.	Property and Equipment	110,000	
	Cash		110,000
15. Depreciation expense provision for the year is $400,000.	Depreciation Expense	400,000	
	Accumulated Depreciation		400,000
16. The current portion of long-term debt is reclassified as current from: Bonds payable $50,000 Mortgage note payable 30,000 Total $80,000	Bonds Payable	50,000	
	Mortgage Note Payable	30,000	
	Current Installment of Long-Term Debt		80,000
17. Professional services donated to the hospital were recognized: Nursing services $17,000 Other professional medical services 3,000	Wages, Salaries, and Benefits	20,000	
	Other Operating Revenue—Unrestricted (contributions)		20,000
18. A provision for medical malpractice costs of $450,000 is recorded. The hospital is self-insured.	Medical Malpractice Costs	450,000	
	Estimated Malpractice Liability		450,000

Event	Entry		
19. A malpractice self-insurance trust at Third Bank is increased by $230,000.	Cash—Limited in Use Under Malpractice Funding Arrangement	230,000	
	Cash		230,000
20. Third-party payor reimbursements of $250,000 are to be set aside for plant replacement.	Cash—Limited in Use by Agreement with Third-Party Payors for Plant	250,000	
	Cash		250,000
21. Columbia received $50,000 cash from a donor to cover operating costs of the student nursing unit.	Cash	50,000	
	Other Operating Revenue—Temporarily Restricted (contributions)		50,000
22. Investment earnings are received in the amount of $75,000 restricted for cancer research.	Cash	75,000	
	Nonoperating Revenue—Temporarily Restricted (investment earnings)		75,000
23. A $500,000 donation was made to Columbia Hospital for investments in long-term securities as a pure endowment.	Cash	500,000	
	Nonoperating Revenue—Temporarily Restricted (endowment contributions)		500,000
24. Securities were purchased.	Endowment Investments	500,000	
	Cash		500,000
25. A term endowment expired. The $150,000 principal is now available for use by the hospital administration.	Reclassifications Out—Temporarily Restricted—Satisfaction of Time Restriction	150,000	
	Reclassifications In—Unrestricted—Satisfaction of Time Restriction		150,000
26. Receipts of $200,000 and an unconditional promise to give $100,000 were recorded. Gifts were to be used for operating room equipment.	Contributions Receivable	100,000	
	Cash	200,000	
	Other Operating Revenues—Temporarily Restricted (contributions)		300,000
27. Operating room equipment was purchased. The hospital elects to release the donor restriction over the useful life of the asset.	Equipment	200,000	
	Cash		200,000
28. The first-year depreciation on the above operating equipment was recorded.	Depreciation Expense	40,000	
	Accumulated Depreciation		40,000
29. The expiration of the donor restriction on the fixed asset is recognized by reclassifying from temporarily restricted to unrestricted. This reclassification "matches" the depreciation expense.	Reclassifications Out—Temporarily Restricted—Satisfaction of Plant Acquisition Restrictions	40,000	
	Reclassifications In—Unrestricted—Satisfaction of Plant Acquisition Restrictions		40,000
30. A $400,000 grant from a local manufacturer to be used for a patient nutritional study was received. Results of the study will be used to educate the public, not for the benefit of the donor.	Cash	400,000	
	Other Operating Revenues—Temporarily Restricted (contributions)		400,000
31. Expenses were incurred for the patient nutritional study. Donor restrictions are expired to match specified expenses. A reclassification entry records the expiration of donor restrictions.	Wages, Salaries, and Benefits	25,000	
	Drugs and Supplies Used	10,000	
	Purchased Services	15,000	
	Cash		50,000
	Reclassifications Out—Temporarily Unrestricted—Satisfaction of Program Restrictions	50,000	
	Reclassifications In—Unrestricted—Satisfaction of Program Restrictions		50,000

(continued)

Event	Entry		
32. At year-end, Columbia allocates natural expenses to the functional areas based upon which program they benefited when incurred.	Nursing Services	1,774,000	
	Other Professional Services	1,240,000	
	General Services	995,000	
	Fiscal Services	283,000	
	Administrative Services	791,000	
	Wages, Salaries, and Benefits		3,045,000
	Drugs and Supplies Used		730,000
	Purchased Services		330,000
	Medical Malpractice Costs		450,000
	Depreciation Expense		440,000
	Interest		66,000
	Provision for Bad Debts		22,000
33. Closing entries. Each class of net assets is closed separately.	Patient Service Revenue—Unrestricted	5,000,000	
	Other Operating Revenue—Unrestricted	222,000	
	Nonoperating Revenue—Unrestricted	720,606	
	Reclassifications In—Unrestricted—Satisfaction of Equipment Acquisition Restrictions	40,000	
	Reclassifications In—Unrestricted—Satisfaction of Time Restrictions	150,000	
	Reclassifications In—Unrestricted—Satisfaction of Program Restrictions	50,000	
	Charity Care		200,000
	Contractual Adjustments		380,000
	Nursing Services		1,774,000
	Other Professional Services		1,240,000
	General Services		995,000
	Fiscal Services		283,000
	Administrative Services		791,000
	Unrestricted Net Assets		**519,606**
	Other Operating Revenue—Temporarily Restricted	750,000	
	Nonoperating Revenue—Temporarily Restricted	75,000	
	Reclassifications Out—Temporarily Restricted—Satisfaction of Equipment Acquisition Restrictions		40,000
	Reclassifications Out—Temporarily Restricted—Satisfaction of Time Restrictions		150,000
	Reclassifications Out—Temporarily Restricted—Satisfaction of Program Restrictions		50,000
	Temporarily Restricted Net Assets		**585,000**
	Nonoperating Revenue—Permanently Restricted Endowment Contributions	500,000	
	Permanently Restricted Net Assets		**500,000**

Financial Statements of a Private Health Care Provider

11

OBJECTIVE

Prepare financial statements for governmental and private health care service providers.

The financial statements of a private health care provider include a statement of activities which presents organization-wide totals for changes in unrestricted net assets, temporarily restricted net assets, and permanently restricted net assets. The form is straightforward, showing operating revenues minus operating expenses as an increase (decrease) in net assets from operations. The nonoperating revenue is added to this amount. Expenses are reported using functional classifications. Further information on natural classifications of expenses is a suggested footnote disclosure. In practice, comparative financial statements would be presented. To conserve space, the results of only one year's activities are shown in Illustration 19-7.

Illustration 19-7
Columbia Hospital
Statement of Activities
For Year Ended December 31, 20X5

	Unrestricted	Temporarily Restricted	Permanently Restricted	Total
Revenues, gains, and other support:				
Patient service revenue (net of adjustments)	$ 4,420,000			$ 4,420,000
Other operating revenue	222,000	$ 750,000		972,000
Net assets released from restrictions:				
Satisfaction of program restrictions	50,000	(50,000)		0
Satisfaction of equipment acquisitions restrictions	200,000	(200,000)		0
Expiration of time restrictions	150,000	(150,000)		0
Total operating revenues and other support	$ 5,042,000	$ 350,000		$ 5,392,000
Expenses and losses:				
Nursing services	$ 1,774,000			$ 1,774,000
Other professional services	1,240,000			1,240,000
General services	995,000			995,000
Fiscal services	283,000			283,000
Administrative services	791,000			791,000
Total expenses and losses	$ 5,083,000			$ 5,083,000
Increase (decrease) in net assets from operations	$ (41,000)	$ 350,000		$ 309,000
Nonoperating revenue	$ 720,606	$ 75,000	$ 500,000	$ 1,295,606
Increase (decrease) in net assets	**$ 679,606**	**$ 425,000**	**$ 500,000**	**$ 1,604,606**
Net assets at beginning of year	**4,538,000**	**879,000**	**3,560,000**	**8,977,000**
Net assets at end of year	**$5,217,606**	**$1,304,000**	**$4,060,000**	**$10,581,606**

In addition to the statement of activities, a private health care organization provides a statement of financial position and a statement of cash flows. The statement of financial position, shown in Illustration 19-8, includes assets and liabilities of all funds. The sequence begins with current assets, assets whose use is limited, property and equipment, and possibly other assets. Also shown are the current and other liabilities of the organization and the three classes of net assets, which represent the equity of the hospital.

The statement of cash flows, shown in Illustration 19-9, follows FASB Statement No. 95 that encourages the use of the direct method to present cash flows, although it does accept the indirect method. FASB Statement No. 117 states that the provisions of FASB Statement No. 95 also should be applied to not-for-profit health care entities amended to include among the list of cash inflows from financing activities receipts from contributions and investment income that by donor stipulation are restricted for the purpose of acquisition, construction, improving property, plant, and equipment, or other long-lived assets, or establishing or increasing a permanent endowment or term endowment.

Illustration 19-8
Columbia Hospital
Statement of Financial Position
As of December 31, 20X5

Assets:	
Cash and cash equivalents	$ 735,000
Accounts and interest receivable	908,000
Inventories	81,000
Contributions receivable	265,606
Short-term investments	400,000
Assets restricted to investment in land, buildings, and equipment	445,000
Assets limited in use under malpractice funding agreement	440,000
Property, plant, and equipment (net of depreciation)	5,250,000
Long-term investments	540,000
Endowment investments	4,060,000
Total assets	**$13,124,606**
Liabilities and net assets:	
Accounts payable	$ 53,000
Current installments of long-term debts	80,000
Accrued expenses	100,000
Notes payable	500,000
Estimated malpractice costs	640,000
Long-term debt	1,170,000
Total liabilities	**$ 2,543,000**
Net assets:	
Unrestricted	**$ 5,217,606**
Temporarily restricted	**1,304,000**
Permanently restricted	**4,060,000**
Total net assets	**$10,581,606**
Total liabilities and net assets	**$13,124,606**

Governmental Health Care Organizations

Governmental health care organizations are classified as special purpose governments engaged only in business-type activities. As such, they will present the financial statements required for organizations that use proprietary fund accounting. Many government health care organizations are also component units of another government, e.g., a university hospital, county health care organization or hospital, and state hospitals. If these organizations issue separate financial statements, the notes should identify the primary government in whose financial reporting entity it is included and describe the nature of the relationship with the primary government. The financial statements required for government health care organizations include a statement of net assets (or balance sheet), a statement of revenue, expenses, and changes in net assets, and a statement of cash flows (direct method). These statements are similar to the balance sheet and operating statements illustrated for the private health care organizations and are not illustrated in this chapter. The statement of cash flows has four parts and follows governmental requirements for an additional section on cash flows from noncapital financing activities, such as unrestricted gifts, investment income, and gifts restricted for future periods.

Illustration 19-9
Columbia Hospital
Statement of Cash Flows
For Year Ended December 31, 20X5

Cash flows from operating activities:	
Cash received from patients and third-party payors	$ 3,800,000
Cash received from contributions	450,000
Interest and dividends received	615,000
Cash paid to employees and suppliers	(3,990,000)
Interest paid	(66,000)
Net cash provided by (used for) operating activities	**$ 809,000**
Cash flows from investing activities:	
Purchases of investments	$ (500,000)
Purchases of land, buildings, and equipment	(310,000)
Net cash provided by (used for) investing activities	**$ (810,000)**
Cash flows from financing activities:	
Payments on notes payable	$ (200,000)
Payments on long-term debt	(80,000)
Contributions received restricted for endowment	500,000
Contributions received restricted for property, plant, and equipment	200,000
Net cash provided by (used for) financing activities	**$ 420,000**
Net increase (decrease) in cash and cash equivalents	**$ 419,000**
Cash and cash equivalents at beginning of year	**316,000**
Cash and cash equivalents at end of year	**$ 735,000**
Reconciliation of change in net assets to net cash provided by (used for) operating activities:	
Change in net assets	$ 1,604,606
Adjustments to reconcile change in net assets to net cash provided by (used for) operating activities:	
Depreciation	440,000
Increase in accounts receivable	(798,000)
Increase in contributions receivable	(265,606)
Decrease in inventories	18,000
Increase in accounts payable and accrued liabilities	60,000
Contributions received restricted for endowment	(500,000)
Contributions received restricted for property, plant, and equipment	(200,000)
Increase in liability for estimated malpractice costs	450,000
Net cash provided by (used for operating activities)	**$ 809,000**

REFLECTION

- Private health care organizations follow FASB standards.
- Governmental health care organizations will report as special purpose governments engaged in business-type activities and, as such, follow FASB standards.

- Contractual agreements, courtesy care, and charity care are reductions from patient services revenue. The provision for bad debts is recorded as an expense.
- Many health care organizations use fund accounting for internal control and decision making, but funds are not required in the external financial reports.

UNDERSTANDING THE ISSUES

1. What measurement focuses (identifying which resources are being measured) and bases of accounting (identifying when the effects of transactions or events should be recognized) are used by not-for-profit colleges and universities? How might the two measurement focuses benefit financial reporting for such entities?
2. Explain the accounting for contributions (of cash, pledges, or investments that may be converted into cash) for a private university. How does this accounting for contributions differ from that of a public university?
3. Explain how restricted gifts and grants are accounted for by public colleges and universities. Compare this with the accounting for restricted gifts and grants by private colleges and universities.
4. Distinguish assets limited as to use from restricted assets.
5. Explain a hospital's rigid adherence to gross revenue determination.
6. What is the special concern over accounting for medical malpractice claims? How does accounting for such claims compare to accounting for contingencies in a for-profit business environment?

EXERCISES

Exercise 1 *(LO 3)* **Private university, contributions.** Indicate (with choices a–f) how the following events are recorded in a private university:

a. Credit Contributions—Unrestricted
b. Credit Contributions—Temporarily Restricted
c. Credit Contributions—Permanently Restricted
d. Credit Refundable Deposits
e. Credit Fund Balance
f. No entry

1. Receipt of an unconditional promise to give. ________
2. Receipt of a fixed asset with donor-specified use for an outreach program. ________
3. Receipt of an unconditional cash contribution. ________
4. Receipt of cash to be used for a specific purpose. ________
5. Receipt of free accounting services. ________
6. Receipt of time of volunteers who helped with fund-raising mailings. ________

7. Receipt of an unconditional promise to give over a 5-year period. ____________
8. Receipt of investments that are to be used to set up an endowment with earnings available for operations. ____________
9. Receipt of a conditional promise to give. ____________
10. Receipt of a fixed asset with no donor restriction. ____________
11. Receipt of a cash contribution to be used next year for a research project. ____________
12. Receipt of a cash contribution to be used next year for general operations at the discretion of management. ____________
13. Receipt of cash as part of a government grant funding a cancer research project. A report with research results will be prepared for the government funding agency. ____________
14. Receipt of a cash contribution to be used for acquisition of fixed assets. ____________
15. Receipt of a permanent collection of geography maps that will be displayed to the public. ____________

Exercise 2 *(LO 1, 2, 3, 4)* **Public and private universities, operating activities.** Record the following operating activities.

a. Student fees of $600,000 were assessed, of which $575,000 has been collected and $4,000 is estimated to be uncollectible.
b. The bookstore operates in rented space and is run on a break-even basis. Revenues totaled $100,000, of which 80% was collected to date. Salaries of $35,000 and rent of $10,000 are paid. Other operating expenses amount to $60,000, of which $15,000 has not been paid.
c. A mandatory transfer of $75,000 was made for a payment due on the gymnasium building mortgage.
d. The Student Aid Committee report showed the following:

Cash scholarships issued.	$25,000
Remission of tuition	10,000

e. A check for $10,000 and a pledge for $4,500 are received from the local medical society to cover part of the cost of research on drug effects, one of the university's educational programs. The educational programs will be conducted and paid for in the next fiscal period.
f. The endowment fund received a check for $12,000 of interest on investments. The premium amortization on the investment is $240. The unrestricted current fund is the recipient of the income.

Exercise 3 *(LO 1, 3, 4)* **Public and private universities, grants, contributions.** Record the following events that affect (1) Public University and (2) Private University.

a. A private grant of $150,000 was received to be used exclusively for defraying costs of holding conferences on the topic of genes.
b. By year-end, $110,000 of the grant mentioned in item (a) had been applied to the purpose stipulated.
c. The grant provided that amounts not awarded by year-end are to be transferred to the endowment fund. The liability to that fund is recorded.
d. An alumnus, who was a former athlete, contributed $20,000 to assist in the search for a basketball coach.

Exercise 4 *(LO 1, 2, 3, 4)* **Public and private universities, loans.** Record the following events that affect the loan activities of Private University.

a. An alumnus donates $420,000 to establish the student loan fund. Students are charged a 5% annual interest rate.
b. Loans of $380,000 are made to students.
c. The remaining $40,000 is deposited in the university credit union, which pays a current interest rate of 7%.
d. Loans of $20,000 are repaid, plus $800 of interest.
e. Interest of $1,400 is received from the university credit union.
f. A student who had borrowed $1,000 was in a serious automobile accident and withdrew from school. The university wrote off the loan as uncollectible.

Exercise 5 *(LO 1, 2, 3, 4)* **Public and private universities, endowments.** Record the following endowment activity events of Private University.

a. An alumnus donates $250,000 to the endowment fund. The cash is fully invested in bonds with a face value of $242,000 which are purchased at an $8,000 premium. The income earned is to be available for the Current Restricted Fund for curriculum improvement.
b. A check for $11,250 for interest is received. The premium amortization is $667.
c. The income is transferred to the restricted current fund.
d. The bonds are sold for $260,500.

Exercise 6 *(LO 1, 4)* **Public and private universities, annuity and life income.** Record the following annuity and life income activities of Private University.

a. On July 1, 20X0, J. H. Stack, Emeritus Professor of Accounting, moved out of the state. Stack donated to the university common stock with a cost basis of $50,000 and a fair value of $90,000. Stack is to receive an annuity of $5,000 each year for life; at death, the securities are to be sold and the remaining cash balance is to be transferred to the student loan fund. At a 10% annual rate and a life expectancy of 12 years, the present value of the annuity payments is $34,068.
b. The stock paid $5,400 in dividends each 12-month period.
c. The annuities payable account is adjusted to present value. At year-end, a payment of $5,000 is made to Professor Stack.
d. The annuities payable account is adjusted to present value. A second payment was made a year later.
e. A month later, Professor Stack died, eliminating the liability for future annuity payments.
f. The common stock was sold for $97,000. The cash balance was transferred to the student loan fund.

Exercise 7 *(LO 1, 4)* **Public and private universities, plant fund transactions.** Record the following capital-related transactions for Private University plant funds.

a. Transfers of $250,000 are received from the current unrestricted fund for the purpose of funding the payment of existing debt principal ($50,000) and building an addition to the science building ($200,000).
b. Contributions of $30,000 restricted for major repairs of university buildings are received. $20,000 is spent for appropriate repairs.
c. A partial payment of $50,000 is made on the debt principal.
d. Work on the science building addition is completed with a total cost of $220,000. Unpaid contract costs total $35,000.
e. New gymnasium equipment costing $25,000 is purchased from funds previously donated by a former Olympic medalist for that purpose.
f. A building with a fair value of $300,000 was donated to the university by an alumnus.

g. Depreciation on all assets totaled $75,000.
h. During a celebration after a basketball victory, $2,000 of gym equipment disappeared.

Exercise 8 *(LO 7, 10)* **Private health care, journal entries, revenue and cash flow.** The following transactions took place in the Brook Private Hospital during the year ending December 31, 20X1:

1. Gross revenues of $7,800,000 were earned for service to Medicare patients.
2. Expected contractual adjustments with Medicare, a third-party payor, are $3,605,000; and allowance for contractual adjustments account is used by Brook.
3. Medicare cleared charges of $7,800,000 with payments of $3,960,800 and contractual allowances of $3,839,200.
4. Interim payments received from Medicare amounted to $260,000.
5. The hospital made a lump-sum payment back to Medicare of $100,000.

a. Record the transactions in the general journal.
b. Calculate the amount of net patient service revenue.
c. What is the net cash flow from transactions with Medicare?
d. What adjustments must be made at year-end to settle up with Medicare and properly report the net patient service revenue after this settlement?

Exercise 9 *(LO 6, 7)* **Health care, revenues.** A hospital has three revenue-controlling accounts: Patient Service Revenue, Other Operating Revenue, and Nonoperating Revenue.

a. State in general terms the type of revenue found in each controlling account.
b. Indicate into which of the three controlling accounts each of the following would be placed by using the symbols PS for Patient Service Revenue, OO for Other Operating Revenue, N for Nonoperating Revenue, and N/A if not a revenue item:

1. Tuition for entry to the nursing school. ____________
2. An unrestricted gift of cash. ____________
3. General nursing fees charged to patients. ____________
4. Charges for physicians' care. ____________
5. A restricted gift used for research on genes. ____________
6. Dividends from the hospital's investments. ____________
7. Revenue from gift shop sales. ____________
8. Patient room and board charges. ____________
9. Proceeds from sales of cafeteria meals. ____________
10. Recovery room fees. ____________
11. Contributions for plant replacement and expansion. ____________

Exercise 10 *(LO 6, 7, 8, 10)* **Health care, revenues, expenses, contributions.** Record the following events of Elmwood Hospital.

a. Patients were billed for the following gross charges:

Room and board	$680,000
Physicians' care.	220,000
Laboratory and radiology	110,000

b. A donation of drugs with a fair value of $12,000 was received from a doctor. The drugs are normally purchased.

c. Revenues were reported from:

Newsstand and snack bar.	$15,800
Parking lot charges	3,200
Vending machines.	9,800

d. A charity allowance of $13,000 was granted to indigent patients.
e. Contractual adjustments granted to patients for Medicare charges totaled $68,000.
f. The hospital recorded an increase in the provision of $26,000 for uncollectible receivables.

Exercise 11 *(LO 11)* **Health care, statement of activities.** The Pure Air Rehabilitation Hospital has the following balances that are extracted from its December 31, 20X7, trial balance:

Account	Debit	Credit
Nursing Services Expense	230,000	
Professional Fees Expense.	340,000	
General and Administrative Expense	150,000	
Depreciation Expense	90,000	
Interest Expense.	13,000	
Asset Whose Use Is Limited	55,000	
Repairs and Maintenance Expense.	110,000	
Provision for Uncollectible Accounts	14,000	
Contractual Adjustments	26,000	
Patient Service Revenue.		740,000
Income, Seminars		23,000
Child Day Care Revenue		15,000
Parking Fees		4,500
Endowment Income—Temporarily Restricted		120,000
Interest Income—Unrestricted		3,000
Donations—Temporarily Restricted.		18,000
Gains (Distributable) on Sale of Endowments—Temporarily Restricted		56,000
Net Assets—Unrestricted (January 1, 20X7)		800,000
Net Assets—Temporarily Restricted (January 1, 20X7).		755,000
Net Assets—Permanently Restricted (January 1, 20X7)		750,000

From the above information, prepare a statement of activities for the year ended December 31, 20X7.

Exercise 12 *(LO 6, 7, 8, 10)* **Health care, financial statement impact of transactions.** Alpha Hospital, a nongovernmental not-for-profit organization, has adopted an accounting policy that does not imply a time restriction on gifts of long-lived assets. For items (1) through (6), indicate the manner in which the transaction affects Alpha's financial statements.

A. Increase in unrestricted revenues, gains, and other support.
B. Decrease in an expense.
C. Increase in temporarily restricted net assets.
D. Increase in permanently restricted net assets.
E. No required reportable event.

1. Alpha's board designates $1,000,000 to purchase investments whose income will be used for capital improvements.
2. Income from investments in item (1) above, which was not previously accrued, is received.
3. A benefactor provided funds for building expansion.

4. The funds in item (3) above are used to purchase a building in the fiscal period following the period the funds were received.
5. An accounting firm prepared Alpha's annual financial statements without charge to Alpha.
6. Alpha received investments subject to the donor's requirement that investment income be used to pay for outpatient services.

(AICPA adapted)

PROBLEMS

Problem 19-1 *(LO 1, 2, 3)* **Public and private schools, multiple-choice.** Select the best answer for each of the following multiple-choice items dealing with universities:

1. For the 20X7 fall semester, Brook Public University assessed its students $4,000,000 (net of refunds), covering tuition and fees for educational and general purposes. However, only $3,700,000 was expected to be realized because tuition remissions of $80,000 were allowed to faculty members' children attending Brook, and scholarships totaling $220,000 were granted to students. What amount should Brook include in educational and general current funds revenues from student tuition and fees?
   a. $4,000,000
   b. $3,920,000
   c. $3,780,000
   d. $3,700,000
2. Private College is sponsored by a religious group. Volunteers from this religious group regularly contribute their skilled services to Private and are paid nominal amounts to cover their commuting costs. If Private did not receive these volunteer services, it would have to purchase similar services. During 20X6, the total amount paid to these volunteers was $12,000. The gross value of services performed by them, as determined by reference to lay-equivalent salaries, amounted to $300,000. What amount should Private record as expenses in 20X6 for these volunteers' services?
   a. $312,000
   b. $300,000
   c. $12,000
   d. $0
3. Abbott Public University's unrestricted current fund comprised the following:

Assets.	$5,000,000
Liabilities (including deferred revenues of $100,000)	3,000,000

   The fund balance of Abbott's unrestricted current fund was
   a. $1,900,000.
   b. $2,000,000.
   c. $2,100,000.
   d. $5,000,000.
4. The following receipts are among those recorded by Curry Private College during 20X9:

Unrestricted gifts	$500,000
Restricted gifts (expended for current operating purposes)	200,000
Restricted gifts (not yet expended).	100,000

   The amount that should be included in revenues is
   a. $800,000.
   b. $700,000.
   c. $600,000.
   d. $500,000.

5. In 20X7, the board of trustees of Burr Private University designated $100,000 from its current funds for college scholarships. Also in 20X7, the university received a bequest of $200,000 from an estate of a benefactor who specified that the bequest was to be used for hiring teachers to tutor handicapped students. None of the bequest has been spent. What amount should be accounted for as restricted net assets?

   a. $0
   b. $100,000
   c. $200,000
   d. $300,000

6. The following information pertains to interest received by Beech Public University from endowment fund investments for the year ended June 30, 20X8:

	Received	Expended for Current Operations
Unrestricted	$300,000	$100,000
Restricted	500,000	75,000

   What amount should be credited to endowment income for the year ended June 30, 20X8?

   a. $800,000
   b. $375,000
   c. $175,000
   d. $100,000

7. On July 31, 20X8, Sabio Public College showed the following amounts to be used for:

Renewal and replacement of college properties	$200,000
Retirement of indebtedness on college properties	300,000
Purchase of physical properties for college purposes, but unexpended at July 31, 20X8	400,000

   What total amount should be included in Sabio's plant funds at July 31, 20X8?

   a. $900,000
   b. $600,000
   c. $400,000
   d. $200,000

8. The following expenditures were among those incurred by Cheviot Public University during 20X7:

Administrative data processing	$ 50,000
Scholarships and fellowships	100,000
Operation and maintenance of physical plant	200,000

   The amount to be included in the functional classification "Institutional Support" expenditures account is

   a. $50,000.
   b. $150,000.
   c. $250,000.
   d. $350,000.

9. Assets that the governing board of a public university, rather than a donor or outside agency, has determined are to be retained and invested for purposes other than loan or plant would be accounted for as

   a. an endowment.
   b. unrestricted net assets.
   c. deposits held in custody for others.
   d. restricted net assets.

10. Which of the following statements usually will not be included in the annual financial report of a public university engaged only in business-type activities?

    a. Statement of activities
    b. Statement of net assets
    c. Statement of cash flows
    d. Statement of revenues, expenses, and changes in net assets

    (AICPA adapted)

Problem 19-2 *(LO 1, 2, 3)* **Public and private schools, multiple-choice.** Select the best answer for each of the following multiple-choice items. (Nos. 1–11 are AICPA adapted.)

1. An alumnus donates securities to Rex Private College and stipulates that the principal be held in perpetuity and revenues be used for faculty travel. Dividends received from the securities should be recognized as revenues in

   a. endowment funds.
   b. quasi-endowment funds.
   c. restricted current funds.
   d. unrestricted current funds.

2. A private college's plant funds group includes which of the following subgroups?

   (1) Renewals and replacement funds
   (2) Retirement of indebtedness funds
   (3) Restricted current funds

   a. 1 and 2
   b. 1 and 3
   c. 2 and 3
   d. None of the above

3. Funds received by a private college from donors who have stipulated that the principal is nonexpendable but the income generated may be expended for current operating needs would be accounted for as

   a. contributions—permanently restricted.
   b. contributions—temporarily restricted.
   c. contributions—unrestricted.
   d. fund balance increases.

4. The following funds were among those held by State College at December 31, 20X1:

Principal specified by the donor as nonexpendable	$500,000
Principal expendable after the year 20X9.	300,000
Principal designated from unrestricted net assets	100,000

   What amount should State College classify as permanently restricted endowments?

   a. $100,000
   b. $300,000
   c. $500,000
   d. $900,000

5. Are public and private colleges and universities required to report depreciation expenses in their financial statements?

	Public	Private
a.	Yes	Yes
b.	Yes	No
c.	No	No
d.	No	Yes

6. In the loan fund of a private or public college, each of the following types of loans would be found *except*

   a. faculty loans.
   b. computer loans.
   c. staff loans.
   d. student loans.

7. In 20X2, State University's board of trustees established a $100,000 fund to be retained and invested for scholarship grants. In 20X2, the fund earned $6,000, which had not been disbursed at December 31, 20X2. What amount should State report as unrestricted investment earnings at December 31, 20X2?

   a. $0
   b. $6,000
   c. $100,000
   d. $106,000

8. On January 2, 20X2, a graduate of Oak Private College established a permanent trust fund and appointed Security Bank as the trustee. The income from the trust fund is to be paid to Oak and used only by the School of Business to support student scholarships. What entry is required on Oak's books to record the receipt of cash from the interest on the trust fund?

   a. Debit Cash and credit Deferred Revenues
   b. Debit Cash and credit Temporarily Restricted Endowment Revenue
   c. Debit Cash and credit Temporarily Restricted Contributions
   d. Debit Cash and credit Unrestricted Endowment Revenue

9. At the end of the year, Cramer Private University's balance sheet comprised $15,000,000 of assets and $9,000,000 of liabilities (including deferred revenues of $300,000). What is the balance of Cramer's net assets?

   a. $5,700,000
   b. $6,000,000
   c. $6,300,000
   d. $15,000,000

10. Financial resources of a college or university that are currently expendable at the discretion of the governing board and that have not been restricted externally nondesignated by the board for a specific purpose should be reported in the balance sheet as

    a. board-designated current funds.
    b. permanently restricted net assets.
    c. unrestricted net assets.
    d. temporarily restricted net assets.

11. Which of the following accounts would appear in the plant fund of a not-for-profit private college?

	Fuel Inventory for Power Plant	Equipment
a.	Yes	Yes
b.	No	Yes
c.	No	No
d.	Yes	No

12. Which of the following is required as part of the complete set of financial statements for a private college or university?

    a. Statement of changes in financial position
    b. Statement of activities
    c. Statement of revenues, expenses, and changes in net assets
    d. None of the above

Problem 19-3 *(LO 1, 5)* **Private vs. public universities reporting.** You have recently been hired as the financial manager of Bloomington University, a private university in a small town. Your previous experience has been with a large state university in a nearby state.

◄◄◄◄◄ **Required**

What key differences did you find between the format of the operating statements of Bloomington University for the year and that of your previous state university? How does the proportion of revenue from various sources differ? What key differences did you find between the format of the balance sheets? The statements of cash flows?

◄◄◄◄◄ **Required**

Problem 19-4 *(LO 3, 4)* **Public and private schools, contributions vs. exchange transactions.** Record the following transactions. Identify each as a contribution agency or an exchange transaction, and prepare any appropriate entries.

1. Private University coordinated its annual special event with the opening of the alumni weekend. Tickets to the special event were $200 and included a buffet (cost, $30), admission to the university symphony (cost, $30), and a reception (cost, $35). A total of 1,000 tickets was sold.
2. A local manufacturing company gave $2,000,000 to Private University to commission a study on the relationship of worker stress to chronic disease. The results of the study will be used to educate the general public.
3. Allen Corporation gave a contribution of $850,000 to Private University. Allen Corporation specifies that the gift is to be invested in perpetuity and that the income may be used by Private University to pay operating costs.
4. Local Corporation donated a building to Private College for use as new office space. The cost to Local was $75,000. The building was appraised by a professional real estate appraiser at $100,000, while another appraiser valued it at $110,000.
5. An alumna of XYZ Private College has notified the school that she will donate to the school any net proceeds in excess of $50,000 from her next novel. She stipulates that the college use her gift to buy new equipment for the writing lab.
6. Cheryl Debit, an accountant, spent Sunday afternoon at Private University sending out to alumni a mailing seeking more contributions for the building fund.
7. A very famous artist notified the local private university that she has included in her will her plans to donate all of her paintings for exhibit at the university art gallery. A copy of her will is included with her letter.
8. A grant in the amount of $400,000 from the U.S. Department of Labor and Economics was received by Private University to fund research on the impact of accounting standards. A report of research findings is to be submitted to the grantor.
9. U.S. government funds amounting to $50,000 flow to Private University to be held for students qualifying for financial aid.

Problem 19-5 *(LO 1, 2, 3, 4, 5)* **Public university, various transactions, statement of current funds revenues, expenses, and other changes.** A partial balance sheet of Greenleaf State University, a public university, as of the end of its fiscal year, July 31, 20X5, is as follows:

Greenleaf State University
Current Funds Balance Sheet
July 31, 20X5

Assets		Liabilities and Fund Balances	
Unrestricted:		Unrestricted:	
Cash	$200,000	Accounts payable	$100,000
Accounts receivable (net of $15,000 allowance)	360,000	Due to other funds	40,000
		Deferred revenues—tuition & fees	25,000
Prepaid expenses	40,000	Fund balance	435,000
Total unrestricted	$600,000	Total unrestricted	$600,000
Restricted:		Restricted:	
Cash	$ 10,000	Accounts payable	$ 5,000
Investments	210,000	Fund balance	215,000
Total restricted	$220,000	Total restricted	$220,000
Total current funds	$820,000	Total current funds	$820,000

The following information pertains to the year ended July 31, 20X6:

a. Cash collected from students' tuition totaled $3,000,000. Of this amount, $362,000 represented accounts receivable outstanding at July 31, 20X5; $2,500,000 was for current-year tuition; and $138,000 was for tuition applicable to the semester beginning in August 20X6.
b. Deferred revenue at July 31, 20X5, was earned during the year ended July 31, 20X6.
c. Accounts receivable at July 31, 20X5, that were not collected during the year ended July 31, 20X6, were determined to be uncollectible and were written off against the allowance account. At July 31, 20X6, the allowance account was estimated at $10,000.
d. During the year, an unrestricted appropriation of $60,000 was made by the state, to be paid to Greenleaf sometime in August 20X6.
e. During the year, unrestricted cash gifts of $80,000 were received from alumni. Greenleaf's board of trustees allocated $30,000 of these gifts to the student loan fund.
f. During the year, restricted fund investments costing $25,000 were sold for $31,000. Restricted fund investments were purchased at a cost of $40,000. Restricted fund investment income of $18,000 was earned and collected during the year. This income is restricted for an ongoing research project.
g. Unrestricted general expenses of $2,500,000 were recorded in the voucher system. At July 31, 20X6, the unrestricted accounts payable balance was $75,000.
h. The restricted accounts payable balance at July 31, 20X5, was paid. The restricted fund paid $10,000 from its investment income for costs of an ongoing research project.
i. The $40,000 due to other funds at July 31, 20X5, was paid to the plant fund as required.
j. One-quarter of the prepaid expenses at July 31, 20X5, expired during the current year and pertained to general education expense. There was no addition to prepaid expenses during the year.

Required ▶ ▶ ▶ ▶ ▶

1. Prepare journal entries in summary form to record the foregoing transactions for the year ended July 31, 20X6. Letter each entry to correspond with the letter indicated in the description of its respective transaction, and omit explanations. Use the following format:

		Current Funds			
Entry		Unrestricted		Restricted	
Letter	Accounts	Debt	Credit	Debit	Credit

2. Prepare a statement of current funds revenues, expenditures, and other changes, including a total column, for the year ended July 31, 20X6, and conclude with the fund balances at year-end.

(AICPA adapted)

Problem 19-6 *(LO 1, 2, 3, 4)* **Public university, various transactions.** The following events occurred as part of the operations of Craig State University, a public university:

a. To construct a new computer complex, the university floated at par a $22,000,000, 7% serial bond issue on October 1, paying interest on June 30 and December 31. Accrued interest is to be transferred to the retirement of indebtedness plant fund when construction begins. Construction costs are to be accumulated in the unexpended plant fund until the unit is completed.
b. Since construction has begun, the accrued interest, which must be used to assist in meeting bond interest payments, is transferred. Payments for construction to date total $5,000,000.
c. On December 31, a mandatory transfer of $385,000 is made from the unrestricted current fund to cover the remainder of the interest due on December 31 on the bond issue.
d. The bond interest due on December 31 is paid.
e. Construction of the complex is completed at an additional cost of $17,000,000. Payment is made for $16,000,000; the balance will be paid in one year under a retained percentage agreement.
f. The cost of the complex is transferred.
g. A required transfer of $2,770,000 is made from the unrestricted current fund to cover redemption of the first serial bond of $2,000,000 plus interest.
h. Payments are made for the bond principal and interest in item (g).
i. Gifts of land and a building were received, appraised at $200,000 and $350,000, respectively. The state's leading industrialist made the gift on condition that the university would assume a $90,000 mortgage on the property.
j. Pledges of $100,000 to be paid in one year were received with the understanding that the funds would be used to remodel the building received in item (i). It is estimated that $5,000 of the pledges will not be collected.
k. A donor contributed $100,000 in cash for the acquisition of rare first editions for the university library. The director of the library located a collection of the first editions that was available for $160,000. The university board transferred $60,000 from the unrestricted current fund to cover the difference.
l. The first edition collection is purchased, and payment is made.

Prepare journal entries to record the events, indicating in which funds the entries are made. ◄◄◄◄◄ **Required**

Problem 19-7 *(LO 1, 2, 3, 4, 5)* **Private university, various transactions, statement of activities.** The balance sheet of Washbush Private University as of the end of its fiscal year, June 30, 20X7, is as follows:

template cd

Washbush Private University
Statement of Financial Position
For Year Ended June 30, 20X7

Assets		Liabilities and Fund Balances	
Cash	$257,000	Accounts payable	$ 40,000
Accounts receivable student tuition and fees less allowance for doubtful accounts of $9,000	311,000	Deferred revenues	66,000
		Long-term debt	100,000
		Total liabilities	$206,000
		Net assets:	
		Unrestricted	$487,000
State appropriations receivable	75,000	Temporarily restricted	40,000
Endowment investments	50,000	Permanently restricted	50,000
Property, plant, and equipment (net)	90,000	Total net assets	$577,000
Total assets	$783,000	Total net assets and liabilities	$783,000

The following transactions occurred during the fiscal year ended June 30, 20X8:

a. On July 7, 20X7, a gift of $90,000 was received from an alumnus. The alumnus requested that one-half of the gift be used for the purchase of equipment for the university athletic department and the remainder be used for the establishment of a permanently restricted endowment. The alumnus further requested that the income generated by the endowment be used annually to award a scholarship to a qualified disadvantaged student. On July 20, 20X7, the board of trustees resolved that the funds of the newly established endowment would be invested in savings certificates. On July 21, 20X7, the savings certificates were purchased.
b. Revenue from student tuition and fees applicable to the year ended June 30, 20X8, amounted to $1,900,000. Of this amount, $66,000 was collected in the prior year, and $1,686,000 was collected during the year ended June 30, 20X8. In addition, at June 30, 20X8, the university had received cash of $158,000 representing fees for the session beginning July 1, 20X8.
c. During the year ended June 30, 20X8, the university had collected $308,000 of the outstanding accounts receivable at the beginning of the year. The remainder was determined to be uncollectible and was written off against the allowance account. At June 30, 20X8, the allowance account was adjusted to $6,000.
d. During the year, interest charges of $6,000 were earned and collected on late student fee payments.
e. During the year, the state appropriation was received. An additional unrestricted appropriation of $40,000 was made by the state, but it had not been paid to the university as of June 30, 20X8.
f. A gift of $30,000 cash restricted was received from alumni of the university for economic research expenses.
g. During the year, endowment investments that cost $21,000 were sold for $24,000. This includes accrued investment income amounting to $1,900. All income was restricted for programs to enhance teaching effectiveness.
h. During the year, unrestricted operating expenses of $1,800,000 were recorded. They include the following:

Instruction	$ 500,000
Research	400,000
Institutional support	100,000
Student aid	100,000
Student services	200,000
Operation and maintenance of plant	500,000
Total	$1,800,000

At June 30, 20X8, $60,000 of these expenses remained unpaid.
i. Temporarily restricted funds of $13,000 were spent for specified economic research described in item (f).
j. The accounts payable at June 30, 20X7, were paid during the year.
k. During the year, $7,000 interest was earned and received on the savings certificates purchased in item (a).
l. In honor of its 25th anniversary, Washbush Private University conducted a fund drive. Contributions of $16,000 were received. Additional unconditional pledges of $14,000 were promised for payment in December 20X8. It is anticipated that $2,000 of the pledges will be uncollectible.

Required ▶ ▶ ▶ ▶ ▶

1. Prepare journal entries to record the transactions. Assume fund accounting is not used.
2. Prepare a statement of activities for the year ended June 30, 20X8, using a column for each of the three net asset classifications and a total column.

Problem 19-8 *(LO 1, 2, 3, 4, 5)* **Private university, various transactions, statement of activities.** The following events occurred as part of the operations of Kronke Private University:

a. To construct a new business building, the university floated at par a $20,000,000, 8% serial bond issued on July 1. Interest is to be paid on December 31 and June 30. In addition, contributions from the community specifically for the new building totaled $5,000,000.
b. Payments for construction to date total $7,000,000.
c. Interest payments are made on December 31.
d. Construction of the building is completed at an additional cost of $18,000,000. Payment is made for $16,000,000; the balance will be paid in one year under a retained percentage agreement. Institutional policy is to release donor restrictions when assets are placed in service.
e. The first bond serial payment of $2,000,000 plus interest is paid.
f. A gift of land and a building was received, appraised at $200,000 and $350,000, respectively. The gift was made on the condition that the university assume a $90,000 mortgage on the property. The university assumed the mortgage.
g. Pledges with a present value of $200,000 to be paid over the next five years were received. The funds will be restricted for remodeling the building received in item (f). It is estimated that $20,000 of the pledges will not be collected.
h. A donation of $500,000 of stock was made by a wealthy citizen. The stock cannot be sold for five years. After the 5-year period, the stock can be sold, and any proceeds are to be used to finance campus construction projects.
i. Dividends of $10,000 on the stock in item (h) were received and were also restricted for construction projects.
j. Depreciation on the building received in item (f) totaled $25,000.

◄◄◄◄◄ **Required**

1. Prepare journal entries to record these events for Kronke Private University. Assume that fund accounting is not used.
2. Prepare a statement of activities.

Problem 19-9 *(LO 4, 5)* **Private college, closing entries, statement of activities.** The pre-closing trial balance of Park Private College has the following balances:

template cd

	Debit	Credit
Expenses—Instruction	1,230,000	
Expenses—Research	840,000	
Expenses—Academic Support	250,000	
Expenses—Student Services	200,000	
Expenses—Institutional Support	225,000	
Expenses—Operation and Maintenance of Plant	400,000	
Expenses—Student Aid	350,000	
Expenses—Auxiliary Enterprises Expenses	475,000	
Reclassifications Out—Temporarily Restricted—Satisfaction of Program Restrictions	75,000	
Reclassifications Out—Temporarily Restricted—Satisfaction of Equipment Acquisitions Restrictions	250,000	
Reclassifications Out—Temporarily Restricted—Expiration of Time Restrictions	50,000	
Tuition and Fees		1,500,000
Contributions—Unrestricted		265,000
Government Appropriations, Grants, and Contracts		800,000
Other Investment Income—Unrestricted		250,000
Sales and Services of Auxiliary Enterprises		500,000

(continued)

	Debit	Credit
Reclassifications In—Unrestricted—Satisfaction of Program Restrictions		75,000
Reclassifications In—Unrestricted—Satisfaction of Equipment Acquisition Restrictions		250,000
Reclassifications In—Unrestricted—Expiration of Time Restrictions		50,000
Contributions—Temporarily Restricted		200,000
Endowment Income—Temporarily Restricted		15,000
Contributions—Permanently Restricted		500,000
Net Realized Gains on Endowment—Temporarily Restricted		25,000
Unrestricted Net Assets, January 1, 20X5		675,000
Temporarily Restricted Net Assets, January 1, 20X5		975,000
Permanently Restricted Net Assets, January 1, 20X5		2,500,000

Required ▶ ▶ ▶ ▶ ▶

1. Prepare closing entries for the three net asset classifications.
2. Prepare a statement of activities for the year ended December 31, 20X5, using a column for each of the net asset classifications.

Required ▶ ▶ ▶ ▶ ▶

Problem 19-10 *(LO 5)* **Private college, statement of financial position.** Using the data in Problem 19-9 and the following additional information, prepare a statement of financial position for Park Private College.

	Debit	Credit
Cash	275,000	
Accounts Receivable (net)	625,000	
Contributions Receivable	85,000	
Inventory of Supplies	55,000	
Student Loans Receivable	300,000	
Land, Buildings, and Equipment (net)	1,000,000	
Long-Term Investments	3,025,000	
Accounts Payable		220,000
Amounts Held on Behalf of Others		250,000
Long-Term Debt		560,000
U.S. Government Grants Refundable		100,000

Problem 19-11 *(LO 6, 7, 8, 10)* **Health care, multiple-choice.** Select the best answer for each of the following multiple-choice items dealing with hospitals.

1. On March 1, 20X8, A. C. Rowe established a $100,000 endowment fund, the income from which is to be paid to Elm Hospital for general operating purposes. Elm does not control the fund's principal. Rowe appointed West National Bank as trustee of this fund. What journal entry is required by Elm to record the establishment of the endowment?

		Debit	Credit
a.	Cash	100,000	
	Nonexpendable Endowment Fund		100,000
b.	Cash	100,000	
	Nonoperating Revenue		100,000
c.	Nonexpendable Endowment Fund	100,000	
	Endowment Fund Balance		100,000

d. A memorandum entry only.

2. In 20X8, Wells Hospital received an unrestricted bequest of common stock with a fair value of $50,000 on the date of receipt of the stock. The testator had paid $20,000 for this stock in 20X6. Wells should record this bequest as

   a. nonoperating revenue of $50,000.
   b. nonoperating revenue of $30,000.
   c. nonoperating revenue of $20,000.
   d. a memorandum entry only.

3. Cedar Hospital has a marketable equity securities portfolio that is included appropriately in noncurrent assets in unrestricted funds. The portfolio has an aggregate cost of $300,000. It had an aggregate fair value of $250,000 at the end of 20X7 and $290,000 at the end of 20X6. If the portfolio was reported properly in the balance sheet at the end of 20X6, the change in the valuation allowance at the end of 20X7 should be

   a. $0.
   b. a decrease of $40,000.
   c. an increase of $40,000.
   d. an increase of $50,000.

4. Ross Hospital's accounting records disclosed the following information:

Net resources invested in plant assets (hospital policy is to release donor restrictions when assets are placed in service)	$10,000,000
Board-designated funds..	2,000,000

   What amount should be included as unrestricted net assets?

   a. $12,000,000
   b. $10,000,000
   c. $2,000,000
   d. $0

5. Under Cura Hospital's established rate structure, patient service revenues of $9,000,000 would have been earned for the year ended December 31, 20X7. However, only $6,750,000 was collected because of charity allowances of $1,500,000 and discounts of $750,000 to third-party payors. For the year ended December 31, 20X7, what amount should Cura record as net patient service revenues?

   a. $6,750,000
   b. $7,500,000
   c. $8,250,000
   d. $9,000,000

6. An organization of high school seniors performs services for patients at Leer Hospital. These students are volunteers and perform services that the hospital would not otherwise provide, such as wheeling patients in the park and reading to patients. These volunteers donated 5,000 hours of service to Leer in 20X7. At the minimum wage rate, these services would amount to $22,500, while it is estimated that the fair value of these services was $27,000. In Leer's 20X7 statement of revenues and expenses, what amount should be reported as nonoperating revenue?

   a. $27,000
   b. $22,500
   c. $6,250
   d. $0

7. In June 20X8, Park Hospital purchased medicines from Jove Pharmaceutical Company at a cost of $2,000. However, Jove notified Park that the invoice was being cancelled and the medicines were being donated to Park. Park should record this donation of medicines as

a. a memorandum entry only.
b. other operating revenue of $2,000.
c. a $2,000 credit to operating expenses.
d. a $2,000 credit to nonoperating expenses.

8. Palma Hospital's patient service revenues for services provided in 20X8, at established rates, amounted to $8,000,000 on the accrual basis. For internal reporting, Palma uses the discharge method. Under this method, patient service revenues are recognized only when patients are discharged, with no recognition given to revenues accruing for services to patients not yet discharged. Patient service revenues at established rates using the discharge method amounted to $7,000,000 for 20X8. According to GAAP, Palma should report patient service revenues for 20X8 of

   a. either $8,000,000 or $7,000,000, at the option of the hospital.
   b. $8,000,000.
   c. $7,500,000.
   d. $7,000,000.

9. In 20X6, Pyle Hospital received a $250,000 pure endowment grant. Also in 20X6, Pyle's governing board designated, for special uses, $300,000 which had originated from unrestricted gifts. What amount of these resources should be accounted for as part of the unrestricted net asset class?

   a. $0
   b. $250,000
   c. $300,000
   d. $550,000

10. Cura Hospital's property, plant, and equipment, net of depreciation, amounted to $10,000,000, with related mortgage liabilities of $1,000,000. What amount should be included in the permanently restricted net asset class?

   a. $0
   b. $1,000,000
   c. $9,000,000
   d. $10,000,000

(AICPA adapted)

Problem 19-12 *(LO 7, 8)* **Health care, multiple-choice.** Select the best answer for each of the following multiple-choice items dealing with health care organizations.

1. Inventory donated for use in a hospital should be reported as
   a. other operating revenue.
   b. nonoperating revenue.
   c. an addition to the unrestricted net assets.
   d. an addition to the restricted net assets.

2. Dee City's community hospital, which uses enterprise fund reporting and chooses to follow FASB guidelines, normally includes proceeds from sale of cafeteria meals in
   a. patient service revenues.
   b. other operating revenues.
   c. ancillary service revenues.
   d. deductions from dietary service expenses.

3. During 20X1, Trained Hospital received $90,000 in third-party reimbursements for depreciation. These reimbursements were restricted as follows:

For replacement of fully depreciated equipment	$25,000
For additions to property	65,000

What amount of these reimbursements should Trained include in revenue for the year ended December 31, 20X1?

a. $0
b. $25,000
c. $65,000
d. $90,000

4. A hospital should report earnings from endowment funds that are restricted to a specific operating purpose as

a. temporarily restricted revenues.
b. permanently restricted revenues.
c. unrestricted revenues.
d. unrestricted revenues when expended.

5. Hospital financial resources are required by a bond indenture to be set aside to finance construction of a new pediatrics facility. In which of the following hospital net asset classes should these resources be reported?

a. Permanently restricted
b. Temporarily restricted
c. Unrestricted
d. Refundable deposits

6. Which of the following sets of financial statements is required for private not-for-profit health care organizations?

a. Balance sheet, statement of revenues, expenses, and changes in fund balances
b. Balance sheet, statement of revenues and expenses, and statement of cash flows
c. Balance sheet, statement of changes in fund balances, and statement of cash flows
d. Balance sheet, statement of operations, and statement of cash flows

7. Land valued at $400,000 and subject to a $150,000 mortgage was donated to Beaty Hospital without restriction as to use. Which of the following entries should Beaty make to record this donation?

a.	Land	400,000	
	Mortgage Payable		150,000
	Endowment Fund Balance		250,000
b.	Land	400,000	
	Mortgage Payable		150,000
	Contributions—Unrestricted		250,000
c.	Land	400,000	
	Debt Fund Balance		150,000
	Endowment Fund Balance		250,000
d.	Land	400,000	
	Mortgage Payable		150,000
	Unrestricted Fund Balance		250,000

8. In hospital accounting, restricted net assets are

a. not available unless the board of directors removes the restrictions.
b. restricted as to use only for board-designated purposes.
c. not available for current operating use; however, the income generated by the funds is available for current operating use.
d. restricted as to use by the donor, grantor, or other source of the resources.

9. Not-for-profit health care organizations are typically sponsored by
   a. community organizations.
   b. religious organizations.
   c. universities.
   d. any of the above.

10. A not-for-profit hospital that follows FASB standards should report investment income from an endowment that is restricted to a specific operating purpose as
    a. general fund revenue.
    b. endowment fund revenue.
    c. unrestricted revenue.
    d. temporarily restricted revenue.

11. Restricted funds are
    a. not available unless the board of directors removes the restrictions.
    b. restricted as to use of the donor, grantor, or other source of the resources.
    c. not available for current operating use; however, the income earned on the funds is available.
    d. restricted as to use only for board-designated purposes.

(AICPA adapted)

Problem 19-13 *(LO 6, 7, 8, 10, 11)* **Health care, various transactions, statement of activities.** The June 30, 20X7, adjusted trial balances of the Bayfield Community Health Care Association follow.

Bayfield Community Health Care Association
Adjusted Current Funds Trial Balances
June 30, 20X7

	Unrestricted		Restricted	
Cash	11,000		29,000	
Bequest Receivable			5,000	
Pledges Receivable	12,000			
Accrued Interest Receivable	1,000			
Investments (at cost, which approximates market)	140,000			
Endowment Investments			250,000	
Accounts Payable and Accrued Expenses		50,000		1,000
Refundable Deposits		2,000		
Allowance for Uncollectible Pledges		3,000		
Net Assets, July 1, 20X6:				
Designated, Unrestricted		12,000		
Undesignated, Unrestricted		26,000		
Temporarily Restricted				3,000
Permanently Restricted				250,000
Endowment Revenue—Temporarily Restricted				20,000
Contributions		300,000		15,000
Membership Dues		25,000		
Program Service Fees		30,000		
Investment Income		10,000		
Auction Proceeds		42,000		
Auction Expenses	11,000			
Deaf Children's Program	120,000			
Blind Children's Program	150,000			
Management and General Services	49,000			
Fund-Raising Services	9,000			

Provision for Uncollectible Pledges	2,000			
Reclassifications In—Satisfaction of Program Restrictions		5,000		
Reclassifications Out—Satisfaction of Program Restrictions			5,000	
	505,000	505,000	289,000	289,000

1. Prepare a statement of activities for the year ended June 30, 20X7.
2. Prepare a statement of financial position as of June 30, 20X7.

◄◄◄◄◄ **Required**

(AICPA adapted)

Problem 19-14 *(LO 11)* **Health care, various transactions, statement of activities.** The following nominal accounts were extracted from the December 31, 20X7, adjusted trial balance of Downs Private Hospital:

	Debit	Credit
Gross patient service revenue		$11,049,200
Research grant revenue to the extent expended		361,000
Revenue from sale of cafeteria meals to guests and employees		108,000
Donated services of nurses and physicians (skilled services otherwise purchased)		145,000
Unrestricted gifts and grants		100,200
Unrestricted endowment income		12,000
Gifts restricted for equipment purchase		540,000
Donor-restricted investments for permanent endowment		150,000
Temporarily restricted endowment income		25,000
Revenue from parking lot		31,000
Revenue from vending machines		68,000
Income on investments whose use is limited by the board for capital improvements		207,000
Contributions restricted by donor for pediatric unit operations		225,000
Reclassifications in—unrestricted—satisfaction of program restrictions		125,000
Reclassifications in—unrestricted—satisfaction of plant acquisition restrictions		220,000
Unrestricted net assets, January 1, 20X7		625,000
Temporarily restricted net assets, January 1, 20X7		825,000
Permanently restricted net assets, January 1, 20X7		2,350,000
Reclassifications out—temporarily restricted—satisfaction of program restrictions	$ 125,000	
Reclassifications out—temporarily restricted—satisfaction of plant acquisition restrictions	220,000	
Administrative services (including $30,000 malpractice cost)	112,500	
Contractual adjustments under third-party reimbursement programs	1,328,500	
Charity care	215,000	
Provision for uncollectibles	341,600	
Nursing services (including $125,000 in pediatric unit)	6,589,100	
Dietary services	1,511,200	
Maintenance services	838,300	
Depreciation and amortization	478,200	
Interest expense	142,200	
Loss on sale of endowment investments	5,300	

Prepare a statement of activities for the year ended December 31, 20X7.

◄◄◄◄◄ **Required**

template cd

Problem 19-15 *(LO 11)* **Health care, statement of cash flows.** You are provided with a summarized version of the cash account of Lakeside Hospital, a not-for-profit organization for 20X7.

Cash Account	Debit	Credit
Cash balance, January 1, 20X7	$ 275,900	
Cash received from: Patients	2,061,900	
Third-party payors	6,500,000	
Operation of gift shop	517,700	
Unrestricted gifts	323,500	
Contributions restricted for endowment	500,000	
Donor-restricted contributions for purchase of property and equipment	183,000	
Early repayment of long-term debt		$ 242,300
Cash paid to: Employees		1,151,000
Suppliers		6,200,000
Providers of consultation services		800,000
Bank for interest		147,000
Contractor for purchase of property and equipment		501,200
Cash balance, December 31, 20X7	$1,320,500	

Required ▶ ▶ ▶ ▶ ▶ Prepare a statement of cash flows, using the direct method, for the year ended December 31, 20X7.

Required ▶ ▶ ▶ ▶ ▶ **Problem 19-16** *(LO 11)* **Health care, reconciliation of change in net assets to net cash provided by operating activities.** Using data from Problem 19-15 and the following additional information, prepare a reconciliation of change in net assets to net cash provided by operating activities that would accompany Lakeside Hospital's statement of cash flows for the year ended December 31, 20X7.

The following condensed statement of activities for the year ended December 31, 20X7, shows the following:

Total operating revenues	$9,312,400
Total operating expenses	8,780,100
Income from operations	$ 532,300
Nonoperating revenue	1,102,900
Excess of revenues over expenses	$1,635,200

Included in the condensed statement of activities were as follows:

Depreciation and amortization	$422,500
Noncash gifts and bequests	37,500
Increase in expense and liability for estimated malpractice costs	12,300

An analysis of comparative balance sheet items showed the following changes in balances during 20X7:

Increase in patient accounts receivable	$266,300
Decrease in supplies inventory	11,800
Increase in accounts payable	10,100

PART

5 Fiduciary Accounting

Chapter 20: *Estates and Trusts: Their Nature and the Accountant's Role*

Chapter 21: *Debt Restructuring, Corporate Reorganizations, and Liquidations*

Effective estate planning continues to be an ever-increasing service provided by practicing accountants. As the value of capital markets continues to grow, more and more individuals find that their estate has increased in value. The desires of those owning an estate may be communicated through a variety of trusts or a will. It is important to properly account for the activity of an estate so that these desires are properly carried out. Furthermore, many estates are subject to an estate tax, and it is important to have a basic knowledge as to how estate taxes may be minimized through gifting and the use of trusts.

Unfortunately, for a variety of reasons, a company may find that it is insolvent and unable to continue its business operations unless certain changes occur. A variety of options is available to such troubled companies. In many instances, it is possible for the company to continue operations by use of a quasi-reorganization, a debt restructuring, or a corporate reorganization. In other instances, it is apparent that the company must declare bankruptcy and liquidate its net assets. Corporate reorganizations and liquidations are subject to a number of legal requirements set forth in the Bankruptcy Code. All these corrective actions must be accounted for according to special principles that have an effect on both the debt and equity interests in a company.

Estates and Trusts: Their Nature and the Accountant's Role

CHAPTER

20

Learning Objectives

When you have completed this chapter, you should be able to

1. **Describe the goals of estate planning.**
2. **Explain the various factors that affect estate principal.**
3. **Explain how one's taxable estate may be minimized.**
4. **Calculate the taxable estate and the resulting estate tax.**
5. **Describe various forms in which an estate may be distributed.**
6. **Account for the principal and income components of an estate.**
7. **Explain what a trust is and what the basic accounting issues are.**

This chapter examines the basic nature of estates and trusts and how the practicing accountant may be involved with them. A tremendous amount of complexity surrounds the legal and tax aspects of estates and trusts; therefore, this chapter provides only a broad overview.

An estate consists of the net assets of an individual at the time of his or her death. Until these net assets are completely distributed or consumed, the estate also exists as a separate, distinct entity that is governed, managed, and accounted for. Often, the net assets of an estate are distributed to a trust, which is also a separate, distinct entity. The trust is an arrangement whereby assets are protected, conserved, and/or distributed by a trustee according to the terms of the trust agreement. Persons who are responsible for the management of the net assets of an estate or trust have a fiduciary responsibility. These persons, called *fiduciaries*, are held accountable by law and are required to prepare specialized reports that account for their actions. The role of the accountant in the preparation of these reports is discussed in this chapter.

THE ROLE OF ESTATE PLANNING

1

OBJECTIVE

Describe the goals of estate planning.

Estate planning has a primary goal of reflecting the desires of the deceased individual, referred to as the *decedent*. Proper estate planning for individuals with sizeable asset values involves income tax and gift-giving strategies. As one's wealth increases, such strategies become more important. Obviously, such planning can become extremely complex since the circumstances and desires of each individual differ. As the net assets of an estate increase in value and nature, so does the complexity of the necessary estate planning. Many attorneys and accountants specialize in estate planning, which requires special knowledge of law, taxation, and accounting.

As the complexity of an estate increases, so do the goals of estate planning, which should include the following:

1. Discover and clearly communicate the desires and wishes of the decedent.
2. Ensure that the estate is administered or managed properly in order to satisfy the desires and wishes of the decedent.
3. Maximize the economic value of the estate's net assets.
4. Minimize the taxes that may be assessed against the assets and income of the estate.
5. Define the necessary liquidity of the estate's assets so that desired conveyances and distributions may be achieved.
6. Provide a proper and timely accounting of the activities of the estate and its fiduciary.

Communicating through a Will

Obviously, a deceased individual is not available to directly communicate his or her intentions regarding the estate. Therefore, it is critical that prior to death the person communicate through the creation of a valid *will*, a legal declaration containing directions as to the disposition of property. When an individual dies having left a will, the decedent is said to have died *testate*. The will must be presented to a *probate* court, which determines the validity of the will and identifies the fiduciary responsible for administering the will. Generally, probate law is developed by each state; therefore, it may vary significantly throughout the United States. While the Uniform Probate Code does exist, its adoption by states has been very limited.

An *inter vivos* trust is a popular way of passing property, without a will, to one's heirs and thereby avoiding the probate process. This type of trust is formed during one's lifetime, and property is transferred to a trust. The individual(s) making the transfer becomes trustee of the trust. Upon his or her death, a successor trustee is appointed and will have the ability to distribute the assets of the trust according to the terms of the trust.

A fiduciary responsible for the administration of a will may be named or nominated in the will. This person is referred to as an *executor* or personal representative and, assuming he or she is able and has the desire to serve, normally will be confirmed by the probate court. If the will does not name an executor or the executor is unable to serve, the court will appoint a party referred to as an *administrator*. Once the will has been probated, the decedent's assets are managed by the fiduciary subject to the oversight or control of court.

If a decedent has no will or an invalid will, the person is said to have died *intestate*. In this situation, the probate court appoints an administrator and distributes the net assets of the estate according to state inheritance laws. Usually, the order of distribution is to spouse, children, grandchildren, parents, grandparents, and then collateral relations such as siblings, aunts, and uncles. In many states, if there is a spouse and children, the estate is split: one half to the spouse and one half to the children.

2

OBJECTIVE

Explain the various factors that affect estate principal.

Identifying the Probate Principal or Corpus of an Estate

One of the first responsibilities of the fiduciary of an estate is to identify the assets of the estate. A decedent may have two types of estates. One, the *probate estate*, is described in this section and includes all of the decedent's assets passing to others by means of the will. The other estate, the *gross estate*, is the one that is used to determine the federal and state estate tax liability. The gross estate includes all assets owned by the decedent at the moment of death, regardless of whether they pass to others by means of the will, by joint tenancy, or by community property laws. These assets vary in nature and must be measured at their fair value. The value of certain assets, such as publicly traded securities, is determined with relative ease, while other assets, such as an interest in a closely held business, require independent appraisals.

The assets of the estate are referred to as the principal or *corpus* of the estate. In identifying the principal, the fiduciary must identify, or inventory, those assets that were the legal property of the decedent at the time of death. Therefore, the assets will include accrued items such as interest and rents. Items frequently comprising the estate principal include the following:

1. Cash on hand and in bank accounts.
2. Investments such as stocks, bonds, mutual funds, retirement accounts, money market funds, and survivorship annuities.
3. Accrued interest and declared dividends on the above investments as of the decedent's death.
4. Capital interests in businesses, such as closely held corporations, partnerships, and/or sole proprietorships.
5. Life insurance proceeds that are receivable by the estate, receivable by another for the benefit of the estate, or the result of the decedent having an ownership interest in the insurance policy. Therefore, if the decedent or the estate has an "incident of ownership," the proceeds are included in the estate.
6. Investments in real estate, including accrued rents at the date of the decedent's death.
7. Intangible assets, such as patents and royalties, including related accrued income at the date of the decedent's death.
8. Loans or notes receivable, including accrued interest at the date of the decedent's death.
9. Unpaid wages and other forms of earned income accruing to the decedent at the date of the decedent's death.
10. Personal valuables, including furniture, fixtures, jewelry, vehicles, boats, and collectible items such as coins, stamps, and artwork.

It is important to note that the preceding inventory of the principal is not reduced by the liabilities of the decedent. These obligations are recognized when they are paid or satisfied through the distribution of estate principal.

Often, it is not possible for the fiduciary to identify all of the assets of an estate initially. Those assets that are discovered subsequently must be included ultimately in the estate principal.

Exempt Property and Special Allowances. Some state probate laws exempt certain real property from the estate principal. These assets pass directly to the designated beneficiary or joint tenant. For example, if the decedent and his or her spouse own property as joint tenants, title to the entire property passes to the surviving tenant and is excluded from the decedent's estate. A surviving spouse's interest in community property is not included in the decedent's estate. However, the decedent's interest in the community property is included. Other assets of the decedent are not included in the estate principal by way of a *homestead allowance* and a *family allowance* and, therefore, are exempt from the probate process. Such assets are intended to support the family homestead and its members. Certain items of personal property (clothing, furniture, automobiles, etc.) are also exempt. However, such allowances differ significantly from state to state.

Accounting for the Inventory of a Probate Estate. After the special exemptions and allowances for estate assets have been provided for, the fiduciary must file a report with the probate court identifying the estate principal, which consists of the initial assets transferred to the estate as well as those assets subsequently discovered. An initial accounting of the estate principal requires an entry debiting the various assets and crediting an estate principal account.

In order to demonstrate the initial accounting for estate principal, assume Jane Jacoby died on June 1, 20X7. Jane's will names her attorney, Howard Wells, as executor of the estate. Through special exemptions and allowances, Jane's residence, $2,000 cash, clothing, and furniture passed to her husband, Walter Jacoby. Life insurance proceeds of $50,000 also were paid to the beneficiary, Robert Williams, Jane's son from a prior marriage. The remaining assets of the estate are subject to probate and are recorded as follows:

Principal Cash	81,000	
Investment in XYZ Stock and Mutual Funds	1,144,000	
Declared Dividend on XYZ Stock	3,000	
Investment in J&D Partnership	155,000	
Automobile	15,000	
Wages Receivable	2,000	
Estate Principal		1,400,000

An investment in Apex bonds valued at $20,000, along with accrued interest of $1,000, was discovered subsequently and is recorded as follows:

Investment in Apex Bonds	20,000	
Accrued Interest	1,000	
Estate Principal: Assets Subsequently Discovered		21,000

After recording the inventory of the estate principal, the fiduciary would submit a listing of the inventory to the probate court.

Subsequent to the initial recording of the inventory, sales or other dispositions of the assets may occur. Gains on such transactions increase the estate principal, while losses reduce principal. Continuing the above examples for the estate of Jane Jacoby, the following entries account for the sale of estate assets:

Principal Cash	165,000	
Investment in J&D Partnership		155,000
Gain on Realization of Principal Asset		10,000
Principal Cash	19,500	
Loss on Realization of Principal Asset	1,500	
Investment in Apex Bonds		20,000
Accrued Interest		1,000
Principal Cash	5,000	
Wages Receivable		2,000
Declared Dividend on XYZ Stock		3,000

Identifying Claims against the Probate Estate

The discovery and identification of claims against the decedent's estate are of equal importance to the discovery and identification of estate principal. Notification of the decedent's death is required by law, and valid claims must be identified within a prescribed period of time. The fiduciary must evaluate the validity of claims and place them in an order of priority for payment purposes. The order of priority varies from state to state. The following order of priority is one example:

1. Claims having a special lien against property, but not to exceed the value of the property.
2. Funeral and administrative expenses.
3. Taxes: income, estate, and inheritance.
4. Debts due the United States and various states.
5. Judgments of any court of competent jurisdiction.
6. Wages due domestic servants for a period of not more than one year prior to date of death and medical claims for the same period.
7. All other claims.

Within a class, each claim is satisfied on a pro rata basis if funds are inadequate to accomplish total payment for that class.

The following claims against the estate of Jane Jacoby are accounted for as follows:

Funeral Expenses	5,000	
Administrative Expenses	3,000	
Debts of Decedent Paid	23,000	
Medical Expenses	7,000	
Principal Cash		38,000

REFLECTION

- Estate planning has many goals, foremost of which is to reflect the wishes of the decedent.
- Estate principal may consist of many assets; claims normally exist against such assets.

TAX IMPLICATIONS OF AN ESTATE

3
OBJECTIVE
Explain how one's taxable estate may be minimized.

A major claim against the assets of an estate may result from the imposition of a federal estate tax and a state inheritance tax. An estate is considered to be a separate, distinct taxable entity during the period of administration or settlement. This period of time may not be unduly prolonged. The estate will be considered terminated after a reasonable period of time is allowed for administration and settlement. Minimizing the taxes imposed on an estate is a very complex topic, and prudent estate tax planning is critical. During one's lifetime, serious consideration should be given to how various divestitures and trusts could be used to manage one's taxable estate. In addition, proper planning should address the following considerations:

1. Maximizing benefits of the marital deduction.
2. Making gifts during one's lifetime.
3. Taking actions to accomplish a step-up in property basis.
4. Taking actions to benefit from a loss in property values.
5. Utilization of charitable deductions.
6. Planning estate liquidity.

To be protected, an estate must have a certain amount of liquid assets to pay taxes and the probate costs of establishing the validity of the will. Otherwise, a forced sale of estate assets might result. Some form of insurance often is recommended to provide liquidity and flexibility.

Federal Estate Taxation

Significant changes regarding gratuitous transfers of property resulted from the *Tax Reform Act of 1976*. Prior to its enactment, transfers of property during the owner's lifetime were subject to the federal gift tax, while property passing as a result of death was subject to the federal estate tax. The rules and rates for these taxes were different. Most of the distinction was removed by the Tax Reform Act, which combined the separate gift tax and estate tax into a unified transfer tax, which addresses both life (gift) and death transfers made after 1976. Therefore, taxable gifts and taxable estates are both taxed at the same rates.

The computation of the federal estate tax may be summarized as follows:

Gross estate	XX
Less deductions allowed	– XX
Taxable estate	XX
Add post-1976 taxable gifts	+ XX
Unified tax base	XX

(continued)

Tentative tax on total transfers	XX
Less tax credits	– XX
Estate tax due.	XX

The starting point for the computation of the federal estate tax is the determination of the gross estate, which includes the fair value of property owned by the decedent at date of death, regardless of the nature of the property or how it passes. Whether it is real or personal, tangible or intangible, business or nonbusiness, the property is includable. The gross estate, for tax purposes, is often greater than the estate for probate purposes due to special tax rules (for example, special rules regarding joint tenancy). The gross estate also includes transfers by the deceased during his or her lifetime in which certain rights are retained by the decedent (such as the right to enjoyment, or possession, the right to designate persons who will possess or enjoy, and of transfers which at the date of the decedent's death were subject to the decedent's power to alter, revoke, terminate, or amend the transfer).

The taxable estate is determined by subtracting the total of the following allowable deductions:

1. Allowable expenses, such as funeral expenses and costs of administrating the estate;
2. Indebtedness against property included in the gross estate, such as a mortgage and other debts of the decedent;
3. Unpaid property and income taxes of the decedent to date of death;
4. Uninsured losses from casualty or theft of estate assets during the period of settlement;
5. Transfers to charitable organizations specified by the will; and
6. Marital deduction, which is unlimited in amount, for estate property that passes to the surviving spouse if he or she is a U.S. citizen.

The unified transfer tax approach requires that the taxable estate be increased by any taxable gifts made after 1976 by the decedent prior to death. Gifts would be taxable to the donor if their fair value per donee exceeded annual exclusion amounts and/or the lifetime unified credit exclusion amount (to be discussed later). Both the annual exclusion amount and the unified credit have changed over time, and such changes are scheduled to continue. Rules regarding what constitutes a gift are complex and subject to exception. For example, tuition payments made directly to an educational organization and/or medical payments made on another's behalf are not considered taxable gifts.

Adding taxable gifts to the taxable estate results in a unified tax base to which the unified transfer tax rates are applied. The tax rates are progressive in nature and have changed over time. The *Economic Growth and Tax Relief Reconciliation Act of 2001* resulted in scheduled reductions in transfer tax rates and increases in the unified credit through the year 2009. In 2010, the estate tax is scheduled to be repealed. In 2011, if Congress does not take further action, estate and gift regulations will revert to what they were prior to passage of the act of 2001. All examples and end-of-chapter materials will be based on rates and amounts applicable for the year 2006. In 2006, rates range from 18% to 46%. Taxable estates up to $10,000 are taxed at 18%, while taxable amounts exceeding $2,000,000 are taxed at 46%. The Unified Transfer Tax Rate Schedule is presented in Exhibit 20-1.

Application of the tax rates to the unified tax base results in a tentative estate tax which is then reduced by certain credits. The two most common credits relate to taxes paid on post-1976 taxable gifts and the unified credit. Recalling that post-1976 taxable gifts are added to the taxable estate to produce a unified tax base, it is apparent that the taxable gifts are again being taxed at the applicable rates. If there were no further adjustment, this would result in double taxation on taxable gifts, once at the time of the gift and again as part of the estate tax calculation. Therefore, a credit for taxes associated with post-1976 gifts is calculated. The credit is equal to the tax that would be imposed on the taxable gift based on unified transfer tax rates that are in effect at the time of the decedent's death. If the credit were merely the amount of tax originally paid on the gift, it is possible that the gift could be currently taxed, as part of the unified tax base, at rates that were different than at the time of the gift. In that case, the credit would not offset the current tax associated with the gift. Therefore, the credit associated with gifts is based on current rates in effect.

The *unified credit* is a significant factor for most estates and in substance results from excluding a portion of taxable estate from taxation. The maximum amount of the credit and excluded amounts are as follows:

For Decedents Dying and Gifts During	Applicable Credit Amount	Applicable Exclusion Amount
2006	$ 780,800	$2,000,000
2007	780,800	2,000,000
2008	780,800	2,000,000
2009	1,455,800	3,500,000

The applicable credit amount corresponds with the unified transfer tax, which would be due on the applicable exclusion amount. For example, if one had a taxable estate of $2,000,000 in the year 2006, the unified transfer tax would be $780,800, which corresponds with the applicable credit. Additional credits against the tax due are based on state death or inheritance taxes paid and foreign death taxes. After recognizing applicable credits, the net tax due is paid out of the principal of the estate. If the estate principal does not have adequate cash to pay the taxes, other principal assets must be liquidated in order to generate the necessary cash.

Exhibit 20-1
Unified Transfer Tax Rate Schedule

Taxable Amount over	Taxable Amount Not over	Tax on Amount in Column A	Rate of Tax on Excess over Amount in Column A
$ 0	$ 10,000	$ 0	18%
10,000	20,000	1,800	20
20,000	40,000	3,800	22
40,000	60,000	8,200	24
60,000	80,000	13,000	26
80,000	100,000	18,200	28
100,000	150,000	23,800	30
150,000	250,000	38,800	32
250,000	500,000	70,800	34
500,000	750,000	155,800	37
750,000	1,000,000	248,300	39
1,000,000	1,250,000	345,800	41
1,250,000	1,500,000	448,300	43
1,500,000	2,000,000	555,800	45
2,000,000		780,800	46

For the years 2007 through 2009, the maximum tax rate will be 45% on amounts in excess of $1,500,000.

Estate Reduction with Gifts

Estate planning is essential to achieving the maximum benefit provided in the law, especially when the impact of continued inflation is considered. One simple way to reduce an estate is to make gifts annually. Currently, the first $11,000 ($22,000 for consenting spouse gifts) to any one person during any calendar year is excluded in determining taxable gifts. This is an annual exclusion and is scheduled to change due to inflation indexing. Based on current annual exclusion amounts, consenting spouses who participate for 10 years in an annual gift program involving six recipients would be able to transfer $1,320,000 ($22,000 × 6 × 10) without incurring any gift tax, thereby preserving the full unified credit for use in their estates. Spouses also can make gifts to each other. No matter what the amount, such gifts between spouses are not subject to gift tax.

In addition to the annual exclusion amount, there is a unified lifetime exclusion amount for gift tax purposes. Currently, a lifetime gift exclusion amount equal to $1 million exists. Therefore, a donor who makes $1 million in gifts during his or her lifetime (prior to death) is exempt from paying taxes on this gift. The benefit of this exclusion amount is that taxes on a $1 million gift, which would otherwise be $345,800 (based on unified transfer tax rates for years 2006 through 2009), are not imposed.

One might ask, "What is the maximum total gift a husband and wife may give to one individual at one time in 2006 without incurring any tax?" For gift tax purposes, a gift made by one person to someone other than his or her spouse is considered as having been made one-half by each spouse. Each spouse is entitled to a unified credit of $345,800 (in 2006), or an exemption equivalent gift of $1 million, plus the annual $11,000 exclusion. Therefore, a husband and wife together could give $2,022,000 (2 × $1,011,000) to one person (assuming none of the exclusion amount had been previously used) without incurring any gift tax. The unified credit is not an annual credit but rather a lifetime credit. Therefore, once used, a unified transfer (gift) tax would be due on gifts above the annual exclusion.

4

OBJECTIVE

Calculate the taxable estate and the resulting estate tax.

Marital Deduction

In the computation of the taxable estate, recall that a marital deduction is allowed for the value of qualifying property passing to a surviving spouse. The amount of the deduction is unlimited. No matter how large the estate, a bequest of all property to one's surviving spouse will completely eliminate federal estate taxes for the decedent. That statement is technically correct but incomplete. It should also state that the deduction may defer estate taxes only until the death of the other spouse. At that point, it may be discovered that use of the unlimited deduction actually increased the overall estate tax. This can result because the tax rates are progressive (the higher the tax base, the higher the rates), and the effect of the unlimited marital deduction is to channel all assets into the estate of the surviving spouse.

To illustrate, assume Ruth Marshall's will stipulated that her husband William was to receive all of her gross estate valued at $3,300,000. Outstanding debts of $150,000 and funeral and administrative expenses totaling $50,000 are paid out of the estate. Also, assume that later in the year (assume 2006) William dies with Ruth's estate assets of $3,100,000 still intact plus other assets of $1,000,000. At the time of William's death, debts of his estate total $80,000, and $20,000 of funeral and administrative costs have been incurred. With an unlimited marital deduction, their estate tax computations are as follows:

	Ruth		William	
Gross estate		$ 3,300,000		$4,100,000
Less deductions:				
Debts	$ 150,000		$80,000	
Funeral and administrative costs	50,000		20,000	
Marital deduction	3,100,000	(3,300,000)	0	(100,000)
Taxable estate		$ 0		$4,000,000
Estate tax before credits				$1,700,800
Less unified credit (available in 2006)				(780,800)
Estate tax due				$ 920,000

As an alternative strategy, Ruth's will could have stipulated that an amount equal to the applicable exclusion amount ($2,000,000) be placed in a trust, with William as the income beneficiary. Such trusts are referred to as credit shelter trusts as they "shelter" a portion of the total estate from estate tax by using the unified credit available to each spouse. Sometimes, these trusts are also referred to as marital deduction trusts or "A-B" trusts. In any case, if these trusts meet IRS guidelines, they are not subject to estate tax when the surviving spouse (William) dies. Therefore, if properly designed, the trust amount would be included in the decedent's taxable estate but offset by the unified credit. The balance of the decedent's (Ruth) net estate would be offset by the marital deduction and avoid estate tax. The balance of the decedent's net estate would pass to the surviving spouse. In our example, Ruth's taxable estate would consist of the amount of the credit shelter trust ($2,000,000), the tax on which would be offset by the unified credit. The balance of Ruth's net estate of $1,100,000 ($3,300,000 − $150,000 debts − $50,000 costs − $2,000,000 trust) would go directly to William and qualify for the marital deduction. Now, their estate computations would be as follows:

	Ruth		William	
Gross estate		$3,300,000		$2,100,000
Less deductions:				
Debts	$ 150,000		$80,000	
Funeral and administrative costs	50,000		20,000	
Marital deduction	1,100,000	1,300,000	0	100,000
Taxable estate		$2,000,000		$2,000,000
Estate tax before credits		$ 780,800*		$ 780,800
Less unified credit (available in 2006)		(780,800)		(780,800)
Estate tax due		$ 0		$ 0

*This amount of tax is based on the unified rate schedule for estates.

Failure to do some estate planning could cost the Marshall family $920,000.

Valuation of Estate Assets

Fair value must be established for assets included in an estate. Some valuations, such as the value of stocks and bonds traded on recognized exchanges, pose no problems. For other assets, such as property, jewelry, art objects, or antiques, a competent appraisal in writing should be obtained. Assets are included in the estate at their fair value on the date of death or on an alternate valuation date, if the executor or administrator so elects. If the alternate valuation date is elected, all estate property must be valued as of six months after the decedent's death, except for property sold, distributed, or otherwise disposed of during the 6-month period. Such property is valued as of the date of disposition. The alternate valuation date may be used only if it would reduce the total gross estate and decrease the estate tax liability. The alternate valuation date protects estates if there should be a significant decrease in property values during the 6-month interval.

Formerly, it would have been possible for a fiduciary, knowing that there would be no estate tax to pay, to select the alternate valuation date if assets increased in value, thereby giving the heirs a higher basis for their inherited property, at no cost to the estate. To prevent this windfall, Congress took an action that permitted election of the alternate valuation date only if it would reduce the total gross estate and decrease the estate tax liability.

Congress felt it was being sufficiently generous by permitting a stepped-up basis. Recall that, to the recipient, the basis of property acquired from a decedent is fair value on the date of death or alternate valuation date. That regulation may result in a step-up of basis. For example, assume Jane Jacoby held stock with a cost of $100,000. At the date of her death, it was worth $500,000 and was willed to her nephew, whose basis now becomes $500,000. A subsequent sale by him for $500,000 would result in no taxable gain. Although the value of the stock must be included in the inventory of the estate, which would be subject to the unified transfer tax only if the estate is large enough, the $400,000 gain would escape *federal income taxation* because of the step-up in basis. If Jane had sold the stock before her death, the gain would have been subject to income tax. Tax planning would suggest that, if possible, property that has appreciated substantially in value should be held as part of an estate because of the advantage of the step-up in basis. The opposite is true if there is a substantial decline in value. If Jane's stock had a value of $5,000 on the valuation date, that would become the basis to her nephew. Neither he nor the estate would derive any income tax benefit from the $95,000 loss in value. If Jane had sold the stock prior to her death, benefits resulting from the deductibility of the loss for income tax purposes would have materialized.

Other Taxes Affecting an Estate

In addition to federal estate taxes, most individual states assess an inheritance tax on the value of estate assets conveyed to heirs. Unlike the estate tax, the inheritance tax is levied on the heirs rather than the estate. Certain transfers of assets are exempt, while other transfers are partially exempt, depending on the amount of the transfer and the relationship of the heir. The taxable amount of nonexempt transfers is reduced further by certain deductions such as funeral and administrative expenses, debts of the decedent, and mortgages on real property.

In certain instances, an estate subsequently will generate income that is not included in the initial estate principal. The estate is viewed as a separate taxable entity. Estate income that is distributed currently and properly to a beneficiary generally is excluded from the taxable income of the estate. Therefore, the estate functions as a conduit through which the income passes to the recipient. Income passing in this manner retains the same character it had in the hands of the estate. For example, if the estate receives and distributes nontaxable income such as interest on municipal bonds, the interest remains tax free in the hands of the recipient. Normally, the beneficiary is taxed on any taxable income that he or she receives, and the estate, as a separate entity, is taxed on any income that it accumulates. Estate income taxes are assessed at rates similar to those used for individual taxpayers except that the levels of income at which rates become effective are much lower for estates than they are for individuals.

Measurement of Estate Income

The tax incidence on estate income suggests the need for the estate fiduciary to distinguish between transactions affecting principal and those affecting income. Furthermore, a decedent's will may stipulate certain provisions regarding estate income that differ from those regarding principal. For example, a will might stipulate that the interest income earned on bonds subsequent to the decedent's death is to accrue to a particular beneficiary for a period of time. The recipient of the income is referred to as an *income beneficiary*, and the party ultimately receiving the principal is referred to as the *remainderman*.

If the will is not clear with respect to the measurement of income, state statutes should be applied. Many states have adopted the *Revised Uniform Principal and Income Act*, which provides guidance as to the measurement of estate principal and income. The determination of estate income does not always parallel generally accepted accounting principles (GAAP). As discussed previously, the gains or losses on the sale of estate assets are considered to be components of principal rather than income. When bonds are a part of the estate at the time of death, the premium or discount on the bonds is not amortized. However, if bonds are purchased subsequently by the fiduciary, a premium is generally amortized, whereas a discount is not amortized.

Unless the will requires it, the common procedure is not to make any charge against income for depreciation. If the decedent wishes to protect principal for the depreciation factor, the will should state that depreciation should be charged against income, and an amount equal to the depreciation should be transferred from income to principal. For the depletion on wasting assets, the general rule is that income should be charged for the depletion because of the possibility of total consumption of principal.

REFLECTION

- One's taxable estate may be reduced in a number of ways, including annual gifting, the creation of trusts, and marital exclusions.
- The taxable estate consists of the gross estate less allowable deductions. The amount of estate tax is also reduced by a unified credit.

SETTLING A PROBATE ESTATE

5

OBJECTIVE

Describe various forms in which an estate may be distributed.

After the debts of an estate and the applicable estate taxes have been determined and paid, the fiduciary must focus on carrying out the remaining provisions of the decedent's will as they relate to principal and income. If the decedent dies intestate, distribution of remaining estate principal is governed by applicable state law.

Distributions of Property

If a decedent dies intestate, real property is distributed according to the laws of descent of the state in which the real property is located. Personal property is distributed according to the laws of distribution of the decedent's home state, called the *state of domicile*. In general, only a spouse or blood relative may receive an intestate distribution.

In a testate situation, a distribution of real property is a *devise*, and the recipient of the property is the *devisee*. Distributions of personal property are called bequests or *legacies*, and the recipient of personal property is called the *legatee*.

A devise is usually a distribution of a specific piece of real property. In contrast, legacies may include one or more of the following types:

1. A *specific legacy* is a gift of a particular, specified thing, distinguishable from others: my 3-carat diamond ring or the 20 bottles of Romanée Conti Burgundy 1991 on the north wall of my wine cellar.
2. A *demonstrative legacy* is a gift of an amount from a specific source, with the will stipulating that if the amount cannot be satisfied from that source, it shall be satisfied from the general estate: $50,000 from several identified insurance policies. If proceeds are inadequate to meet the amount, the difference shall constitute a general legacy.
3. A *general legacy* is a gift of an indicated amount or quantity of something: $5,000 or 20 bottles of wine. However, the specific source of the payment is not designated.
4. A *residuary legacy* is composed of all estate property remaining after assigning the specific, demonstrative, and general legacies.

If the remaining estate principal, after paying debts and expenses, is not adequate to satisfy the various legacies, a process called *abatement* is followed. Abatement requires that the legacies be satisfied to whatever extent possible in the order in which they are presented above [items (1) through (4)]. If the amount of assets designated as a general legacy is not available, the available amount is abated proportionately among the recipients. For example, assume a general legacy calls for $5,000 to be paid to each of two individuals and $2,500 to be paid to each of another two individuals and only $12,000 is available. Abatement would result in two individuals receiving $4,000 each and the other two individuals receiving $2,000 each.

In order to illustrate the accounting for the distribution of property, we continue the earlier example regarding Jane Jacoby's estate. Events (1) through (6) of Illustration 20-1 relate to Jane's estate. Events (7) through (14) relate to the accounting for estate income and property distributions. Events (15) and (16) reflect the closing of estate principal and income.

Illustration 20-1
Accounting for the Estate of Jane Jacoby

	Event	Entry		
1.	Recording of the initial estate inventory after special exemptions and allowances.	Principal Cash	81,000	
		Investment in XYZ Stock and Mutual Funds	1,144,000	
		Declared Dividend on XYZ Stock	3,000	
		Investment in J&D Partnership	155,000	
		Automobile	15,000	
		Wages Receivable	2,000	
		Estate Principal		1,400,000
2.	Subsequent discovery of estate assets.	Investment in Apex Bonds	20,000	
		Accrued Interest	1,000	
		Estate Principal: Assets Subsequently Discovered		21,000
3.	Sale of estate assets: J&D Partnership for $165,000 cash.	Principal Cash	165,000	
		Investment in J&D Partnership		155,000
		Gain on Realization of Principal Asset		10,000
4.	Sale of estate assets: Apex bonds plus accrued interest for $19,500.	Principal Cash	19,500	
		Loss on Realization of Principal Asset	1,500	
		Investment in Apex Bonds		20,000
		Accrued Interest		1,000
5.	Receipt of accrued wages and dividends receivable.	Principal Cash	5,000	
		Wages Receivable		2,000
		Declared Dividend on XYZ Stock		3,000
6.	Payment of claims against the estate.	Funeral Expenses	5,000	
		Administrative Expenses	3,000	
		Debts of Decedent Paid	23,000	
		Medical Expenses	7,000	
		Principal Cash		38,000
7.	Receipt of interest on cash accounts.	Income Cash	1,000	
		Estate Income		1,000
8.	Receipt of dividend declared on XYZ stock subsequent to decedent's death.	Income Cash	3,000	
		Estate Income		3,000
9.	Distribution of specific legacy of automobile to Jane's nephew.	Legacies Distributed	15,000	
		Automobile		15,000
10.	Distribution of general legacy of $25,000 to Jane's sister.	Legacies Distributed	25,000	
		Principal Cash		25,000
11.	Distribution of specific legacy of 5,000 shares of XYZ stock to Riveredge Nature Center.	Legacies Distributed	186,000	
		Investment in XYZ Stock		186,000
12.	Payment of administrative expenses of which $100 is traceable to income.	Administrative Expenses	300	
		Expenses Chargeable against Income	100	
		Principal Cash		300
		Income Cash		100

Event	Entry		
13. Distribution of income cash traceable to dividends received to Jane's brother.	Distribution to Income Beneficiary	3,000	
	Income Cash		3,000
14. Distribution of all estate assets to the Jacoby children's trust administered by First National Trust Company.	Principal Assets Transferred to Trust	1,165,200	
	Income Assets Transferred to Trust	900	
	Principal Cash		207,200
	Investment in XYZ Stock and Mutual Funds		958,000
	Income Cash		900
15. Closing of estate principal.	Estate Principal	1,400,000	
	Estate Principal: Assets Subsequently Discovered	21,000	
	Gain on Realization of Principal Asset	10,000	
	Loss on Realization of Principal Asset		1,500
	Funeral Expenses		5,000
	Administrative Expenses		3,300
	Debts of Decedent Paid		23,000
	Medical Expenses		7,000
	Legacies Distributed		226,000
	Principal Assets Transferred to Trust		1,165,200
16. Closing of estate income.	Estate Income	4,000	
	Expenses Chargeable against Income		100
	Distributions to Income Beneficiary		3,000
	Income Assets Transferred to Trust		900

The Charge and Discharge Statement

Periodically, the fiduciary will prepare a report to the court summarizing the results during the period of stewardship. This report is called a *charge and discharge statement.* The preparation of the report is simplified if a double trial balance has been prepared, since the charge and discharge statement is divided into two parts—one as to principal and one as to income. The statement for the estate of Jane Jacoby on December 31, 20X7, appears as Illustration 20-2.

Illustration 20-2
Charge and Discharge Statement
Estate of Jane Jacoby
Howard Wells, Executor
Charge and Discharge Statement
For Period June 1, 20X7, to December 31, 20X7

As to Principal		
I charge myself with:		
Assets per original inventory	$1,400,000	
Assets subsequently discovered	21,000	
Net gain on realization of principal assets	8,500	
Total charges		$1,429,500

(continued)

As to Principal

I credit myself with:		
Funeral and administrative expenses	$ 8,300	
Medical expenses	7,000	
Debts of decedent paid	23,000	
Legacies distributed	226,000	
Total credits		264,300
Balances as to estate principal, consisting of:		
Cash—principal	$ 207,200	
XYZ stock and mutual funds	958,000	
		$1,165,200

As to Income

I charge myself with:		
Estate income		$ 4,000
I credit myself with:		
Expenses chargeable against income	$ 100	
Distributions to income beneficiaries	3,000	
Total credits		3,100
Balances as to estate income, consisting of:		
Cash—income		$ 900

In a more complex estate, each of the items in the charge and discharge statement would be supported by a schedule providing detail. For example, a supporting schedule for gains and losses on realization of principal assets might appear as follows:

Schedule of Gains and Losses on Realization of Principal Assets

	Inventory Value	Proceeds on Realization	Loss	Gain
J&D Partnership	$155,000	$165,000		$10,000
Apex bonds and accrued interest	21,000	19,500	$(1,500)	
Totals	$176,000	$184,500	$(1,500)	$10,000

If the fiduciary had completed his or her responsibilities to the estate, all assets comprising estate principal and income would have been distributed. In this case, the charge and discharge statement would reflect zero balances as to estate principal and income. Final distributions of estate principal often are made in the form of a residual legacy and/or a trust for the benefit of designated parties. After all final distributions, the estate records are closed with the estate principal and estate income accounts serving as clearing accounts. The final distributions of the estate of Jane Jacoby, along with necessary closing entries, are recorded as events (14) through (16) of Illustration 20-1.

6

OBJECTIVE

Account for the principal and income components of an estate.

Summary of Items Affecting Estate Principal and Income

A variety of items can affect the estate of a decedent, and the presence of a valid will certainly provides direction in this regard. The estate's fiduciary must act in a responsible manner and assume that a proper accounting of the items affecting an estate has taken place. A proper accounting will provide better management of the estate and serve as a basis for statutory reporting requirements. Today's professional accountant can support the fiduciary role by understanding the principles of estate administration and accounting. A review of the items affecting estate principal and income will help to ensure a proper accounting.

The items that are usually chargeable against principal and the account debited when each item is recorded are as follows:

Item	Account Debited
Debts of the decedent incurred prior to death	Debts of Decedent Paid
Funeral and administrative expenses	Funeral and Administrative Expenses
Medical expenses	Medical Expenses
Costs incurred in probating the will	Funeral and Administrative Expenses
Final income taxes of decedent	Debts of Decedent Paid
Federal estate tax* and any state inheritance tax	Funeral and Administrative Expenses
Legal and other professional fees to preserve estate principal	Funeral and Administrative Expenses
Charges applicable to personal property that produces no income	Expenses Chargeable against Principal
Distributions of legacies or devises in a testate distribution	Legacies Distributed or Devices Distributed } often combined in the first account
Distributions to trusts	Principal Assets Transferred to Trust
Disposition of estate assets at a loss	Loss on Realization of Principal Assets (a gain would be credited to Gain on Realization of Principal Assets, with total proceeds on any sale of a principal asset debited to Cash—Principal)

*The Uniform Probate Code provides that where the will does not stipulate treatment of estate taxes, they are to be prorated to the recipients of estate assets on the basis of the value of the asset received relative to the aggregate value of all assets subject to tax.

When income cash is received, Estate Income is credited, and if the estate is large, a subsidiary ledger is maintained that details the types of income. The items for which income cash usually is disbursed and the account debited when each item is recorded are as follows:

Item	Account Debited
Expenses incurred to protect income flow	Expenses Chargeable against Income
Ordinary repairs to income-producing property	Expenses Chargeable against Income
Distributions of income cash to beneficiaries	Distributions to Income Beneficiaries
Distributions of income cash to trusts	Income Assets Transferred to Trust

REFLECTION

- The assets of an estate may be distributed in a number of ways, including charitable transfers, devises, and legacies.
- It is important to separately account for estate principal and income. A charge and discharge statement is used to summarize the disposition of estate principal and income.

TRUST ACCOUNTING ISSUES

7
OBJECTIVE
Explain what a trust is and what the basic accounting issues are.

A trust is a separate, distinct entity that receives assets from an individual for the purpose of managing and distributing them over a period of time. A trust is also recognized as a taxable entity until trust assets have been distributed and the administration of the trust is completed. Trusts may be created for several reasons. It is possible that heirs to an estate currently lack the maturity, sophistication, or prudence necessary to receive substantial assets directly. Therefore, a trust is established to manage the asset for the intended heir(s). Trusts also provide opportunities for assets to be exempt from the probate process and, more important, taxes imposed on an estate. Finally, trusts are used as a means to convey assets to special organizations or causes, such as charities, universities, and other not-for-profit organizations. Rather than conveying estate assets directly to these organizations, a trust presents an opportunity to recognize the needs of individual heirs prior to such distributions.

Trusts may take a variety of forms, and various strategies can be used to create a trust. A *charitable remainder trust* distributes the income from trust assets to individual beneficiaries over a period of time (often for the rest of their lives), at which time the assets go to the remainderman which must be a charitable organization. Under such an arrangement, a charitable deduction is available to the *grantor* when the trust is created. Upon death of the grantor, the property is excluded from the estate, thereby avoiding estate taxes. A *bypass or credit shelter trust* is designed to split assets between a surviving spouse and a trust so that the value of the marital deduction and unified credit are maximized. Generally, the surviving spouse receives income during his or her lifetime after which the trust assets are distributed to surviving children or heirs. A *qualified terminable interest property trust* (QTIP trust) is similar to a bypass or credit shelter trust.

Noting that trusts may be designed to accomplish a variety of purposes, they may become operative while the grantor is alive or they may be created through a will to become effective upon the grantor's death. The former type of trust is an *inter vivos*, or *living, trust*, while the latter is referred to as a *testamentary trust.* In order to carry out the provisions of a trust, a *trustee* must be appointed. The trustee may be an individual; however, banks frequently serve as trustees. Most major banks have a trust department whose services are available for a fee.

Financial Accounting for Trusts

The accounting for a trust is very similar to the accounting for an estate. The distinction between principal and income must be maintained through the use of *trust principal* and *trust income accounts.* The trust agreement should provide direction regarding how income is to be determined. A charge and discharge statement is required periodically for both trust principal and income.

Illustration 20-3 demonstrates the accounting for various events affecting the trust established by Jane Jacoby's will.

Illustration 20-3
Accounting for the Jacoby Children's Trust

Event	Entry		
1. Receipt of distribution from the estate of Jane Jacoby.	Principal Cash	207,200	
	Investment in XYZ Stock and Mutual Funds	958,000	
	Trust Principal		1,165,200
	Income Cash	900	
	Trust Income		900
2. Sale of mutual funds.	Principal Cash	200,000	
	Income Cash	5,000	
	Investment in Mutual Funds		200,000
	Trust Income		5,000
3. Receipt of dividend and interest income.	Income Cash	5,300	
	Trust Income		5,300
4. Payment of trustee's fees and allocation to principal and income.	Administrative Expenses: Principal	400	
	Administrative Expenses: Income	200	
	Principal Cash		400
	Income Cash		200
5. Distribution of income cash to beneficiaries.	Distribution to Income Beneficiary	11,000	
	Income Cash		11,000

To demonstrate adherence to the terms of the trust, the trustee must provide annual, confidential reports to income beneficiaries and remaindermen. For a testamentary trust, a report must also be rendered to the probate court of the county in which the will was admitted to probate. The nature of the report is dependent upon the statutory requirement of the relevant state. Generally, within 30 days after the end of each year, a report must be filed that shows:

1. The trust principal on hand at the beginning of the period.
2. Changes in the trust principal during the period, such as asset acquisitions or dispositions.
3. The trust principal on hand at the end of the period, its composition, and the estimated fair values of all investments.

As to trust income, the report shows:

1. The trust income on hand at the beginning of the period.
2. Trust income received during the period, including its sources and amounts.
3. Distributions of trust income made during the period to income beneficiaries.
4. The trust income on hand at the end of the period and how it is invested.

These requirements may be met by the periodic filing of a charge and discharge statement, provided that sufficient detail as to principal and income is incorporated into the report. At the time the statement is submitted to the court, many trustees prefer to close trust books to have them correspond to the annual time frame used in filing reports. Trust Principal and Trust Income are the clearing accounts used in the closing process, paralleling the procedures for closing an estate.

The trust will terminate when all trust property is distributed in accordance with the trust arrangement. For example, a trust may have been created to provide a beneficiary with income until this beneficiary reaches a specified age, at which time trust principal is released. The trustee's final report will take the same form as the periodic reports but, in addition, will itemize total distribution of trust principal and income to indicate termination of stewardship.

REFLECTION

- A trust is a separate, distinct entity, and its principal and income must be separately accounted for.

UNDERSTANDING THE ISSUES

1. Estate planning is becoming more important to many individuals. Identify several goals of estate planning.
2. Explain why it may be wise for a wealthy spouse to use the unified credit rather than to transfer all of their estate to the surviving spouse in the form of the marital exclusion.
3. Explain why is it important to separately account for the principal and income of an estate and what happens if such assets are not adequate to satisfy demonstrative or general legacies.

EXERCISES

Exercise 1 *(LO 2)* **Recording disbursements of an estate.** Casey Jones died testate on May 1, 20X0. As the approved executor, prepare journal entries to record the following activities related to the estate:

a. The assets are inventoried, and the following listing is filed with the probate court:

Cash	$ 60,000
Stock of Trains, Inc.	40,000
Zip Railroad 10% bonds, interest payable March 1 and September 1, at face value (also fair value)	120,000
Accrued interest on Zip bonds	2,000
Personal and household effects	30,000
Total	$252,000

b. Funeral expenses paid, $2,800.

c. Dividends were declared on May 10 by Trains, Inc., and the check for $800 was received on June 1.

d. Interest on Zip Railroad bonds was collected on September 1.

e. Half of the Zip Railroad bonds were sold on October 1 at 103 plus accrued interest.

f. Casey was a bachelor. The will stipulates that his personal and household effects be given to his housekeeper, Karen Kay. The executor released the items to her.

g. On December 1, the executor's fee of $3,000 was approved by the court and paid. Of the total amount, $200 is to be charged against income of the estate.

Exercise 2 *(LO 1, 3, 7)* **Reducing a taxable estate, accounting for trust principal.** On November 1, 20X0, Alice Nolan, a married woman, was diagnosed with a terminal illness and has approximately six months to live. Her husband is significantly older and has been in poor health for some time. Alice has net assets with a fair value of approximately $4 million. Included in the marital estate are investments in stock, life insurance policies on Alice's life naming her husband as beneficiary, corporate bonds which were purchased at a premium, and a modest timber plantation in southern Georgia. In contemplation of her death, Alice has several questions regarding how to best manage her estate and minimize estate taxes. Assume that the unified credit is $780,800, associated with an exclusion amount of $2 million for estate tax purposes. The annual exclusion amount for gift tax purposes is $11,000, and the lifetime exclusion amount is $1 million.

1. What advice would you give Alice with respect to whether or not she should dispose of certain securities which have and are expected to continue to have a fair value that is less than their original cost?
2. What actions might Alice take in order to exclude the life insurance proceeds from being included in her estate?
3. Assuming that Alice has previously given $450,000 in post-1976 taxable gifts, what is the maximum annual gift that she can make to her three sisters, in total, and avoid gift taxes, assuming that her husband does not consent to the gifts?
4. Assume that the corporate bonds are to be placed in a charitable remainder trust, with her son receiving the income from the bonds for 10 years and the Sierra Club receiving the remainder after that point. Why might including the amortization of the premium on the bonds as a component of determining income be advantageous to the interests of the Sierra Club?
5. If Alice's will bequests the tree plantation to her husband and the income from the plantation to her stepson, in fairness to her husband, should the income from the plantation include the effect of depletion on the timberland?

Exercise 3 *(LO 4, 5)* **Estate tax and distribution, general legacies.** The estate of Marlene Johnson consists of assets having a fair value of $308,785. As of the date of her death, the following claims exist against the estate:

Claims Existing at Date of Death	Amount of Claim
Mortgage balance including principal and accrued interest due on personal residence with a fair value of $180,000	$142,580
Funeral expenses	6,300
Expenses incurred by executor of estate for administration purposes	2,100
Income and estate taxes	12,400
Brokerage commissions associated with the sale of the personal residence	16,000
A lien against the personal residence for unpaid real estate taxes	4,200
Unreimbursed medical claims for the last three months prior to death	27,000
Unpaid balance of personal loan received from her brother	14,700
Unpaid balance of automobile repair expenses. A mechanic's lien has been placed on the automobile which has a fair value of $5,000	750
Unpaid balance of other personal expenses	3,950
Total of all claims	$229,980

Legacies addressed in the decedent's will include the following:

1. Proceeds of $30,000 from the sale of the personal residence, after payment of mortgages, real estate taxes, and sales costs, will be paid to the decedent's nephew.
2. The collection of Edward S. Curtis photographs, valued at $22,000, will be given to the decedent's nephew.
3. Cash of $40,000 will be divided equally among the decedent's two sisters.

Prepare a schedule, in order of priority, indicating how the assets of the estate will be disbursed.

Exercise 4 *(LO 5)* **Distribution of estate.** At his date of death, Robert Quade's estate consisted of the following assets and liabilities measured at fair market value:

Assets	
Cash—checking and savings	$ 15,000
Life insurance death benefit	1,000,000
Personal residence	350,000
Investment in mutual funds	550,000
Automobiles	70,000
Hunting land	440,000
Personal effects	35,000
Collection of rare maps	85,000
Total assets	$2,545,000

Liabilities	
Mortgage on personal residence	$ 55,000
Automobile loan	15,000
Credit card balances	5,000
Total liabilities	$ 75,000

Robert Quade was a single person and his will contained the following provisions:

1. The hunting land was to be donated to the Ozaukee Land Trust, recognized as a charitable organization.
2. The 1966 Pontiac GTO, valued at $32,000, is to be given to his friend, Greg Keltner.
3. Cash of $400,000 was to be given to his sister, Roberta Quade Barnes.

4. The rare maps of the Wisconsin territory, valued at $15,000, are to be given to a close friend and fellow sportsman, Donald Levy. All remaining maps are to be given to Fort Lewis College, recognized as a charitable organization.
5. The personal residence and personal effects were to be deeded to his only brother, Thomas Quade.
6. All remaining assets were to be placed in a trust for the benefit of his minor niece, Pamela Barnes.

Quade's estate incurred final administrative and funeral expenses of $20,000.

1. Explain why Robert Quade's estate was not subject to any federal estate taxes.
2. Prepare a schedule that details the distribution of the estate by devise and legacies. Each category of legacy should be separately set forth.

Exercise 5 *(LO 4)* **Determination of estate tax.** Roger Kamp, a divorced person, died in 20X5 with an estate consisting of assets valued at $4,008,000 and liabilities of $380,000. Roger's will contained the following provisions:

1. Robert Sullivan would serve as executor of the estate and trustee for the Kamp Children Trust.
2. Timberland with a market value of $560,000 would be placed in a charitable remainder trust. The income from the trust would accrue to the benefit of his sister Marsha Kamp Rodriquez. Income would be reduced by the depletion charge associated with the number of board feet of lumber harvested.
3. Securities with a value of $25,000 would be given to the Milwaukee Art Museum, recognized as a charitable organization.
4. Securities with a value of $600,000 would be given to his married daughter, Maria Kamp Wilson.
5. $180,000 to each of his three best hunting friends to be paid from the proceeds of the sale of Roger's investment in hunting land in Alaska. The hunting land was valued at $495,000 and subsequently sold for $500,000.
6. $360,000 to his long-time friend Ernest Kampmeyer.
7. Proceeds from the life insurance policy with a death benefit of $1,200,000 would be placed in a trust for the benefit of Roger's two minor children.

Administrative and funeral expenses associated with Roger's estate totaled $30,000. Roger's income tax returns for the year of death reported unpaid federal and state income taxes of $13,000.

1. Assuming the unified transfer tax rates set forth in the text and a unified credit of $780,800, determine the amount of estate tax due on Roger Kamp's estate.
2. Prepare a schedule showing the amounts and recipients of general legacies.

Exercise 6 *(LO 3)* **Strategies to minimize estate taxes.** Edith Leppert and her husband, Gerald Leppert, have net assets with market values of $3,300,000 and $2,400,000, respectively. The Lepperts have begun to do some estate tax planning and are developing various strategies based on the following assumptions:

1. Due to preexisting health conditions, it is assumed that Edith will precede her husband in death and Gerald will survive Edith by three years.
2. Gerald's net assets, including those assets received upon Edith's death, are expected to appreciate at a compound rate of 5% per year.
3. Administrative and funeral expenses are estimated to be $25,000 per person.
4. Both Edith and Gerald have each earmarked $150,000 of their net assets to be donated to charitable organizations.

Based on the above information, determine the amount of estate tax that both Edith and Gerald Leppert would be exposed to given: (a) that no trusts were established and (b) that a credit shelter trust is created for the benefit of their children. Unified transfer tax rates and the 2006 exclusion amount as set forth in the text should be used.

Exercise 7 *(LO 7)* **Analysis of trust activity.** Jack Mason is a single parent with three minor children. His will provides for the creation of a trust for the benefit of his three children. His entire net estate is to be placed into the trust, and the trustee is authorized to approve disbursements to the children until they reach the age of 25. Upon reaching the age of 25, each child is to receive their proportionate share of the trust principal and income. For example, the first child to reach age 25 will receive one-third of the trust principal and income. The next child to reach age 25 will receive one-half of the trust principal and income at that time.

The following facts relate to the trust:

1. The following assets were transferred to the trust after the settlement of Jack Mason's estate: Cash, $100,000; stock in IBM, $150,000; investment in real estate partnership, $400,000; and forest land, $200,000.
2. Subsequent to Mason's death, an investment in a limited partnership was discovered. The investment was valued at $40,000.
3. One-half of the investment in the real estate partnership was sold for $220,000.
4. Dividends on the IBM stock were received in the amount of $20,000. The dividend was declared prior to Mason's death.
5. All cash balances were invested in a short-term interest-bearing account, and the trust received $5,000 in interest.
6. The trustee for the benefit of the children approved disbursements in the amount of $32,000. Disbursements are first considered to be a distribution of available trust income and then as a distribution of trust principal.
7. Trustee's fees in the amount of $10,000 were paid. All such fees are to be allocated equally between principal and income.
8. Eight percent bonds with a face value of $80,000 were purchased for $84,000. The bonds have a remaining life of five years, and any premium is to be amortized.
9. Income from the harvest of timber in the amount of $22,000 was received. The trust document calls for a charge against income for depletion. Depletion is calculated based on a units-of-output method that is based on board feet of timber harvested. Approximately 11% of the total board feet is represented by this harvest. The land is expected to have a residual value of $60,000 after removal of the timber.
10. Real estate taxes on the land in the amount of $6,000 were paid. Such taxes are considered a component of trust income.
11. The real estate partnership made a distribution of income in the amount of $22,000 to the trust.
12. A semiannual interest payment on the bonds was received by the trust.
13. The trustee paid $6,000 of taxes on trust income.
14. IBM stock with a basis of $60,000 was sold for $80,100.

Prepare a schedule to determine the amount of trust principal to be received by the first child to reach the age of 25. The schedule should show the cash balance available at any point in time.

Exercise 8 *(LO 6)* **Accounting for estate principal and income.** Jason Jackson was killed in a mountain-climbing accident in British Columbia. As Jason's trusted friend and CPA, you have been named executor of his estate and guardian to his minor child, Cody Jackson. Jason's estate consists of the following assets subject to probate:

Cash	$ 15,000
Vacant land in Colorado	130,000
Investment in Merkt stock	54,000
Investment in GTE stock	13,000
Dividends declared on GTE stock	1,000
Investment in Trident bond fund	40,000
Accrued interest on Trident bond fund	2,000
Royalties receivable	17,000

Prepare journal entries to record the above inventory and the following events related to the estate principal and income:

a. Final medical and funeral expenses of $22,000 are paid.
b. An individual retirement account (IRA) naming Jackson's estate as beneficiary and having a value of $37,000 subsequently is discovered.
c. Cash dividends of $1,000 on the GTE stock and $2,700 on the Merkt stock are received.
d. The vacant land in Colorado is sold for $150,000 less accrued property taxes of $2,000 and a broker's commission of $8,000.
e. Interest of $2,400 is received on the Trident bond fund, and the royalty receivable is also collected.
f. Income taxes of $4,000 on the decedent's final tax return are paid, along with $24,000 of other claims against the estate.
g. A legacy of $15,000 is paid to the High Adventure Climbing School.
h. Administrative expenses of $3,200 are paid, of which $100 is traceable to income.

Exercise 9 *(LO 6)* **Charge and discharge statement.** Given the facts of Exercise 8, prepare the charge and discharge statement that would have resulted from the above events and prepare the entries to transfer all estate principal and income amounts to a trust for the benefit of Cody Jackson.

Exercise 10 *(LO 7)* **Recording the activities of a trust.** Prior to his death, Winston Weber placed the following assets in a trust on November 15, 20X8:

Assets	Fair Value
Stock in Norland Medical including a $1,000 declared dividend to shareholders of record on November 1, 20X8. The dividend was paid on December 1, 20X8.	$101,000
8% corporate bonds (originally acquired at a face value of $210,000) including accrued interest of $7,700. Semiannual interest was paid on December 1, 20X8.	217,000
Farmland that is leased to an adjacent landowner for a monthly rent of $500. The lease covers a 12-month period beginning June 1, 20X8. All monthly lease payments are due on the first of the month and have been made when due.	240,000
Cash	5,000

At the date of transfer to the trust, the farmland had an outstanding mortgage that was also transferred to the trust. The principal mortgage balance after the September 1, 20X8, payment was $46,937 and had the following terms: quarterly payments of $2,000 with the next payment due on December 1, 20X8, annual interest of 8% (assume each month represents a 30-day period).

Income from the trust will be paid out to the income beneficiary on the last day of each year. As trustee for the trust, prepare the necessary entries for the trust through the end of 20X8 assuming that the trust uses the cash basis of accounting.

PROBLEMS

Problem 20-1 *(LO 3)* **Strategies to minimize estate tax.** James and Susan Wagner have assets with fair market values of $4,200,000 and $1,800,000, respectively. James has been diagnosed with a terminal illness and is expected to pass away within the current year 20X5. James wants to minimize his estate taxes, and any appropriate planning should consider the following factors:

1. James Wagner has debts of $220,000 against the assets in his estate.
2. It is estimated that administrative and funeral expenses will be $25,000 each for James and Susan.
3. It is estimated that Susan would be able to live comfortably for the balance of her life if she had an estate of $3 million at the time of her husband's death. Susan will make charitable contributions to the extent that her estate exceeds $3 million as a result of her husband's death.
4. Assume that Susan will live for three years after the death of her husband.
5. It is anticipated that at the time of Susan's death her estate would have appreciated by $150,000 per year for years 20X5 through 20X7.
6. Neither James nor Susan has made any gifts during the current year 20X5.
7. The couple has two children and three grandchildren. One of the grandchildren is attending the University of Wisconsin and is expected to graduate in 20X7. Annual tuition costs are $10,000 per year for years 20X5 through 20X7.
8. James has agreed to make a $200,000 charitable contribution to the Sierra Club out of his estate.
9. If any trusts are created, the income from the trust will benefit the surviving spouse, and any corpus will ultimately pass to the children.

Develop an estate plan for the Wagners that would minimize estate taxes and incorporate the above factors. The unified transfer tax rates and the 2006 exclusion amounts set forth in the text should be used. Assume that annual nontaxable gifts up to $11,000 per donor will be made to all children and grandchildren to whatever extent possible. ◄◄◄◄◄ **Required**

Problem 20-2 *(LO 6)* **Recording activities for an estate and a trust.** At the time of Robert Granger's death, his estate consisted of the following assets and liabilities measured at fair market value:

Assets	
Cash	$ 50,000
Personal residence	450,000
Automobile and sailboat	65,000
Investment in mutual funds	1,280,000
Collection of antique duck decoys	85,000
Death benefit of life insurance policy	500,000
Farmland in Ozaukee County	800,000
Total assets	$3,230,000

Liabilities	
Mortgage on personal residence	$ 150,000
Insurance policy loan	50,000
Credit card balances	5,000
Total liabilities	$ 205,000

The following information is relevant to the administration of Robert's estate:

1. Robert is a single person and has two minor children from a previous marriage. After satisfying the other provisions of his will, the balance of Robert's estate is to be transferred to a trust for the benefit of his minor children. Annual trust income in the amount of $15,000 is to be transferred to the children. Upon attaining the age of 21, each child would receive corpus of $25,000. The remaining corpus of the trust and any undistributed income is to be paid out to the children when they both have attained the age of 25.
2. Title to the personal residence, subject to the mortgage, will be transferred to Robert's sister who is to serve as the guardian for his minor children.
3. The collection of antique duck decoys is to be given to Ducks Unlimited which is a qualifying charitable organization.

4. Robert's sailboat, valued at $35,000, is to be given as a charitable contribution to the Milwaukee Community Sailing Center. The automobile will be given to his nephew Roger Stevens.
5. Funeral and administrative expenses of the estate are $25,000.
6. Investments in mutual funds with an estate value of $170,000 were sold for $180,000 to provide necessary liquidity.

Subsequent to the settlement of Robert's estate, the following activity occurred in the children's trust during the first year:

1. The farmland was rented for $25,000. Property taxes and other operating expenses associated with the farmland were incurred in the amount of $8,000.
2. Mutual funds with an estate value of $120,000 were sold for $132,000. Mutual funds with an estate value of $50,000 were sold for $45,000.
3. Income on the mutual fund investments was $22,000.
4. The trustee made a payment of corpus to Robert's daughter upon her turning 21 years of age.
5. After distributing the required amount of trust income, all available cash with the exception of $5,000 of income cash was invested in mutual funds.

Required ▶ ▶ ▶ ▶ ▶ Prepare all necessary entries to record the activities of the estate and the trust. Unified transfer tax rates and the 2006 exclusion amount as set forth in the text should be used.

Problem 20-3 *(LO 7)* **Recording the activities of a trust.** Prior to his death, Gordon Mayer created a trust for the benefit of his two children, Gretta and Gary. At date of his death, all assets of the estate and related liabilities would pass to the trust. The trust contains the following provisions:

1. Fifty percent of the trust income in the year of the decedent's death and for the following calendar year will be paid to Gretta. Payments will be made at year-end.
2. Fifty percent of the trust income in the year of the decedent's death and for the next two calendar years will be held on behalf of Gary. The accumulated trust income, less applicable trust income taxes, will be disbursed to Gary in the month following the end of the final calendar year to which this provision relates.
3. On the one-month anniversary of the decedent's death, $200,000 will be conveyed to the Cedarburg Community Library. In the first month following the year of the decedent's death, 40% of the principal balance measured as of the prior year-end will be conveyed to St. Cecil's Community Hospital.
4. All costs associated with managing the trust's investments in stocks and bonds will be charged to principal.
5. All dividends and interest earned subsequent to the date of the decedent's death will be included in income.
6. Fees and expenses incurred by the trustee for administration purposes will be allocated equally between trust principal and income.
7. All capital improvements to maintain rental properties in good condition will be charged against trust principal.
8. All normal maintenance costs associated with rental properties will be charged against trust income.
9. The interest portion of mortgage payments on rental properties accruing after the date of death will be allocated equally between trust principal and income.
10. Depreciation will not be considered in determining trust income.
11. On November 1 in each of the two calendar years following the year of the decedent's death, $25,000 will be contributed to the Boy Scouts of America.
12. All taxes associated with the decedent's estate and final income are to be paid out of the trust principal.

Gordon Mayer died on September 18, 20X6, when his estate consisted of the following assets at fair value: cash, $32,000; stocks and bonds, $570,000; and rental properties, $1,234,000. The following additional events occurred subsequent to his death during 20X6:

1. Final personal income taxes in the amount of $27,000 were paid in 20X6.
2. Dividends and interest were received on investments in the amounts of $23,000 and $27,000, respectively. Of the dividends, $13,000 was declared as payable to shareholders of record as of September 15, 20X6. The interest received included $8,400 of accrued interest as of the decedent's death. The value of the dividend and accrued interest as of date of death is included in the $570,000 value of the stocks and bonds.
3. Stocks with a fair value of $320,000 at date of death were sold for $335,000.
4. A new roof and siding were installed on rental properties in the amount of $134,000. Ordinary repairs on rental properties were $25,000, of which $6,700 had been incurred prior to the decedent's death.
5. Expenses associated with managing the trust's investment in stocks and bonds totaled $9,200, and the trustee's expenses were $6,000.
6. Mortgage payments on rental property totaled $94,000, of which $45,000 represented interest. Of the interest, $8,200 represented interest that had accrued as of the date of the decedent's death.
7. Gross rents of $124,000 were received.
8. Estimated taxes of $21,434 were paid on trust income which was not distributed.

Prepare all necessary entries to record the activities of the trust subsequent to the decedent's death through the end of 20X6. ◀◀◀◀◀ **Required**

Problem 20-4 *(LO 6)* **Recording estate activities, charge and discharge statement.** Sheri Shannon died on June 1, 20X3, leaving a valid will that named her friend, Steve Chevalier, the executor of the estate.

a. Steve prepared the following inventory of assets, listing their fair values as of June 1:

Cash	$31,000
1,000 shares of Pal Corporation common stock	60,000
2,000 shares of BVD Corporation common stock	40,000
Rapid Transit Corporation (RTC) 8% bonds, interest payable April 1 and October 1, $30,000 face amount	30,300
Time-share condominium unit at Lake Tahoe, used for her two-week vacations	10,000
Sheri's one-half interest in Sheri Limo Service Company	70,000

b. On June 15, after filing the inventory of assets with the probate court, Steve discovered Sheri's gold coin collection that was appraised at $18,000.
c. On June 20, a $250 check was received from Pal Corporation for dividends declared on May 10, 20X3, to owners on record as of May 30.
d. Steve sold the time-share condominium for $14,000 on July 7.
e. The following items were paid between June 1 and July 31:

Sheri's charge card purchases	$1,900
Funeral costs	6,000
Lawyer's fee to probate the will	800
Cost to paint condominium prior to sale	1,100
Payment to executor approved by the court	1,700

f. On July 5, a $15,000 check was received for Sheri's portion of partnership earnings for the quarter ended June 30. Earnings are fairly constant from one month to the next and are available for withdrawal on a monthly basis if a partner so desires. Otherwise, payments are made quarterly.

g. Sheri's partner offered Steve $90,000 for her interest in the partnership. Steve accepted the offer and received full payment.
h. On October 1, a check for interest was received from Rapid Transit Corporation.
i. On December 1, Steve completed Sheri's final income tax return, paying the additional tax due of $18,200.

Required ▶ ▶ ▶ ▶ ▶

1. Prepare journal entries to record the events.
2. Prepare a charge and discharge statement as of December 31, 20X3.

template cd

Problem 20-5 *(LO 6)* **Charge and discharge statement.** Alex Dunn, Jr., died on January 15, 20X7; his records disclose the following estate at fair value:

Cash in bank	$ 3,750
6% note receivable, including $50 accrued interest	5,050
Stocks	50,000
Dividends declared on stocks	600
6% mortgage receivable, including $100 accrued interest	20,100
Real estate—apartment house	35,000
Household effects	8,250
Total	$122,750

Subsequent to recording the inventory of the estate, the executor discovered on July 1, 20X7, the late Alex Dunn, Sr., had created a trust fund that established his son, Alex Dunn, Jr., as life tenant and his grandson as remainderman. The assets in the fund consist solely of the outstanding capital stock of Dunn, Inc., namely, 2,000 shares of common stock. At the creation of the trust, the book value and the fair value of these shares was $400,000. At December 31, 20X7, the fair value was $500,000. On January 2, 20X7, Dunn, Inc., declared a $1.25 per share cash dividend payable February 2, 20X7 to shareholders of record on January 12, 20X7.

The executor's cash transactions from January 15 to January 31, 20X7, were as follows:

Cash receipts:

Jan. 20	Dividends declared	$ 600
25	6% notes receivable collected	5,000
	Interest accrued on note	58
	Stocks sold, inventoried at $22,500	20,900
	6% mortgage sold	20,100
	Interest accrued on mortgage	132
29	Real estate sold	30,250
	Dividends not previously declared	900
		$77,940

Cash disbursements:

Jan. 20	Funeral expenses	$ 750
23	Decedent's debts	8,000
25	Decedent's legacies	10,000
31	Distribution of income to window	500
31	Property taxes assessed January 10, 20X7	1,000
		$20,250

Required ▶ ▶ ▶ ▶ ▶

Prepare a charge and discharge statement for the executor for the period from January 15 to January 31, 20X7.

Problem 20-6 *(LO 6)* **Charge and discharge statement.** Maxwell Stevens, a single person, died on August 12, 20X8. His will indicated the following:

1. His nephew should receive any income from the estate until such time as the estate is liquidated.
2. All assets of the estate should be converted to cash in a timely manner, and the final remaining estate principal should be conveyed to Ducks Unlimited, a not-for-profit organization, with the stipulation that these funds be used for wetland preservation efforts in the state of Colorado.
3. Maxwell's attorney, Janice Edquist, is to serve as executrix of the estate.

The following events occurred regarding the estate of Maxwell Stevens:

1. Various bank accounts totaling $34,000 were consolidated for estate purposes.
2. An insurance policy with a death benefit of $300,000 was discovered subsequent to death. The policy names Maxwell Stevens's niece, Cynthia Townsend, beneficiary of the policy.
3. Stocks with a fair value of $278,000 at date of death were sold for $267,000. Dividends on the above stocks were received in the amount of $3,400, of which $1,200 represented amounts that had been declared to shareholders of record on August 1, 20X8.
4. Bonds with a fair value of $138,000 at date of death were sold for $143,000, including accrued interest. The accrued interest subsequent to the date of death was $850.
5. Real estate with a fair value of $380,000 at date of death was sold for $390,000 less broker's commission of 8% and closing fees of $750. Prior to the closing on the sale of real estate, rental income in the amount of $14,500 was received and expenses (not including interest) totaling $6,550 were paid. Rental income and expenses in the amounts of $6,250 and $3,600, respectively, were traceable to the period prior to the decedent's death.
6. A land contract note on the real estate in the amount of $97,000 was paid off upon sale of the real estate. In addition to the principal amount, accrued interest in the amount of $2,550 was also paid. Of the interest, $1,230 had accrued prior to the decedent's death.
7. The following claims against the estate existed: funeral and administrative expenses, $11,200; decedent's final personal income tax liability, $3,200; and miscellaneous personal bills, $1,300.

◄◄◄◄◄ **Required**

1. Explain why the estate was not subject to any federal estate tax.
2. Assuming that the above information describes the activities of the estate and that all provisions of the decedent's will have been carried out, prepare a charge and discharge statement.

Problem 20-7 *(LO 6)* **Recording estate principal and income.** Laurel Rose has been the executrix of her brother's estate since his death on February 1, 20X6. The following events occurred during her administration:

a. Included in the principal assets were 40, $1,000, 8% City of Pittsburgh bonds paying interest on January 1 and July 1. The bonds had a fair value of 101 on February 1, 20X6. Laurel sold the bonds at 103, plus accrued interest, on March 1, 20X6.
b. On March 1, 20X6, Laurel purchased 50, $1,000, 5% City of Detroit bonds at 98, plus accrued interest. The bonds pay interest on April 1 and October 1. The bonds mature on April 1, 20X8.
c. On March 1, 20X6, she also purchased $10,000 (face value), 7% City of Newark bonds at 102 plus accrued interest. The bonds pay interest on June 1 and December 1. The bonds mature on December 1, 20X7.
d. On April 1, 20X6, she received a check for the interest on the Detroit bonds.
e. On June 1, 20X6, she received a check for the interest on the Newark bonds.
f. On September 1, 20X6, she sold the Detroit bonds at 101, plus accrued interest.

◄◄◄◄◄ **Required**

Prepare journal entries to record each of these events. Use the straight-line method of amortization where applicable.

Problem 20-8 *(LO 6, 7)* **Recording activity of an estate and a trust.** You are given the following trial balance of the estate of Sheri Shannon as of December 31, 20X3. Her will stipulated that the executor should be granted $30,000 from principal cash. The remainder of the estate's principal assets and its income assets are to be transferred to Community Bank, which will act as trustee of an endowment fund. Income from trust assets shall be used for scholarships for accounting majors at a local university.

	Debit	Credit
Cash—Principal	115,950	
Cash—Income	5,800	
Pal Corporation Stock	60,000	
BVD Corporation Stock	40,000	
Rapid Transit Corporation Bonds	30,300	
Coin Collection	18,000	
Estate Principal		241,700
Estate Income		5,800
Assets Subsequently Discovered		28,250
Gain on Realization of Principal Assets		24,000
Funeral and Administrative Expenses	8,500	
Debts of Decedent Paid	20,100	
Expenses Chargeable against Principal	1,100	
Total	299,750	299,750

Required ▶ ▶ ▶ ▶ ▶

1. Record the payment to the executor and the transfer of all remaining assets to the trustee.
2. Prepare journal entries to close the executor's records.
3. Prepare journal entries to record receipt of assets by the trustee. Explain why it was unnecessary to accrue the interest on the Rapid Transit Corporation bonds to the date of actual transfer.

Debt Restructuring, Corporate Reorganizations, and Liquidations

CHAPTER

21

Learning Objectives

When you have completed this chapter, you should be able to

1. **Describe various ways in which debt may be restructured and how it impacts the debtor's financial records.**
2. **Explain why a company may decide to engage in a quasi-reorganization and how it impacts the company and its shareholders.**
3. **Explain various remedies available to a troubled enterprise under bankruptcy law and the steps followed in seeking a remedy.**
4. **Apply the principles of bankruptcy to the preparation of the statement of affairs.**
5. **Apply the principles of bankruptcy to the preparation of the statement of realization and liquidation.**

The principles of accounting are based on several important underlying assumptions, one of which is the going concern assumption. Since this assumption assumes that a business entity will have a long, extended life as a separate, distinct entity, valuation and classification of account balances are significantly influenced by it. For example, both the valuation of a building at depreciated historical cost, rather than net realizable value, and the classification of a building as a noncurrent asset, rather than a current asset, are in recognition of the going concern assumption. Certainly, without this assumption all assets and liabilities would be classified as current in nature.

However, over time, the going concern assumption may not hold true for all business entities. An entity may voluntarily decide to cease its business purpose. For example, a research and development (R&D) venture may cease operations at the completion of a successful or unsuccessful R&D effort. Unfortunately, a business entity also may face difficulties that cause the going concern assumption to be challenged. A business may suffer from several factors, including poor management, poor accounting controls, uncontrolled growth, loss of market share, resistance to change, government intervention, and/or a declining profit margin. Although many businesses may be able to respond to these factors in a positive manner, other businesses may become troubled or insolvent and seek corrective action. A business is considered to be insolvent if it is unable to service its liabilities, or if it technically has liabilities in excess of assets. Businesses experiencing such difficulties often are viewed as *bankrupt*, which is a state of lacking all or part of the means to service debts. This chapter focuses on several corrective actions available to a troubled or insolvent business, including troubled debt restructurings, reorganizations, and liquidations.

No business is immune from the factors that may result in financial difficulty. Large, small, young, and mature companies alike may find themselves having to cope with such difficulties. Along with the expansion of business comes the inevitable fact that some businesses may become troubled and/or fail. These difficulties are an everyday occurrence affecting both young and mature companies. Exhibit 21-1 contains excerpts related to two companies facing financial difficulties.

Exhibit 21-1
Examples of Troubled Businesses

Kmart—Tuesday, January 22, 2002

Kmart Corporation filed for bankruptcy protection today, becoming the largest retailer to seek shelter from creditors under Chapter 11. The company, known for its Bluelight Special and discount prices, has struggled in the competitive discount market against Wal-Mart and Target.

Debt rating agencies, including Standard & Poor's, have in recent weeks lowered their credit ratings for Kmart. The filing comes a day after a major food distributor, Fleming Cos., said it had cut off most shipments to Kmart because the discounter failed to make its regular weekly payment for deliveries. Fleming said Kmart, its largest customer, owes $78 million.

Source: http://creditcollectionsworld.com

Mirant (an energy company that produces and sells electricity)—January 19, 2005

Mirant today filed its proposed Plan of Reorganization and Disclosure Statement, putting into motion a process intended to allow the company to emerge from Chapter 11 protection by mid-year.

If the Disclosure Statement is found by the Court to contain adequate information, then the company will solicit votes on the Plan from those creditors, security holders, and interest holders who are entitled to vote on the Plan.

Under the Plan, Mirant's balance sheet will be materially delevered with over $5 billion of debt, and over $1 billion of other claims, being converted to equity. Current equity would be cancelled. Each holder of current equity would then receive any surplus value after creditors are paid in full, plus the right to a pro rata share of warrants issued by the new company if they vote to accept the Plan (warrants would give each holder the right to purchase new Mirant shares at a set price within a certain period of time).

Source: http://mirant.com

The accounting profession is involved with troubled businesses in a variety of ways. Providing consulting services and sound financial planning and reporting, accountants may be of invaluable service in thwarting or managing the forces leading to financial difficulty. Accountants also provide an important discovery and reporting function for those businesses seeking relief from their financial difficulties.

1
OBJECTIVE

Describe various ways in which debt may be restructured and how it impacts the debtor's financial records.

RELIEF PROCEDURES NOT REQUIRING COURT ACTION

When a business becomes insolvent or is not able to service its debts on a timely basis, there are several remedies available that do not require court approval. Since several of these remedies are discussed in intermediate textbooks, they will only be highlighted in this section. Seeking relief to financial problems outside of bankruptcy court offers several advantages. The time required to implement relief procedures is significantly less than the time required to seek relief through bankruptcy proceedings. Not requiring court action also allows the debtor's financial problems to be less public and more discreet. Knowledge of a company's financial troubles can adversely affect its ability to generate new business and acquire goods and services from vendors.

Troubled Debt Restructurings

A basic approach to resolving an inability to service debt is to seek some concessions or compromises from major creditors. A *troubled debt restructuring* is a process whereby creditors grant concessions to the debtor that they would not consider otherwise. However, both the debtor and creditor are faced with a difficult situation, and a restructuring offers the creditor the best opportunity to recover the debt, as compared to nonrestructuring alternatives.

In a debt restructuring, it is not uncommon for the debtor to recognize a gain on the restructuring activity. Companies often engage in debt restructurings as part of their routine capital risk management and therefore such restructurings are not unusual and/or nonrecurring. Therefore, restructuring gains would not normally be recognized as an extraordinary item unless the criteria for recognition, unusual and nonrecurring in nature, as an extraordinary item are met.[1]

Although not all debt restructurings qualify as troubled debt restructurings, those that do generally take several forms. Troubled debt restructurings are discussed in FASB No. 15. The most common forms of restructuring, along with the appropriate debtor accounting, are summarized as follows:

Transfer of Assets in Full Settlement:

- Form: The debtor transfers assets, such as third-party receivables, real estate, and other assets, to the creditors in order to satisfy the debt either totally or partially.
- Accounting by Debtor: The debtor records a gain on restructuring measured by the excess of the carrying basis of the debt, including related accrued interest, premiums, etc., and the fair value of the transferred assets. The difference between the book value of assets transferred to the debtor and their fair value results in a gain or loss, which is not part of the gain on restructuring.
- Example: Assets with a book value of $100,000 and a fair value of $120,000 are transferred to a creditor in full settlement of a loan of $130,000 plus accrued interest of $2,000.

Loan Payable	130,000	
Accrued Interest Payable	2,000	
Gain on Assets		20,000
Assets		100,000
Gain on Restructuring		12,000

Granting an Equity Interest:

- Form: Excluding existing terms for converting debt into equity (e.g., convertible debt), an equity interest in the company is granted to the creditor in order to satisfy the debt either totally or partially.
- Accounting by Debtor: The debtor records a gain on restructuring measured by the excess of the carrying basis of the debt and the fair value of the equity interest.
- Example: Preferred stock with a par value of $20,000 and a fair value of $120,000 is granted to a creditor in full settlement of a loan of $130,000 plus accrued interest of $2,000.

Loan Payable	130,000	
Accrued Interest Payable	2,000	
Preferred Stock, at Par		20,000
Paid-In Capital in Excess of Par		100,000
Gain on Restructuring		12,000

Modification of Terms:

- Form: The terms of the debt are modified in several possible ways involving interest and/or principal. Interest rates may be reduced and/or accrued interest may be reduced. The principal amount of the debt may be reduced and/or the maturity date of the loan may be extended.
- Accounting by Debtor: If the total future cash payments (both principal and interest) specified by the restructuring are less than the carrying basis of the debt, a gain on

1 FASB Statement No. 145, *Rescission of FASB Statement Nos. 4, 44, and 64, Amendment of FASB Statement No. 13, and Technical Corrections* (Norwalk, CT Financial Accounting Standards Board, 2002).

restructuring is recognized. After recognizing the gain, all subsequent cash payments made per the terms of the restructuring should be accounted for as a reduction of the debt payable. Therefore, no interest expense shall be recognized on the restructured debt. If the total future cash payments (both principal and interest) specified by the restructuring are more than the carrying basis of the debt, no gain on restructuring is recognized. However, interest expense is recognized between restructuring and maturity. The interest recognized should be based on an effective interest rate that equates the present value of restructured future cash payments to the carrying value of the debt.

- Example A: The terms of an outstanding debt of $130,000 plus accrued interest of $2,000 have been modified as follows: payments of $60,000 per year will be made over the next two years in full satisfaction of the debt.

Loan Payable	130,000	
Accrued Interest Payable	2,000	
Restructured Loan Payable		120,000
Gain on Restructuring		12,000
Restructured Loan Payable	60,000	
Cash		60,000
Restructured Loan Payable	60,000	
Cash		60,000

- Example B: Same situation as Example A except that the payments are $76,057 each year, which results in an effective interest rate of 10%.

Loan Payable	130,000	
Accrued Interest Payable	2,000	
Restructured Loan Payable		132,000
Restructured Loan Payable	62,857	
Interest Expense (10% × $132,000)	13,200	
Cash		76,057
Restructured Loan Payable	69,143	
Interest Expense (10% × $69,143)	6,914	
Cash		76,057

Combination Restructurings:

- Form: A restructuring may involve some combination of the above restructuring features.
- Accounting by Debtor: The accounting for a combination restructuring is the same as discussed above except that first, the carrying basis of the debt should be reduced by the fair market value of assets transferred and/or equity interests granted. This step does not result in the recognition of a gain on restructuring. Second, the remaining carrying basis of the debt is compared against the "modification of terms" portion of the restructuring and accounted for accordingly.
- Example: Land with a fair value of $52,000 and a cost basis of $45,000 is transferred to a creditor in partial settlement of a debt of $130,000 plus accrued interest of $2,000. The balance of the debt is satisfied by the payment of $35,000 per year for each of the next two years.

Loan Payable	130,000	
Accrued Interest Payable	2,000	
Gain on Transfer of Land		7,000
Land		45,000
Gain on Restructuring		10,000
Restructured Debt		70,000

Restructured Debt.	35,000	
Cash		35,000
Restructured Debt.	35,000	
Cash		35,000

As seen from the previous examples, a troubled debt restructuring may be accomplished in a variety of ways. Regardless of the method used, a formal agreement must be reached between the debtor and individual creditors. Generally, such agreements take the form of a creditor agreement or a composition agreement. A creditor agreement is used to extend the terms of a debt or make other concessions regarding future interest rates. A composition agreement is used to scale down a creditor's claims against the debtor. For example, creditors might agree to accept $0.70 per dollar of debt owed to them.

Although the above discussion of troubled debt restructuring has focused on the necessary accounting by the debtor, FASB No. 114, as amended by FASB No. 118, discusses the necessary accounting by the creditor. A creditor in a troubled debt restructuring, involving only a modification of terms of a receivable, should measure the loan receivable based on the present value of the expected future cash flows discounted at the loan's effective interest rate. As a practical matter, the creditor may measure the loan receivable at the loan's observable market price or the fair value of the collateral, assuming the loan is collateral dependent. If the measure of the impaired loan receivable is less than the recorded investment in the loan, the difference is charged to bad-debt expense and a valuation allowance is established.[2]

Quasi-Reorganizations

2

OBJECTIVE

Explain why a company may decide to engage in a quasi-reorganization and how it impacts the company and its shareholders.

A corporation may not be insolvent and yet may have accumulated a relatively large deficit as a result of such problems as an excessive investment in plant assets or inventory, or management's inability to recognize and influence market demands. If management is replaced and if profits result from new policies, most state laws still will not permit declaration of dividends until the deficit is eliminated. The turnabout period and deficit elimination may take so long that the investors' interest in the company vanishes, and capital acquisition becomes difficult. To overcome such a handicap, the corporation might seek a *quasi-reorganization*.

Quasi-reorganization does not require court action, nor does it require the consent of creditors since creditor interests are not altered. However, the procedure is described in state laws, many of which require a quasi-reorganization to be approved by two-thirds of the stockholders. The accounting literature is not specific regarding the conditions under which a quasi-reorganization can occur. However, it was most frequently viewed as an approach which would allow for net assets to be reduced to lower fair values and a deficit in retained earnings to be eliminated. The Securities and Exchange Commission has set forth specific criteria which must be satisfied before a quasi-reorganization is accepted. Furthermore, SEC Staff Accounting Bulletin (SAB) No. 78 does not allow registrants to use this procedure just to eliminate a deficit in retained earnings. Net assets must also be restated, and the net result must be a write-down in value versus a write-up.

The primary purpose of a quasi-reorganization is to eliminate a large deficit and take such action as will permit successful operations in the future. Excessive plant capacity and equipment may be sold, and remaining assets and liabilities will be revalued to reflect their fair values. For example, long-lived assets will be written down to reflect an impairment in their value.[3] Such revaluations most often increase the deficit in retained earnings. The deficit remaining after these revaluations must be reduced to zero.

It should be noted that the write-down of the assets increases the deficit, which then will be eliminated by subsequent changes in the capital structure.

The deficit is eliminated by charges against the existing paid-in capital in excess of par or stated values. If no such paid-in capital exists, it may be created by altering the capital structure

2 FASB Statement No.114, *Accounting by Creditors for Impairment of a Loan* (Norwalk, CT: Financial Accounting Standards Board, 1993).

3 FASB Statement No. 121, *Accounting for the Impairment of Long-Lived Assets and for Long-Lived Assets to Be Disposed Of* (Norwalk, CT: Financial Accounting Standards Board, 1995).

and substituting stock with lower par value or lower stated value for existing shares. To illustrate the manner in which the owners' equity section in the balance sheet is revised by a quasi-reorganization, assume the following stockholders' equity:

Common stock ($10 par, 12,000 shares outstanding)	$120,000
Retained earnings (deficit)	(45,000)
Total stockholders' equity	$ 75,000

On March 1, 20X0, the stockholders approve a reduction in par value to $1. Note that such a maneuver has absolutely no effect on the proportionate interests of each stockholder.

The entries to record the quasi-reorganization are as follows:

Common Stock ($10 par)	120,000	
Common Stock ($1 par)		12,000
Paid-In Capital from Reduction in Stock Par Value (or Reorganization Capital)		108,000
To record the reduction in par value.		
Paid-In Capital from Reduction in Stock Par Value	45,000	
Retained Earnings		45,000
To eliminate the deficit.		

Immediately following the quasi-reorganization, the owners' equity section would show the following:

Common stock ($1 par, 12,000 shares outstanding)	$12,000
Paid-in capital from reduction in stock par value	63,000
Retained earnings (subsequent to March 1, 20X0)	0
Total stockholders' equity	$75,000

In future financial statements, retained earnings must be dated to indicate the starting point of new accumulations. The process of dating retained earnings should be continued for as long a period of time as is deemed advisable, but rarely does it exceed 10 years.

Corporate Liquidations

A corporation may decide to liquidate its assets, distribute available amounts to creditors, and terminate the business. Such a liquidation may be accomplished without a formal bankruptcy proceeding through the use of a general assignment for the benefit of creditors, which generally must be agreed to by all creditors. Shareholders of the corporation receive any net assets remaining after fully satisfying the claims of creditors. Usually, assets are not adequate to fully satisfy creditor claims. In this case, creditors share according to the terms of the general assignment.

REFLECTION

- Troubled debt may be restructured in a number of ways, including forgiveness of debt, transfer of assets, granting an equity interest, and/or a modification of terms.
- If a company has a deficit in retained earnings and yet has opportunities for future profits, the deficit may prevent the timely distribution of such profits in the form of dividends. A quasi-reorganization is designed to eliminate the deficit in retained earnings and provide the company with a fresh start.

BANKRUPTCY REFORM ACT OF 1978 AND THE BANKRUPTCY CODE AMENDMENTS

3

OBJECTIVE

Explain various remedies available to a troubled enterprise under bankruptcy law and the steps followed in seeking a remedy.

If a satisfactory solution cannot be reached under the procedures described in the previous paragraphs, the legal proceedings for bankruptcy may be initiated. Modern bankruptcy procedures attempt to give a debtor a fresh start, unburdened by former obligations, while simultaneously accomplishing an equitable distribution of the debtor's property among creditors.

In an attempt to modernize an antiquated system existing under the Bankruptcy Act of 1898, as amended by the Chandler Act of 1938, Congress passed the *Bankruptcy Reform Act of 1978* (Title 11 of the U.S. Code), which became effective on October 1, 1979. In 1982, the U.S. Supreme Court ruled that the section of the Bankruptcy Reform Act of 1978 (hereafter referred to as the Act) giving bankruptcy judges the power to consider and rule on issues that were not directly part of the bankruptcy proceedings was unconstitutional. Under the Act, bankruptcy judges had the power to consider any issue arising in or related to bankruptcy cases. Thus, if a company had filed in bankruptcy court and another company had a damage suit against it, the damage claim could have been heard in bankruptcy court instead of in a federal district or state court. Under the Supreme Court's decision, bankruptcy judges now must limit their rulings to issues directly related to bankruptcy proceedings. In June 1984, Congress passed a bill to overhaul the bankruptcy system. The bill limited the powers of bankruptcy judges to comply with the 1982 Supreme Court decision and created 85 new federal trial and appellate judgeships to assist with cases that spill out of bankruptcy courts. The Bankruptcy Act was amended in 1988, 1990, and, most recently, in 1994.

A bankruptcy case may be filed under one of the following operative chapters of the code:

Chapter 7: Liquidation. A nonbusiness debtor or any business not wishing to remain in operation, except a railroad, governmental unit, bank, insurance company, or savings and loan association, may file a petition under this chapter.

Chapter 9: Adjustments of Debts of a Municipality. This chapter is not covered in this text.

Chapter 11: Reorganization. The purpose of Chapter 11 is to allow a company (or individual) to pay a portion of its debts, discharge remaining debts, and continue in business. This chapter is used primarily by corporate or partnership debtors. Although the chapter may be used by an individual proprietor, the procedures are more cumbersome and more expensive than those of Chapter 13. Only individuals with substantial assets and liabilities resort to Chapter 11 proceedings.

Chapter 13: Adjustment of Debts of an Individual with Regular Income. This chapter is limited exclusively to individuals, including sole proprietors, with less than $250,000 in unsecured debt and less than $750,000 in secured debt. A joint case of debtor and spouse is permissible if their combined debt does not exceed the two limitations.

There are provisions for the movement or conversion of a case from one chapter to another, such as converting an unsuccessful reorganization (Chapter 11) to a liquidation (Chapter 7). Chapters 9 and 13 of the code will not be specifically discussed in this text.

Commencement of a Bankruptcy Case

The Act states that a debtor either must be a person (individual, partnership, or corporation) residing in or having a domicile, business, or property in the United States, or must be a municipality. If a debtor initiates the action of filing a petition with the court of bankruptcy under the appropriate chapter of the Act, it is a *voluntary* case. A voluntary petition may seek relief under Chapters 7, 9, 11, or 13. Filing constitutes an *order for relief,* which represents a stay of action by prohibiting commencement or continuation of legal action against the debtor to recover a claim.

If the petition is filed by someone other than the debtor, an *involuntary* proceeding results. Such proceedings may be filed under *Chapter 7 (Liquidation)* or *Chapter 11 (Reorganization)*, but not under *Chapter 13*, where the individual debtor is willing to make payments to creditors. Certain small businesses are allowed to use streamlined ("fast track") procedures in order to facilitate a solution to bankruptcy issues. Involuntary proceedings may not be initiated against a farmer or a charitable organization. Under Chapters 7 and 11, if a debtor has 12 or more creditors, three or more of them may file an involuntary petition, providing the total of their noncontingent, unsecured claims is $10,000 or more. If there are less than 12 creditors, one or more of them may initiate an involuntary case, but the same limit of $10,000 applies. In an involuntary case, the claims must have arisen before the order for relief was issued. The court will issue such an order if the debtor files no answer to the involuntary petition. If an answer is filed by the debtor, the court will hold a hearing, following which it will either dismiss the case, issue an order for relief, or postpone the decision pending receipt of additional information.

Corporate Reorganizations—Chapter 11

The ultimate goal of a reorganization is to restructure the debt and/or equity of a company so that the company may continue to carry on its business purpose and become a financially sound business. Unfortunately, the vast majority of reorganizations never achieve this goal. Such a reorganization often is more attractive than a debt restructuring not involving a bankruptcy proceeding because the reorganization may be more generous toward the debtor company. Generally, a reorganization reduces debt through forgiveness to a greater extent than a conventional debt restructuring. Furthermore, interest on unsecured debt is not accrued during the period of reorganization. The period of reorganization provides a company with an opportunity to delay creditors from bringing suit for delinquent debts as well as to seek protection from a variety of business risks, which may affect a company's ability to continue as a going concern. Companies have used Chapter 11 procedures to gain court protection for a broad spectrum of purposes.

Recent events have strengthened the position of those who are critical of the manner in which Chapter 11 has been manipulated. It was designed to assist those in difficulty under the conventional interpretation of indebtedness. On the docket of bankruptcy courts have been companies who have filed in order to protect themselves from mass tort litigations (Manville, with its asbestos products, and A.H. Robins Inc., with its Dalkon Shield contraceptive device), to ward off enforcement of huge judgments (Texaco), or to escape funding of pension plans (LTV Corporation). It is doubtful that Congress intended bankruptcy laws to be an umbrella of corporate protection with such serious public consequences.

Developing a Plan of Reorganization

A petition seeking a corporate reorganization may be filed voluntarily or involuntarily to seek an order for relief. Normally, the debtor remains in charge of the business, although in unusual instances, a trustee (receiver) may be appointed to take control of the company. Those unusual instances include management fraud, deceit, and/or gross mismanagement.

After the filing of the petition, the law provides that the debtor shall not be harassed by creditors or stockholders so that the debtor can devote full energy to the reorganization. For the first 120 days, the debtor has the exclusive right to file a plan of reorganization. Thereafter, a plan may be filed by any party of interest. The court appoints a committee of the creditors holding the seven largest claims against the debtor. A committee of equity security holders also may be appointed. Their primary functions are to consult with the debtor in possession (or the trustee) about the administration of the case and to assist in the formulation of a plan of reorganization.

The plan of reorganization must detail the methods and means by which it will achieve its objectives. Possible arrangements will involve eliminating some debt, reducing debt principal and/or interest, reducing interest rates, postponing payment, and exchanging an equity interest for creditor claims or exchanging a lower ranking for a higher equity interest, such as substitution of common stock for preferred stock. The plan identifies the various classes of claims (secured versus unsecured) and classes of interests (stockholders or limited partners). It indicates the claims of interests (stockholders or limited partners). It indicates the claims or interests that are not impaired, as well as the treatment to be accorded those that are impaired. A class is impaired if the plan alters its legal or contractual rights.

If a class is not impaired, it is considered to have accepted the plan. The holder of a claim or interest impaired by the plan may accept or reject it. Parties impaired are provided a description of the reorganizational plan along with a court-approved disclosure statement regarding the plan. After evaluating the plan, the affected parties must vote to approve or reject it. A plan affecting impaired creditors is approved if it is accepted by creditors representing at least two-thirds in amount and more than one-half in number of a class of claims. A plan affecting shareholders or equity interests is approved if it is accepted by holders of such interests representing at least two-thirds in amount of the allowed claims of that class.

Upon approval by the impaired parties, confirmation by the bankruptcy court is sought. Before confirmation, the court verifies that under the plan each holder of a claim or interest will receive or retain property of a value that is not less than the amount such holder would receive under a Chapter 7 liquidation. In certain instances, courts have the authority to approve the plan even though the creditors have not approved it (the cram-down provision).

Once a plan is confirmed by the court, its provisions are binding on the debtor, known as a "debtor in possession," and on all creditors and equity security holders, whether or not they accepted the plan. Confirmation vests property in the debtor company or trustee. Such property is free of all claims of creditors and interests of equity holders, except as stipulated in the provisions of the plan. Under Chapter 11, once a plan is confirmed, the payment obligation on the debtor is fixed, regardless of any subsequent increase in the debtor's net cash inflow. If the reorganization is not accomplishing its intended objectives during the period outlined in the plan, a request for modification may be submitted to the court for approval, or a request may be filed to convert to a Chapter 7 liquidation.

Accounting for the Reorganization

The accounting professional is involved significantly in providing expertise regarding corporate reorganizations. Accountants may help in the discovery of assets and liabilities or in the determination of the impact of a reorganization. Prospective information also must be generated in order to determine the effect of a reorganization plan on future operations of the company. A plan of reorganization includes debt and/or equity restructuring similar to that discussed in the earlier section of this text involving troubled debt restructurings and quasi-reorganizations.

With respect to the restructuring of debt in a bankruptcy reorganization, the principles set forth in FASB Statement No. 15 generally do not apply to a bankruptcy reorganization; therefore, a different approach is used to measure the gain or loss on restructuring involving a modification of terms. In a bankruptcy reorganization, the gain on restructuring is measured as the difference between the fair value of the restructured consideration received (its discounted present value) and the carrying basis of the debt being restructured. In FASB Statement No. 15, the gain on restructuring is measured as the difference between the total future cash payments (both principal and interest) to be received and the carrying basis of the debt being restructured. The gain on restructuring in a bankruptcy reorganization is typically recorded as either an item of income or additional paid-in capital. Recognizing the gain as a component of paid-in capital facilitates the reduction of a deficit balance in retained earnings, if appropriate as part of the reorganization plan.

The recognition of subsequent interest on the restructured debt also differs for a bankruptcy reorganization. In this case, the total interest recognized on the restructured debt is imputed at market rates and represents the difference between the fair value of the new debt (its discounted present value using market rates) and the total of all principal and interest payments. An FASB Statement No. 15 restructuring measures the total interest as the difference between the carrying basis of the debt being restructured and the total of all principal and interest payments. Therefore, under Statement No. 15, no interest is recognized if the total of all principal and interest payments made under the restructuring agreement do not exceed the carrying basis of the original debt being restructured. Other than the above differences, the accounting principles and standards for reorganizations are applicable to both bankruptcy and nonbankruptcy reorganizations.

Companies undergoing corporate reorganizations also are required to submit to the bankruptcy court periodic reports detailing operations, cash flows, and other information that the court may request. The preparation of these statements and reports presents no unusual accounting problems. Balance sheets may distinguish between assets and liabilities existing prior to and subsequent to the approval of the reorganization or appointment of a trustee, if applicable. Generally, the books of record used to account for the company prior to reorganization also are employed during the reorganization. However, if a trustee is appointed, the trustee may elect to establish a new set of books.

If new accounting records are to be established, the assets accepted by the fiduciary are debited at their book values, with a credit to an account called X Corporation in Trusteeship. On the corporate books, the transfer of assets is recorded by debiting an account to charge the fiduciary, such as E. Schenker, Trustee. These new accounts are reciprocal and represent the accountability of the trustee.

The fiduciary is not responsible for commitments made by the corporation prior to the period of stewardship. Therefore, those liabilities remain on the corporate books. However, the courts may direct payment of such liabilities. In this case, the trustee either may directly debit X Corporation in Trusteeship or create a temporary account, such as Accounts Payable—X Corporation, which periodically is closed into the major reciprocal account. The corporation would reflect payment with a debit to Accounts Payable and a credit to the account E. Schenker, Trustee.

The usual accounting procedures are followed by the trustee to record revenues and expenses. At the end of the year or at termination of the period of stewardship, the profit or loss on the trustee's books is closed into the accountability account, X Corporation in Trusteeship. On the corporate books, net income is recorded with a debit to the trustee account and a credit to Retained Earnings, while a net loss is recorded by the reverse procedure. When control is returned to the owners, the trustee eliminates all account balances, including the X Corporation in Trusteeship balance. The corporation records these accounts and eliminates the trustee account.

While the trustee is in control, the corporation's financial story is contained partly in the records of the trustee and partly in those of the corporation. The two records must be combined in order to prepare financial statements. The following skeleton worksheet is designed to accomplish the objective of reuniting the two sets of financial information:

X Corporation in Trusteeship
E. Schenker, Trustee
Worksheet for Combined Trial Balance
For Year Ended June 30, 20X1

Account Title	Trial Balance		Adjustments and Eliminations		Combined Trial Balance
	Trustee	Corporation			
Debits:					
E. Schenker, Trustee		90,000		(a) 90,000	
Total Debits	500,000	420,000			
Credits:					
X. Corp. in Trusteeship	90,000		(a) 90,000		
Total Credits	500,000	420,000			

The worksheet begins with the trial balances of the trustee's records and the corporation's records. These trial balances should be adjusted fully before they are entered on the worksheet. Any additional adjustments discovered subsequently are entered, and the two reciprocal account balances are eliminated. The items then are combined to produce a trial balance from which financial statements may be prepared.

Corporate Liquidations—Chapter 7

The only solution for certain insolvent companies is to liquidate the assets of the company, service its debts, distribute any remaining funds to shareholders, and terminate the business. Unfortunately, corporate reorganizations frequently are not successful and ultimately result in liquidation. Commencement of a plan to liquidate may be voluntary or involuntary. Approval of the plan is subject to the same requirements as a reorganization.

The commencement of a voluntary or involuntary case under Chapter 7 (Liquidation) creates an estate that consists of the assets of the debtor, who must file an inventory of property and debts/claims identified on the following schedules:

- Real Property—at fair value
- Personal Property—at fair value
- Property Claimed as Exempt—at fair value (the nature of exemptions varies from state to state)
- Property Not Otherwise Scheduled—at fair value
- Creditors Holding Secured Claims—amount of claim and fair value of security
- Creditors Holding Unsecured Priority Claims—amount of claim
- Creditors Holding Unsecured Nonpriority Claims—amount of claim

Appointment of a Trustee in Liquidation

As soon as possible after issuing the order for relief, the court appoints an interim trustee to take charge until a permanent trustee is selected, and then a meeting of creditors is called. Creditors either may elect a permanent trustee or have the interim trustee serve in that capacity. Proofs of claim are examined by the trustee, who may accept them or, if they are improper, disallow them. To be considered in the settlement, a claim normally must be filed within 90 days after the date set for the first meeting of creditors.

The debtor is required to be present at the meeting of creditors in order to be subject to examination by the creditors or the trustee and must cooperate with the trustee in the preparation of an inventory of property, the examination of proofs of claim, and the general administration of the estate. To assist the trustee, a debtor files a *statement of affairs*, consisting of answers to a series of stated questions about the identity of the debtor's records and books, transactions, and events affecting the financial condition of the debtor, including any prior bankruptcy proceedings. This legal statement of affairs is not to be confused with the accounting statement of affairs discussed later in the chapter.

Duties of Trustee. The trustee shall:

1. Collect and reduce to money the nonexempt property of the estate.
2. Account for all money and property received, maintaining a record of cash receipts and disbursements.
3. Investigate the financial affairs of the debtor, including a review of the forms filed by the debtor.
4. Examine proofs of claim and disallow any improper claim.
5. Furnish information reasonably requested by a party of interest.
6. Operate the business of the debtor, if any, when so authorized by the court if such operation is in the best interest of the estate and consistent with its orderly liquidation.
7. Pay dividends to creditors as promptly as practicable, with regard for priorities. (The law applies the term "dividend" to any payment made to a creditor.)
8. File reports of progress, with the final report accompanied by a detailed statement of receipts and disbursements.

Disposition of Property. One duty of the trustee is to dispose of property, even if another entity has an allowed claim secured by a lien on the property. The claim is secured to the amount of the value of the property. For example, if a creditor has an allowed claim of $20,000, with a sole lien against real property whose fair value is $30,000, the claim is fully secured. Upon realization of the property, the excess of $10,000 would be available to meet unsecured claims in the order of priority. If the creditor in the example has an allowed claim of $35,000, there is a secured claim of $30,000 and an unsecured claim of $5,000.

Priorities for Unsecured Claims. An order of priority to receive distributions from amounts available to meet unsecured claims has been established by the Act. Each class must be paid in full or provided for before any amount is paid to the next lower class. When the amount is inadequate to pay all claims of a given class, the amount is distributed on a pro rata basis within that class. When the amount is sufficient to pay the claims of all classes, which is highly unlikely, the excess amount is returned to the debtor. The order of priority for allowed unsecured claims is as follows:

Class 1—Expenses to administer the estate. Those who administer the estate should be assured of payment; otherwise, competent attorneys and accountants would not be willing to participate.

Class 2—Debts incurred after the commencement of a case of involuntary bankruptcy but before the order for relief or appointment of a trustee. These items, referred to as "gap" creditors, are granted priority in order to permit the business to carry on its operations during the period of legal proceedings.

Class 3—Wages (salaries or commissions) up to $4,000 per individual, earned within 90 days before the filing of the petition or the cessation of the debtor's business, whichever occurs first.

Class 4—Unpaid contributions to employee benefit plans, arising from services performed up to 180 days prior to filing the petition, to the extent of $4,000 per employee covered by the plan.

Class 5—Deposits up to $1,800 each for goods or services never received from the debtor.

Class 6—Tax claims of a governmental unit. These taxes are nondischargeable (i.e., they still must be met by the debtor after the termination of the case).

Class 7—Claims of general creditors not granted priority. All remaining unsecured claims fall into this category.

For a successful case under Chapter 11 (Reorganization) or Chapter 13 (Individual), the sequence of priority also has significance. In a Chapter 11 case, the plan of reorganization will not be confirmed unless the court has determined that creditors will receive at least as much as they would under Chapter 7. The same idea is used for Chapter 13 cases, for which the Code states that the court will approve the plan only if the value of the property to be distributed on account of each allowed unsecured claim is not less than the amount that would be paid under Chapter 7.

It is important to note that although the goal of a liquidation is to discharge the debts, certain debts are not dischargeable. For example, certain taxes, fines, and/or penalties are nondischargeable.

REFLECTION

- Bankruptcy law provides for various remedies: liquidation and reorganization are the most frequently used solutions. A company must carry out, voluntarily or involuntarily, a number of steps when seeking a remedy. The claims of various parties must be identified and prioritized.

PREPARATION OF THE STATEMENT OF AFFAIRS

4

OBJECTIVE

Apply the principles of bankruptcy to the preparation of the statement of affairs.

Earlier in this chapter, a reference was made to the legal statement of affairs, which consists of responses to questions regarding a debtor's financial condition. The other report with the same name is the accounting statement of affairs, which is discussed in this section of the chapter. The primary purpose of the *accounting statement of affairs* is to approximate the estimated amounts available to each class of claims. It thereby assists all concerned parties in reaching a decision as to what insolvency action is preferable. It is a balance sheet of a potentially liquidating concern rather than of a going concern. Thus, it shifts the emphasis for assets from historical cost to estimated realizable values and the allocation of proceeds to creditors and stockholders. It is important to note that the statement of affairs is based on estimated values available to creditors, and the actual values realized from the liquidation of assets may differ. Although the statement assumes a liquidation of the insolvent company, the statement also is used to evaluate the reasonableness of a corporate reorganization. Plans for a corporate reorganization will not be confirmed by the court unless creditors will receive at least as much as they would under a liquidation.

In the past, the preparation and the format of the statement of affairs have been cumbersome and confusing. Thus, a revised form is recommended in which the statement of affairs is split into two sections, one dealing with the assets and the other with the liabilities and the owners' equity. Before the statement of affairs is prepared, however, the account balances should be adjusted fully, an income statement should be prepared, and owners' equity should be adjusted to include the net profit or net loss to date.

The asset portion of the statement of affairs identifies the assets of the liquidating entity and their book value, estimated net realizable value, and estimated gain or loss upon liquidation. Available assets are identified as follows:

1. Assets pledged with fully secured creditors.
2. Assets pledged with partially secured creditors.
3. Free assets available to unsecured creditors.

For each asset, the net realizable value must be estimated, using whatever information is available. For example, receivables would exclude unrealizable amounts; marketable securities would be based on current market reports; and real estate would reflect current market appraisals. Some assets, such as goodwill, may have no realizable value. For each asset, the difference between realizable value and book value is entered as a gain or loss upon liquidation. The assets available to unsecured creditors also are identified on the asset section of the statement of affairs.

The liability and owners' equity section on the statement of affairs identifies the following components:

1. Fully secured creditors.
2. Partially secured creditors.
3. Unsecured creditors with priority (Class 1 through 6 creditors).
4. Unsecured creditors without priority (Class 7 creditors).
5. Owners' equity deficiency or surplus.

In order to illustrate the statement of affairs, assume Insolve Corporation's adjusted balance sheet as of February 28, 20X2, is as appears in Illustration 21-1 on page 1152.

Prior to liquidation, management has decided to complete the work in process by incurring \$12,000 of additional labor costs and \$4,000 of additional overhead. It is expected that, upon completion, the additional finished goods can be sold for \$94,000. The mortgage payable is secured by the land and building, and the bank loan is secured by the equipment. Accounts payable totaling \$180,000 are secured by inventory with a book value of \$180,000 and an estimated net realizable value of \$160,000.

Illustration 21-1

Insolve Corporation
Balance Sheet
February 28, 20X2

Assets			
Current assets:			
Cash		$ 4,000	
Accounts receivable	$ 84,000		
Less allowance for uncollectible accounts	(14,000)	70,000	
Marketable securities		20,000	
Inventories:			
Raw materials	$ 35,000		
Work in process	63,000		
Finished goods	124,000	222,000	$316,000
Property, plant, and equipment:			
Land		$ 110,000	
Building		340,000	
Less accumulated depreciation—building		(158,000)	
Equipment		290,000	
Less accumulated depreciation—equipment		(140,000)	442,000
Goodwill (net of amortization)			48,000
Total assets			$806,000
Liabilities and Owners' Equity			
Current liabilities:			
Accounts payable		$240,000	
Accrued liabilities—other		12,000	
Accrued income taxes		6,000	
Accrued mortgage interest		24,000	
Accrued liquidation expenses		13,000	
Accrued payroll taxes		14,000	
Accrued payroll (not exceeding $4,000 per person)		33,000	$342,000
Long-term liabilities:			
Mortgage payable		$280,000	
Bank loan payable		200,000	480,000
Total liabilities			$822,000
Owners' equity:			
Common stock		$ 10,000	
Paid-in capital in excess of par		40,000	
Deficit		(66,000)	(16,000)
Total liabilities and owners' equity			$806,000

The statement of affairs for Insolve Corporation is based on assumed net realizable amounts and appears as Illustration 21-2.

Illustration 21-2

Insolve Corporation
Statement of Affairs
February 28, 20X2

Book Value	Assets	Estimated Net Realizable Value	Estimated Amount Available for Unsecured Creditors	Estimated Gain or (Loss) on Liquidation
	Assets pledged with fully secured creditors:			
$110,000	Land	$130,000		$ 20,000
182,000	Building (net)	210,000		28,000
	Total	$340,000	$ 36,000	
	Assets pledged with partially secured creditors:			
150,000	Equipment (net)	$118,000		(32,000)
	Inventory			
35,000	Raw materials	18,000		(17,000)
63,000	Work in process (less estimated completion costs of $16,000)	78,000		15,000
124,000	Finished goods	112,000		(12,000)
	Total	$326,000	48,000	
	Free assets:			
4,000	Cash	$ 4,000	4,000	
70,000	Accounts receivable (net)	70,000	70,000	
20,000	Marketable securities	14,000	14,000	(6,000)
48,000	Goodwill			(48,000)
	Estimated amount available for unsecured creditors with and without priority		$172,000	
	Less unsecured creditors with priority		(66,000)	
	Estimated amounts for unsecured creditors without priority:			
	Net realizable amount available		$106,000	
	Deficiency (to agree with total unsecured amount without priority)		68,000	
$806,000	Totals	$754,000	$174,000	$(52,000)

(continued)

There are several important things to note about the mechanics of the statement of affairs. First, the two major sections of the statement (Assets and Liabilities and Owners' Equity) should be completed in conjunction with each other. For example, when identifying assets pledged with partially secured creditors, the secured and unsecured amounts of liabilities to such creditors should be identified. Second, the statement is constructed to provide crossfootings as a check on the mathematical accuracy and completeness of the schedule. For example, in the asset section the book value of the assets should equal the assets' estimated net realizable value plus (minus) the estimated loss (gain) on liquidation ($806,000 = $754,000 + $52,000). In the liabilities and owners' equity section, the book value total before the owners' deficiency should equal the total of estimated secured and unsecured liabilities ($822,000 = $582,000 + $66,000 + $174,000). Finally, the deficiency traceable to unsecured creditors without priority

Illustration 21-2 *(continued)*

Insolve Corporation
Statement of Affairs
February 28, 20X2

Book Value	Liabilities and Owners' Equity	Estimated Secured Amount	Estimated Unsecured Amount: With Priority	Estimated Unsecured Amount: Without Priority
	Fully secured creditors:			
$ 24,000	Accrued mortgage interest	$ 24,000		
280,000	Mortgage payable	280,000		
	Total	$304,000		
	Partially secured creditors:			
200,000	Bank loan payable	$118,000		$ 82,000
180,000	Accounts payable	160,000		20,000
	Total	$278,000		
	Unsecured creditors with priority:			
6,000	Accrued income taxes		$ 6,000	
13,000	Accrued liquidation expenses		13,000	
14,000	Accrued payroll taxes		14,000	
33,000	Accrued payroll		33,000	
	Unsecured creditors without priority:			
12,000	Accrued liabilities—other			12,000
60,000	Accounts payable			60,000
$822,000	Totals	$582,000	$66,000	$174,000
(16,000)	Owners' deficiency			
$806,000				

($68,000) should equal the difference between the estimated net realizable value of the assets and the total of estimated secured and unsecured amounts due creditors ($68,000) = $754,000 – ($582,000 + $66,000 + $174,000). This deficiency represents the extent to which the net realizable value of assets is inadequate to meet the claims of creditors. Certainly, if the net realizable value of such assets exceeded the creditors' claims, the excess would be available to satisfy the claims of owners/shareholders.

Of interest to the unsecured creditors in Class 7 and the bankruptcy court is a ratio that is referred to as the dividend to general unsecured creditors. This ratio is computed as follows:

$$\text{Dividend} = \frac{\text{Net proceeds available to unsecured creditors in Class 7}}{\text{Total claims of unsecured creditors in Class 7}}$$

The dividend is an estimate of how much will be received by Class 7 unsecured creditors for each dollar owed to them, and it is expressed either in absolute amount or in percentage form.

The approximate dividend in Class 7 unsecured creditors of Insolve Corporation will be computed as follows:

$$\frac{\$106,000}{\$174,000} = \$0.61 \text{ on one dollar, or } 61\%$$

REFLECTION

- The statement of affairs identifies the various assets of a troubled enterprise and their net realizable values. These values are then applied toward the claims of various secured and unsecured creditors.

PREPARATION OF OTHER ACCOUNTING REPORTS

5

OBJECTIVE

Apply the principles of bankruptcy to the preparation of the statement of realization and liquidation.

The trustee appointed to a company in liquidation is expected to make periodic reports to the bankruptcy court regarding the activities of the trustee. In the absence of specific reporting requirements imposed by the Act, each bankruptcy court identifies the type of accounting reports to be submitted by the trustee.

Generally speaking, a court will require the trustee to provide an accounting regarding the following items pertaining to the insolvent company:

1. Unrealized assets assigned to the trustee including those subsequently discovered.
2. Assets that have been realized or liquidated.
3. Liabilities to be liquidated that have been assigned to the trustee.
4. Liabilities that have been liquidated.

Historically, the preceding information was presented in a report called the realization and liquidation account, which employed a rather cumbersome format. Currently, this information is most often presented in a worksheet format that identifies critical balances and relevant cash receipts and disbursements.

The *statement of realization and liquidation* differs from the statement of affairs in the following respects:

1. The statement of realization and liquidation reports the actual liquidation results. In contrast, the statement of affairs is of a pro forma nature and is based on estimated rather than actual results.
2. The statement of realization and liquidation provides an ongoing reporting of the trustee's activities and is updated throughout the liquidation process. The statement of affairs is a summary of the estimated results of a completed liquidation.

In order to illustrate the preparation of a statement of realization and liquidation, the balance sheet of Insolve Corporation, which was presented in Illustration 21-1, will be used as a starting point. Assuming the assets and liabilities contained in Insolve's balance sheet were assigned to the trustee, a statement of realization and liquidation for the period March 1, 20X2, to March 31, 20X2, is presented in Illustration 21-3 on page 1156. In reviewing this illustration, note that it reports actual results rather than estimated amounts, as contained in the statement of affairs. Also note that the statement reports liquidation activity to date and may be updated to reflect subsequent activity.

Illustration 21-3

Insolve Corporation
Statement of Realization and Liquidation
For Period March 1, 20X2, to March 31, 20X2

	Assets		Liabilities				
					Unsecured		
	Cash	Noncash	Fully Secured	Partially Secured	With Priority	Without Priority	Owners' Equity
Beginning balances, assigned March 1, 20X2	$ 4,000	$ 802,000	$304,000	$ 380,000	$66,000	$ 72,000	$(16,000)
Subsequently discovered and other items:							
Assets......................		15,000*					15,000
Loans from officers............						20,000*	(20,000)
Additional liquidation expenses[a]					2,000		(2,000)
Cash receipts:							
Sale of marketable securities....	16,000*	(20,000)					(4,000)
Partial collection of accounts receivable	52,000	(52,000)					
Sale of equipment	124,000*	(150,000)					(26,000)
Sale of inventory[b]	134,000*	(148,000)					(14,000)
Cash disbursements:							
Partial payment of bank loan[c] ...	(124,000)			(200,000)		76,000	
Partial payment of accounts payable[d]	(98,000)			(135,000)		37,000	
Ending balances	$ 108,000	$ 447,000	$304,000	$ 45,000	$68,000	$205,000	$(67,000)

*These amounts differ from the estimated amounts included in the statement of affairs.

[a]Liquidation expenses were originally estimated to be $13,000. However, actual liquidation expenses to date total $15,000.

[b]The sale of inventory consists of the following:

	Book Value	Amount Realized
Raw materials	$ 35,000	$ 18,000
Work in process (less completion costs of $18,000).....................	63,000	76,000
Finished goods	50,000	40,000
	$148,000	$134,000

[c]The bank loan of $200,000 is secured by the equipment, which was disposed of for $124,000, net of expenses. Therefore, $76,000 of the loan is reclassified as an unsecured liability.

[d]The sale of inventory described in footnote b included inventory securing the accounts payable. This inventory had a book value of $135,000 and was sold for $98,000. Therefore, accounts payable with a value of $135,000 were secured only to the extent of $98,000. The unsecured portion of $37,000 ($135,000 – $98,000) is reclassified as such.

The statement also may be used to reassess the effect of a liquidation on various claims of liabilities. For example, as of March 31, 20X2, Insolve Corporation still has $447,000 of noncash assets to be realized. A statement of these assets and their newly revised estimated net realizable values follows:

Noncash Assets	Book Value	Estimated Net Realizable Value
Accounts receivable (net)	$ 18,000	$ 18,000
Inventories	74,000	70,000*
Land	110,000	130,000
Building (net)	182,000	210,000
Goodwill	48,000	0
Assets subsequently discovered	15,000	17,000
Total assets	$447,000	$445,000

*$44,000 of this amount is traceable to partially secured accounts payable.

The estimated net realizable value of noncash assets of $445,000 plus the available existing cash of $108,000 represents a total of $553,000, which would be available to satisfy liabilities and owners' equity. A tentative distribution of this total follows:

Liabilities and Owners' Equity	Book Value	Estimated Distribution	Dividend (Payout) Percentage
Fully secured liabilities	$304,000	$304,000	100%
Partially secured liabilities:			
Book value of $45,000 less unsecured portion of $1,000	44,000	44,000	100
Unsecured liabilities:			
With priority	68,000	68,000	100
Without priority:			
Book value of $205,000 plus unsecured portion of partially secured liabilities	206,000	137,000	67
Owners' equity (deficit)	(67,000)		
Total liabilities and owners'equity	$555,000	$553,000	

Although corporate reorganizations and liquidations are significantly influenced by law, the accounting profession also may be significantly involved in the entire process. Accountants assist in the identification and valuation of assets and liabilities traceable to the insolvent company. The activities of a company involved in a Chapter 11 reorganization or a Chapter 7 liquidation must be periodically reported to the bankruptcy courts. This periodic reporting function is a major area involving the expertise of the accounting profession.

REFLECTION

- The statement of realization and liquidation accounts for various events undertaken to liquidate an enterprise. The statement reports the disposition of assets and the application of proceeds to the settlement of various creditor claims.

UNDERSTANDING THE ISSUES

1. If a debt is restructured through a modification of terms, explain how the gain on restructuring is determined when the restructuring is not under bankruptcy law versus one that is.
2. Distinguish between a corporate reorganization and a liquidation as provided for under bankruptcy law.
3. Explain how the claims of fully secured and partially secured creditors affect the dividend that may be received by unsecured creditors.
4. Explain what purpose the statement of realization and liquidation serves.

EXERCISES

Exercise 1 *(LO 1)* **Effect of various restructuring alternatives.** The Ames Corporation has been experiencing difficulties servicing its long-term debt which has a current balance of $620,000 including accrued interest. Ames is considering two possible alternatives to restructuring the debt. Alternative #1 would consist of conveying vacant land with a fair value of $350,000 and a book value of $275,000 to the creditor. In addition, Ames would make two annual payments of $120,000 each. Alternative #2 would call for Ames to make five annual payments of $135,000. All payments are to be made at the end of the respective years. The market rates of interest for a 2-year and 5-year note are 10% and 12%, respectively.

1. Prepare a schedule to compare the total effect on net income of Alternatives #1 and #2 related to the restructuring.
2. Discuss whether the alternative with the most favorable effect on net income provides the company with the greatest economic advantage.

Exercise 2 *(LO 1, 2)* **Effect of a quasi-reorganization.** For the last several years, the Manion Corporation has encountered a declining market for its major product line. Attempts to diversify have led to additional disappointments. This unfortunate set of circumstances has left the company with significant debt and an inability to service its debt. The existing debt consists of $20,000,000 of principal and $875,000 of accrued interest. Discussions with the creditors have resulted in a proposed restructuring of debt. The restructuring would consist of the following actions:

1. Exchanging preferred stock with a fair value of $5,100,000 and a par value of $5,000,000 in exchange for full settlement of $5,500,000 of principal debt.
2. Exchanging land with a value of $4,000,000 and a book value of $3,000,000 in exchange for $4,500,000 of principal debt.
3. The remaining debt and accrued interest would be repaid over the next 10 years with semiannual payments due every six months. The annual stated rate would be 8.5%.

Past operating losses have resulted in a deficit in retained earnings of $3,400,000. In addition to the deficit, the company's equity includes common stock at par value of $6,000,000 and contributed capital in excess of par value in the amount of $1,000,000.

Prepare a schedule that determines the effect on current income of the debt restructuring and the reduction in par value of the common stock necessary to eliminate any deficit in retained earnings. Assume that the restructuring is not part of a formal bankruptcy filing.

Exercise 3 *(LO 2)* **Benefits of a quasi-reorganization.** Barber Technologies designs and develops software to be used for the management of inventory by both retailers and manufacturing firms. Over the past three years, the company has experienced significant competition and a declining market resulting in a significant deficit in retained earnings. In reponse to this condition, you have suggested that management consider the following:

a. Recognize all asset impairments.
b. Restructure the long-term debt by committing to make future payments that are less than the basis of the original debt.
c. Adjust the par value of common stock to eliminate the deficit in retained earnings.

Discuss how the above actions will likely affect:

1. The current ratio, debt-to-equity ratio, and return on equity.
2. The determination of net income in subsequent periods.

Exercise 4 *(LO 2)* **Record a quasi-reorganization.** Montrose Manufacturing, Inc. has designed and built timber-harvesting equipment for over 25 years. Due to declining demand and increased foreign competition, the company has accumulated significant operating losses. The company has been able to withstand these pressures through the use of heavy debt financing. The company has just completed development of a new product line unrelated to the timber industry and it expects that significant profits will be generated over the next 5 to 10 years. Unfortunately, the income generated from this new line of business will not be available to shareholders in the form of dividends due to the large deficits traceable to prior operations.

In order to provide for dividend opportunities in the near future, the shareholders of the corporation have authorized a quasi-reorganization. A condensed balance sheet and related information prior to the reorganization are as follows:

Assets	Book Value	Fair Value
Cash and cash equivalents	$ 220,000	$ 220,000
Accounts receivable	800,000	740,000
Inventory	1,280,000	1,100,000
Other current assets	240,000	280,000
Depreciable assets (net)	4,300,000	3,800,000
Total assets	$6,840,000	$6,140,000

Liabilities and Equity		
Current liabilities	$ 1,700,000	
Contingent liabilities	580,000	$500,000
Other liabilities	3,700,000	
Common stock at par value	1,000,000	
Contributed capital in excess of par	1,800,000	
Retained earnings (deficit)	(1,940,000)	
Total liabilities and equity	$ 6,840,000	

Prepare the necessary entries to record the quasi-reorganization.

Exercise 5 *(LO 1, 3)* **Cash flows, debt restructuring, effect on income under bankruptcy and nonbankruptcy law.** In an attempt to avoid liquidating the company, the management of Carter, Inc., is considering a reorganization that calls for the restructuring of $2,100,000 of debt maturing in three years and related accrued interest payable of $72,737. The restructuring agreement calls for monthly payments over the next 60 months, a reduction in the interest rate to 8%, and the cancellation of $200,000 of debt. The market rate of interest for such a refinancing would be 13%. In addition to the debt restructuring, management is proposing to reduce the par value of its common stock in order to generate enough paid-in capital in excess of par value to absorb a $500,000 deficit in retained earnings. The present balance of paid-in capital in excess of par value is $80,000.

1. Prepare a schedule to determine the total gain resulting from the forgiveness and restructuring of debt and the amount of future interest expense assuming (a) a nonbankruptcy approach and (b) a bankruptcy approach to the reorganization.
2. Determine by how much the par value of common stock would have to be reduced in order to absorb the deficit in retained earnings assuming (a) a nonbankruptcy approach and (b) a bankruptcy approach.

Exercise 6 *(LO 1, 3)* **Cash flows, debt restructuring, effect on income under bankruptcy and nonbankruptcy law.** Rather than entering into a lengthy bankruptcy proceeding, Peltzer Manufacturing has reached agreement with its long-term creditors to restructure various loans. The restructured loans are described below.

Loan A—This debt has a principal balance of $4,000,000 and accrued interest of $80,000. Under the restructuring agreement, $500,000 of debt would be forgiven, and the balance of the amounts due would be refinanced at a rate of 10% with monthly installment payments of $50,000 and a term of eight years. Assets with a net realizable value of $2,500,000 would also be pledged as additional security against the restructured loan.

Loan B—This debt has a principal balance of $1,000,000 and accrued interest of $25,000. Under the restructuring agreement, the accrued interest would be forgiven, and the principal amount would be exchanged for preferred stock with a par value of $500,000 and a fair value of $900,000.

Loan C—This debt has a principal balance of $2,000,000 and accrued interest of $37,500. Under the restructuring agreement, the creditor would receive a parcel of land with a book value of $200,000 and a net realizable value of $250,000. The remaining unpaid balance would be refinanced over five years at a 9% interest rate. Installment payments would be on a quarterly basis.

1. Determine the total quarterly cash outflows that will be required by Peltzer's debt restructuring.
2. Covering the first quarter subsequent to restructuring, prepare a schedule that compares the effect on Peltzer's net income of accounting for the restructuring as part of a formal bankruptcy filing versus it not being part of such a filing.

Exercise 7 *(LO 4)* **Dividend to unsecured creditors without priority.** The creditors of the Thorel Corporation agreed to a Chapter 7 liquidation which, based on the statement of affairs, suggested that unsecured creditors without priority would receive approximately $0.60 on the dollar. The unsecured creditors are interested in determining whether the preliminary estimate still seems appropriate. The trustee was originally assigned noncash assets of $1,480,000 and creditor claims as follows: fully secured, $670,000; partially secured, $400,000; unsecured with priority, $200,000; and unsecured without priority, $320,000. Assets with a book value of $45,000 and unsecured liabilities (without priority) of $35,000 were subsequently discovered. Assets with a total book value of $740,000 were sold for $715,000 net. Fully secured liabilities of $410,000 and partially secured liabilities of $280,000 were paid. Remaining liquidation expenses were estimated to be $30,000.

Assume the remaining noncash assets have an estimated net realizable value as follows:

Assets traceable to fully secured creditors	$240,000
Assets traceable to partially secured creditors	110,000
Remaining assets	382,000

Determine the revised estimate of the dividend to be received by unsecured creditors without priority.

Exercise 8 *(LO 1, 3)* **Evaluation of restructuring alternatives.** Baxter Manufacturing, Inc. has an outstanding note payable with a balance of $2,000,000. The note calls for 14 semiannual payments of $183,141 based on a 7% interest rate. The company has experienced declining markets and serious cash flow problems. In an attempt to improve cash flows, the company is negotiating a restructuring of the above note. The following alternatives are being considered:

a. Dispose of a parcel of land that the company had purchased as a future plant site. However, given current conditions, the likelihood of a relocation seems remote. The site has a book value of $400,000 and a current market value of $550,000. Transaction costs to dispose of the land are estimated to be $35,000. The net proceeds from the sale of the land would be used to reduce the note payable. The balance of the note would be restructured with 14 semiannual payments of $100,000 each.
b. Dispose of the parcel of land as set forth above and apply $300,000 of the net proceeds to reduce the note. The balance of the note would be restructured with 20 semiannual payments of $90,000 each.

1. Assuming that current borrowing rates are 6%, compare the income statement and balance sheet effect of the two alternatives assuming (a) a nonbankruptcy approach and (b) a bankruptcy approach.
2. Given a nonbankruptcy approach and ignoring the effect on the financial statements, discuss which alternative would be preferred.

Exercise 9 *(LO 3, 4)* **Liquidation, distribution to creditors.** Casper Blueprinting, Inc., has filed under Chapter 7 of the Bankruptcy Code. The estimated net realizable value of its assets is as follows:

Cash and cash equivalents	$ 23,000
Accounts receivable	42,000
Inventory and supplies	15,000
Blueprinting equipment	114,000
Furniture and fixtures	12,000
Computer hardware and software	21,000
Delivery vehicle	14,000
Total assets	$241,000

Creditor's claims are summarized as follows:

a. Bank loan balance of $82,000 plus accrued interest of $3,000 with a first lien against blueprinting equipment.
b. Dealer-financed vehicle loan with an outstanding balance of $18,000 which is secured by the delivery vehicle.
c. Accounts payable due vendors in the amount of $21,000 and secured by the inventory and supplies.
d. A line of credit balance due of $30,000 secured by the accounts receivable.
e. Unpaid payroll and income taxes of $23,000.
f. Accounting and legal fees due in the amount of $12,000 in connection with the administration of the bankrupt estate.
g. Unpaid wages to employees totaling $4,200 ($700 represents the largest amount due any one employee).
h. Loans due shareholders of the corporation totaling $80,000.
i. Other unsecured creditors without priority in the amount of $31,000.

Prepare a schedule to show the estimated amount to be received by each major category of creditor.

Exercise 10 *(LO 5)* **Statement of realization and liquidation, dividend to unsecured creditors without priority.** A partially completed statement of realization and liquidation is as follows:

The Rodak Corporation
Statement of Realization and Liquidation
For Period July 1, 20X9, to August 12, 20X9

	Assets		Liabilities				
					Unsecured		
	Cash	Noncash	Fully Secured	Partially Secured	With Priority	Without Priority	Owners' Equity
Beginning balances, assigned July 1, 20X9 . .	$12,000	$590,000	$200,000	$175,000	$54,000	$150,000	$23,000
Cash receipts: Sale of inventory	30,000	(25,000)					5,000

The following additional transactions have occurred through August 12, 20X9:

a. Receivables collected amount to $39,000. Receivables with a book value of $15,000 that were not allowed for were written off.
b. A $12,000 loan that was fully secured was paid off.
c. A valid claim is received from a leasing company seeking payment of $15,000 for equipment rentals.
d. Securities costing $18,000 are sold for $23,000, minus brokerage fee of $500.
e. Depreciation on machinery is $3,200.
f. Payments on accounts payable total $25,000, of which the entire amount was secured by the inventory sold.
g. Machinery that originally cost $85,000 and has a book value of $45,000 sold for $36,000.
h. Proceeds from the sale of machinery in (g) are remitted to the bank, which holds a $50,000 loan on the machinery.

1. Update the statement of realization and liquidation to properly reflect transactions (a) through (h).
2. Assuming the remaining noncash assets can be realized for $410,000, determine the estimated dividend to be received by unsecured creditors without priority.

PROBLEMS

Problem 21-1 *(LO 1)* **Restructuring versus liquidation.** Atoyo Fabricating, Inc., has not been able to service its debts adequately. The company is a family business which has been in existence for 35 years. The shareholders want to avoid liquidating the business and are seeking your help in formulating a plan of reorganization which

a. Provides creditors with at least as much consideration as, if not more than, they would receive if the company were liquidated.
b. Does not require monthly debt service in excess of $75,000.

Information regarding the various creditor claims and possible restructuring parameters is as follows:

a. Accounts payable due vendors total $134,000. Terms are generally 2/10 net 30, and virtually all accounts are past due. Vendors with balances of $40,000 due have indicated that in satisfaction of the amount due, they would accept equal monthly installment payments bearing no less than 12% and not exceeding three months in duration. These vendors have secured their claims with inventory which has a book value and net realizable value of $55,000 and $42,000, respectively. Vendors with a balance due of $74,000 have a secured interest in inventory with a book value of $60,000 and a net realizable value of $46,000. These vendors would accept three monthly installment payments of $20,000 including interest at the rate of 12% in satisfaction of the amount due. The remaining payables represent unsecured amounts which would be paid $3,000 per month for the next five months including interest at 12%.
b. The equipment note has a balance due of $320,000 plus accrued interest of $18,000. Equipment with a book value of $280,000 and a net realizable value of $325,000 serves as collateral for this loan. The original loan had an interest rate of 11% and a remaining term of 30 months. The creditor will not agree to a change in the interest rate but will accept a revised term of 36 to 42 months in exchange for a personal guarantee of the amount due by each of the shareholders of record.
c. The note due a shareholder in the amount of $20,000 is secured by the cash surrender value of an insurance policy in the amount of $15,000 and is payable on demand. The shareholder would accept four semiannual payments, including interest at 12%, if the present value of these payments is equal to 120% of what would have been received if the company had been liquidated.
d. The mortgage payable of $420,000 plus accrued interest of $28,000 is fully secured by real estate with a book value of $310,000 and a net realizable value of $460,000. The original mortgage has a remaining term of 334 months and an interest rate of 9%. The mortgage company would agree to a restructuring of 360 months and an interest rate of 11%.
e. All other creditors totaling $160,000 are unsecured without priority. Management would like to propose that these creditors receive monthly payments over the next eight months with interest at 12%. The net present value of these payments should equal 110% of what would have been received had the company been liquidated.

The book values and net realizable values of the company's assets are as follows:

	Book Value	Net Realizable Value
Cash and cash equivalents	$ 5,000	$ 5,000
Accounts receivable (net)	120,000	85,000
Inventory	145,000	100,000
Equipment (net)	330,000	345,000
Real property (net)	310,000	460,000
Cash surrender values	25,000	25,000
Licensing agreement	30,000	10,000
Furniture and fixtures	25,000	12,000
	$990,000	$1,042,000

Prepare a schedule which analyzes the proposed restructuring against the goals set by management. ◄◄◄◄◄ **Required**

Problem 21-2 *(LO 1)* **Cash budget during a period of reorganization.** Mayne Manufacturing Company has incurred substantial losses for several years and has become insolvent. On March 31, 20X5, Mayne petitioned the court for protection from creditors and submitted the following statement of financial position:

Mayne Manufacturing Company
Statement of Financial Position
March 31, 20X5

Assets	Book Value	Liquidation Value
Accounts receivable	$100,000	$ 50,000
Inventories	90,000	40,000
Plant and equipment	150,000	160,000
Total assets	$340,000	$250,000

Liabilities and Stockholders' Equity	
Accounts payable—general creditors	$ 600,000
Common stock outstanding	60,000
Deficit	(320,000)
Total liabilities and stockholders' equity	$ 340,000

Mayne's management informed the court that the company has developed a new product. A prospective customer is willing to sign a contract for the purchase of 10,000 units of this product during the year ending March 31, 20X6; 12,000 units of this product during the year ending March 31, 20X7; and 15,000 units of this product during the year ending March 31, 20X8; all at a price of $90 per unit. This product can be manufactured using Mayne's present facilities. Monthly production with immediate delivery is expected to be uniform within each year. Receivables are expected to be collected during the calendar month following sales.

Unit production costs of the new product are expected to be as follows:

Direct materials	$20
Direct labor	30
Variable overhead	10

Fixed costs (excluding depreciation) will amount to $130,000 per year.

Purchases of direct materials will be paid during the calendar month following purchase. Fixed costs, direct labor, and variable overhead will be paid as incurred. Inventory of direct materials will be equal to 60 days' usage. After the first month of operations, 30 days' usage of direct materials will be ordered each month.

The general creditors have agreed to reduce their total claims to 60% of their March 31, 20X5, balances, under the following conditions:

a. Existing accounts receivable and inventories are to be liquidated immediately, with the proceeds turned over to the general creditors.
b. The balance of reduced accounts payable is to be paid as cash is generated from future operations, but in no event later than March 31, 20X7. No interest will be paid on these obligations.

Under this proposed plan, the general creditors would receive $110,000 more than the current liquidation value of Mayne's assets. The court has engaged you to determine the feasibility of this plan.

Required ▶ ▶ ▶ ▶ ▶ Ignoring any need to borrow and repay short-term funds for working capital purposes, prepare a cash budget for the years ending March 31, 20X6, and 20X7, showing the cash expected to be available to pay the claims of the general creditors and payments to general creditors and the cash remaining after payment of claims. Support the cash budget with two schedules showing collections from customers and disbursements for direct materials.

Problem 21-3 *(LO 1, 2)* **Effect of a quasi-reorganization.** Marshall Tool and Die Company has been experiencing significant foreign competition and a declining market. Annual net losses from operations have averaged $250,000 over the last three years. The company's balance sheet as of December 31, 20X7, is as follows:

Assets		Liabilities and Equity	
Cash	$ (15,000)	Accounts payable	$ 320,000
Accounts receivable (net)	500,000	7% Notes payable	1,500,000
Inventory	150,000	Common stock at par	550,000
Plant and equipment (net)	1,560,000	Contributed capital in excess of par	550,000
Goodwill	150,000	Retained earnings	(300,000)
Other assets	35,000	20X7 Net income	(240,000)
Total assets	$2,380,000	Total liabilities and equity	$2,380,000

After analyzing accounts receivable and inventory, it has been determined that the allowance for uncollectibles should be increased by $75,000 and the inventory should be written down by $20,000. Based on recent appraisals, it is estimated that the plant and equipment have a market value of $900,000. The goodwill is traceable to the purchase of a small tooling company in 20X3. Based on an analysis of cash flows associated with that acquisition, it is estimated that the goodwill has an impaired value of $0. Other assets represent a note receivable from officers of the corporation. The note calls for five annual payments of $8,309 including interest at the rate of 6%.

In response to the current situation, the company has decided to take the following actions:

a. Record the suggested impairment in all assets.
b. Restructure the note receivable from the officers to reflect four annual payments and an interest rate of 7.5%.
c. Restructure the note payable, which was due in 20X9, to provide for 12 semiannual payments of $120,000 including interest at the annual rate of 6%.
d. Engage in a quasi-reorganization to eliminate the deficit in retained earnings.

◄◄◄◄◄ **Required**

1. Prepare a revised classified balance sheet to reflect the effect of management's actions.
2. Compute the following ratios before and after management's actions: current ratio and debt-to-equity ratio.
3. Given the above ratio analysis, if the ratios do not suggest an improvement, discuss the benefits of management's actions.

Problem 21-4 *(LO 4)* **Statement of affairs.** A creditor's committee of Carlton Company has obtained the March 31, 20X5, balance sheet shown below:

template cd

Carlton Company
Balance Sheet
March 31, 20X5

Assets		
Current assets:		
Cash		$ 11,250
Marketable securities		28,750
Notes receivable	$ 10,000	
Less notes receivable discounted	10,000	0
Accounts receivable	$ 15,000	
Less allowance for doubtful accounts	1,000	14,000
Subscriptions receivable		20,000

(continued)

Assets			
Inventories:			
Finished goods	$ 27,500		
Work in process	11,250		
Materials	15,000	53,750	
Total current assets			$127,750
Property, plant, and equipment:			
Land and building	$112,500		
Equipment	60,000	$172,500	
Less accumulated depreciation		50,000	
Total property, plant, and equipment			122,500
Total assets			$250,250

Liabilities and Stockholders' Equity			
Current liabilities:			
Notes payable		$ 87,500	
Accounts payable		60,000	
Salaries payable		2,650	
Property tax payable		1,150	
Total current liabilities		$151,300	
Long-term liabilities:			
First mortgage payable	$37,500		
Second mortgage payable	50,000	87,500	
Total liabilities			$238,800
Stockholders' equity:			
Common stock, $100 par (1,000 shares authorized):			
750 shares issued		$ 75,000	
250 shares subscribed		25,000	
Total		$100,000	
Retained earnings (deficit)		(88,550)	
Total stockholders' equity			11,450
Total liabilities and stockholders' equity			$250,250

An analysis of the company's accounts disclosed the following activities through April 30, 20X5:

a. Carlton Company started business on April 1, 20X0, with authorized stock of $100 par. Of the 1,000 authorized shares, 750 were paid for in full at par, and 250 were subscribed at par, with a required 20% down payment and the balance payable upon call. All the subscriptions receivable are due from W. Krueger, president of the company, and are fully collectible.
b. Marketable securities include the $25,000 cost of U.S. Treasury bonds valued at $23,200 and 25 shares of Groves Company common stock, costing $3,750, with a fair value of $3,300.
c. The land originally cost $10,000, and the building was erected at a cost of $102,500. Of the accumulated depreciation, $30,000 is applicable to the building. The realizable value of the real estate is $75,000.
d. Notes receivable were endorsed with recourse when discounted and are expected to be dishonored. Of the accounts receivable, $3,000 are considered collectible.
e. Inventories are shown at cost. Any finished goods are expected to yield 110% of cost. If scrapped, goods in process have a realizable value of only $2,200. It is estimated, however, that the work in process can be completed by the addition of $3,000 of present materials

and an expenditure of $3,500 for labor. The materials deteriorate rapidly and will realize only 20% of cost. (Use the cost completion method illustrated in the text.)

f. Equipment is estimated to have a realizable value of $12,000.

g. Notes payable include a $25,000 note to Aerotex Company and a $62,500 note to B. Williams. Aerotex holds the U.S. Treasury bonds as security for its loans. It also holds the first mortgage of $37,500 on the company's real estate, interest on which is paid through March 31, 20X5. The note payable to Williams is secured by a chattel mortgage on factory equipment. Interest on the note has been paid through March 31, 20X5. Williams also holds the second mortgage on the real estate.

h. Any expenses not specifically mentioned need not be considered. All salaries qualify for priority, including labor to complete the work in process.

Prepare a statement of affairs for Carlton Company. ◀◀◀◀◀ **Required**

Problem 21-5 *(LO 4)* **Dividend to unsecured creditors without priority if corporation liquidation.** Jensen Manufacturing, Inc., has filed under Chapter 11 of the Bankruptcy Act. At the time of filing the plan of reorganization, the company had total assets of $2,040,000 and liabilities and equity as follows:

Accounts payable	$ 210,000
Note payable—officer	120,000
Equipment note payable	500,000
Line of credit payable	360,000
Mortgage payable	625,000
Convertible bonds	200,000
Common stock at par	100,000
Paid-in capital	50,000
Deficit retained earnings	(125,000)

The plan of reorganization contains the following proposals:

a. The accounts payable due vendors will be settled for $180,000, and all subsequent purchases will be on a C.O.D. basis. The payables are secured by inventory with a book value and net realizable value of $165,000.

b. The amount due the officer will be settled by conveying vacant land with a cost basis of $60,000 and a net realizable value of $85,000.

c. The equipment note is collateralized by equipment with a net book value of $410,000 and a net realizable value of $440,000. The proposal calls for servicing the debt as follows: 60 monthly payments of $10,010 including interest at 12% per annum.

d. The line of credit is secured by receivables and inventory which have a combined book value and net realizable value of $400,000, and the line will not be affected by the reorganization.

e. The mortgage will be restructured to provide for 120 monthly payments of $8,590 including interest at 10% per annum. The mortgage is secured by a building and underlying land which has a combined book value and net realizable value of $450,000 and $650,000, respectively.

f. The convertible bonds will be retired in exchange for a promise to make four annual payments of $40,000 each. The market rate for a similar loan is 11%.

g. The par value of the common stock will be reduced to $10,000, and the deficit will be eliminated against the additional paid-in capital.

◀◀◀◀◀ **Required**

Before confirming the plan of reorganization, the bankruptcy court must verify that each holder of a claim or interest will not receive or retain property of a value less than the amount such holder would have received under a Chapter 7 liquidation. Calculate the minimum net realizable value of assets available to unsecured creditors—without priority which would be necessary to meet the Chapter 7 "test" referred to above. Assume that if the company were liquidated, $40,000 of liquidation expenses would be incurred.

Problem 21-6 *(LO 4)* **Evaluation of bankruptcy alternatives for a partially secured creditor.** West Diamond Bank has an outstanding loan to Alpine Construction Company in the amount of $5,000,000. The loan calls for 20 quarterly payments of $305,784 based on an annual interest rate of 8%. The bank's collateral consists of all equipment of the company, except the equipment securing the note payable—officers, and a parcel of land. Alpine's assets at net realizable value and liabilities consist of the following:

Assets		Liabilities	
Cash	$ 50,000	Accounts payable	$ 225,000
Receivables (net)	730,000	Wages payable	50,000
Inventory	320,000	Taxes payable	70,000
Equipment	3,200,000	Pension contribution due	140,000
Vehicles and trucks	250,000	Line of credit	500,000
Parcel of land	1,000,000	Note payable—US Bank	300,000
Note receivable—officers	50,000	Note payable—officers	75,000
Other assets	100,000	Note payable—West Diamond Bank	5,000,000
Total assets	$5,700,000	Total liabilities	$6,360,000

Additional information relating to the liabilities is as follows:

a. The line of credit is fully secured by the receivables of the company.
b. The note payable to US Bank is collateralized by the company's vehicles and trucks.
c. The note payable—officers is secured by the note receivable—officers and a piece of equipment with a net realizable value of $25,000.

Management of the company is considering three possible alternatives to its present situation. The alternatives are as follows:

a. Liquidate under Chapter 7 of the bankruptcy code.
b. Reorganize under Chapter 11 of the bankruptcy code.
c. Restructure debt under a nonbankruptcy approach.

If a Chapter 11 approach were pursued, the company would be proposing that West Diamond Bank accept 24 quarterly payments with a present value equal to 110% of the amount that the bank would receive if liquidation were pursued. If a nonbankruptcy approach were pursued, the company would be proposing that West Diamond Bank restructure its debt to provide for 24 quarterly payments of $250,000.

Required ▶▶▶▶▶

1. Considering that West Diamond Bank is currently earning 7.2% on loans with a duration of five to seven years, prepare a schedule that analyzes the present value of each of the alternatives available to West Diamond Bank. Assume that all unsecured claims with priority are within the legal limits.
2. Prepare a schedule that computes the first year of interest expense for Alpine Construction Company on the West Diamond Bank note under alternatives (b) and (c) above.

Problem 21-7 *(LO 1, 4)* **Creditor's remedy under a liquidation versus a restructuring.** Your client, Imax Financial, originally lent Wiedemeyer Manufacturing $1,000,000. Unfortunately, the loan is in default, and $900,000 of principal and $20,000 of accrued interest remains unpaid. Imax is deciding whether to encourage other creditors to commence an involuntary bankruptcy proceeding against Wiedemeyer or to restructure their unpaid loans.

Details surrounding the assets and liabilities of Wiedemeyer are as follows:

	Book Value			
	Debit	Credit	Estimated Net Realizable Value	Note
Cash and cash equivalents	$ 115,000		$ 115,000	
Accounts receivable	650,000		580,000	1
Inventory	875,000		750,000	2
Other current assets	180,000		177,100	
Property, plant, and equipment (net)	3,500,000		3,600,000	3
Goodwill	250,000			
Accounts payable		$1,100,000		
Other current liabilities		285,000		4
Bank line of credit		400,000		
Mortgage payable		2,800,000		
Loan to Imax		920,000		

Notes:

1. Receivables with a book value of $500,000 and a net realizable value of $460,000 were used to secure the bank line of credit. Under the terms of the line of credit an amount equal to 80% of the qualified receivables could be loaned.
2. Inventory was used to secure $800,000 of accounts payable. The relevant inventory has a book value of $700,000 and a net realizable value of $670,000.
3. Land and buildings with a combined book value of $2,900,000 and a net realizable value of $3,000,000 serve as collateral for the mortgage payable. Additional land with a book value of $300,000 and a net realizable value of $500,000 serves as collateral on the Imax loan.
4. Other current liabilities consist of the following:

   a. A vehicle loan with an unpaid balance of $15,000. The subject vehicle has a book value of $20,000 and a fair value of $12,000.
   b. A $40,000 note due officers of the corporation. The note is unsecured.
   c. Unpaid wages of $160,000.
   d. Unpaid contributions to the corporate pension plan in the amount of $20,000.
   e. Miscellaneous general creditors in the amount of $50,000.

Rather than forcing Wiedemeyer into bankruptcy, Imax would possibly consider restructuring its loan. However, any possible restructuring would have to include a stated interest rate of 8.5% with interest payments due on a quarterly basis. Furthermore, the term of the restructured loan could not exceed five years.

Prepare a schedule that would determine how much of the Imax loan would have to be forgiven in a restructuring in order to place Imax in the same position as it would have been if Wiedemeyer had been liquidated. Also, determine the periodic payment to be made by Wiedemeyer if the loan were restructured. ◄◄◄◄◄ **Required**

Problem 21-8 *(LO 1, 3, 4)* **Restructuring versus liquidation.** FICO Corporation is insolvent, and its board of directors is considering several alternatives being proposed by both creditors and management. The creditors are proposing to seek an involuntary petition to liquidate the corporation. It is estimated that the assets and liabilities of the corporation as of February 1, 20X8, will have the following values:

	Book Value	Fair Value
Assets pledged with fully secured creditors	$2,400,000	$2,809,000
Assets pledged with partially secured creditors	1,640,000	1,580,000
Free assets	870,000	740,000
Fully secured creditors	2,300,000	N/A
Partially secured creditors	1,640,000	N/A
Unsecured creditors:		
With priority	80,000	N/A
Without priority	1,200,000	N/A

In addition to the preceding liabilities, it is estimated that the trustee's expenses in connection with the liquidation of the corporation will be $35,000.

Management is proposing to continue operations under the supervision of a court-appointed trustee. Management's plan consists of the following:

a. Continue operations for the balance of 20X8, which would result in the following:

Sales revenue:	
Collected	$1,480,000
Uncollected	210,000
Cost of sales:	
Beginning inventory decrease	60,000
Current purchases:	
Paid	1,100,000
Unpaid	150,000
Selling, general, and administrative (SG&A) expenses:	
Paid	80,000
Unpaid ($20,000 of Class 3 wages)	30,000

b. Accounts receivable on February 1, 20X8, of $320,000 would be disposed of as follows:

Written off	$ 30,000
Assigned as collateral of a new loan of $250,000	290,000

c. With the exception of (b) above, all accounts receivable are considered free assets. All accounts payable are unsecured.

d. A $600,000 bank loan, which was partially secured by assets with a book value of $540,000, will be satisfied by the payment of $100,000 cash and the substitution of a new 6-month unsecured loan. The new loan calls for principal payments of $400,000 and interest payments of $24,000 based on a market rate of interest.

e. Unsecured creditors with claims of $400,000 on February 1 will accept 4,000 shares of 6.5%, cumulative, preferred stock. The preferred stock has an estimated fair value of $320,000.

f. Equipment with a net book value of $640,000 will be sold for $520,000. This equipment is pledged as collateral on a $550,000 note. Holders of the note will accept the sales proceeds as payment in full. Additional equipment necessary for operations will be leased under operating leases. Applicable lease payments are included in cost of sales.

g. As of December 31, 20X8, management estimated that assets pledged with fully secured creditors will have a net realizable value of $2,750,000, assets pledged with partially secured creditors will have a net realizable value of 110% of the creditors' balances, and free assets will have a net realizable value equal to 90% of book value.

◄◄◄◄◄ **Required**

1. The board of directors of FICO Corporation has retained you to evaluate the two competing proposals. Prepare a schedule for each alternative that identifies for each category of liabilities and owners' equity: book values, assets available to satisfy claims, and dividend (recovery) percentages.
   Hint: The analysis of management's proposal should include schedules that detail the new balances for liabilities, owners' equity, and available assets as of December 31, 20X8.
2. As a common shareholder, discuss which proposal would be most attractive to you.

Problem 21-9 *(LO 1, 3)* **Debt restructuring alternatives.** Torke Manufacturerig has the following interest-bearing debt:

Creditor	Book Value of Debt	Term	Interest Rate per Year	Periodic Payment	Collateral
Bank One	$ 800,000	20 quarters	7.2%	$47,986	Equipment
Bank Two	1,200,000	96 months	6	15,770	Equipment
Bank Three	4,000,000	96 months	8.2	56,954	Land and building
Company officers	250,000	12 months	5	21,402	Unsecured

The company has appraoched each of its creditors to discuss possible debt restructurings. Each of the creditors has agreed to the following possible restructuring alternatives:

Bank One—The bank has agreed to refinance the note at an annual interest rate of 6% with quarterly payments to be amortized over 20 quarters. However, a single balloon payment will be due after receipt of the 16th quarterly payment in the amount of the outstanding balance.

Bank Two—The bank has agreed to two possible options. The first option requires an immediate payment of $300,000 and the balance to be paid with 84 quarterly payments of $10,000 each. The current market rate of interest is 7.2%. The immediate payment of $300,000 will be financed through the sale of an undeveloped piece of land owned by the company. The land has a book value of $200,000 and a net realizable value of $300,000.

Bank Three—The bank will forgive $200,000 of debt and service the balance of the debt over 96 monthly periods with payments of $52,187.14 based on an interest rate of 7.2%.

Company Officers—The officers have agreed to extend the term of the note to 18 months with an annual interest rate of 6%.

The company is attempting to settle on a restructuring plan. However, the plan must fit with several constraints. The company wants to restrict debt service of principal and interest to a monthly average of $95,000 cash over the next 12 months. The company also wants the present value of all remaining debt service payments to be less than 90% of the current balance. Finally, the company wants to reduce the following year's interest expense by 10% and increase reported pretax earnings by the maximum amount.

◄◄◄◄◄ **Required**

Prepare a schedule that evaluates each of the debt restructuring alternatives against the company's constraints and make a final recommendation as to which alternative should be accepted.

Problem 21-10 *(LO 5)* **Statement of realization and liquidation, unsecured creditors with and without priority.** The past several years have been extremely difficult for Avery Manufacturing Company, Inc. During this time, the company lost significant market share and was successfully sued with respect to several product liability cases. In response to those problems, the company filed a voluntary petition to liquidate the company on May 15, 20X9, at which time the company had the following condensed trial balance:

template cd

	Debits	Credits
Cash	$ 30,000	
Noncash assets	2,958,000	
Liabilities:		
Fully secured		$1,720,000
Partially secured		762,000
Unsecured—with priority		20,000
Unsecured—without priority		230,000
Owners' equity		256,000
Total	$2,988,000	$2,988,000

The bankruptcy court issued an order of relief on June 1, 20X9. The following liquidation transactions occurred through July 15, 20X9:

a. The inventory of raw materials was disposed of as follows:

	Cost	Fair Value
Returned to fully secured vendors	$180,000	$180,000
Sold to liquidations broker	70,000	50,000
Transferred to work in process	40,000	40,000
	$290,000	$270,000

b. Work in process with a cost prior to liquidation of $117,000 was completed with the addition of the following costs:

Raw materials per (a)	$40,000
Additional unpaid labor (individually less than $4,000)	17,000
Overhead:	
Depreciation	1,000
Additional liabilities incurred	4,000[a]
	$62,000

[a]These debts were incurred between May 17, 20X9, and May 28, 20X9.

The finished work in process was sold for $160,000.

c. Remaining finished goods with a cost of $204,000 were sold to a liquidation broker for $154,000.

d. The company's Indiana manufacturing facility, which had a net book value of $1,240,000, was sold for $1,000,000. The $800,000 mortgage on the property and related accrued interest of $34,000 were paid off with the sales proceeds.

e. The company's warehouse with a net book value of $430,000 and an appraised value of $380,000 was assigned to the bank that held the $450,000 mortgage on the property.

f. Equipment with a net book value of $450,000 was sold at auction for $330,000. Lenders with equipment loans of $272,000, including accrued interest, received $220,000 upon sale of the equipment. Leased equipment was returned to the lessors and the company forfeited $15,000 in lease deposits.

g. Unassigned accounts receivable were realized as follows:

	Book Value	Fair Value
Collected in full	$ 72,000	$72,000
Written off:		
Against a $30,000 allowance	30,000	0
In excess of allowance	14,000	0
	$116,000	$72,000

h. Assigned accounts receivable totaling $40,000 were disposed of as follows:

Collected in full	$32,000
Returned to the company with recourse	8,000

i. Expenses totaling $14,000 have been incurred by the trustee.
j. The company was just assessed another $15,000 of property taxes, which brings the total amount of taxes owed to governmental units to $35,000.

◀◀◀◀◀ **Required**

1. Prepare a statement of realization and liquidation for the period June 1, 20X9, to July 15, 20X9.
2. Determine the amount to be paid to unsecured creditors with and without priority assuming the remaining noncash assets have a net realizable value of (a) $10,000 and (b) $64,000. If only unsecured creditors with priority will receive a distribution, indicate which specific class of creditors will be paid.

Index of APB and FASB Pronouncements

The following list of pronouncements by the Accounting Principles Board and the Financial Accounting Standards Board (as of June 30, 2005) is provided as an overview of the standards issued since 1962. Some of the pronouncements by the Committee on Accounting Procedure are still authoritative; most of these are summarized in *Accounting Research Bulletin No. 43* issued in June 1953. A number of the APB and FASB pronouncements have been superseded.

FASB Statement No.	Statement Title	Issue Date
1	*Disclosure of Foreign Currency Translation Information*	
2	*Accounting for Research and Development Costs*	10/74
3	*Reporting Accounting Changes in Interim Financial Statements—an amendment of APB Opinion No. 28*	12/74
4	*Reporting Gains and Losses from Extinguishment of Debt—an amendment of APB Opinion No. 30*	3/75
5	*Accounting for Contingencies*	3/75
6	*Classification of Short-Term Obligations Expected to Be Refinanced—an amendment of ARB No. 43, Chapter 3A*	5/75
7	*Accounting and Reporting by Development Stage Enterprises*	6/75
8	*Accounting for the Translation of Foreign Currency Transactions and Foreign Currency Financial Statements*	10/75
9	*Accounting for Income Taxes: Oil and Gas Producing Companies—an amendment of APB Opinions No. 11 and 23*	10/75
10	*Extension of "Grandfather" Provisions for Business Combinations—an amendment of APB Opinion No. 16*	10/75
11	*Accounting for Contingencies: Transition Method—an amendment of FASB Statement No. 5*	12/75
12	*Accounting for Certain Marketable Securities*	12/75
13	*Accounting for Leases*	11/76
14	*Financial Reporting for Segments of a Business Enterprise*	12/76
15	*Accounting by Debtors and Creditors for Troubled Debt Restructurings*	6/77
16	*Prior Period Adjustments*	6/77
17	*Accounting for Leases: Initial Direct Costs—an amendment of FASB Statement No. 13*	11/77
18	*Financial Reporting for Segments of a Business Enterprise: Interim Financial Statements—an amendment of FASB Statement No. 14*	11/77
19	*Financial Accounting and Reporting by Oil and Gas Producing Companies*	12/77
20	*Accounting for Forward Exchange Contracts—an amendment of FASB Statement No. 8*	12/77

FASB Statement No.	Statement Title	Issue Date
21	*Suspension of the Reporting of Earnings per Share and Segment Information by Nonpublic Enterprises—an amendment of APB Opinion No. 15 and FASB Statement No. 14*	4/78
22	*Changes in the Provisions of Lease Agreements Resulting from Refundings of Tax-Exempt Debt—an amendment of FASB Statement No. 13*	6/78
23	*Inception of the Lease—an amendment of FASB Statement No. 13*	8/78
24	*Reporting Segment Information in Financial Statements That Are Presented in Another Enterprise's Financial Report—an amendment of FASB Statement No. 14*	12/78
25	*Suspension of Certain Accounting Requirements for Oil and Gas Producing Companies—an amendment of FASB Statement No. 19*	2/79
26	*Profit Recognition on Sales-Type Leases of Real Estate—an amendment of FASB Statement No. 13*	4/79
27	*Classification of Renewals or Extensions of Existing Sales-Type or Direct Financing Leases—an amendment of FASB Statement No. 13*	5/79
28	*Accounting for Sales with Leasebacks—an amendment of FASB Statement No. 13*	5/79
29	*Determining Contingent Rentals—an amendment of FASB Statement No. 13*	6/79
30	*Disclosure of Information about Major Customers—an amendment of FASB Statement No. 14*	8/79
31	*Accounting for Tax Benefits Related to U.K. Tax Legislation Concerning Stock Relief*	9/79
32	*Specialized Accounting and Reporting Principles and Practices in AICPA Statements of Position and Guides on Accounting and Auditing Matters—an amendment of APB Opinion No. 20*	9/79
33	*Financial Reporting and Changing Prices*	9/79
34	*Capitalization of Interest Cost*	10/79
35	*Accounting and Reporting by Defined Benefit Pension Plans*	3/80
36	*Disclosure of Pension Information—an amendment of APB Opinion No. 8*	5/80
37	*Balance Sheet Classification of Deferred Income Taxes—an amendment of APB Opinion No. 11*	7/80
38	*Accounting for Preacquisition Contingencies of Purchased Enterprises—an amendment of APB Opinion No. 16*	9/80
39	*Financial Reporting and Changing Prices: Specialized Assets-Mining and Oil and Gas—a supplement to FASB Statement No. 33*	10/80
40	*Financial Reporting and Changing Prices: Specialized Assets-Timberlands and Growing Timber—a supplement to FASB Statement No. 33*	11/80

FASB Statement No.	Statement Title	Issue Date
41	*Financial Reporting and Changing Prices: Specialized Assets-Income-Producing Real Estate—a supplement to FASB Statement No. 33*	11/80
42	*Determining Materiality for Capitalization of Interest Cost—an amendment of FASB Statement No. 34*	11/80
43	*Accounting for Compensated Absences*	11/80
44	*Accounting for Intangible Assets of Motor Carriers—an amendment of Chapter 5 of ARB No. 43 and an interpretation of APB Opinions 17 and 30*	12/80
45	*Accounting for Franchise Fee Revenue*	3/81
46	*Financial Reporting and Changing Prices: Motion Picture Films*	3/81
47	*Disclosure of Long-Term Obligations*	3/81
48	*Revenue Recognition When Right of Return Exists*	6/81
49	*Accounting for Product Financing Arrangements*	6/81
50	*Financial Reporting in the Record and Music Industry*	11/81
51	*Financial Reporting by Cable Television Companies*	11/81
52	*Foreign Currency Translation*	12/81
53	*Financial Reporting by Producers and Distributors of Motion Picture Films*	12/81
54	*Financial Reporting and Changing Prices: Investment Companies—an amendment of FASB Statement No. 33*	1/81
55	*Determining whether a Convertible Security is a Common Stock Equivalent—an amendment of APB Opinion No. 15*	2/82
56	*Designation of AICPA Guide and Statement of Position (SOP) 81-1 on Contractor Accounting and SOP 81-2 concerning Hospital-Related Organizations as Preferable for Purposes of Applying APB Opinion 20—an amendment of FASB Statement No. 32*	2/82
57	*Related Party Disclosures*	3/82
58	*Capitalization of Interest Cost in Financial Statements That Include Investments Accounted for by the Equity Method—an amendment of FASB Statement No. 34*	4/82
59	*Deferral of the Effective Date of Certain Accounting Requirements for Pension Plans of State and Local Governmental Units—an amendment of FASB Statement No. 35*	4/82
60	*Accounting and Reporting by Insurance Enterprises*	6/82
61	*Accounting for Title Plant*	6/82
62	*Capitalization of Interest Cost in Situations Involving Certain Tax-Exempt Borrowings and Certain Gifts and Grants—an amendment of FASB Statement No. 34*	6/82
63	*Financial Reporting by Broadcasters*	6/82
64	*Extinguishments of Debt Made to Satisfy Sinking-Fund Requirements—an amendment of FASB Statement No. 4*	9/82
65	*Accounting for Certain Mortgage Banking Activities*	9/82

FASB Statement No.	Statement Title	Issue Date
66	*Accounting for Sales of Real Estate*	10/82
67	*Accounting for Costs and Initial Rental Operations of Real Estate Projects*	10/82
68	*Research and Development Arrangements*	10/82
69	*Disclosures about Oil and Gas Producing Activities—an amendment of FASB Statements 19, 25, 33, and 39*	11/82
70	*Financial Reporting and Changing Prices: Foreign Currency Translation—an amendment of FASB Statement No. 33*	12/82
71	*Accounting for the Effects of Certain Types of Regulation*	12/82
72	*Accounting for Certain Acquisitions of Banking or Thrift Institutions—an amendment of APB Opinion No. 17, an interpretation of APB Opinions 16 and 17, and an amendment of FASB Interpretation No. 9*	2/83
73	*Reporting a Change in Accounting for Railroad Track Structures—an amendment of APB Opinion No. 20*	8/83
74	*Accounting for Special Termination Benefits Paid to Employees*	8/83
75	*Deferral of the Effective Date of Certain Accounting Requirements for Pension Plans of State and Local Governmental Units—an amendment of FASB Statement No. 35*	11/83
76	*Extinguishment of Debt—an amendment of APB Opinion No. 26*	11/83
77	*Reporting by Transferors for Transfers of Receivables with Recourse*	12/83
78	*Classification of Obligations That Are Callable by the Creditor—an amendment of ARB No. 43, Chapter 3A*	12/83
79	*Elimination of Certain Disclosures for Business Combinations by Nonpublic Enterprises—an amendment of APB Opinion No. 16*	2/84
80	*Accounting for Futures Contracts*	8/84
81	*Disclosure of Postretirement Health Care and Life Insurance Benefits*	11/84
82	*Financial Reporting and Changing Prices: Elimination of Certain Disclosures—an amendment of FASB Statement No. 33*	11/84
83	*Designation of AICPA Guides and Statement of Position on Accounting by Brokers and Dealers in Securities, by Employee Benefit Plans, and by Banks as Preferable for Purposes of Applying APB Opinion 20—an amendment FASB Statement No. 32 and APB Opinion No. 30 and a rescission of FASB Interpretation No. 10*	3/85
84	*Induced Conversions of Convertible Debt—an amendment of APB Opinion No. 26*	3/85
85	*Yield Test for Determining whether a Convertible Security is a Common Stock Equivalent—an amendment of APB Opinion No. 15*	3/85

FASB Statement No.	Statement Title	Issue Date
86	*Accounting for the Costs of Computer Software to Be Sold, Leased, or Otherwise Marketed*	8/85
87	*Employers' Accounting for Pensions*	12/85
88	*Employers' Accounting for Settlements and Curtailments of Defined Benefit Pension Plans and for Termination Benefits*	12/85
89	*Financial Reporting and Changing Prices*	12/86
90	*Regulated Enterprises-Accounting for Abandonments and Disallowances of Plant Costs—an amendment of FASB Statement No. 71*	12/86
91	*Accounting for Nonrefundable Fees and Costs Associated with Originating or Acquiring Loans and Initial Direct Costs of Leases—an amendment of FASB Statements No. 13, 60, and 65 and a rescission of FASB Statement No. 17*	12/86
92	*Regulated Enterprises-Accounting for Phase-in Plans—an amendment of FASB Statement No. 71*	8/87
93	*Recognition of Depreciation by Not-for-Profit Organizations*	8/87
94	*Consolidation of All Majority-owned Subsidiaries—an amendment of ARB No. 51, with related amendments of APB Opinion No. 18 and ARB No. 43, Chapter 12*	10/87
95	*Statement of Cash Flows*	11/87
96	*Accounting for Income Taxes*	12/87
97	*Accounting and Reporting by Insurance Enterprises for Certain Long-Duration Contracts and for Realized Gains and Losses from the Sale of Investments*	12/87
98	*Accounting for Leases: Sale-Leaseback Transactions Involving Real Estate, Sales-Type Leases of Real Estate, Definition of the Lease Term, and Initial Direct Costs of Direct Financing Leases—an amendment of FASB Statements No. 13, 66, and 91 and a rescission of FASB Statement No. 26 and Technical Bulletin No. 79-11*	5/88
99	*Deferral of the Effective Date of Recognition of Depreciation by Not-for-Profit Organizations—an amendment of FASB Statement No. 93*	9/88
100	*Accounting for Income Taxes-Deferral of the Effective Date of FASB Statement No. 96—an amendment of FASB Statement No. 96*	12/88
101	*Regulated Enterprises-Accounting for the Discontinuation of Application of FASB Statement No. 71*	12/88
102	*Statement of Cash Flows-Exemption of Certain Enterprises and Classification of Cash Flows from Certain Securities Acquired for Resale—an amendment of FASB Statement No. 95*	2/89
103	*Accounting for Income Taxes-Deferral of the Effective Date of FASB Statement No. 96—an amendment of FASB Statement No. 96*	12/89

FASB Statement No.	Statement Title	Issue Date
104	*Statement of Cash Flows-Net Reporting of Certain Cash Receipts and Cash Payments and Classification of Cash Flows from Hedging Transactions—an amendment of FASB Statement No. 95*	12/89
105	*Disclosure of Information about Financial Instruments with Off-Balance-Sheet Risk and Financial Instruments with Concentrations of Credit Risk*	3/90
106	*Employers' Accounting for Postretirement Benefits Other Than Pensions*	12/90
107	*Disclosures about Fair Value of Financial Instruments*	12/91
108	*Accounting for Income Taxes-Deferral of the Effective Date of FASB Statement No. 96—an amendment of FASB Statement No. 96*	12/91
109	*Accounting for Income Taxes*	2/92
110	*Reporting by Defined Benefit Pension Plans of Investment Contracts—an amendment of FASB Statement No. 35*	8/92
111	*Rescission of FASB Statement No. 32 and Technical Corrections*	11/92
112	*Employers' Accounting for Postemployment Benefits—an amendment of FASB Statements No. 5 and 43*	11/92
113	*Accounting and Reporting for Reinsurance of Short-Duration and Long-Duration Contracts*	12/92
114	*Accounting by Creditors for Impairment of a Loan—an amendment of FASB Statements No. 5 and 15*	5/93
115	*Accounting for Certain Investments in Debt and Equity Securities*	5/93
116	*Accounting for Contributions Received and Contributions Made*	6/93
117	*Financial Statements of Not-for-Profit Organizations*	6/93
118	*Accounting by Creditors for Impairment of a Loan-Income Recognition and Disclosures—an amendment of FASB Statement No. 114*	10/94
119	*Disclosure about Derivative Financial Instruments and Fair Value of Financial Instruments*	10/94
120	*Accounting and Reporting by Mutual Life Insurance Enterprises and by Insurance Enterprises for Certain Long-Duration Participating Contracts—an amendment of FASB Statements 60, 97, and 113 and Interpretation No. 40*	1/95
121	*Accounting for the Impairment of Long-Lived Assets and for Long-Lived Assets to Be Disposed Of*	3/95
122	*Accounting for Mortgage Servicing Rights—an amendment of FASB Statement No. 65*	5/95
123	*Accounting for Stock-Based Compensation*	10/95
123 (revised 2004)	*Share-Based Payment*	12/04
124	*Accounting for Certain Investments Held by Not-for-Profit Organizations*	11/95

FASB Statement No.	Statement Title	Issue Date
125	*Accounting for Transfers and Servicing of Financial Assets and Extinguishments of Liabilities*	6/96
126	*Exemption from Certain Required Disclosures about Financial Instruments for Certain Nonpublic Entities—an amendment to FASB Statement No. 107*	12/96
127	*Deferral of the Effective Date of Certain Provisions of FASB Statement No. 125—an amendment to FASB Statement No. 125*	12/96
128	*Earnings per Share*	2/97
129	*Disclosure of Information about Capital Structure*	2/97
130	*Reporting Comprehensive Income*	6/97
131	*Disclosures about Segments of an Enterprise and Related Information*	6/97
132	*Employers' Disclosures about Pensions and Other Postretirement Benefits—an amendment of FASB Statements No. 87, 88, and 106*	2/98
132 (revised 2003)	*Employers' Disclosures about Pensions and Other Postretirement Benefits—an amendment of FASB Statements No. 87, 88, and 106*	12/03
133	*Accounting for Derivative Instruments and Hedging Activities*	6/98
134	*Accounting for Mortgage-Backed Securities Retained after the Securitization of Mortgage Loans Held for Sale by a Mortgage Banking Enterprise—an amendment of FASB Statement No. 65*	10/98
135	*Rescission of FASB Statement No. 75 and Technical Corrections*	2/99
136	*Transfers of Assets to a Not-for-Profit Organization or Charitable Trust That Raises or Holds Contributions for Others*	6/99
137	*Accounting for Derivative Instruments and Hedging Activities—Deferral of the Effective Date of FASB Statement No. 133—an amendment of FASB Statement No. 133*	6/99
138	*Accounting for Certain Derivative Instruments and Certain Hedging Activities—an amendment of FASB Statement No. 133*	6/00
139	*Rescission of FASB Statement No. 53 and amendments to FASB Statements No. 63, 89, and 121*	6/00
140	*Accounting for Transfers and Servicing of Financial Assets and Extinguishments of Liabilities—a replacement of FASB Statement No. 125*	9/00
141	*Business Combinations*	6/01
142	*Goodwill and Other Intangible Assets*	6/01
143	*Accounting for Asset Retirement Obligations*	6/01
144	*Accounting for the Impairment or Disposal of Long-Lived Assets*	8/01
145	*Rescission of FASB Statements No. 4, 44, and 64, Amendment of FASB Statement No. 13, and Technical Corrections*	4/02

FASB Statement No.	Statement Title	Issue Date
146	*Accounting for Costs Associated with Exit or Disposal Activities*	6/02
147	*Acquisitions of Certain Financial Institutions—an amendment of FASB Statements No. 72 and 144 and FASB Interpretation No. 9*	10/02
148	*Accounting for Stock-Based Compensation-Transition and Disclosure—an amendment of FASB Statement No. 123*	12/02
149	*Amendment of Statement 133 on Derivative Instruments and Hedging Activities*	4/03
150	*Accounting for Certain Financial Instruments with Characteristics of both Liabilities and Equity*	5/03
151	*Inventory Costs—an amendment of ARB No. 43, Chapter 4*	11/04
152	*Accounting for Real Estate Time-Sharing Transactions—an amendment of FASB Statements No. 66 and 67*	12/04
153	*Exchanges of Nonmonetary Assets—an amendment of APB Opinion No. 29*	12/04
154	*Accounting Changes and Error Corrections—a replacement of APB Opinion No. 20 and FASB Statement No. 3*	5/05

Index

A

B

D

E

G

H

I

L

Q

R

S

W

Y

Z

PRESENT VALUE TABLES

Present Value of $1 Due in *n* Periods

$$PV = A\left[\frac{1}{(1+i)^n}\right] = A(PVF_{\overline{n}|i})$$

n	2%	3%	4%	5%	6%	8%	10%	12%	16%	20%
1	0.9804	0.9709	0.9615	0.9524	0.9434	0.9259	0.9091	0.8929	0.8621	0.8333
2	0.9612	0.9426	0.9246	0.9070	0.8900	0.8573	0.8264	0.7972	0.7432	0.6944
3	0.9423	0.9151	0.8890	0.8638	0.8396	0.7938	0.7513	0.7118	0.6407	0.5787
4	0.9238	0.8885	0.8548	0.8227	0.7921	0.7350	0.6830	0.6355	0.5523	0.4823
5	0.9057	0.8626	0.8219	0.7835	0.7473	0.6806	0.6209	0.5674	0.4761	0.4019
6	0.8880	0.8375	0.7903	0.7462	0.7050	0.6302	0.5645	0.5066	0.4104	0.3349
7	0.8706	0.8131	0.7599	0.7170	0.6651	0.5835	0.5132	0.4523	0.3538	0.2791
8	0.8535	0.7894	0.7307	0.6768	0.6274	0.5403	0.4665	0.4039	0.3050	0.2326
9	0.8368	0.7664	0.7026	0.6446	0.5919	0.5002	0.4241	0.3606	0.2630	0.1938
10	0.8203	0.7441	0.6756	0.6139	0.5584	0.4632	0.3855	0.3220	0.2267	0.1615
11	0.8043	0.7224	0.6496	0.5847	0.5268	0.4289	0.3505	0.2875	0.1954	0.1346
12	0.7885	0.7014	0.6246	0.5568	0.4970	0.3971	0.3186	0.2567	0.1685	0.1122
13	0.7730	0.6810	0.6006	0.5303	0.4688	0.3677	0.2897	0.2292	0.1452	0.0935
14	0.7579	0.6611	0.5775	0.5051	0.4423	0.3405	0.2633	0.2046	0.1252	0.0779
15	0.7430	0.6419	0.5553	0.4810	0.4173	0.3152	0.2394	0.1827	0.1079	0.0649
16	0.7284	0.6232	0.5339	0.4581	0.3936	0.2919	0.2176	0.1631	0.0930	0.0541
17	0.7142	0.6050	0.5134	0.4363	0.3714	0.2703	0.1978	0.1456	0.0802	0.0451
18	0.7002	0.5874	0.4936	0.4155	0.3503	0.2502	0.1799	0.1300	0.0691	0.0376
19	0.6864	0.5703	0.4746	0.3957	0.3305	0.2317	0.1635	0.1161	0.0596	0.0313
20	0.6730	0.5537	0.4564	0.3769	0.3118	0.2145	0.1486	0.1037	0.0514	0.0261
25	0.6095	0.4776	0.3751	0.2953	0.2330	0.1460	0.0923	0.0588	0.0245	0.0105
30	0.5521	0.4120	0.3083	0.2314	0.1741	0.0994	0.0573	0.0334	0.0116	0.0042
40	0.4529	0.3066	0.2083	0.1420	0.0972	0.0460	0.0221	0.0107	0.0026	0.0007
50	0.3715	0.2281	0.1407	0.0872	0.0543	0.0213	0.0085	0.0035	0.0006	0.0001